HANDBOOK
OF
ALGORITHMS
FOR
PHYSICAL
DESIGN
AUTOMATION

HANDBOOK OF ALGORITHMS FOR PHYSICAL DESIGN AUTOMATION

EDITED BY

CHARLES J. ALPERT

DINESH P. MEHTA

SACHIN S. SAPATNEKAR

CRC Press
Taylor & Francis Group
Boca Raton London New York

CRC Press is an imprint of the
Taylor & Francis Group, an **informa** business

AN AUERBACH BOOK

Auerbach Publications
Taylor & Francis Group
6000 Broken Sound Parkway NW, Suite 300
Boca Raton, FL 33487-2742

© 2009 by Taylor & Francis Group, LLC, except for Chapter 19, © by Jason Cong and Joseph R. Shinnerl. Printed with permission.
Auerbach is an imprint of Taylor & Francis Group, an Informa business

No claim to original U.S. Government works
Printed in the United States of America on acid-free paper
10 9 8 7 6 5 4 3 2 1

International Standard Book Number-13: 978-0-8493-7242-1 (Hardcover)

Library of Congress Cataloging-in-Publication Data

Handbook of algorithms for physical design automation / edited by Charles J. Alpert, Dinesh P. Mehta, Sachin S. Sapatnekar.
    p. cm.
  Includes bibliographical references and index.
  ISBN-13: 978-0-8493-7242-1
  ISBN-10: 0-8493-7242-9
  1. Integrated circuit layout--Mathematics--Handbooks, manuals, etc. 2. Integrated circuit layout--Data processing--Handbooks, manuals, etc. 3. Integrated circuits--Very large scale integration--Design and construction--Data processing--Handbooks, manuals, etc. 4. Algorithms. I. Alpert, Charles J. II. Mehta, Dinesh P. III. Sapatnekar, Sachin S., 1967- IV. Title.

TK7874.55.H36 2009
621.3815--dc22
                                            2008014182

Visit the Taylor & Francis Web site at
http://www.taylorandfrancis.com

and the Auerbach Web site at
http://www.auerbach-publications.com

Dedications

To the wonderful girls in my life:
Cheryl, Candice, Ciara, and Charlie

Charles J. Alpert

To the memory of my grandparents:
Nalinee and Gajanan Kamat, Radha and Shreenath Mehta

Dinesh P. Mehta

To Ofelia and Arunito

Sachin S. Sapatnekar

Contents

PART I   Introduction

PART II   Foundations

PART III   Floorplanning

PART IV   Placement

PART V   Net Layout and Optimization

PART VI   Routing Multiple Signal Nets

PART VII   *Manufacturability and Detailed Routing*

PART VIII   *Physical Synthesis*

PART IX   *Designing Large Global Nets*

PART X   *Physical Design for Specialized Technologies*

Editors

Charles J. Alpert (Chuck) was born in Bethesda, Maryland, in 1969. He received two undergraduate degrees from Stanford University in 1991 and his doctorate from the University of California, Los Angeles, California in 1996, in computer science. Upon graduation, Chuck joined IBM's Austin Research Laboratory where he currently manages the Design Productivity Group, whose mission is to develop design automation tools and methodologies to improve designer productivity and reduce design cost. Chuck has over 100 conference and journal publications and has thrice received the best paper award from the ACM/IEEE Design Automation Conference. He has been active in the academic community, serving as chair for the Tau Workshop on Timing Issues and the International Symposium on Physical Design. He also serves as an associate editor of *IEEE Transactions on Computer-Aided Design*. He received the Mahboob Khan Mentor Award in 2001 and 2007 for his work in mentoring. He was also named the IEEE fellow in 2005.

Dinesh P. Mehta received his BTech in computer science and engineering from the Indian Institute of Technology, Bombay, India, in 1987; his MS in computer science from the University of Minnesota, Minneapolis, Minnesota, in 1990; and his PhD in computer science from the University of Florida, Gainesville, Florida, in 1992. He was on the faculty at the University of Tennessee Space Institute, Tullahoma, Tennessee from 1992 to 2000, where he received the Vice President's Award for Teaching Excellence in 1997. He was a visiting professor at Intel's Strategic CAD Labs in 1996 and 1997. He has been on the faculty in the mathematical and computer science departments at the Colorado School of Mines, Golden, Colorado since 2000, where he is a professor and currently also serves as department head. He is a coauthor of *Fundamentals of Data Structures in C++* and a coeditor of *Handbook of Data Structures and Applications*. His publications and research interests are in VLSI design automation, and applied algorithms and data structures. He is a former associate editor of the *IEEE Transactions on Circuits and Systems-I*.

Sachin S. Sapatnekar received his BTech from the Indian Institute of Technology, Bombay, India in 1987; his MS from Syracuse University, New York, in 1989; and his PhD from the University of Illinois at Urbana–Champaign, Urbana, Illinois, in 1992. From 1992 to 1997, he was an assistant professor in the Department of Electrical and Computer Engineering at Iowa State University, Ames, Iowa. Since then, he has been on the faculty of the Department of Electrical and Computer Engineering at the University of Minnesota, Minneapolis, Minnesota, where he is currently the Robert and Marjorie Henle Professor. He has published widely in the area of computer-aided design of VLSI circuits, particularly in the areas of timing, layout, and power. He has held positions on the editorial board of the *IEEE Transactions on CAD* (he is currently the deputy editor-in-chief), the *IEEE Transactions on VLSI Systems*, and the *IEEE Transactions on Circuits and Systems II*. He has served on the technical program committee for various conferences, as a technical program co-chair for Design Automation Conference (DAC), and as a technical program and general chair for both the IEEE/ACM Tau Workshop and the ACM International Symposium on Physical Design. He is a recipient of the NSF Career Award, three best paper awards at DAC, and one at International Conference on Computer Design (ICCD), and the Semiconductor Research Corporation Technical Excellence award. He is a fellow of the IEEE.

Contributors

Saurabh N. Adya
Synopsys, Inc.
Sunnyvale, California

Ameya R. Agnihotri
Magma Design Automation
San Jose, California

Christoph Albrecht
Cadence Research Laboratories
Berkeley, California

Charles J. Alpert
IBM Corporation
Austin, Texas

Kia Bazargan
Department of Electrical and Computer
  Engineering
University of Minnesota
Minneapolis, Minnesota

Murat Becer
CLK Design Automation
Littleton, Massachusetts

Ulrich Brenner
Research Institute for Discrete Mathematics
University of Bonn
Bonn, Germany

Yao-Wen Chang
Department of Electrical Engineering
  and Graduate Institute of Electronics
  Engineering
National Taiwan University
Taipei, Taiwan

Charlie Chung-Ping Chen
Department of Electrical Engineering
National Taiwan University
Taipei, Taiwan

Tung-Chieh Chen
Graduate Institute of Electronics Engineering
National Taiwan University
Taipei, Taiwan

Scott Y.L. Chin
Electrical and Computer Engineering
University of British Columbia
Vancouver, British Columbia, Canada

Minsik Cho
Electrical and Computer Engineering
  Department
University of Texas
Austin, Texas

Nathalie Chan King Choy
Electrical and Computer Engineering
University of British Columbia
Vancouver, British Columbia, Canada

Chris Chu
Department of Electrical and Computer
  Engineering
Iowa State University
Ames, Iowa

Jason Cong
Computer Science Department
University of California
Los Angeles, California

Yan Feng
Cadence Design Systems
San Jose, California

Jon Frankle
Cadence Design Systems
San Jose, California

Aki Fujimura
Direct 2 Silicon
San Jose, California

Joseph Ganley
Synopsys, Inc.
Vienna, Virginia

Puneet Gupta
Department of Electrical Engineering
University of California
Los Angeles, California

Bill Halpin
Synopsys, Inc.
Sunnyvale, California

Asmus Hetzel
Magma Design Automation, Inc.
San Jose, California

Nathaniel Hieter
IBM Corporation
East Fishkill, New York

Miloš Hrkić
Magma Design Automation
Austin, Texas

Jiang Hu
Department of Electrical and Computer
 Engineering
Texas A & M University
College Station, Texas

Shiyan Hu
Department of Electrical and Computer
 Engineering
Michigan Technology University
Houghton, Michigan

Yehea I. Ismail
Electrical Engineering and Computer Science
 Department
Northwestern University
Evanston, Illinois

Andrew B. Kahng
Electrical and Computer Engineering and
 Computer Science and Engineering
University of California
San Diego, California

Andrew Kennings
Department of Electrical and Computer
 Engineering
University of Waterloo
Waterloo, Ontario, Canada

Vishal Khandelwal
Synopsys, Inc.
Hillsboro, Oregon

Cheng-Kok Koh
School of Electrical and Computer Engineering
Purdue University
West Lafayette, Indiana

Dorothy Kucar
IBM Corporation
Yorktown Heights, New York

Zhuo Li
IBM Corporation
Austin, Texas

John Lillis
Department of Computer Science
University of Illinois
Chicago, Illinois

Frank Liu
IBM Corporation
Austin, Texas

Zhi-Quan Luo
Department of Electrical and Computer
 Engineering
University of Minnesota
Minneapolis, Minnesota

Patrick H. Madden
Computer Science Department
Binghamton University
Binghamton, New York

Igor L. Markov
Department of Electrical Engineering
 and Computer Science
University of Michigan
Ann Arbor, Michigan

Dinesh P. Mehta
Department of Mathematical and
 Computer Sciences
Colorado School of Mines
Golden, Colorado

Arjen Mets
IBM Corporation
East Fishkill, New York

Joydeep Mitra
Electrical and Computer Engineering
 Department
University of Texas
Austin, Texas

Gi-Joon Nam
IBM Corporation
Austin, Texas

Sani Nassif
IBM Corporation
Austin, Texas

Ralph H.J.M. Otten
Eindhoven University of Technology
Eindhoven, the Netherlands

Muhammet Mustafa Ozdal
Intel Corporation
Hillsboro, Oregon

David Z. Pan
Electrical and Computer Engineering
  Department
University of Texas
Austin, Texas

Min Pan
Cadence Design Systems, Inc.
San Jose, California

Rajendran Panda
Freescale Semiconductor, Inc.
Austin, Texas

Evanthia Papadopoulou
IBM Corporation
Yorktown Heights, New York

Kara K.W. Poon
Electrical and Computer Engineering
University of British Columbia
Vancouver, British Columbia, Canada

Ruchir Puri
IBM Corporation
Yorktown Heights, New York

Lakshmi Reddy
IBM Corporation
East Fishkill, New York

Haoxing Ren
IBM Corporation
Austin, Texas

Gabriel Robins
Department of Computer Science
University of Virginia
Charlottesville, Virginia

Jarrod A. Roy
Department of Electrical Engineering
  and Computer Science
University of Michigan
Ann Arbor, Michigan

Sanghamitra Roy
Department of Electrical and Computer
  Engineering
University of Wisconsin–Madison
Madison, Wisconsin

Jeffrey S. Salowe
Cadence Design Systems
San Jose, California

Kambiz Samadi
Department of Electrical and Computer
  Engineering
University of California
San Diego, California

Sachin S. Sapatnekar
Electrical and Computer Engineering
  Department
University of Minnesota
Minneapolis, Minnesota

Prashant Saxena
Synopsys, Inc.
Hillsboro, Oregon

Louis K. Scheffer
Cadence Design Systems
San Jose, California

Franklin M. Schellenberg
Mentor Graphics Corporation
San Jose, California

Rupesh S. Shelar
Intel Corporation
Hillsboro, Oregon

Joseph R. Shinnerl
Tabula, Inc.
Santa Clara, California

Ankur Srivastava
Department of Electrical and
  Computer Engineering
University of Maryland
College Park, Maryland

Haihua Su
Magma Design Automation, Inc.
Austin, Texas

Susmita Sur-Kolay
Advanced Computing and Microelectronics
    Unit
Indian Statistical Institute
Kolkata, India

William Swartz
InternetCAD.com
Dallas, Texas

Cliff C. N. Sze
IBM Corporation
Austin, Texas

Steve Teig
Tabula, Inc.
Santa Clara, California

Louise Trevillyan
IBM Corporation
Yorktown Heights, New York

Paul G. Villarrubia
IBM Corporation
Austin, Texas

Kristofer Vorwerk
Department of Electrical and
    Computer Engineering
University of Waterloo
Waterloo, Ontario, Canada

Jens Vygen
Research Institute for Discrete Mathematics
University of Bonn
Bonn, Germany

Ting-Chi Wang
Department of Computer Science
National Tsing Hua University
Hsinchu, Taiwan

Steven J.E. Wilton
Electrical and Computer Engineering
University of British Columbia
Vancouver, British Columbia, Canada

Martin D.F. Wong
Department of Electrical and
    Computer Engineering
University of Illinois at Urbana–Champaign
Urbana, Illinois

Xiaojian Yang
Synopsys, Inc.
Sunnyvale, California

Evangeline F.Y. Young
Department of Computer Science and
    Engineering
Chinese University of Hong Kong Shatin
Hong Kong, China

Alexander Zelikovsky
Department of Computer Science
Georgia State University
Atlanta, Georgia

Hai Zhou
Department of Electrical Engineering
    and Computer Science
Northwestern University
Evanston, Illinois

Vladimir Zolotov
IBM Corporation
Yorktown Heights, New York

Part I

Introduction

1 Introduction to Physical Design

Charles J. Alpert, Dinesh P. Mehta,
and Sachin S. Sapatnekar

CONTENTS

1.1 INTRODUCTION

The purpose of VLSI physical design is to embed an abstract circuit description, such as a netlist, into silicon, creating a detailed geometric layout on a die. In the early years of semiconductor technology, the task of laying out gates and interconnect wires was carried out manually (i.e., by hand on graph paper, or later through the use of layout editors). However, as semiconductor fabrication processes improved, making it possible to incorporate large numbers of transistors onto a single chip (a trend that is well captured by Moore's law), it became imperative for the design community to turn to the use of automation to address the resulting problem of scale. Automation was facilitated by the improvement in the speed of computers that would be used to create the next generation of computer chips resulting in their own replacement! The importance of automation was reflected in the scientific community by the formation of the Design Automation Conference in 1963 and both the International Conference on Computer-Aided Design and the *IEEE Transactions on Computer-Aided Design* in 1983; today, there are several other conferences and journals on design automation.

While the problems of scale have been one motivator for automation, other factors have also come into play. Most notably, improvements in technology have resulted in the invalidation of some critical assumptions made during physical design: one of these is related to the relative delay between gates and the interconnect wires used to connect gates to each other. Initially, gate delays dominated interconnect delays to such an extent that interconnect delay could essentially be ignored when computing the delay of a circuit. With technology scaling causing feature sizes to shrink by a factor of 0.7 every 18 months or so, gates became faster from one generation to the next, while wires became more resistive and slower. Early metrics that modeled interconnect delay as proportional to the length of the wire first became invalid (as wire delays scale quadratically with their lengths) and then valid again (as optimally buffered interconnects show such a trend). New signal integrity effects began to manifest themselves as power grid noise or in the form of increased crosstalk as wire cross-sections became "taller and thinner" from one technology generation to the next. Other problems came into play: for instance, the number of buffers required on a chip began to show trends that increased at alarming rates; the delays of long interconnects increased to the range of several clock cycles; and new technologies emerged such as 3D stacked structures with multiple layers of

3

active devices, opening up, literally and figuratively, a new dimension in physical design. All of these have changed, and are continuing to change, the fundamental nature of classical physical design.

A major consequence of interconnect dominance is that the role of physical design moved upstream to other stages of the design cycle. Synthesis was among the first to feel the impact: traditional 1980s-style logic synthesis (which lasted well into the 1990s) used simplified wire-load models for each gate, but the corresponding synthesis decisions were later unable to meet timing specifications, because they operated under gross and incorrect timing estimates. This realization led to the advent of physical synthesis techniques, where synthesis and physical design work hand in hand. More recently, multicyle interconnects have been seen to impact architectural decisions, and there has been much research on physically driven microarchitectural design.

These are not the only issues facing the designer. In sub-90 nm technologies, manufacturability issues have come to the forefront, and many of them are seen to impact physical design. Traditionally, design and manufacturing inhabited different worlds, with minimal handoffs between the two, but in light of* issues related to subwavelength lithography and planarization, a new area of physical design has opened up, where manufacturability has entered the equation. The explosion in mask costs associated with these issues has resulted in the emergence of special niches for field programmable gate arrays (FPGAs) for lower performance designs and for fast prototyping; physical design problems for FPGAs have their own flavors and peculiarities.

Although there were some early texts on physical design automation in the 1980s (such as the ones by Preas/Lorenzetti and Lengauer), university-level courses in VLSI physical design did not become commonplace until the 1990s when more recent texts became available. The field continues to change rapidly with new problems coming up in successive technology generations. The developments in this area have motivated the formation of the International Symposium on Physical Design (ISPD), a conference that is devoted solely to the discipline of VLSI physical design; this and other conferences became the major forum for the learning and dissemination of new knowledge. However, existing textbooks have failed to keep pace with these changes. One of the goals of this handbook is to provide a detailed survey of the field of VLSI physical design automation with a particular emphasis on state-of-the-art techniques, trends, and improvements that have emerged as a result of the dramatic changes seen in the field in the last decade.

1.2 OVERVIEW OF THE PHYSICAL DESIGN PROCESS

Back when the world was young and life was simple, when Madonna and Springsteen ruled the pop charts, interconnect delays were insignificant and physical design was a fairly simple process. Starting with a synthesized netlist, the designer used floorplanning to figure out where big blocks (such as arrays) were placed, and then placement handled the rest of the logic. If the design met its timing constraints before placement, then it would typically meet its timing constraints after placement as well. One could perform clock tree synthesis followed by routing and iterate over these process in a local manner.

Of course, designs of today are much larger and more complex, which requires a more complex physical design flow. Floorplanning is harder than ever, and despite all the algorithms and innovations described here, it is still a very manual process. During floorplanning, the designers plan their I/Os and global interconnect, and restrict the location of logic to certain areas, and of course, the blocks (of which there are more than ever). They often must do this in the face of incomplete timing data. Designers iterate on their floorplans by performing fast physical synthesis and routing congestion estimation to identify key problem areas.

Once the main blocks are fixed in location and other logic is restricted, global placement is used to place the rest of the cells, followed by detailed placement to make local improvements. The placing of cells introduces long wires that increase delays in unexpected places. These delays are then reduced

* Pun unintended.

by wire synthesis techniques of buffering and wire sizing. Iteration between incremental placement and incremental synthesis to satisfy timing constraints today takes place in a single process called physical synthesis. Physical synthesis embodies just about all traditional physical design processes: floorplanning, placement, clock tree construction, and routing while sprinkling in the ability to adapt to the timing of the design. Of course, with a poor floorplan, physical synthesis will fail, so the designer must use this process to identify poor block and logic placement and plan global interconnects in an iterative process.

The successful exit of physical synthesis still requires post-timing-closure fix-up to address noise, variability, and manufacturability issues. Unfortunately, repairing these can sometimes force the designer back to earlier stages in the flow.

Of course, this explanation is an oversimplification. The physical design flow depends on the size of the design, the technology, the number of designers, the clock frequency, and the time to complete the design. As technology advances and design styles change, physical design flows are constantly reinvented as traditional phases are removed or combined by advances in algorithms (e.g., physical synthesis) while new ones are added to accommodate changes in technology.

1.3 OVERVIEW OF THE HANDBOOK

This handbook consists of the following ten parts:

1. Introduction: In addition to this chapter, this part includes a personal perspective from Ralph Otten, looking back on the major technical milestones in the history of physical design automation. A discussion of physical design objective functions that drive the techniques discussed in subsequent parts is also included in this part.
2. Foundations: This part includes reviews of the underlying data structures and basic algorithmic and optimization techniques that form the basis of the more sophisticated techniques used in physical design automation. This part also includes a chapter on partitioning and clustering. Many texts on physical design have traditionally included partitioning as an integral step of physical design. Our view is that partitioning is an important step in several stages of the design automation process, and not just in physical design; therefore, we decided to include a chapter on it here rather than devote a full handbook part.
3. Floorplanning: This identifies relative locations for the major components of a chip and may be used as early as the architecture stage. This part includes a chapter on early methods for floorplanning that mostly viewed floorplanning as a two-step process (topology generation and sizing) and reviews techniques such as rectangular dualization, analytic floorplanning, and hierarchical floorplanning. The next chapter exclusively discusses the slicing floorplan representation, which was first used in the early 1970s and is still used in a lot of the recent literature. The succeeding two chapters describe floorplan representations that are more general: an active area of research during the last decade. The first of these focuses on mosaic floorplan representations (these consider the floorplan to be a dissection of the chip rectangle into rooms that will be populated by modules, one to each room) and the second on packing representations (these view the floorplan as directly consisting of modules that need to be packed together). The penultimate chapter describes recent variations of the floorplanning problem. It explores formulations that more accurately account for interconnect and formulations for specialized architectures such as analog designs, FPGAs, and three-dimensional ICs. The final chapter in this part describes the role of floorplanning and prototyping in industrial design methodologies.
4. Placement: This is a classic physical design problem for which design automation solutions date back to the 1970s. Placement has evolved from a pure wirelength-driven formulation to one that better understands the needs of design closure: routability, white space distribution, big block placement, and timing. The first chapter in this part overviews how the placement

problem has changed with technology scaling and explains the new types of constraints and objectives that this problem must now address.

There has been a renaissance in placement algorithms over the last few years, and this can be gleaned from the chapters on cut-based, force-directed, multilevel, and analytic methods. This part also explores specific aspects of placement in the context of design closure: detailed placement, timing, congestion, noise, and power.

5. Net Layout and Optimization: During the design closure process, one needs to frequently estimate the layout of a particular net to understand its expected capacitance and impact on timing and routability. Traditionally, maze routing and Steiner tree algorithms have been used for laying out a given net's topology, and this is still the case today. The first two chapters of this part overview these fundamental physical design techniques.

Technology scaling for transistors has occurred much faster than for wires, which means that interconnect delays dominate much more than for previous generations. The delays due to interconnect are much more significant, thus more care needs to be taken when laying out a net's topology. The third chapter in this part overviews timing-driven interconnect structures, and the next three chapters show how buffering interconnect has become an absolutely essential step in timing closure. The buffers in effect create shorter wires, which mitigate the effect of technology scaling. Buffering is not a simple problem, because one has to not only create a solution for a given net but also needs to be cognizant of the routing and placement resources available for the rest of the design. The final chapter explores another dimension of reducing interconnect delay, wire sizing.

6. Routing Multiple Signal Nets: The previous part focused on optimization techniques for a single net. These approaches need conflict resolution techniques when there are scarce routing resources. The first chapter explores fast techniques for predicting routing congestion so that other optimizations have a chance to mitigate routing congestion without having to actually perform global routing. The next two chapters focus on techniques for global routing: the former on the classic rip-up and reroute approach and the latter on alternative techniques like network flows. The next chapter discusses planning of interconnect, especially in the context of global buffer insertion. The final chapter addresses a very important effect from technology scaling: the impact of noise on coupled interconnect lines. Noise issues must be modeled and mitigated earlier in the design closure flows, as they have become so pervasive.

7. Manufacturability and Detailed Routing: The requirements imposed by manufacturability and yield considerations place new requirements on the physical design process. This part discusses various aspects of manufacturability, including the use of metal fills, and resolution-enhancement techniques and subresolution assist features. These techniques have had a major impact on design rules, so that classical techniques for detailed routing cannot be used directly, and we will proceed to discuss the impact of manufacturability considerations on detailed routing.

8. Physical Synthesis: Owing to the effects that have become apparent in deep submicron technologies, wires play an increasingly dominant role in determining the circuit performance. Therefore, traditional approaches to synthesis that ignored physical design have been supplanted by a new generation of physical synthesis methods that integrate logic synthesis with physical design. This part overviews the most prominent approaches in this domain.

9. Designing Large Global Nets: In addition to signal nets, global nets for supply and clock signals consume a substantial fraction of on-chip routing resources, and play a vital role in the functional correctness of the chip. This part presents an overview of design techniques that are used to route and optimize these nets.

10. Physical Design for Specialized Technologies: Although most of the book deals with mainstream microprocessor or ASIC style designs, the ideas described in this book are largely

applicable to other paradigms such as FPGAs and to emerging technologies such as 3D integration. These problems require unique solution techniques that can satisfy these requirements. The last part overviews constraints in these specialized domains, and the physical design solutions that address the related problems.

1.4   INTENDED AUDIENCE

The material in this book is suitable for researchers and students in physical design automation and for practitioners in industry who wish to be familiar with the latest developments. Most importantly, it is a valuable complete reference for anyone in the field and potentially for designers who use design automation software.

Although the book does lay the basic groundwork in Part I, this is intended to serve as a quick review. It is assumed that the reader has some background in the algorithmic techniques used and in physical design automation. We expect that the book could also serve as a text for a graduate-level class on physical design automation.

NOTE ABOUT REFERENCES

The following abbreviations may have been used to refer to conferences and journals in which physical design automation papers are published.

ASPDAC	Asian South Pacific Design Automation Conference
DAC	Design Automation Conference
EDAC	European Design Automation Conference
GLSVLSI	Great Lakes Symposium on VLSI
ICCAD	International Conference on Computer-Aided Design
ICCD	International Conference on Computer Design
ISCAS	International Symposium on Circuits and Systems
ISPD	International Symposium on Physical Design
IEEE TCAD	*IEEE Transactions on the Computer-Aided Design of Integrated Circuits*
IEEE TCAS	*IEEE Transactions on Circuits and Systems*
ACM TODAES	*ACM Transactions on the Design Automation of Electronic Systems*
IEEE TVLSI	*IEEE Transactions on VLSI Systems*

2 Layout Synthesis: A Retrospective

Ralph H.J.M. Otten

CONTENTS

2.1 THE FIRST ALGORITHMS (UP TO 1970)

Design automation has a history of over half a century if we look at its algorithms. The first algorithms were not motivated by design of electronic circuits. Willard Van Orman Quine's work on simplifying truth functions emanated from the philosopher's research and teaching on mathematical logic. It produced a procedure for simplifying two-level logic that remained at the core of logic synthesis for decades (and still is in most of its textbooks). Closely involved in its development were the first pioneers in layout synthesis: Sheldon B. Akers and Chester Y. Lee. Their work on switching networks, both combinational and sequential, and their representation as binary decision programs came from the same laboratory as the above simplification procedure, and preceded the landmark 1961 paper on routing.

9

2.1.1 LEE'S ROUTER

What Lee [1] described is now called a grid expansion algorithm or maze runner, to set it apart from earlier independent research on the similar abstract problem: the early paper of Edsger W. Dijkstra on shortest path and labyrinth problems [2] and Edward F. Moore's paper on shortest paths through a maze [3] were already written in 1959. But in Lee's paper the problem of connecting two points on a grid with its application to printed circuit boards was developed through a systematization of the intuitive procedure: identify all grid cells that can be reached in an increasing number of steps until the target is among them, or no unlabeled, nonblocked cells are left. In the latter case, no such path exists. In the former case, retracing provides a shortest path between the source and the target (Figure 2.1).

The input consists of a grid with blocked and nonblocked cells. The algorithm then goes through three phases after the source and target have been chosen, and the source has been labeled with 0:

1. Wave propagation in which all unlabeled, nonblocked neighbors of labeled cells are labeled one higher than in the preceding wave.
2. Retracing starts when the target has received a label and consists of repeatedly finding a neighboring cell with a lower label, thus marking a shortest path between the source and the target.
3. Label clearance prepares the grid for another search by adding the cells of the path just found to the set of blocked cells and removing all labels.

The time needed to find a path is $\mathcal{O}(L^2)$ if L is the length of the path. This makes it worst case $\mathcal{O}(N^2)$ on an $N \times N$ grid (and if each cell has to be part of the input, that is any cell can be initially blocked, it is a linear-time algorithm). Its space complexity is also $\mathcal{O}(N^2)$. These complexities were

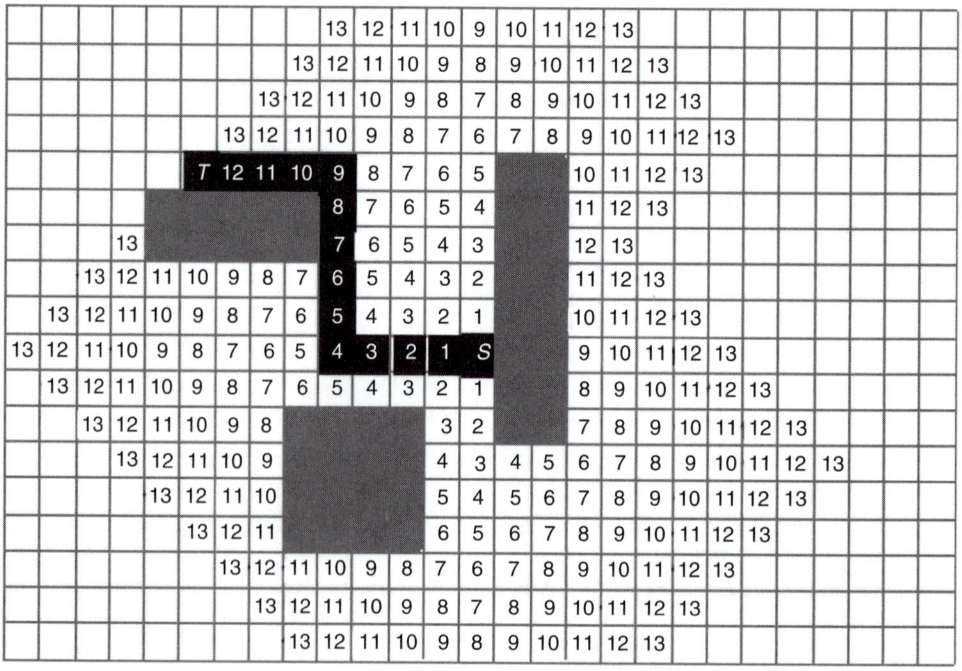

FIGURE 2.1 Wave propagation and retracing. Waves are sets of grid cells with the same label. The source S gets label 0. The target T gets the length of the shortest path as a label (if any). Retracing is not unique in general.

soon seen as serious problems when applied to real-world cases. Some relief in memory use was found in coding the labels: instead of labeling each explored cell with its distance to the source, it suffices to record that number modulo 3, which works for any path search on an unweighted graph. Here, however, the underlying structure is bipartite, and Akers [4] observed that wave fronts with a label sequence in which a certain label bit is twice on and then twice off (i.e., 1, 1, 0, 0, 1, 1, 0, ...) suffice. Trivial speedup techniques were soon standard in maze running, mostly aimed at reducing the wave size. Examples are designating the most off-center terminal as the source, starting waves from both terminals, and limiting the search to a box slightly larger than the minimum containing the terminals.

More significant techniques to reduce complexity were discovered in the second part of the decade. There are two techniques that deserve a mention in retrospective. The first technique, line probing, was discovered by David W. Hightower [5] and independently by Koichi Mikami and Kinya Tabuchi [6]. It addressed both the memory and time aspects of the router's complexity. The idea is for each so-called base point to investigate the perpendicular line segments that contain the base point and extend those segments to the first obstacles on their way. The first base points are the terminals and their lines are called trial lines of level 0. Mikami and Tabuchi choose next as base points all grid points on the lines thus generated. The trial lines of the next level are the line segments perpendicular to the trial line containing their base point. The process is stopped when lines originating from different terminals intersect. The algorithm guarantees a path if one exists and it will have the lowest possible number of bends. This guarantee soon becomes very expensive, because all possible trial lines of the deepest possible level have to be examined. Hightower therefore traded it for more efficiency in the early stages by limiting the base points to the so-called escape points, that is, only the closest grid point that allows extension beyond the obstacle that blocked the trial line of the previous level. Line expansion, a combination of maze running and line probing, came some ten years later [7], with the salient feature of producing a path whenever one existed, though not necessarily with the minimum number of bends.

The essence of line probing is in working with line segments for representing the routing space and paths. Intuitively, it saves memory and time, especially when the search space is not congested. The complexity very much depends on the data structures maintained by the algorithm. The original papers were vague about this, and it was not until the 1980s that specialists in computational geometry could come up with a rigorous analysis [8]. In practice, line probers were used for the first nets with distant terminals. Once the routing space gets congested, more like a labyrinth where trial lines are bound to be very short, a maze runner takes over.

The second technique worth mentioning is based on the observation that from a graph theoretical point of view, Lee's router is just a breadth-first search that may take advantage of special features like regularity and bipartiteness. But significant speed advantage can be achieved by including a sense of direction in the wave propagation phase, preferring cells closer to the target. Frank Rubin [9] implements such an idea by sorting the cells in the wavefront with a key representing the grid distance to the target. It shifts the character of the algorithm from breadth-first to depth-first search.

This came close to what was developed simultaneously, but in the field of artificial intelligence: the A* algorithm [10]. Here the search is ordered by an optimistic estimate of the source–target pathlength through the cell. The sum of the number of steps to reach that cell (exactly as in the original paper of Lee) plus the grid distance to the target (as introduced by Rubin) is a satisfactory estimate, because the result can never be more than that estimate. This means that it will find the shortest route, while exploring the least number of grid cells. See Chapter 23 for a more detailed description of maze routing.

Lee's concept combined with A* is still the basis of modern industrial routers. But many more issues than just the shortest two-pin net have to be considered. An extension to multiterminal nets is easy (e.g., after connecting two pins, take the cells on that route as the initial wavefront and find the shortest path to another terminal, etc.), but it will not in general produce the shortest connecting tree (for this the Steiner problem on a grid has to be solved, a well-known NP-hard problem, which is discussed in Chapter 24). Routing in many wiring layers can also straightforwardly be incorporated by adopting a three-dimensional grid. Even bipartiteness is preserved, but looses its significance because of preferences in layers and usually built-in resistance against creating vias. The latter and some other desirable features can be taken care of by using other cost functions than just distance and tuning these costs for satisfactory results. Also a net ordering strategy has to be determined, mostly to achieve close to full wire list completion. And taking into account sufficient effects of modern technology (e.g., cross talk, antenna phenomena, metal fill, lithography demands) makes router design a formidable task, today even more than in the past. This will be the subject of Chapters 34 through 36 and 38.

2.1.2 ASSIGNMENT AND PLACEMENT

Placement is initially seen as an assignment problem where n modules have to be assigned to at least n slots. The easiest formulation associated a cost with every module assignment to each slot, independent of other assignments. The Hungarian method (also known as Munkres' algorithm [11]) was already known and solved the problem in polynomial time. This was however an unsatisfactory problem formulation, and the cost function was soon replaced by

$$\sum_i a_{i,p(i)} + \sum_{i,j} c_{i,j} d_{p(i),p(j)}$$

where

$d_{p(i),p(j)}$ is the distance between the slots assigned to modules i and j
$a_{i,p(i)}$ is a cost associated with assigning module i to slot $p(i)$
$c_{i,j}$ is a weight factor (e.g., the number of wires between module i and j) penalizing the distance between the modules i and j

With all $c_{i,j}$ equal to zero, it reduces to the assignment problem above and with all a equal to zero, it is called the quadratic assignment problem that is now known to be NP hard (the traveling salesperson problem is but a special case).

Paul C. Gilmore [12] soon provided (in 1962) a branch-and-bound solution to the quadratic assignment problem, even before that approach had got this name. In spite of its bounding techniques, it was already impractical for some 15 modules, and was therefore unable to replace an earlier heuristic of Leon Steinberg [13]. He used the fact that the problem can be easily solved when all $c_{i,j} = 0$, in an iterative technique to find an acceptable solution for the general problem. His algorithm generated some independent sets (originally all maximal independent sets, but the algorithm generated independent sets in increasing size and one can stop any time). For each such set, the wiring cost for all its members for all positions occupied by that set (and the empty positions) was calculated. These numbers are of course independent of the positions of the other members of that set. By applying the Hungarian method, these modules were placed with minimum cost. Cycling through these independent sets continues until no improvement is achieved during one complete cycle. Steinberg's method was repeatedly improved and generalized in 1960s.*

Among the other iterative methods to improve such assignments proposed in these early years were force-directed relaxation [14] and pairwise interchange [15]. In the former method, two modules in a placement are assumed to attract each other with a force proportional to their distance. The proportionality constant is something like the weight factor $c_{i,j}$ above. As a result, a module is subjected to a resultant force that is the vector sum of all attracting forces between pairs it is involved in. If modules could move freely, they would move to the lowest energy state of the system. This

---

* Steinberg's 34-module/36-slot example, the first benchmark in layout synthesis, is only recently optimally solved for Euclidean norm, almost 40 years after its publication in 1961. The wirelength was 4119.74. The best result of the 1960s was by Frederick S. Hiller (4475.28).

is mostly not a desirable assignment because many modules may opt for the same slot. Algorithms therefore are moved one module at a time to a position close to the zero-tension point

$$\left(\frac{\sum_i c_{Mi} x_i}{\sum_i c_{Mi}}, \frac{\sum_i c_{Mi} y_i}{\sum_i c_{Mi}} \right)$$

Of course, if there is a free slot there, it can be assigned to it. If not, the module occupying it can be moved in the same way if it is not already at its zero-tension point. Numerous heuristics to start and restart a sequence of such moves are imaginable, and kept the idea alive for the decennia to come, only to mature around the year 2000 as can be seen in Chapter 18.

A simple method to avoid occupied slots is pairwise interchange. Two modules are selected and if interchanging their slot positions improves the assignment, the interchange takes place. Of course only the cost contribution of the signal nets involved has to be updated. However, the pair selection is not obvious. Random selection is an option, ordering modules by connectedness was already tried before 1960, and using the forces above in various ways quickly followed after the idea got in publication. But a really satisfactory pair selection was not shown to exist.

The constructive methods in the remainder of that decade had the same problem. They were ad-hoc heuristics based on a selection rule (the next module to be placed had to have the strongest bond with the ones already placed) followed by a positioning rule (such as pair linking and cluster development). They were used in industrial tools of 1970s, but were readily replaced by simulated annealing when that became available. But one development was overlooked, probably because it was published in a journal not at all read by the community involved in layout synthesis. It was the first analytic placer [16], minimizing in one dimension

$$\sum_{i,j=1}^{n} c_{ij} \left[p(i) - p(j) \right]^2$$

with the constraints $\mathbf{p}^T \mathbf{p} = 1$ and $\sum_i p(i) = 0$, to avoid the trivial solution where all components of $\mathbf{p}$ are the same. That is, an objective that is the weighted sum of all squared distances. Simply rewriting that objective in matrix notation yields

$$2\mathbf{p}^T \mathbf{A} \mathbf{p}$$

where $\mathbf{A} = \mathbf{D} - \mathbf{C}, \mathbf{D}$ being the diagonal matrix of row sums of $\mathbf{C}$. All eigenvalues of such a matrix are nonnegative. If the wiring structure is connected, there will be exactly one eigenvalue of $\mathbf{A}$ equal to 0 (corresponding to that trivial solution), and the eigenvector associated with the next smallest eigenvalue will minimize the objective under the given constraints. The minimization problem is the same for the other dimension, but to avoid a solution where all modules would be placed on one line we add the constraint that the two vectors must be orthogonal. The solution of the two-dimensional problem is the one where the coordinates correspond with the components of the eigenvectors associated with second and third smallest eigenvalues.

The placement method is called Hall placement to give credit to the inventor Kenneth M. Hall. When applied to the placement of components on chip or board, it corresponds to the quadratic placement problem. Whether this is the right way to formulate the wire-length objective will be extensively discussed in Chapters 17 and 18, but it predates the first analytic placer in layout synthesis by more than a decade!

2.1.3 SINGLE-LAYER WIRING

Most of the above industrial developments were meant for printed circuit boards (in which integrated circuits with at most a few tens of transistors are interconnected in two or more layers) and backplanes (in which boards are combined and connected). Integrated circuits were not yet subject to automation. Research, both in industry and academia, started to get interesting toward the end of the decade. With only one metal layer available, the link with graph planarity was quickly discovered. Lots of effort went into designing planarity tests, a problem soon to be solved with linear-time algorithms. What was needed, of course, was planarization: using technological possibilities (sharing collector islands, small diffusion resistors, multiple substrate contacts, etc.) to implement a circuit using a planarized model. Embedding the planar result onto the plane while accounting for the formation of isolated islands, and connecting the component pins were the remaining steps [17].

Today the constraints of those early chips are obsolete. Extensions are still of some validity in analogue applications, but are swamped by a multitude of more severe demands. Planarization resurfaced when rectangular duals got attention in floorplan design. Planar mapping as used in these early design flows started a whole new area in graph theory, the so-called visibility graphs, but without further applications in layout synthesis.*

The geometry of the islands provided the first models for rectangular dissections and their optimization, and for the compaction algorithms based on longest path search in constraint graphs. These graphs, originally called polar graphs and illustrated in Figure 2.3, were borrowed† from early works in combinatorics (how to dissect rectangles into squares?) [20]. They enabled systematic generations of all dissection topologies, and for each such topology a set of linear equations as part of the optimization tableau for obtaining the smallest rectangle under (often linearized) constraints. The generation could not be done in polynomial time of course, but linear optimization was later proven to be efficient.

A straightforward application of Lee's router for single-layer wiring was not adequate, because planarity had to be preserved. Its ideas however were used in what was a first form of contour routing. Contour routing turned out to be useful in the more practical channel routers of the 1980s.

2.2 EMERGING HIERARCHIES (1970–1980)

Ten years of design automation for layout synthesis produced a small research community with a firm basis in graph theory and a growing awareness of computational complexity. Stephen Cook's famous theorem was not yet published and complexity issues were tackled by bounding techniques, smart speedups, and of course heuristics. Ultimately, and in fact quite soon, they proved to be insufficient. Divide-and-conquer strategies were the obvious next approaches, leading to hierarchies, both uniform requiring few well-defined subproblems and pluriform leaving many questions unanswered.

2.2.1 DECOMPOSING THE ROUTING SPACE

A very effective and elegant way of decomposing a problem was achieved by dividing the routing space into channels, and solving each channel by using a channel router. It found immediate application in two design styles: standard cell or polycell where the channels were height adjustable and channel routing tried to use as few tracks as possible (Figure 2.2 for terminology), and gate arrays where the channels had a fixed height, which meant that channel router had to find a solution within a given number of tracks. If efficient minimization were possible, the same algorithm would suffice, of course. The decision problems, however, were shown to be NP complete.

The classical channel-routing problem allows two layers of wires: one containing the pins at grid positions and all latitudinal parts (branches), exactly one per pin, and one containing all longitudinal parts (trunks), exactly one for each net. This generates two kinds of constraints: nets with overlapping intervals need different tracks (these are called horizontal constraints), and wires that have pins at the same longitudinal height must change layer before they overlap (the so-called vertical constraints).

---

* In this context, they were called horvert representations [18].
† The introduction of polar graphs in layout synthesis [19] was one on the many contributions that Tatsuo Ohtsuki gave to the community.

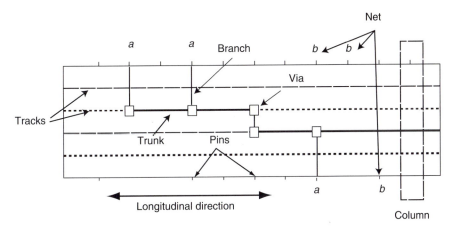

FIGURE 2.2 Terminology in channel routing.

The problem does not always have a solution. If the vertical constraints form cycles, then the routing cannot be completed in the classical model. Otherwise a routing does exist, but finding the minimum number of tracks is NP hard [21].

In the absence of vertical constraints, the problem can be solved optimally in almost linear time by a pretty simple algorithm [22], originally owing to Akihiro Hashimoto and James Stevens, that is known as the left-edge algorithm.* Actually there are two simple greedy implementations both delivering a solution with the minimum number of tracks. One is filling the tracks one by one from left to right each time trying the unplaced intervals in sequence of their left edges. The other places the intervals in that sequence in the first available track that can take it. In practice, the left-edge algorithm gets quite far in routing channels, in spite of possible vertical constraints. Many heuristics therefore started with left-edge solutions.

To obtain a properly wired channel in two layers, the requirements that latitudinal parts are one-to-one with the pins and that each net can have only one longitudinal part are mostly dropped by introducing doglegs.† Allowing doglegs enables in practice always a two-layer routing with latitudinal and longitudinal parts never in the same layer, although in theory problems exist that cannot be solved. It has been shown that the presence of a single column without pins guarantees the existence of a solution [23]. Finding the solution with the least number of tracks remains NP hard [24].

Numerous channel routers have been published, mainly because it was a problem that could be easily isolated. The most effective implementation, without the more or less artificial constraints of the classical problem and its derivations, is the contour router of Patrick R. Groeneveld [25]. It solves all problems although in practice not many really difficult channels were encountered. In modern technologies, with a number of layers approaching ten, channel routing has lost its significance.

2.2.2 NETLIST PARTITIONING

Layout synthesis starts with a netlist, that is, an incidence structure or hypergraph with modules as nodes and nets as hyperedges. The incidences are the pins. These nets quickly became very large,

---

* It is often referred to as an algorithm for coloring an interval graph. This is not correct, because an interval representation is assumed to be available. It is, however, possible to color an interval graph in polynomial time. One year after the publication of the left-edge algorithm, Yanakakis Gavril gave such an algorithm for chordal graphs of which interval graphs are but a special case.

† Originally, doglegs were only allowed at pin positions. The longitudinal parts might be broken up in several longitudinal segments. The dogleg router of that paper was probably never implemented and the presented result was edited. The paper became nevertheless the most referenced paper in the field because it presented the benchmark known as the Deutsch difficult example. Every channel router in the next 20 years had to show its performance when solving that example.

in essence following Moore's law of exponential complexity growth. Partitioning was seen as the way to manage complex design. Familiarity with partitioning was already present, because the first pioneers were involved in or close to teams that had to make sure that subsystems of a logic design could be built in cabinets of convenient size. These subsystems were divided over cards, and these cards might contain replaceable standard units. One of these pioneers, Uno R. Kodres, who had already provided in 1959 an algorithm for the geometrical positioning of circuit elements [26] in a computer, possibly the first placement algorithm in the field, gave an excellent overview of these early partitioners [27]. They started with one or more seed modules for each block in the partitioning. Then, based once more on a selection rule, blocks are extended by assigning one module at a time to one block. Many variations are possible and were tried, but all these early attempts were soon wiped out by module migration methods, and first by the one of Brian W. Kernighan and Shen Lin [28]. They started from a balanced two-partition of the netlist, that is, division of all modules into two nonoverlapping blocks of approximately equal size. The quality of that two-partition was measured in the number of nets connecting modules in both blocks, the so-called cutsize. This number was to be made as low as possible. This was tried in a number of iterations. For each iteration, the gain of swapping two modules, one from each block, was calculated, that is, the reduction in cutsize as a consequence of that swap. Gains can be positive, zero, or negative. The pairs are unlocked and ordered from largest to smallest gain. In that order each unlocked pair is swapped, locked to prevent it from moving back, and its consequence (new blocks and updated gains) is recorded. When all modules (except possibly one) are locked the best cutsize encountered is accepted. A new iteration can take place if there is a positive gain left.

Famous as it is, the Kernighan–Lin procedure left plenty of room for improvement. Halfway in the decade, it was proven that the decision problem of graph partition was NP complete, so the fact that it mostly only produced a local optimum was unavoidable, but the limitations to balanced partitions and only two-pin nets had to be removed. Besides a time-complexity of $O(n^3)$ for an n-module problem was soon unacceptable. The repair of these shortcomings appeared in a 1982 paper by Charles M. Fiduccia and Robert M. Mattheyses [29]. It handled hyperedges (and therefore multipin nets), and instead of pair swapping it used module moves while keeping bounds on balance deviations, possibly with weighted modules. More importantly, it introduced a bucket data structure that enabled a linear-time updating scheme. Details can be found in Chapter 7.

At the same time, one was not unaware of the relation between partitioning and eigenvalues. This relation, not unlike the theory behind Hall's placement [16], was extensively researched by William E. Donath and Alan J. Hoffman [30]. Apart from experiments with simulated annealing (not very adequate for the partitioning problem in spite of the very early analogon with spin glasses) and using migration methods for multiway partitioning, it would be well into the 1990s before partitioning was carefully scrutinized again.

2.2.3 MINCUT PLACEMENT

Applying partitioning in a recursive fashion while at the same time slicing the rectangular silicon estate in two subrectangles according to the area demand of each block is called mincut placement. The process continues until blocks with known layouts or suitable for dedicated algorithms are obtained. The slicing cuts can alternate between horizontal and vertical cuts, or have the direction depend on the shape of the subrectangle or the area demand. Later, also procedures performing four-way partition (quadrisection) along with dividing in four subrectangles were developed. A strict alternation scheme is not necessary and many more sophisticated cut-line sequences have been developed. Melvin A. Breuer's paper [31] on mincut placement did not envision deep partitioning, but large geometrically fixed blocks had to be arranged in a nonoverlapping configuration by positioning and orienting. Ulrich Lauther [32] connected the process with the polar graph illustrated in Figure 2.3. The mincut process by itself builds a series-parallel polar graph, but Lauther also defined three local operations, to wit mirroring, rotating, and squeezing, that more or less preserved the relative positions.

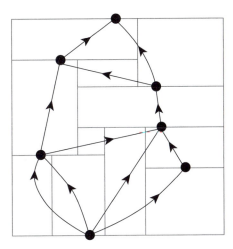

FIGURE 2.3 Polar graph of a rectangle dissection.

The first two are pretty obvious and do not change the topology of the polar graph. The last one, squeezing, does change the graph and might result in a polar graph that is not series parallel.

The intuition behind mincut placement is that if fewer wires cross the first cut lines, there will be fewer long connections in the final layout. An important drawback of the early mincut placers, however, is that they treat lower levels of partitioning independent from the blocks created earlier, that is, without any awareness of the subrectangles to which connected modules were assigned. Modules in those external blocks may be connected to modules in the block to be partitioned, and be forced unnecessarily far from those modules. Al Dunlop and Kernighan [33] therefore tried to capture such connectivities by propagating modules external to the block to be partitioned as fixed terminals to the periphery of that block. This way their connections to the inner modules are taken into account when calculating cutsizes. Of course, now the order in which blocks are treated has an impact on the final result.

2.2.4 CHIP FABRICATION AND LAYOUT STYLES

Layout synthesis provides masks for chip fabrication, or more precisely, it provides data structures from which masks are derived. Hundreds of masks may be needed in a modern process, and with today's feature sizes, optical correction is needed in addition to numerous constraints on the configurations. Still, layout synthesis is only concerned with a few partitions of the Euclidean plane to specify these masks.

When all masks are specific to producing a particular chip, we speak of full-custom design. It is the most expensive setup and usually needs high volume to be cost effective. Generic memory always was in that category, but certain application specific designs also qualified. Even in the early 1970s, the major computer seller of the day saw the advantage of sharing masks over as many as possible different products. They called it the master image, but it became known ten years later as the gate-array style in the literature. Customization in these styles was limited to the connection layers, that is, the layers in which fixed rows of components were provided with their interconnect. Because many masks were never changed in a generation of gate-array designs, these were known as semi-custom designs. Wiring was kept in channels of fixed width in early gate arrays.

Another master-image style was developed in the 1990s that differed from gate arrays by not leaving space for wires between the components. It was called sea-of-gates, because the unwired chip was mostly nothing else than alternating rows of p-type and n-type metal oxide semiconductor (MOS)-transistors. Contacts with the gates were made on either side of the row, although channel contacts were made between the gates. A combination of routers was used to achieve this over-the-cell routing. The routers were mostly based on channel routers developed for full-custom chips.

Early field programmable gate arrays predated (and survived) the sea-of-gates approach, which never became more than niche in the cost-profit landscape of the chip market. It allows individualization away from the chip production plant by establishing or removing small pieces of interconnect.

Academia believed in full-custom, probably biased by its initial focus on chips for analogue applications. Much of their early adventures in complete chip design for digital applications grew out of the experience described in Section 2.1.3 and were encouraged by publications from researchers in industry such as Satoshi Goto [34], and Bryan T. Preas and Charles W. Gwyn [35]. Rather than a methodology, suggested by the award-winning paper in 1978, it established a terminology. Macrocell layout and general-cell assemblies in particular remained for several years names for styles without much of a method behind it.

Standard-cell (or polycell) layout was a full-custom style that lent itself to automation. Cells with uniform height and aligned supply and clock lines were called from a library to form rows in accordance with a placement result. Channel routing was used to determine the geometry of the wires in between the rows. The main difference with gate-array channels was that the width was to be determined by the algorithm. Whereas in gate-array styles, the routers had to fit all interconnect in channels of fixed width, the problem in standard-cell layouts was to minimize the number of tracks, and whatever the result, reserve enough space on the chip to accommodate them.

2.3 ITERATION-FREE DESIGN

By 1980, industrial tools had developed in what was called spaghetti code, depending on a few people with inside knowledge of how it had developed from the initial straightforward idea sufficient for the simple examples of the early 1970s, into a sequence of patches with multiple escapes from where it could end up in almost any part of the code. In the meantime, academia were dreaming of compiling chips. Carver A. Mead and Lynn (or Robert) Conway wrote the seminal textbook [36] on very large scale integration between 1977 and 1979, and, although not spelled out, the idea of (automatically) deriving masks from a functional specification was born shortly after the publication in 1980. A year later, David L. Johannsen defended his thesis on silicon compilation.

2.3.1 FLOORPLAN DESIGN

From the various independent algorithms for special problems grew the layout synthesis as constrained optimization: wirelength and area minimization under technology design rules. The target was functionality with acceptable yield. Speed was not yet an issue. Optimum performance was achieved with multichip designs, and it would take another ten years before single-chip microprocessors would come into their ball park.

The real challenge in those days was the phase problem between placement and routing. Obviously, placement has a great impact on what is achievable with routing, and can even render unroutable configurations. Yet, it was difficult to think about routing without coordinates, geometrical positions of modules with pins to be connected. The dream of silicon compilation and designs scalable over many generations of technology was in 1980 not more than a firm belief in hierarchical approaches with little to go by apart from severe restrictions in routing architecture.* A breakthrough came with the introduction of the concept of floorplans in the design trajectory of chips by Ralph H.J.M. Otten [37]. A floorplan was a data structure capturing relative positions rather than fixed

---

* There was an exception: when in 1970 Akers teamed up with James M. Geyer and Donald L. Roberts [38] and tried grid expansion to make designs routable. It consisted of finding cuts of horizontal and vertical segments of only conductor areas in one direction and conductor free lines in the other. Furthermore, the cutting segment in the conductor area should be perpendicular to all wires cut. The problems that it created were an early inspiration for slicing.

coordinates. In a sense, floorplan design is a generalization of placement. Instead of manipulating fixed geometrical objects in a nonoverlapping arrangement in the plane, floorplan design treats modules as objects with varying degrees of flexibility and tries to decide on their position relative to the position of others.

In the original paper, the relative positions were captured by a point configuration in the plane. By a clever transformation of the netlist into the so-called dutch metric, an optimal embedding of these points could be obtained. The points became the centers of rectangular modules with an appropriate size that led to a set of overlapping rectangles when the point configuration was more or less fit in the assessed chip footprint. The removal of overlap was done by formulating the problem as a mathematical program.

Other data structures than Cartesian coordinates were proposed. A significant related data structure was the sequence pair of Hiroshi Murata, Kunihiro Fujiyoshi, Shigetoshi Nakatake, and Yoji Kajitani in 1997 [39]. Before that, a number of graphs, including the good old-polar graphs from combinatorial theory, were used and especially around the year 2000 many other proposals were published. Chapters 9 through 11 will describe several floorplan data structures.

The term floorplan design came from house architecture. Already in 1960s, James Grason [40] tried to convert preferred neighbor relationships into rectangles realizing these relations. The question came down to whether a given graph of such relations had a rectangular dual. He characterized such graphs in a forbidden-graph theorem. The algorithms he proposed were hopelessly complex, but the ideas found new following in the mid-1980s. Soon simple, necessary, and sufficient conditions were formulated, and Jayaram Bhasker and Sartaj Sahni produced in 1986 a linear-time algorithm for testing the existence of a rectangular dual and, in case of the affirmative, constructing a corresponding dissection [41].

The success of floorplanning was partially due to giving answers that seemed to fit the questions of the day like a glove: it lent itself naturally to hierarchical approaches* and enabled global wiring as a preparation for detailed routing that took place after the geometrical optimization of the floorplan. It was also helped by the fact that the original method could reconstruct good solutions from abstracted data in extremely short computation times even for thousands of modules. The latter was also a weakness because basically it was the projection of a multidimensional Euclidean space with the exact Dutch distances onto the plane of its main axes. Significant distances perpendicular to that plane were annihilated.

2.3.2 Cell Compilation

Hierarchical application of floorplanning ultimately leads to modules that are not further dissected. They are to be filled with a library cell, or by a special algorithm determining the layout of that cell depending on specification and assessed environment. The former has a shape constraint with fixed dimensions (sometimes rotatable). The latter is often macrocells with a standard-cell layout style. They lead to staircase functions as shape constraints where a step corresponds to a choice of the number of rows.

In the years of research toward silicon compilers, circuit families tended to grow. The elementary static complementary metal oxide semiconductor (CMOS)-gate has limitations, specifically in the number of transistors in series. This limits the number of distinct gates severely. The new circuit techniques allowed larger families. Domino logic, for example, having only a pull-down network determining its function, allows much more variety. Single gates with up to 60 transistors have been used in designs of the 1980s. This could only be supported if cells could be compiled from their functional specification.

The core of the problem was finding a linear-transistor array, where only transistors sharing contact areas could be neighbors. This implied that the charge or discharge network needed a topology of an Euler graph. In static cmos, both networks had to be Eulerian, preferably with the same sequence

---

* Many even identified floorplanning with hierarchical layout design, clearly an undervaluation of the concept.

of input signals controlling the gate. The problem even attracted a later fields medallist in the person of Curtis T. McMullen [42], but the final word came from the thesis of Robert L. Maziasz [43], a student of John P. Hayes. Once the sequence was established, the left-edge algorithm could complete the network, if the number of tracks would fit on the array, which was a mild constraint in practice; but an interesting open question for research is to find an Euler path leading to a number of tracks under a given maximum.

2.3.3 LAYOUT COMPACTION

Area minimization was considered to be the most important objective in layout synthesis before 1990. It was believed that other objectives such as minimum signal delay and yield would benefit from it. A direct relation between yield and active area was not difficult to derive and with gate delay dominating the overall speed performance, chips usually came out faster than expected. The placement tools of the day had the reputation of using more chip area than needed, a belief that was based mainly on the fact that manual design often outperformed automatic generation of cell layouts. This was considered infeasible for emerging chip complexities, and it was felt that a final compaction step could only improve the result. Systematic ways of taking a complete layout of a chip and producing a smaller design-rule correct chip, while preserving the topology, therefore became of much interest.

Compaction is difficult (one may see it as the translation of topologies in the graph domain to mask geometries that have to satisfy the design rules of the target technology). Several concepts were proposed to provide a handle on the problem: symbolic layout systems, layout languages, virtual grids, etc. At the bottom, there is the combinatorial problem of minimizing the size of a complicated arrangement of many objects in several related and aligned planes. Even for simple abstractions the two-dimensional problem is complex (most of them are NP hard). An acceptable solution was often found in a sequence of one-dimensional compactions, combined with heuristics to handle the interaction between the two dimensions (sometimes called $1\frac{1}{2}$-compaction). Many one-dimensional compaction routines are efficiently solvable, often in linear time. The basis is found in longest-path problem, already popular in this context during 1970s. Compaction is discussed in several texts on VLSI physical design such as those authored by Majid Sarrafzadeh and Chak-Kuen Wong [44], Sadiq M. Sait and Habib Youssef [45], and Naveed Sherwani [46], but above all in the book of Thomas Lengauer [47].

2.3.4 FLOORPLAN OPTIMIZATION

Floorplan optimization is the derivation of a compatible (i.e., relative positions of the floorplan are respected) rectangle dissection, optimal under a given contour score e.g., area and perimeter that are possibly constrained, in which each undissected rectangle satisfies its shape constraint. A shape constraint can be a size requirement with or without minima imposed on the lengths of its sides, but in general any constraint where the length of one side is monotonically nonincreasing with respect to the length of the other side.

The common method well into the 1980s was to capture the relative positions as Kirchhoff equations of the polar graph. This yields a set of linear equalities. For piecewise linear shape constraints that are convex, a number of linear inequalities can be added. The perimeter can then be optimized in polynomial time. For nonconvex shape constraints or nonlinear objectives, one had to resort to branch-and-bound or cutting-plane methods: for general rectangle dissections with nonconvex shape constraints the problem is NP hard. Larry Stockmeyer [48] proved that even a pseudo-polynomial algorithm does not exist when $P \neq NP$.

The initial success of floorplan design was, beside the facts mentioned in Section 2.3.1, also due to a restraint that was introduced already in the original paper. It was called slicing because the geometry of compatible rectangle dissection was recognizable by cutting lines recursively slicing completely through the rectangle. That is rectangles resulting from slicing the parent rectangle could either be sliced as well or were not further dissected. This induces a tree, the slicing tree, which in an hierarchical approach that started with a functional hierarchy produced a refinement: functional submodules remained descendants of their supermodule.

More importantly, many optimization problems were tractable for slicing structures, among which was floorplan optimization. A rectangle dissection has the slicing property iff its polar graph is series parallel. It is straightforward to derive the slicing tree from that graph. Dynamic programming can then produce a compatible rectangle dissection, optimal under any quasi-concave contour score, and satisfying all shape constraints [49]. Also labeling a partition tree with slicing directions can be done optimally in polynomial time if the tree is more or less balanced and the shape constraints are staircase functions as Lengauer [50] showed. Together with Lukas P.P.P. van Ginneken, Otten then showed that floorplans given as point configurations could be converted to such optimal rectangle dissections, compatible in the sense that slices in the same slice respect the relative point positions [51]. The complexity of that optimization for N rectangles was however $\mathcal{O}(N^6)$, unacceptable for hundreds of modules. The procedure was therefore not used for more than 30 modules, and was reduced to $\mathcal{O}(N^3)$ by simple but reasonable tricks. Modules with more than 30 modules were treated as flexible rectangles with limitations on their aspect ratio.

2.3.5   BEYOND LAYOUT SYNTHESIS

It cannot be denied that research in layout synthesis had an impact on optimization in other contexts and optimization in general. The left-edge algorithm may be rather simple and restricted (it needs an interval representation), simulated annealing is of all approaches the most generic. A patent request was submitted in 1981 by C. Daniel Gelatt and E. Scott Kirkpatrick, but by then its implementation (MCPlace) was already compared (by having Donald W. Jepsen watching the process at a screen and resetting temperature if it seemed stuck in local minimum) against IBM's warhorse in placement (APlace) and soon replaced it [52]. Independent research by Vladimir Cerny [53] was conducted around the same time. Both used the metropolis loop from 1953 [54] that analyzed energy content of a system of particles at a given temperature, and used an analogy from metallurgy were large crystals with few defects were obtained by annealing, that is, controlled slow cooling.

The invention was called simulated annealing but could not be called an optimization algorithm because of many uncertainties about the schedule (begin temperature, decrements, stopping criterion, loop length, etc.) and the manual intervention. The annealing algorithm was therefore developed from the idea to optimize the performance within a given amount of elapsed CPU time to be used [55]. Given this one parameter, the algorithm resolved the uncertainties by creating a Markov chain that enhanced the probability of a low final score.

The generic nature of the method led to many applications. Further research, notably by Sara A. Solla, Gregory B. Sorkin, and Steve R. White, showed that, in spite of some statements about its asymptotic behavior, annealing was not the method of choice in many cases [56]. Even the application described in the original paper of 1983, graph partitioning, did not allow the construction of a state space suitable for efficient search in that way. It was also shown however that placement with wirelength minimization as objective lent itself quite well, in the sense that even simple pairwise interchange produced a space with the properties shown to be desirable by the above researchers. Carl Sechen exploited that fact and with coworkers he created a sequence of releases of the widely used timberwolf program [57], a tool based on annealing for placement. It is described in detail in Chapter 16.

It is not at all clear that simulated annealing performs well for floorplan design where sizes of objects differ in orders of magnitude. Yet, almost invariably, it is the method of choice. There was of course the success of Martin D.F. Wong and Chung Laung (Dave) Liu [58] who represented the slicing tree in polish notation and defined a move set on it (that move set by the way is not unbiased, violating a requirement underlying many statements about annealing). Since then the community has been flooded with innovative representations of floorplans, slicing and nonslicing, each time resorting to annealing as the underlying design engine, without attention for configuring the state space. Nevertheless, it is the structure of the local minima,* determined by the move set that is crucial for a reliable application of annealing.

2.4 CLOSURE PROBLEMS

The introduction of the fruits of design automation of the 1980s in industry generated mostly distrust and disbelief among designers. No longer was it simply computer-aided design limited to liberating them from routine, but tedious tasks that were reliably performed for them with predictable results. Modules were absorbed, duplicated, split, and spread, and signal nets had disappeared. The whole structure of a design might have changed beyond recognition after a single run of retiming. In many places, designers felt insecure and the introduction of new tools hampered production rather than boosting it.

Layout synthesis got its share of this skepticism. One of its pioneers phrased it as layout is on its way out. Yet, there was a solid background in algorithms and heuristics, and a better understanding of the problem and its context. Many of the original approaches were revisited, improved and, above all, compared with others on the basis of a common meaningful set of benchmarks. No longer was it acceptable to publish yet another heuristic for a well-known subtask of the layout synthesis problem with some self-selected examples to suggest effectiveness and efficiency. This book provides ample evidence that tool making for layout synthesis matured after 1995. The perfection and adaptation of these tools for the ongoing evolution of silicon technologies is the major achievement of the 1990s.

Beside reliable tools supported by rigorous proofs and unbiased comparison, additional shifts were needed. The field developed over three decades from translating intuition into (interactive) procedures, over formulation of well-defined optimization problems, toward integral trajectories without global iteration. This was feasible as long as there was a dominant objective: get it on a chip that is manufacturable. Wire-length minimization served as such an objective. There was some intuition that short wires were good for area, speed, and power, but they were not a target. In the pioneering stages, this was surprisingly successful: most designs were faster than expected and power was not yet a problem.

By 1990, this was no longer enough. Certainly, speed became an important performance characteristic, and it was foreseeable that it would not stay the only additional one. It inspired formulations where one characteristic was optimized under constraints for the other characteristics. They were called closure problems: one aspect was to be guaranteed (closed), while others were handled as well as possible.

2.4.1 WIRING CLOSURE

The research aiming at silicon compilation can therefore be viewed as wiring closure. The phase problem of placement and routing where unroutable placements might occur, and, with the increased chip complexity, not easily repaired, was solved by introducing restrained floorplans. Floorplans only captured relative positions, but combined with efficient optimization, they could provide enough information to perform global routing. The technology of that era, which allowed not more than two wiring layers and therefore kept routing separate from the so-called active area, benefited from the decomposition of the wiring space into channels. Global wiring was therefore in essence assigning wires to channels.

When adopting slicing as a restraint, a number of conflicts can be avoided. An important property of slicing structures is that detailed routing can be done with a single algorithm: channel routing.

---

* Sara A. Solla, Gregory B. Sorkin, and Steve R. White [56] proposed a measure for the ultrametricity of the space of local minima and the barriers between them. A good state space should be close to ultrametric. The proposed measure was the correlation between the heights of the higher two barriers in every triple of minima. Placement of equal-sized objects score close to 1, although partitioning typically ends up with 0.6.

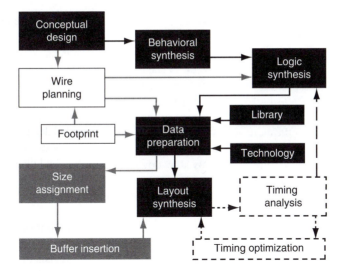

FIGURE 2.4   Modern flows in design automation.

That is, there is a sequence in which channels can be routed with fully specified longitudinal pin positions. Switch boxes are not necessary. Moreover, channels are just rectangles between the slices, with a shape constraint based on the information provided by the global router (almost all channels can be routed close to density, and density can be estimated when there is a good idea of where the pins of the nets are going to be).

Shapes only have to be assessed, and the assessment can be updated whenever more information comes available. Once the cell assemblers (among which channel routers) are called, the shapes become final. Floorplan optimization can then be called to convert the floorplan into a placement with exact coordinates. Slicing floorplans can be optimized quickly. Therefore, there is no harm in calling it whenever convenient. Thus, iteration-free synthesis was enabled. Figure 2.4 shows in the black boxes a generic iteration-free flow. The essence is that each block makes its decisions once and the flow never goes back to it. In the reality of the 1980s, slicing guaranteed wiring when used in a (possibly hierarchical) floorplanning context. With more wiring layers available, the premise of this solution was no longer valid.

2.4.2   Timing Closure

The first reaction to demands concerning speed were to include timing analysis in the tool set. After producing the geometry of the layout, the netlist got extended with parasitics and other network elements to determine its performance. The dynamical tuning of net weights was never a good idea because of convergence problems. Soon wire-load models were developed to obtain more precise estimates and indications where the critical paths were. Transistor sizing, buffer insertion, and fanout tree construction could then improve timing without changing the logic. It did not take long before logic resynthesis entered the scene, using these load models to make another netlist with hopefully better timing properties. In Figure 2.4, this is indicated by the dashed boxes and arrows.

All these measures introduced iteration, the latter even global iteration over almost the complete trajectory. And still it could only produce just another local optimum, not likely to be global. In other words, if timing demands were not met, one was never sure whether that was because the technology of the day could not provide it or the tool set simply did not find it. With Moore's law of unforgiving push behind the chip market, this was not satisfactory.

A paradigm shift was needed and was found by adopting a delay model for gates that had roots in a paper by Ivan E. Sutherland and Robert F. Sproull [59], and was justified in practice by Joel

Grodstein, Eric Lehman, Heather Harkness, William J. Grundmann, and Yoshinori Watanabe [60]. The key observation was that the size of a gate with constant delay varies linearly with the load. Writing this down for a network (not necessarily acyclic) leads to solving a set of linear equations for gate sizes (a so-called Leontieff system), which can be iteratively updated with the sizes to adjust the capacitive loads, and will surely converge if there are no limitations on the gate sizes [61]. Timing could be guaranteed (if feasible) for networks that could be modeled with lumped capacitances, which was true for all networks within the scope of the logic synthesis tools in those days.

With timing no longer the more or less arbitrary outcome of an optimization with area/wire length as its objective, the uncertainty shifted to area. Buffer insertion kept a spot in the flow, but now no longer for improving speed. Buffers can only slow down a path in a network sized by the Leontieff method. Timing can only be kept within the specification when buffers are inserted in noncritical paths with enough slack. That might be beneficial, because it may save area, but it would never make the network faster. In addition, the flow became iteration free again as can be seen in Figure 2.4 with only the black and grey boxes included.

2.4.3 WIRE PLANNING

The complexity of chips in the meantime had developed from a state in which delay was mainly caused by capacitive loads, predominantly gate capacitances, to a situation where most of the global delay was in the wires. Whereas the Sutherland model maintains it salient property as long as resistance between the gate and its load could be neglected, it was of little value when performance critically depends on the distributed resistance and capacitance of wires on today's chips. A delay model published shortly after the Second World War [62], named Elmore delay after the author, was the basis of much of the research on performance of designs in silicon in the second half of the decade of the 1990s. It was pretty accurate for point-to-point connections when it predicted that the delay of long wires depended quadratically on their lengths. It could also be used in combination with the buffer models of Takayasu Sakurai [63] to show that when optimally segmented, the delay became linear in its length (regardless of the size of these buffers). The length of these segments did depend on the layer (or rather on the resistance and capacitance per unit length). An interesting observation however is that the delay of a segment in an optimally segmented and buffered wire (of course also an optimum size can be determined for the buffers) does not depend on the layer: it depends on the properties of the transistors in the buffer. This implies that the delay is known as soon as the process is chosen in which the buffers are going to be made [61].

These theoretical facts open new possibilities for design automation of the backend, and a wealth of opportunities for research. A lot of assumptions are quite idealistic: there is not always place for a buffer at its optimal position, derivations are usually for homogeneous wires, connections are trees in general, etc. But the two observations of delay in length and segment delay independent of layer enable a scenario for wire planning:

1. Assign global wires as connection between modules that synthesis can cope with and therefore so small that buffering does not help in speedup.
2. For given chip performance do time budgeting with convex time-size trade-offs for the modules.
3. Synthesize netlists for the modules with function and delay for all gates.
4. Size the gates for constant delay.

In Figure 2.4, the scenario is depicted (exclude the dashed boxes and arrows) and shows that no global iterations are implied. An initial footprint has to be chosen though, and convex trade-offs (enabling efficient area minimization under timing bounds) have to be available (or extracted). Only after time budgeting is it clear whether the design will fit in the chosen floorplan. Timing closure for large chips is not yet fully solved.

2.5 WHAT DID WE LEARN?

The present goal of design automation has to be design closure, that is, how to specify a function to be implemented on a chip, feed it to an electronic design automation (EDA) tool, and get, without further interaction, a design that meets all requirements concerning functionality, speed, size, power, yield, and other costs. It is the obvious quest of industry and the natural evolution from the sequence of closure problems of the past decennium. Instead of focusing on trade-offs between two or three performance characteristics whenever such a closure problem surfaces such as how to achieve wire-ability in placement of components or modules on a chip, how to allocate resources to optimize schedules, or how to ensure timing convergence with minimal size, a more general approach should be taken that in principle accounts for all combinations of performance characteristics [64].

No doubt the best algorithms developed in layout synthesis in the last 15 years will be key ingredients and will get due attention in this book. Today's practice of offering rigorous background and thorough evaluation, preferably using well-established benchmarks, will be exemplified.

REFERENCES

1. C.Y. Lee, An algorithm for path connections and its applications, *IRE Transactions on Electronic Computers*, EC-10(3): 346–365, September 1961.
2. E.W. Dijkstra, A note on two problems in connexion with graphs, *Numerische Mathematik*, 1: 269–271, 1959.
3. E.F. Moore, Shortest path through a maze, *Annals of the Computation Laboratory of Harvard University*, 30: 285–292, 1959.
4. S.B. Akers, A modification of Lee's path connection algorithm, *IEEE Transactions on Electronic Computers*, EC-16(1): 97–98, February 1967.
5. D.W. Hightower, A solution to line-routing problems on the continuous plane, in *Proceedings of the 6th Design Automation Workshop*, Las Vegas, NV, pp. 1–24, 1969.
6. K. Mikami and K. Kabuchi, A computer program for optimal routing of printed circuit connectors, *IFIPS Proceedings*, H47: 1475–1478, 1968.
7. W. Heyns, W. Sansen, and H. Beke, A line-expansion algorithm for the general routing problem with a guaranteed solution, in *Proceedings of the 17th Design Automation Conference*, Minneapolis, MN, pp. 243–249, 1980.
8. T. Asano, M. Sato, and T. Ohtsuki, Computational geometry algorithms, Chapter 9, in *Layout Design and Verification*, ed. T. Ohtsuki, North-Holland, Amsterdam, the Netherlands, pp. 295–347, 1986.
9. F. Rubin, The lee path connection algorithm, *IEEE Transactions on Computers*, C-23(9): 907–914, September 1974.
10. P.E. Hart, N.J. Nilsson, and B. Raphael, A formal basis for the heuristic determination of minimum cost paths, *IEEE Transactions on Systems Science and Cybernetics*, SSC4(2): 100–107, 1968.
11. J. Munkres, Algorithms for the assignment and transportation problems, *Journal of the Society of Industrial and Applied Mathematics*, 5(1): 32–38, March 1957.
12. P.C. Gilmore, Optimal and suboptimal algorithms for the quadratic assignment problem, *Journal of the Society of Industrial and Applied Mathematics*, 10(2): 305–313, June 1962.
13. L. Steinberg, The backboard wiring problem: A placement algorithm, *Society of Industrial and Applied Mathematics Reviews*, 3(1): 37–50, January 1961.
14. C.J. Fisk, D.L. Caskey, and L.L. West, ACCEL: Automated circuit card etching layout, *Proceedings of the IEEE*, 55(11): 1971–1982, November 1967.
15. M. Hanan and J.M. Kurtzberg, A review of the placement and quadratic assignment problems, *Society of Industrial and Applied Mathematics Reviews*, 14(2): 324–342, April 1972.
16. K.M. Hall, An r-dimensional quadratic placement algorithm, *Management Science*, 17(3): 219–229, November 1970.
17. M.C. van Lier and R.H.J.M. Otten, Automatic IC layout: The model and technology, *IEEE Transactions on Circuits and Systems*, 22(11): 845–855, November 1975.
18. R.H.J.M. Otten and J.G. van Wijk, Graph representations in interactive layout design, in *Proceedings IEEE International Symposium Circuits and Systems*, New York, NY, pp. 914–918, 1978.

19. T. Ohtsuki, N. Sugiyama, and H. Kawanishi, An optimization technique for integrated circuit layout design, in *Proceedings of the ICCST-Kyoto*, Kyoto, Japan, pp. 67–68, September 1970.

20. R.L. Brooks, C.A.B. Smith, A.H. Stone, and W.T. Tutte, The dissection of rectangles into squares, *Duke Mathematical Journal*, 7: 312–340, 1940.

21. A.S. Lapaugh, Algorithms for integrated circuit layout, PhD thesis, MIT, Boston, MA, November 1980.

22. A. Hashimoto and J. Stevens, Wire routing by optimizing channel assignment within large apertures, in *Proceedings of the 8th Design Automation Workshop*, Atlantic City, NJ, pp. 155–169, 1971.

23. P.R. Groeneveld, Necessary and sufficient conditions for the routability of classical channels, *Integration, the VLSI Journal*, 16: 59–74, 1993.

24. T.G. Szymanski, Dogleg channel routing is NP-complete, *IEEE Transactions on CAD of Integrated Circuits and Systems*, 4(1): 31–41, January 1985.

25. P.R. Groeneveld, H. Cai, and P. Dewilde, A contour-based variable-width gridless channel router, in *Proceedings of the International Conference on Computer-Aided Design*, San José, CA, pp. 374–377, 1987.

26. U.R. Kodres, Geometrical positioning of circuit elements in a computer, in *AIEE Fall General Meeting*, Chicago, ILL, No. 59-1172, October 1959.

27. U.R. Kodres, Partitioning and card selection, Chapter 4, in *Design Automation of Digital Systems*, Vol. 1, ed. M.A. Breuer, Prentice Hall, Englewood Cliffs, NJ, pp. 173–212, 1972.

28. B.W. Kernighan and S. Lin, An efficient heuristic procedure for partitioning graphs, *Bell System Technical Journal*, 49(2): 291–307, February 1970.

29. C.M. Fiduccia and R.M. Mattheyses, A linear time heuristic for improving network partitions, in *Proceedings of the 19th Design Automation Conference*, Las Vegas, NV, pp. 175–181, 1982.

30. W.E. Donath and A.J. Hoffman, Algorithms for partitioning of graphs and computer logic based on eigenvectors of connection matrices, *IBM Technical Disclosure Bulletin*, 15: 938–944, 1972.

31. M.A. Breuer, A class of min-cut placement algorithms, in *Proceedings of the 14th Design Automation Conference*, New Orleans, LA, pp. 284–290, 1977.

32. U. Lauther, A min-cut placement algorithm for general cell assemblies based on a graph representation, in *Proceedings of the 16th Design Automation Conference*, San Diego, CA, pp. 1–10, 1979.

33. A.E. Dunlop and B.W. Kernighan, A procedure for placement of standard-cell VLSI circuit, *IEEE Transactions on CAD of Integrated Circuits and Systems*, CAD-4 (1): 92–98, January 1985.

34. S. Goto, An efficient algorithm for the two-dimensional placement problem in electrical circuit layout, *IEEE Transactions on Circuits and Systems*, CAS-28 (1): 12–18, January 1981.

35. B.T. Preas and C.W. Gwyn, Methods for hierarchical automatic layout of custom LSI circuit masks, in *Proceedings of the 15th Design Automation Conference*, pp. 206–212, 1978.

36. C. Mead and L. Conway, *Introduction to VLSI Systems*, Addison-Wesley, Reading, MA, 1980.

37. R.H.J.M. Otten, Automatic floorplan design, in *Proceedings of the 19th Design Automation Conference*, Las Vegas, NV, pp. 261–267, 1982.

38. S.B. Akers, J.M. Geyer, and D.L. Roberts, IC mask layout with a single conductor layer, in *Proceedings of the 7th Workshop on Design Automation*, San Francisco, CA, pp. 7–16, 1970.

39. H. Murata, F. Fujiyoshi, S. Nakatake, and Y. Kajitani, VLSI module placement based on rectangle packing by the sequence-pair, *IEEE Transactions on Computer-Aided Design*, 15: 1518–1524, December 1996. (ICCAD 1995).

40. J. Grason, A dual linear graph representation for space-filling location problems of the floor plan type, in *Emerging Methods in Environmental Design and Planning*, ed. G.T. Moore, Proceedings of the Design Methods Group, 1st International Conference, Cambridge, MA, pp. 170–178, 1968.

41. J. Bhasker and S. Sahni, A linear algorithm to find a rectangular dual of a planar triangulated graph, *Algorithmica*, 3: 247–278, 1988.

42. C.T. McMullen and R.H.J.M. Otten, Minimum length linear transistor arrays in MOS, in *IEEE International Symposium on Circuits and Systems*, Kyoto, Japan, pp. 1783–1786, 1988.

43. R.L. Maziasz and J.P. Hayes, *Layout Minimization of CMOS Cells*, Kluwer Academic Publishers, Boston, MA; Dordrecht, The Netherlands; London, U.K., 1992.

44. M. Sarrafzadeh and C.-K. Wong, *An Introduction to VLSI Physical Design*, McGraw-Hill Companies Inc., Hightstown, NJ, 1996.

45. S.M. Sait and H. Youssef, *VLSI Physical Design Automation*, McGraw-Hill Companies Inc./IEEE Press, Hightstown, NJ, 1995.

46. N. Sherwani, *Algorithms for VLSI Physical Design Automation*, Kluwer Academic Publishers, Boston, MA; Dordrecht, The Netherlands; London, U.K., 1995.

47. T. Lengauer, *Combinatorial Algorithms for Integrated Circuit Layout*, John Wiley & Sons, New York; Berlin, Germany, 1990.

48. L. Stockmeyer, Optimal orientations of cells in slicing floorplan designs, *Information and Control*, 57(2–3): 91–101, May/June 1983.

49. R.H.J.M. Otten, Efficient floor plan optimization, in *Proceedings of International Conference on Computer Design*, Portchester, NY, pp. 499–503, October–November 1983.

50. T. Lengauer and R. Müller, The complexity of floorplanning based on binary circuit partitions, Technical Report 46, Department of Mathematics and Computer Science, University of Paderborn, Paderborn, Germany, 1986.

51. L.P.P.P. van Ginneken and R.H.J.M. Otten, Optimal slicing of plane point placements, *Proceedings of the Conference on European Design Automation*, Glascow, U.K., pp. 322–326, 1990.

52. S. Kirkpatrick, C.D. Gelatt, and M.P. Vecchi, Optimization by simulated annealing, *Science*, 220(4598): 671–680, 1983.

53. V. Cerny, A thermodynamical approach to the travelling salesman problem: An efficient simulation algorithm, *Journal of Optimization Theory and Applications*, 45: 41–51, 1985.

54. N. Metropolis, A.W. Rosenbluth, M.N. Rosenbluth, A.H. Teller, and E. Teller, Equations of state calculations by fast computing machines, *Journal of Chemical Physics*, 21(6): 1087–1092, 1953.

55. R.H.J.M. Otten and L.P.P.P. van Ginneken, *The Annealing Algorithm*, Kluwer Academic Publishers, Boston, MA; Dordrecht, The Netherlands; London, U.K., 1989.

56. S.A. Solla, G.B. Sorkin, and S.R. White, Configuration space analysis for optimization problems, in *Disordered Systems and Biological Organization*, eds. E. Bienenstock et al., NATO ASI Series, F20, Springer Verlag, Berlin, Germany, pp. 283–293, 1986.

57. C. Sechen and A.L. Sangiovanni-Vincentelli, The timberwolf placement and routing package, *IEEE Journal of Solid-State Circuits*, 20: 510–522, 1985.

58. D.F. Wong and C.L. Liu, A new algorithm for floorplan design, in *Proceedings of the 23rd Design Automation Conference*, Las Vegas, NV, pp. 101–107, 1986.

59. I.E. Sutherland and R.F. Sproull, Logical effort: Designing for speed on the back of an envelope, in *Proceedings of the 1991 University of California Santa Cruz Conference on Advanced Research in VLSI*, ed. C. Sequin, MIT Press, Santa Cruz, CA, pp. 1–16, 1991.

60. J. Grodstein, E. Lehman, H. Harkness, W.J. Grundmann, and Y. Watanabe, A delay model for logic synthesis of continuously-sized networks, in *Proceedings of the International Conference on Computer-Aided Design*, San Francisco, CA, pp. 458–462, 1995.

61. R.H.J.M. Otten, A design flow for performance planning: New paradigms for iteration free synthesis, in *Architecture Design and Validation Methods*, ed. E. Böerger, Springer, Berlin, Heidelberg, Germany; New York, pp. 89–139, 2000.

62. W.C. Elmore, The transient analysis of damped linear networks with particular regard to wideband amplifiers, *Journal of Applied Physics*, 19(1): 55–63, January 1948.

63. T. Sakurai, Approximation of wiring delay in MOSFET LSI, *IEEE Journal of Solid-State Circuits*, 18(4): 418–426, August 1983.

64. M.C.W. Geilen, T. Basten, B.D. Theelen, and R.H.J.M. Otten, An algebra of Pareto points, *Fundamenta Informaticae*, 78(1): 35–74, 2007.

3 Metrics Used in Physical Design

Frank Liu and Sachin S. Sapatnekar

CONTENTS

Physical design consists of a number of steps that attempt to optimize one or more specified design objectives, under one or more design constraints. This optimization is based on predictors and metrics that measure the value of the circuit property. These metrics must be computationally efficient, so that they may be embedded in the inner loop of an optimizer and may be called repeatedly during optimization, and yet have sufficient accuracy that is commensurate with the needs of the specific stage of physical design. In this chapter, we overview several metrics that may be used in objective and constraint functions in physical design, used to measure circuit properties such as timing, noise, power, and temperature. It should be noted that although area is also a metric used in optimization, area metrics are generally quite simple, and are not covered in this chapter.

3.1 TIMING

For most of today's VLSI designs, a dominant portion is synchronous in nature. In a synchronous design, a main clock signal is required to coordinate the operation of various logic blocks across the chip. A highly simplified view of a logic block is shown in Figure 3.1. The block consists of a cluster of combinational circuits, surrounded by the input and output latch banks, which may, e.g., be

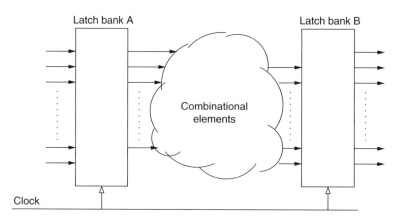

FIGURE 3.1 An illustrative timing diagram of a sequential circuit.

level clocked or edge triggered. A clock signal synchronizes the operations of the latch banks. The input latch bank provides primary inputs, which are computational results of the previous stage, to the combinational cluster, and the results of the logic computation are stored (or latched) by the output latch bank. Because the two latch banks open at a fixed interval, which is determined by the frequency of the clock signal, the time the combinational cluster takes to complete logic computation has to meet this constraint. In a modern VLSI design, the circumstance is much more complicated, but the general principle still holds.

It is quite likely that the combinational cluster will be constructed by the instances of logic gates from a predefined library. The timing performance of the combinational block is a strong function of the physical design, such as the placement of the gates, the routing of signal wires, as well as the sizing of the transistors. Therefore, any of these physical design optimizations must be guided by fast timing evaluators.

In this chapter, we briefly introduce the timing metrics commonly used in physical design. We first review the classic Elmore delay and slew metric, followed by more advanced fast timing estimation metrics. Finally, we review the fundamentals of static timing analysis of combinational circuits.

3.1.1 Elmore Delay and Slew Metrics

The dynamic behavior of an interconnect structure can be described by a system of ordinary differential equations. From a physical design point of view, this behavior can be characterized by two quantities: delay and slew (or rise/fall time), as depicted in Figure 3.2. This section outlines techniques for calculating these two quantities efficiently, with the given parameters of the interconnect structure.

3.1.1.1 Elmore Delay

The Elmore delay was first proposed by W. C. Elmore in 1948 [1], but did not receive much attention for over three decades. It was not until the 1980s, when the wire delays on an integrated circuit became nonnegligible, that it was rediscovered by Rubenstein et al. [2], and today, it is still the most popular timing metric in physical optimization. The reason for its popularity can be attributed not only to its simplicity but also to other important characteristics such as additivity, which we discuss later.

We will proceed under the reasonable assumption that an interconnect structure can be modeled as a set of lumped RLC segments, and we represent the impulse response of a specific node voltage in the circuit by $h(t)$. If we denote the Laplace transformation of $h(t)$ as $H(s)$, we can expand it into a Taylor series at $s = 0$:

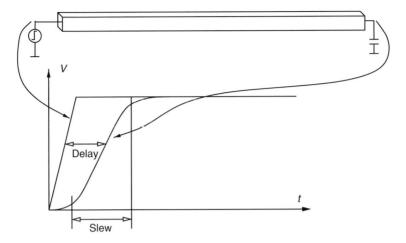

FIGURE 3.2   Delay and slew of a wire segment.

$$H(s) = \int_0^\infty h(t)\, e^{-st} dt = \sum_{k=0}^{\infty} \frac{(-1)^k}{k!} s^k \int_0^\infty t^k h(t) dt \qquad (3.1)$$

Therefore,

$$H(s) = m_0 + m_1 s + m_2 s^2 + m_3 s^3 + \cdots \qquad (3.2)$$

where

$$m_k = \frac{(-1)^k}{k!} \int_0^\infty t^k h(t) dt \quad \text{for} \quad k = 0, 1, 2, \ldots \qquad (3.3)$$

The coefficients of the Taylor expansion is commonly known as the (circuit) moments.

For an RC circuit without resistive path to ground, the impulse response $h(t)$ satisfies the following conditions:

$$\begin{cases} h(t) \geq 0, \quad \forall\, t \\ \int_0^\infty h(t) dt = 1 \end{cases} \qquad (3.4)$$

In probability theory, any continuous real function that satisfies Equation 3.4 is a probability density function (PDF). The integral of a PDF is defined as a cumulative density function:

$$S(t) = \int_0^t h(\tau) d\tau \qquad (3.5)$$

This corresponds to the step response in circuit analysis (Figure 3.3).

Several characteristics are commonly used to describe a statistical distribution. The first is the mean, which is defined as

$$\mu = \int_0^\infty th(t) dt \qquad (3.6)$$

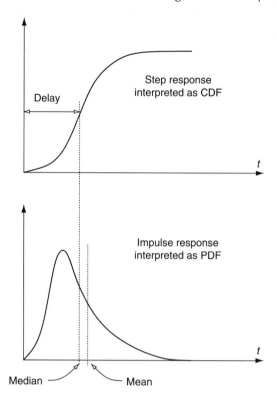

FIGURE 3.3 Elmore delay: approximating the median with the mean.

Another important characteristic is the median, which is defined as the halfway point on a PDF curve:

$$\int_{0}^{M} h(t)\mathrm{d}t = \frac{1}{2} \tag{3.7}$$

The similarity between the impulse response of an RC tree and a statistical PDF is quite clear. Observe that the commonly used 50 percent delay point in circuit analysis actually corresponds to the median of the underlying distribution. This is the keen observation of Elmore in 1948. Moreover, he also made the proposal that as the median was difficult to calculate, one could use the mean, which is much easier to calculate, as an approximation of median:

$$M \approx \mu = -m_1 = \int_{0}^{\infty} t\, h(t)\mathrm{d}t \tag{3.8}$$

3.1.1.2 Elmore Delay for RC Trees

For an RC tree (i.e., an RC network with no direct resistive path to ground), the calculation of Elmore delay can be carried out quite efficiently. In such a case, the Elmore delay between any two nodes can be expressed as

$$\mu = \sum R_i \cdot \sum_{\text{downstream}} C_j \tag{3.9}$$

where
  R_i is the traversal of the resistors on the unique path between two nodes
  C_j permutes all the capacitance seen from resistor R_i

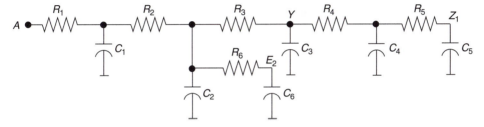

FIGURE 3.4   An example of RC tree to illustrate the process of calculating Elmore delay.

For the simple example shown in Figure 3.4, the Elmore delay from root node A and fan-out node $Z1$ can be calculated by traversing the unique resistive path from $Z1$ to A:

$$\mathrm{ED}_{A \to Z1} = R_5 C_5 + R_4(C_4 + C_5) + R_3(C_3 + C_4 + C_5)$$
$$+ R_2(C_2 + C_3 + C_4 + C_5 + C_6)$$
$$+ R_1(C_1 + C_2 + C_3 + C_4 + C_5 + C_6)$$

The Elmore delay has a nice property: it is additive. In other words, for two nodes A and C on a branch, if node B lies between A and C, we can write:

$$\mathrm{ED}_{A \to C} = \mathrm{ED}_{A \to B} + \mathrm{ED}_{B \to C}$$

For the example shown in Figure 3.4, we can easily verify that

$$\mathrm{ED}_{A \to Y} = R_3(C_3 + C_4 + C_5) + R_2(C_2 + C_3 + C_4 + C_5 + C_6)$$
$$+ R_1(C_1 + C_2 + C_3 + C_4 + C_5 + C_6)$$
$$\mathrm{ED}_{Y \to Z1} = R_5 C_5 + R_4(C_4 + C_5)$$

Thus,

$$\mathrm{ED}_{A \to Z1} = \mathrm{ED}_{A \to Y} + \mathrm{ED}_{Y \to Z1}$$

The Elmore delay of an RC tree has another important property: it can be proven to be the upper bound of the true 50 percent circuit delay under any input excitation [3]. In other words, if a particular RC net is optimized based on the Elmore delay, its real delay is guaranteed to be better. Empirically it has been shown that although the Elmore delay is the upper bound, the error can be quite substantial in some cases, especially for those nodes close to the driving point. The accuracy for far-end nodes (those close to the sink pins) is much better. Note that this property only applies to RC trees, and it does not hold for nontree circuits, e.g., meshes.

The Elmore delay can also be calculated for distributed circuits. For a uniform wire at the length of L, with a unit resistance R, a unit capacitance C, and a loading capacitance C_{L}, it can be shown that the Elmore delay at the far-end of the wire is

$$\mathrm{ED} = \frac{1}{2} RL(CL + C_{\mathrm{L}})$$

3.1.1.3   Elmore Delay for Nontrees

For a nontree RC network, the calculation of Elmore delay is more involved. The simple traversal algorithm for tree-like structures is no longer valid. Instead, we can formulate the circuit into the modified nodal analysis (MNA) formulation and solve for the moments. In this case, a linear circuit can be formulated as

$$\mathbf{G}x(t) + \mathbf{C}\frac{\mathrm{d}}{\mathrm{d}t}x(t) = \mathbf{B}u(t)$$

where
  $\mathbf{G}$ is the conductance matrix
  $\mathbf{C}$ is the capacitance matrix
  matrix $\mathbf{B}$ specifies where the excitations are applied

The entries in unknown vector $x(t)$ consists of node voltages, branch currents of voltage sources, as well as branch currents of inductors. $u(t)$ is the external time-varying excitation. The Laplace transformation of the MNA formulation is

$$\mathbf{G}X(s) + s\mathbf{C}X(s) = \mathbf{B}U(s)$$

The first circuit moment is

$$m_1 = -\mathbf{G}^{-1}\mathbf{C}\mathbf{G}^{-1}\mathbf{B}$$

Therefore, the Elmore delay at a particular node can be calculated by selecting the corresponding entry in the vector of the first moment:

$$ED_i = \mathbf{e}_i^{\mathrm{T}}\mathbf{G}^{-1}\mathbf{C}\mathbf{G}^{-1}\mathbf{B}$$

where vector $\mathbf{e}_i$ is the selection vector with all entries zero except at the ith location.

Computationally, only one LU factorization of the conductance matrix $\mathbf{G}$ is required in the above calculation, and the rest of calculation is merely forward–backward substitution of the prefactorized matrix as well as matrix–vector multiplication, which can be carried out quite efficiently.

It is also worth pointing out that the above procedure is the general description of the Elmore delay calculation for any linear circuit. Thus, it can be used to calculate the Elmore delay of an RC tree as well. However, due to its special topology, the LU factorization of an RC tree can be carried out without explicit formulation of the conductance and capacitance matrices, and a closed-form formula, described earlier, for the Elmore delay can be obtained. More details on how to construct the MNA matrices and the calculation of Elmore delay for a general circuit can be found in Ref. [4].

3.1.1.4 Elmore Slew

In his original paper, Elmore refereed to slew as the gyration. If we follow the probability interpretation of signal transition, it can be shown that just as the delay corresponds to the median of the PDF function, the slew corresponds to the variance of the PDF function. A first-order estimate of variance is the second central moment, which is defined as

$$\sigma^2 = m_1^2 - 2m_2$$

In practice, because quite often slew is defined as the difference of delay between 10 percent and 90 percent delay points, the above metric needs to be scaled accordingly.

$$\mathrm{Slew} = \frac{8}{10}\sqrt{m_1^2 - 2m_2}$$

Note that we need the second circuit moment to calculate the slew. In general, it can be shown that the second circuit moment can be calculated in MNA formulation as

$$m_2 = \mathbf{G}^{-1}\mathbf{C}\mathbf{G}^{-1}\mathbf{C}\mathbf{G}^{-1}\mathbf{B}$$

In practice, the factorized matrix $\mathbf{G}$ during m_1 calculation can be reused to calculate m_2. Therefore, the added computational complexity is only a few matrix–vector multiplications and backward/forward substitutions, which are usually much cheaper than matrix factorization itself. For RC trees, the matrix does not need to be explicitly formulated and factorized at all. The path-tracing algorithm used in m_1 calculation can be applied as well. More details can be found in Ref. [4].

3.1.1.5   Limitations of Elmore Delay

As we have discussed earlier, the Elmore delay has a few very nice properties when applied on RC trees. They are

- Easy to calculate
- Proven to be the upper bound for any node under any input excitation
- Additive along the signal path

During physical design, most on-chip signal wires can be modeled as trees, therefore, the Elmore delay has been quite popular and has been implemented in many physical design algorithms.

However, the Elmore metric also has some limitations, especially in terms of accuracy. Empirically it has been shown that even for RC trees, the accuracy of Elmore delay can be over ten times off at certain nodes, especially for the nodes close to the driving point. The reason for this inaccuracy can be explained as follows: the essence of Elmore delay is to use mean to approximate median for a particular PDF. Such an approximation is only accurate when the PDF is unimodal and has zero skew, e.g., the PDF is symmetric. For an RC tree, this is only true for far-end nodes. For the near-end nodes (the ones which are close to the driving point), the skewness of the impulse response (which we interpreted as a PDF) is quite large. As a consequence, the approximation used in Elmore delay becomes inaccurate.

3.1.2   FAST TIMING METRICS

The essence of Elmore delay is the probability interpretation of the impulse response of a linear circuit. This allows the signal response to be approximated by using a structured continuous function as the template, thus making it possible to quickly extract delay and slew metrics. In the derivation of Elmore delay, it is assumed that the underlying PDF function is symmetric. A natural extension of the idea is to remove this assumption: we can use an asymmetric PDF and hopefully the accuracy can be improved. In the first proposed method [5], the gamma distribution function was used as the template function. Later on, other distribution functions are proposed to be the template function, including the Weibull [6] and lognormal [7] functions. Another benefit of these extended approaches is that we are no longer limited to the 50 percent delay point. Once the parameters of the function template are known, we can calculate any percentile delay point. The price we have to pay to get better accuracy is that more moments are needed. Besides, all of these fast delay metrics cannot be proved to be the upper bound of the true delay, although empirically it has been shown that overall they are more accurate.

3.1.2.1   PRIMO and H-Gamma

The idea of PRIMO [5] was to approximate the circuit impulse response as the PDF function of a gamma distribution. Because only two parameters are needed to determine a gamma distribution, these two parameters can be easily determined by applying the moment-matching principle. Once the coefficients of the gamma distribution are known, we do not need to approximate the median with the mean. Instead, we can directly calculate the median, which corresponds to the 50 percent delay. Later, an improved version of gamma fitting was introduced in H-gamma [8]. Here, we only describe H-gamma.

The gamma statistical distribution is defined on support $x > 0$, with the PDF defined as

$$f(x; k, \theta) = \frac{\theta^k x^{k-1} e^{-\theta x}}{\Gamma(k)}$$

where $\Gamma(k)$ is the gamma function:

$$\Gamma(k) = \int_0^\infty x^{k-1}\,e^{-x}\,dx$$

Each gamma distribution is uniquely determined by two parameters, k and θ, and both of them have to be positive. The mean and the variance of a gamma distribution are

$$\text{mean} = \frac{k}{\theta}$$

$$\text{variance} = \frac{k}{\theta^2}$$

To derive H-gamma, we can rewrite the impulse response of a circuit node as

$$Y(s) = m_0 + m_1 s + m_2 s^2 + m_3 s^3 + \cdots$$

$$= m_0 + m_1 s \left(1 + \frac{m_2}{m_1}s + \frac{m_3}{m_1}s^2 + \cdots\right)$$

The series in parenthesis is referred as the normalized homogeneous function. In H-gamma, the normalized homogeneous function is fit into the PDF of a gamma distribution by matching the first two moments. The results are

$$\frac{k}{\theta} = -\frac{m_2}{m_1}$$

$$\frac{k}{\theta^2} = 2\left(\frac{m_3}{m_1}\right) - \left(\frac{m_2}{m_1}\right)^2$$

Once two parameters k and θ are calculated, we can approximate the step response as

$$y(t) \approx 1 + m_1 \frac{\theta^k t^{k-1}\,e^{-\theta t}}{\Gamma(k)}$$

The delay at any percentile point ϕ can be calculate by setting the left-hand-side of the above equation to ϕ and solve for t. Unfortunately, this process requires a nonlinear iteration method such as Newton–Raphson because this equation cannot be explicitly solved.

To address this issue, the nonlinear iteration process can be simplified to a table look-up procedure by scaling time t with θ, and k with $-m_1$. The scaled response approximation can be shown to be

$$y_{\lambda,k}(x) = 1 - \frac{\lambda x^{k-1}\,e^{-x}}{\Gamma(k)}$$

For any percentile ϕ, a two-dimensional table needs to be preconstructed with λ and k as the input and x as the output. The final delay is then calculated by scaling x with θ: $t = x/\theta$. Empirically it has been shown that H-gamma metric has good accuracy for both near and far-end nodes. One reason for its accuracy is particularly due to the fact that three moments are used to calculate the delay at each node.

3.1.2.2 Weibull-Based Delay

Another proposed delay metric uses Weibull distribution as the underlying function template. The advantage of using the Weibull distribution is that the percentile points are very easy to calculate. A Weibull distribution is defined on the support of $t > 0$ and is determined by two parameters:

$$f(x\colon \alpha, \beta) = \alpha\beta^{-\alpha}x^{\alpha-1}\,e^{-(x/\beta)^\alpha}$$

Both parameters, α and β, must be positive. The mean and variance of a Weibull distribution is

$$\text{Mean} = \beta \Gamma(1 + \theta)$$

$$\text{Variance} = \beta^2 [\Gamma(1 + 2\theta) - \Gamma^2(1 + \theta)]$$

Unlike the gamma distribution, in which the distribution parameters can be easily calculated from moments, the Weibull distribution requires iterative evaluation of gamma functions. To simplify the process, it is proposed that a look-up table be precharacterized. The look-up table requires the first two circuit moments as inputs and it returns the parameter θ:

r	$\text{Log}_{10}(r)$	θ
0.63096	−0.2	0.48837
0.79433	−0.1	0.76029
1.00000	+0.0	1.00000
1.25892	+0.1	1.22371
1.58489	+0.2	1.43757
1.99526	+0.3	1.64467
2.51189	+0.4	1.84678
3.16228	+0.5	2.04507
3.98107	+0.6	2.24031
5.01187	+0.7	2.43305
6.30957	+0.8	2.62371
7.94328	+0.9	2.81262
10.00000	+1.0	3.00000
12.58925	+1.1	3.18607
15.84893	+1.2	3.37098

where $r = m_2/m_1^2$. Note that it is recommended to use $\log_{10}(r)$ value in the interpolation. Once θ is known, the other parameter, β, is calculated by using the following equation:

$$\beta = \frac{-m_1}{\Gamma(1 + \theta)}$$

Although an evaluation of the gamma function is again needed, the following table can be used to avoid the evaluation:

x	Gamma(x)
1.0	1.00000
1.1	0.95135
1.2	0.91817
1.3	0.89747
1.4	0.88726
1.5	0.88623
1.6	0.89352
1.7	0.90864
1.8	0.93138
1.9	0.96176
2.0	1.00000

The table only covers the data range between 1 and 2, and the following recursive property of the gamma function can be used to calculate other x:

$$\Gamma(x+1) = x\Gamma(x) \quad \forall\, x > 1$$

Once α and β are known, the delay at any percentile ϕ can be calculated as

$$t_\phi = \beta \left(\ln \frac{1}{1-\phi} \right)^\theta$$

In particular, the 50 percent delay point can be calculated as

$$t_{0.5} = \beta[\ln(2)]^\theta \approx \beta \cdot (0.693)^\theta$$

3.1.2.3 Lognormal Delay

Another delay metric uses lognormal distribution for probability interpretation of response signal [7]. The lognormal distribution is determined by two parameters μ and σ. Its PDF is defined as

$$f(x; \mu, \sigma) = \frac{1}{x\sigma\sqrt{2\pi}} \exp\left\{ \frac{[\ln(x) - \mu]^2}{2\sigma^2} \right\}$$

Similar to Weibull-based delay, the first two circuit moments are matched to the moments of the distribution to calculate μ and σ. Once they are known, the delay can be calculated by calculating the median of the lognormal distribution. After simplification, it turns out that the 50 percent delay metric is a closed form of the two circuit moments:

$$t_{0.5} = \frac{m_1^2}{\sqrt{2m_2}}$$

The lognormal distribution can also be used to provide a closed-form slew metric. Because slew metric is equivalent to the difference of two delay points (e.g., 10 percent and 90 percent delay), the accuracy requirement is higher. In some cases, especially for the near-end nodes, metrics based on two moments may not be sufficiently accurate. To achieve the balance between the accuracy and complexity, a three-piece approach was proposed, based on the value of $r = m_1/\sqrt{m_2}$:

- $r \le 0.35$:

$$\text{Slew}_{12} = \frac{m_1^2}{\sqrt{2m_2}} \left(e^{kS\sqrt{2}} - e^{-kS\sqrt{2}} \right)$$

  where $S = \sqrt{\ln(2m_2/m_1^2)}$, and the value of k depends on the definition of slew and is explained later.
- $r \ge 1$

$$\text{Slew}_{23} = \sqrt{\frac{2m_2 - m_1^2}{z(z-1)}} \left(e^{k\sqrt{2\ln(z)}} - e^{-k\sqrt{2\ln(z)}} \right)$$

  where $z = (y-1/y)^2 + 1$ and $y = \sqrt[3]{(\gamma + \sqrt{4 + \gamma^2})/2}$, where $\gamma = (-6m_3 + 6m_1m_2 - 2m_1^3)/(2m_2 - m_1^2)^{3/2}$ and k is the function of slew ratio.
- $0.35 < r < 1$

$$\text{Slew} = \left(\frac{20}{13}r - \frac{7}{13} \right) \text{slew}_{23} + \frac{20}{13}(1 - r)\,\text{slew}_{12}$$

The value k is the scaling factor needed to reflect difference in terms of slew definition. It is calculated based on the table below:

Slew Definition	k
10/90	0.9063
20/80	0.5951
25/75	0.4769
30/70	0.3708

3.1.3 FUNDAMENTALS OF STATIC TIMING ANALYSIS

As discussed earlier in this section, a sequential circuit consists of combinational elements and sequential elements and can be represented as a set of combinational blocks that lie between latches. This subsection presents methods that compute the delay of a combinational logic block.

A combinational logic circuit can be represented as a timing graph $G = (V, E)$, where the elements of V, the vertex set, are the logic gates in the circuit and the primary inputs and outputs of the circuit. A pair of vertices, u and $v \in G$, are connected by a directed edge $e(u, v) \in E$ if there is a connection from the output of the element represented by vertex u to the input of the element represented by vertex v. A simple logic circuit and its corresponding graph are illustrated in Figure 3.5a and b, respectively. In this section, we present techniques that are used for the static timing analysis of digital combinational circuits. The word "static" alludes to the fact that this timing analysis is carried out in an input-independent manner, and purports to find the worst-case delay of the circuit over all possible input combinations. The method is often referred to as CPM (critical path method). The computational efficiency of CPM has resulted in its widespread use, even though it has some limitations.

The CPM-based algorithm, applied to a timing graph $G = (V, E)$, can be summarized by the pseudocode shown below:

```
Algorithm CRITICAL_PATH_METHOD
Q = Ø;
for all vertices i ∈ V
    n_visited_inputs [i] = 0;
/* Add a vertex to the tail of Q if all inputs are ready */
for all primary inputs i
    /* Fanout gates of i */
    for all vertices j such that (i → j) ∈ E
        if (++n_visited_inputs [j] == n_inputs [j]) addQ (j,Q);
while (Q ≠ Ø) {
    g = top(Q);
    remove (g,Q);
    compute_delay [g]
    /* Fanout gates of g */
    for all vertices k such that (g → k) ∈ E
        if (++n_visited_inputs[k] == n_inputs [k]) addQ (k,Q);
}
```

The procedure is best illustrated by means of a simple example. Consider the circuit in Figure 3.6, which shows an interconnection of blocks. Each of these blocks could be as simple as a logic gate

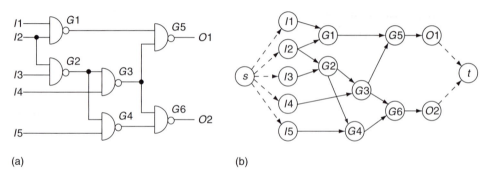

(a)   (b)

FIGURE 3.5   (a) An example combinational circuit and (b) its timing graph. (From Sapatnekar, S. S., *Timing*, Kluwer Academic Publisher, Boston, MA, 2004. With permission.)

or could be a more complex combinational block, and is characterized by the delay from each input pin to each output pin. For simplicity, this example will assume that for each block, the delay from any input to the output is identical. Moreover, we will assume that each block is an inverting logic gate such as a NAND or a NOR, as shown by the "bubble" at the output. The two numbers, d_r/d_f, inside each gate represent the delay corresponding to the delay of the output rising transition, d_r, and that of the output fall transition, d_f, respectively. We assume that all primary inputs are available at time zero, so that the numbers "0/0" against each primary input represent the worst-case rise and fall arrival times, respectively, at each of these nodes. The critical path method proceeds from the primary inputs to the primary outputs in topological order, computing the worst-case rise and fall arrival times at each intermediate node, and eventually at the outputs of a circuit.

A block is said to be ready for processing when the signal arrival time information is available for all of its inputs; in other words, when the number of processed inputs of a gate g, n_visited_inputs[g], equals the number of inputs of the gate, n_inputs[g]. Notationally, we refer to each block by the symbol for its output node. Initially, because the signal arrival times are known only at the primary inputs, only those blocks that are fed solely by primary inputs are ready for processing. In the example, these correspond to the gates i, j, k, and l. These are placed in a queue Q using the function addQ, and are processed in the order in which they appear in the queue.

In the iterative process, the block at the head of the queue Q is taken off the queue and scheduled for processing. Each processing step consists of

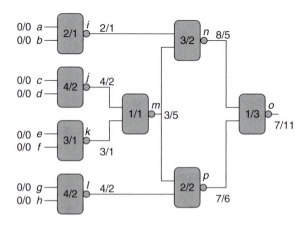

FIGURE 3.6   An example illustrating the application of the CPM on a circuit with inverting gates. The numbers within the gates correspond to the rise delay/fall delay of the block, and the bold numbers at each block output represent the rise/fall arrival times at that point. The primary inputs are assumed to have arrival times of zero, as shown. (From Sapatnekar, S. S., *Timing*, Kluwer Academic Publisher, Boston, MA, 2004. With permission.)

- Finding the latest arriving input to the block that triggers the output transition (this involves finding the maximum of all worst-case arrival times of inputs to the block), and then adding the delay of the block to the latest arriving input time, to obtain the worst-case arrival time at the output. This is represented by function `compute_delay` in the pseudocode.
- Checking all of the block that the current block fans out to, to find out whether they are ready for processing. If so, the block is added to the tail of the queue using function `addQ`.

The iterations end when the queue is empty. In the example, the algorithm is executed as follows:

Step 1: In the initial step gates, i, j, k, and l are placed on the queue because the input arrival times at all of their inputs are available.

Step 2: Gate i, at the head of the queue, is scheduled. Because the inputs transition at time 0, and the rise and fall delays are 2 and 1 units, respectively, the rise and fall arrival times at the output are computed as $0 + 2 = 2$ and $0 + 1 = 1$, respectively. After processing i, no new blocks can be added to the queue.

Step 3: Gate j is scheduled, and the rise and fall arrival times are similarly found to be 4 and 2, respectively. Again, no additional elements can be placed in the queue.

Step 4: Gate k is processed, and its output rise and fall arrival times are computed as 3 and 1, respectively. After this computation, we see that all arrival times at the input to gate m have been determined. Therefore, it is deemed ready for processing, and is added to the tail of the queue.

Step 5: Gate l is now scheduled, and the rise and fall arrival times are similarly found to be 4 and 2, respectively, and no additional elements can be placed in the queue.

Step 6: Gate m, which is at the head of the queue, is scheduled. Because this is an inverting gate, the output falling transition is caused by the latest input rising transition, which occurs at time $\max(4, 3) = 4$. As a consequence, the fall arrival time at m is given by $\max(4, 3) + 1 = 5$. Similarly, the rise arrival time at m is $\max(2, 1) + 1 = 3$. At the end of this step, both n and p are ready for processing and are added to the queue.

Step 7: Gate n is scheduled, and its rise and fall arrival times are calculated as $\max(1, 5) + 3 = 8$ and $\max(2, 3) + 2 = 5$ respectively.

Step 8: Gate p is now processed, and its rise and fall arrival times are found to be $\max(5, 2) + 2 = 7$ and $\max(3, 4) + 2 = 6$, respectively. This sets the stage for adding gate o to the queue.

Step 9: Gate o is scheduled, and its rise and fall arrival times are $\max(5, 6) + 1 = 7$ and $\max(8, 7) + 3 = 11$, respectively. The queue is now empty and the algorithm terminates.

The worst-case delay for the entire block is therefore $\max(7, 11) = 11$ units.

Because there are many paths in a combinational block, it is important to identify the path (or paths) on which the worst-case delay of the whole block is achieved for physical design optimization. The critical path, defined as the path between an input and an output with the maximum delay, can be easily found by using a traceback method. We begin with the block whose output is the primary output with the latest arrival time: this is the last block on the critical path. Next, the latest arriving input to this block is identified, and the block that causes this transition is the preceding block on the critical path. The process is repeated recursively until a primary input is reached.

In the example, we begin with Gate o at the output, whose falling transition corresponds to the maximum delay. This transition is caused by the rising transition at the output of gate n, which must therefore precede o on the critical path. Similarly, the transition at n is affected by the falling transition at the output of m, and so on. By continuing this process, the critical path from the input to the output is identified as being caused by a falling transition at either input c or d, and then progressing as follows: rising $j \rightarrow$ falling $m \rightarrow$ rising $n \rightarrow$ falling o.

3.2 NOISE

Coupling noise is yet another unwanted side effect of the scaling in deep submicron technology, and its impact can be reduced through physical design transformations. The effect arises due to geometric scaling, which requires the wires to be narrower and the spacing between adjacent wires smaller. On the other hand, because the chip size is also getting larger (in terms of multiples of the minimum feature size), it is necessary to reduce wire resistance by increasing the aspect ratio of the wire cross section. The compounded effect is the increase of the coupling capacitance between adjacent signal wires.

When two interconnect networks are capacitively coupled, usually the one with the stronger driving gate is referred to as the aggressor, while the one with the weaker driver is called the victim. It is quite possible that an aggressor can affect multiple victims, and a victim can have more than one aggressors. For simplicity, we only discuss the case with one aggressor and one victim. These ideas can be easily extended to more general cases. The application domain for this analysis is in noise-aware routing. For scalable methods that can be applied to full-chip noise analysis, the reader is referred to Chapter 34.

When the aggressor switches, if the victim is quiet, then the coupling will generate a glitch on the victim wire. If the glitch is sufficiently large and occurs within a certain timing window, the (erroneous) glitch can be latched into a memory storage element and cause a logic error. If the victim is also switching, then depending on the polarities of the signals and the corresponding switching windows, the signal on the victim wire can be slowed down or sped up, which may cause timing violations. Although very elaborate algorithms are available to estimate the coupling effects between the signal wires, (see Refs. [9,10]), it is highly desirable to correct the problem at its root, i.e., during the physical design phase.

The exact amount of noise injected to the victim net from the aggressor is a function of circuit topologies and values of both aggressor and victim nets, as well as the properties of the signal. To accurately estimate the noise, every component of the coupled network is required, which is not realistic during physical design. Fortunately, there is a simple noise metric equivalent to Elmore delay in timing [11].

In Ref. [11], it is assumed that the excitations in the aggressor net are infinite ramps, which are signals whose first derivatives are zero before $t = 0$, and constant afterward. From the circuit analysis point of view, the coupling capacitors act like differentiators. Thus, the coupling node voltage will come to a steady state, whose level can be used as an indicator of the coupling effect. For a circuit of general topology, the noise metric must be solved with circuit analysis techniques, which involves the construction of MNA formulations and solving of the matrices. The MNA matrices of a coupled circuit can be written as

$$\begin{bmatrix} \mathbf{G}_{11} & \mathbf{0} \\ \mathbf{0} & \mathbf{G}_{22} \end{bmatrix} \begin{bmatrix} \mathbf{x}_1 \\ \mathbf{x}_2 \end{bmatrix} + \begin{bmatrix} \mathbf{C}_{11} & \mathbf{C}_c \\ \mathbf{C}_c^T & \mathbf{C}_{22} \end{bmatrix} \begin{bmatrix} \dot{\mathbf{x}}_1 \\ \dot{\mathbf{x}}_2 \end{bmatrix} = \begin{bmatrix} \mathbf{B}_1 \\ \mathbf{0} \end{bmatrix} \mathbf{u}$$

In the above equation, the first partition is the aggressor net while the second partition is the victim net. The submatrices $\mathbf{G}_{11}$ and $\mathbf{C}_{11}$ represent the conductance and capacitance of the aggressor net; and $\mathbf{G}_{22}$ and $\mathbf{C}_{22}$ represent the conductances and capacitances of the victim net; while $\mathbf{C}_c$ represents the coupling between the two nets. According to Ref. [11], simple algebraic manipulations can be employed to estimate the worst case as

$$\mathbf{V}_{2,\max} = \mathbf{G}_{22}^{-1} \mathbf{C}_c \mathbf{G}_{11}^{-1} \mathbf{B}_1 \dot{\mathbf{u}}$$

Note that the worst-case noise is only a function of the resistances of the victim and aggressor nets, as well as the coupling capacitances. It is not a function of the self-capacitances of the two nets (under the assumption that the input is an infinite ramp).

If both aggressor and victim nets have tree-like topologies, then the above noise metric can be calculated with a simple graph traversal, which is similar to the Elmore delay calculation of tree-like RC networks. To illustrate the procedure, we can rewrite the worst-case noise metric as

$$\mathbf{I_c} = \mathbf{C_c G_{11}^{-1} B_1 \dot{u}}$$
$$\mathbf{V_{2,max}} = \mathbf{G_{22}^{-1} I_c} \tag{3.10}$$

Because the excitation in the aggressor net is an infinite ramp, the term $\mathbf{I_c}$ represents the coupling current injected into the victim net. If the aggressor net is properly connected, then it can be shown using simple circuit arguments [11] that the injected current is simply $\mathbf{C_c \dot{u}}$. The calculation of the voltage in the victim net can then be carried out using a procedure similar to Elmore delay propagation, except that we traverse the tree from the root to the leaf nodes. To illustrate the procedure, we give a simple example shown in Figure 3.7.

Because the noise is not a function of the self-capacitance of either the aggressor or the victim, it is not drawn in the diagram. In the first step of the calculation, the equivalent current injections from the aggressor net is calculated, which correspond to evaluating the first equation in Equation 3.10. Because there is no direct resistive path to ground and there is only one independent voltage source in the aggressor, it is trivial to show that

$$I_1 = C_1 \cdot \dot{u}$$
$$I_2 = C_2 \cdot \dot{u}$$
$$I_3 = C_3 \cdot \dot{u}$$

We then replace the coupling capacitors of the victim with those current sources. Because the root of the tree is grounded, we calculate the worst-case noise by a graph traversal, from root to leaves:

$$I_{B,max} = R_1(C_1 + C_2 + C_3)\dot{u}$$
$$I_{D,max} = R_1(C_1 + C_2 + C_3)\dot{u} + R_2(C_2 + C_3)\dot{u}$$
$$I_{E,max} = R_1(C_1 + C_2 + C_3)\dot{u} + R_2(C_2 + C_3)\dot{u} + R_3(C_3)\dot{u}$$
$$I_{F,max} = R_1(C_1 + C_2 + C_3)\dot{u} + R_2(C_2 + C_3)\dot{u}$$

Although Devgan's metric is easy to calculate, its accuracy is limited. For fast transitions, in particular, the metric evaluates to a physically impossible value that exceeds the supply voltage. Note that the evaluation is still correct, as Devgan's noise metric only guarantees an upper bound on the noise; however, the accuracy in such cases is clearly limited.

To improve accuracy, a further improvement of the static noise metric was proposed in Ref. [12], which extended the idea of Devgan's metric through the use of more than one moment. In addition,

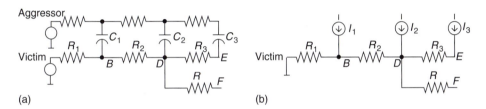

(a)   (b)

FIGURE 3.7 An example of worst-case noise calculation, showing (a) the original circuit and (b) the equivalent circuit when coupling capacitors are replaced by injected noise current sources. (From Sapatnekar, S. S., *Timing*, Kluwer Academic Publisher, Boston, MA, 2004. With permission.)

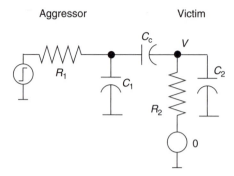

FIGURE 3.8   Circuit diagram for the derivation of the transient noise peak.

the aggressor excitation was assumed to be a first-order exponential function rather than an infinite ramp. To obtain a closed-form noise metric, the response at the victim net was calculated using moment-matching approach.

Another type of noise metric that takes the transient approach is the work in Ref. [13]. Instead of assuming that the excitation at the aggressor is an infinite ramp, it is assumed that the aggressor excitation is a step signal. However, the circuit topology is highly simplified so that a close-form noise metric can be derived. The aggressor–victim pair is simplified as shown in Figure 3.8 [13], where R_1 is the total resistance of the aggressor and R_2 is the total resistance of the victim. Note that the victim is grounded by a zero-valued voltage source. It then can be proved that the noise peak at node V is

$$X_V = \cfrac{1}{1 + \frac{C_2}{C_c} + \frac{R_1}{R_2}\left(1 + \frac{C_1}{C_c}\right)}$$

An alternative two-stage π model is presented in the metric in Ref. [14].

For long global nets, there is also the possibility that two nets are inductively coupled, especially when the the aggressor and victim nets are in parallel, such as in a bus structure. The analysis and estimation of the inductively coupling is much more involved. Because inductive coupling mostly occurs in selected cases, quite often detailed circuit analysis is affordable. In many cases, various types of shielding are implemented to minimize the inductive coupling effect [15,16].

3.3   POWER

With the decreasing transistor channel lengths and increasing die sizes, power dissipation has become a major design constraint. There are three major components of power dissipation: the dynamic power, the short-circuit power, and the static power. Historically, the dynamic power and short-circuit power have been the subject of many studies. In recent years, as the complimentary metal oxide semiconductor (CMOS) devices rapidly approach the fundamental scaling limit, static power has become a major component of the total power consumption. We discuss these components separately in the subsequent subsections.

3.3.1   DYNAMIC POWER

For a CMOS circuit, its states are represented by the charges stored at various metal oxide semiconductor field effect transistors (MOSFETs). When the circuit is operating, the change of the circuit states is realized by charging and discharging of these transistors. This charge/discharge operation can be illustrated in the simple circuit shown in Figure 3.9. When the circuit is in quiescence, inverters INV1, INV2, and INV3 store 1, 0, and 1, respectively. When a falling transition occurs at the input

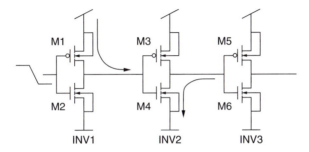

FIGURE 3.9 A simple circuit to illustrate charging and discharging of the gate capacitors.

of INV1, the state of INV2 changes from 0 to 1, by charging the gate capacitor of MOSFET M3 and M4 via transistor M1. In the meantime, the state of INV3 changes from 1 to 0, which is achieved by discharging the gate capacitor of M5 and M6 to ground (via M4).

Consider gate INV1, whose output is being charged from low to high. During this transition, the output parasitic capacitance is charged, and some energy is dissipated in the (nonlinear) positive-channel metal oxide semiconductor (PMOS) transistor resistance. It can be shown that for a single transition, each of these components equals $\frac{1}{2}C_L V_{DD}^2$, where C_L is the load capacitance at the output, and this energy is supplied by the V_{DD} source. In a subsequent cycle, when the output of INV1 discharges, all of the dynamic energy dissipated in the negative-channel metal oxide semiconductor (NMOS) transistor comes from the capacitor C_L, and none comes from V_{DD}. Therefore, for every high-to-low-to-high transition, the energy dissipated in a single cycle can be calculated as

$$P_{\text{dynamic}} = C_{\text{gate}} V_{DD}^2 \qquad (3.11)$$

where C_{gate} is the total capacitance of all gate capacitors involved. If a rising transition occurs next, the energy stored at the gate capacitance of M3 and M4 is simply dissipated to ground.

This concept can be generalized from inverters to arbitrary gates, and the essential idea and the formula remain valid. If the clock frequency is f and the gate switches on every clock transition, then the number of transitions is multiplied by f. The power dissipated can then be calculated as the energy dissipated per unit time. In general, though, a gate does not switch on every single clock transition, and if α is the probability that a gate will switch during a clock transition, the dynamic power of the gate can be estimated as

$$P_{\text{dynamic}} = \alpha C_{\text{gate}} V_{DD}^2 f \qquad (3.12)$$

Here, α is referred to as the switching factor for the gate.

The total power of the circuit can be computed by summing up Equation 3.12 over all gates in the circuit. For a circuit in which the final signal value settles to V_{DD}, as is the case for static CMOS logic, the above calculation is accurate; simple extensions are available for other logic circuits (such as pass transistor logic) where the signal value does not reach V_{DD} [17].

The value of α is dependent on the context of the gate in the circuit. For tree-like structures, this computation is straightforward, but for general circuits with reconvergent fanout, it is quite difficult to accurately calculate the switching factors [18]. Nevertheless, numerous heuristic approaches are available, and are widely used.

From the physical design point of view, usually the supply voltage V_{DD} is determined by the technology and the switching factor α is determined by the logic synthesis. Therefore, only gate capacitance C_{gate} can be optimized during the physical optimization phase. As shown in Equation 3.12, the smaller the overall gate capacitance, the smaller the dynamic power. The minimization of the overall gate size (while maintaining the necessary timing constraints) is actually the same objective of many physical design algorithms. Therefore, an optimal solution of those algorithms is also the optimal solution in terms of dynamic power.

Another approach to reduce dynamic power is to avoid unnecessary toggling of the devices. This is possible for state-storage devices such as latches and flip-flops. A carefully designed clock gating scheme can greatly reduce dynamic power. However, usually these techniques are beyond the scope of physical design flows.

3.3.2 SHORT-CIRCUIT POWER

The mechanism of short-current power can be illustrated in the simple example shown in Figure 3.9. For INV1, when the falling transition occurs at the input, the PMOS device M1 switches from off to on, while the NMOS device M2 switches from on to off. Because of the intrinsic delays of the MOSFET devices as well as the loading effect of the gate capacitance of INV2, the switching cannot occur instantaneously. For a short period during the transition, both M1 and M2 are partially on, thus providing a direct path between the power supply and the ground. Certain amount of power is dissipated by this short-circuit current, which is also referred as the shoot-through current.

The short-circuit power has strong dependence on the capacitive load and the input signal transition time. Although accurate circuit simulation can be applied to calculate the short-circuit power, such an approach is prohibitively expensive. A more realistic approach is to estimate the short-circuit power via empirical equations. Some analysis techniques are proposed in Refs. [19,20]. However, according to many reports, the short-circuit current only accounts for between 5 and 10 percent of total power consumption in a well-designed circuit.

3.3.3 STATIC POWER

In a digital circuit, MOSFET devices function as switches to realize certain logic functions. Ideally, we would like these switches to be completely off when the the controlling gate is off. However, MOSFET devices are far from ideal. Even when the circuit is not operating, the MOSFET devices are "leaking" current between terminals. Although each transistor only leaks a small amount of current, the overall full chip leakage can be substantial due to the sheer number of transistors.

There are two major components of leakage current: subthreshold leakage current and gate tunneling current [21]. These two components are illustrated in Figure 3.10. The subthreshold leakage current (I_1 in Figure 3.10) is the leakage current between the drain and source node when the device is in the off state (the voltage between the gate and source terminal is zero). Historically, in 0.25 μm and higher technology nodes, the subthreshold leakage was small enough to be negligible (several orders of magnitude smaller than the on-current). However, the traditional scaling requires the reduction of supply voltage V_{DD}, along with the reduction of the channel length. As a consequence, the threshold voltage must be scaled accordingly to maintain the driving capability of the MOSFET

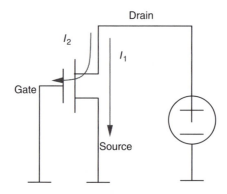

FIGURE 3.10   Two major components of the leakage current.

device. The smaller threshold voltage causes large increase of subthreshold leakage current, so that this is a significant factor in nanometer technologies.

The second component of the static power is the gate tunneling current (I_2 in Figure 3.10), which is also the consequence of scaling. As the device dimensions are reduced, the gate oxide thickness also has to be reduced. An unwanted consequence of thinner gate oxide thickness is the increased gate tunneling leakage current.

Many factors can affect the amount of subthreshold leakage current, including many device and environmental variables. An expression for the subthreshold leakage current density, i.e., the current per unit transistor area, is given by Ref. [22]:

$$J_{sub} = \frac{W}{L_{eff}} \mu \sqrt{\frac{q\epsilon_{si}N_{cheff}}{2\phi_s}} \upsilon_T^2 \exp\left(\frac{V_{gs} - V_{th}}{\eta \upsilon_T}\right)\left[1 - \exp\left(\frac{-V_{ds}}{\upsilon_T}\right)\right] \tag{3.13}$$

The details of the parameters in the above equation can be found in Ref. [22]. Here we would like to mention a few points:

- Term $\upsilon_T = kT/q$ is the thermal voltage, where k is the Boltzmann's constant, q is the electrical charge, and T is the junction temperature. From the equation, we can see that the leakage is an exponential function of the junction temperature T.
- Symbol V_{th} represents the threshold voltage. It can be shown that for a given technology, V_{th} is a function of the effective channel length L_{eff}. Therefore, subthreshold leakage is also an exponential function of effective channel length.
- Drain-to-source voltage, V_{ds}, is closely related to supply voltage V_{DD}, and has the same range in static CMOS circuits. Therefore, subthreshold leakage is an exponential function of the supply voltage.
- Threshold voltage V_{th} is also affected by the body bias V_{BS}. In a bulk CMOS technology, because the body node is always tied to ground for NMOS and V_{DD} for PMOS, the body bias conditions for stacked devices are different, depending on the location of the off device on a stack (e.g., top of the stack or bottom of the stack). As a result, the subthreshold leakage current can quite vary when different input vectors are applied to a gate with stacks.

For the gate tunneling current, a widely used model is the one provided in Ref. [23]:

$$J_{tunnel} = \frac{4\pi m^* q}{h^3} (kT)^2 \left(1 + \frac{\gamma kT}{2\sqrt{E_B}}\right) \exp\left(\frac{E_{F0,Si/SiO_2}}{kT}\right) \exp\left(-\gamma\sqrt{E_B}\right) \tag{3.14}$$

where
T is the operating temperature
$E_{F0,Si/SiO_2}$ is the Fermi level at the Si/SiO_2 interface
m^* depends on the the underlying tunneling mechanism

Parameters k and q are defined as above, and h is Planck's constant: all of these are physical constants. The term $\gamma = 4\pi t_{OX}\sqrt{2m_{OX}}/h$, where t_{ox} is the oxide thickness, and m_{ox} is the effective electron mass in the oxide. Besides physical constants and many technology-dependent parameters, it is quite clear that the gate-tunneling leakage depends on the gate oxide thickness and the operating temperature. The former is a strong dependence, but the latter is more complex: over normal ranges of operating temperature, the variations in gate leakage are roughly linear. In comparison with subthreshold leakage, which shows exponential changes with temperature, these gate leakage variations are often much lower. More details about this model can be found in Ref. [23].

One possible solution to mitigate the negative impact of gate current is to use material with higher dielectric constants (so-called high-k material) in junction with metal gates [24]. In many current technologies, the gate leakage component is non-negligible. Recently, some progress has been reported on the development of high-k material. If successfully deployed, the new technology can reduce gate tunneling leakage by at least an order of magnitude, and at least postpone the point at which gate leakage becomes significant.

Owing to the power consumption limit dictated by the air-cooling technique widely accepted by the industry and market, power consumption, especially static power, has become a major design constraint. In addition to the advancements in manufacturing technology and material science, several circuit level power reduction techniques also have implications on the physical design flow. They include power gating, V_{th} (or effective channel length) assignment, input vector assignment, or any combination of these methods. More details on these topics can be found in Refs. [21,25–27].

3.4   TEMPERATURE

One of the primary effects of increased power dissipation is that it can lead to a higher on-chip operating temperature. High chip temperature is not only a performance issue but also a reliability and cost issue. High channel temperature affects MOSFET device performance by reducing the threshold voltage V_{th} and the mobility. If V_{DD} is unchanged, the lowered threshold voltage usually leads to larger driving current, while reduced mobility leads to smaller driving current. For a normal design with an increase of 100°C, the effect is dominated by mobility reduction, thus higher temperature leads to smaller overall driving capability [28], although inverse temperature dependence, where the speed of a gate increases with temperature, is also seen [29]. For interconnect networks, higher wire temperature will cause larger interconnect delay because metal has positive temperature coefficients. For example, for every 10°C increase, the resistivity of copper will increase by approximately 3 percent. On the reliability side, at elevated temperature, the metal molecules are more prone to electromigration, negative temperature bias instability (NBTI) [30–32], and time-dependent oxide breakdown (TDDB) [33]. Thus, temperature is always an important factor in reliability analysis. From a cost point of view, the cost of a heat sinking solution increases steeply with the total power dissipation of the chip. Air-cooled technologies are the cheapest option, but these can achieve only a certain level of cooling; beyond this level, all available options are substantially more expensive, and in today's commercial world, they are not viable for consumer products.

For many high-performance microprocessors, due to the large size of the die and large power dissipation, it is common to observe a temperature differential of 30°C–50°C between regions with high switching activity levels (e.g., a processor core) and those with low activity levels (e.g., memory). Potentially, these large spatial distributions can cause functional failures.

Before describing the flow of thermal analysis, we briefly describe how heat is dissipated from today's IC product. Figure 3.11 shows a highly simplified cross section of a typical IC product. Most

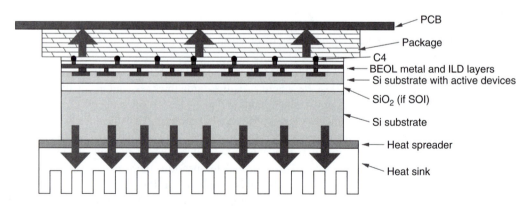

FIGURE 3.11   Simplified cross section to illustrate heat transfer from an IC chip.

high-performance IC designs use C4 technology for I/O and power delivery (versus the cheaper wire-bond technology that is used for lower performance parts). Hundreds to thousands of lead C4's are placed on top of the metal layer, and are connected to the printed circuit board (PCB) via the package. On the substrate side, a heat spreader is mounted next to the die, which is connected to a heat sink. The whole structure actually is "flipped" upside down so that a heat sink is on the top (thus C4 technology is also called flip-chip technology). The heat can be dissipated from both the heat sink side and the C4 side. However, because the heat sink has much smaller thermal resistivity, majority of the heat is dissipated from the heat sink.

There are three major mechanisms for heat transfer: conduction, convection, and radiation [34]. Convection occurs when heat is transferred by fluid movement (e.g., air or water). Radiation is the mechanism when the heat is transferred by photons of light in the spectrum. For modern IC products, convection and radiation only occur at interface of the heat sink, while almost all on-chip heat transfer is through conduction. The heat transfer at the heat sink interface is often described as a macromodel. For on-chip thermal analysis, cooling issues related to the heat sink are often decoupled from on-chip analysis by assuming it to be at the ambient temperature. Therefore, we only focus on conduction in this section.

The fundamental physics law governing heat conduction is the Fourier's law. If uniform material is assumed, it can be described as

$$\nabla^2 T(\mathbf{r}) + \frac{g(\mathbf{r})}{k_{\mathbf{r}}} = \frac{\rho c}{k_{\mathbf{r}}} \frac{\partial T}{\partial t}$$

where
  k is the thermal conductivity at the particular location
  ρ is the density of the material
  c is the specific heat capacity
  g is the volume power density, which is also location dependent

Usually the problem is formulated in three-dimensional space, therefore $\mathbf{r}$ is a three-dimensional array $\mathbf{r} = (x, y, z)$. Because the time constant of on-chip temperature change is usually in the order of milliseconds, while the operating frequency of electric signal is in the picoseconds range, it is often assumed that the thermal dissipation is a steady-state problem. Under this assumption, the heat diffusion equation can be simplified as

$$\nabla^2 T(\mathbf{r}) = -\frac{g(\mathbf{r})}{k_{\mathbf{r}}} \tag{3.15}$$

To solve the above three-dimensional thermal equation, appropriate boundary conditions need to be established. Because many layers of materials are involved and they all have different thermal conductivities, also due to the fact that power density distribution is uneven across the die, usually relatively fine spatial discretization is needed. Overall, it is difficult to solve the problem analytically. Instead a numerical method is applied.

Like other partial differential equations, the heat diffusion problem can be solved using the finite difference method [35,36], the finite element method, or the boundary element method [37]. A commonly used method is the finite difference method. Because $\nabla^2 T(\mathbf{r}) = \frac{\partial^2 T}{\partial x^2} + \frac{\partial^2 T}{\partial y^2} + \frac{\partial^2 T}{\partial z^2}$, if we discretized the space in 3D space, the term $\frac{\partial^2 T}{\partial x^2}$ can be approximated by

$$\frac{\partial^2 T}{\partial x^2} \approx \frac{T_{i+1,j,k} - 2T_{i,j,k} + T_{i-1,j,k}}{\Delta x^2}$$

where i, j, and k are the indexes in the x, y, and t directions, respectively. After some algebraic manipulation, the steady-state thermal diffusion problem can be formulated into the matrix form:

$$\mathbf{GT} = \mathbf{P}$$

where

    $\mathbf{G}$ is the thermal conductance matrix

    unknown vector $\mathbf{T}$ is the steady-state temperature at all mesh points

Depending on the resolution required, the size of the problem can be quite large. The problem can be solved by applying a direct solver or using iterative techniques [35,38,39].

Like the finite difference method, the finite element method also results in a matrix of the type

$$K\mathbf{T} = \mathbf{P} \tag{3.16}$$

although in this case, the left-hand side coefficient matrix is denser (but still qualifies as a sparse matrix). The T variables here are node temperatures in the discretization, and the elements of K can be set up using element stamps. The finite element method essentially uses a polynomial fit within each grid cell, and the element stamps represent this fit. In the finite element parlance, the left-hand side matrix, K, is referred to as the global stiffness matrix. Stamps for boundary conditions can similarly be derived. Conductive boundary conditions simply correspond to fixed temperatures; because these parameters are no longer variables, they can be eliminated and the quantities moved to the right-hand side so that K is nonsingular.

As discussed earlier, a change in temperature will change the threshold voltage and mobility of a MOSFET device [28]. Usually, but not always, an elevated temperature causes the reduction of the overall driving strength of the MOSFET device. However, as the voltage supply V_{DD} gets close to 1-V range, the reduction of mobility may not offset the increase of driving capability due to the lowering of threshold voltage V_{th}. In other words, the higher temperature causes the transistors to have stronger driving capability, which in turn make the temperature increase further. Moreover, the subthreshold leakage increases exponentially with temperature, so that a small change in the temperature can result in a large change in the static power. When this happens, a positive feedback loop is formed between temperature and transistor driving capability. The issue is especially troublesome during "burn-in" testing, when the finished product is stress-tested under a higher supply voltage and an increased ambient temperature. During testing, the phenomenon is often referred as thermal runaway. Once this happens, the usual outcome is the complete destruction of the product. Fortunately, so far there have been no reports that thermal runaway happens for products operating under normal conditions, but nevertheless, thermal effects can cause parts to deviate from their prescribed power and timing specifications.

ACKNOWLEDGMENT

Part of Section 3.1.3 has been published in *Timing*, authored by Sachin Sapatnekar, by Kluwer Academic Publishers in 2004 [40]. (Used with kind permission of Springer Science and Business Media.)

REFERENCES

1. W. C. Elmore. The transient response of damped linear networks with particular regard to wideband amplifiers. *Journal of Applied Physics*, 19:55–63, January 1948.
2. J. Rubenstein, P. Penfield, and M. A. Horowitz. Signal delay in RC tree networks. *IEEE Transactions on Computer-Aided Design of Integrated Circuits and Systems*, pp. 202–211, July 1983.
3. R. Gupta, B. Tutuianu, and L. T. Pileggi. The Elmore delay as a bound for RC trees with generalized input signals. *IEEE Transactions on Computer-Aided Design of Integrated Circuits and Systems*, 16(1):95–104, January 1997.

4. L. T. Pillage and R. A. Rohrer. Asymptotic wavelform evaluation for timing analysis. *IEEE Transactions on Computer-Aided Design of Integrated Circuits and Systems*, 9(4):352–366, April 1990.
5. R. Kay and L. Pileggi. PRIMO: Probability interpretation of moments for delay calculation. In *Proceedings of the ACM/IEEE Design Automation Conference*, San Francisco, CA, pp. 463–468, 1998.
6. F. Liu, C. V. Kashyap, and C. J. Alpert. A delay metric for RC circuits based on the Weibull distribution. In *Proceedings of the IEEE/ACM International Conference on Computer-Aided Design*, San Jose, CA, pp. 620–624, 2002.
7. C. J. Alpert, F. Liu, C. V. Kashyap, and A. Devgan. Close-form delay and skew metrics made easy. *IEEE Transactions on Computer-Aided Design of Integrated Circuits and Systems*, 23(12):1661–1669, December 2004.
8. T. Lin, E. Acar, and L. Pileggi. H-gamma: An RC delay metric based on a gamma distribution approximation of the homogeneous response. In *Proceedings of the IEEE/ACM International Conference on Computer-Aided Design*, San Jose, CA, pp. 19–25, 1998.
9. K. L. Shepard, V. Narayanan, and R. Rose. Harmony: Static noise analysis of deep submicron digital integrated circuits. *IEEE Transactions on Computer-Aided Design of Integrated Circuits and Systems*, 18(8):1132–1150, August 1999.
10. P. Chen, D. A. Kirkpatrick, and K. Keutzer. Miller factor for gate-level coupling delay calculation. In *Proceedings of the IEEE/ACM International Conference on Computer-Aided Design*, San Jose, CA, pp. 68–74, 2000.
11. A. Devgan. Efficient coupled noise estimation for on-chip interconnects. In *Proceedings of the IEEE/ACM International Conference on Computer-Aided Design*, San Jose, CA, pp. 147–153, 1997.
12. M. Kuhlmann and S. S. Sapatnekar. Exact and efficient crosstalk estimation. *IEEE Transactions on Computer-Aided Design of Integrated Circuits and Systems*, 20(7):858–866, July 2001.
13. A. Vittal and M. Marek-Sadowska. Crosstalk reduction for VLSI. *IEEE Transactions on Computer-Aided Design of Integrated Circuits and Systems*, 16(3):290–298, March 1997.
14. J. Cong, D. Z. Pan, and P. V. Srinivas. Improved crosstalk modeling for noise-constrained interconnect optimization. In *Proceedings of the Asia/South Pacific Design Automation Conference*, Yokohama, Japan, pp. 373–378, 2001.
15. L. He and K. M. Lepak. Simultaneous shield insertion and net ordering for capacitive and inductive coupling minimization. In *Proceedings of the ACM International Symposium on Physical Design*, San Diego, CA, pp. 55–60, 2000.
16. Y. Massoud, S. Majors, J. Kawa, T. Bustami, D. MacMillen, and J. White. Managing on-chip inductive effects. *IEEE Transactions on VLSI Systems*, 10(6):789–798, December 2002.
17. N. Weste and K. Eshraghian. *Principles of CMOS VLSI Design*, 2nd edn. Addison-Wesley, Reading, MA, 1993.
18. F. Najm. A survey of power estimation techniques in VLSI circuits. *IEEE Transactions on VLSI Systems*, 2(4):446–455, December 1994.
19. A. Hirata, H. Onodera, and K. Tamaru. Estimation of short-circuit power dissipation for static CMOS gates. *IEICE Transactions on Fundamentals of Electronics*, E00-A(1):304–311, January 1995.
20. K. Nose and T. Sakurai. Analysis and future trend of short-circuit power. *IEEE Transactions on Computer-Aided Design of Integrated Circuits and Systems*, 19(9):1023–1030, September 2000.
21. K. Roy, S. Mukhopadhyay, and H. Mahmoodi-Meimand. Leakage current mechanisms and leakage reduction techniques in deep-micrometer CMOS circuits. *Proceedings of the IEEE*, 91(2):305–327, February 2003.
22. S. Mukhopadhyay, A. Raychowdury, K. Roy, and C. Kim. Accurate estimation of total leakage in nanometer-scale bulk CMOS circuits based on device geometry and doping profile. *IEEE Transactions on Computer-Aided Design of Integrated Circuits and Systems*, 24(3):363–381, March 2005.
23. K. Bowman, L. Wang, X. Tang, and J. D. Meindl. A circuit-level perspective of the optimum gate oxide thickness. *IEEE Transactions on Electron Devices*, 48(8):1800–1810, August 2001.
24. B. H. Lee, L. Kang, W. J. Qi, R. Nieh, Y. Jeon, K. Onishi, and J. C. Lee. Ultrathin hafnium oxide with low leakage and excellent reliability for alternative gate dielectric application. In *Technical Digest of International Electron Devices Meeting (IEDM)*, Washington, D.C., pp. 133–136, 1999.
25. F. Gao and J. P. Hayes. Exact and heuristic approach to input vector control for leakage power reduction. *IEEE Transactions on Computer-Aided Design of Integrated Circuits and Systems*, 25(11):2564–2571, November 2006.

26. S. Mutoh et al. 1-V power supply high-speed digital circuit technology with multithreshold voltage CMOS. *IEEE Journal of Solid-State Circuits*, 30(8):847–854, August 1995.
27. D. Lee, D. Blaauw, and D. Sylvester. Static leakage reduction through simultaneous v_t/t_{ox} and state assignment. *IEEE Transactions on Computer-Aided Design of Integrated Circuits and Systems*, 24(7):1014–1029, July 2005.
28. K. Kanda, K. Nose, H. Kawaguchi, and T. Sakurai. Design impact of positive temperature dependence on drain current in sub-1-V CMOS VLSIs. *IEEE Journal of Solid-State Circuits*, 36(10):1559–1564, October 2001.
29. V. Gerousis. Design and modeling challenges for 90 nm and 50 nm. In *Proceedings of the IEEE Custom Integrated Circuits Conference*, San Jose, CA, pp. 353–360, 2003.
30. D. K. Schroder. Negative bias temperature instability: Road to cross in deep submicron silicon semiconductor manufacturing. *Journal of Applied Physics*, 94(1):1–18, July 2003.
31. M. A. Alam. A critical examination of the mechanics of dynamic NBTI for pMOSFETs. In *IEEE International Electronic Devices Meeting*, Washington, D.C., pp. 14.4.1–14.4.4, 2003.
32. S. V. Kumar, C. H. Kim, and S. S. Sapatnekar. An analytical model for negative bias temperature instability (NBTI). In *Proceedings of the IEEE/ACM International Conference on Computer-Aided Design*, San Jose, CA, pp. 493–496, 2006.
33. A. M. Yassine, H. E. Nariman, M. McBride, M. Uzer, and K. R. Olasupo. Time dependent breakdown of ultrathin gate oxide. *IEEE Transactions on Electron Devices*, 47(7):1416–1420, July 2000.
34. J. H. Lienhard and J. H. Lienhard. *A Heat Transfer Textbook*, 3rd edn. Phlogiston Press, Cambridge, MA, 2005.
35. Y. Cheng and S. M. Kang. A temperature-aware simulation environment for reliable ULSI chip design. *IEEE Transactions on Computer-Aided Design of Integrated Circuits and Systems*, 19(10):1211–1220, October 2000.
36. T. -Y. Wang and C. C. -P. Chen. 3-D thermal-ADI: A linear-time chip level transient thermal simulator. *IEEE Transactions on Computer-Aided Design of Integrated Circuits and Systems*, 21(12):1434–1445, December 2002.
37. Y. Zhan, B. Goplen, and S. Sapatnekar. Electrothermal analysis and optimization techniques for nanoscale integrated circuits. In *Proceedings of the Asia/South Pacific Design Automation Conference*, Yokohama, Japan, pp. 219–222, 2006.
38. H. Qian, S. Nassif, and S. Sapatnekar. Random walks in a supply network. In *Proceedings of the ACM/IEEE Design Automation Conference*, Anaheim, CA, pp. 93–98, 2003.
39. P. Li, L. T. Pileggi, M. Ashehi, and R. Chandra. IC thermal simulation and modeling via efficient multigrid-based approaches. *IEEE Transactions on Computer-Aided Design of Integrated Circuits and Systems*, 25(9):1763–1776, September 2006.
40. S. Sapatnekar, *Timing*, Kluwer Academic Publishers, Boston, MA, 2004.

Part II

Foundations

4 Basic Data Structures

Dinesh P. Mehta and Hai Zhou

CONTENTS

4.1 INTRODUCTION

Physical design automation may be viewed as the process of converting a circuit into a geometric layout. We distinguish between three categories of data structures for the purpose of organizing this chapter:

1. Data structures used to represent the input to physical design: the circuit or the netlist
2. Data structures used during the physical design process
3. Data structures used to represent the output of physical design: the layout

4.2 INPUT DATA STRUCTURES

A circuit consists of components and their interconnections. Each component contains logic that implements some functionality. It also has pins (or terminals) with which it communicates with other components. The entire circuit also needs to be able to communicate with the rest of the world and does so through the use of external pins. An interconnection connects (or makes electrically

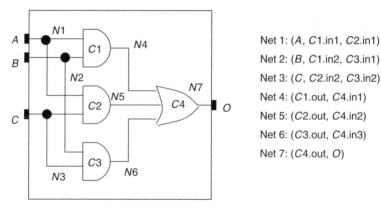

Net 1: (A, C1.in1, C2.in1)

Net 2: (B, C1.in2, C3.in1)

Net 3: (C, C2.in2, C3.in2)

Net 4: (C1.out, C4.in1)

Net 5: (C2.out, C4.in2)

Net 6: (C3.out, C4.in3)

Net 7: (C4.out, O)

FIGURE 4.1   Circuit and its netlist.

equivalent) a set of two or more pins. These pins may be associated with the components or may be external pins. Each interconnection is called a net. The circuit is described by a list of all nets, the netlist. Figure 4.1 shows a simple example, where the components are simple logic gates. Components do not necessarily have to be logic gates. A component could be more complex. For example, it could be a multiplier that was manually designed or designed by some other tool. The chip corresponding to a circuit can itself be a component in a larger circuit.

The mathematical structure that comes closest to representing a circuit is the hypergraph. A hypergraph consists of a set of vertices and a set of hyperedges, where each hyperedge connects a set of $k \geq 2$ vertices. (When $k = 2$ for each edge, the hypergraph reduces to the more familiar graph.) A hypergraph approximates a circuit in that each vertex is mapped to a component and each hyperedge corresponds to a net. Even so, the hypergraph is not a complete representation of a circuit:

1. Components may have associated physical attributes. For example, if the component is a rectangle, its height and width will be provided; locations of pins on the rectangle may also be provided.
2. Nets have an associated direction, which play a role during routing. Consider Net 1 in Figure 4.1 that interconnects three terminals. Pin A is the source of the signal and C1.in1 and C2.in1 are the sinks.
3. Nets connect pins, but hyperedges connect components. You could fix this by having vertices model pins rather than components, but then you lose the property that some pins are associated with a single component. If this component is moved, all of its pins must move with it.

The number of mathematical and algorithmic tools available for hypergraphs is small relative to that for graphs. So, it is unlikely that there is much to be gained even if the hypergraph was a complete representation. As a result, a netlist is sometimes represented by a graph. This is not unreasonable because it turns out that the vast majority of nets are indeed two-terminal nets. There is no well-defined way to convert a net with more than two terminals into one or more graph edges. One approach is to add an edge between every pair of terminals in the net. A netlist converted into a graph is often represented by a connectivity matrix. A matrix element in position $[i][j]$ denotes the number of nets that connect modules i and j.*

The netlist of Figure 4.1 is a complete description of a circuit. It may be read from a circuit file, parsed and used to populate an internal data structure. This internal data structure is the starting point of the physical design process. How should this internal data structure be organized? It

---

* This is actually a multigraph and not a graph because many edges are permitted between a pair of vertices.

seems obvious that at a minimum, the data structure should consist of a list of nets, where each net object contains a list of pins. Should there also be a list of components where each component object also contains a list of pins? Should each component contain a list of nets that are incident on it? Is it necessary to instantiate a pin object? If so, should it contain pointers to the component and net to which it belongs? The answer to these questions depend on what kinds of queries will be posed to the data structure by the particular physical design (PD) tool. One size does not fit all.

4.3 DATA STRUCTURES USED DURING PD

There are too many data structures in this category to describe in this chapter. Fortunately, the vast majority of these are traditional data structures such as arrays, linked lists, search trees, hash tables, and graphs. We do not discuss these structures as they are typically covered in an undergraduate data structures text (e.g., Ref. [1]). Graph algorithms are covered in Chapter 5. Below, we sample some advanced data structures that have either been specifically designed with PD applications in mind or have found widespread application in PD.

4.3.1 FLOORPLANNING DATA STRUCTURES

Several innovative data structures (representations) have been developed for floorplanning. We defer a discussion of these data structures to the floorplanning section of the handbook, where they are discussed in considerable detail (see Chapters 9 through 11).

4.3.2 GEOMETRIC DATA STRUCTURES

Each stage of physical design automation has a significant geometric aspect, with the possible exception of partitioning that is more of a graph-theoretic problem. The computational geometry literature [2] describes a number of geometric data structures. The benefit of using geometric data structures is that a query has a better time complexity than it would on a simple data structure such as an array or a linked list. Implementing geometric data structures can be time consuming, but they may be found in algorithmic or geometric libraries [3,4]. A practitioner should weigh their benefits against the simplicity of arrays and linked lists. Examples of geometric data structures include interval trees, range trees, segment trees, kd trees, and priority search trees. Voronoi diagrams and Delaunay triangulations may also be viewed as geometric data structures. Some of these structures can be extended to higher dimensions although this comes at the cost of simplicity and time complexity. Two or three dimensions are usually sufficient for physical design applications. These data structures are often used in conjunction with the planesweep algorithm technique. Describing all of these data structures is beyond the scope of this chapter. Instead, we pick two, the interval tree and kd tree, and describe these briefly to give the reader a flavor of how they work.

4.3.2.1 Interval Trees

Most physical designs can be represented as a set of axis-parallel rectangles. The boundaries of these rectangles can be viewed as intervals. One common operation needed on these intervals is to find a subset of them that intersect with a perpendicular line. If such a query only happens a limited number of times, it can be efficiently processed by a sweep-line algorithm in $O(n \log n)$ time. However, when such queries need to be done repeatedly, it is better to preprocess the intervals and store them in a data structure that can answer the queries more efficiently. The interval tree is a structure that can be built in $O(n \log n)$ time and then answers the query in $O(\log n + k)$ time, where k is the number of intervals intersecting the perpendicular line.

Even though an interval lies on a line that is a one-dimensional space, it is actually a two-dimensional datum because it has two independent parameters. An interval starting at a and ending at b is represented by $[a, b]$. It is not possible to have a total order over the set of intervals. The idea of

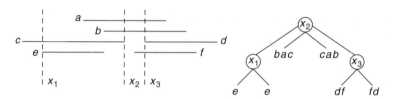

FIGURE 4.2   Set of intervals and its interval tree.

the interval tree is to partition the set of intervals into three groups based on a given point x: intervals to the left of the point $L(x)$, intervals to the right of the point $R(x)$, and intervals overlapping with the point $C(x)$. The subsets $L(x)$ and $R(x)$ of intervals can be recursively represented. The subset $C(x)$ also needs to be organized for the queries. Even though $C(x)$ could include all the intervals in the original set, organizing them is much simpler: they can be ordered both on their left points and on their right points. If the query point $q < x$, only the left points of $C(x)$ need to be checked in increasing order; if $q > x$, only the right points of $C(x)$ need to be checked in decreasing order. To balance $L(x)$ and $R(x)$, thus to have a short tree, it is desired to use the median of all the endpoints as x. Figure 4.2 shows an interval tree for a set of intervals, where the intervals in $C(x)$ are organized in two lists according to their left and right points.

The following result can be easily proved based on the above discussion.

Theorem 1   *For a given set of n intervals, an interval tree can be constructed in $O(n \log n)$ time; with it, a query on the intervals containing a given point can be answered in $O(\log n + k)$ time, where k is the number of covering intervals.*

Applications of interval trees may be found in Refs. [5–7].

4.3.2.2   kd Trees

The query facilitated by a kd tree can be viewed as the reverse of that by an interval tree. In one dimension, a set of points are given and a query by an interval wants to find all the points in it. If the queries happen a limited number of times, they can be efficiently processed by linear scans of the points in $O(n)$ time. When queries need to be done frequently, a sorted array or a binary tree can be built by preprocessing, and a query can be done in $O(\log n + k)$ time where k is the number of points on the interval.

A kd tree is simply an extension of this binary tree to higher dimension space. It first partitions all the points into two groups of almost the same size along one dimension, and then recursively partitions the groups along other dimensions. It follows the same order of dimensions for further partitionings. Figure 4.3 shows a kd tree for a set of points on a plane (two-dimensional space)

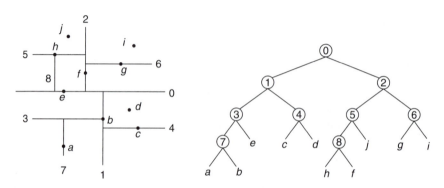

FIGURE 4.3   Set of points on the plane and its kd tree.

```
Algorithm KdTreeQuery(v, R)
if v is a leaf
    then output the point if it is in R
    else {
        if left(v) is fully contained in R
            then output points in left(v)
            else if left(v) intersects R
                then KdTreeQuery (left(v),R)
        // similar code for right (v) omitted
}
```

FIGURE 4.4   Range query algorithm on a kd tree.

with a horizontal partitioning followed by a vertical one. The algorithm for building a kd tree is straightforward, based on recursive bipartitioning of the points along one dimension. Its runtime is in $O(n \log n)$. Given an orthogonal range, a query on a kd tree will give all the points within the range. The range query algorithm is just a simple extension of the interval query on binary trees and it is described in Figure 4.4.

Theorem 2   *A kd tree for n points can be built in $O(n \log n)$ time; a query with an axis-parallel range can be performed in $O(n^{1-1/d} + k)$ where $d > 1$ is the dimension and k is the number of points within the range. In a two-dimensional plane, a query takes $O(\sqrt{n} + k)$ time.*

An application of the kd tree may be found in Ref. [8].

4.3.3   SPANNING GRAPHS: A GLOBAL ROUTING DATA STRUCTURE

Given a set of n points in a plane, a spanning tree is a set of edges that connects all n points and contains no cycles. When each edge is weighted using some distance metric, the minimum spanning tree is a spanning tree whose sum of edge weights is minimum. If Euclidean distance (L_2) is used, it is called the Euclidean minimum spanning tree; if rectilinear distance (L_1) is used, it is called the rectilinear minimum spanning tree (RMST). The RMST is often used as a starting point for constructing a Steiner tree, which is used extensively in global routing (see Chapter 24).

The usual approach for constructing a minimum spanning tree is to first define a complete weighted graph on the set of points and then to construct a spanning tree on it, for example, by running Kruskal's algorithm (see Chapter 5). Given a set of points V, an undirected graph $G = (V, E)$ is called a spanning graph if it contains a minimum spanning tree. The cardinality of a graph is its number of edges. The complete graph has a cardinality of $\Theta(n^2)$, which is expensive. For the L_2 metric, the Delaunay triangulation, a spanning graph of cardinality $O(n)$, can be constructed in $\Theta(n \log n)$ time. However, this approach does not work for the L_1 metric as the Delaunay triangulation may be degenerate. Zhou et al. [9] describe a rectilinear spanning graph of cardinality $O(n)$ that can be constructed in $O(n \log n)$ time [9]. Its use in the construction of a Steiner tree is described in Ref. [10]. We sketch the salient features of this data structure below.

Minimum spanning tree algorithms use two properties to infer the inclusion and exclusion of edges in a minimum spanning tree:

1. Cut property states that an edge of smallest weight crossing any partition of the vertex set into two parts belongs to a minimum spanning tree.
2. Cycle property states that an edge with largest weight in any cycle in the graph can be safely deleted.

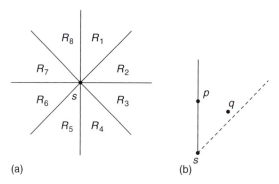

FIGURE 4.5   Octal partition of the plane.

Define the octal partition of the plane with respect to s as the partition induced by the two rectilinear lines and the two 45° lines through s, as shown in Figure 4.5a. Here, each of the regions R_1 through R_8 includes only one of its two bounding half line as shown in Figure 4.5b.

Lemma 1   *Given a point s in the plane, each region R_i, $1 \leq i \leq 8$, of the octal partition has the property that for every pair of points $p, q \in R_i$, $\|pq\| < \max(\|sp\|, \|sq\|)$.*

Here $\|sp\|$ is the L_1-distance between s and p. Consider the cycle on points s, p, and q and suppose $\|sp\| < \|sq\|$. From the cycle property, edge sq can safely be excluded from the spanning graph. This can be extended to excluding edges from s to all points in R_1, except for the nearest one.

A property of the L_1-metric is that the contour of equidistant points from s forms a line segment in each region. In regions R_1, R_2, R_5, and R_6, these segments are captured by an equation of the form $x + y = c$; in regions R_3, R_4, R_7, and R_8, they are described by the form $x - y = c$. This property is used to devise a planesweep algorithm to construct the spanning graph. For each point s, we need to find its nearest neighbor in each octant. We illustrate how to efficiently compute the nearest neighbor in R_1 for each point. Other octants are similarly processed. For the R_1 octant, a sweep line is moved along all points in increasing order of $x + y$. During the sweep, we maintain an active set consisting of points whose nearest neighbors in R_1 are yet to be discovered. When a point p is processed, we identify all points in the active set that have p in their R_1 regions. Suppose s is such a point in the active set. Because points are scanned in increasing $x + y$, p must be the nearest point to s in R_1. Therefore, we add edge sp to the spanning graph and delete s from the active set. After processing these active points, we also add p to the active set. Each point is added and deleted at most once from the active set. The runtime for the sweep is $O(n \log n)$. Each point s has an edge to its nearest neighbor in each octant. This gives a spanning graph of cardinality $\Theta(n)$.

4.3.4   MAX-PLUS LISTS

Max-plus lists are applicable to slicing floorplans [11], technology mapping [12], and buffer insertion [13] problems. Consider a list where each item consists of a pair of elements (m, p). Each item represents a possible solution to an optimization problem that seeks to minimize both m and p (e.g., m and p could represent the height and width of a chip). Solution j is said to be redundant with respect to solution i if $i.m \leq j \cdot m$ and $i \cdot p \leq j \cdot p$ because it is no better than i on either attribute. Consider a list of three solutions: $S_1 = (5, 4)$, $S_2 = (4, 6)$, and $S_3 = (5, 5)$. S_3 is redundant wrt S_1. Neither S_1 nor S_2 is redundant wrt any of the other solutions. Redundant elements are discarded from the list.

Consider an ordered list $A = [(A_1 \cdot m, A_1 \cdot p), \ldots, (A_q \cdot m, A_q \cdot p)]$ such that $A_i \cdot m > A_j \cdot m \wedge A_i \cdot p < A_j \cdot p$ for any $i < j$. Such an ordering of solutions is always possible if redundant solutions are not present in the list. Our example list of three elements above can be rewritten as $[(5,4), (4,6)]$.

These lists arise in the context of dynamic programming, which tries to find an optimal solution to a problem by first finding optimal solutions to subproblems and then merging them to find an optimal solution to the larger problem. Each list represents possible optimal solutions to a subproblem. Merging them gives us a list of possible optimal solutions to the bigger problem.

We next define the list merge. Given two ordered lists A and B as defined above with q and r elements, respectively, compute another list C such that each element c of C is obtained by combining an element a of A with an element b of B using the max-plus operation as follows:

$$c.m = \max(a \cdot m, a \cdot m)$$

$$c.p = a \cdot p + b \cdot p$$

Redundant solutions are not permitted in C. Thus, C only contains the irredundant combinations among the qr possible combinations of elements in A and B. Let the size of C be s.

To illustrate the rationale for the max-plus operation to combine elements, consider two rectangles with dimensions $h_1 \times w_1$ and $h_2 \times w_2$. Suppose one rectangle is stacked on top of the other and we wish to determine the dimensions of the smallest bounding box that encloses both rectangles. The height of this bounding box is the sum of the heights of the two rectangles while its width is the maximum of the two rectangle widths; that is, the max plus operation. In buffer insertion, the two quantities are delay (maximum operation) and downstream capacitance (plus operation).

Stockmeyer [11] proposed an algorithm to perform the list merge in time $O(q + r)$. However, when the merge tree is skewed, it takes r^2 time to combine all the lists even though the total number of items in C is r. Stockmeyer's algorithm is inefficient when the two lists have very different lengths. An extreme case is when a single item is being merged with a big list. In this case, the algorithm reduces to a linear time search to find the location of an element in a sorted list. Balanced binary search trees [14] were used to represent each list so that a search can be done in $O(\log r)$ time. In addition, to avoid updating the p values individually, the update was annotated on a node for the rooted subtree. Shi's algorithm is faster when the merge tree is skewed, with $O(r \log r)$ time relative to Stockmeyer's $O(r^2)$ time. However, Shi's algorithm is complicated and much slower when the merge tree is balanced.

To summarize, the merge of two candidate lists using balanced binary search trees can only speed up the merge of two candidate lists of very different lengths (unbalanced situation), but not the merge of two candidate lists of similar lengths (balanced situation).

Figure 4.6 illustrates the best data structure for maintaining solutions in each of the two extreme cases: the balanced situation requires a linked list that can be viewed as a totally skewed tree; the unbalanced situation requires a balanced binary tree. However, most cases in reality are between these extremes, where neither data structure is the best. The max-plus list is an efficient data structure for the merge operation [15]. As shown in Figure 4.6, it can adapt to the structure of the merge tree: it becomes a linked list in balanced situations and behaves like a balanced binary tree in unbalanced situations. The merge algorithm based on max-plus list has the same asymptotic time complexity as that used in Refs. [14,16] but is easier to implement and more efficient in practice [15].

The max-plus list is based on the skip list [17]. Because a max-plus list is similar to a linked list, its merge operation is just a simple extension of Stockmeyer's algorithm. During each iteration of Stockmeyer's algorithm, the current item with the maximal m value in one list is finished, and the

FIGURE 4.6 Flexibility of max-plus list.

new item is equal to the finished item with its p value incremented by the p value of the other current item. The idea of the max-plus list is to finish a sublist of more than one item at one iteration. Assume that $A_i \cdot m > B_j \cdot m$, we want to find a $i \leq k \leq a$ such that $A_k \cdot m \geq B_j \cdot m$ but $A_{k+1} \cdot m < B_j \cdot m$. These items $A_i, \ldots, A_k$ are finished and put into the new list after their p values are incremented by $B_j \cdot p$. The speedup over Stockmeyer's algorithm comes from the fact that this sublist is processed (identified and updated) in a batch mode instead of item by item. The forward pointers in a max-plus list are used to skip items when searching for the sublist, and an adjust field is associated with each forward pointer to record the incremental amount on the skipped items. Each item is defined by the following C code:

```
struct maxplus_item{
    int level; /* the level*/
    float m, p; /* the two values*/
    float *adjust;
    struct maxplus_item **forward; /*forward pointers*/
}
```

The size of adjust array is equal to the level of this item, and adjust[i] means that the p values of all the items jumped over by forward[i] should add a value of adjust[i].

Two skip lists with sizes q and $r(q \leq r)$ can be merged in $O(q + q \log r/q)$ expected time [18]. This quantity is proportional to the number of jump operations performed on the skip list. Max-plus lists are merged in a similar manner, except that the adjust field need to be updated. The complexity is also proportional to the number of jump operations. However, it can be shown that the number of jump operations in a maxplus merge is within a constant facor of the number of jumps in an ordinary skip list. Thus, the expected complexity of a max-plus merge is identical to that of a skip-list merge, which is the same as that of a balanced binary search tree.

4.4 LAYOUT DATA STRUCTURES

Transistors and logic gates are manufactured in layers on silicon wafers. Silicon's conductivity can be significantly improved by diffusing n- and p-type dopants into it. This layer of the chip is called the diffusion (diff) layer. The source and drain of a transistor are formed by separating two n-type regions with a p-type region (or vice versa) and its gate is formed by sandwiching a silicon dioxide (an insulator) layer between the p-type region and a layer of polycrystalline silicon (a conductor). Because polycrystalline silicon (poly) is a conductor, it is also used for short interconnections (wires). Although poly conducts electricity, it is not sufficient to complete all the interconnections in one layer. Modern chips usually have several layers of aluminum (metal), a conductor, separated from each other by insulators on top of the poly layer. These make it possible for the gates to be interconnected as specified in the design. Note that a layer of material X (e.g., poly) does not mean that there is a monolithic slab of poly over the entire chip area. The poly is only deposited where gates or wires are needed. The remaining areas are filled with insulating materials and for our purposes may be viewed as being empty. In addition to the layers as described above, it is necessary to have a mechanism for signals to pass between layers. This is achieved by contacts (to connect poly with diffusion or metal) and vias (to connect metal on different layers).

A layout data structure stores and manipulates the rectangles on each layer. Some important high-level operations that a layout data structure must support are design-rule checking, layout compaction, and parasitic extraction. Design rules specify geometric constraints on the layout so that the patterns on the processed wafer preserve the topology of the designs. An example of a design rule is that the width of a wire must be greater than a specified minimum. If this constraint is violated, it is possible that for the wire to be discontinuous because of errors in the fabrication process. Additional design rules for CMOS technology may be found in Ref. [19, p. 142]. Capacitance, resistance, and inductance are commonly referred to as parasitics. After a layout has been created, the parasitics must be computed to verify that the circuit will meet its performance goals. The parasitics are computed from the geometry of the layout. For example, the resistance of a rectangular slab of metal is $\frac{\rho l}{tw}$, where ρ is the resistivity of the metal and l, w, and t are the slab's length, width, and thickness, respectively. See Ref. [19, Chapter 4] for more examples. Compaction tries to make the layout as small as possible without violating any design rules. Reducing chip area dramatically reduces cost per chip. (The cost of a chip can grow as a power of five of its area [20].) Two-dimensional compaction is NP-hard, but one-dimensional compaction can be carried out in polynomial time. Heuristics for two-dimensional compaction often iteratively interleave one-dimensional compactions in the x- and y-directions. For more details, see Ref. [21].

4.4.1 CORNER STITCHING

In a layout editor, a user manually designs the layout, by inserting rectangles of the appropriate dimensions at the appropriate layer. The MAGIC system [22] developed at U.C. Berkeley includes a layout editor. The corner-stitching data structure was proposed by Ousterhout [23] to store nonoverlapping rectilinear circuit components in MAGIC. The data structure is obtained by partitioning the layout area into horizontally maximal rectangular tiles. There are two types of tiles: solid and vacant, both of which are explicitly stored in the corner-stitching data structure. Tiles are obtained by extending horizontal lines from corners of all solid tiles until another solid tile or a boundary of the layout region is encountered. The set of solid and vacant tiles so obtained is unique for a given input. The partitioning scheme ensures that no two vacant or solid tiles share a vertical side. Each tile T is stored as a node that contains the coordinates of its bottom left corner, x_1 and y_1, and four pointers N, E, W, and S. N (respectively, E, W, S) points to the rightmost (respectively, topmost, bottommost, leftmost) tile neighboring its north (respectively, east, west, south) boundary. The x and y coordinates of the top right corner of T are $T.E \to x_1$ and $T.N \to y_1$, respectively, and are easily obtained in $O(1)$ time. Figure 4.7 illustrates the corner-stitching data structure.

Corner stitching supports a rich set of operations. These include simple geometric operations like insertion and deletion of rectangles, point finding (search for the tile containing a specified point), neighbor finding (find all tiles that abut a given tile), area searches (do any solid tiles intersect a given rectangular area?), and area enumeration (enumerate all tiles that intersect a given rectangular area). It also supports more sophisticated operations like plowing (move a large piece of a design in a specified direction) and one-dimensional compaction. We describe the point-find operation below to provide the reader with a flavor of the corner-stitching data structure (Figure 4.8). Given a pointer to an arbitrary tile T in the layout, the algorithm seeks the tile in the layout containing the point P.

Figure 4.9 illustrates the execution of the point-find operation on a pathological example. From the start tile T, the while loop of line 5 follows north pointers until tile A is reached. We change

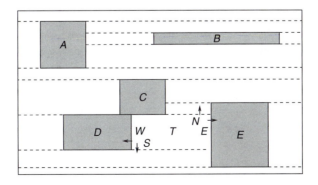

FIGURE 4.7   Corner stitching data structure. Pointers (stitches) are shown for tile T.

Algorithm *Tile Point_Find (Tile T, Point P)*
1. *current* = *T*;
2. **while** (*P* is not contained in *current*)
3.   **while** (*P.y* does not lie in *current*'s y-range)
4.   **if** (*P.y* is above *current*) *current* = *current* → *N*;
5.   **else** *current* = *current* → *S*;
6.   **while** (*P.x* does not lie in *current*'s x-range)
7.   **if** (*P.x* is to the right of *current*) *current* = *current* → *E*;
8.   **else** *current* = *current* → *W*;
9. **return** (*current*);

FIGURE 4.8   Point find in corner stitching.

directions at tile *A* because its *y*-range contains *P*. Next, west pointers are followed until tile *F* is reached (whose *x*-range contains *P*). Notice that the sequence of west moves causes the algorithm to descend in the layout resulting in a vertical position that is similar to that of the start tile. As a result of this misalignment, the outer while loop of the algorithm must execute repeatedly until the point is found (note that the point will eventually be found because the point-find algorithm is guaranteed to converge). *Point_Find* has a worst case complexity is $O(n)$ and its average complexity is $O(\sqrt{n})$. In comparison, a tree-type data structure has an average case complexity of $O(\log n)$. The slow speed may be tolerable in an interactive environment and may be somewhat ameliorated in that it could often take $O(1)$ time because of locality of reference (i.e., two successive points searched for by a user are likely to be near each other requiring fewer steps of the point-find algorithm).

The space requirements of corner stitching must take into account the number of vacant tiles. Mehta [24] shows that the number of vacant tiles is $3n + 1 - k$, where n is the number of solid tiles and k is a quantity that depends on the geometric locations of the tiles.

Expanded rectangles [25] expands solid tiles in the corner-stitching data structure so that each tile contains solid material and the empty space around it. No extra tiles are needed to represent empty space. Marple et al. [26] developed a layout system called tailor that was similar to MAGIC except that it allowed 45° layout. Thus, rectangular tiles are replaced by trapezoidal tiles. Séquin

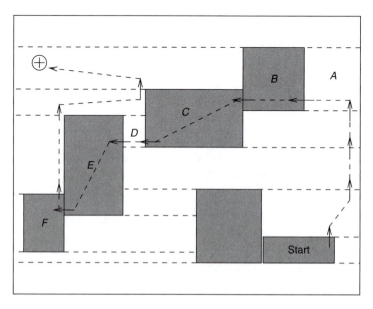

FIGURE 4.9   Illustration of point find operation and misalignment.

and Façanha [27] proposed two generalizations to geometries including circles and arbitrary curved shapes, which arise in microelectromechanical systems. As with its corner-stitching-based predecessors, the layout area is decomposed in a horizontally maximal fashion into tiles. Consequently, tiles have upper and lower horizontal sides. Their left and right sides are represented by parameterized cubic Bezier curves or by composite paths composed of linear, circular, and spline segments. Mehta and Blust [28] extended Ousterhout's corner-stitching data structure to directly represent L-shape and other simple rectilinear shapes without partitioning them into rectangles. This results in a data structure that is topologically different from the other versions of corner stitching described above.

Because, in practice, circuit components can be arbitrary rectilinear polygons, it is necessary to partition them into rectangles to enable them to be stored in the corner-stitching format. MAGIC handles this by using horizontal lines to partition the polygons. Nahar and Sahni [29] studied this problem and presented an algorithm to decompose a polygon that outperforms the standard planesweep algorithm. Lopez and Mehta [30] presented algorithms for the problem of breaking an arbitrary rectilinear polygon into L-shapes using horizontal cuts to optimize its memory requirements.

Corner stitching requires rectangles to be non-overlapping. So, an instance of the corner-stitching data structure can only be used for a single layer. However, corner stitching can be used to store multiple layers in the following way. Consider two layers A and B. Superimpose the two layers. This can be thought of as a single layer with four types of rectangles: vacant rectangles, type A rectangles, type B rectangles, and type AB rectangles. Unfortunately, this could greatly increase the number of rectangles to be stored. It also makes it harder to perform insertion and deletion operations. Thus, in MAGIC, the layout is represented by a number of single-layer corner-stitching instances and a few multiple-layer instances when the intersection between rectangles in different layers is meaningful, for example, transistors are formed by the intersection of poly and diffusion rectangles.

4.4.2 QUAD TREES AND VARIANTS

In contrast to layout editors, industrial layout verification benefits from a more automated approach. This is better supported by hierarchical structures such as the quad tree. The underlying principle of the quad tree is to recursively subdivide the two-dimensional layout area into four quads until a stopping criterion is satisfied. The resulting structure is represented by a tree with a node corresponding to each quad, with the entire layout area represented by the root. A node contains children pointers to the four nodes corresponding the quads formed by the subdivision of the node's quad. Quads that are not further subdivided are represented by leaves in the quad tree.

Ideally, each rectangle is the sole occupant of a leaf node. In general, of course, a rectangle does not fit inside any leaf quad, but rather intersects two or more leaf quads. To state this differently, it may intersect one or more of the horizontal and vertical lines (called bisectors) used to subdivide the layout region into quads. Three strategies have been considered in the literature as to where in the quad tree these rectangles should be stored. These strategies, which have given rise to a number of quad tree variants, are listed below and are illustrated in Figure 4.10:

1. Smallest: Store a rectangle in the smallest quad (not necessarily a leaf quad) that contains it. Such a quad is guaranteed to exist because each rectangle must be contained in the root quad.
2. Single: Store a rectangle in precisely one of the leaf quads that it intersects.
3. Multiple: Store a rectangle in all of the leaf quads that it intersects.

Obviously, if there is only one rectangle in a quad, there is no need to further subdivide the quad. However, this is an impractical (and sometimes impossible) stopping criterion. Most of the quad-tree variants discussed below have auxiliary stopping criteria. Some subdivide a quad until it reaches a specified size related to the typical size of a small rectangle. Others stop if the number of rectangles in a quad is less than some threshold value. Figure 4.11 lists and classifies the quad-tree variants.

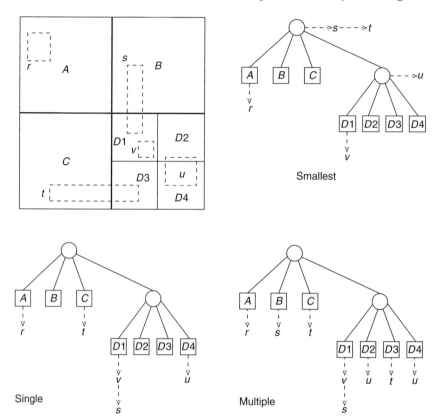

FIGURE 4.10 Quad-tree variations.

4.4.2.1 Bisector List Quad Trees

Bisector list quad trees (BLQT) [31], which was the first quad-tree structure proposed for VLSI layouts, used the smallest strategy. Here, a rectangle is associated with the smallest quad (leaf or nonleaf) that contains it. Any nonleaf quad Q is subdivided into four quads by a vertical bisector and a horizontal bisector. Any rectangle associated with this quad must intersect one or both of the bisectors (otherwise, it is contained in one of Q's children, and should not be associated with Q). The set of rectangles are partitioned into two sets: V, which consists of rectangles that intersect the vertical bisector, and H, which consists of rectangles that intersect the horizontal bisector. Rectangles

Author	Abbreviation	Year of Publication	Strategy
Kedem	BLQT	1982	Smallest
Rosenberg	kd	1985	N/A
Brown	MSQT	1986	Multiple
Weyten et al.	QLQT	1989	Multiple
Pitaksanonkul et al.	BQT	1989	Single
Lai et al.	HV	1993	Smallest
Lai et al.	HQT	1996	Multiple

FIGURE 4.11 Summary of quad-tree variants.

that intersect both bisectors are arbitrarily assigned to one of V and H. These lists were actually implemented using binary trees. The rationale was that because most rectangles in integrated circuit (IC) layouts were small and uniformly distributed, most rectangles will be at leaf quads. A region-search operation identifies all the quads that intersect a query window and checks all the rectangles in each of these quads for intersection with the query window.

4.4.2.2 kd Trees

Rosenberg [32] compared BLQT with kd trees and showed experimentally that kd trees outperformed an implementation of BLQT. Rosenberg's implementation of the BLQT differs from the original in that linked lists rather than binary trees were used to represent bisector lists. It is hard to evaluate the impact of this on the experimental results, which showed that point-find and region-search queries visit fewer nodes when the kd tree is used instead of BLQT. The experiments also show that kd trees consume about 60–80 percent more space than BLQTs.

4.4.2.3 Multiple Storage Quad Trees

In 1986, Brown proposed a variation [33] called multiple storage quad trees (MSQT). Each rectangle is stored in every leaf quad it intersects. (See the quad tree labeled "Multiple" in Figure 4.10.) An obvious disadvantage of this approach is that it results in wasted space. This is partly remedied by only storing a rectangle once and having all of the leaf quads that it intersects contain a pointer to the rectangle. Another problem with this approach is that queries such as region search may report the same rectangle more than once. This is addressed by marking a rectangle when it is reported for the first time and by not reporting rectangles that have been previously marked. At the end of the region-search operation, all marked rectangles need to be unmarked in preparation for the next query. Experiments on VLSI mask data were used to evaluate MSQT for different threshold values and for different region-search queries. A large threshold value results in longer lists of pointers in the leaf quads that have to be searched. On the other hand, a small threshold value results in a quad tree with greater height and more leaf nodes as quads have to be subdivided more before they meet the stopping criterion. Consequently, a rectangle now intersects and must be pointed at by more leaf nodes. A region-search query with a small query rectangle (window) benefits from a smaller threshold because it has to search smaller lists in a handful of leaf quads. A large window benefits from a higher threshold value because it has to search fewer quads and encounters fewer duplicates.

4.4.2.4 Quad List Quad Trees

In 1989, Weyten and De Pauw [34] proposed a more efficient implementation of MSQT called quad list quad trees (QLQT). For region searches, experiments on VLSI data showed speedups ranging from 1.85 to 4.92 over MSQT, depending on the size of the window. In QLQT, four different lists (numbered 0–3) are associated with each leaf node. If a rectangle intersects the leaf quad, a pointer to it is stored in one of the four lists. The choice of the list is determined by the relative position of this rectangle with respect to the quad. The relative position is encoded by a pair of bits xy. x is 0 if the rectangle does not cross the lower boundary of the leaf quad and is 1, otherwise. Similarly, y is 0 if the rectangle does not cross the left boundary of the leaf quad and is 1, otherwise. The rectangle is stored in the list corresponding to the integer represented by this two bit string. Figure 4.12 illustrates the concept. Notice that each rectangle belongs to exactly one list 0. This corresponds to the quad that contains the bottom left corner of the rectangle. Observe, also, that the combination of the four lists in a leaf quad gives the same pointers as the single list in the same leaf in MSQT. The region search of MSQT can now be improved for QLQT by using the following procedure for each quad that intersects the query window. If the query window's left edge crosses the quad, only the quad's lists 0 and 1 need to be searched. If the window's bottom edge crosses the quad, the quad's lists 0 and 2 need to be searched. If the windows bottom left corner belongs to the quad, all four lists must

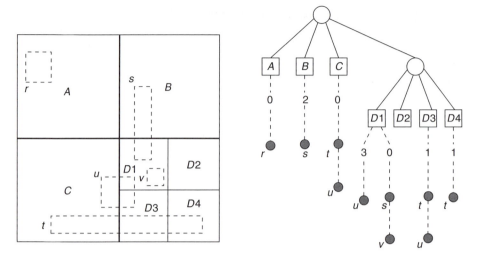

FIGURE 4.12 Leaf quads are A, B, C, $D1$, $D2$, $D3$, and $D4$. The rectangles are r–v. Rectangle t intersects quads C, $D3$, and $D4$ and must appear in the lists of each of the leaf nodes in the quad tree. Observe that t does not cross the lower boundaries of any of the three quads and $x = 0$ in each case. However, t does cross the left boundaries of $D3$ and $D4$ and $y = 1$ in these cases. Thus, t goes into list 1 in $D3$ and $D4$. Because t does not cross the left boundary of C, it goes into list 0 in C. Note that the filled circles represent pointers to the rectangles rather than the rectangles themselves.

be searched. For all other quads, only list 0 must be searched. Thus, the advantages of the QLQT over MSQT are as follows:

1. QLQT has to examine fewer list nodes than MSQT for a region-search query.
2. Unlike MSQT, QLQT does not require marking and unmarking procedures to identify duplicates.

4.4.2.5   Bounded Quad Trees

Later, in 1989, Pitaksanonkul et al. proposed a variation of quad trees [35] that we refer to as bounded quad trees (BQT). Here, a rectangle is only stored in the quad that contains its bottom left corner (see the quad tree labeled "Single" in Figure 4.10). This may be viewed as a version of QLQT that only uses list 0. Experimental comparisons with kd trees show that for small threshold values, quad trees search fewer nodes than kd trees.

4.4.2.6   HV Trees

Next, in 1993, Lai et al. [36] presented a variation that once again uses bisector lists. It overcomes some of the inefficiencies of the original BLQT by a tighter implementation. An HV tree consists of alternate levels of H-nodes and V-nodes. An H-node splits the space assigned to it into two halves with a horizontal bisector, while a V-node does the same by using a vertical bisector. A node is not split if the number of rectangles assigned to it is less than some fixed threshold.

Rectangles intersecting an H-node's horizontal bisector are stored in the node's bisector list. Bisector lists are implemented using cut trees. A vertical cutline divides the horizontal bisector into two halves. All rectangles that intersect this vertical cutline are stored in the root of the cut tree. All rectangles to the left of the cutline are recursively stored in the left subtree and all rectangles to the right are recursively stored in the right subtree. So far, the data structure is identical to Kedem's binary

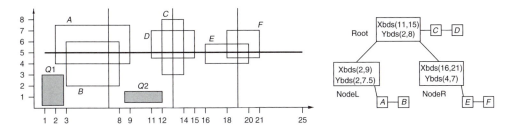

FIGURE 4.13   Bisector list implementation in HVT. All rectangles intersect the thick horizontal bisector line ($y = 5$). The first vertical cutline at $x = 13$ corresponding to the root of the tree intersects rectangles C and D. These rectangles are stored in a linked list at the root. Rectangles A and B are to the left of the vertical cutline and are stored in the left subtree. Similarly, rectangles C and D are stored in the right subtree. The X bounds associated with the root node are obtained by examining the x coordinates of rectangles C and D, while its Y bounds are obtained by examining the y coordinates of all six rectangles stored in the tree. The two shaded rectangles are query rectangles. For $Q1$, the search will start at root, but will not search the linked list with C and D because $Q1$'s right side is to the left of root's lower x bound. The search will then examine nodeL, but not nodeR. For $Q2$, the search will avoid searching the bisector list entirely because its upper side is below root's lower y bound.

tree implementation of the bisector list. In addition to maintaining a list of rectangles intersecting a vertical cutline at the corresponding node n, the HV tree also maintains four additional bounds that significantly improve performance of the region-search operation. The bounds y_upper_bound and y_lower_bound are the maximum and minimum y coordinates of any of the rectangles stored in n or in any of n's descendants. The bounds x_lower_bound and x_upper_bound are the minimum and maximum x coordinates of the rectangles stored in node n. Figure 4.13 illustrates these concepts. Comprehensive experimental results comparing HVT with BQT, kd, and QLQT showed that the data structures ordered from best to worst in terms of space requirements were HVT, BQT, kd, and QLQT. In terms of speed, the best data structures were HVT and QLQT followed by BQT and finally kd.

4.4.2.7   Hinted Quad Trees

In 1997, Lai et al. [37] described a variation of the QLQT that was specifically designed for design-rule checking. Design-rule checking requires one to check rectangles in the vicinity of the query rectangle for possible violations. Previously, this was achieved by employing a traditional region query whose rectangle was the original query rectangle extended in all directions by a specified amount. Region searches start at the root of the tree and proceed down the tree as discussed previously. The hinted quad tree is based on the philosophy that it is wasteful to begin searching at the root, when, with an appropriate hint, the algorithm can start the search lower down in the tree. Two questions arise here: at which node should the search begin and how does the algorithm get to that node? The node at which the design rule check for rectangle r begins is called the owner of r. This is defined as the lowest node in the quad tree that completely contains r expanded in all four directions. Because the type of r is known (e.g., whether it is n-type diffusion or metal), the amount by which r has to be expanded is also known in advance. Clearly, any rectangle that intersects the expanded r must be referenced by at least one leaf in the owner node's subtree. The owner node may be reached by following parent pointers from the rectangle. However, this could be expensive. Consequently, in HQT, each rectangle maintains a pointer to the owner virtually eliminating the cost of getting to that node. Although this is the main contribution of the HQT, there are additional implementation improvements over the underlying QLQT that are used to speed up the data structure. First, the HQT resolves the situation where the boundary of a rectangle stored in the data structure or a query rectangle coincides with that of a quad. Second, HQT sorts the four lists of rectangles stored in each leaf node with one of their x or y coordinates as keys. This reduces the search time at the leaves and consequently makes it possible to use a higher threshold than that used in QLQT. Experimental results showed that HQT outperforms QLQT, BQT, HVT, and kd on neighbor-search queries by at least 20 percent. However, its build time and space requirements were not as good as some of the other data structures.

ACKNOWLEDGMENT

Section 4.4 was reproduced with permission of Taylor & Francis Group, LLC, from Chapter 52 (Layout Data Structures), in *Handbook of Data Structures and Applications*, Chapman and Hall/CRC Press, edited by Dinesh P. Mehta and Sartaj Sahni.

REFERENCES

1. E. Horowitz, S. Sahni, and D. Mehta. *Fundamentals of Data Structures in C++*, Second Edition. Summit, NJ: Silicon Press, 2007.
2. M. de Berg, M. van Kreveld, M. Overmars, and O. Schwarzkopf. *Computational Geometry: Algorithms and Applications*, Second Edition. Berlin, Germany: Springer-Verlag, 2000.
3. K. Mehlhorn and S. Naher. *LEDA: A Platform for Combinatorial and Geometric Computing*. Cambridge, United Kingdom: Cambridge University Press, 1999.
4. http://www.cgal.org/.
5. S.C. Maruvada, K. Krishnamoorthy, F. Balasa, and L.M. Ionescu. Red-black interval trees in device-level analog placement. *IEICE Transactions on Fundamentals of Electronics, Communications and Computer Sciences*, E86-A (12): 3127–3135, Japan, December 2003.
6. J. Cong, J. Fang, and K.-Y. Khoo. An implicit connection graph maze routing algorithm for ECO routing. *Proceedings of the International Conference on Computer-Aided Design*, San Jose, California, 1999.
7. H.-Y. Chen, Y.-L. Li, and Z.-D. Lin. NEMO: A new implicit connection graph-based gridless router with multi-layer planes and pseudo-tile propagation. *International Symposium on Physical Design*, San Jose, California, 2006.
8. S. Liao, N. Shenoy, and W. Nicholls. An efficient external-memory implementation of region query with application to area routing. *Proceedings of the International Conference on Computer Design*, Freiburg, Germany, 2002.
9. H. Zhou, N. Shenoy, and W. Nicholls. Efficient spanning tree construction without Delaunay triangulation. *Information Processing Letters*, 81(5), 2002.
10. H. Zhou. Efficient steiner tree construction based on spanning graphs. *IEEE Transactions on Computer Aided Design*, 23(5): 704–710, May 2004.
11. L. Stockmeyer. Optimal orientations of cells in slicing floorplan designs. *Information and Control*, 59: 91–101, 1983.
12. K. Keutzer. Dagon: Technology binding and local optimization by dag matching. In *Proceedings of the Design Automation Conference*, Miami Beach, Florida, pp. 617–623, June 1987.
13. L.P.P.P. van Ginneken. Buffer placement in distributed RC-tree networks for minimal Elmore delay. In *Proceedings of the International Symposium on Circuits and Systems*, New Orleans, Louisiana, pp. 865–868, 1990.
14. W. Shi. A fast algorithm for area minimization of slicing floorplans. *IEEE Transactions on Computer Aided Design*, 15: 550–557, 1996.
15. R. Chen and H. Zhou. A flexible data structure for efficient buffer insertion. In *Proceedings of the International Conference on Computer Design*, pp. 216–221, San Jose, CA, October 2004.
16. W. Shi and Z. Li. An $o(n \log n)$ time algorithm for optimal buffer insertion. In *Proceedings of the Design Automation Conference*, pp. 580–585, Anaheim, CA, June 2003.
17. W. Pugh. Skip lists: A probabilistic alternative to balanced trees. *Communications of the ACM*, 33(6), 1990.
18. W. Pugh. *A Skip List Cookbook*. Technical Report CS-TR-2286.1. College Park, MD: University of Maryland, 1990.
19. N.H.E. Weste and K. Eshraghian. *Principles of CMOS VLSI Design: A Systems Perspective*, Second Edition. New York: Addison Wesley, 1993.
20. J.L. Hennessy and D.A. Patterson. *Computer Architecture: A Quantitative Approach*, Third Edition. New York: Morgan Kaufmann, 2003.

21. D.G. Boyer. Symbolic layout compaction review. In *Proceedings of 25th Design Automation Conference*, Anaheim, California, pp. 383–389, 1988.
22. J. Ousterhout, G. Hamachi, R. Mayo, W. Scott, and G. Taylor. Magic: A VLSI layout system. In *Proceedings of 21st Design Automation Conference*, pp. 152–159, 1984.
23. J.K. Ousterhout. Corner stitching: A data structuring technique for VLSI layout tools. *IEEE Transactions on Computer-Aided Design*, 3(1): 87–100, 1984.
24. D.P. Mehta. Estimating the memory requirements of the rectangular and L-shaped corner stitching data structures. *ACM Transactions on the Design Automation of Electronic Systems*, 3(2), April 1998.
25. M. Quayle and J. Solworth. Expanded rectangles: A new VLSI data structure. In *Proceedings of the International Conference on Computer-Aided Design*, pp. 538–541, 1988.
26. D. Marple, M. Smulders, and H. Hegen. Tailor: A layout system based on trapezoidal corner stitching. *IEEE Transactions on Computer-Aided Design*, 9(1): 66–90, 1990.
27. C.H. Séquin and H. da Silva Façanha. Corner stitched tiles with curved boundaries. *IEEE Transactions on Computer-Aided Design*, 12(1): 47–58, 1993.
28. D.P. Mehta and G. Blust. Corner stitching for simple rectilinear shapes. *IEEE Transactions on Computer-Aided Design of Integrated Circuits and Systems*, 16: 186–198, February 1997.
29. S. Nahar and S. Sahni. A fast algorithm for polygon decomposition. *IEEE Transactions on Computer-Aided Design*, 7: 478–483, April 1988.
30. M. Lopez and D. Mehta. Efficient decomposition of polygons into L-shapes with applications to VLSI layouts. *ACM Transactions on Design Automation of Electronic Systems*, 1: 371–395, 1996.
31. G. Kedem. The quad-CIF tree: A data structure for hierarchical on-line algorithms. In *Proceedings of the 19th Design Automation Conference*, Washington, pp. 352–357, 1982.
32. J.B. Rosenberg. Geographical data structures compared: A study of data structures supporting region queries. *IEEE Transactions on Computer-Aided Design*, 4(1): 53–67, 1985.
33. R.L. Brown. Multiple storage quad trees: A simpler faster alternative to bisector list quad trees. *IEEE Transactions on Computer-Aided Design*, 5(3): 413–419, 1986.
34. L. Weyten and W. de Pauw. Quad list quad trees: A geometric data structure with improved performance for large region queries. *IEEE Transactions on Computer-Aided Design*, 8(3): 229–233, 1989.
35. A. Pitaksanonkul, S. Thanawastien, and C. Lursinsap. Comparison of quad trees and 4-D trees: New results. *IEEE Transactions on Computer-Aided Design*, 8(11): 1157–1164, 1989.
36. G. Lai, D.S. Fussell, and D.F. Wong. HV/VH trees: A new spatial data structure for fast region queries. In *Proceedings of the 30th Design Automation Conference*, Dallas, Texas, pp. 43–47, 1993.
37. G. Lai, D.S. Fussell, and D.F. Wong. Hinted quad trees for VLSI geometry DRC based on efficient searching for neighbors. *IEEE Transactions on Computer-Aided Design*, 15(3): 317–324, 1996.

5 Basic Algorithmic Techniques

Vishal Khandelwal and Ankur Srivastava

CONTENTS

This chapter provides a brief overview of some commonly used general concepts and algorithmic techniques. The chapter begins by discussing ways of analyzing the complexity of algorithms, followed by general algorithmic concepts like greedy algorithms and dynamic programming. This is followed by a comprehensive discussion on graph algorithms including network flow techniques. This is followed by discussions on NP completeness and computational geometry. The chapter ends with the description of the technique of simulated annealing.

5.1 BASIC COMPLEXITY ANALYSIS

An algorithm is essentially a sequence of simple steps used to solve a complex problem. An algorithm is considered good if its overall runtime is small and the rate at which this runtime increases with the problem size is small. Typically, this runtime complexity is analytically measured/modeled as a function of the total number of elements in the input problem. To make this analysis simpler, several notations and conventions have been developed.

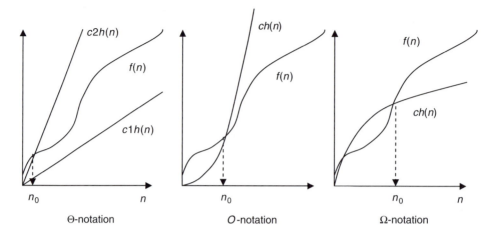

FIGURE 5.1   Complexity analysis.

Θ-Notation

For a function $h(n)$, $\Theta[h(n)]$ represents the set of all functions that satisfy the following:

$$\Theta[h(n)] = \{f(n): \text{there exist positive constants } c1 \text{ and } c2 \text{ and an } n_0 \text{ such that}$$

$$0 \leq c1h(n) \leq f(n) \leq c2h(n) \quad \forall\, n \geq n_0\}$$

Conceptually, the set of functions $f(n)$ are sandwiched between $c1h(n)$ and $c2h(n)$. In such scenarios, $h(n)$ is said to be the asymptotically tight bound (see Figure 5.1) for $f(n)$. Therefore, if an algorithm has a complexity of $f(n)$ (takes $f(n)$ steps to execute), then its complexity could be classified as $\Theta[h(n)]$.

O-Notation

For a function $h(n)$, $O[h(n)]$ represents a set of functions that satisfy the following:

$$O[h(n)] = \{f(n): \text{there exist positive constants } c \text{ and an } n_0 \text{ such that}$$

$$0 \leq f(n) \leq ch(n) \quad \forall\, n \geq n_0\}$$

The O-notation represents an upper bound (see Figure 5.1) for the set of functions $f(n)$. Therefore, an algorithm with complexity $f(n)$ could be classified as an algorithm with complexity $O[h(n)]$.

Ω-Notation

For a function $h(n)$, $\Omega[h(n)]$ represents a set of functions that satisfy the following:

$$\Omega[h(n)] = \{f(n): \text{there exist positive constants } c \text{ and an } n_0 \text{ such that}$$

$$0 \leq ch(n) \leq f(n) \quad \forall\, n \geq n_0\}$$

The Ω-notation represents a lower bound (see Figure 5.1) for the set of functions $f(n)$.

EXAMPLE

Analysis of the Complexity of Sort

```
Sort (Array:A, size:N):
last = N
While last >= 1
```

```
                max = A[1]
                max-location = 1
                For i = 1 to last
                        If (A[i] > max)
                                max = A[i]
                                max-location = i
                temp = A[max-location]
                A[max-location] = A[last]
                A[last] = temp
                last = last - 1
        Return A
```

The outer while loop runs N times. For the first time the inner loop runs N times, followed by $N - 1$ and then $N - 2$, etc. So the total number of iterations in this algorithm become $N + N - 1 + N - 2 + \cdots + 1 = N(N + 1)/2$.

Now it can be seen that the algorithmic complexity of sort, $f(N) = N(N + 1)/2$ is $O(N^2)$ and also $\Theta(N^2)$.

5.2 GREEDY ALGORITHMS

An algorithm is defined as a sequence of simple steps that solves a more complicated problem. At each step, the algorithm makes a decision from a set of choices. Greedy algorithms [1] have the property of making a choice that looks the best at that time. This may or may not guarantee the optimality of the final solution. The key advantage of greedy algorithms is simplicity. In this section, we will discuss the basic properties that a problem must have for greedy strategies to yield the optimal solution. If we can demonstrate the following properties in a problem, then greedy methods will yield the optimal solution:

1. Problem can be modeled as a combination of a greedy choice and a smaller subproblem.
2. There exists an optimal solution to the problem in which the greedy choice has been made.
3. Combination of the optimal solution to the subproblem and the greedy choice results in the optimal solution to the overall problem.

EXAMPLE

Fractional Knapsack Problem

Given a knapsack of a certain size W *and* n *items, with the* i*th item having a value of* v_i *and a quantity of* w_i*. We would like to fill the knapsack with the maximum valued goods.*

The algorithm is as follows:

1. Sort the items in decreasing order of v_i/w_i.
2. Start from the first item in the list and pick as much as you can.
3. If space still left, then go to the next item and repeat.

Note that we select as much as possible of the most valuable item (largest v_i/w_i). This is a greedy step. The remaining space in the knapsack is filled by the remaining items. This constitutes the subproblem. It can be shown that the above three properties hold for the fractional knapsack problem and therefore it is solvable optimally using greedy strategies.

There are many problems (including the 0–1 generalization of the knapsack problem where we are forced to choose the entire item or none at all) where a greedy scheme cannot guarantee optimality. In

such scenarios, greedy schemes are usually employed as heuristics resulting in quick but good solutions
to the problem, although not provably optimal.

5.3 DYNAMIC PROGRAMMING

The technique of dynamic programming (DP) [1] essentially is a way of utilizing the availability
of cheap memory to improve the runtime of algorithms. This technique was invented by Richard
Bellman in 1953. Before we go into the details of this technique, let us discuss the following sequence
of steps for solving a problem:

1. Break the problem into smaller subproblems.
2. Solve the smaller subproblems optimally.
3. Combine the optimal solutions to the smaller subproblems to get a solution to the original
   problem.

Now the term optimal substructure means that the optimal solution to the subproblems can be
used to generate the optimal solution to the overall problem. If indeed this is true then the above-
mentioned sequence of steps for solving a problem must generate the optimal solution to the overall
problem. DP also generates the optimal solution using the same principle. Let us illustrate the DP
philosophy using an example.

EXAMPLE

Generation of the Nth Fibonacci Number

Solution

A simple way of generating the Nth Fibonacci number could be as follows:

```
FIBONACCI(N)
        If N = 0 or 1
                then return N
        Else
                return FIBONACCI(N − 1) + FIBONACCI(N − 2)
```

Note that this problem demonstrates optimal substructure because the optimal solution to the
problem of size N can be generated by the optimal solution for subproblem of size $N − 1$ and $N − 2$.
The complexity of this algorithm could be analyzed as follows. Let $T(N)$ represent the complexity
of optimally solving a problem of size N. So

$$T(N) = T(N − 1) + T(N − 2) \quad \text{for } N > 1$$

It could be shown that $T(N)$ is an exponential function of N, which clearly is impractical for
large problems. Nonetheless, from close inspection, we find that to solve the subproblem of size
$N − 1$, we will inevitably solve a subproblem of size $N − 2$. This property is called overlapping
subproblems. Existence of overlapping subproblems could be utilized to improve the complexity of
the above algorithm. Basically, every time a subproblem of a certain size is encountered for the first
time, its optimal solution could be stored. Next time, if the optimal solution to this subproblem is
needed, it could simply be accessed from memory. Using such techniques, a modified algorithm for
Fibonacci numbers is as follows:

```
MODIFIED FIBONACCI(N)
For i = 1 to N
        M[i] = −1
Function Fib(N)
```

```
If M[N] ! = -1
        M[N] = Fib(N-1) + Fib(N-2)
return M[N]
```

In this algorithm, the array M stores the optimal solution (Fibonacci values). Whenever the solution of a subproblem is needed, it could be simply read from this array without having to perform the whole computation again from scratch. This technique is called memoization. It could be seen that the complexity of this algorithm is no longer exponential.

Although the Fibonacci example is not an optimization problem, it illustrates the concept behind DP quite well. DP is essentially a divide-and-conquer approach in which larger complex problems are subdivided in simpler subproblems. The existence of the optimal substructure property ensures that optimality of the overall problem will be maintained. Furthermore, overlapping subproblems could be stored in memory (memoization) for improving the runtime complexity of the algorithm. DP-based approaches for a given problem could be developed as follows:

1. Express the overall problem in the form of subproblems.
2. Investigate if the optimal substructure property holds.
3. Investigate the existence of overlapping subproblems.
4. Develop a memoization-based approach in which the solutions to overlapping subproblems are stored in memory, hence improving the computational complexity.

Several physical design/synthesis problems including buffer insertion for wiring trees and technology mapping could be solved optimally using DP [5].

5.4   INTRODUCTION TO GRAPH THEORY

Graph theory [1,2] is believed to have begun in the year 1736 with the publication of the solution to the Konigsberg bridge problem, developed by Euler. A graph is characterized by $G = (V, E)$, where V is the set of vertices and E is the set of edges between them (see Figure 5.2). These edges could either be directed (leading to a directed graph) or undirected (undirected graph). Graphs provide an excellent way to abstract various problems in physical synthesis and design. Combinational circuits are typically modeled as directed acyclic graphs and placement netlists are also modeled as graphs.

Definition 1   *Path: A sequence of vertices and edges in which no vertex is repeated.*

Definition 2   *Cycle: A sequence of vertices $v_0, v_1, v_2, \ldots, v_n$ where $v_n = v_0$ and all other vertices are different.*

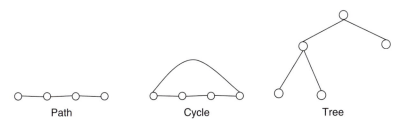

Path   Cycle   Tree

FIGURE 5.2   Examples of graphs.

5.4.1 GRAPH TRAVERSAL/SEARCH

Searching a graph is the process of hopping from one vertex to the other in search for the appropriate
vertex or edge. Graph search is used extensively in physical synthesis and design problems when
a gate of a specific characteristic is being searched. It also finds widespread application in timing
analysis. Two schemes for searching on a graph have been developed

5.4.1.1 Breadth First Search

Given a graph $G = (V, E)$ and a source vertex s, breadth first search (BFS) systematically investigates
all the vertices that can be reached from s. The algorithm is outlined below:

```
BFS(G(V,E),s)
For each vertex u ∈ V − {s}
    Status[u] = untouched
    Distance[u] = ∞
Distance[s] = 0
QUEUE = {s}
While QUEUE! = NULL
    u = FRONT(QUEUE) /* The function FRONT returns the front
        of a queue */
    For each vertex v that can be directly reached from u
        If Status[v] = untouched
                Status[v] = touched
                Distance[v] = Distance[u] + 1
                ENQUEUE(QUEUE, v)
    DEQUEUE(QUEUE)  /* Remove the Front Vertex from the Queue */
    Status[u] = Finished
```

In this algorithm, the frontier between the discovered and undiscovered vertices proceeds like
a wavefront. Starting from the source, all vertices immediately adjacent to it are investigated. This
is followed by investigation of all vertices adjacent to these and so on. This algorithm finds the
minimum number of edges between the source s and the vertices that are reachable from s (this
information gets stored in the array Distance). If a vertex cannot be reached then its distance from
the source is infinity.

5.4.1.2 Depth First Search

Unlike BFS that proceeds as a wavefront, depth first search (DFS) investigates deeper in the graph
till it cannot go any further. At this point, it backtracks to the nearest vertex and investigates its
neighbors once again in a depth first manner. This process continues till no further vertices can be
explored. The algorithm is outlined below:

```
DFS(G(V,E))                        Touch-DFS(u)
For each vertex u                      Status[u] = touched
      Status[u] = untouched        Time = Time + 1
Time = 0                               Starting-Time[u] = Time
For each vertex u                      For each v that can be reached from u
   If Status[u] = untouched                If Status[v] = untouched
```

```
Touch-DFS(u)                              Touch-DFS(v)
                              Status[u] = finished
                              Time = Time + 1
                              Finishing-Time[u] = Time
```

As indicated in the algorithm above, we start with a vertex and investigate deeper into the neighborhood till we cannot go any further. At this point, we go one level above to the previous vertex and investigate deep into the graph once again. A vertex is deemed finished if all the vertices adjacent to it have been touched in a depth first manner. Note that Starting-Time and Finishing-Time, respectively, indicate the time stamp at which we begin investigating a vertex and at which we have investigated its entire neighborhood.

The runtime complexity of both BFS and DFS is $O(|V| + |E|)$.

5.4.1.3 Topological Ordering

Definition 3   *Directed Acyclic Graph (DAG): A directed graph $G = (V, E)$ in which there are no directed cycles.*

Directed acyclic graphs can be used to model most combinational circuits and therefore are particularly important for VLSI computer-aided design (CAD). Topological ordering in DAGs is an ordering $v_0, \ldots, v_n$ of all vertices in V such that for a given vertex v_i, all the vertices in V that have a path either directly or indirectly to v_i must come before v_i in this ordering.

Topological ordering can be generated using DFS by sorting the nodes in decreasing order of their finishing times.

5.4.2 MINIMUM SPANNING TREE

Let us suppose we have an undirected graph $G = (V, E)$ where each edge (u, v) has a weight $w(u, v)$. A spanning tree on such a graph is defined as follows:

Definition 4   *Spanning tree: A spanning tree of a graph $G = (V, E)$ is a subgraph $G' = (V, E')$, which has the same vertices as G and the edges $E' \subseteq E$ such that G' forms a tree.*

A minimum spanning tree (MST) of a graph G is a spanning tree with the minimum total weight (of all edges) among all possible spanning trees of G (see Figure 5.3). There are two popular algorithms for finding the MST of a graph: Kruskal's algorithm and Prim's algorithm.

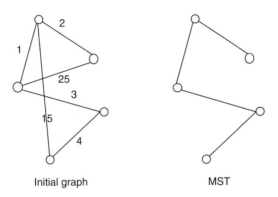

Initial graph   MST

FIGURE 5.3   Minimum spanning tree.

5.4.2.1 Kruskal's Algorithm

Kruskal's algorithm proceeds by starting with a set of disconnected trees (a forest) of vertices in G and merges them in such a way that we eventually get the MST of G. The algorithm is as follows:

```
Kruskal(G=(V,E))
Each node in G represents a trivial Tree.
Sort all edges in E in non-decreasing order of weights
For each edge (u,v) ∈ E in the non-decreasing order
    If u and v are in separate trees
            Merge the two trees into one by connecting them
                 through the edge (u,v)
```

The algorithm starts by assigning all nodes to separate trees. Then it traverses the edges in nondecreasing order of their weights. If an edge merges two separate trees then it is used to create a larger tree otherwise it is discarded. The algorithm terminates after generating the MST.

5.4.2.2 Prim's Algorithm

Unlike Kruskal's algorithm, that maintains multiple trees and merges them iteratively, Prim's algorithm has only one tree and merges more vertices in this tree till the MST is created. The algorithm is outlined as follows:

```
Prim(G=(V,E))
Start with any vertex in V and assign it to a Tree T
While there exist vertices in G not in T
        Find a vertex in G-T which is closest to T
        Expand T by including this vertex
```

MSTs are used extensively in physical design to predict the wirelengh of interconnects when the placement information is available and routing is not known.

5.4.3 Shortest Paths in Graphs

The problem of shortest paths in graphs has several important practical applications. Given a graph $G = (V, E)$ (directed or undirected) and edge weights, try to find the shortest weighted path from a given source s to all other vertices (single-source shortest path problem) or between all pair of vertices. The overall weight of a path is simply the sum of all the edge weights on it.

Let us start the discussion with the single-source shortest path problem. Given a source s, we would like to find the shortest path to all other vertices in the graph. Definition of a shortest path between two vertices becomes ambiguous when there exists a negative weight cycle between the source and the destination. We can simply find a shorter route by indefinitely going around this negative cycle (and therefore reducing the overall path weight). We describe two algorithms for finding the shortest paths: Dijkstra's algorithm and Bellman Ford algorithm. Dijkstra's algorithm assumes all the edge weights are positive and therefore there are no negative weighted cycles either. On the other hand, Bellman Ford algorithm can handle negative weighted edges and also detect the existence of negative weighted cycles (a case where shortest path is not defined).

5.4.3.1 Dijkstra's Algorithm

This algorithm takes a weighted graph G with positive edge weights, a source vertex, and generates the shortest weighted path solution. It initializes two sets S and S'. The set S consists of all vertices in G whose shortest path from s has been calculated and the set S' consists of all the remaining vertices. Initially, $S = \{s\}$ and $S' = V - \{s\}$. We also initialize a label array L, which stores the labeling for the vertices. The moment a vertex u is included in the set S, its labeling $L[u]$ is exactly the weight of the shortest path between s and u. Initially, $L[s] = 0$ and $L[u] = \infty \ \forall \ u \in V - \{s\}$. In the next step, the labels of all the vertices v in S', which are adjacent to a vertex u in S are updated as follows. If $L[u] + weight(u, v) \leq L[v]$ then $L[v] = L[u] + weight(u,v)$. After updating all the labels, the vertex in S' that has the smallest label is chosen and moved to the set S. At this point, the label of this node corresponds to the weight of the shortest path from s. These sequence of steps are continued till S' is null. The algorithm is formally outlined below:

```
Dijkstra(G=(V,E))
S = {s}, S' = V - {s}
L[s] = 0, L[u] = ∞ ∀ u ∈ V - {s}
L[u] = weight[su] ∀ u adjacent to s
While S' ! = NULL
        Find Minimum L[u] ∀ u in S'
        S = S U {u}
        S' = S' - {u}
        For each v in S' that is adjacent to u
                If L[v] ≥ L[u] + weight(uv)
                        L[v] = L[u] + weight(uv)
```

It could be seen that this is a greedy algorithm because at each step a greedy choice is executed (the vertex with the smallest labeling is chosen). This greedy algorithm indeed results in the optimal solution.

5.4.3.2 Bellman Ford Algorithm

Dijkstra's algorithm cannot handle edge weights that are negative. Bellman Ford algorithm not only handles negative edge weights but also detects the existence of negative weighted cycles (that are reachable from the source s). The algorithm is iterative in nature. Once again it has a label array L. $L[s]$ is initializes to 0 and infinity for all other vertices. The algorithm is outlined below:

```
Bellman Ford (G=(V,E))
L[s] = 0, L[u] = ∞ ∀ u ∈ V - {s}
For i = 1 to Number of Vertices
        For each edge (u,v) ∈ E
                If L[v] ≥ L[u] + weight(uv)
                        L[v] = L[u] + weight(uv)
```

The algorithm is quite self-explanatory. It could be proved that if there are no negative weighted cycles reachable from s then the array L has the shortest path to each vertex in the graph. Detection of negative weighted cycles (reachable from s) can be done by the following simple procedure:

```
Negative Cycle Detection
Let L be the labeling of all nodes after application
        of Bellman Ford
```

```
For each edge (u,v) ∈ E
    If L[v] > L[u] + weight(uv)
        Return: Negative Weighted Cycle Exists
```

The all pair shortest path problem tries to find the shortest paths between all vertices. Of course, one approach is to execute the single-source shortest path algorithm for all the nodes. Much faster algorithms like Floyd Warshall algorithm, etc. have also been developed.

5.5 NETWORK FLOW METHODS

Definition 5   A network *is a directed graph G* $= (V, E)$ *where each edge* $(u, v) \in E$ *has a capacity* $c(u, v) \geq 0$. *There exists a node/vertex called the source, s and a destination/sink node, t. If an edge does not exist in the network then its capacity is set to zero.*

Definition 6   A flow *in the network G is a real value function* $f: VXV \rightarrow R$. *This has the following properties:*

1. *Capacity constraint: Flow* $f(u, v) \leq c(u, v) \quad \forall\, u, v \in V$
2. *Flow conservation:* $\forall\, u \in V - \{s, t\},\ \Sigma_{v \in V} f(u, v) = 0$
3. *Skew symmetry:* $\forall\, u, v \in V, f(u, v) = -f(v, u)$

The value of a flow is typically defined as the amount of flow coming out of the source to all the other nodes in the network. It can equivalently be defined as the amount of flow coming into the sink from all the other nodes in the network. Figure 5.4 illustrates an example of network flow.

Definition 7   Maximum flow problem *is defined as the problem of finding a flow assignment to the network such that it has the maximum value (note that a flow assignment must conform to the flow properties as outlined above).*

Network flow [4] formulations have large applicability in various practical problems including supply chain management, airline industry, and many others. Several VLSI CAD applications like low power resource binding, etc. can be modeled as instances of network flow problems. Network flow has also been applied in physical synthesis and design problems like buffer insertion.

Next, an algorithm is presented that solves the maximum flow problem optimally. This algorithm was developed by Ford and Fulkerson. This is an iterative approach and starts with $f(u, v) = 0$ for

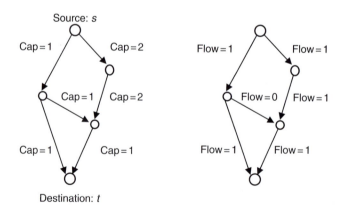

FIGURE 5.4   Network flow.

all vertex pairs (u, v). At each step/iteration, the algorithm finds a path from s to t that still has available capacity (this is a very simple explanation of a more complicated concept) and augments more flow along it. Such a path is therefore called the augmenting path. This process is repeated till no augmenting paths are found. The basic structure of the algorithm is as follows:

```
Ford-Fulkerson (G,s,t)
     For each vertex pair (u,v)
          f(u,v) = 0
     While there is an augmenting path p from s to t
          Send more flow along this path without violating
               the capacity of any edge
     Return f
```

At any iteration, augmenting path is not simply a path of finite positive capacity in the graph. Note that capacity of a path is defined by the capacity of the minimum capacity edge in the path. To find an augmenting path, at a given iteration, a new graph called the residual graph is initialized. Let us suppose that at a given iteration all vertex pairs uv have a flow of $f(u, v)$. The residual capacity is defined as follows:

$$c_f(u, v) = c(uv) - f(u, v)$$

Note that the flow must never violate the capacity constraint. Conceptually, residual capacity is the amount of extra flow we can send from u to v. A residual graph G_f is defined as follows:

$$G_f = (V, E_f) \quad \text{where } E_f = \{(u, v), \in V X V : c_f(u, v) > 0\}$$

The Ford Fulkerson method finds a path from s to t in this residual graph and sends more flow along it as long as the capacity constraint is not violated. The run-time complexity of Ford Fulkerson method is $O(E^* f_{max})$ where E is the number of edges and f_{max} is the value of the maximum flow.

Theorem 1 *Maximum Flow Minimum Cut: If f is a flow in the network then the following conditions are equivalent*

1. *f is the maximum flow*
2. *Residual network contains no augmenting paths*
3. *There exists a cut in the network with capacity equal to the flow f*

A cut in a network is a partitioning of the nodes into two: with the source s on one side and the sink t on another. The capacity of a cut is the sum of the capacity of all edges that start in the s partition and end in the t partition.

There are several generalizations/extensions to the concept of maximum flow presented above.

Multiple sources and sinks: Handling multiple sources and sinks can be done easily. A super source and a super sink node can be initialized. Infinite capacity edges can then be added from super source to all the sources. Infinite capacity edges can also be added from all the sinks to the super sink. Solving the maximum flow problem on this modified network is similar to solving it on the original network.

Mincost flow: Mincost flow problems are of the following type. Assuming we need to pay a price for sending each unit of flow on an edge in the network. Given the cost per unit flow for all edges in the network, we would like to send the maximum flow in such a way that it incurs the minimum total cost. Modifications to the Ford Fulkerson method can be used to solve the mincost flow problem optimally.

Multicommodity flow: So far the discussion has focused on just one type of flow. Several times many commodities need to be transported on a network of finite edge capacities. The sharing of the same network binds these commodities together.

These different commodities represent different types of flow. A version of the multicommodity problem could be described as follows. Given a network with nodes and edge capacities/costs, multiple sinks and sources of different types of flow, satisfy the demands at all the sinks while meeting the capacity constraint and with the minimum total cost. The multicommodity flow problem is NP-complete and has been an active topic of research in the last few decades.

5.6 THEORY OF NP-COMPLETENESS

For algorithms to be computationally practical, it is typically desired that their order of complexity be polynomial in the size of the problem. Problems like sorting, shortest path, etc. are examples for which there exist algorithms of polynomial complexity. A natural question to ask is "Does there exist a polynomial complexity algorithm for all problems?". Certainly, the answer to this question is no because there exist problems like halting problem that has been proven to not have an algorithm (much less a polynomial time algorithm). NP-complete [3] problems are the ones for which we do not know, as yet, if there exists a polynomial complexity algorithm. Typically, the set of all problems that are solvable in polynomial time is called P. Before moving further, we would like to state that the concept of P or NP-complete is typically developed around problems for which the solution is either yes or no, a.k.a., decision problems. For example, the decision version for the maximum flow problem could be "Given a network with finite edge capacities, a source, and a sink, can we send at least K units of flow in the network?" One way to answer this question could be to simply solve the maximum flow problem and check if it is greater than K or not.

Polynomial time verifiability: Let us suppose an oracle gives us the solution to a decision problem. If there exists a polynomial time algorithm to validate if the answer to the decision problem is yes or no for that solution, then the problem is polynomially verifiable. For example, in the decision version of the maximum flow problem, if an oracle gives a flow solution, we can easily (in polynomial time) check if the flow is more than K (yes) or less than K (no). Therefore, the decision version of the maximum flow problem is polynomially verifiable.

NP class of problems: The problems in the set NP are verifiable in polynomial time. It is trivial to show that all problems in the set P (all decision problems that are solvable in polynomial time) are verifiable in polynomial time. Therefore, $P \subseteq NP$. But as of now it is unknown whether $P = NP$.

NP-complete problems: They have two characteristics:

1. Problems can be verified in polynomial time.
2. These problems can be transformed into one another using a polynomial number of steps.

Therefore, if there exists a polynomial time algorithm to solve any of the problems in this set, each and every problem in the set becomes polynomially solvable. It just so happens that to date nobody has been able to solve any of the problems in this set in polynomial time. Following is an procedure for proving that a given decision problem is NP-complete:

1. Check whether the problem is in NP (polynomially verifiable).
2. Select a known NP-complete problem.
3. Transform this problem in polynomial steps to an instance of the pertinent problem.
4. Illustrate that given a solution to the known NP-complete problem, we can find a solution to the pertinent problem and vice versa.

If these conditions are satisfied by a given problem then it belongs to the set of NP-complete problems.

The first problem to be proved NP-complete was Satisfiability or SAT by Stephen Cook in his famous 1971 paper "The complexity of theorem proving procedures," in *Proceedings of the 3rd Annual ACM Symposium on Theory of Computing*. Shortly after the classic paper by Cook, Richard Karp proved several other problems to be NP-complete. Since then the set of NP-complete problems has been expanding. Several problems in VLSI CAD including technology mapping on DAGs, gate duplication on DAGs, etc. are NP-complete.

EXAMPLE

Illustrative Example: NP-Completeness of 3SAT

3SAT: Given a set of m clauses anded together $F = C_1 \cdot C_2 \cdot C_3 \cdots \cdots C_m$. Each clause C_i is a logical OR of at most three boolean literals $C_i = (a + b + \bar{o})$ where $\bar{o}$ is the negative phase of boolean variable o. Does there exist an assignment of 0/1 to each variable such that F evaluates to 1? (Note that this is a decision problem.)

Proof of NP-Completeness: Given an assignment of 0/1 to the variables, we can see if each clause evaluates to 1. If all clauses evaluate to 1 then F evaluates to 1 else it is 0. This is a simple polynomial time algorithm for verifying the decision given a specific solution or assignment of 0/1 to the variables. Therefore, 3SAT is in NP. Now let us transform the well-known NP-complete problem SAT to an instance of 3SAT.

SAT: Given a set of m clauses anded together $G = C_1 \cdot C_2 \cdot C_3 \cdots \cdots C_m$. Each clause C_i is a logical OR of boolean literals $C_i = (a + b + \bar{o} + e + f + \cdots)$. Does there exist an assignment of 0/1 to each variable such that G evaluates to 1. (Note that this is a decision problem.)

To perform this tranformation, we look at each clause C_i in the SAT problem with more than three literals. Let $C_i = (x_1 + x_2 + x_3 + \cdots + x_k)$. This clause is replaced by $k-2$ new clauses each with length 3. For this to happen, we introduce $k-3$ new variables $u_i, \ldots, u_{k-3}$. These clauses are constructed as follows.

$$P_i = (x_1 + x_2 + u_1)(x_3 + \bar{u}_1 + u_2)(x_4 + \bar{u}_2 + u_3)(x_5 + \bar{u}_3 + u_4) \cdots (x_{k-1} + x_k + \bar{u}_{k-3})$$

Note that if there exists an assignment of 0/1 to $x_1, \ldots, x_k$ for which C_i is 1, then there exists an assignment of 0/1 to $u_1, \ldots, u_{k-3}$ such that P_i is 1. If C_i is 0 for an assignment to $x_1, \ldots, x_k$, then there cannot exist an assignment to $u_1, \ldots, u_{k-3}$ such that P_i is 1. Hence, we can safely replace C_i by P_i for all the clauses in the original SAT problem with more than three literals. An assignment that makes C_i 1 will make P_i 1. An assignment that makes C_i as 0 will make P_i as 0 as well. Therefore, replacing all the clauses in SAT by the above-mentioned transformation does not change the problem. Nonetheless, the transformed problem is an instance of the 3SAT problem (because all clauses have less than or equal to three literals). Also, this transformation is polynomial in nature. Hence, 3 SAT is NP-complete.

5.7 COMPUTATIONAL GEOMETRY

Computational geometry deals with the study of algorithms for problems pertaining to geometry. This theory finds application in many engineering problems including VLSI CAD, robotics, graphics, etc.

5.7.1 CONVEX HULL

Given a set of n points on a plane, each characterized by its x and y coordinates. Convex hull is the smallest convex polygon P for which these points are either in the interior or on the boundary of the polygon (see Figure 5.5). We now present an algorithm called Graham's scan for generating a convex hull of n points on a plane.

```
Graham Scan(n points on a plane)
Let p₀ be the point with minimum y coordinate
Sort the rest of the points p₁, ..., pₙ₋₁ by the polar
    angle in counterclockwise order w.r.t. p₀
```

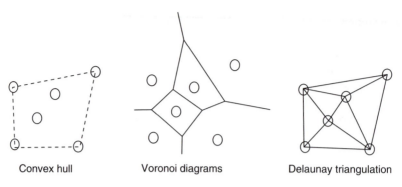

| Convex hull | Voronoi diagrams | Delaunay triangulation |

FIGURE 5.5 Computational geometry.

```
Initialize Stack S
Push(p₀,S)
Push(p₁,S)
Push(p₂,S)
For i = 3 to n−1
        While (the angle made by the next to top point on S,
                top point on S and pᵢ makes a non left turn)
                    Pop(S)
        Push(pᵢ, S)
Return S
```

The algorithm returns the stack S that contains the vertices of the convex hull. Basically, the algorithm starts with the bottom-most point p_0. Then it sorts all the other points in increasing order of the polar angle made in counterclockwise direction w.r.t p_0. It then pushes p_0, p_1, and p_2 in the stack. Starting from p_3, it checks if top two elements and the current point p_i forms a left turn or not. If it does then p_i is pushed into the stack (implying that it is part of the hull). If not then that means the current stack has some points not on the convex hull and therefore needs to be popped. Convex hulls, just like MSTs, are also used in predicting the wirelength when the placement is fixed and routing is not known.

5.7.2 VORONOI DIAGRAMS AND DELAUNAY TRIANGULATION

A Voronoi diagram is a partitioning of a plane with n points (let us call them central points) into convex polygons (see Figure 5.5). Each convex polygon has exactly one central point. Also, any point within the convex polygon is closest to the central point associated with the polygon.

Delaunay triangulation is simply the dual of Voronoi diagrams. This is a triangulation of central points such that none of the central points are inside the circumcircle of a triangle (see Figure 5.5).

Although we have defined these concepts for a plane, they are easily extendible to multiple dimensions as well.

5.8 SIMULATED ANNEALING

Simulated annealing is a general global optimization scheme. This technique is primarily inspired from the process of annealing (slow cooling) in metallurgy where the material is cooled slowly to form high quality crystals. The simulated annealing algorithm basically follows a similar principle. Conceptually, it has a starting temperature parameter that is usually set to a very high quantity. This temperature parameter is reduced slowly using a predecided profile. At each temperature value, a set of randomly generated moves span the solution space. The moves basically change the current solution randomly. A move is accepted if it generates a better solution. If a move generates a solution quality that is worse than the current one then it can either be accepted or rejected depending on a random criterion. Essentially, outright rejection of bad solutions may result in the optimization process getting stuck in local optimum points. Accepting some bad solutions (and remembering the best solution found so far) helps us get out of these local optimums and move toward the global optimum. At a given temperature, a bad solution is accepted if the probability of acceptance is greater than the randomness associated with the solution. The pseudocode of simulated annealing is as follows:

```
Simulated Annealing
s := Initial Solution s0; c = Cost(s); T = Initial Temperature Tmax
current best solution = s
While (T > Final Temperaure Tmin)
    K = 0
    While (K <= Kmax)
        Accept = 0
        s1 = Randomly Perturb Solution(s)
        If(cost(s1) < cost(s))
            Accept = 1
        Else
            r = random number between [0,1] with uniform
                probability
            if (r < exp(-L(cost(s) - cost(s1))/T))
                \* Here L is a constant *\
                Accept = 1
        If Accept = 1
            s = s1
            If (cost(s1) < cost(current best solution))
                current best solution = s1
        k = k + 1
    T = T* (scaling á)
```

Simulated annelaing has found widespread application in several physical design problems like placement, floorplanning, etc. [6]. Many successful commerical and academic implementations of simulated annealing-based gate placement tools have made a large impact on the VLSI CAD community.

REFERENCES

1. T.H. Cormen, C.L. Leiserson, R.L. Rivest, and C. Stein, *Introduction to Algorithms*, The MIT Press, Cambridge, Massachusetts, 2001.
2. G. Chartrand and O.R. Oellermann, *Applied and Algorithmic Graph Theory*, McGraw-Hill, Singapore, 1993.
3. M.R. Garey and D.S. Johnson, *Computers and Intractability: A Guide to the Theory of NP-Completeness*, W.H. Freeman and Company, New York, 1999.
4. R.K. Ahuja, T.L. Magnanti, and J.B. Orlin, *Network Flows: Theory, Algorithms and Applications*, Prentice Hall, Englewood Cliffs, New Jersey, 1993.
5. G. De Micheli, *Synthesis and Optimization of Digital Circuits*, McGraw-Hill, New York, 1994.
6. M. Sarrafzadeh and C.K. Wong, *An Introduction to VLSI Physical Design*, McGraw-Hill, New York, 1996.

6 Optimization Techniques for Circuit Design Applications

Zhi-Quan Luo

CONTENTS

6.1 INTRODUCTION

This chapter describes fundamental concepts and theory of optimization that are most relevant to physical design applications. The basic convex optimization models of linear programming (LP), second-order cone programming, semidefinite programming (SDP), and geometric programming are reviewed, as are the concept of convexity, optimality conditions, and Lagrangian relaxation. Finally, the concept of robust optimization is introduced and a circuit optimization example is used to illustrate its effectiveness.

The goal of this chapter is to provide an overview of these developments and describe the basic optimization concepts, models, and tools that are most relevant to circuit design applications, and in particular, to expose the reader to the types of nonlinear optimization problems that are "easy." Generally speaking, any problem that can be formulated as a linear program falls into this category. Thanks to the results of research in the last few years, there are also classes of nonlinear programs that can now be solved in computationally efficient ways.

Until recently, the work-horse algorithms for nonlinear optimization in engineering design have been the gradient descent method, Newton's method, and the method of least squares. Although these algorithms have served their purpose well, they suffer from slow convergence and sensitivity to the algorithm initialization and stepsize selection, especially when applied to ill-conditioned or nonconvex problem formulations. This is unfortunate because many design and implementation problems in circuit design applications naturally lead to nonconvex optimization formulations, the solution of which by the standard gradient descent or Newton's algorithm usually works poorly. The main problem with applying the least squares or the gradient descent algorithms directly to the nonconvex formulations is slow convergence and local minima. One powerful way to avoid these problems is to derive an exact convex reformulation of the original nonconvex formulation. Once a convex reformulation is obtained, we can be guaranteed of finding the globally optimal design efficiently without the usual headaches of stepsize selection, algorithm initialization, and local minima. There has been a significant advance in the research of interior point methods [8] and conic optimization [11] over the last two decades, and the algorithmic framework of interior point algorithms for solving these convex optimization models are presented.

For some engineering applications, exact linear or convex reformulation is not always possible, especially when the underlying optimization problem is NP-hard. In such cases, it may still be possible to derive a tight convex relaxation and use the advanced conic optimization techniques to obtain high-quality approximate solutions for the original NP-hard problem. One general approach to derive a convex relaxation for an nonconvex optimization problem is via Lagrangian relaxation. For example, some circuit design applications may involve integer variables that are coupled by a set of complicating constraints. For these problems, we can bring these coupling constraints to the objective function in a Lagrangian fashion with fixed multipliers that are changed iteratively. This Lagrangian relaxation approach removes the complicating constraints from the constraint set, resulting in considerably easier to solve subproblems. The problem of optimally choosing dual multipliers is always convex and is therefore amenable to efficient solution by the standard convex optimization techniques.

To recognize convex optimization problems in engineering applications, one must first be familiar with the basic concepts of convexity and the commonly used convex optimization models. This chapter starts with a concise review of these optimization concepts and models including linear programming, second-order cone programming (SOCP), semidefinite cone programming, as well as geometric programming, all illustrated through concrete examples. In addition, the Karush–Kuhn–Tucker optimality conditions are reviewed and stated explicitly for each of the convex optimization models, followed by a description of the well-known interior point algorithms and a brief discussion of their worst-case complexity. The chapter concludes with an example illustrating the use of robust optimization techniques for a circuit design problem under process variations.

Throughout this chapter, we use lowercase letters to denote vectors, and capital letters to denote matrices. We use superscript ^{T} to denote (vector) matrix transpose. Moreover, we denote the set of n by n symmetric matrices by $\mathcal{S}^n$, denote the set of n by n positive (semi) definite matrices $(\mathcal{S}^n_{++})\mathcal{S}^n_+$. For two given matrices X and Y, we use "$X \succ Y$" ($X \succeq Y$) to indicate that $X - Y$ is positive (semi)-definite, and $X \bullet Y := \sum_{i,j} X_{ij} Y_{ij} = \mathrm{tr}\, XY^T$ to indicate the matrix inner product. The Frobenius norm of X is denoted by $\|X\|_F = \sqrt{\mathrm{tr}\, XX^T}$. The Euclidean norm of a vector $x \in \mathfrak{R}^n$ is denoted $\|x\|$.

6.2 OPTIMIZATION CONCEPTS

6.2.1 CONVEX SETS

A set $S \subset \mathfrak{R}^n$ is said to be convex if for any two points $x, y \in S$, the line segment joining x and y also lies in S. Mathematically, it is defined by the following property

$$\theta x + (1 - \theta)y \in S, \quad \forall \theta \in [0, 1] \quad \text{and} \quad x, y \in S.$$

Many well-known sets are convex. For example, the unit ball $S = \{x \mid \|x\| \leq 1\}$. However, the unit sphere $S = \{x \mid \|x\| = 1\}$ is not convex because the line segment joining any two distinct points is no longer on the unit sphere. In general, a convex set must be a solid body, containing no holes, and always curved outward. Other examples of convex sets include ellipsoids, hypercubes, and so on. In the context of linear programming, the constraining inequalities geometrically form a polyhedral set, which is easily shown to be convex.

In the real line $\Re$, convex sets correspond to intervals (open or closed). The most important property about convex set is the fact that the intersection of any number (possibly uncountable) of convex sets remains convex. For example, the set $S = \{x \mid \|x\| \leq 1, x \geq 0\}$ is the intersection of the unit ball with the nonnegative orthant ($\Re_+^n$), both of which are convex. Thus, their intersection S is also convex. The unions of two convex sets are typically nonconvex.

6.2.2 CONVEX CONES

A convex cone $\mathcal{K}$ is a special type of convex set that is closed under positive scaling: for each $x \in \mathcal{K}$ and each $\alpha \geq 0$, $\alpha x \in \mathcal{K}$. Convex cones arise in various forms in engineering applications. The most common convex cones are

1. Nonnegative orthant $\Re_+^n$
2. Second-order cone (also known as ice-cream cone):

$$\mathcal{K} = \text{SOC}(n) = \{(t, x) \mid t \geq \|x\|\}$$

3. Positive semidefinite matrix cone

$$\mathcal{K} = \mathcal{S}_+^n = \{X \mid X \text{ symmetric and } X \succeq 0\}$$

For any convex cone $\mathcal{K}$, we can define its dual cone

$$\mathcal{K}^* = \{x \mid \langle x, y \rangle \geq 0, \quad \forall\, y \in \mathcal{K}\}$$

where $\langle \cdot, \cdot \rangle$ denotes the inner product operation. In other words, the dual cone $\mathcal{K}^*$ consists of all vectors y that form a nonobtuse angle with all vectors in $\mathcal{K}$. We will say $\mathcal{K}$ is self-dual if $\mathcal{K} = \mathcal{K}^*$. It can be shown that the nonnegative orthant cone, the second-order cone, and the symmetric positive semidefinite matrix cone are all self-dual. Notice that for the second-order cone, the inner product operation $\langle \cdot, \cdot \rangle$ is defined as

$$\langle (t, x), (s, y) \rangle = ts + x^\mathrm{T} y, \text{ for all } (t, x) \text{ and } (s, y) \text{ with } t \geq \|x\| \text{ and } s \geq \|y\|$$

and for the positive semidefinite matrix cone

$$\langle X, Y \rangle = X \bullet Y = \sum_{i,j} X_{ij} Y_{ij}$$

6.2.3 CONVEX FUNCTIONS

A function $f(x)\colon \Re^n \to \Re$ is said to be convex if for any two points $x, y \in \Re^n$

$$f(\theta x + (1 - \theta)y) \leq \theta f(x) + (1 - \theta)f(y), \quad \forall \theta \in [0, 1]$$

Geometrically, this means that, when restricted over the line segment joining x and y, the linear function joining $(x, f(x))$ and $(y, f(y))$ always dominates the function f.

There are many examples of convex functions. Any linear function is convex. Other examples include the commonly seen univariate functions $|x|$, e^x, x^2 as well as multivariate functions $a^\mathrm{T}x + b$, $\|Ax\|^2$, where A, a, and b are given data matrix/vector/constant. We say f is concave if $-f$ is convex. The entropy function $-\sum_i x_i \log x_i$ is a concave function over $\mathfrak{R}^n_+$. If f is continuously differentiable, then the convexity of f is equivalent to

$$f(y) \geq f(x) + \nabla f(x)^\mathrm{T}(y - x), \quad \forall x, y \in \mathfrak{R}^n$$

In other words, the first-order Taylor series expansion serves as a global under-estimator of f. In addition, if f is twice continuously differentiable, then the convexity of f is equivalent to the positive semidefiniteness of its Hessian matrix:[*]

$$\nabla^2 f(x) \succeq 0, \quad \forall x \in \mathfrak{R}^n$$

The above criterion shows that a linear function is always convex, while a quadratic function $x^\mathrm{T}Px + a^\mathrm{T}x + b$ is convex if and only if $P \succeq 0$. Notice that the linear plus the constant term $a^\mathrm{T}x + b$ do not have any bearing on the convexity (or the lack of) of f. A function f is said to be concave if $-f$ is convex. One can think of numerous examples of functions which are neither convex nor concave. For instance, the function x^3 is convex over $[0, \infty)$ and concave over the region $(-\infty, 0]$, but is neither convex nor concave over $\mathfrak{R}$.

The most important property about convex functions is the fact that they are closed under summation, positive scaling, and the point-wise maximum operations. In particular, if the $\{f_i\}$'s are convex, then so is $\max_i\{f_i(x)\}$ (even though it is typically nondifferentiable). A notable connection between convex set and convex function is the fact that the level sets of any convex function $f(x)$ are always convex, that is, $\{x \mid f(x) \leq c\}$ is convex for any $c \in \mathfrak{R}$. The converse is not true, however. For example, the function $f(x) = \sqrt{|x|}$ is nonconvex, but its level sets are convex.

6.2.4   CONVEX OPTIMIZATION PROBLEMS

Consider a generic optimization problem (in the minimization form)

$$
\begin{aligned}
\text{minimize} \quad & f_0(x) \\
\text{subject to} \quad & f_i(x) \leq 0, \quad i = 1, 2, \ldots, m \\
& h_j(x) = 0, \quad j = 1, 2, \ldots, r \\
& x \in S
\end{aligned}
\tag{6.1}
$$

where
   f_0 is called the objective function (or cost function)
   $\{f_i\}_{i=1}^m$ and $\{h_j\}_{j=1}^r$ are called the inequality and equality constraint functions, respectively
   S is called a constraint set

In practice, S can be implicitly defined by an oracle such as a user-supplied software. The optimization variable $x \in \mathfrak{R}^n$ is said to be feasible if $x \in S$ and it satisfies all the inequality and equality constraints. A feasible solution x^* is said to be globally optimal if $f(x^*) \leq f(x)$ for all feasible x. In contrast, a feasible vector $\bar{x}$ is said to be locally optimal if there exists some $\epsilon > 0$ such that $f(\bar{x}) \leq f(x)$ for all feasible x satisfying $\|x - \bar{x}\| \leq \epsilon$.

The optimization problem (Equation 6.1) is said to be convex if (1) the functions f_i ($i = 0, 1, 2, \ldots, m$) are convex; (2) $h_j(x)$ are affine functions (i.e., h_j is of the form $a_j^\mathrm{T}x + b_j$ for some $a_j \in \mathfrak{R}^n$ and $b_j \in \mathfrak{R}$); and (3) the set S is convex. Violating any one of the above three conditions will result in a nonconvex problem. Notice that if we "minimize" to "maximize" and change direction

---

[*] The Hessian is essentially the second derivative for a multivariate function.

of the inequalities from "$f_i(x) \leq 0$" to "$f_i(x) \geq 0$," then Equation 6.1 is convex if and only if all $f_i(x)(i = 0, 1, 2, \ldots, m)$ are concave.

A linear programming problem is one where all of $f_i(x)$, $\{x \in 0, \ldots, m\}$ and $h_j(x), j \in \{0, \ldots, r\}$ are linear functions, and this is trivially a convex formulation. Linear programs are generally solved using the simplex method, or by interior point methods. In specific cases, where the linear program has a specific structure, domain-specific algorithms may be used. For example, the shortest path problem can be written as a linear program, but is most efficiently solved using graph algorithms. Other linear programming problems with specific structures are the network flow problem, and an example of applying network flows to physical design can be seen in Chapter 32.

For a more general example of a convex optimization problem, consider the following entropy maximization problem:

$$\text{maximize} \quad \sum_{i=1}^{n} x_i \log x_i$$
$$\text{subject to} \quad \sum_{i=1}^{n} x_i = 1, x_i \geq 0, \quad i = 1, 2, \ldots, n$$
$$Ax = b, \quad j = 1, 2, \ldots, r$$

where the linear equalities $Ax = b$ may represent the usual moment matching constraints.

Let us now put in perspective the role of convexity in optimization. It is well known that, for the problem of solving a system of equations, linearity is the dividing line between the easy and difficult problems.[*] Once a problem is formulated as a solution to a system of linear equations, the problem is considered done because we can simply solve it either analytically or using existing numerical softwares. In fact, there are many efficient and reliable softwares available for solving systems of linear equations, but none for nonlinear equations. The lack of high-quality softwares for solving nonlinear equations is merely a reflection of the fact that they are intrinsically difficult to solve.

In contrast, the dividing line between the easy and difficult problems in optimization is no longer linearity, but rather convexity. Convex optimization problems are the largest subclass of optimization problems that are efficiently solvable, whereas nonconvex optimization problems are generically difficult. The theories, algorithms, and software tools for convex optimization problems have advanced significantly over the last 50 years. There are now (freely downloadable) high-quality software that can deliver accurate solutions efficiently and reliably without the usual headaches of initialization, stepsize selection, or the risk of getting trapped in a local minimum. Once an engineering problem is formulated in a convex manner, it is reasonable to consider it "solved" (or game over), at least from the engineering perspective.

For any convex optimization problem, the set of global optimal solutions is always convex. Moreover, every local optimal solution is also a global optimal solution, so there is no danger of being stuck at a local solution. There are other benefits associated with a convex optimization formulation. For one thing, there exist highly efficient interior point optimization algorithms whose worst-case complexity (i.e., the total number of arithmetic operations required to find an ϵ-optimal solution) grows gracefully as a polynomial function of the problem data length and $\log 1/\epsilon$. In addition, there exists an extensive duality theory for convex optimization problems, a consequence of which is the existence of a computable mathematical certificate for infeasible convex optimization problems. As a result, well-designed software for solving convex optimization problems typically return either an optimal solution, or a certificate (in the form of a dual vector) that establishes the infeasibility of the problem. The latter property is extremely valuable in engineering design because it enables us to identify constraints which are very restrictive.

---

[*] These notions can be made precise using the computational complexity theory; for example, NP-hardness results.

6.3 LAGRANGIAN DUALITY AND THE KARUSH–KUHN–TUCKER CONDITION

Consider the following (not necessarily convex) optimization problem:

$$
\begin{aligned}
\text{minimize} \quad & f_0(x) \\
\text{subject to} \quad & f_i(x) \le 0, \quad i = 1, 2, \ldots, m \\
& h_j(x) = 0, \quad j = 1, 2, \ldots, r \\
& x \in S
\end{aligned}
\tag{6.2}
$$

Let p^* denote the global minimum value of Equation 6.2. For symmetry reason, we will call Equation 6.2 the primal optimization problem and x the primal vector. Introducing a dual variable $\lambda \in \Re^m$ and $\nu \in \Re^r$, we can form the Lagrangian function

$$
L(x, \lambda, \nu) := f_0(x) + \sum_{i=1}^{m} \lambda_i f_i(x) + \sum_{j=1}^{r} \nu_j h_j(x)
$$

The so-called dual function $d(\lambda, \nu)$ associated with Equation 6.2 is defined as

$$
d(\lambda, \nu) := \min_{x \in S} L(x, \lambda, \nu)
$$

Notice that, as a point-wise minimum of a family of linear functions (in (λ, ν)), the dual function $d(\lambda, \nu)$ is always concave. We will say (λ, ν) is dual feasible if $\lambda \ge 0$ and $d(\lambda, \nu)$ is finite. The well-known weak duality result says the following.

Proposition 1 *For any primal feasible vector x and any dual feasible vector (λ, ν), there holds*

$$
f(x) \ge d(\lambda, \nu)
$$

In other words, for any dual feasible vector (λ, ν), the dual function value $d(\lambda, \nu)$ always serves as a lower bound on the primal objective value $f(x)$. Notice that x and (λ, ν) are chosen independent of each other (so long as they are both feasible). Thus, $p^* \ge d(\lambda, \nu)$ for all dual feasible vector (λ, ν). The largest lower bound for p^* can be found by solving the following dual optimization problem:

$$
\begin{aligned}
\text{maximize} \quad & d(\lambda, \nu) \\
\text{subject to} \quad & \lambda \ge 0, \nu \in \Re^r
\end{aligned}
\tag{6.3}
$$

Notice that the dual problem (Equation 6.3) is always convex regardless of the convexity of the primal problem (Equation 6.2), because $d(\lambda, \nu)$ is concave. Let us denote the maximum value of Equation 6.3 by d^*. Then, we have $p^* \ge d^*$. Interestingly, for most convex optimization problems (satisfying some mild constraint qualification conditions, such as the existence of a strict interior point), we actually have $p^* = d^*$ (strong duality).

In general, the dual function $d(\lambda, \nu)$ is difficult to compute. However, for special classes of convex optimization problems (see Section 6.4), we can derive their duals explicitly. Below is a simple example illustrating the concept of duality for linear programming.

EXAMPLE

Let us consider the following linear programming problem

$$
\begin{aligned}
\text{minimize} \quad & x_1 + x_2 \\
\text{subject to} \quad & x_1 + 2x_2 = 2, \\
& (x_1, x_2)^{\mathrm{T}} \in \Re_+^2
\end{aligned}
\tag{6.4}
$$

The primal optimal solution is unique and equal to $(x_1^*, x_2^*) = (0, 1)$, with $p^* = x_1^* + x_2^* = 1$. The Lagrangian function is given by $L(x, v) = x_1 + x_2 + v(2 - x_1 - x_2)$, and the dual function is given by

$$d(v) = \min_{(x_1, x_2)^T \in \Re_+^2} [x_1 + x_2 + v(2 - x_1 - 2x_2)]$$

$$= 2v + \min_{(x_1, x_2)^T \in \Re_+^2} [(1 - v)x_1 + (1 - 2v)x_2]$$

$$= \begin{cases} 2v & \text{if } v \leq \frac{1}{2} \\ -\infty & \text{otherwise} \end{cases}$$

Thus, the dual linear program can be written as

$$\text{maximize} \quad d(v) = 2v$$
$$\text{subject to} \quad v \leq \tfrac{1}{2}$$

Clearly, the dual optimal solution is given by $v^* = 1/2$ and the dual optimal objective value is $d^* = 1$. Thus, we have in this case $p^* = d^*$. In light of Proposition 1, the dual optimal solution $v^* = 1/2$ serves as a certificate for the primal optimality of (x_1^*, x_2^*).

Next, we present a local optimality condition for the optimization problem (Equation 6.2). For ease of exposition, let us assume $S = \Re$. Then, a necessary condition for x^* to be a local optimal solution of Equation 6.2 is that there exists some (λ^*, v^*) such that

$$f_i(x^*) \leq 0, \quad \forall i = 1, 2, \ldots, m \tag{6.5}$$

$$h_j(x^*) = 0, \quad \forall j = 1, 2, \ldots, r \tag{6.6}$$

$$\lambda^* \geq 0 \tag{6.7}$$

$$\nabla f_0(x^*) + \sum_{i=1}^{m} \lambda_i^* \nabla f_i(x^*) + \sum_{j=1}^{r} v_j^* \nabla h_j(x^*) = 0 \tag{6.8}$$

$$\lambda_i^* f_i(x^*) = 0, \quad \forall i = 1, 2, \ldots, m \tag{6.9}$$

Collectively, the conditions given by Equations 6.5 through 6.9 are called the Karush–Kuhn–Tucker (KKT) condition for optimality. Notice that the first two conditions given by Equations 6.5 and 6.6 represent primal feasibility of x^*, condition given by Equation 6.7 represents dual feasibility, condition given by Equation 6.8 is equivalent to $\nabla_x L(x^*, \lambda^*, v^*) = 0$, while the last condition given by Equation 6.9 signifies the complementary slackness for the primal and dual inequality constraint pairs: $f_i(x) \leq 0$ and $\lambda_i \geq 0$.

For the above linear programming example, we can easily check whether the vector $(x_1^*, x_2^*) = (0, 1)$ and the Lagrangian multipliers $(\lambda_1^*, \lambda_2^*, v^*) = (\frac{1}{2}, 0, \frac{1}{2})$ satisfy the above KKT condition. Moreover, they are the unique solution of Equations 6.5 through 6.9. Thus, $(x_1^*, x_2^*) = (0, 1)$ is the unique primal optimal solution for Equation 6.4.

In general, the KKT condition is necessary but not sufficient for optimality. However, for convex optimization problems (and under mild constraint qualification conditions), the KKT condition is also sufficient. If the constraints in Equation 6.2 are absent, the corresponding KKT condition simply reduces to the well-known stationarity condition for unconstrained optimization problem: $\nabla f_0(x^*) = 0$. That is, the unconstrained local minimums must be attained at stationary points (at which the gradient of f_0 vanishes). However, in the presence of constraints, local optimal solutions of Equation 6.2 are no longer attained at a stationary point; instead, they are attained at a KKT point x^*, which together with some dual feasible vector (λ^*, v^*) satisfies the KKT condition (Equations 6.5 through 6.9).

6.3.1 Lagrangian Relaxation

Lagrangian duality theory presented above can also be used to derive convex relaxations of nonconvex optimization problems. An example of its application in physical design is provided in Chapter 32.

To understand the idea, consider the following (not necessarily convex) optimization problem:

$$
\begin{aligned}
\text{minimize} \quad & f_0(x) \\
\text{subject to} \quad & f_i(x) \le 0, \quad i = 1, 2, \dots, m \\
& h_j(x) = 0, \quad j = 1, 2, \dots, r \\
& x \in S
\end{aligned}
\tag{6.10}
$$

where the explicit constraints $f_i(x) \ge 0$ and $h_j(x) = 0$ are assumed to be the complicating constraints. All other easy constraints are implicitly modeled by the membership condition $x \in S$. Lagrangian relaxation is a powerful approach to approximately solve the (possibly nonconvex) optimization problem given by Equation 6.10. Its basic procedure can be described as follows. For any fixed dual multipliers $\lambda \in \Re_+^m$ and $v \in \Re^r$, we dualize the complicating constraints and compute the dual function

$$
d(\lambda, v) = \min_{x \in S} L(x, \lambda, v) = \min_{x \in S} \left(f_0(x) + \sum_{i=1}^{m} \lambda_i f_i(x) + \sum_{j=1}^{r} v_j h_j(x) \right)
\tag{6.11}
$$

Because the membership condition $x \in S$ consists of only easy constraints, the computation of $d(\lambda, v)$ can be much simpler than the original problem (Equation 6.10). In fact, for many applications, the constraint functions f_i and h_j are separable (e.g., linear functions):

$$
f_i(x) := \sum_{k=1}^{n} f_{ik}(x_k), \quad h_j(x) := \sum_{k=1}^{n} h_{jk}(x_k), \quad 0 \le i \le m, \ 1 \le j \le r
$$

and the constraint set S has a Cartesian product form

$$
S := S_1 \times S_2 \times \cdots \times S_n
$$

In this case, the minimization of $L(x, \lambda, v)$ over S can be decomposed naturally along each variable x_i, and the corresponding Lagrangian relaxation procedure is known as Lagrangian decomposition:

$$
\begin{aligned}
d(\lambda, v) &= \min_{x \in S} L(x, \lambda, v) \\
&= \min_{x \in S} \left(f_0(x) + \sum_{i=1}^{m} \lambda_i f_i(x) + \sum_{j=1}^{r} v_j h_j(x) \right) \\
&= \min_{x \in S_1 \times S_2 \times \cdots \times S_n} \sum_{k=1}^{n} \left(f_{0k}(x_k) + \sum_{i=1}^{m} \lambda_i f_{ik}(x_k) + \sum_{j=1}^{r} v_j h_{jk}(x_k) \right) \\
&= \sum_{k=1}^{n} \min_{x_k \in S_k} \left(f_{0k}(x_k) + \sum_{i=1}^{m} \lambda_i f_{ik}(x_k) + \sum_{j=1}^{r} v_j h_{jk}(x_k) \right)
\end{aligned}
$$

In this way, the computation of dual function $d(\lambda, v)$ and its sub differential is decomposed along each coordinate and therefore greatly simplified.

Lagrangian relaxation aims to

$$
\begin{aligned}
\text{maximize} \quad & d(\lambda, v) \\
\text{subject to} \quad & \lambda \ge 0
\end{aligned}
\tag{6.12}
$$

by repeatedly updating the dual multipliers λ, v. As noted earlier, the dual problem (Equation 6.12) is always convex and the weak duality implies $f(x) \geq d(\lambda, v)$ for any pair of primal–dual feasible solutions x and (λ, v). Thus, the maximum dual objective value d^* serves as a lower approximation of primal optimal value p^*.

The updating of dual parameters (λ, v) can be accomplished by any of the standard convex optimization procedures. A popular approach is to make the adjustment along the gradient ascent direction of $d(\lambda, v)$. This requires the computation of $\nabla d(\lambda, v)$ which may not exist because the dual objective function is often non differentiable (whenever the primal objective function contains flat pieces). Fortunately, we can easily obtain a subgradient of the dual function $d(\lambda, v)$, and adjust the multipliers along a subgradient direction.* In particular, for any $\lambda \in \mathfrak{R}_+^m$ and $v \in \mathfrak{R}^r$, let us use $x(\lambda, v)$ to denote a minimizer of Equation 6.11. Then, a subgradient of the dual objective function at (λ, v) is

$$g[x(\lambda, v)] = \{f_1[x(\lambda, v)], \ldots, f_m[x(\lambda, v)], h_1[x(\lambda, v)], \ldots, h_r[x(\lambda, v)]\} \qquad (6.13)$$

The convex hull of all subgradients of dual function d at (λ, v) is called the subdifferential of $d(\lambda, v)$ which we denote by

$$\partial d(\lambda, v) := \text{Conv}\{g[x(\lambda, v)] \mid x(\lambda, v) \text{ is a minimizer of Equation 6.11}\}$$

Thus, at each iteration k, we can adjust the multipliers according to

$$\lambda_i^{k+1} := \left[\lambda_i^k + \alpha^k f_i(x(\lambda^k, v^k))\right]_+, \quad i = 1, 2, \ldots, m$$

$$v_j^{k+1} := v_j^k + \alpha^k h_j(x(\lambda^k, v^k)), \quad j = 1, 2, \ldots, r$$

where $[\cdot]_+$ denotes the projection to the set of nonnegative real numbers and $\{\alpha^k\}$ is a sequence of stepsizes satisfying

$$\alpha^k > 0, \quad \sum_{k=1}^{\infty} \alpha^k = \infty, \quad \sum_{k=1}^{\infty} (\alpha^k)^2 < \infty$$

Moreover, if (λ^*, v^*) is a maximizer of the dual problem (Equation 6.12), then the optimality condition implies the existence of a subgradient $g^* \in \partial d(\lambda^*, v^*)$ such that

$$\begin{cases} g_i^* \leq 0, \text{ and } g_i^* < 0 \text{ implies } v_i^* = 0, & \text{for } i = 1, 2, \ldots, m \\ g_j^* = 0, & \forall j = 1, 2, \ldots, r \end{cases} \qquad (6.14)$$

In general, there may not be a maximizer $x(\lambda^*, v^*)$ of Equation 6.11 such that $g^* = g(x(\lambda^*, \mu^*))$. If this is the case, then there is a positive duality gap between the primal and dual pair (Equations 6.10 through 6.12). Otherwise, if there exists an $x(\lambda^*, v^*)$ such that $g^* = g[x(\lambda^*, \mu^*)$ (which is the case when $\partial d(\lambda^*, \mu^*)$ is a singleton), then there is no duality gap and $x(\lambda^*, \mu^*)$ is an optimal solution of the primal nonconvex problem (Equation 6.10). Indeed, the feasibility of $x(\lambda^*, v^*)$ can be seen from the dual optimality condition Equation 6.14, which requires the subgradient vector g^* at (λ^*, v^*) to satisfy

$$g_i^* \leq 0, \ i = 1, 2, \ldots, m; \quad g_j^* = 0, \ j = 1, 2, \ldots, r$$

In light of Equation 6.13, this is further equivalent to the primal feasibility of $x(\lambda^*, v^*)$

$$f_i[x(\lambda^*, v^*)] \leq 0, \ i = 1, 2, \ldots, m; \quad h_j[x(\lambda^*, v^*)] = 0, \ j = 1, 2, \ldots, r$$

---

* A vector g is a subgradient of a concave function f at x if $f(y) \leq f(x) + g^T(y - x) \ \forall y$.

For an integer linear programming problem, we can use $x \in S$ to model the integer constraints. The remaining linear constraints (inequalities and equalities) can be brought to the objective function in a Lagrangian fashion via fixed multipliers. In this case, the resulting Lagrangian relaxation is known to yield a tighter lower bound for the original problem than the straightforward linear programming relaxation (i.e., simply dropping the integer constraint $x \in S$).

6.3.2 DETECTING INFEASIBILITY

Efficient detection of infeasibility is essential in engineering design applications. However, the problem of detecting and removing the incompatible constraints is NP-hard in general, especially if the constraints are nonconvex. However, for convex constraints, we can make use of duality theory to prove inconsistency. Let us consider the following example.

EXAMPLE

Determine if the following linear system is feasible or not:

$$x_1 + x_2 \le 1$$
$$x_1 - x_2 \le -1$$
$$-x_1 \le -1$$

Let us multiply the last inequality by 2 and add it to the first and the second inequalities. The resulting inequality is $0 \le -1$, which is a contradiction. This shows that the above linear system is infeasible.

In general, a linear system of inequalities

$$Ax \le b \tag{6.15}$$

is infeasible if and only if there exists some $\lambda \ge 0$, such that

$$\lambda^\mathrm{T} A = 0, \quad \lambda^\mathrm{T} b < 0 \tag{6.16}$$

Clearly, the existence of a such λ serves as a certificate for the incompatibility of the linear inequalities in Equation 6.15. What is interesting (and nontrivial) is the fact that the converse is also true. That is, if the system (Equation 6.15) is infeasible, then there always exists a mathematical certificate λ satisfying Equation 6.16. Results of this kind are called the theorems of alternatives, and are related to the well-known Farkas' lemma for the linear feasibility problem.

The above result can also be extended to the nonlinear context. For instance, consider a system of convex (possibly nonlinear) inequality system:

$$f_1(x) < 0, f_2(x) < 0, \ldots, f_m(x) < 0 \tag{6.17}$$

Then, either Equation 6.17 is feasible or there exists some $\lambda \ne 0$ satisfying

$$\lambda \ge 0, \quad g(\lambda) = \inf_x \{\lambda_1 f_1(x) + \lambda_2 f_2(x) + \cdots + \lambda_m f(x)\} \ge 0 \tag{6.18}$$

Exactly one of the above two conditions holds true. The existence of a $\lambda \ne 0$ satisfying Equation 6.18 proves the infeasibility of Equation 6.17. Such a λ serves as a certificate of infeasibility. Modern software (e.g., SeDuMi [9]) for solving convex optimization problems either generate an optimal solution or a certificate showing infeasibility. In contrast, software for nonconvex optimization problems cannot detect infeasibility. They typically fail to converge when the underlying problem is infeasible, either due to data overflow or because the maximum number of iterations is exceeded.

6.4   LINEAR CONIC OPTIMIZATION MODELS

We now review several most commonly used convex optimization models in engineering design applications. Consider a primal–dual pair of linear conic optimization problems:

$$
\begin{aligned}
\text{minimize} \quad & C \bullet X \\
\text{subject to} \quad & \mathcal{A}X = b, \quad X \in \mathcal{K}
\end{aligned}
\tag{6.19}
$$

and

$$
\begin{aligned}
\text{maximize} \quad & b^\mathsf{T} y \\
\text{subject to} \quad & \mathcal{A}^* y + S = C, \quad S \in \mathcal{K}^*
\end{aligned}
\tag{6.20}
$$

where
   $\mathcal{A}$ is a linear operator mapping an Euclidean space onto another Euclidean space
   $\mathcal{A}^*$ denotes the adjoint of $\mathcal{A}$
   $\mathcal{K}$ signifies a pointed, closed convex cone
   $\mathcal{K}^*$ is its dual cone

The problems given by Equations 6.19 and 6.20 include many well-known special cases listed below.

6.4.1   LINEAR PROGRAMMING

$$
\mathcal{K} = \mathfrak{R}_+^n
$$

In this case, the linear conic optimization problem reduces to

$$
\begin{aligned}
\text{minimize} \quad & c^\mathsf{T} x \\
\text{subject to} \quad & Ax = b, \quad x \geq 0
\end{aligned}
\tag{6.21}
$$

and its dual becomes

$$
\begin{aligned}
\text{maximize} \quad & b^\mathsf{T} y \\
\text{subject to} \quad & A^\mathsf{T} y + s = c, \quad s \in 0
\end{aligned}
\tag{6.22}
$$

The optimality condition is given by

$$
Ax = b, \ x \geq 0, \quad A^\mathsf{T} y + s = c, \ s \in 0, \quad x^\mathsf{T} s = 0.
$$

6.4.2   SECOND-ORDER CONE PROGRAMMING

$$
\mathcal{K} = \prod_{i=1}^{n} \mathrm{SOC}(n_i)
$$

Let $\tilde{x} = (\tilde{x}_1, \tilde{x}_2, \ldots, \tilde{x}_k)^\mathsf{T}$ with $\tilde{x}_i = (t_i, x_i)^\mathsf{T} \in \mathrm{SOC}(n_i)$ (namely, $t_i \geq \|x_i\|$). Similarly, we denote $\tilde{x} = (\tilde{s}_1, \tilde{s}_2, \ldots, \tilde{s}_k)^\mathsf{T}$ with $\tilde{s}_i = (\tau_i, s_i)^\mathsf{T} \in \mathrm{SOC}(n_i)$. The data vector $\tilde{c} = (\tilde{c}_1, \tilde{c}_2, \ldots, \tilde{c}_k)^\mathsf{T}$ with $\tilde{c}_i \in \mathfrak{R}^{n_i}$, and the data matrix $\tilde{A} \in \mathfrak{R}^{m \times (n_1 + \cdots + n_k)}$. In this case, the linear conic optimization problem (Equation 6.19) reduces to

$$
\begin{aligned}
\text{minimize} \quad & \tilde{c}^\mathsf{T} \tilde{x} \\
\text{subject to} \quad & \tilde{A}\tilde{x} = b, \quad \tilde{x}_i \in \mathrm{SOC}(n_i), \quad \forall i
\end{aligned}
\tag{6.23}
$$

and its dual becomes

$$
\begin{aligned}
\text{maximize} \quad & b^{\mathsf{T}} y \\
\text{subject to} \quad & \tilde{A}^{\mathsf{T}} y + \tilde{s} = \tilde{c}, \quad \tilde{s}_i \in \text{SOC}(n_i), \quad \forall i
\end{aligned}
\tag{6.24}
$$

The optimality condition is given by

$$
\tilde{A}\tilde{x} = b, \; \tilde{x} \in \prod_{i=1}^{n} \text{SOC}(n_i), \quad \tilde{A}^{\mathsf{T}} y + \tilde{s} = \tilde{c}, \; \tilde{s} \in \prod_{i=1}^{n} \text{SOC}(n_i), \quad \tilde{x}^{\mathsf{T}} \tilde{s} = 0
$$

6.4.3 SEMIDEFINITE PROGRAMMING

$$
\mathcal{K} = \mathcal{S}_{+}^{n} \text{ or } (\mathcal{H}_{+}^{n})
$$

In this case, the linear conic optimization problem reduces to

$$
\begin{aligned}
\text{minimize} \quad & C \bullet X \\
\text{subject to} \quad & A_i \bullet X = b_i, \quad i = 1, 2, \ldots, m, \quad X \geq 0
\end{aligned}
\tag{6.25}
$$

and its dual becomes

$$
\begin{aligned}
\text{maximize} \quad & b^{\mathsf{T}} y \\
\text{subject to} \quad & \sum_{i=1}^{m} A_i{}^{\mathsf{T}} y_i + S = C, \quad S \geq 0
\end{aligned}
\tag{6.26}
$$

The optimality condition is given by

$$
A_i \bullet X = b_i, \; X \geq 0, \quad \sum_{i=1}^{m} A_i{}^{\mathsf{T}} y_i + S = C, \; S \geq 0, \quad X \bullet S = 0
$$

6.5 INTERIOR POINT METHODS FOR LINEAR CONIC OPTIMIZATION

For ease of exposition, we focus on the SDP case with $\mathcal{K} = \mathcal{S}_{+}^{n}$. The other cases can be treated similarly (in fact, they are special case of SDP). In practice, sometimes it is more convenient to work with the so-called rotated second order cone: $\{(t, s, x) \in \mathfrak{R}^{n} \mid ts \geq \|x\|^2, t \geq 0, s \geq 0\}$. This cone is equivalent to the standard SOC(n) via a simple linear transformation.

Assume that the feasible regions of the SDP pair (Equations 6.19 and 6.20) have nonempty interiors. Then we can define the central path of Equations 6.19 and 6.20 as $\{(X(\mu), S(\mu))\}$ satisfying

$$
\begin{aligned}
\mathcal{A}^{*} y(\mu) + S(\mu) &= C \\
\mathcal{A} X(\mu) &= b \\
X(\mu) S(\mu) &= \mu I
\end{aligned}
\tag{6.27}
$$

where μ is a positive parameter. By driving $\mu \to 0$ and under mild assumptions, the central path converges to an optimal primal–dual solution pair for Equations 6.19 and 6.20. Notice that the central path condition (Equation 6.27) is exactly the necessary and sufficient optimality condition for the following convex problem:

$$
\begin{aligned}
\text{minimize} \quad & C \bullet X - \mu \log \, \det(X) \\
\text{subject to} \quad & \mathcal{A} X = b, \quad X \in \mathcal{S}_{+}^{n}
\end{aligned}
\tag{6.28}
$$

In other words, the points on the central path corresponds to the optimal solution of Equation 6.28 and the associated optimal dual solution. Here the function $- \log \det(X)$ is called the barrier function for the positive semidefinite matrix cone $\mathcal{S}_{+}^{n}$.

Many interior point algorithms follow (approximately) the central path to achieve optimality. As a result, the iterates are required to remain in a neighborhood of the central path that can be defined as

$$\mathcal{N}(\gamma) = \left\{ (X, y, S) \mid \mathcal{A}X = b, \mathcal{A}^*y + S = C, X \geq 0, S \geq 0, \left\| X^{1/2}SX^{1/2} - \frac{X \bullet S}{n} I \right\|_F \leq \gamma \frac{X \bullet S}{n} \right\}$$

With this definition, a generic interior point path-following algorithm can be stated as follows:

Generic Path-Following Algorithm

Given a strictly feasible primal-dual pair $(X^0, y^0, S^0) \in \mathcal{N}(\gamma)$ with $0 < \gamma < 1$. Let $k = 0$.
REPEAT (main iteration)
  Let $X = X^k, y = y^k, S = S^k$, and $\mu_k = X \bullet S/n$.
  Compute a search direction $(\Delta X^k, \Delta y^k, \Delta S^k)$.
  Compute the largest step t_k such that

$$(X + t^k \Delta X^k, y + t^k \Delta y^k, S + t^k \Delta S^k) \in \mathcal{N}(\gamma).$$

  Set $X^{k+1} = X + t^k \Delta X^k, y^{k+1} = y + t^k \Delta y^k, S^{k+1} = S + t^k \Delta S^k$.
  Set $k = k + 1$.
UNTIL convergence.

There are many choices for the search direction $(\Delta X, \Delta y, \Delta S)$. For example, we can take it as the solution of the following linear system of equations:

$$\mathcal{A}^* \Delta y + \Delta S = C - S - \mathcal{A}^* y$$
$$\mathcal{A} \Delta X = b \tag{6.29}$$
$$\mathcal{H}_P(\Delta X S + X \Delta S) = \mu I - \mathcal{H}_P(XS)$$

where P is a nonsingular matrix and

$$\mathcal{H}_P(U) = \frac{1}{2}[PUP^{-1} + (PUP^{-1})^\mathsf{T}]$$

Different choices of P lead to different search directions. For example, $P = I$ corresponds to the so-called AHO direction [11].

The standard analysis of path-following interior point methods shows that a total of $O(\sqrt{n} \log(\mu_0/\epsilon))$ main iterations are required to reduce the duality gap $X \bullet S$ to less than ϵ. Each main iteration involves solving the linear system of equations (Equation 6.29) whose size depends on the underlying cone $\mathcal{K}$. If $\mathcal{K} = \mathfrak{R}^n_+$ (linear programming), the linear system is of size $O(n)$, implying each main iteration has an arithmetic complexity of $O(n^3)$. In the case where $\mathcal{K} = \prod_{i=1}^n \mathrm{SOC}(n_i)$ (SOCP), the linear system (Equation 6.29) will have size $O(\Sigma_i n_i)$, so the complexity of solving Equation 6.29 is $O((\Sigma_i n_i)^3)$. For the SDP case where $\mathcal{K} = \mathcal{S}^n_+$, the size of the linear system (Equation 6.29) is $O(n^2)$, so the amount of work required to solve Equation 6.29 is $O(n^6)$. Combining the estimates of the number of main iterations with the complexity estimate per each iteration yields the overall complexity of interior point methods. In general, the computational effort required to solve SDP is more than that of SOCP, which in turn is more than that of LP. However, the expressive power of these optimization models rank in the reverse order.

6.6 GEOMETRIC PROGRAMMING

For circuit design applications, we often encounter optimization problems with design variables corresponding to the geometry of the circuit. Such problems naturally take the form of a geometric program (GP) whose definition is described below. An example of a geometric program in the context of physical design is described in Chapter 29.

6.6.1 BASIC DEFINITIONS

A monomial function is defined as

$$f(x) = cx_1^{\alpha_1} x_2^{\alpha_2} \cdots x_n^{\alpha_n}$$

where
$c \geq 0$
$\alpha_j \in \Re$
domain of $f(x)$ is $\{x \mid x_i \geq 0\}$

For example, $f(x) = 5x_1^{2.3} x_2^{-0.7} x_3^{2.5}$ is a monomial. The nonnegativity of variables $\{x_i\}$ follow from the fact that they correspond to geometric sizing parameters. Notice that a monomial function is nonconvex in general. For instance, $f(x_1, x_2) = x_1 x_2$ is a nonconvex monomial.

A posynomial function is defined as the sum of monomial functions

$$f(x) = \sum_{k=1}^{r} c_k x_1^{\alpha_{1k}} x_2^{\alpha_{2k}} \cdots x_n^{\alpha_{nk}}$$

where
$c_k \geq 0$
$\alpha_{ik} \in \Re$
and again the domain of $f(x)$ is $\{x \mid x_i \geq 0\}$

An example of posynomial is given by $f(x_1, x_2, x_3) = x_1^2 x_2^{-1} x_3^{0.5} + 2x_1^{2.1} x_2^3$.
A GP is an optimization problem in the form

$$
\begin{aligned}
\text{minimize} \quad & f_0(x) \\
\text{subject to} \quad & f_i(x) \leq 1, \quad i = 1, \ldots, m \\
& h_i(x) = 1, \quad i = 1, \ldots, p
\end{aligned}
\tag{6.30}
$$

where
$f_0, \ldots, f_m$ are posynomial functions
$h_1, \ldots, h_p$ are monomial functions

In this original form, GP is not a convex problem in general because the constraint functions $\{f_i\}$'s are not convex and the equality functions $\{h_j\}$'s are not affine. However, there exists a nonlinear transformation under which the GP problem (Equation 6.30) can be reformulated as an equivalent convex optimization problem.

6.6.2 CONVEX REFORMULATION OF A GP

Consider the following nonlinear transformation:

$$y_i = \log x_i, \quad x_i = e^{y_i}$$

Under this transformation, a monomail function $f(x) = cx_1^{\alpha_1}x_2^{\alpha_2}\cdots x_n^{\alpha_n}$ can be written as

$$\log f(e^{y_1},\dots,e^{y_n}) = \alpha_1 y_1 + \cdots + \alpha_n y_n + \beta$$

which is affine in y, where $\beta = \log c$. Moreover, if $f(x) = \sum_{k=1}^r c_k x_1^{\alpha_{1k}} x_2^{\alpha_{2k}} \cdots x_n^{\alpha_{nk}}$ is posynomial then

$$\log f(e^{y_1},\dots,e^{y_n}) = \log \sum_{k=1}^r \exp(\alpha_{1k}y_1 + \cdots + \alpha_{nk}y_n + \beta_k)$$

which is convex in y, where $\beta_k = \log c_k$. Consequently, under this transformation, the geometric program (Equation 6.30) in convex form in terms of variables $\{y_i\}$ is

$$
\begin{aligned}
\text{minimize} \quad & \log f_0(e^{y_1},\dots,e^{y_n}) \\
\text{subject to} \quad & \log f_i(e^{y_1},\dots,e^{y_n}) \leq 0, \quad i = 1,\dots,m \\
& \log h_i(e^{y_1},\dots,e^{y_n}) = 0, \quad i = 1,\dots,p
\end{aligned}
$$

Once this convex reformulation is solved, say, using interior point methods, we can recover the original design variables $\{x_i\}$ using the inverse transform $x_i = e^{y_i}$. In this way, every GP, even though nonconvex in its original form, can be efficiently solved using interior point methods in polynomial time. More details can be found in Refs. [3,4].

6.6.3 GATE SIZING AS A GP

The conventional gate sizing problem is formulated as

$$
\begin{aligned}
\text{minimize} \quad & \text{area} = \sum_{i=1}^n a_i W_i L_i \\
\text{subject to} \quad & \text{delay} \leq T_{\text{spec}} \\
& W_{\min} \leq W_i, L_{\min} \leq L_i, \quad \forall i = 1,\dots,n
\end{aligned}
\tag{6.31}
$$

where
  W_i and L_i are, respectively, the width and the effective channel length of gate i
  a_i is some weight factor

Using the Elmore delay model,* which is used for simplicity, each gate i in the circuit can be replaced by an equivalent $R_{\text{on}_i}C_i$ element, where R_{on_i} represents the effective on resistance of the pull-up or the pull-down network, and the term C_i subsumes the source, drain, and gate capacitances of the transistors in the gate. The expressions for R_{on_i} and C_i for a gate i are given by

$$R_{\text{on}_i} = \frac{\alpha L_i}{W_i}, \quad C_i = \beta L_i W_i + \gamma \tag{6.32}$$

where α, β, and γ are known constants.

From Equation 6.32, we see that both the capacitances and the on resistance of the transistors in a gate are posynomial functions of the vectors $W = (\dots,W_i,\dots)^{\text{T}}$ and $L = (\dots,L_i,\dots)^{\text{T}}$. Consequently, the term $R_{\text{on}_i}C_i$, which is the equivalent delay contribution of gate i in the circuit, is also a posynomial function of W and L. By breaking the circuit into a series of RC trees, and applying the Elmore delay computations at each node of the circuit graph, we see that the delay constraint of Equation 6.31 at the primary outputs of the circuit can be replaced by m posynomial delay constraints of the form

$$\sum_l K_l \prod_j W_j^{a_j} L_j^{b_j} \leq t_i \tag{6.33}$$

---

* Other more accurate convex gate delay models may be used instead of the Elmore model.

where

   m is the number of nodes in the circuit graph

   K_l is a constant coefficient of the lth monomial term that can be derived from Equation 6.32,

   t_i is the arrival time at gate i

   $a_j, b_j \in \{-1, 0, 1\}$ are the exponents of the jth components of the W and L vectors

By substituting Equation 6.33 in Equation 6.31 for all gates in the circuit, the transistor sizing problem is formulated as a GP having a posynomial objective function and posynomial inequality constraints. The resulting GP can be solved using standard convex optimization techniques. In Section 6.7, we show how the robust version of the standard GP formulation (Equation 6.31) can be converted to another GP.

6.7   ROBUST OPTIMIZATION

Robust optimization models in mathematical programming have received much attention recently (see, e.g., Refs. [1,2,5]). In this subsection we briefly review some of these models and some extensions.

Consider a convex optimization for the form

$$
\begin{aligned}
\text{minimize} \quad & f_0(x) \\
\text{subject to} \quad & f_i(x) \leq 0, \quad i = 1, 2, \ldots, m
\end{aligned}
\tag{6.34}
$$

where each f_i is convex. In many engineering design applications, the data defining the constraint and the objective functions may be inexact, corrupted by noise or may fluctuate with time around a nominal value. In such cases, the traditional optimization approach simply solves Equation 6.34 by using the nominal value of the data. However, an optimal solution for the nominal formulation (Equation 6.34) may yield poor performance or become infeasible when each f_i is perturbed in the actual design. In other words, optimal solutions for Equation 6.34 may be misleading or even useless in practice. A more appropriate design approach is to seek a high-quality solution that can remain feasible and deliver high-quality performance in all possible realizations of unknown perturbation. This principle was formulated rigorously in Refs. [1,2,5]. Specifically, the data perturbation can be modeled using a parameter vector δ, with $\delta = 0$ representing the nominal unperturbed situation. In other words, we consider a family of perturbed functions parameterized by δ: $f_i(x; \delta)$, with δ taken from an uncertainty set Δ containing the origin. Then a robustly feasible solution x is the one that satisfies

$$
f_i(x; \delta) \leq 0, \quad \forall \, \delta \in \Delta \quad \text{or equivalently} \quad \max_{\delta \in \Delta} f_i(x; \delta) \leq 0
$$

Thus, a robustly feasible solution x is, in a sense, strongly feasible because it is required to satisfy all slightly perturbed version of the nominal constraint $f_i(x; 0) = f_i(x) \leq 0$. The robust optimal solution can now be defined as a robust feasible solution that minimizes the worst-case objective value $\max_{\delta \in \Delta} f_0(x; \delta)$. This gives rise to the following formulation:

$$
\begin{aligned}
\text{minimize} \quad & \max_{\delta \in \Delta} f_0(x; \delta) \\
\text{subject to} \quad & f_i(x; \delta) \leq 0, \quad \forall \, \delta \in \Delta, \quad i = 1, 2, \ldots, m
\end{aligned}
\tag{6.35}
$$

Let us assume that the perturbation vector δ enters the objective and the constraint functions f_i in such a way that preserves convexity, that is, each $f_i(x; \delta)$ remains a convex function for each $\delta \in \Delta$. As a result, the robust counterpart (Equation 6.35) of the original (nominal case) convex problem (Equation 6.34) remains convex because its constraints are convex (for each i and δ) and the objective function $\max_{\delta \in \Delta} f_0(x; \delta)$ is also convex.

Much of the research in robust optimization is focused on finding a finite representation of the feasible region of Equation 6.35, which is defined in terms of infinitely many constraints (one for each $\delta \in \Delta$). Assume that the uncertainty parameter δ can be partitioned as $\delta = (\delta_0, \delta_1, \delta_2 \ldots, \delta_m)^{\mathsf{T}}$ and that the uncertainty set has a Cartesian product structure $\Delta = \Delta_0 \times \Delta_1 \times \cdots \times \Delta_m$, with $\delta_i \in \Delta_i$. Moreover, assume that δ enters $f_i(x; \delta)$ in an affine manner. Under these assumptions, it is possible to characterize the robust feasible set of many well-known classes of optimization problems in a finite way. In particular, consider the robust linear programming model proposed by Ben-Tal and Nemirovskii [2]:

$$
\begin{aligned}
\text{minimize} \quad & \max_{\|\Delta c\| \leq \epsilon_0} (c + \Delta c)^{\mathsf{T}} x \\
\text{subject to} \quad & (a_i + \Delta a_i)^{\mathsf{T}} x \geq (b_i + \Delta b_i), \\
\text{for all} \quad & \|(\Delta a_i, \Delta b_i)\| \leq \epsilon_i, \quad i = 1, 2, \ldots, m
\end{aligned}
\tag{6.36}
$$

where each $\epsilon_i > 0$ is a prespecified scalar. In the above formulation, we have $\delta_i = (\Delta a_i, \Delta b_i)$ and $\Delta_i = \{(\Delta a_i, \Delta b_i) \mid \|(\Delta a_i, \Delta b_i)\| \leq \epsilon_i\}$. It is known that the above robust LP can be reformulated as a SOCP [2]. Refs. [1,2,5] have shown that the robust counterpart of some other well-known convex optimization problems can also be reformulated in a finite way as a conic optimization problem, often as an SOCP or SDP. Next we consider a robust formulation of a geometric program.

6.7.1 ROBUST CIRCUIT OPTIMIZATION UNDER PROCESS VARIATIONS

We use a simple example to explain the procedure to incorporate the process variation effects in the delay constraints set. We use the toy circuit of Figure 6.1, comprising just one driver gate and one load gate, for this illustration. The main idea can be generalized to arbitrarily large circuits.

For simplicity we neglect the interconnect delay and the effect of drain and source capacitances of the driver gate. Applying the Elmore delay model to the gates of circuit of Figure 6.1, we can write the delay constraint for the circuit as

$$
\frac{k_1 l_1 l_2 w_2}{w_1} + \frac{k_2 l_2}{w_2} \leq t_{\text{spec}}
\tag{6.37}
$$

where k_1 and k_2 are constants. To ensure that the delay constraint of Equation 6.37 is met under the effect of random process variations, we impose the following condition

$$
\max_{(l - l_0, w - w_0) \in \Delta} \left(\frac{k_1 l_1 l_2 w_2}{w_1} + \frac{k_2 l_2}{w_2} \right) \leq t_{\text{spec}}
\tag{6.38}
$$

where

w_0 and l_0 represent, respectively, the nominal values of the transistor w and l

Δ signifies the uncertainty region

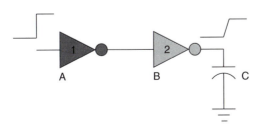

FIGURE 6.1   Simple example circuit.

To simplify the above robust constraint, we approximate the constraint function by the first-order Taylor series expansion around the nominal value (w_0, l_0) and arrive at the following simplified robust constraint:

$$
\frac{k_1 l_{1_0} l_{2_0} w_{2_0}}{w_{1_0}} + \frac{k_2 l_{2_0}}{w_{2_0}}
$$

$$
+ \max_{(\delta l, \delta w) \in \Delta} \left(\frac{k_1 l_{1_0} l_{2_0} \delta w_2}{w_{1_0}} + \frac{k_1 l_{2_0} w_{2_0} \delta l_1}{w_{1_0}} + \frac{k_1 l_{1_0} w_{2_0} \delta l_2}{w_{1_0}} \right.
$$

$$
\left. + \frac{k_2 \delta l_2}{w_{2_0}} - \frac{k_1 l_{1_0} l_{2_0} w_{2_0} \delta w_1}{w_{1_0}^2} - \frac{k_2 l_{2_0} \delta w_2}{w_{2_0}^2} \right) \leq t_{\text{spec}} \tag{6.39}
$$

where $\delta w = w - w_0$ and $\delta l = l - l_0$ denote, respectively, the random variations in w and l. Employing the ellipsoid uncertainty model

$$
\Delta = \{(\delta l, \delta w) : (\delta l^{\text{t}}, \delta w^{\text{t}}) P^{-1} (\delta l^{\text{t}}, \delta w^{\text{t}})^{\text{t}} \leq 1\} \tag{6.40}
$$

for the random parameter variations, we are led to

$$
\begin{bmatrix} \delta w_1 \\ \delta w_2 \\ \delta l_1 \\ \delta l_2 \end{bmatrix} = \begin{bmatrix} (P^{1/2} \mathbf{u})_1 \\ (P^{1/2} \mathbf{u})_2 \\ (P^{1/2} \mathbf{u})_3 \\ (P^{1/2} \mathbf{u})_4 \end{bmatrix} \tag{6.41}
$$

where

P is the covariance matrix of the random vector (l, w) of the driver and the load gate of Figure 6.1

$\mathbf{u}$ is the vector characterizing the variation within the four-dimensional ellipsoid centered at the nominal values of w and l, with $\|\mathbf{u}\| \leq 1$

We introduce two vectors ϕ_1 and ϕ_2 to collect the positive and negative coefficients of the variational parameters of Equation 6.39 respectively:

$$
\phi_1 = \begin{bmatrix} 0 \\ \frac{k_1 l_{1_0} l_{2_0}}{w_{1_0}} \\ \frac{k_1 l_{2_0} w_{2_0}}{w_{1_0}} \\ \frac{k_1 l_{1_0} w_{2_0}}{w_{1_0}} + \frac{k_2}{w_{2_0}} \end{bmatrix}, \quad \phi_2 = \begin{bmatrix} \frac{-k_1 l_{1_0} l_{2_0} w_{2_0}}{w_{1_0}^2} \\ \frac{-k_2 l_{2_0}}{w_{2_0}^2} \\ 0 \\ 0 \end{bmatrix} \tag{6.42}
$$

From the definitions in Equations 6.41 and 6.42, the linearized robust constraint Equation 6.39 can be rewritten as

$$
\frac{k_1 l_{1_0} l_{2_0} w_{2_0}}{w_{1_0}} + \frac{k_2 l_{1_0}}{w_{2_0}} + \max_{\|\mathbf{u}\| \leq 1} \left(\langle P^{1/2} \phi_1, \mathbf{u} \rangle + \langle P^{1/2} \phi_2, \mathbf{u} \rangle \right) \leq t_{\text{spec}} \tag{6.43}
$$

where $\langle \cdot, \cdot \rangle$ represents the standard inner product. By the Cauchy–Schwartz inequality, a sufficient condition for Equation 6.43 is

$$
\frac{k_1 l_{1_0} l_{2_0} w_{2_0}}{w_{1_0}} + \frac{k_2 l_{1_0}}{w_{2_0}} + \|P^{1/2} \phi_1\| + \|P^{1/2} \phi_2\| \leq t_{\text{spec}} \tag{6.44}
$$

We then introduce two auxiliary variables r_1 and r_2 as

$$r_1 = \|P^{1/2}\phi_1\|, \text{ i.e., } r_1^2 = \phi_1^T P \phi_1$$
$$r_2 = \|P^{1/2}\phi_2\|, \text{ i.e., } r_2^2 = \phi_2^T P \phi_2 \tag{6.45}$$

The inequality of Equation 6.44 can then be replaced by the following equivalent constraints:

$$\frac{w_1 l_{1_0} l_{2_0} w_{2_0}}{w_{1_0}} + \frac{k_2 l_{1_0}}{w_{2_0}} + r_1 + r_2 \le t_{spec} \tag{6.46}$$

$$\phi_1^T P \phi_1 r_1^{-2} \le 1 \tag{6.47}$$

$$\phi_2^T P \phi_2 r_2^{-2} \le 1 \tag{6.48}$$

The inequality of Equation 6.46 is clearly a posynomial in terms of l, w, and the auxiliary variables r_1 and r_2. By construction, all the elements of ϕ_1 are posynomials, and all the nonzero elements of ϕ_2 are negative of posynomials. The covariance matrix P has all nonnegative elements, because a negative correlation between random variables representing the W and L variations would not have any physical meaning. Thus, the quadratic terms $\phi_1^T P \phi_1 = \sum_{i,j} P_{ij}\phi_{1_i}\phi_{1_j}$ and $\phi_2^T P \phi_2 = \sum_{i,j} P_{ij}\phi_{2_i}\phi_{2_j}$ are a summation of monomials with positive coefficients. Consequently, the constraints of Equations 6.47 and 6.48 are also posynomials. Note that the inequality in Equations 6.47 and 6.48 will be forced to equality at optimality, because the auxiliary variables r_1 and r_2 (which represent

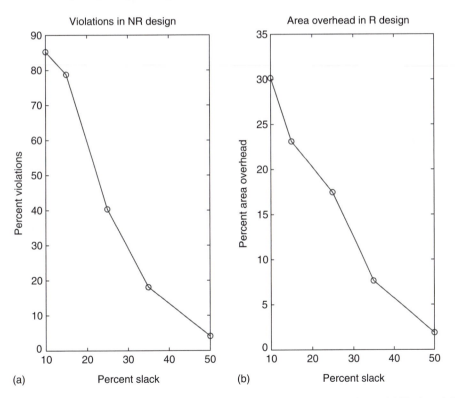

FIGURE 6.2 Nonrobust and robust designs for C499 circuit for different values of T_{spec}. (a) Timing violations for nonrobust designs. (b) Area overhead for robust designs. (From Singh, J., et al., Robust gate sizing by geometric programming, Proceedings of 2005 IEEE Design and Automation Conference, Anaheim, California, 2005.)

the maximum variation in the uncertainty ellipsoid) are to be minimized. Hence, by following the procedure outlined above, we have converted the robust posynomial constraint of Equation 6.38 to a set of posynomial constraints of Equations 6.46 through 6.48.

For a general circuit, the procedure described for the example circuit of Figure 6.1 can be repeated for each constraint. Thus, by adding at most two auxiliary variables for each constraint j, we can explicitly account for the robustness against the process uncertainties while still maintaining the desirable posynomial structure of the original constraints (Equation 6.37). By this procedure, we can convert a conventional GP formulation of the gate sizing problem to a robust gate sizing problem, which is also a GP itself. The latter can be efficiently solved using the standard convex optimization techniques (e.g., Ref. [7]).

We have applied the robust gate sizing technique to a ISCAS 85 benchmark circuit (C499). The cell library selected consists of inverters and two and three input NAND and NOR gates. We use a TSMC 180 nm technology parameter [10] to estimate the constants for the on resistance and the source, drain, and gate capacitances. We assume capacitive loading for the gates. The objective function chosen for the optimization is to minimize Area $= \sum_i m_i w_i l_i$, where m is the number of transistors in gate i. We have implemented the proposed robust gate sizing procedure in a C program, and used an optimization software [7] to solve the final GP. The final result is illustrated in Figure 6.2.

ACKNOWLEDGMENT

The text in Section 6.7 is based on a joint work [6] with Dr. Jaskirat Singh and Professor Sachin Sapatnekar. The author hereby gratefully acknowledges their contribution to this work.

REFERENCES

1. Ben-Tal, A., El Ghaoui, L., and Nemirovskii, A., Robust semidefinite programming, in *Handbook of Semidefinite Programming*, edited by Wolkowicz, H., Saigal, R., and Vandenberghe, L., Kluwer Academic Publishers, March 2000.
2. Ben-Tal, A. and Nemirovskii, A., Robust convex optimization, *Mathematics of Operations Research*, 23, 769–805, 1998.
3. Boyd, S. and Vandenberghe, L., *Convex Optimization*, Cambridge University Press, Cambridge, United Kingdom, 2003.
4. Chiang, M., Geometric programming for communication systems, *Foundations and Trends in Communications and Information Theory*, 2005.
5. El Ghaoui, L., Oustry, F., and Lebret, H., Robust solutions to uncertain semidefinite programs, *SIAM Journal on Optimization*, 9(1), 1998.
6. Singh, J., Nookala, V., Luo, Z.-Q., and Sapatnekar, S., Robust gate sizing by geometric programming, Proceedings of 2005 IEEE Designa and Automation Conference, June 13–17, 2005, Anaheim, California.
7. Mosek Software, Available at http://www.mosek.com.
8. Nesterov, Y. and Nemirovskii, A., *Interior Point Polynomial Methods in Convex Programming, SIAM Studies in Applied Mathematics* 13, Philadelphia, PA, 1994.
9. Sturm, J.F., Using SeDuMi 1.02, A Matlab toolbox for optimization over symmetric cones, *Optimization Methods and Software*, 11–12, 625–653, 1999. See http://fewcal.kub.nl/sturm/software/sedumi.html for updates.
10. TSMC: 180 nm Test Data, Available at http://www.mosis.org/Technical/Testdata/tsmc-018-prm.html.
11. Wolkowicz, H., Saigal, R., and Vandenberghe, L., *Handbook of Semidefinite Programming: Theory, Algorithms and Applications*, Kluwer Academic Press, pp. 163–188, 1999.

7 Partitioning and Clustering

Dorothy Kucar

CONTENTS

Modern standard cell placement techniques must handle huge and ever-increasing design sizes. It is computationally infeasible to place flattened representations of designs of this scale. A key step in cell placement is obtaining a smaller representation of the design that captures the global connectivity of the original design. This is what is known as partitioning and clustering. Partitioning is typically used to divide a netlist into two or four blocks, then recursively applied to the subregions such that the wiring cost between blocks is minimized. Clustering, on the other hand, is inherently a bottom-up approach, where cells are initially assigned to their own block, then they are gradually merged into larger and larger blocks. The purpose of clustering is to reduce the problem size to more manageable proportions and to recover structural information implicit in the original netlist. Modern placers use a combination of clustering and partitioning to reduce runtimes and preserve structure that was present in the original netlist. The very large scale integrated (VLSI) design automation community has added several twists to the original graph-theoretic formulation, including fixing vertices to specific blocks, assigning weights to vertices, and introducing timing constraints into the formulation.

This survey consists of five sections. Section 7.1 introduces the basic concepts and notations relevant to partitioning and clustering. Section 7.2 describes move-based partitioning techniques. Section 7.3 describes mathematical partitioning formulations. Section 7.4 describes clustering techniques, which are employed in multilevel partitioners, described in Section 7.5.

7.1 PRELIMINARIES

In this chapter, a circuit is a collection of elementary switching elements called standard cells and possibly larger macroblocks, connected to one another by wires at the same electrical potential called signal nets enclosed by some sort of boundary. The points at which signal nets come into contact with cells are called pins. If a pin connects cells to areas outside the circuit boundary, it is referred to as a terminal (Figure 7.1). Standard cell connectivity information is provided in the form of a netlist, which contains net names followed by the names of cells they are connected to.

The combinatorial nature of VLSI physical design problems lends itself nicely to formulations involving graphs or matrices. Most often, a circuit is represented as a hypergraph where cells are represented as weighted vertices. The weight is typically proportional to the number of pins or the area of the cell. A hypergraph is the most natural representation of a circuit because, in a circuit, more than two vertices may be connected by the same signal net. Circuit hypergraphs have certain desirable properties as far as algorithm development is concerned. They are nearly planar because chips are typically printed on seven to ten metal layers. The nets of the circuit hypergraph are also of reasonably bounded degree—algorithms that deal with nets of high degree like power, ground, or clock nets are not discussed here. In this chapter, a hypergraph comprises $|V|$ vertices, $|E|$ nets, $|P|$ pins, and k blocks, the set of vertices in the ith block is denoted by C_i, and a net consists of $|e|$ vertices. Although a hypergraph is the natural representation of a circuit, it is very difficult to work with. Often, nets are modeled as cliques or stars as in Figure 7.2b.

Definition 1 *A clique is a subgraph of graph G(V, E) in which every vertex is connected to every other vertex.*

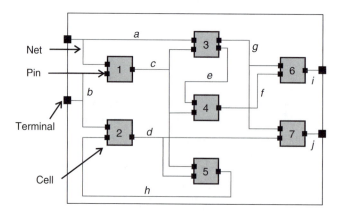

FIGURE 7.1 Schematic diagram of a circuit illustrating terminals, cells, and nets.

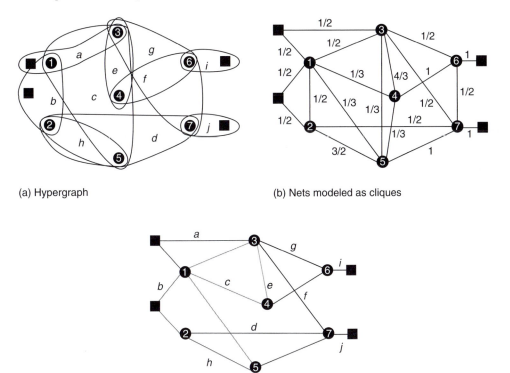

(a) Hypergraph   (b) Nets modeled as cliques

(c) Nets modeled as stars

FIGURE 7.2   Net representations.

It follows that a net connected to $|e|$ vertices will be represented by $\binom{|e|}{2}$ edges. Another way of representing nets is a star graph model.

Definition 2   *A star graph is a subgraph of graph $G(V, E)$ in which every vertex except for one is a leaf vertex. The nonleaf-vertex connects all leaf vertices as in Figure 7.2c.*

In the star graph model, each vertex induces one edge, thus a net consisting of $|e|$ vertices will be represented by $|e| - 1$ edges. Using this representation, the problem of edge weights is alleviated, but the root vertex must be chosen sensibly. Some placers use an alternate star model where an auxiliary root vertex connecting all of the net's original vertices is inserted (described in Chapter 17).

7.1.1   NET MODELS

Many of the techniques described in this work require that nets be represented in terms of edges. If a net on $|e|$ vertices is represented as a complete graph on $|e|$ vertices and if $|e|$ is large, the $|e|$ vertices will likely be placed in the same block after bipartitioning. The result is that nets with small numbers of vertices may be cut because of the predominance of large nets [SK72]. The solution to this problem is to weight the graph edges of the net so that regardless of how vertices in the graph are partitioned, the sum of the weights of the edges cut should be as close to 1 as possible. Generally, it will not be possible for this sum to be exactly 1 as the theorem below states.

Theorem 1   *There is no consistent edge weighting scheme such that when some edges are removed (to split the hypergraph into several parts), their weight is exactly 1 for $|e|$ vertices where $|e| \geq 4$ [IWW93].*

For example, a net consisting of four vertices is represented by an equivalent six-edge complete graph. To cut off one vertex from the rest requires cutting three edges, so the weight should be 1/3 (for a total edge weight of 1). However, to cut off two vertices from the rest requires cutting four edges (each with weight 1/4). Because some of the edges assigned weights of 1/3 and 1/4 may be the same, this weighting scheme is inconsistent.

Lengauer [Len90] proves that no matter what weighting scheme is selected, there will always exist an exact graph bipartition with a deviation of $\Omega(\sqrt{|e|})$ from the cost of cutting a single net. Additionally, Ihler et al. [IWW93] conjecture that a clique graph model is the best in terms of deviation from the true cost of cutting one net.

In the generic clique model, a net on $|e|$ vertices induces a complete graph where each edge has weight

$$w_i = \frac{1}{|e| - 1}$$

This weighting scheme arises from linear placements into fixed slots separated by a unit distance. The denominator indicates the minimum total wirelength used to connect the $|e|$ vertices. Vannelli and Hadley [VH90] propose the following metric that guarantees the weight of edges cut under a k-way partitioning has an upper bound of 1.

$$w_i = \frac{1}{\left\lfloor \frac{|e|}{k} \right\rfloor \left\lceil \frac{|e|}{k} \right\rceil}$$

Huang [HK97] proposes a weight of

$$w_i = \frac{4}{|e|(|e| - 1)}$$

that distributes the weight of one net evenly across two edges and gives an expected cut weight of 1. The following weighting scheme distributes the edge weight evenly across $|e| - 1$ edges:

$$w_i = \frac{2}{|e|}$$

In Ref. [AY95], the authors use a variant of Huang's metric:

$$w_i = \frac{4}{|e|(|e| - 1)} \frac{2^{|e|} - 2}{2^{|e|}}$$

7.1.2 PARTITIONING AND CLUSTERING METRICS

In this section, we give some definitions relevant to hypergraph partitioning and use them to describe metrics used in hypergraph partitioning.

Definition 3 *Given a hypergraph, $G(V, E)$, nets that have vertices in multiple blocks belong to the cutset, E^c, of the hypergraph. Given k blocks, the cutset between the ith pair of blocks where $i = 1 \cdots \binom{k}{2}$ is denoted by E_i^c.*

Definition 4 *A partition, $f(V, k)$, of the set of vertices, V, into k blocks, $\{C_1, \ldots, C_k\}$ is given by $C_1 \cup C_2 \cup \cdots \cup C_k = V$ where $C_i \cap C_j = \emptyset$ and $\alpha|V| \leq |C_i| \leq \beta|V|$ for $1 \leq i < j \leq k$ and $0 \leq \alpha, \beta \leq 1$.*

Definition 5   *The weight of the ith block is denoted by $w(C_i)$. Usually, it is equal to the number of vertices in the ith block, $|C_i|$*

Definition 6   *Given a clustering solution $\{C_1, C_2, \ldots, C_k\}$, where C_i indicates a group of vertices, construct a clustered hypergraph $H'(V', E')$ such that for every $e \in E$, there is a hyperedge $e' \in E'$ with $e' = \{C | \exists v \in e \cap C\}$.*

Mincut partitioning: This metric counts the number of nets running between pairs of blocks

$$\min \quad f(V, k) = \sum_{i=1}^{k} |E_i^c|$$

$$\text{s.t.} \quad \alpha|V| \le w(C_i) \le \beta|V|$$

For example, if a net spans three blocks then it would be counted three times in the objective [Alp96]. A slightly different objective is one that counts the number of entire nets that are cut (this is formally called the **netcut**). These objectives are identical if the number of blocks is two. Typically, $\alpha = 0.45$ and $\beta = 0.55$ for bipartitioning. For k-way partitioning, some authors favor the following constraints:

$$\frac{|V|}{\alpha k} \le w(C_i) \le \frac{\alpha|V|}{k}$$

where $\alpha > 1$ [KK99].

Min-ratiocut bipartitioning: The ratiocut metric, r_c, is used in Refs. [WC91], [RDJ94] and others as a way of incorporating balance constraints into the objective. The objective is

$$\min \ f(V, 2) = r_c = \frac{|E^c|}{w(C_1)w(C_2)}$$

where the numerator indicates the netcut. For a given netcut, this metric is minimized when the two blocks are of equal size. However, as Alpert and Kahng [AK95] point out, the weakness in this metric is that r_c is very sensitive to change in $|E^c|$ and relatively unaffected by changes in $w(C_1)$ or $w(C_2)$. Thus, given a small enough netcut, it is possible to obtain a minimal ratio cut even if the block sizes are uneven.

In the analytic bipartitioning technique described in Ref. [RDJ94], vertices are assigned to positions along the x-axis, simultaneously. Block assignments are then derived from the coordinates in some fashion. Thus, it is not possible to move individual vertices from one block to another as is the case with iterative-based partitioners. Consequently, vertices may be assigned positions along the x-axis that do not satisfy even fairly loose balance constraints in which a block is allowed to have between 45 and 55 percent of the cells (or total cell area).

Min-ratiocut k-way partitioning: Chan et al. [CSZ94] generalize the ratiocut metric for k blocks to

$$\sum_{i=1}^{k} \left[\frac{|E_i^c|}{w(C_i)} \right] \le \sum_{i=1}^{k} \lambda_i$$

where λ_i is the ith smallest eigenvalue of the Laplacian matrix of $G(V, E)$.

Scaled cost: Another metric that combines the usual minimum cut objective with block size constraints is

$$f(V, k) = \frac{1}{|V|(k-1)} \sum_{i=1}^{k} \frac{|E_i^c|}{w(C_i)}$$

This metric is used in Refs. [AK93,AK94,AK96,KK98,AKY99].

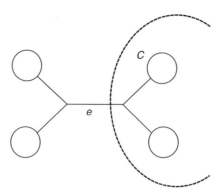

FIGURE 7.3   Absorption metric.

Absorption: The absorption metric measures the sum of nets, as a fraction, that are absorbed by blocks [SS95].

$$\max \sum_{i=1}^{k} \sum_{\{e \in E \mid e \cap C_i \neq \emptyset\}} \frac{|e \cap C_i| - 1}{|e| - 1}$$

At the two extremes, nets that have one vertex in a block C add 0 to the absorption metric; nets that have all vertices in a block C add 1 to the absorption metric. In Figure 7.3, $|e \cap C| = 2$, $\frac{|e \cap C| - 1}{|e| - 1} = \frac{1}{3}$.

In addition to the usual balance constraints, partitioning formulations may include constraints for vertices that are assigned to a specific block. The presence of fixed terminals adds some convexity to this otherwise highly nonconvex problem, making it computationally less expensive [EAV99]. In Ref. [ACKM00], the authors point out that the presence of fixed vertices makes the problem trivial in the sense that only one or two passes of an iterative improvement engine are required to approach a good solution.

7.2 MOVE-BASED PARTITIONING METHODS

In this section, we will outline the most significant developments in the field of iterative improvement-based partitioning. Iterative improvement forms the basis of multilevel partitioning, which represents the state of the art as far as partitioning is concerned.

7.2.1 KERNIGHAN–LIN HEURISTIC

Kernighan and Lin's work was the earliest attempt at moving away from exhaustive search in determining the optimal netcut subject to balance constraints. In Ref. [KL70], they propose a $O(|V|^2 \log |V|)$ heuristic for graph bipartitioning based on exchanging pairs of vertices with the highest gain between two blocks, C_1 and C_2. They define the gain of a pair of vertices as the number of edges by which the netcut decreases if vertices x and y are exchanged between blocks. Assuming a_{ij} are entries of a graph adjacency matrix, the gain is given by the formula

$$g(v_x, v_y) = \left(\sum_{v_j \notin C_1} a_{xj} - \sum_{v_j \in C_1} a_{xj} \right) + \left(\sum_{v_j \notin C_2} a_{yj} - \sum_{v_j \in C_2} a_{yj} \right) - 2a_{xy}$$

The terms in parentheses count the number of vertices that have edges entirely within one block minus the number of vertices that have edges connecting vertices in the complementary block.

TABLE 7.1

Gain Computations

Previous State	Next State	Gain
A	B	$|AB_A| + |OAB_A| - |IA| - |OA|$
B	A	$|IAB_A| + |OAB_A| - |IA| - |OA|$

The procedure works as follows: vertices are initially divided into two sets, C_1 and C_2. A gain is computed for all pairs of vertices (v_i, v_j) with $v_i \in C_1$ and $v_j \in C_2$; the pair of vertices, (v_x, v_y), with the highest gain is selected for exchange; v_x and v_y are then removed from the list of exchange candidates. The gains for all pairs of vertices, $v_i \in (C_1 - \{v_x\})$ and $v_j \in (C_2 - \{v_y\})$, are recomputed and the pairing of vertices with the highest gain are exchanged. The process continues until $g(v_x, v_y) = 0$, at which point, the algorithm will have found a local minimum. The algorithm can be repeated to improve upon the current local minimum. Kernighan and Lin observe that two to four passes are necessary to obtain a locally optimal solution.

In Ref. [SK72], Schweikert and Kernighan introduce a model that deals with hypergraphs directly. They point out that the major flaw of the (clique) graph model is that it exaggerates the importance of nets with more than two connections. After bipartitioning, vertices connecting large nets tend to end up in the same block, whereas vertices connected to two point nets end up in different blocks. They combine their hypergraph model in the Kernighan–Lin partitioning heuristic and obtain much better results on circuit partitioning problems.

7.2.2 FIDUCCIA–MATTHEYSES HEURISTIC

The Fiduccia–Mattheyses (FM) [FM82] method is a linear-time, $[O(|P|)]$ per pass, hypergraph bipartitioning heuristic. Its impressive runtime is due to a clever way of determining which vertex to move based on its gain and to an efficient data structure called a bucket list.

Borrowing the terminology and notation from Ref. [KN91], a critical net is one that is connected to a single vertex in one of the blocks (so that the removal of that vertex removes the net from that block). A net state is a combination of subnetworks that contain a net as well as the subnetworks in which the net is critical. Let A indicate that a net is entirely within block A; let A_A indicate that a net in block A is critical to block A. Let the prefix I or O indicate that the net is an input or output to the vertex, thus IAB_A indicates the input net has vertices in blocks A and B but that is critical to block A. The gain equations are computed with respect to vertices and are given in Table 7.1.

In Figure 7.4, if we move vertex u from A to B, the gain is computed in the following way. $|AB_A| = 2$ because nets 1 and 2 are critical to A, $|OAB_A| = 2$ refers to nets 1 and 2 as well, $|IA| = 3$

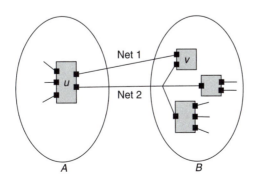

Net 1

Net 2

u

v

A

B

FIGURE 7.4 Example of gain computations.

because there are three inputs to u in A, and $|OA| = 2$ because there are two outputs to u in A. The gain is given by $|AB_A| + |OAB_A| - |IA| - |OA| = 2 + 2 - 3 - 2 = -1$, which implies moving vertex u will result in the netcut increasing by 1. On the other hand, moving vertex v from B to A implies $|IAB_A| = 1$ because v has one input that is critical to A, $|OAB_A| = 0$ because v has no outputs critical to A, $|IA| = 0$ because v has no inputs in A, and $|OA| = 0$ because v has no outputs in A, for a total gain of 1.

The gains are maintained in a $[-|P|_{max} \cdots |P|_{max}]$ bucket array whose ith entry contains a doubly linked list of free vertices with gains currently equal to i. The maximum gain, $|P|_{max}$, is obtained when a vertex of degree $|P|_{max}$ (i.e., a vertex that is incident on $|P|_{max}$ nets) is moved across the block boundary and all of its incident nets are removed from the cutset (Figure 7.5).

The free vertices in the bucket list are linked to vertices in the main vertex array so that during a gain update, vertices are removed from the bucket list in constant time (per vertex). Superior results are obtained if vertices are removed and inserted from the bucket list using a last-in-first-out (LIFO) scheme (over first-in-first-out [FIFO] or random schemes) [HHK97]. The authors of Ref. [HHK97] speculate that a LIFO implementation is better because vertices that naturally block together will tend to be listed sequentially in the netlist. Care must be exercised to compute gains correctly for situations where a cell has two inputs on the same net.

7.2.3 IMPROVEMENTS ON THE FIDUCCIA–MATTHEYSES HEURISTIC

This section discusses a few noteworthy improvements to the original FM implementation that have helped the acceptance of FM as the most popular partitioning technique.

The first improvement to FM is Krishnamurthy's look-ahead scheme [Kri84], in which a vertex belonging to a multivertex net, which is in the cutset, is considered for a move. Moving this vertex may not necessarily remove the net from the cutset in the current pass, but may do so in a future pass. Kirshnamurthy's method calculates a gain vector consisting of a sequence of r gain values, which are likely to result in r moves from the current move. The rth level gain counts the reduced netcut after r moves. If there are ties in the current gain value, gain vectors are calculated for those configurations; ties at the ith move are broken by looking at the possible gains at the $(i + 1)$st iteration.

Sanchis [San89] extends the FM concept to deal with multiway partitioning. Her method incorporates Fiduccia and Mattheyses' gain bucket structure (modified for multiway partitioning) with Krishnamurthy's look-ahead scheme. One pass of the algorithm consists of examining moves that result in the highest gain among all $k(k-1)$ bucket lists. The vertex with the highest gain that satisfies the balance criterion is then moved. After a move, all $k(k-1)$ bucket lists are updated.

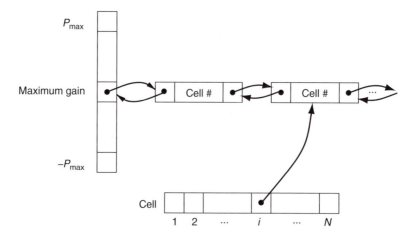

FIGURE 7.5 Bucket-list data structure used in FM iterative improvement partitioning algorithm.

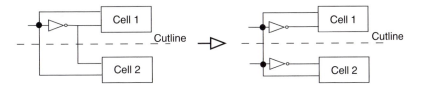

FIGURE 7.6 On the left side, the netcut is 2; on the right side, the inverter has been replicated so the netcut is only 1.

An extension to the FM algorithm works by replicating cells across blocks to reduce the netcut as in Figure 7.6 [KN91]. Replication is useful in the context of field programmable gate array (FPGA) partitioning where there are hard limits on the number of I/O resources. The concept of replication is depicted in Figure 7.6.

The principal modification to the FM algorithm is the insertion of gain equations that model cell replication. Again, using the notation from Ref. [KN91] and the previous section, the gains are given in Table 7.2, where the last four lines are due to vertex replication or unreplication. Notice that there is very little change to the algorithm, thus the asymptotic complexity is equivalent to that of FM.

Dutt and Deng [DD96] observe that iterative improvement engines such as FM or look-ahead do not identify blocks adequately, and consequently, miss locally optimal solutions with respect to the netcut. They point out that in FM, the total gain of a vertex is composed of the sum of an initial gain component and an updated gain component. They propose to make the decision regarding which subsequent vertices to move based on the updated gain component exclusively.

In Ref. [CL98], the authors propose a k-way FM-based partitioning method that does not rely on recursive subdivision of the solution space. Up until that point, a k-way partitioning solution meant partitioning into two blocks, then four, and so on in a recursive fashion. The problem with this approach is that vertices can only be moved between the two blocks within the current partitioning level, so the partitioning solution is fairly localized, as is illustrated on the left in Figure 7.7. In their approach, two blocks form a pair when the cutsize between them is maximum or minimum during the last several passes. FM-type partitioning is then performed on vertices within the two selected blocks as on the right in Figure 7.7.

7.2.4 SIMULATED ANNEALING

In the late 1980s, simulated annealing emerged as a viable means to solve difficult combinatorial problems. The nomenclature comes from the process of crystal growth, called annealing. A material is initially heated to molten state. If it is cooled slowly enough, the molecules gradually fall into a state of minimal energy and the material assumes a beautiful crystalline shape. The mathematical analogy is that state corresponds to a feasible solution, energy corresponds to solution cost, and

TABLE 7.2

More Detailed set of Gain Computations

Previous State	Next State	Gain Equation
A	B	$|AB_A| + |OAB_A| - |IA| - |OA|$
B	A	$|IAB_A| + |OAB_A| - |IA| - |OA|$
A	AB	$|OAB| + |OAB_A| - |IA|$
B	AB	$|OAB| + |OAB_B| - |IB|$
AB	A	$|IAB_B| - |OAB_A| - |OAB|$
AB	B	$|IAB_A| - |OAB_B| - |OAB|$

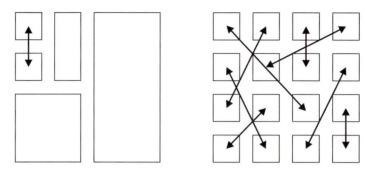

FIGURE 7.7   Recursive versus pairwise k–way partitioning.

minimal energy corresponds to an optimal solution. The principal advantage of simulated annealing over other methods is its ability to accept moves that will increase the cost function, initially with a reasonably high probability, but with decreasing probability as the temperature decreases. In this way, it is possible to climb out of local optima. The details of the simulated annealing algorithm are given in Ref. [KGV83].

Simulated annealing is applied to the problem of graph partitioning in Ref. [JAMS89]. Any partition of vertices into two sets, C_1 and C_2, is a valid solution, where C_1 and C_2 are not necessarily the same size. The algorithm attempts to even out partition sizes by moving the vertex that results in the least increase in cutsize from the larger set to the smaller set using the cost function

$$\text{cost}(C_1, C_2) = |\{\{u, v\} \in E : u \in C_1 \quad \text{and} \quad v \in C_2\}| + \alpha(|C_1| - |C_2|)^2$$

The temperature is embedded in the α parameter, thus at higher temperatures, imbalanced block sizes are penalized according to the square of the difference in block sizes. As the temperature decreases, block sizes become more balanced. Simulated annealing tends to produce smaller netcuts than iterative methods, albeit with much greater runtimes [JAMS89].

7.3   MATHEMATICAL PARTITIONING FORMULATIONS

Analytical partitioning methods use equation solving techniques to assign vertices to one of the two blocks so that the number of edges with endpoints in both blocks is minimized. In this section, we use the notation C_1 and C_2 to denote the sets of vertices in each block. In Ref. [CGT95], the authors use spectral bipartitioning to bipartition the vertices about the median of the entries in the second eigenvector of the Laplacian matrix. In Ref. [AK94], the authors use a space-filling curve traversal of the space spanned by a small set of eigenvectors to determine where to split the ordering induced by the set of eigenvectors. This section discusses analytical approaches to partitioning in more detail. The formulations in this section use the definitions given below.

Definition 7   *Given a graph on $|V|$ vertices and $|E|$ edges where w_{ij} indicates the weight of the edge connecting vertices i and j, the adjacency matrix, **A**, is defined as*

$$a_{ij} = \begin{cases} w_{ij} > 0 & \text{if vertices } i \text{ and } j \text{ are adjacent } i \neq j \\ 0 & \text{otherwise} \end{cases}$$

Note that usually, w_{ij} is set to 1.

We denote the ith eigenvalue of **A** by α_i

Definition 8   *Given an adjacency matrix of a graph on $|V|$ vertices, the diagonal degree matrix,* **D***, is defined as*

$$d_{ii} = \sum_{j=1}^{|V|} a_{ij}$$

Definition 9   *Given a graph on $|V|$ vertices, define the corresponding $|V| \times |V|$ Laplacian matrix,* **L** $=$ **D** $-$ **A**.

7.3.1   QUADRATIC PROGRAMMING FORMULATION

Given a graph $G(V, E)$, vertices $u \in V$ and $v \in V$, let $x_v = 1$ if vertex v belongs to block 1 and $x_v = -1$ if vertex v belongs to block 2. We wish to minimize the number of edges with endpoints in both blocks. Because $x_v = \pm 1$, this is equivalent to minimizing the one-dimensional (integer) distance between all pairs of connected vertices [HK91].

$$\min \sum_{(u,v) \in E} (x_u - x_v)^2 \qquad (7.1)$$

The nonzero pattern in the summand results in the matrix formulation:

$$\min_{x} (\mathbf{P}^{\mathrm{T}} \mathbf{x})^{\mathrm{T}} (\mathbf{P}^{\mathrm{T}} \mathbf{x}) = \min \mathbf{x}^{\mathrm{T}} \mathbf{P} \mathbf{P}^{\mathrm{T}} \mathbf{x} = \min \mathbf{x}^{\mathrm{T}} \mathbf{L} \mathbf{x} \qquad (7.2)$$

where **P** is the $|V| \times |E|$ node-arc incidence matrix defined as [NW88]

$$p_{v,e} = \begin{cases} +1 & \text{if vertex } v \text{ is the head of edge } e \\ -1 & \text{if vertex } v \text{ is the tail of edge } e \\ 0 & \text{otherwise} \end{cases}$$

and where **L** is the Laplacian matrix of the graph. To accommodate nonunit weights on the edges, one forms the product $\mathbf{PWP}^{\mathrm{T}}$, where **W** is a diagonal matrix with the nonzero entries representing the weights of edges [GM00]. We list the properties of **L** here.

Property 1   **L** *is a symmetric, positive semi definite matrix.*

Proof   Using Equations 7.1 and 7.2, we have

$$\mathbf{x}^{\mathrm{T}} \mathbf{L} \mathbf{x} = \frac{1}{2} \sum_{i=1}^{|V|} \sum_{j=1}^{|V|} (x_i - x_j)^2 \geq 0, \quad \forall\, x_i \neq x_j \qquad \square$$

By Property *1*, the eigenvalues are all real and nonnegative.

Property 2   *The sum of elements in each row of* **L** *equal* 0

Proof   Recall that $\mathbf{L} = \mathbf{D} - \mathbf{A}$ and that $d_{ii} = \sum_{j=1}^{|V|} a_{ij}$, thus

$$\sum_{j=1}^{|V|} \ell_{ij} = d_{ii} - \sum_{j=1}^{|V|} a_{ij} = \sum_{j=1}^{|V|} a_{ij} - \sum_{j=1}^{|V|} a_{ij} = 0 \qquad \square$$

The graph partitioning formulation includes block assignment constraints on the vertices [Hal70, PSL90]:

$$\min_{\mathbf{x}} \quad \mathbf{x}^T \mathbf{L} \mathbf{x}$$

$$\text{s.t.} \quad x_v = \pm 1$$

Because of its discrete nature, this problem is very difficult to solve exactly. The discrete constraints can be modeled by n ith order constraints [TK91]. In practice, the integer constraints are approximated by first- and second-order constraints only. The second-order constraints in Equation 7.4 spread vertices about the median. The first-order constraints in Equation 7.5 dictate that there are an approximately equal number of vertices on both sides of the median. For convenience, we define $\mathbf{e}$ as the vector of all ones. Thus, the optimization problem is

$$\min_{\mathbf{x}} \quad \mathbf{x}^T \mathbf{L} \mathbf{x} \tag{7.3}$$

$$\text{s.t.} \quad \mathbf{x}^T \mathbf{x} = 1 \tag{7.4}$$

$$\mathbf{x}^T \mathbf{e} = 0 \tag{7.5}$$

This formulation essentially replaces the solution space consisting of the vertices of the ± 1 unit hypercube with the points on the surface of the Euclidian unit sphere.

Theorem 2   *[PSL90] A globally optimal solution to Equations 7.3 through 7.5 is* $\mathbf{x} = \mathbf{u}_2$, *where* $\mathbf{u}_2$ *is the eigenvector corresponding to the second smallest eigenvalue of* **L**.

$\mathbf{u}_2$ is formally known as the Fiedler vector [Fie73]. The components of the Fiedler vector that are negative valued represent the coordinates of vertices in the first block; components of the second eigenvector that are greater than or equal to 0 represent the coordinates of vertices in the second block. The effect is that the eigenvector components of strongly (weakly) connected vertices are close (far away), thus strongly connected vertices are more likely to be assigned to the same block. Because it minimizes the distance between pairs of vertices, the technique we have just described can be used as a one-dimensional placement of vertices [TK91]. Unfortunately, there is no guarantee that the optimal solution obtained by the continuous optimization problem closely approximates the discrete optimum [CGT95].

7.3.1.1   Lower Bounds on the Cutset Size

The Laplacian matrix used in the bipartitioning quadratic programming formulation is, in fact, the discretized version of the Laplace operator from partial differential equation (PDE) theory. If the PDE is solved exactly, one can obtain theoretical bounds on the number of edges cut for a line graph fixed at both ends. The canonical graph used to obtain lower bounds is a line graph of length L with tethered endpoints, as in Figure 7.8. We represent the string by $|V| = n$ weighted masses connected by $n + 1$ pieces of string such that each piece is $\Delta x = \frac{L}{n}$ units long.

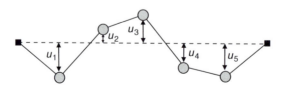

FIGURE 7.8   Line graph.

The bipartitioning problem for the line graph has an exact solution, which is given by the second eigenvalue of $\mathbf{L}$, $\lambda_2 = \frac{2a\pi}{L}$ and the second eigenvector of $\mathbf{L}$ is given by

$$\mathbf{u}_2 = \left(\sin \left[\frac{2\pi(\Delta x)}{n+1} \right] \quad \sin \left[\frac{2\pi(2\Delta x)}{n+1} \right] \cdots \sin \left\{ \frac{2\pi[(n-1)\Delta x]}{n+1} \right\} \quad \sin \left[\frac{2\pi(n\Delta x)}{n+1} \right] \right)$$

when $n = 2$ (i.e., the case with bipartitioning), the string vibrates such that the u-coordinate at the midpoint is always 0. The area to the left of the midpoint (thus, half of the vertices) has $u > 0$ and the area to the right of the midpoint has $u < 0$ (the other half of vertices).

Some of the earliest theoretical developments in eigenvector bipartitioning were concerned with finding lower bounds on the size of the cutset. First, we give two definitions:

Definition 10   *A block assignment matrix, $\mathbf{X}$, is defined as*

$$x_{is} = \begin{cases} 1 & \text{if vertex i is in block s} \\ 0 & \text{otherwise} \end{cases}$$

A related matrix describes whether two vertices are in the same block.

Definition 11   *A block adjacency matrix, $\mathbf{B} = \mathbf{X}\mathbf{X}^{\mathrm{T}}$, is defined as*

$$b_{ij} = \begin{cases} 1 & \text{if vertex } i \text{ is in the same block as vertex } j \\ 0 & \text{otherwise} \end{cases}$$

The eigenvalues of $\mathbf{B}$ are $\{\beta_1, \beta_2, \ldots, \beta_k, 0, \ldots, 0\}$ where k indicates the desired number of blocks. Donath and Hoffman [DH73] provide lower bounds on the number of edges cut:

$$|E^c| \geq -\frac{1}{2} \sum_{j=1}^{k} \lambda_j \beta_j$$

where λ_j is an eigenvalue of the adjacency matrix plus a diagonal matrix $\mathbf{U}$, such that $\sum_{i=1}^{|V|} u_{ii} = -\sum_{j=1}^{|V|} \sum_{i=1}^{|V|} a_{ij}$.

Barnes [Bar82] restated k-way graph partitioning in terms of finding a block assignment matrix, $\mathbf{B}$, so that the distance (in a two-norm sense) between $\mathbf{B}$ and the adjacency matrix, $\mathbf{A}$, is as small as possible. The rationale is that if vertices i and j are adjacent (i.e., $a_{ij} = 1$), then they should end up in the same block (i.e., $b_{ij} = 1$). He shows that

$$\min |E^c| \equiv \min \|\mathbf{A} - \mathbf{B}\|^2$$

Hagen and Kahng [HK92] proved that

$$|E^c| \geq \frac{|C_1| \cdot |C_2|}{|V|} \lambda_2$$

which agrees with Boppana's [Bop87] bounds of

$$|E^c| \geq \frac{|V|}{4} \lambda_2$$

when $|V_1| = |C_2| = \frac{|V|}{2}$. Other bounds are found in Ref. [FRW92].

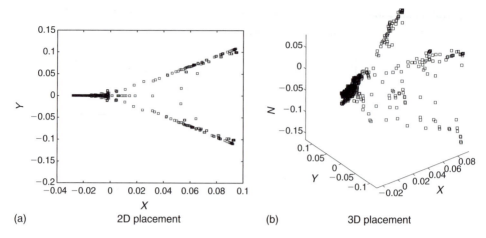

(a)   2D placement   (b)   3D placement

FIGURE 7.9   Placements of `prim1` using (a) two eigenvectors and (b) three eigenvectors.

7.3.1.2   Partitioning Solutions from Multiple Eigenvectors

It is also possible to use multiple eigenvectors to determine arrangements of vertices that minimize the number of cuts. Hall [Hal70] suggests that the location of the vertices in r-dimensional space can be used to identify blocks (see Section 7.3.1 for a description of his method). Two- and three-dimensional placements of `prim1` are shown in Figure 7.9. The three branches in the two-dimensional plot indicate three blocks should be formed. On the other hand, it is not as obvious how to cluster vertices in the three-dimensional plot.

Instead of minimizing the squared distance between two vertices as in Equations 7.3 and 7.4, Frankle and Karp [FK86] transform the distance minimization problem to one of finding the point emanating from the projection of **x** onto all eigenvectors that is furthest from the origin. The vector induced by this point will give a good ordering with respect to the wirelength.

Chan et al. [CSZ94] use the cosine of the angle between two rows of the $|V| \times k$ eigenvector matrix, **V**, to determine how close the vertices are to each other. If the cosine between two vectors is close to 1, then the corresponding vertices must belong to the same block. Their k-way partitioning heuristic constructs k prototype vectors with distinct directions (to represent blocks) and places into the corresponding block the vertices that have corresponding vectors within $\frac{\pi}{8}$ radians of the prototype vector.

This approach was the starting point for a method devised by Alpert et al. The idea behind multiple eigenvector linear orderings (MELO) [AY95], [AKY99] is after removing the first column (which corresponds to the zero eigenvalue) from **V** (call this matrix **V′**), the partition that satisfies the usual mincut objective and balance constraints is obtained by finding a permutation of the rows of **V′** that results in the maximum possible two-norm sum of the rows. Alpert and Yao [AKY99] prove that when the number of eigenvectors selected is n, then maximizing the vector sum is equivalent to minimizing netcut.

7.3.2   Linear Programming Formulations

In paraboli, Riess et al. [RDJ94], [AK95] use the eigenvector technique of Section 7.3.1 to fix the vertices corresponding to the ten smallest eigenvector components and ten largest eigenvector components to locations 1.0 and 0.0, respectively. The center of gravity of the remaining vertices is fixed at location 0.5. They use a mathematical programming technique to reposition the free vertices so the overall wirelength is reduced. The mathematical formulation is given by

$$\min \quad \sum_{i=1}^{|V|} \sum_{j=1}^{|V|} \frac{a_{ij}}{|x_i - x_j|}(x_i - x_j)^2$$

$$\text{s.t.} \quad \sum_{i=1}^{|V|} x_i = f$$

In the next pass of the algorithm, the 5 percent of vertices with the largest (smallest) resulting coordinate are moved so their center of gravity is at $x_i = 0.95$ and $x_i = 0.05$. After performing the optimization and repositioning, the process is repeated at center of gravity of $x_i = 0.9$ and $x_i = 0.1$, etc. The process is repeated ten times so there are ten different orderings. The best ordering is the one among the ten orderings with the best ratiocut metric.

In Ref. [LLLC96], the authors point out that linear cost functions spread out dense blocks of vertices, whereas quadratic cost functions naturally identify blocks of vertices, making it easier to assign discrete locations to otherwise closely packed vertices. They incorporate the merits of both linear and quadratic methods in a modified α-order cost function:

$$\min \quad \sum_{i>j}^{|V|} \sum_{j=1}^{|V|} \frac{a_{ij}}{|x_i - x_j|^{2-\alpha}}(x_i - x_j)^2$$

$$\text{s.t.} \quad \sum_{i=1}^{|V|} x_i = f$$

where $1 \le \alpha \le 2$. If $\alpha = 1$, the cost function becomes the linear cost function; for $\alpha = 2$, the cost function becomes the quadratic cost function. They observe that $\alpha = 1.2$ best incorporates the benefits of linear and quadratic cost functions.

7.3.3 INTEGER PROGRAMMING FORMULATIONS

In Ref. [AK95], the authors formulate bipartitioning as an integer quadratic program. Let x_{is} indicate that vertex i belongs to block s. Let a_{ij} represent the cost of the edge connecting vertices i and j. Let **B** be a matrix with $b_{ii} = 0$, $\forall i$ and $b_{ij} = 1$, $\forall i \ne j$. The optimization problem that minimizes the number of edges that have endpoints in more than one block is given by

$$\min \quad \sum_{i,j=1}^{k} \sum_{s,\ell=1}^{m} a_{ij} x_{is} b_{s\ell} x_{j\ell} \qquad (7.6)$$

$$\text{s.t.} \quad \sum_{s=1}^{k} x_{is} = 1 \quad \forall i \qquad (7.7)$$

$$\sum_{i=1}^{m} x_{is} = u_s \quad \forall s \qquad (7.8)$$

$$x_{ij} = \{0, 1\} \qquad (7.9)$$

Constraint given in Equation 7.7 indicates each vertex belongs to exactly one block and constraint given in Equation 7.8 denotes block sizes. The rationale behind the objective function is that when the edge (i, j) is cut, $a_{ij} \sum_{s,\ell=1}^{k} x_{is} b_{s\ell} x_{j\ell} = a_{ij}$—in effect the cost of cutting the edge (i, j) appears only once in the summation. On the other hand, if edge (i, j) is uncut, then $s = \ell$ and $b_{s\ell} = 0$, which implies that $a_{ij} \sum_{s,\ell=1}^{k} x_{is} b_{s\ell} x_{j\ell} = 0$.

In Refs. [AV93], [Kuc05], the authors formulate the k-way partitioning problem as a 0–1 integer linear program (INLP). Assume there are $j = 1 \cdots k$ blocks, $i = 1 \cdots |V|$ vertices, $s = 1 \cdots |E|$ nets, and $i' = 1 \ldots |e|_s$ vertices per net s. Let $s(i')$ denote the index of the i'th vertex of edge s in the set of vertices, V. Define x_{ij} to be an indicator variable such that

$$x_{ij} = \begin{cases} 1 & \text{vertex } i \text{ is in block } j \\ 0 & \text{otherwise} \end{cases}$$

The crux of the model is in the way we represent uncut edges. If a specific net consists of vertices 1 through 4, then it will be uncut if

$$x_{1j}x_{2j}x_{3j}x_{4j} = 1 \quad \text{for some } j$$

Introduce the indicator variable

$$y_{sj} = \begin{cases} 1 & \text{if net } s \text{ has all of its vertices entirely in block } j \\ 0 & \text{otherwise} \end{cases}$$

These constraints enable us to write the partitioning problem as an integer program. To understand how these constraints work, consider a net consisting of vertices 1 and 5. Thus, for this net to be uncut, $x_{ij}x_{5j} = 1$. Because $x_{1j}, x_{5j} \in \{0, 1\}$ then it is true that $x_{1j}x_{5j} \le x_{1j}$ and $x_{1j}x_{5j} \le x_{5j}$.

The objective function maximizes the sum of uncut nets (hence, minimizing the sum of cutnets)

$$\max \quad \sum_{j=1}^{k} \sum_{s=1}^{n} y_{sj} \tag{7.10}$$

$$\text{s.t.} \quad y_{sj} \le x_{s(i')j} \quad \forall\, i', j, s \tag{7.11}$$

$$\sum_{j=1}^{n} x_{ij} = 1 \quad \forall\, i \tag{7.12}$$

$$l_j \le \sum_{i=1}^{m} a_i x_{ij} \le u_j \quad \forall\, j \tag{7.13}$$

$$x_{pq} = 1 \quad p \in V, q \in B \tag{7.14}$$

$$x_{ij} = \{0, 1\} \tag{7.15}$$

$$y_{sj} = \{0, 1\} \tag{7.16}$$

Constraint given in Equation 7.11 is the net connectivity constraint. Constraint given in Equation 7.12 has each vertex assigned to exactly one block. Constraint given in Equation 7.13 imposes block size limits, given nonunit cell sizes a_i. The bounds for bipartitioning are typically $l_j = [0.45 \sum_{i=1}^{m} a_i]$ and $u_j = [0.55 \sum_{i=1}^{m} a_i]$. Constraint given in Equation 7.14 indicates that vertex p is in block q.

7.3.4 NETWORK FLOW

Given a directed graph G, each directed edge (or arc) (x, y) has an associated nonnegative number $c(x, y)$ called the capacity of the arc. The capacity can be viewed as the maximal amount of flow that

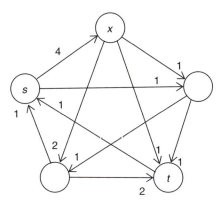

FIGURE 7.10   Flow network. (From Ford, L. R. and Fulkerson, D. R., *Flows in Networks*, Princeton University Press, Princeton, NJ, 1962.)

leaves x and ends at y per unit time [FF62]. Let s indicate a starting node and t a terminating node. A flow from s to t is a function f that satisfies the equations

$$\sum_{\text{from } y} f(x,y) - \sum_{\text{to } y} f(y,x) = \begin{cases} k, & x = s \\ 0, & x \neq s, t \\ -k, & x = t \end{cases} \tag{7.17}$$

$$f(x,y) \leq c(x,y) \quad \forall\, (x,y) \tag{7.18}$$

Equation 7.17 implies the total flow k out of s is equal to $-k$ out of t and there is no flow out of intermediate nodes (as with Kirchoff's law).

Equation 7.18 implies the flow is not allowed to exceed the capacity value. Borrowing the example from Ref. [FF62], in Figure 7.10, we see that the flow out of s is $-1 - 1 + 1 + 4 = 3$, the flow out of intermediate node x is $-4 + 2 + 1 + 1 = 0$ and the flow out of t is $-2 + 1 - 1 - 1 = -3$.

The idea behind bipartitioning is to separate G into two blocks (not necessarily the same size) such that $s \in C_1$ and $t \in C_2$ where the netcut is given by $\sum_{x \in C_1, y \in C_2} c(x,y)$. The following theorem links computing the maximum flow to the netcut.

Theorem 3   MinFlow MaxCut: *For any network, the maximum flow value from s to t is equal to the minimum cut capacity for all cuts separating s and t*

If we can find the maximum flow value from s to t, we will have found the partition with the smallest cut. In Figure 7.10, the maximum flow is 3. In Ref. [FF62], the authors prove the maximum flow computation can be solved in polynomial time. The problem is that partitions can be very unbalanced.

In Ref. [YW94], the authors propose a maximum flow algorithm that finds balanced partitions in polynomial time. Because nets are bidirectional, to apply network flow techniques, the net is transformed into an equivalent flow network and the flow representation shown in Figure 7.11 is used.

The idea is that all vertices in net 1 are connected toward vertex x and away from vertex y. The next step is to solve the maxflow-mincut problem in $O(|V\|E|)$ time, which obtains the minimal cutset, E^c, for the unbalanced problem. Finally, if the balance criterion is not satisfied, vertices in C_1 (or C_2) are collapsed into s (or t), a vertex $v \in C_1$ (or in C_2) incident on a net in E^c is collapsed into s (or t) and the cutset, E^c, is recomputed. The procedure has the same time complexity as the unbalanced mincut algorithm.

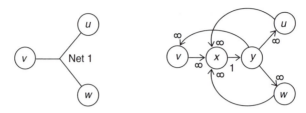

FIGURE 7.11 Efficient flow representation.

7.3.5 DYNAMIC PROGRAMMING

In a series of two papers [AK94], [AK96], the authors discuss clustering methods that form blocks by splitting a linear ordering of vertices using dynamic programming. It can be shown that dynamic programming can be used to optimally split the ordering into blocks [AK94].

In Ref. [AK94], the authors embed a linear ordering obtained from multiple eigenvectors in multidimensional space and use a traveling-salesman problem (TSP) heuristic to traverse the points. The idea is that points that are close together in the embedding are in proximity to one another in the linear ordering. A space-filling curve is then used as a good TSP heuristic because it traverses the points that are near to each other before wandering off to explore other parts of the space. They construct k blocks by splitting the tour into $2, 3, \ldots, k - 1$, up to k segments using dynamic programming.

7.4 CLUSTERING

Partitioning is implicitly a top-down process in which an entire netlist is scanned for the separation of vertices into a few blocks. The complementary process to partitioning is clustering in which a few vertices at a time are grouped into a number of blocks proportional to the number of vertices [Alp96].

A block can be defined in a number of ways. Intuitively, a block is a dense region in a hypergraph [GPS90]. The clique is the densest possible subgraph of a graph. The density of a graph $G(V, E)$ is $\frac{|E|}{\binom{|V|}{2}}$ and by this definition, clustering is the separation of V into k dense subgraphs, $\{C_1, C_2, \ldots, C_k\}$ in which each of C_i have density equal to ϵ: $0 < \epsilon \leq 1$. However, this problem is NP-complete [AK95].

A less formal way of defining a block is simply a region where vertices have multiple connections with one another. This forms the basis of clustering techniques that use vertex matchings. Normally, matchings apply to graphs, but here, we apply them to hypergraphs. A matching of $G = (V, E)$ is a subset of hyperedges with the property that no two hyperedges share the same vertex. A heavy-edge matching means edges with the heaviest weights are selected first. A maximum matching means as many vertices as possible are matched [PS98], [Ten99]. For a hypergraph that consists of two-point hyperedges only, a maximum matching consists of $\frac{|V|}{2}$ edges (Figure 7.12). In more general case, a maximum matching contracts fewer than $\frac{|V|}{2}$ edges.

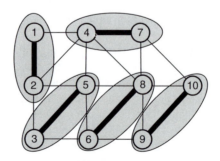

FIGURE 7.12 Maximum matching of two-point hyperedges.

The clustering process tends to decrease the sparsity of the netlist, which is fortunate because FM-based algorithms perform best when the average vertex degree is larger than 5 [AK95]. Walshaw [Wal03] suggests clustering filters out irrelevant data from the partitioning solution space so that subsequent iterative improvement steps look for a minimum in a more convex space.

We have divided clustering methods into three categories roughly in chronological order. Clustering techniques block many vertices simultaneously in a hierarchical fashion [KK98,AK98] or one vertex at a time in an agglomerative fashion, based on physical connectivity information [AK96,CL00, HMS03,LMS05,AKN+05]. In cell placers, information such as cell names (i.e., indicating which presynthesized objects cells belonged to) may be incorporated to speed up the clustering heuristic.

7.4.1 HIERARCHICAL CLUSTERING

Hierarchical techniques merge all vertices into clusters at the same time. Candidate vertices for hierarchical clustering are based on the results of vertex matchings [BS93,HL95,AK98,KK98,Kar03]; matched vertices are then merged into clusters of vertices. Matchings are used extensively because they tend to locate independent logical groupings of vertices, thus avoiding the buildup of vertices of excessively large degree. Matchings may be selected randomly or by decreasing netsize, called heavy-edge matching. After clustering, the average vertex weight increases, but the average net degree decreases. Karypis and Kumar [Kar03] use the following clustering schemes, assuming unit weights on nets:

1. Select pairs of vertices that are present in the same nets by finding a maximum matching of vertices based on a clique-graph representation (edge clustering).
2. Find a heavy-edge matching of vertices by nonincreasing net size; after all nets have been visited, merge matched vertices (net clustering).
3. After nets have been selected for matching, for each net that has not been contracted, its (unmatched) vertices are contracted together (modified net clustering).
4. To preserve some of the natural clustering that may be destroyed by the independence criterion of the previous three schemes, after an initial matching phase, for each vertex $v \in V$, consider vertices that belong to nets with the largest weight incident on v, whether they are matched or not (first choice clustering).

The clustering schemes are depicted in Figure 7.13.

Karypis [Kar03] points out that there is no consistently better clustering scheme for all netlists. Examples can be constructed for any of the above clustering methods that fail to determine the correct partitions [Kar03]. Karypis [Kar03] also suggests that a good stopping point for clustering is when there are $30k$ vertices where k indicates the desired number of blocks.

After the clustering phase, an initial bipartition that satisfies the balance constraint is performed. It is not necessary at this point to produce an optimal bipartition because that is ultimately the purpose of the refinement phase. Recently, several new clustering algorithms have been devised.

7.4.2 AGGLOMERATIVE CLUSTERING

Agglomerative methods form clusters one at a time based on connectivity of nets adjacent to the vertices being considered. Once a cluster is formed, its vertices are removed from the remaining pool of vertices. The key to achieving a good clustering solution is in somehow capturing global connectivity information.

7.4.2.1 Clustering Based on Vertex Ordering

In Ref. [AK96], the authors introduce the concept of an attraction function and a window to construct a linear ordering of vertices. Given a starting vertex, v_i^*, and an initially empty set of ordered vertices, S,

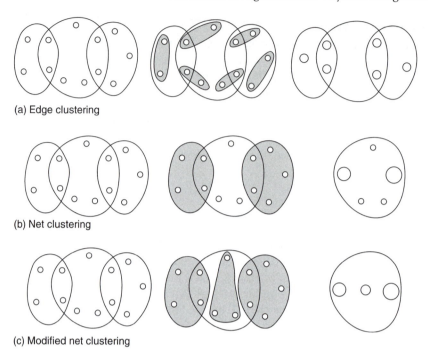

(a) Edge clustering

(b) Net clustering

(c) Modified net clustering

FIGURE 7.13 Clustering schemes. (From Karypis, G., *Multilevel Optimization in VLSICAD*, Kluwer Academic Publishers, Boston, MA, 2003.)

they compute the attraction function for v_i^* at step i in $V - S$. Various attraction functions are described. For example, one using the absorption objective is given by

$$\text{Attract}(i) = \sum_{e \in E(i) | e \cap S \neq \emptyset} \frac{1}{|e| - 1}$$

where $E(i)$ indicates the set of edges at step i. They then select the vertex v_i^* in $V - S$ with optimal attraction function and add it to S. Finally, they update the attraction function for every vertex in $V - S$ and repeat until $V - S$ becomes empty. The order in which vertices are inserted into S defines blocks, where vertices that were recently inserted into S have more attraction on v_i^* than vertices that were inserted many passes earlier (called windowing in Ref. [AK96]). Dynamic programming is ultimately used to split S into blocks. The authors report that windowing produced superior results with respect to the absorption metric over other ordering techniques.

7.4.2.2 Clustering Based on Connectivity

In Ref. [CL00], the authors use the concept of edge separability to guide the clustering process. Given an edge $e = (x, y)$, the edge separability, $\lambda(e)$, is defined as the minimum cutsize among cuts separating vertices x and y. To determine the set of nets to be clustered, $Z(G)$, they solve a maximum flow problem (because computing edge separability is equivalent to finding the maximum flow between x and y). To assess in what order the nets in $Z(G)$ should be contracted, the authors use a specialized ranking function related to the separability metric. Nets are contracted until the maximum cluster limit size of $\log_2 |V|$ is reached.

In Refs. [HMS03], [HMS04], the authors use a clique representation of nets, the weight of a connection is given by

$$w(c) = \frac{w(e)}{(|e| - 1)|e|}$$

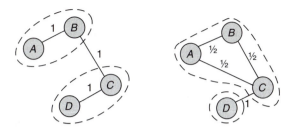

FIGURE 7.14   Clique net model (with edge weights $1/(|e| - 1)$) favors absorption better.

where $w(c)$ is the weight of a cluster and $w(e)$ is the weight of a net segment (determined by the net model used). The rationale behind using a clique model for nets is that it favors configurations where the net is absorbed completely into a cluster. In Figure 7.14, net 1 consists of vertices $\{A, B, C\}$ and net 2 consists of vertices $\{C, D\}$. On the left side, using a star net model, the cost of cutting any edge is 1 so clusters can be formed in three ways. On the right side, the cost of cutting the edge connecting C and D is highest, so clusters like these are formed.

The cost of each of a fine cluster, f, is given by $\sum_{c \in f} w(c)$ and the overall cost of a fine clustering solution is given by $\sum_{f} \sum_{c \in f} w(c)$, where the goal is to maximize the overall cost of the fine clustering solution.

In Ref. [LMS05], the authors propose clustering technique based on physical connectivity. They define an internal force of a block C as a summation of weights of all internal block connections.

$$F_{\text{int}}(C) = \sum_{i,j \in C} w(i,j)$$

As well, they define an external force of a block C as the summation of weights of nets with at least one vertex located outside C and at least one vertex inside C.

$$F_{\text{ext}}(C) = \sum_{i \in C, j \ni C} w(i,j)$$

The measure that best reflects physical connectivity is the ratio of external to internal forces.

$$\ell(C) = \frac{F_{\text{ext}}(C)}{F_{\text{int}}(C)}$$

Where the goal is to maximize $\ell(C)$. F_{ext} can be measured in other ways as well. In Ref. [LMS05], the authors use a local Rent's exponent of a block

$$p = \log_G \left(\frac{T}{t} \right)$$

where
   G is the number of nodes in the block
   T is the number of nets that have connections inside the block and outside the block
   t is the average node degree of the circuit

The seed growth algorithm works by constructing a block with strong physical connectivity starting from a seed node with large net degree. The connectivity between neighbor node u and block C is given by $\text{conn}(u, C) = \sum_{i \in C} w(u, i)$. In subsequent passes, neighbor nodes with the largest possible connectivity are added to the block while keeping the internal force as large as possible.

When the block size exceeds some threshold value, an attempt is made to minimize the local Rent exponent to reduce the external force. Experimental results indicate the seed growth algorithm produces placements with improved wirelength over placers that use clustering techniques described in Section 7.4.1.

7.4.2.3 Clustering Based on Cell Area

In Ref. [AKN+05], the authors propose a clustering scheme tailored specifically to large-scale cell placement. Their method is different from methods described in Section 7.4.1 in that those methods block vertices indiscriminately, whereas best choice clustering considers only the best possible pair of vertices among all vertex pairs. The main idea behind best choice clustering is to identify the best possible pair of clustering candidates using a priority-queue data structure with pair-value key the tuple $(u, v, d(u, v))$ where u and v are the vertex pair and $d(u, v)$ is the clustering score. The pair-value keys are sorted, in descending order, by clustering score. The idea is to block the pair at the top of the priority queue.

The clustering score is given by

$$ d(u, v) = \sum_e \frac{1}{|e|} \left[\frac{1}{a(u) + a(v)} \right] $$

The first term is the weight of hyperedge e, which is inversely proportional to the number of vertices incident on hyperedge e. The $a(u) + a(v)$ term is the total area of cells u and v. Thus, this method favors cells with small area, connected by nets of small degree. The above area function is necessary to prevent the formation of overly large blocks. The authors propose using other score functions including one that uses the total number of pins instead of cell area, because the total number of pins is more indicative of block size (via Rent's rule described in Section 7.4.2).

Once a (u, v) pair with the highest clustering score is merged into vertex u', the clustering score for all of u's neighbors must be recalculated. This represents the most time-consuming stage of the best choice clustering algorithm. For this reason, the authors introduce the concept of the lazy-update clustering score technique, in which the recalculation of clustering scores is delayed until a vertex pair reaches the top of the priority queue.

The best choice clustering algorithm is shown to produce better quality placement solutions than edge coarsening and first-choice clustering. The lazy-update scheme is shown to be particularly effective at reducing runtime, all with almost no change in half-perimeter wirelength. Studies are under way as of this writing into incorporating fixed vertices (corresponding to input/output terminals) into the best choice algorithm.

7.5   MULTILEVEL PARTITIONING

The gist of multilevel partitioning is to construct a sequence of successively coarser graphs, to partition the coarsest graph (subject to balance constraints) and to project the partitions onto the next level finer graph while performing numerical or FM-type iterative improvement to further improve the partition [BJ93,BS93,HL95,Alp96,KAKS97] (Figure 7.15).

7.5.1   MULTILEVEL EIGENVECTOR PARTITIONING

The basis of multilevel partitioning with eigenvectors is described in Ref. [BS93] and consists of clustering, interpolation, and refinement steps. Contraction consists of selecting a subgraph, $G'\colon V' \subset V$, of the original graph such that V' is a maximum matching with respect to G. The Lanczos algorithm [Dem97] is then applied to the reduced bipartitioning problem.

Interpolation consists of the following: given an $|V'| \times 1$ Fiedler vector, $\mathbf{x}'$, of a contracted graph G', an interpolation step constructs a $|V| \times 1$ vector $\mathbf{x}_0$ out of $\mathbf{x}'$. This is accomplished by remembering

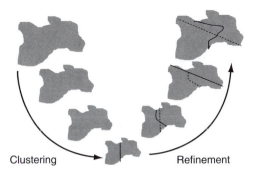

FIGURE 7.15   Essence of multilevel partitioning.

that the ith component of $\mathbf{x}'$ was derived by contracting vertex $m(i)$ of $\mathbf{x}$ and upon reconstructing a new $|V| \times 1$ vector, $\mathbf{x}_0$, inserting component $x_{m(i)}$ into the $m(i)$th slot of $\mathbf{x}_0$, initially filling all empty slots in $\mathbf{x}_0$ with zeros. For example, if

$$\mathbf{x}_0 = [x_1 \ 0 \ 0 \ x_4 \ 0 \ x_6 \ 0 \ 0 \ 0 \ x_{10}]$$

then the zero components are then assigned the average values of their left and right nonzero neighbors

$$\mathbf{x}_0 = \left[x_1 \ \frac{x_1 + x_4}{2} \ \frac{x_1 + x_4}{2} x_4 \ \frac{x_4 + x_6}{2} x_6 \ \frac{x_6 + x_{10}}{2} \ \frac{x_6 + x_{10}}{2} \ \frac{x_6 + x_{10}}{2} x_{10} \right]$$

Refinement consists of using $\mathbf{x}_0$ as a good starting solution for the Fiedler optimization problem Equations 7.3 through 7.5. The authors use a cubically converging numerical technique called Rayleigh quotient iteration to solve for $\mathbf{x}$ [Wat91].

7.5.2   MULTILEVEL MOVE-BASED PARTITIONING

One of the original works on multilevel partitioning in the VLSI domain [AHK96] applied techniques that were previously employed on finite element meshes [HL95], [KK95]. The authors converted circuit netlists to graphs, using a clique representation for individual nets, and ran the multilevel graph partitioner, Metis [KK95], to obtain high-quality bipartitions. Using a graph representation, however, has the pitfall that removing one edge from the cutset does not reflect the true objective that is to remove an entire net from the cutset. Subsequent works [AHK97], [KAKS97] partitioned hypergraphs directly using the two-stage approach of clustering and refinement. They obtained optimal or near-optimal mincut results on the set of test cases listed. Multilevel partitioning, to this day, remains the de facto partitioning technique.

Multilevel move-based partitioning consists of clustering and iterative improvement steps. The power of multilevel partitioning becomes evident during the iterative improvement phase, where moving one vertex across the block boundary corresponds to moving an entire group of clustered vertices.

The refinement process consists of repeatedly applying an iterative improvement phase to successively finer hypergraphs, while declustering after each pass of the interchange heuristic. Because of the space complexity of Sanchis' k-way FM algorithm and because vertices are clustered into the proper blocks, Karypis et al. [KK99] use a downhill-only search variant of FM that does not require the use of a bucket list. Their refinement method visits vertices in random order and moves them if they result in a positive gain (and preserve the balance criterion). If a vertex v is internal to the block being considered, then it is not moved; if v is a boundary vertex, it can be moved to a block that houses v's neighbors. The move that generates the highest gain is effectuated. In experiments, the refinement method converges to a high-quality solution in only a few passes.

7.5.3 NEW INNOVATIONS IN MULTILEVEL PARTITIONING

With increasing design sizes, it is becoming increasingly difficult to place an entire design flat using one processor. A novel partitioning approach [Ma07] is applied to placement such that the computing effort is spread across several processors. The approach consists of a rough initial flat placement, a partitioning step, followed by detailed placement within the partition blocks where each block is assigned to its own processor. The novelty of this technique lies in the way the blocks are determined. Normally, an engineering change in one block will affect all other blocks. However, this is not the case if the block boundary is determined by elements such as latches, flip-flops, or fixed objects. Once these objects are identified, block boundaries that minimize the number of nets running between blocks are determined. Finally, detailed placement is applied to blocks, each block assigned to its own processor.

7.6 CONCLUSION

This chapter has presented a historical survey of partitioning and clustering techniques ranging from move-based methods to multilevel techniques to mathematical formulations including quadratic, linear, and integer programming approaches. Multilevel methods have proven to be the partitioning technique of choice in the VLSI community owing to the quality of results they produce with very small runtimes. A consequence of which is that partitioning is currently viewed as a solved problem. However, as problem sizes continue to increase, multilevel partitions may no longer be near optimal. Recent works [Ma07] revisit the partitioning problem and offer new solutions for very large-scale netlists.

ACKNOWLEDGMENTS

I would like to thank my colleagues, especially Ulrich Finkler and Chuck Alpert for giving their comments and suggestions, and James Ma for helpful discussions regarding new innovations in multilevel partitioning.

REFERENCES

[ACKM00] C. J. Alpert, A. E. Caldwell, A. B. Kahng, and I. L. Markov, Hypergraph partitioning with fixed vertices, *IEEE Transactions on Computer-Aided Design of Circuits and Systems* **19**(2): 267–272, 2000.

[AHK96]   C. J. Alpert, L. W. Hagen, and A. B. Kahng, A hybrid multilevel/genetic approach for circuit partitioning, *Proceedings of the Physical Design Workshop*, 1996, Reston, VA, pp. 100–105.

[AHK97]   C. J. Alpert, J. -H. Huang, and A. B. Kahng, Multilevel circuit partitioning, *Proceedings of the ACM Design Automation Conference*, Anaheim, CA, 1997, pp. 530–533.

[AK93]   C. J. Alpert and A. B. Kahng, Geometric embeddings for faster and better multi-way netlist partitioning, *Proceedings of the ACM Design Automation Conference*, Dallas, TX, 1993, pp. 743–748.

[AK94]   _____ , Multi-way partitioning via spacefilling curves and dynamic programming, *Proceedings of the ACM Design Automation Conference*, San Diego, CA, 1994, pp. 652–657.

[AK95]   _____ , Recent directions in netlist partitioning: A survey, *Integration: The VLSI Journal* **19**: 1–813, 1995.

[AK96]   _____ , A general framework for vertex orderings, with applications to circuit clustering, *IEEE Transactions on VLSI Systems* **4**(2): 240–246, 1996.

[AK98]   _____ , Multilevel circuit partitioning, *IEEE Transactions on Computer-Aided Design of Circuits and Systems* **17**(8): 655–667, 1998.

[AKN+05] C. J. Alpert, A. B. Kahng, G. -J. Nam, S. Reda, and P. G. Villarrubia, A semi-persistent clustering technique for VLSI circuit placement, *Proceedings of the International Symposium on Physical Design*, San Francisco, CA, 2005, pp. 200–207.

[AKY99]   C. J. Alpert, A. B. Kahng, and S. Z. Yao, Spectral partitioning with multiple eigenvectors, *Discrete Applied Mathematics* **90**(1–3): 3–26, 1999.

[Alp96]   C. J. Alpert, Multi-way graph and hypergraph partitioning, PhD thesis, University of California, Los Angeles, CA, 1996.

[AV93]   S. Areibi and A. Vannelli, Advanced search techniques for circuit partitioning, DIMACS Series in *Discrete Mathematics and Theoretical Computer Science*, American Mathematical Society, Rutgers, NJ, 1993, 77–97.

[AY95]   C. J. Alpert and S. -Z. Yao, Spectral partitioning: The more eigenvectors, the better, *Proceedings of the ACM Design Automation Conference*, San Francisco, CA, 1995, pp. 195–200.

[Bar82]   E. R. Barnes, An algorithm for partitioning the nodes of a graph, *SIAM Journal of Algebraic and Discrete Methods* **3**(4): 541–550, 1982.

[BJ93]   T. N. Bui and C. Jones, A heuristic for reducing fill-in in sparse matrix factorization, *Proceedings of the Sixth SIAM Conference on Parallel Processing for Scientific Computing*, Portsmouth, VA, Vol. 1, 1993, pp. 445–452.

[Bop87]   R. B. Boppana, Eigenvalues and graph bisection: An average-case analysis, *Proceedings of the IEEE Symposium on Foundations of Computer Science*, Los Angeles, CA, 1987, pp. 280–285.

[BS93]   S. T. Barnard and H. D. Simon, A fast multilevel implementation of recursive spectral bisection for partitioning unstructured problems, *Proceedings of the Sixth SIAM Conference on Parallel Processing for Scientific Computing*, Portsmouth, VA, 1993, pp. 711–718.

[CGT95]   T. F. Chan, J. R. Gilbert, and S. -H. Teng, Geometric Spectral Partitioning, Technical report, Xerox PARC, 1995.

[CL98]   J. Cong and S. K. Lim, Multiway partitioning with pairwise movement, *Proceedings of the International Conference on Computer-Aided Design*, San Jose, CA, 1998, pp. 512–516.

[CL00]   _____ , Edge separability based circuit clustering with application to circuit partitioning, *Asia South Pacific Design Automation Conference*, Yokohama, Japan, 2000, pp. 429–434.

[CSZ94]   P. K. Chan, M. Schlag, and J. Zien, Spectral k-way ratio-cut partitioning, *IEEE Transactions on Computer-Aided Design of Integrated Circuits and Systems* **13**(9): 1088–1096, 1994.

[DD96]   S. Dutt and W. Deng, VLSI circuit partitioning by cluster-removal using iterative improvement techniques, *Proceedings of the International Conference on Computer-Aided Design*, San Jose, CA, 1996, pp. 194–200.

[Dem97]   J. W. Demmel, *Applied Numerical Linear Algebra*, Philadelphia, PA, SIAM, 1997.

[DH73]   W. E. Donath and A. J. Hoffman, Lower bounds for the partitioning of graphs, *IBM Journal of Research and Development* **17**(9): 420–425, 1973.

[EAV99]   H. Etawil, S. Areibi, and A. Vannelli, ARP: A convex optimization based method for global placement, IEEE/ACM, International Conference on Computer Aided Design, San Jose, CA, 1999, pp. 20–24.

[FF62]   L. R. Ford and D. R. Fulkerson, *Flows in Networks*, Princeton University Press, Princeton, NJ, 1962, p. 11.

[Fie73]   M. Fiedler, Algebraic connectivity of graphs, *Czechoslovak Mathematics Journal*, 23, 298–305, 1973.

[FK86]   J. Frankle and R. M. Karp, Circuit placements and cost bounds by eigenvector decomposition, *Proceedings of the International Conference on Computer-Aided Design*, Santa Clara, CA, 1986, pp. 414–417.

[FM82]   C. M. Fiduccia and R. M. Mattheyses, A linear-time heuristic for improving network partitions, *Proceedings of the ACM Design Automation Conference*, Washington D.C., 1982, pp. 175–181.

[FRW92]   J. Falkner, F. Rendl, and H. Wolkowicz, A Computational Study of Graph Partitioning, Technical Report CORR 92–95, Department of Combinatorics and Optimization, University of Waterloo, August 1992, Waterloo, Ontario, Canada.

[GM00]   S. Guattery and G. L. Miller, Graph embeddings and Laplacian eigenvectors, *SIAM Journal on Matrix Analysis and Applications* **22**(3): 703–723, 2000.

[GPS90]   J. Garbers, J. Promel, and A. Steger, Finding clusters in VLSI circuits, *Proceedings of the International Conference on Computer-Aided Design*, Santa Clara, CA, 1990, pp. 520–523.

[Hal70]   K. M. Hall, An r-dimensional quadratic placement algorithm, *Management Science* **17**(11): 219–229, 1970.

[HHK97] L. Hagen, D. J. -H. Huang, and A. B. Kahng, On implementation choices for iterative improvement partitioning algorithms, *IEEE Transactions on Computer-Aided Design of Circuits and Systems* **16**(10): 1199–1205, 1997.

[HK91]   L. Hagen and A. B. Kahng, Fast spectral methods for ratio cut partitioning and clustering, *Proceedings of the International Conference on Computer-Aided Design*, Santa Clara, CA, 1991, pp. 10–13.

[HK92]   _____ , New spectral methods for ratio cut partitioning and clustering, *IEEE Transactions on Computer-Aided Design* **11**(9): 1074–1085, 1992.

[HK97]   D. J. -H. Huang and A. B. Kahng, Partitioning-based standard-cell global placement with an exact objective function, *Proceedings of the International Symposium on Physical Design*, Napa Valley, CA, 1997, pp. 18–25.

[HL95]   B. Hendrickson and R. Leland, A multilevel algorithm for partitioning graphs, *Proceedings of the 1995 Supercomputing Conference*, Los Alamitos, CA, 1995, pp. 485–500.

[HMS03] B. Hu and M. Marek-Sadowska, Fine granularity clustering for large scale placement problems, *Proceedings of the International Symposium on Physical Design*, San Diego, CA, 2003, pp. 67–74.

[HMS04] _____ , Fine granularity clustering–based placement, *IEEE Transactions on Computer-Aided Design of Integrated Circuits and Systems* **23**(4): 527–536, 2004.

[IWW93] E. Ihler, D. Wagner, and F. Wagner, Modelling hypergraphs by graphs with the same mincut properties, *Information Processing Letters* **45**(4): 171–175, 1993.

[JAMS89] D. S. Johnson, C. R. Aragon, L. A. Mcgeoch, and C. Schevon, Optimization by simulated annealing: An experimental evaluation Part I, Graph partitioning, *Operations Research* **37**, 865–892, 1989.

[KAKS97] G. Karypis, R. Aggarwal, V. Kumar, and S. Shekhar, Multilevel hypergraph partitioning: Application in VLSI domain, *Proceedings of the IEEE/ACM Design Automation Conference*, Anaheim, CA, 1997, pp. 526–529.

[Kar03] G. Karypis, Multilevel hypergraph partitioning, *Multilevel Optimization in VLSICAD*, Kluwer Academic Publishers, Boston, MA, 2003.

[KGV83] S. Kirkpatrick, C. D. Gelatt, and M. P. Vecchi, Optimization by simulated Annealing, *Science* **220**(4598): 671–680, 1983.

[KK95]   G. Karypis and V. Kumar, A fast and high quality multilevel scheme for partitioning irregular graphs, *Proceedings of the International Conference on Parallel Processing*, Urbana-Champaign, IL, 1995, pp. 113–122.

[KK98]   _____ , *hMETIS: A Hypergraph Partitioning Package, Version 1.5.3*, Department of Computer Science/Army HPC Research Center University of Minnesota, Minneapolis, MN, 1998.

[KK99]   _____ , Multilevel k-way hypergraph partitioning, *Proceedings of the IEEE/ACM Design Automation Conference*, New Orleans, LA, 1999, pp. 343–348.

[KL70]   B. W. Kernighan and S. Lin, An efficient heuristic procedure for partitioning graphs, *Bell System Technical Journal*, 49, 291–307, 1970.

[KN91]   C. Kring and R. Newton, A cell-replication approach to mincut-based circuit partitioning, *Proceedings of the International Conference on Computer-Aided Design*, Santa Clara, CA, 1991, pp. 2–5.

[Kri84] B. Krishnamurty, An improved min-cut algorithm for partitioning VLSI networks, *IEEE Transactions on Computers* **C-33**(5): 438–446, 1984.

[Kuc05] D. Kucar, New insights into hypergraph partitioning, PhD thesis, University of Waterloo, Waterloo, Ontario, Canada, 2005.

[Len90] T. Lengauer, *Combinatorial Algorithms for Integrated Circuit Layout*, John Wiley & Sons, New York, 1990.

[LLLC96] J. Li, J. Lilis, L. -T. Liu, and C. -K. Cheng, New spectral linear placement and clustering approach, *Proceedings of the ACM Design Automation Conference*, 1996, pp. 88–93.

[LMS05] Q. Liu and M. Marek-Sadowska, Pre-layout physical connectivity prediction with applications in clustering, placement and logic synthesis, *Proceedings of the IEEE International Conference on Computer Design*, San Jose, CA, 2005.

[Ma07]   J. Ma, private communications, 2007.

[NW88]   G. L. Nemhauser and L. A. Wolsey, *Integer and Combinatorial Optimization*, John Wiley & Sons, New York, 1988.

[PS98]   C. Papadimitriou and K. Steiglitz, *Combinatorial Optimization*, Dover Publications, Mineola, NY, 1998.

[PSL90]   A. Pothen, H. D. Simon, and K. P. Liou, Partitioning sparse matrices with eigenvectors of graphs, *SIAM Journal on Matrix Analysis and Applications* **11**(3): 430–452, 1990.

[RDJ94]   B. M. Riess, K. Doll, and F. M. Johannes, Partitioning very large circuits using analytical placement techniques, *Proceedings of the ACM Design Automation Conference*, San Diego, CA, 1994, pp. 646–651.

[San89]   L. A. Sanchis, Multi-way network partitioning, *IEEE Transactions on Computers* **38**(1): 62–81, 1989.

[SK72]   D. G. Schweikert and B. W. Kernighan, A proper model for the partitioning of electrical circuits, *Proceedings of the ACM Design Automation Conference*, San Diego, CA, 1972, pp. 57–62.

[SS95]   W. -J. Sun and C. Sechen, Efficient and effective placement for very large circuits, *IEEE Transactions on Computer-Aided Design of Integrated Circuits and Systems* **14**(3): 349–359, 1995.

[Ten99]   S. H. Teng, *Coarsening, Sampling, and Smoothing: Elements of the Multilevel Method*, Vol. 105, Springer Verlag, New York, NY, 1999, pp. 247–276.

[TK91]   R. -S. Tsay and E. S. Kuh, A unified approach to partitioning and placement, *IEEE Transactions on Circuits and Systems* **38**: 521–533, 1991.

[VH90]   A. Vannelli and S. W. Hadley, A Gomory–Hu cut tree representation of a netlist partitioning problem, *IEEE Transactions on Circuits and Systems* **37**(9): 1133–1139, 1990.

[Wal03]   C. Walshaw, An exploration of multilevel combinatorial optimisation, *Multilevel Optimization in VLSICAD*, Kluwer Academic Publishers, Boston, MA, 2003.

[Wat91]   D. S. Watkins, *Fundamentals of Matrix Computations*, John Wiley & Sons, New York, NY, 1991.

[WC91]   Y. -C. Wei and C. -K. Cheng, Ratio cut partitioning for hierarchical designs, *IEEE Transactions on Computer-Aided Design* **10**(7): 911–921, 1991.

[YW94]   X. Yang and D. F. Wong, Efficient network flow based min-cut balanced partitioning, *Proceedings of the International Conference on Computer-Aided Design*, San Jose, CA, Vol. 6–10, Nov. 1994, pp. 50–55.

Part III

Floorplanning

8 Floorplanning: Early Research

Susmita Sur-Kolay

CONTENTS

8.1 INTRODUCTION

In physical design, floorplanning determines the topology of the layout, i.e., the relative positions of modules on the chip, based on the interconnection requirements of the circuit and estimates for area. A floorplan can provide a guideline in the detailed design of functional modules or blocks when the aspect ratios and pin positions of some of the modules on the chip are still unconstrained. Thus, floorplanning is important not only for physical design, but even more for choosing design alternatives in the early stages that are likely to produce optimal designs.

Placement was originally seen as a special case of floorplanning where the sizes and shapes of all the modules are known. In the history of computer-aided design (CAD) for very large scale integration (VLSI) circuits, the placement problem was addressed both for printed circuit boards as well as large scale integration (LSI) circuits. With the rapid increase in the scale of integration, the role of floorplanning came into the picture, particularly for the custom layout design style with variable width and height of modules. Some of the major techniques that were originally proposed for placement have subsequently been tailored for floorplanning.

The most significant difference between floorplanning and placement is in the modeling of the cells or modules.* The extra degree of freedom in floorplanning, arising from the flexibililty of the interface and shape of modules that constitute the design, enlarges the portion of the chip available for placing the components. The floorplanning algorithm may have to deal with three types of modules: modules from a library with design and interface fixed, modules with known design but flexible layout, and modules with designs not completely known or certain. With respect to the physical design flow, area estimation also has to handle all these three types of modules.

Floorplan optimization has conventionally been achieved by two steps: (1) feasible topology generation and (2) sizing (determining the aspect ratios of the rectangular modules to optimize objective functions such as chip area, total wirelength, etc.). Topology generation focuses on computing the relative locations of modules based on their interconnections without restriction on their exact shapes; an estimate of the area of each module may however be known. The sizing step then determines the shape, i.e., the aspect ratio of a module in tune with that of its neighbors to attain a globally optimal floorplan solution.

This chapter concentrates on the early approaches to the floorplanning phase in the context of full-custom design or semicustom design styles such as building blocks, standard cells, and gate arrays. The early floorplanning methods may be classified into constructive, iterative, and knowledge-based techniques. Constructive algorithms are primarily used for topology generation and are discussed in Sections 8.2 through 8.5. Iterative techniques, on the other hand, mainly tackle the second task of floorplanning, namely sizing, and are discussed in Sections 8.6 through 8.8. Knowledge-based approaches [1–4] are considered in Section 8.9 and algorithms for a unified approach to topology generation and sizing are sketched in Section 8.10.

8.2 FLOORPLAN TOPOLOGY GENERATION

Some of the commonly used terms in floorplanning literature are defined first. For graph-theoretic terminologies used without definition in this chapter, the reader is referred to an appropriate text (e.g., Ref. [5]).

A floorplan is a rectangle dissection of an enveloping rectangle by horizontal (parallel to x-axis) and vertical (parallel to y-axis) line segments, termed cuts, into a finite number of indivisible nonoverlapping rectangles (Figure 8.1a and b), which correspond to the modules in the floorplan. If the exact shape of the modules are not considered, then such a rectangle dissection depicts a floorplan topology. A floorplan with n cuts has exactly $n + 1$ modules. Conventionally, two perpendicular cuts are allowed to meet to form T-junctions only, but not a cross ($+$).

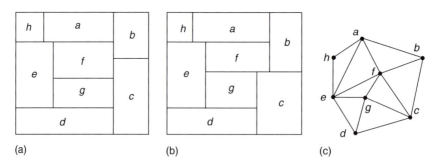

(a)   (b)   (c)

FIGURE 8.1   (a) Slicible floorplan F_s, (b) nonslicible floorplan F_n, and (c) both floorplans have the same adjacency graph R.

---

* In the context of this handbook, placement is defined as the narrower problem of placing standard cells (each cell has the same height) in rows.

A floorplan is slicible if its rectangular dissection can be obtained by recursively dividing rectangles into smaller rectangles until each nonoverlapping rectangle is indivisible. Slicible floorplans (Figure 8.1a) are also termed slicing structures, or simply slicings. All floorplans may not be slicible (Figure 8.1b). A summary of the major approaches to topology generation is presented next.

1. Slicing embedding [6,7]: This is a constructive method generating a special type of floorplan only. A point embedding is first determined by relying on the netlist information. The relative positions of the modules are depicted in the form of a slicing tree or equivalently a series-parallel polar graph [8]. Then a floorplan is obtained in polynomial time by cutting the embedding into a slicing structure as the slicing tree is traversed appropriately. The approach neglects the actual building block dimensions. Additional discussions on slicings appear in Chapters 2 and 9.

2. Partitioning and slicing [9–11]: The divide-and-conquer approach is employed by adapting a mincut approach (details appear in Chapter 15) for the placement of building blocks [9] to the floorplanning problem. In the Mason system [10], mincut bipartitioning is combined with the slicing tree representation in an effort to ensure routability. Global improvement of a partition is obtained by in-place partitioning based on the slicing tree. A scheme for global channel assignment and I/O pin assignment aids in floorplan evaluation. The system provides an interactive environment and can act as a human designer's assistant.

3. Dual graph method [12–15]: Among the most important floorplanning paradigms, the dual graph method of floorplanning deserves special mention. This is a constructive method based on graph algorithms. The topology of the modules is extracted from the adjacency relations with respect to circuit interconnections, given as a neighborhood graph. At first, this graph is planarized by deleting a minimum number of connections and adding crossover vertices. Then the optimal rectangular dual is sought for the planar graph. Rectangular dualization is of particular interest because of its algorithmic efficiency and the fact that the components are guaranteed to have rectangular layout. It emphasizes the proximity of heavily connected modules. A performance-driven version [15] was designed, where a dual is first generated considering routing constraints and then compacted by a linear programming-based heuristic method. A significant amount of research has been carried out on the dual graph method, including extension to rectilinear modules. The next section elaborates on many elegant results on rectangular dual floorplans.

4. Hierarchical enumeration [16]: This method falls into the group of connectivity clustering methods; the basis is circuit connectivity. For clusters of cells, floorplan templates having simplified topologies are used. Recursion is applied to obtain floorplan for large, complex circuits. There is a limit on the number of rectangular, arbitrary-sized blocks at each hierarchy level to enable simple pattern enumeration and exhaustive search later on. The novelty of this approach is that information about global routing can be maintained during floorplanning. The details of hierarchical floorplanning appear later in Section 8.5.

8.3   RECTANGULAR DUALS

A floorplan generated by rectangular dualization is often referred to as a rectangular dual. Given such a floorplan F, a rectangular graph $R = (V, E)$ representing the adjacency of modules in F has a vertex for each module and an edge $(u, v) \in E$ if and only if the modules denoted by vertices u and v are adjacent (i.e., share a common boundary). The graph R is also known as the adjacency or neighborhood graph [12,17]. For a given floorplan, a unique rectangular graph always exists, but the converse is not necessarily true as illustrated in Figure 8.1, where both the floorplans have the same rectangular graph of Figure 8.1c. Although there may be exponentially many different rectangular

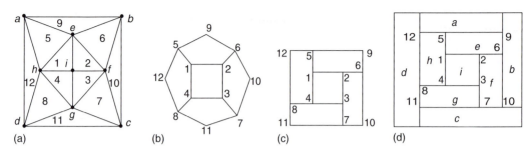

FIGURE 8.2 (a) Rectangular graph N, (b) its geometric dual without the vertex for the exterior face, (c) its inner dual, and (d) its rectangular dual. (Figure a, b, and c from Sur-Kolay, S. and Bhattacharya, B.B., *Lecture Notes in Computer Science*, 338, 88, 1988.)

duals for a given R, the strength of the dualization method lies in the fact that a solution, if one exists, can nevertheless be found in linear time [14].

A graph embedding is a particular drawing of a graph on a surface (which may often be a two-dimensional plane) such that its edges may intersect only at their endpoints. A graph is planar if there exists an embedding of it on a plane, whereas a plane graph is an embedding of a planar graph on a plane [5]. By definition, a rectangular floorplan is embedded on a plane, which therefore implies that its rectangular graph is a plane graph. As all intersections of cuts of F form T-junctions, all the internal faces of R, the rectangular graph of F, are triangles bounded by three edges. Hence, a rectangular graph is a plane triangulated graph [12,13].

Given an n-vertex plane triangulated graph G, its rectangular dual R_d, [12,13] consists of n nonoverlapping rectangles, where a rectangle in R_d corresponds to a distinct vertex $i \in G$, and rectangles i and j in R_d share at least a portion of a side if and only if there is an edge (i, j) in G. The rectangular dual of G, if it exists, corresponds to a valid rectangular floorplan where the rectangles represent the modules of the floorplan. Because all faces of G are triangles, no more than three rectangular faces in the rectangular dual of G meet at a vertex and thus the floorplan has only T-junctions and no cross junctions.

A rectilinear embedding of a plane graph is an embedding in which all the edges of the graph are either horizontal or vertical. Thus, a cycle in the plane graph is embedded as a rectilinear polygon. Next, let G be a given plane triangulated graph and G_d be its geometric dual [5] whose vertices correspond to the faces of G and there is an edge between two vertices in G_d if and only if the corresponding faces in G share an edge. An inner dual D [16,33] of G is a rectilinear embedding of G_d, excluding the vertex corresponding to the exterior face of G, such that each internal face of D is bounded by four or more edges and embedded as a rectangle. All the internal vertices of D have degree 3. Thus, we can obtain the rectangular dual of G (Figure 8.2) by placing the inner dual of G within an enveloping rectangle, because the exterior face of G is not reflected in D, and then projecting each degree 2 (respectively, degree 1) vertex of D onto the side (respectively, two sides) of the enveloping rectangle nearest to it. A vertex in D has degree 1 if two of the edges of the corresponding triangular face in G lie on its exterior face and only the third edge is shared with another internal triangular face of G. But the key question is whether a rectangular dual exists and if so, how it can be constructed efficiently.

8.3.1 DUALIZABILITY

A plane triangulated graph that is a rectangular graph has a rectangular dual, by definition. Every plane triangulated graph however does not have a rectangular dual. A triangle (or cycle of length 3) in a plane triangulated graph G, which is not the boundary of an internal face, is called a complex triangle [13,18]. In the graph shown in Figure 8.3a, the triangles ABD, BDC, and CDA are internal

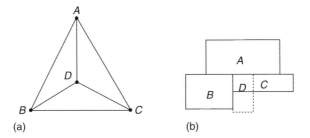

FIGURE 8.3 (a) Plane triangulated graph with a complex triangle and (b) conflict in constructing its rectangular dual.

faces, but triangle ABC is not and is therefore a complex triangle. So in the rectangular dual, if rectangles A, B, and C have to share edges pairwise, then there is no room for rectangle D to share edges with all the three rectangles A, B, and C and yet not overlap with any of these three rectangles (Figure 8.3b).

One of the necessary conditions for G to have a rectangular dual is that G has no complex triangles. Formally, a graph G is said to be a properly triangulated plane (PTP) graph, if it is a connected plane graph and satisfies the following properties [12]:

P_1: Every face (except the exterior) is a triangle (i.e., bounded by three edges).
P_2: All internal vertices have degree ≥ 4.
P_3: All cycles that are not faces and the exterior face have length ≥ 4.

Further, every planar graph that satisfies P_1 and P_3 also satisfies P_2 [17]. The necessary and sufficient conditions under which a PTP graph G has a rectangular dual were established in Refs. [12,13]. A few definitions are needed for the statement of these conditions. A chord of a cycle in G is an edge between two nonconsecutive vertices on the cycle (so it is not part of the cycle). A chord (u, v) of the outermost cycle S of G is said to be critical if one of the two paths between u and v on the cycle has no end vertices of any other chord of S. Such a path is called a corner implying path. For instance, the edge (a, e) in Figure 8.1c is a chord, and a critical one as well where the path $\{a, h, e\}$ is corner implying. The implication of this is that in the rectangular dual of R, the rectangle corresponding to vertex h has to be in a corner of the bounding rectangle of the dual.

A graph G is said to be biconnected if between any two vertices u and v in G there exist two paths in G with no common vertices except u and v. Biconnected components of a graph are commonly called blocks, and a vertex shared by two blocks is an articulation point. So, the block neighborhood graph (BNG) of a graph G is a graph in which there is a distinct vertex for each block of G and there is an edge between two vertices if and only if the two corresponding blocks share a vertex. A corner implying path in a block of G is said to be critical if it contains no articulation points of G.

Corner implying path criteria [12]: A PTP graph G has a rectangular dual if and only if one of the following is true:

1. G is biconnected and has no more than four corner implying paths.
2. G has $k, k > 1$, biconnected components; the BNG of G is a path itself; the biconnected components that correspond to the ends of this path have at most two critical corner implying paths; and no other biconnected component contains a critical corner implying path.

Intuitively, a biconnected rectangular graph should have no more than four vertices having degree 2 and these, if at all present, should appear on the outermost cycle because a rectangular dual can have at most four rectangles at the four corners of its bounding rectangle.

It can be shown that biconnectivity and the properties P_1 and P_3 of a rectangular graph imply that its embedding is unique. Kozminski and Kinnen gave an $O(n^2)$ time algorithm for constructing such a dual.

Bipartite matching criteria: Another elegant characterization of rectangularity based on the perfect matching problem in bipartite graphs was established in Ref. [13]. Each T-junction may be uniquely associated with the module whose side (wholly or partially) forms the crosspiece (defined later in Section 8.3.2.1) of the T-junction. As the T-junctions in the rectangular dual correspond to the triangular faces in the PTP graph, each triangular face in the PTP graph is assigned to one of its three vertices (indicated by arrows in Figure 8.4) for construction of a floorplan. Although there may be more than one such assignment for a given R (Figure 8.4a and b), an arbitrary assignment may not guarantee a feasible rectangular dual. Further, to take into account the T-junctions along the boundary of the rectangular dual, the graph R is extended by adding four special vertices t, r, b, and l to represent the four sides of the boundary and all vertices on the outermost cycle of R are connected appropriately to these four sides to retain the PTP property. Each corner vertex has two extra edges and each of the remaining vertices on the outermost cycle has one extra edge. A bipartite graph $B = (X \cup Y, E)$ is derived thus from the PTP graph R, where (1) each vertex in X corresponds to a triangular face of R, (2) Y is a set of vertices associated with each vertex v of R such that if degree of v is $d(v)$, then there are exactly $d(v) - 4$ instances of v, and (3) there is an edge between a vertex $x \in X$ and a vertex $y \in Y$ if the PTP face corresponding to x is adjacent to the PTP vertex represented by y. In the PTP of Figure 8.4, the outermost cycle has six vertices of which vertices h, b, c, and d are chosen as corners. and therefore each of these has two extra edges in the extended graph and vertices a and e have only one extra edge each. The dualizability criteria [13] are as follows:

1. PTP graph admits a rectangular dual if and only if each triangular face can be assigned to one of its adjacent vertices such that each vertex y with degree $d(v)$ has $d(v) - 4$ triangular faces assigned to it.
2. PTP graph admits a rectangular dual if and only if there is a perfect matching in the bipartite graph associated with it.

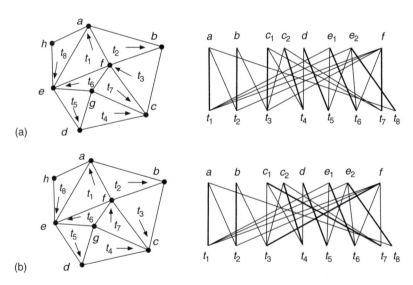

(a)

(b)

FIGURE 8.4 (a) Rectangular graph R with a feasible assignment of triangular faces to vertices, and the maximum matching in its bipartite graph B that corresponds to the floorplan in Figure 8.1a; (b) another feasible assignment for R and the maximum matching in B that corresponds to the floorplan in Figure 8.1b. Matched edges are indicated by thick lines.

Steps of rectangular dualization

Input: A block-level circuit connectivity graph C.
Output: A floorplan F.
1. Planarization of C by edge deletion or dummy node addition
2. Triangulation of the planar graph
3. Elimination of complex triangles from the plane triangulated graph to obtain a PTP graph
4. Construct and report a rectangular dual of the PTP graph

At this juncture, the steps of floorplanning by rectangular dualization [19] of a circuit are summarized above as an analysis of its time complexity is in order. The first step of planarization of the logical network of the circuit by deleting a minimum number of edges or a set of edges with minimum total weight is known to be NP-complete [20]. The second step of triangulating a planar graph can be done in linear time. But, there is neither a polynomial time optimum algorithm nor a NP-completeness proof [18] for the third step of eliminating all complex triangles from the plane triangulated graph. Efficient polynomial time algorithms for constructing a rectangular dual for a given PTP graph have been proposed in Refs. [12,13,17]. This has been improved by Bhasker and Sahni to a linear time algorithm [14] to check existence of a rectangular dual for a given planar triangulated graph and construct it, if it exists. An outline of this algorithm appears below in Algorithm I and the major steps are demonstrated in Figure 8.5. The limitation of rectangular dualization stems from its requirement of a PTP graph, but this can be overcome as discussed in Section 8.4.4. The algorithmic efficacy of rectangular dualization often leads to employing this method to generate a good topology on which other iterative floorplanning methods can be applied to obtain very good solutions quickly.

Algorithm 1   Linear time algorithm to find a rectangular dual [14]

Algorithm *RD_Floorplan*
begin
1. For each biconnected component of given PTP graph
     Embed it on a plane such that
        P_1 and P_3 are satisfied and all its articulation points are on the outermost cycle;
     If no embedding exists, then report 'NOT DUALIZABLE' and halt;
2. Find the critical corner implying paths and assign four corners *NW, NE, SE, SW*
        to vertices on the outermost cycle;
3. Add to the graph a special vertex *Head-node* and new directed edges from it
        to all the vertices on the outermost cycle between *NW* and *NE*;
4. Starting from *NW*, traverse downward from *Head-node*;
5. For each directed path from *Head-node* starting with the leftmost one
     for each vertex in the directed path order
        place a new rectangle below its predecessor such that the adjacency
           with rectangles for vertices on the path immediately to its left is maintained.
end.

8.3.2   SLICIBILITY OF RECTANGULAR DUALS

Several investigators have advocated that in top-down hierarchical circuit design, slicing structures have advantages over general nonslicing ones. Slicible floorplans can be represented by elegant data structures such as series-parallel polar graphs [6,8], slicing trees [7], and normalized Polish postfix

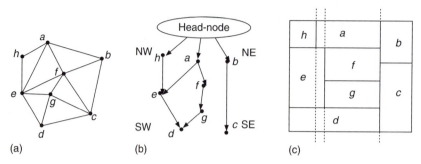

FIGURE 8.5   (a) Rectangular graph R, (b) its path directed graph with a special head-node and the four corners marked, and (c) rectangular dual construction by traversing each directed path from the special head-node in left to right order as indicated by dashed lines.

expressions [21]. These types of floorplans are computationally easier to deal with because they allow a natural partition of the design into partially independent subproblems, hence the divide-and-conquer strategy succeeds.

The problem of optimal orientations of modules is solvable in polynomial time for a slicible floorplan, but remains NP-complete in the strong sense for general floorplans [22]. Slicing facilitates not only floorplanning but also wiring. Optimal wiring of a single net in a slicing structure, minimizing the overall area instead of wirelength, can be done in $O(n \log n)$ time [23]. This problem is far more complicated in the general nonslicible case. In fact, the next chapter of this handbook dwells exclusively on slicing floorplans.

Notwithstanding the fact that slicible floorplan topologies have enjoyed preference owing to their divide-and-conquer algorithms, nonslicible floorplans are better as far as optimal sizing is concerned, and hence their intriguing properties are addressed later in this chapter.

The distinguishing criterion between slicibility and nonslicibility of a floorplan succinctly epitomized in Ref. [24] is presented next. The issue of representing nonslicible floorplans is addressed in Section 8.4. The salient question whether a slicible floorplan exists for a given neighborhood graph for modules of a circuit is also taken up thereafter.

8.3.2.1   Four-Cycle Criterion for Slicibility of a Floorplan

A graph-theoretic characterization of slicible floorplans [24] is based on the concept of a channel graph, where a channel in a floorplan is a cutline. From the convention of T-junctions, no two channels overlap. If two perpendicular channels a and b intersect at a point p, then p is an endpoint of either a or b, but not both; the one of which p is an endpoint is called the base of the T-junction and the other is called the crosspiece. The two parts of the crosspiece channel on either side of the junction are called arms. The same cut may be the base of one T-junction and crosspiece of another T-junction. A channel graph of a floorplan is a directed graph $C = (V, A)$ where there is a distinct vertex in V for each channel and there is an arc (a, b) from a to b in A if and only if there is a T-junction of which channel a is the base and channel b the crosspiece. Figure 8.6b and d shows the respective channel graphs of the slicible and nonslicible floorplan in Figure 8.6a and c. The following two crucial theorems about channel graphs of floorplans were proved in Ref. [24]:

1. Four-cycle theorem: A channel graph has a directed cycle if and only if it has a cycle of length 4.
2. Slicing theorem: A channel graph of a floorplan is acyclic if and only if the floorplan is a slicible floorplan.

Essentially, by detecting directed four-cycles in the channel graph of a given floorplan, its nonslicibility can be decided and this is achievable in linear time. There are two possible arrangements

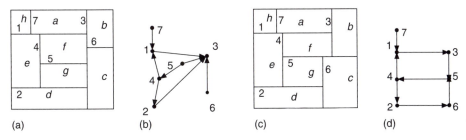

FIGURE 8.6 (a) Slicible floorplan F_s and (b) its channel graph; (c) nonslicible floorplan F_n and (d) its channel graph containing a directed four-cycle.

of channels in a floorplan that produce directed four-cycles in the channel graph. This property can also be employed in a polynomial time heuristic for converting a nonslicible floorplan to a slicible one with minimal alterations [25].

A few more properties of channel graphs have been observed [26,27]. A channel graph C is (1) connected, (2) planar but not necessarily embeddable on a planar grid, (3) bipartite, (4) outdegree of any vertex in $C \leq 2$, (5) at least four vertices in C have outdegree 1, (6) every internal face of C is bounded by exactly four arcs, (7) the number of arcs shared by two adjacent directed four-cycles is less than or equal to 1, and (8) C has no bridges [5]. The channel graph of a given floorplan is unique, but there may be more than one floorplan with the different neighborhood relations corresponding to a given channel graph. The existence of a floorplan corresponding to a planar, bipartite digraph with maximum outdegree of 2 and at least four vertices having outdegree 1 was raised in Ref. [27], and the affirmative answer was proven in Ref. [28]. The next section addresses certain important features of nonslicible floorplans.

8.4 NONSLICIBILE FLOORPLAN TOPOLOGIES

8.4.1 MAXIMAL RECTANGULAR HIERARCHY

The several efficient representation schemes that follow naturally from the recursive definition of slicible floorplans are not directly applicable to nonslicible floorplans. Nevertheless, a general non-slicible floorplan has a unique representation based on the concept of maximal rectangular hierarchy (MRH) [25] and above all, this representation is supportive of divide-and-conquer algorithms. Similar representations have been proposed independently in Refs. [29–32], although they mostly assume that at each level there can be a branching of at most five as is the case for the basic nonslicible pattern. A close relation between the strongly connected components of the channel graph of a nonslicible floorplan and its MRH was established [26], which leads to a simple depth-first search based $O(n)$ algorithm for extraction of MRH where the floorplan has n modules.

A maximal rectangle in a floorplan can be defined as one which is not contained in any rectangle other than the envelope of the floorplan, or does not partially overlap with any other rectangle. A nonslicible floorplan can be decomposed uniquely into a nonempty set of mutually exclusive (nonoverlapping) and collectively exhaustive maximal rectangles. This is demonstrated in Figure 8.7. If the floorplan is slicible and has a single through cut at the top level of the slicing tree, then the two rectangles on either side of the through cut are the only maximal rectangles. In the case of multiple through cuts in the same direction at the top level, the boundary is the only maximal rectangle; all indivisible blocks within it are its children in the MRH. The usual slicing tree may be utilized for processing within this maximal rectangle.

Maximal rectangles can be defined recursively to produce a hierarchy of maximal rectangles, called the maximal rectangular hierarchy. A maximal rectangle may contain a slicible or a nonslicible pattern of rectangles. At the top level, we have just the bounding rectangle of the floorplan. Each

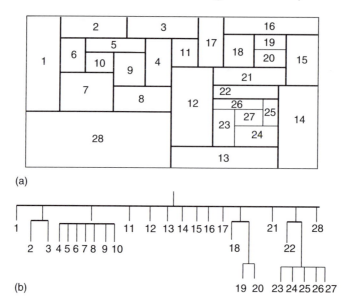

(a)

(b)

FIGURE 8.7 (a) Maximal rectangular hierarchy of a floorplan topology and (b) the corresponding hierarchy tree. Each level of the hierarchy is marked by a different line thickness. (From Sur-Kolay, S., Studies on nonslicible floorplans in VLSI layout design, Doctoral dissertation, Jadavpur University, 1991.)

level of the MRH has a rectangular boundary and a set of mutually exclusive and collectively exhaustive maximal rectangles. This hierarchy can be represented by a tree. Because the set of maximal rectangles at each level is unique, the MRH of a nonslicible floorplan is also unique.

8.4.2 INHERENT NONSLICIBILITY

The fact that a rectangular graph can have more than one nonisomorphic dual brings us to the fundamental question about the existence of rectangular graphs that have no slicible duals. This is equivalent to characterizing slicibility of rectangular graphs.

A rectangular graph is inherently nonslicible if there exists no slicible rectangular dual of it, consequently no slicible floorplan. It turns out that [33] there exists an inherently nonslicible graph N, having nine vertices. N is a minimum (in the number of vertices and edges) inherently nonslicible rectangular graph.

The inherently nonslicible graph, N, is a maximal rectangular graph (MRG) (i.e., no edge can be added without violating rectangularity) of 9 vertices and $20(=3*9-7)$ edges. An MRG of n vertices is not unique. For all $n \geq 4$, there exists an MRG with $(3n-7)$ edges that has a slicible dual. It follows that any rectangular graph with 8 or fewer vertices has a slicible rectangular dual. Moreover, the minimum rectangular graph that is inherently nonslicible is unique.

There exists a family of inherently nonslicible floorplans, named INS [25]. Besides the first member N, (Figure 8.2a), few more are shown in Figure 8.8a through d, and in fact, there are an infinite number of members in INS. The peculiarity of inherent nonslicibility can be demonstrated by examining a few pairs of similar floorplans. Consider the one in Figure 8.8a. The cut β acts like a lock and blocks slicibility. But addition of another vertical cut to divide the block below it produces a slicible floorplan so this new cut acts like a handle aiding slicibility. With this insight, pseudomaximality at any level of the MRH is defined so that if any maximal rectangle has more than four T-junctions around it externally, then the next level of the MRH within it cannot be ignored. The intuition behind this is that the inner level may provide a handle and produce an equivalent slicing. This idea is applicable for deciding membership in INS. Although nonslicibility of given floorplan can be easily decided as mentioned earlier in Section 8.3.2.1, the necessary and sufficient conditions

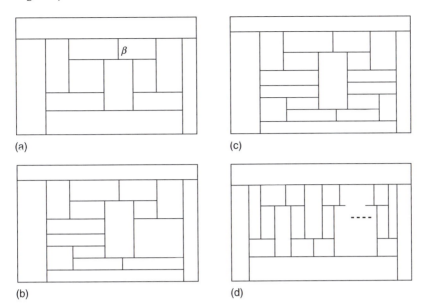

FIGURE 8.8 Members of family INS: (a) second smallest having two 5-wheels, (b) third smallest having three 5-wheels, (c) fourth smallest having four 5-wheels, and (d) template for a general member. (Figure a, c, and d from Sur-Kolay, S. and Bhattacharya, B.B., in *Proc. Inter. Symp. Circuits and Systems*, Singapore, 1991, pp. 2850–2853.)

for INS are still an open problem. But few sufficient conditions for slicibility of rectangular graphs that have been proven [26,28] are listed next.

Slicibility and vertex degree pattern: In a floorplan F, an indivisible rectangular module has $k \geq 4$ T-junctions (including corners) on it, which is called a facial k-cycle. First, F is pseudomaximally reduced to F', then extracting the dual of F' gives a reduced rectangular graph R'. If R' satisfies any of these conditions that can be checked quickly, then we can guarantee the existence of a slicible equivalent of F', hence F. A reduced rectangular graph is slicible if (1) all its internal vertices have degree 5 or more, or (2) none of its internal vertices have degree 5. Hence, all facial cycles in F' have length 4 or more than 5, but not 5. In the members of INS discovered, there is always a vertex of degree 4 with at least two adjacent vertices having degree 5.

Slicibility and three-chromaticity: A rectangular graph is slicible if it is (1) three-chromatic or (2) outerplanar [5].

Checking whether a given rectangular graph is three-chromatic as well as determining a valid vertex coloring with three colors can be done in linear time.

Tighter criterion of slicibility: A fairly recent result on slicibility [34] states that a rectangular graph R with n vertices, $n > 4$, is slicible if it satisfies either of the following conditions:

1. Its outermost face is a four-cycle and not all four exterior vertices are required to be corners.
2. All the complex four-cycles in R are maximal (i.e., not contained in any other four-cycle).

8.4.3 CANONICAL EMBEDDING OF RECTANGULAR DUALS

Nonuniqueness of the rectangular dual of a neighborhood graph has associated with it the notion of equivalence of two rectangular duals with isomorphic neighborhood graphs being isomorphic. Equivalent floorplans are not isomorphic in terms of definition of the channels. Nonisomorphic floorplans correspond to different rectangular dissections, so the associated cutlines are different. Any floorplan with n modules has $n - 1$ channels and $(2n - 2)$ T-junctions. Hence, the number of

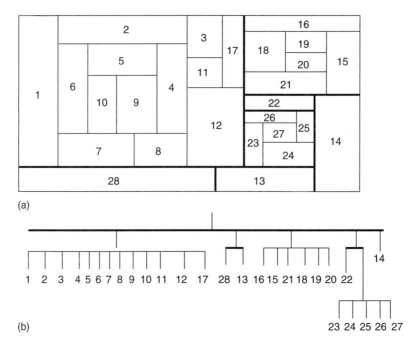

(a)

(b)

FIGURE 8.9 (a) Canonical embedding of the floorplan in Figure 8.7a and (b) its MRH tree. Each level is marked with different line thickness. (From Sur-Kolay, S., Studies on nonslicible floorplans in VLSI layout design, Doctoral dissertation, Jadavpur University, 1991.)

nodes and arcs in the two channel graphs are equal, but the difference lies in the set of arcs. This leads to the concept of a canonical rectangular dual or a canonical embedding for a class of equivalent floorplans.

A canonical embedding of a rectangular dual is a rectilinear embedding, which (1) is a valid equivalent floorplan and (2) the corresponding channel graph has the minimum number of directed four-cycles.

A maximal rectangle at any level of the MRH is said to be strongly maximal (smr) if it has exactly four T-junctions around it externally. It has been shown that any level of the strong MRH (i.e., MRH with smr's) can have at most one smr in the canonical form [35] of the rectangular dual (Figure 8.9).

The properties of nonslicible rectangular duals in this section are useful in producing desired floorplan topologies, and are also relevant to the subsequent routing phase.

8.4.4 DUALIZATION WITH RECTILINEAR MODULES

If a given adjacency graph is not dualizable, then one approach discussed earlier is to convert it to a PTP graph by planarizing and eliminating all forbidden complex triangles [18]. But this very often ends up in large wasted space because of the introduction of several dummy modules. An alternative approach is to introduce L-shaped modules [36], or even two-concave rectilinear modules with shapes like Z, T, W, or U [37] (Figure 8.10). The necessary and sufficient conditions under which a plane triangulated graph admits a dual with such rectilinear modules appear in Ref. [37] and their construction algorithm for a dual with n modules requires $O(n)$ time.

The origin of L-shaped modules is in the complex triangles in the adjacency graph. A floorplan, or the dual of the graph, is now seen as a dissection of a bounding rectangle into L-shaped regions where a rectangle is a special type of L-shaped region. A plane triangulated graph with a complex triangle (Figure 8.3a) is no longer forbidden because one of the three vertices of the complex triangle, say C,

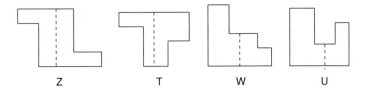

FIGURE 8.10 Four possible two-concave rectilinear shapes of module and each can be decomposed into two L-shaped modules as indicated by the dashed line. (From Yeap, G. and Sarrafzadeh, M., *SIAM J. Comput.*, 22, 500, 1993.)

can be realized as an L-shaped module having a concave corner to satisfy all adjacency conditions. As a matter of fact, for each complex triangle, at least one of its three vertices must have an L-shaped module in the dual, i.e., the floorplan topology. An assignment of a complex triangle to a vertex needs to be made to accommodate a concave corner in the corresponding module. A conflict is said to occur if a vertex is simultaneously assigned to two complex triangles where one is not contained in the other. An adjacency graph is said to be fully assigned if all its complex triangles can be assigned without any conflicts. The set of vertices assigned is termed as the assignment set. The characterization of graphs that admit L-shaped duals is given by the following criteria.

A plane triangulated adjacency graph G has an L-shaped dual D_e if and only if it satisfies the following two properties [37]:

1. G has at least five vertices and the exterior face of G is a cycle of length greater than 4.
2. G can be fully assigned and the corresponding assignment set A does not include the four vertices on the exterior face.

An algorithm to find a geometric dual containing both rectangular and L-shaped duals has been designed based on finding an assignment set using maximum matching [36]. This has also been generalized to the case where the input graph is not biconnected. The time complexity to test whether a given G admits an L-shaped dual is $O(n^{3/2})$ and to construct one, if it exists, is $O(n^2)$, where n is the number of modules. Incidentally, given such a topology, a simulated annealing-based algorithm for floorplan sizing with L-shaped modules was designed and implemented by Wong and Liu [38].

Further generalization to two-concave rectilinear modules with eight sides, six convex corners, and two concave corners has also been proposed in Ref. [37]. The necessity for these arises from the fact that conflicts may arise during assignment of vertices to complex triangles. A perfect assignment of a plane triangulated graph G is a set of assignments of all its complex triangles where (1) every complex triangle is assigned to a vertex, (2) no vertex has more than two assignments, and (3) the four vertices t, l, b, and r on the exterior face are unassigned. The necessary condition for the existence of a dual, i.e., floorplan topology with two-concave rectilinear modules for a given G is finding a perfect assignment. Such an assignment and thus a floorplan can be constructed in time linear in the number of modules.

The key result is that every biconnected planar triangulated graph admits a floorplan with two-concave rectilinear modules. Hence, these modules are the ultimate, i.e., necessary and sufficient for floorplanning by graph dualization.

8.5 HIERARCHICAL FLOORPLANNING

As finding an optimal solution to the floorplanning problem is computationally expensive, hierarchical approach for handling larger instances is a natural choice. The fundamental idea is to divide and conquer with a very small branching factor at each level. Although the number of possible floorplans for a given problem is exponential, enumeration of all possible floorplans for only three or four modules/rectangles at any level with their given connectivity and size specifications takes constant time.

Another strong motivation for employing a hierarchical approach is that because floorplanning decisions affect the subsequent phases of placement or global routing, it is desirable to integrate these phases as much as possible. A hierarchical method makes this computationally feasible as designed and implemented by Dai et al. [16,39] and Lengauer et al. [40].

As part of the macrocell based layout system called BEAR, the hierarchical floorplanner by Dai et al. consists of three steps:

> *Step 1—Bottom-up clustering*: A hierarchical tree is constructed in a bottom-up fashion by clustering strongly connected modules greedily. Each cluster has a limited number of modules, typically upto four. For each cluster, the shapes of the blocks are also considered so that there is no mismatch within the cluster. Issues with size incompatibility at higher levels between two neighboring clusters with fewer connections may arise, but these can be resolved by limiting the sizes of the clusters at the higher levels so that the smaller sized clusters are dealt with earlier, thereby reducing the percentage of wasted area.
>
> *Step 2—Top-down placement*: The cluster tree is traversed from the root, which has its desired shape and terminals specified. These requirements are propagated to the children clusters and their respective shape and terminals are determined. The small number of possible floorplan templates (Figure 8.11) are enumerated and clusters are assigned to rectangles or rooms in a template to obtain a floorplan topology. In most cases, the winning topology is determined by computing the estimated routing space for each of the possible topologies. This is continued till the orientations of the leaf modules are decided. It may be pointed out that this method works well when the leaf level modules can be of flexible shape. A certain amount of look ahead to the grandchild level is also added during top-down shape determination. The system allows the user to monitor the trade-off among shape, area, and connections costs.
>
> *Step 3—Floorplan optimization*: This step improves the solution obtained above by iteratively selecting certain blocks and resizing them. The blocks selected usually lie on the longest paths through the placement based on the routing estimates. Such paths are either between the left and right sides of the chip or the top and bottom sides. The routing cost is computed by adding the edge weights (number of net connections) between pairs of clusters multiplied by the distance between their centers in the current placement. The global routing information is updated incrementally after each iteration. The stopping criterion is that the longest paths contain fixed size blocks only or flexible blocks that belong to the longest path in the perpendicular direction as well. Although this method is very efficient for small circuits, it needs to be executed in a two-pass mode iteratively, one for each direction, to achieve fast convergence for larger circuits.

In the hierarchical approach taken by Lengauer et al. [40], the hierarchy or cut-tree is generated in a top-down manner by recursive mincut method initially and then the bottom levels of the tree are obtained by bottom-up clustering. Once again the degree of the cut-tree is restricted to 4. Floorplan

FIGURE 8.11   Some templates used in hierarchical floorplanner BEAR with at most degree 4 branching at any node of the hierarchy.

sizing is done by bottom-up traversal of the cut-tree to compute the floorplan alternatives based on the shape function for the children modules/rectangles. Finally, a particular floorplan alternative and its corresponding global routing are constructed simultaneously. For a floorplan topology, there exists a breadth-first top-down labeling of the nodes of the cut-tree with a particular pattern. The pattern selection performed at each node is guided by the external wiring costs computed for the previous cut-tree level without the need for penalty functions à la Dai et al. for assigning modules to rectangular regions smaller than the requirement. Moreover, the number of patterns is bounded by a small integer. The sizing algorithm employs shape function instead of the penalty-oriented method by Dai et al. Thus, this method implemented in the system FRODO reports better results over BEAR.

8.6 FLOORPLAN SIZING METHODS

Given a floorplan topology, the second task is to obtain the aspect ratios of the modules so that the overall area, total netlength, and maximum netlength is optimal. Some of the major techniques are listed below and more details of two important ones appear in the subsequent sections.

1. Force-directed with slicing [41]: The PIONEER system is an iterative method. It provides two capabilities: extraction of initial layout from a user-specified data and interactive graphics for improving the initial layout. The improvement of initial layout proceeds in three steps. First, macrocenters are determined, then a slicing structure is generated, and finally the layout is expanded.

2. Relaxation method [42,43]: This iterative floorplanning method is different from improvement by interchange because relaxation implies an obvious next state. In Ref. [42], dimensional relaxation is used to improve a floorplan. It consists of modifying the shapes of cells as well as the topology of the horizontal and vertical line segments that define the floorplan.

3. Simulated annealing: Timber Wolf [44] is one of the first floorplanning systems based on simulated annealing technique. It produces not only the relative positions of the modules but also their aspect ratios and pin positions. The algorithms for optimal floorplan design, reported in Ref. [21,38], also use simulated annealing. The first algorithm can generate slicing structures with rectangular modules only, whereas the second one can produce non-slicing floorplans and even L-shaped modules. A new representation of floorplans using normalized Polish expressions facilitates selection during iterative improvement by pairwise interchange (see Chapter 9 for details). The major disadvantages of these systems are that they are computation intensive and may not be readily adapted to deal with various constraints on floorplan.

4. Genetic algorithm [45]: This stochastic iterative method requires appropriate encoding of a floorplan and its associated cost function along with the definition of effective crossover and mutation operators for iterative moves. Each move has an activation probability. It can handle large floorplans and the quality of the solutions are comparable with simulated annealing-based methods.

5. Analytic force-directed method with packing [46,47]: Iterative floorplanning by this method consists of two subtasks. First, an initial placement is obtained either by potential energy method, or by attractive and repulsive force method as in the CHAMP system. Then a semiautomatic block packing process is undertaken by relocating and reshaping modules as well as the chip boundary. Constraint-based analytic sizing methods have also been proposed [48–50]; further details are elaborated in the following section.

6. Branch-and-bound [29]: Layouts occupying minimum area can be obtained by this method using graph-theoretic representation of floorplan and suitably formulating a network flow optimization problem. Graph-theoretic representation can also yield optimal aspect ratios of modules in any floorplan by a branch-and-bound heuristic.

8.7 ANALYTIC SIZING

The floorplan sizing algorithms that adopt an analytical approach essentially model the problem as a set of constraints on the dimensions and connectivities of the rectangular modules such that a certain objective function is minimized. Among these, a method based on potential energy modeling of overlap and separation was proposed by Ying et al. [48]. The shape constraints are met by bounding penalty functions. An unconstrained minimization problem is then solved heuristically. As the time complexity is high, the authors mention incorporating hierarchical floorplanning by using the method recursively.

　　The most effective and widely referred analytic floorplan sizing algorithm based on mixed integer programming formulation was proposed by Sutanthavibul et al. [49]. The essence of this is described next. The assumption is that the area of a rectangular module is known a priori, but its actual shape may be either fixed or flexible within certain limits for the aspect ratios (width to height ratio). The variables in the mixed integer programming are of two types, namely integer variables (x_i, y_i) indicating the x- and y-coordinates of the lower left corner of module i, and certain 0–1 variables that primarily take care of different constraints. The width and height of module i is denoted by (w_i, h_i).

Constraints for nonoverlap of modules i and j: If both modules are rigid, we have the four linear inequalities (I.a). Typically, the bounds on the width W and height H of the chip may be specified. By employing two 0–1 integer variables x_{ij} and y_{ij}, we can ensure that at least one of the four inequalities (I.b) holds for any pair of modules i and j. Thus for any one of the four possible values of (x_{ij}, y_{ij}), only one of the four inequalities is applicable, the other three being vacuously true. It is assumed that for all i, the values of (x_i, y_i) are nonnegative and definitely less than the chip width or height as the case may be.

Constraints for nonoverlap of two rigid modules i and j

$x_i + w_i \leq x_j, i$ left of j	$x_i + w_i \leq x_j + W(x_{ij} + y_{ij})$
$x_i - w_j \geq x_j, i$ right of j	$x_i - w_j \geq x_j - W(1 - x_{ij} + y_{ij})$
$y_i + h_i \leq y_j, i$ below j	$y_i + h_i \leq y_j + H(1 + x_{ij} - y_{ij})$
$y_i - h_j \geq y_j, i$ above j	$y_i - h_j \geq y_j - H(2 - x_{ij} - y_{ij})$
(I.a) Variable-size chip	(I.b) Fixed-size chip

If rotation by 90° is to be permitted for the rigid modules, then an additional 0–1 integer variable z_i is introduced and the constraints are modified to the following where $M = \max(W, H)$:

$$x_i + z_i h_i + (1 - z_i)w_i \leq x_j + M(x_{ij} + y_{ij})$$
$$x_i - z_j h_j + (1 - z_j)w_j \geq x_j - M(1 - x_{ij} + y_{ij})$$
$$y_i + z_i w_i + (1 - z_i)h_i \leq y_j + M(1 + x_{ij} - y_{ij})$$
$$y_i - z_j w_j + (1 - z_j)h_j \geq y_j - M(2 - x_{ij} - y_{ij})$$

Next, modules with flexible shapes but fixed area s_i are considered in the inequalities (I.c and I.d) by converting the quadratic relation $w_i h_i = s_i$ to a linear one, i.e., by expressing h_i as a linear function of w_i based on the first two terms of the Taylor series expansion about the point $w_{i\,\max}$ as given below:

$$h_i = \frac{s_i}{w_{i\,\max}} + (w_{i\,\max} - w_i)\frac{s_i}{w_{i\,\max}^2} \text{ or, } h_i = h_{i0} + \Delta w_i \lambda_i$$

where $h_{i0} = \frac{s_i}{w_{i\,max}}$, $\lambda_i = \frac{s_i}{w_{i\,max}^2}$, and $\Delta w_i = w_{i\,max} - w_i$

Constraints for nonoverlap of a flexible module i

$x_i + w_{i\,max} - \Delta w_i \leq x_j$	$x_i + w_{i\,max} - \Delta w_i \leq x_j$
$y_i + h_{i0} + \Delta w_i \lambda_i \leq y_j$	$y_i + h_{i0} + \Delta w_i \lambda_i \leq y_j$
$x_i - w_j \geq x_j$	$x_j + w_{j\,max} - \Delta w_j \leq x_i$
$y_i - h_i \geq y_j$	$y_j + h_{j0} \mid \Delta w_j \lambda_j \leq y_i$
(I.c) With rigid module j	**(I.d) With flexible module j**

Constraints on interconnection length can also be thrown in with few continuous positive variables per net and the half-perimeter metric is used. The complexity of the entire mixed integer linear programming problem may be reduced by considering the constraints for critical nets only as this number is far smaller. Routability is modeled by linear constraints based on the rule that the total net length is 0.5 times the length of the routing tracks in the chip. This ensures that enough empty space around each module is reserved for routing. For each pair of modules, two continuous and one integer variable is introduced.

The package LINDO is used to solve for the values of the variables and arrive at a floorplan solution. If the topology is given, then all the 0–1 integer variables acquire specific values and the problem of determining the shapes of the modules reduces to standard linear programming one and is hence polynomially solvable. The number of continuous variables and the linear constraints are respectively $2n$ and $O(n)$ where the floorplan has n modules.

The major drawback of this approach is the huge solution time for mixed integer linear programming. For example, a floorplan with 25 modules may need about 600 integer variables. The technique devised to overcome this is to consider very few, typically 10–12, modules at a time and then successively augment the floorplan in a locally optimal way by adding a new group of modules each time till all modules have been processed. The selection of the groups of modules can be performed either by clustering based on connectivity or linear ordering depending on the I/O connections. The key to reducing the complexity is to have fewer number of variables, thus the already positioned modules in a partial floorplan are replaced by fewer number of covering rectangles. The floorplanning algorithm by analytical method [49] is given in Algorithm 2.

Algorithm 2   Floorplanning algorithm by mixed integer linear programming [49]

Algorithm *MILP_Floorplan*
begin
 Select a group S of k modules as seed;
 Formulate MILP for S;
 Solve to generate partial floorplan for S;
 while $(k \leq n)do/ * n$ is total number of modules $*/$
  Select a new group of e modules based on connections to already positioned modules;
  Find a set of d covering rectangles for the present partial floorplan where $d \leq k$;
  Formulate MILP for d covering rectangles and e unpositioned modules;
  Solve to obtain new partial floorplan;
  $k = k + e$;
 endwhile;
end.

8.8   BRANCH-AND-BOUND STRATEGY FOR SIZING

One of the early algorithms for optimal sizing of general floorplans with rigid modules was devised by Wimer et al. [29]. The input to this algorithm is a floorplan topology represented by a pair of dual polar graphs, also known as the x-graph or horizontal constraint graph, and the y-graph or vertical constraint graph. Each graph is planar, directed acyclic with a single source and a single sink corresponding to the left (top) and right (bottom) edges of the bounding rectangle of the floorplan. A vertex in the x-graph corresponds to a vertical side of a rectangular module in the floorplan. There is a directed arc from a vertex i to a vertex j if there is a rectangular module in the floorplan whose left and right edges correspond to i and j, respectively. In the y-graph, the vertices denote the horizontal edges of the modules and the directed arc goes from the top edge i lying above the bottom edge j of a module. Each module M_k in the floorplan topology has a set of one or more specified dimensions, so in the x-graph the directed edge from the left to the right vertical edge of M_k has an associated weight denoting the width w_k of M_k. Similarly, in the y-graph the weight of a directed edge corresponds to the height of the module whose top and bottom edges form the endpoints of the edge.

In the floorplan sizing problem, the goal is to determine the positions of all the modules for a given topology such that the total area of the bounding rectangle is minimized. For slicing topologies, the two graphs belong to the special class called series parallel. If each leaf has finitely many possible shapes, then Stockmeyer's bottom-up sizing algorithm [22] becomes applicable. However, for the general case the problem is NP-hard so a branch and strategy is chosen. It proceeds as follows:

First, a module is chosen based on some criterion for a particular level. In other words, if there are n modules, then there are n levels in the branch-and-bound tree and the degree of a node in the ith level is equal to the number of possible shapes of module M_i. A linear order of the modules is obtained so that along any directed path of x- or y-graph, the predecessors of a module appear in the linear order before the module. At the root, each edge of the x- and y-graphs is assigned the smallest possible value it may take among all given shapes for the first module in the linear order. While going from the ith level to the $(i + 1)$th, appropriate values are assigned to the edges corresponding to the module M_{i+1} in the two graphs. At each node of the tree, the width and height of the partial floorplan is computed. When going down along a path in the tree from root to a leaf, the area is nondecreasing in the number of already positioned modules. Let A_{min} denote the minimum value of area achieved thus far. The forward processing is performed in level order from the root. If at a node in ith level, the area A is greater than the current A_{min} of the $(i + 1)$th level processed thus far from left, then this node is not expanded any further (Figure 8.12) and the process backtracks upward till it finds a suitable node for branching downward.

The efficiency of the method is influenced by the following factors: (1) the value of A_{min} as early backtracks are desirable; (2) the area of a partial floorplan obtained is a lower bound on the area of the complete floorplan, hence if the lower bound is raised, early backtracks will occur; and (3) the order in which the possible dimensions of module M_i are examined at the ith level of the branch-and-bound tree.

Intuitively, a module whose size is likely to have greater effect on the area of the complete floorplan, such as one with large size or one which lies on a critical (longest) path or many directed paths in the polar dual graphs, should be considered earlier. Along with a branching strategy that guarantees attainment of global minimum, a very effective bounding value for the area of the remaining modules is computed to guide the search.

Additional efficiency of the method is attained by decomposing the floorplan topology into maximal slicible structures for which series-parallel algorithm is applied. Branch-and-bound strategy is used only for the maximal rectangles as discussed in Section 8.4.1.

Another constraint-based floorplanning algorithm proposed by Vijayan et al. [50] also can handle flexible, fixed (rigid), and preplaced modules. The input is specified as two sets of constraints in the form of the two directed acyclic horizontal and vertical constraint graphs. A linear time algorithm for topological sorting of directed acyclic graphs is used to find the critical (longest) paths in the

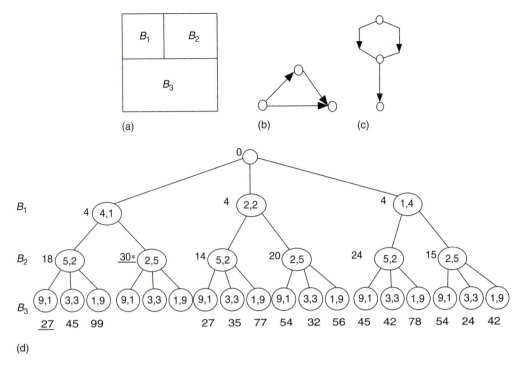

(d)

FIGURE 8.12   (a) Example floorplan topology with three modules, (b) its *x*-graph, (c) its *y*-graph, and (d) its branch-and-bound tree where shape lists are B_1: (4,1),(2,2),(1,4), B_2: (5,2),(2,5), and B_3: (9,1),(3,3),(1,9). The width–height pair appears inside the node and the area of the subfloorplan at that level, outside it. A node marked "∗" has area greater than minimum bound at that stage and hence no further branching from it is required. (From Wimer, S., Koren, I., and Cederbaum, I., *IEEE Trans. Computer-Aided Design*, 8, 139, 1989.)

two graphs. Redundant constraints are removed and flexible blocks on the more critical paths are reshaped. Certain criteria to characterize two different notions of redundancy among constraints are formulated and utilized to reduce the time complexity. This heuristic is iterated until a floorplan solution of desired dimensions is obtained.

8.9   KNOWLEDGE-BASED FLOORPLANNING APPROACHES

Floorplanning is meaningful for very large designs tackled in a top-down fashion. There is generally a vast amount of design data and the optimization problems are computatinally hard. Often more than one objective has to be optimized. Thus, artificial intelligence techniques have been attempted by a few researchers, especially when details of modules are not known.

FLOYD, one of the early rule-based expert systems for floorplanning, was designed and implemented by Dickinson [1]. The key idea in another system FLUTE [2] is to produce a rectangular topology by placing the modules on a rectangular grid graph using a set of rules that take shape and connectivity constraints into account. Then sizing or geometric realization is achieved by a heuristic method to solve a system of linear and quadratic inequalities. Like many artificial intelligence systems, this is implemented in LISP.

Jabri and Skellern [4] adopt a combination of algorithmic and knowledge-based approach for a top-down floorplanning system called PIAF. Rectangular dualization method is used to generate topologies and then other constraints are introduced for knowledge-based estimation and prediction of dimensions and areas of modules. The final phase consists of a greedy algorithm for determining the exact shapes and locations of the modules. The system FLAIR developed by Brück et al. [3] employs a band of expert systems for estimating a broad range of design parameters relevant to transforming an architectural plan to a geometric one in two steps—first producing a rough or postulative plan and then a final one.

In general, these systems are fairly complex to design, implement, and validate. Accurate definition of the rule base and its fine tuning are required for attaining optimality. These have greater potential in interactive design environments.

8.10 UNIFIED METHOD FOR TOPOLOGY GENERATION AND SIZING

With exponentially many feasible topologies for a given neighborhood graph, design space exploration and optimality are limited if the sizing is performed on a particular feasible topology. Among the very few methods that integrate the two subtasks of floorplanning, two are notable.

The first one is a dynamic programming based method [51] that can handle slicible floorplans only. A set of slicing trees is enumerated by top-down partitioning of the adjacency graph and represented by an enumeration tree model. Size optimization is carried out simultaneously by Stockmeyer's method [22] for each topology enumerated. The role of dynamic programming is to reduce the time complexity to polynomial time by memoization of optimal solutions for subfloorplans.

The second method [52] is a two-phase technique applicable to nonslicible floorplans including inherently nonslicible ones. Canonical embedding results of Section 8.4.3 are applied to establish that a binary tree representation for general floorplans exists where the internal nodes correspond to either straight cutlines or Z-cuts having two monotonic staircase bends. The possible topologies are derived by top-down partitioning and kept in an AND–OR graph. A bottom-up sizing phase finally reports the optimal floorplan. The slicibility criterion in Ref. [34] can provide additional improvement in the speed of the floorplanner with negligible sacrifice of solution quality.

ACKNOWLEDGMENTS

The author would like to thank all her floorplanning research collaborators, especially Professors Bhargab B. Bhattacharya of Indian Statistical Institute and Parthasarathi Dasgupta of Indian Institute of Management, Kolkata. Part of the Sections 8.3, 8.3.1, 8.4.2, and 8.7 has been published in Sur-Kolay, S. and Bhattacharya, B.B., *Foundations of Software Technology and Theoretical Computer Science*, LCNS 338, 88, 1988; Bhasker, S. and Sahni, S., *Algorithmica*, 3, 274, 1988; Sur-Kolay, S. and Bhattacharya, B.B., Proceedings of the ISCAS, pp. 2850–2853, 1991; Sutanthavibul, E., et al., *IEEE Trans. Computer-Aided Design*, 10, 761, 1991, respectively. With permission.

REFERENCES

1. A. Dickinson. Floyd: A knowledge-based floorplan designer. In *Proceedings of the IEEE International Conference on Computer Design (ICCD)*, San Jose, CA, October 1–4, pp. 176–179, 1986.
2. B. Ackland and H. Watanabe. Flute: An expert floorplanner for full-custom VLSI design. *IEEE Design and Test of Computers*, 4:32–41, 1987.
3. R. Brück, K.-H. Temme, and H. Wronn. FLAIR: A knowledge-based approach to integrated circuit floorplanning. In *Proceedings of the International Workshop on Artifical Intelligence for Industrial Applications*, Hitachi City, Japan, May 25–27, pp. 194–199, 1988.
4. M.A. Jabri and D.J. Skellern. PIAF: A knowledge-based/algorithmic top-down floorplanning system. In *Proceedings of the 26th ACM/IEEE Design Automation Conference (DAC)*, Las Vegas, NV, June 25–29, pp. 582–585, June 1989.
5. F. Harary. *Graph Theory*. Addison-Wesley Publishing Co., Reading, MA, 1969.
6. R.H.J.M. Otten. Automatic floorplan design. In *Proceedings of the 19th ACM/IEEE Design Automation Conference (DAC)*, Las Vegas, NV, June 14–16, pp. 261–267, June 1982.
7. R.H.J.M. Otten. Efficient floorplan optimization. In *Proceedings of the IEEE International Conference on Computer Design (ICCD)*, Port Chester, NY, pp. 499–502, October 1983.
8. R.L. Brooks, C.A.B. Smith, A.H. Stone, and W.T. Tutte. The dissection of rectangles into squares. *Duke Mathematical Journal*, 7: 312–340, 1940.

9. U. Lauther. A min-cut placement algorithm for general cell assemblies based on a graph representation. In *Proceedings of the 16th ACM/IEEE Design Automation Conference (DAC)*, San Diego, CA, June 25–27, pp. 1–10, June 1979.

10. D.P. LaPotin and S.W. Director. MASON: A global floorplanning approach for VLSI design. *IEEE Transactions on Computer-Aided Design*, CAD-5(4): 477–489, October 1986 (ICCAD 1985).

11. H. Modarres and A. Kelapure. An automatic floorplanner upto 100,000 gates. *IEEE Transactions on Computer-Aided Design*, VLSI Systems Design, pp. 38–44, December 1987.

12. K. Kozminski and E. Kinnen. Rectangular duals of planar graphs. *Networks*, 15: 145–157, 1985.

13. S.M. Leinwand and Y.T. Lai. Algorithms for floorplan design via rectangular dualization. *IEEE Transactions on Computer-Aided Design*, 7(12), December 1988. (DAC 1984).

14. J. Bhasker and S. Sahni. A linear time algorithm to find a rectangular dual of a planar triangulated graph. *Algorithmica*, 3(2): 274–278, 1988 (DAC 1986).

15. B. Lokanathan and E. Kinnen. Performance optimized floorplanning by graph planarization. In *Proceedings of the 26th ACM/IEEE Design Automation Conference (DAC)*, Las Vegas, NV, June 25–29, pp. 116–121, June 1989.

16. W.M. Dai and E.S. Kuh. Simultaneous floor planning and global routing for hierarchical building-block layout. *IEEE Transactions on Computer-Aided Design*, 6: 828–837, September 1987 (DAC 1986).

17. J. Bhasker and S. Sahni. A linear time algorithm to check for the existence of rectangular dual of a planar triangulated graph. *Networks*, 17: 307–317, 1987.

18. K. Koike, S. Tsukiyama, and I. Shirakawa. An algorithm to eliminate all complex triangles in a maximal planar graph for usein VLSI floorplan. In *Proceedings of the International Symposium on Circuits and Systems (ISCAS)*, San Jose, CA, May 5–7, pp. 321–324, IEEE, 1986.

19. G. Sorkin, W.R. Heller, and K. Maling. The planar package planner for system designers. In *Proceedings of the 19th ACM/IEEE Design Automation Conference (DAC)*, Las Vegas, NV, June 14–16, pp. 253–260, June 1982.

20. M.J. Garey and D.J. Johnson. *Computers and Intractability: A Guide to the Theory of NP-Completeness*. W.H. Freeman & Co., San Francisco, CA, 1979.

21. D.F. Wong and C.L. Liu. A new algorithm fir floorplan design. In *Proceedings of the 23rd ACM/IEEE Design Automation Conference (DAC)*, Las Vegas, NV, June 29–July 2, pp. 101–107, June 1986.

22. L.J. Stockmeyer. Optimal orientation of cells in slicing floorplan designs. *Information and Control*, 57: 187–192, 1983.

23. P. Sipala, W.K. Luk, and C.K. Wong. Minimum area wiring for slicing structures. *IEEE Transactions on Computer-Aided Design*, C-36(6): 745–760, June 1987.

24. K.J. Supowit and E.F. Slutz. Placement algorithms for custom VLSI. In *Proceedings of the 20th ACM/IEEE Design Automation Conference (DAC)*, Miami Beach, FL, June 27–29, pp. 164–170, June 1983.

25. S. Sur-Kolay and B.B. Bhattacharya. On the family of inherently nonslicible floorplans in VLSI design. In *Proceedings of the International Symposium on Circuits and Systems (ISCAS)*, pp. 2850–2853, Singapore, June 1991.

26. S. Sur-Kolay and B.B. Bhattacharya. The cycle structure of channel graphs for nonslicible floorplans and a unified algorithm for feasible routing order. In *Proceedings of the IEEE International Conference on Computer Design (ICCD)*, pp. 524–527, Boston, October 1991.

27. Y. Cai and D.F. Wong. A channel/switchbox definition algorithm for building-block layout. In *Proceedings of the 27th ACM/IEEE Design Automation Conference (DAC)*, Orlando, FL, June 24–28, pp. 638–641, June 1990.

28. S. Sur-Kolay. *Studies on Nonslicible Floorplans in VLSI Layout Design*, Doctoral dissertation, Jadavpur University, Calcutta, 1991.

29. S. Wimer, I. Koren, and I. Cederbaum. Optimal aspect ratios of building blocks in VLSI. *IEEE Transactions on Computer-Aided Design*, 8(2): 139–145, February 1989.

30. D.F. Wong and P.S. Sakhamuri. Efficient floorplan area optimization. In *Proceedings of the 26th ACM/IEEE Design Automation Conference (DAC)*, Las Vegas, NV, June 25–29, pp. 586–589, June 1989.

31. C.-H. Chen and I.G. Tollis. Area optimization of spiral floorplans. *Journal of Circuits, Systems and Computers*, 3(4): 833–857, 1993 (ICCD 1991).

32. K. Chong and S.Sahni. Optimal realizations of floorplans. *IEEE Transactions on Computer-Aided Design*, 12(6): 793–804, June 1993.

33. S. Sur-Kolay and B.B. Bhattacharya. Inherent nonslicibility of rectangular duals in VLSI floorplanning. *Foundations of Software Technology and Theoretical Computer Science*, LCNS 338: 88–107, 1988.

34. P.S. Dasgupta and S. Sur-Kolay. Slicibility conditions of rectangular graphs and their applications to floorplan optimization. *ACM Transactions on Design Automation of Electronic Systems*, 6(4): 447–470, October 2001.

35. S. Sur-Kolay and B.B. Bhattacharya. Canonical embedding of rectangular duals. In *Proceedings of the 29th ACM/IEEE Design Automation Conference (DAC)*, Anaheim, CA, June 8–12, pp. 69–74, June 1992.

36. S. Sun and M. Sarrafzadeh. Floorplanning by graph dualization: L-shaped modules. *Algorithmica*, 10: 429–456, 1993.

37. G. Yeap and M. Sarrafzadeh. Floor-planning by graph dualization: 2-concave rectilinear modules. *SIAM Journal of Computing*, 22(3): 500–526, June 1993.

38. D.F. Wong and C.L. Liu. Floorplan design for rectangular and L-shaped modules. In *Digest of ACM/IEEE International Conference on Computer Aided Design (ICCAD)*, Santa Clara, CA, November 9–12, pp. 520–523, 1987.

39. W. Dai, B. Eschermann, E.S. Kuh, and M. Pedram. Hierarchical placement and floorplanning in BEAR. *IEEE Transactions on Computer-Aided Design*, 8(12): 1335–1349, December 1989.

40. T. Lengauer and R. Muller. Robust and accurate hierachical floorplanning with integrated global wiring. *IEEE Transactions on Computer-Aided Design*, 12(6): 802–809, June 1993.

41. L.S. Woo, C.K. Wong, and D.T. Tang. Pioneer: A macro-based floorplanning design system. *VLSI System Design*, CAD-4: 32–43, August 1986.

42. E. Berkcan and E. Kinnen. Ic layout planning and placement by dimensional relaxation. In *Proceedings of the IEEE International Conference on Computer Design (ICCD)*, San Jose, CA, October 1–4, pp. 223–234, 1986.

43. M.J. Cieselski and E. Kinnen. Digraph relaxation for 2-dimensional placement of IC blocks. *IEEE Transactions on Computer-Aided Design*, CAD-6(1): 55–66, January 1987.

44. C. Sechen and A.L. Sangiovani-Vincentelli. The timberwolf placement and routing package. *IEEE Journal of Solid-State Circuits*, SC-20(2): 510–522, 1985.

45. M. Rebaudengo and M.S. Reorda. Gallo: A genetic algorithm for floorplan area optimization. *IEEE Transactions on Computer-Aided Design*, 15(8): 943–951, August 1996.

46. Y.C. Hsu and W.J. Kubitz. A procedure for chip floorplanning. In *Proceedings of the International Symposium on Circuits and Systems (ISCAS)*, Philadelphia, PA, May 4–7, pp. 568–571, 1987.

47. K. Ueda, H. Kitazawa, and I. Harada. Champ: Chip floorplan for hierarchical VLSI layout design. *IEEE Transactions on Computer-Aided Design*, CAD-4: 12–22, January 1985.

48. C. Ying and J.S. Wong. An analytical approach to floorplanning for hierarchical building blocks layout. *IEEE Transactions on Computer-Aided Design*, 8(4): 403–412, April 1989.

49. S. Sutanthavibul, E. Shragowitz, and J.B. Rosen. An analytical approach to floorplan design and optimization. *IEEE Transactions on Computer-Aided Design*, 10(6): 761–769, June 1991. (DAC 1990).

50. G. Vijayan and R.S. Tsay. A new method for floor planning using topological constraint reduction. *IEEE Transactions on Computer-Aided Design*, 10(12): 1494–1501, December 1991.

51. G. Yeap and M. Sarrafzadeh. A unified approach to floorplan sizing and enumeration. *IEEE Transactions on Computer-Aided Design*, 12(12): 1858–1867, December 1993.

52. P.S. Dasgupta, S. Sur-Kolay, and B.B. Bhattacharya. A unified approach to topology generation and optimal sizing of floorplans. *IEEE Transactions on Computer-Aided Design*, 17(2): 126–135, February 1998.

9 Slicing Floorplans

Ting-Chi Wang and Martin D.F. Wong

CONTENTS

9.1 INTRODUCTION

A floorplan is a dissection of an enveloping rectangle R by horizontal and vertical line segments into a set of nonoverlapping basic rectangles (or rooms) such that each room is large enough to accommodate the module assigned to it. Note that in some situations, there may be some basic rectangles without any modules assigned to them. We call them empty rooms.

An important class of floorplans is the set of all slicing floorplans [1,2]. A slicing floorplan is one that can be obtained by recursively cutting a rectangle into two smaller rectangles by either a vertical or horizontal line segment. Typically, a slicing floorplan for n modules has n rooms each of which

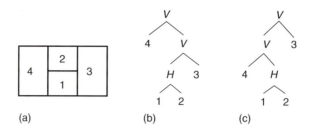

FIGURE 9.1 Slicing floorplan and its two slicing trees. (a) A slicing floorplan for four modules, (b) and (c) two slicing trees for the floorplan in (a).

accommodates a different module. Figure 9.1a shows a slicing floorplan for four modules. There are advantages of using slicing floorplans. For example, focusing on slicing floorplans significantly reduces the search space and, thus, the runtime. Moreover, the shape flexibilities of modules can be fully utilized to pack modules tightly [3–5]. Consequently, existing slicing floorplan algorithms in general run very efficiently and yet can pack modules tightly.

In Section 9.2, we give some necessary preliminaries with respect to the floorplan design problem. In Section 9.3, we present two schemes for representing slicing floorplans. In Section 9.4, we study several important optimization problems, including the well-known area optimization problem, and their solutions for slicing floorplans. These optimization algorithms are typically embedded into a slicing floorplanner. We then turn our attention to classical slicing floorplan design, and introduce different solutions in Section 9.5. In Section 9.6, we focus on modern slicing floorplan design that takes placement constraints into account. Several placement constraints are addressed, and their solutions are described. Finally, we highlight more recent advances in slicing floorplan design for field programmable gate arrays (FPGAs) and three-dimensional integrated circuits (3D ICs), in addition to several interesting theoretical results, in Section 9.7, and draw a conclusion in Section 9.8.

9.2 PRELIMINARIES

In the floorplan design problem, we are given a set of n modules, named $1, 2, \ldots, n$, and a list of n triplets of numbers, $(a_1, p_1, q_1), (a_2, p_2, q_2), \ldots, (a_n, p_n, q_n)$ with $p_i \leq q_i$, $1 \leq i \leq n$. For each module i, (a_i, p_i, q_i) specifies its area and shape constraint. That is, if module i has width w_i and height h_i, the following conditions must hold:

1. $w_i \times h_i = a_i$
2. $p_i \leq (h_i/w_i) \leq q_i$, if $i \in M_1$
3. $p_i \leq (h_i/w_i) \leq q_i$ or $(1/q_i) \leq (h_i/w_i) \leq (1/p_i)$, if $i \in M_2$

We define (h_i/w_i) to be the aspect ratio of module i. Module i is said to be a hard module if $p_i = q_i$, otherwise it is said to be a soft module. The two disjoint module sets M_1 and M_2 are given with $M_1 \cup M_2 = \{1, 2, \ldots, n\}$, where M_1 specifies the set of modules with fixed orientation, and M_2 specifies the set of modules with free orientation (i.e., they can be rotated). Given a floorplan, if x_i and y_i are the width and the height, respectively, of the basic rectangle that accommodates module i, we must have $x_i \geq w_i$ and $y_i \geq h_i$. The shape curves in Figure 9.2 specify different kinds of shape constraints for a module where each shaded region (including the shape curve) is called the bounded area. A point in the bounded area gives the dimensions of the basic rectangle that can accommodate the module. (The x and y coordinates of the point give the width and the height of the room.) Figure 9.2a and b correspond to the case where the module is rigid; in addition, the module in Figure 9.2a has fixed orientation while the one in Figure 9.2b can be rotated. Figure 9.2c and d both correspond to the case where the module is flexible (soft); similarly the module in Figure 9.2c has fixed orientation while the one in Figure 9.2d has free orientation. Let H, L_1, L_2, L_3, and L_4 be the

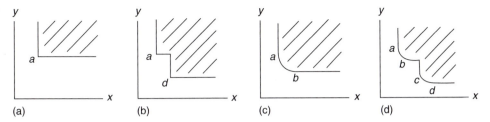

FIGURE 9.2 Different shape curves. (a) The shape curve for a hard module with fixed orientation, (b) the shape curve for a hard module with free orientation, (c) the shape curve for a soft module with fixed orientation, and (d) the shape curve for a soft module with free orientation.

hyperbola $xy = a_i$, the line $y = q_i x$, the line $y = p_i x$, the line $y = (1/p_i)x$, and the line $y = (1/q_i)x$, respectively. In these figures, the intersections between H and L_1, L_2, L_3, L_4 are points a, b, c, d, respectively.

To describe the wiring information between each pair of modules, an $n \times n$ matrix C can be provided, where element c_{ij}, $1 \leq i, j \leq n$, denotes the number of wires between modules i and j. Given a floorplan, its quality is typically measured by the area of the enveloping rectangle, the center-to-center total wirelength, or a weighted sum of the area and the wirelength. If d_{ij} denotes the center-to-center Manhattan distance between basic rectangles (or modules) i and j, $1 \leq i, j \leq n$, the total wirelength can be defined to be $\sum_{1 \leq i,j \leq n} d_{ij}c_{ij}$. Therefore, the floorplan design problem asks to find a floorplan that minimizes a given cost measure subject to the area and shape constraints imposed on each module. Moreover, a designer can also specify the range of the aspect ratio of the chip to constrain the final floorplan to have a certain shape.

9.3 SLICING FLOORPLAN REPRESENTATIONS

In this section, we describe two well-known and frequently used representations, slicing tree [1,3] and Polish expression [2], for slicing floorplans. Their details are given in Sections 9.3.1 and 9.3.2.

9.3.1 SLICING TREE

The hierarchical structure of a slicing floorplan can be described by an oriented rooted binary tree, called slicing tree[*] [1,3]. Figure 9.1b shows a slicing tree for the slicing floorplan given in Figure 9.1a. Each internal node of a slicing tree is labeled with either V or H, denoting either a vertical or a horizontal cut. Each leaf denotes a room (or module) and is labeled by a number between 1 and n. A slicing tree is said to be skewed if no node and its right child have the same label [2]. Figure 9.1c is a skewed slicing tree while Figure 9.1b is not, although both slicing trees represent the same floorplan. From Figure 9.1, it is clear that a slicing floorplan may be represented by more than one slicing tree. These slicing trees correspond to different orders in which consecutive horizontal and vertical cuts are made. In fact, a skewed slicing tree is obtained by making consecutive horizontal cuts from top to bottom, and consecutive vertical cuts from right to left. It can be proved that the skewed slicing tree is unique for a given slicing floorplan.

It should be noted that a slicing tree is only a top-down description of the cut types (horizontal or vertical) for a given slicing floorplan, and no dimensional information is associated with each cut. Therefore, a slicing tree may represent more than one slicing floorplan. These floorplans differ in the dimensions for the rooms. An equivalence relation can be defined on the set of all slicing floorplans with n modules. Given two different floorplans, they are said to be equivalent iff they

---

[*] There are slicing floorplans that can be also represented by trees such that internal nodes in these trees have more than two children. These trees can always be transformed into binary trees. Therefore, using a binary tree to represent a slicing floorplan causes no loss of generality.

are represented by the same skewed slicing tree. As a result, the set of slicing floorplans can be partitioned into equivalence classes, where each equivalence class of slicing floorplans corresponds to a different slicing structure. Therefore, we can use the set of skewed slicing trees with n leaves to represent the set of slicing structures with n modules without causing any redundancies. As we shall see in Section 9.4, there are efficient algorithms for selecting a "best" floorplan (e.g., measured by the floorplan area) among the floorplans with the same slicing structure.

9.3.2 POLISH EXPRESSION

Given a slicing tree, we can obtain the corresponding Polish expression by performing the postorder traversal of the tree [2]. For example, the Polish expressions for the two slicing trees shown in Figure 9.1b and c are 412H3VV and 412HV3V, respectively. Clearly, there may be more than one Polish expression that represents the same slicing floorplan. This makes the Polish expression representation (or equivalently the slicing tree representation) an undesirable choice for representing solutions at least for the following reasons. First, the solution space is unnecessarily increased. Second, the set of slicing structures is not evenly distributed over the set of Polish expressions, causing undesirable biases toward some slicing structures. Because there is always only one skewed slicing tree for representing a slicing structure, the corresponding normalized Polish expression is thus defined and obtained by performing the postorder traversal of the skewed slicing tree [2]. Because no internal node and its right child have the same cut type in a skewed slicing tree, there are no consecutive V's or H's in the corresponding normalized Polish expression. Besides, it can be also proved that there is a one-to-one correspondence between the set of normalized Polish expressions of length $2n - 1$ and the set of slicing structures with n modules.

9.4 OPTIMIZATIONS ON SLICING FLOORPLANS

One approach to floorplan design is to first determine a floorplan topology (the slicing structure for a slicing floorplan), that is, the relative positions of the modules by using the wiring information among the modules. On the basis of the floorplan topology, various optimization problems are then solved to minimize a given cost measure. Among them, the area optimization determines a shape for each module such that the area of the resultant floorplan is minimized [3–6]. Besides, if each module is also given a power consumption value associated with each allowable shape, the area/power optimization problem can be defined to select a shape as well as its associated power consumption value for each module such that the power (obtained by summing up the power consumption values of all modules) and the area of the resultant floorplan are optimized simultaneously [7]. In this section we address several variants of the area optimization problem and the area/power optimization problem for slicing floorplans, and introduce their efficient solutions.

9.4.1 AREA OPTIMIZATION

In this subsection, our focus is on slicing floorplan area optimization. We assume that the given slicing structure is specified by a slicing tree. Two variants of slicing floorplan area optimization are addressed. The first one assumes that the given slicing tree is oriented in the sense that the cut type of each internal node is explicitly specified. Such an oriented tree complies exactly with the definition of a slicing tree as given in Section 9.3. On the other hand, to increase the chance of further minimizing floorplan area, the second variant assumes that the given tree is unoriented, which means that the cut type of each internal node is not specified and thus needs to be determined as well.

9.4.1.1 Oriented Slicing Tree

For the case where an oriented slicing tree is given, we describe three algorithms by Stockmeyer [3], Shi [4], and Otten [5].

9.4.1.1.1 Stockmeyer's Algorithm

In Ref. [3], Stockmeyer considers the module orientation problem where each module is rigid but may be rotated. Therefore, each module has at most two possible shapes. The shape curve for each such module looks like the one shown in Figure 9.2a or b. Given an oriented slicing tree and the possible shapes of each module, Stockmeyer gives an efficient algorithm to select a shape for each module such that the resulting floorplan has the smallest area among all equivalent floorplans represented by the given slicing tree.

Let T be the given slicing tree, u be a node of T, and $L(u)$ be the set of leaves in the subtree rooted at u. Stockmeyer's algorithm constructs a list of pairs, $\{(w_1, h_1), (w_2, h_2), \ldots, (w_k, h_k)\}$, with $k \leq |L(u)| + 1, w_1 > w_2 > \cdots > w_k$ and $h_1 < h_2 < \cdots < h_k$ for u. The first and second numbers in each pair denote the width and the height of a module (if u is a leaf) or a subfloorplan (if u is an internal node), respectively. Besides, two pointers are kept for each pair in the list to facilitate the determination of the shape for each module that achieves the minimum-area floorplan.

The construction is done in bottom-up manner. For a leaf of T, the algorithm constructs a list to store the shapes of the corresponding module. If a module has dimensions w and h with $w > h$, the list is $\{(w, h), (h, w)\}$. On the other hand, if $w = h$ or the module has a fixed orientation, only one pair (w, h) is stored in the list. The two pointers of each pair are null. For an internal node u of T with children u_1 and u_2, let $\{(w_1, h_1), (w_2, h_2), \ldots, (w_m, h_m)\}$ and $\{(w'_1, h'_1), (w'_2, h'_2), \ldots, (w'_k, h'_k)\}$ be the two lists of pairs which have been constructed for u_1 and u_2, respectively. Besides, we have $m \leq |L(u_1)| + 1$ and $k \leq |L(u_2)| + 1$. Suppose u corresponds to a horizontal cut. Then a pair (w_i, h_i) from u_1 and a pair (w'_j, h'_j) from u_2 can be combined to get a pair $(\max(w_i, w'_j), h_i + h'_j)$ in the list for u. It is clear that that not all mk such new pairs need consideration if some of them are redundant. For example, with $w_i > w'_j$, there is no need to combine (w_i, h_i) and (w'_z, h'_z) for any $z > j$ because $\max(w_i, w'_j) = \max(w_i, w'_z) = w_i$, and $h_i + h'_j < h_i + h'_z$. (Note that in this case $(\max(w_i, w'_z), h_i + h'_z)$ is redundant.) Therefore, the following procedure, similar to merging two sorted lists, is used for combining the two lists to obtain the list for u.

1. $i \leftarrow 1, j \leftarrow 1$.
2. If $i > m$ or $j > k$ then terminate.
3. Add $(\max(w_i, w'_j), h_i + h'_j)$ to the list for u with pointers to (w_i, h_i) and (w'_j, h'_j).
4. If $w_i > w'_j$, then $i \leftarrow i + 1$ and goto (2).
5. If $w_i < w'_j$, then $j \leftarrow j + 1$ and goto (2).
6. If $w_i = w'_j$ then $i \leftarrow i + 1, j \leftarrow j + 1$, and goto (2).

Clearly, the time complexity of the procedure is linear, that is, $O(m + k)$, and the length of the list produced for u is at most $m + k - 1 \leq |L(u_1)| + 1 + |L(u_2)| + 1 - 1 = |L(u)| + 1$. The procedure can be easily modified if u corresponds to a vertical cut.

After the list for the root of T is constructed, a pair producing the minimum area (and satisfying the given chip aspect ratio constraint) is chosen and the corresponding pointers are used to determine the shape of each module in a top-down manner. The time complexity of the whole algorithm is $O(n^2)$ in the worst case, where n is the number of modules. It should be pointed out that the algorithm can be naturally applied to handle the general case where modules may have more than two possible shapes.

9.4.1.1.2 Shi's Algorithm

In Ref. [4], Shi considers the same area optimization problem as in Ref. [3] and presents a faster algorithm that runs in $O(m \log m)$ time, where m is the total number of possible shapes of all modules. This complexity does not depend on the number of modules, the depth of the slicing tree, or the distribution of the m shapes among the modules. He also proves that $O(m \log m)$ is the lower bound on the time complexity for any area minimization algorithm, which implies that his algorithm has an optimal runtime.

Instead of using a list to store the set of possible shapes for each node u of a slicing tree, Shi's algorithm uses a balanced binary tree (e.g., AVL tree [8] or red–black tree [9]), denoted by $BBT(u)$. We call $BBT(u)$ the shape tree for u. For every irredundant shape s of u, there is a node $v(s)$ in $BBT(u)$ having the following four major fields:

$w[v(s)]$: to be used for computing the width of s
$h[v(s)]$: to be used for computing the height of s
$w^+[v(s)]$: to be added to the widths of all descendents of $v(s)$
$h^+[v(s)]$: to be added to the heights of all descendents of $v(s)$

$BBT(u)$ has the height and the width as two keys, and a search, insertion, or deletion can be performed on either key. However, the width $w(s)$ and the height $h(s)$ of s are not explicitly stored in the corresponding node $v(s)$. Instead, they are stored in the path from the root of $BBT(u)$ to $v(s)$. Let $P(s)$ be the set of nodes on the path from the root of $BBT(u)$ to $v(s)$. The width and the height of s are computed as follows:

$$w(s) = w[v(s)] + \sum_{v' \in P(s)} w^+[V']$$

$$h(s) = h[v(s)] + \sum_{v' \in P(s)} h^+[V']$$

For example, a balanced binary tree storing five shapes (5,5), (4,6), (3,7), (2,8), and (1,9) are shown in Figure 9.3. The reason for introducing the two fields h^+ and w^+ is as follows. Suppose u is an internal node of the slicing tree T, has two children u_1 and u_2, and corresponds to a horizontal cut. Suppose that we want to combine k shapes $s_1, s_2, \ldots, s_k$ of u_1 with a shape t of u_2 to get k shapes of u. Let $BBT(u_1)$ denote the tree storing the list of shapes, $s_1, s_2, \ldots, s_k$ of u_1. Also assume that the widths of $s_1, s_2, \ldots, s_k$ are all greater than the width of t. To combine s_i's and t, Stockmeyer's algorithm will add the height of t to the heights of $s_1, s_2, \ldots, s_k$ and take $O(k)$ time. However, it takes only $O(1)$ time for Shi's algorithm to add the height of t to the h^+ field of the root of $BBT(u_1)$. Now $BBT(u_1)$ becomes a shape tree for u. The h^+ value will be propagated down and added to the height of a node in $BBT(u_1)$ as soon as the corresponding shape is accessed in the future. As a result, repeated and unnecessary updates can be avoided by postponing the propagation until future access happens.

We next explain how to construct the irredundant shapes for an internal node u of T with children u_1 and u_2 and store them in a shape tree $BBT(u)$. Assume the irredundant shapes of u_1 and u_2 have

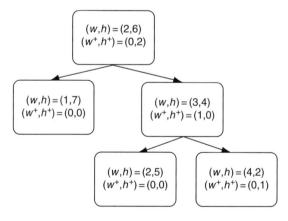

FIGURE 9.3   Balanced binary tree storing five shapes.

been obtained and stored in the shape trees $BBT(u_1)$ and $BBT(u_2)$, respectively. Let the number of shapes in $BBT(u_1)$ and $BBT(u_2)$ be m_1 and m_2. Without loss of generality, we assume $m_1 \geq m_2$. The shape tree $BBT(u)$ is constructed in the following three steps. The first step is to find irredundant shapes of u such that their widths are decided by u_2, or by u_1 and u_2, and to store them in a list L for later use. The second step is to find irredundant shapes of u such that their heights are decided by u_1. The last step is to insert the list L generated in the first step into the shape tree obtained in the second step. The three steps are implemented by performing search, insertion, and deletion operations on $BBT(u_1)$ in an efficient way such that $BBT(u_1)$ becomes the shape tree for u at the end.

9.4.1.1.3 Otten's Algorithm

Recall from Section 9.2 that each point on the shape curve of a module denotes a possible shape of the module. The shape curve of a module can be naturally generalized to a subfloorplan that corresponds to an internal node of a slicing tree. Let u be an internal node of a given slicing tree with children u_1 and u_2. Let $C(u)$, $C(u_1)$, and $C(u_2)$ denote the shape curves of u, u_1, and u_2, respectively. Let $C(u_1) + C(u_2)$ be the shape curve obtained by adding $C(u_1)$ and $C(u_2)$ along the y-direction; that is, $C(u_1) + C(u_2) = \{(x, y + y')|(x, y) \in C(u_1) \text{ and } (x, y') \in C(u_2)\}$ (Figure 9.4a). Let $C(u_1)^*C(u_2)$ be the shape curve obtained by adding $C(u_1)$ and $C(u_2)$ along the x-direction; that is, $C(u_1)^*C(u_2) = \{(x + x', y)|(x, y) \in C(u_1) \text{ and } (x', y) \in C(u_2)\}$. Otten in Ref. [5] observes that if u corresponds to a horizontal cut, $C(u)$ can be obtained from $C(u_1) + C(u_2)$. On the other hand, if u is a vertical cut, $C(u)$ can be obtained from $C(u_1)^*C(u_2)$. It is easy to see that $C(u)$ produced in either way is also a shape curve. Moreover, $C(u)$ is piecewise linear if both $C(u_1)$ and $C(u_2)$ are piecewise linear. The shape curves shown in Figure 9.2a and b (both are also called staircase shape curves) and Figure 9.4b are all piecewise linear. Any piecewise linear shape curve can be completely characterized by an ordered list of all its corners. (For example, $\{a\}$, $\{a, d\}$ and $\{a, b, c, d, e\}$ are the ordered lists of corners of the curves shown in Figures 9.2a,b and 9.4b, respectively.) For piecewise linear shape curves, Otten gives an efficient algorithm that computes $C(u)$ by adding $C(u_1)$ and $C(u_2)$ at the corners along a corresponding direction.

It should be pointed out although Stockmeyer's algorithm originally only targets the set of staircase shape curves (which is a subset of all piecewise linear curves), it is also directly applicable to piecewise linear curves because it adopts the same idea as Otten's algorithm (though both algorithms were developed independently).

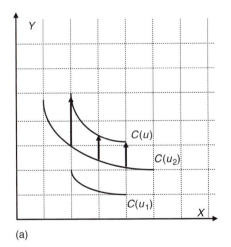
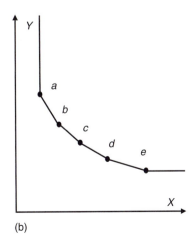

(a)   (b)

FIGURE 9.4 (a) Adding two shape curves along the y-direction. (b) Piecewise linear shape curve.

9.4.1.2 Unoriented Slicing Tree

In Ref. [6], Zimmermann studies a variant of the area optimization problem in which no assumption is made about the cut type of each internal node in a slicing tree. He presents an algorithm that first computes the two shape curves for each internal node, one for a vertical cut and the other for a horizontal cut. See Figure 9.5 for an illustration, where the shape curves in Figure 9.5c and d are obtained by adding the two shape curves in Figure 9.5a and b along the y-direction (corresponding to a horizontal cut) and the x-direction (corresponding to a vertical cut), respectively. Then the lower bound of the two shape curves is chosen at each x coordinate to produce the final shape curve of this internal node (see Figure 9.5e where the final shape curve is shown in boldface). In addition, each segment of the final shape curve can be marked to represent the chosen cut type. This algorithm has exponential-time complexity in the worst case even if the shape curve of each module is piecewise linear, but has pseudopolynomial complexity when each module has integer dimensions.

9.4.2 AREA/POWER OPTIMIZATION

In Ref. [7], Chao and Wong study an optimization problem that considers both area and power. For each possible shape of a module in the problem, a power consumption value is also given and associated with the shape. Each possible shape together with its associated power consumption value are called an implementation. Given a slicing tree, the problem asks to select an implementation for each module based on the power and geometrical information such that both the area and the power consumption of the resultant floorplan are optimized. The power consumption of a floorplan is obtained by adding up the power consumption value of the selected implementation of each module.

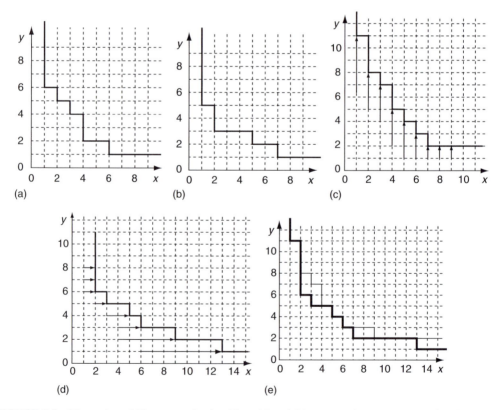

FIGURE 9.5 Illustration of Zimmerman's algorithm. (a) and (b) are two shape curves, (c) the shape curve obtained by adding the two shape curves in (a) and (b) along the y-direction, (d) the shape curve obtained by adding the two shape curves in (a) and (b) along the x-direction, and (e) the shape curve (in boldface) obtained by choosing the lower bound of the two shape curves in (c) and (d) at each x coordinate.

Two versions of the optimization problem are considered. The first one is to minimize the floorplan power consumption subject to a given upper bound on the floorplan area. Another one is to minimize the floorplan area subject to a given upper bound on the floorplan power consumption. Both versions can be solved by almost the same algorithm. The only difference is the criterion for selecting a best implementation for the floorplan after the set of implementations is constructed for the floorplan.

Suppose each implementation of a module is denoted by a triple (w, h, e) where w, h, e represent the width, the height, and the power consumption value, respectively. Also assume that each implementation is irredundant. (An implementation (w, h, e) is redundant if there is another implementation (w', h', e') of the same module such that $x \geq x', y \geq y'$, and $e \geq e'$.) Let Q be the set of possible implementations of a module, and $\{e_1, e_2, \ldots, e_k\}$ be the set of distinct power consumption values in Q. Q is first partitioned into k disjoint sets, $Q_1, Q_2, \ldots, Q_k$ such that each implementation in Q_i has the same power consumption value p_i, $1 \leq i \leq k$. The geometric information of the implementations in Q_i is denoted by the set $\{(w, h) | (w, h, e) \in Q_i\}$, which is assumed to be specified by a piecewise linear shape curve C_i. The pair (p_i, C_i) is called a power-indexed shape curve. Let C and C' denote two piecewise linear shape curves. Given two power-indexed shape curves (C, e) and (C', e'), $(C, e) + (C', e')$ $((C, e)^*(C', e'))$, respectively) is defined to be the power-indexed shape curve $(C + C', e + e')$ $((C^*C', e + e'))$, respectively). (Recall that both $C + C'$ and C^*C' can be efficiently computed [3–5].) Let $S = \{(C_1, e_1), (C_2, e_2), \ldots, (C_l, e_l)\}$ and $S' = \{(C'_1, e'_1), (C'_2, e'_2), \ldots, (C'_k, e'_k)\}$ be two sets of power-indexed shape curves. We define $S + S'$ $(S + S'$, respectively) to be $\{(C_i + C'_j, e_i + e'_j) | 1 \leq i \leq l, 1 \leq j \leq k\}$ $(\{(C_i^*C'_j, e_i + e'_j) | 1 \leq i \leq l, 1 \leq j \leq k\}$, respectively).

The algorithm constructs a set of power-indexed shape curves for every internal node in a bottom-up fashion. Let u be an internal node with children u_1 and u_2. Let $S(u)$, $S(u_1)$, and $S(u_2)$ denote the sets of power-indexed shape curves of u, u_1, and u_2, respectively. $S(u)$ can be constructed by $S(u_1) + S(u_2)$ (if u is a horizontal cut) or $S(u_1)^*S(u_2)$ (if u is a vertical cut). Besides, if there exist two power-indexed shape curves in $S(u)$ having the same power consumption value, they can be combined into one by merging their shape curves. Once the set of power-indexed shape curves for the root, say $S = \{(C_1, e_1), (C_2, e_2), \ldots, (C_l, e_l)\}$, is computed, the area of every irredundant implementation of the root can be calculated from a corner on each C_i. Among those implementations whose power consumption (area, respectively) satisfies the given power (area, respectively) bound, the one with minimum area (minimum power, respectively) is selected.

The algorithm has exponential-time complexity in the worst case, but if each implementation of any module has integer power consumption value and dimensions, the algorithm runs in pseudopolynomial time.

9.5   CLASSICAL SLICING FLOORPLAN DESIGN

The slicing floorplan design problem in general can be solved by the following two typical approaches. The first approach is to derive the final solution in two stages. It first determines a slicing structure (or an initial floorplan) using wiring information among modules (and possibly area information of modules), and then uses the geometric shape information of the modules to solve some optimization problems, for example, those introduced in the previous section, on the slicing structure and to produce the final solution. The mincut-based methods [10,11] and the point-configuration based methods [1,12] fall into this type of approach. Another approach to solve the floorplan design problem is by simultaneously considering the interconnection information as well as the area and shape information. This approach starts with an initial floorplan and iteratively improves solutions by taking both interconnect and shape information into account until the convergence is reached or the runtime exceeds. The simulated annealing based algorithm [2], which uses the set of normalized Polish expressions as the solution space, belongs to this type of approach.

It will require more than a single chapter to review all existing methods for slicing floorplan design. Therefore, our focus in this section is on introducing some classical methods, including the mincut-based methods [10,11], the point-configuration based methods [1,12], and the simulated annealing based method [2], which fall into the above-mentioned two types of approaches.

9.5.1 MINCUT-BASED SLICING FLOORPLAN DESIGN

A typical mincut-based method is to first apply a mincut partitioning algorithm (e.g., [13–15]) to generate a slicing structure (or an initial floorplan) and then use various optimization techniques to generate the final solution. During the mincut partitioning process, the shape of each module is ignored, and only its area is taken into account. This process is equivalent to a sequence of partitioning steps each of which divides a set of modules into two subsets such that the number of nets connecting modules from both subsets and the area difference between the two subsets are small. The partitioning process terminates when each subset contains only one module. The algorithms in Refs. [10,11] are classified as this type of approach, and are described below.

The mincut-based algorithm given in Ref. [10] assumes that the modules to be placed are all hard modules, but can be rotated and reflected. Throughout the mincut partitioning process, the chip layout is represented by a pair of dual graphs $G_x = (V_x, E_x)$ and $G_Y = (V_x, E_y)$. Each of G_x and G_y is a planar, directed acyclic graph (DAG) containing one source and one sink, and may have parallel edges. There is a one-to-one correspondence between the edges of G_x and G_y, and each corresponding pair of edges (e_x, e_y) represents a rectangle with width $l(e_x)$ and height $l(e_y)$, where $l(e)$ denotes the length associated with edge e. Besides, each pair of edges (e_x, e_y) also corresponds to a subset of modules; the area $l(e_x) \times l(e_y)$ equals the total area of the modules in the subset. At the beginning, both G_x and G_y contain one edge each, e_x and e_y, and this pair of edges corresponds to the set of all modules. The chip layout covered by the modules is assumed to be square, and therefore both $l(e_x)$ and $l(e_y)$ are set to be $\sqrt{A}$, where A is the total area of the modules. The set of all modules is then partitioned into two subsets using a modified Kernighan–Lin algorithm [13,14] such that the number of nets incident to modules in different subsets is as small as possible and the area difference in the two subsets does not exceed a predefined value. This step also corresponds to a splitting of the edge pair into two new edge pairs each of which represents one subset. The length of each edge in G_x is adjusted according to the total module area of the corresponding subset. The partitioning procedure is applied to both of the subsets, but the cut direction is changed and therefore the edge lengths in G_y need adjusting afterward. The partitioning algorithm is applied recursively to the new subsets until each subset contains one module. Now each edge pair of G_x and G_y corresponds to a module, but the shape of the module is not correctly represented. To fix it, the lengths of each edge pair are first replaced by the dimensions of the corresponding module, and then in both graphs a longest path from the source to each node is calculated to get the position of the corresponding module.

It is clear that the mincut partitioning process induces a slicing floorplan due to the nature of recursive mincut partitioning. To further reduce the area or wirelength of the floorplan, three methods, rotation, squeezing, and reflecting, are applied. To rotate a module, the width and height of the module are exchanged. The squeezing technique splits a node into two nodes and inserts a zero-length edge pair. The reflection technique flips a module with respect to the x- or y-axis. Reflection of a module only influences the wirelength. Note that squeezing causes local changes in a graph, and therefore may destroy the slicing structure.

In contrast to the above-mentioned algorithm, another mincut partitioning based method, called Mason [11] allows each module to have a number of possible shapes (i.e., soft module), and uses a slicing tree (instead of a pair of dual graphs) to represent the partitioning hierarchy. At each partitioning step, an in-place partitioning scheme is applied together with a combined exhaustive and heuristic partitioning method. The idea behind in-place partitioning is to perform partitioning by taking external connections into account, resulting in a better global positioning of modules. The exhaustive partitioning procedure enumerates all possible solutions to find the optimal solution. On the other hand, the heuristic partitioning method adopts the Fiduccia–Mattheyses method [15]. Whether the exhaustive or heuristic method is used for a partitioning step is based on the number of modules to be partitioned. Once the slicing tree is constructed, the dimensions and position of each module are determined by an area optimization method similar to those in Refs. [3–5].

9.5.2   Point-Configuration Based Slicing Floorplan Design

The point-configuration based approach treats each module as a point by ignoring the area of the module. It is based on using the interconnection information as the only measure of the mutual proximity between modules, and uses a mathematical method involving matrix manipulation to position the modules as points in the plane. From this point configuration, a slicing structure is constructed by taking module areas and shapes into consideration. Finally, various optimization procedures are applied to produce the positions and orientations (or dimensions) of the modules realizing the final floorplan under a cost measure. The algorithms in Refs. [1,12] are classified as this type of approach, and are introduced below.

The algorithm in Ref. [12] combines the advantages of force-directed placement and mincut algorithm. A force-directed placement algorithm solves a system of differential equations that considers interconnection information. It is fast in calculating a point configuration, but modules may overlap in the solution because it ignores the size and shape information of the modules. On the other hand, a mincut algorithm can effectively consider module areas during the partitioning process, but due to its sequential nature, the partitioning result depends on the starting solution and the amount of nets cut is minimized only locally. Therefore, the algorithm in Ref. [12] uses a modified Newton–Raphson method [16] to calculate a point configuration, and a cut algorithm to calculate a slicing floorplan based on the point configuration as well as the shapes of the modules. In fact, the cut algorithm does not need a partitioning algorithm like the ones in Refs. [13–15]; instead it uses the point configuration produced by the force-directed algorithm. Each cutline (which carries the position information on the fixed-area chip and thus geometrically separates modules into two parts) is determined with respect to the constraints such as the sizes and shapes of the modules, the number of modules per subset, and the minimization of critical signal nets. The cut algorithm terminates when each subset (corresponding to a basic rectangle on the chip plane) contains only one module. A slicing structure is implied by the cut algorithm, but due to the shape mismatches between basic rectangles and modules, modules may overlap. To eliminate module overlaps, modules are moved and rotated by taking module shapes into consideration.

Another point-configuration based algorithm is given in Ref. [1]. To get a point configuration, the algorithm in Ref. [1] first defines a dutch metric D which is an $n \times n$ matrix with each off-diagonal element d_{ij} being $1 - c_{ij}$, and each diagonal element being 0, where $c_{ij} = \frac{\Sigma\{w_k | p_{ik}=1 \text{ and } p_{jk}=1\}}{\Sigma\{w_k | p_{ik}=1 \text{ or } p_{jk}=1\}}$. Note that w_k is the weight given for net k (the higher the weight of a net, the closer the modules connected by the net should be), and $p_{ik} = 1$ if module i is connected to net k, otherwise $p_{ik} = 0$. With the matrix D, the Schoenberg matrix $-(1/2)ZDZ$ is formed and the partial eigensolution containing the two largest eigenvalues are obtained, where Z, I, J are $n \times n$ matrices, $Z = J - (1/n)I$, I has all elements being 1, and J has each diagonal element being 1 and the other elements being 0. The corresponding two-dimensional point configuration of the modules is now specified by the two eigenvectors. Next, using the information on module areas and assuming that all modules are flexible, but their shapes are close to square, a slicing structure is constructed based on deformation calculation. The consequence of this construction is that modules with points relatively far from each other are separated after a few cutlines while modules with points at a relatively short distance are together in many nested cutlines. Moreover, the relative positions of the modules in the slicing structure will closely resemble those of the corresponding points in the Schoenberg construction. Finally, the wiring space in the structure can be estimated and translated into a set of constraints for an optimization procedure to produce the position and orientation of each module that realizes the best final floorplan subject to these constraints.

9.5.3   Simulated Annealing Based Slicing Floorplan Design

Wong and Liu in Ref. [2] present a slicing floorplan design algorithm that simultaneously minimizes the chip area and the total wirelength. Their algorithm is referred to as the Wong–Liu algorithm

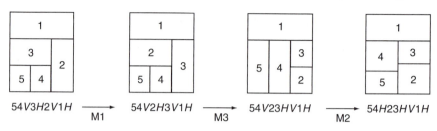

$$54V3H2V1H \xrightarrow{M1} 54V2H3V1H \xrightarrow{M3} 54V23HV1H \xrightarrow{M2} 54H23HV1H$$

FIGURE 9.6 Illustration of three types of moves.

in the rest of this chapter. It employs the technique of simulated annealing [17], and uses the set of normalized Polish expressions as the solution space to avoid an unnecessarily large number of states and thus enables the speedup of the search procedure significantly. The following three types of moves, M1, M2, and M3, are used to modify a normalized Polish expression to get a neighboring one.

> M1: Swap two adjacent modules. (Two modules are adjacent iff there is no other module between them in the expression.)
> M2: Complement a chain of cuts. (A chain of cuts is a sequence of consecutive elements in the expression such that each element is a cut [i.e., V or H]. V and H are complements of each other.)
> M3: Swap adjacent module and cut. (A module and a cut are adjacent iff they are consecutive elements in the expression.)

It is clear that M1 and M2 each always produce a normalized Polish expression. M3, however, might not produce a normalized Polish expression. To generate an M3 move, a pair of adjacent module and cut is repeatedly chosen until swapping them will lead to a normalized Polish expression. It is claimed that the three types of moves are sufficient to ensure that any normalized Polish expression can be reached from any other via a finite number of moves. Figure 9.6 gives a demonstration of the three types of moves.

Each normalized Polish expression generated in the annealing process will be evaluated as follows. Let T_f denote the corresponding slicing structure for a normalized Polish expression f. The area A and the total wirelength W of f are defined to be the area and the total wirelength of a minimum-area floorplan of T_f. The cost function for measuring the quality of a normalized Polish expression is $A + \lambda W$, where λ is a user-specified constant to control the relative importance of A and W. The minimum-area floorplan can be computed efficiently by the slicing floorplan area optimization algorithms [3–5]. In fact, it is observed that the calculation of a minimum-area floorplan can be done in an incremental manner because the calculation only needs to be performed on tree nodes that are changed after a move of type M1, M2, or M3.

9.6 SLICING FLOORPLAN DESIGN CONSIDERING PLACEMENT CONSTRAINTS

In floorplan design, it is useful if a designer is allowed to specify some placement constraints to be satisfied in the final floorplan. Typical placement constraints that have been addressed for slicing floorplans are boundary constraints [18–20], range constraints [21], abutment constraints [22], and clustering constraints [23]. In this section, we describe each type of placement constraint, and highlight existing techniques to handle it during floorplan design. As a matter of fact, most of the techniques are extensions of the Wong–Liu algorithm [2].

9.6.1 BOUNDARY CONSTRAINTS

A boundary constraint forces some modules to be positioned along one of the four sides of a floorplan. It is particularly useful when a designer wants to place some modules along the boundaries for shorter input–output connections. Besides, floorplan design is usually done in a hierarchical manner in which modules are grouped into different units and the floorplan of each unit is independently determined. For this case, it helps if some modules are constrained to be placed along a boundary of the unit so that they are closer to other modules in neighboring units.

Boundary constraints can be specified as follows. The set of all modules is divided into five disjoint module sets M_F, M_L, M_R, M_T, M_B. Each module in M_F is a free module that can be placed anywhere in a floorplan. On the other hand, each module in M_L (M_R, M_T, M_B, respectively) is a boundary-constrained module with the left (right, top, bottom, respectively) boundary constraint and has to be placed along the left (right, top, bottom, respectively) boundary of the floorplan. Note that M_L (M_R, M_T, M_B, respectively) may be an empty set if no module must be placed along the left (right, top, bottom, respectively) boundary. For example, for the two slicing floorplans shown in Figure 9.7a and b, if module 2 is constrained to be placed along the left boundary, then the one in Figure 9.7a is infeasible while the one in Figure 9.7b is feasible.

A result on the boundary-constrained problem is reported by Young and Wong in Ref. [18]. They enhance the Wong–Liu algorithm [2] to handle boundary constraints. Their main idea is to check the normalized Polish expression in each iteration of the simulated annealing process to see whether the given boundary constraints are satisfied. Then their algorithm fixes the violated constraints (if any) as much as possible, and includes a term in the cost function to penalize the remaining violations.

A linear-time method is used to find the boundary information for each module in a normalized Polish expression. The boundary information of a module tells whether there are modules on the left of, on the right of, above, and below the module. Because a Polish expression or a slicing tree has the relative position information among modules (e.g., the Polish expression ijH means that module i is below module j, while the expression ijV means that module i is on the left of module j), the following facts can be observed. If module i must be placed on the right (left, respectively) boundary of the final floorplan, i cannot be in the left (right, respectively) subtree of any internal node labeled with V. On the other hand, if module i must be placed at the top (bottom, respectively) boundary of the final floorplan, i cannot be in the left (right, respectively) subtree of any internal node labeled with H. On the basis of these facts, the boundary information of each module can be obtained by scanning the Polish expression once from right to left and by using a stack.

Once the boundary information is known, all the modules violating their boundary constraints can be determined, and the algorithm fixes as many violations as possible by shuffling the modules. If module i is not placed along the required boundary, it will be shuffled with another module j which is closest to i in the Polish expression and is placed at a position satisfying the boundary constraint of i. This fixing procedure takes $O(mn)$ for each expression, where m is the number of constrained modules and n is the total number of modules. If there are still some constraints that cannot be satisfied after all possible shufflings, a penalty term is included in the cost function. The

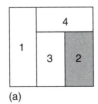
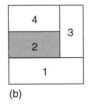

(a)   (b)

FIGURE 9.7 Illustration of infeasible and feasible floorplans with a boundary constraint. (a) An infeasible floorplan where module 2 cannot be placed along the left boundary and (b) a feasible floorplan where module 2 can be placed along the left boundary.

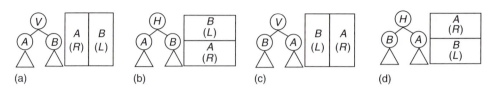

FIGURE 9.8 Examples of feasible and infeasible topologies. (a) A floorplan having an infeasible topology, (b) a floorplan having a feasible topology, obtained by performing an O_1 operation on the root of the tree in (a), (c) a floorplan having a feasible topology, obtained by performing an O_2 operation on the root of the tree in (a), and (d) a floorplan having a feasible topology, obtained by performing an O_3 operation on the root of the tree in (a).

penalty term is measured by the total distance of the modules from the boundaries of the floorplan along which they are required to be placed.

Because the above-mentioned algorithm [18] also adopts the same set of moves as the Wong–Liu algorithm (i.e., M1, M2, and M3 described in Section 9.5.3) to generate a neighboring normalized Polish expression, it is very likely that only a subset of modules has changed the boundary information in the new normalized Polish expression, and therefore only the boundary information for those modules needs to be recomputed. On the basis of this observation, three speedup methods capable of performing incremental calculation of boundary information are given in Ref. [19].

A drawback with the algorithm in Ref. [18] is that the shuffling method may not always resolve all constraint violations even though a penalty term is added to the cost function to account for those violations. This has been empirically confirmed in Ref. [20], implying that the algorithm in Ref. [18] cannot guarantee that a floorplan satisfying all given boundary constraints is always obtainable unless the annealing process is long enough. To cope with this difficulty, Liu et al. developed a quadratic-time method that transforms a normalized Polish expression with constraint violations into another one with all violations eliminated [20]. The main idea is to examine each internal node of a slicing tree (constructed from a normalized Polish expression) in a bottom-up fashion and determine if the node has a feasible topology or not. (An internal node has a feasible topology if it is feasible to place each boundary-constrained module along the required boundary in its corresponding subfloorplan.) If the node has an infeasible topology, the tree will be modified such that the node ends up with a feasible topology. Three operations, O_1, O_2, and O_3, are given to perform modifications. An O_1 operation changes the cut direction of a node, an O_2 operation swaps the left and the right subtrees of a node, and an O_3 operation performs an O_1 operation followed by an O_2 operation. For example, suppose subfloorplan A contains modules having the right boundary constraint (denoted by R), subfloorplan B contains modules having the left boundary constraint (denoted by L), and both A and B have feasible topologies. Figure 9.8a produces a floorplan having an infeasible topology, but the floorplans in Figure 9.8b through d all have feasible topologies. It is clear that Figure 9.8b through d can be transformed from Figure 9.8a by performing an O_2, an O_1, and an O_3 operation on the root, respectively. Although in most cases the three basic operations can transform nodes into ones having feasible topologies, there are also some cases where they fail. Besides, even if an internal node has a feasible topology, the tree needs to be modified as well for some cases to ensure that the root has a feasible topology later on. To handle these difficult cases, additional transformation operations are provided [20].

9.6.2 RANGE CONSTRAINTS

A range constraint forces a module to be placed within a given rectangular region in the final floorplan. It is less restrictive than a preplaced constraint, which requires a module to be placed at a fixed position in the final floorplan.[*] In fact, the range constraint problem is a more general problem because any preplaced constraint for a module can be written as a range constraint by specifying

---

[*] Note that the problem of floorplan design with obstacles can be solved by treating the obstacles as preplaced modules.

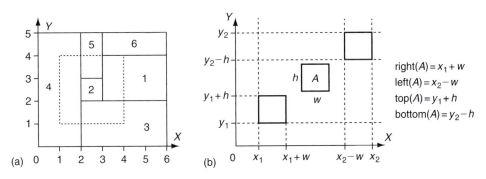

FIGURE 9.9 (a) Preplaced and range constraints. (b) Range constraint representation.

the rectangular region whose dimensions are the same as those of the module. Figure 9.9a gives an example where module 1 with a preplaced constraint must be placed with its lower left corner at $(3, 2)$ and module 2 with a range constraint must be placed within the dotted-line region. The floorplan shown in Figure 9.9a satisfies both constraints.

The preplaced constraint problem for slicing floorplans is considered in Ref. [24] which extends the Wong–Liu algorithm [2] by using the notion of reference point to construct shape curves in the presence of preplaced constraints. Young and Wong also present a slicing floorplanner with range constraints in Ref. [21], and empirically observe that when their floorplanner is specified to handle preplaced constraints, it outperforms the one in Ref. [24]. Therefore in this subsection we only introduce the algorithm in Ref. [21].

In the range constraint problem, two sets of modules, M_F and M_{Range}, are given, where each module in M_F does not have any placement constraint and each module in M_{Range} is a hard module and has a specified range constraint. The algorithm in Ref. [21] extends the Wong–Liu algorithm [2] to handle range constraints. The main contribution is a novel shape curve computation, which takes range constraints into consideration. When vertically or horizontally combining two modules, if at least one of them has a range constraint, the resultant subfloorplan will also have a range constraint. Therefore, the range constraint information will be propagated upward from the leaves to the root during the bottom-up shape curve construction process, and both the dimensional information, that is, the height and the width, and the range constraint information, need to be kept.

Let A be a subfloorplan (containing one or more modules) with a range constraint, the following four variables are used to represent the constraint:

- Top(A): Shortest distance of the upper boundary of A from the x-axis
- Bottom(A): Longest distance of the lower boundary of A from the x-axis
- Right(A): Shortest distance of the right boundary of A from the y-axis
- Left(A): Longest distance of the left boundary of A from the y-axis

We use Figure 9.9b to explain the four variables. In Figure 9.9b, A has width w and height h, and it is constrained to be placed inside the rectangle $\{(x, y)|x_1 \leq x \leq x_2, y_1 \leq y \leq y_2\}$. Then top($A$) = $y_1 + h$, bottom(A) = $y_2 - h$, right(A) = $x_1 + w$, and left(A) = $x_2 - w$. With a range constraint represented in such a manner, the traditional shape curve construction methods [3–5] are enhanced to compute the range constraint and dimensional information of a subfloorplan X from those of its two children subfloorplans A and B. In addition, if a normalized Polish expression does not satisfy all range constraints, the algorithm adds into the cost function a penalty term, which is measured by the total distance of the modules having range constraints from their desired regions.

9.6.3 ABUTMENT CONSTRAINTS

In foorplan design, a designer may want to have some modules abut one another to favor the transmission of data among those modules. This abutment problem is common in practice, but few

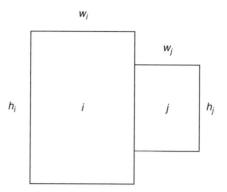

FIGURE 9.10   Horizontal abutment.

floorplanning algorithms can handle it. In this subsection, we describe a solution [22] to this problem for slicing floorplans. Although the floorplanning algorithm given in Ref. [22] is capable of handling L-shaped and T-shaped modules as well, a discussion of this is beyond the scope of this chapter.

Two modules i and j are said to abut horizontally (Figure 9.10), denoted by Habut(i, j), iff a vertical boundary L_i of module i and a vertical boundary L_j of module j abut such that L_i is immediately on the left of L_j and the abutment length is $\min\{l(L_i), l(L_j)\}$, where $l(L_i)$ is the length of L_i and $l(L_j)$ is the length of L_j. The vertical abutment constraint Vabut(i, j) can be defined similarly. Abutment constraints can be also generalized to involve more than two modules.

The algorithm extends the Wong–Liu algorithm [2] to handle abutment constraints. In each step of the simulated annealing process, through the use of a stack, a normalized Polish expression is scanned once to find the top, bottom, left, and right neighbors of every module. These topological relationships are independent of the dimensions of the modules, and can be derived based on the following observation. Let $L[X]$, $R[X]$, $T[X]$, and $B[X]$ denote the set of modules lying along the left boundary, right boundary, top boundary, and bottom boundary of a subfloorplan X. Consider putting X to the left of Y to get a new subfloorplan. If both $R[X]$ and $L[Y]$ have more than one module, the top module in $R[X]$ will abut horizontally with the top module in $L[Y]$ and the bottom module in $R[X]$ will abut horizontally with the bottom module in $L[Y]$. On the other hand, if either $R[X]$ or $L[Y]$ has only one module, every module in $R[X]$ will abut horizontally with every module in $L[Y]$. The vertical neighborhood relationship can be observed similarly.

Once the neighbors of each module are known, each abutment constraint can be checked. If the normalized Polish expression does not satisfy all abutment constraints, the algorithm will swap modules to satisfy the abutment constraints as much as possible. When a vertical abutment constraint for modules i and j, Vabut(i, j), is violated, the algorithm will first try to move j to the top of i by swapping j with the closest top neighbor of i in the Polish expression. If it fails, for example, all the top neighbors of i are fixed in their positions, the algorithm will try to move i to the bottom of j by swapping i with the closest bottom neighbor of j. The fixing procedure for a horizontal abutment constraint is defined similarly. It is likely that some constraints are still violated after all the possible swappings, and therefore a penalty term is added in the cost function to penalize those violations.

Scanning a Polish expression once to find the neighbors of every module takes $O(n)$ time, and swapping modules to fix violated abutment constraints takes $O(mn)$ time, where n is total number of modules and m is the total number of abutment constraints.

9.6.4   CLUSTERING CONSTRAINTS

A clustering constraint is to enforce some modules to be placed geometrically adjacent to each other in the final floorplan. By imposing the clustering constraint on modules that are heavily connected,

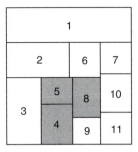

FIGURE 9.11 Feasible floorplan having three modules involved in a clustering constraint.

the routing cost among those modules can be reduced. In this subsection, we describe a recent work on slicing floorplan design considering clustering constraints [23].

A clustering constraint can be specified by a subset of modules such that all the modules in this subset are geometrically adjacent to each other in the final floorplan. Figure 9.11 shows an example of the clustering constraint, where modules 4, 5, and 8 are the modules to be clustered and they are placed adjacent to each other in the feasible floorplan as shown. In Ref. [23], an extension of the Wong–Liu algorithm [2] is presented to handle the clustering constraint problem. The extension includes a linear-time method to locate neighbors of a module from a normalized Polish expression and a method to swap the modules to satisfy the given clustering constraint. In each iteration of the annealing process, these two methods are used to transform a normalized Polish expression into another one that satisfies the given cluster constraint. A term measured by the sum of the center-to-center distances between the modules with the same cluster constraint is added to the cost function such that those modules can be placed more closely.

9.7   OTHER ADVANCES IN SLICING FLOORPLANS

We next address two important advances, one in the theoretical study on area-optimal slicing floorplans [25], and the other in the completeness of the slicing tree representation for general floorplans [26]. We then describe the respective algorithms [27,28] that make modern heterogeneous FPGAs and 3D ICs realizable in slicing floorplans.

9.7.1   THEORETICAL RESULTS FOR AREA-OPTIMAL SLICING FLOORPLANS

One possible concern about slicing floorplans is that even the slicing floorplan with optimal area may still be not good at packing modules tightly as a nonslicing one, and hence may introduce a larger chip area. Although, there is empirical evidence showing that comparable slicing floorplan results can be obtained using much less runtime [18], it is important to have a mathematical analysis to guarantee their performance.

In Ref. [25], the following area-optimal slicing floorplan design problem is addressed. Given n soft modules each with the same shape flexibility $r(\geq 1)$, what is the minimum area among all possible slicing floorplans? Note that a module is said to have shape flexibility r iff the module can be represented by any rectangle with the same area as long as the aspect ratio of the rectangle is between $1/r$ and r. It is proved that if $r \geq 2$, then there exists a slicing floorplan F such that area$(F) \leq \min\{1 + (1/\lfloor\sqrt{r}\rfloor), 5/4, (1+\theta)\}A_{\text{total}}$, where A_{total} is the total area of all the modules, $A_{\max}$ is the maximum module area, and $\theta = \sqrt{2A_{\max}/(rA_{\text{total}})}$. The shape of such a slicing floorplan closely resembles a square. The first term in the upper bound, that is, $(1 + (1/\lfloor\sqrt{r}\rfloor))A_{\text{total}}$, favors larger r; for example, if $r = 25$, the first term is $1.2A_{\text{total}}$. The second term gives a better bound than the first one if $r \leq 16$. The third term considers the ratios of the module areas and gives a good bound when all the module areas are small as compared with the total module area; for example, if $r = 2$ and

$A_{max} = A_{total}/100$, the third term is $1.1 A_{total}$. In fact, the experimental results reported in Ref. [25] show that by applying the Wong–Liu slicing floorplanner [2] to more than 20 test cases each with 100 soft modules of shape flexibility 2, slicing floorplans with areas smaller than the above-mentioned mathematical bound can be produced.

To get each term in the upper bound, a slicing floorplan is constructed such that its area will meet the bound. Each construction uses a different method to classify modules into groups based on module areas, and modules in different groups are represented by rectangles of different widths (while modules in the same group have the same width). Then modules are placed one at a time from the one with largest area to the one with smallest area by putting a module on the lowest possible level and moving it to the leftmost position on that level.

In addition, when r is slightly less than 2, that is, $r = 2 - \varepsilon$ with ε being a small positive number, it can be also proved that there exists a slicing floorplan whose area is upper bounded by $\min\{(5/4)[1 + (\varepsilon/2)], [1 + \theta + (\varepsilon/2)]\} A_{total}$.

9.7.2 COMPLETENESS OF SLICING TREE REPRESENTATION

Although it can be mathematically proved that a slicing floorplan capable of packing modules closely is achievable, there are constraints (e.g., the same shape flexibility for modules) that must be satisfied beforehand. On the other hand, it is still commonly believed that an area-optimal slicing floorplan may still suffer from a poor utilization of space when all modules are hard. For this reason, many efforts have been devoted for creating nonslicing floorplan representations. These representations are effective and efficient for handling hard modules, but many of them are still unable to fully exploit the shape flexibility of soft modules.

In Ref. [26], it is proved that when augmented with a simple compaction procedure, the slicing tree representation can generate all maximally compact placements of modules. (Note that no module in a maximally compact placement (or called admissible placement in Ref. [29]) can be moved horizontally to the left or vertically downward without moving any other modules.) As a result, slicing tree is a complete representation of both slicing and nonslicing floorplans. We now describe the idea behind the proof.

Given a slicing tree, its corresponding slicing placement is defined to be the area-optimal floorplan such that no vertical cutlines can be moved to the left, no horizontal cutlines can be moved downward, and each module is placed in the lower left corner of a basic rectangle. For example, Figure 9.12f shows a slicing placement of the slicing tree in Figure 9.12d.

A horizontal adjacency graph $G = (V, E)$ can be constructed from a placement of modules. The set V of vertices corresponds to the set of modules. There is an edge (u, v) in the edge set E iff the left boundary of v is immediately adjacent to the right boundary of u. It is clear that G is a DAG. A vertex u in G is said to be a left-boundary vertex iff u is a module placed along the left boundary of the placement. Clearly all left-boundary vertices have in-degree 0. In general the converse may not be true, but it is true for maximally compact placements. Another key fact is that for a maximally compact placement, all vertices in G are connected to the set of left-boundary vertices.

Given any maximally compact placement P, let G_P be the horizontal adjacency graph of P, and $B = \{b_1, b_2, \ldots, b_k\}$ be the set of left-boundary vertices in G. Because every vertex in G is reachable from at least one vertex in B, a spanning forest $Q = \{T_1, T_2, \ldots, T_k\}$ of G can be found, where T_i is a tree rooted at $b_i, i = 1, 2, \ldots, k$. For example, Figure 9.12a gives a maximally compact placement of nine modules and Figure 9.12b shows the horizontal adjacency graph, where vertices 7, 4, 1 are left-boundary vertices. Figure 9.12c shows a spanning forest containing three trees rooted at 7, 4, 1, respectively.

Now for the trees rooted at $b_1, b_2, \ldots, b_k, k - 1$ horizontal cutlines dividing a floorplan into k parts are constructed. For each tree, the transformations shown in Figure 9.13 are then recursively applied to its child subtrees to further expand the slicing structure. Figure 9.12d and e show the final slicing tree and floorplan. From the slicing floorplan, the corresponding slicing placement P' can

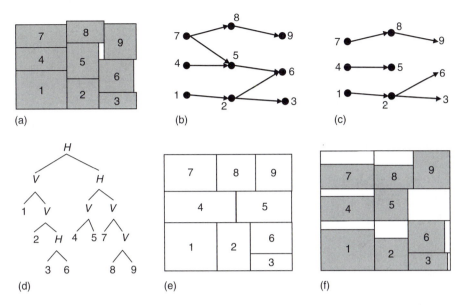

(a)   (b)   (c)

(d)   (e)   (f)

FIGURE 9.12 Generating a slicing placement from a maximally compact placement. (a) A maximally compact placement of 9 modules, (b) the horizontal adjacency graph of (a), (c) a spanning foust of (b), (d) the slicing tree derived from (c), (e) the slicing floorplan derived from (c), and (f) the slicing placement derived from (d) (or (e)).

be constructed (Figure 9.12f). Because the positions of the modules in the x-direction in P' are the same as those in P, performing a compaction along y-direction, which moves modules downward as far as possible, transforms P' into P. This concludes that slicing tree is a complete representation of floorplans in the sense that by an augmenting compaction step, all maximally compact placements can be produced as well.

9.7.3 HETEROGENEOUS FPGA FLOORPLANNING

Modern FPGAs can accommodate multimillion gates and their future generations will be even more complex. As a result, a hierarchical approach based upon partitioning and floorplanning becomes necessary to successfully realize a design on an FPGA. Owing to the heterogeneous logic and routing resources on a modern FPGA, FPGA floorplanning is very different from floorplanning for application-specific integrated circuits (ASICs). Although there are also some previous works, for

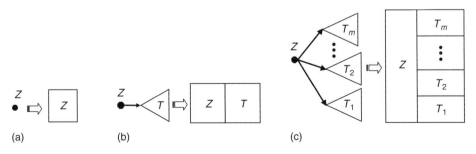

(a)   (b)   (c)

FIGURE 9.13 Three types of transformations for expanding a slicing structure. (a) Type 1 transformation, applied when Z has no child, (b) Type 2 transformation, applied when Z has only one child, and (c) Type 3 transformation, applied when Z has two or more children.

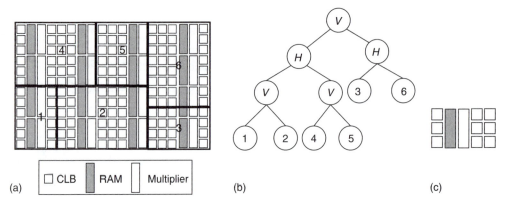

FIGURE 9.14 (a) Slicing floorplan. (b) Slicing tree. (c) Pattern.

example, Ref. [30], on FPGA floorplanning, they all target at older generations of FPGAs consisting of configurable logic blocks (CLBs) only. In this subsection, we consider modern heterogeneous FPGA chips that consist of columns of CLBs, with column pairs of RAMs and multipliers interleaved between them (Figure 9.14a). The Xilinx Spartan3 family and Vertex-II family conform to this architecture [31]. For such an FPGA architecture, the first slicing floorplan design algorithm is given in Ref. [27]. The algorithm uses slicing trees to represent floorplans during a simulated annealing process similar to Ref. [2], but it nontrivially extends the slicing floorplan area optimization algorithms [3,5] to find the optimal realization for each slicing tree. The main idea behind this extension is explained below.

Assume that a set of modules is given, where each module has an associated resource requirement vector $\varphi = (m_1, m_2, m_3)$, indicating that this module requires m_1 CLBs, m_2 RAMs, and m_3 multipliers. The FPGA floorplanning problem is to place modules on the chip such that each region assigned to a module satisfies the resource requirements of the module, regions for different modules do not overlap, and a given cost function is optimized. For example, if there are six modules, and their resource requirement vectors are $\varphi_1 = (12, 2, 1), \varphi_2 = (30, 4, 4), \varphi_3 = (15, 1, 1), \varphi_4 = (24, 4, 4), \varphi_5 = (18, 2, 2)$, and $\varphi_6 = (30, 2, 2)$, then Figure 9.14a is a feasible slicing floorplan for these modules (see Figure 9.14b for the corresponding slicing tree). For easier illustration, a coordinate system is adopted on the chip. In Figure 9.14a the horizontal unit is the width of a CLB, and the vertical unit is the height of a CLB. The lower left CLB has coordinate $(0, 0)$, the lower left RAM occupies coordinates $(1, 0)$ through $(1, 2)$, and the lower left multiplier occupies coordinates $(2, 0)$ through $(2, 2)$. Let H and W be the height and the width of the chip, respectively.

Any rectangular region r in the chip is denoted by a four-tuple (x, y, w, h), where (x, y), w, and h are the lower left coordinate, the width, and the height of r, respectively. The $x(r)$, $y(r)$, $w(r)$, and $h(r)$ each denote a corresponding field of r. Let R_i denote the set of rectangular regions in the chip that satisfy the resource requirements of module i. Each region in R_i is said to be a realization of module i because it is feasible to place module i in that region. A realization r_1 in R_i is redundant if there is another realization r_2 in R_i such that both realizations have the same lower left coordinate (i.e., $r_1(x) = r_2(x)$, $r_1(y) = r_2(y)$) and r_2 is not larger than r_1 in both dimensions (i.e., $r_2(w) \leq r_1(w)$ and $r_2(h) \leq r_1(h)$). Clearly all redundant realizations can be discarded. Let $L(i, x, y)$ denote the irreducible realization list (IRL) for module i starting at coordinate (x, y) and it contains all the irredundant realizations in R_i with (x, y) being their lower left coordinate. Therefore, all irredundant realizations of a module are organized into different IRLs for different starting coordinates. Each IRL is sorted in the decreasing height order, and hence it is also sorted in the increasing width order.

The definition of an IRL can be extended to the nodes in a slicing tree. Given two rectangles r_1 and r_2, the bounding rectangle of r_1 and r_2 is a rectangle r with $r(x) = \min\{r_1(x), r_2(x)\}$, $r(y) = \min\{r_1(y), r_2(y)\}$, $r(w) = \max\{r_1(w) + r_1(x), r_2(w) + r_2(x)\} - r(x)$, and

$r(h) = \max\{r_1(h) + r_1(y), r_2(h) + r_2(y)\} - r(y)$. Given a tree node u, if u represents module i, $R_u = R_i$. On the other hand, if u is an internal node, let u_1, u_2 be the left and the right children of u. If u is a vertical cut (a horizontal cut, respectively), R_u consists of all bounding rectangles of r_1 in R_{u_1} and r_2 in R_{u_2}, where r_1 is to the left side of (below, respectivly) r_2. The IRL for a tree node u starting at coordinate (x, y) is defined as $L(u, x, y) = \{r | r$ is irredundant in $R_u, x(r) = x,$ and $y(r) = y\}$. Therefore, the set of all irredundant realizations of a tree node is also organized into different IRLs for different starting coordinates.

Given a slicing tree, the IRLs of each node are calculated from leaves to the root. Obviously, the IRLs of each module only need to be calculated once, right at the beginning of the simulated annealing process. Suppose u is the internal node under consideration, and is a vertical cut. Let u_1, u_2 be the left and the right children of u. Assume $L(u_1, x, y) = \{r_1, r_2, \ldots, r_k\}$ is sorted as expected. It can be shown that it is enough to combine every realization r_i in $L(u_1, x, y)$ with realizations in $L(u_2, x + w(r_i), y)$ to generate $L(u, x, y)$. Moreover, when combining r_i with realizations in $L(u_2, x + w(r_i), y)$, we may not need to consider all combinations. For those realizations in $L(u_2, x + w(r_i), y)$ with heights not larger than $h(r_i)$, we only need to consider the highest one to get a minimum width. We also do not need to combine r_i with a realization r' in $L(u_2, x + w(r_i), y)$ if $h(r') \geq h(r_{i-1})$. The procedure to construct $L(u, x, y)$ can be derived similarly when u is a horizontal cut. It takes $O(l \log l)$ time to construct $L(u, x, y)$, where $l = \max\{H, W\}$.

The above-mentioned method, however, should not be implemented directly on the chip, because finding IRLs for every coordinate makes the space complexity formidable. Fortunately, a real FPGA chip is very regular with repetitions of a basic pattern. Consider the example chip in Figure 9.14a whose basic pattern is shown in Figure 9.14c. It turns out that this repetition property can be utilized such that only computation on the pattern instead of the whole chip needs to be done. As a result, evaluating a slicing tree takes $O(nml \log l)$ time and needs $O(nlm)$ memory space, where n is the number of modules and m is the number of points on the pattern.

9.7.4 3D Floorplanning

Complementary metal oxide semiconductor (CMOS) technology has continuously scaled into nanometer regime, and it has become more difficult to improve the chip performance by just size shrinking in a planar wafer. 3D ICs is a promising technology to keep the speed of an IC advancing. 3D ICs provide significant performance benefits over two-dimensional integrated circuits (2D ICs) mainly by reducing the interconnect lengths and introducing new geometrical arrangement of modules [32]. To improve the performance, circuit modules will not be confined in only one layer in 3D ICs. This produces a problem for current 2D floorplanning tools. As a result, 3D floorplanning algorithms are required for 3D IC design.

A 3D slicing floorplan design problem is addressed in Ref. [28]. This problem is formulated as that of placing a given set of 3D rectangular modules without overlapping while a given cost function is optimized. Assuming each 3D module is a hard module but with free rotation, an algorithm for solving the 3D slicing floorplan design problem is reported in Ref. [28], which generalizes slicing trees to represent different 3D floorplans, and uses simulated annealing to search for a good slicing floorplan. The main idea of the algorithm is highlighted below.

A 3D slicing floorplan can be obtained by cutting a 3D block by 2D planes (which are perpendicular to the x-, y-, or z-axis) into a set of 3D subblocks such that each 3D subblock is large enough to accommodate the 3D module assigned to it (Figure 9.15a). Slicing trees can be generalized to represent 3D slicing floorplans such that each internal node of a slicing tree is now labeled by X, Y, or Z. The label X (Y, Z, respectively) means that the corresponding subfloorplan is cut by a plane that is perpendicular to the x-axis (y-axis, z-axis, respectively). Figure 9.15b gives a slicing tree to represent the 3D floorplan shown in Figure 9.15a.

Because a slicing tree is a full binary tree (due to the fact that each internal node of the tree has two children), a static array with $2n - 1$ elements can be used to represent all the nodes of the tree,

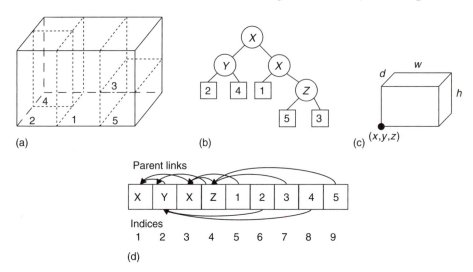

FIGURE 9.15 (a) 3D slicing floorplan with five modules. (b) Corresponding slicing tree. (c) Dimensions of a 3D block. (d) Static array.

where n is the number of modules. Each of the first $n - 1$ elements in the array represents an internal node, and the first element always represents the root of the tree. The last n elements represent the leaves. Each element of the array is associated with a ten-tuple $(t, p, l, r, x, y, z, w, d, h)$. The t is the tag information and its value is X, Y, or Z for each internal node and a module name for a leaf. p, l, and r denote the element indices in the array for the parent, the left child, and the right child of a node, respectively. The x, y, z, w, d, h are the dimensional information of a module or a subfloorplan, and (x, y, z) is called the base point (see Figure 9.15c). Figure 9.15d is the static array for the slicing tree shown in Figure 9.15b, where only the parent link of each element is drawn for simplicity. Given the static array of a slicing tree, the position of each module and the dimensions of the corresponding floorplan can be calculated by a recursive procedure starting from the root.

Two kinds of moves, exchange and rotation, are used during the annealing process for generating neighboring solutions. An exchange move randomly chooses two subtrees and swaps them; as a result, the two corresponding elements in the static array will be updated accordingly. On the other hand, a rotation move randomly selects a subtree and rotates the corresponding subfloorplan along x-, y-, or z-axis; as a result, the elements of the static array corresponding to the internal nodes contained in the subtree will be updated accordingly. It can be proved that the two neighborhood moves are complete in the sense that each slicing tree can be reached from another one via at most $10n - 6$ moves.

This 3D floorplanner can be specialized to solve the 2D problem as well, and according to Ref. [28], it is able to produce 2D slicing floorplans with the smallest areas for the two largest MCNC benchmarks, ami33 and ami49, among all 2D slicing and nonslicing floorplanning algorithms ever reported in the literature. Besides, this 3D floorplanner can be extended to handle various types of placement constraints and thermal distribution.

9.8   CONCLUSION

In this chapter, we have introduced two slicing floorplan representations, that is, slicing tree and Polish expression, on which many existing slicing floorplan design/optimization algorithms are based. We have presented efficient/effective area and power optimization algorithms for slicing floorplans. These optimization algorithms are typically embedded into a slicing floorplanner. We have discussed the problem of slicing floorplan design with or without placement constraints, and highlighted existing solutions. Finally we have described some more recent results in slicing floorplans for FPGAs and 3D ICs, in addition to the mathematical analysis on area upper bound and the completeness of slicing tree representation.

Before concluding this chapter, we would like to point out that since 1970s, slicing floorplans have been an active research topic, and therefore it is very difficult to discuss all existing solutions of this area in a single chapter. Instead, we have chosen to present the results, including the most recent ones in the past ten years, which we think will interest readers the most.

REFERENCES

1. R. H. J. M. Otten. Automatic floorplan design. *Proceedings of Design Automation Conference*, pp. 261–267, 1982.
2. D. F. Wong and C. L. Liu. A new algorithm for floorplan design. *Proceedings of Design Automation Conference*, Las Vegas, Nevada, pp. 101–107, 1986.
3. L. J. Stockmeyer. Optimal orientation of cells in slicing floorplan designs. *Information and Control*, 57(2):91–101, 1983.
4. W. Shi. An Optimal algorithm for area minimization of slicing floorplans. *Proceedings of International Conference on Computer-Aided Design*, San Jose, California, pp. 480–484, 1995.
5. R. H. J. M. Otten. Efficient floorplan optimization. *Proceedings of International Conference on Computer Design*, Las Vegas, Nevada, pp. 499–502, 1983.
6. G. Zimmermann. A new area and shape function estimation technique for VLSI layouts. *Proceedings of Design Automation Conference*, Atlantic City, New Jersey, pp. 60–65, 1988.
7. K.-Y. Chao and D. F Wong. Floorplanning for low power designs. *Proceedings of International Symposium on Circuits and Systems*, Seattle, Washington, pp. 45–48, 1995.
8. R. E. Tarjan. *Data Structures and Network Algorithms*. SIAM Press, Philadelphia, Pennsylvania, 1983.
9. T. Corman, C. E. Leiserson, and R. Rivest. *Introduction to Algorithms*. MIT Press, Cambridge, Massachusetts, 1990.
10. U. Lauther. A min-cut placement algorithm for general cell assemblies based on a graph representation. *Proceedings of Design Automation Conference*, San Diego, California, pp. 1–10, 1979.
11. D. P. La Potin and S. W. Director. Mason: A global floorplanning approach for VLSI design. *IEEE Transactions of Computer-Aided Design of Integrated Circuits and Systems*, CAD-5(4):477–489, 1986.
12. G. J. Wipfler, M. Wiesel, and D. A. Mlynski. A combined force and cut algorithm for hierarchical VLSI layout. *Proceedings of Design Automation Conference*, pp. 671–677, 1982.
13. B. W. Kernighan and S. Lin. An efficient heuristic procedure for partitioning graphs. *Bell System Technical Journal*, 49(2):291–307, 1970.
14. D. G. Schweikert and B. W. Kernighan. A proper model for the partitioning of electrical circuits. *Proceedings of Design Automation Workshop*, pp. 56–62, 1972.
15. C. M. Fiduccia and R. M. Mattheyses. A linear-time heuristic for improving network partitions. *Proceedings of Design Automation Conference*, pp. 175–181, 1982.
16. B. Quinn. A force directed component placement procedure for printed circuit boards. *IEEE Transactions on Circuits and Systems*, CAS-26(6):377–388, 1979.
17. S. Kirkpatrick, C. D. Gelatt, and M. P. Vecchi. Optimization by simulated annealing. *Science*, 220, 671–680, 1983.
18. F. Y. Young and D. F. Wong. Slicing floorplans with boundary constraints. *Proceedings of Asia and South Pacific Design Automation Conference*, Hong Kong, pp. 17–20, 1999.
19. E.-C. Liu, T.-H. Lin, and T.-C. Wang. On accelerating slicing floorplan design with boundary constraints. *Proceedings of International Symposium on Circuits and Systems*, Geneva, Switzerland, pp. III-339–III-402, 2000.
20. E.-C. Liu, M.-S. Lin, J. Lai, and T.-C. Wang. Slicing floorplan design with boundary-constrained modules. *Proceedings of International Symposium on Physical Design*, Sonoma County, California, pp. 124–129, 2001.
21. F. Y. Young and D. F. Wong. Slicing floorplans with range constraints. *Proceedings of International Symposium on Physical Design*, Monterey, California, pp. 97–102, 1999.
22. F. Y. Young, H. H. Yang, and D. F. Wong. On extending slicing foorplans to handle L/T-shaped modules and abutment constraints. *IEEE Transactions of Computer-Aided Design of Integrated Circuits and Systems*, 20(6):800–807, 2001.

23. W. S. Yuen and F. Y. Young. Slicing floorplan with clustering constraints. *Proceedings of Asia and South Pacific Design Automation Conference*, Yokohama, Japan, pp. 503–508, 2001.

24. F. Y. Young and D. F. Wong. Slicing floorplans with pre-placed modules. *Proceedings of International Conference on Computer-Aided Design*, San Jose, California, pp. 252–258, 1998.

25. F. Y. Young and D. F. Wong. How good are slicing floorplans? *Proceedings of International Symposium on Physical Design*, Napa Valley, California, pp. 144–149, 1997.

26. M. Lai and D. F. Wong. Slicing tree is a complete floorplan representation. *Proceedings of Design, Automation, and Test in Europe*, Munich, Germany, pp. 228–232, 2001.

27. L. Cheng and D. F. Wong. Floorplan design for multi-million gate FPGAs. *Proceedings of International Conference on Computer-Aided Design*, San Jose, California, pp. 292–299, 2004.

28. L. Cheng, L. Deng, and D. F. Wong. Floorplanning for 3-D VLSI design. *Proceedings of Asia and South Pacific Design Automation Conference*, Shanghai, China, pp. 405–411, 2005.

29. P. Guo, C.-K. Cheng, and T. Yoshimura. An O-Tree representation of non-slicing floorplan and its applications. *Proceedings of Design Automation Conference*, New Orleans, Louisiana, pp. 268–273, 1999.

30. J. M. Emmert and D. Bhatia. A methodology for fast FPGA floorplanning. *Proceedings of International Symposium on Field Programmable Gate Arrays*, Monterey, California, pp. 47–56, 1999.

31. Xilinx Inc. http://www.xilinx.com.

32. K. Banerjee, S. J. Souri, P. Kapur, and K. C. Saraswat. 3-D ICs: A novel chip design for improving deep submicrometer interconnect performance and systems-on-chip integration. *Proceedings of the IEEE*, 89(5):602–633, 2001.

10 Floorplan Representations

Evangeline F.Y. Young

CONTENTS

10.1 INTRODUCTION

A floorplan representation is a data structure that captures the relative positions of the rooms in a dissection of a rectangular region. It differs from a packing representation, which captures the relative positions of the blocks to be packed into a rectangular region. In this chapter, we will study different rectangular dissection representations (with the exception of the slicing representation which was discussed in the last chapter). There are several graph-based representations for rectangular dissections in the early floorplanning literature, e.g., polar graph, neighborhood graphs, etc. In this chapter, we will only focus on recent representations for floorplans, which are mainly string-based. Unlike the slicing representation, these representations can characterize any dissection of a rectangle into rooms. We begin by formally defining a floorplan (which is also often referred to as a mosaic floorplan in the literature). A rectangular dissection is a floorplan if and only if it observes the following three properties:

1. Each room is assigned exactly one block.
2. The internal line segments (segs) of the dissection are only permitted to form T-junctions (Figure 10.1). "+"-shaped junctions, where two distinct T-junctions meet at the same point, are considered to be degenerate. The representational power of floorplans is not impacted by this because the two T-junctions can be separated by sliding the noncrossing segment of one of the two T-junctions by a very small distance (Figure 10.2).

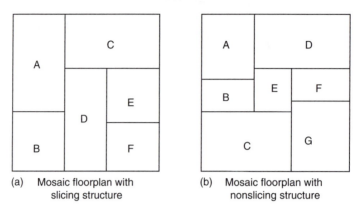

(a)   Mosaic floorplan with   (b)   Mosaic floorplan with
       slicing structure   nonslicing structure

FIGURE 10.1 Examples of floorplans, showing (a) a mosaic floorplan with slicing structure and (b) a mosaic floorplan with nonslicing structure.

3. The topology is defined in terms of room–seg adjacency relationships rather than room–room adjacency relationships. The distinction between the two is described below.

A floorplan can be defined in terms of relationships between adjacent rooms (i.e., rooms whose boundaries share a line segment) or in terms of adjacency relationships between a room and a seg (one of the boundaries of a room is the seg). In either case, it is necessary to specify the nature of the adjacency relationship (e.g., room A is to the left of room B or room B is above segment s in Figure 10.3). Two floorplans are equivalent with respect to the room–seg relation if and only if it is possible to label the rooms and the segments in such a way that the two sets of room–seg relations are identical. Similarly, two floorplans are equivalent with respect to the room–room relationship if and only if there is a labeling of the rooms such that the two sets of room–room relations are identical. Figure 10.3 shows two floorplans that are identical with respect to the room–seg relationship, but

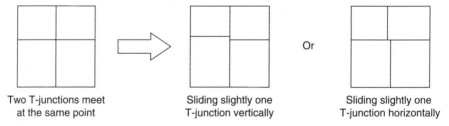

Two T-junctions meet   Sliding slightly one   Sliding slightly one
at the same point   T-junction vertically   T-junction horizontally

FIGURE 10.2 Degenerated case modeled by slightly moved T-junctions.

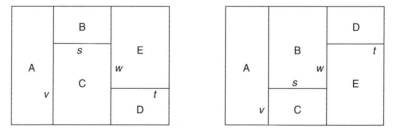

FIGURE 10.3 Room–seg relation and room–room relation.

not with respect to the room–room relationship. In this chapter, floorplans are defined with respect to the room–seg relation.

10.2 CORNER BLOCK LIST

The corner block list (CBL) [1] was one of the first representations proposed for the class of mosaic floorplans. CBL is a topological representation and the topological relationship between two rooms as described by a CBL is independent of the modules contained in those rooms. We will see later in this section that the time complexity to transform a CBL to a placement is $O(n)$ where n is the number of rooms. It just takes $n(3 + \lceil \lg n \rceil)$ bits to describe a packing in CBL and the size of the solution space is $O(n!2^{3n-3})$.

10.2.1 CORNER BLOCK

In a mosaic floorplan F, the room* in the top-right corner is called the corner block. The orientation for a corner block B is defined according to the T-junction at the bottom-left corner of the room containing B. There are only two kinds of T-junctions, a T rotated by 90° anticlockwise or a T rotated by 180°. In the first case, B is said to be vertically oriented and is denoted by a "0" bit. For the other case, B is said to be horizontally oriented and is denoted by a "1" bit. The two possible orientations of a corner block are illustrated in Figure 10.4. To obtain the CBL of a floorplan, or to construct the floorplan from a CBL, the concepts of deleting and inserting a corner block are needed.

If the corner block B of a given mosaic floorplan F is vertically oriented, B is deleted by sliding the bottom segment of B up along its left segment until it reaches the upper boundary of F. Similarly, if B is horizontally oriented, it is deleted by sliding its left segment along its bottom segment until reaching the right boundary of F. An example to illustrate this deletion process is shown in Figure 10.5. It is

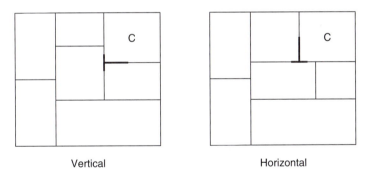

FIGURE 10.4 Different orientations of a corner block.

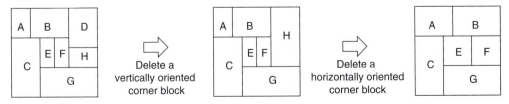

FIGURE 10.5 Deletion of the corner block in a mosaic floorplan.

---

* The term "block" is a physical entity with a width and a height, whereas a "room" is a topological entity without specified dimensions. We use the two terms interchangeably in this section to be consistent with the original CBL paper.

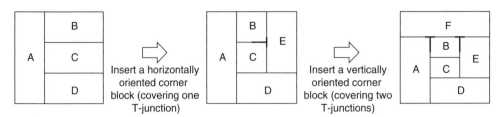

FIGURE 10.6 Insertion of a corner block to a mosaic floorplan.

not difficult to see that a mosaic floorplan will remain mosaic after deleting the corner block. The corner block insertion process is the reverse of the deletion process. To insert a new corner block B' to a mosaic floorplan F horizontally, a vertical segment (covering a certain number of 270° rotated T-junctions) at the right boundary of F is pushed to the left to create a room at the top-right corner of F for B'. Similarly, to insert a new corner block B' to a mosaic floorplan F vertically, a horizontal segment (covering a certain number of 0° rotated T-junctions) at the upper boundary of F is pushed downward to create a room at the top-right corner of F for B'. An example to illustrate this insertion process is shown in Figure 10.6.

10.2.2 DEFINITION OF CORNER BLOCK LIST

The CBL of a mosaic floorplan F containing n blocks is a three-tuple (S, L, T) where $S = s_1 \cdots s_n$ is a sequence of the block names, $L = l_1 \cdots l_{n-1}$ is a bit string denoting the corner block orientations, and $T = t_1 t_2 \cdots t_{n-1}$ is a bit string denoting some T-junction information. The CBL of F is constructed by recursively deleting corner blocks from F until only one block is left. We define a sequence of mosaic floorplans $F_i, i = 0, \ldots, n-1$, where $F_0 = F$ and F_{i+1} is obtained from F_i by deleting the corner block in F_i. Then, s_i is the corner block of F_{n-i}; l_i is a bit denoting the orientation of s_{i+1} ("0" ["1"] for a vertically [horizontally] oriented block); and t_i is a sequence of k_i "1"s followed by a "0," where k_i is the number of T-junctions covered by the bottom (left) segment of the vertically (horizontally) oriented corner block of s_{i+1}. Notice that F_{n-1} has only one block and the orientation of or the number of T-junctions covered by it is undefined, so the indices i of l_i and t_i only run from 1 to $n-1$. An example of the CBL of a mosaic floorplan is shown in Figure 10.7.

It takes no more than $n(3 + \lceil \lg n \rceil)$ bits to represent a floorplan by a CBL where $n \times \lceil \lg n \rceil$ bits are used to record the block names in the list S, $n-1$ bits are used to record the orientations in the list L and no more than $2n - 1$ bits are used to record the T-junction information in the list T.

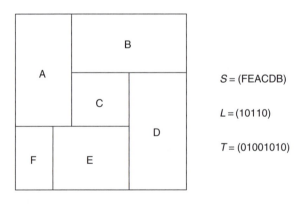

$S = (FEACDB)$

$L = (10110)$

$T = (01001010)$

FIGURE 10.7 Corner block list of a mosaic floorplan.

Transformation from floorplan to CBL

1. **While** there is a corner block B, **repeat**
2.   Delete B.
3.   **If** B is not the last block, record (B, orientation, T-subsequence).
4.   Add the last block to the block name list and concatenate all records in a reversed order to obtain the lists (S, L, T).

FIGURE 10.8 Transformation from floorplan to CBL.

Transformation from CBL to floorplan

1. Initialize the floorplan with block $S[1]$.
2. **For** $i = 2$ to n **do**
3.   Add block $S[i]$ to the floorplan with orientation $L[i-1]$, covering a number of T-junctions according to list T.
4.   **If** the number of T-junctions required to be covered is more than the number of T-junctions available, report error and exit.

FIGURE 10.9 Transformation from CBL to floorplan.

10.2.3 TRANSFORMATION BETWEEN CORNER BLOCK LIST AND FLOORPLAN

The linear-time transformations between CBL and floorplan are described in Figures 10.8 and 10.9. A drawback of CBL is that an arbitrary three-tuple (S, L, T), where S is a permutation of n block names, L is an $n-1$-bit string, and T is a bit string starting and ending with "0"s and having $n-1$ "0"s in total, may not correspond to a floorplan, because of the constraints on the composition of the list T.

10.2.4 FLOORPLANNING ALGORITHM

This CBL representation can be used in search-based optimization technique like simulated annealing. Neighboring solutions can be generated by the following moves:

1. Randomly exchange two blocks in S
2. Randomly toggle a bit in L
3. Randomly toggle a bit in T
4. Randomly pick a block and rotate it by 90°, 180°, or 270°
5. Randomly pick a soft block and change its shape

Notice that the second and the third move may result in an infeasible CBL, i.e., one that does not correspond to any floorplan. Therefore, checking and appropriate correction steps are needed.

10.2.5 EXTENDED CORNER BLOCK LIST STRUCTURE

The extended CBL, ECBL$_\lambda$, was proposed by Zhou et al [2] to represent general floorplans that may include empty rooms. Like the CBL, ECBL$_\lambda$ represents a rectangular dissection and assigns blocks

---

Transformation from floorplan to ECBL

1. Insert a false block to each empty room.
2. **While** there is a corner block B, **repeat**
3.   Delete B.
4.   **If** B is not a false block, record (B, orientation, T-subsequence),
      else record (false block, orientation, T-subsequence).
5. Add the last block to the block name list and concatenate all records in a reversed
   order to obtain the lists (S, L, T).

FIGURE 10.10   Transformation from floorplan to ECBL.

Transformation from ECBL to floorplan

1. Initialize the floorplan with block $S[1]$.
2. **For** $i = 2$ to $\lfloor \lambda n \rfloor$ **do**
3.   **If** all real blocks are added already, output the floorplan and exit,
4.   **else**
5.   Add block $S[i]$ to the floorplan with orientation $L[i - 1]$ covering a number of
         T-junctions according to list T.
6.   **If** the number of T-junctions required to be covered is more than the number of
         T-junctions available, report error and exit.

FIGURE 10.11   Transformation from ECBL to floorplan.

to rooms, but it contains more rooms than there are blocks, leaving some of the rooms empty. In block assignment, a false block of zero width and height is assigned to an empty room. An extended CBL, $ECBL_\lambda$, is defined as follows:

Definition 1   *Given n blocks, an* extended corner block list *with an extending factor λ, denoted by* $ECBL_\lambda$, *is a corner block list (S, L, T) of a floorplan with $\lfloor \lambda n \rfloor$ rooms, of which $\lfloor \lambda n \rfloor - n$ rooms are empty and occupied by false blocks and the remaining n rooms hold the n given blocks.*

The transformation algorithms between floorplan and ECBL are updated to account for the introduction of false blocks (Figures 10.10 and 10.11). Similar to the analysis of CBL, the complexities of these algorithms are both $O(\lfloor \lambda n \rfloor)$, and the number of combinations of $ECBL_\lambda$ is $O(C^n_{\lfloor \lambda n \rfloor} n! 2^{3\lfloor \lambda n \rfloor - 4})$. There is an additional factor of $C^n_{\lfloor \lambda n \rfloor}$ in the total number of combinations because there are $C^n_{\lfloor \lambda n \rfloor}$ ways to select n rooms from $\lfloor \lambda n \rfloor$ rooms to accommodate the n real blocks.

The solution space of $ECBL_\lambda$ is guaranteed to contain the optimal solution when $\lambda = n$. It can be shown that the bounded sliceline grid (a packing representation discussed in the next chapter) $BSG_{n \times n}$ can be represented by an $ECBL_n$, i.e., λ is set to n. From the optimum solution theorem of bounded sliceline grids, there exists a $BSG_{n \times n}$-based packing corresponding to the optimal solution, so the solution space of $ECBL_n$ must also contain the optimal solution. However, setting λ to n will significantly increase the size of the solution space and the complexities of the transformation algorithms from linear to quadratic. Fortunately, it has been shown experimentally that fairly good results can be obtained by setting λ to a real number constant in the range [1.5,3], which agrees with a fact proven later that $\Theta(n - 2\sqrt{n})$ empty rooms are enough to generate any packing.

10.3 Q-SEQUENCE

A new data structure called the Quarter-state sequence (abbreviated as Q-sequence) was proposed by Sakanushi et al. [3,4] to represent a floorplan. A Q-sequence is a string of room labels and two positional symbols with a total length of $3n$ where n is the number of rooms. Both encoding and decoding of the Q-sequence representation can be done in linear time.

To construct the Q-sequence of a floorplan, the following terms are defined. A room is called the tail room if it lies at the bottom-right corner of the floorplan. A room r that is not a tail room has a bottom-right corner, which is either a 180° or a 270° rotated T-junction. In either case, the noncrossing segment of the T-junction is called the prime seg of r. If the prime seg l of a room r is vertical (horizontal), the rooms that touch l from the right (below) are called the associated rooms of r, and the topmost (leftmost) associated room is called the next room of r. The Q-state of room r is a string starting with the room label r followed by n_r "R"s ("B"s) if the prime seg of r is vertical (horizontal), where n_r is the number of associated rooms of r. The subQ-sequence Y is constructed by concatenating the Q-states of all the rooms in the order of $r_1, r_2, \ldots, r_n$, where r_1 is the room at the top-left corner of the packing, and r_{i+1} is the next room of r_i, for $i = 1, \ldots, n - 1$. We define string X as consisting of p "R"s with q "B"s, where p and q are the numbers of rooms touching the left-wall and the top-wall of the whole floorplan. The final Q-sequence is obtained by concatenating X with the subQ-sequence Y. An example is shown in Figure 10.12. Henceforth, we assume that the rooms are always labeled from 1 to n in the Q-sequence (i.e., $r_i = i$).

Given a Q-sequence Q, we can obtain an RQ-sequence by deleting all the "B"s and replacing every "R" by an open parenthesis and every room label by a close parenthesis. We can construct a BQ-sequence similarly by interchanging the roles of "B" and "R". There are two necessary and sufficient properties:

1. Single: The subsequence of Q between any two rooms contains a string with at least one "R" or at least one "B."
2. Parenthesis: The RQ-sequence and BQ-sequence of Q are well formed.

It can be shown that the number $F(n)$ of distinct Q-sequences for n blocks is upper bounded by $2^{(3n-1)} \times n!$. Given a Q-sequence, vertical and horizontal constraint graphs can be constructed directly from the sequence and floorplan realization can be done in linear time. A decoding algorithm will be given in the next section. Besides, boundary constraint can also be handled efficiently by using the Q-sequence representation.

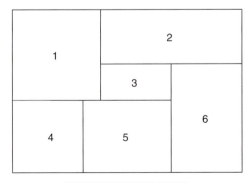

RRBB1RR2BB3BB4R5R6

FIGURE 10.12 Example of the Q-sequence representation.

Transformation from Q-sequence to floorplan

1. Initialize the floorplan with block n.
2. **For** $i = n - 1$ to 1 **do** /* Let $I(i)$ be the Q-state of block i. */
3.   **If** $I(i)$ contains 'R's,
4.   Add block i from the left of the chip pushing aside top m_i blocks, where m_i is the number of 'R's in $I(i)$, that are adjacent to the left boundary of the chip.
5.   **If** $I(i)$ contains 'B's,
6.   Add block i from the top of the chip pushing down leftmost m_i blocks, where m_i is the number of 'B's in $I(i)$, that are adjacent to the top boundary of the chip.

FIGURE 10.13 Transformation from Q-sequence to floorplan.

10.3.1 EXTENDED Q-SEQUENCE

The Q-sequence representation is extended [5] to allow empty room insertion to include the optimal packing in the solution space. It is proven that at most $n - \lfloor\sqrt{4n-1}\rfloor$ empty rooms are needed to represent any packing and the size of the solution space will become $2^{6n}(2n)!/n!$ if empty rooms are included. A new move to perturb a floorplan by making use of a parenthesis tree pair is introduced to improve the packing performance. A linear-time decoding algorithm to realize a floorplan from a Q-sequence is given in Figure 10.13 and an example that illustrates the decoding steps is shown in Figure 10.14.

10.3.1.1 New Move Based on Parenthesis Constraint Tree

The R parenthesis tree of a Q-sequence is obtained by representing the corresponding RQ-sequence in the form of a tree such that each node represents a pair of parentheses corresponding to a room. We label the "R" corresponding to the open parenthesis of room i by R_i for $i = 1, \ldots, n$. An example is shown in Figure 10.15. The B parenthesis tree can be constructed similarly from the BQ-sequence and the "B"s are also labeled from 1 to n accordingly. Parenthesis trees have the following properties:

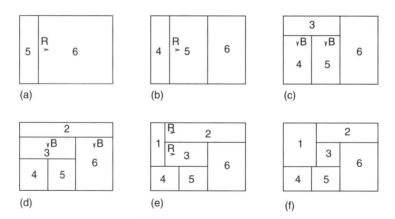

FIGURE 10.14 Example of realizing a floorplan from its Q-sequence RRBB1RR2BB3BB4R5R6, showing (a) the floorplan after adding block 5, (b) the floorplan after adding block 4, (c) the floorplan after adding block 3, (d) the floorplan after adding block 2, (e) the floorplan after adding block 1, and (f) the final floorplan.

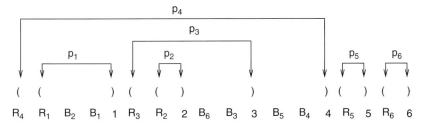

FIGURE 10.15   Q-sequence and its R parenthesis system.

Property 1   *Given two rooms i and j corresponding to node i and node j, respectively, in the R parenthesis tree, if node i is an ancestor (the left sibling) of node j, room i is below (on the left of) room j in the packing.*

Property 2   *Given two rooms i and j corresponding to node i and node j, respectively, in the B parenthesis tree, if node i is an ancestor (the left sibling) of node j, room i is on the right of (above) room j in the packing.*

Property 3   *The rooms corresponding to the nodes whose parent is the root in the R (B) parenthesis tree are placed along the bottom (right) boundary of the packing.*

The R and B parenthesis trees of the floorplan in Figure 10.14f are shown in Figure 10.16. The Q-sequence can be perturbed by moving the positional symbols "R"s and "B"s back and forth as long as the corresponding RQ-sequence and BQ-sequence are still well formed. Parenthesis trees can help to constrain the movement such that the resulting Q-sequence will remain feasible. For example, when an R_i is moved to the left, some of node i's siblings in the R parenthesis tree will become node i's children, but we cannot move R_i to the left of R_j where node j is the parent of node i. Similarly, when R_i is moved to the right, some of node i's children in the R parenthesis tree will become node i's left siblings, but we cannot move R_i to the right of the label of room i. If moving a positional symbol "R" will result in a blank subsequence between two room labels i and j where $j > i$, one can place the positional symbol B_j between the labels i and j to restore a feasible Q-sequence.

In the annealing process, four perturbation operations can be applied to change a Q-sequence: (1) rotate a module, (2) swap the modules in two rooms, (3) move an "R" randomly and feasibly in

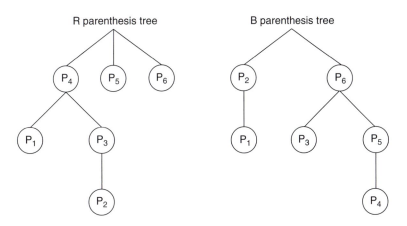

FIGURE 10.16   Parenthesis trees of the packing in Figure 10.14f.

the Q-sequence, and (4) move a "B" randomly and feasibly in the Q-sequence. It can be shown that starting from any arbitrary initial floorplan, we can transform it to any other floorplan by applying at most $O(n)$ perturbation operations.

10.4 TWIN BINARY TREES

Yao et al. [6] proposed another representation for floorplans and derived the exact number of floorplan configurations. Let $M(n)$ be the number of floorplans with n rooms. These floorplans can be analyzed in terms of the numbers of T-junctions on the top and right boundaries of the floorplan. Let $F_n(i,j)$ denote the number of floorplans with n rooms, with i T-junctions on the top boundary and j T-junctions on the right boundary. $M(n)$ where $n \geq 1$ can be computed by the following equation:

$$M(n) = \sum_{i,j>0} F_n(i,j)$$

When $n = 1$, $F_n(0,0) = 1$, and when $n > 1$, $F_n(0,0) = 0$, because there is at least one T-junction on either the top or the right boundary when the floorplan has two or more rooms. Also, $F_n(i,j) = 0$ when $i + j \geq n$, because there are at most $n - 1$ T-junctions on the top and right boundaries for a floorplan with n rooms. A recurrence for $F_n(i,j)$ can be obtained by deleting the top-right room in the floorplan as described in the section on CBL.

$$F_{n+1}(i+1,j+1) = \sum_{k=1}^{\infty} [F_n(i+k,j) + F_n(i,j+k)], \quad n \geq 1$$

It turns out that the base cases and the recurrence for $F_n(i,j)$ are identical to those used for generating the Baxter number $B(n)$ [7]. The Baxter number $B(n)$ has been shown by Chung et al. [8] to have the form

$$B(n) = \binom{n+1}{1}^{-1} \binom{n+1}{2}^{-1} \sum_{k=1}^{n} \binom{n+1}{k-1} \binom{n+1}{k} \binom{n+1}{k+1} \tag{10.1}$$

Therefore, the number of floorplans with n rooms is given by Equation 10.1. By borrowing the concept of the Baxter permutation, an efficient representation for floorplans is developed. A bijection between Baxter permutations and twin binary trees (TBTs) was introduced in Ref. [9], where TBTs are defined as follows:

Definition 2   The set of twin binary trees $TBT_n \subset Tree_n \times Tree_n$ is the set $TBT_n = \{(b_1, b_2)|b_1, b_2 \in Tree_n \cap \Theta(b_1) = \Theta^c(b_2)\}$ where $Tree_n$ is the set of all binary trees with n nodes, and $\Theta(b)$ is the labeling of a binary tree b obtained as follows. Beginning with an empty sequence, perform an in-order traversal on the tree. Whenever encountering a node with no left (right) child, a bit "0" ("1") is appended to the sequence. The first "0" and the last "1" are omitted. Θ^c is the complement of Θ in which the bits "0" and "1" are interchanged.

Except for the four corners of a floorplan, all block corners are formed by T-junctions. There are four possible orientations for the T-junctions: 0°, 90°, 180°, and 270° as shown in Figure 10.17. To construct the TBT representation of a mosaic floorplan, the following terminologies concerning mosaic floorplan are defined:

Definition 3   If room A is not at the top-right corner of a floorplan, the T-junction at the top-right corner of A is either a 0° T-junction or a 270° T-junction. Let B be the room adjacent to A by the noncrossing segment of that T-junction, B is called the C^+-neighbor of A.

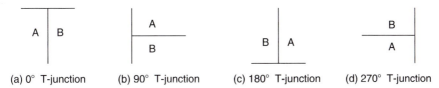

(a) 0° T-junction   (b) 90° T-junction   (c) 180° T-junction   (d) 270° T-junction

FIGURE 10.17   Four different types of T-junctions, with (a) 0° rotaion, (b) 90° rotation, (c) 180° rotation, and (d) 270° rotation.

Definition 4   *If room A is not at the bottom-left corner of a floorplan, the T-junction at the bottom-left corner of A is either a 90° T-junction or a 180° T-junction. Let B be the room adjacent to A by the noncrossing segment of that T-junction, B is called the C^--neighbor of A.*

Every room, except the top-right corner room, has exactly one C^+-neighbor. Similarly, every room, except the bottom-left corner room, has exactly one C^--neighbor. If we represent each room by a node and connect each node to its C^+-neighbor, we can construct a tree whose root is the top-right corner room of the floorplan. Similarly, if we connect each node to its C^--neighbor, we can construct a second tree whose root is the bottom-left corner block of the floorplan. The algorithm for obtaining the TBT representation of a floorplan is shown in Figure 10.18 and an example of the TBT representation of a floorplan is shown in Figure 10.19. The complexity of this algorithm is $O(n)$ where n is the total number of rooms and the pair of trees so generated is a pair of TBTs. Moreover, there is a one-to-one mapping between TBTs (τ_1, τ_2) and all floorplans. This property makes the TBT a nonredundant representation for floorplans.

Theorem 1   *The pair of trees (τ_1, τ_2) generated by the algorithm in Figure 10.18 is a pair of twin binary trees.*

Theorem 2   *Given a floorplan, there exists a unique twin binary tree representation for the floorplan. Similarly, a twin binary tree represents a unique floorplan.*

Transformation from floorplan F to TBT

1. $E^+ = E^- = \emptyset$.
2. Let $V^+ = V^- = \{i|\ \text{block}\ i \in F\}$.
3. **For** each block i:
4.   **If** i is not the top-right corner block of F,
5.   Get C^+-neighbor j of i. Put $E^+ = E^+ \cup (j, i)$.
6.   **If** block j is on the right of i, set i be the left child of j,
7.   **else** set i be the right child of j.
8.   **If** i is not the bottom-left corner block of F,
9.   Get C^--neighbor j of i. Put $E^- = E^- \cup (j, i)$.
10.   **If** block j is on the left of i, set i be the right child of j,
11.   **else** set i be the left child of j.
12. $\tau_+ = (V^+, E^+), \tau_- = (V^-, E^-)$.
13. Output (τ_-, τ_+).

FIGURE 10.18   Transformation from floorplan to TBT.

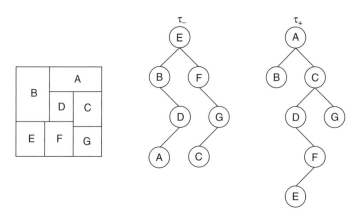

FIGURE 10.19   TBT representation of a mosaic floorplan.

10.5   TWIN BINARY SEQUENCES

Twin binary trees can represent floorplans uniquely, but it is not known how to use them effectively to generate different floorplans. The Twin binary sequence (TBS) is proposed in Ref. [10] to effectively encode TBT with four-tuples $s = (\pi, \alpha, \beta, \beta')$ such that necessary and sufficient conditions for the feasibility of an encoding can be identified, and feasible encodings can be generated effectively according to these conditions. Each four-tuple $s = (\pi, \alpha, \beta, \beta')$ represents a floorplan with n modules, where π is a permutation of the module names, α is a sequence of $n-1$ bits, and β and β' are sequences of n bits. These four-tuples can be one-to-one mapped to pairs of binary trees t_1 and t_2 such that t_1 and t_2 are twin binary to each other and can uniquely describe a floorplan. In addition, empty rooms can be inserted to include the optimal solution in the solution space. Instead of including an excessive number of dummy blocks in the set of modules, which will increase the size of the solution space significantly, the TBS representation allows us to insert an exact number of irreducible empty rooms in a floorplan such that every packing can be obtained uniquely from one and only one floorplan. The size of the solution space is $O(n!2^{3n}/n^{1.5})$, which is the size with no empty room insertions, but every packing can be generated uniquely and efficiently from one floorplan in the solution space in linear time without any redundancy. A lower bound of $\Omega(n - 2\sqrt{n})$ empty rooms are needed to obtain any packing. Together with the upper bound from Ref. [5], the number of empty rooms required is exactly $\Theta(n - 2\sqrt{n})$.

The definition of TBS is based on an observation that an arbitrary pair of binary trees t_1 and t_2 is a TBT representation of a floorplan if and only if they are twin binary to each other and their inorder traversals are the same. However, the labeling and the inorder traversal are not sufficient to identify a unique pair of t_1 and t_2. Given a permutation of n module names π and a labeling α of $n - 1$ bits, there can be more than one valid pairs of t_1 and t_2 such that their inorder traversals are π and $\Theta(t_1) = \Theta^c(t_2) = \alpha$. To specify a pair of trees uniquely, two additional bit sequences β and β' can be used for t_1 and t_2, respectively. In $\beta(\beta')$, the ith bit is equal to "1" if the ith module in the inorder traversal of $t_1(t_2)$ is the right child of its parent and is "0" otherwise. These bits are called directional bits. Notice that any $n - 1$ bit sequence $\alpha = \alpha_1\alpha_2 \cdots \alpha_{n-1}$ and n bit sequence $\beta = \beta_1\beta_2 \cdots \beta_n$ will correspond to the labeling and the directional bit sequence of a binary tree t if and only if the sequence $\beta_1\alpha_1\beta_2\alpha_2 \cdots \alpha_{n-1}\beta_n$ has one "0" more than "1," and for any prefix of this sequence, the number of "0"s is not less than the number of "1"s. Now we can use a four-tuple $(\pi, \alpha, \beta, \beta')$ to represent a floorplan where π is a permutation of n module names, α is an $n - 1$ bit sequence, and β and β' are n bit sequences such that the pairs α and β, and α^c and β' satisfy the above conditions of representing the labeling and the directional bit sequence of a binary tree.

Transformation from TBS $(\pi, \alpha, \beta, \beta')$ to floorplan

1. Initialize the floorplan with block π_n.
2. **For** $i = n - 1$ to 1:
3.   **If** α_i is zero,
4.   Find the smallest k where $i < k \leq n$ and β_k is equal to one.
5.   Add block π_i to the floorplan from the left, pushing aside the set
          $S = \{\pi_j | i < j \leq k$ and β_j not deleted yet$\}$ of blocks.
6.   Delete $\beta_{i+1}, \beta_{i+2} \cdots \beta_k$ from β.
7.   **If** α_i is one,
8.   Find the smallest k where $i < k \leq n$ and β'_k is equal to one.
9.   Add block π_i to the floorplan from the top, pushing down the set
          $S = \{\pi_j | i < j \leq k$ and β'_j not deleted yet$\}$ of blocks.
10.   Delete $\beta'_{i+1}, \beta'_{i+2} \cdots \beta'_k$ from β'.

FIGURE 10.20   Transformation from TBS to floorplan.

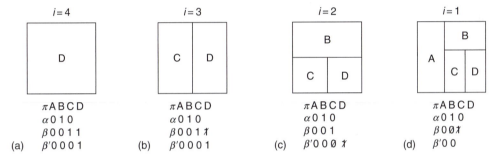

FIGURE 10.21   Example of constructing a floorplan from its TBS.

This four-tuple representation is called TBS and the mapping between TBS and floorplans is one-to-one. Therefore, there is no redundancy in the TBS representation, and the size of the solution space for n modules is equal to the Baxter number $B(n)$ [6] and can be shown to be bounded by $O(n! 2^{3n}/n^{1.5})$. An algorithm to realize a floorplan from a given TBS representation $(\pi, \alpha, \beta, \beta')$ in linear time by scanning the sequences only once is given in Figure 10.20 with an example shown in Figure 10.21.

To include the optimal solution in the solution space, empty rooms can be inserted. In TBS, empty rooms can be inserted exactly into the representation such that every nonslicing structure can be generated from one and only one mosaic floorplan nonredundantly. In a packing, there are two kinds of empty rooms. One results because the room assigned to a module is too large. This type of empty room is called reducible and is not considered because the topological relationship is not affected. The other type is called irreducible and refers to rooms that cannot be removed by merging with the neighboring rooms. Examples of reducible and irreducible empty rooms are shown in Figure 10.22. The T-junctions at the four corners of an irreducible empty room must form a wheel shape and the neighboring rooms at those T-junctions must not be irreducible empty rooms themselves.

To construct a packing from a floorplan, we only need to consider the insertion of those irreducible empty rooms (called "X" in the following). Irreducible empty rooms can only be of the two forms shown in Figure 10.23.

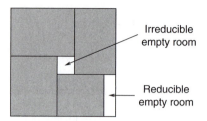

FIGURE 10.22   Examples of reducible and irreducible empty rooms.

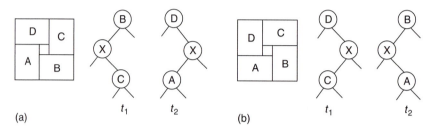

FIGURE 10.23   Two types of irreducible empty rooms, with (a) an anticlockwise wheel and (b) a clockwise wheel.

In the construction, a vertical sliceline with a T-junction on each side will be mapped to an anticlockwise "X," while a horizontal sliceline with a T-junction on each side will be mapped to a clockwise "X." This mapping and the corresponding changes needed to be made to the TBTs are shown in Figure 10.24. This mapping is unique, i.e., every packing can be obtained by this mapping from one and only one floorplan.

The empty room insertion process is based on two observations. First, it is known that the adjacent rooms of an irreducible empty room must be occupied by some blocks, so the "X"s must be inserted between some module nodes as in Figure 10.25. Initially, as many "X"s as possible will be inserted into the two TBTs (Figure 10.25b) according to the two possible forms of insertions (Figure 10.24). The invalid ones will then be deleted. This deletion is based on the second observation that a pair of TBT can represent a floorplan if and only if their inorder traversals are equivalent. By tracing the inorder traversal of the two trees after inserting all the possible "X"s, we can match those "X"s easily because there must be an equal number of "X"s between any two consecutive module names. There

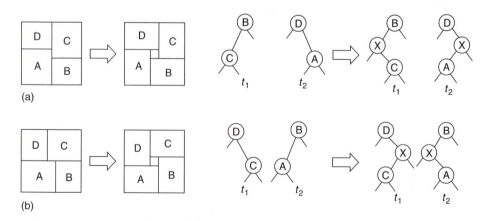

FIGURE 10.24   Mapping between mosaic floorplan and nonslicing floorplan, showing (a) mapping to an anticlockwise wheel and (b) a mapping to a clockwise wheel.

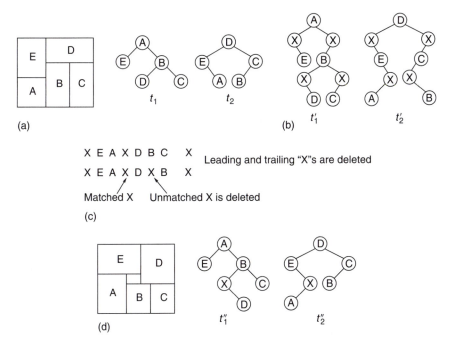

FIGURE 10.25 Constructing a packing from a floorplan, showing (a) the original mosaic floorplan, (b) the twin binary trees before and after inserting irreducible empty rooms, (c) the inorder traversals of the twin binary trees, and (d) the final floorplan with its twin binary tree representation.

may be choices in the mapping but each different choice will correspond to a different nonslicing floorplan. In this way, we can insert an exact number of irreducible empty rooms at the right places to produce different nonslicing structures. This empty room insertion step can be implemented directly on a TBS efficiently.

It is shown that at most $n - 1$ irreducible empty rooms are needed to construct any packing structure from a floorplan. On the other hand, a lower bound of $n - 2\sqrt{n} + 1$ irreducible empty rooms is proven with an example. Together with the upper bound from Ref. [5], the number of empty rooms required is $\Theta(n - 2\sqrt{n})$.

10.6   PLACEMENT CONSTRAINTS IN FLOORPLAN DESIGN

The CBL representation has been extended to handle boundary constraints, abutment constraints, and rectilinear block packing. Boundary constraints are useful for satisfying I/O requirements and the abutment requirements between neighboring units in modern designs. The necessary and sufficient conditions for a module satisfying boundary constraints in a floorplan represented by a CBL have been derived [11]. By making use of these conditions, the required boundary constraints can be checked in linear time by scanning the CBL. The CBL can be fixed as much as possible in case some constraints are violated. A penalty function is derived to measure the degree of violation of the constraints. The conditions are based on the observation that in the process of transforming a CBL to a floorplan, if a module is required to be placed on the left (bottom) boundary of the floorplan, the module should be placed on top (the right hand side) of all the previously placed modules when it is being processed. On the other hand, if a module is required to be placed along the right (top) boundary, no modules processed afterward should be placed on its right (above it). These conditions can be checked very efficiently for a given CBL $= (S, L, T)$ by computing two lists of numbers, R_i^{tn} and T_i^{tn} for $i = 1, \ldots, n$, associated with the n insertion steps in the transformation process from CBL to floorplan as follows:

$$R_1^{tn} = T_1^{tn} = 0$$

$$L_{i-1} = 1 \Rightarrow \begin{cases} R_i^{tn} = R_{i-1}^{tn} - TN_{i-1} \\ T_i^{tn} = T_{i-1}^{tn} + 1 \end{cases}$$
$$L_{i-1} = 0 \Rightarrow \begin{cases} R_i^{tn} = R_{i-1}^{tn} + 1 \\ T_i^{tn} = T_{i-1}^{tn} - TN_{i-1} \end{cases} \quad (10.2)$$

where TN_i is the number of "1"s before the ith "0" in the list T. The necessary and sufficient conditions for a module M_i to satisfy boundary constraint are stated in the following theorem:

Theorem 3   *A module M_i in list S is along the left (bottom) boundary of the final chip if and only if $T_i^{tn} = 0 (R_i^{tn} = 0)$. A module M_i in list S is along the top (right) boundary of the final chip if and only if $T_k^{tn} > T_i^{tn} (R_k^{tn} > R_i^{tn})$ for all $k = i + 1, \ldots, n$.*

The algorithm for boundary constraint checking given a CBL is shown in Figure 10.26. In this boundary checking algorithm, the CBL is scanned twice, one from left to right and once from right to left, so the complexity of this algorithm is $O(n)$. In case some constraints are violated, the corresponding CBL can be fixed as much as possible by swapping the modules that violate

---

Scan a CBL (S, L, T) to find all the modules lying along the boundaries and compute the penalty cost

1.   *penalty* $= 0, P^{tn} = T_1^{tn} = 0$ and $B^T = B^B = B^L = B^R = \emptyset$.
2.   **For** $i = 2$ to n **do**:
3.   Find R_i^{tn} and T_i^{tn} according to equation (2).
4.   **If** $T_i^{tn} = 0, B^L = B^L \cup \{M_i\}$.
5.   **If** $R_i^{tn} = 0, B^B = B^B \cup \{M_i\}$.
6.   **If** M_i is constrained to the left boundary,
7.   *penalty* $=$ *penalty* $+ T_i^{tn}$.
8.   **If** M_i is constrained to the bottom boundary,
9.   *penalty* $=$ *penalty* $+ R_i^{tn}$.
10.   Find kt where M_{kt} is the last module whose T^{tn} equals 0.
11.   Find kr where M_{kr} is the last module whose R^{tn} equals 0.
12.   *min_rtn* $=$ *min_ttn* $= \infty$.
13.   **For** $i = n$ to min$\{kt, kr\}$ **do**:
14.   **If** M_i is constrained to the top boundary,
15.   *penalty* $=$ *penalty* $+ \max\{0, T_i^{tn} -$ *min_ttn* $+ 1\}$.
16.   **If** M_i is constrained to the right boundary,
17.   *penalty* $=$ *penalty* $+ \max\{0, R_i^{tn} -$ *min_rtn* $+ 1\}$.
18.   **If** $R_i^{tn} <$ *min_rtn*,
19. $B^R = B^R \cup \{M_i\}$.
20.   *min_rtn* $= R_i^{tn}$.
21.   **If** $T_i^{tn} <$ *min_ttn*,
22. $B^T = B^T \cup \{M_i\}$.
23.   *min_ttn* $= T_i^{tn}$.
24.   *penalty* $=$ *penalty*$+$ number of modules before M_{kt} and M_{kr} in S and limited by the top or right boundary constraint.
25.   Output *penalty*, B^T, B^B, B^L and B^R.

FIGURE 10.26   Boundary check.

TABLE 10.1

Comparisons between Different Representations

Representation	Solution Space	Packing Time	Flexibility
CBL	$O(n!2^{3n-3})$	$O(n)$	Mosaic
Q-sequence	$O(n!2^{3n-1})$	$O(n)$	Mosaic
TBT	$\Theta(n!2^{3n}/n^4)$	$O(n)$	Mosaic
TBS	$\Theta(n!2^{3n}/n^4)$	$O(n)$	Mosaic

the constraints with free modules in the sets B^{T}, B^{L}, B^{R}, and B^{B}. If there are still violations after this swapping step, the corresponding floorplan does not have enough positions along the boundary to satisfy all the requirements, and a penalty term will be included in the cost function of the annealing process to penalize the remaining violated constraints. This penalty term will drop to zero as the annealing process proceeds.

A similar approach can be used to handle abutment constraints [12]. Abutment constraints are useful in practice as designers may want the logic blocks in a pipeline of a circuit to abut with one another to favor the transmission of data between them. By scanning the CBL of a candidate floorplan solution, the abutment information of all the blocks can be obtained efficiently in linear time. The CBL can be fixed as much as possible in case some constraints are violated. Based on this approach, L-shaped and T-shaped blocks can also be handled by partitioning a rectilinear block into a few abutting rectangular subblocks. Besides abutment constraints and rectilinear blocks, rotation and reflection of L-shaped and T-shaped blocks have also been considered [12].

10.7   CONCLUDING REMARKS

We have discussed four different types of representations for floorplans, including CBL, Q-sequence, TBT, and TBS. These representations are compared in Table 10.1. (A similar table compares packing representations in the next chapter.) They exhibit some interesting relationships with each other [6]. For example, given a floorplan F, the inorder traversal of the trees in its TBT representation is identical to the sequence S in the CBL representation (S, L, T) of the floorplan obtained by rotating F by 90°. All of these representations are practically useful because there are efficient linear-time algorithms for floorplan realization and encoding. However, CBL and Q-sequence have redundancy in their representations and the sizes of their solution space are both upper bounded by $O(n!2^{3n})$. TBT and TBS are nonredundant representations and the size of their solution space is $\Theta(n!2^{3n}/n^4)$ according to the analysis in Ref. [13] on the exact number of floorplans with n modules. All these representations can be extended to generate any general packing structure by including dummy empty blocks. According to the results from Refs. [5,10], the exact number of dummy empty blocks needed to generate any general packing structure is $\Theta(n - 2\sqrt{n})$. However, if these extra dummy blocks are added, the size of the solution space will be increased significantly. For TBS, it is possible to identify the exact locations in the representation where dummy empty blocks should be inserted such that every packing structure can be generated from exactly one floorplan. By using this property, Zion et al. [13] obtained a tighter upper bound for the total number of general packings of $O(n!2^{5n}/n^{4.5})$ by bounding the number of ways to insert dummy empty rooms into a TBS.

REFERENCES

1. X. Hong, S. Dong, G. Huang, Y. Cai, C. K. Cheng, and J. Gu. Corner block list representation and its application to floorplan optimization. *IEEE Transactions on Circuits and Systems II*, 51(5): 228–233, 2004. (ICCAD 2000).

2. S. Zhou, S. Dong, C. K. Cheng, and J. Gu. ECBL: An extended corner block list with solution space including optimum placement. *International Symposium on Physical Design*, Sonoma, California, 2001.

3. K. Sakanushi and Y. Kajitani. The quarter-state sequence (Q-sequence) to represent the floorplan and applications to layout optimization. *Proceedings of IEEE Asia Pacific Conference on Circuits and Systems*, Tianjin, China, pp. 829–832, 2000.

4. K. Sakanushi, Y. Kajitani, and D. P. Mehta. The quarter-state-sequence floorplan representation. *IEEE Transactions on Circuits and Systems I*, 50(3): 376–386, 2003.

5. C. Zhuang, K. Sakanushi, L. Jin, and Y. Kajitani. An enhanced Q-sequence augmented with empty room insertion and parenthesis trees. *Design, Automation and Test in Europe Conference and Exhibition*, Paris, France, pp. 61–68, 2002.

6. B. Yao, H. Chen, and C. K. Cheng. Floorplan representations: Complexity and connections. *ACM Transactions on Design Automation of Electronic Systems*, 8(1): 55–80, 2003. (ISPD 2001).

7. G. Baxter. On fixed points of the composite of commuting functions. *Proceedings of American Mathematics Society*, 15: 851–855, 1964.

8. F. R. K. Chung, R. L. Graham, J. E. E. Hoggatt, and M. Kleiman. The number of Baxter permutations. *Journal of Combinatorial Theory, Series A*, 24(3): 382–394, 1978.

9. S. Dulucq and O. Guibert. Baxter permutations. *Discrete Mathematics*, 180: 143–156, 1998.

10. E. F. Y. Young, C. C. N. Chu, and Z. C. Shen. Twin binary sequences: A non-redundant representation for general non-slicing floorplan. *IEEE Transactions on Computer-Aided Design of Integrated Circuits and Systems*, 22(4): 457–469, 2003. (ISPD 2002).

11. Y. Ma, S. Dong, X. Hong, Y. Cai, C. -K. Cheng, and J. Gu. VLSI floorplanning with boundary constraints based on corner block list. *IEEE Asia and South Pacific Design Automation Conference*, Yokohama, Japan, pp. 509–514, 2001.

12. Y. Ma, X. Hong, S. Dong, Y. Cai, C. K. Cheng, and J. Gu. Floorplanning with abutment constraints and L-shaped/T-shaped blocks based on corner block list. *Proceedings of the 38th ACM/IEEE Design Automation Conference*, Las Vegas, NV, pp. 770–775, 2001.

13. Z. C. Shen and C. C. N. Chu. Bounds on the number of slicing, mosaic and general floorplans. *IEEE Transactions on Computer-Aided Design of Integrated Circuits and Systems*, 22(10): 1354–1361, 2003.

11 Packing Floorplan Representations

Tung-Chieh Chen and Yao-Wen Chang

CONTENTS

11.1 INTRODUCTION

As technology advances, design complexity is increasing and the circuit size is getting larger. To cope with the increasing design complexity, hierarchical design and IP modules are widely used. This trend makes module floorplanning/placement much more critical to the quality of a VLSI design than ever.

A fundamental problem to floorplanning/placement lies in the representation of geometric relationship among modules. The representation profoundly affects the operations of modules and the complexity of a floorplan/placement design process. It is thus desired to develop an efficient, flexible, and effective representation of geometric relationship for floorplan/placement designs.

Many floorplan representations have been proposed in the literature. We can represent a floorplan as a rectangular dissection of the floorplan region, and classify the representations based on the floorplan structures that the representations can model. Preceding chapters have covered the slicing structure [1,2], which can be obtained by repetitively subdividing rectangles horizontally or vertically into smaller rectangles, and the mosaic structure [3] for which the floorplan region is dissected into rooms so that each room contains exactly one module. The mosaic structure is more general than the slicing structure in the sense that the former can model more floorplan structures.

This chapter focuses on the representations for the packing structure, the most general floorplan representation that can model a floorplan with empty rooms. There is a special type of the packing structure, the compacted structure, for which modules are compacted to some corner of the floorplan region, say the bottom-left corner, and no module can further be shifted down or left. The compacted structure induces much smaller solution spaces than the general one. Unlike the general packing representation, which can fully model the topological relationship among modules [4–8], however, the compacted packing representations [9–11] can model only partial topological information, and thus the module dimensions are required to construct an exact floorplan.

In this chapter, we shall detail the modeling, properties, and operations of the popular packing floorplan representations in the literature: compacted floorplan representations such as O-tree, B^*-tree, and corner sequence (CS), and general packing ones such as sequence pair (SP) [6], bounded-sliceline grid (BSG), transitive closure graph (TCG), transitive closure graph with a sequence (TCG-S), and adjacent constraint graph (ACG) [8].

11.1.1 PROBLEM DEFINITION

To make this chapter self-contained, we shall start with the definition of the floorplanning problem. Let $B = \{b_1, b_2, \ldots, b_m\}$ be a set of m rectangular modules whose width, height, and area are denoted by w_i, h_i, and a_i, $1 \leq i \leq m$. Each module is free to rotate. Let (x_i, y_i) denote the coordinate of the bottom-left corner of module b_i, $1 \leq i \leq m$, on a chip. A placement $\mathcal{P}$ is an assignment of (x_i, y_i) for each $b_i, 1 \leq i \leq m$, such that no two modules overlap. The goal of floorplanning/placement is to optimize a predefined cost metric such as a combination of the area (i.e., the minimum bounding rectangle of $\mathcal{P}$) and wirelength (i.e., the summation of half bounding box of interconnections) induced by a placement.

In the following sections, we first introduce the compacted packing floorplanning representations, O-tree [10], B*-tree [9], and CS [11], and then the general ones, SP [6], BSG [7], TCG [4,12], TCG-S [5,13], and ACG [8].

11.2 O-TREE

An O-tree is used to model an admissible placement defined in Ref. [10]. A placement is said to be admissible if and only if all modules are compacted in both x- and y-directions; i.e., no module can shift left or down with other modules being fixed. Figure 11.1a gives an example of an admissible placement.

11.2.1 RELATIONSHIP BETWEEN A PLACEMENT AND AN O-TREE

An O-tree is a rooted ordered tree structure with an arbitrary number of branches (children) for each node. There are two types of O-trees, horizontal O-trees and vertical O-trees. Given an admissible placement, a horizontal O-tree T can be constructed as follows. The root represents the left boundary of the placement. The children are adjacent to and on the right-hand side of their parent with zero separation distance in the x-direction. See Figure 11.1b for a horizontal O-tree of the admissible placement shown in Figure 11.1a. A vertical O-tree can similarly be defined by making the root represent the bottom boundary of the placement and an edge represent the vertical geometrical relationship between two modules. An O-tree is encoded by the two-tuple (S, π), where the $2(n-1)$-bit string S identifies the branching structure of the n-node tree, and the permutation π denotes the module sequence for the depth-first search (DFS) traversal of the tree. A "0" ("1") represents a traversal which descends (ascends) an edge in the tree. An example is shown in Figure 11.1b for the two-tuple $(S, \pi) = (001100011101, abcdef)$ that encodes the placement/floorplan shown in Figure 11.1a.

Because the root of a horizontal O-tree represents the left boundary of the placement/floorplan, we set its coordinate $(x_{\text{root}}, y_{\text{root}}) = (0, 0)$. Let node n_i be the parent of node n_j, we have $x_j = x_i + w_i$. For each module b_i, let $L(i)$ be the set of modules b_k's on the left of b_i in π, and interval $(x_k, x_k + w_k)$ overlaps interval $(x_i, x_i + w_i)$ by a nonzero length. If $L(i)$ is nonempty, we have

$$y_i = \begin{cases} \max_{k \in L(i)}\{y_k + h_k\}, & L(i) \neq \emptyset \\ 0, & \text{otherwise} \end{cases}$$

We can find a placement by visiting the tree in the DFS order from an horizontal O-tree.

To efficiently compute the y-coordinate from a horizontal O-tree, we can adopt the contour data structure [10] to facilitate the operations on modules. The contour structure is a doubly linked list for modules, describing the contour curve in the current compaction direction. A horizontal

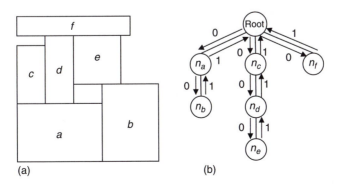

(a)   (b)

FIGURE 11.1   (a) Admissible placement and (b) O-tree for the placement shown in (a).

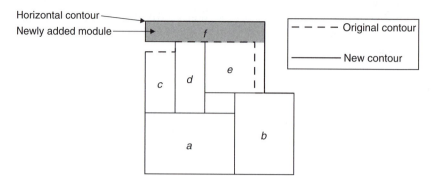

FIGURE 11.2 To add a new module on top, we search the horizontal contour from left to right and update it with the top boundary of the new module.

contour (Figure 11.2) can be used to reduce the running time for finding the y-coordinate of a newly inserted module. Without the contour, the running time for determining the y-coordinate of a newly inserted module would be linear to the number of modules. However, the y-coordinate of a module can be computed in amortized $O(1)$ time by maintaining the contour structure [10], making the overall packing time for a floorplan to be linear to the number of modules. Figure 11.2 illustrates how to update the horizontal contour after inserting a new module.

11.2.2 O-TREE PERTURBATIONS

An O-tree can be perturbed by the following steps: (1) select a module b_i in the original O-tree (S, π), (2) delete a module b_i from the O-tree (S, π), and (3) insert a module b_i in the position with the best value of the cost function among all possible external positions in (S, π). Figure 11.3 gives the definition of the internal and external positions.

Given an O-tree with n nodes, there are $2n - 1$ possible inserting positions as external nodes. In Figure 11.3, there are 13 possible inserting positions in the 7-node tree. The operation of finding these positions on (S, π) is simply adding a string 01 to any position in bit string S and adding the label to its related position in π.

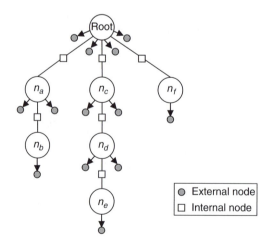

FIGURE 11.3 Internal and external insertion positions. To facilitate updating the encoding tuple, the O-tree allows a node to be inserted only at the external positions.

11.3   B*-TREE

B*-trees, proposed by Chang et al. [9], are based on ordered binary trees and the admissible placement. Inheriting from the nice properties of ordered binary trees, B*-trees are very easy for implementation and can perform the respective primitive tree operations search, insertion, and deletion in only constant, constant, and linear times.

There exists a unique correspondence between an admissible placement and its induced B*-tree. Given an admissible placement $\mathcal{P}$, in other words, we can construct a unique B*-tree corresponding to $\mathcal{P}$, and the packing corresponding to the B*-tree is the same as $\mathcal{P}$. Therefore, an optimal placement (in terms of packing area)—an admissible placement—always corresponds to some B*-tree. The nice property of the unique correspondence between an admissible placement and its induced B*-tree prevents the search space from being enlarged with redundant solutions and guarantees that an optimal placement can be found by searching on B*-trees.

11.3.1   FROM A PLACEMENT TO A B*-TREE

Given an admissible placement $\mathcal{P}$, we can represent it by a unique (horizontal) B*-tree T. Figure 11.4b gives an example of a B*-tree representing the placement of Figure 11.4a. A B*-tree is an ordered binary tree whose root corresponds to the module on the bottom-left corner. Similar to the DFS procedure, we construct the B*-tree T for an admissible placement P in a recursive fashion: Starting from the root, we first recursively construct the left subtree and then the right subtree. Let R_i denote the set of modules located on the right-hand side and adjacent to b_i. The left child of the node n_i corresponds to the lowest module in R_i that is unvisited. The right child of the node n_i represents the lowest module located above and with its x-coordinate equal to that of b_i. Following the aforementioned DFS procedure and definitions, we can guarantee the One-to-one correspondence between an admissible placement and its induced B*-tree.

As shown in Figure 11.4, it makes the module a the root of T because a is on the bottom-left corner. Constructing the left subtree of n_a recursively, it makes n_b the left child of n_a. Because the left child of n_b does not exist, it then constructs the right subtree of n_b. The construction is recursively performed in the DFS order. After completing the left subtree of n_a, the same procedure applies to the right subtree of n_a. The resulting B*-tree for the placement of Figure 11.4a is shown in Figure 11.4b. The construction takes only linear time.

11.3.2   FROM A B*-TREE TO A PLACEMENT

Given a B*-tree T, we shall compute the x- and y-coordinates for each module associated with a node in the tree. The x- and y-coordinates of the module associated with the root $(x_{root}, y_{root}) = (0, 0)$

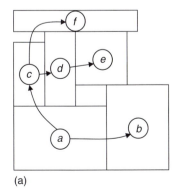

(a)

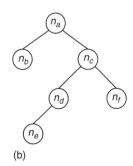

(b)

FIGURE 11.4   (a) Admissible placement and (b) the (horizontal) B*-tree representing the placement.

because the root of T represents the bottom-left module. The B*-tree keeps the geometric relationship between two modules as follows. If node n_j is the left child of node n_i, module b_j must be located on the right-hand side and adjacent to module b_i in the admissible placement; i.e., $x_j = x_i + w_i$. Besides, if node n_j is the right child of n_i, module b_j must be located above, with the x-coordinate of b_j equal to that of b_i; i.e., $x_j = x_i$. Therefore, given a B*-tree, the x-coordinates of all modules can be determined by traversing the tree once. Similar to the O-tree, the contour data structure is adopted to efficiently compute the y-coordinate from a B*-tree (Section 11.2.1). Overall, given a B*-tree, we can determine the corresponding packing (i.e., compute the x- and y-coordinates for all modules) in linear time.

11.3.3 B*-TREE PERTURBATIONS

Given an initial B*-tree (a feasible solution), we perturb the B*-tree to another using the following three operations.

- Op1: rotate a module
- Op2: move a module to another place
- Op3: swap two modules

Op1 rotates a module, and the B*-tree structure is not changed. Op2 deletes and inserts a node. Op2 and Op3 need to apply the deletion and insertion operations for deleting and inserting a node from and to a B*-tree. We explain the two operations in the following.

Deletion: There are three cases for the deletion operation.

- Case 1: a leaf node
- Case 2: a node with one child
- Case 3: a node with two children

In Case 1, we simply delete the target leaf node. In Case 2, we remove the target node and then place its only child at the position of the removed node. The tree update can be performed in $O(1)$ time. In Case 3, we replace the target node n_t by either its right child or its left child n_c. Then we move a child of n_c to the original position of n_c. The process proceeds until the corresponding leaf node is handled. Such a deletion operation requires $O(h)$ time, where h is the height of the B*-tree. Note that in Cases 2 and 3, the relative positions of the modules might be changed after the operation, and thus we might need to reconstruct a corresponding placement for further processing.

Insertion: While adding a module, we can place it around some module. We define two types of positions as follows.

- Internal position: a position between two nodes in a B*-tree
- External position: a position pointed by a NULL pointer

We can insert a new node into either an internal or an external position.

11.4 CORNER SEQUENCE

Corner Sequence (CS) = $\langle (S_1, D_1)(S_2, D_2) \cdots (S_m, D_m) \rangle$ uses a packing sequence S of the m modules as well as the corresponding bends D formed by the modules to describe a compacted placement [11]. Each two-tuple (S_i, D_i), $1 \le i \le m$, is referred to as a term of the CS. We first show how to derive a CS representation from a compacted placement.

11.4.1 FROM A PLACEMENT TO A CS

A module b_i is said to cover another module b_j if b_i is higher than b_j and their projections in the x axis overlap, or b_i is right to b_j and their projections in the y axis overlap (i.e., $y'_j \leq y_i, x'_j > x_i$ and $x_j < x'_i$, or if $x'_j \leq x_i, y'_j > y_i$ and $y_j < y'_i$). Here, $x'_i = x_i + w_i$ and $y'_i = y_i + h_i$. Given an admissible placement [10] (a left and bottom compacted placement), we first pick the dummy modules b_s and b_t, and make $R = \langle st \rangle$ for the two chosen modules. The module b_i on the bottom-left corner of $\mathcal{P}$ is picked (i.e., $S_1 = b_i$ and $D_1 = [s, t]$) because it is the unique module at the bend of R, and the new R becomes $\langle sit \rangle$. When there exists more than one module at bends, we pick the left-most module that does not cover other unvisited modules at the bends. Therefore, the module b_j at the bend $[s, i]$ is picked if b_j exists and b_j does not cover the other unvisited module b_k at the bend $[i, t]$; otherwise, b_k is picked. This process continues until no module is available. On the basis of above procedure, there exists at least one module at a bend of the current R before all modules are chosen because the placement is compacted. Therefore, there exists a unique CS corresponding to a compacted placement.

Figure 11.6a through h show the process to build a CS from the placement $\mathcal{P}$ of Figure 11.5a. R initially consists of s and t. Module a at bottom-left corner is chosen first because it is the unique module at the bend of $R(S_1 = a$ and $D_1 = [s, t])$. Figure 11.6a shows the resulting R (denoted by heavily shaded areas). Similarly, module b is chosen ($S_2 = b$ and $D_2 = [a, t]$) and the new R is shown in Figure 11.6b. After module b_d in Figure 11.6b is chosen, a and b are removed from R because the corner formed by a and b is already occupied (see Figure 11.6c for the new R). As shown in Figure 11.6d, there exist two modules b_f and b_c at bends. Although b_f is left to b_c, we pick b_c first because b_f covers b_c. This process repeats until no module is available, and the resulting CS is shown in Figure 11.6i.

11.4.2 FROM A CS TO A PLACEMENT

The dynamic sequence packing (DSP for short) scheme [11] is used to transform a CS into a placement. For DSP, a contour structure is maintained to place a new module. Let L be a doubly linked list that keeps modules in a contour. Given a CS, we can obtain the corresponding placement in $O(m)$ time by inserting a node into L for each term in the CS, where m is the number of modules.

L initially consists of n_s and n_t that denote dummy modules s and t, respectively. For each term $(i, [j, k])$ in a CS, we insert a node n_i between n_j and n_k in L for module b_i, and assign the $x(y)$ coordinate of module b_i as $x'_j(y'_k)$. This corresponds to placing module b_i at the bend $[j, k]$. Then, those modules that are dominated by b_i in the $x(y)$ direction should be removed from R. This can be done by deleting the predecessor (successor) n_p's of n_i in L if y'_p's (x'_p's) are smaller than $y'_i(x'_i)$. The

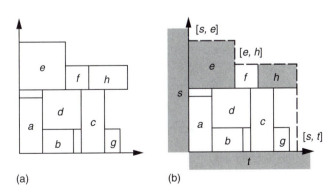

(a) (b)

FIGURE 11.5 (a) Placement $\mathcal{P}$ in a chip. (b) Contour R of $\mathcal{P}$. (From Lin, J.-M., Chang, Y.-W., and Lin, S.-P., *IEEE Trans. VLSI Syst.*, 4, 679, 2003. With permission.)

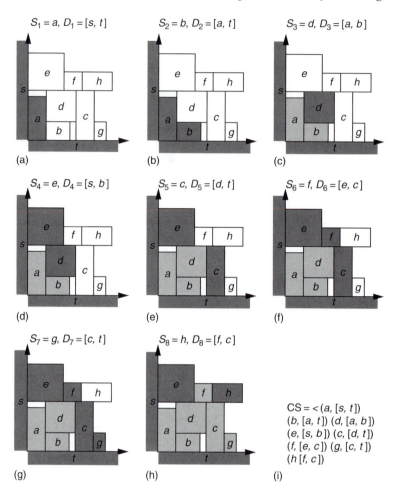

FIGURE 11.6 (a–h) Process to build a CS from a placement. (Note that the heavily shaded modules denote those in R and the lightly shaded ones denote the visited modules.) (i) Resulting CS. (From Lin, J.-M., Chang, Y.-W., and Lin, S.-P., *IEEE Trans. VLSI Syst.*, 11, 679, 2003. With permission.)

process repeats until no term in the CS is available. Let $W(H)$ denote the width (height) of a chip. $W = x'_u(H = y'_v)$ if $n_u(n_v)$ is the node right before (behind) $n_t(n_s)$ in the final L.

Figure 11.7 gives an example of the packing scheme for the CS shown in Figure 11.7a. L initially consists of n_s and n_t. We first insert a node n_a between n_s and n_t because $S_1 = a$ and $D_1 = [s, t]$. The $x(y)$ coordinate of b_a is $x'_s(y'_t)$. Figure 11.7b shows the resulting placement and L. Similarly n_b is inserted between n_a and n_t in L of Figure 11.7b because $S_2 = b$ and $D_2 = [a, t]$ (see Figure 11.7c for the resulting placement and L). After we insert a node n_d between the two nodes n_a and n_b in L of Figure 11.7c for the third term $(d, [a, b])$ in the CS, the predecessor n_a (successor n_b) of n_d is deleted because $y'_a \leq y'_d(x'_b \leq x'_d)$ (see Figure 11.7d). The process repeats for all terms in the CS, and the resulting placement and L are shown in Figure 11.7i. The width (height) of a chip is $W = x'_h(H = y'_e)$ because the node right before (behind) $n_t(n_s)$ is $n_h(n_e)$ in L. The DSP packing scheme packs modules correctly in $O(m)$ time, where m is the number of modules.

The solution space of CS is bounded by $(m!)^2$, where m is the number of modules. It should be noted that, in addition to the number of modules, the solution space of CS also depends on the dimensions of the modules. The above theorem considers the worst case for CS—all modules appear

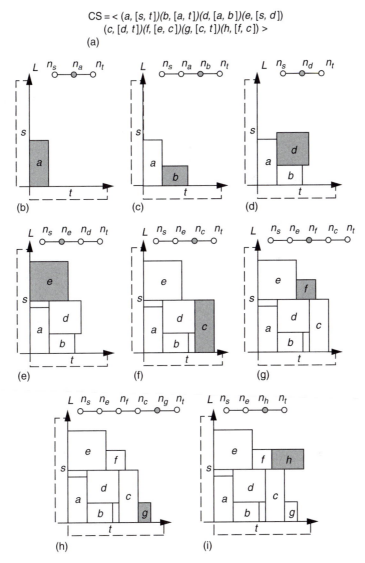

FIGURE 11.7 (b–i) DSP packing scheme for the CS shown in (a), where $CS = \langle(a,[s,t])(b,[a,t]) (d,[a,b])(e,[s,d])(c,[d,t])(f,[e,c])(g,[c,t])(h,[f,c])\rangle$. (From Lin, J.-M., Chang, Y.-W., and Lin, S.-P., *IEEE Trans. VLSI Syst.*, 11, 679, 2003. With permission.)

in the contour all the time during packing. Obviously, it is quite often that only part of the modules are in the contour. Therefore, the practical solution space of CS is significantly smaller than $(m!)^2$.

11.4.3   CS PERTURBATIONS

A CS can be perturbed by the following four perturbations to obtain a new CS:

- Exchange: exchange two modules in S_i and S_j.
- Insert: insert the ith term between the jth and $(j+1)$th terms.
- Rotate: rotate a module in S_i.
- Randomize: randomize a new D_i for the module in S_i by choosing arbitrary neighboring nodes in L.

For the exchange and insert (rotate and randomize) operations, the first l terms of the given CS will not be changed during perturbation, where $l = \min\{i,j\} - 1 (l = i - 1)$. Therefore, for each perturbation, we only need to consider the modules after the lth term and perform incremental update on the existing packing (solution). The coordinate of module b_i in $S_i, i = l + 1, \ldots, m$, can be obtained by inserting a node n_i into two neighboring nodes n_j and n_k in L if $D_i = [j,k]$. However, if the designated nodes do not exist in L, we randomly insert the node n_i into two arbitrary neighboring nodes n_q and n_r in L, and thus $D_i = [q,r]$. Note that we can guarantee a feasible solution after each perturbation by applying this process.

Figure 11.8 illustrates the procedure to perturb the CS using the exchange operation. If two modules f and h in S_6 and S_8 are exchanged, we have the new CS shown in Figure 11.8a. Figure 11.8b shows the placement and L for the CS before perturbation. Modules $a, b, c, d,$ and e are in the first five terms of the CS, and will not be changed for this perturbation because $l = \min\{6,8\} - 1 = 5$ here. The coordinates of the modules in the last three terms of CS can be obtained by their corresponding bends. (We insert nodes between two designated neighboring nodes according to their bends). Figure 11.8c shows the resulting placement and L after we insert the node n_h between the nodes n_e and n_c in the L of Figure 11.8b. Then, for module g, we cannot place it at the designated bend $[c,t]$ because there do not exist two adjacent nodes n_c and n_t in the L of Figure 11.8c. Therefore, we randomly insert n_g into two arbitrary neighboring nodes in L. There are three candidate bends for placing module g: $[s,e], [e,h],$ and $[h,t]$ (see the L and the placement). If we insert n_g between n_e and n_h (the new bend of module g becomes $[e,h]$), the resulting placement and L is given in Figure 11.8d. Similarly, we intend to insert n_f between nodes n_f and n_c for the module f in the L of Figure 11.8d. However,

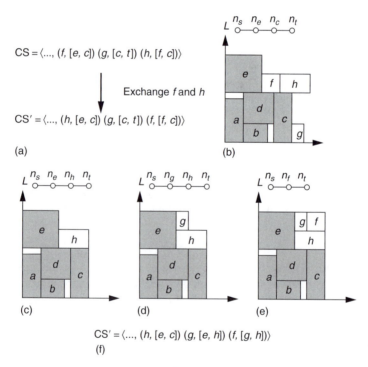

FIGURE 11.8 Example of exchanging two modules b_f and b_h in S_6 and S_8 for the CS. (a) CS after the modules in S_6 and S_8 have been exchanged. (b) L for those modules $a, b, c, d,$ and e whose coordinates remain the same. (c)–(e) Resulting placement and L after the modules $h, g,$ and f have been packed, respectively. (f) Resulting CS after the operation. (From Lin, J.-M., Chang, Y.-W., and Lin, S.-P., *IEEE Trans. VLSI Syst.*, 11, 679, 2003. With permission.)

there do not exist two neighboring nodes n_f and n_c in the L of Figure 11.8d, we thus randomly insert it between the nodes n_g and n_h. See Figure 11.8e for the resulting placement and L. Finally, we have the resulting CS shown in Figure 11.8f.

11.5 SEQUENCE PAIR

Sequence pair (SP) is proposed by Murata et al. [6]. An SP is an ordered pair of module name sequences to model general floorplans.

11.5.1 FROM A PLACEMENT TO AN SP

Figure 11.9 gives an example placement $\mathcal{P}$ on a chip. The following procedure encodes $\mathcal{P}$ to an SP. For each module b_i, we draw two lines, up-right locus and down-left locus. The up-right locus of module b_i is initially located at the upper-right corner of b_i and starts to move upward. It turns its direction alternately right and up until it reaches the upper-right corner without crossing: (1) boundaries of other modules, (2) previously drawn lines, and (3) the boundary of the chip. The down-left locus of b_i can be drawn in the similar method. The union of these two loci and the connecting diagonal line of b_i is called the positive locus of b_i. They are referred to by the corresponding module names. An example of resulting positive loci is shown in Figure 11.10a.

With the construction of positive loci, we have that no two positive loci cross each other. Thus, these positive loci can be linearly ordered, as well as the corresponding modules. Here we order the positive loci from left. Let Γ_+ be the module name sequence in this order. In Figure 11.10a, $\Gamma_+ = ecadfb$ is obtained.

Negative loci are drawn similarly as the positive loci. The difference is that a negative locus is the union of the left-up locus and right-down locus. Let Γ_- be the module name sequence in the order of the negative loci from left. An example of negative loci is shown in Figure 11.10b. Observing it from left, $\Gamma_- = fcbead$ is obtained. Finally, the SP (Γ_+, Γ_-) is obtained.

11.5.2 FROM AN SP TO A PLACEMENT

Given an SP (Γ_+, Γ_-), the geometric relation of modules can be derived from an SP as follows. Module b_i is left (right) to module b_j if b_i appears before (after) b_j in both Γ_+ and Γ_-. Module b_i is below (above) module b_j if b_i appears after (before) b_j in Γ_+ and b_i appears before (after) b_j in Γ_-.

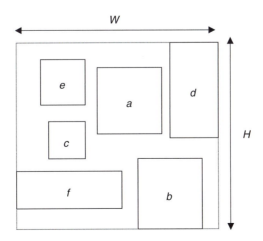

FIGURE 11.9 Placement $\mathcal{P}$ on a chip. (From Murata, H., Fujiyoshi, K., Nakatake, S., and Kajitani, Y., *IEEE Trans. Comput. Aided Des. Integr. Circuits Syst.*, 15, 1518, 1996. With permission.)

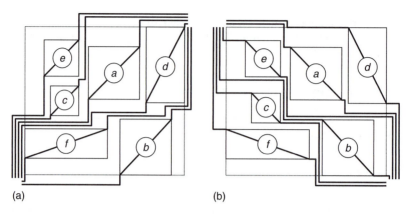

FIGURE 11.10 (a) Positive loci and (b) negative loci. (From Murata, H., Fujiyoshi, K., Nakatake, S., and Kajitani, Y., *IEEE Trans. Comput. Aided Des. Integr. Circuits Syst.*, 15, 1518, 1996. With permission.)

To obtain the placement from an SP, we construct an $m \times m$ grid. Label the horizontal grid lines and vertical grid lines with module names along Γ_+ and Γ_- from top and from left, respectively. A cross point of the horizontal grid line of label i and the vertical grid line of label j is referred to by (i, j). Then, rotate the resulting grid by 45° counterclockwise to get an oblique grid. (Figure 11.11) Put each module b_i with its center being on (i, i). Expand the separation of grid lines enough to eliminate overlapping of modules. The resulting packing trivially satisfies the constraint implied by the given SP. An example is shown in Figure 11.11.

Given an SP (Γ_+, Γ_-), the optimal packing under the constraint can be obtained in $O(m^2)$ time, where m is the number of modules, by applying the well-known longest path algorithm for node-weighted directed acyclic graphs. The process is given below. We first construct the horizontal-constraint graph, a directed and node-weighted graph $G_H(V, E)$ (where V is the set of nodes, and E is the set of edges), based on the "left of" constraint of (Γ_+, Γ_-).

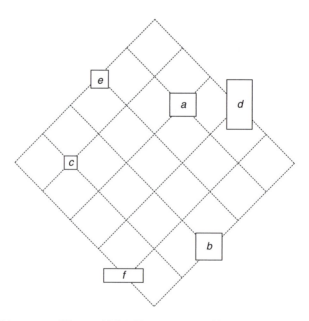

FIGURE 11.11 Packing on an oblique grid for $(\Gamma_+, \Gamma_-) = (ecadfb, fcbead)$. (From Murata, H., Fujiyoshi, K., Nakatake, S., and Kajitani, Y., *IEEE Trans. Comput. Aided Des. Integr. Circuits Syst.*, 15, 1518, 1996. With permission.)

1. V: source s, sink t, and m nodes labeled with module names
2. E: (s, i) and (i, t) for each module b_i, and (i, j) if and only if b_i appears before (after) b_j in both Γ_+ and Γ_- (the "left of" constraint)
3. Node-weight: zero for s and t, width of module b_i for the remaining nodes

Similarly, the vertical-constraint graph $G_V(V, E)$ is constructed using the "below" constraint and the height of each module.

There should be no directed cycle in both graphs. We set the x-coordinate of b_i to be the longest path length from s to i in G_H. The y-coordinate of b_i is set independently using G_V. If two modules b_i and b_j are in horizontal relation, then there is an edge between i and j in G_H, and thus they do not overlap horizontally in the resulting placement. Similarly, if b_i and b_j are in vertical relation, they do not overlap vertically. Because any pair of modules are either in horizontal or vertical relation, no two modules overlap each other in the resulting placement.

The width (height) of the chip is determined by the longest path length between the source and the sink in $G_H(G_V)$. The longest path length calculation on each graph can be done in $O(m^2)$ time, proportional to the number of edges in the graph. For the G_H and G_V shown in Figure 11.12, we have $(\Gamma_+, \Gamma_-) = (ecadfb, fcbead)$. The resulting placement after the longest path length calculation is shown in Figure 11.13.

On the basis of the longest common subsequence (LCS), two faster packing algorithms with respective time complexities $O(\lg n)$ and $O(\lg \lg n)$ to transform a SP to its placement are proposed by Tang, Tian, and Wong [14] and Tang and Wong [15]. Given an SP (Γ_+, Γ_-), let Γ_+^R denotes the reverse of Γ_+, and define $lcs(X, Y)$ as the length of the LCS of X and Y. That is, if $Z = \langle z_1, z_2, \ldots, z_n \rangle$ is the LCS of two weighted sequences X and Y, $lcs(X, Y) = \sum_{i=1}^{n} w(z_i)$, and $w(z_i)$ is the weight of z_i. If an SP $(\Gamma_+, \Gamma_-) = (X_1 b X_2, Y_1 b Y_2)$, then $lcs(X_1, Y_1)$ is the x coordinate of the block b, where $w(i)$ is the width of the block i, and $lcs(\Gamma_+, \Gamma_-)$ is the width of the placement. For the y coordinate, if an SP $(\Gamma_+, \Gamma_-) = (X_1 b X_2, Y_1 b Y_2)$, then $(\Gamma_+^R, \Gamma_-) = (X_2^R b X_1^R, Y_1 b Y_2)$ and $lcs(X_2^R, Y_1)$ is the y coordinate of the block b, where $w(i)$ is the height of the block i, and $lcs(\Gamma_+, \Gamma_-)$ is the width of the placement. Thus, given an SP, we can compute the LCS to determine the x and y coordinates of all blocks and the width/height of the placement. The packing times are $O(\lg n)$ and $O(\lg \lg n)$ when the balanced search tree and host tree are used to compute the LCS [14], respectively.

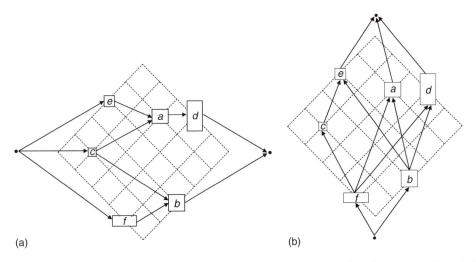

(a)   (b)

FIGURE 11.12   (a) Constraint graph G_H and (b) constraint graph G_V (transitive edges are not shown in both graphs for simplicity). (From Murata, H., Fujiyoshi, K., Nakatake, S., and Kajitani, Y., *IEEE Trans. Comput. Aided Des. Integr. Circuits Syst.*, 15, 1518, 1996. With permission.)

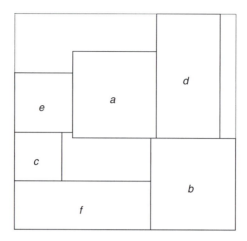

FIGURE 11.13 Best packing with the minimum area induced by $(\Gamma_+, \Gamma_-) = (ecadfb, fcbead)$. (From Murata, H., Fujiyoshi, K., Nakatake, S., and Kajitani, Y., *IEEE Trans. Comput. Aided Des. Integr. Circuits Syst.*, 15, 1518, 1996. With permission.)

11.5.3 SP PERTURBATIONS

There are three types of pair-interchanges: (1) two module names in Γ_+, (2) two module names both in Γ_+ and Γ_-, and (3) the width and the height of a module, where the last one is for orientation optimization.

11.6 BOUNDED-SLICELINE GRID

A BSG structure [7] contains rooms, horizontal unit segments, and vertical unit segments. Figure 11.14 shows an example of a BSG of dimension $p \times q$, $\mathrm{BSG}_{p \times q}$. When using a BSG structure to represent a placement, $p \times q$ must be larger or equal to the number of modules. A rectangular space surrounded by an adjacent pair of vertical and horizontal units is called the room. Vertical unit

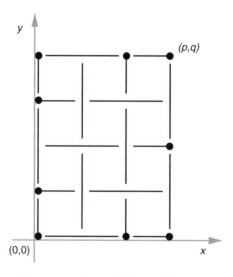

FIGURE 11.14 BSG of dimension $p \times q$, $\mathrm{BSG}_{p \times q}$. (From Nakatake, S., Fujiyoshi, K., Murata, H., and Kajitani, Y., *Proceedings of International Conference on Computer-Aided Design*, 1996. With permission.)

segments define the vertical relations, while horizontal unit segments define the horizontal ones. The placement of m modules is formulated as the room assignment of m modules by placing m modules into different rooms. The next section describes an algorithm to transform the BSG room assignment to the corresponding placement.

11.6.1 FROM A BSG ASSIGNMENT TO A PLACEMENT

Given a set of modules M, where $|M| = n$. Assuming that $p \times q \geq n$, an assignment of M is a one-to-one mapping of modules into the rooms of $\text{BSG}_{p \times q}$. A room to which no module is assigned is called an empty room.

We use the example shown in Figure 11.15 to explain the process of transforming the BSG to the corresponding placement. Given four modules (Figure 11.15a) and the assignment of four modules in the BSG (Figure 11.15b), we construct a horizontal unit adjacency graph $G_h(V_h, E_h)$ and a vertical unit adjacency graph $G_v(V_v, E_v)$ according to the BSG, and assign the weight of the edges in the unit adjacency graphs. If $e \in E_h$ and e crosses a nonempty room, $w(e) =$ height of the module assigned there. If $e \in E_v$ and e crosses a nonempty room, $w(e) =$ width of the module assigned there. Otherwise, if e crosses an empty room or is incident on the source or the sink, $w(e) = 0$. The corresponding horizontal unit adjacency graph $G_h(V_h, E_h)$ and the vertical unit adjacency graph $G_v(V_v, E_v)$ to the assignment are shown in Figure 11.15c and d, respectively.

Let $G_h(V_h, E_h)$ be the horizontal unit adjacency graph. For each vertex $u \in V_h$, $l_h(u)$ denotes the length of the longest path from the source s_h to u. Similarly in G_v, $l_v(u)$ denotes the longest path length from s_v to $u \in V_v$. We use a longest-path algorithm to determine the positions of modules. The longest-path algorithm works in linear time of the number of edges when the input G is a directed acyclic graph. The total number of edges of the unit adjacency graphs is between $2(pq + p + q)$ and $2(pq + p + q) - 4$. So, the time complexity to find the longest path is $O(pq)$.

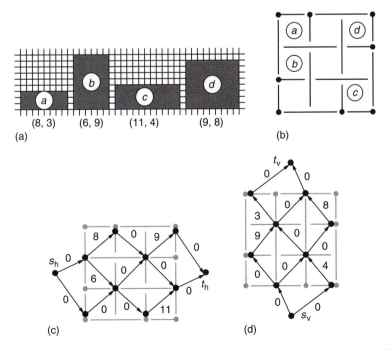

FIGURE 11.15   (a) Input modules, (b) BSG assignment, (c) horizontal unit adjacency graph $G_h(V_h, E_h)$, and (d) vertical unit adjacency graph $G_v(V_v, E_v)$. (From Nakatake, S., Fujiyoshi, K., Murata, H., and Kajitani, Y., *Proceedings of International Conference on Computer-Aided Design*, 1996. With permission.)

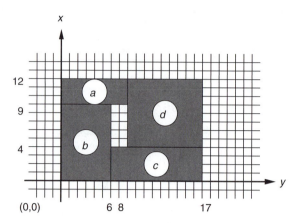

FIGURE 11.16 Corresponding placement of the example in Figure 11.15. (From Nakatake, S., Fujiyoshi, K., Murata, H., and Kajitani, Y., *Proceedings of International Conference on Computer-Aided Design*, 1996. With permission.)

The following BSG-PACK procedure transforms a BSG with a given assignment to the corresponding placement [7]:

> Given an assignment of M to $BSG_{p \times q}$, let m be a module assigned to a room whose left (vertical) boundary unit is V_m and bottom (horizontal) boundary unit is H_m. Then, place m such that its left bottom is at $(l_v(u_{V_m}), l_h(u_{H_m}))$ where u_{V_m} and u_{H_m} are the vertices corresponding to the units V_m and H_m in the vertical unit and horizontal unit adjacency graphs, respectively. The area of the packing is $(l_v(t_v) \times l_h(t_h))$.

Figure 11.16 gives the resulting placement for the assignment of Figure 11.15.

11.6.2 BSG PERTURBATIONS

It is very simple to perturb one BSG assignment to get another BSG assignment. We can first choose two different rooms, and then interchange (swap) the contents of them to generate a new BSG assignment.

11.7 TRANSITIVE CLOSURE GRAPH

The transitive closure of a directed acyclic graph G is defined as the graph $G' = (V, E')$, where $E' = \{(n_i, n_j)$: there is a path from node n_i to node n_j in $G\}$. The representation, proposed by Lin and Chang in Refs. [4,12], describes the geometric relations among modules based on two graphs, namely a horizontal TCG C_h and a vertical TCG C_v. In this section, we first introduce the procedure for constructing C_h and C_v from a placement. Then, we describe how to pack modules from TCG.

11.7.1 FROM A PLACEMENT TO A TCG

For two nonoverlapped modules b_i and b_j, b_i is said to be horizontally (vertically) *related* to b_j, denoted by $b_i \vdash b_j (b_i \perp b_j)$, if b_i is on the left (bottom) side of b_j and their projections on the $y(x)$ axis overlap. Note that two modules cannot have both horizontal and vertical relations unless they overlap. For two nonoverlapped modules b_i and b_j, b_i is said to be diagonally related to b_j if b_i is on the left side of b_j and their projections on the x and the y axes do not overlap. In a placement, every two modules must bear one of the three relations: horizontal relation, vertical relation, and diagonal relation. To simplify the operations on geometric relations, we treat a diagonal relation for modules b_i and b_j as a horizontal one, unless there exists a chain of vertical relations from $b_i(b_j)$, followed by

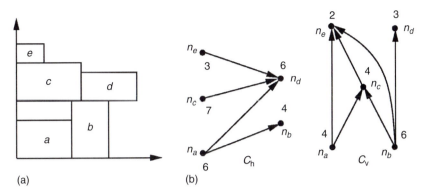

FIGURE 11.17   (a) Placement in a chip and (b) the corresponding TCG. (From Lin, J.-M., and Chang, Y.-W., *IEEE Trans. VLSI Syst.*, 13, 288, 2005. With permission.)

the modules enclosed with the rectangle defined by the two closest corners of b_i and b_j, and finally to $b_j(b_i)$, for which we make $b_i \perp b_j(b_j \perp b_i)$.

Figure 11.17a shows a placement with five modules b_a, b_b, b_c, b_d, and b_e whose widths and heights are (6, 4), (4, 6), (7, 4), (6, 3) and (3, 2), respectively. In Figure 11.17a, $b_a \vdash b_b, b_a \perp b_c$, and module b_e is diagonally related to module b_b. There exists a chain of vertical relations formed by modules b_e, b_c, and b_b between the two modules b_e and b_b (i.e., $b_b \perp b_c$ and $b_c \perp b_e$). Therefore, we make $b_b \perp b_e$. Also, module b_e is diagonally related to module b_d. However, there does not exist a chain of vertical relations between modules b_e and b_d, and thus we make $b_e \vdash b_d$.

TCG can be derived from a placement as follows. For each module b_i in a placement, we introduce a node n_i with the weight being the width (height) in $C_h(C_v)$. If $b_i \vdash b_j$, we construct a directed edge from node n_i to node n_j (denoted by (n_i, n_j)) in C_h. Similarly, we construct a directed edge (n_i, n_j) in C_v if $b_i \perp b_j$. Given a placement with m modules, we need to perform the above process $m(m - 1)/2$ times to capture all the geometric relations among modules (i.e., C_h and C_v have $m(m - 1)/2$ edges in total).

As shown in Figure 11.17b, for each module $b_i, i \in \{a, b, c, d, e\}$, we introduce a node n_i in C_h and also in C_v. For each node n_i in $C_h(C_v), i \in \{a, b, c, d, e\}$, we associate the node with a weight equal to the width (height) of the corresponding module b_i. Because $b_a \vdash b_b$, we construct a directed edge (n_a, n_b) in C_h. Similarly, we construct a directed edge (n_a, n_c) in C_v because $b_a \perp b_c$. This process is repeated until all geometric relations among modules are defined. As shown in Figure 11.17b, each TCG has five nodes, and there are totally ten edges in C_h and C_v (four in C_h and six in C_v).

11.7.2   FROM A TCG TO A PLACEMENT

We now present the packing method for a TCG. Given a TCG, its corresponding placement can be obtained in $O(m^2)$ time by performing a well-known longest path algorithm on the TCG, where m is the number of modules. To facilitate the implementation of the longest path algorithm, we augment the given two closure graphs as follows. We introduce two special nodes with zero weights for each closure graph, the source n_s and the sink n_t, and construct an edge from n_s to each node with in-degree equal to zero, and also from each node with out-degree equal to zero to n_t. (Note that the TCG augmentation is performed only for packing. It will be clear later that such augmentation is not needed for other operations such as solution perturbation.)

Let $L_h(n_i)(L_v(n_i))$ be the length of the longest path from n_s to n_i in the augmented $C_h(C_v)$. $L_h(n_i)(L_v(n_i))$ can be determined by performing the single source longest path algorithm on the augmented $C_h(C_v)$ in $O(m^2)$ time, where m is number of modules. The coordinate (x_i, y_i) of a module b_i is given by $(L_h(n_i), L_v(n_i))$. Because the respective width and height of the placement for the given TCG are $L_h(n_t)$ and $L_v(n_t)$, the area of the placement is given by $L_h(n_t)L_v(n_t)$.

11.7.3 TCG Properties

A feasible TCG has the following three properties: (1) C_h and C_v are acyclic (2) each pair of nodes must be connected by exactly one edge either in C_h or in C_v and (3) the transitive closure of $C_h(C_v)$ is equal to $C_h(C_v)$ itself.

Property 1 ensures that a module b_i cannot be both left and right to (below and above) another module b_j in a placement. Property 2 guarantees that no two modules overlap because each pair of modules have exactly one of the horizontal or vertical relation. Property 3 is used to eliminate redundant solutions. It guarantees that if there exists a path from n_i to n_j in one closure graph, the edge (n_i, n_j) must also appear in the same closure graph. For example, there exist two edges (n_i, n_j) and (n_j, n_k) in C_h, which means that $b_i \vdash b_j$ and $b_j \vdash b_k$, and thus $b_i \vdash b_k$. If the edge (n_i, n_k) appears in C_v instead of in C_h, b_k is not only left to b_i but also above b_i. The resulting area of the corresponding placement must be larger than or equal to that when the edge (n_i, n_k) appears in C_h.

On the basis of the properties of TCG, there exists a unique placement corresponding to a TCG, and the size of the solution space for TCG is $(m!)^2$, where m is the number of modules [4].

11.7.4 TCG Perturbations

To ensure the correctness of the new TCG after perturbation, as described in the preceding section, the new TCG must satisfy the aforementioned three feasibility properties. To identify a feasible TCG for perturbation, we introduce the concept of transitive reduction edges of TCG.

An edge (n_i, n_j) is said to be a reduction edge if there does not exist another path from n_i to n_j, except the edge (n_i, n_j) itself; otherwise, it is a closure edge. Because TCG is formed by directed acyclic TCGs, given an arbitrary node n_i in one TCG, there exists at least one reduction edge (n_i, n_j), where $n_j \in F_{out}(n_i)$. Here, we define the fan-in (fan-out) of a node n_i, denoted by $F_{in}(n_i)(F_{out}(n_i))$, as the nodes n_j's with edges $(n_j, n_i)(n_i, n_j)$. For nodes $n_k, n_l \in F_{out}(n_i)$, the edge (n_i, n_k) cannot be a reduction edge if $n_k \in F_{out}(n_l)$. Hence, we remove those nodes in $F_{out}(n_i)$ that are fan-outs of others. The edges between n_i and the remaining nodes in $F_{out}(n_i)$ are reduction edges. For the C_v shown in Figure 11.17a, $F_{out}(n_a) = \{n_c, n_e\}$. Because n_e belongs to $F_{out}(n_c)$, edge (n_a, n_e) is a closure edge while (n_a, n_c) is a reduction one.

We apply the following four operations to perturb a TCG:

- Rotation: rotate a module
- Swap: swap two nodes in both of C_h and C_v
- Reverse: reverse a reduction edge in C_h or C_v
- Move: move a reduction edge from one TCG (C_h or C_v) to the other

Rotation and swap do not change the topology of a TCG while reverse and move do. To maintain the properties of the TCG after performing the reverse and move operations, we may need to update the resulting graphs.

Rotation. To rotate a module b_i, we only need to exchange the weights of the corresponding node n_i in C_h and C_v. TCG is closed under the rotation operation, and such an operation takes $O(1)$ time.

Swap. To swap two nodes n_i and n_j, we only need to exchange two nodes in both C_h and C_v. TCG is closed under the swap operation, and such an operation takes O(1) time.

Reverse. The reverse operation reverses the direction of a reduction edge (n_i, n_j) in a TCG, which corresponds to changing the geometric relation of the two modules b_i and b_j. For two modules b_i and b_j, $b_i \vdash b_j (b_i \perp b_j)$ if there exists a reduction edge (n_i, n_j) in $C_h(C_v)$; after reversing the edge (n_i, n_j), we have the new geometric relation $b_j \vdash b_i (b_j \perp b_i)$. Therefore, the geometric relation among modules is transparent not only to the TCG representation but also to the reverse operation (i.e., the effect of such an operation on the change of the geometric relation is known before packing); this property can facilitate the convergence to a desired solution.

To reverse a reduction edge (n_i, n_j) in a TCG, we first delete the edge from the graph, and then add the edge (n_j, n_i) to the graph. For each node $n_k \in F_{in}(n_j) \cup \{n_j\}$ and $n_l \in F_{out}(n_i) \cup \{n_i\}$ in the new graph, we shall check whether the edge (n_k, n_l) exists in the new graph. If the graph contains the edge, we do nothing; otherwise, we need to add the edge to the graph and delete the corresponding edges (n_k, n_l) (or (n_l, n_k)) in the other TCG, if any, to maintain the properties of the TCG.

To maintain the properties of a TCG, we can only reverse a reduction edge. Further, for each edge introduced in a TCG, we remove its corresponding edge from the other graph. Therefore, there is always exactly one relation between each pair of modules. TCG is closed under the reverse operation, and such an operation takes $O(m^2)$ time, where m is the number of modules in the placement.

Move. The move operation moves a reduction edge (n_i, n_j) in a TCG to the other, which corresponds to switching the geometric relation of the two modules b_i and b_j between a horizontal relation and a vertical one. For two modules b_i and b_j, $b_i \vdash b_j (b_i \perp b_j)$ if there exists a reduction edge (n_i, n_j) in $C_h(C_v)$; after moving the edge (n_i, n_j) to $C_v(C_h)$, we have the new geometric relation $b_i \perp b_j (b_i \vdash b_j)$. Therefore, the geometric relation among modules is also transparent to the move operation.

To move a reduction edge (n_i, n_j) from a TCG G to the other G' in a TCG, we first delete the edge from G and add it to G'. Similar to the reverse operation, for each node $n_k \in F_{in}(n_i) \cup \{n_i\}$ and $n_l \in F_{out}(n_j) \cup \{n_j\}$, we shall check whether the edge (n_k, n_l) exists in G'. If G' contains the edge, we do nothing; otherwise, we need to add the edge to G' and delete the corresponding edge (n_k, n_l) (or (n_l, n_k)) in G, if any, to maintain the properties of the TCG.

To maintain the properties of a TCG, we can only move a reduction edge. If we move a closure edge (n_i, n_k) associated with the two reduction edges (n_i, n_j) and (n_j, n_k) in one TCG to the other, then there exist a path from n_i to n_k in the two graphs, implying that $b_i \vdash b_k$ and $b_i \perp b_k$, which gives a redundant solution. Further, for each edge introduced in a TCG, we remove its corresponding edge from the other graph. Therefore, there is always exactly one relation between each pair of modules. TCG is closed under the move operation, and such an operation takes $O(m^2)$ time, where m is the number of modules in the placement.

11.8 TCG-S

TCG-S representation, also proposed by Lin and Chang in Refs. [5,13], combines TCG $= (C_h, C_v)$ and SP $= (\Gamma_+, \Gamma_-)$, which uses a horizontal and a vertical TCGs as well as the packing sequence Γ_- to represent a placement. TCG-S tries to combine the advantages of SP and TCG and at the same time eliminate their disadvantages. With the property of SP, faster packing and perturbation schemes are possible. Inheriting some nice properties from TCG, the geometric relations among modules are transparent to TCG-S (implying faster convergence to a desired solution), placement with position constraints becomes much easier, and incremental update for cost evaluation can be realized.

With the characteristics of TCG and SP, TCG-S has the following four feasibility *properties*:

1. C_h and C_v are acyclic.
2. Each pair of nodes must be connected by exactly one edge either in C_h or in C_v.
3. Transitive closure of $C_h(C_v)$ is equal to $C_h(C_v)$ itself.
4. Packing sequence Γ_- is the topological order of both C_h and C_v.

11.8.1 FROM A PLACEMENT TO TCG-S

For two nonoverlapped modules b_i and b_j, they could bear one of the horizontal, vertical, and diagonal relations as defined in Section 11.7. If b_i is horizontally (vertically) related to b_j, denoted by $b_i \vdash b_j (b_i \perp b_j)$, then b_i is left to (below) b_j and their projections on the $y(x)$ axis overlap. The diagonal relation between two modules b_i and b_j is also defined in Section 11.7, and is treated as a horizontal one unless there exists a chain of vertical relations from $b_i(b_j)$, followed by the modules overlapped with the rectangle defined by the two closest corners of b_i and b_j, and finally to $b_j(b_i)$, for which it is considered as $b_i \perp b_j(b_j \perp b_i)$.

Given a placement, Γ_- can be extracted as follows. We first extract the module on the bottom-left corner. At each iteration, we extract the left-most unvisited module b with all the modules below b having been extracted. The process repeats until no module is left. Figure 11.18a through f illustrate the procedure to extract a Γ_- from the placement of Figure 11.24a. We first extract the module b_a on the bottom-left corner (Figure 11.18a), and then b_b because it is the left-module with all the modules below b_b having been extract (Figure 11.18b). This process continues until no module is left, resulting in $\Gamma_- = \langle abcdegf \rangle$.

After extracting Γ_-, we can construct C_h and C_v based on Γ_-. For each module b_i in Γ_-, we introduce a node n_i with the weight being b_i's width (height) in $C_h(C_v)$. Also, for each module b_i before b_j in Γ_-, we introduce an edge (n_i, n_j) in $C_h(C_v)$ if $b_i \vdash b_j(b_i \perp b_j)$. As shown in Figure 11.18b and g, for the first two modules b_a, b_b in Γ_-, we introduce the nodes n_a and n_b in $C_h(C_v)$ and assign the

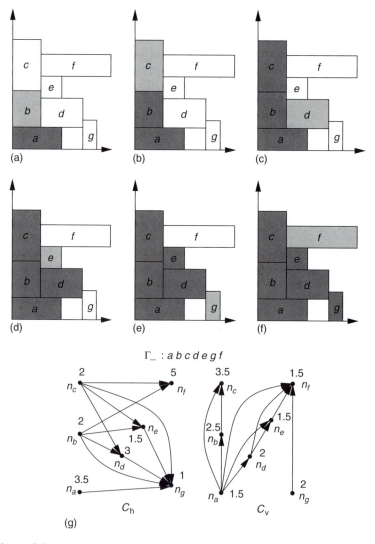

FIGURE 11.18   (a–f) Process to extract a Γ_- from the placement and (g) resulting TCG-S. (From Lin, J.-M. and Chang, Y.-W., *IEEE Trans. Comput. Aided Des. Integr. Circuits Syst.*, 23, 968, 2004. With permission.)

weights as their widths (heights). Also, we construct a directed edge (n_a, n_b) in C_v because module b_a is before b_b and $b_a \perp b_b$. The process repeats for all modules in Γ_-, resulting in the TCG-S shown in Figure 11.18g. Each TCG has seven nodes and 21 edges in total (eleven in C_h and ten in C_v). Note that there exists a unique TCG-S corresponding to a placement.

11.8.2   FROM TCG-S TO A PLACEMENT

Lin and Chang propose an $O(m \lg m)$-time packing scheme for TCG-S based on Γ_- as well as a horizontal and a vertical contours R_h and R_v, where m is the number of modules. The basic idea is to process the modules based on the sequence defined in Γ_-, and then pack the current module to a corner formed by two previously placed modules in $R_h(R_v)$ according to the geometric relation defined in $C_h(C_v)$.

11.8.3   TCG-S PERTURBATIONS

Four operations rotation, swap, reverse, and move in TCG are extended to perturb C_h and C_v. During each perturbation, we must maintain the three feasibility properties for C_h and C_v. Unlike the rotation operation, swap, reverse, and move may change the configurations of C_h and C_v and thus their properties. Further, we also need to maintain Γ_- to conform to the topological ordering for new C_h and C_v.

Rotation. To rotate a module b_i, we exchange the weights of the corresponding node n_i in C_h and C_v. Because the configurations of C_h and C_v do not change, so does Γ_-. Figure 11.19b shows the resulting TCG-S and placement after rotating the module g shown in Figure 11.19a. Notice that the new Γ_- is the same as that in Figure 11.19a. TCG-S is closed under the rotation operation, and such an operation does not change the topology of the TCG and Γ_-.

Swap. Swapping n_i and n_j does not change the topologies of C_h and C_v. Therefore, we only need to exchange b_i and b_j in Γ_-. Figure 11.19c shows the resulting TCG-S and placement after swapping the nodes n_c and n_g shown in Figure 11.19b. Notice that the modules b_c and b_g in Γ_- in Figure 11.19c are exchanged. TCG-S is closed under the Swap operation, and such an operation takes $O(1)$ time.

Reverse. To reverse a reduction edge (n_i, n_j) in one TCG, we first delete the edge (n_i, n_j) from the graph, and then add the edge (n_j, n_i) to the graph. To keep C_h and C_v feasible, for each node $n_k \in F_{in}(n_j) \cup \{n_j\}$ and $n_l \in F_{out}(n_i) \cup \{n_i\}$ in the new graph, we have to keep the edge (n_k, n_l) in the new graph. If the edge does not exist in the graph, we add the edge to the graph and delete the corresponding edge (n_k, n_l) (or (n_l, n_k)) in the other graph. To make Γ_- conform to the topological ordering of new C_h and C_v, we delete b_i from Γ_- and insert b_i after b_j. For each module b_k between b_i and b_j in Γ_-, we shall check whether the edge (n_i, n_k) exists in the same graph. We do nothing if the edge (n_i, n_k) does not exist in the same graph; otherwise, we delete b_k from Γ_- and insert it after the most recently inserted module. Figure 11.19d shows the resulting TCG-S and placement after reversing the reduction edge (n_d, n_e) of the C_v in Figure 11.19c. Because there exists no module between b_d and b_e in Γ_-, we only need to delete b_d from Γ_- and insert it after b_e, and the resulting Γ_- is shown in Figure 11.19d. TCG-S is closed under the reverse operation, and such an operation takes $O(m)$ time, where m is the number of modules.

Move. To move a reduction edge (n_i, n_j) from a TCG G to the other G', we delete the edge from G and then add it to G'. Similar to reverse, for each node $n_k \in F_{in}(n_i) \cup \{n_i\}$ and $n_l \in F_{out}(n_j) \cup \{n_j\}$ in G', we must move the edge (n_k, n_l) to G' if the corresponding edge (n_k, n_l) (or (n_l, n_k)) is in G. Because the operation changes only the edges in C_h or C_v but not the topological ordering among nodes, Γ_- remains unchanged. Figure 11.19e shows the resulting TCG-S and placement after moving the reduction edge (n_a, n_e) from C_v to C_h in Figure 11.19d. Notice that the resulting Γ_- is the same as that in Figure 11.19d. TCG-S is closed under the move operation, and such an operation takes $O(m)$ time, where m is the number of modules. In particular, Γ_- remains the same after the operation.

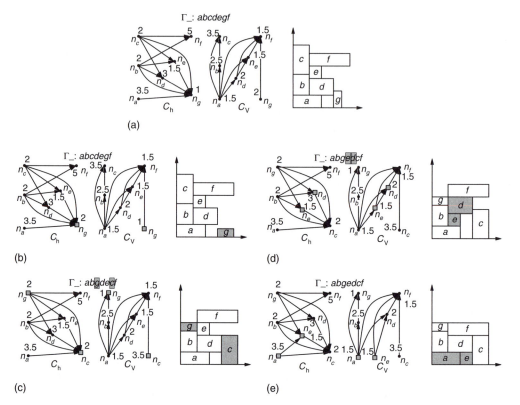

FIGURE 11.19 Four types of perturbation. (a) The initial TCG-S and placement, (b) resulting TCG-S and placement after rotating the module b_g shown in (a), (c) resulting TCG-S and placement after swapping the nodes n_c and n_g shown in (b), (d) resulting TCG-S and placement after reversing the reduction edge (n_d, n_e) shown in (c), and (e) resulting TCG-S and placement after moving the reduction edge (n_a, n_e) from the C_v of (d) to C_h. (From J.-M. Lin and Y.-W. Chang, *IEEE Trans. Comput. Aided Des. Integr. Circuits Syst.*, 23, 968, 2004. With permission.)

11.9 ADJACENT CONSTRAINT GRAPH

The ACG is proposed by Zhou and Wang [8] to model general floorplans. It tries to incorporate the advantages of both the adjacency graph and the constraint graph of a floorplan: edges in an ACG are between modules close to each other, thus the physical distance of two modules can be measured directly in the graph; the floorplan area and module positions can be simply found by longest path computations because an ACG is a constraint graph.

The idea behind the constraint graph is simple: a node represents a module and an edge in the horizontal graph represents the "left to" relation and an edge in the vertical graph represents the "below" one. The adjacency graph, on the other hand, is an undirected graph and has one edge between each pair of adjacent modules. As an illustration, for a floorplan given in Figure 11.20a, its constraint graphs are shown in Figure 11.20b, and its adjacency graph in Figure 11.20c.

ACG is defined as a constraint graph that has exactly one relation (horizontal or vertical) between every pair of nodes and has no transitive edge or cross to prevent redundancy. Here, a cross is defined as a subgraph on four nodes a, b, c, d such that edges (a, b), (c, d) are of one type (e.g., vertical edges) while (a, c), (b, c), (a, d), (b, d) are of the other type (e.g., horizontal edges). The edges in an ACG can be grouped according to the relations they represent, called groups H and V. From the definition, there are paths between any two modules within exact one group. Figure 11.20d shows the ACG of the placement in Figure 11.20a.

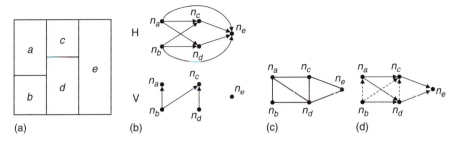

FIGURE 11.20 (a) Floorplan, (b) constraint graph, (c) adjacency graph, and (d) ACG. (From Zhou, H. and Wang, J., *Proceedings of International Conference on Computer Design*, 2004. With permission.)

11.9.1 ACG PROPERTIES

The directed edges in an ACG form a total order on the nodes. In other words, the nodes can be arranged in a line such that all the edges are from left to right. The nodes can be doubly linked in a linear order (the total order). Edges are all directed from left to right. Each edge keeps its two end nodes and is kept in one edge list at each end node. Each node maintains four linked lists of edges: one for incoming H edges, one for outgoing H edges, one for incoming V edges, and one for outgoing V edges. The edges in each list are ordered according to the distances between end nodes: shorter edges come first. The structure is illustrated by an example in Figure 11.21a, where edges are shown in arcs: the edges above the node line are in group H and those below are in group V. Notice that node n_d has one incoming H edge from n_a, one outgoing H edge to n_e, two incoming V edges from n_b and n_c, and no outgoing V edge. These four lists of edges have direct geometrical meanings, each connects to constraining modules in one direction: left, right, top, or bottom. And the edge orders in the lists will be either clockwise or counterclockwise, based on how H and V edges are interpreted. For example, if the H edges are interpreted as "left to" and the V edges as "below," the geometrical interpretation of Figure 11.21a is illustrated in Figure 11.21b, where H edges are ordered counterclockwise and V edges are ordered clockwise.

On the basis of the ACG data structure, it is simple and efficient to check and eliminate crosses. The patterns of a cross in the data structure are shown in Figure 11.22. Note that any node has edges to the three other nodes.

If the cross formed on n_a, n_b, n_c, n_d is minimal, that is, no other cross exists on nodes between n_a and n_d, the nodes n_b, n_c, n_d are consecutive among the neighbors of n_a; that is, except n_c, no node between n_b and n_d is connecting to n_a. Thus, if we follow the edges of the node n_a in consecutive order, an edge type pattern VHH or HVV implies a cross. We can verify that no cross exists by running the checking process on edges starting from every node. Verifying that no cross exists can be done in linear time in terms of the number of edges.

Total symmetry is another property of ACG. Given an ACG data structure, it is still a valid ACG when the node order is reversed or the edge groups H and V are swapped. This symmetry comes directly from the symmetry in the geometrical relations represented. The four geometrical

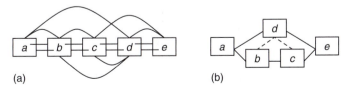

FIGURE 11.21 (a) ACG structure and (b) geometrical relations. (From Zhou, H. and Wang, J., *Proceedings of International Conference on Computer Design*, 2004. With permission.)

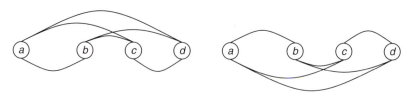

FIGURE 11.22 Patterns of a cross in an ACG. (From Zhou, H. and Wang, J., *Proceedings of International Conference on Computer Design*, 2004. With permission.)

relations, left, right, up, and down, are symmetrical with each other. On the basis of symmetry, every provable result concerning edges in an ACG also implies the other three dual results. It simplifies our presentation in the sequel. If a result concerning edges in an ACG is correct, the result by exchanging left and right (and forward and backward) or H and V is also correct. Given the order on nodes, the information represented by V edges is redundant to that represented by H edges. For example, in Figure 11.21a, with the node order, one group of edges can be constructed from the other group to satisfy the ACG definition. However, keeping both groups of edges facilitates the maintenance and operations on ACG. For example, without one group of edges, it is very hard to check whether the other group belongs to a valid ACG. In an ACG, any two consecutive V neighbors from a given node are connected by an H edge.

11.9.2 ACG Perturbations

There are two types of perturbations for ACG, appending and swap.

Appending.   Appending is an operation to add a new node to the left or the right of a given ACG. We only discuss appending a node to the left of an ACG, and appending a node to the right of an ACG can be done in a similar method. This operation takes constant time for adding one edge and works as follows. First, the new node is added to the left of the node linked list. Then edges from the new node to some other nodes are added iteratively. In each iteration, the closest node that does not have a relation with the new node is identified and a suitable type of edge is then added between them. Because the type pattern *VHH* or *HVV* gives a cross, once the edge type changes, it needs to keep changing. The key operation in each iteration, that is, identifying the closest node not yet having a relation with the new node, can be done in constant time. At the beginning, when no edge is on the new node, it has no relation with its right node. During the iterations, when the new node has already some edges, a relation may be implied by a path from the new node to another node.

When the new node has only V edges, the first H neighbor of its furthest V neighbor is the closest node not having a relation with it. When the new node has last two edges of types V, H, there must be an H edge from the V neighbor to the H neighbor, and the closest node not having a relation with the new node is connected to the V neighbor next to that H edge. The appending process costs linear time and storage complexity is the number of added edges.

Swap.   Swap is an operation that exchanges the positions of two adjacent nodes in the node list. Because an ACG requires edges directed from left to right, the original edge must be removed and a new edge is added to the other group. Because edges in one group represent horizontal relations and those in the other group represent vertical relations, swap will change the geometrical relation of two modules from horizontal to vertical, or vice versa. Suppose a swap is done on nodes n_a, n_b and the original edge (n_a, n_b) is of type H. After the swap, edge (n_a, n_b) is deleted from group H and a new edge (n_b, n_a) is added to group V. All H paths through (n_a, n_b) are then broken, which may leave some node pairs without any relation. On the other hand, with the new edge (n_b, n_a) is added, new V paths may formed, which may make some V edges become transitive. The swap operation will repair these damages and make the ACG valid again. First, consider the transitive edges formed in V group. Based on the way the swap operation is defined, the transitive edges only appear locally. When edge (n_b, n_a) is swapped into group V, transitive edges may only be formed from n_b's left V neighbors to n_a or from n_b to n_a's right V neighbors.

On the basis of the result, we only need to check n_b's V left neighbors to see whether they have V edges to n_a. If so, these edges need to be deleted. Similarly, we will also check n_a's V neighbors to see whether they have V edges from n_b, and if so, delete them. Then, the effects of deleting edge (n_a, n_b) from group H are considered. Two nodes will lose their relation if originally there is only one H path that goes through edge (n_a, n_b). The repair can also be done locally. It is easy to see that a path broken by deleting (n_a, n_b) can be restored by connecting b_a with the node after n_b or n_b with the node before n_a. Furthermore, the path is the only one between the two nodes if and only if the path between n_a and the node after n_b and the path between n_b and the node before n_a are the only paths. Therefore, we need only to consider n_a with n_b's right H neighbors and n_b with n_a's left H neighbors. However, before adding an H edge between two nodes, we must make sure that there is no other H path between them. For each left H neighbor of n_a, we will find its right H neighbor before n_a and check whether that node has n_b as its V neighbor. If so, we will add an H edge from the current left neighbor of n_a to n_b. Similar thing can be done with n_b's right H neighbors. It should be noted that a swap may introduce crosses in the graph.

11.10 DISCUSSIONS

Like the NPE (normalized polished expression) to the skewed slicing tree [2], B*-tree is equivalent to O-tree, and TCG is equivalent to SP. Nevertheless, their neighborhood structures and operations distinguish them from each other in floorplan design.

11.10.1 COMPARISONS BETWEEN O-TREES AND B*-TREES

B*-tree is equivalent to O-tree, yet with faster operations, simpler data structures, and greater flexibility in handling various placement constraints (and higher scalability for very large-scale designs; see Refs. [16–18].

To transform an O-tree into the corresponding B*-tree, we first represent the O-tree using the left-child, right-sibling binary tree [19]. Figure 11.23b shows an example of the left-child, right-sibling tree representing the O-tree in Figure 11.23a. Then, we delete the root and make the left child of the root as the root of the B*-tree, and the resulting B*-tree is obtained as shown in Figure 11.23c. Similarly, given a B*-tree, we can add a root and transform the B*-tree (left-child, right-sibling tree) to the corresponding O-tree.

Despite the equivalence, there is an intrinsic difference between these two representations. A B*-tree can directly model a two-dimensional packing in a single binary tree while an O-tree only

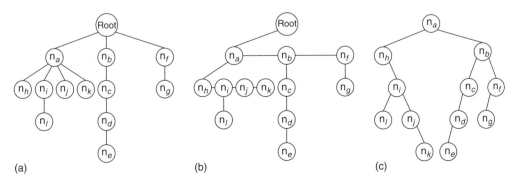

FIGURE 11.23 (a) O-tree modeled, (b) O-tree, by using the left-child, right-sibling binary tree, and (c) corresponding B*-tree.

explicitly represents a one-dimensional packing. Therefore, as mentioned earlier, only one B*-tree is sufficient for floorplan design while the O-tree operates on both a horizontal and a vertical trees. Further, the operation on an O-tree is not as efficient as that on a B*-tree because the O-tree is not a binary tree and needs to keep the encoded tuple (S, π).

The floorplan design algorithm presented in Ref. [10] is deterministic by perturbing an O-tree systematically. The perturbation procedure is to delete a module from the O-tree, and then insert it into the best position based on its evaluation. Owing to the irregular structure, the candidate positions for inserting a node are limited to the external nodes (see Figure 11.3) to facilitate the updations of the encoding tuple. Inserting a node to a position other than external positions makes the update of the encoding tuple more difficult and time consuming. The inflexibility might cause the O-tree to deviate from the optimal during solution perturbations, and thus inevitably limit the quality of a floorplan design. This inflexibility might be a major drawback of the O-tree representation, yet it can be fixed in B*-trees.

Further, searching and updating the encoding tuple, which are basic operations for the primitive search, insertion, and deletion in an O-tree, all takes linear time. In contrast, the search and insertion operations in an B*-tree take only constant time.

11.10.2 EQUIVALENCE OF SP AND TCG

SP and TCG are equivalent, too. We can transform between TCG and SP as follows: Let the fan-in (fan-out) of a node n_i, denoted by $F_{in}(n_i)(F_{out}(n_i))$, be the nodes n_j's with edges $(n_j, n_i)((n_i, n_j))$. Given a TCG, we can obtain a sequence Γ_+ by repeatedly extracting a node n_i with $F_{in}(n_i) = \emptyset$ in C_h and $F_{out}(n_i) = \emptyset$ in C_v, and then deleting the edges (n_i, n_j)'s $((n_j, n_i)$'s) from $C_h(C_v)$ until no node is left in $C_h(C_v)$. Similarly, we can transform a TCG into another sequence Γ_- by repeatedly extracting the node n_i with $F_{in}(n_i) = \emptyset$ both in C_v and C_h, and then deleting the edges (n_i, n_j)'s from both C_h and C_v until no node is left in C_h and C_v. Given an SP $= (\Gamma_+, \Gamma_-)$, we can obtain a unique TCG $= (C_h, C_v)$ from the two constraint graphs of the SP by removing the source, sink, and associated edges. For example, the SP of Figure 11.24b is equivalent to the TCG of Figure 11.24c. It is proved in Ref. [4] that there exists a one-to-one correspondence between TCG and SP.

Although TCG and SP are equivalent, their properties and induced operations are significantly different. Both SP and TCG are considered very flexible representations and construct constraint graphs to evaluate their packing cost. Γ_- of an SP corresponds to the ordering for packing modules to the bottom-left direction and thus can be used for guiding module packing. However, like most existing representations, the geometric relations among modules are not transparent to the operations of SP (i.e., the effect of an operation on the change of module relation is not clear before packing),

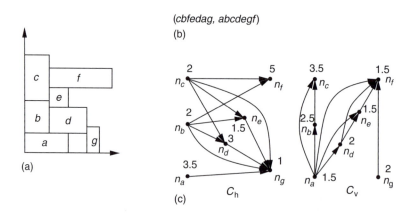

FIGURE 11.24 (a) Placement, (b) corresponding SP of (a), and (c) corresponding TCG of (b).

and thus we need to construct constraint graphs from scratch after each perturbation to evaluate the packing cost; this deficiency makes SP harder to converge to a desired solution and to handle placement with constraints (e.g., boundary modules, preplaced modules, etc).

In contrast to SP, the geometric relations among modules are transparent to TCG as well as its operations, facilitating the convergence to a desired solution. Further, TCG supports incremental update during operations and keeps the information of boundary modules as well as the shapes and the relative positions of modules in the representation. Unlike SP, nevertheless, we need to perform extra operations to obtain the module packing sequence and an additional $O(m^2)$ time to find the reduction edges in the constraint graph for some operations.

For both SP and TCG, the packing scheme by applying the longest path algorithm is time consuming because all edges in the constraint graphs are processed, even though they are not on the longest path. As shown in C_h of Figure 11.24c, if we add a source with zero weight and connect it to those nodes with zero in-degree, the x coordinate of each module can be obtained by applying the longest path algorithm on the resulting directed acyclic graph. Therefore, we have $x_g = \max\{x'_a, x'_b, x'_c, x'_d, x'_e\}$. To reduce the number of modules considered for placing a module, the concept of a horizontal (vertical) contour, denoted by $R_h(R_v)$, is proposed by-Lin and Chang in Refs. [5,13]. $R_h(R_v)$ is a list of modules b_i's for which there exists no module b_j with $y_j \geq y'_i (x_j \geq x'_i)$ and $x'_j \geq x'_i (y'_j \geq y'_i)$; that is, $R_h(R_v)$ is a list of modules in the horizontal (vertical) contour. For the placement of Figure 11.24a, for example, $R_h = \langle b_c, b_f \rangle$ and $R_v = \langle b_g, b_d, b_e, b_f, b_c \rangle$. To place a new module, we only need to consider the bends (and thus the modules) in the contour, and thus the packing time can be improved.

Suppose we have packed the modules b_a, b_b, b_c, b_d, and b_e based on the sequence Γ_-. Then, the resulting horizontal contour $R_h = \langle b_c, b_e, b_d \rangle$. Keeping R_h, we only need to traverse the contour from b_e, the successor of b_e (in terms of in-order search tree traversal), to the last module b_d, which have a horizontal relation with b_g (because there is an edge (n_d, n_g) in C_h). Thus, we have $x_g = x'_d$. Packing modules in this way, we only need to consider x_e and x_d, and can get rid of the computation for a maximum value, leading to a faster packing scheme.

11.11 3D FLOORPLAN REPRESENTATIONS

Recently, dynamically reconfigurable FPGAs are developed to improve logic capacity by time-sharing mechanism. We may use 3D-space (x, y, t) to model a dynamically reconfigurable system. The x and y coordinates represent the 2D-plane of FPGA resources (spatial dimension), while the t coordinate represents the time axis (temporal dimension). Each reconfigurable unit operations (RFUOP) (or task) (the execution unit in a reconfigurable FPGA) is modeled by a rectangular box (module). We may denote each module as a 3D box with spatial dimensions x and y and the temporal dimension t.

Figure 11.25a shows a program with four parts of codes mapped into RFUOPs. Because of the placement constraint, we may not load all the modules into the device at the same time. Therefore, how to place these modules into the reconfigurable unit (RFU) becomes a 3D placement problem as shown in Figure 11.25b. The objective is to allocate modules to optimize the area and execution time and to satisfy specified constraints.

To deal with the 3D floorplanning problem, a few 3D floorplan representations extending the 2D floorplan ones are proposed. For example, sequence triple [20] and sequence quintuple [20] are extensions of sequence pair for 2D-packing. K-tree [21], T-tree [22], and 3D-sub TCG [23] are extensions of O-tree, B*-tree, and TCG for 2D-packing, respectively. In the following sections, we briefly introduce T-tree, sequence triplet, and 3D-subTCG for 3D-packing.

11.11.1 T-TREE

T-trees are inspired by B*-trees, allowing each node with at most three children that represent the dimensional relationship among modules, as shown in Figure 11.26a. The key insight why it uses a

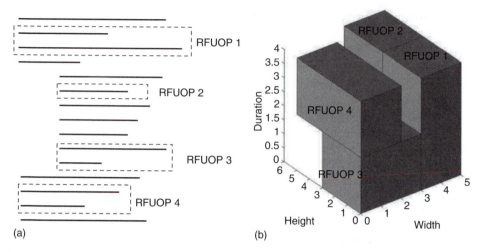

FIGURE 11.25 (a) Running program and (b) 3D-placement of the running program. (From Yuh, P.-H., Yang, C.-L., Chang, Y.-W., and Chen, H.-L., *Proceedings of Asia and South Pacific Design Automation Conference*, 2004. With permission.)

ternary tree is that for a 3D space, a task v_i may have at most three tasks, one in each dimension, that are adjacent to v_i. That is, task v_j in the X^+ direction of v_i, task v_k in the Y^+ direction of v_i, and task v_l in the T^+ direction of v_i, as shown in Figure 11.26b. Thus, to model the relationship among these tasks, we treat v_i as the root and v_j, v_k, and v_l are the children of v_i. Because we have at most three relations in the 3D space, each parent has at most three children.

The T-tree represents the geometric relationships between two modules as follows. If node n_j is the left child of node n_i, module v_j must be placed adjacent to module v_i on the T^+ direction, i.e., $t_j = t_i + T_i$. If node n_k is the middle child of node n_i, module v_k must be placed in the Y^+ direction of module v_i, with the t-coordinate of v_k equal to that of v_i, i.e., $t_k = t_i$ and $y_k \geq y_i + H_i$. If node n_l is the right child of node n_i, module v_l must be placed on the X^+ direction of module v_i, with the t- and y-coordinates equal to those of v_i, i.e., $t_l = t_i$ and $y_l = y_i$.

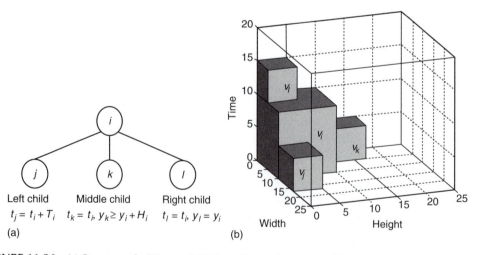

FIGURE 11.26 (a) Structure of a T-tree and (b) three direct relations in a 3D space. (From Yuh, P.-H., Yang, C.-L., and Chang, Y.-W., *Proceedings of International Conference on Computer-Aided Design*, 2004. With permission.)

11.11.2 SEQUENCE TRIPLET

Sequence triplet ST $= (\Gamma_1, \Gamma_2, \Gamma_3)$ is an extension of sequence pair. In sequence triplet, every pair of modules is assigned with a unique topology. Let the function $\Gamma_i^{-1}(n)$ denote the position of module n in sequence Γ_i. The topology of modules a and b is assigned by the following rules:

RL-topology:
$\Gamma_1^{-1}(a) < \Gamma_1^{-1}(b)$ and $\Gamma_2^{-1}(a) > \Gamma_2^{-1}(b)$ and $\Gamma_3^{-1}(a) < \Gamma_3^{-1}(b) \rightarrow b$ is right of a
$\Gamma_1^{-1}(a) > \Gamma_1^{-1}(b)$ and $\Gamma_2^{-1}(a) > \Gamma_2^{-1}(b)$ and $\Gamma_3^{-1}(a) < \Gamma_3^{-1}(b) \rightarrow b$ is right of a

FR-topology:
$\Gamma_1^{-1}(a) < \Gamma_1^{-1}(b)$ and $\Gamma_2^{-1}(a) < \Gamma_2^{-1}(b)$ and $\Gamma_3^{-1}(a) < \Gamma_3^{-1}(b) \rightarrow b$ is rear of a

AB-topology:
$\Gamma_1^{-1}(a) < \Gamma_1^{-1}(b)$ and $\Gamma_2^{-1}(a) > \Gamma_2^{-1}(b)$ and $\Gamma_3^{-1}(a) > \Gamma_3^{-1}(b) \rightarrow b$ is below of a

To find the corresponding 3D placement for a sequence triplet, we first decode it to RL-, FR-, and AB-topology according to the above rules. Similar to the packing of sequence pair, then, three constraint graphs G_{RL}, G_{FR}, and G_{AB} are constructed. Then, all module locations can be determined by the longest path length to corresponding nodes. As an example, Figure 11.27 illustrates the 3D-packing with the topology decoded from the sequence triplet (bac, acb, abc).

11.11.3 3D-SubTCG

3D-subTCG contains three transitive graphs, C_h, C_v, and C_t. For each module v_i, it introduces one node n_i in each graph. If $v_i \vdash v_j (v_i \perp n_j)$, it constructs one edge (n_i, n_j) in $C_h(C_v)$. If v_i must be executed before v_j, it introduces an edge (n_i, n_j) in C_t.

Figure 11.28 shows a placement with six modules b_a, b_b, b_c, b_d, b_e, and b_f whose widths, heights, and durations are $(5, 1, 4), (3, 5, 4), (3, 2, 3), (3, 2, 1), (2, 2, 1)$, and $(2, 2, 3)$, respectively. Figure 11.29 shows the 3D-subTCG corresponding to the placement of Figure 11.28. The value associated with a node in C_h (C_v or C_t) gives the width (height or duration) of the corresponding module, and the edge (n_i, n_j) in C_h (C_v or C_t) denotes the horizontal (vertical or temporal) relation of v_i and v_j. In Figure 11.29, because module $v_c(v_a)$ is left to (below) $v_b(v_f)$, there exists an edge $(n_c, n_b)(n_a, n_f)$ in $C_h(C_v)$. Similarly, because module v_a must be executed before task v_d, there exists an edge (n_a, n_d) in C_t. To obtain the coordinate of each module, we apply the longest path algorithm to the three graphs in a 3D-subTCG.

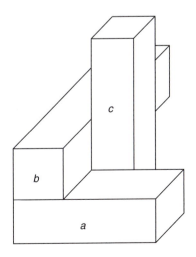

FIGURE 11.27   3D packing of the sequence triplet (bac, acb, abc).

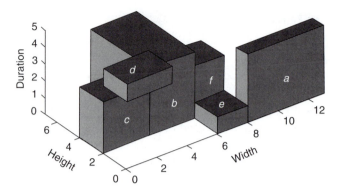

FIGURE 11.28 3D placement. The corresponding 3D-subTCG is given in the Figure 11.29. (From Yuh, P.-H., Yang, C.-L., Chang, Y.-W., and Chen, H.-L., *Proceedings of Asia and South Pacific Design Automation Conference*, 2004. With permission.)

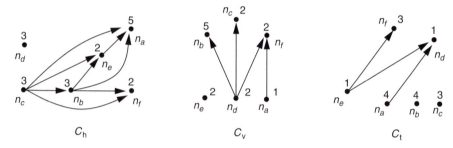

FIGURE 11.29 Corresponding 3D-subTCG of Figure 11.28. (From Yuh, P.-H., Yang, C.-L., Chang, Y.-W., and Chen, H.-L., *Proceedings of Asia and South Pacific Design Automation Conference*, 2004. With permission.)

On the basis of previous works [22,23], the T-tree and 3D-subTCG outperform sequence triplet. Further, the T-tree outperforms the 3D-subTCG in terms of packing efficiency and volume optimization, due to its relatively simpler tree representation and good neighborhood structure. Nevertheless, the 3D-subTCG has the following three advantages over the T-tree:

- 3D-subTCG is a fully topological representation that can represent the general topological modeling of tasks, and thus contains a complete solution structure for searching the optimal floorplan/placement solution. In contrast, T-tree is a partially topological representation and can only represent part of the compacted 3D floorplans where each task must be compacted to the origin.
- Because the relation between each pair of tasks is defined in the representation, the geometric relation of each pair of tasks is transparent to both the 3D-subTCG representation and its induced operations. Thus, we can perform the feasibility detection before perturbation to guarantee the satisfaction of precedence constraints. In contrast, T-tree is a partially topological representation where some geometric relations among tasks cannot be obtained directly from representation. Thus, it is harder to detect the violations of the precedence constraints before packing and a postprocessing is required to guarantee the feasibility of the solutions after packing.
- Because the geometric relations among tasks can be directly obtained from the representation, 3D-subTCG may be more suitable for handling various practical placement constraints. For example, because the input/output blocks are on the boundary of the reconfigurable devices, such as the Xilinx Virtex, some tasks are desired to be placed on the boundary

of a device. We can easily detect if a task is on the boundary of the device by observing the in-degree/out-degree of its corresponding node in C_h or C_v. We can also detect if a task starts at time step zero on an RFU by observing the in-degree/out-degree of its corresponding node in C_t.

11.12 APPLICATION IN HANDLING OTHER CONSTRAINTS IN FLOORPLAN DESIGN

A few floorplan constraints have been studied in the literature, and the B*-tree representation has been shown to be successful for handling these constraints. As it is not our intension here to exhaust all floorplan constraints, we shall in the following subsections give the handling of two example popular floorplan constraints: boundary constraints [24] and rectilinear modules [25] based on the B*-tree representation.

11.12.1 BOUNDARY CONSTRAINTS

The boundary-constrained modules are modules that must be placed along boundaries in the final placement. A module can be placed along the bottom (left) boundary if there exists no module below (left to) the module in the final placement. Similarly, a module can be placed along the top (right) boundary if there exists no module above (right to) the module in the final placement. By the definition of a B*-tree, the left child n_j of a node n_i represents the lowest adjacent module b_j to the right of b_i (i.e., $x_j = x_i + w_i$). The right child n_k of n_i represents the lowest visible module b_k above b_i and with the same x coordinate as b_i (i.e., $x_k = x_i$). Therefore, we have the following four properties [24] to guarantee that there exists no module below, left to, right to, and above the module along the bottom, left, right, and top boundaries, respectively.

1. Node corresponding to a bottom boundary module cannot be the right child of others
2. Node corresponding to a left boundary module cannot be the left child of others
3. Node corresponding to a right boundary module cannot have a left child
4. Node corresponding to a top boundary module cannot have a right child

The aforementioned properties must be satisfied to guarantee a feasible B*-tree with boundary-constrained modules. However, they only describe the necessary conditions for a B*-tree with the boundary constraints, that is, a module may not be placed along the designated boundary if the corresponding property is satisfied. To guarantee that modules are placed at designated boundaries, sufficient conditions are studied in Ref. [25] for a B*-tree with boundary constraints. The following conditions show the feasibility conditions of a B*-tree with the bottom, left, top, and right constraints (Figure 11.30):

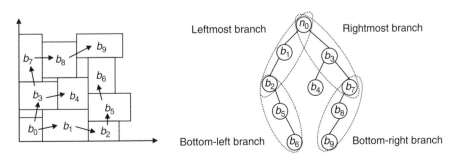

FIGURE 11.30 Boundary modules and their corresponding B*-tree branches.

- Bottom-boundary condition: The nodes corresponding to the bottom boundary modules must be in the leftmost branch of a B*-tree.
- Left-boundary condition: The nodes corresponding to the left boundary modules must be in the rightmost branch of a B*-tree.
- Right-boundary condition: For the right boundary modules, their corresponding nodes are in the bottom-left branch of a B*-tree with the left child for each node in the path being deleted.
- Top-boundary condition: For the top boundary modules, their corresponding nodes are in the bottom-right branch of a B*-tree with the right child for each node in the path being deleted.

Given an initial B*-tree, the simulated annealing algorithm perturbs the B*-tree to get a new one. Then, the four feasibility conditions of B*-trees are checked. If any condition is violated, it transforms an infeasible B*-tree into a feasible one. As a result, a placement satisfying the boundary constraints can be obtained.

11.12.2 RECTILINEAR MODULES

First, we show how to apply B*-tree to find a feasible placement with L-shaped modules. Let b_L denote an L-shaped module. b_L can be partitioned into two rectangular submodules by slicing b_L along its middle vertical boundary. As shown in Figure 11.31a, b_1 and b_2 are the submodules of b_L, and we say $b_1, b_2 \in b_L$.

To ensure that the left submodule b_1 and the right submodule b_2 of an L-shaped module b_L abut, Wu, Chang, and Chang impose the following location constraint (LC for short) for b_1 and b_2 in Ref. [26]:

LC: Keep b_2 as b_1's left child in the B*-tree.

The LC relation ensures that the x-coordinate of the left boundary of b_2 is equal to that of the right boundary of b_1.

The contour data structure is kept carefully to solve the misalignment problem. When transforming a B*-tree to its corresponding placement, it updates the contour to maintain its top profile sequence as follows. Assume that b_1 and b_2 are the respective left and right submodules of an L-shaped module b_L, and they are misaligned. When processing b_2, b_1 must have been placed. We can classify the misalignment into two categories and adjust them as follows:

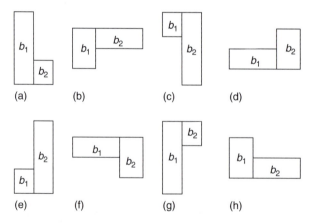

FIGURE 11.31 Eight situations of an L-shaped module. Each is partitioned into two parts by slicing it along the middle vertical boundary.

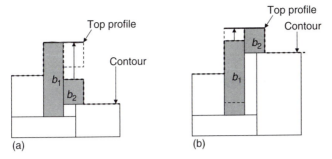

(a)   (b)

FIGURE 11.32 Placing two submodules b_1 and b_2 of an L-shaped module. (a) If the contour is lower than the top profile sequence at b_2, then we pull b_2 up to meet the top profile sequence. (b) If the contour is higher than the top profile sequence at b_2, then we pull b_1 up to meet the top profile sequence.

1. Basin: The contour is lower than the top profile sequence at the position of the current submodule b_2 (Figure 11.32a). In this case, we pull b_2 up to conform to the top profile sequence of the L-shaped module b_L.
2. Plateau: The contour is higher than the top profile sequence at the position of the current submodule b_2 (Figure 11.32b). In this case, we pull b_1 up to conform to the top profile sequence of b_L. (Note that b_2 cannot be moved down because the compaction operation makes b_2 be placed right above another module.)

It is clear that each of the adjustment can be performed in constant time with the contour data structure.

For each L-shaped module b_i, there are eight orientations by rotation and flip, as shown in Figure 11.31. To preserve the LC relation and keep it in the B*-tree, we repartition b_i into two submodules after it is rotated or flipped and keep the LC relation between them. Figure 11.31 shows the submodules after repartitioning. As shown in the figure, an L-shaped module is always partitioned by slicing it along the middle vertical boundary. After repartitioning, we should update the top profile sequence for the module.

To handle general rectilinear module blocks, a rectilinear module can be partitioned into a set of rectangular submodules. Let b_i denote an arbitrarily shaped rectilinear module. b_i can be partitioned into a set of rectangular submodules by slicing b_i from left to right along every vertical boundary of b_i, as shown in Figure 11.33a. Figure 11.33b shows the module of Figure 11.33a after rotating by 90° clockwise; there are six submodules in it after the repartition.

There are two types of rectilinear modules: convex and concave modules. A rectilinear module is convex if any two points within the module can be connected by a shortest Manhattan path, which also

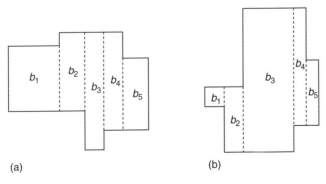

(a)   (b)

FIGURE 11.33 (a) Partition a convex module along every vertical boundary from left to right. (b) Repartition the module of (a) after it rotates.

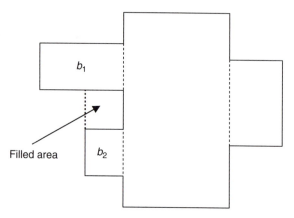

FIGURE 11.34 Filling approximation for a rectilinear module.

lies within the module; the module is concave, otherwise. Figures 11.33 and 11.34 show two convex and a concave modules, respectively. A convex module b_C can be partitioned into a set of submodules $b_1, b_2, \ldots, b_n$ ordered from left to right. Considering the LC relation, we keep the submodule b_{i+1} as b_i's left child in the B*-tree to ensure that they are placed side by side along the x-direction, where $1 \leq i \leq (n-1)$. To ensure that $b_1, b_2, \ldots, b_n$ are not misaligned, we modify the processing for basin and plateau as follows:

- Basin: The contour is lower than the top profile sequence at the position of a submodule. We pull the submodule up to conform to the top profile sequence.
- Plateau: The top boundary of a submodule $b_i (1 \leq i \leq n)$ in the contour is higher than the top profile sequence at the position of b_i. Assume that b_i has the largest top boundary. We pull all submodules, except b_i, up to conform to the top profile sequence.

For a concave module, there might be empty space between two submodules. As shown in Figure 11.34, the submodule b_1 is placed above the submodule b_2, which cannot be characterized by an LC relation in the B*-tree. Nevertheless, we can fill the concave holes of a concave module and make it a convex module. This operation is called a filling approximation for the rectilinear module. For any concave module, we treat it as a convex module after applying appropriate filling.

11.13 SUMMARY

Table 11.1 summarizes the sizes of the solution spaces, packing times, perturbation properties, and flexibility of the floorplan representations discussed in this chapter. Among the representations, SP, TCG, TCG-S, and ACG are fully topological representations and can represent the general floorplans; in contrast, O-tree, B*-tree, and CS are partially topological representations and can model only compacted floorplans. Therefore, SP, TCG, TCG-S, and ACG are intrinsically more flexible than O-tree, B*-tree, and CS because they keep more information in their representations (i.e., data structures). On the other hand, because SP, TCG, TCG-S, and ACG keep more information in their representations, they are typically less efficient than O-tree, B*-tree, and CS. As a result, SP, TCG, TCG-S, ACG have larger solution spaces than O-tree, B*-tree, and CS.

Further, for the compacted floorplan representations, O-tree, B*-tree, and CS, their representation might change after packing, which will not occur for the general floorplan representations. For example, given a B*-tree, the resulting placement might not correspond to the original B*-tree due to the compaction operation during packing. We thus denote this situation by $\otimes$ to distinguish it from the purely feasible cases (denoted by $\bigcirc$) for the general floorplan representations.

TABLE 11.1
Comparisons between Various Packing Floorplan Representations

Represent.	Solution Space Size	Packing Time	Generate Feasible Perturbations	Flexibility
O-tree	$O(n!2^{2n}/n^{1.5})$	$O(n)$	$\otimes$	Compacted
B*-tree	$O(n!2^{2n}/n^{1.5})$	$O(n)$	$\otimes$	Compacted
CS	$\leq (n!)^2$	$O(n)$	$\otimes$	Compacted
SP	$(n!)^2$	$O(n^2)^a$	$\bigcirc$	General
BSG	$O(n!C(n^2,n))$	$O(n^2)$	$\bigcirc$	General
TCG	$(n!)^2$	$O(n^2)$	$\bigcirc$	General
TCG-S	$(n!)^2$	$O(n \lg n)$	$\bigcirc$	General
ACG	$O((n!)^2)$	$O(n^2)$	$\bigcirc$	General

a   Note that $O(n \lg \lg n)$ packing time for SP is known in Ref. [15]. Also, given a TCG, a TCG-S, or an ACG, it can first be transformed into an SP in linear time, and then performs the packing with the corresponding SP in $O(n \lg \lg n)$ time by using the method in Ref. [15].

For the packing time, SP and TCG require $O(n^2)$ time to generate a floorplan, where n is the number of modules. (Note that SP can reduce its packing time to $O(n \lg \lg n)$ time based on the longest common subsequence technique, as mentioned in Section 11.5.) With an additional packing sequence, TCG-S can reduce its packing time to $O(n \lg n)$. For the partial topological representations (the tree-based representations—O-tree and B*-tree—and CS), the packing time is only linear time because they keep relatively simpler information in their data structures. (It should also be noted that, given a TCG, a TCG-S, or an ACG, it can first be transformed into an SP in linear time, and then performs the packing with the corresponding SP in $O(n \lg \lg n)$ time by using the method in Ref. [15].)

As a final remark for floorplan representation, the evaluation of a floorplan representation should be made from at least the following three aspects: (1) the definition/properties of the representation, (2) its induced solution structure (not merely its solution space), and (3) its induced operations. We shall avoid the pitfall that judges a floorplan representation by only one of the aforementioned three aspects alone; for example, claiming a floorplan representation A is superior to another floorplan representation B simply because A has a smaller solution space and a faster packing time. Here is an analogy: the representation itself is like the body of an automobile while the induced operations is like the wheels of the automobile and the solution structure is like the highway network. An automobile with its body alone can go nowhere. For a comprehensive study of floorplan representations, similarly, we shall evaluate them from at least all the aforementioned three aspects.

REFERENCES

1. R.H.J.M. Otten. Automatic floorplan design. In *Proceedings of ACM/IEEE Design Automation Conference*, pp. 261–267, 1982.
2. D.F. Wong and C.L. Liu. A new algorithm for floorplan design. In *Proceedings of ACM/IEEE Design Automation Conference*, Las Vegas, NV, pp. 101–107, 1986.
3. X. Hong, G. Huang, T. Cai, J. Gu, S. Dong, C.-K. Cheng, and J. Gu. Corner block list: An effective and efficient topological representation of non-slicing floorplan. In *Proceedings of ACM/IEEE Design Automation Conference*, Los Angeles, CA, pp. 8–12, 2000.
4. J.-M. Lin and Y.-W. Chang. TCG: A transitive closure graph-based representation for non-slicing floorplans. In *Proceedings of ACM/IEEE Design Automation Conference*, Las Vegas, NV, pp. 764–769, 2001.
5. J.-M. Lin and Y.-W. Chang. TCG-S: Orthogonal coupling of P*-admissible representations for general floorplans. In *Proceedings of ACM/IEEE Design Automation Conference*, New Orleans, LA, pp. 842–847, 2002.

6. H. Murata, K. Fujiyoshi, S. Nakatake, and Y. Kajatani. Rectangle-packing based module placement. In *Proceedings of IEEE/ACM International Conference on Computer-Aided Design*, San Jose, CA, pp. 472–479, 1995.

7. S. Nakatake, K. Fujiyoshi, H. Murata, and Y. Kajitani. Module placement on BSG-structure and IC layout applications. In *Proceedings of IEEE/ACM International Conference on Computer-Aided Design*, San Jose, CA, pp. 484–491, 1996.

8. H. Zhou and J. Wang. ACG-adjacent constraint graph for general floorplans. In *Proceedings of IEEE International Conference on Computer Design*, San Jose, CA, pp. 572–575, 2004.

9. Y.-C. Chang, Y.-W. Chang, G.-M. Wu, and S.-W. Wu. B*-trees: A new representation for non-slicing floorplans. In *Proceedings of ACM/IEEE Design Automation Conference*, Los Angeles, CA, pp. 458–463, 2000.

10. P.-N. Guo, C.-K. Cheng, and T. Yoshimura. An O-tree representation of non-slicing floorplan and its applications. In *Proceedings of ACM/IEEE Design Automation Conference*, New Orleans, LA, pp. 268–273, 1999.

11. J.-M. Lin, Y.-W. Chang, and S.-P. Lin. Corner sequence: A P-admissible floorplan representation with a worst case linear-time packing scheme. *IEEE Transactions on Very Large Scale Integration (VLSI) Systems*, 11(4):679–686, August 2003.

12. J.-M. Lin and Y.-W. Chang. TCG: A transitive closure graph based representation for general floorplans. *IEEE Transactions on Very Large Scale Integration (VLSI) Systems*, 13(2):288–292, February 2005.

13. J.-M. Lin and Y.-W. Chang. TCG-S: Orthogonal coupling of P*-admissible representations for general floorplans. *IEEE Transactions on Computer-Aided Design of Integrated Circuits and Systems*, 24(6):968–980, June 2004.

14. X. Tang, R. Tian, and D. F. Wong. Fast evaluation of sequence pair in block placement by longest common subsequence computation. In *Proceedings of IEEE/ACM Design, Automation and Test in Europe Conference*, Paris, France, pp. 106–111, 2000.

15. X. Tang and D. F. Wong. FAST-SP: A fast algorithm for block placement based on sequence pair. In *Proceedings of IEEE/ACM Asia South Pacific Design Automation Conference*, Yokohama, Japan, pp. 521–526, 2001.

16. T.-C. Chen, Y.-W. Chang, and S.-C. Lin. IMF: Interconnect-driven multilevel floorplanning for large-scale building-module designs. In *Proceedings of IEEE/ACM International Conference on Computer-Aided Design*, San Jose, CA, pp. 159–164, 2005.

17. H.-C. Lee, Y.-W. Chang, and H. Yang. MB*-tree: A multilevel floorplanner for large-scale building-module design. *IEEE Transactions on Computer-Aided Design of Integrated Circuits and Systems*, 26(8):1430–1444, 2007.

18. H.-C. Lee, J.-M. Hsu, Y.-W. Chang, and H. Yang. Multilevel floorplanning/placement for large-scale modules using B*-trees. In *Proceedings of ACM/IEEE Design Automation Conference*, Anaheim, CA, pp. 812–817, 2003.

19. T. Cormen, C. Leiserson, R. Rivest, and C. Stein. *Introduction to Algorithms*, 2nd edn. The MIT Press/McGraw-Hill Book Company, Cambridge, MA, 2001.

20. H. Yamazaki, K. Sakanushi, S. Nakatake, and Y. Kajitani. The 3D-packing by meta data structure and packing heuristics. *IEICE Transcations on Fundamentals*, E82-A(4):639–645, 2003.

21. H. Kawai and K. Fujiyoshi. 3D-block packing using a tree representation. In *Proceedings of the 18th Workshop on Circuits and Systems in Karuizawa*, pp. 199–204, 2005.

22. P.-H. Yuh, C.-L. Yang, and Y.-W. Chang. Temporal floorplanning using the T-tree representation. In *Proceedings of IEEE/ACM International Conference on Computer-Aided Design*, San Jose, CA, pp. 300–305, 2004.

23. P.-H. Yuh, C.-L. Yang, Y.-W. Chang, and H.-L. Chen. Temporal floorplanning using 3D-subTCG. In *Proceedings of IEEE Asia-Pacific Conference on Circuits and Systems*, Yokohama, Japan, pp. 725–730, 2004.

24. J.-M. Lin, H.-E. Yi, and Y.-W. Chang. Module placement with boundary constraints using B*-trees. *IEE Proceedings–Circuits, Devices and Systems*, 149(4):251–256, 2002.

25. M.-C. Wu and Y.-W. Chang. Placement with alignment and performance constraints using the B*-tree representation. In *Proceedings of IEEE International Conference on Computer Design*, San Jose, CA, pp. 300–305, 2004.

26. G.-M. Wu, Y.-C. Chang, and Y.-W. Chang. Rectilinear block placement using B*-trees. *ACM Transactions on Design Automation of Electronics Systems*, 8(2):188–202, 2003.

12 Recent Advances in Floorplanning

Dinesh P. Mehta and Yan Feng

CONTENTS

12.1 INTRODUCTION

Conversations with industry practitioners suggest that there is currently a disconnect between the practice of floorplanning in industry and classical academic floorplanning focused on area minimization. There is, however, a significant and growing body of literature in floorplanning that attempts to bridge this divide. The goal of this chapter is to collect and present some of these efforts in a unified manner. Much of this work builds on one or more of the representations discussed in the three preceding chapters. We refer the reader to these chapters for a comprehensive review of these representations and to the original papers for a more detailed study. The chapter is organized as follows. Section 12.2 presents the latest trends in floorplanning problem formulations. Fixed-outline floorplanning is discussed in Section 12.3. Several approaches for considering interconnect planning during floorplanning are described in Section 12.4. Floorplanning for specialized architectures such as field programmable gate arrays (FPGAs) and analog integrated circuits (ICs) are discussed in Section 12.5. Statistical floorplanning and floorplanning for manufacturability are described in Sections 12.6 and 12.7, respectively. Section 12.8 concludes this chapter.

12.2 REFORMULATING FLOORPLANNING

Recall that in classical floorplanning, the input consists of a set of modules and module connectivity information. The objective is to minimize the area and the estimated wirelength. Kahng [1] was the first to explicitly question the assumptions made in classical floorplanning in 2000 and argued that several of these are not relevant to industrial floorplanning. We begin this chapter by examining these and other issues below.

12.2.1 OUTLINE-FREE VERSUS FIXED-OUTLINE FLOORPLANNING

This first issue pertains to the floorplan or chip boundary. Classical floorplanning operates under the outline-free model wherein no bounding rectangle is specified. Instead, the floorplanning algorithm typically based on simulated annealing (SA) attempts to minimize chip area subject to (usually fairly generous) aspect ratio constraints. In contrast, in the fixed-outline version, the dimensions of the bounding chip rectangle are fixed before floorplanning; in other words, the chip boundary is an input constraint rather than an optimization criterion. The fixed-outline model is considered to be more realistic because floorplanning is only carried out after the die size and the package have been chosen in most design methodologies.

How does this change in formulation impact floorplanning technology? Because the dimensions of the bounding rectangle are now part of the input, the modules have to be organized so that they fit inside this rectangle. Does this make the problem easier or harder? It depends on the bounding rectangle. If this is much larger than necessary, it makes the problem easier. If the bounding rectangle is tight, it makes the problem harder.

Another way to look at the two formulations is that the outline-free formulation is an optimization problem (we are trying to minimize area) and the fixed-outline formulation is a decision problem (we are trying to meet area constraints). This relationship between an optimization and the decision versions of a problem arises in the study of NP-completeness in theoretical computer science. NP-completeness theory is based on decision problems, whereas real-world problems are usually optimization problems. The argument that is made in this context is that the two versions are essentially equivalent; specifically, one can solve the constrained version of the problem by running an optimizer and returning a "yes" or a "no" depending on whether the value returned by the optimizer (e.g., the chip area) is respectively less or greater than the constraint (e.g., the available area in the fixed-outline). This argument does not work here because of the two-dimensional (2D) nature of the constraint. Fixed-outline floorplanning does not merely require the floorplan to meet a single (area) constraint; rather, it requires the floorplan to meet both width and height criteria. It is precisely the trade-off between height and width that makes the problem challenging when the bounding rectangle is tight. We make this more concrete with an example. Suppose the desired outline is 10×10 and a classical floorplanning optimizer obtains a solution with area $90 < 100$. If the resulting floorplan dimensions are (say) 15×6, this is still a failure because a 15×6 rectangle cannot fit inside a 10×10 rectangle.

12.2.2 MODULE SHAPE AND FLEXIBILITY

Classical floorplanning has mostly used rectangular modules and sometimes other simple shapes such as L- and T-shapes. We are not aware of a technical reason for shapes to be restricted to rectangles and believe that this arose because rectangles are easier to work with than other rectilinear shapes. (Imagine how much easier it would be to play Tetris if all shapes were rectangles.) Classical floorplanning does allow flexible modules (modules whose dimensions are not fixed); however, in the context of rectangular modules, this is limited to allowing a module to have any aspect ratio in a range. Current designs consist of a mixture of blocks and cells. Blocks are components that have typically already been designed and therefore have fixed shapes and dimensions. Cells can be grouped together to form flexible blocks that can take on arbitrary rectilinear shapes.

How does this impact floorplanning? Clearly, having fixed nonrectangular shapes complicates the problem. For example, writing a program that merely figures out whether two arbitrary rectilinear polygons intersect or not is more complex than asking the same question for a pair of rectangles. Literature that considers the graph dualization approach to floorplanning with simple rectilinear shapes confirms this as does work on extending corner stitching to simple rectilinear shapes. The use of arbitrary rectilinear polygons also clearly increases the solution space relative to solely using rectangles (the latter is a special case of the former). On the other hand, having malleable rectilinear shapes increases the opportunity for obtaining better solutions: intuitively, this is because flexible rectilinear shapes can be massaged and squeezed in between fixed-shape blocks. However, if this flexibility is taken too far, it could result in long stringy shapes that may not be suitable for routing (assuming that interconnections connecting cells within a block must stay within the block boundary). In short, the use of flexible, arbitrary rectilinear shapes is a bit of a double-edged sword.

12.2.3   WHITESPACE: TO MINIMIZE OR NOT TO MINIMIZE?

Whitespace is defined as the fraction of chip area that does not contain silicon devices. Minimizing area (or whitespace) has traditionally been a key objective of floorplanning. Hennessy and Patterson point out in their classic computer architecture text that die cost is proportional to the square of die area [2, p. 24].

Although area minimization is still an important cost-metric, it alone is no longer sufficient in modern floorplan design. One reason is that true chip area depends on both the area used for logic and the area used for interconnect. Module areas represent area used for logic and short interconnects, but do not account for area needed by power and ground lines, nor for longer and wider interconnects, nor space between interconnects, etc. Thus, area minimization should also take into account sources of area that have traditionally been ignored. A second reason is the realities of deep-submicron design: timing requirements and routing congestion are becoming more problematic, both of these are exacerbated by insufficient area. Therefore, the floorplan must contain some whitespace by design to alleviate these problems so that feasible solutions can be obtained. We also need to reserve whitespace for buffer insertion for high-performance designs. (Buffer insertion is discussed separately in Chapters 26 through 28.)

Finally, we note that in the fixed-outline formulation, the provided outline essentially determines the amount of whitespace available, transforming whitespace minimization to a constraint. However, the floorplanning algorithm's strategy may depend on how much whitespace is provided. If the bounds are tight, the algorithm can declare victory if it manages to fit the blocks in the outline. If the bounds are loose and there is plenty of whitespace, the floorplanning algorithm can reasonably be expected to do more (e.g., optimize other criteria such as wirelength).

12.2.4   INTERCONNECT

Classical floorplanning algorithms focus on minimizing wirelength estimates (in addition to area). This does not take into account the actual routes of long-distance connections and therefore (somewhat) ignores timing and congestion. More recent floorplanning algorithms attempt to rectify this by using more relevant criteria to judge the quality of the solution from an interconnect standpoint.

12.2.5 MODULE LOCATIONS: KNOWN OR UNKNOWN?

The whole point of floorplanning is to find suitable locations for modules and so it would seem that this information would be unknown at the start of the process. However, there are scenarios when locations may be approximately known. For example, if a chip is based off of an earlier generation of the same chip, a floorplan architect who was familiar with the design of the original chip may wish to place modules in the same approximate locations (manual or interactive floorplanning). Or, if the floorplan is the result of engineering change order modifications (i.e., incremental floorplanning), the floorplan architect may not want to radically change the locations of the modules. Alternatively, the approximate locations may be the result of a preceding step such as dualization or force directed placement (Chapter 8), or a quick rough placement as described in the next chapter. There is a substantial body of research related to the addition of location constraints such as range and boundary constraints (discussed in Chapters 9 through 11), and symmetry constraints (discussed later in this chapter) to SA-based algorithms that address situations where there is some insight into module locations.

12.2.6 HUMAN INTERVENTION

The preceding section brings up another question. Should floorplanning be completely automated? This is the ideal scenario, but may be unrealistic because of the number of issues involved. Therefore, it may be necessary to build tools that enable an interactive type of floorplanning paradigm that involves interaction between the architect and the tool.

12.3 FIXED-OUTLINE FLOORPLANNING

12.3.1 AUTOMATED FLOORPLANNING WITH RECTANGULAR MODULES

Adya and Markov [3] present a fixed-outline floorplanning algorithm based on SA using sequence pairs. (We refer to this as automated fixed-outline floorplanning to differentiate it from the incremental/interactive formulation described in the next section.)

An enabling idea in this work is the use of slack-based moves. The concept of slack is illustrated in Figure 12.1. Consider the horizontal and vertical constraint graphs corresponding to a sequence pair. The longest path from source to sink in these graphs gives the width and height of the chip, respectively. The (x, y) location of each module is obtained from the constraint graph by compacting modules toward the left and the bottom. A module's (x, y) location may also be obtained by compacting modules to the right and the top. The difference in the two x (y) values of a module is its slack in the x (y) dimension. The slack is an indicator of the flexibility available to place the module

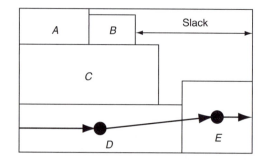

FIGURE 12.1 Slacks shown in the X direction: Module B has a significant amount of slack, the width of the chip will not be impacted if a block is placed to its right. In contrast, modules D and E have zero slack and belong to a critical path. One of these will have to be moved out of the critical path to reduce the chip's width.

without violating the sequence pair and without increasing chip size. The strategy is to move blocks with zero slack (in one or both dimensions) and place them next to blocks with large slack. The rationale is that a dimension of the chip can only be reduced by removing a zero-slack block from its critical path in the constraint graph. Blocks are placed next to blocks with large slack as there is more likely to be room there. The cost function includes a penalty for violations of the fixed-outline constraint in the horizontal and vertical directions. The experiments in this chapter show that the use of slack-based moves results in substantially higher success rates relative to approaches that only penalize fixed-outline violations.

The resulting floorplanning tool called Parquet (http://vlsicad.eecs.umich.edu/BK/parquet/) has been widely used in several research projects involving fixed-outline floorplanning. The authors have released several improvements to the software. The following quotation from the website describes the major algorithmic improvements (as of July 2007).

> The main difference between Parquet-2 and Parquet-3 is that Parquet-3 has an alternative floorplan representation (B*-Trees) ... Parquet-4.5 also introduces the "Best" floorplanning representation which chooses between "SeqPair" and "BTree" depending upon the input instance and optimization objectives. It has been found empirically that B*-Trees are better at packing than Sequence Pairs, so if wirelength is not being optimized or available whitespace is lower than 10%, "Best" chooses the B*-Tree representation. We have also found empirically that B*-Trees are faster than Sequence Pairs on instances with 100 or more blocks, so "Best" chooses B*-Tree over Sequence Pair in these cases as well.

Lin et al. present a fixed-outline algorithm based on evolutionary search [4]. Chen and Chang [5] present a fixed-outline algorithm based on B* trees that uses an alternative annealing schedule called fast SA that consists of three stages (high-temperature random search, pseudogreedy local-search, and hill-climbing search). The goal is to arrive at a solution faster than traditional annealing schedules. The authors report better experimental results than Ref. [4] and Parquet-4.5 (both sequence pair and B*-tree versions).

12.3.2 INCREMENTAL/INTERACTIVE FLOORPLANNING WITH RECTILINEAR MODULES

The research described in this section differs from that in the previous section in two respects: (1) flexible blocks are allowed, at least in theory, to take embarrassingly rectilinear shapes and (2) approximate locations for blocks are known. This permits the algorithm to ignore interconnect-related issues because it assumes that interconnect was considered when the locations were decided.

Mehta and Sherwani [6] considered a formulation where the approximate centers of flexible modules and the exact location of fixed modules are given. A zero whitespace formulation is assumed (i.e., the fixed-outline includes exactly as much area as necessary to contain the blocks). The objective is to compute exact shapes and locations for each flexible block such that the number of sides in the corresponding rectilinear polygons is minimized as is the displacement from the center specified for each module. The algorithm discretizes the floorplan area into a grid; grid squares are assigned to each flexible block by using variations of breadth-first traversal (Figure 12.2).

However, such a traversal may disconnect available grid squares making it impossible for blocks to remain connected. This was overcome by splitting each grid square into four smaller subsquares and traversing a subgrid in a twice-around-the-tree traversal. This guarantees that flexible blocks can be made to fit within the fixed-outline without being disconnected. Experimental results confirm this and also examine trade-offs between various grid square assignment methods. This algorithm processes blocks iteratively and consequently the quality of the shapes and locations assigned to them depends on the order in which they are processed. This approach is also computationally expensive in that its time complexity is a function of the number of grid squares created during the discretization step.

Feng et al. [7] considered an improvement to this that overcomes the two problems cited above; namely, the sequential processing of blocks and the expensive discretization step in an approach

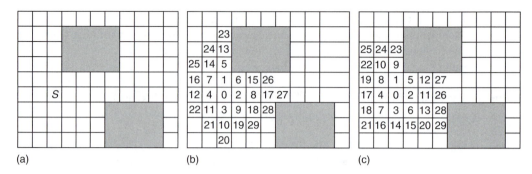

(a)   (b)   (c)

FIGURE 12.2   (a) Floorplan grid and the location in the center square S for a flexible block, (b) allocation of 30 grid squares to the flexible block using a strict breadth-first traversal, and (c) allocation of 30 grid squares using a modified breadth-first traversal.

called interactive floorplanning. Once again, the outline is fixed, approximate locations for modules are known, modules may be fixed or flexible and can have arbitrary rectilinear shapes. However, the formulation differs in that each module is constrained; i.e., a constraining rectangle is specified for each module so that the module cannot be assigned area outside the constraining rectangle (Figure 12.3). This is a very constrained formulation, making it likely that there is no solution for a given input. The idea is that if a solution does not exist, the algorithm should indicate this to the user, and the user should then accordingly adjust the constraints (hence the term "interactive floorplanning"). A zero or near-zero whitespace formulation is addressed in Ref. [7]. A max-flow network flow algorithm is used to determine feasibility. If the input is feasible, a min-cost max-flow algorithm is used to actually assign area to each module. A postprocessing step is needed to clean up the output. Feng and Mehta [8] also consider the situation where white space is relatively plentiful. In this case, the problem objectives are made more stringent by assigning shapes to modules so that the extents and number of sides of modules are minimized. The postprocessing step of Ref. [7] is not needed, making the solution cleaner. Instead, an iterative refinement step is used to make the modules provably more compact. Finally, Feng and Mehta provide automated mechanisms to adjust constraining rectangles based on minimizing the standard deviation of density over the floorplan area [9].

In Ref. [10], Liao et al. explicitly consider the incremental floorplanning problem: Given an initial floorplan with precise locations and shapes for its modules specified. Suppose the area requirements

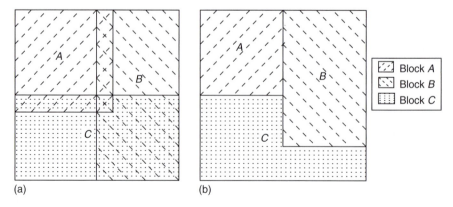

(a)   (b)

FIGURE 12.3   (a) Constraining rectangles for modules A, B, and C. Each constraining rectangle contains enough area for the corresponding module. Note that constraining rectangles may overlap. (b) Actual area allocation to modules A, B and, C. Each module is allocated area within its constraining rectangle.

of some of the blocks change. How can the floorplan be reconstituted so that all modules have their updated areas without disrupting their locations in the floorplan (and preferably without increasing the overall area of the floorplan). The available whitespace must be distributed among the competing modules in the vicinity. Geometric algorithms based on planesweep were used to simultaneously expand each module's boundary until it encounters another module or the floorplan boundary. These algorithms take polynomial time and were designed to work with arbitrary rectilinear shapes.

12.4 FLOORPLANNING AND INTERCONNECT PLANNING

This section is concerned with interconnect planning, an activity that goes hand in hand with floorplanning. We further classify the research activity in this area based on the type of interconnect planning. Congestion-based methods primarily impact routability, while buffer-based methods primarily impact timing and performance. We also discuss bus-driven methods and close this section with a description of relatively recent research on constructing floorplans with a view to improving microarchitecture performance.

12.4.1 CONGESTION CONSIDERATIONS DURING FLOORPLANNING

Traditional floorplanning considers interconnect by including a wirelength term in the cost function used to guide SA. However, this does not provide the accuracy needed to ensure that the floorplan is routable. Routability is related to congestion. If more nets must pass through a region in the chip than there is room for, the design will be unroutable. Here we discuss strategies for congestion evaluation during floorplanning. One extreme is to use a global router to evaluate routability. Although this is accurate, it is computationally expensive because it has to be run within the SA loop.

Most congestion evaluation metrics use a grid-based approach. The idea here is to divide the floorplan area into rectangular tiles and then estimate the number of nets that cross tile boundaries. An issue with the grid-based approach is to select how coarse it is. A coarse grid will result in more efficient, but less accurate, computation. Another concern is how to determine precisely which tile boundaries a net will cross. Because there are typically several possible routes for a net, we do not know a priori which ones it will cross. One approach is to perform coarse global routing. Another approach is to compute a probabilistic map (Figure 12.4): First compute the probability (under some assumptions) that a net will cross a tile boundary. Next, for each tile boundary, add up the probabilities over all the nets.

Chen et al. [11] propose two techniques for interconnect analysis during SA-based floorplanning using a slicing tree representation. The first only allows a single bend (L-shaped route), while the second allows two bends (Z-shaped route). The floorplan is subdivided into grids. Given the two

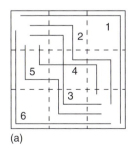
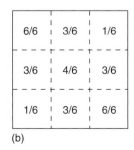

(a)   (b)

FIGURE 12.4 A two-pin net is to be routed from the upper left grid square to the bottom right grid square. Six possible routes are shown in (a). If each of these routes is equally likely, we are able to compute the probability that the net passes through a given grid square. For example, four out of six routes (2, 3, 4, and 5) pass through the middle square, resulting in a probability of 4/6.

endpoints of a net, the L-shaped routing scheme only permits two types of routes. Each is considered to be equally likely with 0.5 probability. This probability is associated with the grid boundaries crossed by the route. Each net is routed one at a time using a routing path that minimizes a cost term that contains a penalty term for congestion, a prevention term that discourages the router from using bin boundaries that are nearing saturation, and a term that rewards a route if it reuses existing routes for the same net. The overflow (excess congestion) is added to the SA cost term. Using Z-shapes (two bends) results in a greater choice of routing paths, resulting in a more accurate, but computationally expensive, estimate. Because this computation takes place within the SA loop, the L-shape routes are used at medium temperature, while Z-shapes routes are used at low temperatures.

Lai et al. [12] argue that grid-based approaches (as described above) to computing congestion are expensive, given that this computation is carried out repeatedly inside the floorplaning SA loop. They propose evaluating the congestion on the half-perimeter boundary of several regions in the floorplan. One of the novelties of this work is that region definitions are naturally tied to the twin binary tree (TBT) representation (the floorplan representation used in this work), making their definition of congestion easier to compute. Although the definition of regions is, in some sense, arbitrary, it provides statistical samples of wire density in different areas of the floorplan. The chapter also considers a mirror TBT representation that increases the number of regions considered (and therefore increases the number of samples considered). Experimental results show improved routability when congestion is considered relative to when it is not. Shen and Chu [13] observe that although the approach in Ref. [12] is efficient, it also only provides a coarse evaluation of congestion. They also observe that a probability map-based approach to evaluating congestion could differ significantly from that of a global router. (Once a route has been chosen for a net, its associated tile boundaries are less available than the probability map suggests, while the other possible routes and the associated tile boundaries are more available than the probability map suggests.) Instead, they propose an approach based on the maximum concurrent flow problem. (This is a multicommodity flow problem in which every pair of entities can send and receive flow concurrently. The objective is to maximize throughput, subject to capacity constraints, where throughput is the actual flow between the pair of entities divided by the predefined demand for that pair. A concurrent flow is one in which the throughput is identical for all entity pairs [14].) For a given floorplan, the goal is to estimate the best maximum congestion over all possible global routing solutions. This approach uses twin binary sequences.

Sham and Young [15] develop a floorplanner that simultaneously incorporates routability and buffer planning. They observe that congestion depends on the routes chosen for the wires, which in turn depends on the availability of buffer resources. Accordingly, their congestion model based on probability maps takes into account where buffers will be needed along the length of the wire and where white space is available in the floorplan to accommodate buffers. A two-phase SA algorithm is used. The cost function used in the first phase is the traditional combination of area and wirelength. The second phase incorporates a congestion metric (the average number of wires in the top ten percent most congested grids) in addition to area and wirelength. Ma et al. [16] also simultaneously consider buffer planning and routability during floorplanning. Their algorithm uses the corner block list (CBL) representation.

12.4.2 INTEGRATED BUFFER PLANNING AND FLOORPLANNING

The insertion of buffers reduces delay along the interconnect. One can only determine whether and where to insert buffers after the modules have been placed and the interconnect lengths have been somewhat established. On the other hand, buffers can only be inserted where white space is available in the floorplan. This points to a need to integrate floorplanning and buffer planning, a research area that has been addressed in the literature [16–19]. However, we omit discussing this important area here because it is covered in considerable detail in Chapter 33.

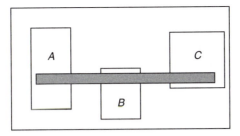

FIGURE 12.5 The shaded rectangle is a bus that must pass through modules A, B, and C. For this to work, they must be positioned so that the intersection of their y-intervals is wider than the bus's y-interval.

12.4.3 BUS-DRIVEN FLOORPLANNING

A bus is a group of wires that is required to pass through a set of specified modules. It is specified by the set of macroblocks through which it must go and a width. The width is determined by the number of wires it contains. In Ref. [20], each bus is realized by a rectangular strip. For a bus to be feasible, the macroblocks must be located such that it is indeed possible for a horizontal/vertical rectangular strip of the required width to pass through the blocks (Figure 12.5). The sequence pair representation is used. This result was extended by Law and Young [21] to allow buses with one or two bends. Chen and Chang [5] also explore bus-driven floorplan using B^* trees and a fast SA schedule and report better results than Ref. [20].

12.4.4 FLOORPLAN/MICROARCHITECTURE INTERACTIONS

The execution time of a program is the product of the number of (machine) instructions executed (the dynamic instruction count), the average number of clock cycles required per instruction (CPI), and the clock cycle time. Reducing instruction count and CPI has traditionally been within the purview of compiler technology and architecture, while reducing the clock cycle time (the reciprocal of the clock frequency) has been the responsibility of logic and physical design. This separation existed because any block-to-block communication on a chip took less than a cycle, an assumption that is no longer true. Consequently, there is a growing body of work that explores the interaction between microarchitecture and physical design. This interaction specifically focuses on floorplanning, because floorplanning is the first high-level physical design step that determines the locations of blocks on the chip, which is needed to determine interconnection lengths.

A key strategy used here is interconnect or wire pipelining, which introduces latches (flip-flops) on interconnects to break them into smaller segments so that signal propagation time on these segments takes less than one clock cycle. However, although wire pipelining keeps clock cycle time low, it increases block-to-block latency, which could result in an increase in CPI. A metric that simultaneously captures both of these entities is throughput, which is the number of instructions executed per second = clock frequency/CPI. Several of the papers described below develop algorithms to obtain floorplans that optimize throughput. A key challenge here is to measure the CPI. The traditional method for doing this is to use a cycle-accurate simulator on a large number of benchmarks. However, cycle-accurate simulators are extremely time consuming making them impossible to include in the inner loop of a floorplan optimization algorithm. They are also sufficiently time consuming that they can only be used sparingly offline (i.e., outside the floorplanning loop). All of the methods below work by plugging in a term into the Parquet floorplanner SA cost function that in one way or the other approximates throughput. What distinguishes the methods is the accuracy with which throughput is approximated and the effort (in terms of number of cycle accurate simulations) required to generate the throughput approximation.

Cong et al. [22] developed an SA algorithm that is integrated with Parquet that seeks to minimize the sum of weighted netlengths divided by the IPC (IPC = instructions executed per cycle = 1/CPI). This quantity approximates maximizing the throughput. Netweights are based on the slacks of their pins (computed by performing a static timing analysis). The algorithm evaluates alternative block implementations and uses an interconnect performance estimator.

Long et al. [23] consider a version that minimizes CPI. Their contribution is to use a trajectory piecewise-linear model to estimate CPI. This estimate, based on table lookup, is much faster than a cycle-accurate simulation, and has an error of about 3 percent. When this estimate is incorporated in Parquet's SA objective function, it results in a significant reduction in CPI with a modest increase in floorplan area.

Casu and Macchiarulo [24] focus on the impact of loops in the logic netlist on throughput. The throughput is not explicitly included in the cost function, but is approximated as follows: Each net is assigned a weight that is the inverse of the shortest loop the net belongs to. The Manhattan distance between pins is divided by the maximum length admissible between clocked elements. The weighted sum over all nets is included as the throughput term in the Parquet SA objective function.

Casu and Macchiarulo [25] extended their earlier work by taking into account the fact that a channel will contribute to the overall throughput degradation of the system at most up to its activation time. They introduce an additional channel activation ratio, which is defined as the time fraction in which a block communication channel is active. The weighting factor is used to multiply the throughput term so that the channel communication properties are taken into account.

Ekpanyapong et al. [26] profiled architectural behavior on several applications and obtained frequencies on global interconnect usage; this is used to determine the weight of each wire (the greater the frequency, the greater the weight). These weights are incorporated into a mixed integer nonlinear program (MINP) floorplanner whose goal is to minimize weighted global wirelength. The MINP formulation is relaxed to a more tractable linear programming (LP) formulation. The final results are fed back into a cycle-accurate simulator, which shows a 40 percent improvement in CPI relative to a floorplanner that does not take architectural behavior into account.

Jagannathan et al. [27] cite limitations in Ref. [22] in that the cycle time for interconnect may not match the cycle time for blocks because the latter did not consider wire pipelining. It also differs from previous work in that it only considers systemwide critical paths and loops rather than all two-pin nets. They also argue that it is sufficient to use relative changes to the IPC (as opposed to an exact computation of IPC) to guide floorplanning. To this end, they develop an IPC sensitivity model to track changes in IPC because of different layouts. IPC sensitivity is computed as follows: the latency of one critical path is varied while keeping the others fixed and the degradation of IPC with each additional cycle of latency on that path computed. Parquet is used with a weighted combination of area and 1/IPC. The approach used here is to fix a target frequency, and then floorplan to optimize IPC (as opposed to simultaneously optimizing IPC and frequency).

Nookala et al. [28] focus specifically on the throughput objective and identify throughput-critical wires based on the theory of multifactorial design (a statistical design technique). They argue that if each of n buses in a design can have k different latencies, the number of simulations that would normally be needed to sample the search space is $O(k^n)$. Whereas, with multifactorial design theory, the number of simulations needed is $O(n)$. The throughput-critical wires so obtained are emphasized during floorplanning, by replacing the total wirelength objective in Parquet with a weighted sum of factor latencies. These are input to the floorplanner along with a target frequency. The performance of the obtained layout is validated using cycle-accurate simulations. They subsequently [29] refine this work to significantly speed up cycle-accurate simulations that preserve the quality of the solution.

Wu et al. [30] propose a thermal-aware architectural floorplanning framework. By adopting adaptive cost function and heuristic-guided pertubation in their SA algorithm, their floorplanner is able to obtain a high-performance chip layout with significant thermal gains compared to the layout obtained by the traditional performance-driven floorplanner.

12.4.5 FLOORPLAN AND POWER/GROUND COSYNTHESIS

Voltage (IR) drop in power/ground networks is an important problem in IC design. The resistance in power wires is increasing substantially. As a result, the reference supply voltage in chip components may be less than it should be. This can weaken the driving capability in logic gates, reduce circuit performance, reduce the noise margin, etc. Yim et al. [31] show that it is advantageous to consider power network and clock distribution issues at the early floorplanning stage rather than after detailed layout.

How does this relate to floorplanning? Power-hungry modules draw larger currents. If these modules are placed far away from the power pad (on the boundary of the chip), then the combination of the larger current and greater resistance because of increased wirelength exacerbates the IR drop for that module. Such modules should be placed nearer the power pad. Liu and Chang [32] propose a methodology to simultaneously carry out floorplanning and synthesize the power network. They use SA with the B*-tree representation. The SA cost function is modified to include penalties for violating power integrity constraints and the power/ground mesh density cost function. In addition, the B*-tree representation is constrained so that the most power-hungry modules (the ones that draw the most current) are on the boundary near the power pads. (In experiments, this reduction in solution space caused a factor of three improvement in runtime.) The proposed methodology was successfully integrated into a commercial design flow.

12.5 FLOORPLANNING FOR SPECIALIZED ARCHITECTURES

This section considers variants of the floorplanning problem for specialized architectures such as FPGAs, three-dimensional (3D) ICs, and analog circuits.

12.5.1 FPGA FLOORPLANNING

Cheng and Wong [33] introduced FPGA floorplanning. The floorplanning problem in modern FPGAs is heterogeneous because it consists of different types of components that are arranged in columns at specified locations on the chips. These consist of configurable logic blocks (CLBs), multipliers, RAMs, etc. (Figure 12.6). In application specific integrated circuit (ASIC) floorplanning, a module is simply specified by its area or by its height and width. (ASIC floorplanning may be viewed as homogeneous floorplanning because the area throughout the chip is of the same type and an ASIC

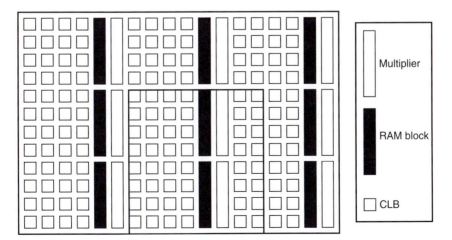

FIGURE 12.6 Illustration of the heterogeneous resources on an FPGA. The vector corresponding to the resources contained in the highlighted block is (48,2,2).

module can be placed anywhere on the chip.) In FPGA floorplanning, a module is specified by the number of resources of each type that it requires. Cheng and Wong introduced the notion of a resource requirement vector (n_1, n_2, n_3) to characterize each module, where n_1, n_2, and n_3 are the number of CLBs, RAMs, and multipliers, respectively. They then define FPGA floorplanning to be the placement of modules on the chip so that (1) each region assigned to a module satisfies its resource requirements, (2) regions for different modules do not overlap, and (3) a given cost function is optimized. The problem is solved by a two-step strategy. In the first step, the authors use an approach based on slicing trees and SA. This involves computing irreducible realization lists, which specify all of the locations that a module can be placed in so that it meets its resource requirements. An irreducible list is computed for each node in the floorplan tree in a bottom-up manner. At this stage, each node in the tree corresponds to a rectangle. Once these lists are computed, it is possible to evaluate the given floorplanning tree. This evaluation is used in the SA algorithm. The second step consists of compaction followed by postprocessing.

Another two-step solution to the FPGA floorplanning problem is presented in Ref. [34]. The first step is a resource-aware floorplanning step based on Parquet. An FPGA is a bounded rectangle making it more natural to use a fixed-outline algorithm than area-minimization. In addition, the SA cost function contains a resource term that penalizes each module by the amount of mismatch between its resource requirements and the resources available in its current location. This step is expected to place modules at locations that are close to their resources. Even so, it is unlikely that each module meets its resource requirements. This is addressed by deploying a second step based on constrained floorplanning. The purpose of this step is to ensure that each module meets its resource requirements without substantially changing the location and shape that were obtained as a result of the first step. The underlying algorithm is based on a min-cost max-flow network formulation. Thus, it results in a solution that takes a global view of resource demand and supply across the chip. The constrained floorplanning techniques, originally designed for homogeneous floorplans, were modified to account for heterogeneity in FPGAs. In addition, this algorithm can incorporate trade-off between resources. For example, each CLB in a Xilinx Vertex-II FPGA can implement 32 bits. If a module needs memory, it can acquire this resource from the RAM on the FPGA or from CLBs. The flow network in the constrained floorplanner can incorporate this modification to the formulation.

12.5.2 3D Floorplanning

Three-dimensional floorplanning [35–37] has become an active area of research because of the possibility of 3D integrated circuits. We refrain from discussing this area here because it is covered elsewhere: Chapter 9 on slicing floorplans and Chapter 11 on packing representations contain detailed discussions on 3D floorplan representations, while Chapter 47 discusses the state of the art with respect to 3D IC technologies.

12.5.3 Analog Floorplanning

High-performance analog circuits require layouts where groups of devices are placed symmetrically with respect to one or more axes. This is done to match layout-related parasitics in both halves of a group of devices.

A symmetry pair consists of two modules with the same dimensions. Without loss of generality, we define symmetry with respect to a vertical axis $x = X_A$. Let (x_L, y_L, w, h) and (x_R, y_R, w, h) denote the left and right modules, respectively. Then, $y_L = y_R$ and $(x_L + w + x_R)/2 = x_A$ must be true for modules L and R to be symmetric. A self-symmetric module is one which is symmetric with respect to itself; i.e., $x_L = x_R$ and $y_L = y_R$. This means that the module must be bisected by the axis of symmetry. A symmetry group may consist of several symmetry pairs and self-symmetric modules. All of these must share the same axis of symmetry (Figure 12.7).

The challenge that arises during floorplanning based on SA is how to search the state space efficiently. One approach is to search the state space as before, ignoring states that do not meet the

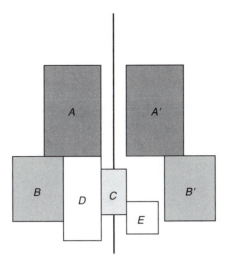

FIGURE 12.7   Symmetry group in an analog floorplan consisting of (A, A') and (B, B'). C is self-symmetric. D and E have no symmetry constraints.

symmetry requirement. However, the majority of states are of this type. This means that the SA process wastes a lot of time on infeasible solutions. The research [38–44] in this area explores how to improve on floorplan representations such as sequence pairs, O trees, and B* trees, so that they are symmetric feasible; i.e., each state visited and evaluated by SA does indeed correspond to a floorplan that satisfies symmetry. The original work mainly considers a single axis of symmetry. More recent research explicitly considers several axes of symmetry simultaneously and involves converting the sequence-pair constraint graphs into a set of linear expressions, which are then solved using linear programming. Most recently, Lin and Lin [45] propose automatically symmetric-feasible B* trees (ASF-B* trees), which can handle not only 1D but also 2D symmetry constraints. A hierarchical B* tree (HB* tree) is constructed by incorporating ASF-B* trees into traditional B* trees to handle the simultaneous placement of modules in symmetry group and nonsymmetry modules for analog placement.

12.6   STATISTICAL FLOORPLANNING

The basis for this line of research is that precise module dimensions may not be known during floorplanning, because floorplanning can be used very early in the design process by an architect as an estimation tool. At this stage, the modules have not yet been created and therefore their dimensions are unavailable. Suppose that, instead, the architect is able to supply an input consisting of module height and width distribution lists. For example, a module's width may be represented as $\{(4, .2), (5, .5), (6, .3)\}$, meaning that the module has widths of 4, 5, and 6 with probabilities .2, .5, and .3, respectively.

Bazargan et al. [46] approach this problem by using SA with the slicing-tree representation. The main novelty of their work is the way in which floorplan area is evaluated. Recall that in slicing floorplans, the area of a larger rectangle is obtained from its two slice rectangles by adding widths and computing the max of their heights (assuming the two rectangles are separated by a vertical cut). In the statistical version, this computation takes the height and width distribution lists of the two modules as input and produces height and width distribution lists of the resulting rectangle as the output. We describe this using an example.

$$M1 : W = \{(3, .2), (5, .5), (6, .3)\}, H = \{(5, .5), (6, .5)\}$$
$$M2 : W = \{(2, .3), (3, .6), (4, .1)\}, H = \{(4, .4), (5, .6)\}$$

Suppose these modules are separated by a horizontal cut (i.e., heights must be added and widths must be maxed). The width distribution list of the new rectangle is $\{(3,.18),(4,.02),(5,.5),(6,.3)\}$ and its height list is $\{(9,.2),(10,.5),(11,.3)\}$.

Repeating this process as the area evaluation algorithm traverses the slicing tree in a bottom-up fashion finally results in distribution lists for chip height and width. The authors use these quantities to compute a cost function that is the combination of expected area and standard deviation of area. Including standard deviation in the cost function makes it more likely that the area of the floorplan obtained by statistical floorplanning is close to the area of the final solution (i.e., after module dimensions have all been finalized) relative to minimizing expected area alone. The paper also considers a combined height/width distribution list (e.g., $\{(4,5,.3),(6,3,.7)\}$ means that a module has height 4 and width 5 with a probability of .3 and a height of 6 and a width of 3 with probability of .7). This is a more realistic formulation, but experimental results have been more promising with the separate distribution lists.

12.7 FLOORPLANNING FOR MANUFACTURABILITY

Floorplanning, as we have defined it so far, is concerned with the arrangement of components within a single chip. In this section, we discuss a floorplanning-like problem that arises because of the economics associated with manufacturing a chip. Recall that several chips can be manufactured from a single wafer. To do this, a mask set has to be prepared for the wafer. The cost of creating a mask set is substantial. For high-volume manufacturing (i.e., when many chips of the same type are to be produced), this one-time cost (X) is amortized over the number of chips (c) produced. For low-volume manufacturing (few chips have to be produced), the cost per chip X/c becomes prohibitive. The multiple project reticle concept addresses this problem for low-volume manufacturing by departing from the assumption that all of the chips on a wafer have to be of the same type. Instead, different chips (possibly sent to the fabrication facility by different companies) are placed in a reticle. Several copies of the reticle are arranged in rows and columns on a single wafer. The mask cost X can now be spread out among the different companies. Suppose there are ten different chips from different companies on a wafer, then the mask cost for each company is $X/10$. This is amortized over the number of chips resulting in a cost per chip of $X/10c$.

However, this approach presents some new challenges. These different chips have to be extracted from the wafer by cutting (dicing) the wafer. Existing wafer dicing technologies are somewhat restrictive, making chip locations on the reticle vital to optimizing the chip yield. For example, the side-to-side wafer dicing technology cuts the wafer using horizontal and vertical cutlines that traverse the entire length of the wafer (Figure 12.8). Within a given reticle, these lines may either cut through dies rendering them useless or might leave large margins making the dies unacceptably large.

There are several associated algorithmic problems. The reticle floorplanning formulation proposes that we compute a floorplan and positions of the cutlines assuming a side-to-side wafer dicing technology. In Ref. [47], both reticle area and wafer yield were optimized using SA. In Ref. [48], the yield was treated as a constraint and the reticle area was optimized. This strategy, coupled with a branch-and-bound algorithm, resulted in better solutions than those in Ref. [47]. To further reduce fabrication cost, projects requiring different numbers of metal layers can be put on the same shuttle. In Ref. [49], Chen et al. proposed an integer linear programming (ILP)-based floorplanner shuttle runs consisting of projects of different desired processes.

Another problem associated with reticle floorplanning was considered by Xu et al. [50]. In this variation, the objective is to compute a floorplan that optimizes area and a quantity called postCMP oxide topography variation. Minimizing this quantity provides the process with a larger margin. PostCMP oxide topography variation is closely related to the feature density. One technique for reducing the variation in feature density is to insert dummy features into the design. The floorplanning algorithm uses SA on slicing floorplans with a cost function that approximates the topography variation. (Topography variation minimization can be formulated as a linear programming problem,

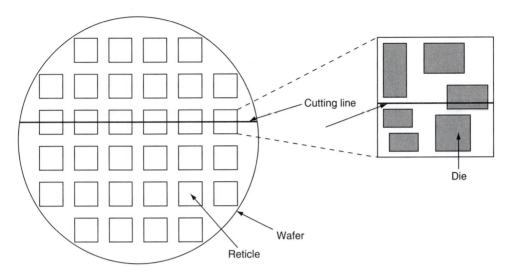

FIGURE 12.8 Illustration of reticle floorplanning. A wafer contains many reticles, each of which contains several dies in an identical configuration. The reticle floorplanning problem asks how these dies should be configured in the reticle, given that the wafer will be diced using horizontal and vertical lines that cut through the entire wafer.

but this is too time consuming to include in the SA loop.) SA is followed by a step that slides or rotates the chip and by a third step that inserts a dummy feature.

12.8 CONCLUDING REMARKS

This chapter has been an effort to try and capture as much floorplanning research as possible with a bias toward newer and interesting problem formulations that are likely to be significant in practice. We apologize in advance for any omissions.

ACKNOWLEDGMENTS

The authors thank Yao-Wen Chang, Tung-Chi Chen, Igor Markov, and Sachin Sapatnekar for carefully reviewing the manuscript and suggesting improvements.

REFERENCES

1. A.B. Kahng, Classical floorplanning harmful? *Proceedings of the 2000 International Symposium on Physical Design*, April 9–12, San Diego, CA, pp. 207–213, 2000.
2. J.L. Hennessy and D. Patterson, *Computer Architecture: A Quantitative Approach*, Fourth edn. Morgan Kaufman, 2007.
3. S.N. Adya and I.L. Markov, Fixed-outline floorplanning: Enabling hierarchical design, *IEEE Transactions on Very Large Scale Integration Systems*, Vol. 11, No. 6, pp. 1120–1135, 2003. (ICCD 2001).
4. C.-T. Lin, D.-S. Chen, and Y.-W. Wang, Modern floorplanning with boundary and fixed-outline constraints via genetic clustering algorithm, *Journal of Circuits, Systems, and Computers*, Vol. 15, pp. 107–128, Feb. 2006. (ASPDAC 2004).
5. T.-C. Chen and Y.-W. Chang, Modern floorplanning based on B*-tree and fast simulated annealing, *IEEE Transactions on Computer-Aided Design of ICs and Systems*, Vol. 25, pp. 637–650, Apr. 2006. (ISPD 2005).
6. D. Mehta and N. Sherwani, On the use of flexible, rectilinear blocks to obtain minimum-area floorplans in mixed block and cell designs, *ACM Transactions on Design Automation of Electronic Systems*, Vol. 5, pp. 82–97, Jan. 2000.

7. Y. Feng, D. Mehta, and H. Yang, Constrained floorplanning using network flows, *IEEE Transactions on Computer-Aided Design of ICs and Systems*, Vol. 23, No. 4, pp. 572–580, 2004. (ISPD 2003).

8. Y. Feng and D. Mehta, Constrained floorplanning with whitespace, in *VLSI India*, 17th International Conference on VLSI Design, Mumbai, India, 2004.

9. Y. Feng and D. Mehta, Module relocation to obtain feasible constrained floorplans, *IEEE Transactions on Computer-Aided Design of ICs and Systems*, Vol. 25, pp. 856–866, 2006.

10. S. Liao, M. Lopez, and D. Mehta, Constrained polygon transformations for incremental floorplanning, *ACM Transactions on Design Automation of Electronic Systems*, Vol. 6, Jul. 2001.

11. H.-M. Chen, H. Zhou, D.F. Wong, H.H. Yang, and N. Sherwani, Integrated floorplanning and interconnect planning, in *International Conference on Computer-Aided Design*, San Jose, CA, pp. 54–57, 1999.

12. S.T.W. Lai, E.F.Y. Young, and C.C.N. Chu, A new and efficient congestion evaluation model in floorplanning: Wire density control with twin binary trees, in *Design Automation and Test in Europe*, in Europe Conference and Exposition, 3–7 March, Munich, Germany, pp. 856–861, 2003.

13. C. Shen and C. Chu, Accurate and efficient flow based congestion estimation in floorplanning, in *Asian and South Pacific Design Automation Conference*, pp. 671–676, 2004.

14. F. Shahrokhi and D.W. Matula, The maximum concurrent flow problem, *Journal of the ACM*, 37(2), 318–334, 1990.

15. C.W. Sham and F.Y. Young, Routability-driven floorplanner with buffer block planning, *IEEE Transactions on Computer-Aided Design of ICs and Systems*, Vol. 22, pp. 470–480, Apr. 2003. (ISPD 2002).

16. Y. Ma, X. Hong, S. Dong, S. Chen, C.-K. Cheng, and J. Gu, Buffer planning as an integral part of floorplanning with consideration of routing congestion, *IEEE Transactions on Computer-Aided Design of ICs and Systems*, Vol. 24, pp. 609–621, Apr. 2005. (ISPD 2003).

17. J. Cong, T. Kong, and Z. Pan, Buffer block planning for interconnect planning and prediction, *IEEE Transactions on Very Large Scale Integration Systems*, Vol. 9, pp. 929–937, Dec. 2001. (ICCAD 1999).

18. X. Tang and D.F. Wong, Network flow based buffer planning, *Integration*, Vol. 30, No. 2, pp. 143–155, 2002. (ISPD 2000).

19. P. Sarkar, V. Sundararaman, and C.-K. Koh, Routability-driven repeater block planning for interconnect-centric floorplanning, *IEEE Transactions on Computer-Aided Design of ICs and Systems*, Vol. 20, pp. 660–671, May 2001. (ISPD 2000).

20. H. Xiang, X. Tang, and M.D.F. Wong, Bus-driven floorplanning, *IEEE Transactions on Computer-Aided Design of ICs and Systems*, Vol. 23, No. 11, pp. 1522–1530, 2004. (ICCAD 2003).

21. J.H.Y. Law and E.F.Y. Young, Multi-bend bus driven floorplanning, in *International Symposium on Physical Design*, San Francisco, CA, pp. 113–120, 2005.

22. J. Cong, A. Jagannathan, G. Reinman, and M. Romesis, Microarchitecture evaluation with physical planning, in *Proceedings of the 40th Design Automation Conference*, Anaheim, CA, June 2–6, 2003.

23. C. Long, L.J. Simonson, W. Liao, and L. He, Floorplanning optimization with trajectory piecewise-linear model for pipelined interconnects, in *Design Automation Conference*, San Diego, CA, June 7–11, pp. 640–645, 2004.

24. M.R. Casu and L. Macchiarulo, Throughput-driven floorplanning with wire pipelining, *IEEE Transactions on Computer-Aided Design of ICs and Systems*, Vol. 24, pp. 663–675, May 2005. (ISPD 2004).

25. M.R. Casu and L. Macchiarulo, Floorplan assisted data rate enhancement through wire pipelining: A real assessment, in *International Symposium on Physical Design*, pp. 121–128, 2005.

26. M. Ekpanyapong, J.R. Minz, T. Watewai, H.-H. Lee, and S.K. Lim, Profile-guided microarchitectural floorplanning for deep submicron processor design, *IEEE Transactions on Computer-Aided Design of ICs and Systems*, Vol. 25, No. 7, pp. 1289–1300, 2006. (DAC 2004).

27. A. Jagannathan, H. Yang, K. Konigsfeld, D. Milliron, M. Mohan, M. Romesis, G. Reinman, and J. Cong, Microarchitecture evaluation with floorplanning and interconnect pipelining, in *Asian and South Pacific Design Automation Conference*, Shanghai, China, January 18–21, 2005.

28. V. Nookala, Y. Chen, D.J. Lilja, and S.S. Sapatnekar, Microarchitecture-aware floorplanning using a statistical design of experiments approach, in *Design Automation Conference*, San Diego, CA, June 13–17, 2005.

29. V. Nookala, Y. Chen, D.J. Lilja, and S.S. Sapatnekar, Comparing simulation techniques for microarchitecture-aware floorplanning, in *IEEE International Symposium on Performance Analysis of Systems and Software*, Austin, TX, March 20–22, 2006.

30. Y.-W. Wu, C.-L. Yang, P.-H. Yuh, and Y.-W. Chang, Joint exploration of architectural and physical design spaces with thermal consideration, in *International Symposium on Low Power Electronics and Design*, San Diego, CA, August 8–10, pp. 123–126, 2005.

31. J.-S. Yim, S.-O. Bae, and C.-M. Kyung, A floorplan-based planning methodology for power and clock distribution in ASICs, in *Proceedings of Design Automation Conference*, New Orleans, LA, June 21–25, pp. 766–771, 1999.

32. C.-W. Liu and Y.-W. Chang, Power/ground network and floorplan cosynthesis for fast design convergence, *IEEE Transactions on Computer-Aided Design of ICs and Systems*, Vol. 26, pp. 693–704, Apr. 2007. (ISPD 2006).

33. L. Cheng and M.D.F. Wong, Floorplan design for multimillion gate FPGAs, *IEEE Transactions on Computer-Aided Design of ICs and Systems,* Vol. 25, pp. 2795–2805, Dec. 2006. (ICCAD 2004).

34. Y. Feng and D. Mehta, Heterogeneous floorplanning for FPGAs, in *VLSI India*, Hyderabad, India, 3–7 January 2006.

35. K. Bazargan, R. Kastner, and M. Sarrafzadeh, 3-D floorplanning: Simulated annealing and greedy placement methods for reconfigurable computing systems, in *Design Automation for Embedded Systems*, 2000. (RSP 99).

36. L. Cheng, L. Deng, and M.D.F. Wong, Floorplanning for 3D VLSI design, in *Asian and South Pacific Design Automation Conference*, Shanghai, China, January 18–21, 2005.

37. J. Cong, J. Wei, and Y. Zhang, A thermal-driven floorplanning algorithm for 3D ICs, in *International Conference on Computer-Aided Design*, San Jose, CA, November 7–11, 2004.

38. F. Balasa and K. Lampaert, Symmetry within the sequence-pair representation in the context of placement for analog design, *IEEE Transactions on Computer-Aided Design of ICs and Systems*, Vol. 19, pp. 721–731, July. 2000. (DAC 1999).

39. F. Balasa and S.C. Maruvada, Using non-slicing topological representations for analog placement, *IEICE Transactions on Fundamentals of Electronics, Communications and Computer Sciences*, Vol. E84-A, pp. 2785–2792, Nov. 2001. (ASPDAC 2001).

40. S.C. Maruvada, K. Krishnamoorthy, F. Balasa, and L.M. Ionescu, Red-black interval trees in device-level analog placement, *IEICE Transactions on Fundamentals of Electronics, Communications and Computer Sciences*, Vol. E86-A, pp. 3127–3135, Dec. 2003. (ASPDAC 2003).

41. F. Balasa, S.C. Maruvada, and K. Krishnamoorthy, On the exploration of the solution space in analog placement with symmetry constraints, *IEEE Transactions on Computer-Aided Design of ICs and Systems*, Vol. 23, pp. 177–191, Feb. 2004. (ICCAD 2002).

42. J.-M. Lin, G.-M. Wu, Y.-W. Chang, and J.-H. Chang, Placement with symmetry constraints for analog layout design using TCG-S, in *Proceedings of ACM/IEEE Asia South Pacific Design Automation Conference*, Shanghai, China, January 18–21, pp. 1135–1138, 2005.

43. S. Kouda, C. Kodama, and K. Fujiyoshi, Improved method of cell placement with symmetry constraints for analog IC layout design, in *Proceedings of ACM International Symposium on Physical Design*, San Jose, CA, April 9–12, 2006.

44. Y.-C. Tam, E.F.-Y. Young, and C. Chu, Analog placement with symmetry and other placement constraints, in *International Conference On Computer Design*, Las Vegas, NV, June 26–29, pp. 349–354, 2006.

45. P.-H. Lin and S.-C. Lin, Analog placement based on novel symmetry-island formulation, in *Design Automation Conference*, San Diego, CA, June 4–8, 2007.

46. K. Bazargan, S. Kim, and M. Sarrafzadeh, Nostradamus: A floorplanner of uncertain design, *IEEE Transactions on Computer-Aided Design of ICs and Systems*, Vol. 18, pp. 389–397, Apr. 1999. (ISPD 1998).

47. A.B. Kahng, I.I. Mandoiu, Q. Wang, X. Xu, and A. Zelikovsky, Multiproject reticle floorplanning and wafer dicing, in *International Symposium on Physical Design*, Phoenix, AZ, pp. 70–77, 2004.

48. A.B. Kahng and S. Reda, Reticle floorplanning with guaranteed yield for multi-project wafers, in *International Conference On Computer Design*, San Jose, CA, October 11–13, pp. 106–110, 2004.

49. C.-C. Chen and W.-K. Mak, A multi-technology-process reticle floorplanner and wafer dicing planner for multi-project wafers, in *Asian and South Pacific Design Automation Conference*, Yokohama, Japan, January 24–27, pp. 777–782, 2006.

50. G. Xu, R. Tian, D.Z. Pan, and M.D.F. Wong, CMP aware shuttle mask floorplanning, in *Asian and South Pacific Design Automation Conference*, Shanghai, China, January 18–21, pp. 1111–1115, 2005.

BIBLIOGRAPHY

1. S.N. Adya and I.L. Markov, Consistent placement of macro-blocks using floorplanning and standard-cell placement, *ACM Transactions on Design Automation of Electronic Systems*, Vol. 10, Jan. 2005. (ISPD 2002).
2. J. Cong, M. Romesis, and J. Shinnerl, Fast floorplanning by look-ahead enabled recursive bipartitioning, *IEEE Transactions on Computer-Aided Design of ICs and Systems*, Vol. 25, pp. 1719–1732, Sept. 2006. (ASPDAC 2005).
3. J. Crenshaw, M. Sarrafzadeh, P. Bannerjee, and P. Prabhakaran, An incremental floorplanner, in *GLSVLSI*, Ann Arbor, MI, pp. 248–251, 1999.
4. A. Ranjan, K. Bazargan, and M. Sarrafzadeh, Fast hierarchical floorplanning with congestion and timing control, *IEEE Transactions on Very Large Scale Integration Systems*, Vol. 9, No. 2, pp. 341–351, 2001. (ICCD 2000).
5. F. Rafiq, M. Chrzanowska-Jeske, H.H. Yang, and N. Sherwani, Bus-based integrated floorplanning, in *Proceedings of the IEEE Symposium on Circuits and Systems*, Scottsdale, AZ, pp. 875–878, 2002.
6. F. Rafiq, M. Chrzanowska-Jeske, H.H. Yang, M. Jeske, and N. Sherwani, Integrated floorplanning with buffer/channel insertion for bus-based designs, *IEEE Transactions on Computer-Aided Design of ICs and Systems*, Vol. 22, No. 6, pp. 730–741, 2003. (ISPD 2002).
7. Y.M. Fang and D.F. Wong, Simultaneous functional-unit binding and floorplanning, in *International Conference on Computer-Aided Design*, San Jose, CA, pp. 317–321, 1994.
8. M. Moe and H. Schmit, Floorplanning of pipelined array modules using sequence pairs, in *International Symposium on Physical Design*, Monterey, CA, April 6–9, 2003.

13 Industrial Floorplanning and Prototyping

Louis K. Scheffer

CONTENTS

13.1 INTRODUCTION

Industrial floorplanning and prototyping consist of the steps needed after the chip logic is defined, but before the final detailed implementation of a production chip. Several of the steps, such as pure block placement and mixed block and cell placement (also called the boulders and dust problem), have received considerable academic interest and are covered in other sections. This chapter instead concentrates on the practical problems that must be solved in the floorplanning of large industrial chips.

In this chapter we assume the chips to be designed consist of predefined blocks and standard cells. Predefined blocks (commonly called IP blocks, where IP stands for intellectual property) commonly include memories, processors and analog functions, and are presented to the designer as givens. Their placement and orientation must be decided, but their contents cannot be changed. IP blocks come in a wide variety of shapes and sizes, but are typically relatively large, perhaps the equivalent of a few thousand to a few million gates. Standard cells, by contrast, are very small, usually incorporating just one to a few logic gates. Usually they are of a uniform height (hence standard) and designed to be abutted into rows. A crucial distinction in a typical design flow is that the IP blocks are selected by the designer, and cannot be changed by the automatic tools, whereas the standard cells, are normally generated by logic synthesis [1], and can be freely modified by the tools as long as the logical function specified by the RTL is preserved.

A floorplan and a prototype are two different approximate versions of a chip, at different levels of abstraction. The floorplan is the more abstract of the two, consisting of just a chip outline, placement and orientation of the hard blocks, an IO placement, sites where the standard cells can go, and an approximate power grid design. The blocks may be hard, or fully defined, or may be blocks that are still under construction. These are commonly called soft if their size or aspect ratio is not fully decided, or black or gray boxes if their size is fixed but their contents unknown. (In the terminology of floorplanning, a black box is a cell where only the inputs, outputs, and function are known. By analogy, white and gray boxes have contents fully and partially defined, respectively. Note that the color of a box may vary according to purpose—the same block may be a black box for placement, a gray box for timing, but a white box for logic verification.)

A prototype consists of everything from the floorplan, plus a detailed placement and at least a rough route (normally including at least layer and track assignment). The goal is to enable reasonably accurate extraction and timing verification, and hence show a design is feasible and ready for the more time-consuming steps of final placement and routing. The final detailed implementation may or may not follow the prototype.

Like placement, a good floorplan or prototype is not unique. Typically, there are many different possible floorplans for the same design, of comparable quality. One of the major questions, as in placement, is how do you know you have got a good floorplan, compared with what might be possible? This situation is even worse than the situation in placement, where there are at least a few examples where the optimum solution is known [2].

13.1.1 FLOORPLANNING IN THE DESIGN FLOW

Design of a modern chip involves many steps. First, the exact function of the chip must be defined, and shown to be correct. The formal definition of the function is usually specified in RTL, and proving it correct is done by simulation, formal verification, and a host of other techniques. These steps are collectively referred to as front-end design.

The RTL from the front-end process then goes to the back end where it is turned into a detailed implementation. Normally, this involves mapping the function into an interconnected set of logic gates (by logic synthesis), followed by placement, routing, extraction, timing analysis, and design rule checking, and ultimately the fabrication of the masks, and then ICs.

In cases where engineering margins of performance, power, and cost are large, the front and back ends can be largely independent. In many cases, however, they interact fairly strongly, particularly when some feature of the RTL is difficult or impossible to implement in the back end. This interaction is made worse by the differing expertises involved. Most front-end designers are not familiar with the back-end tools, and do not have time to run them in any case. Most back-end designers do not have the expertise to change the RTL, even if they were allowed to do so. Floorplanners are an attempt to bridge this gap with a tool accessible to both sides.

Floorplanning decides the overall layout of the chip, and is used early in the chip design flow [3], when the design is malleable and all fixes are possible. Normally it is used by a front-end user, or a back-end expert working in close cooperation with a front-end group. One of the main objectives of floorplanning is helping both the front- and back-end users understand the design. Which constraints are easy, and which hard? Does it meet timing? Routability? Has enough routing resource been allocated to the power supplies? Will the RTL work as is, or are changes needed to make it feasible to meet the design constraints using the specified process and library? Because one of the main tasks of a floorplanner is diagnostics (where is the routing hard, and why? Why is the timing hard to meet?), easy-to-use graphical user interfaces (GUIs) and easy-to-understand feedback are critical.

Because one of the main points of floorplanning is to understand the design as early as possible, a crucial feature of a floorplanner is the ability to work with incomplete designs. Missing blocks, incomplete constraints, and even missing technology information must be handled, often by allowing designers to enter estimates for the missing data.

Once the RTL is deemed complete, or nearly so, the next step is prototyping. This is a fast (and often rough) pass through the entire physical design process of synthesis, placement, routing, extraction, and timing analysis. This quick pass is meant to verify feasibility and completeness before starting on the lengthy production-quality physical design steps. The prototype design produced may or may not form the basis of the final implementation. Normally prototyping is done by a back-end user, or at least someone with experience in placement and routing. Because one of the main reasons for prototyping is to ensure that everything is ready, it is much less tolerant of missing data than a floorplanner. The prototyper will perform at least a rough version of the final implementation steps, including place and route, extraction and timing analysis, so all required inputs must be present and consistent. This includes libraries, the input hardware description language (or HDL), constraints, IP blocks, and so on. Completion of a successful prototype shows the RTL should no longer need major changes.

Prototyping is also part of a business model for ASIC handoff. In this business model, responsibility for a chip is split among the end customer, who wishes to logically design and sell a chip, and the ASIC house, who does the detailed implementation and manufacturing. Several costs and responsibilities are contractually obligated in such a relationship:

- The designer, usually working at the end customer, must supply an RTL that can be practically implemented in the specified process (even though they do not do this implementation themselves).
- The ASIC house must quote a price for the detailed implementation. There are normally additional charges if the RTL changes after implementation starts.
- The ASIC house must quote a price for each chip produced.

Prototyping (and to a lesser extent, floorplanning) helps a great deal with this interface between companies. The designer uses prototyping to make sure their RTL can be implemented in the specified process with the needed performance, and to ensure that all is ready for implementation, to avoid additional charges for later changes. Also, a prototype serves as a concrete example of at least one way to meet the design goals, though the ASIC house is not normally constrained to follow it. On the other side, the ASIC house uses prototyping for QA on incoming designs, to make sure all required information is there, and for cost estimates for both the detailed implementation process and the final chip cost. A prototype, as a physically accurate model, also helps ensure that the chip will fit in the specified package and can be bonded successfully.

Finally, a floorplanner or prototyper also serves as a central repository for data, especially in the hierarchical design style. The input is the RTL for all groups, libraries, IO files, SDC constraints, and so on. The output is a similar set of files for each physical block. This implies the use and reading of many languages: LEF/DEF, IO specifications, Verilog or VHDL, delay constraints, and so on.

13.1.2 EVOLUTION OF BLOCK-BASED DESIGNS [4]

Floorplanners were originally built for designs with relatively few blocks, with the chip area dominated by standard cells, as shown in Figure 13.1a. However, as chips have gotten larger, designers have incorporated larger and larger fractions of blocks. The remaining standard cells, increasing in number but decreasing in terms of percentage, must be placed into the spaces between the blocks. An example of such a floorplan is shown in Figure 13.1b. This change in design style has several implications for the algorithms and methods used in today's floorplanners.

13.2 HISTORY

When chips were small, and tools primitive, what we currently call a floorplan could be drawn by hand on a piece of paper. Place and route tools, when used, were only run after the netlist was

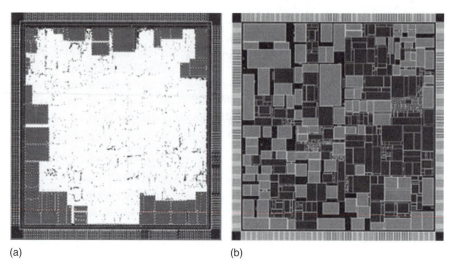

(a)   (b)

FIGURE 13.1   (a) Standard cell-dominated design on the left and (b) block-dominated design on the right. (From Wein, E. and Benkoski, J., *Electronics Engineering Times*, August 20, 2004. With permission.)

finalized. Performance was verified by taking the final placed and routed results, running extraction, then delay calculation, then timing analysis. Any performance optimizations, or corrections of errors and omissions, were done using the place or route tool directly.

As chips grew past a few thousand gates, an additional tool began to make sense. Some of tasks that were not well addressed by the old flow include:

- Designers wished to know if a design was feasible before (or without) doing the final layout tasks such as a fully detailed power grid.
- Designers wanted to examine the feasibility of a design before all parts were complete.
- Designers wanted to divide a design up into two or more sections, each of which could be treated separately.
- Designers wanted to understand where there design was easily implemented, and where there were problems, early in the design cycle when RTL changes are still relatively easy.

Floorplanners were invented to address these needs. Many of the initial uses of floorplanning envisioned it as part of a suite of integrated tools, such as VIVID [5,6], or the internal tools of DEC [7], or CHEOPS [8]. By 1986, standalone floorplanners such as Mason were available [9].

In the late 1990s, as designs became bigger yet, they often ran into problems in detailed implementation even though they had what appeared to be a good floorplan. In particular, problems often only showed up after detailed routing, extraction, and timing were complete, because many characteristics of the final design are heavily influenced by the details of the routing. However, detailed placement, routing, extraction, and verification often took a week or more—not unreasonable for the final implementation, but too long for effective feedback to the earlier stages of the design process. The technical solution was to do a very fast but fully detailed placement, followed by a very fast (but rough) detailed route, and a fast approximate RC extract. If timing analysis on this indicated all was well, then the relatively lengthy detailed implementation process could begin. A floorplan that was verified through these additional steps was sometimes called a virtual silicon prototype, and the process called prototyping. See Goering for an early reference [10], Chao and Lev [11] for an informal explanation of the importance of detailed wiring, and Dai et al. [12] for a more formal description of the process.

13.2.1 HISTORY OF PIN ASSIGNMENT

Early on, printed wiring boards (PWBs) served as modules. Assigning pins on these modules was the equivalent of pin assignment in IC floorplanners. This was does as early as 1972 [13]. For ICs, this problem was only seriously addressed in the 1980s.

By 1984, the pin assignment problem was explicitly addressed [14]. By 1989, pin assignment was being combined with global routing [15,16]. By 1990, it was combined with floorplanning [17,18], and by 2002 with buffer planning [19]. See Section 13.4 for more details.

13.2.2 HISTORY OF TIMING BUDGETS

Time budgeting was first addressed in the context of breaking a path delay into individual net delays, as in Ref. [20]. Many other approaches to this have been developed [21]. Then budgeting was extended to hierarchical design, for example, by Venkatesh [22] or Kuo and Wu [23]. In a floorplanner, it makes sense to use the hierarchy information as well [24].

13.2.3 ACADEMIC VERSUS INDUSTRIAL FLOORPLANNING

Although they both have activities called floorplanning, industry and academia mean very different things by this term. In academia, floorplanning refers primarily to automatic placement of pure block designs, or designs including large fractions of blocks, with objectives of good packing and minimum wirelength. A related term, floorplacement, refers to the automatic simultaneous placement of blocks and standard cells [25,26].

In contrast, in industrial floorplanning, manual input is allowed if not encouraged, and the main goals are timing and routability, with area and wirelength treated as means to an end, and not an objective by themselves. Industrial floorplanning includes, and is often dominated by, practical concerns such as power grid design, dealing with partially specified or contradictory data, multivoltage support for power reduction, buffer insertion, ease of clock tree design, and so on.

13.3 USE OF HIERARCHY

Floorplanning and prototyping may be flat or hierarchical. In a flat floorplan, the entire design is treated as a single problem, and any cell or block can be placed at any location in the design. There is no need to assign cells and pins to the blocks, or create block budgets for timing or power. This flat design style is conceptually straightforward and provides maximum implementation flexibility. However, it has several disadvantages, especially for large designs. It may stress the limits of tools (which often cannot handle a large design flat) as well as humans, who may not be able to easily understand such a design. Because every detail of the design interacts, there may be no easy way to divide the work among teams. Flat design may well make changes more difficult, because they are less localized, which can also impact design closure [27]. For these and other reasons, many chips are designed hierarchically. In this case, the chip surface is divided into areas, commonly called blocks. Each block represents an independent design problem—all cells assigned to the block must be placed inside it, and all wires purely internal to the block must be routed within its boundary. Signals that connect to the rest of the design are brought to pins, where the routing from the rest of the design will connect. These pins must be assigned locations and layers for each block, and each block must be assigned a definite size and location within the chip. All design constraints must be budgeted among the blocks. Foremost among these constraints are timing and power. The budgeting process is crucial, in particular, one infeasible budget (among tens of thousands of pins) can make the whole design infeasible, where it might be easily completed using a flat flow.

There are also intermediate design styles, intended to combine the advantages of flat and hierarchical design. For example, placement might be hierarchical, to limit the scope of changes, but routing done flat, to avoid the need for pin assignment. A similar approach is a flat floorplan with regions. In this particular case, the cells are confined to specific regions as in a hierarchical design, but again the routing is done flat. In the same spirit, many floorplanners support operations such as edit in context to enable the user to treat a hierarchical design as flat where this is beneficial, without actually flattening the design.

13.3.1 IS HIERARCHICAL DESIGN LESS EFFICIENT?

It is sometimes argued that a hierarchical design is intrinsically less efficient than a flat design, in terms of area or performance. While this has some basis in practice, it is not true in theory, if arbitrary rearrangement of the hierarchy is allowed. This can be shown as follows [28]: take the result of the hypothetically more efficient flat tool or procedure. Then divide this flat design, cookie cutter style, to create a hierarchical design. This design, if fabricated, would be exactly the same as the flat design, and have exactly the same size and performance.

This exact procedure is only useful as an existence proof, because there is no point in building a hierarchical design that is exactly the same as an existing flat design. Furthermore, the cookie cutter approach will almost surely result in a completely incomprehensible hierarchy. There may be no easy way to express high-level constraints on the block pins; indeed even the pins may be split into subpieces. But this procedure does show that the problem is the limitations of hierarchical tools, not the use of hierarchy itself.

A very similar procedure has been used to limit the scope of changes during ECOs [29]. This showed empirically that this procedure not only generate hierarchical designs with the same efficiency as the corresponding flat designs, but also that under normal conditions (no huge cells) this can be done even when restricted to slicing floorplans.

13.3.2 LOGICAL VERSUS PHYSICAL HIERARCHY

Normally, the input to an industrial floorplanner is a netlist defined in structural Verilog or VHDL. Usually, any hierarchy present in the original Verilog or VHDL files was developed for ease of proving logical correctness. Often, it not appropriate for physical design.

One typical difference is that the input logical hierarchy is deep, whereas the preferred physical hierarchy is shallow, with as few levels as practical. Physical design is typically most efficient when gates are combined into blocks that are relatively large (a million gates or so is typical as of 2006).

The usual solution is to match the top level of hierarchy exactly, with further hierarchy underneath on the logical side but a flat structure on the physical side. Generating this hierarchy automatically does not usually work because partitioning the top level design constraints normally requires knowledge of design intent. It is almost always better for the designer to specify the high-level hierarchy decomposition, with the help of the floorplanner

One of the most common ways for the floorplanner to assign the designer in finding a good physical hierarchy is based on the relationship between a truly flat design and a corresponding hierarchical design, as discussed above. A floorplanner will typically perform a full flat placement, see where the cells "want" to be, and use this to help define the partitioning into blocks. Visually, this is often done by displaying the results of a flat placement, coloring each cell according to its source block in the hierarchy, as shown in Figure 13.2. Blobs of similar color cells then define a potential partitioning—which cells should be grouped together, and where the resulting block should be placed on the chip. Because a good partitioning also needs to take many other factors into account, such as the ease of dividing constraints, divisions into work groups, and so on, the partitioning is normally an interactive operation, using the color map as a guide.

In practice, many variations of this idea are used:

- Use of an earlier version of the design to decide the partitioning. Assuming the differences are small, this may give a good partitioning for the final design.
- Use of a faster, but lower quality, algorithm for the flat design. This may include placement, routing, and extraction. The hope is that if the quickly produced flat design is feasible, and

FIGURE 13.2   These figures show flat placements of a design, with each cell color coded to show what portion of the input hierarchy it came from. All have similar quality, but are quite different. Note also that cells from the same logical hierarchy are often, but not always, grouped together. (Courtesy of David Shen, Cadence.)

then used to generate the hierarchy, then each piece, when fully implemented by the final tool, will be at least as good as the result of the quick tool. This is not guaranteed, but is a reasonable guess, especially when the fast tool is tuned to mimic the behavior of the final production-quality tool.

- Use the same principle with routing to decide pin positions. Route it once flat, then use where the routes cross the block boundaries as pin positions.
- Use the same principle for timing budgeting. Route the chip (flat or with assigned pins), then look at when the signals propagate through the pin locations, and assign timing budgets based on those times.

13.4   PIN ASSIGNMENT AND TIMING BUDGETING

Once the gates have been assigned to blocks, designers often wish to develop the blocks in parallel. This implies making the block into a self-contained unit. Each pin must be assigned a position (often but not always on the periphery), and a layer. This is called the pin assignment problem. This is closely related to the problem of terminal propagation [30], which is an internal decision made by the placer when dividing a large problem into two or more subproblems. Another closely related problem is the assignment of the entire chip's external IO pins. This is a particularly hard problem because it not only involves the chip physical design but also the package parasitics and logical design (the possibility of simultaneous switching). This chip-package codesign problem, and the pin assignments that result from it, are beyond the scope of this chapter, but many discussions and considerable research are available [31–38].

Pin assignment interacts strongly with routing. By definition, a feasible pin position assignment allows both the top level and the block routing to complete, so routability must be taken into account. Pin placement also interacts with the router to determine the timing of the global interconnects, the ease of the implementation of the blocks, and wirelength. Many approaches to combine pin assignment and routing have been tried. Pin assignment was combined with global routing by Cong in Ref. [15], and updated in Ref. [16]. The basic idea is to construct a redundant graph of needed connections and then iteratively remove the worst edges, until only a tree remains for each net. Wang et al. [39] approach the same problem by searching for steiner trees among the graph of possible connections, with capacities on each edge. Pin assignment can also be attacked as part of the even more general problems of floorplanning—deciding the placements and shapes of each block. This approach, studied by Pedram, et al. [17] and Koide et al. [40], has not been followed up in industrial floorplanning, because the scale of the individual problems makes it hard to consider them all in combination. An additional complication became evident during the late 1990s—long lines, such as those considered in global routing and pin assignment, almost always require buffer insertion. Albrecht et al. [19] and Xiang et al. [41,42] have combined pin assignment and buffer planning, both by casting the assignment as a flow problem (multicommodity flow and min-cost flow, respectively).

However, industrial floorplanners do not typically use any of these methods. More typical is to create a flat instance of the hierarchical design, then place it and (roughly) route it. Then pins are assigned where routes cross the block boundaries. This approach has some practical advantages. Routability and timing are taken into account, provided the flat placement and routing tools do so. The resulting pin assignment is guaranteed to be feasible, because the design was routed at least once with those positions. The main drawback is that often the pin positions cannot be assigned until a complete block design is available, meaning that in practice they are often determined with an early version of the design. The hope is that later changes will not upset the pin assignment too much.

Next, the timing constraints for each pin must be specified. Normally this is an arrival time for each input, and a required time for each output. The process of assigning a sufficient and feasible timing constraint to each pin, given the overall constraints on the chip, is called time budgeting. Most of the work is based on the zero slack algorithm (ZSA) as described by Hauge at al. [43,44] and in Ref. [20].

In practice, assigning the timing constraints must be done very carefully. A typical design, as of 2006, many have hundreds blocks, each with thousands of pins. If a single one of these hundreds of thousands of pins is assigned an infeasible objective, the entire design process may fail. Thus, ensuring that all timing constraints are feasible is critically important.

If the whole design exists, at least in preliminary form, a procedure very similar to the pin assignment described above is often used. A complete prototype of the design is constructed, with a full placement and at least a rough routing. Then extraction, delay calculation, and static timing will result in, for each signal, a time when the signal is available, and a time when it is required. The difference between these is the slack, and as long as the timing objective is within this interval, the assignment should be feasible.

13.5   ROUTABILITY ANALYSIS

A placement is not useful if a design cannot be routed, and a timing budget computed from a placement can be wildly off if the routing is not as expected. Hence floorplanners must have a fairly accurate picture of how the routing will turn out, even though they do not do the routing themselves. Such an understanding is obtained through routability analysis.

Commercial detailed routers typically have certain characteristics that need to be taken into account by floorplanners. If the design is un-congested, they can usually route every route in very nearly the theoretical minimum length. As the design becomes congested, the routes increase in length compared with the theoretical minimums, as nets must detour to complete their wiring. Finally, if the congestion is too great, the design becomes infeasible and cannot be routed at all. Importantly, the exact point where a design becomes unroutable is hard to predict. The router can often compensate for a few over-full regions by rerouting other nets. In this case, the wirelength will grow slightly, and the execution time may increase considerably, as many passes of rip-up and reroute are required to complete the routing. Eventually, as the density increases still more, the router will fail and the routes cannot be completed.

Estimates of routing congestion may be based on a global route [45], or a trial route [46]. In a global route, all routes are mapped to a coarse grid defined over the chip. Each net is assigned a path through this grid, either by explicit routing or probabilistically (see Chapter 23 or Ref. [45], for more details). After all nets are routed, if all the global cells are under capacity, then the design can almost surely be detail routed. If at most a few percent of the global routing cells are just slightly over capacity, the design is still likely to route. If any cells are far over capacity, or if there are clusters of over-capacity cells, then detailed routing will most likely fail.

Because the marginal cases are hard to resolve, one common technique is to have the floorplanner produce a color map of congestion. Then the user can apply their domain-specific knowledge or experience to decide if the final design is likely to route successfully. Often the decision to accept or try again is determined by the available time to market.

13.6 BUFFER AND FLIP-FLOP INSERTION

In modern IC processes, a long wire (or a large wiring tree) cannot simply be driven from the source. As a wire gets longer, both the resistance and capacitance scale linearly with the length. Therefore, the delay in a wire of length L scales as $O(L^2)$, and quickly dominates all other sources of delay. Furthermore, the output of such a wire will have a very poor slew rate, leading to noise and power problems.

To avoid these problems, buffers are inserted into long wires, dividing them into shorter segments. If done properly, this makes the total delay a linear function of length, and fixes the slew rate problems. The questions of where to place these buffers, how they interact with routing tree construction, and how big the buffers should be, have received a great deal of attention (see Refs. [47–53] for just a few examples). On the basis of the original Van Ginneken algorithm [54], most of these algorithms work from the leaves to the root, keeping some combination of the arrival time required, driving point capacitance, slew rate, or power. Each step closer to the root creates new combinations, which are pruned by dynamic programming, heuristics, or both.

Even if the desired locations for buffers are known, many purely practical problems remain. Do the buffers go into each block, or are they grouped into buffer banks between the blocks? In a multivoltage chip, are there sites of the right voltage available? If blocks are power-switched, is the domain of a proposed buffer site compatible with the power domain of the source and destination? How do you account for the congestion (especially on lower metal and vias) caused by the buffers that are inserted later? How do you back-annotate delays on components the front-end design does not know about? Industrial floorplanners spend a lot of time and effort trying to make buffer insertion as painless as possible.

One saving grace of buffer insertion is that by and large it does not affect logic function, and therefore does not much affect the front-end design (except for the incorporation of delays, which is needed for all signals in any case). However, a long wire on a fast chip may take more than one cycle to traverse the die, and then it becomes advantageous to pipeline the wire. This is a much more difficult problem, as the insertion of a clocked element requires significant changes to both the logical and physical designs. Although automatic methods have been proposed [55–58], they are seldom if ever used. In practice, the floorplan is used to identify the long wires, extra clocked elements are added to those wires in the RTL, and then mapped into available locations in the layout. This manual process is tedious and assumes the existence of a fairly static floorplan, and hence is applied only to the highest performance chips such as microprocessors [59].

13.7 ESTIMATING PARASITICS AND TIMING

One of the most important jobs of a floorplanner is estimating the timing of an implementation. The timing is composed of inherent gate delays and delays induced by parasitics, including incremental gate delay due to loading and delays through the interconnect itself. The gate delay portion of the total delay is normally well characterized, expressed as functions of output load and input slope, and included as part of a standard cell library or IP block. Therefore, almost all of the uncertainty to be resolved during the implementation revolves around the interconnect parasitics. The process normally proceeds in three steps: estimate the route, then estimate the electrical parasitics of the route, then estimate the delay from the parasitics.

Because the level of physical details known varies throughout the process of floorplanning and prototyping, there are many different ways to calculate estimate the parasitics, and hence the timing.

- During the first synthesis runs, when no physical design yet exists, parasitics are estimated by wire load models. These are estimates of parasitics based only on features from the logical design—fanout, hierarchy crossings, and so on. Lacking physical data, wire load models are at most statistically correct. They can accurately predict characteristics that are the sum or average over many nets, such as total wirelength or power. They are not very good at predicting the length or delays of individual nets or paths [60].
- Once a placement is available, the accuracy goes up dramatically. The exact pin positions can be determined from the placement, then the parasitic estimator can construct a Steiner tree for each net. Although creating an optimal steiner tree is NP-complete [61], there are many fast approximations available [62,63]. Then the horizontal and vertical connections of the Steiner tree can be assigned parasitic values, normally based on the average properties of horizontal and vertical layers. Missing in this formulation is any interaction between nets, and any effects due to layer assignment.
- The next level of detail is global routing. Here the surface of the chip is divided into regions, typically 10–20 tracks on a side and one layer thick. Connections are routed on this course grid, trying to respect the capacity of each edge between regions. The estimates are much better, because layer assignment and net–net interaction are now taken into account. However, effects due to adjacency cannot be estimated, because this is not known at this time.
- The next level is a trial route, where each net on the global routing grid is assigned a track, but the portions of each route within a global routing grid cell remain estimated. Now much better capacitance estimates are possible, in particular, the effects of adjacent track occupancy are now accounted for. This may seem minor, but today's relatively smart routers often count on these effects when optimizing designs, using such tricks are distributing empty tracks adjacent to critical signals. Unless these tendencies are included in the analysis, the timing may be off considerably.
- Next, an actual router may be used to connect the pins. This gives the most accurate estimates, at the expense of longer runtimes. Even here, however, there are speed/accuracy trade-offs. Often a fast, incremental, but less accurate extractor is used in optimization and ECO loops, even if a real router is used to rewire any changes. Then a slower but sign-off quality extractor may be used once the design is believed to be in a near-final state.

Driven by the same speed versus accuracy trade-off, many floorplanners also calculate interconnect delay differently at different stages of the flow. Early on, a simple lumped-C approximation may be sufficient. When higher quality estimates are available, Elmore delay can be used. As the design approaches timing closure, accuracy is crucial, and the full arsenal of multimoment methods, detailed consideration of cross coupling, slope propagation, and all the other intricacies of sign-off timing analysis must be employed.

13.8 POWER SUPPLY DESIGN

Because of constant changes during the early stages of floorplanning, power supply wiring is usually specified as a power supply plan, which is used to generate an actual power supply network. The plan can be executed (or reexecuted) after changes to regenerate the power supply wires and vias.

Power supply wires are normally pushed down from the top, with possible cutouts for memory and other IP cells. A typical sequence includes

1. Define a main power supply grid. This will include the layers, spacing of wires, and width of wires. In modern (less than 100 nm processes) the maximum width of wires may be severely restricted. Therefore, wide wires must be implemented as a parallel bundle of smaller wires.
2. Define cutouts in the main grid for IP blocks, and build rings around them. This is needed because most IP blocks have their own power supply defined.
3. Perform stub routing. This routes all IP block power supply pins, and all standard cell rows, to the closest point on the power supply network. This is often done with a specialized line probe or maze router.

The advent of chips with multiple different supply voltages has led to new problems, and hence new features, in industrial floorplanners. See, for example, voltage islands in Ref. [64].

A prototyper must also include power supply network analysis, as well as power supply design. Power supply wiring changes are more disruptive than almost any other types of changes—they always involve making the power supply wires larger, which requires rerouting signal lines, which normally causes overcongestion and hence problems with routing, timing, and design closure. Fixing these problems certainly requires extensive routing changes, often placement changes, and maybe even RTL changes if the problem is serious enough. Combined with sign-off tools for IR-drop and electromigration that can only be run at the very end of the design cycle, after all detailed routing is complete, there is the potential for fatal errors, discovered very late and requiring extensive fixes. This is exactly the type of problem prototyping is designed to prevent, so it is crucial that a prototyper construct a power supply network that will survive the scrutiny of the final sign-off tools. This involves doing the same types of analysis as the sign-off tools [65]: estimate the power consumption of the cells/blocks, create an electrical model of the power supply network, and evaluate the voltage drops and branch currents. Because a high-priority goal is quick turnaround, the analysis algorithms often make (conservative) approximations to gain analysis speed.

13.9   ECOs AND ACCOUNTING FOR CHANGES

A major constraint on the design and capabilities of industrial floorplanners is that the design is constantly changing as the floorplan is finalized. Every step must be designed with this in mind. The input netlist changes, blocks change size and shape, pins come and go, and timing constraints prove easy or infeasible. Each of these must be accommodated without losing any previous manual work, where possible. This problem is not unique to floorplanning, it also occurs in other steps of the design flow as well, such as synthesis and detailed routing. See Refs. [66,67] for general discussions of the problems of incremental CAD, and Ref. [27] for a discussion of design closure.

Some of the more common changes, and their implications, are

- Netlist changes: This can range from trivial to extremely difficult, depending on how much work has been done on the original netlist. If the changes are minor, and the synthesis tool cooperates by keeping instance and signal names consistent, then finding the gates to be deleted and added is easy, basically just a text compare. For minor changes, a good location for the new gates can often be determined from the gate's connections. The placement must then be modified, either using techniques specifically developed for placement ECOs [29], or perhaps using techniques that have been developed by the placement community to create a legal layout from an approximate solution [68–74].

  On the other hand, if buffers and inverters have been inserted and removed, and the clock restructured, or if logic paths have been restructured, then the process of mapping the changes into the existing design is very hard. This problem, trying to determine the smallest set of changes that will turn an existing design A into something with the function of new design B, is a difficult superset of formal equivalence checking [75]. As a result, a more common approach is to try to make all operations replayable. Then the designers can start with the new netlist, and reperform all the same optimizations they performed the first time. If the circuit is suitably similar, with luck similar optimizations will yield similar results.

- Block size changes: Block size changes almost always result in the block getting bigger (if the block gets smaller, it is much less of a problem). In this case, the design will surely require new routing (or new estimated routing for a floorplan), almost surely require a new placement, and maybe a new floorplan. Again the ability replay previous optimizations and operations is helpful.
- Pin changes: Removal of a pin presents no particular problem. Addition of a pin requires finding a location for it and wiring to it.
- Constraint changes: These may require anywhere between no changes and massive changes to implement. If the constraint is on a block pin, both the block and the top level must be checked, and if necessary modified.

Note that replay options should not depend, in general, on physical coordinates, because these may change if a block size changes. Instance names can often be used, if the proceeding software is careful, but netlist comparison functionality may be needed in the floorplanner if it is not.

13.10   WORKING WITH INCOMPLETE AND INCONSISTENT DESIGNS

Because one of the main goals of a floorplanner is to find problems early, it is crucial that floorplanners work with early versions of a design. These designs may be incomplete, or in an inconsistent state, but designers still expect to find problems in the portions that are complete, where possible. This strongly implies all operations should be as forgiving as practical, performing as much analysis as they can even in the presence of obvious errors and omissions. Input reading and parsing should continue wherever possible even when errors are found. Analysis of a placed design should continue even though overlapping cells are discovered, though with a warning to the user. Estimated routing parasitics should be available if the net is unrouted, partially routed, completely routed, or even shorted to an adjoining net. This accommodating spirit, though hard to quantify, is crucial in making a floorplanner a useful tool.

One of the most common problems in an incomplete design is inclusion of a block that does not yet exist. This may be an IP block that has not yet been acquired, or a block that has not yet been designed. Such a missing block must have at least an area specified, and perhaps pin locations, layer usage, timing constraints, and other properties. Floorplanners allow the block to be specified as hard (specific dimensions) or soft, where the area is fixed but the floorplanner can determine the aspect ratio. Pin locations and timing constraints, if needed, can be specified through graphic interfaces, spreadsheets, text files, or scripts. Once the real data is available, the floorplanner will replace the estimated cell characteristics with the real ones.

Any estimated cell model is faced with strongly conflicting constraints. Because it will be thrown away, it should be simple and quick to create. However, because it will factor into the size and cost of the chip, and help determine the implementation of the rest of the design, it should be reasonably accurate. Clearly this a tall order, and experience with similar designs is the only realistic hope for reasonable estimates. However, when coupled with experienced designers, this feature is very helpful, and all industrial floorplanners include this ability.

13.11   CONCLUSIONS AND FUTURE WORK

Floorplanning and prototyping have evolved from "nice to have" to crucial parts of today's (as of 2006) design flows. The gap between RTL and working silicon is quite large, and it is almost impossible to predict the performance or cost of a design expressed in RTL alone without a floorplan or prototype. Probably every large chip today, with the possible exception of purely memory or analog chips, goes through a floorplanner on its way to production.

In the future, we can expect that designs will become even more block dominated. In 2006, for example, a chip can hold 100 million gates, but typical schedules only permit designers to design perhaps 1 million gates from scratch. There are two ways designers can still take advantage of the larger chip capacity. First, they can include many copies of a single subdesign, the path taken by multicore processors and graphics chips. However, only parallelizable designs can easily use this strategy, so more common is to use a large percentage of prebuilt IP blocks. Memories, processors, and analog blocks are most common.

This shift from area dominated by standard cells to area dominated by blocks has several implications for floorplanners. Some of these implications are shown in Figure 13.3. Placement now includes a packing component, not just wirelength and timing. A rigorous treatment of obstacles is required for estimated routes, global routing, buffer insertion, and congestion analysis. If a grid power supply is used, it must be on the layers not used by the blocks. A good placement and partitioning, from a user point of view, may now need rectilinear blocks, not just rectangles. Floorplanning, partitioning, and placement are now strongly interacting problems and may need to be combined. These, and many other points, are discussed in Refs. [25,26,76].

Power is also becoming a much larger issue for many designs. A floorplan does not much influence the total amount of power used by a design (the RTL and the semiconductor processing have much larger impacts), but it does affect issues such as thermal gradients and hot spots. Also, floorplanning must be aware of techniques used to reduce power, such as multiple supplies and voltage islands.

A third trend is that as chips get larger, many more chip schedules are dominated by logic verification and not physical design. Because time to market is, if anything, becoming even more important, the goal is then to produce the final physical design as soon as possible after the logic is declared correct. This has two implication for floorplanners. Clearly, the programs must execute quickly—within a day is strongly preferred so little time is lost in case of problems. The next implication is that each operation must be automatic, or can be copied from a similar operation done on a previous version of the design.

FIGURE 13.3 Block-dominated design, including a few very large blocks that make placement and partitioning very challenging. (Courtesy of Jarrod Roy and the authors of Ref. [26].)

Finally, floorplanners and prototypers are large and complex programs, working on large and complex designs. Better user-interfaces, able to work at higher levels of abstraction, are always needed, as are better software engineering techniques.

ACKNOWLEDGMENTS

The author would like to thank Dave Noice of Cadence and Raymond Nijssen of Tabula for helpful conversations.

REFERENCES

1. S. Khatri and N. Shenoy. Logic synthesis. *Electronic Design Automation for Integrated Circuits Handbook*, volume II, CRC Press, Boca Raton, FL, 2006.
2. J. Cong, M. Romesis, and M. Xie. Optimality, scalability and stability study of partitioning and placement algorithms. In *ISPD'03, Proceedings of the International Symposium on Physical Design 2003*, pp. 88–94. ACM Press, NY, 2003.
3. L. Stok, D. Hathaway, K. Keutzer, and D. Chinnery. Design flows. *Electronic Design Automation for Integrated Circuits Handbook*, volume II, CRC Press, Boca Raton, FL, 2006.
4. E. Wein and J. Benkoski. Hard macros will revolutionize SoC design. *Electronics, Engineering Times*, August 20, 2004.
5. J. Rosenberg. Vertically integrated VLSI circuit design. *Dissertation Abstracts International Part B: Science and Engineering*, 44(5), 1983.
6. J. Rosenberg, D. Boyer, J. Dallen, S. Daniel, C. Poirier, J. Poulton, D. Rogers, and N. Weste. A vertically integrated VLSI design environment. In *DAC '83, Proceedings of the 20th Conference on Design Automation*, pp. 31–38. IEEE Press, Piscataway, NJ, 1983.
7. A. Hutchings, R. Bonneau, and W. Fisher. Integrated VLSI CAD systems at Digital Equipment Corporation. In *Proceedings of the Design Automation Conference 1985*, pp. 543–548. ACM Press, NY, 1985.
8. C. Masson, D. Barbier, R. Escassut, D. Winer, G. Chevallier, P. F. Zeegers, B. SA, and L. Clayes-sous Bous. CHEOPS: An integrated VLSI floor planning and chip assembly system implemented in object oriented Lisp. In *Proceedings of the 1990 European Design Automation Conference (EDAC)*, pp. 250–256. IEEE Press, Piscataway, NJ, 1990.
9. D. La Potin and S. Director. Mason: A global floorplanning approach for VLSI design. *IEEE Transactions on CAD*, 5(4):477–489, 1986.
10. R. Goering. EDA vendors redraw chip-design process. *EE Times*, 10:49, 1999.
11. P. Chao and L. Lev. Down to the wire-requirements for nanometer design implementation. *EE Design*, August 15, 2002.
12. W. Dai, D. Huang, C. Chang, and M. Courtoy. Silicon virtual prototyping: The new cockpit for nanometer chip design [SoC]. In *ASP-DAC 2003*, pp. 635–639. ACM Press, NY, 2003.
13. N. L. Koren. Pin assignment in automated printed circuit board design. In *DAC '72, Proceedings of the 1972 Design Automation Conference*, pp. 72–79. ACM Press, NY, 1972.
14. H. Brady. An approach to topological pin assignment. *IEEE Transactions on CAD*, 3(3):250–255, 1984.
15. J. Cong. Pin assignment with global routing. In *ICCAD '89, Proceedings of the International Conference on Computer-Aided Design 1989*, pp. 302–305. ACM Press, NY, 1989.
16. J. Cong. Pin assignment with global routing for general cell designs. *IEEE Transactions on CAD*, 10(11):1401–1412, 1991.
17. M. Pedram, M. Marek-Sadowska, and E. Kuh. Floorplanning with pin assignment. In *ICCAD '90, Proceedings of the International Conference on Computer Aided Design 1990*, pp. 98–101, NY, 1990. ACM Press.
18. M. Pedram and B. Preas. A hierarchical floorplanning approach. In *ICCD '90, Proceedings of the 1990 IEEE International Conference on Computer Design: VLSI in Computers and Processors*, pp. 332–338. IEEE Press, Piscataway, NJ, 1990.
19. C. Albrecht, A. B. Kahng, I. Mandoiu, and A. Zelikovsky. Floorplan evaluation with timing-driven global wireplanning, pin assignment, and buffer/wire sizing. In *ASP-DAC '02, Proceedings of Asia and South Pacific Design Automation Conference 2002*, pp. 580–587, NY, 2002. ACM Press.

20. R. Nair, C. Berman, P. Hauge, and E. Yoffa. Generation of performance constraints for layout. *IEEE Transactions on CAD*, 8(8):860–874, 1989.

21. M. Sarrafzadeh, D. Knol, and G. Tellez. A delay budgeting algorithm ensuring maximum flexibility in placement. *IEEE Transactions on CAD*, 16(11):1332–1341, 1997.

22. S. Venkatesh. Hierarchical timing-driven floorplanning and place and route using a timing budgeter. In *CICC '95, Proceedings of the Custom Integrated Circuits Conference 1995*, pp. 469–472. IEEE Press, Piscataway, NJ, 1995.

23. C. Kuo and A. Wu. Delay budgeting for a timing-closure-driven design method. In *ICCAD '00, Proceedings of the International Conference on Computer-Aided Design 2000*, pp. 202–207. IEEE Press, Piscataway, NJ, 2000.

24. X. Yang, B. K. Choi, and M. Sarrafzadeh. Timing-driven placement using design hierarchy guided constraint generation. In *ICCAD '02, Proceedings of the International Conference on Computer-Aided Design 2002*, p. 42. ACM Press, NY, 2002.

25. J. Roy, S. Adya, D. Papa, and I. Markov. Min-cut Floorplacement. *IEEE Transactions on CAD*, 25(7):1313–1326, 2006.

26. A. Ng, I. Markov, R. Aggarwal, and V. Ramachandran. Solving hard instances of floorplacement. In *ISPD '06, Proceedings of the International Symposium on Physical Design 2006*, pp. 170–177. ACM Press, NY, 2006.

27. P. Osler and J. Cohn. Design closure. *Electronic Design Automation for Integrated Circuits Handbook*, volume II, CRC Press, Boca Raton, FL, 2006.

28. L. Scheffer. A methodology for improved verification of VLSI designs without loss of area. In *Proceedings of the Caltech Conference on Very Large Scale Integration*, Caltech Pasadena, CA, 1981.

29. J. Roy and I. Markov. ECO-system: Embracing the change in placement. Technical Report CSE-TR-519-06, University of Michigan, Ann Arbor, Michigan, June 20, 2006.

30. A. Dunlop and B. Kernighan. A procedure for placement of standard-cell VLSI circuits. *IEEE Transactions on CAD*, 4(1):92–98, 1985.

31. U. Shrivastava and B. Bui. Inductance calculation and optimal pin assignment for the design of pin-grid-array and chip carrier packages. *IEEE Transactions on Components, Hybrids, and Manufacturing Technology*, 13(1):147–153, 1990.

32. T. Pförtner, S. Kiefl, and R. Dachauer. Embedded pin assignment for top down system design. In *Proceedings of the Conference on European Design Automation*, pp. 209–214. IEEE Computer Society Press, Los Alamitos, CA, 1992.

33. N. Hirano, M. Miura, Y. Hiruta, and T. Sudo. Characterization and reduction of simultaneous switching noise for a multilayer package. In *Proceedings of the 44th Electronic Components and Technology Conference 1994*, pp. 949–956. IEEE Press, Piscataway, NJ, 1994.

34. N. Sugiura. Effect of power and ground pin assignment and inner layer structure on switching noise. *IEICE Transactions on Electronics E Series C*, 78:574–574, 1995.

35. X. Aragones, J.L. Gonzalez, and A. Rubio. *Analysis and Solutions for Switching Noise Coupling in Mixed-Signal ICs*. Kluwer Academic Publishers, Dordrecht, the Netherlands, 1999.

36. R. Ravichandran, J. Minz, M. Pathak, and S. Easwar. Physical layout automation for system-on-packages. In *ECTC '04, Proceedings of the Electronic Components and Technology 2004*, volume 1, pp. 41–48. IEEE Press, Piscataway, NJ, 2004.

37. M. Shen, J. Liu, L. R. Zheng, and H. Tenhunen. Chip-package co-design for high performance and reliability off-chip communications. In *HDP '04, Proceedings of the 6th IEEE CPMT Conference on* High Density Microsystem Design and Packaging and Component Failure Analysis 2004. pp. 31–36. IEEE Press, Piscataway, NJ, 2004.

38. P. Franzon. Tools for chip-package codedesign. *Electronic Design Automation for Integrated Circuits Handbook*, volume II, CRC Press, Boca Raton, FL, 2006.

39. L. Wang, Y. Lai, and B. Liu. Simultaneous pin assignment and global wiring for custom VLSI design. In *IEEE International Symposium on Circuits and Systems* 1991, pp. 2128–2131. IEEE Press, Piscataway, NJ, 1991.

40. T. Koide, S. Wakabayashi, and N. Yoshida. Pin assignment with global routing for VLSI building block layout. *IEEE Transactions on CAD*, 15(12):1575–1583, 1996.

41. H. Xiang, X. Tang, and M.D.F. Wong. Min-cost flow-based algorithm for simultaneous pin assignment and routing. *IEEE Transactions on CAD*, 22(7), 2003.

42. H. Xiang, X. Tang, and M.D.F. Wong. An algorithm for integrated pin assignment and buffer planning. *ACM Transactions on Design Automation of Electronic Systems (TODAES)*, 10(3):561–572, 2005.

43. P. Hauge, R. Nair, and E. Yoffa. Circuit placement for predictable performance. In *ICCAD '87, Proceedings of the International Conference on Computer-Aided Design 1987*, pp. 88–91. ACM Press, NY, 1987.

44. P. Hauge, R. Nair, and E. Yoffa. *Circuit Placement for Predictable Performance*. IBM Thomas J. Watson Research Center, Yorktown Heights, NY, 1987.

45. J. Hu and S. Sapatnekar. A survey on multi-net global routing for integrated circuits. *Integration: The VLSI Journal*, 31(1):1–49, November 2001.

46. C. Lee. An algorithm for path connections and its applications. *IRE Transactions on Electronic Computers*, EC-10:346–365, September 1961.

47. L. John, C. Cheng, and T. Lin. Simultaneous routing and buffer insertion for high performance interconnect. In *GLSVLSI '96, Proceedings of the 6th Great Lakes Symposium on VLSI*, p. 148. Washington, DC, IEEE Computer Society, 1996.

48. M. Kang, W. Dai, T. Dillinger, and D. LaPotin. Delay bounded buffered tree construction for timing driven floorplanning. In *ICCAD '97, Proceedings of the 1997 IEEE/ACM International Conference on Computer-Aided Design*, pp. 707–712. IEEE Press, Piscataway, NJ, 1997.

49. J. Cong and X. Yuan. Routing tree construction under fixed buffer locations. In *DAC '00, Proceedings of the 37th Conference on Design Automation*, pp. 379–384. ACM Press, New York, 2000.

50. F. Dragan, A. Kahng, I. Mandoiu, S. Muddu, and A. Zelikovsky. Provably good global buffering by multi-terminal multicommodity flow approximation. In *ASP-DAC '01, Proceedings of the 2001 Conference on Asia South Pacific Design Automation*, pp. 120–125. ACM Press, New York, 2001.

51. C. Alpert, M. Hrkic, J. Hu, A. Kahng, J. Lillis, B. Liu, S. Quay, S. Sapatnekar, A. Sullivan, and P. Villarrubia. Buffered Steiner trees for difficult instances. In *ISPD '01, Proceedings of the 2001 International Symposium on Physical Design*, pp. 4–9. ACM Press, New York, 2001.

52. W. Chen, M. Pedram, and P. Buch. Buffered routing tree construction under buffer placement blockages. In *ASP-DAC '02, Proceedings of the 2002 Conference on Asia South Pacific Design Automation/VLSI Design*, p. 381. IEEE Computer Society Washington, DC, 2002.

53. C. J. Alpert, G. Gandham, M. Hrkic, J. Hu, and S. T. Quay. Porosity aware buffered steiner tree construction. In ISPD '03, Proceedings of the 2003 International Symposium on Physical Design, pp. 158–165. ACM Press, New York, 2003.

54. L. van Ginneken. Buffer placement in distributed RC-tree networks for minimal Elmore delay. In *Proceedings of IEEE International Symposium on Circuits and Systems*, pp. 865–868. IEEE Press, Piscataway, NJ, 1990.

55. R. Lu, G. Zhong, C. Koh, and K. Chao. Flip-flop and repeater insertion for early interconnect planning. In *DATE'02, Proceedings of the Conference on Design, Automation and Test in Europe*, p. 690, IEEE Computer Society, Washington, DC, 2002.

56. L. Scheffer. Methodologies and tools for pipelined on-chip interconnect. In *Proceedings of the 2002 IEEE International Conference on Computer Design: VLSI in Computers and Processors*, pp. 152–157. IEEE Press, Piscataway, NJ, 2002.

57. V. Chandra, A. Xu, and H. Schmit. A low power approach to system level pipelined interconnect design. In *SLIP'04, Proceedings of the 2004 International Workshop on System Level Interconnect Prediction*, pp. 45–52. ACM Press, New York, 2004.

58. J. Cong, Y. Fan, and Z. Zhang. Architecture-level synthesis for automatic interconnect pipelining. In *DAC '04, Proceedings of the Design Automation Conference*, pp. 602–607. ACM Press, New York, 2004.

59. R. McInerney, K. Leeper, T. Hill, H. Chan, B. Basaran, and L. McQuiddy. Methodology for repeater insertion management in the RTL, layout, floorplan and fullchip timing databases of the Itanium microprocessor. In *ISPD'00, Proceedings of the International Symposium on Physical Design 2000*, pp. 99–104. ACM Press, New York, 2000.

60. L. Scheffer and E. Nequist. Why interconnect prediction doesn't work. In *SLIP'00, Proceedings of the 2000 International Workshop on System-Level Interconnect Prediction*, pp. 139–144. ACM Press, New York, 2000.

61. M. R. Garey and D. S. Johnson. The rectilinear Steiner tree problem is NP complete. *SIAM Journal of Applied Math*, 32:826–834, 1977.

62. H. Chen, C. Qiao, F. Zhou, and C. Cheng. Refined single trunk tree: a rectilinear steiner tree generator for interconnect prediction. In *SLIP'02, Proceedings of the 2002 International Workshop on System-Level Interconnect Prediction*, pp. 85–89. ACM Press, New York, 2002.

63. C. Chu. Fast and accurate rectilinear Steiner minimal tree algorithm for VLSI design. In *ISPD'05, Proceedings of the International Symposium on Physical Design 2005*, pp. 28–35. ACM Press, NY, 2005.

64. J. Hu, Y. Shin, N. Dhanwada, and R. Marculescu. Architecting voltage islands in core-based system-on-a-chip designs. In *ISLPED'04, Proceedings of the 2004 International Symposium on Low Power Electronics and Design 2004*, pp. 180–185. ACM Press, NY, 2004.

65. D. Blaauw, S. Pant, R. Chanda, and R. Panda. Design and analysis of power supply networks. *Electronic Design Automation for Integrated Circuits Handbook*, volume II, CRC Press, Boca Raton, FL, 2006.

66. O. Coudert, J. Cong, S. Malik, and M. Sarrafzadeh. Incremental CAD. In *ICCAD'00, Proceedings of the International Conference on Computer-Aided Design 2000*, pp. 236–243. ACM Press, NY, 2000.

67. J. Cong and M. Sarrafzadeh. Incremental physical design. In *ISPD'00, Proceedings of the International Symposium on Physical Design 2000*, pp. 84–92. ACM Press, NY, 2000.

68. Z. Li, W. Wu, X. Hong, and J. Gu. Incremental placement algorithm for standard-cell layout. In *ISCAS 2002, IEEE International Symposium on Circuits and Systems 2002*, volume 2. IEEE Press, Piscataway, NJ, 2002.

69. W. Choi and K. Bazargan. Incremental placement for timing optimization. In *ICCAD '03, Proceedings of the International Conference on Computer-Aided Design 2003*, pp. 463–466. ACM Press, NY, 2003.

70. U. Brenner and J. Vygen. Legalizing a placement with minimum total movement. *IEEE Transactions on CAD*, 23(12):1597–1613, 2004.

71. U. Brenner, A. Pauli, and J. Vygen. Almost optimum placement legalization by minimum cost flow and dynamic programming. In *ISPD'04, Proceedings of the International Symposium on Physical Design 2004*, pp. 2–9. ACM Press, NY, 2004.

72. A.B. Kahng, I.L. Markov, and S. Reda. On legalization of row-based placements. In *Proceedings of the 14th ACM Great Lakes Symposium on VLSI*, pp. 214–219. ACM Press, NY, 2004.

73. T. Luo, H. Ren, C. Alpert, and D. Pan. Computational geometry based placement migration. In *ICCAD '05, Proceedings of the International Conference on Computer-Aided Design 2005*, pp. 41–47. ACM Press, NY, 2005.

74. H. Ren, D. Z. Pan, C. J. Alpert, and P. Villarrubia. Diffusion-based placement migration. In *DAC '05, Proceedings of the Design Automation Conference*, pp. 515–520. ACM Press, NY, 2005.

75. A. Kuehlmann and F. Somenzi. Equivalence checking. *Electronic Design Automation for Integrated Circuits Handbook*, volume II, CRC Press, Boca Raton, FL, 2006.

76. S. Adya, S. Chaturvedi, J. Roy, D. Papa, and I. Markov. Unification of partitioning, placement and floorplanning. In *ICCAD '04, Proceedings of the International Conference on Computer-Aided Design 2004*, pp. 550–557. ACM Press, NY, 2004.

Part IV

Placement

14 Placement: Introduction/ Problem Formulation

Gi-Joon Nam and Paul G. Villarrubia

CONTENTS

14.1   INTRODUCTION

Placement is a physical synthesis task that transforms a block/gate/transistor-level netlist into an actual layout for timing convergence. It is a crucial step that assembles the basic building blocks of logic netlist and establishes the overall timing characteristic of a design by determining exact locations of circuit elements within a given region. In modern VLSI designs, the size of chip becomes larger and the required clock frequency keeps increasing due to higher performance and more complex functional requirements on a single chip. Moreover, with aggressive technology scaling into the deep submicron (DSM) era, interconnect delays become the dominant factor for overall chip performance. Because the locations of circuit elements and corresponding interconnect delays are determined during the placement stage, it has significant impact on the final performance of the design. Moreover, if a design is placed poorly, it is virtually impossible to close timing, no matter how much other physical synthesis and routing optimizations are applied to it. Hence, placement is regarded as one of the most important and effective optimization techniques in the physical synthesis flow. Today, placement is no longer a point tool in modern timing closure flow [1]. Significant portions of logic and physical optimization algorithms have to interact with placement to improve timing of a design and to guarantee a legal placement solution after optimizations. Consequently, most industrial and academic physical synthesis tools are developed around a placement infrastructure.

The typical objective function of placement is to minimize total wirelength of a design. This is because wirelength can be easily modeled and serve as a good first-order approximation of real objective functions such as timing, power, and routability of a design. There also exist various forms of wirelength. For example, quadratic wirelength, linear wirelength, or some approximation of linear wirelength are popular models that are employed in many placement tools. Recently, Steiner wirelength, which is considered as the most accurate estimator of the routed wirelength, was also used as the placement objective function in some academic placement tools. Whatever wirelength form is used, producing a good placement wirelength is critical for timing closure of modern designs because the wirelength directly affects the interconnect delays of electrical signals. The wirelength also affects the routability of a design, which is another important aspect of physical synthesis. The routing is performed right after the placement and there is no point in producing an unroutable placement solution.

14.2 PROBLEM FORMULATION

Because the primary task of placement is to determine the locations of circuit elements in a design, the placement region P needs to be defined first. Usually, a placement region is a rectangle area defined by coordinates (xlow, ylow, xhigh, yhigh). This is not a necessity for modern placement and actually a wider variety of placement regions such as L-shapes or T-shapes have been observed recently in special problem instances such as region constraint* (movebound) placement. However, for global placement, a rectangular placement region is still the norm. The circuit netlist is represented as a graph $G = (V, E)$, where V is a set of circuit elements in a design and E is a set of connections (nets) among them. The vertex set V consists of two disjoint subsets, MV and FV where MV/FV represents a set of movable/fixed circuit elements respectively. For each $v \in$ FV, the location (x, y) of v is already determined and the placement should not change them. The location of each $v \in$ MV needs to be determined by placement and their locations must fall within the given placement region P.

Each net $e_i \in E$ is a hyper-edge and conveniently represented as a subset of circuit elements, which are electrically connected each other, i.e., $e_i = \{v_{i1}, v_{i2}, \ldots, v_{im}\}, \forall v_{ij} \in V$. Hence, $|e|$, the cardinality of net e, denotes the number of pins on the net. Figure 14.1 shows a simple example of a placement problem. The big rectangle in Figure 14.1a represents a placement region P and each circle represents a movable circuit element to be placed within P. Small rectangles on the boundary of the placement region are I/O pins that are considered as fixed circuit elements. These movable and fixed circuit elements are connected to each other by nets. The goal of placement is to find a legal location for each movable circuit element while minimizing the given objective function. In this example, only one movable circuit element (circle) is assumed to be placed within a placement grid (slot) that is defined by dotted lines.

Some class of global placement algorithms, such as a partitioning-based algorithms or simulated annealing, is effective in directly handling hyper-edge nets. Others, particularly analytical placement algorithms, require a hyper-edge to be transformed into a set of clique edges. For example, quadratic optimization-based analytic placement needs a clique-edge model to solve a symmetric positive definite linear system equation. A net usually has a source-pin (driver) and multiple sink pins, which make it a directed hyper-edge.[†] The current state-of-the-art global placement algorithms still ignore the directions of the hyper-edges and treat a netlist graph G as a undirected graph. However, the directions of hyper-edges can be utilized to better handle certain types of nets. A high fan-out clock

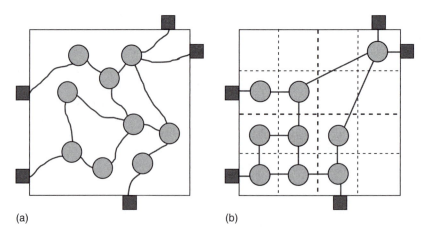

(a)   (b)

FIGURE 14.1 Simple placement instance. (a) Before placement and (b) after placement.

---

* More discussion of region constraints and movebounds are provided in Section 14.3.
† There exists a bidirectional net such as a bus signal. In this case, one pin can be considered as a source pin while the others are regarded as sink pins.

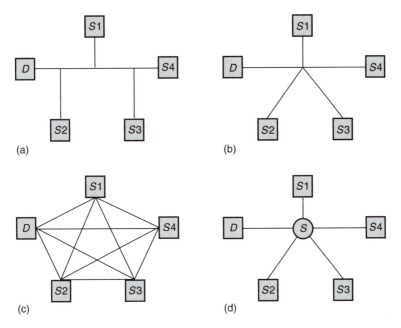

FIGURE 14.2 Net model: hyper-edge model, clique-edge model, and star. (a) Original net with a driver and four sinks, (b) hyper-edge, (c) clique edge, and (d) star.

net, for example, can be better placed by representing it as a star model with a source pin in the center. Figure 14.2 shows a hyper-edge net and corresponding clique/star models. A more detailed circuit netlist representation discussion can be found in Chapter 7.

The typical objective function of a placement is the sum of net wirelengths, i.e., $\Sigma WL(e), \forall e \in E$. For a given net, different types of wirelength $WL(e)$ can be measured. A net half-perimeter (NHP) wirelength model (Figure 14.3b) measures the smallest bounding box, which surrounds all sinks of the net. A minimum spanning tree (MST) model (Figure 14.3c) calculates a minimum tree length, which connects all pins of the net. However, only a direct connection of a pair of pins on the net is considered to build a tree. A Steiner tree (ST) model (Figure 14.3d) is also a tree connecting all pins of the net, but any arbitrary point (not pin) in a tree segment is also considered to branch off other tree segments to reduce the tree length. Therefore Steiner tree length is always equal to or better than that of MST. Because the routes of nets are implemented with horizontal and vertical metal layers,[*] a rectilinear minimum spanning tree or rectilinear Steiner tree is a more accurate estimation of real net wirelengths and these rectilinear versions of MST and ST are popularly used in physical design research (see Chapter 24 for more detailed discussion on MST and ST). Simple NHP bounding box is the most popular model used in placement today simply because it is efficient to compute and also it is a good approximation of routed wirelength for the majority of nets. For some difficult nets, Steiner tree wirelength might be necessary to optimize for better routability, but the number of these nets is marginal in most cases.

A net e can have a weight $w(e)$ associated with it. In a timing-driven placement (Chapter 21), a net is assigned a weight based on its timing criticality. The more critical a net is for timing closure, the higher the weight assigned to the net so that a placement algorithm can try harder to reduce its wirelength leading to less signal delay. When a net weight is present, the common objective function of a placement is the weighted sum of wirelengths, i.e., $\Sigma w(e)^*WL(e), \forall e \in E$.

---

[*] X-route with 45° angle metal layer is available in advanced technology. However, horizontal and vertical metal layers are still more common as of today.

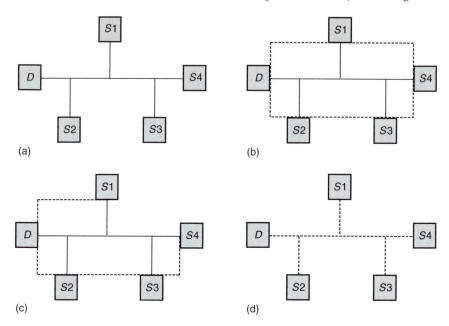

FIGURE 14.3 Net wirelength model: NHP, MST, and ST. Net model is drawn in dotted line. (a) Routed net with a driver and four sinks, (b) NHP model, (c) rectilinear MST model, and (d) rectilinear ST model.

Suppose that there are n movable circuit elements $[v_1, v_2, \ldots, v_n]$ and m nets $[e_1, e_2, \ldots, e_m]$ in a given netlist graph $G = (V, E)$, i.e., $|V| = n$ and $|E| = m$. Let each movable circuit element v_i's location be (x_i, y_i). Then, the placement problem can be formulated as follows [2–4]: Given a placement region P with width W and height H, a netlist graph $G = (V, E)$, and objective function $f(V, E)$, find the location (x_i, y_i) of each $v_i \in$ MV such that (1) each $v_i \in$ MV is placed completely within P, (2) no overlap exists between any pair of (v_i, v_j), $\forall v_i, v_j \in V$, and (3) the objective function $f(V, E)$ is minimized. In the case of the standard cell placement problem, an additional circuit row constraint must be honored and each standard cell must be placed within a circuit row boundary.

The intuition of the wirelength based placement objective function is to reduce signal delays of the design and enhance routability simply by minimizing the total (weighted) wirelength. With the aggressive advance of technology, placement starts to model other important aspects of the design directly, such as power, signal integrity, thermal distribution, clocking, placement congestion, or even optical proximity correction effects for better design manufacturability. However, the fundamental formulation of the placement problem tends to stay the same, even in these new variants of placement algorithms. New issues can be addressed by factoring in the corresponding modeling component into the wirelength based objective function. For example, those additional factors are modeled into net weights and the weighted wirelength objective function can be minimized during placement. Chapter 22 elaborates on how these modern issues are addressed in placement algorithms.

Placement is an NP-complete problem [5]. Consequently, the placement problem is usually divided into subproblems—global placement, legalization, and detailed placement—and each sub-problem is attacked separately. Global placement determines the approximate distributions of circuit elements while optimizing a given objective function, typically wirelength. Usually global placement allows some degree of overlapping among circuit elements leading to an illegal placement solution. The legalization step then transforms an illegal global placement solution into a legal one (i.e., no overlap is allowed) while minimizing the perturbation to the original global placement solution. Figure 14.4 shows a placement example before and after the legalization process. Detailed placement finally improves the objective function further by performing local refinements. It is also important to

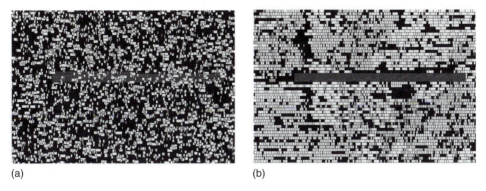

(a)   (b)

FIGURE 14.4   Before and after legalization of placement. (a) Before legalization, i.e., illegal solution and (b) after legalization, i.e., legal solution.

keep a legal, nonoverlapping placement state during detailed placement. Sometimes, the legalization process is viewed as part of the detailed placement process. A variety of global placement algorithms are further described in Chapters 15 through 19, and Chapter 20 presents detailed placement algorithms.

14.3   MODERN ISSUES IN PLACEMENT

In this section, we review several important issues in modern placement problem.

1. Fixed layout region placement: Placement has been actively researched for a long time as a fundamental problem in design automation. The classical placement problem typically focused on minimizing the overall placement area by packing circuit elements more compactly. This packing-driven area optimization is still a dominant theme in the floorplanning domain. In a modern chip synthesis flow for timing closure, however, placement optimization is executed almost always after the die size and package have been chosen. Thus, placement should be formulated as an (wirelength) optimization problem with a fixed layout region, rather than a packing-driven area minimization problem [6]. In fixed region placement, the layout area is already determined and the circuit elements and its netlist are also determined. Thus, the amount of white space is a constant. This implies that the management of white space during placement becomes more important than before, to minimize placement objective functions such as wirelength and routing congestion.

2. White space management for congestion control: One thing noticeably different in modern IC designs is the increasing amount of white space available in a design [7]. As design complexity continues to increase while time-to-market decreases, IP reuse and semihierarchical or full-hierarchical designs are becoming increasingly pervasive leading to more chunky design footprints with memory arrays, IP blocks, etc., as opposed to pure standard cell designs. Consequently, today's placement instances resemble the problem of arranging "dust" logic (standard cells) around these large blocks. Because the large blocks tend to dictate the design footprint, one can no longer assume that the placeable area in some way matches the total cell area of the design; one must recognize the trend of the increasing percentage of free space available on the chip. One might think increased free space, or design sparsity, might make placement easier. However, even though the dust logic is a small percentage of the chip area, there can still be millions of cells in the dust logic that have profound effects on timing and routability. In other words, packing all the cells in a design can yield the minimum wirelength solution, but create enough congestion to make

the design unroutable. A strategy of simple uniform spreading of the design may work well for dense designs, but can unnecessarily hurt timing for sparse designs. Thus, white space management is absolutely required in modern placement algorithms to achieve better timing and routability.

3. Mixed-size placement: For the past few decades, standard cell placement is considered as the norm. A standard cell based design consists of circuit elements called standard cells whose heights remain the same, and the placement problem is to place these circuit elements within regular circuit row boundaries (Figure 14.5a). In today's design methodology, designers are encouraged to take hierarchical or semihierarchical design approaches with reusable internal/third-party IPs to reduce design turnaround time. As a result, a wider distribution of circuit element sizes is observed during placement. In some sense, mixed-size placement (Figure 14.5b), as opposed to uniform-height placement of standard cells, is a more complicated problem because these large macro blocks can cause a serious challenge during placement legalization. Also, these chunky blocks play an important role in determining final timing performance. Hence, the early placement of large macros (during floorplanning or flat placement) is an important problem in a modern timing closure flow. To provide further flexibility in floorplanning and placement, sometimes all the standard cells as well as large macros are considered as movable objects and are placed simultaneously. This new problem is called floorplacement [8]. In general, today's placement algorithms must be able to handle a wide range of object sizes, because the trend indicates that more IP blocks are included in a design.

4. Region constraints (movebounds): In a hierarchical design methodology, the functionality of a design is logically partitioned first and floorplanning is executed on the set of logically partitioned blocks to determine the approximate locations of those logical blocks. Circuit elements belonging to the same logical partition are grouped together and need to be placed in the vicinity of the layout region. This is in contrast to the top-down flat physical design process where logical partitioning is flattened and circuit elements are freely placed and routed at the leaf level of the logical hierarchy. In flat physical synthesis, physical partitions do not necessarily correlate with logical partitions. Although flat physical synthesis usually produces a better quality of result, the tight turnaround time requirement makes hierarchical synthesis a more viable solution in today's environment. In a hierarchical synthesis flow,

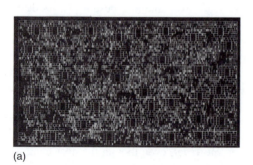

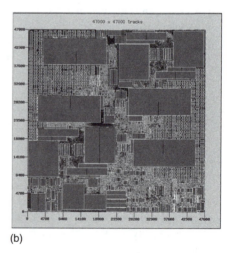

(a)   (b)

FIGURE 14.5 Standard cell placement versus mixed-size placement. (a) Standard cell placement and (b) mixed-size placement.

a region constraint (also known as a movebound) is usually employed to force circuit elements belonging to the same logic partition to be placed within a predetermined layout area. Essentially, a region constraint is a predetermined boundary where a set of circuit elements has to be placed and routed. Multiple region constraints may exist in a design, but not all the circuit elements are constrained by a region constraint either. Some circuit elements can be placed anywhere in layout area while others must be placed within the corresponding boundary defined by region constraints. Another motivation for region constraints is multiple clock/voltage domains in a design. In modern circuit design, multiple clock domains or voltage domains are frequently used due to performance and power dissipation trade-offs. For example, computationally unimportant parts in a chip can be slowed down to lower clock frequency while critical path computations have to be executed at the highest clock frequency. The lowered clock frequency results in the saving of unnecessary power consumption. The clock network typically consumes a significant portion of the overall chip power [9] and the size of the clock network can serve as a first-order approximation of the clock network power consumption. Hence, a smaller clock domain area is always preferred, if possible, to reduce clock network power dissipation. These clock domains are similar to logical partitions and region constraints can facilitate to define and reduce the size of clock domain. However, region constraints can make the placement algorithm complicated and modern placement algorithms must be capable of handling these unforeseen constraints without affecting the quality of results.

5. Clock-aware placement: Clock nets typically have much more sink pins to drive than normal data signal nets. This is because any sequential circuit elements (latches or flip-flops) require global clock signals to synchronize with each other. Sometimes, there are multiple clock domains in a design due to performance and power consumption trade-offs. Because of the high fan-out nature of clock nets, in a typical placement process, clock nets are ignored during the optimization as they tend to degrade the quality of placement solution. Moreover, the higher frequency design constraint forces a design to include more sequential circuit elements resulting in larger clock domain and higher clock power consumption. Recent studies show that the power budget of clock nets and networks amounts to more than 40 percent of overall chip power [9]. Even worse, each sink of a clock net needs to have the same signal propagation delay from the clock source. In reality, each sink has different clock signal propagation delay and the maximum delay difference of pairs of two sink pins is called clock skew. One of the objectives of clock network construction is to minimize the clock skew. Because clock nets are sensitive to technology variations due to their large network size and high frequency constraint, the placement of sequential circuit elements affects the clock network performance significantly. Postplacement clock network construction tends to fail more frequently due to the tighter skew, latency, and power constraints. Recent research [10] also shows that by considering these clock network constraints during quadratic placement, higher clock network performance (less skew, clock latency, and power consumption) can be achieved without almost any loss of data signal performance. Essentially, they tried to reduce clock network wirelengths by navigating potential locations of sequential circuit element during placement via register contraction techniques. More advanced technology and corresponding design paradigms will require higher clock frequency and more robustness to technology variations. Thus, the combined placement and clock network construction optimization has great promises for better layout solutions.

6. Scalability: As the complexity of a design grows exponentially, the corresponding number of gates in a design is expected to grow at a steep rate. Hierarchical design and the design reuse paradigm can help to manage the size of a design. Yet, a multimillion gate count is considered a norm in modern IC design [11,12]. Owing to large design sizes, placement runtime tends to be the bottleneck of the overall timing closure flow and the reduction of placement runtime, i.e., scalable placement algorithms, arises as a critical problem.

Recently, the multilevel paradigm shows great promise to make placement algorithms more scalable with design size [13]. The multilevel method consists of three processes: coarsened abstract structure generation (coarsening or aggregation), optimization on the coarsened structure (relaxation), and transforming optimized solutions to an uncoarsened structure (interpolation). The simplest method of applying multilevel optimization in placement is a so-called "V-cycle" [13] approach where consecutive coarsenings are executed to obtain the most reduced design, then iterative relaxation, interpolation, and uncoarsening are applied to convert it to an optimized, flattened level. Combined with netlist clustering algorithms, multilevel optimization was demonstrated to provide a significant runtime reduction without almost any degradation of (sometimes even improved) quality of solutions [12]. Chapter 19 addresses multilevel techniques and their application in placement.

7. Stability: To achieve timing closure and design convergence, typically several instances of placement have to be run. Placement can help to identify needed changes in the logic, required buffering, gate sizing, routing congestion, etc. Once these problems are fixed, placement may have to be run again. Ideally, after each subsequent placement run, the problems that were fixed during the last iteration stay fixed and new problems do not crop up. However, if a placement algorithm returns a dramatically different solution from the last solution, entirely new problems could emerge. In other words, a placement algorithm needs to produce similar solutions when almost the same input instance (albeit with a slightly different netlist or constraints) is given. This stability is a particularly important issue in a timing closure flow where multiple invocations of placement are necessary. The quantification of the degree of stability of placement algorithms is also an important topic for further research [14,15].

8. Macroblock (random logic module) placement versus ASIC placement: In microprocessor design, blocks with tight timing constraints such as data-paths, floating point units, etc. are still custom designed and layouts are produced by a human being. However, significant portion of macroblocks, for example, control logic modules, consist of random logic. These random logic modules are typically designed in HDL (high-level description language), synthesized and laid out via design automation tools. The characteristics of these random logic modules are quite different from those of ASIC designs. Owing to the high-performance nature of microprocessor design, the target timing constraint is extremely tight compared with that of ASIC design. The latches and leaf level clock distribution buffers are much larger than standard cells and the locations of these objects tend to affect final timing performance considerably. The number of circuit elements to be placed is order of magnitude smaller than ASIC placement problems. Thus, scalability is not an issue in macroblock placement. Rather more accurate modeling of timing with enhanced optimization techniques (at the cost of runtime, of course) is more important in this placement problem domain.

9. Three-dimensional placement: Traditionally, placement is formulated as a two-dimensional problem that places circuit elements in a 2D plane. Recent advances in package technology, however, enable chips to be piled up and interconnected together so that more functional blocks and logics can be inserted to chip designs [16]. Including more logics is not only a predominant advantage of 3D chip integration but also introduces new technical problems. The primary concern of 3D integration is a thermal issue. Because multiple circuit planes are stacked up tightly, it is more difficult to dissipate heat, particularly in the middle planes. Hot spots of integrated circuits in modern technology have adverse impacts on circuit performance because temperature directly affects the subthreshold voltage of transistors, resulting in slower responses and signal propagations. Heat dissipation can be addressed via thermal gradient consideration during floorplanning/placement [17] or inserting thermal vias to facilitate heat flow [18]. Another principal concern of 3D integration is the signal propagation among different circuit planes. The signal delay from one plane to another is an order-of-magnitude higher than that of the same plane. Because the circuit performance,

i.e., maximum frequency of a design, is limited by the maximum delay of timing critical paths in a design, reducing plane-to-plane signal delay is an important issue in 3D placement. Therefore, partitioning and placement of logics for planes have consequential effects on the final performance of design and plane-to-plane interconnect needs to be considered during placement. These unforeseen concerns of 3D integration require a new formulation of 3D placement and open new opportunities for placement research.

In addition to these issues, more and more technology constraints are being considered during placement, such as power/thermal constraints, power/ground network, IR drop constraints, etc. [17, 19–21]. This is because a placement solution can directly affect the final quality of solution of design closure. This trend will carry on as long as technology scaling continues, and it confirms that placement remains the most important problem in design closure.

14.4 GENERAL APPROACHES TO PLACEMENT

Placement algorithms are typically based on a simulated annealing, top-down cut-based partitioning, or analytical paradigm (or some combination thereof). Simulated annealing is an iterative optimization method that mimics the physical metal cooling process. With the given objective function, the process tries to achieve a better solution via a set of predefined moves. If a move improves the objective function, it is always accepted. If a move produces a worse solution, it is accepted based on some probability function. At early stages (with high temperature), a bad move has higher chance to get accepted while at later stages of placement (with lower temperature), the probability goes down exponentially. These worse-yet-accepted moves are essential for a simulated annealing placement algorithm to overcome a local optimum solution in which a placement might be stuck. A greedy move-based placement tool cannot escape from this local optimum once it steps into one. The typical set of moves in a simulated annealing placement algorithm are (1) relocation of a circuit element into new position, (2) exchanges of two circuit elements' locations or (3) mirroring/rotation of a circuit element at the same location, etc. As mentioned earlier, the typical objective function is total wirelength. Recently, other factors such as routability, power, area, and even signal integrity metrics are directly modeled in the objective function of simulated annealing placement tools, because an iterative optimization approach is very flexible to model these nonconventional multidimensional objective functions. However, simulated annealing placement is regarded as a rather slow method compared with other placement algorithms as the design size grows. Chapter 16 provides more detailed discussion of simulated annealing placement algorithms.

The advent of flat/multilevel partitioning as a fast and effective algorithm for min-cut partitioning has helped to spawn off a new generation of top-down cut-based placement tools. A placer in this class partitions circuit elements into either two (bisection) or four (quadrisection) regions of the chip, then recursively (following breadth-first search order) partitions each region until a good coarse placement solution is achieved [22]. When each region is partitioned, circuit elements outside the region are assumed to be fixed at the current locations and pseudopins are created around the region under consideration. This is called a terminal propagation [23]. Because the basic algorithm is based on partitioning, the typical objective function is the number of netcuts between subregions. Finding a good partitioning indicates that good logical clustering of circuit elements are found with less communications among them that can lead to a better total wirelength. To speed up the algorithm, multilevel clustering can be combined with a partitioning-based placement. In general, cut-based multilevel partitioning placement can be performed quite well particularly when designs are dense. Also, partitioning-based placement is a relatively fast placement algorithm. Partitioning-based placement algorithms are discussed in Chapter 15, and the fundamental partitioning concept and algorithm itself can be found in Chapter 7.

Analytical placement algorithms typically solve a relaxed placement formulation (e.g., minimum total squared wirelength) optimally, allowing cells to temporarily overlap. Legalization is achieved by removing overlaps via either partitioning or by introducing additional forces or constraints to generate a new optimization problem. The formulation of these methods models the mechanical spring network. Each net represents a spring that attracts circuit elements connected to the net. The optimum solution represents the equilibrium state of the given spring network. Analytic placers can perform poorly when the data is naturally degenerate (which occurs when no fixed object exists) because it becomes difficult to legalize a placement where thousands of circuit elements are placed virtually at the same location. Also, analytical methods may have difficulties in dense designs where legalization is forced to significantly alter the analytic solution. The new breed of analytic placement algorithm, dubbed as forced-based placement showed great promise recently. Force-based placement adds additional forces to the formulation that pull circuit elements from high-density regions to low ones. The key point is to achieve a better distributed placement solution by integrating these spreading forces into a formulation, instead of relying on explicit partitioning or other techniques. There are a variety of techniques for cell spreading in force-based analytic placement techniques. During placement, some form of density analysis is performed to calculate spreading forces. Once the spreading forces are determined, these forces can be applied to each circuit element via constant forces, or explicit fixed-point methods. Sometimes, a density (overlapping) penalty function is included in the placement objective function explicitly so that nonlinear optimization can minimize total wirelengths and overlapping simultaneously. In this nonlinear optimization framework, linear wirelength approximation can also be included to minimize half-perimeter bounding box wirelength directly. To speed up the convergence of optimization, circuit clustering techniques can be combined with these analytic placement algorithms. These clustering techniques can not only reduce the runtime of placement but also improve the quality of placement solutions. The general analytical placement algorithm is presented in Chapter 17 and the new force-directed methods are discussed in Chapter 18.

Recently, the ISPD (International Symposium on Physical Design) Conference hosted two placement contests in 2005 and 2006 for the academic placement research community. The contests provided a common platform where various placement algorithms can be evaluated on the same set of realistic large-scale ASIC designs. Particularly, the new placement benchmark circuits that were released during the contests have set a new bar for requirements of modern placement capability. By providing a common basis for quantitative measurements of contemporary placement algorithms, researchers were able to publicize their placement tools and results and discuss the pros and cons of different breeds of placement algorithms. For more serious placement researchers, ISPD placement contests can serve as a good starting point for further in-depth discussions of placement algorithms and implementations [11,24].

REFERENCES

1. P. G. Villarrubia, Important placement considerations for modern VLSI chips, invited talk at International Symposium on Physical Design, San Diego, CA, 2000.
2. S. M. Sait and H. Youssef, *VLSI Physical Design Automation: Theory and Practice*, World Scientific, River Edge, NJ, 1999.
3. M. Sarrafzadeh and C. K. Wong, *An Introduction to VLSI Physical Design*, McGraw-Hill, NY, 1996.
4. N. A. Sherwani, *Algorithms for VLSI Physical Design Automation*, Kluwer Academic Publishers, Norwell, MA, 1999.
5. M. R. Garey and D. S. Johnson, *Computers and Intractability: A Guide to the Theory of NP-Completeness*, W. H. Freeman and Company, NY, 1979.
6. A. B. Kahng, Classical floorplanning harmful? in *Proceedings of International Symposium on Physical Design*, 2000, San Diego, CA, pp. 207–213.
7. C. Alpert, G. -J. Nam, and P. G. Villarrubia, Effective free space management for cut-based placement via analytical constraint generation, *IEEE Transactions on Computer-Aided Design*, 22(10): 1343–1353, 2003 (ICCAD 2002).
8. S. N. Adya and I. L. Markov, Combinatorial techniques for mixed-size placement, *ACM Transactions on Design Automation of Electronic Systems*, 10(5): 2005.

9. D. E. Duate, N. Vijaykrishnan, and M. J. Irwin, A clock power model to evaluate impact of architectural and technology optimization, *IEEE Transactions on VLSI*, 10(6): 844–855, December 2002.
10. Y. Lu, C. -N. Sze, X. Hong, Q. Zhou, Y. Cai, L. Huang, and J. Hu, Navigating registers in placement for clock network minimization, in *Proceedings of Design Automation Conference*, Anaheim, CA, 2005, pp. 176–181.
11. G. -J. Nam and J. Cong (Eds.), *Modern Circuit Placement: Best Practices and Results*, Springer Verlag, NY, 2007.
12. G.-J. Nam, S. Reda, C. J. Alpert, P. G. Villarrubia, and A. B. Kahng, A fast hierarchical quadratic placement algorithm, *IEEE Transactions on Computer-Aided Design of Circuits and Systems*, 25(4): 678–691, April, 2006 (ISPD 2005).
13. J. Cong and J. Shinnerl (Eds.), *Multilevel Optimization in VLSI CAD*, Kluwer Academic Publishers, AA Dordrecht, the Netherlands, 2003.
14. S. N. Adya, I. L. Markov, and P. G. Villarrubia, On whitespace and stability in physical synthesis, *Integration: The VLSI Journal*, 39(4): 340–362, 2006 (ICCAD 2003).
15. C. Alpert, G. -J. Nam, P. G. Villarrubia, and M. Yildiz, Placement stability metrics, in *Proceedings of Asia South Pacific Design Automation Conference*, Shanghai, China, 2005, pp. 1144–1147.
16. R. Montoye, The four degrees of 3D, invited talk at International Symposium on Physical Design, Phoenix, AZ, 2004.
17. B. Goplen and S. Sapatnekar, Efficient thermal placement of standard cells in 3D ICs using a force directed approach, in *Proceedings of International Conference on Computer-Aided Design*, 2003, pp. 86–90.
18. J. Cong and Y. Zhang, Thermal via planning for 3-D ICs, in *Proceedings of International Conference on Computer-Aided Design*, San Jose, CA, 2005, pp. 745–752.
19. Y. Cheon, P. -H. Ho, A. B. Kahng, S. Reda, and Q. Wang, Power-aware placement, in *Proceedings of Design Automation Conference*, Anaheim, CA, 2005, pp. 795–800.
20. A. B. Kahng, B. Liu, and Q. Wang, Supply voltage degradation aware analytical placement, in *Proceedings of International Conference on Computer Design*, San Jose, CA, 2005, pp. 437–443.
21. J. Lou and W. Chen, Crosstalk-aware placement, *IEEE Design and Test of Computers*, 21(1): 24–32, 2004.
22. A. E. Caldwell, A. B. Kahng, and I. L. Markov, Can recursive bisection alone produce routable placement? in *Proceedings of Design Automation Conference*, Los Angeles, CA, 2000, pp. 477–482.
23. A. E. Dunlop and B. W. Kernighan, A procedure for placement of standard cell VLSI circuits, *IEEE Transactions on Computer-Aided Design of Integrated Circuits*, 4(1): 92–98, 1985.
24. Available at http://www.ispd.cc/contests.

15 Partitioning-Based Methods

Jarrod A. Roy and Igor L. Markov

CONTENTS

Over the years, partitioning-based placement has seen many revisions and enhancements, but the underlying framework illustrated in Figures 15.1 and 15.2 remains much the same. Top-down partitioning-based placement algorithms seek to decompose a given placement instance into smaller instances by subdividing the placement region, assigning modules to subregions, and cutting the

```
Variables: queue of placement bins
Initialize queue with top-level placement bin
1  While (queue not empty)
2     Dequeue a bin
3     If (bin small enough)
4        Process bin with end-case placer
5     Else
6        Choose a cut-line for the bin
7        Build partitioning hypergraph from netlist and cells
            contained in the bin
8        Partition the bin into smaller bins (generally via min-cut
            bisection or quadrisection)
9        Enqueue each child bin
```

FIGURE 15.1   Top-down partitioning-based placement.

netlist hypergraph [7,19]. The top-down placement process can be viewed as a sequence of passes where each pass examines all bins and divides some of them into smaller bins. The division step is commonly accomplished with balanced mincut partitioning, which minimizes the number of signal nets connecting modules in multiple regions [7]. These techniques leverage well-understood and scalable algorithms for hypergraph partitioning and typically lead to routable placements [9]. Recent work offers extensions to block placement, large-scale mixed-size placement [15,18,31] and robust incremental placement [33].

15.1   TOP-DOWN PARTITIONING-BASED PLACEMENT FRAMEWORK

Using mincut partitioning in placement was presented by Breuer in 1977 [7]. The underlying framework remains mostly the same and is illustrated in Figures 15.1 and 15.2. The core area is comprised of a series of placement bins which represent (1) a placement region with allowed module locations (sites), (2) a collection of circuit modules to be placed in this region, (3) all signal nets incident to the modules in the region, and (4) fixed cells and pins outside the region that are connected to modules in the region (terminals).

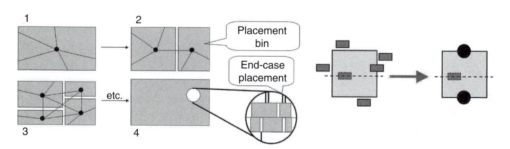

FIGURE 15.2   The overall process of top-down placement is shown on the left. The placement area and netlist are successively divided into placement bins until the bins are small enough for end-case placement. One important enhancement to top-down placement is terminal propagation, shown on the right. The net in question has five fixed terminals: four above and one below the cutline. It also has movable cells, which are represented by the cell with a dashed outline. The four fixed terminals above the cutline are propagated to the black circle at the top of the bin while the one fixed terminal below the cutline is propagated to the black circle below the cutline. The movable cells remain unpropagated. Note that the net is inessential because terminals are propagated to both sides of the cutline. (From Roy, J. A. and Markov, I. L., *IEEE Trans. CAD*, 26, 632, 2007.)

Mincut partitioning-based placers proceed by dividing the netlist and placement area into successively smaller pieces until the pieces are small enough to be handled efficiently by optimal end-case placers [11]. State-of-the-art placers generally use a wide range of hypergraph partitioning techniques to best fit partitioning problem size—optimal (branch-and-bound [11]), middle-range (Fiduccia–Mattheyses [20]), and large-scale (multilevel Fiduccia–Mattheyses [10,26]). Mincut placement is highly scalable (due in large part to algorithmic advances in mincut partitioning [10,20,26]) and typically produces routable placements.

In this section, we introduce topics relevant to top-down partitioning-based placement that must be addressed by all modern mincut placers. Specifically these include terminal propagation, bipartitioning versus multiway partitioning, cutline selection, and whitespace (or free space) allocation.

15.1.1 TERMINAL PROPAGATION AND INESSENTIAL NETS

Proper handling of terminals is essential to the success of top-down placement approaches [11,19, 21,37]. When a placement bin is split into multiple subregions, some of the cells inside may be tightly connected to cells outside of the bin. Ignoring such connections can adversely affect the quality of a placement because they can account for significant amounts of wirelength. On the other hand, these terminals are irrelevant to the classic partitioning formulation as they cannot be freely assigned to partitions. A compromise is possible by using an extended formulation of partitioning with fixed terminals, where the terminals are considered to be fixed in (propagated to) one or more partitions, and assigned zero areas (original areas are ignored). Nets propagated to both partitions in bipartitioning are considered inessential because they will always be cut and can be safely removed from the partitioning instance to improve runtime [11]. Terminal propagation is typically driven by geometric proximity of terminals to subregions/partitions. Figure 15.2 (right) depicts terminal propagation for a net with several fixed terminals. This particular net is inessential for bipartitioning as it has terminals propagated to both sides of the cutline.

15.1.2 BIPARTITIONING VERSUS MULTIWAY PARTITIONING

In his seminal work on mincut placement, Breuer introduced two forms of recursive mincut placement: slice/bisection and quadrature [7]. The style of mincut placement most commonly used today has grown from the quadrature technique, which advocated the use of horizontal and vertical cuts; the slice/bisection technique used only horizontal cuts and exhibited worse performance than quadrature [7].

Since that time, horizontal and vertical cutlines have been standard in all placement techniques, but there has been debate as to whether there should be an ordering to the cuts (i.e., horizontally bisect a bin then vertically bisect its children as in quadrature [7]) or both cuts should be done simultaneously as in quadrisection [37]. Quadrisection has been shown to allow for the optimization of techniques other than mincut (such as minimal spanning tree length [21]), but terminal propagation is more complex when splitting a bin into four child bins instead of two. Also, bisection can simulate quadrisection with added flexibility in cutline selection and shifting (see Section 15.1.3) [31]. There are currently no known implementations that use greater than four-way partitioning and the majority of partitioning-based placement techniques involve mincut bipartitioning.

15.1.3 CUTLINE SELECTION AND SHIFTING

Breuer studied two types of cutline direction selection techniques and found that alternating cutline directions from layer to layer produced better half-perimeter wirelength (HPWL) than using only horizontal cuts [7]. The authors of Ref. [40] studied this phenomenon further by testing 64 cutline direction sequences. Their experiments did not find that the two cut-sequences that alternate at each layer were the best, but did find that long sequences of cuts in the same direction during placement were detrimental to performance [40]. The authors of Ref. [43] not only developed a dynamic programming technique to choose optimal cut sequences for partitioning-based placement but also found that nearly optimal cut sequences could be determined from the aspect ratio of the bin to be split. This technique has been independently used in the Capo placer [30–35].

After the cutline direction is chosen, partitioning-based placers generally choose the cut-line that best splits a placement bin in half in the desired direction. Usually cutlines are aligned to placement row and site boundaries to ease the assignment of standard-cells to rows near the end of global placement [9]. After a bin is partitioned, the initial cutline may be shifted to satisfy objectives such as whitespace allocation or congestion reduction.

15.1.4 WHITESPACE ALLOCATION

Management of whitespace (also known as free space) is a key issue in physical design as it has a profound effect on the quality of a placement. The amount of whitespace in a design is the difference between the total placeable area in a design and the total movable cell area in the design. A natural scheme for managing whitespace in top-down placement, uniform whitespace allocation, was introduced and analyzed in Ref. [12]. Let a placement bin to be partitioned have site area S, cell area C, absolute whitespace $W = \max\{S - C, 0\}$, and relative whitespace $w = W/S$. A bipartitioning divides the bin into two child bins with site areas S_0 and S_1 such that $S_0 + S_1 = S$ and cell areas C_0 and C_1 such that $C_0 + C_1 = C$. A partitioner is given cell area targets T_0 and T_1 as well as a tolerance τ for a bipartitioning instance. τ defines the maximum percentage by which C_0 and C_1 are allowed to differ from T_0 and T_1, respectively. In many cases of bipartitioning, $T_0 = T_1 = \frac{C}{2}$, but this is not always true [5].

The work in Ref. [12] bases its whitespace allocation techniques on whitespace deterioration: the phenomenon that discreteness in partitioning and placement does not allow for exact uniform whitespace distribution. The whitespace deterioration for a bipartitioning is the largest α, such that each child bin has at least αw relative whitespace. Assuming nonzero relative whitespace in the placement bin, α should be restricted such that $0 \leq \alpha \leq 1$ [12]. The authors note that $\alpha = 1$ may be overly restrictive in practice because it induces zero tolerance on the partitioning instance but $\alpha = 0$ may not be restrictive enough as it allows for child bins with zero whitespace, which can improve wirelength but impair routability [12].

For a given block, feasible ranges for partition capacities are uniquely determined by α. The partitioning tolerance τ for splitting a block with relative whitespace w is $\frac{(1-\alpha)w}{1-w}$ [12]. The challenge is to determine a proper value for α. First assume that a bin is to be partitioned horizontally n times more during the placement process. n can be calculated as $\lceil \log_2 R \rceil$ where R is the number of rows in the placement bin [12]. Assuming end-case bins have $\alpha = 0$ because they are not further partitioned, the relative whitespace of an end-case bin, $\overline{w}$, is determined to be $\frac{\overline{\tau}}{\overline{\tau}+1}$ where $\overline{\tau}$ is the tolerance of partitioning in the end-case bin [12].

Assuming that α remains the same during all partitioning of the given bin gives a simple derivation of $\alpha = \sqrt[n]{\frac{\overline{w}}{w}}$ [12]. A more practical calculation assumes instead that τ remains the same over all partitionings. This leads to $\tau = \sqrt[n]{\frac{1-\overline{w}}{1-w}} - 1$ [12]. $\overline{w}$ can be eliminated from the equation for τ and a closed form for α based only w and n is derived to be $\alpha = \frac{\sqrt[n+1]{1-w}-(1-w)}{w\left(\sqrt[n+1]{1-w}\right)}$ [12].

15.1.4.1 Free Cell Addition

One relatively simple method of nonuniform whitespace allocation in placement was presented in Ref. [3]. To achieve a nonuniform allocation of whitespace, free cells (standard cells that have no connections in the netlist) are added to the design that is placed using uniform whitespace allocation. Care must be taken not to add too many cells to the design that can complicate the work of many placement algorithms, increasing interconnect length or leading to overlapping circuit modules [18].

Several other whitespace allocation techniques have been published in the literature, many of which have the objective of congestion reduction [28,32,38,39,42]. These techniques that deal specifically with congestion reduction are covered in Chapter 22.

15.2 ENHANCEMENTS TO THE MINCUT FRAMEWORK

This section describes several techniques that are recent improvements to the to the mincut partitioning-based framework presented in Section 15.1. These techniques range from fairly simple yet effective techniques such as repartitioning and placement feedback to changes in the optimization goals of mincut placement as in weighted netcut.

15.2.1 BETTER RESULTS THROUGH ADDITIONAL PARTITIONING

Huang and Kahng introduced two techniques for improving the results of quadrisection-based placement known as cycling and overlapping [21]. Cycling is a technique whereby results are improved by partitioning every placement bin multiple times each layer [21]. After all bins are split for the first time in a layer of placement, a new round of partitioning on the same bins is done using the results of the previous round for terminal propagation. These additional rounds of partitioning are repeated until there is no further improvement of a cost function [21]. A similar type of technique was presented for mincut bisection called placement feedback. In placement feedback, bins are partitioned multiple times, without requiring steady improvement in wirelength, to achieve more consistent terminal propagation [25].

Placement feedback serves to reduce the number of ambiguously propagated terminals. Ambiguity in terminal propagation arises when a terminal is nearly equidistant to the centers of the child bins of the bin being partitioned. In such cases it is unclear as to what side of the cutline the terminal should be propagated. Traditional choices for such terminals are to propagate them to both sides or neither side of the cutline in fear of making a poor decision [25]. Ambiguously propagated terminals introduce indeterminism into mincut placement as they may be propagated differently based on the order in which placement bins are processed [25].

To reduce the number of ambiguously propagated terminals, placement feedback repeats each layer of partitioning n times. Each successive round of partitioning uses the resulting locations from the previous partitioning for terminal propagation. The first round of partitioning for a particular layer may have ambiguous terminals, but the second and later rounds will have reduced numbers of ambiguous terminals making terminal propagation more robust [25]. Empirical results show that placement feedback is effective in reducing HPWL, routed wirelength and via count [25].

The technique of overlapping also involves additional partitioning calls during placement [21]. While doing cycling in quadrisection, pieces of neighboring bins can be coalesced into a new bin and split to improve solution quality [21]. Brenner and Rohe introduced a similar technique that they called repartitioning which was designed to reduce congestion [6]. After partitioning, congestion was estimated in the placement bins of the design. Using this congestion data, new partitioning problems were formulated with all neighbors of a congested area. Solving these new partitioning problems would spread congestion to neighboring areas of the placement while possibly incurring an increase in net length [6].

Capo [30–35] repartitions bins similarly for the improvement of HPWL. After the initial solution of a partitioning problem is returned from a mincut partitioner, Capo has the option of shifting the cutline to fulfill whatever whitespace requirements may be asked of it. A shift of the cutline, though, represents a change in the partitioning problem formulation: the initial partitioning problem was built assuming a different cutline that can have a significant effect on terminal propagation. Thus, the partitioning problem is rebuilt with the new cutline and solved again to improve wirelength. The repartitioning does not come with a significant run time penalty because the initial partitioning solution is reused and modified by flat passes of a Fiduccia–Mattheyses [20] partitioner.

15.2.2 FRACTIONAL CUT

When a placement bin is split with a vertical cutline, there can be many possible cutlines that split the bin roughly equally because the size of sites in row-based placement is generally small. Conversely, row heights are generally nontrivial as compared to the height of the core placement area. Because standard cells are ultimately placed in rows, most mincut placers choose to align cutlines to row boundaries [9]. The authors of Ref. [4] argue that this causes the "narrow region" problem, which leads to instability in mincut placement. The narrow region problem becomes an issue when bins become tall and narrow. In such cases, total cell area may be able to fit into a given narrow bin, but it may not be possible to assign cells into these rows legally due to row area constraints or the number of legal solutions is so small that netcut is artificially increased as a result [4]. A simple example of this phenomenon is shown in Figure 15.3.

To remedy this situation, the authors of Ref. [4] propose using a fractional cut: a horizontal cutline that is allowed to pass through a fraction of a row. As horizontal cutlines do not necessarily align with rows, cells must be assigned to rows before optimal end-case (typically single row) placers can be used [4]. To legalize the placement, one proceeds on a row-by-row basis. Each cell is tentatively assigned to a preferred height in the placement: the center of its placement bin. Starting with the topmost row, cells are greedily assigned to rows so as to minimize the cost of assigning cells. If a cell is assigned to the current row, its cost is the squared distance from its preferred position to the current row. If a cell is not assigned to the current row, its cost is the squared distance from its preferred position to the next lower row [4]. The assignment of cells to rows is achieved efficiently by a dynamic programming formulation [4]. After all cells are assigned to rows, they are sorted by their x coordinates and packed in rows to remove any overlaps. Experimental results show considerable improvements in terms of HPWL reduction in placement, but packing of cells in rows does not generally produce routable placements [32].

15.2.3 ANALYTICAL CONSTRAINT GENERATION

The authors of Ref. [5] note that mincut placement techniques are effective at reducing HPWL of designs that are heavily constrained in terms of whitespace, but do not perform nearly as well as analytical techniques when there are large amounts of whitespace. They suggest that one reason for the discrepancy is that mincut placers try to divide placement bins exactly in half with a relatively small tolerance. This tends to spread cell area roughly uniformly across the core area. Increasing the

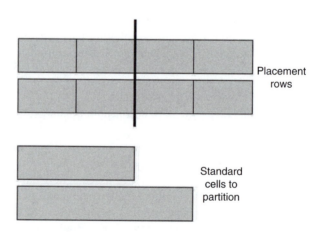

FIGURE 15.3 Even though capacity constraints are satisfied, no legal vertical cutline exists to partition the standard cells into the placement rows.

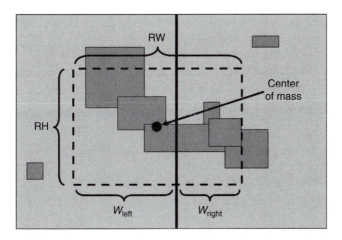

FIGURE 15.4 Analytical constraint generation in a placement bin. Movable objects are placed with an analytical technique. Their placements and areas are used to determine the center of mass of the placement. A rectangle with the same aspect ratio of the placement bin and same area as the total movable objects is superimposed on the bin, and is centered at the center of mass. In this case, movable object area will be allocated in the ratio $W_{\text{left}} : W_{\text{right}}$.

tolerance for partitioning a bin can allow for less uniformity in placement and lower HPWL due to tighter packing, but still does not reproduce the performance of analytical techniques [5].

To improve the HPWL performance of mincut placement techniques on designs with large amounts of whitespace (which are becoming increasingly popular in real-world designs), while still retaining the good performance of mincut techniques when there is limited whitespace, the authors of Ref. [5] suggest integrating analytical techniques and mincut techniques. Before constructing a partitioning instance for a given placement bin, an analytical placement technique is run on the objects in the bin to minimize their quadratic wirelength [5]. Next, the center of mass of the placement of the objects of the bin is calculated. This points to roughly where the objects should go to reduce their wirelength. One then constructs a rectangle having the same aspect ratio as the placement bin and the same area as the total movable object area in the bin. This is illustrated in Figure 15.4. Let A be the total movable object area in the bin, H be the height of the bin, and W the width of the bin. The height and width of such a rectangle are calculated as: rectangle height $\text{RH} = \sqrt{\frac{AH}{W}}$ and rectangle width $\text{RW} = \sqrt{\frac{AW}{H}}$ [5]. One centers this rectangle at the center of mass of the analytical placement and intersects the rectangle with the proposed cutline of the bin. The amount of area of the rectangle that falls on either side of the cutline is used as a target for mincut partitioning [5]. In Figure 15.4, the target area for the left-hand side of the partitioning is $\text{RH} \cdot W_{\text{left}}$; similarly, the target for the right-hand side of the partitioning is $\text{RH} \cdot W_{\text{right}}$. As most mincut partitioners choose to split cell area equally, this is a significant departure from traditional mincut placement.

Empirical results suggest that analytical constraint generation (ACG) is effective at improving the performance of mincut placement on designs with large amounts of whitespace while retaining the good performance and routability of mincut placers on constrained designs. This performance comes at the cost of approximately 28 percent more runtime [5].

15.2.4   BETTER MODELING OF HPWL BY PARTITIONING

It is well known that the mincut objective in partitioning does not accurately represent the wirelength objective of placement [21,36]. Optimizing HPWL and other objectives directly through partitioning can provide improvements over mincut. Huang and Kahng showed that net weighting and quadrisection can be used to minimize a wide range of objectives such as minimal spanning tree cost [21]. Their technique consists of computing vectors of weights for each net (called net vectors) and using these weights in quadrisection [21]. Although this technique can represent a wide range of cost functions to minimize, it requires the discretization of pin locations into the centers of bins and requires that 16 weights must be calculated per net for partitioning [21].

The authors of Ref. [36] introduce a new terminal propagation technique in their placer THETO that allows the partitioner to better map netcut to HPWL. Terminal propagation in THETO differs from traditional terminal propagation in that each original net may be represented by one or two nets in the partitioned netlist, depending on the configuration of the net's terminals. This technique is simplified in Ref. [15] and reduced to the calculation of costs wirelengths per net per partitioning instance, which completely determine the connectivity and weights of all nets in the derived partitioning hypergraph. For each net in each partitioning instance, one must calculate the cost of all nodes on the net being placed in partition $1(w_1)$, the cost of all nodes on the net being placed in partition $2(w_2)$, and the cost of all nodes on the net being split between partitions 1 and 2 (w_{12}). Up to two nets can be created in the partitioning instance, one with weight $|w_1 - w_2|$ and the other with weight $w_{12} - \max(w_1, w_2)$. The only assumption made in Ref. [15] is that $w_{12} \geq \max(w_1, w_2)$. Using these costs and proper connectivity in the derived hypergraph, minimizing weighted netcut directly corresponds to minimizing HPWL.

15.3 MIXED-SIZE PLACEMENT

Mixed-size placement, the placement of large macros in addition to standard cells, has become a relevant challenge in physical design and is poised to dominate physical design in the near future as we move from traditional "sea of cells" ICs to "sea of hard macros" SoCs [41]. To keep up with this shift in physical design, several techniques for partitioning-based mixed-size placement have been proposed and are described in this section. These techniques include floorplacement, PATOMA, and mixed-size placement with fractional cut.

15.3.1 FLOORPLACEMENT

From an optimization point of view, floorplanning and placement are very similar problems–both seek nonoverlapping placements to minimize wirelength. They are distinguished by scale and the need to account for shapes in floorplanning, which calls for different optimization techniques. Netlist partitioning is often used in placement algorithms, where geometric shapes of partitions can be adjusted. This considerably blurs the separation between partitioning, placement, and floorplanning, raising the possibility that these three steps can be performed by one CAD tool. The authors of Ref. [31] develop such a tool and term the unified layout optimization floorplacement following Steve Teig's keynote speech at ISPD 2002.

The traditional mincut placement scheme breaks down when modules are comparable in size to their bins. When such a module appears in a bin, recursive bisection cannot continue, or else will likely produce a placement with overlapping modules. In floorplacement, one switches from recursive bisection to local floorplanning where the fixed outline is determined by the bin. This is done for two main reasons: (1) to preserve wirelength [8], congestion [6], and delay [23] estimates that may have been performed early during top-down placement and (2) to avoid legalizing a placement with overlapping macros.

Although deferring to fixed-outline floorplanning is a natural step, successful fixed-outline floorplanners have appeared only recently [1]. Additionally, the floorplanner may fail to pack all modules within the bin without overlaps. As with any constraint-satisfaction problem, this can be for two reasons: either (1) the instance is unsatisfiable or (2) the solver is unable to find any of existing solutions. In this case, the technique undoes the previous partitioning step and merges the failed bin with its sibling bin, then discards the two bins. The merged bin includes all modules contained in

```
   Variables: queue of placement bins
   Initialize queue with top-level placement bin
1  While (queue not empty)
2    Dequeue a bin
3    If(bin has large/many macros or is marked as merged)
4    Cluster std-cells into soft macros
5    Use fixed-outline floorplanner to pack all macros (soft+hard)
6    If fixed-outline floorplanning succeeds
7      Fix macros and remove sites underneath the macros
8    Else
9      Undo one partition decision. Merge bin with sibling
10      Mark new bin as merged and enqueue
11   Else if (bin small enough)
12      Process end case
13   Else
14      Bipartition the bin into smaller bins
15      Enqueue each child bin
```

FIGURE 15.5   Mincut floorplacement. Boldfaced lines 3–10 are different from traditional mincut placement. (From Roy, J. A., Adya, S. N., Papa, D. A., and Markov, I. L., *IEEE Trans. CAD*, 25, 1313, 2006.)

the two smaller bins, and its rectangular outline is the union of the two rectangular outlines. This bin is floorplanned, and in case of failure can be merged with its sibling again. The overall process is summarized in Figure 15.5 and an example is depicted in Figure 15.6.

It is typically easier to satisfy the outline of a merged bin because circuit modules become relatively smaller. However, simulated annealing takes longer on larger bins and is less successful in minimizing wirelength. Therefore, it is important to floorplan at just the right time, and the algorithm determines this point by backtracking. Backtracking incurs some overhead in failed floorplan runs, but this overhead is tolerable because merged bins take considerably longer to floorplan. Furthermore, this overhead can be moderated somewhat by careful prediction.

For a given bin, a floorplanning instance is constructed as follows. All connections between modules in the bin and other modules are propagated to fixed terminals at the periphery of the

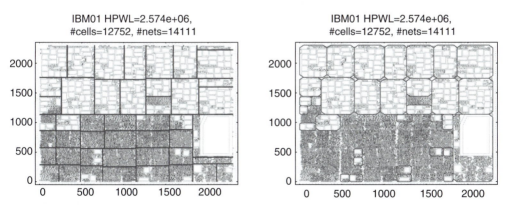

FIGURE 15.6   Progress of mixed-size floorplacement on the IBM01 benchmark from IBM-MSwPins. The picture on the left shows how the cutlines are chosen during the first six layers of mincut bisection. On the right is the same placement but with the floorplanning instances highlighted by "rounded" rectangles. Floorplanning failures can be detected by observing nested rectangles. (From Roy, J. A., Adya, S. N., Papa, D. A., and Markov, I. L., *IEEE Trans. CAD*, 25, 1313, 2006.)

bin. As the bin may contain numerous standard cells, the number of movable objects is reduced by conglomerating standard cells into soft placeable blocks. This is accomplished by a simple bottom-up connectivity-based clustering [26]. Large modules in the bin are kept out of this clustering. To further simplify floorplanning, soft blocks consisting of standard cells are artificially downsized, as in Ref. [3]. The clustered netlist is given to the fixed-outline floorplanner Parquet [1], which sizes soft blocks and optimizes block orientations. After suitable locations are found, the locations of large modules are returned to the top-down placer and are considered fixed, and the rows below them are fractured. At this point, mincut placement resumes with a bin that has no large modules in it, but has somewhat nonuniform row structure. When mincut placement is finished, large modules do not overlap by construction, but small cells sometimes overlap (typically below 0.01 percent by area). Those overlaps are quickly detected and removed with local changes.

Because the floorplacer includes a state-of-the-art floorplanner, it can natively handle pure block-based designs. Unlike most algorithms designed for mixed-size placement, it can pack blocks into a tight outline, optimize block orientations, and tune aspect ratios of soft blocks. When the number of blocks is very small, the algorithm applies floorplanning quickly. However, when given a larger design, it may start with partitioning and then call fixed-outline floorplanning for separate bins. As recursive bisection scales well and is more successful at minimizing wirelength than annealing-based floorplanning, the proposed approach is scalable and effective at minimizing wirelength.

15.3.2   PATOMA AND POLARBEAR

PATOMA 1.0 [17] pioneered a top-down floorplanning framework that utilizes fast block-packing algorithms (ROB or ZDS [16]) and hypergraph partitioning with hMETIS [26]. This approach is fast and scalable, and provides good solutions for many input configurations. Fast block-packing is used in PATOMA to guarantee that a legal packing solution exists, at which point the burden of wirelength minimization is shifted to the hypergraph partitioner. This idea is applied recursively to each of the newly created partitions. In end-cases, when a partitioning step leads to unsatisfiable block-packing, the quality of the result is determined by the quality of its fast block-packing algorithms. The placer PolarBear [18] integrates algorithms from PATOMA to increase the robustness of a top-down mincut placement flow. Similar to PATOMA, the floorplanner IMF [15] utilizes top-down partitioning, but allows overlaps in the initial top-down partitioning phase. A bottom-up merging and refinement phase fixes overlaps and further optimizes the solution quality.

15.3.3   FRACTIONAL CUT FOR MIXED-SIZE PLACEMENT

The work in Ref. [27] advocates a two-stage approach to mixed-size placement. First, the mincut placer FengShui [4] generates an initial placement for the mixed-size netlist without trying to prevent overlaps between modules. The placer only tracks the global distribution of area during partitioning and uses the fractional cut technique (see Section 15.2.2), which further relaxes book keeping by not requiring placement bins to align to cell rows. While giving mincut partitioners more freedom, these relaxations prevent cells from being placed in rows easily and require additional repair during detail placement. This may particularly complicate the optimization of module orientations, not considered in Ref. [27].

The second stage consists of removing overlaps by a fast legalizer designed to handle large modules along with standard cells. The legalizer is greedy and attempts to shift all modules toward the left or right edge of the chip. The implementation reported in Ref. [27] can lead to horizontal stacking of modules and sometimes yields out-of-core placements, especially when several very large modules are present (the benchmarks used in Ref. [27] contain numerous modules of medium size). See Figure 15.10 in Ref. [31] and Figure 15.6 in Ref. [30] for examples of this behavior. Another concern about packed placements is the harmful effect of such a strategy on routability [42]. Overall, the work in Ref. [27] demonstrates very good legal placements for common benchmarks,

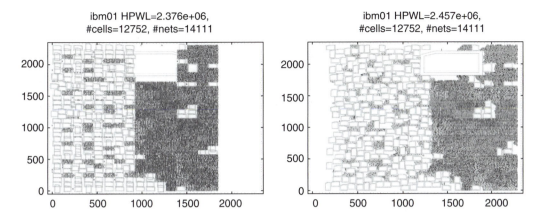

FIGURE 15.7 A placement of the IBM01 benchmark from `IBM-MSwPins` by FengShui before (left) and after (right) legalization and detail placement.

but questions remain about the robustness and generality of the proposed approach to mixed-size placement. Example FengShui placements before and after legalization are shown in Figure 15.7.

15.3.4 MIXED-SIZE PLACEMENT IN DRAGON2006

The traditional Dragon flow does not take macros into consideration during placement. To account for macros, partitioning, bin-based annealing and legalization must be modified. Dragon2006 makes two passes on a design with obstacles; the first pass finds locations for macros and the second treats macros as fixed obstacles [39] (similar to Ref. [2]).

In the first pass, partitioning is modified to handle large movable macros. The traditional Dragon flow alternates cut directions at each layer and chooses the cutline to split a bin exactly in half in order to maintain a regular grid structure. In the presence of large macros, the requirement of a regular bin structure is relaxed. The cutline of the bin is shifted to allow the largest macro to fit into a child bin after partitioning. If macros can only fit in one bin, they are preassigned to the child bin in which they can fit and not involved in partitioning [38,39].

Bin-based simulated annealing after partitioning is also modified as bins may not all have the same dimensions. Horizontal swaps between adjacent bins are only allowed if they are of the same height. Similarly, vertical swaps between adjacent bins are only allowed if they are of the same width. Lastly, diagonal bin swaps are only legal if the bins have the same height and width. After all bins have fewer than a threshold of cells, partitioning stops, and macro locations are legalized. Once legal, macros are considered fixed and partitioning begins again at the top level to place the standard cells of the design [38,39].

15.4 ADVANTAGES OF MINCUT PLACEMENT

This section presents recent techniques that give mincut placement a significant advantage over other placement algorithms in whitespace allocation, floorplacement, routed wirelength, and incremental placement.

15.4.1 FLEXIBLE WHITESPACE ALLOCATION

The mincut bisection based placement framework offers much flexibility in whitespace allocation. Section 15.1.4 describes uniform allocation of whitespace for mincut bisection placement and a trivial preprocessing step to allow for nonuniform allocation. This section outlines two more sophisticated whitespace allocation techniques, minimum local whitespace and safe whitespace, that can be used for nonuniform whitespace allocation and satisfying whitespace constraints [35].

Minimum local whitespace. If a placement bin has more than a user-defined minimum local whitespace (minLocalWS), partitioning will define a tentative cutline that divides the bin's placement area in half. Partitioning targets an equal division of cell area, but is given more freedom to deviate from its target. Tolerance is computed so that with whitespace deterioration, each descendant bin of the current bin will have at least minLocalWS [35].

The assumption that the whitespace deterioration, α, in end-case bins is 0 presented in Section 15.1.4 no longer applies, so the calculation of α must change. Because we want all child bins of the current bin to have minLocalWS relative whitespace, end-case bins, in particular, must have at least minLocalWS and thus we may set $\overline{w} = $ minLocalWS, instead of a function of τ. Using the assumption that α remains constant during partitioning, α can be calculated directly as $\alpha = \sqrt[n]{\frac{\overline{w}}{w}}$ [12]. With the more realistic assumption that τ remains constant, τ can be calculated as $\tau = \sqrt[n]{\frac{1-\overline{w}}{1-w}} - 1$ [12]. Knowing τ, α can be computed as $\alpha = (\tau + 1) + \frac{\tau}{w}$ [12].

After a partitioning is calculated, the cutline is shifted to ensure that minLocalWS is preserved on both sides of the cutline. If the minimum local whitespace is chosen to be small, one can produce tightly packed placements, which greatly improve wirelength.

Safe whitespace. This whitespace allocation mode is designed for bins with large quantities of whitespace. In safe whitespace allocation, as with minimum local whitespace allocation, a tentative geometric cutline of the bin is chosen, and the target of partitioning is an equal bisection of the cell area. The difference in safe whitespace allocation mode is that the partitioning tolerance is much higher. Essentially, any partitioning solution that leaves at least safeWS on either side of the cutline is considered legal. This allows for very tight packing and reduces wirelength, but is not recommended for congestion-driven placement [35].

Figure 15.8 illustrates uniform and nonuniform whitespace allocation. Figure 15.8a shows global placements with uniform (top) and nonuniform (bottom) whitespace allocation on the ISPD 2005 contest benchmark adaptec1 (57.34 percent utlization) [29]. In the nonuniform placement shown, the minimum local whitespace is 12 percent and safe whitespace is 14 percent Figure 15.8b and c shows intensity maps of the local utilization of each placement. Lighter areas of the intensity maps signify violations of a given target placement density; darker areas have utilization below the target. Regions completely occupied by fixed obstacles are shaded as if they exactly meet the target density. The target densities for columns in Figure 15.8b and c are 90 percent and 60 percent. Note that uniform whitespace produces almost no violations when the target is 90 percent and relatively few when the target is 60 percent. The nonuniform placement has more violations as compared to the uniform placement especially when the target is 60 percent, but remains largely legal with the 90 percent target density.

15.4.2 SOLVING DIFFICULT INSTANCES OF FLOORPLACEMENT

Floorplacement (see Section 15.3.1) appears promising for SoC layout because of its high capacity and the ability to pack blocks. However, as experiments in Ref. [30] demonstrate, existing tools for floorplacement are fragile—on many instances they fail, or produce remarkably poor placements.

To improve the performance of mincut placement on mixed-size instances, the authors of Ref. [30] propose three synergistic techniques for floorplacement that in particular succeed on hard instances: (1) selective floorplanning with macro clustering, (2) improved obstacle evasion for B*-tree, and (3) ad hoc look-ahead in top-down floorplacement. Obstacle evasion is especially important for top-down floorplacement, even for designs that initially have no obstacles. The techniques are called SCAMPI, an acronym for scalable advanced macro placement improvements. Empirically, SCAMPI shows significant improvements in floorplacement success rate (68 percent improvement as compared

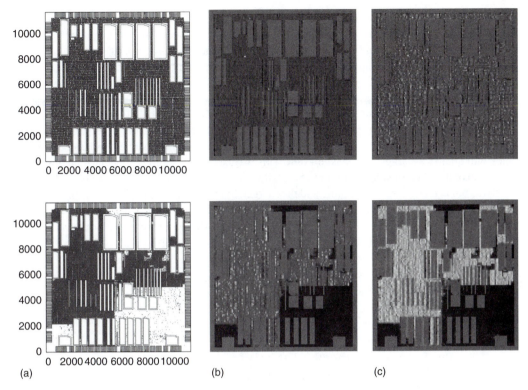

FIGURE 15.8 Columns in (a) show global placements of the ISPD 2005 placement contest bench mark adaptecl (57.34 percent utilization) with uniform white space allocation (top) and nonuniform whitespace allocation (bottom). Fixed obstacles are drawn with double lines. To indicate orientation, north west corners of blocks are truncated. Columns in (b) and (c) depict the local utilization of the placements. Lighter areas of the placement signify placement regions with density above a given target (90 percent for columns in (b) and 60 percent for columns in (c)) whereas darker areas have utilization below the target. (From Ng, A. N., Markov, I. L., Aggarwal, R., and Ramachandran, V., *ISPD*, pp. 170–177, April 2006. With permission.)

to the floorplacement technique presented in Section 15.3.1) and HPWL (3.5 percent reduction compared to floorplacement in Section 15.3.1).

15.4.2.1 Selective Floorplanning with Macro Clustering

In top-down correct-by-construction frame works like Capo (Section 15.3.1 and PATOMA [17] (Section 15.3.2), a key bottleneck is in ensuring ongoing progress—partitioning, floorplanning, or end-case processing must succeed at any given step. Both frameworks experience problems when floorplanning is invoked too early to produce reasonable solutions—PATOMA resorts to solutions with very high wirelength, and Capo times out because it runs the annealer on too many modules. To scale better, the annealer clusters small standard cells into soft blocks before starting simulated annealing. When a solution is available, all hard blocks are considered placed and fixed—they are treated as obstacles when the remaining standard cells are placed. Compared to other multilevel frameworks, this one does not include refinement, which makes it relatively fast. Speed is achieved at the cost of not being able to cluster modules other than standard cells because the floorplanner does not produce locations for clustered modules. Unfortunately, this limitation significantly restricts scalability of designs with many macros [30].

The proposed technique of selective floorplanning with macro clustering allows to cluster blocks before annealing, and does not require additional refinement or cluster-packing steps (which are among the obvious facilitators)—instead, certain existing steps in floorplacement are skipped. This improvement is based on two observations: (1) blocks that are much smaller than their bin can be treated like standard cells and (2) the number of blocks that are large relative to the bin size is necessarily limited. For example, there cannot be more than nine blocks with area in excess of 10 percent of a bin's area [30].

In selective floorplanning, each block is marked as small or large based on a size threshold. Standard cells and small blocks can be clustered, except that clusters containing hard blocks have additional restrictions on their aspect ratios. After successful annealing, only the large blocks are placed, fixed, and considered obstacles. Normal top-down partitioning resumes, and each remaining block will qualify as large at some later point. This way, specific locations are determined when the right level of detail is considered (Figure 15.10). If floorplanning fails during hierarchical placement, the failed bin is merged with its sibling and the merged bin is floorplanned (Figure 15.9). The blocks marked as large in the merged bin include those that exceed the size threshold and also those marked as large in the failed bin (because the failure suggests that those blocks were difficult to pack). After the largest macros are placed, the flow resumes [30].

```
     Variables: queue of placement partitions
     Initialize queue with top-level partition
1    While (queue not empty)
2      Dequeue a partition
3      If (partition is not marked as merged)
4        Perform look-ahead floorplanning on partition
5        If look-ahead floorplanning fails
6          Undo one partition decision
7          Merge partition with sibling
8          Mark new partition as merged and enqueue
9      Else if (partition has large macros or
             is marked as merged)
10       Mark large macros for placement after floorplanning
11       Cluster remaining macros into soft macros
12       Cluster std-cells into soft macros
13       Use fixed-outline floorplanner to pack
             all macros (soft+hard)
14       If fixed-outline floorplanning succeeds
15         Fix large macros and remove sites beneath
16       Else
17         Undo one partition decision
18         Merge partition with sibling
19         Mark new partition as merged and enqueue
20     Else if (partition is small enough and
             mostly comprised of macros)
21       Process floorplanning on all macros
22     Else if (partition small enough)
23       Process end case std cell placement
24     Else
25       Bipartition netlist of the partition
26       Divide the partition by placing a cut-line
27       Enqueue each child partition
```

FIGURE 15.9 Modified mincut floorplacement flow. Boldfaced lines are new. (From Ng, A. N., Markov, I. L., Aggarwal, R., and Ramachandran, V., *ISPD*, 2006.)

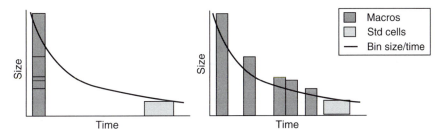

FIGURE 15.10 The plot on the left illustrates traditional floorplacement. Whenever a floorplanning threshold is reached, all macros in the bin are designated for floorplanning. Then, the floorplacement flow continues down until detailed placement, where the standard cells will be placed. The plot on the right illustrates the SCAMPI flow. Macros are selectively placed at the appropriate levels of hierarchy. (From Ng, A. N., Markov, I. L., Aggarwal, R., and Ramachandran, V., *ISPD*, 2006.)

The proposed technique limits the size of floorplanning instances given to the annealer by a constant and does not require much extra work. However, it introduces an unexpected complexity. The floorplacement framework does not handle fixed obstacles in the core region, and none of the public benchmarks have them. When Capo fixes blocks in a particular bin, it fixes all of them and never needs to floorplan around obstacles. Another complication due to newly introduced fixed obstacles is in cutline selection. Reliable obstacle-evasion and intelligent cutline selection may be required by practical designs, even without selective floorplanning (e.g., to handle prediffused memories, built-in multipliers in FPGAs, etc.). Therefore, they are viewed as independent but synergistic techniques [30]. When satisfying area constraints is difficult, it is very important to increase the priority of area optimization so as to achieve legality [14]. Because of this, the authors of Ref. [30] select the B*-tree [13] floorplan representation for its amenability to packed configurations and add obstacle evasion into B*-tree evaluation.

15.4.2.2 Ad Hoc Look-Ahead Floorplanning

The sum of block areas may significantly underestimate the area required for large blocks. Better estimates are required to improve the robustness of floorplacement and look-ahead area-driven floorplanning appears as a viable approach [30].

SCAMPI performs look-ahead floorplanning to validate solutions produced by the hypergraph partitioner, and check that a resulting partition is packable, within a certain tolerance for failure. Look-ahead floorplanning must be fast, so that the amortized runtime overhead of the look-ahead calls is less than the total time saved from discovering bad partitioning solutions. Therefore, look-ahead floorplanning is performed with blocks whose area is larger than 10 percent of the total module area in the bin, and soft blocks containing remaining modules. For speed, the floorplanner is configured to perform area-only packing, and the placer is configured to only perform look-ahead floorplanning on bins with large blocks. Dealing with only the largest blocks is sufficient because floorplanning failures are most often caused by such blocks [30].

15.4.3 OPTIMIZING STEINER WIRELENGTH

Weighted terminal propagation as described in Ref. [15], and summarized in Section 15.2.4, is sufficiently general to account for objectives other than HPWL such as Steiner wirelength (StWL) [32]. StWL is known to correlate with final routed wirelength (rWL) more accurately than HPWL and the authors of Ref. [32] hypothesize that if StWL could be directly optimized during global placement, one may be able to enhance routability and reduce routed wirelength.

The points required to calculate w_1 for a given net are the terminals on the net plus the center of partition 1. Similarly, the points required to calculate w_2 are the terminals plus the center of

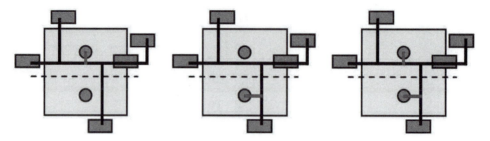

FIGURE 15.11 Calculating the three costs for weighted terminal propagation with StWL: w_1 (left), w_2 (middle), and w_{12} (right). The net has five fixed terminals: four above and one below the proposed cutline. For the traditional HPWL objective, this net would be considered inessential. Note that the structure of the three Steiner trees may be entirely different, which is why w_1, w_2, and w_{12} are evaluated independently. (From Roy, J. A. and Markov, I. L., *IEEE Trans. CAD*, 26, 632, 2007.)

partition 2. Lastly, the points to calculate w_{12} are the terminals on the net plus the centers of both partitions. See Figure 15.11 for an example of calculating these three costs. Clearly, the HPWL of the set of points necessary to calculate w_{12} is at least as large as that of w_1 and w_2 because it contains an additional point. By the same logic, StWL also satisfies this relationship because RSMT length can only increase with additional points. Because StWL is a valid cost function for these weighted partitioning problems, this is a framework whereby it can be minimized [32].

The simplicity of this framework for minimizing StWL is deceiving. In particular, the propagation of terminal locations to the current placement bin and the removal of inessential nets [11]—standard techniques for HPWL minimization—cannot be used when minimizing StWL. Moving terminal locations drastically changes Steiner-tree construction and can make StWL estimates extremely inaccurate. Nets that are considered inessential in HPWL minimization (where the x- or y-span of terminals, if the cut is vertical or horizontal respectively, contains the x- or y-span of the centers of child bins) are not necessarily inessential when considering StWL because there are many Steiner trees of different lengths that have the same bounding box. Figure 15.11 illustrates a net that is inessential for HPWL minimization but essential for StWL minimization. Not only computing Steiner trees but also traversing all relevant nets to collect all relevant point locations can be very time consuming. Therefore, the main challenge in supporting StWL minimization is to develop efficient data structures and limit additional runtime during placement [32].

15.4.3.1 Pointsets with Multiplicities

Building Steiner trees for each net during partitioning is a computationally expensive task. To keep runtime reasonable when building Steiner trees for partitioning, the authors of Ref. [32] introduce a simple yet highly effective data structure—pointsets with multiplicities. For each net in the hypergraph, two lists are maintained. The first list contains all the unique pin locations on the net that are fixed. A fixed pin can come from sources such as terminals or fixed objects in the core area. The second list contains all the unique pin locations on the net that are movable, that is, all other pins that are not on the fixed list. All points on each list are unique so that redundant points are not given to Steiner evaluators. To do so efficiently, the lists are kept in sorted order. For both lists, in addition to the location of the pin, the number of pins that correspond to a given point is also saved [32].

Maintaining the number of actual pins that correspond to a point in a pointset (the multiplicity of that point) is necessary for efficient update of pin locations during placement. If a pin changes position during placement, the pointsets for the net connected to the pin must be updated. First, the original position of the pin must be removed from the movable point set. As multiple pins can have the same position, especially early in placement, the entire net would need to be traversed to see if any other pins share the same position as the pin that is moving. Multiplicities allow to know this information in constant time. To remove the pin, one performs a binary search on the pointset and decreases the multiplicity of the pin's position by 1. If this results in the position having a multiplicity of 0, the position can be removed entirely. Insertion of the pin's new position is similar: first, a binary search is performed on the pointset. If the pin's position is already present in the pointset, the multiplicity is increased by 1. Otherwise, the position is added in sorted order with a multiplicity of 1. Empirically, building and maintaining the pointset data structures takes less than 1 percent of the runtime of global placement [32].

15.4.3.2 Performance

The authors of Ref. [32] compared three Steiner evaluators in terms of runtime impact and solution quality. They chose the FastSteiner [24] evaluator for global placement based on its reasonable runtime and consistent performance on large nets. Empirical results show the use of FastSteiner leads to a reduction of StWL by 3 percent on average on the IBMv2 benchmarks [42] (with a reduction of routed wirelength up to 7 percent) while using less than 30 percent additional runtime [32].

15.4.4 INCREMENTAL PLACEMENT

To develop a strong incremental placement tool, ECO-system, the authors of Ref. [33] build upon an existing global placement framework and must choose between analytical and top-down. The main considerations include robustness, the handling of movable macros, and fixed obstacles, as well as consistent routability of placements and the handling of density constraints. On the basis of recent empirical evidence [30,32,35], the top-down framework appears a somewhat better choice. However, analytical algorithms can also be integrated into ECO-system when particularly extensive changes are required. ECO-system favorably compares to recent detail placers in runtime and solution quality and fares well in high-level and physical synthesis.

15.4.4.1 General Framework

ECO-system can be likened to reverse engineering the mincut placement process. The goal is to reconstruct the internal state of a mincut placer that could have produced the given initial placement. Given this state, one can choose to accept or reject its previous decisions based on their own criteria and build a new placement for the design. If many of the decisions of the placer were good, one can achieve a considerable runtime savings as compared to placement from scratch. If many of the decisions are determined to be bad, one can do no worse in terms of solution quality than placement from scratch. The overall algorithm in the framework of mincut placement is shown in Figure 15.12. An overview of the application of ECO-system to an illegal placement is depicted in Figure 15.13.

To rebuild the state of a mincut placer, one must reconstruct a series of cutlines and partitioning solutions efficiently. One must also determine criteria for the acceptability of the derived partitioning and cutline. To extract a cutline and partitioning solution from a given placement bin, all possible cutlines of the bin as well as the partitions they induce must be examined. Starting at one edge of the placement bin (left edge for a vertical cut and bottom edge for a horizontal cut) and moving toward the opposite edge, for each potential cutline encountered, one maintains the cell area on either side of the cutline, the partition induced by the cutline and its netcut.

Once a cutline and partitioning have been chosen, they must be evaluated. To evaluate the partitioning, the authors of Ref. [33] use it as input to a Fiduccia–Mattheyses partitioner and see how much it can be improved by a single pass (if the bin is large enough, a multilevel Fiduccia–Mattheyses partitioner can be used). The intuition is that if the constructed partitioning is not worthy of reuse, a single Fiduccia–Mattheyses pass could improve its cut nontrivially. If the Fiduccia–Mattheyses pass improves the cut beyond a certain threshold, the solution is discarded and the entire bin is bisected from scratch. If a partition is accepted by this criterion, one performs a legality test: if the partitioning overfills a child bin, the cutline is discarded and the bin is bisected from scratch.

```
Variables: queue of placement bins
Initialize queue with top-level placement bin
1  While (queue not empty)
2    Dequeue a bin
3    If (bin not marked to place from scratch)
4     If(bin overfull)
5       Mark bin to place from scratch, break
6      Quickly choose the cut-line which has the smallest
        net-cut considering cell area balance constraints
7      If(cut-line causes overfull child bin)
8        Mark bin to place from scratch, break
9      Induce partitioning of bin's cells from cut-line
10     Improve net-cut of partitioning with
        single pass of Fiduccia-Mattheyses
11     If(% of improvement > threshold)
12       Mark bin to place from scratch, break
13     Create child bins using cut-line and partitioning
14     Enqueue each child bin
15   If(bin marked to place from scratch)
16     If (bin small enough)
17       Process end case
18     Else
19       Bipartition the bin into child bins
20        Mark child bins to place from scratch
21       Enqueue each child bin
```

FIGURE 15.12 Incremental mincut placement. Boldfaced lines 3–15 and 20 are different from traditional mincut placement. (From Roy, J. A. and Markov, I. L., *IEEE Trans. CAD*, 20, 2173, 2007.)

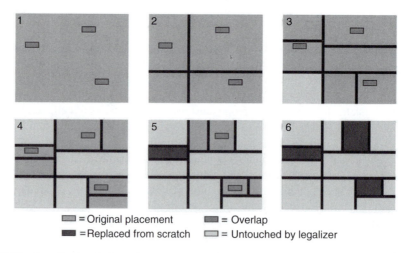

= Original placement   ▬ = Overlap
▬ = Replaced from scratch   = Untouched by legalizer

FIGURE 15.13 Legalization during mincut placement. Placement bins are subdivided until (i) a bin contains no overlap and is ignored for the remainder of the legalization process or, (ii) the placement contained in the bin is considered too poor to be kept (too many overlaps or does not meet the solution quality requirements) and is replaced from scratch using mincut or analytical techniques. (From Roy, I. A. and Markov, I. L., *IEEE Trans. CAD*, 20, 2173, 2007.)

Empirically, the runtime of the cutline selection procedure (which includes a single pass of a Fiduccia–Mattheyses partitioner) is much smaller than partitioning from scratch. On large benchmarks, the cutline selection process requires 5 percent of ECO-system runtime time whereas mincut partitioners generally require 50 percent or more of ECO-system runtime. ECO-system as a whole requires approximately 15 percent of original placement runtime.

15.4.4.2   Handling Macros and Obstacles

With the addition of macros, the flow of top-down placement usually becomes more complex. The authors of Ref. [33] adopt the style of floorplacement from Refs. [30,31] (see Sections 15.3.1 and 15.4.2). For legalization with macros, a new criterion for floorplanning is added: if a placement bin has nonoverlapping positions for macros (i.e., no macros in the placement bin overlap each other) the macros are placed in exactly their initial positions; if some of the macros overlap, other floorplanning criteria are used to decide. If any of the macros are moved, the placement of all cells and macros in the bin must be discarded and placement and proceeds as described in Ref. [31].

15.5   STATE-OF-THE-ART MINCUT PLACERS

In this section, we present partitioning-based placement techniques that are used in cutting-edge placers. For each placer, we describe its overall flow, how this differs from the generic mincut flow, and how it handles challenges in placement such as fixed obstacles and mixed-size instances. In particular, we describe the techniques used by the placers Dragon [38,39,42], FengShui [4,27], NTUPlace2 [22], and Capo [30–35].

15.5.1   DRAGON

The most recent version of Dragon, Dragon2006 [39], combines mincut bisection with simulated annealing for placement. In its most basic flow, Dragon2006 utilizes recursive bisection with the hMETIS partitioner [26]. Each bin is partitioned multiple times with a feedback mechanism to allow for more accurate terminal propagation (see Section 15.2.1 for more details on placement feedback). Partitioning is followed by simulated annealing on the placement bins where whole bins are swapped with one another to improve HPWL [38,39]. After a number of layers of interleaved partitioning and simulated annealing, each bin contains only a few cells and the partitioning phase terminates. Next, bins are aligned to row structures and cell-based simulated annealing is performed wherein cells are swapped between bins to improve HPWL [38,39]. Lastly, cell overlaps are removed and local detail placement improvements are made.

15.5.2   FENGSHUI

FengShui [4,27] is a recursive bisection mincut placer that uses the hMETIS partitioner [26]. FengShui implements the fractional cut technique (see Section 15.2.2) and packs its placements to either side of the placement region, which has a serious affect on the routability of its placements [32]. FengShui also supports mixed-size placement (see Section 15.3.3)

15.5.3   NTUPLACE2

NTUPlace2 [22] is a hybrid placer that uses both mincut partitioning and analytical techniques for standard-cell and mixed-size designs. NTUPlace2 uses repartitioning (see Section 15.2.1), cutline shifting (see Section 15.1.3), and weighted netcut (see Section 15.2.4) [22].

NTUPlace2 uses analytical techniques to aid partitioning, which are different from those in ACG (see Section 15.2.3). Before partitioning calls to the hMETIS partitioner [26], objects in a placement bin are placed by an analytical technique to reduce quadratic wirelength [22]. These objects that are placed far from the proposed cutline are considered fixed in their current locations for the partitioning process. This technique helps to make terminal propagation more exact, and, with the weighted netcut technique, has resulted in very good solution quality [22].

To handle mixed-size placement, macro locations are legalized at each layer. Macros become fixed at different layers of placement according to their size relative to placement bin size. Thus, larger macros are placed earlier in placement [22]. Macros are legalized using a linear programming technique that attempts to minimize the movement of macros during legalization [22].

15.5.4 CAPO

Capo [30–35] is a mincut floorplacer. As such, it implements the floorplacement flow as described in Section 15.3.1 and further improved by SCAMPI (Section 15.4.2) rather than the traditional mincut flow and implicitly handles mixed-size placement and fixed obstacles in the placement area. Capo can use either MLPart [10] or hMETIS [26] for hypergraph partitioning. Whitespace allocation in Capo is done per placement bin: either uniform (see Section 15.1.4), minimum local or safe whitespace allocation (see Section 15.4.1) is chosen based on the bin's whitespace and user-configurable options. To improve the quality of results, Capo also implements repartitioning (see Section 15.2.1), placement feedback (see Section 15.2.1), weighted net-cut (see Section 15.2.4), and several whitespace allocation techniques. Capo has also been used to optimize Steiner wirelength in placement (see Section 15.4.3) and can be used for incremental placement (see Section 15.4.4).

REFERENCES

1. S. N. Adya and I. L. Markov, Fixed-outline floorplanning: Enabling hierarchical design, *IEEE Transactions on VLSI*, 11(6) 1120–1135, December 2003 (*ICCD* 2001, pp. 328–334).
2. S. N. Adya and I. L. Markov, Combinatorial techniques for mixed-size placement, *ACM Transactions on Design Automation of Electronic Systems*, 10(5), 58–90, January 2005 (*ISPD* 2002, pp. 12–17).
3. S. N. Adya, I. L. Markov, and P. G. Villarrubia, On whitespace and stability in physical synthesis, *Integration: The VLSI Journal*, 25(4), 340–362, 2006 (*ICCAD* 2003, pp. 311–318).
4. A. Agnihotri et al., Fractional cut: Improved recursive bisection placement, *ICCAD*, San Jose, CA, pp. 307–310, 2003.
5. C. J. Alpert, G. -J. Nam, and P. G. Villarrubia, Effective free space management for cut-based placement via analytical constraint generation, *IEEE Transactions on CAD*, 22(10), 1343–1353, 2003 (*ICCAD* 2002, pp. 746–751).
6. U. Brenner and A. Rohe, An effective congestion driven placement framework, *IEEE Transactions on CAD*, 22(4), pp. 387–394, 2003 (*ISPD* 2002, pp. 6–11).
7. M. Breuer, Min-cut placement, *Journal of Design Automation and Fault Tolerant Computing*, 1(4), 343–362, October 1977 (*DAC* 1977, pp. 284–290).
8. A. E. Caldwell, A. B. Kahng, S. Mantik, I. L. Markov, and A. Zelikovsky, On wirelength estimations for row-based placement, *IEEE Transactions on CAD*, 18(9), 1265–1278, 1999.
9. A. E. Caldwell, A. B. Kahng, and I. L. Markov, Can recursive bisection alone produce routable placements? *DAC*, pp. 477–482, Los Angeles, June 2000.
10. A. E. Caldwell, A. B. Kahng, and I. L. Markov, Design and implementation of move-based heuristics for VLSI hypergraph partitioning, *ACM Journal of Experimental Algorithms*, 5, 2000.
11. A. E. Caldwell, A. B. Kahng, and I. L. Markov, Optimal partitioners and end-case placers for standard-cell layout, *IEEE Transactions on CAD*, 19(11), 1304–314, 2000 (*ISPD* 1999, pp. 90–96).
12. A. E. Caldwell, A. B. Kahng, and I. L. Markov, Hierarchical whitespace allocation in top-down placement, *IEEE Transactions on CAD*, 22(11), 716–724, November 2003.
13. Y. C. Chang et al., B*-trees: A new representation for non-slicing floorplans, *DAC*, Los Angeles, CA, pp. 458–463, 2000.

14. T. C. Chen and Y. W. Chang, Modern floorplanning based on fast simulated annealing, *ISPD*, San Francisco, CA, pp. 104–112, 2005.
15. T. C. Chen, Y. W. Chang, and S. C. Lin, IMF: Interconnect-driven multilevel floorplanning for large-scale building-module designs, *ICCAD*, San Jose, CA, pp. 159–164, November 2005.
16. J. Cong, G. Nataneli, M. Romesis, and J. Shinnerl, An area-optimality study of floorplanning, *ISPD*, Phoenix, AZ, pp. 78–83, 2004.
17. J. Cong, M. Romesis, and J. Shinnerl, Fast floorplanning by look-ahead enabled recursive bipartitioning, *IEE Transactions on CAD*, 25(9), 1719–1732, 2006 (*ASPDAC*, 2005 pp. 1119–1122).
18. J. Cong, M. Romesis, and J. Shinnerl, Robust mixed-size placement under tight white-space constraints, *ICCAD*, San Jose, CA, pp. 165–172, 2005.
19. A. E. Dunlop and B. W. Kernighan, A procedure for placement of standard cell VLSI circuits, *IEEE Transactions on CAD*, 4(1), 92–98, 1985.
20. C. M. Fiduccia and R. M. Mattheyses, A linear time heuristic for improving network partitions, *DAC*, Washington, D.C., pp. 175–181, 1982.
21. D. J. -H. Huang, and A. B. Kahng, Partitioning-based standard-cell global placement with an exact objective, *ISPD*, Napa Valley, CA, pp. 18–25, 1997.
22. Z. -W. Jiang et al., NTUPlace2: A hybrid placer using partitioning and analytical techniques, *ISPD*, San Jose, CA, pp. 215–217, 2006.
23. A. B. Kahng, S. Mantik, and I. L. Markov, Min-max placement for large-scale timing optimization, *ISPD*, San Diego, CA, pp. 143–148, April 2002.
24. A. B. Kahng, I. I. Mandoiu, and A. Zelikovsky, Highly scalable algorithms for rectilinear and octilinear Steiner trees, *ASPDAC*, Kitakyushu, Japan, pp. 827–833, 2003.
25. A. B. Kahng and S. Reda, Placement feedback: A concept and method for better min-cut placement, *DAC*, San Diego, CA, pp. 357–362, 2004.
26. G. Karypis, R. Aggarwal, V. Kumar, and S. Shekhar, Multilevel hypergraph partitioning: applications in VLSI domain, *DAC*, Anaheim, CA, pp. 526–629, 1997.
27. A. Khatkhate, C. Li, A. R. Agnihotri, M. C. Yildiz, S. Ono, C. -K. Koh, and P. H. Madden, Recursive bisection based mixed block placement, *ISPD*, Phoenix, AZ, pp. 84–89, 2004.
28. C. Li, M. Xie, C. K. Koh, J. Cong, and P. H. Madden, Routability-driven placement and white space allocation, *ICCAD*, San Jose, CA, pp. 394–401, 2004.
29. G. -J. Nam, C. J. Alpert, P. Villarrubia, B. Winter, and M. Yildiz, The ISPD2005 placement contest and benchmark suite, *ISPD*, San Francisco, CA, pp. 216–220, 2005.
30. A. N. Ng, I. L. Markov, R. Aggarwal, and V. Ramachandran, Solving hard instances of floorplacement, *ISPD*, San Jose, CA, pp. 170–177, April 2006.
31. J. A. Roy, S. N. Adya, D. A. Papa, and I. L. Markov, Min-cut floorplacement, *IEEE Transactions on CAD*, 25(7), 1313–1326, 2006 (*ICCAD* 2004, pp. 550–557).
32. J. A. Roy and I. L. Markov, Seeing the forest and the trees: Steiner wirelength optimization in placement, *IEEE Transactions on CAD* 26(4), 632–644, 2007 (*ISPD* 2006, pp. 78–85).
33. J. A. Roy and I. L. Markov, ECO-system: Embracing the change in placement, *IEEE Transactions on CAD*, 26(12), 2173–2185, 2000 (*ASP-DAC* 2007, pp. 147–152).
34. J. A. Roy, D. A. Papa, S. N. Adya, H. H. Chan, J. F. Lu, A. N. Ng, and I. L. Markov, Capo: Robust and scalable open-source min-cut floorplacer, *ISPD*, San Francisco, CA, pp. 224–227, April 2005.
35. J. A. Roy, D. A. Papa, A. N. Ng, and I. L Markov, Satisfying whitespace requirements in top-down placement, *ISPD*, San Jose, CA, pp. 206–208, April 2006.
36. N. Selvakkumaran and G. Karypis, Theto—A fast, scalable and high-quality partitioning driven placement tool, Technical report, University of Minnesota, 2004.
37. P. R. Suaris and G. Kedem, An algorithm for quadrisection and its application to standard cell placement, *IEEE Transactions on Circuits and Systems*, 35(3), 294–303, 1988 (*ICCAD* 1987, pp. 474–477).
38. T. Taghavi, X. Yang, B. -K. Choi, M. Wang, and M. Sarrafzadeh, Dragon2005: Large-scale mixed-size placement tool, *ISPD*, San Francisco, CA, pp. 245–247, April 2005.
39. T. Taghavi, X. Yang, B. -K. Choi, M. Wang, and M. Sarrafzadeh, Dragon2006: Blockage-aware congestion-controlling mixed-size placer, *ISPD*, San Jose, CA, pp. 209–211, April 2006.
40. K. Takahashi, K. Nakajima, M. Terai, and K. Sato, Min-cut placement with global objective functions for large scale sea-of-gates arrays, *IEEE Transactions on CAD*, 14(4), 434–446, 1995.

41. E. Wein and J. Benkoski, Hard macros will revolutionize SoC design, *EE Times*, August 20, 2004. http://www.eetimes.com/news/design/showArticle.jhtml?articleID=26807055.
42. X. Yang, B. K. Choi, and M. Sarrafzadeh, Routability driven white space allocation for fixed-die standard-cell placement, *IEEE Transactions on CAD*, 22(4), 410–419, April 2003 (*ISPD* 2002, pp. 42–49).
43. M. C. Yildiz and P. H. Madden, Improved cut sequences for partitioning based placement, *DAC*, Las Vegas, NV, pp. 776–779, 2001.

16 Placement Using Simulated Annealing

William Swartz

CONTENTS

16.1 INTRODUCTION

Simulated annealing is a technique for finding an optimal or near-optimal solution for combinatorial optimization problems, or problems that have discrete variables. This technique was proposed by Kirkpatrick, Gelatt, and Vecchi in 1983 [1] and has been successfully applied to circuit partitioning, placement, and routing in the physical design of integrated circuits.

The goal of a combinatorial optimization algorithm is to find the state of lowest cost (or energy) from a discrete space of admissible configurations S. For each problem, a cost function must be defined that maps each state to a real number denoting its cost. For many problems, the number of possible states grows exponentially with the size of the input. Optimizing becomes the process of searching for the state of lowest cost in a hyper-dimensional space. With a large number of possible states to visit, the brute force method of visiting all configurations becomes impractical. Clearly, we need a search strategy to uncover the lowest cost solution in the jungle of states.

For many problems, the states of the configuration space are related. A problem exhibits optimal substructure if an optimal solution to the problem contains within it optimal solutions to subproblems. These cases may be solved by either a greedy or a dynamic programming algorithm. In a greedy-choice problem, a globally optimal solution can be found by making a locally optimal (greedy) decision. The best choice is made at each moment; at each step, we solve the ramifications of the previous choice. The choice made by a greedy algorithm cannot depend on future decisions or solutions to subproblems. In dynamic programming, a choice is made at each step that may depend on the solutions to the subproblems.

```
Algorithm simulated_annealing(void)
1 T ← T₀                                      /* Initial Temperature */
2 do
3   do
4       j = generate(i)                       /* Move Strategies */
5       if accept (ΔC, T) then                /* Metropolis function */
6           i = j
7   until cost is in equilibrium              /* Temperature equilibrium */
8 update (T)                                  /* Temperature decrement */
9 until cost cannot be reduced
    any further                               /* Stopping criteria */
```

FIGURE 16.1   Basic simulated annealing algorithm.

Unfortunately, the placement problem described here does not exhibit optimal substructure. If we apply the greedy algorithm search strategy, we will usually get stuck in a local minimum. This means that

$$c(i) \geq c(j_{min}), \quad \forall j \in S(j_{min}) \tag{16.1}$$

where j_{min} is the local minimum state, and $S(j_{min})$ is the set of states reachable from the state j_{min}.

In many cases, there is a large disparity between the local minimum and the global minimum cost. We need a search strategy that avoids local minima and finds the global minimum. Simulated annealing is such a search strategy.

At the heart of the simulated annealing algorithm is the Metropolis Monte Carlo procedure that was introduced to provide an efficient simulation of a collection of atoms in equilibrium at a given temperature [2]. The Metropolis procedure is the inner loop of the simulated annealing algorithm as shown in Figure 16.1. Although the greedy algorithm forbids changes of state that increase the cost function, the Metropolis procedure allows moves to states that increase the cost function. Kirkpatrick et al. suggested that the Metropolis Monte Carlo method can be used to simulate the physical annealing process and to solve combinatorial optimization problems [1]. They suggested adding an outer loop that lowers the temperature from a high melting temperature in slow stages until the system freezes, and no further changes occur. At each temperature, the simulation must proceed long enough for the system to reach a steady state. The sequence of temperatures and the method to reach equilibrium at each temperature is known as annealing schedule. They showed that this same technique can be applied to combinatorial optimization problems if a cost function is used in place of energy, and the temperature is used as a control parameter.

16.2   ANNEALING SCHEDULES

It has been shown that the simulated annealing algorithm, when started in an arbitrary state and given an appropriate annealing schedule, will eventually converge to a global optimum [3]. Although these results required an infinite amount of computation time for the convergence guarantee, in practice, simulated annealing has been extremely successful when applied to circuit partitioning and placement problems. It has outperformed all other known algorithms if given sufficient time resources.

The essential elements of the simulated annealing algorithm are summarized below in Figure 16.1. The algorithm consists of two loops. Each execution of the inner loop generates new configurations to be evaluated at constant temperature. The acceptance of a new configuration j depends on the current temperature T and the change in cost between the current configuration i and the proposed configuration j as presented in Figure 16.2. All configuration changes that do not increase the cost are accepted as in any-iterative improvement algorithm, but moves with $\Delta C > 0$

```
Algorithm accept(ΔC, T)
1     if ΔC ≤ 0 then /*new cost is less than or equal to the old cost */
2            return(ACCEPT) /*accept the new configuration */
3     else
4            randomly generate a number r between 0 and 1
5            if r < e⁻ᴬᶜ/ᵀ then return(ACCEPT)
6            else return (REJECT)
```

FIGURE 16.2 Acceptance function for the simulated annealing algorithm.

are accepted depending on the value of ΔC and the value of T. The Boltzmann distribution $\left(e^{\frac{-\Delta C}{T}}\right)$ that governs physical annealing is used as the criteria for determining acceptance of states with increased cost.

In this simple formulation of simulated annealing, we designate that the inner loop is repeated until the average value of the cost appears to have converged. As T is lowered from a high value, large uphill moves are mostly rejected. As T is lowered further, moves with yet lower values of $\Delta C > 0$ become largely rejected. In some sense, critical decisions are made for those values of $\Delta C > 0$ which are on the order of the value of T. Hence, simulated annealing operates in a pseudohierarchical fashion with respect to $\Delta C > 0$ values as T is decreased.

16.3   SIMULATED ANNEALING AND PLACEMENT

The critical ingredients for a implementing a successful placer based on simulated annealing are the simulated annealing cooling schedule, the cost function to be evaluated, and the generation of new state configurations or move strategies. Although simulated annealing placers are quite straightforward to implement, the best results in terms of quality and execution time have been obtained with careful attention to these details. We discuss each of these aspects of simulated annealing in turn.

16.4   SIMULATED ANNEALING COOLING SCHEDULES

A simulated annealing cooling schedule is differentiated by the implementation of four lines of the basic annealing schedule presented in Figure 16.1: initial temperature selection, temperature equilibrium criteria, temperature update, and stopping criteria. A common implementation is easily coded as shown in Figure 16.3. Here, iterations is a variable which counts the number of Metropolis cycles or inner loop executions, numberOfMoves is a variable which counts the number of generated new configurations in an iteration, I_{max} is the predetermined maximum number of iterations, N_{max} is the predetermined maximum number of moves generated per iteration, and α is the temperature multiplier.

Although the previous implementation is simple, effective, and easily programmed, it has a major drawback: at low temperatures, the running time is very long because many candidates for moves are rejected before each move to a different configuration. To remedy this inefficiency, various approaches have been proposed to speed the algorithm including parallel implementations [4–6] as well as rejectionless hill climbing [7]. Lam studied the problem and proposed a statistical annealing schedule [8]. Lam's schedule is based on the observation that annealing is successful if the system is kept close to thermal equilibrium as the temperature is lowered. However, to keep the system in equilibrium at all times requires that the temperature decrements be infinitesimal; a long time would have passed before the system is frozen, and annealing is stopped. From a practical standpoint, a good annealing schedule must, therefore, achieve a compromise between the quality of the final solution and the computation time. To determine when the system is in equilibrium so that the

```
1  T ← largeNumber                        /* Initial Temperature */
1b iterations ← 0
2  do
2b   numberOfMoves ← 0
3    do
4       j = generate(i)                    /* Move Strategies */
4b      increment numberOfMoves
5       if accept(ΔC, T) then              /* Metropolis function */
6          i = j
7    while numberOfMoves ≤ N_max           /* Temperature equilibrium */
8    T ← αT, 0.8 ≤ α ≤ 0.99                /* Temperature decrement */
8b   increment iterations
9  while iterations ≤ I_max                /* Stopping criteria */
```

FIGURE 16.3   Simple simulated annealing algorithm.

temperature could be lowered, we need an equilibrium criterion [9]. A system is close to equilibrium at temperature T if the following condition is satisfied

$$\mu(s) - \lambda\sigma(s) \leq \bar{c} \leq \mu(s) + \lambda\sigma(s) \tag{16.2}$$

where
   $\bar{c}$ is the average cost of the system
   $s = 1/T$ is the inverse temperature
   $\mu(s)$ and $\sigma(s)$ are the mean and standard deviation of the cost if the system were in thermal equilibrium at temperature T

The parameter λ, which can be made as small as desired to ensure a good approximation of equilibrium, realizes the compromise between the quality of the final solution and the computation time: the smaller the λ, the better is the quality of the final solution and the longer is the computation time.

Simulated annealing has been applied to the placement problem in the TimberWolf system. Complete accounts of the implementations of simulated annealing for earlier versions of the TimberWolf placement programs have been published [10–18]. The inclusion of the results of a theoretically derived statistical annealing schedule have been responsible for the very significant reduction in the CPU time required by TimberWolf.

We now present the adapation of Lam's statistical annealing schedule [8] found in TimberWolf. In his work, Lam showed theoretically that the optimum acceptance rate of proposed new configurations is approximately 44 percent. In Lam's algorithm, a range limiter window (first described in Ref. [10]) is used to keep the acceptance rate (denoted as ρ) as close as possible to 44 percent. (The range limiter window bounds the magnitude of the perturbation (or move distance) from the current state. The range limiter window size is designed to increase the acceptance rate at a given temperature. Changes in cost are on the order of the move distance. Therefore, reducing the move distance yields smaller values and hence an elevated acceptance rate.) In the beginning of the execution of this algorithm, the temperature T is set to a very high value (effectively infinity). Even with the range limiter dimensions encompassing the entire chip, the acceptance rate ρ approaches 100 percent. Because a further increase in range limiter dimensions cannot decrease ρ, there clearly must be a region of operation for the algorithm in which ρ is above the ideal value of 44 percent. Also, as T gets sufficiently low, the range limiter dimensions reduce to their minimum values. Then, as ρ drops below 44 percent, there is no way for it to return to a higher level. It is therefore apparent

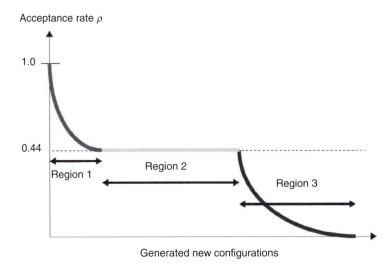

FIGURE 16.4 Anticipated plot of the acceptance rate versus generated new configurations.

that there is a region of operation in which ρ falls from 44 percent toward zero as T approaches zero. The anticipated three regions of operation (ρ above 0.44, ρ equals 0.44, and ρ below 0.44) are illustrated in Figure 16.4. One disadvantage of the schedule developed by Lam is its inability to accurately predict when the execution of the algorithm will end from the beginning of the run. That is, it is not known how many new configurations will be generated during the course of the execution of the algorithm. In an effort to gain a different perspective on Lam's theory, the authors of TimberWolf measured ρ versus generated new configurations for executions on several industrial circuits. One objective was to determine the percentage of the run (i.e., the percentage of the total new configurations generated) devoted to each of the three regions of operation.

These percentages were remarkably similar for the very wide range of circuit sizes which were tested. A typical plot is shown in Figure 16.5.

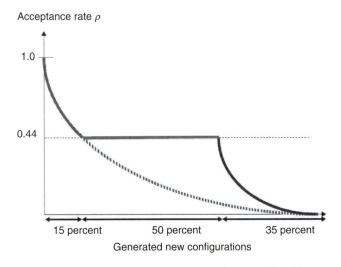

FIGURE 16.5 Typical measured acceptance rate versus generated new configurations as obtained from experiments conducted on several industrial circuits, showing the percentage of the run spent in each region of operation.

They discovered that for region 1 (which encompasses approximately 15 percent of the run), ρ versus generated new configurations could be modeled by an exponential function. This function has a peak value of 1.0, and passes through the point where ρ first reduces to 0.44. Furthermore, they found that region 3 could also be modeled by an exponential function with peak value 0.44 and minimum value 0.0. In region 2, the acceptance rate is flat, but they discovered that the decrease in the range limiter window dimensions as a function of generated new configurations can also be modeled by exponential functional form. That all three regions can be modeled by exponential functions is not surprising in light of the use of the (exponential) Boltzmann-like factor used to govern acceptance or rejection of new configurations. Here they define an iteration (represented by I where $1 \leq I \leq I_{max}$) to correspond to an interval along the horizontal axis in Figure 16.6. That is, N_{max} new configurations are generated during iteration I. An iteration defines a set of N_{max} moves during which the range limiter window dimensions remain constant.

In simulated annealing, the more new configurations generated during the course of a run, the higher the probability of achieving a better solution. However, extensive experimentation suggested the existence of a diminishing return on the number of new configurations generated. Therefore, a default number of moves can be determined for which the best results can be obtained with high probability. The default total number of moves during a run is set to

$$\text{total}_{\text{moves}} = 1500N_{\text{c}}^{4/3} \tag{16.3}$$

where N_{c} is the number of cells. In TimberWolf implementations, they set I_{max} equal to 150 iterations. Therefore:

$$N_{\text{max}} = 10N_{\text{c}}^{4/3} \tag{16.4}$$

Note that the range limiter dimensions are actually changed 50 percent of 150 times, or 75 times during the course of a run (i.e., its dimensions only change during region 2 of the operation of the annealing algorithm).

Because we know that the acceptance rate behavior described in Figure 16.5 along with the default values of I_{max} and N_{max} yield close to the best possible results for simulated annealing, the algorithm

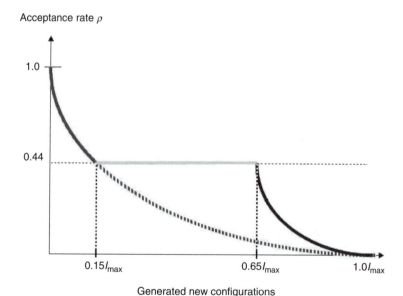

FIGURE 16.6   Target acceptance rate versus iteration.

is forced to strictly obey that acceptance rate behavior through the use of a feedback mechanism. That is, for each iteration I (I varies from 1 to $I_{\max}$), one can compute the target acceptance rate (ρ_I^T) as shown in Figure 16.6. To ensure that significant further reductions in the cost are not possible, the target acceptance rate is set to be below 1 percent at the last iteration ($I_{\max}$).

One can force the actual acceptance rate to track the target acceptance rate by using negative feedback control on the temperature T:

$$T = \left[1 - \frac{\rho_I - \rho_I^T}{K}\right] T \tag{16.5}$$

where K is a damping constant used to stabilize the control of the value of T (in TimberWolf implementations, a very suitable value of K is 40). T is updated every update_limit moves (as defined in the description of our simulated annealing algorithm in Figure 16.7). Note that T can increase as well as decrease as the execution of the algorithm proceeds, and the range limiter window dimensions decrease exponentially as a function of the number of iterations. In Lam's schedule by contrast, T decreases monotonically but the range limiter window dimensions fluctuate up or down. Clearly these two parameters are closely related. It is sufficient to dictate the functional form for either one, and let the other parameter adapt to monitored conditions.

```
Algorithm simulated_annealing(X₀)
1  X ← X₀                              /* set current configuration equal
                                          to initial configuration */
2  T ← set_initial_T()                 /* sufficiently sample configuration
                                          space to ascertain value of T yielding
                                          an initial acceptance rate slightly
                                          below 100 percent */

3  I ← 1
4  while I ≤ Imax do
5     N ← 0                            /* N is the number of moves attempted
                                          so far during iteration I */
6     set_range_limiter_size(I)        /* sets range limiter window dimensions */
7     up ← 0                           /* update counter */
8     while N ≤ Nmax do
9        N ← N + 1
10       up ← up + 1
11       if up = update_limit then     /* we need to update the temperature T */
12          up ← 0                      /* reset the counter */
13          if ρI < ρIᵀT then
14             raise_temp(T)
15          else if ρI > ρIᵀT then
16             lower_temp(T)
17       Y = generate(X)               /* propose a new configuration */
18       ΔC = C(Y) − C(X)              /* compute the cost change */
19       if accept(ΔC, T) then
20             X ← Y                    /* accept the new configuration to be
                                          the current config. */
21 I ← I + 1
```

FIGURE 16.7   Advanced simulated annealing algorithm.

The heuristic adaptation of Lam's schedule shown in Figure 16.7 did not show a difference in placement quality for a given execution time as compared to Lam's original version and was adopted as the annealing schedule in TimberWolf. The TimberWolf approach generates a fixed number of moves for a circuit of a given size, and therefore, the number of iterations is known a priori.

16.5 COST FUNCTIONS

One of the advantages of the simulated annealing algorithm is its ability to accommodate any cost function. In fact, there are no constraints on the form of the cost function. However, recent research has shown that the best results are linear or logarithmically related terms or variables. Siarry et al. have "noticed improved convergence toward the correct results when using normalized variables instead of unnormalized real variables range exploration with the same simulated annealing algorithm" [19].

Traditionally, a common cost function for simulated annealing row-based placers is the weighted summation of total half-perimeter wirelength, timing penalty, overlap penalty, row length control penalty, and congestion penalty:

$$C = \beta_w W + \beta_t P_t + \beta_o P_o + \beta_r P_r + \beta_c P_c \tag{16.6}$$

where

$$W = \sum_{n=1}^{N_N} \max_{v_i, v_j \in n} |x_i - x_j| + \max_{v_i, v_j \in n} |y_i - y_j| \tag{16.7}$$

$$P_t = \sum_{p=1}^{N_P} D_p \tag{16.8}$$

$$D_p = f(R, C, l, t_g) \tag{16.9}$$

$$P_o = \sum_{k \neq l} O_x(k, l)^2 \tag{16.10}$$

$$P_r = \sum_{r=1}^{N_R} |L(r) - L_d(r)| \tag{16.11}$$

$$P_c = \sum_{m=1}^{N_x} \sum_{n=1}^{N_y} C_g(m, n) \tag{16.12}$$

$$C_g(m, n) = \begin{cases} 0, & (d_{mn} \leq s_{mn}) \\ d_{mn} - s_{mn}, & (d_{mn} > s_{mn}) \end{cases} \tag{16.13}$$

The wirelength term W is the summation over all nets where each net consists of a set of terminals v_i, and (x_i, y_i) is the coordinate of v_i. The constant N_N represents the total number of nets present in the design.

The timing penalty P_t is the summation of all N_P path delays in the circuit. The generalized delay function D_p is shown as a complex function of resistance R, capacitance C, wirelength l of path, and propagation delay t_g through the circuit. The timing model may utilize lookup tables, Elmore delay calculations, or simple lumped capacitance calculations.

The overlap penalty function $O_x(k, l)$ returns the amount of overlap of cells k and l in the x direction of the row (as we assume horizontal rows). The overlap term is used to insure a legal placement at the end of annealing, that is, no two cells overlap in a row or area.

The row length penalty function is present to ensure that each row in a standard cell placement is filled to a desire length. The function $L(r)$ returns the length of row r and the function $L_d(r)$ returns the desired length of row r.

The congestion cost P_C is calculated by overlaying a two-dimensional global bin structure over the design. Global routing is performed on each net by mapping each terminal vertex v_i to its corresponding bin (m, n), collapsing the terminals within a bin, and interconnecting the terminals spanning the bins. Each time a net crosses a bin, the demand for an bin edge is incremented. The total demand for a bin is the sum of all bin edges. The geometry of the design determines the routing supply s_{mn} available for the bin. An overflow occurs if the demand of a bin d_{mn} exceeds its supply s_{dm}. The congestion is the sum overflows over all global routing bins.

Each of the terms of the cost function are multiplied by a scaling factor β_i to balance the relative importance of the term. To achieve good results over many different circuits and conditions, a feedback mechanism was proposed to control the individual β_i [12]:

$$\beta_{i_{I+1}} = \max \left\{ 0, \beta_{i_I} + \frac{P_i - P_i^{\mathrm{T}}}{P_i^{\mathrm{T}}} \right\} \tag{16.14}$$

where the scaling factor at the next iteration $\beta_{i_{I+1}}$ is calculated from the current scaling factor β_{i_I} (at the Ith iteration) and an error term representing the deviation of penalty P_i from the ideal target penalty P_i^{T}. While this does help improve the final result and drive the penalty terms to zero, this method does not adequately determine the initial scaling factor β_{i_0} and may require a damping factor similar to Equation 16.5 to prevent numerical large oscillations of the scaling factor. Furthermore, to achieve satisfactory results, this method requires a significant tuning effort.

Nevertheless, many simulated annealing placers used cost functions of this general form. In fact, the early versions of TimberWolfSC, the row-based simulated annealing placer used the following cost function [12]:

$$C = W + \beta_o P_o + \beta_r P_r \tag{16.15}$$

For floorplanning or macrocell placement problems, the overlap penalty becomes two dimensional and an additional term is sometimes added to minimize wasted area between cells known as white space:

$$P_S = \frac{A_C(s)}{A_T} \tag{16.16}$$

where $A_c(s)$ is the total area of the chip including white space and A_T is the sum of all of the cell areas. In this case, the scaling factor has been defined as [4]:

$$\beta_s = \begin{cases} K_0 & P_s < 1 \\ K_1 e^r & P_s \geq 1 \end{cases} \tag{16.17}$$

where K_0 and K_1 are two constants such that $K_0 \gg K_1 e^r$ to ensure feasibility.

However, these straightforward functions suffer in that they fail dimensional analysis as the individual terms are not unit compatible. This makes the cost function unfit for general use and susceptible to problems tuning the weight factors. While one can attempt to optimize the weight factors using a set of benchmark circuits, constant weighting factors precludes optimal solutions over a sufficiently large dynamic range. In addition, the feedback control of these weighting factors becomes more unstable as the dynamic range increases; it will become increasingly difficult to balance the linear terms again quadratic terms. Clearly, as problems change in size and topology, the relative attention paid to individual terms of the cost function will vary enormously. Yet most published works on placement have cost functions of the mixed form of Equation 16.6. This is due to an over reliance on benchmarks as a performance measure. Benchmarks offered at given technology node are similar in terms of scale and mask the mixed unit cost function problem.

One can avoid the problematic mixed unit cost function by rewriting the cost function in terms of a single dimension, length, making all terms unit compatible. The timing penalty can be rewritten in terms of a path length penalty where the bounds are given or derived from timing analysis [17]:

$$P_p = \begin{cases} \text{length}(p) - \text{upperBound}(p) & \text{length}(p) > \text{upperBound}(p) \\ \text{lowerBound}(p) - \text{length}(p) & \text{length}(p) < \text{lowerBound}(p) \\ 0 & \text{otherwise} \end{cases} \qquad (16.18)$$

$$\text{length}(p) = \sum_{\forall n \in p} W_n \qquad (16.19)$$

The cell overlap penalty may be completely eliminated through the use of cell shifting and the row length control penalty may be eliminated by careful attention to row bounds during new state generation [15]. The floorplanning area term can be rewritten as the square root of its area and this was utilized in TimberWolfMC [18].

The congestion penalty is more challenging but it can be rewritten in terms of detour length or the additional length needed by a net to avoid a congested area. Kahng and Xu have shown how to effectively calculate the detour length from a congestion map [20]. Sun and Sechen [15] proposed just two terms in their cost function for Timberwolf version 7 whereas the commercial version of TimberWolf (aka InternetCAD itools) uses the following strict length-based cost function which utilizes half-perimeter, timing, and detour costs:

$$C = W + \beta_t P_t + \beta_d P_d \qquad (16.20)$$

16.6 MOVE STRATEGIES

Most simulated annealing placement algorithms predominately use two new configuration strategies or moves: a relocation of a single cell to a new position and a pairwise exchange of cells. Sechen and Lee [12] proposed a bin structure to automatically control the ratio of single cell relocations to pairwise exchanges. Each standard cell row is divided into bins. The center of each cell is assigned to a bin. A new move is proposed as follows: A cell a is randomly chosen. A new position is chosen which resides within the range limiter window and its corresponding bin is calculated. If the bin is empty, a single cell move to this position is performed. Otherwise, randomly pick cell b from the cells in the bin. Cells a and b are exchanged as shown in Figure 16.8.

Although the primary new state strategy is the single and pairwise exchange of cells, other new state generators have been proposed and adopted. In row-based standard cell placement algorithms, cell orientation and exchange of adjacent cells are common moves at low temperatures. Floorplanning or macrocell placers are augmented with aspect ratio modification, and pin optimization moves. Simulated annealing device placement algorithms are further enhanced with transistor folding, diffusion merging, cell grouping, and symmetry operations. Hustin and Sangiovanni-Vincentelli proposed a dynamic and adaptive move strategy that optimizes the amount of work performed at each temperature. They compute a quality factor for each type of move m for a given temperature T [21]:

$$Q_m^T = \frac{\sum_{j \in A_m} |\Delta C_j|}{\|G_m\|} \qquad (16.21)$$

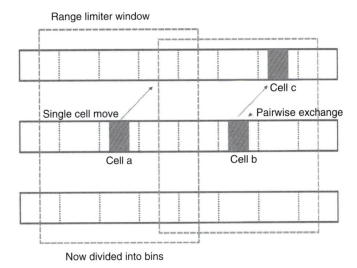

FIGURE 16.8   Automatic move strategy.

where

    $\|G_m\|$ is the number of generated moves
    A_m is subset of accepted moves of type m, that is, $A_m \subseteq G_m$
    $|\Delta C_j|$ is absolute value of the change in cost due to the accepted move m

The probability of proposing the move m at a given temperature is then given by

$$p_m^T = \frac{Q_m^T}{\sum_m Q_m^T} \qquad (16.22)$$

As you can see, the quality factor and hence probability of selecting a move m will be high when moves of this type are frequently accepted or when the average change in cost is large at the current temperature. This method discourages small delta cost moves at high temperatures where they would have little impact on the progress of exploring the state space and discourages large delta cost moves at low temperatures where such moves would drastically perturb the current state and have little chance of acceptance.

Sechen and Lee's work describes many of the details of implementing a simulated annealing placer. It is the basis for many of the advanced works in the field. It is available in source code in the SPEC CPU2000 benchmark set [22].

16.7   MULTILEVEL METHODS

To reduce the execution time of simulated annealing placement, multilevel methods were introduced. Mallela and Grover were the first to introduce a two-step annealing process to standard cell placement to reduce runtime [23]. The execution time is reduced by effectively reducing the size of the problem through clustering of the standard cells. First they form clusters of cells based on their interconnections. Cells that are highly interconnected will be placed into the same cluster. The execution time of the clustering algorithm is only a small fraction of simulated annealing placement time. The clustered netlist is then placed using simulated annealing placement. Because the number of total cells has been reduced, the execution time of the simulated annealing problem is reduced. Next, the clusters are broken up and the original netlist is restored. Then a final low temperature simulated annealing is performed where the range of cell movement is limited and the number of moves per cell is greatly reduced; thereby the overall execution time is reduced. This resulted in a factor of 2–3 speedup in execution time and a 6–17 percent improvement in half-perimeter wirelength.

Sun and Sechen increased the number of levels of clustering to three [15]. They were able to achieve up to 7.5× speedup on designs containing 25,000 placeable objects. They also saw an improvement in half-perimeter wirelength due to clustering although some of the improvement may be due to their new cost function and wire estimation model. In this work, the cost function used only contained the sum of the half-perimeter wirelengths and timing constraints. All penalty functions were removed so that there would be no need for the sophisticated negative feedback controller used to weigh the penalty terms. Instead only moves that generated no overlap were allowed.

16.8 PARTITION-BASED METHODS

Simulated annealing placers have also incorporated partitioning techniques to achieve better quality and speed. NRG [24] and Tomus [25] convert the placement problem to a partitioning problem that is solved using simulated annealing. The placement problem is reduced by dividing the row topology into uniform grids or bins. Each standard cell or field programmable gate array lookup table (FPGA LUT) is assigned to a bin. A penalty term is introduced to maintain uniform cell density among the bins. Standard cells are exchanged by picking two cells in different bins and swapping them. Because the number of bins is much smaller than the possible standard cell positions, the search space is reduced resulting in a speedup. A second or detailed placement phase ensues, which removes any residual overlap and legalizes the placement of the cells. Both of these algorithms worked on a flat netlist and did not scale well for larger netlists. The NRG work was enhanced to overcome these shortcomings in the Dragon 2000 placer and derivatives and is the subject of Chapter 15.

16.9 GENETIC PROGRAMMING

Genetic programming is a related stochastic algorithm. Genetic programming is an attempt to mimic the known processes of evolution to solve problems [26,27]. A solution to the problem is represented by a string of symbols. Each solution has an associated cost or score. New solutions known as offspring are generated by combining parts of the solutions from two parent solutions in what is known as a crossover operation. In addition, a new solution may be formed by mutating a string by randomly changing one or more symbols in the string. Initially, a large number of solutions known as the population are constructed. This population is evolved by creating new offspring solutions and maintaining only the fittest solutions. The final solution is the best solution found at a fixed number of generations. A genetic placement algorithm was proposed by Cohoon and Paris [26] and results were furnished for small examples.

The advantage of genetic approach is that large number of possible solutions are maintained increasing the likeliness of a good final solution. It is often stated that simulated annealing is a special case of genetic programming where the population is one. This is not true. In genetic programming, there is not a stationary Boltzmann distribution to manipulate, which would allow the algorithm to converge. This lack of convergence guarantee is the biggest disadvantage of genetic programming.

Several works [28,29] were proposed to overcome this weakness. SAGA [28] attempted to rectify the problem by starting with a genetic algorithm and then slowly convert to a simulated annealing algorithm by pruning the population. Mahfoud and Goldberg [29] sought a parallel simulated annealing algorithm. They proposed an algorithm that manipulates a population of simulated annealing solutions rather than a single solution. It employs crossover and mutation operators like standard genetic programming but holds Boltzmann trials between children and parents to determine the fittest members. It slowly lowers the temperature to achieve convergence. Unfortunately, this work has not been applied to standard cell placement.

16.10 PARALLEL ALGORITHMS

To further reduce the execution time of the simulated annealing placement algorithm, several multiple processor algorithms were proposed. A parallel algorithm may be characterized by the computer organization for which it is designed (multiple instruction, multiple data architecture [MIMD] or single instruction, multiple data architecture [SIMD]) and its granularity (fine or coarse). There have been four general strategies utilized in parallel simulated annealing programs: single move acceleration, parallel moves, multiple Markov chains, and speculative computation [30]. The single move acceleration strategy attempts to break up an individual move into subtasks, which are evaluated on separate processors. Such strategies require shared memory and do no scale well. In the parallel move strategy, each processor generates and evaluates moves independent of any other processor. Unfortunately, care must be taken so that the moves do not interact and give erroneous results. The multiple Markov chain approach uses concurrent but separate simulated annealing chains, which are periodically exchanged. Finally, the speculative computation strategy attempts to predict the future behavior of simulated annealing moves.

Kravitz and Rutenbar [6] proposed an adaptive parallel simulated annealing placement algorithm where in the high-temperature regime, a move is decomposed into subtasks and distributed across different processors and in the low-temperature regime, multiple complete moves are performed in parallel. The authors introduced the concept of "serializable subset" of moves to prevent interaction between processors. A serializable subset is an ordered subset of moves that, if evaluated serially, would produce the same accept and reject decisions as a parallel evaluation of moves. Unfortunately, it is prohibitively expensive to maintain a large serializable set and the authors seek a simple set of one accepted move and the remainder rejected moves. Although this guarantees that no conflict arises between the processors, it is only applicable at low temperatures where the acceptance rate is low.

Cassotto et al. used clustering on a 8 processsor shared memory computer to achieve six times improvement in speed without loss of quality [4]. Sun and Sechen achieve near linear speedup for on a network of workstations using the parallel move approach [16].

Other algorithms [5] have been proposed on hypercube multiprocessors. The lack of access to such specialize hardware has made this work less practical. Chandy et al. attempted to overcome these problems by proposing a framework for implementing parallel simulate annealing placement on a wide range of parallel architectures [30].

16.11 MACHINE LEARNING

Over time there have been many advancements in the evolution of the simulated annealing placer. These include clustering, hierarchy, annealing schedules, range limiters, and move sets. Each of these improvements was introduced on a trial-and-error basis using empirical tests. Su et al. [31] proposed statistical learning techniques to learn and discover strategies to improve and speed the execution of simulated annealing placers. The researchers created a response model that comprised of seven normalized parameters for each of ten temperature regions:

$$y = B_0 + \sum_{i=1}^{r} \sum_{j=1}^{q} B_j^i p_j^i \qquad (16.23)$$

where
$r = 10$
$q = 7$

The parameters were drawn from placement literature and included force-directed placement and quadratic placement features. The linear regression algorithm was trained using a set of examples to correlate the model with the final solution quality measured with the half-perimeter wirelength metric. After training, the 70 parameter value coefficients were examined and those close to zero were eliminated. The trained annealing algorithm was then run on a set of new examples to determine the efficiency of the new placement algorithm. Remarkably, the trained algorithm had discovered the range window limiter algorithm automatically. The trained algorithm outperformed the base algorithm in both speed and quality. Although the regression analysis is limited by the quality of input parameters, this technique is unique in its ability to tune simulated annealing algorithms to their proper values. When new parameters or techniques are discovered, this methodology allows these parameters to be incorporated easily into the simulated annealing framework.

16.12 FUTURE

Although other placement methods have supplanted simulated annealing in the computed-aided design community, these new methods do not compare favorably with simulated annealing on small designs, that is, designs under 25,000 placeable objects. The state-of-the-art placement algorithms are foremost focused on capacity so much that the placement problem was redefined to encompass two stages: global and detailed placement. In the global placement phase, cell positions are not necessarily legal and may overlap. This phase serves only to minimize wirelength, timing, and congestion constraints. A second phase known as detail placement is performed to legalize the placement such that cell overlaps are removed and each cell is mapped to a valid position in the row. Traditional simulated annealing placers do not make this distinction. Simulated annealing placement has not scaled well as design sizes have increased compared with the latest state-of-the-art placement algorithms. Simulated annealing placers dominate results at small design sizes. Perhaps applying newer multilevel clustering techniques may further improve the performance of simulated annealing placers.

REFERENCES

1. Kirkpatrick S, Gelatt C., and Vecchi M., Optimization by simulated annealing, *Science*, 220(4598), 671, 1983.
2. Metropolis N., Rosenbluth A., Rosenbluth M., Teller A., and Teller E., Equations of state calculations by fast computing machines, *Journal of Chemical Physics*, 21, 1087, 1953.
3. Mitra D., Romeo F., and Sangiovanni-Vincentelli A., Convergence and finite-time behaviour of simulated annealing, Electronics Research Laboratory, College of Engineering, University of CA, Berkeley, 1985.
4. Casotto A., Romeo F., and Sangiovanni-Vincentelli A., A parallel simulated annealing algorithm for the placement of macro-cells, *IEEE Transactions on CAD*, 6(5), 838, 1987.
5. Banerjee P., Jones H. M., and Sargent J. S., Parallel simulated annealing algorithms for cell placement on hypercube multiprocessors, *IEEE Transactions of Parallel and Distributed Systems*, 1(1), 91, 1990.
6. Kravitz S. A. and Rutenbar R. A., Placement by simulated annealing on a multiprocessor, *IEEE Transactions on CAD* 6(4), 534, 1987.
7. Green J. W. and Supowit K. J. Simulated annealing without rejected moves, *IEEE Transactions on CAD*, 5(1), 221, 1986.
8. Lam J. and Delosme J. M., Performance of a new annealing schedule, *Proceedings of the 25th Design Automation Conference*, Anaheim, CA, 306, 1988.
9. Rose J., Klebsch W., and Wolf J., Temperature measurement and equilibrium dynamics of simulated annealing placements, *IEEE Transactions on CAD*, 9(3), 253, 1990.
10. Sechen C. and Sangiovanni-Vincentilli A., The TimberWolf placement and routing package, *IEEE Journal of Solid-State Circuits*, 20(2), 432, 1985.
11. Sechen C. and Sangiovanni-Vincentelli A., TimberWolf3.2: A new standard cell placement and global routing package, *Proceedings of the Design Automation Conference*, Las Vegas, NV, 432, 1986.
12. Sechen C. and Lee K. L., An improved simulated annealing algorithm for row-based placement, *Proceedings of ICCAD*, Las Vegas, NV, 478, 1987.
13. Sechen C., Chip-planning, placement, and global routing of macro/custom intergrated circuits using simulated annealing, *Proceedings of the Design Automation Conference*, Atlantic City, NJ, 73, 1988.

14. Sechen C., *VLSI Placement and Global Routing Using Simulated Annealing*, Kluwer Academic Publishers, Boston, MA, 1988.
15. Sun W. J. and Sechen C., Efficient and effective placement for very large circuits, *Proceedings of ICCAD*, Santa Clara, MA, 170, 1993.
16. Sun W. and Sechen C., A loosely coupled parallel algorithm for standard cell placement, *Proceedings of ICCAD*, San Jose, CA, 137, 1994.
17. Swartz W. and Sechen C., Timing driven placement for large standard cell circuits, *Proceedings of Design Automation Conference*, San Francisco, CA, 211, 1995.
18. Swartz W. and Sechen C., New algorithms for the placement and routing of macro cells, *Proceedings of ICCAD*, Santa Clara, CA, 336, 1990.
19. Siarry P., Berthiau P. G., Durbin F., and Haussy J., Enhanced simulated annealing for globally minimizing functions of many-continuous variables, *ACM Transactions on Mathematical Software*, 23, 209, 1997.
20. Kahng A. B. and Xu X., Accurate pseudo-constructive wirelength and congestion estimation, International Workshop on System-Level Interconnect Prediction, Monterey, CA, 61, 2003.
21. Hustin S. and Sangiovanni-Vincentelli A., TIM, a new standard cell placement program based on the simulated annealing algorithm, paper 4.2, International Workshop on Placement and Routing, Research Triangle Park, NC, May 10–13, 1988.
22. Available at http://www.spec.org/benchmarks.html.
23. Mallela S. and Grover L., Clustering based simulated annealing for standard cell placement, *Proceedings of 25th Design Automation Conference*, Atlantic City, NJ, 312, 1988.
24. Sarrafzadeh M. and Wang M., NRG: Global and detailed placement, *Proceedings of ICCAD*, San Jose, CA, 532, 1997.
25. Roy K. and Sechen C., A timing driven n-way chip and multi-chip partitioner, *Proceedings of ICCAD*, Santa Clara, CA, 240, 1993.
26. Cohoon J. P. and Paris W. D., Genetic placement, *Proceedings of ICCAD*, Santa Clara, CA, 422, 1986.
27. Kling R. M. and Banerjee P., ESP: A new standard cell placement package using simulated evolution, *Proceedings of the IEEE Design Automation Conference*, Miami Beach, FL, 60, 1987.
28. Esbensen H. and Mazumder P., SAGA: A unification of the genetic algorithm with simulated annealing and its application to macro-cell placements, *Proceedings of the 7th International Conference on VLSI Design*, Calcutta, India, 211, 1994.
29. Mahfoud S. and Goldberg D., Parallel recombinative simulated annealing: A genetic algorithm, *Parallel Computing*, 21(1), 1, 1995.
30. Chandy J. A., Kim S., Ramkumar B., Parkes S., and Banerjee P., An evaluation of parallel simulated annealing strategies with application to standard cell placement, *IEEE Transactions on CAD*, 16(4), 398, 1997.
31. Su L., Buntine W., Newton A. R., and Peters B.S., Learning as applied to stochastic optimization for standard cell placement, *IEEE Transactions on CAD*, 20(4), 516, 2001.

17 Analytical Methods in Placement

Ulrich Brenner and Jens Vygen

CONTENTS

17.1   INTRODUCTION

The basic idea of analytical placement consists of first placing the cells optimally in terms of an appropriate netlength estimation (but without considering disjointness constraints) and then working toward disjointnesss. For the second step, we can distinguish two main approaches. One method consists of modifying the objective function in small steps to force cells to move away from each other. Such force-directed approaches will be described in Chapter 18. In this chapter, we consider methods that reduce overlaps by recursive partitioning of the chip area and the set of cells to be placed. This partitioning is done in such a way that no subregion of the chip area contains more cells than fit into it. Consequently, when the regions are small enough, the cells will be spread over the chip area.

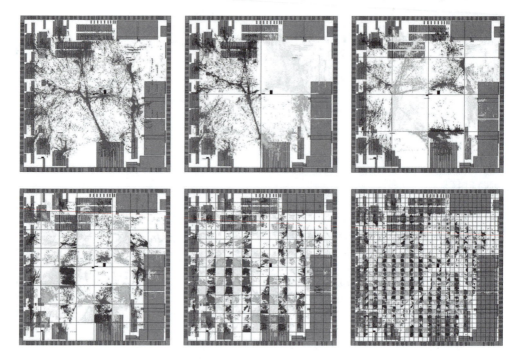

FIGURE 17.1   First six steps of an analytical placer.

Such an analytical placer is illustrated in Figure 17.1. The large objects are preplaced macros. The first picture shows a placement of the movable cells with minimum squared netlength (with many overlaps). Then, in each partitioning step, the regions and the sets of cells are divided into four parts, indicated by different gray scales. We will explain the details later in this chapter.

Analytical placement is based on the ability to minimize netlength efficiently. Therefore, we first discuss this in Section 17.2. We define various measures for netlength and show how to minimize linear and quadratic netlengths. For reasons that we will discuss, most analytical placers use quadratic netlength. Important properties of placements with minimum quadratic netlength are summarized in Section 17.3.

Minimizing quadratic netlength goes back to Tutte (1963) who used it for finding straight-line embeddings of planar graphs. Then, this technique has been applied to placement by Fisk, et al. (1967), Quinn (1975), and Quinn and Breuer (1979). They tried to reduce overlaps between cells by computing iteratively repulsing forces (see Chapter 18).

Probably, the first approach to combine algorithms for minimizing netlength with recursive partitioning has been presented by Wipfler et al. (1982). They adapt the approach by Quinn and Breuer (1979) and used the result as a guideline for recursive bisection steps. We explain bisection and the more sophisticated approaches used today in Section 17.4.

In Section 17.5, we describe methods how the partitioning results can be incorporated in the ensuing netlength optimization steps. Section 17.6 deals with practical aspects of analytical placement implementations.

17.2   HOW TO MINIMIZE NETLENGTH

17.2.1   WHAT IS NETLENGTH?

As discussed in Chapter 14, it is not easy to say what a good placement is. The main design objectives timing, power consumption, and manufacturing cost can be influenced only indirectly by placement, as later design steps such as timing optimization or routing follow. Nevertheless, there is a need for objective functions that can be evaluated fast.

The most widely adopted quality measure is netlength. Netlength can be defined in various ways, but the idea is always to estimate the wirelength after routing a given placement. Timing is typically taken into account by giving critical nets a higher weight (see Chapter 21).

To allow for fast estimation (and possibly optimization) of wirelength, one considers each net individually. This assumes that each net can be wired optimally, disregarding other nets. Of course, this is not the case, but it is a reasonable approximation, at least for the majority of the nets and in particular for the most critical ones, unless there is serious routing congestion (which one should avoid anyway; cf. Chapter 22).

For each net we can consider a shortest rectilinear Steiner tree connecting the pins (see Chapter 24), but we shall also consider other estimates. Formally, we define

Definition 1   *Given a set $\mathcal{N}$ of disjoint nets, each of which is a set of pins, netweights $w : \mathcal{N} \to \mathbb{R}_{\geq 0}$, pin positions $(x, y) : \bigcup \mathcal{N} \to \mathbb{R}^2$, and a function $\mathcal{M} : \{V \subseteq \mathbb{R}^2 | 2 \leq |V| < \infty\} \to \mathbb{R}_{\geq 0}$ (a net model), the (weighted) netlength with respect to $\mathcal{M}$ is*

$$\sum_{N \in \mathcal{N}} w(N)\mathcal{M}(\{(x, y)(p) : p \in N\}).$$

Typically, a pin shape consists of several rectangles, but this is largely ignored during placement, and a representative point is chosen for each pin. As pin shapes are relatively small, the error resulting from this simplification is also rather small, at least in global placement. Detailed placement (legalization; cf. Chapter 20) can improve by considering the actual pin shapes.

The most natural net model, which is closest to the actual wirelength to be expected after routing, is the minimum length of a rectilinear Steiner tree.

However, computing a shortest rectilinear Steiner tree for a given set of points in the plane is NP-hard (Garey and Johnson, 1977). This is one reason why other net models are useful. The following net models have been considered in placement (see also Chapters 7 and 14). Let $V \subseteq \mathbb{R}^2$ be a finite set of points in the plane.

- Steiner(V) is the length of a shortest rectilinear Steiner tree for V.
- BB(V) is half the perimeter of the bounding box of V, that is,

$$\max_{(x,y)\in V} x - \min_{(x,y)\in V} x + \max_{(x,y)\in V} y - \min_{(x,y)\in V} y.$$

- Clique(V) is $\frac{1}{|V|-1}$ times the sum of rectilinear distances over all pairs of points in V, that is,

$$\frac{1}{|V| - 1} \sum_{(x,y),(x',y')\in V} (|x - x'| + |y - y'|).$$

- Star(V) is the minimum total rectilinear distance of an auxiliary point to all elements of V, that is,

$$\min_{(x',y')\in\mathbb{R}^2} \sum_{(x,y)\in V} (|x - x'| + |y - y'|).$$

The factor $\frac{1}{|V|-1}$ in the clique estimate is standard to avoid that nets with many pins dominate the netlength, but other factors (like $\frac{2}{|V|}$) have also been used (see, e.g., Alpert et al., 1999).

The bounding box and the star estimate can both be determined in linear time: the auxiliary point for a star can be found by two median searches (Blum et al., 1973). The clique estimate can be computed in $O(|V| \log |V|)$ time by scanning the points after sorting in each coordinate.

TABLE 17.1

Bounds on the Ratios of Different Net Models

	BB(V)	Steiner(V)	Clique(V)	Star(V)
BB(V)	1	1	1	1
Steiner(V)	$\dfrac{\lceil\sqrt{n-2}\rceil}{2}+\dfrac{3}{4}$	1	$\begin{cases}\dfrac{9}{8} & \text{for } n = 4 \\[2pt] 1 & \text{for } n \neq 4\end{cases}$	1
Clique(V)	$\dfrac{\lceil\frac{n}{2}\rceil\lfloor\frac{n}{2}\rfloor}{n-1}$	$\dfrac{\lceil\frac{n}{2}\rceil\lfloor\frac{n}{2}\rfloor}{n-1}$	1	1
Star(V)	$\left\lfloor\dfrac{n}{2}\right\rfloor$	$\left\lfloor\dfrac{n}{2}\right\rfloor$	$\dfrac{n-1}{\lceil\frac{n}{2}\rceil}$	1

The following result tells how well the other three net models approximate the length of an optimum rectilinear Steiner tree. For two-terminal nets, all the net models are identical.

Theorem 1 *Let V be a finite set of points in $\mathbb{R}^2$ and $n := |V| \geq 3$. Then Table 17.1 shows an upper bound on $\frac{\mathcal{M}_1(V)}{\mathcal{M}_2(V)}$ for net models $\mathcal{M}_1$ (row) and $\mathcal{M}_2$ (column) from BB, Steiner, Clique, and Star.*

As an example how to read Table 17.1, the entry in the second row and third column says that Steiner(V) $\leq \frac{9}{8}$ Clique(V) for all V and Steiner(V) $\leq$ Clique(V) if $n \neq 4$. All inequalities are essentially tight for all n. This result is due to Brenner and Vygen (2001).

In particular, Theorem 1 yields Steiner(V) $\leq$ Clique(V) $\leq$ Star(V) for $n \neq 4$. Hence, the clique model is superior to the star model as it estimates the length of an optimum rectilinear Steiner tree more accurately. Indeed, a clique is an optimum graph with fixed topology in this respect:

Theorem 2 *Let $n \in \mathbb{N}, n \geq 2$. Let G be a connected undirected graph with $V(G) \supseteq \{1,\ldots,n\}$, and with edge weights $w : E(G) \to \mathbb{R}_{>0}$. For $x, y : \{1,\ldots,n\} \to \mathbb{R}$ let*

$$\mathcal{M}_{(G,w)}(x,y) := \min\left\{\sum_{e=\{u,v\}\in E(G)} w(e)(|x(u)-x(v)|+|y(u)-y(v)|)|\right.$$

$$\left. x,y : V(G)\setminus\{1,\ldots,n\} \to \mathbb{R}\right\}.$$

Now define $r(G,w)$ to be the ratio of supremum over infimum of the set

$$\left\{\mathcal{M}_{(G,w)}(x,y) \mid x,y : \{1,\ldots,n\} \to \mathbb{R},\ \text{Steiner}(\{[x(1),y(1)],\ldots,[x(n),y(n)]\}) = 1\right\}.$$

Then this ratio is minimum for the complete graph on $\{1,\ldots,n\}$ with uniform weights; it equals $\frac{3}{2}$ for $n = 4$ and $\dfrac{\lceil\frac{n}{2}\rceil\lfloor\frac{n}{2}\rfloor}{n-1}$ for $n \neq 4$. In this sense, the clique model is optimal for all n.

This is also a result of Brenner and Vygen (2001). A special case that is interesting in the context of net models for mincut approaches was considered before by Chaudhuri et al. (2000).

How fast a net model can be computed and how good it approximates the shortest rectilinear Steiner tree are not the only criteria for net models. Another important issue is how well we can optimize netlength with respect to a given net model, assuming that we do not care about overlaps. This is discussed in the following sections.

17.2.2 MINIMIZING NETLENGTH

A key step in analytical placement is to find a placement that minimizes netlength (with respect to a certain net model), disregarding overlaps. This step assumes that there are some fixed pins, because otherwise one can achieve netlength close to zero by placing everything on the same position.

The netlength depends on the pin positions. Each pin either belongs to a movable cell or has a fixed position. We write $\gamma(p)$ to denote the cell that p belongs to, and $\gamma(p) := \square$ if p is fixed. We denote by $[x_{\text{offs}}(p), y_{\text{offs}}(p)]$ the offset of p with respect to $\gamma(p)$, or the absolute position of p if p is fixed.

A placement is a pair of coordinates $[x(c), y(c)]$ for each $c \in C := \{\gamma(p) | p \in P\} \setminus \{\square\}$. It implies pin positions $[x(p), y(p)] = \{x[\gamma(p)] + x_{\text{offs}}(p), y[\gamma(p)] + y_{\text{offs}}(p)\}$ for all $p \in P$, where $x(\square) := 0$ and $y(\square) := 0$.

Thus, for a given net model $\mathcal{M}$, and given netweights $w : \mathcal{N} \to \mathbb{R}_{>0}$, minimizing netlength is the problem of finding a placement minimizing $\sum_{N \in \mathcal{N}} w(N) \mathcal{M}(\{(x(\gamma(p)) + x_{\text{offs}}(p), y(\gamma(p)) + y_{\text{offs}}(p)) : p \in N\})$. Let us stress once more that we do not care about overlaps here.

Many net models are the sum of two independent parts, one depending on x-coordinates only, and the other one depending on y-coordinates only. Examples are BB, Clique, and Star, but also common quadratic models (see Section 17.2.4). For such net models, x- and y-coordinates can be optimized separately. This results in two independent one-dimensional problems.

17.2.3 HOW TO MINIMIZE LINEAR NETLENGTH

Netlength with respect to any of the net models BB, Clique, or Star can be minimized efficiently (if we do not care about overlaps). As discussed above, the coordinates can be considered separately, and we use only x-coordinates in our exposition.

The problem of minimizing weighted bounding box netlength can be written as a linear program (LP) by introducing two variables l_N and r_N for the leftmost and rightmost coordinate of a pin of each net N (i.e., the edges of the bounding box), and writing

$$\min \sum_{N \in \mathcal{N}} w(N)(r_N - l_N)$$

subject to

$$l_N \leq x(\gamma(p)) + x_{\text{offs}}(p) \leq r_N \quad \text{for all } p \in N \in \mathcal{N}.$$

This is an LP with $2|\mathcal{N}| + |C|$ variables and $2|P| + |C|$ linear inequality constraints. Fortunately, one does not have to use generic LP solvers but can exploit the special structure of this LP. As noted first by Cabot et al. (1970), this LP is the dual of a transshipment problem (uncapacitated minimum cost flow problem), with a vertex for each variable and two arcs for each pin. More precisely, let G be the digraph with vertex set $V(G) := \{l_N, r_N \mid N \in \mathcal{N}\} \cup C \cup \{\square\}$ and arc set $E(G) := \{[l_N, \gamma(p)], [\gamma(p), r_N] \mid p \in N \in \mathcal{N}\}$. The cost of an arc $[l_N, \gamma(p)]$ is $x_{\text{offs}}(p)$, and the cost of $[\gamma(p), r_N]$ is $-x_{\text{offs}}(p)$. Then we look for a minimum cost flow carrying one unit out of l_N and one unit into r_N for each $N \in \mathcal{N}$.

Given a minimum cost flow, it is easy to obtain an optimum dual solution (a feasible potential in the residual graph) by a shortest path computation.

The theoretically fastest known algorithm for transshipment problems, because of Orlin (1993), has a running time of $O[n \log n(m + n \log n)]$, where n is the number of vertices and m is the number of arcs. In our case, we have $n = |C| + 2|\mathcal{N}|$ and $m = 2|P|$. With the realistic assumption $|\mathcal{N}| \geq |C|$, we get a running time of $O[|\mathcal{N}| \log |\mathcal{N}|(|P| + |\mathcal{N}| \log |\mathcal{N}|)]$. See Korte and Vygen (2008) for more details on minimum cost flows.

The star and the clique model (and any other linear model with fixed topology in the sense of Theorem 2) can be reduced to the bounding box model by adding a cell with a single pin for each auxiliary point and replacing each net equivalently by an appropriate set of two-terminal nets. Of course, this may increase the number of nets substantially.

The converse is also true: optimizing the bounding box netlength as above is equivalent to minimizing netlength in a certain netlist containing two-terminal nets only, computable as follows. Introduce fixed pins at the leftmost possible position L and at the rightmost possible position R. Moreover, introduce cells l_N and r_N, each with a single pin, for each net N, and replace the net N by $2|P| + 2$ two-terminal nets, one connecting L and l_N with weight $w(N)(|N| - 1)$, another one connecting r_N and R with weight $w(N)(|N|-1)$, and for each pin $p \in N$ a net connecting l_N and p and a net connecting p and r_N, each of weight $w(N)$. For any placement of the pins, the weighted netlength of the new netlist is $\sum_{N \in \mathcal{N}} w(N)((|N| - 1)(|R - x(r_N)| + |x(l_N) - L|) + \sum_{p \in N}(|x(p) - x(l_N)| + |x(r_N) - x(p)|))$. For a solution minimizing this expression, we have $x(l_N) = \min_{p \in N} x(p)$ and $x(r_N) = \max_{p \in N} x(p)$, and the above expression reduces to $\sum_{N \in \mathcal{N}} w(N)((|N| - 1)(R - L) + (x(r_N) - x(l_N)))$. Except for a constant additive term this is the weighted bounding box netlength.

For netlists with two-terminal nets only and zero pin offsets, an instance is essentially an undirected graph G with edge weights w, a subset $C \subset V(G)$ of movable vertices and coordinates $x(v)$ for $v \in V(G) \setminus C$. Minimizing bounding box netlength then means finding coordinates $x(c)$ for $c \in C$ such that $\sum_{e=(v,w) \in E(G)} w(e)|x(v) - x(w)|$ is minimized. For this special case, Picard and Ratliff (1978) and later also Cheung (1980) proposed an alternative solution, which may be faster than the minimum cost flow approach described above. Their algorithms solve $|V(G) \setminus C| - 1$ minimum s–t-cut problems in an auxiliary digraph with at most $|C| + 2$ vertices (including s and t) and at most $|E(G)| + |C|$ arcs. Finding a minimum s–t-cut can be accomplished by any maximum flow algorithm. In a digraph with n vertices and m edges, the theoretically fastest one, because of King et al. (1994), runs in $O[nm \log_{2+m/(n \log n)} n]$ time. This approach may be faster than any transshipment algorithm in some cases, in particular if there are only few fixed pin positions and significantly more two-terminal nets than cells. However, it is unclear whether nonzero pin offsets can be incorporated.

17.2.4 How to Minimize Quadratic Netlength

Quadratic netlength is a widely used objective function in analytical placement (see Kleinhans et al., 1991 (Gordian); Alpert et al., 1997; Vygen, 1997; Brenner et al. 2008 (BonnPlace)). It is also in use as a starting point for many force-directed approaches (see Chapter 18).

For quadratic optimization, any net model that replaces each net by a graph with fixed topology may be applied. We will describe quadratic netlength optimization for Clique, the generalization to other graphs is straightforward. Because x- and y-coordinates can be computed independently, we again restrict our description to x-coordinates. We ask for x-coordinates $x(c)$ for each $c \in C$ minimizing

$$\sum_{N \in \mathcal{N}} \frac{w(N)}{|N| - 1} \sum_{p,q \in N} \left((x(\gamma(p)) + x_{\text{offs}}(p)) - (x(\gamma(q)) + x_{\text{offs}}(q)) \right)^2.$$

Thus, up to constant terms the objective function is

$$\sum_{N \in \mathcal{N}} \frac{w(N)}{|N| - 1} \sum_{p,q \in N} \left(x(\gamma(p)) \Big(x(\gamma(p)) + 2x_{\text{offs}}(p) - x(\gamma(q)) - 2x_{\text{offs}}(q) \Big) \right.$$

$$\left. + x(\gamma(q)) \Big(x(\gamma(q)) + 2x_{\text{offs}}(q) - x(\gamma(p)) - 2x_{\text{offs}}(p) \Big) \right).$$

Minimizing this function is equivalent to solving the quadratic program (QP)

$$\min_x x^{\mathsf{T}} A x - 2b^{\mathsf{T}} x \tag{17.1}$$

where $A = (a_{c_1,c_2})_{c_1,c_2 \in C}$ and $b = (b_c)_{c \in C}$ with

$$
a_{c_1,c_2} := \begin{cases} \displaystyle\sum_{N \in \mathcal{N}} \sum_{\substack{p,q \in N: \\ \gamma(p)=c_1, \gamma(q) \neq c_1}} \frac{w(N)}{|N|-1} & : \quad c_1 = c_2 \\[3em] \displaystyle\sum_{N \in \mathcal{N}} \sum_{\substack{p,q \in N: \\ \gamma(p)=c_1, \gamma(q)=c_2}} -\frac{w(N)}{|N|-1} & : \quad c_1 \neq c_2 \end{cases}
$$

and

$$
b_c := \sum_{N \in \mathcal{N}} \sum_{\substack{p,q \in N: \\ \gamma(p)=c, \gamma(q) \neq c}} \frac{w(N)}{|N|-1}(x_{\text{offs}}(q) - x_{\text{offs}}(p)).
$$

Here, the notation x^T denotes transposition of x.

If the netlist is connected, then the matrix A is positive definite, and the function $x \mapsto x^T Ax - 2b^T x$ is convex and has a unique minimum x, namely the solution of the linear equation system $Ax = b$. Moreover, the matrix A is sparse because the number of nonzero entries is linear in the number of pins. With these additional properties, Equation 17.1 can be solved efficiently, for example, by the conjugate gradient method (Hestenes and Stiefel, 1952).

We describe its idea for minimizing $f(x) = x^T Ax - 2b^T x$. The algorithm starts with an initial vector x_0. In each iteration $i (i = 1, 2, \ldots)$ we choose a direction d_i and a number $t_i \in \mathbb{R}_{\geq 0}$ such that $f(x_{i-1} + t_i d_i) = \min\{f(x_{i-1} + td_i)|t \in \mathbb{R}\}$, so we have to solve a one-dimensional quadratic optimization problem to compute t_i. Then, we set $x_i := x_{i-1} + t_i d_i$. For iteration 1, we just set $d_1 := -\nabla f(x_0) = -2Ax_0 + 2b$, that is, we search for a minimum in the direction of the gradient. Obviously, we have $d_1^T \nabla f(x_0 + t_1 d_1) = d_1^T \nabla f(x_1) = 0$. The idea of the conjugate gradient method is to choose the directions d_i in such a way that we have in each iteration $i : d_j^T \nabla f(x_i) = 0$ for all $j \in \{1, \ldots, i\}$. This will be the case if all directions are A-conjugate, that is, if they are nonzero and if for all pairs of directions d_j, d_i we have $d_j^T Ad_i = 0$. Then, because the search directions are linearly independent, the gradient $\nabla f(x_i)$ will be 0 after at most n iterations because it is orthogonal to n linearly independent vectors in $\mathbb{R}^n$. The A-conjugacy of the search vectors can be achieved by setting $d_i := -\nabla f(x_i) + \alpha_i d_{i-1}$ for an appropriate value of $\alpha_i \in \mathbb{R}$.

In each iteration of the conjugate gradient method, one multiplication of the $n \times n$-matrix A and an n-dimensional vector are necessary. The number of iterations is bounded by n, but in practice much less iterations are necessary. Generally, if x^* is the optimum solution of Equation 17.1, we have for $i \in \mathbb{N}$:

$$
\|x_{i+1} - x^*\|_A \leq \frac{\text{cond}_2(A) - 1}{\text{cond}_2(A) + 1}\|x_i - x^*\|_A
$$

where $\|x\|_A = \sqrt{x^T Ax}$ and $\text{cond}_2(A) := \|A\|_2 \cdot \|A^{-1}\|_2 \left(\text{with } \|A\|_2 := \left(\sum_{c_1 \in C} \sum_{c_2 \in C} a_{c_1,c_2}^2\right)^{\frac{1}{2}}\right)$.

In other words, the difference between the vectors x_i and the optimum solution decreases exponentially, and the smaller the condition $\text{cond}_2(A)$ of matrix A is, the faster the algorithm converges. Thus, often preconditioning methods are applied to matrix A that reduce the condition. Note that such a preconditioning only makes sense for our problems if the resulting matrix is still sparse.

According to Theorem 2, Clique is the most accurate approximation of a rectilinear Steiner tree among the net models with fixed topology, and it seems to be reasonable to use this model even when minimizing quadratic netlength. However, for quadratic netlength, Clique may be replaced equivalently by Star. Indeed one can easily show that replacing a clique of n pins with uniform edge weights w by a star with uniform weights nw does not change the optimum; this will reduce memory consumption and running time when applied to cliques exceeding a certain cardinality.

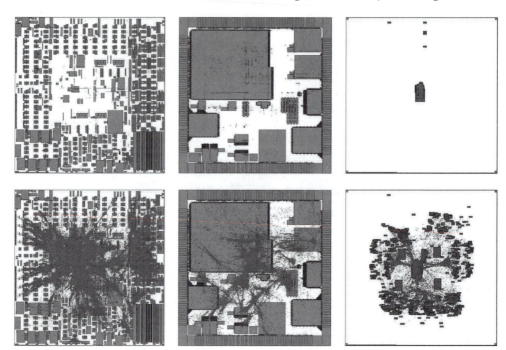

FIGURE 17.2 Placements minimizing linear netlength (upper pictures) and quadratic netlength (lower pictures).

17.2.5 EXAMPLES

For analytical placers, the existence of some preplaced pins is mandatory. Without preplaced pins all cells would be placed at almost the same position in the global optimization (with any reasonable objective function), so we would not get any useful information. Input/output (I/O) pins of the chip will usually be preplaced, and often some of the larger macros will be placed and fixed before placement.

The connections to preplaced pins help to pull cells away from each other but their effect is different for quadratic and linear netlengths. This is illustrated for three chips in Figure 17.2. The first two chips contain some preplaced macros while in the third one, only the I/O pins are fixed and all cells are movable. For each chip, we present two optimum placements for the movable cells minimizing either linear or quadratic netlength. Obviously, in quadratic placement, the connections to the preplaced pins are able to pull the movable cells away from each other, while with the linear objective function, the cells are concentrated at only a very small number of different locations.

17.2.6 OTHER OBJECTIVE FUNCTIONS

Though most analytical placement algorithms optimize quadratic netlength, there are some approaches that use different objective functions. Most of them try to approximate linear netlength by smooth differentiable functions.

The objective functions that we consider in this section consist again of a part for the x-coordinate and a part for the y-coordinate that can be computed independently. We will present again only the part for the x-coordinate.

Sigl et al. (1991) (GordianL) try to combine advantages of linear and quadratic netlength optimizations. Applying the star model, they minimize quadratic netlength but approximate linear netlength by setting netweights that are reciprocally proportional to an estimation of the linear netlength. More precisely, they iteratively compute sequences of locations $[x_i(p), y_i(p)] (i = 0, 1, \ldots)$ for all pins p, and in iteration $i + 1$ they estimate the length of a net N by

$$
\frac{\sum_{p \in N} \left[x_{i+1}(p) - \frac{1}{|N|} \sum_{q \in N} x_{i+1}(q) \right]^2}{\sum_{p \in N} \left| x_i(p) - \frac{1}{|N|} \sum_{q \in N} x_i(q) \right|}
$$

They stop as soon as the locations of the pins do not change significantly anymore. However, there is no proof of convergence.

The single iterations can be performed quite efficiently but because the computations have to be repeated several times, this method is more time consuming than just minimizing quadratic netlength. In the experiments presented by Sigl et al. (1991), the running time of GordianL is about a factor of five larger than the running time of Gordian (but GordianL produces better results).

Alpert et al. (1998) approximate the linear netlength $\sum_{p,q \in N} |x(p) - x(q)|$ of a net N by the so-called β-regularization (for $\beta > 0$):

$$
\text{Clique}_\beta^x(N) = \sum_{p,q \in N} \sqrt{(x(p) - x(q))^2 + \beta}.
$$

$\text{Clique}_\beta^x(N)$ is obviously differentiable and an upper bound of $\sum_{p,q \in N} |x(p) - x(q)|$. Moreover, we have $\text{Clique}_\beta^x(N) \to \sum_{p,q \in N} |x(p) - x(q)|$ for $\beta \to 0$. Of course, net models using other graphs with fixed topology than cliques can be handled analogously. Alpert et al. (1998) apply the primal-dual Newton method that converges to the optimum of this convex objective function.

Kennings and Markov (2002) present a differentiable approximation of the bounding-box netlength. For a net N and parameters $\beta > 0$ and $\eta > 0$, they use

$$
\text{BB}_{\beta,\eta}^x(N) = \left(\sum_{p,q \in N} |x(p) - x(q)|^\eta + \beta \right)^{\frac{1}{\eta}}.
$$

We have $\text{BB}_{\beta,\eta}^x(N) + \text{BB}_{\beta,\eta}^y(N) \geq \text{BB}(N)$ and $\lim_{\eta \to \infty} \lim_{\beta \to 0} [\text{BB}_{\beta,\eta}^x(N) + \text{BB}_{\beta,\eta}^y(N)] = \text{BB}(N)$.

This function if strictly convex (if each connected component of the netlist contains a preplaced pin) and hence can be optimized by the Newton method.

Kahng and Wang (2004) (APlace) and Chan et al. (2005) (mPL) propose to minimize a differentiable approximation to the bounding-box netlength. For a parameter α, they define

$$
\text{BB}_\alpha^x(V) := \alpha \left(\ln \left(\sum_{p \in V} e^{\frac{x(p)}{\alpha}} \right) + \ln \left(\sum_{p \in V} e^{\frac{-x(p)}{\alpha}} \right) \right).
$$

It is easy to see that $\text{BB}_\alpha^x(V) + \text{BB}_\alpha^y(V) \to \text{BB}(V)$ for $\alpha \to 0$. Kahng and Wang (2004) combine this function with a smooth potential function that penalizes placement overlaps to a differentiable objective function that they try to optimize by a conjugate gradient method. However, the resulting objective function is not convex anymore. Moreover, the authors do not show if this method converges to any local minimum. For a more detailed description of the approach, we refer to Chapter 18.

17.3 PROPERTIES OF QUADRATIC PLACEMENT

17.3.1 RELATION TO ELECTRICAL NETWORKS AND RANDOM WALKS

Quadratic placement has a very nice interpretation in terms of random walks. For our exposition, we assume the simplest case that all pin offsets are zero.

Proposition 1   *Given a netlist with zero pin offsets, we define a weighted graph as follows: The vertices are the movable objects (cells) and the fixed pins. For each net N and each pair of pins $p, q \in N$ belonging to different cells c, c' we have an edge with endpoints $\{c, c'\}$ and weight $\frac{w(N)}{|N|-1}$. For each net N and each pair of pins $p, q \in N$, where p belongs to cell c and q is fixed, we have an edge with endpoints $\{c, q\}$ and weight $\frac{w(N)}{|N|-1}$. We assume that some fixed pin is reachable from each cell in this graph.*

We consider random walks in this graph. We always start at a cell, and we stop as soon as we reach a fixed pin. Each step consists of moving to a randomly chosen neighbor, where the probabilities are proportional to the edge weights.

For each cell c, let x_c be the expectation of the x-coordinate of the fixed pin where a random walk started in c ends. Then x_c is precisely the position of c in the quadratic placement.

Proof   It is easy to see that the numbers x_c satisfy the linear equation system $Ax = b$ defined in Section 17.2.4. As it has a unique solution, it is equal to the quadratic placement.   □

This has been generalized to arbitrary pin offsets by Vygen (2007).

Another interpretation of quadratic placement is in the context of electrical networks. Interpret the graph defined above as an electrical network, where edges correspond to connections whose resistance is inversely proportional to the weight, and where a potential of $x(q)$ is applied to each fixed pin q, where $x(q)$ is its x-coordinate. By Ohm's law, a current of $x(c) - x(c')$ is flowing from c to c', where $x(c)$ is the resulting potential of c in this network. By Kirchhoff's law, the numbers x also satisfy the above linear equation system.

17.3.2 STABILITY

In practice, the final netlist of a chip is not available until very late in the design process. Of course, results obtained with preliminary netlists should allow conclusions on results for the final netlist. Therefore, stability is an essential feature of placement algorithms—it is much more important than obtaining results that are close to optimum. When stable placement algorithms are unavailable, one has to enforce stability, for example, by employing a hierarchical design style, dividing the chip into parts and fixing the position of each part quite early. Clearly, such an unflexible hierarchical approach entails a great loss in quality.

For precise statements, we have to formalize the term stability. This requires answers to two questions: When are two placements similar? And what elementary netlist changes should lead to a similar placement?

We first consider the first question. We are not interested in the relative position of two cells unless they are connected. Moreover, if all pins of a net move by the same distance into the same direction, this does not change anything for this net. Therefore, the following discrepancy measure was proposed by Vygen (2007). Again we restrict to zero pin offsets for a simpler notation.

Definition 2   *Let a netlist be given, where $\mathcal{N}$ is the set of its nets and $w: \mathcal{N} \to \mathbb{R}_{\geq 0}$ are netweights. Let two placements be given, and let $[x(p), y(p)]$ and $[x'(p), y'(q)]$ be the position of pin p with respect to the first and second placement, respectively.*

Then the discrepancy of these two placements is defined to be

$$\sum_{N \in \mathcal{N}} \frac{w(N)}{|N| - 1} \sum_{p, q \in N} \left((x(p) - x'(p) - x(q) + x'(q))^2 + (y(p) - y'(p) - y(q) + y'(q))^2 \right).$$

We apply this measure to estimate the effect of small netlist changes on the quadratic placement. The most elementary operation is increasing the weight of a net. As discrepancy is symmetric, this covers also reducing the weight of a net, and deleting or inserting a net. Thus, arbitrary netlist changes can be composed of this operation.

Theorem 3   *Let a netlist be given. We assume that each connected component of the netlist graph contains a fixed pin. Let $[x(p), y(p)]$ be the position of pin p in the quadratic placement of this netlist, and let $[x'(p), y'(p)]$ be its position in the quadratic placement after increasing the weight of a single net N by δ. Then the discrepancy of the two placements is at most $\delta \frac{\lceil \frac{n}{2} \rceil \lfloor \frac{n}{2} \rfloor}{2(n-1)} (X_N^2 + Y_N^2)$, where $n := |N|$ and*

$$X_N := \max\{x(p) \mid p \in N\} \quad \min\{x(p) \mid p \in N\},$$
$$Y_N := \max\{y(p) \mid p \in N\} - \min\{y(p) \mid p \in N\}.$$

This and similar results are proved in Vygen (2007). Roughly speaking, they say that small local changes to a netlist do not change the quadratic placement significantly. In this sense, quadratic placement is stable.

We now argue that other approaches are instable. Even for identical input we can obtain placements with large discrepancy.

Theorem 4   *There exists a constant $\alpha > 0$ such that for each even $n \geq 4$ there is a netlist with n cells and the following properties: Each cell has width $\frac{1}{n}$ and height 1. The chip area in which the cells must be placed is the unit square. Each cell has three, four, or five pins. All pin offsets are zero. All nets have two terminals. There are two optimum placements (with respect to netlength), which have discrepancy at least αn.*

As each optimum placement is a possible result of any local search algorithm, such algorithms are instable. Similarly, Vygen (2007) shows the instability of mincut approaches: there are netlists for which a mincut approach, depending on a tie-breaking rule at the first cut, can produce placements whose discrepancy is proportional to the number of nets (and thus only a constant factor better than the maximum possible discrepancy). Hence, these approaches lack any stability.

This is a reason to favor quadratic placement approaches. Of course, quadratic placements usually contain many overlapping cells, and further steps have to be applied to remove overlaps (cf. Figure 17.2). So far, nobody has succeeded to prove stability of an overall algorithm that produces a feasible placement for any netlist. But at least the basic ingredient, quadratic placement, is stable. Analytical placement algorithms like the ones described in the following, as well as force-directed placement approaches like Eisenmann and Johannes (1998) (cf. Chapter 18) try to modify this placement as little as possible while removing overlaps.

17.4   GEOMETRIC PARTITIONING

17.4.1   Objectives

After minimizing quadratic (or linear) netlength without considering any disjointness constraints, analytical placers start to remove overlaps by partitioning the chip area into regions and by assigning cells to regions such that no region contains more cells than fit into it. As we have a well-optimized placement (but with overlaps), it seems to be reasonable to change it as little as possible, that is, to minimize the total distance that cells move.

More formally, the following problems has to be solved. We are given a set C of movable cells and a set R of regions. Each cell $c \in C$ has a size, denoted by $\text{size}(c)$, and each region $r \in R$ has a capacity, denoted by $\text{cap}(r)$. Moreover, for each pair $(c, r) \in C \times R$ we know the cost $d((c, r))$ of moving cell c to region r. The task is to find a mapping $g : C \rightarrow R$ such that $\sum_{c \in C: g(c) = r} \text{size}(c) \leq \text{cap}(r)$ for all $r \in R$, minimizing $\sum_{c \in C} d((c, g(c)))$.

Unfortunately, to decide if this problem has any feasible solution is NP-complete even if $|R| = 2$ (Karp, 1972). Hence, it is natural to relax the problem by allowing cells to be distributed to different regions. Then we arrive at the following problem:

Fractional assignment problem

Instance: • Finite sets C and R
         • size: $C \to \mathbb{R}_{>0}$
         • cap: $R \to \mathbb{R}_{>0}$
         • $d : C \times R \to \mathbb{R}_{\geq 0}$

Task: Find a mapping $h : C \times R \to [0, 1]$ with $\sum_{r \in R} h((c, r)) = 1$ for all $c \in C$ and $\sum_{c \in C} h((c, r)) \cdot \text{size}(c) \leq \text{cap}(r)$ for all $r \in R$, minimizing $\sum_{c \in C} \sum_{r \in R} h((c, r)) \cdot d((c, r))$.

Considering this fractional version is sufficient because of the following theorem.

Theorem 5 *There is always an optimum solution h of the fractional assignment problem where the set $\{c \in C | \exists r \in R : h((c, r)) \neq \{0, 1\}\}$ has at most $|R| - 1$ elements.*

For a proof, we refer to Vygen (2005). If any optimum solution is given, such an almost integral optimum solution can be computed efficiently.

17.4.2 BIPARTITIONING

If $|R| = 2$, then the fractional assignment problem is equivalent to the fractional knapsack problem (cf. Korte and Vygen, 2008). The unweighted version of this problem (i.e., size$(c) = 1$ for all $c \in C$) can be solved in linear time by using the linear-time algorithm for the median problem described by Blum et al. (1973). Adolphson and Thomas (1977), Johnson and Mizoguchi (1978), and Balas and Zemel (1980) show how the algorithm for the unweighted version can be used as a subroutine for a linear time algorithm of the fractional knapsack problem with weights (cf. Vygen 2005; Korte and Vygen 2008).

Given a nondisjoint placement with minimum (quadratic) netlength, a straightforward partitioning approach consist of bipartitioning the cells set alternately according to the x- and y-coordinates. Indeed, early analytical placement algorithms that have been presented by Wipfler et al. (1982), Cheng and Kuh (1984), Tsay et al. (1988) (Proud), and Jackson and Kuh (1989) apply such a method.

Another analytical placement algorithm based on bipartitioning is Gordian (Kleinhans et al., 1991). The authors try to improve the result of a partitioning step by reducing the number of nets that are cut without increasing the cell movement too much. To this end, they vary the capacities of the subregions (within a certain range), compute cell assignments for the different capacity values, and keep the one with the smallest cut. Moreover, cells may be interchanged between the two subsets after bipartitioning if this reduces the number of nets that are cut.

Sigl et al. (1991) (GordianL) describe an iterative method for bipartitioning. They cope with the problem that if many cells have very similar locations before a partitioning step, the decision to which subset they are assigned is more or less arbitrary. Their heuristic works in two phases, as illustrated in Figure 17.3. Assume that a set of cells (Figure 17.3a) has to be divided into two parts and that we ask for a vertical cut. First, cells with very small or very big x-coordinates are assigned to the left or to the right subset of the partition. In Figure 17.3b, the cells that reach out to the left of coordinate x_1 are assigned to the left part, and the cells that reach out to the right of coordinate x_2 are assigned to the right part. The idea is that the assignment of these cells can hardly be wrong and that the connectivity to them should be used when assigning the remaining cells. The preassigned cells are forced to move further to the left or to the right depending on their assignment. With these additional constraints, new positions for all cells to be partitioned are computed (in GordianL minimizing an

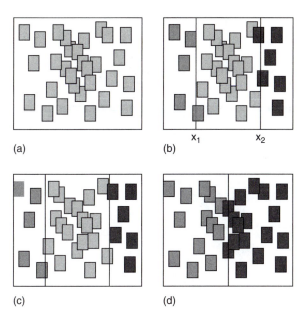

FIGURE 17.3   Iterative partitioning as described by Sigl et al. (1991).

approximation of linear netlength, cf. Section 17.2.6), as shown in Figure 17.3c. Finally, these new positions are used to compute the assignment of the cells (Figure 17.3d).

17.4.3   QUADRISECTION

BonnPlace, an analytical placer proposed by Vygen (1997), makes use of a linear-time algorithm for a special case of the fractional assignment problem. If R consist of four elements r_1, r_2, r_3, and r_4 such that $d((c, r_1)) + d((c, r_3)) = d((c, r_2)) + d((c, r_4))$ for all $c \in C$, then the fractional assignment problem can be solved in time $O(|C|)$ (see Vygen [2005] for a proof). This condition is met if R is the set of the four quadrants of the plane and $d((c, r))$ is the L_1 distance between c and r. Such a partitioning is shown in Figure 17.4 where the gray scales of the cells reflect the region that they are assigned to (e.g., the darkest cells will go to the lower left quadrant). The borderlines between the cell subsets are horizontal, vertical, and diagonal lines that form a geometric structure that is called American map. Vygen (2005) proves that an American map corresponding to an optimum partitioning can be computed in linear time. The algorithm can be seen as a two-dimensional generalization of the median algorithm by Blum et al. (1973).

17.4.4   GRID WARPING

Xiu et al. (2004) (see also Xiu and Rutenbar, 2005) start with a placement that minimizes quadratic netlength but partition the set of cells by borderlines that do not have to be horizontal or vertical.

Assume, for example, that we want to partition the set of cells (and the chip area) into four parts. The chip area is partitioned by a horizontal and a vertical cut running through the whole chip area, thus forming four rectangular regions. To partition the set of cells, Xiu et al. (2004) compute a borderline l_1 connecting the upper edge of the chip area to the lower edge and two borderlines l_2 and l_3 connecting the left (right) edge of the chip area to l_1 (Figure 17.5).

These three borderlines partition the set of cells into four subsets C_1, C_2, C_3, and C_4, and each subset is assigned in the obvious way to a subregion.

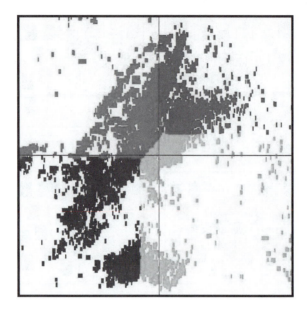

FIGURE 17.4   Set of cells partitioned by quadrisection (according to an American map).

The borderlines used to partition the set of cells shall be chosen such that capacity constraints are met for the subregions and such that routing congestion and netlength are minimized when the cells are moved to their regions. Because it seems to be hard to find optimal cutlines with these optimization goals, the authors apply local search to compute the borderlines. They argue that this is good enough as the number of variables is small (two variables for each cutline). As the algorithm does not only use vertical and horizontal cutlines for the partitioning of the cells and warps the placement in a partitioning step, the authors call it grid-warping partitioning.

17.4.5 MULTISECTION

The fractional assignment problem is solvable in polynomial time because it can be seen as a Hitchcock transportation problem, as special version of a minimum-cost flow problem.

An efficient algorithm for the unbalanced instances that occur in placement (where often $|C|$ is much larger than $|R|$) has been proposed by Brenner (2005) who proved the following theorem:

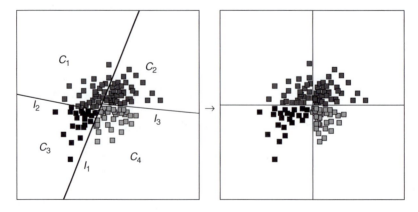

FIGURE 17.5   Grid-warping partitioning step.

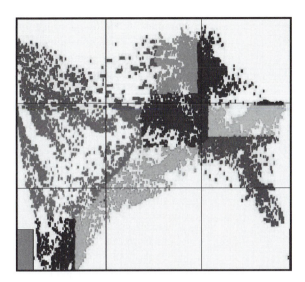

FIGURE 17.6 Set of cells partitioned by multisection.

Theorem 6   *The fractional assignment problem can be solved in time $O[nk^2(\log n + k \log k)]$ where $n := |C|$ and $k := |R|$.*

Thus, for fixed k, the fractional assignment problem can be solved in time $O(n \log n)$. This multisection is slower than the linear-time algorithm for quadrisection proposed by Vygen (2005), but the algorithm is more flexible because it can handle an arbitrary number of regions and an arbitrary costs function. This flexibility can be used, for example, for reducing the number of partitioning steps, and for a more intensive local optimization in repartitioning (see Section 17.6.1; Brenner and Struzyna, 2005). Moreover, movement costs are not restricted to L_1-distances. For example, they could take blocked areas (e.g., used by preplaced macros) into consideration.

An example for multisection with nine regions and L_1-distances as movement costs is shown in Figure 17.6. Again, the gray scales of the cells indicate the region that they are assigned to. As expected, American map structures reappear.

17.5   HOW TO USE THE PARTITIONING INFORMATION

After a partitioning step, each cell is assigned to a region of the chip area. Before the regions (and the corresponding sets of cells) are partitioned further, we have to ensure that the cells are placed (approximately) within their regions. For linear netlength, it is quite obvious how upper and lower bounds on the coordinates of single cells may be added to the LP formulation described in Section 17.2.3. The LP with such additional constraints is still the dual of a minimum-cost flow problem.

If we want to add linear upper and lower bounds for cell positions to the QP (Equation 17.1), this leads to a quadratic objective function that has to be minimized over a convex set. This problem is solvable in polynomial time, but not efficient enough for large instances. Hence, different approaches are used to take the partitioning information into account. We discuss the two main techniques in the following sections.

17.5.1   CENTER-OF-GRAVITY CONSTRAINTS

To move each group of cells toward the region that it has been assigned to, Kleinhans et al. (1991) prescribe the center of gravity of each group as the center of the region that this group is assigned to. For each region, this introduces an equation as an additional constraint on the solution of the QP (Equation 17.1). Kleinhans et al. (1991) show how this constrained quadratic program can be reduced elegantly to an unconstrained QP with the following transformation. For n movable cells and k additional constraints, the constrained QP may be written in the form

$$\min \quad x^T A x - 2b^T x$$
$$\text{s.t.} \quad (I\ S)x = t$$

where the $k \times n$-matrix $(I\ S)$ consists of the $k \times k$-identity matrix I and a $k \times (n-k)$-matrix S. With $x = \begin{pmatrix} x_1 \\ x_2 \end{pmatrix}$ (where $x_1 \in \mathbb{R}^k$ and $x_2 \in \mathbb{R}^{n-k}$), the linear constraints can be written as $x_1 = t - Sx_2$. Hence, we only have to compute the entries of x_2 by solving the following unconstrained problem on $n - k$ variables:

$$\min \quad \begin{pmatrix} t - Sx_2 \\ x_2 \end{pmatrix}^T A \begin{pmatrix} t - Sx_2 \\ x_2 \end{pmatrix} - 2b^T \begin{pmatrix} t - Sx_2 \\ x_2 \end{pmatrix}.$$

By ignoring all constant summands in the objective function, we get the equivalent problem

$$\min \quad x_2^T U^T A U x_2 - 2v^T x_2 \tag{17.2}$$

where $U := \begin{pmatrix} -S \\ I \end{pmatrix}$ and $v := U^T \left[b - A \begin{pmatrix} t \\ 0 \end{pmatrix} \right]$. The matrix $U^T A U$ is positive definite if A is positive definite, but usually $U^T A U$ will not be sparse. Therefore, for an efficient solution, an explicit computation of $U^T A U$ must be avoided. Fortunately, the conjugate gradient method (see Section 17.2.4) only requires to multiply $U^T A U$ with a vector, which can be done by three single multiplications of a sparse matrix and a vector. Hence, provided that the number of constraints is small compared to the number of cells, the conjugate gradient method will efficiently solve the problem (Equation 17.2).

Prescribing the centers of gravity of the cell groups is an efficient way to spread the cells over the chip area. However, we cannot be sure that all cells are placed inside their region, which can be a problem for ensuing partitioning steps. Moreover, the constraints may be too strong if we do not demand an even distribution of the cells. If we allow a higher area utilization in some regions, it will often be reasonable to place cells in their region in such a way that their center of gravity is far away from the center of the region.

17.5.2 SPLITTING NETS

A second way to reflect the result of partitioning in the QP, proposed by Vygen (1997), consists of splitting nets at the borders of regions. In this approach, we assume that the chip area is partitioned in a grid-like manner by vertical and horizontal cutlines that cross the whole chip.

Suppose that we have bounds $\mu \leq x(c) \leq v$ for the x-coordinate of a cell c. For each cell c' that is connected to c but is placed in a window to the right of b (i.e., v is a lower bound on the x-coordinate of c'), we replace the connection to c' by an artificial connection between c and a fixed pin with x-coordinate v. Analogously, connections to cells c' that will be placed to the left of μ are replaced by connections to a fixed pin with x-coordinate μ. Connections to fixed pins outside the bounds of a cell are also split.

Note that this splitting is done for x- and y-coordinate independently, so for x-coordinates only the vertical borderlines and for the y-coordinates only the horizontal borderlines between the windows are considered. In particular, in contrast to standard terminal propagation, it is possible (and in fact will happen quite often) that a connection has to be split for the computation of the x-coordinates but not the y-coordinates, and vice versa. This splitting of the nets forces each cell to be placed inside the region that it is assigned to.

However, a problem that has to be addressed in this approach is the following: it may happen that in a region all cells (or most of them) have their external connection to only one direction. In

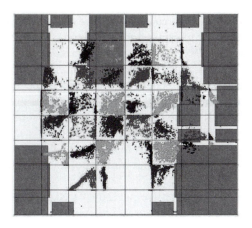 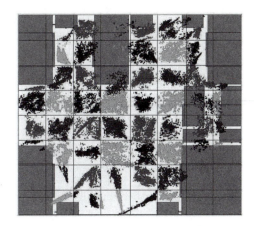

FIGURE 17.7   Effect of the constrained QP before the partitioning step.

that case, a QP solution will place all of them at one border or even in one corner of the region. Such a placement is obviously useless for the next partitioning step based on cell positions. Vygen (1997) proposes to make use of center-of-gravity constraints (see Section 17.5.1) to modify the placements in these cases. Figure 17.7 illustrates how this works. The left picture shows the placement with minimum quadratic netlength (splitting connections at the borderlines as described above) without any additional center-of-gravity constraints.

Based on this we compute a new center of gravity for each region in which the current center of gravity of the cells in the region is closer to the border than it would be possible in any disjoint placement. The new center of gravity is (approximately) the closest possible position in a disjoint placement. Then, a new global QP is solved forcing the centers of gravity of the cell groups in these regions to the new prescribed positions. The right-hand side of Figure 17.7 shows the result. It demonstrates that in particular in the outer regions of the chip area this step changes the placement significantly.

17.6   FURTHER TECHNIQUES

17.6.1   REPARTITIONING

In a pure recursive partitioning approach, cells may never leave their regions. However, especially cell assignments in the first paritioning steps may be suboptimal because they are based on placements in which the cell positions may not differ enough. Therefore, there is need for techniques that are able to correct bad decisions in partitioning. Most analytical placers contain some local optimization methods that are executed between the partitioning steps and that allow cells to leave the regions they are assigned to.

In Gordian (see Kleinhans et al., 1991), cells are moved toward their regions by solving a constrained QP (see Section 17.5.1). As this constrained QP does not force the cells to be placed inside their window, groups of cells that are assigned to different windows may be mixed with each other. In such situations, Kleinhans et al. (1991) reassign cells locally. Let us consider the case when a window is partitioned by a vertical cutline (the case of a horizontal cutline is handled analogously). If after the constrained QP one of the cells assigned to the left window is placed to the right of a cell assigned to the right window, then the two cell subsets are merged and are partitioned once again (using this time the positions of the constrained QP). The old assignment is always replaced by the new assignment. Note that only pairs of cell groups are considered that belong to the same window before the previous partitioning, so this reassignment is the last chance for a cell to leave its window.

After all these new assignments have been computed, a new constrained QP is solved. According to the description by Kleinhans et al. (1991), it is not necessary to iterate this method.

To allow cells to leave their windows even at a late stage, Vygen (1997) proposes a repartitioning technique that tries to find local improvements of the placement. It considers arrays of 2×2 regions (i.e., sets of four regions intersecting in one point) and tries to find a better placement in them. In each such region, the cells are placed with minimum quadratic netlength and are then assigned to the four subregions with a quadrisection step. Finally, a local QP is solved where nets are split according to the new assignment. The new placement is accepted if the total netlength has decreased.

This step is done for all 2×2 arrays of regions. This loop is called repeatedly (with different orders of the arrays of regions) as long as it yields a considerable improvement of the weighted netlength.

Repartitioning enables the cells to leave the region in which they are currently placed. It has also been used by Huang and Kahng (1997) in a minimum-cut-based placer and by Xiu and Rutenbar (2005) in their warping approach.

17.6.2 PARALLELIZATION

Analytical placement methods that use recursive partitioning allow a parallel implementation of most parts of the algorithm. Sometimes, placement and partitioning in one region does not depend on another region, so both regions can be handled in parallel. However, it should be mentioned that many analytical placers apply a global optimization before a partitioning step where all cells are placed simultaneously. For example, in Gordian (Kleinhans et al., 1991), the placements with minimum quadratic netlength (with different center-of-gravity constraints) can hardly be parallelized.

Nevertheless, even some parts of these global optimization steps allow a parallel computation if the assignment of the cells to their windows is used as hard constraints. Assume, for example, that we want to compute the x-coordinate of a cell c for which we have the constraints $\mu \leq x(c) \leq \nu$ for some numbers μ and ν. Then, if we minimize linear netlength, the x-coordinate of c can be computed without knowing the x-coordinates of the cell that have to be placed to the left of μ or to the right of ν. Thus, the x-coordinates in different columns given by the regions can be computed in parallel (and analogously for the y-coordinates).

Such a parallel computation is possible as well if quadratic netlength is minimized and connections are split at the borderlines of regions (see Section 17.5.2).

Also multisection can be done in parallel for separate regions. Moreover, local optimization steps like repartitioning that are often quite time consuming can be performed efficiently in parallel (see Brenner and Struzyna, 2005).

17.6.3 DEALING WITH MACROS

Analytical placers can handle cells of different sizes and shapes. However, recursive partitioning has to stop when cells are too big compared to the region size. Hence, for larger macros only a few partitioning steps can be made. Then, macros have to stay more or less at their position.

In Gordian (Kleinhans et al., 1991), a region is only partitioned if it contains a sufficient number of cells, so in the presence of macros the region sizes may differ over a large range at the end of global placement. Finally, macros are legalized together with the standard cells.

Other analytical placers such as BonnPlace (Vygen, 1997; Brenner and Struzyna, 2005) place the macros legally as soon as they are too big compared to the region size and fix them before continuing with the recursive partitioning.

17.7 CONCLUSION

Analytical placement is the dominant strategy for placement today. Decomposing the task into minimizing netlength and partitioning with respect to area constraints is natural. Using quadratic placement and multisection as the two main components has the advantage that both subproblems can be solved almost optimally very efficiently even for the largest netlists. Moreover, this approach has nice stability features and works well in a timing-closure framework. Therefore, this approach is widely used in industry for many of the hardest placement problems.

REFERENCES

Adolphson, D.L. and Thomas, G.N. A linear time algorithm for a $2 \times n$ transportation problem. *SIAM Journal on Computing* 6: 481–486, 1977.

Alpert, C.J., Chan, T., Huang, D.J.-H., Markov, I., and Yan, K. Quadratic placement revisited. *Proceedings of the 34th IEEE/ACM Design Automation Conference*, Anaheim, CA, 1997, pp. 752–757.

Alpert, C.J., Chan, T.F., Kahng, A.B., Markov, I.L., and Mulet, P. Faster minimization of linear wirelength for global placement. *IEEE Transactions on Computer-Aided Design of Integrated Circuits and Systems* 17: 3–13, 1998.

Alpert, C.J., Kahng, A.B., and Yao, S.-Z. Spectral partitioning: The more eigenvectors, the better. *Discrete Applied Mathematics* 90: 3–26, 1999. (DAC 1995).

Balas, E. and Zemel, E. An algorithm for large zero-one knapsack problems. *Operations Research* 28: 1130–1154, 1980.

Blum, M., Floyd, R.W., Pratt, V., Rivest, R.L., and Tarjan, R.E. Time bounds for selection. *Journal of Computer and System Sciences* 7: 448–461, 1973.

Brenner, U. A faster polynomial algorithm for the unbalanced Hitchcock transportation problem. *Operations Research Letters* 36: 408–413, 2008.

Brenner, U. and Struzyna, M. Faster and better global placement by a new transportation algorithm. *Proceedings of the 42nd IEEE/ACM Design Automation Conference*, Anaheim, CA, 2005, pp. 591–596.

Brenner, U. and Vygen, J. Worst-case ratios of networks in the rectilinear plane. Networks 38: 126–139, 2001.

Brenner, U., Struzyna, M., and Vygen, J. BonnPlace: Placement of leading-edge chips by advanced combinatorial algorithms. To appear in: *IEEE Transactions on Computer-Aided Design of Integrated Circuits and Systems*, 2008.

Cabot, A.V., Francis, R.L., and Stary, A.M. A network flow solution to a rectilinear distance facility location problem. *AIIE Transactions* 2: 132–141, 1970.

Chan, T.F., Cong, J., and Sze, K. Multilevel generalized force-directed method for circuit placement. *Proceedings of the IEEE/ACM International Symposium on Physical Design*, San Francisco, CA, 2005, pp. 227–229.

Chaudhuri, S., Subrahmanyam, K.V., Wagner, F., and Zaroliagis, C.D. Computing mimicking networks. *Algorithmica* 26: 31–49, 2000.

Cheng, C.-K. and Kuh, E.S. Module placement based on resistive network optimization. *IEEE Transactions on Computer-Aided Design of Integrated Circuits and Systems* 3: 218–225, 1984.

Cheung, T.-Y. Multifacility location problem with rectilinear distance by the minimum-cut approach. *ACM Transactions on Mathematical Software* 6: 387–390, 1980.

Eisenmann, H. and Johannes, F.M. Generic global placement and floorplanning. *Proceedings of the 35th IEEE/ACM Design Automation Conference*, San Francisco, CA, 1998, pp. 269–274.

Fisk, C.J., Caskey, D.L., and West, L.E. ACCEL: Automated circuit card etching layout. *Proceedings of the IEEE* 55: 1971–1982, 1967.

Garey, M.R. and Johnson, D.S. The rectilinear Steiner tree problem is *NP*-complete. *SIAM Journal on Applied Mathematics* 32: 826–834, 1977.

Hestenes, M.R. and Stiefel, E. Methods of conjugate gradients for solving linear systems, *Journal of Research of the National Bureau of Standards* 49: 409–439, 1952.

Huang, D.J.-H. and Kahng, A.B. Partitioning based standard cell global placement with an exact objective. *Proceedings of the IEEE/ACM International Symposium on Physical Design*, Napa Valley, CA, 1997, pp. 18–25.

Jackson, M.B. and Kuh, E.S. Performance-driven placement of cell-based ICs. *Proceedings of the 26th IEEE/ACM Design Automation Conference*, Las Vegas, NV, 1989, pp. 370–375.

Johnson, D.B. and Mizoguchi, T. Selecting the Kth element in $X + Y$ and $X_1 + X_2 + \cdots + X_m$. *SIAM Journal on Computing* 7: 147–153, 1978.

Kahng, A.B. and Wang, Q. Implementation and extensibility of an analytic placer. *Proceedings of the IEEE/ACM International Symposium on Physical Design*, Phoenix, AZ, 2004, pp. 18–25.

Karp, R.M. Reducibility among combinatorial problems. In: Miller, R.E. and Thatcher, J.W. (editors), *Complexity of Computer Computations*. Plenum Press, New York, 1972, pp. 85–103.

Kennings, A. and Markov, I. Smoothening max-terms and analytical minimization of half-perimeter wirelength. *VLSI Design* 14: 229–237, 2002.

King, V., Rao, S., and Tarjan, R.E. A faster deterministic maximum flow algorithm. *Journal of Algorithms* 17: 447–474, 1994.

Kleinhans, J.M., Sigl, G., Johannes, F.M., and Antreich, K.J. GORDIAN: VLSI placement by quadratic programming and slicing optimization. *IEEE Transactions on Computer-Aided Design of Integrated Circuits and Systems* 10: 356–365, 1991. (ICCAD 1988).

Korte, B. and Vygen, J. *Combinatorial Optimization: Theory and Algorithms*, Fourth edition. Springer, Berlin, Germany, 2008.

Orlin, J.B. A faster strongly polynomial minimum cost flow algorithm. *Operations Research* 41: 338–350, 1993. (STOC 1988).

Picard, J.C. and Ratliff, H.D. A cut approach to the rectilinear distance facility location problem. *Operations Research* 26: 422–433, 1978.

Quinn, N.R. The placement problem as viewed from the physics of classical mechanics. *Proceedings of the 12th IEEE/ACM Design Automation Conference*, Minneapolis, MN, 1975, pp. 173–178.

Quinn, N.R. and Breuer, M.A. A force directed component placement procedure for printed circuit boards. *IEEE Transactions on Circuits and Systems CAS-26*, 1979, pp. 377–388.

Sigl, G., Doll, K., and Johannes, F.M. Analytical placement: A linear or quadratic objective function? *Proceedings of the 28th IEEE/ACM Design Automation Conference*, San Francisco, CA, 1991, pp. 427–432.

Tsay, R.-S., Kuh, E., and Hsu, C.-P. Proud: A sea-of-gate placement algorithm. *IEEE Design and Test of Computers* 5: 44–56, 1988.

Tutte, W.T. How to draw a graph. *Proceedings of the London Mathematical Society* 13: 743–767, 1963.

Vygen, J. Algorithms for large-scale flat placement. *Proceedings of the 34th IEEE/ACM Design Automation Conference*, Anaheim, CA, 1997, pp. 746–751.

Vygen, J. Geometric quadrisection in linear time, with application to VLSI placement. *Discrete Optimization* 2: 362–390, 2005.

Vygen, J. New theoretical results on quadratic placement. *Integration, the VLSI Journal* 40: 305–314, 2007.

Wipfler, G.J., Wiesel, M., and Mlynski, D.A. A combined force and cut algorithm for hierarchical VLSI layout. *Proceedings of the 19th IEEE/ACM Design Automation Conference*, Las Vegas, NV, 1982, pp. 671–677.

Xiu, Z. and Rutenbar, R.A. Timing-driven placement by gridwarping. *Proceedings of the 42nd IEEE/ACM Design Automation Conference*, Anaheim, CA, 2005, pp. 585–590.

Xiu, Z., Ma, J.D., Fowler, S.M., and Rutenbar, R.A. Large-scale placement by grid-warping. *Proceedings of the 41st IEEE/ACM Design Automation Conference*, San Diego, CA, 2004, pp. 351–356.

18 Force-Directed and Other Continuous Placement Methods

Andrew Kennings and Kristofer Vorwerk

CONTENTS

18.1 INTRODUCTION

Force-directed methods have been studied over the past four decades as a means of placing cells. These methods employ forces to move cells into positions of shorter wirelength or smaller delay. The use of forces was borne out of the physical analogy with Hooke's law in which cells connected by nets can be viewed as exerting attractive spring forces on one another. If the cells in such a system could move freely, they would move in the direction of their forces until the system achieved equilibrium at a minimum energy state. Unfortunately, a minimum energy placement is most often not valid as cells have physical dimensions that are ignored in the spring analogy. Consequently, additional repulsive forces are applied to perturb the cell positions and remove overlap. Force-directed methods, in general, purge cell overlap over many placement iterations, while trading off attractive and repulsive forces to achieve a placement in which cells are placed with little overlap. For example, the progress made by a force-directed placer on circuit IBM04 from the ICCAD04 mixed-size placement benchmark suite [1] is illustrated in Figure 18.1.

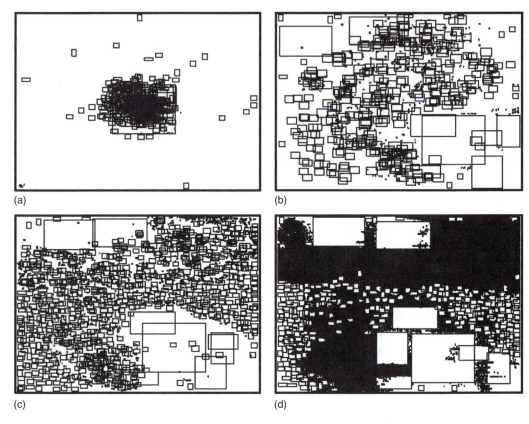

(a)　　　　　　　　　　　　　　(b)

(c)　　　　　　　　　　　　　　(d)

FIGURE 18.1 Typical progression of a force-directed placement method for the circuit IBM04 from the ICCAD04 mixed-size placement benchmark suite: (a) initial placement, (b) after roughly 1/3 through placement, (c) after roughly 2/3 through placement, and (d) before legalization and detailed improvement. The fairly nonoverlapping placement before legalization is obtained without the use of partitioning.

Force-directed methods differ from other placement methods, including simulated annealing, minimum-cut, and analytic methods. Simulated annealing typically begins with an initial feasible (or nearly feasible) placement and applies iterative improvement. Conversely, force-directed methods typically begin with no initial placement and construct the placement as they progress. Minimum-cut and analytic methods are also constructive, but rely on partitioning of the placement area to remove cell overlap. Force-directed methods, however, do not use partitioning, but rather eliminate cell overlap through the introduction of repulsive forces.

The earliest implementations of force-directed methods were examined in the 1960s [2], and many adaptations of these methods remain in use today. Although many variations exist, it is a proper understanding of the similarities and differences between the methods that can lead to either a successful or unsuccessful implementation.

In this chapter, we examine force-directed methods by considering how some of these work. We do not make comparisons between the methods, but rather attempt to illustrate the issues, similarities, and differences between the various implementations described in the literature. We also examine other continuous placement methods (i.e., methods that do not rely on partitioning to remove cell overlap) that, although not seemingly force-directed, still share characteristics with force-directed methods. This chapter is organized as follows. In Section 18.2, we describe the traditional force-directed method that employs quadratic optimization to minimize wirelength and additional constant forces to remove cell overlap. We describe methods that use techniques other than constant forces to eliminate cell overlap in Section 18.3. This includes fixed-point and frequency-based methods. Quadratic optimization is not the best choice for high-quality placements. Many force-directed methods are used in combination with other optimization strategies—we touch upon these interleaved optimizations in Section 18.4. In Section 18.5, we describe other continuous placement techniques and describe their relationships with force-directed methods. Section 18.6 describes several issues facing force-directed methods, and Section 18.7 offers concluding remarks.

18.2 BASIC ELEMENTS OF FORCE-DIRECTED PLACEMENT

Placement typically begins with a circuit netlist modeled as a hypergraph $G_h(V_h, E_h)$ with vertices $V_h = \{v_1, v_2, \ldots, v_n, v_{n+1}, \ldots, v_{n+p}\}$ representing circuit cells and hyperedges $E_h = \{e_1, e_2, \ldots, e_m\}$ representing circuit nets. The set $\{v_1, v_2, \ldots, v_n\}$ represents movable cells and the set $\{v_{n+1}, \ldots, v_{n+p}\}$ represents preplaced cells and I/O pads. Each vertex v_i has dimensions w_i and h_i that represent the width and height of its corresponding circuit cell, respectively. Let (x_i, y_i) denote the coordinates of the center of vertex v_i. Placement information is then captured in the x- and y-directions by two placement vectors $\mathbf{x} = (x_1, x_2, \ldots, x_n)$ and $\mathbf{y} = (y_1, y_2, \ldots, y_n)$.

Placement seeks to optimize objectives, including the minimization of total interconnect length, routing congestion, power consumption, and timing requirements, subject to the constraint that cells cannot overlap. Of course, the simultaneous optimization of these different objectives is difficult. Wirelength is one of the most commonly employed measures of quality—the minimization of wirelength tends to be simpler and also aids in the minimization of other objectives. The most commonly used measurement of wirelength in modern placement is the half-perimeter wirelength (HPWL), which, for any given net $e \in E_H$, is the minimum rectangle that encloses all cells on net e and can be written as

$$\text{HPWL}(e) = \max_{i,j \in e, i<j} |x_i - x_j| + \max_{i,j \in e, i<j} |y_i - y_j| \tag{18.1}$$

The total wirelength of the circuit is given by $\sum_{e \in E_H} \text{HPWL}(e)$. Although HPWL is a convex function, it is neither strictly convex nor differentiable because of the absolute distances $|x_i - x_j|$ and $|y_i - y_j|$—its direct and efficient minimization is difficult. Placement focuses on minimizing an approximation of HPWL subject to the constraint that no cells may overlap. In practice, HPWL is a reasonably close approximation to the final, routed wirelength [3].

18.2.1 QUADRATIC OPTIMIZATION PRELIMINARIES

Kraftwerk [4], perhaps the best-known force-directed placer, introduced a quadratic approximation [5] to HPWL and many other placers have since followed its lead. In quadratic placement, the circuit hypergraph is transformed into a weighted graph. Such a transformation necessitates that each hyperedge be modeled as a set of two-pin nets using a suitable net model. Typical net models include clique or star models, as shown in Figure 18.2 for a five-pin net. In the clique model, each k-pin net is replaced by $k(k-1)/2$ two-pin nets. In the star model, a star node is added for each net to which all pins of the nets are connected. If the weight of a k-pin hyperedge is W, it is common to weight the set of two-pin nets using a weight such as $W/(k-1)$ [6].

The selection of the net model is an implementation decision. It is typical to use a clique model for small nets with few pins, but to switch to the star model for nets with a large number of pins. The clique model results in a denser quadratic optimization problem, whereas the star model tends to improve the sparsity of the problem, but requires additional dummy cells to represent the star nodes. At first glance, it might appear that the choice of net model can influence the solution to the placement problem and this observation is generally true. However, it has been demonstrated [7–9] that weights for the clique and star models can be selected such that the placement solutions are

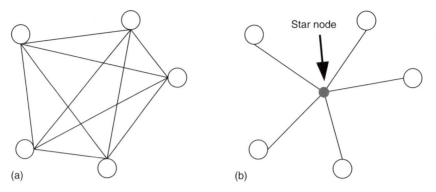

FIGURE 18.2   Models for a five-pin net in which the net is modeled as a (a) clique or as a (b) star. In both cases, the edges in the net model can be weighted. (From Viswanathan, N. and Chu, C.C.-N., *IEEE Trans. CAD 24*, 5, 722, 2005. Copyright IEEE 2005. With permission.)

identical regardless of the model used. Without any loss of generality, we will assume a clique model for all nets in the remainder of our discussion.*

A quadratic placement can be obtained by minimizing the unconstrained objective function given by

$$\Phi(x, y) = \sum_{i,j} w_{i,j}[(x_i - x_j)^2 + (y_i - y_j)^2] \tag{18.2}$$

where w_{ij} represents the weight on the two-pin edge connecting cells i and j in the circuit's weighted graph representation. This objective function is separable into $\Phi(x, y) = \Phi(x) + \Phi(y)$ and can be written in matrix notation (x-direction only) given by

$$\Phi(x) = \frac{1}{2}x^T Q_x x + c_x^T x + \text{const} \tag{18.3}$$

The $n_x \times n_x$ Hessian matrix Q_x encapsulates the connections between pairs of movable cells and is symmetric positive definite.† Vector c_x encapsulates connections between movable cells and fixed cells. Finally, the constant is a result of connections to and between fixed cells. Equation 18.3 is minimized by solving the positive definite system of linear equations given by

$$Q_x x + c_x = 0 \tag{18.4}$$

and is typically solved using any number of iterative solvers including CG, SYMMLQ, GMRES, BICGSTAB, and so forth [10]. Matrix preconditioning is also used to improve the overall efficiency of the iterative solver, including ILU, drop tolerance, and random walk preconditioners [10,11].

Quadratic optimization is often referred to as force-directed placement. Such an analogy follows if the weighted two-pin nets in the circuit's graph approximation are viewed as springs. We can consider the netlist as a system of objects connected by springs with different spring constants (weights). Minimizing the quadratic objective is equivalent to putting the system into a force-equilibrium state in which the resultant force on each movable cell owing to all of the connected spring forces is zero. This result stems from Equation 18.4, in which the ith row of the system of linear equations represents the resultant force on cell i being set to zero.

---

* We note that models based on Steiner trees [12], multipin net decomposition [13], and bounding box [14] have also been suggested in the literature; we refer interested readers to these sources for more information.
† Positive definiteness requires the presence of fixed cells [5,15]. Further, fixed cells are required for a unique solution to the optimization problem.

Unfortunately, solving Equation 18.4 results in a cell placement with significant cell overlap. For example, Figure 18.1a shows the placement for circuit `IBM04` from the `ICCAD04` mixed-size placement benchmark suite [1] after the solution of an unconstrained quadratic program—significant cell overlap clearly exists.

18.2.2 FORCE-BASED SPREADING

Both `Kraftwerk` and `FDP` [16] apply additional constant forces to reduce cell overlap. The force Equation 18.4 is extended with an additional constant force vector $\mathbf{f}_x$ yielding

$$\mathbf{Q}_x\mathbf{x} + \mathbf{c}_x + \mathbf{f}_x = 0 \qquad (18.5)$$

The vector $\mathbf{f}_x$ is used to perturb the placement such that cell overlap is reduced. It is easy to show that the additional forces do not restrict the solution space and that any given placement can satisfy Equation 18.5 by proper selection of $\mathbf{f}_x$ [4].

Cell overlap is not removed just by solving a single perturbation of Equation 18.4 by Equation 18.5. Instead, the cell overlap is removed over numerous iterations with the additional constant forces being updated at each iteration to reflect the changing distribution of cells throughout the placement area. Hence, the additional constant forces are accumulated over iterations and the force equation at any given iteration i can be written as

$$\mathbf{Q}_x\mathbf{x}_i + \mathbf{c}_x + \sum_{k=1}^{i-1} \mathbf{f}_x^k + \mathbf{f}_x^i = 0 \qquad (18.6)$$

The additional constant force is divided into two parts, namely those forces accumulated over previous placement iterations 1 through $i-1$ and a current constant force computed at iteration i. Equivalently, the additional constant force computed at any given iteration is broken into two specific components, namely (1) a stabilizing force that holds the current placement in equilibrium (represented by the accumulation of forces from previous iterations) and (2) a perturbing force computed for a given placement to further reduce cell overlap.

In addition to the requirement that the additional forces be used to distribute cells evenly throughout the placement area, Ref. [4] specifies additional requirements that the forces must satisfy:

1. Force on a cell depends only on its position.
2. Overutilized regions of the placement area are sources of forces.
3. Under-utilized regions of the placement area are sinks of forces.
4. Forces should not form circles.
5. Forces should be zero at infinity.

Given these requirements, the force $f(x, y)$ acting on a cell at position (x, y) within the placement region is computed using Poisson's equation given by

$$\frac{\partial^2 \phi(x, y)}{\partial x^2} + \frac{\partial^2 \phi(x, y)}{\partial y^2} = \kappa d(x, y) \qquad (18.7)$$

where
  $d(x, y)$ is a measure of density at position (x, y)
  κ is a constant of proportionality
  $\phi(x, y)$ is a scalar function such that $\nabla \phi(x, y) = f(x, y)$

Given that forces tend to zero at infinity, a closed form solution for $f(x, y)$ exists and is given by

$$f(x, y) = \kappa \int\limits_{-\infty}^{\infty} \int\limits_{-\infty}^{\infty} d(x', y') \frac{\vec{r}(x, y) - \vec{r}(x', y')}{|\vec{r}(x, y) - \vec{r}(x', y')|^2} dx'dy' \qquad (18.8)$$

where $\vec{r}(x, y)$ is the vector representation of position (x, y). Clearly, there is an analogy to electrostatics where cell area is interpreted as electric charge, $\phi(x, y)$ is electric potential, and $f(x, y)$ represents an electric force field. In practice, the force computation is accomplished using a set of discrete bins superimposed over the placement region. The Poisson equation is solved using discretization and finite differences to determine the values of $\phi(x, y)$ at the centers of bins in the grid. Finally, forces are computed approximately using the difference of $\phi(x, y)$ between adjacent bins.

An alternative approach for force computation was proposed in Ref. [16], where the force computation was based on an analogy with the n-body problem. In this method, the continuous integral in Equation 18.8 is replaced with a bin structure based on a Barnes–Hut quad-tree [17] and the forces are computed using a particle–mesh–particle approach.

The magnitudes (or strength) of the constant forces at each iteration must be determined in relationship to the spring forces representing the quadratic wirelength. The spreading of cells should not be too fast, otherwise the quality of the placement will be compromised. Conversely, the forces should not be weighted too small, otherwise their impact will be negligible and many placement iterations will be required for convergence. Hence, proper force weighting is a significant implementation decision. In Kraftwerk, it is advocated that the maximum strength of all constant forces should be equivalent (normalized) to the force of a net with wirelength $K(W + H)$ where W and H are the width and height of the placement region, respectively. The constant K is a user parameter that can be used to trade-off speed of convergence and the quality of results. However, in Ref. [16], a dynamic weighting is advocated to obtain better placements. Empirically, it was observed that weighting should be (1) small in the early iterations of placement; (2) gradually increased as placement proceeds, but reduced if too much reduction in overlap occurs in any given placement iteration; and (3) large near the end of placement when the final cell positions are effectively determined. In Ref. [16], it was discovered that, at least in the context of mixed-size placement, a further weighting of forces on cells was useful and required due to a large distribution of force weights that depended on the area of the cell. This particular observation is interesting, and also a consequence of how forces were computed Ref. [16].

18.3 ALTERNATIVE TECHNIQUES FOR SPREADING CELLS

Kraftwerk and FDP are examples of force-directed placers that use additional constant forces at each placement iteration to reduce cell overlap. The forces are constant because their calculated magnitudes and directions remain unchanged during a placement iteration, while cell positions are updated through the solution of Equation 18.5. Notwithstanding, constant forces are not the only means by which cells can be spread evenly throughout the placement area. In this section, we consider several proposed alternatives to the use of constant forces.

18.3.1 Fixed Points and Bin Shifting

Fixed points are an alternative approach to remove cell overlap and can be used both to stabilize and to perturb a placement. To understand fixed points and their similarities and differences with constant forces, we begin by defining a pseudocell and a pseudonet in terms of a circuit netlist.

Definition 1   *A pseudocell f is a dimensionless cell fixed at a position (x_f, y_f) that does not exist in the circuit netlist.*

Definition 2 *A pseudonet c(f,i) is a weighted two-pin connection between a pseudocell f and a cell i in the circuit netlist. The pseudonet has a weight equal to $w_{f,i}$ and does not exist in the circuit netlist.*

A fixed point f is defined as a pseudocell connected to exactly one cell $H(f)$ in the netlist through the use of a pseudonet $c(f, H(f))$. The connection is weighted by $w_{f,H(f)}$. Fixed points are used by the placers ARP [18], mFAR [19] and `FastPlace` [8,9].

18.3.1.1 Fixed Points in mFAR

The relationship between fixed points and constant forces was best explained in mFAR [19], where two fixed points are introduced for each cell in the netlist at each placement iteration. The first fixed point for each cell is used to stabilize the position of each cell in force equilibrium, while the second fixed point is used to perturb the cell toward a specific direction aimed at reducing cell overlap.

Any placement with fixed and movable cells (including I/Os) can be transformed into a force-equilibrium state by adding one fixed point to each movable cell. Figure 18.3 illustrates the use of a fixed point versus a constant force to stabilize one cell in a placement. The cell positioned at $(0, 0)$ is connected to two other cells in the netlist. These two connections exert quadratic spring forces on the cell positioned at $(0, 0)$ resulting in a net force of $\overrightarrow{(-3, 0)}$. To stabilize the placement, a constant force of $\overrightarrow{(3, 0)}$ is added in Figure 18.3a to the cell to achieve a resultant net force of zero. Figure 18.3b and c shows two alternatives for achieving force equilibrium using a single fixed point with a weighted connection. Through a combination of the selection for the position of each fixed point f and the weight of the pseudonet connecting the fixed point to its associated cell $H(f)$, the fixed point in Figure 18.3 can be placed anywhere along the x-axis. Any placement can be transformed into force equilibrium in an infinite number of ways using one fixed point for each cell [18].

One additional fixed point per cell can be used to perturb a placement. Figure 18.4 illustrates the use of a fixed point to perturb a placement; in Figure 18.4a, the cell at position $(0, 0)$ is in force equilibrium because of the addition of one fixed point positioned at $(3, 0)$. A perturbing fixed point is added at position $(2, 2)$ as shown in Figure 18.4b and serves to pull the cell in the direction of $(2, 2)$. Finally, Figure 18.4c shows the resulting position of the cell because of the perturbing fixed point. This particular perturbation assumes that the other cells are fixed.

With the addition of fixed points, the objective function for quadratic placement becomes

$$\Phi(x) = \sum_{i,j} w_{i,j}(x_i - x_j)^2 + \sum_f w_{f,H(f)}[x_{H(f)} - x_f]^2 \tag{18.9}$$

where each fixed point f introduces an additional quadratic term, namely $w_{f,H(f)}[x_{H(f)} - x_f]^2$. (A similar term is introduced in the y-direction). Each fixed point f is indistinguishable from fixed cells and I/Os in the original netlist and there remains a trade-off in quadratic wirelength versus the spreading of cells throughout the placement area—the selection of the positions of fixed points and the weight of the pseudonets requires careful consideration.

It is clear that fixed points serve the same purpose as constant forces. However, fixed points stabilize and perturb the placement using spring forces. In Ref. [19], it is claimed that fixed points are a generalization of constant forces, which follows from the observation that a fixed point f is able to mimic a constant force applied to cell $H(f)$ by using a combination of an infinitely large distance between the fixed point f and the cell $H(f)$ and an infinitely small weight on the pseudonet $w_{f,H(f)}$. Specifically, we can let the spring force introduced by the fixed point—$w_{f,H(f)}[x_{H(f)} - x_f]$—be equal to some constant force applied to the cell. As the fixed point moves to a distance of infinity, we simply adjust the weight of the pseudonet. As the fixed point approaches infinity, the angle between the fixed point f and the cell $H(f)$ becomes negligible and any movement of cell $H(f)$ has no effect on the spring force. Hence, the spring force remains constant in both its magnitude and direction.

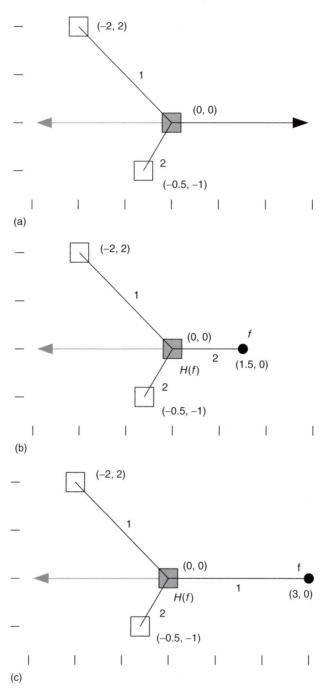

FIGURE 18.3 Illustration of a stabilizing constant force versus stabilizing fixed points. In (a), a constant force is calculated to stabilize the shown cell by countering the spring forces. In (b) and (c), two alternatives for stabilizing the cell with a fixed point are shown. In fact, a fixed point can be positioned anywhere along the *x*-axis to stabilize the placement given an appropriate choice for the weight of the pseudonet. The direction of the spring force exerted by the fixed point on the cell is not constant, but varies as the cell changes position.

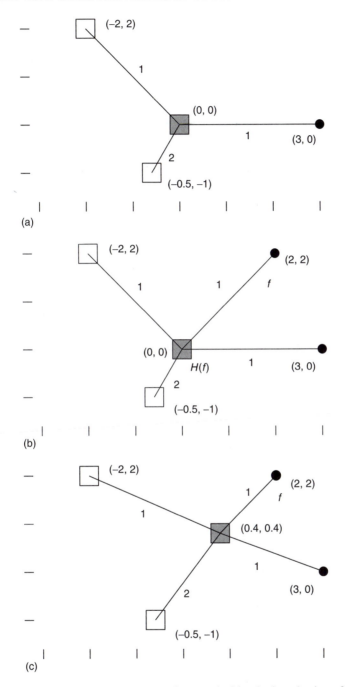

FIGURE 18.4 Illustration of how a placement can be perturbed by the introduction of a perturbing fixed point. The placement in (a) is in equilibrium through the use of a fixed point. In (b), a perturbing fixed point is added at position (2, 2) to pull the cell in this direction. Finally, (c) shows the resulting placement because of the perturbing fixed point.

Fixed points offer other potential benefits compared to constant forces if consideration is given to the overall controllability and stability of each placement iteration. Specifically, using only fixed points, the position of cells at each placement iteration are guaranteed to be within the convex hull of the fixed points, fixed cells, and I/O pads. Hence, it is guaranteed that cells will remain within the placement area if the position of the fixed points are placed within the placement area. This same controllability does not exist for constant forces that can push cells outside the placement region. Finally, the linear system of equations used to determine cell positions becomes better conditioned and the stability problems observed in Ref. [16] are less likely to be observed.

The means by which the position and weighting of the fixed points is determined is key to the success of mFAR. The direction of the stabilizing fixed point is easily determined according to the quadratic spring forces. Perturbing fixed points must be positioned in locations that reduce cell overlap and are computed as follows.

Given a placement, mFAR imposes a $H_g \times W_g$ grid bin structure on the placement area such that each grid bin contains a small number of cells. Here, H_g and W_g are the number of grid bins in the vertical and horizontal directions, respectively. Cells are inserted into bins in the grid based on their current positions. A grid bin is indexed as $b_{r,c}$ where r and c are its row and column indices, respectively. Let $C(b)$ denote the capacity of a grid bin b and let $A(b)$ denote the total cell area assigned to bin b. Any bin b has an overflow if its utilization $U(b) = A(b)/C(b)$ is > 1. A well-distributed placement requires that no bins overflow. Hence, perturbing fixed points should be selected such that cells are pulled away from those bins with overflow to those bins without.

Let us consider the vertical boundary between two adjacent grid bins $b_{r,c}$ and $b_{r,c+1}$. Further, let $C_{r(0,c)}$ and $C_{r(x+1,W_g)}$ be the total row capacity on the left and right sides of the vertical boundary in row r, respectively. Finally, let $A_{r(0,c)}$ and $A_{r(x+1,W_g)}$ be the total cell area assigned to the bins to the left and right of the vertical boundary in row r, respectively. The amount of cell area $x_{r,(c,c+1)}$ that must migrate across the vertical boundary between the grid bins $b_{r,c}$ and $b_{r,c+1}$ can be computed by

$$\frac{A_{r(0,c)} - x_{r,(c,c+1)}}{C_{r(0,c)}} = \frac{A_{r(c+1,W_g)} + x_{r,(c,c+1)}}{C_{r(c+1,W_g)}} \tag{18.10}$$

where $x_{r,(c,c+1)} > 0$ indicates that cells should migrate from left to right across the boundary, while a negative value indicates the reverse. Cells are not shifted across boundaries, but rather the position of the vertical boundary is shifted and the distance moved by the boundary is decided upon by the magnitude of $x_{r(c,c+1)}$ as

$$S_{r,(c,c+1)} = \frac{x_{r,(c,c+1)}}{h(b_{r,c})} \tag{18.11}$$

where
$S_{r,(c,c+1)}$ indicates the amount of the shift
$h(b_{r,c})$ is the height of the grid bin $b_{r,c}$

After the shifts for all grid boundaries are calculated, the new position of any cell i is given by the linear mapping

$$x_i^{new} = x_{min}^{new} + \frac{x_i^{old} - x_{min}^{old}}{x_{max}^{old} - x_{min}^{old}} \times (x_{max}^{new} - x_{min}^{new}) \tag{18.12}$$

A similar operation is performed in the y-direction. The values x_{min}^{old} and x_{max}^{old} are the left and right coordinates of the grid bin before boundary shifting, while values x_{min}^{new} and x_{max}^{new} are the left and right boundaries after the shifting.

The perturbing fixed points should be positioned such that cells are pulled toward their new target positions meaning that the perturbing fixed point f for a cell $H(f)$ is in the direction of $\alpha \mathbf{d}$ where $\mathbf{d}$ is the vector $\overrightarrow{(x_{H(f)}^{new} - x_{H(f)}^{old}, y_{H(f)}^{new} - y_{H(f)}^{old})}$ and α is a design-specific parameter used to control the overall strength of the perturbation. Note that only the direction of the perturbing force and its strength are determined. The actual position of the fixed point f and the weight of the pseudonet such that $\alpha \mathbf{d} = w_{i,j}(\overrightarrow{f} - \overrightarrow{H(f)})$ are not yet determined.

Fixed points and perturbing points may either be placed on-chip (located within the placement area) or off-chip (located outside the placement area) [20]. As previously mentioned, when the quadratic program is solved, cells will always remain within the convex hull defined by the fixed points. Thus, as long as the fixed points are placed within the placement area, the cells will not escape from the placement area. Numerical studies presented in Ref. [20] demonstrated that stabilizing fixed points should be kept off-chip to minimize their impact on wirelength, while perturbing fixed points should be kept along the boundary of the placement area with their edge weights w_{ij} kept as small as possible. Hence, initially all fixed points are positioned along the boundary of the placement area and, as placement progresses, the strength of the stabilizing fixed points are reduced, while their lengths (and positions) are increases such that they are placed off-chip.

18.3.1.2   Fixed Points in FastPlace

The description of fixed points thus far has focused on the implementation used by mFAR. FastPlace also uses fixed points and a bin shifting strategy to reduce cell overlap. However, unlike mFAR that used two fixed points per cell to stabilize and perturb a placement at any given iteration, FastPlace uses only one fixed point per cell.

In any placement iteration, FastPlace skips the calculation of stabilizing fixed points and immediately imposes a $H_g \times W_g$ regular grid structure on the placement area. For each grid bin b, the bin utilization $U(b)$ is calculated. Subsequently, cells are shifted first in the x-direction and then in the y-direction. Similar to mFAR, the shifting in each direction is a two-step process. Grid boundaries are first shifted based on the current utilization of the bins, which yields an uneven bin structure. Subsequently, cells are linearly mapped from their positions in the regular bin structure to a target position in the uneven bin structure thereby yielding a target position for each cell. The shifting of bin boundaries in FastPlace is illustrated in Figure 18.5. The positions of the bin boundaries in

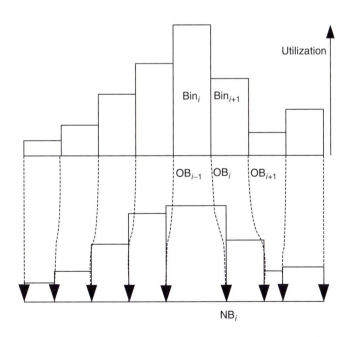

FIGURE 18.5   Illustration of the shifting of bin boundaries used in FastPlace in either the x- or y-direction. The utilization of each bin is calculated based on the current placement and is then used to shift boundaries converting a regular bin structure into an uneven bin structure in which cell overlap is removed. (From Viswanathan, N. and Chu, C.C.-N., *IEEE Trans. CAD 24*, 5, 722, 2005. Copyright IEEE 2005. With permission.)

the x-direction (a similar operation can occur in the y-direction) are computed as follows. Let OB_i be the x-position of the boundary for bin i in the original regular bin structure. Similarly, let NB_i be the x-position of the boundary for bin i in the uneven bin structure. The position of NB_i is calculated via the equation

$$\mathrm{NB}_i = \frac{\mathrm{OB}_{i-1}[U(i+1)+\delta] + \mathrm{OB}_{i+1}[U(i)+\delta]}{U(i) + U(i+1) + 2\delta} \tag{18.13}$$

The idea is that the bin shifting should average out the utilization of adjacent bins. Hence, the intuition behind Equation 18.13 is that it averages the utilization of bins i and $i+1$. The parameter δ is required for the following reasons. Let $\delta = 0$ and $U(i+1) = 0$. From Equation 18.13, it can be seen that $\mathrm{NB}_i = \mathrm{OB}_{i+1}$ and $\mathrm{NB}_{i+1} = \mathrm{OB}_i$ and is a crossover of adjacent bin boundaries that results in an improper mapping of cell positions from the regular to the uneven grid structure. The inclusion of $\delta = 1.5$ prevents this crossover from occurring.

The bin shifting yields a target position for each cell, but it is possible that the displacement of each cell is too large—the cell should not be positioned exactly at its target position, although it should move toward its target position. FastPlace attempts to pull each cell $H(f)$ in the direction of $\mathbf{d} = \left(x_{H(f)}^{\mathrm{new}} - x_{H(f)}^{\mathrm{old}}, y_{H(f)}^{\mathrm{new}} - y_{H(f)}^{\mathrm{old}}\right)$, which is similar to mFAR. However, in FastPlace, movement in this direction is controlled separately in the x- and y-directions using movement control parameters α_x and $\alpha_y (<1)$, respectively. To control the actual distance moved by any cell, α_x and α_y are increasing functions that are inversely proportional to the maximum bin utilization. Consequently, during early placement iterations where there is a large amount of cell overlap (and the maximum bin utilization is large), the movement control parameters are small and cells are shifted very small distances toward their target positions. In later iterations, as cells are well distributed throughout the placement area, α_x and α_y take on larger values to accelerate convergence. In Refs. [8,9], the values for the movement control parameters are given by

$$
\begin{aligned}
\alpha_y &= 0.02 + \frac{0.5}{\max_b U(b)} \\[2ex]
\alpha_x &= 0.02 + \frac{0.5}{\max_b U(b)} \left(\frac{\text{Average cell width}}{\text{Cell height}}\right)
\end{aligned}
\tag{18.14}
$$

which, once again, represent a trade-off in the spreading of cells and the wirelength as measured by the quadratic objective. Finally, the target position for a cell $H(f)$ is taken to be a displacement of $\alpha_x |x_{H(f)}^{\mathrm{new}} - x_{H(f)}^{\mathrm{old}}|$ and $\alpha_y |y_{H(f)}^{\mathrm{new}} - y_{H(f)}^{\mathrm{old}}|$ in the x- and y-directions from its original position, respectively.

The bin shifting, linear mapping, and scaling according to the movement control parameters yields a target position for each cell $H(f)$. It is necessary to calculate a position for each fixed point f and weight the pseudonet $c(f, H(f))$ such that cell $H(f)$ is pulled toward its target position. The approach taken by FastPlace is illustrated in Figure 18.6. Each fixed point f is placed on the boundary of the placement area with its position calculated as follows. Each cell $H(f)$ is moved to its target position as calculated above, while other movable cells are considered fixed. Spring forces will be exerted on cell $H(f)$ because of connections to other cells and will result in a nonzero spring force, because cell $H(f)$ is out of force equilibrium. The constant force that would put cell $H(f)$ back into force equilibrium is calculated, and its ray is intersected with the boundary of the placement area. Fixed point f for cell $H(f)$ is then placed at the intersection of the ray and the boundary of the placement area. By combining bin shifting and force calculations, FastPlace uses a single fixed point per cell placed on the boundary of the placement area to both stabilize and perturb the current placement.

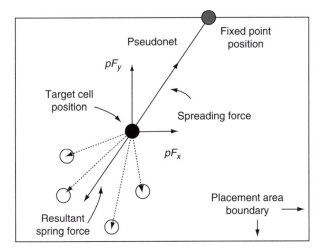

FIGURE 18.6 Illustration of fixed points in `FastPlace`. Given a target location for each cell after the bin stretching, the spring force because of other cells (which are assumed to be fixed) is computed. The perturbing force is in the opposite direction and serves to pull the cell toward its target location. The fixed point is positioned on the boundary of the chip and the weight of the pseudonet is computed according to Equation 18.15.

Finally, the weight of the pseudonet connecting the fixed point f to cell $H(f)$ must be computed. The weight of the pseudonet is computed from the following equation:

$$w_{f,H(f)} = \frac{\sqrt{pF_x^2 + pF_y^2}}{\sqrt{pD_x^2 + pD_y^2}} \qquad (18.15)$$

where
  $pF_x(pF_y)$ is the x-component (y-component) of the stabilizing constant force
  $pD_x(pd_y)$ is the x-component (y-component) of the distance between the fixed point f and the
    target position for cell $H(f)$

18.3.2 FREQUENCY-BASED METHODS

An alternative frequency-based approach to spreading cells was described in Ref. [21] and employed in `UPlace` [13]. In this method, the spreading forces are computed by minimizing the uneven density distribution of cells in the placement area. A regular $N \times N$ grid structure is imposed on the placement area. The density of each bin $b_{i,j}$ in the grid is associated with a matrix element $d_{ij} = D(i,j)$ computed as

$$d_{ij} = U(b_{i,j}) = \frac{A(b_{i,j})}{C(b_{i,j})} \qquad (18.16)$$

where
  $A(b_{i,j})$ is the cell area in the bin $b_{i,j}$
  $C(b_{i,j})$ is the capacity of bin $b_{i,j}$

Thus, matrix **D** represents the density distribution of cell area. The frequency domain representation of this matrix allows the cell distribution to be viewed as the rate at which the magnitudes of the densities change.

The matrix $\mathbf{D}$ can be converted into its frequency-domain representation $\mathbf{F}$ for all elements i, j using a discrete cosine transform, DCT [22], whose formula is given by

$$f_{ij} = \frac{2}{N} e(i) e(j) \sum_{x=0}^{N-1} \sum_{y=0}^{N-1} d_{xy} \cos\left[\frac{(2x+1)i\pi}{2N}\right] \cos\left[\frac{(2y+1)j\pi}{2N}\right] \tag{18.17}$$

where
$\quad x$ and y are coordinates in the spatial domain
$\quad i$ and j are coordinates in the frequency domain

and

$$e(i) = \begin{cases} \frac{1}{\sqrt{2}}, & i = 0 \\ 1, & 1 \le i \le N-1 \end{cases} \tag{18.18}$$

The distribution of all frequencies can then be defined as

$$\text{Dist} = \sum_{i,j} u_{ij} \cdot f_{ij}^2 \tag{18.19}$$

where u_{ij} is the weight of the distribution at the frequency (i, j).* When the placement of cells is totally even, all frequencies f_{ij} become 0, and Dist is minimized.

In UPlace, the quadratic objective $\Phi(x)$ is used to minimize wirelength during placement. Because Dist is complicated and difficult to minimize directly, it is approximated by a quadratic form taken as a function of the cell positions such that $\text{Dist} = \sum_i \text{Dist}_i$, where for each cell i, we have

$$\text{Dist}_i = \frac{1}{2} a_i x_i^2 + b_i x_i + \text{const} \tag{18.20}$$

To determine the coefficients a_i and b_i, the current solution of the placement is disturbed one cell at a time, and the changes in the values of Dist are observed. For a given cell i (considering the x-direction only), the value of Dist is computed for the current placement. The cell i is then shifted left by a distance δ, and $\text{Dist}_{i-\delta}$ is recomputed. The cell i is then shifted right by δ, and $\text{Dist}_{i+\delta}$ is computed. This testing yields three sampled tuple values $\{(i, \text{Dist}_i), (i - \delta, \text{Dist}_{i-\delta}), (i + \delta, \text{Dist}_{i+\delta})\}$ for each cell, which allows the values of a_i, b_i in Equation 18.20 to be interpolated for each i. The coefficients from the quadratic approximation to Dist can be reexpressed in matrix form, added together with the quadratic wirelength $\Phi(x)$, differentiated and set to zero to yield the system of equations given by

$$(\mathbf{Q}_x + \mathbf{A}_x)\mathbf{x} = -\mathbf{c}_x - \mathbf{b}_x \tag{18.21}$$

Here, $\mathbf{A}_x$ is a diagonal matrix defined as $\mathbf{A}_x = \text{diag}(a_1, a_2, \ldots, a_n)$, and $\mathbf{b}_x = [b_1, b_2, \ldots, b_n]^\mathrm{T}$. Note that the constant term in Equation 18.20 disappears as a result of the differentiation. Neither $\mathbf{Q}_x$ nor $\mathbf{c}_x$ are affected by changes to the distribution function Dist; only matrix $\mathbf{A}_x$ and vector $\mathbf{b}_x$ are modified. A similar equation is established for the y-direction.

Equation 18.21 can be likened to the force equation used in Kraftwerk in the following manner. By determining the distribution function Dist, the technique finds an additional force formulation $\mathbf{f}_x = \mathbf{A}_x \mathbf{x} + \mathbf{b}_x$, which equals the first-order derivative of the quadratic approximation to the cell distribution, Dist. Thus, the equilibrium state of the system corresponds to the optimum solution to the combined objective function of both wirelength and cell distribution components [13].

---

* In Ref. [13], $u_{ij} = \frac{1}{i+j+1}$ so that lower-frequency distributions are given higher weights because they are more expensive to eliminate.

18.4 ENHANCEMENTS

Quadratic force-directed placers are generally not as competitive with methods based on simulated annealing or minimum-cut partitioning. This is a consequence of the use of a quadratic wirelength objective. In particular, quadratic wirelength does a poor job of approximating routed wirelength, which is better approximated by a linear objective such as HPWL. Consequently, it is common to interleave the placement iterations with other heuristic strategies to improve the overall quality of the placements. In this section, we review the strategies used in several tools, including FDP, mFAR, and FastPlace.

18.4.1 INTERLEAVED OPTIMIZATIONS

In Ref. [23], Goto proposed an algorithm that can be used to move a cell at (or near) the position that minimizes the wirelength of its connected nets, while assuming other cells are fixed. The algorithm can be applied iteratively to each cell to obtain an improved placement. Central to Goto's idea is the concept of the median of a cell. Goto defines the median of a cell as the position of the cell at which the HPWL of its connected nets is minimum.

The median of cell C is computed as follows. Let E_C denote the set of nets connected to cell C. For each $e \in E_C$, compute the enclosing rectangle of all pins on e, while excluding those connections to cell C; the dimensions of this rectangle can be denoted by coordinates (x_e^{min}, y_e^{min}) and (x_e^{max}, y_e^{max}), where x_e^{min} and x_e^{max} are the minimum and maximum values in the x-direction, respectively. The same definitions hold for y_e^{min} and y_e^{max} in the y-direction. Given these definitions, the total wirelength for all nets connected to cell C at position (x, y) is given by

$$f_C = \sum_{e \in E_C} [f_e(x) + f_e(y)] \tag{18.22}$$

where

$$f_e(x) = \begin{cases} x_e^{min} - x, & x < x_e^{min} \\ 0, & x_e^{min} \le x \le x_e^{max} \\ x - x_e^{max}, & x > x_e^{min} \end{cases} \tag{18.23}$$

$$f_e(y) = \begin{cases} y_e^{min} - y, & y < y_e^{min} \\ 0, & y_e^{min} \le y \le y_e^{max} \\ y - y_e^{max}, & y > y_e^{min} \end{cases} \tag{18.24}$$

The optimal position (x, y) for cell C can be calculated separately in both the x- and y-directions. Goto showed that Equation 18.22 can be written (x-direction only) as

$$f_C = \sum_{e \in E_C} \left(|x - x_e^{min}| + |x - x_e^{max}| \right) \tag{18.25}$$

with the optimal solution given by a median computation. In practice, medians are computed simply by inserting x_e^{min} and x_e^{max} for all $e \in E_C$ into a vector and sorting the entries of the vector. For a vector of length n indexed 1 to n, a suitable minimizing value for x is any value within the range of values stored at the indices $\lfloor n/2 \rfloor$ and $\lfloor n/2 \rfloor + 1$ of the sorted vector. Figure 18.7 shows the computation of the median rectangle for a cell connected to three nets.

Goto observed that the total cost of placing cell C in any position outside of the median is piecewise strictly convex. This fact helps to identify alternative positions for cell C that are perhaps outside of the optimal positions. Goto encapsulates these alternative positions through the use of the ϵ-neighborhood, which is defined as the set of ϵ positions for the cell where the wirelength is one of the ϵ smallest values.

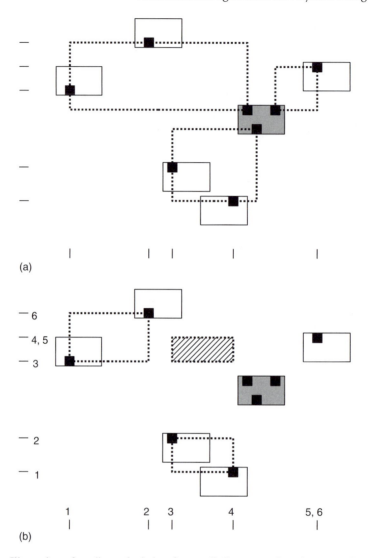

FIGURE 18.7 Illustration of median calculation for a cell C connected to three nets. In (a), the original placement of cells is shown. In (b), the median or optimal range of (x, y) values for cell C is shown. Six x- and y-positions are used for the median computation because three nets are involved. Note that two-pin nets degenerate to a single point. A larger set of position for cell C can be computed and is best done by expanding the median rectangle outward according to the points used in the median computation and corresponds to the concept of ϵ-neighborhoods described by Goto in Ref. [23].

Median improvement was implemented within the force-directed placer, FDP. Specifically, multiple passes of median improvement are performed as cell overlap is reduced. Because median improvement attempts to reposition each cell within its median rectangle, the use of median improvement can reintroduce cell overlap into the placement. To alleviate the cell overlap, FDP attempts to carefully monitor the distribution of cell area when placing a cell inside its median rectangle, it is positioned such that a minimum of overlap is reintroduced. Further, if at any point during the algorithm too much cell overlap is reintroduced, the algorithm is terminated.

In Ref. [16], it was empirically observed that the use of median improvement is most effective near the beginning of placement when a large amount of cell overlap is prevalent and less effective toward the end of placement. To this end, the median rectangle used in FDP is enlarged when it is discovered

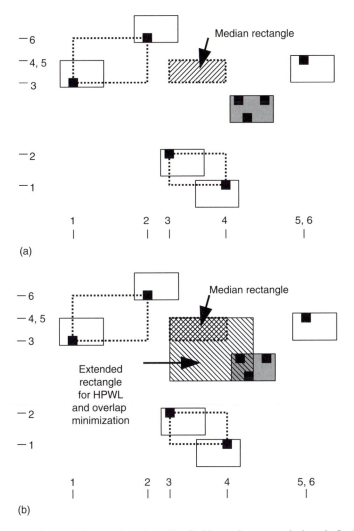

FIGURE 18.8 Rectangles used in FDP based on Goto's idea to improve wirelength. In (a) the median or optimal range for replacing a cell. In (b) the extended range for replacing the cell that improves wirelength while providing more placement flexibility in order to avoid the reintroduction of overlap.

that the algorithm is reintroducing too much cell overlap—this extension of the search rectangle for repositioning a cell is similar to the notion of an ϵ-neighborhood described by Goto. The rectangles considered by the median improvement algorithm used in FDP are illustrated in Figure 18.8. Finally, the median improvement heuristic is used in yet another way in FDP. Specifically, at each iteration, median improvement is applied to determine a new position for each cell. However, the cell positions are not updated. Rather, the cell positions obtained by calling median improvement are used to compute an additional force on each cell. It was found, in FDP, that this additional force can be used to deflect the constant forces and lead to an improved overall quality of placement. In Ref. [16], the use of interleaved median improvement during quadratic force-directed placement was shown to improve wirelength by 10–15 percent when measured in terms of HPWL.

Another interleaved optimization is the iterative local refinement used in FastPlace. In this approach, a regular bin structure is imposed over the placement area to estimate the current utilization of a placement region. The netlist is traversed and the source bin for each cell is determined. Cells are then moved from source to target bins based on both the amount of wirelength improvement and the target bin's utilization. For every cell present in a bin, four scores are computed corresponding to

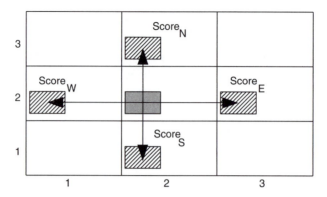

FIGURE 18.9   Illustration of iterative local refinement used in `FastPlace`. A regular bin structure is imposed over the placement area. Cells in source bins are tentatively moved from source bins in the north, east, south, and west directions into adjacent target bins. Scores for each of the four moves are calculated based on reduction in wirelength and change in bin utilization. The best movement is chosen unless all scores are negative, in which case the cell is left in its source bin. (From Viswanathan, N. and Chu, C.C.-N., *IEEE Trans. CAD 24*, 5, 722, 2005. Copyright IEEE 2005. With permission.)

the four possible movements of a cell. For computing scores, it is assumed that a cell moves from its current position in the source bin to the same position in each target bin that is adjacent to the source bin. That is, cells are tentatively moved by one bin width (or bin height). Each score is a weighted summation of two components, namely the resulting wirelength reduction and resulting utilization of the source and target bins. Because this refinement scheme is used primarily to reduce wirelength, the first term of the scoring function is more heavily weighted. If, for any cell, the four computed scores are all negative, the cell is kept in its source bin. This refinement strategy is illustrated in Figure 18.9. Several iterations of iterative local refinement are performed until there is no significant improvement in wirelength. By not using iterative local refinement in Ref. [24], a reduction of 32.2 percent in total runtime was observed, but final wirelengths were 15.1 percent worse. Further, the wirelength increase was more prominent as circuit size increased. Thus, the iterative local refinement is significant in improving the final quality of result.

18.4.2   MULTILEVEL OPTIMIZATION

Netlist clustering is an attractive means of improving the runtime and quality of placements produced by force-directed methods. Clustering coarsens a netlist by merging cells together to form larger groups of cells, or clusters, with the hyperedges adjusted to reflect the possible absorption of circuit connections into clusters. Placement is performed on the coarsened netlist and, as the algorithm progresses, netlists are repeatedly uncoarsened and placed. Unclustering and reclustering is sometimes performed at intermediate steps during placement to allow the placer to escape from earlier bad clustering decisions [16,25]. After placement, detailed improvement is usually performed on the flat netlist to improve final results.

Clustering methods have been used successfully in a number of force-based methods [20,24, 26–29], including many of those methods described in this chapter. Clustering has been shown to significantly improve the runtime and quality of placement results. Much of this improvement stems from the fact that clustering helps to keep tightly connected cells together and prevents placement algorithms from being trapped in local minima. For additional information on clustering, we refer the reader to the cited works and Chapter 7. For additional information on the use of clustering to improve placement, we refer the reader to Chapter 19.

18.5 NONQUADRATIC, CONTINUOUS METHODS

As previously mentioned, force-directed placers tend to rely on quadratic optimization and interleaved improvement heuristics that directly minimize an approximation of wirelength. Although the quadratic wirelength can be linearized using, for example, reweighting [30] and function regularization [31], these schemes require more computational effort when compared to simple quadratic optimization with interleaved improvement. Further, the linearization of quadratic wirelength still requires the conversion of the circuit hypergraph to its weighted graph representation, which serves to further abstract the wirelength model.

Rather than using a quadratic wirelength objective and a hypergraph-to-graph transformation, several placers including `APlace` [32], `mPL` [28], and `LSD` [24] work directly with the circuit hypergraph and attempt to simultaneously minimize a linear wirelength estimate and distribute cells throughout the placement area. These methods implement an objective function that consists, in part, of minimizing a metric of quality such as wirelength and a measure of infeasibility such as overlap. This can be encapsulated in the generic form given by

$$\Phi = \beta \times f_{\text{quality}} + (1 - \beta) \times f_{\text{overlap}} \tag{18.26}$$

where β is an adjustable parameter that represents a trade-off between the quality of result and the amount of cell overlap during any point of the placement method. Typically, the trade-off constant, β, is set close to 1 early in placement (where the focus is on placement quality), and is reduced throughout the placement method to encourage the distribution of cells throughout the placement area.

Placement methods that work directly with the circuit hypergraph, upon first glance, do not appear to be force-directed methods. At a minimum, however, they are similar in that these methods reduce cell overlap without partitioning. We shall see that there are additional similarities.

18.5.1 PLACEMENT VIA LINE SEARCH

`LSD` [24] performs placement with an objective function similar to Equation 18.26 and works with the circuit netlist directly to minimize HPWL. However, it still relies on force-directed methods that use constant additional forces such as `Kraftwerk` and `FDP`.

Specifically, each placement iteration of `LSD` works as follows: Given a placement, additional constant forces are computed to both stabilize and perturb the given placement that is identical to `Kraftwerk` and `FDP`. The particular weights for the perturbing forces are less significant in LSD and the forces are normalized to unity. Subsequently, a QP identical to Equation 18.5 is solved and yields a new placement of cells. However, unlike `Kraftwerk` and `FDP`—which consider this to be the new placement—LSD considers this placement as only a suggested placement of cells. Cells are not actually moved to these new positions. Rather, the new cell positions are subtracted from their original positions to yield a suggested search direction. Movement in this suggested direction reduces cell overlap while accounting for quadratic wirelength.

Within a placement iteration, LSD employs a median improvement heuristic. The initial placement provided to the heuristic is the original placement and not that obtained from the QP. Similar to the QP, the median improvement heuristic returns a new placement of cells. However, this new placement is aimed at reducing the HPWL of the circuit netlist directly, and does not take into account quadratic wirelength or cell overlap. This new placement, however, is not used as a placement—similar to the placement from the QP, the new cell positions from median improvement are subtracted from their original positions to yield another suggested search direction. This search direction aims to minimize HPWL.

Finally, in each placement iteration, LSD performs a two-dimensional line search within the cone produced by the two search directions computed from the QP and application of median improvement. This search cone is illustrated in Figure 18.10. For each position sampled by the

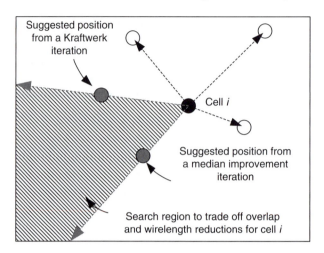

FIGURE 18.10 Illustration of the search cone used in LSD. For each cell, a new placement is computed along the lines of Kraftwerk, which yields a search direction that tends to reduce cell overlap. Similarly, for each cell, a call to median improvement yields a new placement that tends to reduce HPWL directly. LSD uses a line search to explore the region between these two search directions to find the placement of cells that best serves to trade off HPWL and cell overlap according to Equation 18.26.

two-dimensional search, the placement quality and placement overlap are assessed according to the normalized function given by

$$\text{score} = \beta \times \frac{\text{New\_HPWL}}{\text{Orig\_HPWL}} + (1 - \beta) \times \frac{\text{New\_Overlap}}{\text{Orig\_Overlap}} \qquad (18.27)$$

where β controls the preference between HPWL and cell overlap. The values New_HPWL and Old_HPWL represent the HPWL of the current placement being considered by the line search and the original placement, respectively. Similarly, New_Overlap and Old_Overlap represent a measure of the amount of cell overlap for the current placement being considered by the line search and the original placement, respectively. Once all placements have been tested by the line search, the placement with the best normalized score is selected and cell positions are updated. The value of β is a control parameter, which is initially set close to unity to encourage wirelength improvement and is slowly lowered as cells are spread to accelerate convergence. Placement terminates once there exists relatively little cell overlap, as in Ref. [16].

The line search offers a significant advantage over Kraftwerk-like methods [4,16,24], because it implements an easily tunable objective function that can be geared toward speed (by encouraging faster spreading) or toward quality (by preferring lower HPWL). The line search can be also be extended to account for additional objectives simply by computing new forces and modifying the objective function and line search accordingly. Nevertheless, the similarities between LSD and more traditional force-directed placers are clear.

18.5.2 APLACE AND THE LOG-SUM-EXP APPROXIMATION

In the patent by Naylor et al. [33], the HPWL of a hyperedge is approximated using a log-sum-exp formula, given by

$$\text{HPWL}_{\lambda}(e) = \alpha \left[\ln \left(\sum_{v_j \in e_i} e^{\frac{x_j}{\alpha}} \right) + \ln \left(\sum_{v_j \in e_i} e^{\frac{-x_j}{\alpha}} \right) + \ln \left(\sum_{v_j \in e_i} e^{\frac{y_j}{\alpha}} \right) + \ln \left(\sum_{v_j \in e_i} e^{\frac{-y_j}{\alpha}} \right) \right] \qquad (18.28)$$

where α is defined as a smoothing parameter. The smaller the value of α, the more accurate the approximation to Equation 18.1. However, α cannot be chosen to be too small because of machine precision and numerical stability. In effect, the use of the log-sum-exp formula picks the dominant cell positions to approximate the exact HPWL for each edge as specified in Equation 18.1. Despite its use of transcendental functions, the approximation in Equation 18.28 is both differentiable and strictly convex, which makes it fairly simple to minimize.

To spread cells, it is desirable to augment the log-sum-exp form with a penalty function that penalizes the uneven distribution of cells. To this end, based on the patent in Ref. [33], `APlace` [32,34,35] imposes a grid on the placement area and attempts to equalize the total cell area in every grid bin. The straightforward penalty for an uneven cell distribution is given by

$$\rho = \sum_b [A(b) - \text{Average cell area}]^2 \tag{18.29}$$

where $A(b)$ is the cell area in bin b. This penalty is neither smooth nor differentiable and is difficult to optimize. `APlace` approximates the total cell area in each grid bin by area potentials for each cell. The area potential uses a bell-shaped function, as shown in Figure 18.11, to model the effect of a cell's area on nearby grid bins. It is described by the equation given by

$$\text{Potential}(c, b) = \alpha(c) \cdot f(|c_x - b_x|) \cdot f(|c_y - b_y|) \tag{18.30}$$

for grid bin b with center (x_b, y_b), cell c with center (x_c, y_c), and $f(\cdot)$ representing the bell-shaped function. Here, $\alpha(c)$ is a proportionality factor used to ensure that the sum of the potentials for a cell equals the cell's area. That is,

$$\sum_b \text{Potential}(c, b) = \text{Area}(c) \quad \forall \, c \in V$$

In Equation 18.30 and illustrated in Figure 18.11, the bell-shaped function is given by

$$p(d) = \begin{cases} 1 - \frac{2d^2}{r^2}, & 0 \le d \le \frac{r}{2} \\ \frac{2(d-r)^2}{r^2}, & \frac{r}{2} \le d \le r \end{cases} \tag{18.31}$$

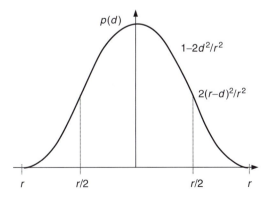

FIGURE 18.11   Bell-shaped penalty function that is used to remove overlap between cells. r controls the range of interaction (the radius) of any given cell's potential. In standard cell placement, the value of r can be set constant, but in mixed-size placement, it is typically adjusted on a per-cell basis (with larger values of r employed for larger cells). (From Kaling, A.B. and Wang, Q., *IEEE Trans. CAD* 24, 5, 734, 2005. Copyright 2005. With permission.)

where r represents the radius of the cells' potentials. The use of piecewise quadratic functions makes the potential function simple to differentiate. Given the notion of cell potential, the expected potential of a grid bin b is one in which the total cell area is evenly distributed over all grid bins. That is,

$$\text{Expected potential}(b) = \frac{\text{Total cell area}}{\text{Num grid bins}} \tag{18.32}$$

Thus, to minimize cell overlap, it suffices to minimize the difference of the potential of cells within each bin and the corresponding expected potential of each bin using a penalty function given by

$$\text{Penalty} = \sum_b \left[\sum_{\text{cell } c} \text{Potential}(c, b) - \text{Expected potential}(b) \right]^2 \tag{18.33}$$

which is smooth and differentiable because of the selection of the bell-shaped potential function.

In APlace, the penalty term in Equation 18.33 is combined with the log-sum-exp approximation to wirelength in Equation 18.28 to arrive at a linearly weighted objective function that represents a trade-off in linear wirelength minimization and the quadratic overlap penalty. This objective function is given by

$$\min \Phi_{sc} = \zeta \cdot \text{HPWL}_\lambda + \omega \cdot \text{Penalty} \tag{18.34}$$

In Equation 18.34, the constant ζ controls the weight associated with wirelength minimization, while ω is used to weight the overlap removal. Too large a value of ω can cause cells to spread hastily and lead to poor wirelength; too large a value of ζ can contract cells together and prevent them from spreading out. To counteract these effects, APlace keeps the value of ω fixed, and sets ζ to be large in the beginning; as the solver slows down (or as a solution appears), ζ is divided by two. The equation is solved repeatedly (and the balance of the weight tipped toward the penalty objective) until cells are spread evenly across the placement area. Because of its smooth and differentiable nature, this objective function can be solved efficiently using the Polak–Ribierre method [10]. To address runtime performance, the placement grid is initially made very coarse, which leads to cells spreading more quickly early on. A progressively finer grid is used as cells spread to ensure a more even distribution of area.

The bell-shaped function previously described is most applicable to standard cells, which are roughly the same size. A modification to the bell-shaped penalty term is described in Ref. [34] to allow for the placement of larger macrocells like those found in mixed-size circuits. In this modification, the scope of the area potential is extended according to the block size so that a larger block has a nonzero potential with respect to nearby grid bins. Given a module v with width w_v, located in bin b, the scope of the module's x-potential is given by $\frac{w_v}{2} + 2w_b$. That is to say, every grid bin within a horizontal distance of $\frac{w_v}{2} + 2w_b$ from the module's center has a nonzero x-potential contribution from the module. Consequently, the bell-shaped potential of a cell v and grid bin b become (x-direction only)

$$p_{v_x}(d) = \begin{cases} 1 - \alpha \cdot d^2, & 0 \le d \le \dfrac{w_v}{2} + w_b \\[2ex] \beta\left(d - \dfrac{w_v}{2} - 2w_b\right), & \dfrac{w_v}{2} + w_b \le d \le \dfrac{w_v}{2} + 2w_b \end{cases} \tag{18.35}$$

where $\alpha = \frac{4(w_v + 4w_b)}{w_v + 2w_b}$ and $\beta = \frac{2(w_v + 4w_b)}{w_b}$. The function is formulated in this fashion so that it is smooth when $d_x = \frac{w_v}{2} + w_b$. (A similar formula is employed in the y-direction.)

One of the benefits of the formulation employed in APlace is its extensibility. In Ref. [32], geometric constraints are considered as additional penalty terms. For example, to handle alignment constraints (in the x-dimension), a penalty function such as $\sum_{i \in |V_H|} (x_i - \bar{x})^2$ can be added.

Numerous additional details are presented in Ref. [29] to improve the overall quality and performance of `APlace`. One improvement to quality stems from the use of multilevel clustering. An adaptive grid size is also described in which the coarseness of the grid is modified based on average cluster size, as this was found to lead to better wirelengths with reduced runtime. Several other implementation-specific details are mentioned therein, and we refer interested readers to Ref. [29] for more information.

`APlace` does not share a direct analogy with the concept of a force—its relationship to other force-directed methods is limited to the removal of cell overlap without the need to partition the placement area and, perhaps, its use of the conjugate gradient method for minimization. It is reasonable to interpret the gradient of the objective function used in `APlace` as a force that specifies a direction for cell movements.

18.5.3 MPL AND ITS GENERALIZATION OF FORCE-DIRECTED PLACEMENT

Like `APlace`, mPL [28] works directly with the circuit hypergraph and minimizes wirelength through the use of the log-sum-exp form in Equation 18.28. The log-sum-exp form was chosen from among two other objective function candidates: the first was the quadratic approximation to wirelength given in Equation 18.2 and the second was the L_p-norm approximation [15] given by

$$\text{HPWL}_{L_p} = \sum_{e \in E_H} \left[\left(\sum_{v_k \in e} x_k^p \right)^{\frac{1}{p}} - \left(\sum_{v_k \in e} x_k^{-p} \right)^{-\frac{1}{p}} + \left(\sum_{v_k \in e} y_k^p \right)^{\frac{1}{p}} - \left(\sum_{v_k \in e} y_k^{-p} \right)^{-\frac{1}{p}} \right] \quad (18.36)$$

In the L_p-norm, the first and second terms tend to max x_k and min x_k as p tends to infinity [28], which results in a tight approximation of the HPWL similar to the log-sum-exp form. However, experimental evidence presented in Ref. [28] suggests that the log-sum-exp form offers HPWL results, which are 3 and 61 percent better than the $L_p (p = 32)$ and quadratic approximations, respectively. Moreover, the log-sum-exp approximation was solvable 67 percent faster than the L_p-norm but 23 percent slower than the quadratic model, and was therefore deemed to offer the best balance of runtime and quality.

Unlike `APlace`, which uses the bell-shaped function to spread cells evenly in localized regions, mPL spreads cells globally via the Helmoltz equation (which is similar to the Poisson equation used in `Kraftwerk` and other placers). mPL imposes a grid structure over top of the placement region. For every bin $b_{i,j}$ in the grid, its density $d_{i,j}$ is computed at each placement iteration. New positions for cells are determined by solving the optimization problem given by

$$\min \left\{ W = \sum_{e \in E_H} \text{HPWL}_\lambda(e) | d_{i,j} = K \quad \forall \text{ bins } b_{i,j} \right\} \quad (18.37)$$

where K is a target density. (K can be specified differently for each $b_{i,j}$ in situations when a nonuniform distribution of cells is desired [28].) This optimization problem is difficult to solve because of the nondifferentiability of the constraints. Thus, mPL uses the Helmholtz equation to arrive at a continuous density representation of $\mathbf{D} = (d_{i,j})$.

The solution to the Helmholtz equation (with boundary conditions) can be used to model diffusion processes, and thus makes an ideal candidate for modeling the spreading of cells in a two-dimensional grid. (The Poisson equation can be considered a special case of the Helmholtz equation.) Applied to the density distribution, the Helmholtz equation can be rewritten as

$$\frac{\partial^2 \phi(x,y)}{\partial x^2} + \frac{\partial^2 \phi(x,y)}{\partial y^2} - \epsilon\phi(x,y) = d(x,y), \quad (x,y) \in R$$
$$\frac{\partial \phi}{\partial v} = 0, \qquad\qquad (x,y) \text{ on the boundary of } R \quad (18.38)$$

where

$\epsilon > 0$

v is an outer unit normal

R represents the placement region, and $d(x, y)$ represents the continuous density function

The boundary conditions, encapsulated in the term $\frac{\partial \phi}{\partial v} = 0$, specify that forces pointing outside of the placement region be set to zero (i.e., Neumann boundary conditions)—this is a key difference with the Poisson method used in `Kraftwerk`, which assumes that forces become zero at infinity.

Because the solution of Equation 18.38 gains two more derivatives than $d(x, y)$, ϕ is a smoothed version of the density function [28]. To solve this problem using the densities $d_{i,j}$, the problem is first discretized using the finite difference method [36] (while employing the Neumann boundary conditions). If $\phi_{i,j}$ represents the value of ϕ at the center of bin $b_{i,j}$, and h_x, h_y represent the width and height of a bin, the discrete approximation to Equation 18.38 can be expressed as

$$\frac{\phi_{i+1,j} - 2\phi_{i,j} + \phi_{i-1,j}}{h_y^2} + \frac{\phi_{i,j+1} - 2\phi_{i,j} + \phi_{i,j-1}}{h_x^2} - \epsilon \phi_{i,j} = d_{i,j} \tag{18.39}$$

for all $1 \le i \le m$ and $1 \le j \le n$, subject to

$$\begin{aligned} \phi_{0,j} &= \phi_{1,j}, & \forall 1 \le j \le n \\ \phi_{m+1,j} &= \phi_{m,j}, & \forall 1 \le j \le n \\ \phi_{i,0} &= \phi_{i,1}, & \forall 1 \le i \le m \\ \phi_{i,n+1} &= \phi_{i,n}, & \forall 1 \le i \le m \end{aligned} \tag{18.40}$$

Once this linear system of equations is solved for ϕ, the optimization problem Equation 18.37 can be reexpressed in terms of ϕ yielding the problem given by

$$\min \left\{ W = \sum_{e \in E_H} \text{HPWL}_\lambda(e) \mid \phi_{i,j} = \hat{K} \quad \forall \text{ bins } b_{i,j} \right\} \tag{18.41}$$

where $\hat{K}$ is a scaled constant representation of K. This optimization problem is solved using Uzawa's algorithm [37]. One iteration of Uzawa's algorithm is given by

$$\nabla W^{k+1} + \sum_{i,j} \lambda_{i,j}^k \nabla \phi_{i,j} = 0$$

$$\lambda_{i,j}^{k+1} = \lambda_{i,j}^k + \alpha(\phi_{i,j} - \hat{K}) \tag{18.42}$$

where

λ^k is the Lagrange multiplier at the kth iteration

α is a parameter to control convergence

Recall that the wirelength portion of the objective W is a function of the cell positions in each iteration. Thus, the term W^{k+1} is a function of the positions of cells in x and y in iteration $k + 1$. The gradient of $\phi_{i,j}$ can be approximated using the difference scheme

$$\nabla_{x_k} \phi_{i,j} = \frac{\phi_{i,j+1} - \phi_{i,j}}{h_x} \tag{18.43}$$

$$\nabla_{yk} \phi_{i,j} = \frac{\phi_{i+1,j} - \phi_{i,j}}{h_y} \tag{18.44}$$

In Ref. [23], one iteration of a `Kraftwerk` placement iteration is shown to be related to an iteration of Uzawa's algorithm. Given the force equation used by `Kraftwerk` in Equation 18.5, a change of variable names shows that the incremental change in cell positions for a quadratic system can be reexpressed as

$$\begin{pmatrix} \mathbf{C} & 0 \\ 0 & \mathbf{C} \end{pmatrix} \begin{pmatrix} \mathbf{x}^{k+1} \\ \mathbf{y}^{k+1} \end{pmatrix} + \begin{pmatrix} \mathbf{p}_x \\ \mathbf{p}_y \end{pmatrix} + \tau_k \begin{pmatrix} \mathbf{f}_x^k \\ \mathbf{f}_y^k \end{pmatrix} = 0 \tag{18.45}$$

In this equation, the quadratic wirelength approximation is used in place of the log-sum-exp model for W in Equations 18.37 and 18.41. The values of $\mathbf{C}$, $\mathbf{p}_x$, and $\mathbf{p}_y$ are derived from ∇W. The scalar τ_k controls the weighting in each iteration, while the forces $\mathbf{f}_x$ and $\mathbf{f}_y$ are computed based on the placement in the kth iteration. In `Kraftwerk`, this equation is iteratively solved until cells are well spread across the placement area. This equation is a special case of the Uzawa iteration in Equation 18.42, achieved by fixing $\lambda_{ij}^k = \tau_k$. The λ^k values are known to be the Lagrange multipliers of Equation 18.41, and must be large enough to spread cells but small enough to achieve convergence. Whereas force weighting is an issue in `Kraftwerk`, `mPL` offers the possibility of dynamically adjusting the weights for all forces individually at each iteration by updating the Lagrangian multipliers. Consequently, `mPL` does not require the ad hoc force scaling typically employed in methods based on Ref. [4] and represents a generalization of `Kraftwerk`.

18.6 OTHER ISSUES

Several important issues have not been addressed in the previous description of force-directed placement methods and we touch upon some of these issues here, including I/O placement, fixed obstacles, and heterogeneous resource placement.

Force-directed methods, including `Kraftwerk`, `FDP`, `mFAR`, and `FastPlace`, require I/Os to be preplaced before force-directed placement because of the need for $\Phi(x)$ to be positive definite. However, in some circumstances, the placement of I/Os can be another degree of freedom, as their placement can impact overall quality. Despite some efforts in the literature (c.f., [24,38]), it is possible that placeable I/Os can be handled more effectively within the context of force-directed and continuous placement methods.

Another difficulty for force-directed methods potentially lies in the handling of fixed obstacles within the placement area. Figure 18.12a shows the `adaptec2` circuit from the `ISPD05` benchmark suite [39]. This circuit contains a large number of preplaced macrocells. In particular, there is a very large preplaced macrocell in the middle of the placement area. Several heuristic strategies (c.f., [19]) have been presented for positioning fixed points on the boundaries of fixed obstacles to encourage cells to be pulled through fixed obstacles and to prevent other cells from remaining inside of fixed obstacles. Figure 18.12b shows the positions of movable cells immediately after the solution to an unperturbed quadratic objective—the cells are highly overlapping, and many are located to the right of the large macro. In practice, it may be difficult for the movable cells in this example to push through or "move around" the obstacles. If one considers the various incarnations of force-directed methods, there is nothing explicit, which indicates that the methods would fail to properly handle fixed obstacles. In fact, placers including `APlace`, `mPL`, `mFAR`, `FastPlace`, and `Kraftwerk` successfully placed the circuits in the `ISPD05` benchmark suite, all of which contain a number of fixed obstacles. However, it is possible that the handling of fixed obstacles can be improved.

Another issue for force-directed methods pertains to the proper handling of heterogeneous resources that commonly appear in the context structured ASIC placement. Such resources correspond to specialized macroblocks (like RAM blocks, multiplier blocks, and IP cores) [40], which are generally much fewer in number than the remaining core (standard) cells. Such blocks require placement at discrete positions inside of the structured ASIC and their placement imposes discrete

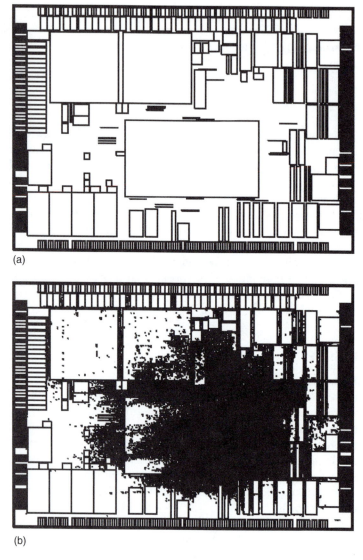

FIGURE 18.12 Illustration of the `adaptec2` circuit from the `ISPD05` benchmark suite [39] where (a) shows the circuit's fixed obstacles and I/O pads before placement and (b) shows that after the placement of cells after a single QP, many cells may become trapped (or blocked) by fixed obstacles.

slot constraints on the placement problem. An illustration of heterogeneous resources within Altera's HC230 structured ASIC is shown in Figure 18.13.

Although `APlace` [32] handles geometric constraints, slot constraints represent another type of constraint not properly handled geometrically. So, the question arises as to what is the best method to handle discrete slot constraints during force-directed placement. Traditional force-directed placers cannot compel heterogeneous cells to be placed at discrete slots—in the best case, these methods can coerce heterogeneous cells toward discrete slots. In Ref. [41], an extension to a force-directed placer to handle heterogeneous resources is presented. In effect, the cell distributions for different types of cells are maintained in separate layers—spreading forces for different types of cells are computed in the appropriate layer. This enhancement was shown to yield placements where cells are placed reasonably closely to the appropriate type of resource. Once again, however, it is worthwhile to ask if

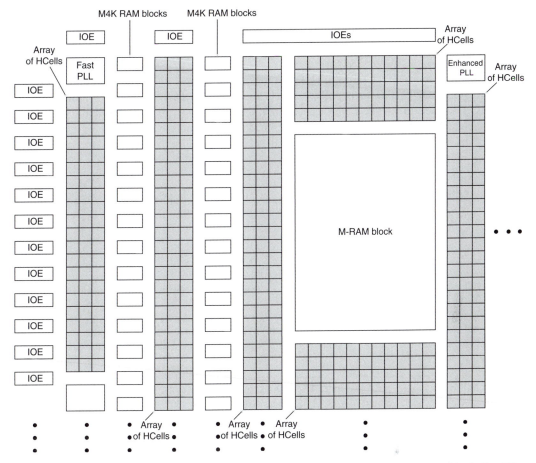

FIGURE 18.13 Partial floorplan of an HC230 structured ASIC [42]. Heterogeneous resources including I/Os, M4K RAMs, PLLs, and mega-RAMs must be placed into disjoint slots. (From Altera corporation, *Hard Copy Series Handbook*, Altera, 2005. With permission.)

even more effective techniques for dealing with heterogeneous resources can be developed because the placement of these resources can have a large impact on the overall quality of the placement.

18.7 CONCLUSIONS

With the advent of `Kraftwerk` in the late 1990s, force-directed placement methods have received a great deal of attention from academia and industry. These methods have been used successfully to place multimillion gate designs, and have continually improved in quality, scalability, and robustness each year.

In this chapter, we have examined force-directed methods by highlighting the similarities and differences between the various implementations described in the literature. We have also examined continuous methods that, like force-directed methods, do not rely on partitioning to remove cell overlap and share similarities with the more traditional force-directed methods. Many of the methods presented in this chapter have been extended to accommodate other practical VLSI placement objectives, which were beyond the scope of the discussion in this chapter. These objectives include timing-, congestion-, and thermal-driven placements. For the interested reader, force-directed placers incorporating timing constraints through netweighting are described in Refs. [32,43,44], while a timing-oriented hypergraph model based on Steiner trees is described in Ref. [45]. Congestion minimization within force-directed methods have also been examined in the context of cell bloating [32]. Force-directed methods for thermal placement in three-dimensional architectures have been examined [46].

The future of force-directed methods is a promising area of research in the field of VLSI CAD. The ease with which the placement problem can be analogized to spreading forces continues to spur research and advancement—new approaches that raise the bar in terms of performance and quality are being conceived at a tremendous pace. Continued improvements in force-directed methods will no doubt serve to strengthen the prominence of these methods.

REFERENCES

1. Adya, S. N., Chaturvedi, S., Roy, J. A., Papa, D. A., and Markov, I. L. Unification of partitioning, placement and floorplanning. In *Proc. ICCAD*, November 2004, pp. 550–557, San Jose, CA.
2. Fisk, C., Caskey, D., and West, L. Automated circuit card etching layout. In *Proc. IEEE*, 55: 1971–1982, 1967.
3. Kahng, A. B. and Reda, S. A tale of two nets: Studies of wirelength progression in physical design. In *Proc. System-Level Interconnect Prediction*, March 2006, pp. 17–24, Munich, Germany.
4. Eisenmann, H. and Johannes, F. M. Generic global placement and floorplanning. In *Proc. DAC*, June 1998, pp. 269–274, San Francisco, CA.
5. Hall, K. M. An *r*-dimensional quadratic placement algorithm. *Manage. Sci. 17* (November): 219–229, 1970.
6. Vygen, J. Algorithms for large-scale flat placement. In *Proc. DAC*, June 1997, pp. 746–751, Anaheim, CA.
7. Kennings, A. and Markov, I. L. Smoothing max-terms and analytical minimization of half-perimeter wire length. *VLSI Design 14*, 3: 229–237, 2002.
8. Viswanathan, N. and Chu, C. C. -N. Fastplace: Efficient analytical placement using cell shifting, iterative local refinement and a hybrid net model. *IEEE Trans. CAD 24*, 5 (May): 722–733, 2005. (ISPD 2004).
9. Viswanathan, N., Pan, M., and Chu, C. C. -N. Fastplace: An analytical placer for mixed-mode designs. In *Proc. ISPD*, April 2005, pp. 221–223, San Francisco, CA.
10. Saad, Y. *Iterative Methods for Sparse Linear Systems*. SIAM, 2003.
11. Qian, H. and Sapatnekar, S. S. A hybrid linear equation solver and its application in quadratic placement. In *Proc. ICCAD*, November 2005, pp. 905–909, San Jose, CA.
12. Obermeier, B. and Johannes, F. M. Quadratic placement using an improved timing model. In *Proc. DAC*, June 2004, pp. 705–710, San Diego, CA.
13. Yao, B., Chen, H., Cheng, C. -K., Chou, N. -C., Liu, L. -T., and Suaris, P. Unified quadratic programming approach for mixed mode placement. In *Proc. ISPD*, April 2005, pp. 193–199, San Francisco, CA.
14. Spindler, P. and Johannes, F. M. Fast and robust quadratic placement combined with an exact linear net model. In *Proc. ICCAD*, November, 2006, pp. 179–186, San Jose, CA.
15. Kennings, A. and Markov, I. L. Analytical minimization of half-perimeter wire-length. In *Proc. ASPDAC*, January 2000, pp. 179–184, Yokohama, Japan.
16. Vorwerk, K., Kennings, A., and Vannelli, A. Engineering details of a stable analytic placer. In *Proc. ICCAD*, November 2004, pp. 573–580, San Jose, CA.
17. Barnes, J. and Hut, P. A hierarchical $O(n \log n)$ force calculation algorithm. *Nature 324*, 4: 446–449, 1986.
18. Etawil, H., Areibi, S., and Vannelli, A. Attractor-repeller approach for global placement. In *Proc. ICCAD*, November 1999, pp. 20–24, San Jose, CA.
19. Hu, B. and Marek-Sadowska, M. Multilevel expansion-based VLSI placement with blockages. In *Proc. ICCAD*, November 2004, pp. 558–564, San Jose, CA.
20. Hu, B. and Marek-Sadowska, M. Multilevel fixed-point-addition-based VLSI placement. *IEEE Trans. CAD 24*, 8 (August): 1188–1203, 2005.
21. Chaudhary, K. and Nag, S. K. Method for analytical placement of cells using density surface representations. United States Patent 6,415,425, July 2002.
22. Nussbaumer, H. J. *Fast Fourier Transform and Convolution Algorithms*. Springer-Verlag, New York, 1982.
23. Goto, S. An efficient algorithm for the two-dimensional placement problem in electrical circuit layout. *IEEE Trans. Circuits Syst. CAS-28*, 1: 12–18, 1981.
24. Vorwerk, K. and Kennings, A. An improved multi-level framework for force-directed placement. In *Proc. DATE*, March 2005, pp. 902–907, Munich, Germany.

25. Karypis, G. *Multilevel Optimization and VLSICAD*. Kluwer Academic Publishers, Boston, MA, 2002, ch. 3.

26. Alpert, C., Kahng, A. B., Nam, G. -J., Reda, S., and Villarubia, P. A semi-persistent clustering technique for VLSI circuit placement. In *Proc. ISPD*, April 2005, pp. 200–207, San Francisco, CA.

27. Chan, T. F., Cong, J., Kong, T., Shinnerl, J. R., and Sze, K. An enhanced multilevel algorithm for circuit placement. In *Proc. ICCAD*, November 2003, pp. 299–306, San Jose, CA.

28. Chan, T., Cong, J., and Sze, K. Multilevel generalized force-directed method for circuit placement. In *Proc. ISPD*, April 2005, pp. 185–192, San Francisco, CA.

29. Kahng, A. B., Reda, S., and Wang, Q. Architecture and details of a high quality, large-scale analytical placer. In *Proc. ICCAD*, November 2005, pp. 891–898, San Jose, CA.

30. Sigl, G., Doll, K., and Johannes, F. M. Analytical placement: A linear or a quadratic objective function? In *Proc. DAC*, June 1991, pp. 427–432, San Francisco, CA.

31. Alpert, C. J., Chan, T., Huang, D. J. -H., Markov, I. L., and Yan, K. Quadratic placement revisited. In *Proc. DAC*, June 1997, pp. 752–757, Anaheim, CA.

32. Kahng, A. B. and Wang, Q. Implementation and extensibility of an analytic placer. *IEEE Trans. CAD 24*, 5 (May): 734–747, 2005. (ISPD 2004).

33. Naylor, W., Donelly, R., and Sha, L. Non-linear optimization system and method for wire length and density within an automatic electronic circuit placer. United States Patent 6,662,348, July 2001.

34. Kahng, A. B. and Wang, Q. An analytic placer for mixed-size placement and timing-driven placement. In *Proc. ICCAD*, November 2004, pp. 565–572, San Jose, CA.

35. Kahng, A. B., Reda, S., and Wang, Q. Aplace: A general analytic placement framework. In *Proc. ISPD*, April 2005, pp. 233–235, San Francisco, CA.

36. Ames, W. F. (ed.). *Numerical Methods for Partial Differential Equations*. Academic Press, New York, 1977.

37. Arrow, K. J., Hurwicz, L., and Uzawa, H. (eds.). *Studies in Nonlinear Programming*. University Press, Stanford, CA, 1958.

38. Westra, J. and Groeneveld, P. Towards integration of quadratic placemnt and pin assignment. In *Proc. IEEE Symp. VLSI*, May 2005, pp. 284–286, Tampa, FL.

39. Nam, G. -J., Alpert, C. J., Villarrubia, P., Winter, B., and Yildiz, M. The ISPD2005 placement contest and benchmark suite. In *Proc. ISPD*, April 2005, pp. 216–220, San Francisco, CA.

40. Selvakkumaran, N., Ranjan, A., Raje, S., and Karypis, G. Multi-resource aware partitioning algorithms for FPGAS with heterogeneous resources. In *Proc. DAC*, June 2004, pp. 741–746, San Diego, CA.

41. Hu, B. Timing-driven placement for heterogeneous field programmable gate array. In *Proc. ICCAD*, November 2006, pp. 383–388, San Jose, CA.

42. Altera Corporation. *HardCopy Series Handbook, Volume 1—Section 1: HardCopy II Device Family Data Sheet*. Altera, 2005.

43. Mo, F., Tabbara, A., and Brayton, R. K. A timing-driven macro-cell placement algorithm. In *Proc. ICCAD*, November 2001, pp. 322–327, San Jose, CA.

44. Hur, S. -W., Cao, T., Rajagopal, K., Parasuram, Y., Chowdhary, A., Tiourin, V., and Halpin, B. Force directed Mongrel with physical net constraints. In *Proc. DAC*, June 2003, pp. 214–219, Anaheim, CA.

45. Obermeier, B., Ranke, H., and Johannes, F. M. Kraftwerk: A versatile placement approach. In *Proc. ISPD*, April 2005, pp. 242–244, San Francisco, CA.

46. Goplen, B. and Sapatnekar, S. S. Efficient thermal placement of standard cells in 3D ICs using a force directed approach. In *Proc. ICCAD*, November 2003, pp. 86–89, San Jose, CA.

19 Enhancing Placement with Multilevel Techniques

Jason Cong and Joseph R. Shinnerl

CONTENTS

The increased importance of interconnect delay on VLSI circuit performance has spurred rapid progress in algorithms for large-scale global placement. The new algorithms often generalize previously studied heuristics or embed them within a hierarchical framework, either top-down recursive partitioning or multilevel (a.k.a. multiscale) optimization. This chapter presents a brief tutorial on the multilevel approach and describes some leading contemporary multiscale algorithms for large-scale global placement.

Multiscale methods have emerged as a means of generating scalable solutions to many diverse mathematical problems in the gigascale range. However, multiscale methods for partial differential equations (PDEs) [1,2] are not readily transferred to large-scale combinatorial optimization problems like placement. Lack of continuity presents one obstacle; myriad local extrema present another. Lack of a natural grid structure presents a challenge as well. Although there has been progress in the so-called algebraic multigrid (AMG) PDE solvers over general, unstructured graphs, extensions of these methods to hypergraphs are not generally available.

Hierarchical levels of abstraction are indispensable in the design of gigascale complex systems, but hierarchies must properly represent physical relationships, viz., interconnects, among constituent parts. The flexibility of the multiscale heuristic provides the opportunity both to merge previously distinct phases in the design flow and to simultaneously model very diverse, heterogeneous kinds of objectives and constraints. Adaptability to complex formulations of standard objectives and constraints such as timing (Chapter 21) [3,4], routability (Chapter 22) [5–7], and power (Chapter 22) [8] is a demonstrated core attribute of the multilevel approach. For simplicity, however, attention in this chapter is restricted to the standard model problem in which weighted half-perimeter wirelength (HPWL) is minimized subject to upper-bounds on the module area density in every bin of a superimposed rectangular grid (Chapter 14).

This chapter has the following aims:

1. Introduce basic ideas and vocabulary.
2. Summarize known basic principles of general multiscale algorithms for global optimization.
3. Summarize properties of leading contemporary multiscale placement algorithms.
4. Compare current practice to the known theory and identify likely areas of research opportunity.

Each of these aims is addressed below in its own section.

19.1 INTRODUCTION TO PLACEMENT BY MULTISCALE OPTIMIZATION

By multiscale optimization [9], we mean (1) the use of optimization at every level of a hierarchy of problem formulations, wherein (2) each variable at any given coarser level represents a subset of variables at the adjacent finer level. In particular, each coarse-level formulation can be viewed directly as a coarse representation of the original problem. Therefore, coarse-level solutions implicitly provide approximate solutions at the finest level as well.

19.1.1 CHARACTERIZATION OF MULTISCALE ALGORITHMS

A generic schematic of the classic V-cycle multiscale-optimization paradigm is shown in Figure 19.1. A generic example of multiscale placement is illustrated in Figures 19.2 and 19.6.

Multiscale algorithms share the following common components. Each is discussed in more detail below.

1. Hierarchy construction (coarsening, aggregation). Although the construction is usually from the bottom-up by recursive aggregation, top-down constructions based on recursive netlist partitioning are sometimes used. On hypergraphs or graphs, aggregation typically amounts to some form of clustering. On graphs, less restrictive forms have been successful, in which a finer-level variable is directly associated with multiple coarse-level variables (see the discussion of weighted aggregation below).
2. Relaxation. In placement, the purpose of intralevel optimization is efficient, iterative exploration of the solution space at that level. Continuous, discrete, local, global, stochastic, and

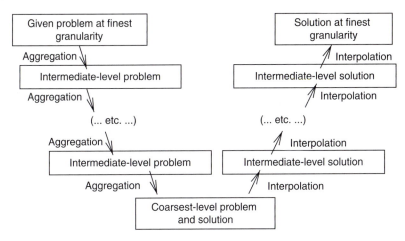

FIGURE 19.1 Multiscale formulation of global optimization.

deterministic formulations may be used in various combinations. The critical requirement is that the iterations make rapid progress by changing variables in amounts proportionate to the modeling scale at the given level. The starting configuration is the solution obtained at an adjacent level, either coarser or finer.

3. Interpolation. A coarse-level solution can be transferred to and represented at its adjacent finer level in a variety of ways. The simplest and most common is simply the placement of all components of a cluster concentrically at the cluster's center. More sophisticated approaches are discussed in Section 19.3.5 below. In the placement literature, interpolation is variously referred to as declustering, disaggregation, or uncoarsening. See Figure 19.5 for an illustration.

4. Iteration flow. The levels of the hierarchy may be traversed in different ways. A single pass of successive top-down refinement from the coarsest to the finest level is still the

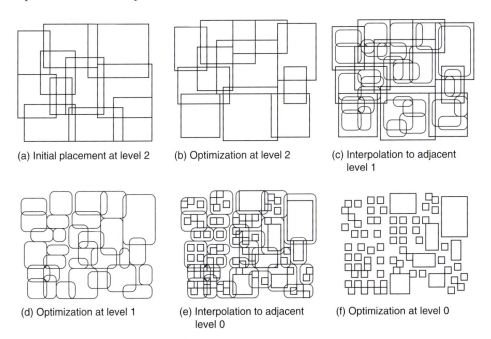

(a) Initial placement at level 2   (b) Optimization at level 2   (c) Interpolation to adjacent level 1

(d) Optimization at level 1   (e) Interpolation to adjacent level 0   (f) Optimization at level 0

FIGURE 19.2 Multiscale placement by successive top-down refinement.

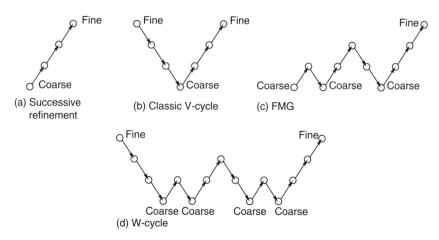

FIGURE 19.3 Some iteration flows for multiscale optimization. Points nearer the bottom of each diagram represent coarser levels of approximation.

most common. It is illustrated schematically in Figure 19.3a and graphically in Figure 19.2. Alternatives include standard flows such as a single V-cycle, multiple V-cycles, W-cycles, and the full multigrid (FMG) F-cycle (see Figure 19.3). In these more general flows, the outcome of relaxation at finer levels is often used to construct the next set of coarser levels. That is hierarchies may be constructed dynamically and adaptively rather than a priori.

The forms taken by these components are usually tightly coupled with the diverse objective and constraint models used by different algorithms.

When the hierarchy is defined by recursive bottom-up clustering, the combined flow of recursive clustering followed by recursive top-down optimization and interpolation is traditionally referred to as a V-cycle (Figure 19.3; the bottom of the V corresponds to the coarsest or top level of the hierarchy). While the usual iteration flow in VLSICAD proceeds top down, from coarsest to finest level, in the elementary theory of convergence of multigrid PDE solvers [1,2], the use of relaxation in the coarsening phase plays a vital role. In placement, such usage translates to location-based or physical clustering, an active area of placement research discussed in Sections 19.2 and 19.3.

19.2 BASIC PRINCIPLES OF MULTISCALE OPTIMIZATION

Multiscale methods originated as geometric multigrid methods in the context of uniformly discretized PDEs, where the resolution and regularity of the discretization make the notion of modeling scale obvious. Although at first glance it might appear that multiscale methods are limited to explicitly discretized problems, subsequent research on algebraic multigrid for general problems lacking any obvious, geometrically regular discretization has borne out the generality and applicability of the multiscale metaheuristic. The important requirement is not the geometric regularity, but the locality of the coupling among the variables. (The locality assumption can also be weakened [9].)

In this section, we define a simple model problem for quadratic placement and use it to draw connections to elementary general properties of multiscale optimization.

19.2.1 Multiscale Model Problem for Quadratic Placement

General formulations of placement are described in Chapter 14. The following simplified form is used here only for exposition of basic principles and techniques. As illustrated in Section 19.3, multiscale algorithms for placement are not limited to this form.

Let vector $s = (x, y) \in \mathbf{R}^n$ denote the 2D coordinates of all movable modules to be placed (n is twice the number of movable modules). Let matrix $Q \in \mathbf{R}^{n \times n}$ denote the (weighted) graph Laplacian satisfying, e.g.,

$$q(s) = \frac{1}{2}s^{\mathrm{T}}Qs - b^{\mathrm{T}}s = \frac{1}{2}\sum_{\text{net} \in e}\sum_{i,j \in e} w_{ij}[(x_i - x_j)^2 + (y_i - y_j)^2] \tag{19.1}$$

where vector $b \in \mathbf{R}^n$ captures connections between fixed terminals and movable objects. (The simplified notation above suggests but need not be limited to a clique model of each net.) Matrix Q is symmetric positive semidefinite.

The quadratic model problem is simply to find an unconstrained minimizer s^* of $q(s)$. As described in Chapter 18, this problem forms a template for one iteration to many force-directed algorithms [10–14].[†] In the presence of fixed terminals, Q is positive definite, and the quadratic function $q(s)$ has a unique minimizer s^* satisfying

$$Qs^* = b \tag{19.2}$$

That is, the simplified quadratic model reduces placement to a linear system of linear equations. In this form, multiscale algorithms for placement are more readily examined in the context of general multiscale algorithms for global optimization or PDEs.

Iterative relaxation on the linear-system model problem (Equation 19.2) may proceed, e.g., by the Gauss–Seidel iterations, i.e., one variable at a time,

$$s_i = \frac{1}{q_{ii}}\left(b_i - \sum_{j \neq i} q_{ij}s_j\right) \tag{19.3}$$

for each $i = 1, \ldots, n$. Such iterations are known to converge on symmetric positive-definite linear systems [15]. Because real netlists for placement are dominated by low-degree nets, placement exhibits local structure; i.e., for most i, $q_{ij} = 0$ for all but a small subset of $j \neq i$. Hence, an entire sweep of Gauss–Seidel relaxation proceeds in runtime essentially linear in the number of movable components.

Next, consider the representation of formulation (Equation 19.2) at an adjacent coarser level in a multiscale flow. Mathematically, it is convenient to proceed as follows:

1. Formulate the coarse-level problem in terms of the *error* $e = s^* - \tilde{s}$ in a given approximate solution $\tilde{s}$ at the finer level.
2. Define interpolation before defining coarsening (see examples in Section 19.2.2).

First, following step 1 above, rewrite Equation 19.2 in terms of the desired perturbation e to the given approximate solution $\tilde{s}$ as $Q(\tilde{s} + e) = b$, or, equivalently, as the residual equation

$$Qe = r \tag{19.4}$$

where the $r = b - Q\tilde{s} = r(\tilde{s})$ is the residual of Equation 19.2 associated with $\tilde{s}$.

Second, following step 2 above, suppose the finer-level variables $e \in \mathbf{R}^n$ are interpolated from coarse-level variables $e_c \in \mathbf{R}^m$ by the linear map $P\colon \mathbf{R}^m \to \mathbf{R}^n$ as follows ($m < n$):

$$e = Pe_c \tag{19.5}$$

[†] Iteratively computed, artificial, fixed, target terminals defined by spreading forces are typically used to produce a sequence of such models whose solutions converge to a sufficiently uniform density profile.

Finally, consider minimization of $q(s)$ in Equation 19.1 at the coarser level under these assumptions 1 and 2, i.e.,

$$\min_{e_c \in \mathbf{R}^m} \tilde{q}(e_c) \equiv q(\tilde{s} + Pe_c) = \frac{1}{2}(\tilde{s} + Pe_c)^{\mathrm{T}} Q(\tilde{s} + Pe_c) - b^{\mathrm{T}}(\tilde{s} + Pe_c)$$

It is easily shown that e_c minimizes $\tilde{q}(e_c)$ if and only if it satisfies

$$P^{\mathrm{T}} Q P e_c = P^{\mathrm{T}} r \tag{19.6}$$

Galerkin coarsening thus defines the linear coarsening operator $P^{\mathrm{T}}: \mathbf{R}^n \to \mathbf{R}^m$ as the transpose of the linear interpolation operator P, as simple substitution of Equation 19.5 into Equation 19.4 yields Equation 19.6 on premultiplication by P^{T}.

By confining coarse-level iterative improvement to the perturbation $e = Pe_c$ to $\tilde{s}$, relaxation at the coarse-level is in effect decoupled from relaxation at the adjacent finer level. The combined approximation $\tilde{s} + e$ is thus not restricted to the range of P and can represent a broader set of solution candidates for fixed P than is possible if relaxation at the coarser level and subsequent interpolation are applied to the entire coarse-level solution s_c rather than just its perturbation e_c.

In both theory and practice, coarsening and interpolation are so closely related that defining one essentially characterizes the other, even if nonlinear or discrete methods are used.

19.2.2 SIMPLE EXAMPLES OF INTERPOLATION

To give the simplified model concreteness for placement, consider the sample netlist H illustrated in Figure 19.4. The coarsening of H on the right-hand side of the figure shows modules 1, 2, and 3 mapped to cluster 0, module 4 mapped to cluster 1, and modules 0 and 5 mapped to cluster 2. For the moment we ignore the algorithm used to define the coarsening and concentrate just on the question of how to place the modules, once a placement of their parent clusters has been computed.* Because in this example there are six modules at the finer level and three modules at the adjacent coarse level, linear interpolation operators for this example are represented as constant 6×3 matrices. Let P_{const} denote the matrix for piecewise-constant linear interpolation, in which each module simply inherits its parent cluster's position. Alternatively, let P_{avg} denote the matrix for linear interpolation in which each module is placed at some linear combination of its parent's position and the positions of other clusters containing modules with which it shares nets; let w_{ij} denote the weight that module

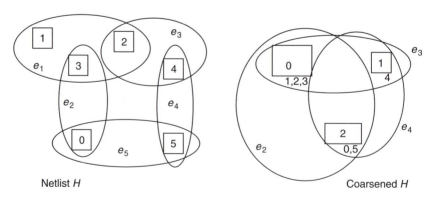

Netlist H Coarsened H

FIGURE 19.4 Simple six module netlist H with five nets and its coarsened approximation.

---

* For concreteness in this example, we describe finer-level objects as modules and coarser-level objects as clusters, but the example applies to any two adjacent levels of hierarchy—the finer-level objects might also be clusters of still finer-level objects, etc.

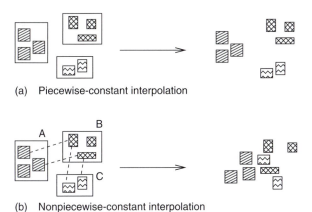

(a) Piecewise-constant interpolation

(b) Nonpiecewise-constant interpolation

FIGURE 19.5 Piecewise constant versus nonpiecewise-constant interpolation (declustering). Each component within a cluster is placed at a weighted average of the locations of all clusters containing other components to which it is connected.

i assigns to the position of cluster j, and assume weights are normalized such that $w_{ij} = 1$ if module i is contained by cluster j. With modules indexed 0, 1, 2, …, 5 and clusters indexed 0, 1, 2, as shown in the figure, P_{const} and P_{avg} take the following forms.

$$P_{\text{const}} = \begin{pmatrix} 0 & 0 & 1 \\ 1 & 0 & 0 \\ 1 & 0 & 0 \\ 1 & 0 & 0 \\ 0 & 1 & 0 \\ 0 & 0 & 1 \end{pmatrix} \quad \text{and} \quad P_{\text{avg}} = \begin{pmatrix} w_{0,0} & 0 & 1 \\ 1 & 0 & 0 \\ 1 & w_{2,1} & 0 \\ 1 & 0 & w_{3,2} \\ 0 & 1 & w_{4,2} \\ 0 & w_{5,4} & 1 \end{pmatrix}$$

Each is applied separately to the x_c and y_c coordinate vectors of the coarse placement to obtain corresponding x and y coordinate vectors of the fine placement, e.g., $x = P_{\text{avg}}x_c$ and $y = P_{\text{avg}}y_c{}^*$ (see also Figure 19.5).

19.2.3 STRICT AGGREGATION VERSUS WEIGHTED AGGREGATION

A common objection to clustering is that its associations may be incorrect and therefore lead subsequent iterations to the wrong part of the solution space. To reduce the likelihood of poorly chosen clusters, the notion of a cluster can be generalized by weighted aggregation. Rather than assign each cell to just one cluster, we can break it into a small number of weighted fragments and assign the fragments to different coarse-level vertices; these are no longer simple clusters and are instead called aggregates. During interpolation, a cell's initial, inherited position is then typically determined by that of several aggregates as a weighted average [16]. Clustering, also called strict aggregation, is a special case of weighted aggregation. To our knowledge, weighted aggregation is not currently used by any published placement algorithm.

19.2.4 SCALABILITY

The scalability of the multilevel approach is straightforward to obtain and understand. Provided relaxation at each level has order linear in the number N_a of aggregates at that level, and the number

---

* Formally, the matrix for the interpolation operator on $s = (x, y) \in \mathbf{R}^n$ is $P = \text{diag}(P_x, P_y)$, where P_x is the interpolation matrix for the x coordinates, and P_y for y. In these examples, $P_x = P_y$.

of aggregates per level decreases by factor $r < 1$ at each level of coarsening, say $N_a(i) = r^i N$ at level i, the total order of a multilevel method is at most $cN(1 + r + r^2 + \cdots) = cN/(1 - r)$. Higher-order (nonlinear) relaxations can still be used, as long as at least one of the following restrictions is enforced.

1. Their use is limited to subsets of bounded size, e.g., by sweeps over overlapping windows of contiguous clusters at the current aggregation level.
2. Starting placement for iterations at each level is good enough that the termination criteria for relaxation at that level can be satisfied after a strictly controlled number of iterations.

In general, unstructured global optimization problems, these restrictions might sharply limit an algorithm's ability to explore the solution space in any scalable way. Placement, however, exhibits sparse local structure, where most variables are related through the objectives and constraints to only a small constant number of other variables. In the presence of such structure, both analysis and results obtained in practice have confirmed that these restrictions need not impair final quality of results [9].

19.2.5 Convergence Properties

Consider a Fourier decomposition of the error $e = \hat{x} - x^*$ in a system of equations $N(x) = 0$ (x^* denotes an exact solution, $\hat{x}$ is a computed approximation to x^*). By localized relaxation, we mean iterative optimization over a small subset of coupled variables, assuming all other variables are held fixed; e.g., Gauss Seidel (Equation 19.3). The fundamental observation is as follows [2]:

Observation 1 *Localized relaxation tends to rapidly reduce high-frequency components of the error in the system of equations. Lower-frequency components of the error are reduced much more slowly.*

There are two key consequences of the observation, both of which stem from the fact that the very notion of high-frequency comes from the modeling scale. First, different frequency-range Fourier components of the error are most efficiently targeted by relaxation at different scales. By coarsening the modeling scale, we can target a coarser scale of the error in the system—simply apply the same relaxation algorithm at the coarser scale. Recursion over all scales of relevance produces highly accurate solutions in extremely fast and scalable runtime. Second, both the outcome of relaxation and the convergence rates of individual variables during relaxation can be used to guide the construction of interpolation or aggregation operators. This connection underlies the basic principles of successful multiscale algorithms for systems of linear and nonlinear differential equations, where a robust convergence analysis has been obtained [2].

In this way, analysis and practice in both linear and nonlinear systems of equations have established a link between relaxation and interpolation for problems with local structure [9].

19.2.5.1 Error-Correcting Algorithm MG/Opt

Elementary local convergence properties of a general error-correcting multiscale optimization algorithm have been established by Lewis and Nash [17]. For simplicity, their consideration of constraints is omitted here. The error being corrected (to first-order) is introduced by transferring approximations from finer level to coarser levels.

Consider the unconstrained minimization of a smooth nonlinear function $F(s)$ over variables $s \in \mathbf{R}^n$ within a modeling system which generates multiple resolutions of F and s as specified by subscripts h (finer scale) and H (coarser scale). In placement, a resolution is primarily a selection of bin-grid dimensions used to enforce density constraints.

A convergent, continuous nonlinear relaxation algorithm R is assumed given, along with continuous interpolation operator I_H^h and continuous coarsening operator $I_h^H = \left(I_H^h\right)^{\mathrm{T}}$.

The following steps comprise on single iteration (at level h) of a multiscale optimization algorithm called MG/Opt [17]. The algorithm makes explicit use of first-order coarse-grid corrections. Given a resolution

$$\min_{s_h} F_h(s_h) \tag{19.7}$$

with initial estimate $s_h^{(0)}$. If this (h) is the coarsest resolution level, solve Equation 19.7 to the fullest possibly accuracy by means of relaxation R. Otherwise, apply the following steps.

1. Apply $N_1 > 0$ iterations of R directly to Equation 19.7, obtaining improved estimate $s_h^{(1)}$. Compute corresponding coarse-level estimate $s_H^{(1)} \equiv I_h^H s_h^{(1)}$.
2. Compute coarse-level gradient correction $v_H = \nabla F_H(s_{H,1}) - I_h^H \nabla F_h(s_{h,1})$.
3. Using initial point $s_{H,1}$, recursively apply this algorithm to the corrected coarse-level problem $\min_{s_H} F_H(s_H) - v_H^T s_H$ to obtain next iterate $s_{H,2}$.
4. Interpolate the coarse-grid step $s_{H,2} - s_{H,1}$ back to a finer-level search direction $e_h = I_H^h(s_{H,2} - s_{H,1})$.
5. Perform line search (for scalar α) at level h to obtain next iterate $s_{h,2} = s_{h,1} + \alpha e_h$.
6. Apply $N_2 > 0$ iterations of relaxation R to Equation 19.7 with initial point $s_{h,2}$ to obtain $s_{h,3}$.
7. Finally, discrete (noncontinuous) refinement steps may be used to transform $s_{h,3}$ to next iterate $s_h^{(1)}$.

At least one of N_1, N_2 must be strictly positive; the other may be positive or zero.

The algorithm is designed to be easy to implement from a given flat nonlinear relaxation and the ability to (a) model the problem at multiple resolutions and (b) transfer approximations between those resolutions.

It is shown by Lewis and Nash [17] that MG/Opt converges under the given assumptions. In particular, they establish the following facts rigorously.

1. Corrected coarse-level model approximates the fine-level model to first order in $\|e_h\|$.
2. Multiscale search direction e_h is a descent direction at the fine level: $e_h^T \nabla F_h(s_h^{(1)}) < 0$.
3. $\lim_{k \to \infty} \|\nabla F_h(s_h^{(k)})\| = 0$, i.e., algorithm MG/Opt converges.
4. Search directions e_h is well scaled; i.e., the natural step $\alpha = 1$ is likely to be accepted close to a solution s^*. The latter property is necessary for fast convergence.

19.3 MULTISCALE PLACEMENT IN PRACTICE

To design and implement a multiscale algorithm, one would like to know what requirements should be imposed on its coarsening and interpolation, relaxation, and iteration flow, and what trade-offs among them can be reasonably expected. In this section, we summarize characteristics of some leading multiscale algorithms and attempt to illustrate the trade-offs they create and the ways they manage them.

19.3.1 CLUSTERING-BASED PRECURSORS

Placement by multilevel optimization can be viewed as the natural recursive extension of clustering-based approaches considered in earlier work. Schuler and Ulrich [18] compared top-down and bottom-up approaches to clustering for linear placement. They observed large speedups compared to flat algorithms. They also observed that balancing cluster sizes (size incorporating both area and connectivity) was important. Mallela and Grover [19] studied clustering as a means of accelerating placement by simulated annealing. They maintained a priority-queue-like structure for cluster candidates. Sechen and Sun [20] employed three levels of clustering in an annealing-based flow. Hur and Lillis [21] used three levels of clustering in linear placement. Cong and Xu [22] studied clustering-based placement, where clustering is first performed based on MFFCs (maximum fanout-free cones) that consider signal directions and logic dependency. These clusters are then placed for timing optimization using TimberWolf6.0 [23], a well-known simulated-annealing-based placement package at that time.

To our knowledge, Ultrafast VPR [24] is the first published work to recursively cluster a circuit model into a hierarchy of models for placement by multiscale optimization. Ultrafast VPR is used to accelerate the annealing-based VPR algorithm (versatile packing, placement and routing [25]) to reduce design times on field-programmable gate arrays (FPGAs) at some expense in placement quality. (FPGA placement quality in Ultrafast VPR is measured by the area used.)

19.3.2 COARSENING

An aggregation strategy defines a recursive transformation of the data functions (objectives and constraints) from finer-level to coarser-level representations. These transformations reduce the numbers of variables and constraints but sometimes increase their complexity as information is compressed. Although some results exist for the accuracy of these transformations as approximations to the original problem in the graph context [2], formal results are, to our knowledge, not yet known in the hypergraph setting. For this reason, contemporary convergence criteria in practice rely on heuristics and empirical observations.

General clustering algorithms are described in Chapter 7. Typically, clustering algorithms for placement merge tightly connected cells in a way that eliminates as many nets at the adjacent coarser level as possible while satisfying some constraint on variation in cluster areas. A class of coarsening algorithms more general than clustering is described briefly in Section 19.2.3.

Important questions for coarsening in practice include the following:

1. How accurately do coarsened objectives and constraints approximate their corresponding finer-level counterparts? What error is incurred?
2. How much coarser than its finer-level source should a coarsened problem be?
3. How much variation in cluster areas should be allowed?
4. How coarse is too coarse? That is, when should recursive coarsening stop?
5. What trade-offs exist between (a) coarsening and relaxation and (b) coarsening and iteration flow? For example, how often can an algorithm afford to revise or completely reconstruct its coarsening hierarchy, and by what means?
6. Should the coarsening model the solution at the finer level, or the change in a given approximation to that solution? Why?

The questions are interdependent, and precise answers for placement are not yet known. Leading academic multiscale placers model the full placement problem at coarser levels rather than the change in a given placement as described in Sections 19.2.1 and 19.2.5. Only force directed placement (FDP)/line search directed placement (LSD) changes its coarsening/interpolation operators over its flow (Section 19.3.3).

The following classifications of coarsening algorithms for multiscale placement are sometimes used.

1. Connectivity-based versus location-based: Although netlist connectivity is always used to some extent, location-based algorithms also require a given current placement as input and attempt to keep neighboring modules together (see Section 19.3.2.2).
2. Transient versus persistent [26]: Transient clusters appear as part of the inner steps of an algorithm but are not associated with coarse-level variables. For example, clusters are formed in multiscale partitioning algorithms used in top-down bisection-based placement, but they are not separately placed. Persistent clusters, on the other hand, are computed a-priori and are actually placed.

3. Score-based versus scoreless [27]: In scoreless algorithms, clusters are committed as soon as they are formed. Examples described in Chapter 7 include edge coarsening, heavy-edge matching, and first choice. In score-based algorithms, alternative candidates are assigned scores and iteratively refined. As the refinement proceeds, the clustering scores are updated, eventually only candidates with sufficiently high scores are selected to serve as clusters. Examples described below include Best choice [26], Fine-granularity [28], and Net cluster [27].

Leading multiscale algorithms limit variation of cluster areas at each level of hierarchy. APlace [29] and NTUPlace3 [30] limit cluster areas to at most 1.5 times the target cluster area. FastPlace3 limits its cluster areas to at most 5 times the target.

Among connectivity-based algorithms, experiments to date suggest that local-connectivity-driven greedy strategies like first-choice vertex matching [31,32] and best choice [26] may be more effective than global-connectivity-driven approaches like edge-separability clustering (ESC) [33]. How best to define coarse-level netlists without explosive growth in the number and degree of coarsened hyperedges relative to coarsened vertices is particularly challenging [27,28,32]; Sections 19.3.2.3 and 19.3.2.4 describe recently proposed solutions.

Although various forms of clustering dominate the recent multiscale placement literature, Rent's rule and the importance of limiting cutsize also make recursive partitioning an attractive means of generating the multiscale hierarchy [7]. Hybrid algorithms for floorplanning or placement that combine clustering with netlist partioning in some form continue to be developed [7,12,34–38].

19.3.2.1   Best-Choice Clustering

As described in Chapter 7 and briefly summarized here, best-choice clustering [26] is the method used by the leading multiscale tools APlace [29], mPL [39], FastPlace 3.0 [40], and RQL [14]. Best choice is a netlist-based, score-based algorithm typically used in placement for persistent or semipersistent clustering.

A graph is defined on the netlist vertices (modules) with each edge weighted by the affinity of the given two vertices. The affinity may represent some weighted combination of complex objectives, such as hypergraph connectivity, spatial proximity, timing delay, area balance, coarse-level hyperedge elimination, etc. The affinities $s(i,j)$ between vertices i and j used by APlace, mPL, FastPlace3, RQL, and NTUPlace3* for connectivity-based clustering are all equal to or slightly modified from the basic affinity formula

$$s(i,j) = \frac{\sum_{e \in N_{ij}} w(e)}{a_i + a_j} \tag{19.8}$$

where
   N_{ij} is the set of nets containing both module i and module j
   a_i and a_j are the respective areas of modules i and j
   $w(e)$ denotes the weight of hyperedge e, typically taken proportional to $1/(|e| - 1)$

An affinity-ordered priority queue (heap) of the vertices (including clusters and partial clusters) is formed; each vertex in the heap is associated with its nearest neighbor under the given affinity metric. At each step, the pair of vertices (u, v) with the highest affinity is removed from the heap and clustered, if its total area does not violate the maximum-area constraint. For efficiency, a lazy-update strategy is then employed: the affinities of the netlist neighbor vertices of u and v are marked as invalid rather than being immediately updated. Affinities of invalid vertices are updated only when they arrive at the top of the heap.

---

* NTUPlace3 uses first choice rather than best choice.

Compared with earlier pass-based algorithms lacking a heap-order organization, the priority-queue formulation consistently improves HPWL of final placements. In experiments reported by the authors [26], final HPWL obtained by the multiscale placer hATP using best choice improves by 4.3 percent over edge coarsening and by 3.2 percent over first choice. Similar improvements have been reported for APlace [41] and mPL [39].

19.3.2.2 Location-Based Clustering

Location-based clustering is also called layout-based clustering or physical clustering. After an initial placement has been obtained as a starting configuration, spatial proximity can be incorporated into the vertex-affinity metric used for clustering [12,16]. A simple three-level illustration is given in Figure 19.6.

Earlier versions of mPL [16] incorporated distance as a reciprocal factor in a second V-cycle.* FDP [12] uses an (additive) convex combination of connectivity and spatial proximity for its vertex affinity function in hybrid first-choice clustering. Specifically, the affinity score $s(i,j)$ between vertices i and j is defined for a given placement as

$$s_{\text{FDP}}(i,j) = \lambda \left(\sum_{e \in N_{ij}} \frac{1}{1 + |x_i - x_j| + |y_i - y_j| - \zeta} \right) + (1 - \lambda) \sum_{e \in N_{ij}} \frac{1}{|e| - 1}$$

where
N_{ij} is the set of nets containing both vertex i and vertex j
$|e|$ is the number of vertices in e
ζ specifies the minimum displacement possible between nonoverlapping modules i and j

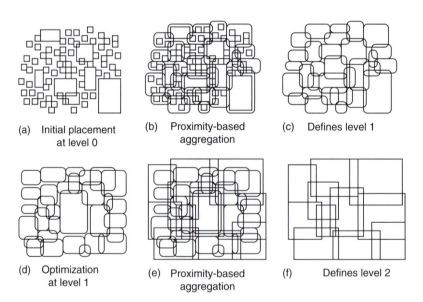

(a)   Initial placement at level 0   (b)   Proximity-based aggregation   (c)   Defines level 1

(d)   Optimization at level 1   (e)   Proximity-based aggregation   (f)   Defines level 2

FIGURE 19.6 Location-based clustering in a three-level multiscale-placement flow. Given an initial placement at the finest level, clusters at each subsequent coarser level are determined from a combination of netlist connectivity and spatial proximity.

---

* Later versions of mPL, however, abandoned the location-based approach in favor of a single V-cycle derived by purely connectivity-driven best-choice clustering [42].

The authors report best results for $\lambda \approx 0.25$. The effect stabilizes iterations and supports multiple V-cycles.

Location-constrained clustering is used in a somewhat different way to define the coarsest level of a three-level formulation used in FastPlace 3.0 [40]. While the first level of fine-grain clustering (cf. Section 19.3.2.3) relies solely on netlist affinities (Equation 19.8) and best choice, the second coarse-grain clustering imposes the added restriction that vertices must be closer than a certain parametrized limit in order to be clustered. In FastPlace 3.0, that limit is set to 10 percent of the maximum chip dimension.

A similar hybrid approach to clustering, using only netlist-connectivity at finer levels but both connectivity and proximity at the coarsest level, is used by mFar [11,43].

The work of Chen et al. [44] describes a more radical approach.* A cluster hierarchy is derived from four separate preliminary placements. Several iterations of the successive-overrelaxation (SOR) variant of coordinate-wise relaxation [15] are applied to the linear equations for the optimality of flat, unconstrained quadratic HPWL perturbed by density-balancing forces computed by a Poisson solver [10]. In each of four separate trials, the cells are initially placed all at the same point: one of the four corners of the placement region. Clusters are selected according to cells' average final proximity over the results of all four trials. Although this iterative, empirical approach to clustering requires significant runtime, it is a fixed initial cost that can be amortized over the cost of subsequent iterations. Numerical results confirm the scalability of this approach.

19.3.2.3 Mutual Contraction and Fine-Granularity Clustering

A central obstacle to multilevel placement of netlists is that, in the course of recursive clustering, modules tend to be eliminated far more rapidly than nets. The result is often extremely densely interconnected coarse-level netlists with very different structure from the original finest-level netlists they are intended to approximate. The problem has been partly addressed in the literature by clustering schemes that strive to eliminate as many nets as possible [32], in particular, nets of low degree. To this end, the mutual contraction formulation [28] models the relative strength of a connection between modules u and v relative to u's total connectivity as

$$w_r(u, v) = \frac{w'(u, v)}{\sum_x w'(u, x)}$$

where the weight $w'(e) = 2/\{[d(e) - 1]d(e)\}$ comes from clique-model (graph-based) approximations of hyperedges in the netlist. The contraction of two modules is defined as the symmetrized product $c_p(x, y) = w_r(x, y)w_r(y, x)$; a pair of modules with a large contraction relative to other pairs is a good candidate for clustering. The notion is readily extended to arbitrary subsets of modules.

In fine-granularity clustering [28], the contraction metric is used to order connections between modules in a priority queue. The modules at the front of the queue are grouped together if their grouping does not violate area-balance or other constraints. A target cluster limit is set a priori; clustering typically stops with most clusters containing two or three modules of average area.

19.3.2.4 Net Cluster

The above strategies share a dependence on metrics derived from pairs of vertices but are largely oblivious to netlist structure involving more than two vertices. The net–cluster study [27] shows that aggregation criteria defined over local subsets broader than simple pairs of vertices can be used to improve quality and runtime of existing multiscale placers. In particular, clustering the vertices of a single multipin net is shown in many instances to improve quality of results over what can be

---

* The hierarchy is used by Chen et al. to solve the linear system of equations for a flat, Poisson-based analytical placement formulation rather than to directly support multilevel placement.

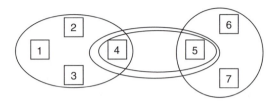

FIGURE 19.7 Netlist with a natural clustering the vertex-pair-based algorithms typically fail to find. The natural clustering most appropriate for placement (or netlist partitioning) groups vertices 1–4 in one cluster and vertices 5–7 in another. Vertex-pair-based algorithms overwhelmingly prefer to cluster vertices 4 and 5, precluding the natural clustering.

obtained with pairwise strategy; cf. Figure 19.7. Another advantage of net cluster is that it reduces the number of nets at approximately the same rate as the number of vertices.

The net cluster algorithm consists of five distinct steps partitioned into two phases.

Phase 1. Candidate cluster (a) identification, (b) refinement, and (c) scoring
Phase 2. Net-cluster (a) scoring and (b) final formation

Initial cluster candidates for phase 1 are simply the nets in the netlist; note that these are not disjoint. Refinement of the candidates proceeds one by one on each of them. For each one, several iterations of FM bipartitioning (Chapter 7) are performed, the cluster candidate used as one subset of the netlist and the rest of the netlist as the other. That is, this step attempts to determine whether each vertex in a cluster candidate is more strongly connected to other vertices in the cluster or to the vertices external to it. After this refinement step, each candidate cluster C_i is scored by

$$s_c(C_i) = \frac{\#\text{nets inside the cluster}}{\#\text{modules inside the cluster}} \times \frac{1}{\text{cluster area}}$$

That is, the score prefers candidate clusters that (1) absorb many nets, (2) aggregate many modules, and (3) have low area. At the end of phase 1, candidate clusters still are not disjoint.

In phase 2, each *net* N_i is then also assigned a score equal to the sum of the scores of the candidate clusters containing it minus the sum of the scores of the candidate clusters cutting it (see Ref. [27] for the precise form). Nets are then visited in descending score order, with one of the four following possible cases applied to each net.

1. If clustering the cells violates cluster-area constraints, then this net is ignored, and the next net is considered.
2. Otherwise, the cells in the net are clustered if none of them have already been clustered.
3. Otherwise, if just one cell in the net has already been clustered, the net can be merged with an existing cluster, if doing so does not violate cluster-area constraints.
4. Otherwise, if at least two cells in the net have already been assigned to different clusters, a merge of all these overlapping clusters and the cells in the current net is made, if doing so does not violate cluster-area constraints.

The net cluster study supports the view that considerable improvement in both runtime and QoR of existing multilevel algorithms may be attainable through a more accurate modeling of local netlist structure during aggregation. On ICCAD2004 test cases of up to approximately 200,000 objects, a single pass of net cluster improves final HPWL of leading multiscale placers mPL6 [39] and NTUPlace3 [30] by 2–5 percent on average.

TABLE 19.1

Approximate Numbers of Clusters $N_{coarsest}$ at Coarsest Levels of Leading Academic Multiscale Placers

Placer	APlace	Dragon	FastPlace3	FDP/LSD	mPL	NTUPlace3
$N_{coarsest}$	2000	4	$N_{finest}/4$	1000	500	6000

Note: The finest-level netlist has N_{finest} modules.

19.3.2.5 Coarsest Level

Because the initial placement at the coarsest level may have a large influence at subsequent iterations, and because the coarsest-level problem is relatively small, the placement at this level is typically performed with great care, to the highest quality possible. For example, mPL [39] uses nonlinear programming while mPG [5] uses simulated annealing. How to judge the coarse-level placement quality is not necesssarily obvious, however, as the coarse-level objective may not correlate strictly with the ultimate fine-level objectives. Under such circumstances, multiple iterations over the entire hierarchical flow may sometimes be important [6,16], evaluation of objectives and constraints at the finest level providing feedback to the representation and optimization at all coarser levels.

Coarsest-level problem sizes of some leading multiscale algorithms are shown in Table 19.1. From the table it is evident that an enormous range of coarsest-level problem sizes exists, from just four movable objects in Dragon [7] to $N/4$ in FastPlace3, where N is the number of modules in the original netlist. The observation that flat (non-multiscale) algorithms, e.g., [13,45] remain competitive suggests that there is no inherent upper limit to best coarsest-level problem size. Similarly, Dragon's results [7] and results from other problem domains [46,47] strongly suggest the absence of any hard lower bound. The complexity of integer nonconvex nonlinear programming, to which placement belongs, is high enough that multiscaling can sometimes produce superior solutions to flat algorithms even when fewer than 100 variables are present.

19.3.2.6 Numbers of Levels

Netlist-driven clustering by variations of best choice or first choice seems to allow a rapid reduction in the number of modeling levels, by allowing a large cluster-size target, without loss of final placement quality. In APlace, each coarse cluster level has about 1/10 the number of movable objects of its adjacent finer level; from Section 19.3.2.5, this rule produces just four levels of hierarchy for APlace on a 1M-module test case. In NTUPlace3, this ratio is approximately 1/5, and in mPL6 it is approximately 1/4.

In contrast, in the location-based clustering used by FDP/LSD [12,48], at most 35 percent of modules are aggregated in one pass of clustering, leaving a much larger number of levels. From Section 19.3.2.5, this rule produces 20 levels of hierarchy for FDP/LSD on a 1M-module test case.

19.3.3 ITERATION FLOW

Of all the leading multiscale placers cited in this chapter, FDP/LSD [48] is the only one known to rely on more than a single pass of successive refinement from coarsest to finest level (cf. Figure 19.3). After each such pass of successive refinement in FDP/LSD, the entire hierarchy is reconstructed, using location-based clustering (Section 19.3.2.2), with one less level of clustering than used in the preceding pass. On a 1M-module test case, this flow constructs a total of $20 + 19 + \cdots + 1 \approx 200$ distinct problem formulations over its history.

19.3.4 RELAXATION

Iterative improvement at each level may employ various techniques—network flows, simu-lated annealing, nonlinear programming, force-directed models—provided that it can support incorporation of complex constraints appropriate to the modeling scale at the current level.

Important considerations for relaxation include the following:

1. Should it be local (e.g., annealing-based) or global (e.g., force-directed)?
2. How should net models (objectives) and density models be adapted to different modeling scales?
3. To what extent should relaxation be expected to change the starting configuration it inherits from an adjacent level?
4. What termination criteria should be used?
5. How scalable must the relaxation be?
6. How easily can it be implemented?
7. How readily can it be adapted to accomodate additional complex constraints?

For example, in both mPL and APlace, the density grid sizes, and log-sum-exp HPWL smoothing parameter, and bin-grid density smoothing parameters are chosen to match the scale of resolution implied by the average cluster size. For this reason, both these engines carefully control the variation in cluster sizes during coarsening.

19.3.4.1 mPL6

In mPL5 [49] and mPL6 [39], fast numerical PDE solvers are used in a generalization of the Eisenmann–Johannes force-directed model [10,13] at each level of hierarchy (Chapter 18). The global NLP relaxations in mPL6 are observed to dramatically improve quality over the earlier implementations [50] relying more on localized iterations. In mPL6 [39], iterations at each level terminate when the average area–density overflow over all bins is sufficiently small. Convergence to nonuniform area–density distributions is enabled by the introduction of filler cells [51] unconnected to modules in the netlist. These are introduced hierarchically from the top-down in proportion to the white space available in each rectangular subregion region following the initial unconstrained placement. In addition, these filler cells are periodically redistributed from scratch from the top-down.

Adjustment of relative weights assigned to the log-sum-exp HPWL objective and the density constraints in mPL6 is intriguing. Modules do not simply spread monotonically toward their final positions. Instead, at every level of hierarchy, the HPWL term is given a large enough weight at early iterations to allow modules to contract together tightly enough to alter relative positions before sub-sequent increase of the density weight and re-expansion of the modules toward a more area-uniform configuration. These alternating contracting and expanding motions seem to confer additional hill-climbing ability to mPL6 and improve its final solution quality significantly compared with simpler and faster monotonic spreading.

19.3.4.2 APlace

In APlace [29,41], nonlinear conjugate gradients is used to iteratively improve a penalty function obtained for analytical approximations of a HPWL objective and bell-shaped bin-based area–density constraints (Chapter 18).

Relaxation at each level of APlace proceeds by the Polak–Ribiere variant of nonlinear conjugate gradients [52] with golden-section linesearch [53]. A hard iteration limit of 100 is imposed. The grid size $|G|$, objective weight, wirelength smoothing parameter α, and area–density potential radius r are selected and adjusted at each level to guide the convergence. Bin size and α are taken proportional to the average cluster size at the current level. The density-potential radius r is set to 2 on most grids but is increased to 4 at the finest grid to prevent oscillations in the maximum cell-area density of any bin. The density-potential weight is fixed at one. The wirelength weight is initially set rather large and is subsequently decreased by 0.5 to escape from local minima with too much overlap. As iterations proceed, the relative weight of the area–density penalty increases, and a relatively uniform cell-area distribution is obtained.

Termination in APlace is based on discrepancy, defined for a given window size A as the maximum ratio of module area in any circumscribing rectangle of area A. Compared with other tools, this measure of density control is quite strict and may account in part for APlace's relatively long runtimes [54].

19.3.4.3 FDP/LSD

In the FDP/LSD [12,48] placer, a multilevel formulation is seen as a way of improving the relative positions of modules following an analytic, unconstrained quadratic HPWL-minimizing initial placement. In particular, clustering of tightly connected modules forces them to remain spatially close, even as other modules less strongly connected to those in the cluster are allowed to migrate away. After the initial analytical placement, netlist partitioning is also incorporated as a means of further separating modules in congested regions before subsequent quadratic placement steps. In contrast to most earlier work, the FDP authors specifically cite large quality improvements due solely to the multilevel formulation.

Termination in FDP is controlled by normalized Klee measure [55], in which the total amount of core area occupied by overlapping modules is accurately computed by a segment-tree technique and then divided by the sum of all module areas. This spread-metric fraction is strictly less than 1 when overlap exists and approaches 1 as overlap is removed. The FDP multiscale flow terminates, and legalization commences, when approximately 30 percent overlap remains according to this metric; i.e., when the spread-metric fraction is approximately 0.7.

19.3.4.4 Dragon

In Dragon [7,37], an initial cutsize-minimizing quadrisection is followed by a bin-swapping-based refinement, in which entire partition blocks at the given level are interchanged in an effort to reduce total wirelength. Recursive quadrisection and bin-swapping proceeds to the finest level. At all levels except the last, low-temperature simulated annealing is used to swap partition blocks. At the finest level, a more detailed and greedy strategy is employed. Dragon has been successfully adapted to incorporate complex constraints such as timing and routability.

19.3.5 INTERPOLATION

Interpolation (a.k.a declustering, uncoarsening) maps a placement at a given coarser level to a placement at the adjacent finer level. The most common interpolation functions used in placement are piecewise constant, wherein each module at the finer level simply inherits the current position of its parent cluster at the coarser level.

Simple declustering and linear assignment can be effective, particularly in contexts with uniformly sized modules [56]. With this approach, each component cluster is initially placed at the center of its parent's location. If an overlap-free configuration is needed, a uniform bin grid can be laid down, and clusters can be assigned to nearby bins or sets of bins. The complexity of this assignment can be reduced by first partitioning clusters into smaller windows, e.g., of 500 clusters each. If clusters can be assumed to have uniform size, then fast linear assignment can be used. Otherwise, approximation heuristics are needed.

Under AMG-style weighted disaggregation, interpolation proceeds by weighted averaging: each finer-level cluster is initially placed at the weighted average of the positions of all coarser-level clusters with which its connection is sufficiently strong [16,57]. Finer-level connections can also be used: once a finer-level cluster is placed, it can be treated as a fixed, coarser-level cluster for the purpose of placing subsequent finer-level clusters. Weighted aggregation is described further in Section 19.2.3.

A constructive approach, as in Ultrafast VPR [24], can also lead to extremely fast and scalable algorithms. At each level, clusters are initially placed in the following sequence: (i) clusters directly connected to output pads, (ii) clusters directly connected to input pads, and (iii) other clusters.

19.3.6 MULTISCALE LEGALIZATION AND DETAILED PLACEMENT

Multiscale algorithms and ideas are featured in recent studies of legalization of mixed-size placements, where the largest objects may be several orders of magnitude larger than the smallest modules. In this setting, the transition from GP to legalization takes on increased importance, as final legalization at the finest level may be difficult or impossible without massive disruption of the given global placement, unless the global placer's estimates of constraint satisfiability are sufficiently precise.

In mPL6 [42], the largest modules at each cluster level are legalized before interpolation to the adjacent finer level. In this way, the multiscale framework is used to smooth the transition between levels and increase the predictability at coarse levels of the final quality of results at the finest level. The multiscale flow essentially decomposes mixed-size legalization into a sequence of legalizations of clusters sizes balanced to within the tolerance prescribed during coarsening. In this way, it efficiently supports look-ahead legalization [36,58] of difficult-to-legalize test cases [30], which can improve QoR on high-utilization designs.

Multiscale ideas are also used in detailed placement [21,59,60]; cf. Chapter 20.

19.4   CONCLUSION

In practice, there is no single, simple, generic prescription for transforming a flat algorithm for placement into a multilevel algorithm. Consistent improvement from one level to the next depends on close coordination of coarsening, relaxation, and interpolation; this coordination depends in turn on the specific ways in which aggregates are defined and a given placement is improved. Intralevel stopping criteria, limits on variation in cluster size, the ratio of problem sizes at adjacent levels, and the number of variables and constraints at the coarsest level may vary across different implementations. Ultimately, the precise settings of these parameters are generally derived empirically. In practice, intralevel termination criteria are designed so that relaxation ends soon after reduction in objectives and relaxed constraint violations slows. Intralevel and outer-flow convergence criteria must complement each other to enable iterative identification of the best solutions.

Nevertheless, in recent years some trends have emerged following the 2005 and 2006 ISPD placement contests [61,62]. Although clustering has long been viewed as a straightforward means to speed and scalability [18–20,24], recent results demonstrate clearly that leading multilevel optimization implementations also produce superior quality [4,12,37,49]. Improved priority-queue-based greedy clustering [26] increases the accuracy of coarse-level representations. Monotonic decrease at coarser levels generally amounts to hill climbing at the finest level, the corresponding large-scale moves of aggregates bypassing local variations en route to globally improved configurations. Clustering errors must be reversible by sufficiently powerful forms of relaxation, interpolation, and iteration flow (e.g., multiple or recursive V-cycles). However, relaxation at finer levels must be scalable, and it must both respect its starting solution inherited from coarser levels and also be able to improve it rapidly.

Netlist-driven priority-queue-based greedy clustering [26] enables rapid reduction in problem size, up to 10 times per level, at no apparent cost in solution quality. Vertex-affinity heuristics such as fine-granularity clustering and net cluster, designed to aggressively reduce net counts at coarser levels, are widely used. Location-based or physical clustering can be used to support multiple traversals over multiple hierarchies. However, best results published to date are still attained by algorithms using just one pass of succesive refinement, from coarsest to finest level, with relatively powerful global relaxation at each level.

Improved formulations of flat analytical placement [10,63,64] have served as superior forms of relaxation in several recent leading multilevel placement implementations [4,49,65], possibly in part because the global view in iterative improvement complements the locality of clustering.

Finally, we note that variants of multiscale placement have also played a significant role in recent advances in hybrid methods for partitioning-based placement (Chapter 15) and floorplanning (Chapter 12).

ACKNOWLEDGMENT

Partial support for this work has been provided by Semiconductor Research Consortium Contract 2003-TJ-1091 and National Science Foundation Contracts CCF 0430077 and CCF-0528583. This chapter is derived from the article in Ref. [50].

REFERENCES

1. A. Brandt. Multi-level adaptive solutions to boundary value problems. *Mathematics of Computation*, 31(138):333–390, 1977.
2. W. L. Briggs, V. E. Henson, and S. F. McCormick. *A Multigrid Tutorial*, 2nd edn. SIAM, Philadelphia, 2000.
3. J. Cong and X. Yuan. Multilevel global placement with retiming. In *Proceedings of Design Automation Conference*, pp. 208–213, New York, 2003. ACM Press.
4. A. B. Kahng and Q. Wang. Implementation and extensibility of an analytic placer. *IEEE Transactions on Computer-Aided Design of Integrated and Systems*, 24(5):734–747, 2005. ISPD 2004–2006, ICCAD 2004–2005.
5. C. -C. Chang, J. Cong, D. Pan, and X. Yuan. Multilevel global placement with congestion control. *IEEE Transactions on Computer-Aided Design of Integrated and Systems*, 22(4):395–409, Apr 2003.
6. C. Li, M. Xie, C. K. Koh, J. Cong, and P. Madden. Routability-driven placement and white space allocation. In *Proceedings of International Conference on Computer-Aided Design*, San Jose, CA, pp. 394–401, Nov 2004.
7. T. Taghavi, X. Yang, B. -K. Choi, M. Wang, and M. Sarrafzadeh. Congestion minimization in modern placement circuits. In G. -J. Nam and J. Cong (editors), *Modern Circuit Placement: Best Practices and Results*, pp. 135–165. Springer, New York, 2007.
8. Y. Cheon, P. -H. Ho, A. B. Kahng, S. Reda, and Q. Wang. Power-aware placement. In *Proceedings of Design Automation Conference*, Anaheim, CA, pp. 795–800, 2005.
9. A. Brandt and D. Ron. Multigrid solvers and multilevel optimization strategies. In J. Cong and J. R. Shinnerl (editors), *Multilevel Optimization and VLSICAD*. Kluwer Academic Publishers, Boston, 2003, pp.1–69.
10. H. Eisenmann and F. M. Johannes. Generic global placement and floorplanning. In *Proceedings of 35th ACM/IEEE Design Automation Conference*, San Franscisco, CA, pp. 269–274, 1998.
11. B. Hu and M. Marek-Sadowska. mFar: Multilevel fixed-points addition-based VLSI placement. In G. -J. Nam and J. Cong (editors), *Modern Circuit Placement: Best Practices and Results*, pp. 229–246. Springer, New York, 2007.
12. K. Vorwerk and A. A. Kennings. An improved multi-level framework for force-directed placement. In *DATE*, Munich, Germany, pp. 902–907, 2005.
13. P. Spindler and F. M. Johannes. Kraftwerk: A fast and robust quadratic placer using an exact linear net model. In G. -J. Nam and J. Cong (editors), *Modern Circuit Placement: Best Practices and Results*, pp. 59–95. Springer, NY, 2007.
14. N. Viswanathan, G. -J. Nam, C. J. Alpert, P. Villarrubia, H. Ren, and C. Chu. RQL: Global placement via relaxed quadratic spreading and linearization. In *Proceedings of Design Automation Conference*, San Diego, CA, pp. 453–458, 2007.
15. G. H. Golub and C. F. Van Loan. *Matrix Computations*, 3rd edn. The Johns Hopkins University Press, Baltimore, Maryland, 1996.

16. T. F. Chan, J. Cong, T. Kong, J. Shinnerl, and K. Sze. An enhanced multilevel algorithm for circuit placement. In *Proceedings of International Conference on Computer-Aided Design*, San Jose, CA, pp. 299–306, Nov 2003.

17. R. M. Lewis and S. Nash. Practical aspects of multiscale optimization methods for VLSICAD. In J. Cong and J. R. Shinnerl (editors), *Multilevel Optimization and VLSICAD*. Kluwer Academic Publishers, Boston, 2003, pp. 265–291.

18. D. M. Schuler and E. G. Ulrich. Clustering and linear placement. In *Proceedings Design Automation Conference*, pp. 50–56, New York, 1972. ACM Press.

19. S. Mallela and L. K. Grover. Clustering based simulated annealing for standard cell placement. In *Proceedings of Design Automation Conference*, Atlantic City, NJ, pp. 312–317. IEEE Computer Society Press, 1988.

20. W. -J. Sun and C. Sechen. Efficient and effective placement for very large circuits. *IEEE Transactions on Computer-Aided Design*, 14(3):349–359, 1995.

21. S. -W. Hur and J. Lillis. Relaxation and clustering in a local search framework: Application to linear placement. In *Proceedings of ACM/IEEE Design Automation Conference*, pp. 360–366, New Orleans, 1999.

22. J. Cong and D. Xu. Exploiting signal flow and logic dependency in standard cell placement. In *Proceedings of Asia South Pacific Design Automation Conference*, p. 63, New York, 1995. ACM Press.

23. C. Sechen and K. W. Lee. An improved simulated annealing algorithm for row-based placement. In *Proceedings of International Conference on Computer-Aided Design*, San Jose, CA, pp. 478–481, 1987.

24. Y. Sankar and J. Rose. Trading quality for compile time: Ultra-fast placement for FPGAs. In *FPGA '99, ACM Symposium on FPGAs*, Monterey, CA, pp. 157–166, 1999.

25. V. Betz and J. Rose. VPR: A new packing, placement, and routing tool for FPGA research. In *Proceedings of International Workshop on FPL*, London, U.K., pp. 213–222, 1997.

26. G. J. Nam, C. Reda, C. J. Alpert, P. Villarrubia, and A. B. Kahng. A fast hierarchical quadratic placement algorithm. *IEEE Transactions on Computer-Aided Design of Integrated and Systems*, 25(4):678–691, 2006 (ISPD 2005).

27. J. Li, L. Behjat, and J. Huang. An effective clustering algorithm for mixed-size placement. In *Proceedings International Symposium on Physical Design*, Austin, TX, pp. 111–118, 2007.

28. B. Hu Marek-Sadowska, M. Fine granularity clustering based placement. *IEEE Transactions on Computer-Aided Design of Integrated and Systems*, 23(4): 527–536, 2004 (ISPD 2003: pp. 67–74, San Diego, CA and DAC 2003: pp. 800–805, Anaheim, CA).

29. A. Kahng, S. Reda, and Q. Wang. APlace: A high quality, large-scale analytical placer. In G. -J. Nam and J. Cong (editors), *Modern Circuit Placement: Best Practices and Results*, pp. 163–187. Springer, NY, 2007.

30. T. -C. Chen, Z. -W. Jiang, T. -C. Hsu, H. -C. Chen, and Y. -W. Chang. NTUPlace3: An analytical placer for large-scale mixed-size designs. In J. Cong and G. -J. Nam (editors), *Modern Circuit Placement: Best Practices and Results*, pp. 289–310. Springer, New York, 2007.

31. G. Karypis. Multilevel algorithms for multi-constraint hypergraph partitioning. Technical Report 99-034, Department of Computer Science, University of Minnesota, Minneapolis, 1999.

32. G. Karypis. Multilevel hypergraph partitioning. In J. Cong and J. R. Shinnerl (editors), *Multilevel Optimization and VLSICAD*. Kluwer Academic Publishers, Boston, 2003, pp. 125–154.

33. J. Cong and S. K. Lim. Edge separability based circuit clustering with application to circuit partitioning. In *Asia South Pacific Design Automation Conference*, Yokohama, Japan, pp. 429–434, 2000.

34. S. N. Adya, S. Chaturvedi, J. A. Roy, D. A. Papa, and I. L. Markov. Unification of partitioning, placement and floorplanning. In *Proceedings of International Conference on Computer-Aided Design*, San Jose, CA, pp. 12–17, 2004.

35. T. -C. Chen, Y. -W. Chang, and S. -C. Lin. Imf: Interconnect-driven multilevel floorplanning for large-scale building-module designs. In *Proceedings of International Conference on Computer-Aided Design*, pp. 159–164, Washington, DC, 2005. IEEE Computer Society.

36. A. N. Ng, I. L. Markov, R. Aggarwal, and V. Ramachandran. Solving hard instances of floorplacement. In *Proceedings of International Symposium on Physical Design*, pp. 170–177, New York, 2006. ACM Press.

37. M. Sarrafzadeh, M. Wang, and X. Yang. *Modern Placement Techiques*. Kluwer, Boston, 2002.

38. J. A. Roy, D. A. Papa, and I. L. Markov. Capo: Congestion-driven placement for standard-cell and RTL netlists with incremental capability. In G. -J. Nam and J. Cong (editors), *Modern Circuit Placement: Best Practices and Results*, pp. 97–134. Springer, New York, 2007.

39. T. F. Chan, J. Cong, J. R. Shinnerl, K. Sze, and M. Xie. mPL6: Enhanced multilevel mixed-size placement with congestion control. In G. -J. Nam and J. Cong (editors), *Modern Circuit Placement: Best Practices and Results*, pp. 247–288. Springer, NY, 2007.

40. N. Viswanathan, M. Pan, and C. Chu. FastPlace 3.0: A fast multilevel quadratic placement algorithm with placement congestion control. In *Proceedings of Asia South Pacific Design Automation Conference*, Yokohama, Japan, pp. 135–140, 2007.

41. A. B. Kahng, S. Reda, and Q. Wang. Architecture and details of a high quality, large-scale analytical placer. In *Proceedings of International Conference on Computer-Aided Design*, San Jose, CA, pp. 891–898, Nov 2005.

42. T. F. Chan, J. Cong, M. Romesis, J. R. Shinnerl, K. Sze, and M. Xie. mPL6: Enhanced multilevel mixed-size placement. In *Proceedings of International Symposium on Physical Design*, San Jose, CA, pp. 212–214, Apr 2006.

43. B. Hu and M. Marek-Sadowska. Multilevel fixed-point-addition-based VLSI placement. *IEEE Transactions on Computer-Aided Design of Integrated and Systems*, 24(8):1188–1203, 2005.

44. H. Chen, C. -K. Cheng, N. -C. Chou, A. B. Kahng, J. F. MacDonald, P. Suaris, B. Yao, and Z. Zhu. An algebraic multigrid solver for analytical placement with layout-based clustering. In *Proceedings of IEEE/ACM Design Automation Conference*, Anaheim, CA, pp. 794–799, 2003.

45. T. Luo and D. Z. Pan. DPlace: Anchor-cell-based quadratic placement with linear objective. In G. -J. Nam and J. Cong (editors), *Modern Circuit Placement: Best Practices and Results*, pp. 39–58. Springer, New York, 2007.

46. A. Brandt. Multiscale scientific computation: Review 2001. In T. Barth, R. Haimes, and T. Chan (editors), *Multiscale and Multiresolution Methods*. Springer Verlag, NY, 2001, pp. 3–95.

47. J. Cong and J. R. Shinnerl (editors). *Multilevel Optimization in VLSICAD*. Kluwer Academic Publishers, Boston, 2003.

48. K. Vorwerk and A. Kennings. Mixed-size placement via line search. In *Proceedings of International Conference on Computer-Aided Design*, San Jose, CA, pp. 899–904, 2005.

49. T. F. Chan, J. Cong, and K. Sze. Multilevel generalized force-directed method for circuit placement. In *Proceedings of International Symposium on Physical Design*, San Francisco, CA, pp. 185–192, 2005.

50. J. Cong, J. R. Shinnerl, M. Xie, T. Kong, and X. Yuan. Large-scale circuit placement. *ACM Transactions on Design Automation of Electronic Systems*, 10(2):389–430, 2005.

51. S. N. Adya, I. L. Markov, and P. Villarrubia. On whitespace and stability in mixed-size placement and physical synthesis. In *Proceedings of International Conference on Computer-Aided Design*, San Jose, CA, pp. 311–319, 2003.

52. S. G. Nash and A. Sofer. *Linear and Nonlinear Programming*. McGraw Hill, New York, 1996.

53. P. E. Gill, W. Murray, and M. H. Wright. *Practical Optimization*. Academic Press, London and New York, 1981. ISBN 0-12-283952-8.

54. http://www.sigda.org/ispd2006/contest.html.

55. K. Vorwerk, A. Kennings, and A. Vannelli. Engineering details of a stable force-directed placer. In *Proceedings of International Conference on Computer-Aided Design*, San Jose, CA, pp. 573–580, Nov 2004.

56. T. F. Chan, J. Cong, T. Kong, and J. Shinnerl. Multilevel optimization for large-scale circuit placement. In *Proceedings of International Conference on Computer-Aided Design*, pp. 171–176, San Jose, CA, Nov 2000.

57. I. Safro, D. Ron, and A. Brandt. Graph minimum linear arrangement by multilevel weighted edge contractions. *Journal of Algorithms*, 60(1): 24–41, 2006.

58. J. Cong, M. Romesis, and J. Shinnerl. Robust mixed-size placement under tight white-space constraints. In *Proceedings of International Conference on Computer-Aided Design*, San Jose, CA, pp. 165–172, Nov 2005.

59. A. B. Kahng, P. Tucker, and A. Zelikovsky. Optimization of linear placements for wirelength minimization with free sites. In *Proceedings Asia South Pacific Design Automation Conference*, Wanchai, Hong Kong, pp. 241–244, 1999.

60. M. Pan, N. Viswanathan, and C. Chu. An efficient and effective detailed placement algorithm. In *Proceedings of International Conference on Computer-Aided Design*, San Jose, CA, pp. 48–55, 2005.

61. G. -J. Nam, C. J. Alpert, P. Villarrubia, B. Winter, and M. Yildiz. The ISPD2005 placement contest and benchmark suite. In *Proceedings of International Symposium on Physical Design*, San Francisco, CA, pp. 216–220, Apr 2005.
62. G. -J. Nam. ISPD 2006 placement contest: Benchmark suite and results. In *Proceedings of International Symposium on Physical Design*, pp. 167–167, New York, 2006. ACM Press.
63. B. Hu and M. Marek-Sadowska. FAR: Fixed-points addition & relaxation based placement. In *Proceedings of International Symposium on Physical Design*, pp. 161–166, New York, 2002. ACM Press.
64. W. C. Naylor, D. Ross, and S. Lu. Nonlinear optimization system and method for wire length and delay optimization for an automatic electric circuit placer, Oct 2001.
65. B. Hu, Y. Zeng, and M. Marek-Sadowska. mFAR: Fixed-points-addition-based VLSI placement algorithm. In *Proceedings of International Symposium on Physical Design*, San Francisco, CA, pp. 239–241, Apr 2005.

20 Legalization and Detailed Placement

Ameya R. Agnihotri and Patrick H. Madden

CONTENTS

20.1 INTRODUCTION

In this chapter, we survey work on space management, legalization, and detailed placement, the design flow steps normally falling between global placement and the start of routing. Over the past few years, the traditional physical design flow has evolved. Where there was once a sequence of discrete steps, one now sees a blurring of activities and a great deal of iterative improvement. The methods described here should not be viewed as standalone optimizations; rather, they should be considered as components in a more complex multifaceted approach.

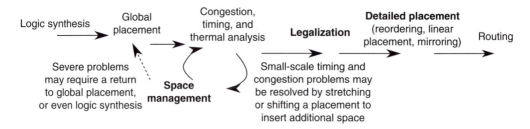

FIGURE 20.1 Traditional linear design flow has been replaced by a more iterative process. Legalization and detailed placement may reveal problems with routing or timing performance, necessitating changes to the placement, and repeated steps. To enable design convergence, it is desirable to have these changes incremental, with each new placement being similar to the prior one. This chapter focuses on the topics indicated in boldface text.

In early design flows, the transition from global placement to detailed placement was relatively simple. The logic elements were aligned to cell rows, and then small local optimizations were performed. With changes to routing models, and the dominance of interconnect delay, space management has fundamentally changed the design flow, and has emerged as a key element of successful strategies.

Figure 20.1 illustrates a current approach; following global placement, a number of methods can be used to analyze a placement. Congestion estimation [1] can identify regions where routing demand will likely exceed the available resources; an effective technique is to insert additional white space between logic elements, spreading out the circuit and gaining more room for wiring. Similarly, timing analysis may find slow paths that can be improved through buffer insertion or gate sizing; again, spreading out of the circuit may be required to provide room for the new logic elements. Thermal hot spots are also a major concern on high-performance devices, and additional space is yet again needed.

A primary motivation for using a space management-based approach is that it provides a measure of stability [2] in the design flow. If one were to return to global placement each time a routing or timing problem was encountered, it would be difficult to achieve design closure; a new placement might eliminate previous problems, but new problems are likely to arise. By shifting and adjusting an existing placement, it is easier to achieve design closure.

For most of the discussion, we focus on the simple objective of half-perimeter wirelength (HPWL) minimization. It should be noted, however, that HPWL is only an estimate of routing demand, and in many cases, this can be far off. For nets with up to three pins, HPWL is the best possible length that could be achieved; for higher degree nets, both minimum spanning trees and Steiner trees can have higher lengths.

The actual length of the interconnect wiring can be increased greatly by the insertion of detours; for dense, congested designs, it may not be possible to avoid detours. The routability of a circuit can be enhanced considerably by adding additional space into a placement; while this can increase HPWL, it may be necessary for successful routing, and can actually improve routed wirelength by reducing the number of detours.

Even if one were to be able to accurately estimate routing lengths, this is not in itself a meaningful metric. Far more important is the delay of the circuitry, which impacts the maximum operating frequency. Similarly, the length of the interconnect impacts switching capacitance and power consumption, but the actual switching behavior must be considered to have an accurate estimate. Although low HPWL correlates with good performance, it should not be viewed as the sole metric for evaluating a placement.

We attempt to highlight how various optimization techniques interact with each other. Although the mixing of techniques results in better overall circuit designs, it also becomes more difficult to quantify the effect of each component.

Our discussion begins with a brief summary of routing models, and how they have changed over the years. With modern designs, space management is essential for achieving routability; the semiconductor industry has switched from a variable-die design style to a fixed-die model, resulting in the distinct possibility that a dense design will fail to route successfully (Figure 20.2). Some optimization methods performed during detail placement may seem counterintuitive unless one considers the routing constraints. After discussing the routing models, we then focus on methods to distribute space within a global placement; this has been an active area over the past few years, and a great deal of progress has been made.

Successful routing is not the only reason that space insertion is of interest. High-performance designs commonly face problems with power delivery and heat removal, spacing out active devices spreads heating, resulting in lower peak temperatures. Yet another application of space insertion methods is as a way to reserve area for timing optimization. As part of an iterative improvement process, individual logic gates may be resized, and buffers can be inserted into long wires. Designs that are not densely packed can accomodate these changes without a great deal of disruption in the overall structure.

After space insertion, a placement must be legalized. Standard cells must align into rows, and may also need to follow a column grid. Overlaps between both standard cells and macroblocks macro must be removed. For legalization, some problems are easy, allowing a remarkably simple method to be used; one objective of space management methods can be to make legalization problems easy.

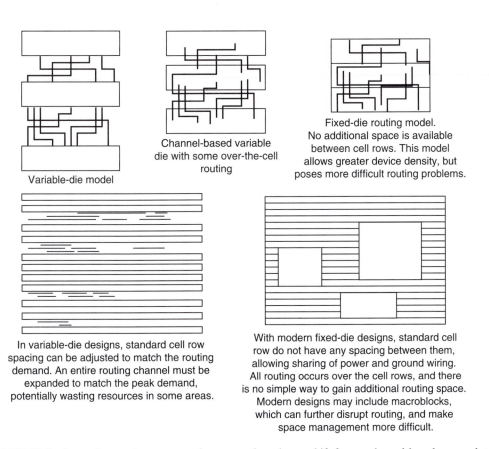

Variable-die model

Channel-based variable die with some over-the-cell routing

Fixed-die routing model. No additional space is available between cell rows. This model allows greater device density, but poses more difficult routing problems.

In variable-die designs, standard cell row spacing can be adjusted to match the routing demand. An entire routing channel must be expanded to match the peak demand, potentially wasting resources in some areas.

With modern fixed-die designs, standard cell row do not have any spacing between them, allowing sharing of power and ground wiring. All routing occurs over the cell rows, and there is no simple way to gain additional routing space. Modern designs may include macroblocks, which can further disrupt routing, and make space management more difficult.

FIGURE 20.2 Increasing routing resources have caused routing to shift from a channel-based approach to over-the-cell. In the fixed-die, over-the-cell model, it may not be possible to shift logic elements apart to gain additional routing resources.

For designs that are dense, legalization is difficult, and more robust methods are necessary if one is to obtain good results.

For legalization of designs that contain both macroblocks and standard cells, there are two distinct approaches. One method first first fixes the positions of macroblocks, and then fills the space between them with standard cells. A second approach is to legalize macroblocks and standard cells simultaneously.

Once a placement is legal, with all overlaps removed and logic elements properly aligned, optimizations that are traditionally classified as detailed placement can be applied. Small groups of standard cells can be shifted or reordered—these local optimizations can have a dramatic impact on wirelength. To maximize the size of an optimization window with acceptable runtimes, dynamic programming is frequently used.

20.1.1 NOTATION

When presenting specific algorithms, we utilize the following notation. For an integrated circuit, the netlist will contain a set of cells $C = \{c_1, c_2, c_3, \ldots, c_n\}$, connected by a set of signal nets $N = \{n_1, n_2, n_3, \ldots, n_m\}$. Each net connects a subset of the cells.

A placement P of a netlist consists of precise x and y positionings for each cell c_i. We focus on transformations of P to another similar placement P' such that the placement has lower overlap, becomes legal, has better wirelength, and so on.

For simplicity, in most cases we assume that the nets connect to the centers of the cells, and we treat macroblocks and standard cells in the same way. Extending the methods described to use exact pin positions is trivial.

20.1.2 ROUTING MODELS

Over the years, the increasing numbers of interconnect layers has driven changes in routing models. This has impacted detail placement in interesting ways.

In earlier variable-die designs, routing success could almost always be assured (given sufficient space). In standard cell designs, the spacing between rows can be adjusted as needed. In earlier fabrication technologies, there were relatively few layers of interconnect metal, and thus most routing occurred in channels between rows. For a congested design, where more routing resources are needed, one would simply need to expand the space between a pair of rows, thereby gaining the necessary resources. If more routing resource was required between rows, a "feedthrough" could be inserted into the row.

With the growth in the number of available metal interconnect layers came the ability to route some connections over cells. For a period, there were T-shaped channels. Some connections were made between rows, but a portion was made directly above. As with variable-die designs, there was flexibility to adjust row spacing.

As the number of interconnect layers further increased, progressively more routing was done above the cells, with cell row spacing decreasing until the traditional channel was eliminated entirely. This is known as the fixed-die routing model. The fixed-die model brings cells closer together, lowering overall wirelengths.

Fixed-die routing now dominates the industry, but faces the problem of routing failure. If a portion of the design has excessive routing demand, there is no simple way to provide additional routing space; space management methods described later in this chapter are gaining popularity as a means to combat routing failure.

Although adding space to a fixed-die design is not trivial, one can in fact leverage a number of techniques found in analytic placement. Figure 20.3 shows an intermediate step in analytic placement, and the congestion map as might be produced by Liu's model [1]. Spreading methods that are applied to an analytic placement can also be applied to gain routing space.

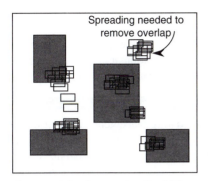
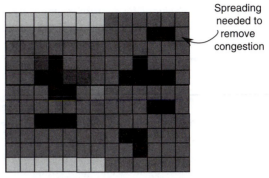

In an analytic placement method, it is common for intermediate steps to have a high degree of cell overlap. Methods to spread apart dense regions are well studied.

Routing congestion is a significant problem; spreading logic elements apart is a common solution. There are many parallels between analytic spreading methods, and modern congestion reduction methods.

FIGURE 20.3 Analytic placement tools face a problem similar to those faced in routing; some portions of a design are excessively dense, and the logic elements need to be separated to obtain a feasible or routable solution.

20.2 SPACE MANAGEMENT

Global placement tools perform a rough positioning of logic elements across the core region. Frequently, this rough placement contains a considerable amount of overlap between logic elements, and there are regions that are excessively dense. This is particularly common with analytic placement methods, but some forms of recursive bisection also exhibit this behavior.

To evaluate a global placement, one common measure is the utilization of different regions of the placement. If the total area of the logic elements assigned to a region is greater than the area of the region itself, it is overutilized or dense. To obtain a legal solution, logic elements must be moved away from dense areas; ideally, this movement should be done with minimum change to the overall structure of the placement.

Figure 20.4 illustrates the issue; initially, a portion of the placement has more circuit elements assigned than there is physical space. Through a variety of space management or placement migration

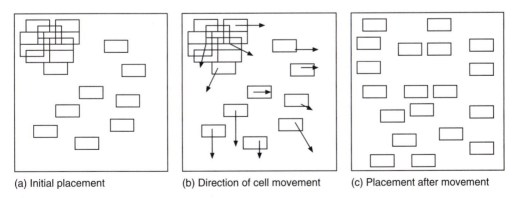

(a) Initial placement   (b) Direction of cell movement   (c) Placement after movement

FIGURE 20.4 Global placement techniques may produce solutions with a significant amount of overlap, or regions with high utilization. Spreading logic elements apart is neccessary for placement legalization. Algorithms that remove overlap can also be effective for adding in additional space for routing.

techniques, new locations for some of the logic elements can be found, resulting in a new placement with better utilization.

Although the most obvious application of space management is in the removal of overlaps and density reduction (making legalization possible), there are other motivations as well. Circuit routing is difficult; additional space makes routing easier, and it is common for large designs to have maximum density constraints on portions of the layout. Space management is also an effective way of adjusting to changes resulting from gate sizing or buffer insertion. Rather than running the placement tool again (possibly obtaining a completely different result), an existing placement can be stretched to accomodate resynthesis. Yet annother use for space management algorithms is in spreading apart devices with high activity—the power dissipated during switching can create thermal hot spots, and spreading can reduce peak on-chip temperatures.

In this section, we discuss a variety of space management techniques; which is best depends a great deal on the initial placement, and on the objectives of designer. We begin with a classic approach based on minimum cost flow, and then consider more recent geometric methods. We also include in the discussion some methods in use in analytic placement tools; in particular, the methods used by FastPlace [3] and Warp [4] can achieve deisred results.

20.2.1   FLOW-BASED OVERLAP REMOVAL

An early approach to placement spreading, which can be used directly on standard cell designs, is a technique that iteratively improves the quality of a placement using network flow optimization. This technique is used by the placement tool Domino [5] and can not only optimize but also remove overlaps in the placement. Vygen [6] also discusses related ideas.

The approach is relatively intuitive. The placement region can be divided into a set of regions; these are normally arranged in a rectangular grid. Each region corresponds to a vertex v_i in a graph. Figure 20.5 illustrates a simple example.

If a region contains more circuit area than physical space, the corresponding vertex forms a supply for a maximum flow problem. Similarly, if a region is not excessively dense, it is a sink. Edges between each pair of vertices can be created, with the cost of the edge being related to the distance between the regions.

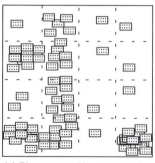

(a) Placement with some overly
dense regions

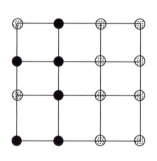

(b) Maximum flow graph, with
supply vertices in black

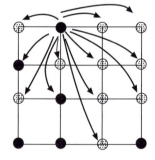

(c) Subset of the edges
considered in maximum flow;
the cost of any edge is related
to the physical distance traveled

FIGURE 20.5   If a placement contains regions that are excessively dense, one can determine an appropriate way to move some logic elements using a minimum cost flow algorithm. Regions of the placement can be modeled as vertices in a graph; edges are placed between regions, with a cost relative to the distance between regions. A flow in the graph corresponds to a ripple of logic elements from one region to another.

Solving the minimum cost flow problem results in a strategy to move circuit elements from dense regions to sparse regions. By keeping the cost of the flow small, the physical displacement of logic elements is also kept small. A flow of x along an edge from vertex v_i to v_j indicates that x units of logic should be moved from the region i to region j; normally, the logic elements closest to region j are selected.

Flow-based improvements are sometimes referred to as ripple moves; one can see chains of regions, where logic elements move in sequence through, from dense regions to sparse. It is common for flow-based methods to be used on only a portion of the placement region at a time; the algorithms used can be computationally expensive.

Algorithm 1 gives a high-level description of this approach. The input to the algorithm is any placement with or without overlaps. The output is an optimized placement with reduced overlaps, and sometimes reduced wirelength.

The first step is to partition the placement area into several small rectangular subregions. This is done to create small subproblems that can be solved efficiently. In Ref. [5], the subregions are allowed to overlap with each other, allowing movement between regions. The subproblems are solved iteratively until the solution quality converges.

Once partitioned, the rest of the algorithm works on individual subregions. Cells are assigned to the subregions that contain their geometric coordinates. For each subregion, a transportation problem is set up and solved to get the improved subplacement.

Algorithm 1 Outline of flow-based space management tool such as Domino [5]

```
Partition the placement region into smaller rectangular
subregions;
while there is an improvement do
    for each subregion ρ do
        Assign cells to ρ depending on their initial locations;
        Set up and solve a transportation problem;
        Move cells to new locations;
    end for
end while
```

20.2.1.1 Setting Up and Solving the Transportation Problem

A transportation problem can be represented in the form of a bipartite graph, as shown in Figure 20.6. The graph has two disjoint sets of nodes known as the supply nodes and the demand nodes. There are edges between the nodes in the two sets with a certain cost w and capacity u associated with each such edge. In our case, the supply nodes are the cells in a subregion, say C_ρ, and demand nodes are placement locations within a subregion, say L_ρ. We need to transport cells in C_ρ to unique locations in L_ρ minimizing the transportation cost. One problem here is that standard cells have fixed heights but variable widths. To account for this, each cell c is broken down into multiple subcells (say s_c). In Ref. [5], width of a subcell is chosen as the the greatest common divisor of the width of all cells within a subregion.

The transportation problem can be converted into a minimum cost maximum flow problem, which can be solved using a variety of techniques. This conversion is done as follows:

- We add two extra nodes in the graph; a super-source node S and a super-sink node T.
- We add $|C_\rho|$ edges between S and each cell node c_i $(\in C_\rho)$. The cost of each such edge is 0 and the capacity is s_{c_i}, that is, the total number of subcells of c_i.

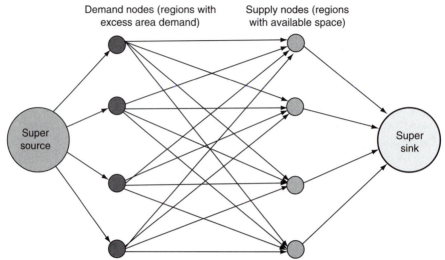

Edges used to find a flow of logic elements from dense to sparse regions.
The cost of each edge is dependent on physical displacement
and approximations of net cost.

FIGURE 20.6   Flow-based methods normally construct a bipartite graph for a portion of the placement region. Edges indicate the possibility of shifting logic elements (or portions thereof) from one area to another; the cost of each edge is based on an estimate of wirelength.

- We add $|L_\rho|$ edges between each location node l_j $(\in L_\rho)$ and T. The cost of each such node is 0 and the capacity is 1 (which indicates that each location can hold at most one subcell).
- Capacity of each edge (c_i, l_j) (where $c_i \in C_\rho$ and $l_j \in L_\rho$) is ∞. The cost calculation of each such edge is complex and is described in detail in the next subsection.

Once the transportation problem is solved, one must then deduce each cell location from the subcell locations. One method is to assign each cell to the row that contains the majority of its subcells. Ties are broken in favor of the row that contains a subcell with the least transportation cost. X-coordinates of cells are determined by calculating the center of gravity of the X-coordinates of corresponding subcells.

20.2.1.2   Calculation of Transportation Cost

In this section, we discuss how to calculate the cost of transporting a cell c $(\in C_\rho)$ to a location l $(\in L_\rho)$ with coordinates (x_l, y_l). This is given by

$$w_{cl} = \sum_{v \in N_c} \Gamma_{clv}$$

where
    N_c is the set of nets of cell c
    Γ_{clv} is the contribution of net v to w_{cl} when cell c is placed at location l

Our objective is the following:

$$\text{minimize} \sum_{c \in C_\rho} w_{cl}$$

For a net v, let C_v^I and C_v^E denote the cells in v that are, respectively, internal and external to the region under consideration. The locations of cells in C_v^E are fixed, where as, the locations of cells in C_v^I are unpredictable during solving the problem. Note that the half-perimeter netlength model can not be directly used in this case to calculate the transportation costs, as cells within the region might be connected to each other; the cost for each cell is dependent on the locations of other cells. Three cases could occur for net v:

1. Case 1: $|C_v^I| = 1$
2. Case 2: $1 < |C_v^I| < |C_v|$
3. Case 3: $|C_v^I| = |C_v|$

For Case 1, the half-perimeter model can be applied directly. For Cases 2 and 3, Ref. [5] suggests two net models to approximate the half-perimeter net model. Let,

$$x_{max}^E = \max |_{c \in C_v^E} (x_c)$$
$$x_{min}^E = \min |_{c \in C_v^E} (x_c)$$

y_{max}^E, y_{min}^E are defined similarly.

1. Net model I:
   For Case 2, the connectivity between the cells in C_v^I is ignored. We have

   $$\Gamma_{clv} = \max(x_{max}^E, x_l) - \min(x_{min}^E, x_l) + \max(y_{max}^E, y_l) - \min(y_{min}^E, y_l)$$

   For Case 3, a dummy cell δ is created at the center of mass of the locations of cells in C_v^I. We have

   $$\Gamma_{clv} = \max(x_\delta, x_l) - \min(x_\delta, x_l) + \max(y_\delta, y_l) - \min(y_\delta, y_l)$$

2. Net model II:
   Let,

   $$\underline{x}_{max}^{I'} = \max |_{c \in I'} (\underline{x}_c)$$
   $$\underline{x}_{min}^{I'} = \min |_{c \in I'} (\underline{x}_c)$$

   where, $I' = C_v^I \setminus \{c\}$ and $(\underline{x}_c, \underline{y}_c)$ is the initial location of cell c. $\underline{y}_{max}^{I'}$ and $\underline{y}_{min}^{I'}$ are defined similarly.
   For Case 2,

   $$\Gamma_{clv} = \max\left(x_{max}^E, x_l, \underline{x}_{max}^{I'}\right) - \min\left(x_{min}^E, x_l, \underline{x}_{min}^{I'}\right) + \max\left(y_{max}^E, y_l, \underline{y}_{max}^{I'}\right) - \min\left(y_{min}^E, y_l, \underline{y}_{min}^{I'}\right)$$

   For Case 3, dummy cell δ is again created as above.

   $$\Gamma_{clv} = \max\left(x_\delta, x_l, \underline{x}_{max}^{I'}\right) - \min\left(x_\delta, x_l, \underline{x}_{min}^{I'}\right) + \max\left(y_\delta, y_l, \underline{y}_{max}^{I'}\right) - \min\left(y_\delta, y_l, \underline{y}_{min}^{I'}\right)$$

A detailed analyis of the two net models described above can be found in Ref. [5]. The flow-based approach of Domino is a classic technique, and one can find the basic elements showing up in a variety of other places (e.g., a legalization method described later in this chapter).

20.2.2 DIFFUSION-BASED PLACEMENT MIGRATION

Conceptually related to flow-based methods is a recent diffusion-based placement migration technique by Ren [7]. The placement area is again decomposed into a set of bins; areas with high utilization are considered high pressure.

A physics-based model can be used to compute particle velocities between bins with different pressures. The approach in Ref. [7] is to calculate pressure differentials between adjacent bins, and then to use this to compute velocities for elements in each region. Through a series of time steps, logic elements move from dense bins to sparse, and achieve a more uniform distribution across the placement area. The approach is illustrated at a high level in Algorithm 2.

The approach requires less computation than flow-based methods, and is perhaps more intuitive. In terms of solution quality, however, it is difficult to draw conclusions: to our knowledge, there has been no direct comparison of the two methods.

An apparent shortcoming of the diffusion approach is that it may spread logic elements apart, even when this is not required. For designs that have a great deal more available space than logic area, this spreading can result in higher wirelength. Methods to insert dummy space are being investigated, but these are heuristic in nature.

Algorithm 2 Diffusion-based placement migration
Map cells onto bins and compute initial bin densities
repeat
    Compute horizontal and vertical velocities for each bin
    Compute new positions and velocities for each cell
    Update bin densities using the new cell positions
until Density constraints are met

20.2.3 WHITE SPACE ALLOCATION

Although flow-based methods are effective, they can be computationally expensive and may also be difficult to implement. Recently, a number of methods that are geometric in nature have been developed. One such technique, white space allocation (WSA), has been used to improve routability [8,9], and also to remove overlap created by gate sizing [10]. WSA in some sense reverses the approach of recursive bisection-based placement tools.

Given an input placement, cutlines in alternating directions can be inserted; this is shown in Figure 20.7a. The method used to generate the initial placement is irrelevant.

The placement is then modified by shifting the cutlines to meet area constraints of each side. In the first column of Figure 20.7a, the vertical cutline is positioned halfway across the placement region. If the distribution of area demand is unbalanced, with a greater portion of the area being on the right, the WSA approach shifts the vertical cutline to the left. Positions of all logic elements are scaled linearly, and the process recurses.

The method is extremely fast, and is also easy to implement. Excessively dense regions are spread out easily, and the relative positions of most logic elements are preserved. Pseudocode for the approach is shown in Algorithm 3.

In Ref. [8], the WSA method was used in conjunction with an estimate of routing congestion. Areas where routing was expected to be difficult were spread out, while areas with low routing demand were contracted. By applying WSA as a postprocessing step to the placements of a variety of tools, experiments showed vast improvement in almost all cases.

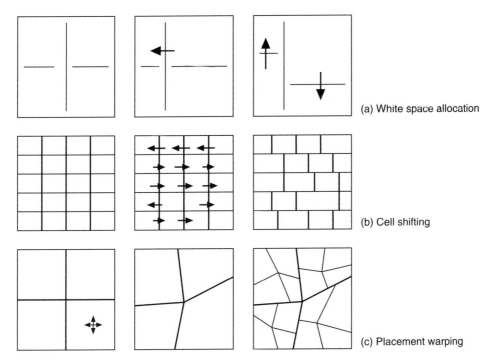

(a) White space allocation

(b) Cell shifting

(c) Placement warping

FIGURE 20.7 Geometric methods for space management; each involves the physical stretching or shifting of a portion of the design. By utilizing simple geometry (rather than a flow computation), overlap can be removed quickly and easily, although with a potential increase in wirelength.

```
Algorithm 3 Outline of the WSA algorithm; recursion continues until
each region contains only a single element
Given a rectangular region r that is h high and w wide
if h ≥ w then
     Insert a horizontal cut line
     Compute the area of cells above and below the cut line
     Shift the cut line vertically to match the relative areas
     Scale the y positions of all cells to match the cut line position
else
     Insert a vertical cut line
     Compute the area of cells to the left and right of the cut line
     Shift the cut line horizontally to match the relative areas
     Scale the x positions of all cells to match the cut line
     position
end if
Recursively process each half
```

The method was used again in Ref. [10], as a means to adjust a placement to changes from gate sizing and buffer insertion. The simplicity of the approach has resulted in its adoption in other placement tools [9].

20.2.4 COMPUTATIONAL GEOMETRY-BASED PLACEMENT MIGRATION

A shortcoming of the WSA approach is that there may be significant sheer along the cutlines; logic elements on either side of a boundary may shift in opposite directions. The effect of this shift is

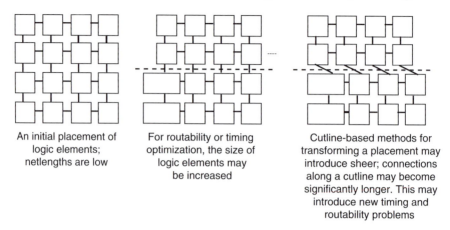

An initial placement of logic elements; netlengths are low

For routability or timing optimization, the size of logic elements may be increased

Cutline-based methods for transforming a placement may introduce sheer; connections along a cutline may become significantly longer. This may introduce new timing and routability problems

FIGURE 20.8 In geometric space allocation methods that use cutlines of some sort, it is possible that logic elements on opposite sides of a cutline have a significant relative displacement after shifting. The optimization objectives of global placement are not preserved, and this can negatively impact both routability and operating frequencies.

that some interconnections may become significantly longer, degrading the overall performance and potentially introducing routing congestion. The sheer problem is illustrated in Figure 20.8.

An alternative method by Luo [11] uses computational geometry-based methods to stretch the placement more uniformly. In one method, a rectilinear grid of bins are adjusted, such that each bin becomes an arbitrary quadrilateral; cell positions are then interpolated. A second approach performs a Delaunay triangulation of the placement area, with cell positions being interpolated within each region.

20.2.5 Cell Shifting

Although not initially envisioned in this manner, the cell shifting technique used in the analytic placement tool FastPlace [3] can be also used for space management.

In cell shifting, the placement region is divided into either horizontal or vertical stripes; this is illustrated in Figure 20.7b. Each stripe is divided into a set of bins, and these bins can expand or contract to meet area constraints. In the figure, the first column corresponds to the initial bin structure. On the basis of the area of logic elements within the bin and the total area of all bins in a row or column, the size of each bin can expand or contract.

When a dense bin expands, the coordinates of any contained logic element are scaled accordingly. The total height or width of a stripe is constrained by the placement area; it is trivial to adjust the sizes of bins such that they equally share the available space.

By iterating alternating horizontally and vertically, new positions can be found for the logic elements, distributing them more uniformly across the chip. The placement tool FastPlace uses these locations as added forces to the analytic formulation, it is by this means that an analytic solution with low overlap can be found. In principle, however, there is nothing that would prevent one from using the approach in the same manner as WSA.

20.2.6 Grid Warping

Yet another geometric technique found in analytic placement is grid warping [4]. This is illustrated in Figure 20.7c. Starting from an initial rectilinear quadrisection, the boundaries of the four regions can be adjusted such that they meet the area demands.

As with the computational geometry approach of Luo [11], the division lines are not restricted to be rectilinear. Rather, the placement area is stretched like a rubber sheet, with positions of the logic elements being scaled.

As with WSA, the grid warping method is applied recursively; each subregion is divided by a rectilinear quadrisection, and then the boundries of these subregions are adjusted.

20.2.7 SPACE MANAGEMENT SUMMARY

Driven primarily by the complications of routing in a fixed-die environment, there has been an explosion of interest in space management techniques. Additionally, advanced fabrication technologies are providing more silicon real estate to work with, and designers are rarely under pressure to pack circuitry as tightly as was once done.

Balancing space is a difficult task. If a design becomes spread too far apart, wires become longer than necessary; this increases power consumption, and lowers the achievable clock rates. A design that is too dense suffers from routing failures, excessive routing detours, and may not be amenable to buffer insertion or gate sizing. At this point, there is no simple method to determine how much space is "enough."

The methods used are frequently reminiscent of overlap removal methods in analytic placement, and one can expect continued cross-fertilization of ideas.

When adjusting a placement to meet eliminate overlap, or to improve routability, cutline-based methods such as WSA may encounter a sheer problem. When evaluating space management approaches, one should consider the magnitude of changes required. For small changes, simple geometric techniques may be sufficient; for larger changes, more robust flow-based methods may be a superior choice.

20.3 LEGALIZATION TECHNIQUES

Placement legalization is a key step in a successful analytic placement flow, and has become important in recursive bisection as well. In a legal placement, all cells must be aligned with row boundaries (and potentially column grids), and no cells may overlap.

Our discussion begins with a flow-based method, leveraging off of the space management methods described in Section 20.2.1. If a design has been spread out effectively, so that no area has demand higher than the available space, legalization is trivial.

The discussion continues, with a relatively recent method by Hill [12], and extensions to it by Agnihotri [13]. This method, known as Tetris, is remarkably simple and easy to implement; it should provide good intuition for the problem. While the method works well for some problems, it can fail dramatically in others; this gives intuition to why more robust methods such as those based on minimum cost flow are necessary.

20.3.1 FLOW AND DIFFUSION-BASED LEGALIZATION

Using either a minimum cost flow formulation [14], or diffusion [7], a placement that has small localized areas of overlap can be obtained. For designs that contain only standard cells (or in which macroblocks are fixed), placement legalization can be easily accomplished.

By creating zones, bins, or regions that are a single cell row tall, and then ensuring that each zone meets a density constraint, a legal placement can be found by packing cells into each zone. A legal solution is guaranteed to exist; distributing cells within a zone can further improve results.

Although we have discussed flow and diffusion-based methods within the context of space management, it is also appropriate to think of them as legalization techniques. Good space management makes placement legalization trivial.

20.3.2 Tetris-Based Legalization

Rather than distributing logic elements with flow-like methods, an alternate approach based on packing is possible. The Tetris legalization method by Hill [12] is remarkably simple, and trivial to implement. We first discuss the approach in the context of standard cell design, and then show how it extends to handle a mix of standard cells and macroblocks. For each cell c_i, we have a desired position (x_i, y_i); the cells must be legalized into standard cell rows $R = \{r_1, r_2, \ldots, r_k\}$, and assume that the left-most open position in each row is known.

The legalization method first sorts the cells C by their x position, and then inserts them into the left side of a row in a greedy manner, such that the displacement of each cell is minimized.

Algorithm 4 The Tetris legalizer by Hill
```
{C}=All cells to be legalized;
Sort the cells in C by their X-coordinates to get L_s;
l_j = left-most position of each row r_j;
for i=1 to the number of cells do
    best=lim sup;
    for j=1 to the number of rows do
        cost=displacement of moving cell i in L_s to l_j;
        if cost ≤ best then
            best=cost;
            best_row=j;
        end if
    end for
    Move cell i in L_s to the row best_row;
    l_best_row=l_best_row + width_i;
end for
```

Pseudocode for the approach is shown in Algorithm 4. If one were to rotate the placement region counterclockwise, the legalization process might look very much like a game of Tetris, for which the algorithm is named.

Our example code can be made to run more quickly by only considering rows close to the desired position of a cell; in practice, runtimes are linear with the number of cells to be legalized. Our example also packs cells to the left, but this is not in general necessary; if space has been reserved for routability, it may be perferable to legalize into a position that is not to the left.

Other obvious variants are to legalize from both the left and right sides, and to sort the cells by their leftmost boundary, rather than their center. The method can also be adapted to designs that contain macroblocks; [13] simply added a check for each row spanned by a macroblock, to find the leftmost position that did not result in an overlap.

Although the Tetris method works well in practice for global placements that have the logic elements distributed evenly, even small areas with overlap can cause significant trouble. When a block must be displaced during legalization, it may cause a ripple effect, resulting in the displacements of many other blocks. In some cases, wirelengths can jump by 30 percent or more; the method is fast and effective for easy legalization problems, but performs poorly on more difficult cases.

20.3.3 Single-Row Dynamic Programming-Based Legalization

Contrast to the simple Tetris legalization method is one which operates on a row-by-row basis [15], single-row dynamic programming-based legalization was developed for standard cell placements, and selects a subset of cells to place in a row using dynamic programming.

The outline of the technique is given in Algorithm 5. Legalization is done from the bottom row to the top row (although the reverse is also possible). Cells are first sorted by their initial Y-coordinates in nondecreasing order. Let L_s denote this sorted list of cells. A set of candidate cells C_{cand}^i are then selected for assignment to a particular row, say R_i. The total width of cells in C_{cand}^i is greater than the capacity of R_i and satisfies the following relation:

$$\lceil k_1 * \text{width}(R_i) \rceil \leq \text{width}(c_{cand}^i) = \sum_{j=1}^{m} \text{width}(c_j) \leq \lceil k_2 * \text{width}(R_i) \rceil$$

where
$k_1, k_2 \in \Re$ and are constants such that $1 < k_1 \leq k_2$
$\text{width}(R_i)$ is the width of row R_i
$\text{width}(C_{cand}^i)$ is the total width of cells in C_{cand}^i
$\text{width}(c_j)$ is the width of cell $c_j \in C_{cand}^i$
$m = |C_{cand}^i|$

Note that cells in C_{cand}^i are always the lowermost m cells in L_s that satisfy the above relation.

The Tetris algorithm packs a single cell at a time onto one side of the placement region, whereas this approach finds a set of cells to fill an entire standard cell row. The method used to find this set of cells is similar to the dynamic programming technique of solving the classic 0–1 knapsack problem [16].

In the knapsack problem, there is a limit on the weight of the knapsack; the analogue of this constraint is the limit on total cell width in the row. Similarly, the value of an item in the knapsack problem is modeled by the physical displacement of each cell.

After identifying the set of candidate cells C_{cand}^i, they are sorted by their X-coordinates in nondecreasing order. These cells are considered for assignment to R_i in this sorted order. The knapsack-like problem is solved using dynamic programming, with the selected cells being packed in, and the remaining cells being considered for legalization in the next row. This process is repeated until all cells have been legalized. Algorithm 5 illustrates the approach.

Algorithm 5 Row-by-row dynamic programming based legalization.
(The overall approach is a variation of the classic method for
the 0-1 knapsack problem)
{C}=All cells to be legalized;
Sort the cells in C by their Y-coordinates to get L_s;
for $i = 1$ to N_{r-1} **do**
    Select a set of candidate cells (C_{cand}^i) from L_s;
    Assign a subset of cells C_{assign}^i from C_{cand}^i to row R_i;
    $L_s = L_s \setminus C_{assign}^i$;
end for
Assign the remaining cells in L_s to row R_{N_r};

Every cell c_j has two factors associated with it: (1) the cost of assigning c_j to row R_i, denoted by w_j^i and (2) the penalty of *not* assigning c_j to R_i, denoted by p_j^i. Obviously, if c_j is assigned to R_i then, $p_j^i = 0$ and if it is not assigned to R_i, then $w_j^i = 0$.

If cell c_j is to be assigned to row R_i, then the cost of assignment is given by the following equation:

$$w_j^i = (x_j^i - x_j)^2 + (y_j^i - y_j)^2$$

where
(x_j^i, y_j^i) is the location in R_i where c_j is going to be placed
(x_j, y_j) is $c_j's$ initial location

On the other hand, the penalty of not assigning c_j to R_i is given by

$$p_j^i = (y_j^{i+1} - y_j)^2$$

where

y_j^{i+1} is the y-coordinate of the center of row R_{i+1}

y_j is $c_j's$ initial y-coordinate

20.4 LOCAL IMPROVEMENTS

Following legalization, a large number of well-studied techniques can be used to optimize a circuit placement. The computational complexity of many useful algorithms is exponential; $O(2^n)$ or $O(n!)$ are common, where n is the number of logic elements being optimized. Even on the fastest available computer, the practical values of n are small—far smaller than the number of elements in a placement problem.

For this reason, only a small number of elements are processed in any given step: those under the sliding window. If the size of the sliding window can accomodate six cells, one might optimize the first six cells in a single row, and then move on to the third through ninth cell. With only six elements, a $O(n!)$ algorithm is practical. Overlaps between optimization windows help minimize the impact of the local nature of this step. Sliding window optimization is shown in Figure 20.9.

20.4.1 CELL MIRRORING AND PIN ASSIGNMENT

The first class of local improvements we consider is cell mirroring; this technique is easy to understand. Each cell in a design contains a set of input and output pins, and these are not usually symmetrically placed. By mirroring a cell around its X axis, interconnect lengths can be improved in many cases. An illustration of this is shown in Figure 20.10.

An early study of the problem by Cheng [17] showed that finding optimal orientations is in fact NP-complete; as such, we cannot hope to find an optimal solution to the problem. In practice, however, relatively simple heuristic methods can be quite effective. One approach is to simply evaluate each orientation on a cell-by-cell basis, selecting the better choice in a greedy manner. Within a few passes, solution quality converges.

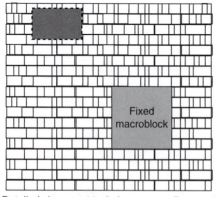

Detailed placement techniques normally operate on a small window into the circuit, making local improvements. Most techniques assume macroblocks are fixed, and optimize around them.

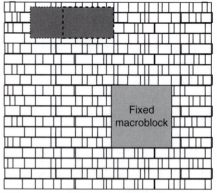

Sliding window optimization is common; windows typically overlap slightly. Optimization windows may be single- or multirow. Multiple passes of optimization are also commonplace.

FIGURE 20.9 Detailed placement techniques are normally applied on a subset of the design, moving from one area to another with a sliding window approach.

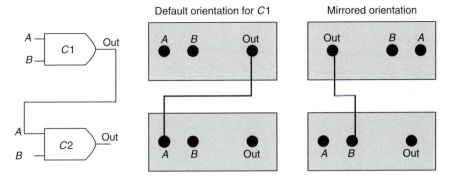

FIGURE 20.10   Standard cells can normally be mirrored along the Y axis. This can reduce the length of some interconnect segments, and may be used to slightly shift routing demand from one area to another. Macroblocks frequently allow mirroring along both axis, as well as rotation.

For typical standard cell design, mirroring is only possible along the X axis; power and ground lines are integrated into the cell design, and mirroring along the Y axis might not be possible. When implementing a detailed placement approach, one should consider the nature of the standard cells; similarly, the detailed placement tool should be considered in cell design.

For macroblocks, mirroring around both the X and Y axes may be possible; it may also be possible to rotate a block.

Related to cell mirroring is the technique of pin assignment. For many logic elements, there may be functionally equivalent pins, for example, the inputs of a NAND gate are equivalent. A circuit designer may specify that signal net n_i is connected to input pin a, while signal net n_j is connected to input pin b; some detailed placement tools support optimization of the assignment. Individual pins may have differing delay characteristics (due to the internal layout of transistors), so optimization of a pin assignment may benefit wirelength, delay, or both.

Finally, cell mirroring and pin assignment may be beneficial in improving the routability of a design. In channel routing tools, an internal data structure known as a vertical constraint graph is frequently used; the data structure reveals an ordering of interconnect segments that will allow easy routing. Depending on precise locations of individual pins, there may be cycles in the constraint graph—significantly complicating routing. Slight changes to pin locations, which can be achieved with mirroring or pin assignment, may eliminate cycles and simplify routing greatly.

Early works by Her [18] and Swartz [19] illustrate a tight coupling between detailed placement and routing. Slight adjustments at a local level can improve routing, and these adjustments are difficult to make without actually performing the detail routing step.

20.4.2   REORDERING OF CELLS

A second common detailed placement method, sometimes integrated with cell mirroring, is improving a design through the reordering of small groups of cells using a sliding window approach. Figure 20.11 shows two cases; in the first, wirelength can be improved by swapping the positions of a pair of a cells. In the second, the optimization window size required to find a better placement is three cells.

For standard cell design, it is common to see optimization window sizes ranging from three to eight. Much larger windows carry a heavy runtime cost, while windows of size two have relatively small wirelength benefit.

Brute force enumeration is easy to implement; some speed improvements can be obtained using branch-and-bound techniques. Caldwell [20] presented an extensive study of the topic, considering different ways to to enumerate permutations, and to bound the solution space. Pseudocode for a simple branch-and-bound approach to cell reordering is shown in Algorithm 6.

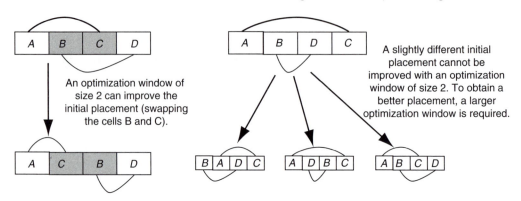

FIGURE 20.11 Order of cells in a row (or group of rows) can be refined using small optimization windows; the size of the window limits the improvement possible, and also impacts runtime considerably.

With designs that are densely packed, evaluating any given permutation is relatively simple; cells of different sizes are simply placed in the order, with the position of cell c_i being immediately after cell c_{i-1}. When there is open space, however, the problem is slightly more difficult.

```
Algorithm 6 A recursive implementation of cell reordering; by computing
partial wirelengths, the number of solutions explored can be reduced
{C} = cells in the optimization window;
{F} = empty set;
left = left side of optimization window;
reorder(C, F, left) {
if C is empty then
    Evaluate current configuration;
    Store configuration if improved;
else
    for each c_i in C do
        place c_i at left;
        reorder(C - c_i, F + c_i, left + width(c_i));
    end for
end if
}
```

Consider a simple case with cells c_i and c_j, and a small open space. There are two different possible permutations of the cells ($c_i c_j$ and $c_j c_i$), but a potentially infinite number of ways to divide the available space between the cells. The optimal amount of space to be inserted before the first cell, between the first and second cell, and after the second cell can be determined (see Section 20.4.4), but this complicates the reordering process.

Reordering of cells across multiple rows is also fairly common. When cells are of different sizes, not all permutations may be valid.

One method of implementing a multiple row reordering function is to first divide the available space on a row-by-row basis. For any given permutation, each cell is inserted into the top-most open row; when a row is filled, processing moves to the next row. If the permutation does not fit, this will be discovered along the way, and the potential solution can be discarded.

When implementing a reordering technique, a number of performance trade-offs must be considered.

- If the size of the optimization window is small, brute force enumeration may be the best approach. Branch-and-bound methods require incremental wirelength computations, and this has a runtime overhead that may outweigh the benefits of solution space pruning.
- If the size of the optimization window is large, branch-and-bound method can have significant benefit. Many permutations can be eliminated easily, with the savings outweighing the extra cost for incremental wirelength computation.
- If the design contains space between cells, one must decide how to handle it. Optimal space allocation can be done, but with a runtime cost; for large optimization windows, this is unlikely to be practical. Space can be treated as a single monolithic unit, or divided equally between cells; what is best may depend on the design itself.
- For optimization across multiple rows, many permutations may be eliminated if cells are of different sizes. This can increase the size of a practical optimization window in some cases. When the design contains space, this may make more permutations possible, thereby lowering the practical optimization window size.

20.4.3 OPTIMAL INTERLEAVING

Another method of altering the order of a group of cells is optimal interleaving by Hur [21]. The approach utilizes dynamic programming to allow for large window sizes with low runtimes. We suggest the text by Cormen [16] as a good reference for dynamic programming (Figure 20.12).

To begin with, let us assume the following:

- C is a given set of cells.
- $A_{initial}$ is an overlap free initial linear arrangement of cells in C. By linear arrangement, we mean the placement of cells within a single row. Here we use the terms arrangement and placement synonymously.
- $C_1 = c_{11}, c_{12}, \ldots, c_{1n}$ and $C_2 = c_{21}, c_{22}, \ldots, c_{2m}$ are two proper subsets of C of size $|C_1| = n$ and $|C_2| = m$ such that, $C_1 \cup C_2 = C$ and $C_1 \cap C_2 = \emptyset$.
- p_{ij} denotes the position of cell c_{ij}.
- $p_{ij} < p_{kl}$ means that c_{ij} precedes c_{kl} in some arragement. Note that c_{kl} may not be immediately next to c_{ij}.

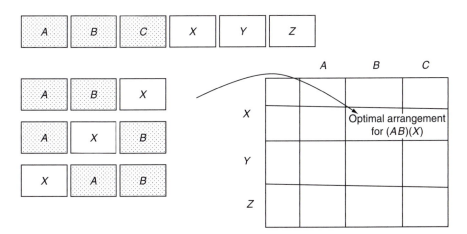

FIGURE 20.12 Interleaving of two groups of standard cells can be done in an efficient manner with dynamic programming. In this figure, we have two sets of cells that are to be interleaved; optimal partial solutions are stored in a matrix.

We are now ready to define interleaving. An interleaving $I_{n,m}$ of C_1 and C_2 is an arrangement of cells in C_1 and C_2 satisfying the following conditions:

$$\text{If } p_{1i} < p_{1j} \text{ in } A_{\text{initial}}, \quad \text{then } p_{1i} < p_{1j} \text{ in } I_{n,m}$$
$$\text{If } p_{2k} < p_{2l} \text{ in } A_{\text{initial}}, \quad \text{then } p_{2k} < p_{2l} \text{ in } I_{n,m}$$

where,

$$i \neq j \quad \text{and} \quad 1 \leq i, j \leq n$$
$$k \neq l \quad \text{and} \quad 1 \leq k, l \leq m$$

Note that there are $\binom{n+m}{n}$ different ways of interleaving C_1 and C_2. An optimal interleaving is the one with minimum cost. The cost of an interleaving $I_{i,j}$ denoted by $w(I_{i,j})$ $(1 \leq i \leq n$ and $1 \leq j \leq m)$ is its total linear wirelength, ignoring the cells in $\{C \backslash I_{i,j}\}$. Because placement rows are typically horizontal, by linear wirelength we mean the wirelength in X-dimension.

Hur and Lillis [21] proposed a polynomial time algorithm for solving the optimal interleaving problem that utilizes dynamic programming. The recurrence equation is stated as follows:

$$I_{0,0} = \varnothing, w(I_{0,0}) = 0$$
$$I_{i,j} = \begin{cases} I_{i-1,j}c_{1i} & \text{if } w(I_{i-1,j}c_{1i}) < w(I_{i,j-1}c_{2j}) \\ I_{i,j-1}c_{2j} & \text{otherwise} \end{cases}$$

Note that a dynamic programming formulation is only possible because for any subsequence $I_{i,j}, w(I_{i,j})$ is independent of the ordering of cells in $\{C \backslash I_{i,j}\}$. The runtime of the algorithm is $O(nm + n_p(n + m))$ where n_p is the number of pins belonging to the nets of cells in C, which is typically proportional to the number of cells.

Optimal interleaving can be applied to the entire legalized placement using the sliding window technique described above. In Ref. [21], the subsets C_1 and C_2 are chosen arbitrarily.

20.4.4 LINEAR PLACEMENT WITH FIXED ORDERINGS

The placement problem is NP-complete, even for the one-dimensional case [22]. The one-dimensional problem is commonly known as linear placement. In this problem, candidate cells belonging to a single placement row are given and we need to find a placement that minimizes the wirelength. Note that we are only allowed to change the X-locations of cells; hence the name linear placement. A restricted variant of this problem, in which we cannot alter the cell ordering, can be solved optimally in polynomial time. One solution method was proposed by Kahng [23], and later on improved on by Brenner [24].

First, to formally state the problem, we assume that we are given the following:

- Set of cells $\{c_1, c_2, \ldots, c_n\}$ with the width of cell c_i denoted by $\text{width}(c_i)$
- Placement row of width $\mathcal{W} : \mathcal{W} \geq \sum_{i=1}^n \text{width}(c_i)$
- Legal initial placement $\underline{P} = \{\underline{p}_1, \underline{p}_2, \ldots, \underline{p}_n\}$, where $\underline{p}_i + \text{width}(c_i) \leq \underline{p}_{i+1}$ for $i = 1, \ldots, n-1, 0 \leq \underline{p}_1$ and $\underline{p}_n \leq [W - \text{width}(c_n)]$

The optimization objective is to find a legal placement $P = \{p_1, p_2, \ldots, p_n\}$ with the minimum possible bounding box wirelength such that if $\underline{p}_i < \underline{p}_j$ in $\underline{P}$ then $p_i < p_j$ in P.

It should be obvious that to impact wirelength, white space must be present. If the cells are densely packed, there is only a single possible placement, and no improvement is possible.

20.4.4.1   Notations and Assumptions

- We are only concerned with nets with at least one movable cell. Let m be the total number of such nets.
- Let c_L^N and c_R^N be the leftmost and rightmost movable cells of net N with locations denoted by p_L^N and p_R^N (recall that we are only dealing with X-location here). Note that c_L^N and c_R^N are known beforehand and do not change during the course of solving the problem as we are not allowed to change the ordering of cells.
- Let f_L^N and f_R^N stand for the locations of the leftmost and rightmost fixed pins of net N (A net without a fixed pin can be broken down into two nets; one that connects c_L^N with a dummy cell at location W and another one that connects c_R^N with a dummy cell at location 0).
- For the sake of simplicity, let us assume that all pins are located at the left edge of their cells.

Our objective is the following:

$$\text{minimize} \sum_N \left(\max \left\{ f_R^N, p_R^N \right\} - \min \left\{ f_L^N, p_L^N \right\} \right)$$

or equivalently,

$$\text{minimize} \sum_N \left(f_R^N - f_L^N \right) + \sum_{i=1}^{n} w_i$$

where w_i is the contribution of cell c_i to the objective function and is given by:

$$w_i = \sum_{N:c_i=c_L^N} \max \left\{ f_L^N - p_i, 0 \right\} + \sum_{N:c_i=c_R^N} \max \left\{ p_i - f_R^N, 0 \right\}$$

A careful observation of the function w_i indicates that cells that are neither c_L^N nor c_R^N for any net N can be placed arbitrarily, as they do not contribute anything to our objective function. These cells can be merged with their predecessors. The remainder of our discussion is valid only for cells that do not fall in this category.

Because every net under consideration has a unique c_L^N and c_R^N and it is possible to have $c_L^N = c_R^N$ for a net (a net that has a single movable cell), we have the relation $n \le 2m$.

20.4.4.2   Analysis of the Cost Function

One can observe that the function w_i is convex piecewise linear. This can be deduced as follows: take a cell c_i and create a sorted list of the f_L^N and f_R^N values of all nets for which $c_i = c_L^N$ or $c_i = c_R^N$, respectively, and mark them on a number line. For any location x, let a (b) denote the number of f_R^N (f_L^N) locations to the right (left) of x. Three possibilities occur

- $a < b$: w_i is linear and decreasing in this interval as x increases
- $a = b$: w_i is constant and minimum
- $a > b$: w_i is linear and increasing as x increases

20.4.4.3   Dynamic Programming Algorithm

Solutions to the linear placement with fixed ordering problem are based on dynamic programming. We use the following notations for this section:

- Let S_i denote the set of sites where cell c_i can be placed without overlapping with any of its neighboring cells.
- Let P_i^j be an optimal prefix placement for cell c_i where all cells to the left of c_i have been placed optimally and $p_i \leq s_j (\in S_i)$.
- Let W_i^j be the total cost of P_i^j and w_i^j denote the cost of placing c_i at $s_j (\in S_i)$.

Our goal is to find $P_n^{\mathcal{W}-\text{width}(c_n)}$.

The dynamic programming formulation can be stated as follows:

$$P_0^j = \emptyset, \quad W_0^j = 0$$

$$P_i^j = \begin{cases} P_{i-1}^{j-\text{width}(c_{i-1})} \cup \{p_i = s_j\} & \text{if } W_{i-1}^{j-\text{width}(c_{i-1})} + w_i^j < W_i^{j-1} \\ P_i^{j-1} & \text{otherwise} \end{cases}$$

20.5 LIMITS OF LEGALIZATION AND DETAILED PLACEMENT

All of the operations performed in legalization and detailed placement are in some sense local, and thus fail to address global optimization objectives. These algorithms are typically applied in an interative manner, in ad hoc mixtures. Many groups have experimented with different legalizers, window sizes for reordering, methods to perform space allocation, and so forth.

There is no simple method to obtain the right strategy. Fortunately, most placement tools from academic groups can be run in a legalization or detailed placement mode, making it easy to test out different techniques. When compared with the runtimes for global placement, detailed placement times are usually low; it is worthwhile to explore different combinations.

The first optimization normally applied would be space insertion to reduce routing congestion. As a rule of thumb, one might wish to keep the routing demand in any area less than about 70 percent of the available routing resource. Dense routing frequently results in the failure to complete all nets, or in large net detours. The achievable routing density depends on the specific routing tool used. The wirelength increase due to space insertion may be less than what one might anticipate. If the logic elements are spread apart, with the placement area increasing by 10 percent, the actual spreading performed is less than 5 percent in horizontal directions. For this case, the worst one should expect would be a 5 percent increase in total wirelength.

Going from an abstract global placement to a legal one typically incurs a small wirelength increase (perhaps a few percent); abstract placements with relatively little overlap generally have smaller increases. If there is excess space for routing, it is quite possible that the legalized placement could actually reduce wirelengths. If there is an increase, reordering, cell mirroring, and optimized linear placement can normally recover some of the wirelength loss.

Within a few iterations, however, the improvements of any technique become asymptotically small. The first few percent of wirelength improvements come easily; afterward, the progress is slow. In many respects, it is a decision of the circuit designer as to how long to carry out detailed placement. For some, a minor improvement in wirelength might have a great deal of value, warranting the extra compute time. For others, a quick-and-dirty solution may be sufficient.

It should be stressed that one of the most crucial considerations is to minimize the amount of overlap during global placement, and ensure that there are no large sections of the design that have area demands that exceed the space available. Legalization methods handle space distribution imperfectly; if the problems can be solved in global placement, the results will almost certainly be better. Comparing the locations of placements before and after legalization can provide a great deal of insight. There are a number of visualization tools for placements; any area that changes significantly during legalization should be examined carefully.

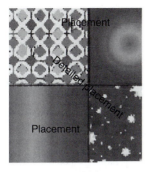

By mapping a graphic image to the cells in a design, it is possible to compare two different placements.
The original image on the left is mapped to placements from Capo and Feng Shui for the benchmark
Peko01 (which has a known optimal solution). Both placements are clearly suboptimal; as the benchmark
lacks pads, the images are rotated.
It is frequently useful to compare images before and after legalization, and at various stages of detailed
placement. Large distortions can identify problems with legalization, or areas where global placement
has performed poorly.

FIGURE 20.13 Detailed placement techniques can resolve local problems, but placement suboptimality
is both a local and global phenomena. In experiments with synthetic designs, one can compare an optimal
configuration with the output of a placement tool by mapping an image. The distortions of the image reveal
how the placement deviates from the desired result.

Although there have been significant advances in placement, the solutions obtained are far from
optimal. Recently, Chang presented a set of benchmark circuits with known optimal configurations [25]. These placement examples with known optimal (PEKO) circuits attracted a great deal of
attention, and the results of many placement tools on the benchmarks was surprising. In Figure 20.13,
we illustrate the results by mapping an image onto the optimal placement of a synthetic PEKO
benchmark, and then rearranging the placements to match results of a number of academic tools.

The PEKO benchmarks contain no pads; thus, there are multiple optimal configurations, corresponding to mirroring or flipping of the design. From the distortions of the images, it should be
clear that many placement tools are globally correct; at a very high level, the placements resemble
the optimal result. At a local level, however, there is a great deal of suboptimality; sections of each
placement are stretched or warped, resulting in higher interconnect lengths.

While there is some question as to how closely the synthetic PEKO benchmarks resemble real
circuitry, it is obvious that placement results could be improved, and that this improvement must
span both the local and global levels.

REFERENCES

1. J. Lou, S. Krishanmoorthy, and H. S. Sheng. Estimating routing congestion using probabilistic analysis. In *Proceedings of International Symposium on Physical Design*, pp. 112–117, 2001.
2. C. J. Alpert, G. -J. Nam, P. G. Villarrubia, and M. C. Yildiz. Placement stability metrics. In *Proceedings of Asia South Pacific Design Automation Conference*, pp. 1144–1147, 2005.
3. N. Viswanathan and C. C. -N. Chu. Fastplace: Efficient analytical placement using cell shifting, iterative local refinement and a hybrid net model. In *Proceedings of International Symposium on Physical Design*, pp. 26–33, 2004.
4. Z. Xiu and R. A. Rutenbar. Timing-driven placement by grid-warping. In *Proceedings of Design Automation Conference*, pp. 585–591, 2005.
5. K. Doll, F. M. Johannes, and K. J. Antreich. Iterative placement improvement by network flow methods. *IEEE Transactions on Computer-Aided Design of Integrated Circuits and Systems*, 13(10):1189–1200, 1994.

6. J. Vygen. Algorithms for detailed placement of standard cells. In *Proceedings of Design, Automation and Test in Europe Conference*, pp. 321–324, 1998.

7. H. Ren, D. Z. Pan, C. J. Alpert, and P. Villarrubia. Diffusion-based placement migration. In *Proceedings of Design Automation Conference*, pp. 515–520, 2005.

8. C. Li, M. Xie, C. -K. Koh, J. Cong, and P. H. Madden. Routability-driven placement and white space allocation. In *Proceedings of International Conference on Computer Aided Design*, pp. 394–401, 2004.

9. J. A. Roy, J. F. Lu, and I. L. Markov. Seeing the forest and the trees: Steiner wirelength optimization in placement. In *Proceedings of International Symposium on Physical Design*, pp. 78–85, 2006.

10. C. Li, C. -K. Koh, and P. H. Madden. Floorplan management: Incremental placement for gate sizing and buffer insertion. In *Proceedings of Asia South Pacific Design Automation Conference*, pp. 349–354, 2005.

11. T. Lou, H. Ren, C. J. Alpert, and D. Z. Pan. Computational geometry based placement migration. In *Proceedings of International Conference on Computer Aided Design*, pp. 41–47, 2005.

12. D. Hill. US Patent 6,370,673: Method and system for high speed detailed placement of cells within an integrated circuit design, 2002.

13. A. R. Agnihotri, S. Ono, C. Li, M. C. Yildiz, A. Khatkhate, C. -K. Koh, and P. H. Madden. Mixed block placement via fractional cut recursive bisection. *IEEE Transactions on Computer-Aided Design of Integrated Circuits and Systems*, 24(5):748–761, 2005.

14. U. Brenner, A. Pauli, and J. Vygen. Almost optimum placement legalization by minimum cost flow and dynamic programming. In *Proceedings of International Symposium on Physical Design*, pp. 2–9, 2004.

15. A. R. Agnihotri, M. C. Yildiz, A. Khatkhate, A. Mathur, S. Ono, and P. H. Madden. Fractional cut: Improved recursive bisection placement. In *Proceedings of International Conference on Computer Aided Design*, pp. 307–310, 2003.

16. T. H. Cormen, C. E. Leiserson, and R. L. Rivest. *Introduction to Algorithms*. MIT Press, Cambridge, MA, 1990.

17. C. K. Cheng, S. Z. Yao, and T. C. Hu. The orientation of modules based on graph decomposition. *IEEE Transactions on Computers*, 40(6):774–780, 1991.

18. T. W. Her and D. F. Wong. On over-the-cell channel routing with cell orientations consideration. *IEEE Transactions on Computer-Aided Design of Integrated Circuits and Systems*, 14(6):766–772, 1995.

19. W. Swartz and C. Sechen. A new generalized row-based global router. In *Proceedings of Design Automation Conference*, pp. 491–498, 1993.

20. A. E. Caldwell, A. B. Kahng, and I. L. Markov. Optimal partitioners and end-case placers for standard-cell layout. *IEEE Transactions on Computer-Aided Design of Integrated Circuits and Systems*, 19(11): 1304–1313, 2000.

21. S. -W. Hur and J. Lillis. Mongrel: Hybrid techniques for standard cell placement. In *Proceedings of International Conference on Computer Aided Design*, pp. 165–170, 2000.

22. M. R. Garey and D. S. Johnson. *Computers and Intractibility: A Guide to the Theory of NP-Completeness*. W. H. Freeman and Co., San Francisco, CA, 1979. p. 209.

23. A. B. Kahng, P. Tucker, and A. Zelikovsky. Optimization of linear placements for wirelength minimization with free sites. In *Proceedings of Asia South Pacific Design Automation Conference*, pp. 241–244, 1999.

24. U. Brenner and J. Vygen. Faster optimal single-row placement with fixed ordering. In *Proceedings of Design, Automation and Test in Europe Conference*, pp. 117–122, 2000.

25. C. C. Chang, J. Cong, and M. Xie. Optimality and scalability study of existing placement algorithms. In *Proceedings of Asia South Pacific Design Automation Conference*, pp. 621–627, 2003.

21 Timing-Driven Placement

David Z. Pan, Bill Halpin, and Haoxing Ren

CONTENTS

21.1 INTRODUCTION

The placement algorithms presented in the previous chapters mostly focus on minimizing the total wirelength (TWL). Timing-driven placement (TDP) is designed specifically targeting wires on timing critical paths. It shall be noted that a cell is usually connected with two or more cells. Making some targeted nets shorter during placement may sacrifice the wirelengths of other nets that are connected through common cells. While the delay on critical paths decreases, other paths may become critical. Therefore, TDP has to be performed in a very careful and balanced manner.

Timing-driven placement has been studied extensively over the last two decades. The drive for new methods in TDP to maximize circuit performance is from multiple facets because of the technology scaling and integration: (1) growing interconnect versus gate delay ratios; (2) higher levels of on-die functional integration, which makes global interconnects even longer; (3) increasing chip operating frequencies, which make timing closure tough; and (4) increasing number of macros and standard cells for modern system-on-chip (SOC) designs. These factors create continuing challenges to better TDP.

Timing-driven placement can be performed at both global and detailed placement stages (see previous chapters on placement). Historically, TDP algorithms can be roughly grouped into two classes: net-based and path-based. The net-based approach deals with nets only, with the hope that if we handle the nets on the critical paths well, the entire critical path delay may be optimized implicitly. The two basic techniques for net-based optimization are through netweighting [1–4] and net constraints [5–10]. The path-based approach directly works on all or a subset of paths [11–14]. The majority path-based approaches formulate the problem into a mathematical programming framework (e.g., linear programming [LP]). There are pros and cons for both net-based and path-based approaches in terms of runtime/scalability, ease of implementation, controllability, etc. Modern TDP techniques tend to use some hybrid manner of both net-based and path-based approaches [15].

In this chapter, we discuss fundamental algorithms as well as recent trends of TDP. Because of the large amount of works in TDP, it is not possible to exhaust all of them in this chapter. Instead, we describe the basic ideas and fundamental techniques, and point out recent researches and possible future directions. We first cover the basic building blocks for TDP. Then the next two sections discuss net-based approaches, i.e., through netweighting and net constraints. Then we survey the basic formulations and algorithms behind the path (or timing graph)-based approach. Additional techniques and issues in the context of TDP are discussed, followed by conclusions.

21.2 BUILDING BLOCKS AND CLASSIFICATION

21.2.1 NET MODELING

Given a placement, net modeling answers a fundamental question how the net is modeled for its routing topology and wirelength computation/estimation. Figure 21.1 shows different net modeling strategies for a multiple-pin net.

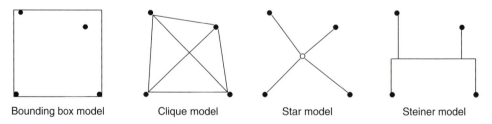

    Bounding box model   Clique model   Star model   Steiner model

FIGURE 21.1   Different net models that can be used for placement.

The simplest and most widely used method to compute wirelength is the half-perimeter wire-length (HPWL) of its bounding box. For a net i, let l_i, r_i, u_i, and b_i represent the left, right, top, and bottom locations of its bounding box. Then the HPWL of net i is

$$HPWL_i = r_i - l_i + u_i - b_i \qquad (21.1)$$

HPWL is the lower bound for wirelength estimation, and it is accurate for two- and three-pin nets, which account for the majority nets.

In analytical placement engines, wirelength is often modeled as a quadratic term (or pseudolinear term as in recent literature [16,17]). In those engines, clique and star models are often used. In the clique model, an edge is introduced between every pin pair of the net. In the star model, an extra star point located at the geometric center is created and each pin is connected to the star point. In general, small nets (e.g., less than five pins) can use the clique model, but for large nets with a lot of pins, clique model is not friendly to the matrix solvers because it creates dense matrices. Star models are preferred for large nets. For the clique model, because it is a complete graph with far more edges than necessary to connect the net, each edge is usually assigned a weight of $2/n$ (where n is the number of pins of the net) [18].

The bounding box, clique, and star models are three most popular net models. There are other net models, such as Steiner trees, which are more accurate for nets with four or more pins. However, in most designs two- and three-pin nets are the majority of the entire netlist. For example, in the industry circuit suite from Ref. [19], two- and three-pin nets constitute 64 and 20 percent of the total nets, respectively [20]. With exception of very few placers [21], Steiner-tree-based models are seldom used because they are computationally expensive. There are some recent works trying to link Steiner tree with placement, e.g., in a partition-based placer [22]. More research is needed to evaluate or make Steiner-based placement mainstream.

21.2.2 TIMING ANALYSIS AND METRICS

As its name implies, TDP has to be guided by some timing metrics, which in turn need delay modeling and timing analysis. TDP algorithms can use different levels of timing models to trade off accuracy and runtime. In general, the switch level resistance-capacitance (RC) model for gates and Elmore delay model for interconnects are fairly sufficient. There are more accurate models [23], but they are not extensively used in placement. One main reason is the higher runtime. The other reason is that during placement, routing is not done yet. It is not very meaningful to use more accurate models if errors from those uncertainties are even greater.

Based on the gate and interconnect delay models, static timing analysis (STA) or even path-based* timing analysis can be performed. STA [24] computes circuit path delays using the critical path method [25]. From the set of arrival times (Arr) asserted on timing starting points and required arrival times (Req) asserted on timing endpoints, STA propagates (latest) arrival time forward and (earliest) required arrival time backward, in the topological order. Then the slack at any timing point t is the difference of its required arrival time minus its arrival time.

$$Slk(t) = Req(t) - Arr(t) \qquad (21.2)$$

Static timing analysis can be performed incrementally if small changes in the netlist are made. For more details on delay modeling and timing analysis, the reader is referred to Chapter 3.

Timing convergence metrics measure the extent to which a placement satisfies timing constraints. They also give an indication of how difficult it would be for a design engineer to

---

* In most cases, STA is sufficient for TDP. The path-based timing analysis is more accurate, e.g., to capture false paths. But it is very time consuming, and one may do it only if necessary, e.g., on a set of critical paths.

manually fix timing problems. The most commonly used timing closure metric is the worst negative slack (WNS)

$$\text{WNS} = \min_{t \in P_o} \text{Slk}(t) \tag{21.3}$$

where P_o is the set of timing endpoints, i.e., primary outputs (POs) and data inputs of memory elements. To achieve timing closure, WNS should be nonnegative. For nanometer designs with growing variability, one may set the slack target to be a positive value to safe guard variations from process, voltage, or thermal issues. The WNS, however, only gives information about the worst path. It is possible that two placement solutions have similar WNS values, but one has only a single critical path while the other has thousands of critical and near critical paths. The figure of merit (FOM) is another very important timing closure metric [4]. It can be defined as follows:

$$\text{FOM} = \sum_{t \in P_o, \text{Slk}(t) < \text{Slk}_t} [\text{Slk}(t) - \text{Slk}_t] \tag{21.4}$$

where Slk_t is the slack target for the entire design. If $\text{Slk}_t = 0$, the FOM is reduced to the total negative slack (TNS) [8].

21.2.3 Overview of Timing-Driven Placement

The overview of TDP is shown in Figure 21.2. It has three basic components: timing analysis, core placement algorithms, and interfaces between them by translating timing analysis/metrics into certain weights or constraints for core placement engines to drive and guide TDP.

The previous section discusses the basics of timing analysis and metrics from a given netlist. However, which netlist to start with so that we can have a meaningful timing analysis to guide TDP is a very important yet open question. For example, shall we start from an unplaced netlist or some initial placement? For modern timing closure, many buffers also need to be inserted for high-fanout nets and long interconnects to get a reasonable timing picture (otherwise, there may be many loading/slew violations that make timing reports meaningless). On the other hand, those buffers will change the netlist structure for TDP. Shall they be kept or stripped out during TDP? There is very little literature covering this netlist preparation step. A reasonable strategy can be as follows: First, we start with some initial placement (e.g., wirelength driven), then perform some rough buffering/fanout optimization to get a reasonable timing estimation for the entire chip to guide TDP engine. Whether to keep those buffers during TDP may vary among different physical synthesis systems.

Placement has been one of the most heavily studied physical design topics. Some of the most popular placement algorithms include analytical/force-directed placement, partition-based placement, simulated-annealing (SA) based placement, and LP-based placement. The reader is referred to Chapters 15 through 18 for detailed discussions.

The most interesting aspect of the TDP is the mechanism to translate timing metrics into actions to drive the core placement engines. The focus of the rest of this chapter is on this aspect. Based on that, the TDP can be roughly classified into net-based and path-based approaches. The net-based approach,

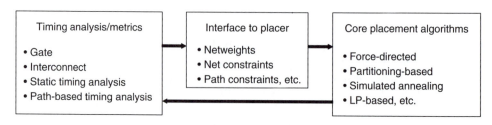

FIGURE 21.2 Basic building blocks and overview of TDP.

as its name implies, deals with individual nets. Because timing analysis inherently deals with paths (with timing propagation), the timing information is then translated into either net constraints or netweights [1–4] to guide TDP engines. The main idea of net constraint generation (or delay budgeting) is to distribute slack for each path to its constituent nets such that a zero-slack solution is obtained. The delay budget for each net is then translated into its wirelength constraint during placement. The main idea of netweighting is to assign higher netweights to more timing-critical nets while minimizing the total weighted wirelength objective. Netweighting gives direction for timing optimization through shortening critical nets, but it does not have exact control because the objective is the total weighted wirelength; the net constraint approach specifies that, but it may be too much constrained in terms of global optimization. Net weighting and net constraint processes can be iteratively refined as more accurate timing information is obtained during placement. A systematic way of explicit perturbation control is important for net-based algorithms.

The path-based approach directly works on all or a subset of paths. The majority of this approach formulate the problem into mathematical programming framework (e.g., LP). It usually maintains an accurate timing view during the placement optimization [26]. However, its drawback is its poor scalability and complexity because of possible exponential number of paths to be simultaneously optimized [26]. An effective technique is to embed timing graph/constraint through auxiliary variables [11]. The mathematical programming-based approach needs to deal with cell overlapping issues, e.g., through partitioning. The path-based timing can also be evaluated in a simulated annealing framework [13].

Both net-based and path-based approaches have pros and cons. Path-based in general has more accurate timing view and control, but it suffers from poor scalability. The net-based approaches, in particular netweighting, have low computational complexity and high flexibility. Thus, they are suitable for large application specific integrated circuits/system-on-chip (ASIC/SOC) designs with millions of placeable objects. Recent research shows that hybrid of these two basic approaches are promising [15].

21.3   NETWEIGHTING-BASED APPROACH

Classic placement algorithms optimize the TWL. They can be easily modified to be timing-driven using the netweighting technique, which assigns different weights to different nets such that the placer minimizes the total weighted wirelength (if all the weights are the same, it degenerates into the classic wirelength-driven placement). Intuitively, a proper netweighting should assign higher weights on more timing-critical nets, with the hope that the placement engine will reduce the lengths of these critical nets and thus their delays to achieve better overall timing.

Netweighting-based TDP is very simple to implement and less computational intensive. As modern very large scale integration (VLSI) designs have millions placeable objects (gates/cells/macros), netweighting is attractive because of its simplicity. Almost all placement algorithms support netweighting. Quadratic placement can optimize the weighted quadratic wirelength, partition-based placement can optimize the weighted cutsize (see Chapter 8), and simulated-annealing-based placement can optimize the weighted linear wirelength, etc.

Although netweighting appears to be straightforward, it is not easy to generate a good netweighting. Higher netweights on a set of critical nets in general shall reduce their wirelengths and delays, but other nets may become longer and more critical. In this section, we will review two basic sets of netweighting algorithms: static netweighting and dynamic netweighting. Static netweighting assigns weights once before TDP and the weights do not change during TDP. Dynamic netweighting updates weights during the TDP process.

21.3.1   STATIC NETWEIGHTING

Static netweighting computes the netweights once before TDP. It can be divided into two categories: empirical netweighting and sensitivity-based netweighting. Empirical netweighting methods compute weights based on certain criticality factors, such as slack, cycle time, and fanout. Critical nets are assigned higher netweights. Sensitivity-based netweighting computes weights based on the sensitivity analysis of netweights to factors such as WNS and FOM. The key difference of these two netweighting schemes is that sensitivity-based approach has some look-ahead mechanism that can estimate the impact of netweighting on key factors. Therefore, it assigns higher netweights on those nets that have bigger impacts on the overall timing closure goal.

21.3.1.1 Slack-Based Netweighting

Empirical netweighting assigns netweight based on the critically of the net, which indicates how much the placer should reduce the wirelength on this net. The criticality computation can be computed based on the static timing analysis (STA). Assuming there is only one clock period, the net criticality can often be measured by slack. Nets with negative slacks are critical nets and are assigned higher netweights than those nets with positive slacks.

$$w = \begin{cases} W_1, & slack < 0 \\ W_2, & slack \geq 0 \end{cases} \tag{21.5}$$

where W_1 and W_2 are positive constants and $W_1 > W_2$. Among the critical nets that have negative slacks, higher weights can also be given to those which are more negative. One can either use a continuous model [1] or a step-wise model [2] to compute weights based on the slack distribution, as shown in Figure 21.3.

It shall be noted that netweights shall not continue to increase when slack is less than certain threshold. This is because slack can be very negative because of invalid timing assertions. Usually, placers do not need very high netweights to pull nets together.

For some placers, one might add an exponential component into netweighting [27] to further emphasize critical nets.

$$w = \left(1 - \frac{slack}{T}\right)^\alpha \tag{21.6}$$

where
T is the longest path delay
α is the criticality exponent

If there are multiple clocks in the design, the clock cycle time can be considered during netweighting. Nets on paths of shorter cycle time should have higher weights than those of longer cycle time with the same slack. For example, we can use T in Equation 21.6 to represent different cycle times. Nets of long cycle clocks get a larger T than those of short cycle clocks.

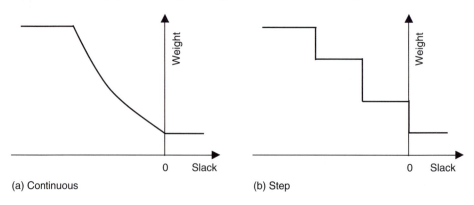

(a) Continuous   (b) Step

FIGURE 21.3 Netweight assignment based on slack using continuous or step model.

$$w = \left(1 - \frac{\text{slack}}{T_{\text{clk}}}\right)^{\alpha} \qquad (21.7)$$

where T_{clk} is the clock cycle time for a particular net.

There are other empirical factors that can be considered for netweighting, e.g., path depth and driver strength [28]. A deep path, which has many stages of logic, is more likely to have longer wirelength. The endpoints of this path could be placed far away from each other, therefore worse timing is expected than a path with less number of stages. A net with a weak driver would have longer delay than a strong driver with the same wirelength. Therefore, netweight should be proportional to the longest path depth (which can be computed by running breadth first search twice: once from PIs and second time from POs), and inversely to slack and driver strength, i.e.,

$$w \approx D_1 \times R_d \qquad (21.8)$$

where
  D_1 is the longest path depth
  R_d is the driver resistance

A weaker driver has a larger effective driving resistance, thus the net it drives will have a bigger netweight.

One could also consider path sharing during netweighting. Intuitively, a net on many critical paths should be assigned a higher weight because reducing the length of such net can reduce the delay on many critical paths.

$$w \approx \text{slack} \times \text{GP} \qquad (21.9)$$

where GP is the number of critical paths passing this net. Suppose we assign two variables for each net p on the timing graph: $F(p)$ the number of different critical paths starting from timing beginning point (PI) to net p; and $B(p)$ the number of different critical paths from net p to timing endpoints (PO). The total number of critical paths passing through net p is then $\text{GP}(p) = F(p) \times B(p)$. This netweighting assignment only considers the sharing effect of critical paths, and each path has the same impact of the netweight. Kong proposed an accurate, all path counting algorithm PATH [3], which considers both noncritical and critical paths during path counting. It can properly scale the impact of all paths by their relative timing criticalities.

To perform netweighting for unplaced designs, STA can use the wire load model, e.g., based on fanout, to estimate the delay (compared to placed designs, STA can use the actual wire load to compute delay). Normally, it is not accurate with wire load models. Therefore, for an unplaced design, an alternative way of generating weights is to use fanout and delay bound [29] instead of slack. Fanout is used to estimate wirelength and wire delay [30], and delay bound is the estimated allowable wire delay, i.e., any wire delay above this bound would result in negative slack. The weight can be computed as the ratio of fanout and delay bound.

$$w \approx \frac{\text{fanout}}{\text{net delay bound}} \qquad (21.10)$$

In general, as the impact of netweight assignment is not very predictable, extensive parameter tuning may be needed to make it work on specific design styles.

21.3.1.2 Sensitivity-Based Netweighting

Netweighting can help improve timing on critical paths. However, it may have negative effects on TWL. Assigning higher netweights on too many nets may result in significant degradation of wirelength, thus may introduce routing congestion and new critical paths. To apply high netweights only on those nets that will result in large gain in timing, we can reduce wirelength degradation and other side effects of netweighting.

Sensitivity-based netweighting tries to predict the netweighting impact on timing and use that sensitivity to guide netweighting [4,31]. The question that sensitivity analysis tries to address is as follows: Given an initial placement from an initial netweighting scheme, if we increase the weight for a net i by certain nominal amount, how much improvement net i will get for its worst slack (WNS) and the overall FOM (or in a more familiar term, TNS when the slack threshold for FOM is 0). With detailed sensitivity analysis, larger weights could be assigned to a net whose weight change can have a larger impact to delay. In this section, we will explain how to estimate both slack sensitivity and TNS sensitivity to netweights and how to use those sensitivities to compute netweights.

First, one needs to estimate the impact of netweight change to wirelength, i.e. the wirelength sensitivity to netweight. This sensitivity depends on the characteristics of a placer. It is not easy to estimate such sensitivity for mincut or simulated-annealing-based algorithms. But for quadratic placement, one can come up with an analytical model to estimate it. Based on Tsay's analytical model [6], the wirelength sensitivity to netweight can be derived [4] as

$$S_W^L(i) = \frac{\Delta L(i)}{\Delta W(i)} = -L(i) \cdot \frac{W_{\text{src}}(i) + W_{\text{sink}}(i) - 2W(i)}{W_{\text{src}}(i) W_{\text{sink}}(i)} \qquad (21.11)$$

where
  $L(i)$ is the initial wirelength of net i
  $W(i)$ is the initial weight of net i
  $W_{\text{src}}(i)$ is the total initial weight on the driver/source of net i (simply the summation of all nets that intersect with the driver)
  $W_{\text{sink}}(i)$ is the total initial weight on the receiver/sink of net i

Intuitively, Equation 21.11 implies that if the initial wirelength $L(i)$ is longer, for the same amount of nominal weight change, it expects to see bigger wirelength change. Meanwhile, if the initial weight $W(i)$ is relatively small, its expected wirelength change will be bigger. The negative sign means that increasing netweight will reduce wirelength.

The next step is to estimate the wirelength impact on delay. Using the switch level RC device model and the Elmore delay model [32], the delay sensitivity to wirelength can be estimated as

$$S_L^T(i) = \frac{\Delta T(i)}{\Delta L(i)} = rcL(i) + cR_{\text{d}} + rC_l \qquad (21.12)$$

where
  r and c are the unit length wire resistance and capacitance, respectively
  R_{d} is the output resistance of the net driver
  C_l is the load capacitance

It implies that for a given technology (fixed r and c), the delay of a long wire with a weak driver and large load will be more sensitive to the same amount of wirelength change.

With wirelength sensitivity and delay sensitivity, one can compute the slack sensitivity to netweight as

$$S_W^{\text{Slk}}(i) = \frac{\Delta \text{Slk}(i)}{\Delta W(i)} = -\frac{\Delta T(i)}{\Delta L(i)} \cdot \frac{\Delta L(i)}{\Delta W(i)} = -S_L^T(i) S_W^L(i) \qquad (21.13)$$

Total negative slack is an important timing closure objective. The TNS sensitivity to netweight is defined as follows:

$$S_W^{\text{TNS}}(i) = \Delta \text{TNS}/\Delta W(i) \qquad (21.14)$$

Note that TNS improvement comes from the delay improvement of this net, Equation 21.14 can be decomposed into

$$S_W^{\text{TNS}}(i) = \frac{\Delta\text{TNS}}{\Delta T(i)} \cdot \frac{\Delta T(i)}{\Delta W(i)} = -K(i)S_W^{\text{Slk}}(i) \qquad (21.15)$$

where $K(i) = \frac{\Delta\text{TNS}}{\Delta T(i)}$, which means how much TNS improvement it can achieve by reducing net delay $T(i)$. It has been shown in Ref. [4] that $K(i)$ is equal to the negative of the number of critical timing endpoints whose slacks are influenced by net i with a nominal $\Delta T(i)$ and can be computed efficiently as shown in the following algorithm:

Algorithm 1 Counting the number of influenced timing critical endpoints for each net
1. decompose nets with multiple sink pins into sets of driver-to-sink nets
2. initialize $K(i) = 0$ for all nets and timing points
3. sort all nets in topological order from timing end points to timing start points
4. **for all** P_o pin t **do**
5.   set $K(t)$ to be 1 if t is timing critical (i.e., $Slk(t) < Slk_t$; otherwise set $K(t)$ to be 0
6. **for all** net i in the above topologically sorted order **do**
7.   **for all** sink pin j of net i **do**
8. $K(i) = K(i) + K(j)$
9.   propagate $K(i)$ of net i to its driver input pins: only the most critical input pin gets $K(i)$; other pins will have $K = 0$ because they are not on the critical path of net i, thus cannot influence the timing end points from net i

As an example, Figure 21.4 shows two paths from a timing begin point P_i to timing endpoints P_{o1} and P_{o2}. Net $n3.1$ and $n3.2$ are the decomposed driver-to-sink nets from the original net $n3$. The pairs in the figure such as $(-3, 1)$ have the following meaning: the first number is the slack, and the second number is the K value. Because the slacks at P_{o1} and P_{o2} are -3ns and -2ns, respectively (worse than the slack target of 0), the K values for P_{o1} and P_{o2} are both 1. We can see how the K values are propagated from PO to PI. Note that for gate C, the upper input pin has slack of -2ns while the lower input pin has slack of -1ns, thus the upper pin is the most timing critical pin to gate C and it will influence the slack of P_{o2}. The lower pin of C does not influence P_{o2}.

The sensitivity-based netweighting scheme starts from a set of initial netweights (e.g., uniform netweighting at the beginning), and computes a new set of netweights that would maximize the slack

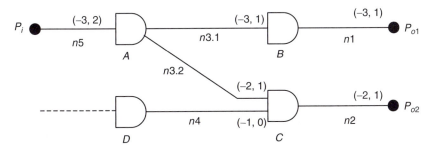

FIGURE 21.4   Counting the number of influenced timing endpoints.

and TNS gain. Because the sensitivity analysis works best when the netweights are updated in small steps from their initial values, it also adds a constant of total change to bound the netweights. The netweight can be computed as

$$
W(i) = \begin{cases} W_{\text{org}}(i), & \text{Slk}(i) > 0 \\ W_{\text{org}}(i) + \alpha\, [\text{Slk}_t - \text{Slk}(i)]\, S_W^{\text{Slk}}(i) + \beta S_W^{\text{TNS}}(i), & \text{Slk}(i) \le 0 \end{cases}
\tag{21.16}
$$

where

$W_{\text{org}}(i)$ is the original netweight

α and β set the bound of netweight changes, and control the balance between WNS and TNS

21.3.2 Dynamic Netweighting

Static netweighting computes netweights once and does not update them during TDP. However, wirelengths change during and after placement, and the original timing analysis may not be valid. To overcome this problem, dynamic netweighting methods were proposed to adjust weights during placement based on timing information available at the current placement stage.

A simple dynamic netweighting scheme is to run multiple placement and netweighting iterations. This scheme can be applied on any placement and netweighting algorithms. This simple scheme, however, is often hard to converge without careful netweighting assignment. This is the so-called oscillation problem [33]. Weights are assigned by performing timing analysis for some given placement solution at the nth iteration [28]. Critical nets receive higher weights. At next iteration, the lengths of those critical nets are reduced, while the lengths of some noncritical nets may be increased, resulting in a different set of critical and noncritical nets. If a net alternates between critical and noncritical nets, we have an oscillation problem. To mitigate this problem, one needs to either periodically recompute timing during the placement process [13,27] or use historical netweighting information to achieve stability [34,35].

21.3.2.1 Incremental Timing Analysis

To periodically update weights during placement, one needs to recompute timing during placement. One could incrementally update timing like Ref. [2], which only computes the incremental slack caused by wirelength increments using delay sensitivity to wirelength.

$$
s^k(n) = s^{k-1}(n) - \Delta d^k(n) = s^{k-1}(n) - S_L^T(n)\Delta l\,(n)
\tag{21.17}
$$

where

$s^k(n)$ is the estimated slack for net n at the k step

$s^{k-1}(n)$ is the slack at $k-1$ step

$\Delta d^k(n)$ is the delay change on net n

S_L^T is the delay to wirelength sensitivity

$\Delta l(n)$ is the wirelength increment

Using sensitivity analysis can provide a fast estimation for incremental timing analysis. One can also perform a more accurate incremental timing analysis. For example, Ref. [34] uses a star net model for placement and netlist changes. The main advantage of this model is that it can calculate individual delay between the source pin and every sink pin of star net more accurately. From given gate coordinates, the star net node is computed as the center of gravity of all pins of the net, and the lengths of all arcs in x and y directions can be obtained. These lengths are used to compute the equivalent lumped elements as used in the derived electrical model. Note that one normally does not perform a full-blown static timing analysis during placement, which would do false path detection, early–late mode analysis, etc.

21.3.2.2 Incremental Net Weighting

To make placement stable with updated weights, we can make use of the historical weights, the so-called incremental netweighting. Different from static netweighting, this method relies on iterations to get the appropriate weights and drives the placement engine along that way.

There are two such algorithms in published literature. One only makes use of the history data of the previous step, the other uses the previous two steps.

In Ref. [35], at each step, it first computes the criticality for a net i as

$$c_i^k = \begin{cases} \left(c_j^{k-1} + 1\right)/2 & \text{if net } i \text{ is among the 3 percent most critical nets} \\ c_j^{k-1}/2 & \text{otherwise} \end{cases} \tag{21.18}$$

The criticality describes how critical a net tends to be in general. For example, if a net was never critical, its criticality is 0 whereas an always critical net has a criticality of 1. This scheme effectively reduces oscillations of weights.

Once the criticality is computed, the netweight then can be updated as

$$w_i^k = w_i^{k-1} \times (1 + c_i^k) \tag{21.19}$$

Therefore, the net with criticality 1 will have its weight doubled at every iteration, while noncritical netweights will stay the same.

The other netweighting scheme uses the criticality information from the previous two steps [34]. In this approach, the criticality number is simplified to either 1 or 0. Nets on critical paths get 1, while nets on noncritical paths get 0. The netweight is updated as follows:

$$w_i^k = \begin{cases} w_i^{k-1} + W & \text{if } c_i^k = 1 \\ 1 & \text{if } c_i^k = 0 \wedge c_i^{k-1} = 0 \wedge c_i^{k-2} = 0 \\ \lceil w_i^{k-1}/2 \rceil & \text{if } c_i^k = 0 \wedge c_i^{k-1} = 0 \wedge c_i^{k-2} = 1 \\ w_i^{k-1} & \text{if } c_i^k = 0 \wedge c_i^{k-1} = 1 \end{cases} \tag{21.20}$$

In this case, the minimum netweight is 1. If the current criticality is 1, its netweight will be increased by W (>1), which determines how fast the weight would increase because of criticality. Using the number of pins of a net to set W is a reasonable choice because delays of nets with high fanouts are usually larger and more likely to be critical. If the current step net criticality is 0, the netweight may change depending on the criticalities of the previous two steps.

21.3.2.3 Placement Implementation

Dynamic netweighting algorithms can be applied to most placement algorithms, e.g., partition-based placement [2,36,37], quadratic placement [34], and force-directed placement [35].

The implementation of dynamic netweighting on quadratic and force-directed placements can be straightforward. Because both placement algorithms provide intermediate gate coordinates at each step, it is easy to estimate wire loads and timing based on those gate coordinates. It is also effective to use the incremental netweighting methods such as Equations 21.19 and 21.20 to drive those placement engines because the matrix solvers for those placers usually respond well to weight changes.

For pure partitioning-based placement, one can also use similar method, i.e. update weights between each partitioning step [2,36]. However, the timing analysis in general is not as accurate because partitioning-based placement does not assign exact gate coordinates inside a partition. Thus, the weights may not effectively control the partitioning process, which aims at minimizing the number of weighted crossings, but not wirelength directly.

One can enforce some cutting constraints to the partitioning algorithm, e.g., the maximum number of times a path can be cut during the iterative partitioning steps [38]. For partitioning-based placement, controlling the cut number on paths in addition to weights helps reduce the wirelength on critical nets more efficiently. It is also a dynamic netweighting approach in that it updates the timing criticality during partitioning process and recomputes weight as well. Unlike previous timing analysis methods that recalculate timing based on gate coordinates, it estimates the critical path by the number of cuts a path has been cut during partitioning. Starting from an initial set of most critical nets, it adds some number of critical nets that has been cut to this set. All the critical nets will be limited to be cut only a maximum number of times by setting a higher weight that is equal to the summation of the weights of noncritical nets in a partition.

In Ref. [39], the minimization of the maximal path delay problem is formulated in the min–max, top-down partition-based placement for timing optimization. The main technique is the iterative net reweighting. In another work [40], the concept of boosting factors is introduced, which adjusts netweights according to net spans, so that the quadratic wirelength can be reduced. The method skews the netlength distribution produced by a mincut placer so as to decrease the number of long nets, with minimal impact on the overall wirelength.

21.4 NET-CONSTRAINT-BASED APPROACH

21.4.1 NET-CONSTRAINT GENERATION

Because interconnect delay is predominately determined by its netlength, a natural choice for controlling delay is through netlength constraint (NLC), which limits the maximum length of a net. The net-constraint-based approach is another popular net-based interface between timing analysis and placement to drive the TDP. The net-constraint approach has several attractive qualities compared to the common netweighting approach. It is not possible to predict the exact timing response to a netweight. Because many nets may have weight changes, there may be conflicts with each other. Sometimes, it is not even certain that the length of a net will be reduced if it is given a higher netweight. Net-constraint approach has more accurate control. The problem then is how to generate a good set of net constraints that are not overly constrained to limit solution space. A common combined flow may be combining netweighting and net constraints, e.g., having netweighting to guide global TDP and net-constraint generation for incremental/iterative improvement.

The two main steps of net-constraint-driven placement are

1. To generate an effective set of NLC bounds
2. To create placers that meet, or nearly meet, these bounds

The following sections will explore these two net-constraint-driven goals.

21.4.1.1 Generating Effective NLCs

Many techniques have been proposed for generating NLCs and many are similar with the approaches for creating netweights. Many of the original methods attempted to create, in a single shot, a set of NLCs, which when met would result in a design that meets timing requirements. More recently, several works have suggested that NLCs should be generated so that the design's target frequency is incrementally improved. The single-shot approaches are described first.

21.4.1.2 Single-Shot NLC Generation

The goal of single-shot NLC generation is to perform a slack budgeting giving timing constraint for each net, which when realized will meet the timing frequency goal. These timing budgets are then used to generate a physical bound for the NLC using silicon process parasitic parameters.

In Ref. [41], the zero-slack algorithm (ZSA) is proposed. This algorithm computes delay bounds for each net based on a tentative set of connection delays chosen so that all timing requirements are met. ZSA chooses maximal delays bounds so that a delay increase on any net connection would produce a timing violation. Based on the delay upper bounds, the wirelength constraints can be generated. Net-constraint generation is formulated as a LP problem, which maximizes the range of permissible length for each net, subject to the LP constraints that timing requirements are met. Intuitively, ZSA will distribute extra slacks uniformly among connections on that path. After that, slacks are updated on other paths that are affected, and the process is repeated until every connection has zero slack. An improvement is suggested in Ref. [42], where a weighted slack budgeting is performed based on the delay per unit load function. A larger weight is assigned to nets that are more sensitive and the slack distribution is allocated proportionally to the weight.

Runtime improvement to slack budgeting using the nonzero slack allocation in intermediate steps is suggested in Ref. [30]. It omits recomputing slacks on connections whose slacks are altered by delay increase on the minimum-slack segment, and thus it converges faster than Ref. [41]. In practice, all slacks converge to near zero in a few iterations. In Ref. [43], the iterative-minmax-PERT [42] procedure is generalized to guarantee the slacks go monotonically to 0.

In Refs. [7,44] the delay budgeting problem is formulated as a convex-programming problem with a special structure, thus efficient graph-based algorithm is proposed. It showed an average of 50 percent reduction in NLC violations over the well-known ZSA [41]. In addition, different delay budgeting objective functions are studied and showed that performance improvements can be made without loss of solution quality. In a recent work [45], a new theoretical framework is presented, which unifies several previous timing budget problems including timing budgeting for maximizing total weighted delay relaxation, minimizing maximum relaxation, and min-skew time budget distribution. Dragon [46] uses design hierarchy information to compute NLCs and it is evaluated using an industrial place and route flow.

21.4.1.3   Incremental NLC Generation

Some NLC generation heuristics have taken an incremental approach to create NLCs [5,47]. These heuristics are used with incremental or iterative placement techniques. Initially, a loose set of NLC on a subset of nets is created, which may not yield a placement that meets timing requirements. Further iterations refine NLCs, tightening the bounds on nets critical at each iteration, so the slack is incrementally improved. Proponents of this approach argue that it is better than deriving a single-shot NLC set. During an industry design flow, timing constraints are often unmeetable, even if every interconnect length is 0. Furthermore, a set of NLCs that guarantee performance requirements may not be achievable by any placement.

An incremental transfer function that uses a LP-based net-constraint generation technique is proposed in Ref. [47]. The technique incrementally generates net constraints and iteratively reduces the length of critical nets by small increments. The goal of this LP-based technique is to derive a set of net constraints that will improve critical path delay d_{initial} by a small amount, Δt. The k longest paths, p_i with delay $d_i > d_{\text{goal}}$ are selected, where $d_{\text{goal}} = d_{\text{initial}} - \Delta t$. For each path, p_i with delay d_i, the delay must be reduced by $d_i - d_{\text{goal}}$. Because the algorithm begins with an initial placement, the current horizontal and vertical lengths, Bx_i and By_i, of bounding box wirelength of each net n_i are known. In each iteration, the horizontal and vertical reduction goals, Δx_i and Δy_i, are computed. The objective function is to minimize the total horizontal and vertical wirelength reductions.

$$\min : \sum_{i \in \text{Nets}} (\Delta x_i + \Delta y_i) \qquad (21.21)$$

For each path, a constraint is created in the LP. For example, if path p_1 is composed of nets n_1, n_2, and n_3, the constraint would be

$$\left(c_{1x} \cdot \Delta x_1 + c_{1y} \cdot \Delta y_1\right) + \left(c_{2x} \cdot \Delta x_2 + c_{2y} \cdot \Delta y_2\right) + \left(c_{3x} \cdot \Delta x_3 + c_{3y} \cdot \Delta y_3\right) < d_1 - d_{\text{goal}} \quad (21.22)$$

where c_{1x} and c_{1y} estimate the delay change per unit horizontal and vertical length of net n_1, etc.

Additional constraints are imposed on each Δx_i and Δy_i reduction goal

$$\Delta x_i < p \cdot Bx_i$$
$$\Delta y_i < p \cdot By_i$$

where p is a parameter $(0 < p < 1)$, usually chosen to start with small value and increased if no solution is found to the LP. Because a net may be shared by more than one path, these constraints may limit the reduction goal of a shared net and force larger improvement goals in other nets.

A convex-programming approach to net-constraint generation is employed by Ref. [5]. Similar to the previous approach [47], it enumerates a set of critical paths to be considered and forms a set of linear constraints on the net delay of these paths. Unlike Ref. [47], each path must have an arrival time that is less than the required time. The result is a set of constraints that, if met, will result in zero slack for the paths considered.

21.4.2 Net-Constraint Placement

Once net constraints are generated, placers must efficiently meet the constraints while generating legal placements and optimizing wirelength. Net-constraint placement algorithms have been proposed for many global and detail placement algorithms. This section explores two global placement approaches: partitioning and force-directed, a several detailed placement approaches.

21.4.2.1 Partition-Based Net-Constraint Placement

Several adaptations of the popular partitioning approach to global placement have been made for net-constraint placement [5,6,9,48]. This section examines a mincut-based approach [5] and two analytical partitioning-based approaches [6,9].

A modified mincut partitioning-based net-constraint global placer is presented in Ref. [5]. The placer modifies the common mincut partitioner using cut weights on constrained nets to change their cut cost. The weights are computed at each partitioning iteration based on the estimated netlengths. For each constrained net, the maximum and minimum estimated lengths, max_i and min_i, are computed, which are the half perimeter of the smallest bounding box enclosing all the cells in n_i in their worst and best assignments to their partition choices. A netweight, w_i, is assigned based on a comparison of these estimates to the bound of the net, b_i. If $b_i < \text{min}_i$, then $w_i = \text{maxcrit}$ is assigned to the net because any increase in the netlength is undesirable. If $b_i > \text{max}_i$, $w_i = 0$ because regardless of assignment choices, the net will not exceed its bound. For nets with $\text{max}_i \geq b_i \geq \text{min}_i$, the weight is computed as

$$\left\lfloor \frac{(\text{max}_i - b_i)}{(\text{max}_i - \text{min}_i)} \cdot \text{maxcrit} + 0.5 \right\rfloor \quad (21.23)$$

The Fiduccia–Mattheyses algorithm [49] is used to make the partition assignments. The algorithm does not guarantee that the net constraints will be met.

One of the first net-constraint-based global placers was published in Ref. [6]. Its general flow follows Proud [50], a partitioning placer that uses mathematical programming to determine partition assignments. Net constraints are created using the ZSA [41] discussed in Section 21.4.1.2. To meet the NLCs, an iterative-solving approach is used. At each iteration, a Lagrange multiplier is computed for each net. For each pin of a net, the multiplier is based on the length constraint, the nets current length, the previous pin weight, and the sum of the weights of the other pins of its cell. It should be noted that the other connectivity of a cell is important in computing pin weight.

Although most net-constraint partitioning placers model the NLCs directly in the partitioning assignment, a different approach is taken in Ref. [9]. This placer assumes that a preliminary wirelength-driven partitioning assignment has been made already and it uses a LP formulation to make minimal reassignment to meet NLCs. Each net is modeled using a bounding-box formulation. The location of each cell is restricted to lie within the boundaries of its parent partition and a reassignment variable is used to indicate if the cell is moved from its currently assigned partition or the other child partition of its parent. If the reassignment causes area violation, unconstrained cells are reassigned from the over capacity partition to the other child partition of its parent. The placer uses the analytical partitioning flow from Gordian [51].

21.4.2.2   Force-Directed Net-Constraint Placement

A force-directed placer that optimizes for net constraints is presented in Ref. [8]. As with the other net constraint placers, this too builds on a strong wirelength-driven placer, Kraftwerk [35]. Kraftwerk uses a quadratic programming (QP) model to generate cell locations. Net constraints are met by generating a higher netweight for nets that are not meeting their NLCs. The increased weights are allocated to the pins that determine the current boundary of the net. The outer pins, in both the X and Y dimensions, are given higher weights to reduce its length as long as it does not meet its NLC. Another idea presented in this chapter is to constrain the net segment connecting the nets driver to its critical receiver.

21.4.2.3   Net-Constraint-Based Detailed Placement

Several net-constraint detailed placement algorithms have been proposed [10,47,52]. In Ref. [10], the ripple-move algorithm from Mongrel [53] is adapted to include the cost of nets that are violating their constraints. In Ref. [52], net-constraint-driven versions of simulated annealing [13,54–56] and Domino [57] are proposed. The change to simulated annealing is a very simple addition to the simulated annealing (SA) cost function which reflects the cost of nets not meeting their NLC. The Domino-transportation cost function is changed and several new techniques to recombine the fractured subcells are proposed.

A local-movement approach that employs LP to reduce nets with constraints while minimizing the movement of unconstrained nets is presented in Ref. [47]. The objective function minimizes the squared movement of the center of a net's bounding box. This approach will create overlaps that must be resolved through a legalization phase that is not net constraint aware.

21.5   PATH (OR TIMING GRAPH)-BASED APPROACH

Historically, path-based TDP refers to those algorithms that directly model the timing constraints (which are inherently path-based) during placement. It ensures that all the paths under consideration will meet their timing requirements after placement. The benefit of path-based approach is that it is explicitly timing driven, unlike net-based approaches which are implicitly timing driven by converting timing constraints into netweights or wirelength constraints. The downside of this approach is the complexity of directly modeling timing in placement, as the number of paths may be prohibitive [26]. Except some early works such as simulated annealing [13], enumerating all paths are not widely adopted. To make the problem size small, one can select only the near-critical paths, but even that could still be huge. The potential problem of only selecting a set of critical paths is that some noncritical paths may become critical.

A more powerful technique is to embed timing graph (through a built-in simplified version of static timing analyzer) into the TDP formulation. It implicitly considers all topological paths and formulates them into some mathematical programming framework by introducing intermediate auxiliary variables (such as arrival times). It eliminates the need to enumerate/optimize a limited set of paths. The LP-based formulation is popular as the HPWL model can be formulated exactly into an LP framework. To explicitly write down the delay modeling and timing propagation with respect to the cell locations (x,y), simple/linearized models are often used. In this section, we first review the general LP-based formulation (which can easily be extended to handle nonlinear mathematical programming). Then we discuss various techniques such as partitioning-based overlap removal and Lagrangian relaxation to complement the general LP-based formulation. We also discuss the simulated annealing technique for path-based TDP and a recent technique using differential timing analysis.

21.5.1 LP-Based Formulation

The general LP-based formulation consists of two sets of variables and constraints: physical and electrical. The physical variables/constraints deal with variables and equations representing cell locations and netlengths (e.g., computed through the HPWL model). The electrical variables/constraints deal with gate and net delay models, arrival time propagation through the critical path method, and constraints that all required arrival times at timing endpoints are met. The objective function may be maximizing either WNS or TNS, or weighted wirelength, etc.

21.5.1.1 Physical Constraints

For cell i, its center coordinates (x_i, y_i) are the variables of the LP program. For a net e_j, let l_j, r_j, t_j, and b_j represent its left, right, top, and bottom locations of its bounding box. Let N_j denote the set of cells connected to net e_j, then we have

$$
\begin{aligned}
l_j &\leq x_i + \text{pin}_x(i,j) \\
r_j &\geq x_i + \text{pin}_x(i,j) \\
t_j &\leq y_i + \text{pin}_y(i,j) \\
b_j &\geq y_i + \text{pin}_y(i,j), \quad \forall\, i \in N_j
\end{aligned}
\tag{21.24}
$$

where $\text{pin}_x(i,j)$ and $\text{pin}_y(i,j)$ are the pin offsets of cell i for its pin connecting to net e_j in horizontal and vertical directions, respectively. The HPWL of net e_j is represented by L_j

$$
L_j = r_j - l_j + t_j - b_j
\tag{21.25}
$$

21.5.1.2 Electrical/Timing Constraints

Let the gate delay $\text{GDelay}_i(k, o)$ represent the pin delay from an input pin k to output pin o of cell i. It can be modeled as a linear function of the load capacitance at the output pin and the slope (transition time) at the input pin with a reasonably high degree of accuracy. Similarly, the slope at the output pin of cell i can be described by a linear function.

$$
\begin{aligned}
\text{GDelay}_i(k,o) &= a_0 + a_1 \cdot \text{CLoad}_i(o) + a_2 \cdot \text{Slope}_i(k) \\
\text{Slope}_i(o) &= b_0 + b_1 \cdot \text{CLoad}_i(o) + b_2 \cdot \text{Slope}_i(k)
\end{aligned}
$$

where
   $\text{Slope}_i(k)$ is the slope at the input pin k of cell i
   $\text{Slope}_i(o)$ is the slope at the output pin o of cell i
   $\text{CLoad}_i(o)$ is the capacitance load seen by the output pin o

The constants a_0, a_1, a_2, b_0, b_1, and b_2 are determined by standard cell library characterizations. These delay and output slope equations can be defined for every feasible signal transition for the cell.

The delay for net e_j, $\text{NDelay}_j(i_1, o, i_2, k)$ from output pin o of cell i_1 to the input pin k of cell i_2 is modeled in the LP using a simplified Elmore model [58] by the following equation:

$$\text{NDelay}_j(i_1, o, i_2, k) = K_D \cdot r \cdot L_j \cdot \left[\frac{c \cdot L_j}{2} + \text{CLoad}_{i_2}(k) \right] \tag{21.26}$$

where
  r is the unit resistance of the interconnect
  c is the unit capacitance constant
  K_D is a constant, 0.69 [14]

If the resistance and capacitance in the horizontal and vertical directions are not equal, an alternate model can be used that replaces L_j with individual variables for the horizontal and vertical lengths.

The arrival time at each pin is modeled through timing propagation and critical path method. Two types of equations are used, the first for input pins and the second for output pins. For input pin k of cell i_2, its arrival time is

$$\text{Arr}_{i2}(k) = \text{Arr}_{i1}(o) + \text{NDelay}_j(i_1, o, i_2, k) \tag{21.27}$$

The arrive time at an output pin o of cell i is represented by the LP variable $\text{Arr}_i(i, o)$ and a set constraints, one for each input pin of cell i. Assuming two input pins k_1 and k_2 for cell i, the equations would be

$$\text{Arr}_i(k_1) + \text{GDelay}_i(k_1, o) \leq \text{Arr}_i(o) \tag{21.28}$$

$$\text{Arr}_i(k_2) + \text{GDelay}_i(k_2, o) \leq \text{Arr}_i(o) \tag{21.29}$$

Most implementations assume the arrival time at the output of a sequential cell to be 0.

Each library cell has a maximum drive strength, limiting the total capacitance the cell can drive. This drive strength limit is incorporated in the LP through length limits on the driven net. This limit is a precomputed constant to the LP formulation.

$$L_j < \text{CMax}(e_j) \tag{21.30}$$

21.5.1.3 Objective Functions

The required time at input pin k of sequential cell v_i, $\text{Req}_i(k)$, is a constant input. The negative slack at these timing endpoints is represented by variable $\text{Slk}_i(k)$ and equations

$$\text{Slk}_i(k) <= \text{Req}_i(k) - \text{Arr}_i(k) \tag{21.31}$$

$$\text{Slk}_i(k) \leq 0 \tag{21.32}$$

The second constraint is needed so that paths are not optimized beyond what is required to meet timing. This constraint can be adapted so that a slight positive margin is created for each path.

The path-based TDP can optimize the TNS, i.e.,

$$\max: \sum_{i \in \text{sequential}} \text{Slk}_i(k) \tag{21.33}$$

To optimize the WNS, a variable representing the WNS is introduced, WNS, i.e.,

$$\text{WNS} < \text{Slk}_i(k) \tag{21.34}$$

And the objective function is simply

$$\text{max: WNS} \tag{21.35}$$

The LP-based objective function can also be a combination of wirelength and slack [11], e.g.,

$$\text{min:} \sum L_j - \alpha \cdot \text{WNS} \tag{21.36}$$

where α is the weight to trade off wirelength and WNS.

To summarize, the complete LP formulation for TDP can be written in the following generic term:

$$\begin{aligned} \text{minimize} \quad & f(\mathbf{X}) \\ \text{subject to} \quad & A\mathbf{X} \leq D \end{aligned} \tag{21.37}$$

where

$\mathbf{X}$ is the set of variables including gate coordinates and auxiliary variables
$f(\mathbf{X})$ is the objective function which can be Equation 21.33, 21.35, or 21.36
$A\mathbf{X} \leq D$ includes all the physical and electrical constraints such as net bounding-box constraints, delay constraints, slack constraints, and other possible additional constraints (such as the center of gravity constraints as in Ref. [11])

21.5.2 PARTITIONING-BASED OVERLAP REMOVAL

The LP-based formulation may create a lot of overlaps. Partitioning-based approach can be used together with LP-based formulation to remove the cell overlaps, as proposed in the original timing graph-based placer Allegro [11]. At each partitioning step, it formulates a LP problem to determine locations of cells. Each partition is divided into two subpartitions, and its cells are sorted based on the LP locations to determine the new partition assignment. The LP model is similar to Section 21.5.1. The objective function is similar to Equation 21.36. The factor α is used to trade off timing optimization versus wirelength. Additional physical constraints includes center-of-gravity constraint and partition-boundary constraint. The center-of-gravity constraint, as shown in Equation 21.38, tries to place the center of gravity of all the gates in the same partition to be in the center of the partition, while the boundary constraints prevent gates being placed outside the partition boundaries.

$$\bar{x} = \frac{\sum m_i x_i}{m_i} \tag{21.38}$$

where

$\bar{x}$ represents the center of the partition in x direction
x_i is the position of gate i
m_i is the equivalent mass of gate i, approximated by the gate width

21.5.3 LAGRANGIAN RELAXATION METHOD

The number of constraints in the general LP-based formulation in Equation 21.37 can be enormous, even for moderate size circuits. Lagrangian relaxation is a very effective technique to transform the original constrained LP-formulation into a set of unconstrained problems in an iterative manner, e.g., as in Ref. [12]. Although the objective function used in Ref. [12] is the quadratic wirelength, the principle of Lagrangian relaxation method is the same. For the general mathematical programming formulation in Equation 21.37, suppose A has m constraint equations. We can define a size-m vector Lagrange multipliers λ and add the nonnegative term $\lambda \cdot (D - AX)$ to the objective function:

$$\max_\lambda \min_X f(\mathbf{X}) + \lambda \cdot (D - A\mathbf{X}) \tag{21.39}$$

When λ is fixed, minimizing $f(\mathbf{X}) + \lambda(D - A\mathbf{X})$ is an unconstrained mathematical programming problem, which can be solved efficiently. Then the Lagrange multiplier λ will be updated to solve a new unconstrained optimization problem. This process is iterated to obtain the constrained optimal solution.

21.5.4 SIMULATED ANNEALING

The simulated annealing is a generic probabilistic algorithm for global optimization. It randomly moves gates, and accepts or rejects the move based on certain cost function. It is very flexible, i.e., it can take any objective function and consider accurate timing models, if needed. In Ref. [13], the simulated annealing algorithm is used for TDP by augmenting the cost function to include path-based timing information. Because efficient runtime of the cost evaluation step is critical in SA, great care has to be taken in implementing the timing cost function. Rather than updating the static timing graph whenever a cell is moved, the approach in Ref. [13] uses an enumerated set of critical paths, P_{critical}. During a move cost evaluation, the paths impacted can be directly updated by adding the change in delay for the nets connected moved cells. The SA engine has two loops. The outer loop identifies P_{critical}, and the inner loop runs a number of annealing iterations. In each outer loop of the annealing process, P_{critical} is chosen as the K most critical paths using Dreyfus method [59]. In the inner loop, the nets impacted by a move will update the slack of paths, and the total timing cost is the sum of the path slacks in P_{critical}. When the inner loop finishes, the outer loop updates the critical paths with new gate locations, and continues the inner loop. The simulated annealing cost function is a combination of wirelength cost and timing cost function.

21.5.5 GRAPH-BASED DIFFERENTIAL TIMING

A recent work by Chowdary et al. [14] addresses the correlation problem of graph-based placers with final sign-off timers. Rather than modeling and computing delays and arrival times as was presented above, this approach optimizes an initial global placement based on the differences in delays, arrival, and required times at all pins of a circuit, relative to a reference static timing analysis. It terms this approach differential timing analysis [14]. This differential timing analyzer is almost exact in the neighborhood of the reference static timing, including modeling of setup time and latch transparency. It also introduces another improvement to graph timing-based placement. The constants used in the delay and slope Equation 21.26 are only accurate for a range of values of output loads and input slopes. To maintain the validity of the differential timing model, placement changes are limited to a local neighborhood. It then solves several iterations of the LP adjusting model constants and the neighborhood limits in each iteration. Differential timing is optimized using LP. A set of LP equations that parallel the static timing graph equations are used. For example, the delta wirelength can be obtained by

$$\Delta L_j = r_j - l_j + t_j - b_j - L_j^{\text{old}} \tag{21.40}$$

where L_j^{old} is the wirelength of net j in the current placement. The equations for Δdelay, Δslope, Δarrival, and Δslack can be formed similarly [14].

21.6 ADDITIONAL TECHNIQUES

There are many additional TDP algorithms in the literature that do not fall exactly into the previous classifications. As mentioned earlier, net-based and path-based algorithms all have pros and cons. A hybrid approach is proposed recently [15] to combine the netweighting and net constraints together with LP-based formulations. Furthermore, because of the complexity of modern placement problems and the iterative refinement nature from global placement to detailed/legal placement, it is very important to have stability between placement iterations. In this section, we present several representative and recent techniques for TDP and timing-aware placement.

21.6.1 HYBRID NET AND PATH-BASED APPROACH

In Ref. [15], a hybrid approach is proposed to combine the netweighting and net constraints together with LP-based formulations. The net-based approaches, especially the netweighting, have low computational complexity and high flexibility/scalability. Therefore, net-based approaches have more advantages as the circuit complexity continues to increase. However, netweighting often completely ignores slew propagation. Because timing is inherently path based, an effective netweighting algorithm should be based on path analysis and consider timing propagation. Furthermore, net-based approaches are often done in an ad hoc manner and may have problems with convergence. For instance, while the delay on critical paths decrease, other paths become critical, and this leads to a convergence problem. A systematic way of explicit perturbation control is important for netweighting-based algorithms. The hybrid approach in Ref. [15] uses a hybrid net and path-based delay sensitivity with limited-stage slew propagation as basis for netweighting. The objective function is the weighted wirelength for a set of critical paths. The LP formulation considers not only cells on the timing-critical paths, but also cells that are logically adjacent to the critical paths in a unified manner, through weighted LP objective function and net-bound constraints. This approach is suitable for incremental timing improvement.

21.6.2 HIPPOCRATES: A DETAILED PLACER WITHOUT DEGRADING TIMING

Another timing-driven incremental placement algorithm [60] helps to reduce TWL and improve timing at the same time. It specifically maintains the timing constraints while reducing wirelength during detailed placement. The detailed placement algorithms it uses can be any commonly used move-based transforms, i.e., cell swapping, cell moving, etc. Instead of modeling path constraints, it models the timing constraints at each input pin. The advantage of this is that it reduces the computation complexity, which allows it to model timing constraints on every timing path. Therefore, the output of this algorithm guarantees no timing degradation. The timing constraint on each pin is called delta arrival time constraint, which is defined as the difference of arrival time at this pin to the arrival time of the most critical input pin on this gate. By constraining the delta delay changed by moving cells to be less than the delta arrival time on each pin, it guarantees that the final arrival time at timing endpoints would not degrade. It also models slew and load capacitance constraints. Experimental results [60] show that Hippocrates helps improve wirelength and timing significantly, in particular on TNS, while conventional detailed placement algorithms fail to maintain the original timing.

21.6.3 ACCURATE NET-MODELING ISSUE

While most timing driven placers assume simple net models, some use specialized net models for timing critical nets, e.g., during global placement [61] or detailed placement [21]. The first, [61], based on force-directed global placement [35], proposes a more accurate tree net model to replace the ubiquitous clique/star net models normally used in quadratic placers. A Steiner tree net model is constructed and the length of each tree segment is controlled by weighting the individual segments to improve timing. This new model does not increase numerical complexity. This net model is not specific to the force-directed formulation and could be used in other QP-based placers. To determine the weight of each Steiner segment, the segment sensitivity is computed by determining the net delay derivative with respect to the segment length. In this way, the segments that produce the most slack improvement are shortened the most.

Another work [21] proposes simultaneous detailed placement and routing to optimize timing. The algorithm is stable and incremental, and it reduces WNS by 9–14 percent, although the runtime is quite high. It begins with a placed and global-routed netlist and optimizes the k most critical paths using a nonconvex mathematical programming model that optimizes slack while capturing the timing impact of cell movements and Steiner point changes of the global route. In this approach, cell movements may change the Steiner tree topology. Within the solving steps, each net is analyzed to ensure that its Steiner tree is correct, otherwise a new topology is generated. Because routing changes are modeled, this is a more accurate net model than those commonly used net models discussed in previous sections.

21.7 CONCLUSIONS

Although TDP has been studied extensively in the past two decades, the problem is still far away from being solved [62]. Many challenges still remain due to the ever-growing problem size and complexity. On the one hand, modern system-on-chip designs have millions of placeable cells and hundreds/thousands of macros [63]; on the other hand, stringent timing requirements and physical effects pose increasing challenges to the timing closure where TDP plays a key role.

It shall be noted that to achieve the overall timing closure, TDP needs to work closely with synthesis/optimization tools (such as buffer insertion and gate sizing) and routing (in particular global routing). The entire physical design/synthesis closure is an extremely complex task. Furthermore, modern complex SOC designs usually have multiple clock domains, or even multiple cycle paths, which make the TDP problem even more complicated. Because of the infrastructure limitation, the academia has not been able to fully push the state of the art and limits of TDP. With the availability of OpenAccess [64] and the OpenAccess gear timer [65,66], it is possible to push the frontier of the very successful International Symposium on Physical Design (ISPD) placement contest [63] for university researchers to work on more realistic timing objectives. As technology scales into sub100 nm regimes, new physical and manufacturing effects, in particular leakage/power and variations, have to be considered together with timing closure during TDP [67,68], which requires continuous innovations for better quality and productivity.

REFERENCES

1. A.E. Dunlop, V.D. Agrawal, D.N. Deutsch, M.F. Jukl, P. Kozak, and M. Wiesel. Chip layout optimization using critical path weighting. In *Proceedings of the Design Automation Conference*, Las Vegas, NV, pp. 133–136, 1985.
2. M. Burstein and M.N. Youssef. Timing influenced layout design. In *Proceedings of the Design Automation Conference*, Albuquerque, NM, pp. 124–130, 1984.
3. T. Kong. A novel net weighting algorithm for timing-driven placement. In *Proceedings of the International Conference on Computer Aided Design*, San Jose, CA, pp. 172–176, 2002.
4. H. Ren, D.Z. Pan, and D. Kung. Sensitivity guided net weighting for placement driven synthesis. *IEEE Transactions on Computer-Aided Design of Integrated Circuits and Systems*, Phoenix, AZ, pp. 711–721, May 2005. (ISPD 2004).
5. T. Gao, P.M. Vaidya, and C.L. Liu. A performance driven macro-cell placement algorithm. In *Proceedings of the Design Automation Conference*, Anaheim, CA, pp. 147–152, 1992.
6. R.S. Tsay and J. Koehl. An analytic net weighting approach for performance optimization in circuit placement. In *Proceedings of the Design Automation Conference*, San Francisco, CA, pp. 636–639, 1991.
7. M. Sarrafzadeh, D. Knol, and G. Tellez. Unification of budgeting and placement. In *Proceedings of the Design Automation Conference*, Anaheim, CA, pp. 758–761, 1997.
8. K. Rajagopal, T. Shaked, Y. Parasuram, T. Cao, A. Chowdhary, and B. Halpin. Timing driven force directed placement with physical net constraints. In *Proceedings of the International Symposium on Physical Design*, San Diego, CA, pp. 60–66, 2003.
9. B. Halpin, C.R. Chen, and N. Sehgal. Timing driven placement using physical net constraints. In *Proceedings of the Design Automation Conference*, Las Vegas, NV, pp. 780–783, 2001.

10. S. Hur, T. Cao, K. Rajagopal, Y. Parasuram, A. Chowdhary, V. Tiourin, and B. Halpin. Force directed mongrel with physical net constraints. In *Proceedings of the Design Automation Conference*, Anaheim, CA, pp. 214–219, 2003.

11. M.A.B. Jackson and E.S. Kuh. Performance-driven placement of cell based ic's. In *Proceedings of the Design Automation Conference*, Las Vegas, NV, pp. 370–375, 1989.

12. A. Srinivasan, K. Chaudhary, and E.S. Kuh. Ritual: A performance driven placement algorithm for small cell ics. In *Proceedings of the International Conference on Computer Aided Design*, Santa Clara, CA, pp. 48–51, 1991.

13. W. Swartz and C. Sechen. Timing driven placement for large standard cell circuits. In *Proceedings of the Design Automation Conference*, San Francisco, CA, pp. 211–215, 1995.

14. A. Chowdhary, K. Rajagopal, S. Venkatesan, T. Cao, V. Tiourin, Y. Parasuram, and B. Halpin. How accurately can we model timing in a placement engine. In *Proceedings of the Design Automation Conference*, Anaheim, CA, pp. 801–806, 2005.

15. T. Luo, D. Newmark, and D.Z. Pan. A new LP based incremental timing driven placement for high performance designs. In *Proceedings of the Design Automation Conference*, San Francisco, CA, pp. 1115–1120, 2006.

16. A.B. Kahng and Q. Wang. Implementation and extensibility of an analytic placer. *Proceedings of the International Symposium on Physical Design*, Phoenix, AZ, pp. 18–25, April 2004.

17. T. Chan, J. Cong, and K. Sze. Multilevel generalized force-directed method for circuit placement. In *Proceedings of the International Symposium on Physical Design*, pp. 185–192. ACM Press, New York, 2005.

18. M.A. Breuer, M. Sarrafzadeh, and F. Somenzi. Fundamental CAD algorithms. *IEEE Transactions on Computer-Aided Design*, 19(12): 1449–1475, 2000.

19. K.D. Boese, A.B. Kahng, and S. Mantik. On the relevance of wire load models. In *Proceedings of the 2001 International Workshop on System-Level Interconnect Prediction*, Rohnert Park, CA, pp. 91–98. ACM Press, 2001.

20. P. Saxena and S. Gupta. Shield count minimization in congested regions. In *Proceedings of 2002 International Symposium on Physical Design*, Del Mar, CA, pp. 78–83. ACM Press, 2002.

21. A.H. Ajami and M. Pedram. Post-layout timing-driven cell placement using an accurate net length model with movable steiner points. In *Proceedings of the Asia and South Pacific Design Automation Conference*, Yokohama, Japan, pp. 595–600, 2001.

22. J.A. Roy, J.F. Lu, and I.L. Markov. Seeing the forest and the trees: Steiner wirelength optimization in placemen. In *ISPD '06: Proceedings of the 2006 International Symposium on Physical Design*, pp. 78–85. ACM Press, New York, 2006.

23. L.T. Pillage and R.A. Rohrer. Asymptotic waveform evaluation for timing analysis. *IEEE Transactions on Computer Aided Design of Integrated Circuits and Systems*, 9: 352–366, April 1990.

24. N. Maheshwari and S. Sapatnekar. *Timing Analysis and Optimization of Sequential Circuits*. Kluwer Academic Publishers, 1999.

25. Sr. R.B. Hitchcock. Timing verification and the timing analysis program. In *Proceedings of the Design Automation Conference*, pp. 594–604, 1982.

26. C.C. Chang, J. Lee, M. Stabenfeldt, and R.S. Tsay. A practical all-path timing-driven place and route design system. In *Asia-Pacific Conference on Circuits and Systems*, pp. 560–563. IEEE/ACM, 1994.

27. A. Marquardt, V. Betz, and J. Rose. Timing driven placement for FPGA. In *ACM Symposium on FPGA*, Monterey, CA, pp. 203–213, 2000.

28. M. Marek-Sadowska and S.P. Lin. Timing driven placement. In *Proceedings of the International Conference on Computer Aided Design*, San Jose, CA, pp. 94–97, 1989.

29. H. Chang, E. Shragowitz, J. Liu, H. Youssef, B. Lu, and S. Sutanthavibul. Net criticality revisited: An effective method to improve timing in physical design. In *Proceedings of the International Symposium on Physical Design*, Del Mar, CA, pp. 155–160, April 2002.

30. W.K. Luk. A fast physical constraint generator for timing driven placement. In *Proceedings of the Design Automation Conference*, pp. 626–631, 1991.

31. B. Halpin, C.Y.R. Chen, and N. Sehgal. A sensitivity based placer for standard cells. In *Proceedings of the 10th Great Lakes Symposium on VLSI*, Chicago, IL, pp. 193–196, 2000.

32. J. Cong, L. He, C.-K. Koh, and P.H. Madden. Performance optimization of VLSI interconnect layout. *Integration, the VLSI Journal*, 21: 1–94, 1996.

33. J. Cong, J.R. Shinnerl, M. Xie, T. Kong, and X. Yuan. Large-scale circuit placement. In *ACM Transactions on Design Automation of Electronic Systems*, pp. 389–430, 2005.

34. B.M. Riess and G.G. Ettelt. SPEED: Fast and efficient timing driven placement. In *Proceedings of the IEEE International Symposium on Circuits and Systems*, Seattle, WA, pp. 377–380, 1995.

35. H. Eisenmann and F.M. Johannes. Generic global placement and floorplanning. In *Proceedings of the Design Automation Conference*, San Francisco, CA, pp. 269–274, 1998.

36. D.J.H. Huang and A.B. Kahng. Partition-based standard-cell global placement with an exact objective. In *Proceedings of the International Symposium on Physical Design*, Napa Valley, CA, pp. 18–25, 1997.

37. S. Ou and M. Pedram. Timing-driven placement based on partitioning with dynamic cut-net control. In *Proceedings of the Design Automation Conference*, Los Angeles, CA, pp. 472–476, 2000.

38. S. Ou and M. Pedram. Timing-driven bipartitioning with replication using iterative quadratic programming. In *Proceedings of the Asia and South Pacific Design Automation Conference*, Wanchai, Hong Kong, pp. 105–108, 1999.

39. A.B. Kahng, S. Mantik, and I.L. Markov. Min–max placement for large-scale timing optimization. In *Proceedings of the International Symposium on Physical Design*, Del Mar, CA, pp. 143–148, 2002.

40. A.B. Kahng, I.L. Markov, and S. Reda. Boosting: Min-cut placement with improved signal delay. In *Proceedings of the Design, Automation and Test in Europe*, Paris, France, pp. 1098–1103, 2004.

41. R. Nair, L. Berman, P.S. Hauge, and E.J. Yoffa. Generation of performance constraints for layout. *IEEE Transactions on Computer-Aided Design of Integrated Circuits and Systems*, 8(8): 860–874, 1989. (ICCAD 1987).

42. H. Youssef and E. Shragowitz. Timing constraints for correct peformance. In *Proceedings of the International Conference on Computer Aided Design*, Santa Clara, CA, pp. 24–27, 1990.

43. J. Frankle. Iterative and adaptive slack allocation for performance-driven layout and FPGA routing. In *Proceedings of the Design Automation Conference*, Anaheim, CA, pp. 539–532, 1992.

44. M. Sarrafzadeh, D. Knol, and G. Tellez. A delay budgeting algorithm ensuring maximum flexibility inplacement. *IEEE Transactions on Computer-Aided Design of Integrated Circuits and Systems*, 16(11): 1332–1341, November 1997.

45. S. Ghiasi, E. Bozorgzadeh, S. Choudhuri, and M. Sarrafzadeh. A unified theory of timing budget management. In *Proceedings of the International Conference on Computer Aided Design*, San Jose, CA, pp. 653–659, 2004.

46. X. Yang, B. Choi, and M. Sarrafzadeh. Timing-driven placement using design hierarchy guided constraint generation. In *Proceedings of the International Conference on Computer Aided Design*, San Jose, CA, pp. 177–180, 2002.

47. W. Choi and K. Bazargan. Incremental placement for timing optimization. In *Proceedings of the International Conference on Computer Aided Design*, San Jose, CA, pp. 463–466, 2003.

48. M. Terai, K. Takahashi, and K. Sato. A new min-cut placement algorithm for timing assurance layout design meeting net length constraint. In *DAC '90: Proceedings of the 27th ACM/IEEE Conference on Design Automation*, pp. 96–102. ACM Press, New York, 1990.

49. C.M. Fiduccia and R.M. Mattheyses. A linear-time heuristic for improving network partitions. In *Proceedings of the Design Automation Conference*, pp. 175–181, 1982.

50. R.-S. Tsay, E.S. Kuh, and C.-P. Hsu. Proud: A fast sea-of-gates placement algorithm. In *Proceedings of the Design Automation Conference*, Atlantic City, NJ, pp. 318–323. IEEE Computer Society Press, 1988.

51. J.M. Kleinhans, G. Sigl, F.M. Johannes, and K.J. Antreich. Gordian: VLSI placement by quadratic programming and slicing optimization. *IEEE Transactions on Computer-Aided Design*, 10(3): 356–365, 1991.

52. B. Halpin, C.Y.R. Chen, and N. Sehgal. Detailed placement with net length constraints. In *Proceedings of the 3rd International Workshop System on Chip*, Alberta, Canada, p. 22, 2003.

53. S. Hur and J. Lillis. Mongrel: Hybrid techniques for standard cell placement. In *Proceedings of the International Conference on Computer-Aided Design*, San Jose, CA, pp. 165–170. IEEE, 2000.

54. C. Sechen. *VLSI Placement and Global Routing Using Simulated Annealing*. Kluwer, B.V., 1988.

55. C. Sechen and A.S. Vincentelli. The Timberwolf placement and routing package. In *IEEE Custom Integrated Circuits Conference*, pp. 522–527, 1984.

56. W.J. Sun and C. Sechen. A loosely coupled parallel algorithm for standard cell placement. In *Proceedings of the International Conference on Computer-Aided Design*, San Jose, CA, pp. 137–144. IEEE, 1994.

57. K. Doll, F.M. Johannes, and K.J. Antreich. Iterative placement improvement by network flow methods. *IEEE Transactions on Computer-Aided Design*, 13: 1190–1200, 1994.

58. W.C. Elmore. The transient response of damped linear networks with particular regard to wide-band amplifiers. *Journal of Applied Physics*, 19(1): 55–63, January 1948.

59. S.E. Dreyfus. An appraisal of some shortest-path algorithms. *Operations Research*, 17: 395–412, 1969.

60. H. Ren, D.Z. Pan, C. Alpert, G.-J. Nam, and P. Villarrubia. Hippocrates: First-do-no-harm detailed placement. In *Proceedings of the Asia and South Pacific Design Automation Conference*, Yokohama, Japan, January 2007.

61. B. Obermeier and F.M. Johannes. Quadratic placement using an improved timing model. In *Proceedings of the Design Automation Conference*, San Diego, CA, pp. 705–710, 2004.

62. J. Cong, M. Romesis, and M. Xie. Optimality and stability study of timing-driven placement algorithms. In *Proceedings of the International Conference on Computer Aided Design*, p. 472. IEEE Computer Society, Washington DC, 2003.

63. G.-J. Nam. ISPD 2006 placement contest: Benchmark suite and results. In *Proceedings of the International Symposium on Physical Design*, pp. 167–167. ACM Press, New York, 2006.

64. http://openeda.si2.org/.

65. Z. Xiu and R.A. Rutenbar. Timing-driven placement by grid-warping. In *Proceedings of the Design Automation Conference*, Anaheim, CA, pp. 585–590, 2005.

66. Z. Xiu, D.A. Papa, P. Chong, C. Albrecht, A. Kuehlmann, R.A. Rutenbar, and I.L. Markov. Early research experience with openaccess gear: An open source development environment for physical design. In *Proceedings of the International Symposium on Physical Design*, pp. 94–100. ACM Press, New York, 2005.

67. Y. Cheon, P.-H. Ho, A.B. Kahng, S. Reda, and Q. Wang. Power-aware placement. In *Proceedings of the Design Automation Conference*, pp. 795–800. ACM Press, New York, 2005.

68. A.B. Kahng, C.-H. Park, P. Sharma, and Q. Wang. Lens aberration aware timing-driven placement. In *Proceedings of the Design, Automation and Test in Europe*, pp. 890–895, 3001. European Design and Automation Association, Leuven, Belgium, 2006.

22 Congestion-Driven Physical Design

Saurabh N. Adya and Xiaojian Yang

CONTENTS

22.1   INTRODUCTION

This chapter discusses the impact and optimization of placement on the routing stage. This is commonly referred as congestion-driven placement. Although a placer that produces unroutable designs will be of little use, historically optimization to directly reduce routing congestion has received less attention than wirelength and timing optimization. Often placement papers fail to report any information on congestion and routability. Over the last decade, with design sizes increasing dramatically and limited number of metal layers available for routing of signals and power, routability has become a paramount issue. This has driven the recent research interest in placement techniques to mitigate congestion while optimizing other placement objectives.

Congestion-driven placement techniques can be classified into the following groups: netlist-connectivity-based methods, pin-density-based methods, and routing-estimation-based methods. Netlist-connectivity-based methods use a priori information about the netlist characteristics to influence the placement process. Pin-density-based methods seek to limit the average pin density in local regions to indirectly address the routability concerns. Routing-estimation-based methods are frequently used during and after the placement process when sufficient routing congestion information is available. Global routers or probabilistic route estimators are often used to drive the various congestion mitigation techniques. Other notable techniques for addressing congestion in the design process include congestion-driven logic synthesis and global-placement density control. Several of these techniques are applied separately during global placement and detail placement, the details of each approach change according to the specific context. Often a placement flow will employ one or several of these methods.

22.2 NETLIST-CONNECTIVITY-BASED APPROACHES

Recent advances in placement technology have attempted to alleviate the problem of wiring congestion during very large scale integration (VLSI) chip design. Classically, placement algorithms find the optimal location of the logic without attempting to change the structure of the logic netlist itself. However, the inherent structure of the logic netlist has a significant impact on the routability, irrespective of the placement algorithm used. With the advent of physical synthesis techniques, there have been several attempts to combine placement transformations of the netlist in conjunction with logic synthesis transforms. Such efforts [14,15,31] have concentrated mainly in improving the delay or area characteristics of the final implementation of the design. Significant decisions regarding the circuit structure are made early in the synthesis stages such as register transfer level (RTL) decomposition, technology-independent logic optimization, technology mapping, etc. For deep submicron (DSM) technologies, the wiring capacitance dominates the gate capacitance and the delay estimation based on fanout, and design legacy statistics (wireload tables) can be highly inaccurate. In addition, logic block size is no longer dictated solely by total cell area, and is often limited by routing resources. For these reasons, wiring congestion is an extremely important design metric and should be taken into consideration at the earliest possible stage of the design flow. In physical design, the required routing resources are captured in terms of routing congestion. Placement or routing can sometimes fix, or avoid, potential congestion problems. However, the netlist structure determined during logic synthesis may mean that it is too late in the flow to target congestion problems. In the following subsections, we detail several recent approaches to target placement congestion by netlist transformations during the logic synthesis stage or by using inherent netlist properties to influence congestion-driven placement.

22.2.1 METRICS FOR STRUCTURAL LOGIC SYNTHESIS

The work in Ref. [26] motivates that a property of the network structure called adhesion can make a significant contribution to routing congestion. The work targets the technology-independent logic optimization stage. Classically, in this stage, literal count is used as a metric for optimization. However, this does not adequately capture the intrinsic entanglement of the netlist. Two circuits with identical literal counts may have significantly different congestion characteristics postplacement. It is shown that by optimizing the adhesion metric in addition to literal count during technology-independent optimization, postrouting congestion can be improved.

The adhesion metric of a logic network is defined as follows:

Definition 1 *The adhesion of a logic network represented by an undirected graph G(V,E) can be measured by the minimum number of edges between all pairs $s, t \in V$ that if removed from the graph would disconnect the graph.*

For measuring connectivity in a technology-independent netlist, the authors propose use of the all-pairs minimum-cut problem to determine the minimum cutsize of all pairs of nodes of a graph. The metric used to describe adhesion of a graph is sum of all-pairs mincut (SAPMC). The following lemma is hence proposed.

Lemma 1 *The adhesion in an undirected graph representing a logic network as given by Definition 1, can be measured by the SAPMC for the graph.*

The authors propose the following conjectures to apply the property of adhesion during logic synthesis optimization. This conjecture is then evaluated empirically.

Conjecture 1   *Networks with lower adhesion value will on the average have better routability postplacement.*

Conjecture 2   *Using adhesion during logic synthesis transformations will result on the average in better routability postplacement.*

As an example of adhesion, the authors give the example in Figure 22.1. Figure 22.1a is an unoptimized network. Two possible optimizations are applied to the original unoptimized network to obtain two implementations, opt 1 in Figure 22.1b and opt 2 in Figure 22.1c. The opt1 circuit has a SAPMC cost of 173, while the opt2 optimized circuit has a SAPMC cost of 152. According to Conjecture 2, opt 2 is a better optimization for the same connection cost of 18 for the two implementations.

The authors perform extensive experiments to validate their conjecture that optimizing the adhesion metric during logic synthesis does indeed reduce congestion postplacement of the mapped netlist. First, they show a strong corelation between SAPMC metric and postplacement congestion by changing the fast extraction, f_x, logic synthesis transform to randomly select an improvement rather than operate in a greedy fashion. Such choices to optimize adhesion as a metric could also be made during other logic synthesis optimizations like cloning, buffer insertion, rewiring, and factorization. The results show a correlation of adhesion as measured by SAPMC to average, and maximum wirelength. Adhesion can be used in conjunction with traditional properties like literal count, number of cells, and cell count as logic synthesis metrics.

22.2.2   CONGESTION-AWARE LOGIC SYNTHESIS

The work by Pandini et al. [31] proposes several techniques to incorporate congestion minimization within logic synthesis. Modern logic synthesis systems are typically divided into two phases: technology-independent optimization and technology mapping. The first phase is concerned with finding a representation of the Boolean equations with the minimum number of literals in the factored form. Technology mapping is the task of transforming a technology-independent logic network into a technology-dependent gate-level netlist. A popular approach to technology mapping implemented in DAGON [12] and MIS [24] is to reduce the problem to directed acyclic graph (DAG) covering problem. The DAG covering problem was approximated by a sequence of tree coverings, which can be solved optimally using dynamic programming. The technology mapping is usually divided into three stages: DAG partitioning, matching, and covering. During DAG partitioning, the network DAG is partitioned into a forest of trees. Subsequently, for each tree, a matching algorithm identifies

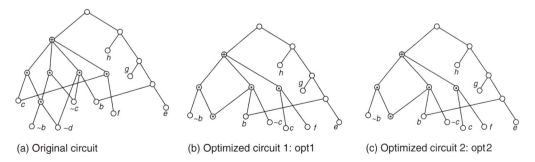

(a) Original circuit   (b) Optimized circuit 1: opt1   (c) Optimized circuit 2: opt2

FIGURE 22.1   Example of adhesion in a logic network. (From Kudva, P. and Dougherty, A., *ICCAD*, 2002.)

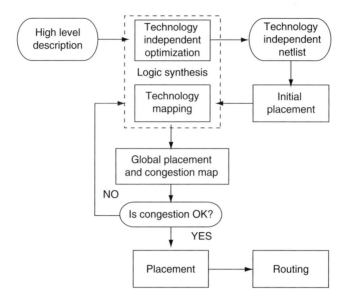

FIGURE 22.2   Application specific integrated circuit (ASIC) design flow to account for congestion in logic synthesis. (From Pandini, D., Pileggi, L. T., and Strojwas, A. J., *DATE*, 2002.)

all possible matches, corresponding to instances of a cell library, for each subnetwork. Finally, an optimal choice according to a cost factor is selected among the matches. The work in Ref. [31] targets the DAG partitioning and covers steps to improve congestion of the final implementation.

The proposed approach in Ref. [31] for congestion-aware technology mapping can be integrated into traditional ASIC design flow, as shown in Figure 22.2. A technology-independent netlist and its initial placement is obtained. If congestion is deemed as a problem for the netlist, technology mapping is carried out in a congestion-aware manner as explained below.

Placement-driven DAG partitioning algorithm proposed in Ref. [31] is shown in Figure 22.3 and is based on depth-first search (DFS) traversal from the circuit primary outputs to the primary inputs. The difference from classical DAG partitioning is that partitioning at multifanout vertices is carried out by taking into account the physical location of the corresponding base gates obtained from placement of the technology-independent netlist. The partitioning is based on the following property: the father of every internal vertex is always the nearest vertex on the chip layout image according to some distance metric. The function distance() uses the placement information to compute the geometric distance between two adjacent vertices. The performance of the partitioning algorithm is not dependent on the order the DAG roots are processed, but it depends only on the physical locations of the technology-independent gates. Also, subject trees that cluster vertices placed in the same neighborhood are obtained by means of this DAG partitioning algorithm.

For the tree-covering stage of the DAG covering problem, the authors propose only a change in the cost function to the original tree-covering algorithm proposed in Ref. [24]. The optimization objective is expanded by including the wirelength contribution into the cost function.

22.2.3 PERIMETER-DEGREE: A PRIORI INTERCONNECTION COMPLEXITY METRIC

Several of the popular congestion mitigation techniques can be classified as a priori congestion techniques (preplacement), online methods (during placement), and posteriori methods (postplacement). Most of existing congestion minimization techniques are posteriori. The work in Ref. [34] present several techniques for a priori congestion minimization using the concept of perimeter-degree. They show that the number of external nets is not a desirable candidate for identifying potential regions of high-interconnect density. Alternatively, they propose perimeter-degree as an effective metric for

```
procedure DAG_Partitioning (graph DAG, array COORD)
    for_each v inDAG do
        v.father = nil;
    od;
    for_each v in DAG.roots() do
        PDP (DAG, v, COORD);
    od;
procedure PDP (graph DAG, vertex v, array COORD)
    v.visited = true;
    for_each e in DAG. outedges(v) do
        w = DAG.target(e);
        if (not w.visited) then
            dist = INFINITY;
            for_each f in DAG. inedges(w) do
                u = DAG.source(f);
                this_dist = distance(COORD[u], COORD[w]);
                if (this_dist < dist) then
                    dist = this_dist;
                    w.father = u;
                fi;
            od;
            PDP (DAG, w, COORD);
        fi;
    od;
```

FIGURE 22.3 Placement-driven DAG partitioning algorithm. PDP stands for placement-driven partitioning. (From Pandini, D., Pileggi, L. T., and Strojwas, A. J., *DATE*, 2002.)

identifying congested regions on a chip. perimeter-degree (P_{peri}) is defined as follows. A region represents a placement bin on the die or a cluster of cells. The degree of a region is the number of nets exposed from the region. The perimeter-degree of the region is the region degree divided by the region perimeter. The bin degree and pin density are two common metrics used for simple congestion control [44]. However, it is misleading to compare just degrees of two regions with dissimilar area. The degree needs to be normalized. Because the degree of a region represents the routing demand at the edges of a region, it is natural to use the perimeter of the region as the normalizing factor. Figure 22.4 shows how two regions with the same degree can have different perimeter degrees. Naturally, region A would have a higher routing supply demand compared to region B.

The authors of Ref. [34] detail simple ways to incorporate the perimeter-degree objective in a multilevel partitioning-based placement tool. The first is to use the perimeter-degree at every cell to compute the cell inflation before placement starts. The rational is to inflate cells with higher perimeter degree before the clustering phase of multilevel placement. This has the effect of diluting the inherently high-density portions of the netlist. There are different thresholds for higher utilization designs compared to lower utilization designs. The second technique is to inflate the clusters formed during the clustering stage with respect to their perimeter-degree. This is done to prevent dense

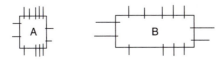

FIGURE 22.4 Equal degree but different perimeter-degree. (From Selvakkumaran, N., Parakh, P., and, Karypis, G., *SLIP*, 2003.)

interconnect regions as a result of clustering. The third approach is to balance the perimeter-degree of the partitions during the partitioning phase of the multilevel placement. One could use a multi-constraint partitioner to solve this problem of balancing area and perimeter-degree simultaneously. Alternatively, one could satisfy both the constraints in a sequential manner by first balancing the perimeter-degree and then balancing the areas of the partitions.

The authors present extensive empirical data to validate their claims about fidelity of perimeter-degree as a simple and effective metric to homogenize interconnection complexity.

22.3 GLOBAL-PLACEMENT CONGESTION IMPROVEMENT

There have been several studies on incorporating the congestion metric during global-placement stage of the physical implementation flow. Local wiring has a big impact on final congestion characteristics of a design. Hence historically, it has been difficult to robustly address congestion during the global-placement stage. There have been major advances in addressing congestion during global placement over the past decade. In this section, we detail some of these approaches.

22.3.1 INCORPORATING CONGESTION ESTIMATION DURING GLOBAL PLACEMENT

The placement algorithms need to have a good and fast estimation of wiring requirements if they intend to target congestion as a metric during the placement process. Other chapters in this book detail several of these wiring density estimation approaches [10,19,27,39]. Works [6,29] have proposed to incorporate congestion estimation techniques within partitioning-driven quadratic placers in interesting ways.

The authors of Ref. [29] base their work on quadratic placement engine that solves an unconstrained minimization problem, the objective function of which is the squared wirelength of the netlist. Because the quadratic solution in general has many overlapping cells, the overlap is resolved by partitioning the solution and iterating over the partitioned solutions [23]. The quadratic wirelength minimum solution serves to guide a mincut partitioning routine. After each round of partitioning, the cells in a region are constrained to the particular region by introducing a center of gravity constraint for each region for subsequent quadratic minimization formulations. Figure 22.5a illustrates the proposed congestion-driven placement methodology. Before each successive placement, internal route estimation and a region-based global route are performed on each region to estimate routing supply-demand ratios. These ratios are used to influence the placer into growing or shrinking the partitioned regions based on resource demand and supply. The region router estimates the routing demand of wires spanning multiple regions. The region router is implemented using a A^* algorithm [5] on the region-based graph. Once routing demand is computed, this information is used to grow or shrink the regions of the current placement. Regions with higher routing demand are allocated more white space by growing them. For q regions in a placement stage, a growth matrix G is defined as an $(n - q \times n - q)$ diagonal matrix with entry g_{ii} equal to the region weight of the independent cell x_i. The growth matrix is computed as follows. After a round of quadratic minimization and partitioning, a set of new regions is generated. Congestion analysis based on the router is performed on this new set of regions. The routing cost is divided into two parts: (1) external cost computed using the region

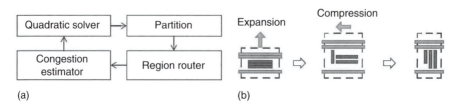

(a)   (b)

FIGURE 22.5   (a) Congestion-driven placement methodology and (b) example of region growth relieving congestion. (From Parakh, P. N., Brown, R. B., and Sakallah, K. A., *DAC*, 1998.)

router for nets spanning multiple regions and (2) internal cost computed using a line-probe router for intraregion routes. The difference between routing supply and demand of a region determine the extra routing tracks required and hence, the growth required by the region. The reader is referred to the original publication [29] for details on how the growth matrix is embedded in the quadratic formulation of the center-of-gravity constraints. The effect of the growth matrix terms in the quadratic formulation is to effectively grow and shrink the regions based on the growth matrix. Reduction in congestion occurs due to the ability to transform horizontal routes into vertical and vice versa. This is shown in Figure 22.5b, where for a vertically congested region vertical expansion is produced.

The work in Ref. [6] also targets a flow to avoid routing congestion during the global placement. The main contribution is to use a fast but reliable way to detect routing criticalities and then use the information effectively in a partitioning-driven placer. The techniques are tested on real-world large industrial design with very good results. The framework for their studies is based on a four-way partitioning (quadrisection)-based quadratic placer, BonnPlace [37]. The placement begins by solving a quadratic wirelength minimum solution as describe in the previous paragraph. This overlapping placement is then used by a quadrisection routine to generate four partitions of the netlist. The objective of the quadrisection is to divide the area of the die into approximately equal regions and assign cells to each region such that density requirements for each region are not violated and the displacement of the cells from their initial quadratic wirelength minimum locations is minimized. Center-of-gravity constraints are then imposed on the cells assigned to their particular regions for subsequent quadratic wirelength minimization. This process is iterated till the number of cells in a region is small enough for detail placement techniques to place. Like the work in Ref. [29], the authors of Ref. [6] also try to relieve congestion during global-placement iterations by allocating more white space to perceived congested areas. However, the mechanism is very different. First, we describe the measurement of congestion of a placement as it appears during the placement algorithm as proposed in Ref. [6]. Given a chip that is partitioned into $k \times k$ regions (forming a $(k+1) \times (k+1)$ placement grid), pin density for each region (for local congestion cost) and a congestion estimation for each edge in the dual graph of the placement grid (for the intraregion congestion cost) is computed. For a fast estimation of a global route, probabilistic global router is used to route the intraregion nets. During a placement level (iteration), the current status of the placement grid is used as the global routing partition. Figure 22.6b shows the routing grid as a dual of the placement grid. Multiterminal nets are split into sets of two-terminal nets using Steiner tree decomposition of the net. For each two point connection in the Steiner tree of a net, probabilistic routing similar to the algorithms proposed in Refs. [27,39] is used. These probabilities are then added over all nets for each routing grid box to give the expected usage $p(e)$. Figure 22.6c shows how probabilities are calculated for two

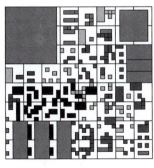

(a) Placement grid

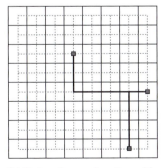

(b) Steiner tree and routing grid

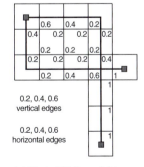

0.2, 0.4, 0.6
vertical edges

0.2, 0.4, 0.6
horizontal edges

(c) Probabilistic weights

FIGURE 22.6 Calculation of routing congestion using probabilistic routing analysis. Given a placement of a chip partitioned into $k \times k$ grid shown in (a), the nets are decomposed into two pin connections using Steiner tree decomposition as shown in (b). Each two pin connection is then routed probabilistically as shown in (c). (From Brenner, U. and Rohe, A., *ISPD*, 2002.)

connections and then added for each grid box. The fraction $\text{cong}(e) = \frac{p(e)}{\text{cap}(e)}$ ($\text{cap}(e)$ is the routing capacity) is defined as the estimated congestion for an edge $e \in E(G)$ in the dual of the placement grid as shown in Figure 22.6b. To account for routability problems inside a routing grid, the pin density pin – $\text{dens}(R)$ inside a region R is used as a second metric. To use the computed congestion data, the authors rely on the popular technique of inflating groups of cells that are deemed to be in a congested region. The size of a congested cell is increased from the normal geometric area of $s(c) = x(c) \cdot y(c)$ to an increased value of $s'(c) = [1 + b(c)] \cdot s(c)$, with $b(c) \geq 0$. During the partitioning stage, the new sizes of cells are used to satisfy the density requirements such that for set $C(R)$ being partitioned in subsets $C(R_1), \ldots, C(R_4)$, the condition $\Sigma_{c \in C(R_i)} s'(c) \leq s(R_i)$ is satisfied for $i = 1, \ldots, 4$. The numbers $b(c)$ depend upon an input parameter $\tau \geq 0$, which is an upper bound on the total increment of $b(c)$ for each placement level. The initial value $b(c)$ for each cell is proportional to pin density of the cell. During placement, if a cell is deemed to be in a congested region R, then $b(c)$ is increased by $\min\{1, 2[\text{cong}(e_i) - 1]\}$. Once the cells in congested regions are inflated, they are spread around using a repartitioning method in the placer, which respects the new inflated sizes of the cells and moves cells out of regions that are too full. Repartitioning is called after normal partitioning stage. It considers 2×2 windows of adjacent regions $R_1, \ldots, R_4$ and forms a larger region $R = R_1 \cup, \ldots, \cup, R_4$. The larger region is then repartitioned to obey new density limits and improve wirelength. This is done for all 2×2 windows repeatedly over all the regions till it yields reasonable improvement in wirelength. Because the windows are overlapping, it allows the inflated cells to move away from congested regions, in effect reducing the demand for routing in these regions.

The work in Ref. [30] also proposes a white-space allocation (WSA) technique based on congestion estimates during mincut global placement. The techniques are based on the (WSA) technique proposed in Ref. [28] and discussed in Section 22.4.2. The difference is that Ref. [28] proposes to apply the technique after placement as a detail placement optimization, while Ref. [30] uses it during partitioning-based global placement. The framework used for the studies in Ref. [30] is a top-down mincut bipartitioning-based placer. Unlike Ref. [6], which uses a quadrisection-based fixed grid placer, Ref. [30] use a bisection-based variable grid placer in which the cutline is allowed to shift after each round of partitioning. The objective for postpartitioning cutline shifting can be based on equalizing densities or congestion estimates. In Ref. [30], before each round of partitioning, the entire placement region is overlayed on a grid. Congestion maps [39] are built using last updated locations of all pins. When cells are partitioned and their positions are changed, the congestion value for their nets are updated. The routing demands and supplies for either side of the cutline are estimated using the congestion map. Using these estimates, cutline is shifted after partitioning to equalize the ratio of demand to supply on either side of the cutline. This effectively allocates more white space to potentially congested areas without having to artificially change the sizes of individual cells.

22.3.2 STEINER WIRELENGTH OPTIMIZATION DURING GLOBAL PLACEMENT

Taking an orthogonal approach to traditional works on congestion-driven placement, the work in Ref. [30] shows that congestion characteristics of a placement can be improved by modifying the objective of the placer to optimize Steiner tree wirelength (StWL) and not the traditional half-perimeter wirelength (HPWL). The contention is that StWL correlates much better with routed wirelength in comparison to HPWL. The placement framework for the study is based on the top-down mincut partitioning algorithm implemented in the well-known Capo placer [1] and is called rooster. Mincut placers generally use either bisection or quadrisection to divide the placement area and the netlist. The objective of the partitioning is to minimize the number of connections between the partitions and also to obey area constraints in the partitions. This is done iteratively till the number of cells in a region is small. When bipartitioning is used, the careful choice of vertical or horizontal cut direction influence wirelength, wirelength ratio between horizontal and vertical components, and also routing congestion in resulting placement solution [36]. Proper handling of terminals [13] is essential to the success of top-down placement approaches. When partitioning a placement bin (region) cells inside the bin may connect to cells and fixed points outside the particular bin. These connections need to be properly accounted for by formulating the problem as partitioning cells in a bin with fixed terminals. The terminals are propagated to boundaries of the bin being partitioned and are considered fixed in one or more partitions. Traditional mincut objective during placement does not accurately represent the wirelength objective [35]. The authors of Ref. [35] introduce a new terminal propagation technique that allows the partitioner to better map netcut to HPWL. Each original net can be represented by one or two weighted nets for the partitioning problem, depending upon the configuration of the net's terminals relative to bin's center. The weighted netcut formulation better represents the HPWL objective. This formulation is later simplified in Ref. [9]. The work in Ref. [30] extends this formulation to facilitate minimization of wirelength estimates other than HPWL, in particular, StWL minimization. The authors of Ref. [30] show that StWL is a valid cost function for the weighted partitioning problems. However, several assumptions for minimizing traditional HPWL objective do not hold anymore. Moving terminal locations changes Steiner tree construction making StWL estimates inaccurate. Additionally, nets that were considered inessential in HPWL minimization cannot be considered so during StWL minimization because there are many Steiner trees of different lengths having same bounding box unlike the HPWL objective. To limit the addition runtime during placement, an efficient data structure called pointset with multiplicities is proposed to aid fast building and maintaining of Steiner trees for partitioning. At the beginning of the mincut placement, all movable cells are placed at the center of the first placement bin that represents the full core placeable area. When constructing the partitioning instance for a bin, a Steiner tree evaluator is called for each essential net of the bin. The weighted partitioning problem is formed based on the Steiner tree segments. The weighted mincut partitioner runs and produces a solution. A cutline is selected based on the partitioning result, new bins are created and cells are placed at the center of their respective bins. Three different Steiner tree evaluators, batched iterated 1-Steiner (BI1ST) [20], FastSteiner [21] and fast lookup table based wirelength estimation technique (FLUTE) [11] are tested in the flow. In addition, Ref. [30] also suggests using the StWL objective in detail placement techniques. Two types of sliding window optimizers targeting StWL are proposed. The first one exhaustively checks all possible linear orderings of a group of cells in row and the second one uses dynamic programming algorithm for an interleaving optimization like the one proposed in Ref. [17].

22.3.3   Free Space Management during Global Placement

Traditional works on congestion-driven placement in the context of high-utilization designs have focused on redistributing the available limited white space toward the congested areas. However, for modern system on chip (SoC) design styles with several big intellectual property (IP) blocks, large macrocells, the available free space has increased for dust logic. For such low-utilization designs, in addition to solving the problem of local high-congestion spots, it is also important to ensure that the design is not overspread over the die and also that it has a good natural distribution of cells in the layout. Addressing these concerns improves the overall quality of the physical design in terms of performance of the circuit, wirelength, power consumed, congestion owing to global nets, etc. However, even for low-utilization designs, care must be taken to ensure that every local region of the die has enough routing resources to accomodate routing demand created by cells in that region. Hence, the free space management techniques during global placement need to be cognizant of maintaining enough white space in the local regions while ensuring that the design is not overspread for other placement objectives.

Hierarchical WSA during top-down partitioning-based placement flows is discussed in Ref. [7] and implemented in the placer Capo. The available white space is uniformly spread throughout the core region. This ensures that every local region of the die has enough available white space and helps routing. At every level of partitioning during the top-down flow, the tolerances during the partitioning of an individual bin are determined by the white space deterioration factor α. α is determined by the available white space in the bin and the number of partitioning levels away to leaf level in the partitioning tree (approximated by $\log_2 N$, where N is the number of cells in the bin). Hierachical WSA allows higher tolerances during partitioning and shifting cutlines after each partitioning to equalize the relative white space in the child bins and to ensure a uniform white space distribution. This simple strategy is very good for high-utilization designs but produces circuits with high wirelength and worse performance for sparse designs.

The work in Ref. [4] argues that top-down placement based on recursive bisection with multilevel partitioning does poorly on low-utilization designs and tends to produce excessive wirelength when large amounts of white space are present. On the other hand, analytical placement algorithms have a global view of the placement problem and can better manage large amounts of white space. To address this, analytical constraint generation (ACG) [4] proposes to combine a mincut-based placer with a quadratic placement engine. In ACG, during top-down recursive bisection-based mincut placement flow, the partitioning capacities for each placement bin to be partitioned are generated based on quadratic wirelength minimum placement at that level. At each level during the top-down flow, the quadratic wirelength minimization engine produces a placement subject to the respective placement bin constraints for each cell. For each placement bin to be partitioned, the capacities of each child bin are determined by the center of mass of the quadratic wirelength minimum solution. The tolerances for the partitioning problem are kept fairly rigid. Care is taken to ensure that none of the child partitioning bins overflow their target utilizations. ACG gets the hint from a quadratic wirelength minimum solution on the natural placement of the design and uses powerful multilevel mincut partitioning techniques to produce lower wirelength solutions that are not overspread.

The techniques proposed in Refs. [2,3], to handle the issue of sparse designs take a different approach. Their techniques are not dependent on the type of the placer. A black-box placer that uniformly distributes the available white space across the core area is assumed. By preprocessing the netlist, it can be ensured that (1) there is minimum local white space through the core area and (2) better allocation of the remaining white space. The constraint of minimum local white space is required to ensure that local regions in the die do not become highly congested. The technique consists of adding small disconnected free cells to the design in an amount not exceeding the white space that remains after the local white space requirement is satisfied. Because the free cells are disconnected and small, the black-box placer is free to place the cells so as to improve the relevant design objectives. After the placement process is complete, the free cells are removed from the design and the underlying cell sites are empty. This causes high cell density (which respects the minimum local white space requirement) in certain areas, with empty sites occupying the vacant areas of the chip. In addition, the work in Ref. [3] describes a low-overhead implementation of filler cells in a mincut placer, because explicit modeling of free cells in the placement problem impacts the runtime and memory footprint of the placer. In contrast to the ACG work where partitioning capacities for each partitioning problem are determined by quadratic wirelength minimum solution and the partitioning tolerances are kept fairly strict, in Ref. [3], the partitioning tolerances for a low-utilization placement bins are increased sufficiently so that the partitioner can find the optimum mincut solution subject to the capacity and tolerance constraints. The increase in tolerances is done keeping in mind the minimum local white space requirements. Figure 22.7 shows the placement of the same design by different mincut placement approaches as discussed above.

22.4 DETAILED PLACEMENT CONGESTION IMPROVEMENT

Congestion-driven detailed placement approaches have been studied extensively in literature. In general, these approaches tend to be more effective compared to congestion-driven global placement, because a relatively more accurate congestion information can be achieved at the detailed placement level. The global-placement step determines rough locations of the majority of the cells, as well as the local area density and pin density. After global placement completes, a pass of congestion estimation can be applied. The congestion distribution of the entire design, or congestion map, is usually the guide of the postglobal-placement congestion-reduction algorithms.

The goal of congestion-reduction algorithms is to reduce the congestion in the peak congestion spots, at the cost of increasing the routing demand in noncongested area, thus averaging out the

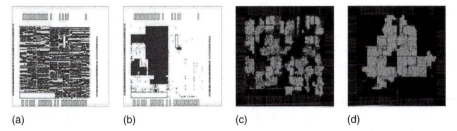

(a) (b) (c) (d)

FIGURE 22.7 Ckt4 design from IBM has 74 percent white space. (a) Placement produced by Capo with uniform white space distribution. (b) Another placement produced by Capo free filler cells (not shown in the picture) was added to reduce the placer white space from 74 to 15 percent. This reduces the wirelength from 15.32e6 to 8.77e6. (c) Placement obtained from a mincut placer from IBM with 70 percent target density. (d) Placement obtained by the ACG technique with 70 percent target density. (From Adya, S. N. and Markov, I. L., *International Conference on Computer Aided Design (ICCAD)*, San Jose, CA, 2003; Alpert, C. J., Nam, G. -J., and Villarrubia, P. G., *Proceedings of the 2002 IEEE/ACM International Conference on Computer-Aided Design*, San Jose, CA, 2002.)

routing demand over the die. For the detailed placement stage, there are typically following three ways to reduce the routing demands in congested area.

First, traditional HPWL improvement, either globally or locally, can reduce the routing demand in the congested area by having smaller wires in the design. In this sense, the conventional wirelength minimization is of value for congestion control. This is particularly true for high-utilization designs, where little room can be used for manipulating the available white space of congestion control. Wang et al. [38] illustrate the relationship between total wirelength and congestion, based on the edge overflow congestion model. They observe a strong correlation between wirelength and congestion in experiments. Recent work on mincut placement [22] or analytical placement [28] also suggests that reducing total HPWL helps producing routable placements.

Second, in congested regions, replacing cells with accurate routing topology information can yield significant congestion reduction. This type of approaches include cell swapping integrated with Steiner tree routing update in the simulated annealing algorithm [38], cell replacement with an exact congestion objective obtained by global routing or routing estimator [28,30], optimal interleaving with trunk tree decomposition [17], and sliding window optimization with StWL objective [30]. The incremental routing approach in Ref. [38] can be runtime prohibitive because both incremental routing and annealing are computationally expensive. A good control of the working area is paramount for the approach. Usually, the working area grows from a highly congested spot and is subject to some maximum area constraints. If the congestion is mainly caused by entangled routing topologies, the cell replacement approach in Ref. [28] can be very effective for moderate congest reduction. The exploration space, however, is rather limited because fewer cells are touched comparing to other methods. Both approaches failed to address the congestion from global interconnects, nets that pass through the congested area. Accounting for global interconnects in routing congestion reduction is fundamentally a very hard problem for detailed placement. The approach in Ref. [30] uses a fast Steiner tree estimator in mincut placement. It is a promising technique as it improves the StWL at almost no cost on runtime.

Third, low-design utilization, or the abundance of whitespace, for many modern ASIC designs allows cell spreading, the most effective way to reduce the routing congestion. By spreading the cells in the core placeable area, the routing resources can be significantly increased. In other words, the average routing demand in the congested area can be reduced to meet the routing resource constraints. Theoretically, if the utilization continues to decrease, the routability goal will be achieved for any given design. In reality, however, spreading the placement inevitably deteriorates the circuit performance and increases the power consumption, because of increased average interconnect length.

We will go through the details of several techniques in the following sections:

22.4.1 ROUTER INTEGRATION

An early approach on cell replacing with routing information was proposed in Ref. [38]. In this work, the detailed placement step is based on low-temperature simulated annealing. Traditionally, the cost function in simulated annealing is total HPWL, or some form of weighted total HPWL. Here the congestion cost is incorporated into the objective function. To obtain congestion cost, a fast Steiner tree router is called for every single move in simulated annealing algorithm. The routing supply/demand information for all the region edges need to be incrementally updated. This approach is computationally expensive because incremental routing and congestion update are much more time consuming than simple bounding-box computation. The advantage is on the fidelity side—congestion improvement achieved in placement can be mostly carried on to the routing. Several techniques can be used to speed up this approach and make it practically feasible, such as routing estimation or lazy update on nets with large fanouts. Using appropriate sizes of the congested regions in optimization is another key step for this approach. The idea is to avoid applying the expensive computation on noncongested areas. The modeling of congestion cost greatly affects the final placement quality. One basic question is should we penalize the moves only when the routing demand is higher than the supply, or we start giving some cost once the demand is close to the supply, i.e., look-ahead approach. The authors tried many different congestion modeling functions and suggest that look-ahead congestion cost combined with total wirelength is most effective.

A typical problem in congestion minimization is that reducing the peak congestion of one region is often at the cost of increasing the congestion of its surrounding area. Classic congestion removal approaches work in expanded area, which is the peak congestion region plus the surrounding less congested area. Furthermore, these approaches work on one expanded area at a time. This results in conflicting congested areas. The authors in Refs. [42,43] suggest conflict resolving techniques before starting congestion optimization. The basic idea is to exploit the flexibility when growing the peak congestion spot to an expanded area, and obtain the best combined expanded areas for multiple peak congestion spots. The problem can be formulated as a linear program or an integer linear program. A simpler heuristic is to start from greedy expansion and gradually adjust the expanded area to avoid conflicts.

Jariwala and Lillis [17] proposed a detailed placement method to integrate trunk decomposition-based routing into optimal interleaving algorithm. Optimal interleaving is a detailed placement wire-length minimization technique proposed in Ref. [17]. It is a powerful intrarow optimization technique. The basic idea is to collect a group of cells in a single-row window, partition them into two groups, and optimally interleave two groups with the same cell order of each group. A dynamic programming algorithm ensures the optimal wirelength can be found in $O(n^2)$ time complexity. In Ref. [17], the routing information is considered in the interleaving process. The routes associated with cells are also interleaved and the number of nets crossing a channel is taken into account. The algorithm is successful on field programmable gate array (FPGA) benchmarks. It reduces the number of congested routing channels (defined as the channels with maximum routing density) by 45 percent on average.

22.4.2 WHITESPACE MANAGEMENT

Because modern cell-based designs usually have utilizations lower than their precedences, recent research work has been focused on congestion improvement in the context of whitespace. Early research on whitespace handling techniques include Ref. [7], in which the whitespace control is used primarily for improving the quality of mincut partitioning, and Ref. [29], which implicitly uses whitespace for area expansion.

Yang et al. [40,41] proposed a WSA approach for the purpose of reducing congestion. The experiment flow in this chapter is complete, including global/detailed routing with a widely used commercial router, on a set of benchmarks based on a 0.18 μm library. After global-placement stage, the chip area is divided into rectangular areas (bins) and the congestion estimation is conducted to obtain a congestion degree for each bin. At this point, all the bins have the same amount of whitespace.

Next, a two-step whitespace reallocation is performed to adjust the amount of whitespace, or cell utilization in each bin. This is accomplished by first computing the desired whitespace distribution based on the current congestion map, and then moving cells between adjacent bins to meet the whitespace requirement. Moving cells for meeting the target whitespace distribution inevitably degrades the quality of the placement. A wirelength improvement stage is introduced to recover the loss. During this low-temperature annealing stage, the latest WSA map is maintained. Cell moving/swapping are allowed only if they do not violate the whitespace requirements by a certain amount. The key factor that determines the performance of this approach is the conversion from congestion map to target whitespace map. Because of the lack of detailed congestion information and uncertainty in cell movement, it is extremely hard to accurately estimate how much whitespace needs to be injected into a bin to make a congested bin routable. What this approach is able to do is to relieve the congestion hot spot to some extent. In reality, because congestion often conflicts with other placement objectives (timing, wirelength, etc.), neither underdoing nor overdoing of congestion removal is desired. Multiple runs with different scaling factor will help to achieve the best trade-off. Another uncertainty of this approach lies in the convergence issue. The target whitespace map is derived from the initial congestion map. However, after cell movement the congestion map will be changed and the target WSA is out of sync, i.e., a previous noncongested spot may pop up with less whitespace allocated. Performing iterations of this approach multiple times may help, but it could cause oscillation problem or considerable loss of quality of the input placement.

An enhancement of the above approach was proposed in Ref. [16]. In this work, the congestion estimation and WSA are similar to that of Ref. [40,41]. A flow-based algorithm called placement migration is devised to guide the cell movement for achieving the whitespace map. This algorithm can minimize the amount of movement (total moving distance of all the moved cells), given an original whitespace map (uniform distribution) and a target whitespace map. Less cell movement means smaller perturbation from the input placement and usually lower wirelength loss.

Another interesting approach named whitespace allocation is proposed by Li et al. [28]. The algorithm starts with a global placement and the derived congestion map. The placement is then modified using a recursive bipartitioning, or slicing tree method. In a preprocessing step, a congestion degree number is computed for every cell in the design, based on current placement congestion map. In the first step, the placement is recursively partitioned until every region contains a small number of cells. For each partitioning step, the cut direction is determined by the aspect ratio of the region to be partitioned. Each cutline geometrically bisects a region evenly and tries to maintain a square shape of the regions. A slicing tree is constructed completely at the end of recursive bipartitioning. Each node of the slicing tree corresponds to a region that is bipartitioned. The left child and right child of the node corresponds to the two subregions after partitioning. A list of cells is saved in each node, representing all the cells placed inside the region. Next, the slicing tree is evaluated in a bottom-up fashion. A congestion level is given to each node of the tree. The congestion level of a node is simply the summation of the congestion level of its two children. For a leaf node, the congestion level is the summation of the congestion degree of all the cells in the end region. A cutline adjustment step is then performed. The cutlines in the nodes are shifted by traversing the tree in a top-down fashion. For each node, the amounts of whitespace allocated to the two child nodes are linearly proportional to their congestion levels. Consider a region r with lower-left corner (x_0, y_0), upper-right corner (x_1, y_1), and the original vertical cut direction at $x_{cut} = (x_0 + x_1)/2$. The area of this region is $A_r = (x_1 - x_0)(y_1 - y_0)$. Assume that the total area of cells for left subregion r_0 and right subregion r_1 are S_0 and S_1, and corresponding congestion levels are OVL_0 and OVL_1, respectively. The total amount of whitespace, $(A_r - S_0 - S_1)$, is to be allocated into two subregions such that the amounts of whitespace in the two subregions are linearly proportional to their congestion levels (Figure 22.8). Thus, the amount of whitespace allocated to subregion r_0 is

$$r_0 = (A_r - S_0 - S_1) \frac{OVL_0}{OVL_0 + OVL_1}$$

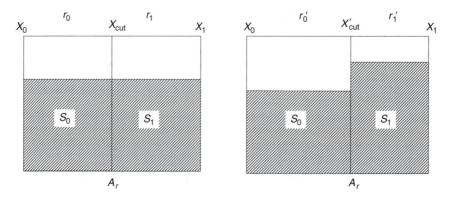

FIGURE 22.8 Subregion r_0 is more congested than subregion r_1. Cutline is shifted from x_{cut} to x'_{cut}, resulting more whitespace in subregion r'_0.

Then the new cutline location x'_{cut} can be derived as follows:

$$\gamma = \frac{S_0 + (A_r - S_0 - S_1)\frac{OVL_0}{OVL_0 + OVL_1}}{A_r}$$

$$x'_{cut} = \gamma x_1 + (1 - \gamma) x_0$$

where γ is the ratio of the left subregion area to A_r after the cutline adjustment.

This step is similar to a top-down partitioning-based global placement except that the cut direction, the cut location, and subnetlists are all known. The cells stay at the center of the region to which they belong during the top-down flow. The placement is then legalized with minimum perturbation and a cell-swapping-based detailed placement is performed. Li et al. showed that this step alone can considerably reduce the postrouting congestion (measured by percentage of overflowed bins) by 72 percent on average. Furthermore, the similar approach was adopted in Ref. [30] for improving congestion by improving the routed total wirelength. The difference is that in Ref. [30] the congestion-estimate-based cutline adjustment is performed during the global-placement stage, which is a top-down partitioning framework.

The limitation of these whitespace adjustment approaches is they can do little on the part of congestion that is originated from global interconnects. If we consider a congested region on the globally routed layout, the congestion of the area can be classified into three types: local nets, the interconnects within the region; semiglobal nets, the interconnects coming in/out the region; and the global nets, the interconnects passing through the region. WSA can relieve the congestion for local or semiglobal nets. However, it cannot reduce the routing demands coming from global nets. Therefore, the effectiveness of the WSA approaches is greatly dependent on the composition of these different types of congestion sources. Generally, the proportions of the congestion sources are determined by two factors: the netlist structure and the global-placement quality. It is thus desirable to make the netlist structure more congestion friendly (reducing global nets at no cost of increasing local nets) or improve the global-placement quality (reducing the total wirelength).

In summary, congestion reduction in detailed placement can be very effective because the congestion spots have been detected with high fidelity after global placement. If enough whitespace is given, most congestion can be relieved by intelligently spreading the cells to achieve a routable design. However, other objectives in placement, such as timing and power, are likely to be degraded during the spreading. Also, more whitespace means less density and more silicon area. In that sense, congestion reduction should not be addressed only in detailed placement. It is an objective throughout the entire placement flow and should be considered as early as possible, even in floorplanning stage.

22.5 SIMULATED ANNEALING FOR CONGESTION IMPROVEMENT

Simulated annealing as an effective placement algorithm has been studied for over two decades [25,32,33]. As circuit sizes increase, simulated annealing is no longer a good choice as an global-placement algorithm because of its weak scalability. However, during detailed placement stage, annealing is still an attractive approach in many cases. For instance, simulated annealing can be applied on a particular region to further optimize the local placement. One flexibility of annealing approach is that it can incorporate virtually any cost into its objective function, as long as the cost can be modeled and incrementally updated. It is then natural to extend simulated annealing from optimizing classic HPWL to optimizing congestion.

A number of publications have presented methods to apply simulated annealing for congestion alleviation. They vary in congestion modeling and objective cost function. In this section, we review several cost functions to represent congestion. Once the right cost function is selected, both low temperature or greedy algorithm can be used as the optimization framework.

22.5.1 RISA

Cheng proposed a routability model named RISA [10] and for the first time integrated the routability model in simulated annealing algorithm. The basic idea of RISA can be explained using Figure 22.9.

The entire chip is divided into $M \times N$ rectangular regions. R represents one such region. There are two nets whose bounding boxes overlap with region R. Let W_R (H_R) be the width (height) of region R, W_1 (H_1) be the width (height) of net N_1s bounding box, w_1 (h_1) be the width (height) of overlapping box between R and net N_1s bounding box. For region R, the horizontal and vertical congestion contributed by net N_1 are

$$C_h = q \frac{w_1 h_1}{H_1 W_R}$$

$$C_v = q \frac{w_1 h_1}{W_1 H_R}$$

where q is the netweight that is a function of net pin count. q is obtained by randomly building optimal Steiner tree within net's bounding box and statistically deriving the probability of net crossings. Table 22.1 shows the precomputed value for q.

Congestion cost computed by RISA model is integrated into simulated annealing algorithm. Experiments show that with RISA model, routing congestion as measured by number of overcongested grids is considerably reduced. The runtime cost is about $2X$ comparing to the original simulated annealing algorithm.

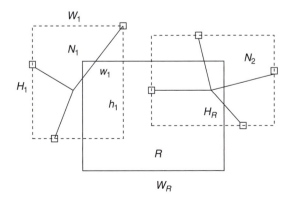

FIGURE 22.9 RISA routability model.

TABLE 22.1
Netweighting for RISA Routability Model

Pin Count	Netweight q	Pin Count	Netweight q
1–3	1.0000	15	1.6899
4	1.0828	20	1.8924
5	1.1536	25	2.0743
6	1.2206	30	2.2334
7	1.2823	35	2.3895
8	1.3385	40	2.5356
9	1.3991	45	2.6625
10	1.4493	50	2.7933

22.5.2 OVERFLOW WITH LOOK-AHEAD

Wang et al. tried a number of cost functions that cover both congestion and wirelength objectives [38].
Let WL be the total wirelength and OF be the total overflow of the current placement. The total
overflow is the sum of overflow for all the placement bins. The overflow is the difference between
routing demand and routing supply of the bin, if demand is larger. The following seven cost functions
are proposed (Figure 22.10):

1. WL: total HPWL (Figure 22.10a)
2. OF: total overflow (Figure 22.10b)
3. Hybrid: $(1 - \alpha)$WL $+ \alpha$OF, $0 \le \alpha \le 1$ (Figure 22.10c)
4. TimeHybrid: $(1 - \alpha_\mathrm{T})$WL $+ \alpha_\mathrm{T}$OF, α is changing during the placement process
   (Figure 22.10d)
5. QL: quadratic function when demand is smaller than supply; linear function when demand
   is greater than supply (Figure 22.10e)

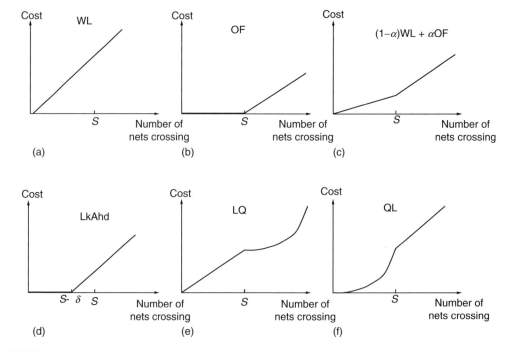

FIGURE 22.10   Cost function versus number of crossing nets on each global bin.

6. LQ: linear function when demand is smaller than supply; quadratic function when demand is greater than supply (Figure 22.10f)
7. Look-Ahead: start considering congestion cost when demand is close enough to supply

All these cost functions are experimented in both global placement and detailed placement stages. The authors found that during global placement, none of the objectives works well except total wirelength. However, in detailed placement stage, several cost functions are reasonably good and LookAhead gives the best result in terms of congestion.

22.5.3 A-TREE ROUTER

Chang et al. integrate a fast A-tree router into a multilevel simulated-annealing global-placement engine called mPG [8]. mPG is inspired by the recent success of the multilevel methods in efficiently handling bipartitioning problem [18]. It consists of three stages: coarsening by clustering, initial placement on the top level, and uncoarsening with refinement. The A-tree router is based on a fast, congestion avoidance two-bend router (LZ-router). The rational behind that is the dominance of LZ-shaped routes in the actual layout. Multipin nets are decomposed to two-pin nets. An incremental A-tree algorithm is developed to efficiently update the routing topology for any pin location change. This A-tree router can be used in conjunction with HPWL at any level of refinement. In practice, the authors find that it is most effective to consider routing cost at the finest level. This is consistent with the conclusion in Ref. [38] that minimizing congestion cost early in the placement flow may have negative effect.

The cost function for congestion-driven mPG is the quadratic sum of the wire usages of all the bins. The wire usage for each bin is the sum of the routed wirelength of the nets that pass through, start from, or end at this bin. Unlike the overflow method, there is no threshold for routing supply in the cost function. This cost function encourages the simulated annealing moves that can lead shorter routed length and less congestion. If the wire usage of a bin increases from W to $W+d$, the congestion cost change is $d^2 + 2Wd$. For a long wire-segment crossing multiple bins, the delta congestion cost can be quickly computed using the sum of the current wire usages of the involved bins.

22.5.4 SPARSE PARAMETER

Hu and Marek-Sadowska [16] proposed a congestion cost function named sparse parameter. With this cost function, the congestion-driven placement does not follow the traditional estimate-and-eliminate strategy. Instead, it tries to reduce the excessive usage of routing resources caused by local nets so that more routing resources are available for the uncertain global nets.

The idea of sparse-parameter cost function originates from two facts. First, the local nets that coming in/out a region vastly determine the congestion situation of the region. This is verified with empirical data. Second, minimizing the number of local nets alone could be wrong, because the cost is often the longer wirelength and the congestion caused by global nets. The authors derive the following function as the wire cost $WS(b)$ for a placement bin b:

$$WS(b) = \sum_{i \in LC(b)} \frac{w_i BB(i)}{d(i)}$$

where
   $LC(b)$ is all the nets that enter or leave the region b
   w_i is the weights to translate half-perimeter length to estimated routed length for net i
   $BB(i)$ is the HPWL for net i
   $d(i)$ is the degree of net i

Once $WS(b)$ is computed for all the bins, a mapping function is used to convert $WS(b)$ to the sparse parameter $P(b)$:

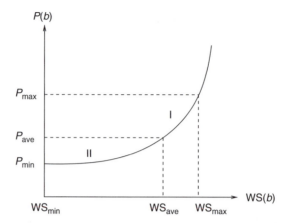

FIGURE 22.11   Sparse function $WS(b)$ to $P(b)$.

$$P(b) = a^{WS(b)} + b$$

where a and b are constants obtained from three points: (WS_{min}, P_{min}), (WS_{ave}, P_{ave}), and (WS_{max}, P_{max}). WS_{min}, WS_{ave}, and WS_{max} are minimum, average, and maximum $WS(b)$ over all the bins, respectively. P_{min}, P_{ave}, and P_{min} are user defined values. The curve of this conversion indicates a sharper slope from WS_{ave} to WS_{max}, meaning higher cost when the congestion of a region is above the average (Figure 22.11).

The above function works well when integrated in simulated annealing algorithm. Particularly, the wirelength increase is negligible compared to pure half-perimeter optimization. The runtime with the sparse parameter is about 2.5 or 3 times slower.

Because of lack of access to real industry router, there is no detailed routing step in the experimental flow. Consequently, the internal routes within the bin are not modeled in the cost function, because they do not contribute to the global routing results (the global router used in Ref. [19] works on bin level and ignore the internal nets). The authors suggest to use some sort of pin-density metric to adjust the sparse parameter.

22.6   CONCLUSION

In this chapter, we reviewed various techniques for reducing congestion and achieving routable designs. Placement-independent techniques use information from netlist connectivity to guide logic synthesis or placement. Addressing congestion in the early design has deep impact on the final design routability. In global-placement stage, congestion modeling is paramount for achieving the appropriate distribution. Pin density and fast routing estimation can be used to guide the placement engine. Detailed placement stage has more accurate routing information. Cell spreading, cell moving, or swapping should consider routing congestion and are very effective for alleviating local congestion.

In summary, placement is the most important stage to achieve routable design. Many studies have shown that congestion problem can be and should be solved in placement stage by applying the right techniques at the right place.

REFERENCES

 1. S. N. Adya, S. Chaturvedi, J. A. Roy, D. Papa, and I. L. Markov, Unification of partitioning, floorplanning and placement, *International Conference of Computer Aided Design (ICCAD)*, San Jose, CA, 2004, pp. 550–557.
 2. S. N. Adya and I. L. Markov, On whitespace and stability in mixed-size placement and physical synthesis, *International Conference on Computer Aided Design (ICCAD)*, San Jose, CA, 2003, pp. 311–318.

3. S. N. Adya, I. L. Markov, and P. G. Villarrubia, On whitespace and stability in physical synthesis, *Integration: The VLSI Journal*, 39(4): 340–362, 2006.

4. C. J. Alpert, G. -J. Nam, and P. G. Villarrubia, Free space management for cut-based placement, *Proceedings of the 2002 IEEE/ACM International Conference on Computer-Aided Design*, San Jose, CA, 2002, pp. 746–751.

5. K.D. Boese, A.B. Kahng, and G. Robins, High-performance routing trees with identified critical sinks, *DAC, Proceedings of the 30th International Conference on Design Automation Conference* (DAC), Dallas, TX, pp. 182–187, 1993.

6. U. Brenner and A. Rohe, An effective congestion driven placement framework, *Proceedings of the 2002 International Symposium on Physical Design* (ISPD), San Diego, CA, pp. 6–11, 2002.

7. A. E. Caldwell, A. B. Kahng, and I. L. Markov, Can recursive bisection alone produce routable placements? *Proceedings of the 37th Conference on Design Automation Conference* (DAC) Los Angeles, CA, pp. 477–482, 2000.

8. C. -C. Chang, J. Cong, Z. Pan, and X. Yuan, Multi-level global placement with congestion control, *IEEE Transactions on Computer-Aided Design of Integrated Circuits and Systems* (TCAD), 22(4):395–409, 2003.

9. T. -C. Chen, Y. -W. Chang, and S. -C. Lin, IMF: Interconnect-driven multilevel floorplanning for large-scale building-module designs, *Proceedings of the 2005 IEEE/ACM International Conference on Computer-Aided Design* (ICCAD), San Jose, CA, pp. 159–164, 2005.

10. C. L. Cheng, RISA: Accurate and efficient placement routability modeling, *Proceedings of the 1994 IEEE/ACM International Conference on Computer-Aided Design* (ICCAD), San Jose, California, pp. 690–695, 1994.

11. C. C. N. Chu. FLUTE: Fast lookup table based wirelength estimation technique, *Proceedings of the 2004 IEEE/ACM International Conference on Computer-Aided Design* (ICCAD), San Jose, CA, pp. 696–701, 2004.

12. E. Detjens, G. Gannot, R. Rudell, A. Sangiovanni-Vincentelli, and A. Wang, Technology mapping in MIS, *ICCAD*, 1987, pp. 116–119.

13. A. E. Dunlop and B. W. Kernighan, A procedure for placement of standard cell VLSI circuits, *IEEE Transactions on Computer-Aided Design of Integrated Circuits*, 4(1): pp. 92–98, January 1985.

14. P. Gopalkrishnan, A. Odabasioglu, L. T. Pillleggi, and S. Raje, Overcoming wireload model uncertainty during physical design, *Proceedings of the 2001 International Symposium of Physical Design* (ISPD) Sonoma, CA, pp. 182–189, 2001.

15. S. Hojat and P. Villarrubbia, An integrated placement and synthesis approach for timing closure of power PC microprocessors, *ICCD*, 1997, pp. 206–210.

16. B. Hu and M. Marek-Sadowska, Congestion minimization during placement without estimation, *Proceedings of the 2002 IEEE/ACM International Conference on Computer-Aided Design* (ICCAD), San Jose, CA, pp. 739–745, 2002.

17. D. Jariwala and J. Lillis, On interactions between routing and detailed placement, *Proceedings of the 2004 IEEE/ACM International Conference on Computer-Aided Design* (ICCAD), San Jose, CA, pp. 387–393, 2004.

18. G. Karypis, R. Aggarwal, V. Kumar, and S. Shekhar, Multilevel hypergraph partitioning: Applications in VLSI domain, *Proceedings of the 34th Annual Conference on Design Automation* (DAC) Anaheim, CA, pp. 526–529, 1997. Available at http://glaros.dtc.umn.edu/gkhome/metis/hmetis/overview.

19. R. Kastner, E. Bozorgzadeh, and M. Sarrafzadeh, Predictable routing, *Proceedings of the 2000 IEEE/ACM International Conference on Computer-Aided Design* (ICCAD), San Jose, CA, pp. 110–114, 2000. Available at http://www.ece.ucsb.edu/kastner/labyrinth/.

20. A. B. Kahng and G. Robins, A new class of iterative Steiner tree heuristics with good performance, *IEEE Transactions on Computer-Aided Design*, 11(7): 893–902, 1992.

21. A. B. Kahng, I. I. Mandoiu, and A. Zelikovsky. Highly scalable algorithms for rectilinear and octilinear Steiner trees, *Proceedings of the 2003 Conference on Asia South Pacific Design Automation Conference* (ASPDAC), Kitakyushu, Japan, pp. 827–833, 2003.

22. A. Kahng and S. Reda, Placement feedback: A concept and method for better min-cut placement, *Proceedings of the 41st Annual Conference on Design Automation* (DAC) San Diego, CA, pp. 357–362, 2004.

23. J. M. Kleinhans, G. Sigl, F.M. Johannes, and K.J. Antreich, VLSI placement by quadratic programming and slicing optimization, *IEEE Transactions on Computer-Aided Design of Integrated Circuits and Systems*, 10(3): 356–361, 1991.

24. K. Keutzer, DAGON: Technology binding and local optimization by DAG matching, *Proceedings of the 24th ACM/IEEE Conference on Design Automation Conference* (DAC) Miami Beach, FL, pp. 341–347, 1987.

25. S. Kirkpatrick, C. D. Gelatt, and M. P. Vecchi, Optimization by simulated annealing, *Science*, 220 (4598): 671–680, May 1983.

26. P. Kudva and A. Dougherty, Metrics for structural logic synthesis, *Proceedings of the 2002 IEEE/ACM International Conference on Computer-Aided Design* (ICCAD) San Jose, CA, pp. 551–556, 2002.

27. J. Lou, S. Krishnamoorthy, and H. S. Sheng, Estimating routing congestion using probabilistic analysis, *Proceedings of the 2001 International Symposium on Physical Design* (ISPD) Sonoma, CA, pp. 112–117, 2001.

28. C. Li, M. Xie, C. -K. Koh, J. Cong, and P. H. Madden, Routability-driven placement and white space allocation, *Proceedings of the 2004 IEEE/ACM International Conference on Computer-Aided Design* (ICCAD), pp. 394–401, 2004.

29. P. N. Parakh, R. B. Brown, and K. A. Sakallah, Congestion driven quadratic placement, *Proceedings of the 35th Annual Conference on Design Automation Conference* (DAC) San Francisco, CA, pp. 275–278, 1998.

30. J. A. Roy, J. F. Lu, and I. L. Markov, Seeing the forest and the trees: Steiner wire-length optimization in placement, *Proceedings of the 2006 International Symposium on Physical Design* (ISPD), San Jose, CA, pp. 78–85, 2006.

31. D. Pandini, L. T. Pileggi, and A. J. Strojwas, Congestion-aware logic synthesis, *Proceedings of the Conference on Design, Automation and Test in Europe* (DATE), p. 664, 2002.

32. C. Sechen, The TimberWolf3.2 standard cell placement and global routing program, *User's Guide for Version 3.2, Release 2*.

33. C. Sechen, Chip-planning, placement, and global routing macro/custom cell integrated circuits using simulated annealing, *Proceedings of the 25th ACM/IEEE Conference on Design Automation Conference* (DAC), Atlantic City, NJ, pp. 73–80, 1998.

34. N. Selvakkumaran, P. Parakh, and G. Karypis, Perimeter-degree: A priori metric for directly measuring and homogenizing interconnection complexity in multilevel placement, *Proceedings of the 2003 International Workshop on System-Level Interconnect Prediction* (SLIP), Monterey, CA, pp. 53–59, 2003.

35. N. Selvakkumaran and G. Karypis, Theto-A fast, scalable and high quality partitioning driven placement tool, Technical report, University of Minnesota, 2004.

36. K. Takahashi, K. Terai, M. Nakajima, and K. Sato, Min-cut placement with global objective functions for large scale sea-of-gates arrays, *IEEE Transactions on Computer-Aided Design of Integrated Circuits and Systems*, 14(4): 434–446, 1995.

37. J. Vygen, Algorithms for large-scale flat placement, *Proceedings of the 34th Annual Conference on Design Automation Conference* (DAC), Anaheim, CA, pp. 746–751, 1997.

38. M. Wang, X. Yang, and M. Sarrafzadeh, Congestion minimization during placement, *IEEE Transactions on Computer-Aided Design of Integrated Circuits and Systems*, 19(10): 1140–1148, 2000.

39. J. Westra, C. Bartels, and P. Groeneveld, Probabilistic congestion prediction, *Proceedings of the 2004 International Symposium Physical Design* (ISPD), Phoenix, A2, pp. 204–209, 2004.

40. X. Yang, B. -K. Choi, and M. Sarrafzadeh, Routability driven white space allocation for fixed-die standard-cell placement, *Proceedings of the 2002 International Symposium on Physical Design* (ISPD) San Diego, CA, pp. 42–47, 2002.

41. X. Yang, B. -K. Choi, and M. Sarrafzadeh, Routability driven white space allocation for fixed-die standard-cell placement, *IEEE Transactions on CAD*, 22(4): 410–419, April 2003.

42. X. Yang, R. Kastner, and M. Sarrafzadeh, Congestion reduction during placement based on integer programming, *Proceedings of the 2001 IEEE/ACM International Conference on Computer-Aided Design* (ISPD), San Jose, CA pp. 573–576, 2001.

43. X. Yang, M. Wang, R. Kastner, S. Ghiasi, and M. Sarrafzadeh, Congestion reduction during placement with provably good approximation bound, *ACM Transactions on Design Automation of Electronic Systems* (TODAES), 8(3): 316–333, 2003.

44. K. Zhong and S. Dutt, Algorithms for simultaneous satisfaction of multiple constraints and objective optimization in a placement flow with application to congestion control, *Proceedings of the 39th Conference on Design Automation Conference* (DAC), New Orleans, Louisiana, pp. 854–859, 2002.

Part V

Net Layout and Optimization

23 Global Routing Formulation and Maze Routing

Muhammet Mustafa Ozdal and Martin D. F. Wong

CONTENTS

23.1 INTRODUCTION

Global routing is an important step in the physical design process. Because of the complexity of the overall routing problem, it is typically solved in two steps: global routing and detailed routing. During global routing, nets are routed on a coarse-grain grid structure with the objective of determining the regions within which each net will be routed. After an approximate routing solution is determined for each net, the second step is to perform detailed routing to find the exact routes of all nets. Because detailed routing is performed based on the global routes, the quality of the final interconnects depends largely on the quality of the global routing solutions.

Typically, detailed routing grids are much larger than the coarse-grain grids of global routing, and the solution space for individual nets is much larger because of the fine-grain modeling of routing resources. On the other hand, the resource model used in global routing is simplified, and the complexity of global routing one net is typically much smaller than the corresponding complexity of detailed routing. Hence, global routing helps detailed routing in two ways. First, the complexity of detailed routing can be reduced by confining its search space to the regions identified by the global routes. Second, it is usually prohibitive to use expensive sophisticated algorithms during detailed routing because of the high problem complexity. Furthermore, the order in which nets are routed can significantly impact the routing quality. Hence, it is the objective of global routing to find a solution such that several metrics (such as routability, wirelength, timing) can be optimized for all nets.

In this chapter, we discuss the basics of global routing formulation, and a high-level overview of global routing algorithms. The rest of the chapter is organized as follows. Section 23.2 presents a global routing grid model, and Section 23.3 describes how to set the edge capacities in such a model. The common objectives of global routing algorithms are discussed in Section 23.4. Section 23.5 describes algorithms to route a single net, with a particular focus on maze routing and its extensions. Finally, Section 23.6 provides a high-level overview of algorithms to route multiple nets.

23.2 GRID MODEL

Global routing is typically represented as a graph problem to capture the adjacencies and capacities of the routing region. A channel-based global routing model has been used for many years. This model is appropriate for circuits with limited number of routing layers, where standard cells or macroblocks occupy most of the routing space. However, as the number of routing layers is increasing, aggressive over-the-cell routing has become more popular in the recent years. In this model, the global routing problem is represented as a grid graph. In the following subsections, we describe these models in more detail.

23.2.1 Channel-Based Graph Model

A typical layout contains a set of cells or macroblocks of which terminals need to be routed to each other. If the number of routing layers is small, the routing space is limited to the channels between these cells or macroblocks. Figure 23.1a illustrates a set of macroblocks and the available routing resources between them. The most natural representation of this routing model is a channel intersection graph, G, where there exists a vertex v_i in G corresponding to each channel intersection i, and an edge exists between vertices v_i and v_j if and only if there exists a channel between intersections i and j. In other words, each edge in graph G corresponds to a channel in the routing area. Figure 23.1b illustrates the graph model corresponding to the macroblocks given in Figure 23.1a.

In this model, each channel c is defined to have channel capacity and channel length. The channel capacity indicates the number of nets that can use this channel without overflow, and the channel length indicates the amount of wirelength necessary to pass through this channel. The global routers using this graph model include Refs. [1–4]. A related problem here is the assignment of feedthrough space between channels of standard cell rows with the objective of wirelength and

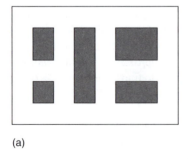
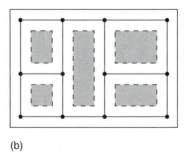

(a) (b)

FIGURE 23.1 (a) Set of macroblocks and the channels between them and (b) its corresponding channel intersection graph.

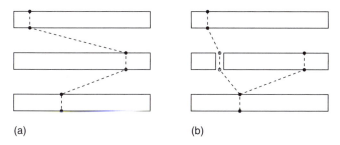

(a)   (b)

FIGURE 23.2 Net with terminals on three standard cell rows. The best topology of this net is illustrated (a) without feedthroughs and (b) with feedthroughs. The dark circles represent the net terminals, and the hollow circles represent the feedthrough terminals created.

congestion minimization [5,6]. This concept is illustrated in Figure 23.2. After the global routing is completed, detailed routing within each channel is done using a channel routing algorithm [7–12] or a river routing algorithm [13–17].

23.2.2 TILE-BASED GRAPH MODEL

As the number of available routing layers is increasing in the current technology, over-the-cell routing model is becoming more and more popular. In this model, the lower layers that contain the cells or macroblocks are used as escape-only layers, and routing between terminals is accomplished mainly on the upper layers. Because the routing resources in the upper layers are not restricted to channels, the layout is partitioned into rectangular regions, and a grid graph G is created as illustrated in Figure 23.3. Here, there exists a vertex in G corresponding to each rectangular tie, and edges exist

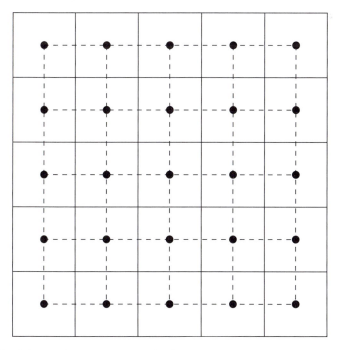

FIGURE 23.3 Circuit is partitioned into rectangular tiles (solid lines), and a grid graph is created. The dark circles and dashed lines represent the vertices and the edges of the grid graph, respectively.

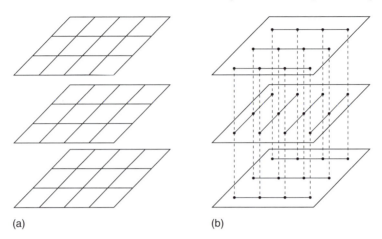

(a)   (b)

FIGURE 23.4   (a) Three-dimensional grid model for a three-layer circuit and (b) its corresponding grid graph, where solid lines represent intralayer connections and dashed lines represent interlayer connections.

in G between vertices that correspond to neighboring ties. Here, each terminal is assumed to lie at the center of the grid cell that contains the terminal.

In this model, edge capacities are set based on the number of routing tracks available passing through the tile boundaries, as will be discussed with more detail in Section 23.3. If a two-dimensional grid model is used (as in Figure 23.3), the routing tracks on every layer are lumped together to compute edge capacities. On the other hand, a three-dimensional grid graph can capture the characteristics of different layers more accurately. For example, there can be routing blockages on specific layers, and different layers can have different wire width and spacing requirements based on the technology being used. Although the three-dimensional grid model can capture the capacity differences in different layers, it requires layer assignment to be performed during global routing. Figure 23.4 illustrates a three-dimensional grid graph, where each layer has either horizontal or vertical preferred orientation. Observe here that there are only horizontal edges on a horizontal layer, and only vertical edges on a vertical layer. The global routing algorithms using tile-based graph model include Refs. [18–25].

23.3   CAPACITY COMPUTATION

As discussed earlier, a graph model G is used for global routing to capture the adjacencies and the capacities of the routing regions. Let u and v represent two vertices in G, corresponding to two adjacent routing regions. The capacity of the edge $e \in G$ between u and v is set so as to reflect the available routing resources between the corresponding routing regions. A common capacity metric for edge e is the number of available routing tracks between the routing regions corresponding to u and v. In other words, capacity of e reflects the number of nets that can be routed between u and v.

It is also possible to extend this simple track-based capacity metric to consider specific locations of blockages, pins, and preroutes. Furthermore, for the three-dimensional graph model described in Section 23.2.2, the routing resources consumed by the utilized vias can be modeled as well. For example, in Refs. [26,27], three types of edge capacities are defined: wiring capacity, through capacity, and interlayer capacity. The wiring capacity is computed by dividing the routing tile into slices based on the available routing resources, as shown in Figure 23.5. Then, the width (W_i) and the depth (D_i) of each slice i is computed. Based on these, the wiring capacity is simply defined as $\sum_i (W_i \times D_i)/D$, where D is the depth of the tile. Similarly, the through capacity is based on the number of nets that can pass straight through the tile. It is computed as the sum of $(W_i \times D_i)$ values for each slice i that spans the entire tile (i.e., $D_i = D$). Finally, interlayer capacitance corresponds to

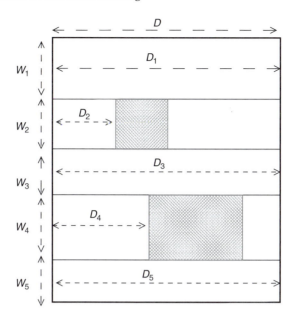

FIGURE 23.5 Capacity estimation model. Here, W_i and D_i represent the width and depth of slice i in the given tile. (From Cong, J., Fang, J., and Khoo, K. -Y., *IEEE Trans. Comput.-Aided Des. Integr. Circuits Syst.*, 20, 633, 2001; Cong, J., Fang, J., Xie, M., and Zhang, J., *IEEE Trans. Comput.-Aided Des. Integr. Circuits Syst.*, 24, 382, 2005.)

the number of vias that can be created within the tile, and is computed as the sum of empty spaces in the tile.

In practice, high-precision capacity estimation can be complex, especially in the presence of arbitrary preroutes, varying wire pitches, and complex design rules. Furthermore, it can also be necessary to model the effect of interlayer connections (i.e., vias) on the horizontal/vertical wire capacities during global routing. In general, considering different factors during capacity estimation can lead to better correlation between global routing and detailed routing in the expense of increased algorithmic complexity.

23.4 ROUTING METRICS

The key objective of global routing is to maximize routability in the consequent detailed routing step, while satisfying various routability constraints. In this section, we give an overview of the commonly used global routing metrics.

23.4.1 CONGESTION

As described in Section 23.3, each global routing tile has a specific capacity. If the total resource usage of the nets assigned to a tile is more than its capacity, then the tile is defined to be congested. Clearly, the detailed router will not be able to route all the nets assigned to a congested tile because of lack of routing resources. However, in practice, detailed routers typically can tolerate some degree of congestion by spreading the wires to nearby not congested tiles, if any.

A good congestion metric needs to consider not only the edge capacities, but also through capacities, as described in Section 23.3. Furthermore, an even spread of congestion throughout the routing region usually leads to better detailed routing solutions.

Typically, global routers assign higher costs for congested-routing resources to discourage nets using these resources. For an even spreading of congestion throughout the routing region, some

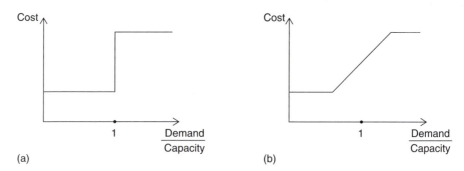

(a)   (b)

FIGURE 23.6 (a) Congestion cost function that penalizes congested resources only and (b) congestion cost function that promotes an even spreading of congestion.

routers use cost functions that are linear functions of resource usage [20,28,29]. These cost functions are reported [20] to give better results than step functions, which only penalize congested resources. Figure 23.6 illustrates sample cost functions corresponding to these two types.

23.4.2 BEND COUNT

As described in Section 23.2, each interconnect layer is used for either horizontal or vertical connections. If a routing path makes a change in its direction (e.g., from horizontal to vertical), this necessitates a layer change, as illustrated in Figure 23.7. So, each bend in a routing path indicates the need for the usage of a via, which connects adjacent interconnect layers. Typically, vias are undesirable because of their negative effects on signal integrity, delay, routing area, and manufacturing yields. Hence, a good global router needs to minimize the number of bends in the routing paths.

23.4.3 WIRELENGTH

Another important metric for global routing is wirelength minimization. Increased wirelengths typically imply larger power consumption and larger delays. Although routing nets with the minimum wirelengths are desirable, a global router may need to introduce detours to avoid blockages or congested regions.

Inherently, congestion minimization metrics can conflict with the wirelength and bend-count minimization metrics, as illustrated in Figure 23.8. So, the trade-off between these metrics should be carefully tuned based on the requirements of the global router.

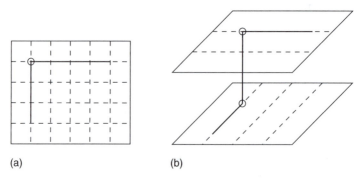

(a)   (b)

FIGURE 23.7 (a) Bend in a routing path is illustrated in the two-dimensional grid model and (b) the via corresponding to the bend is illustrated in the three-dimensional grid model.

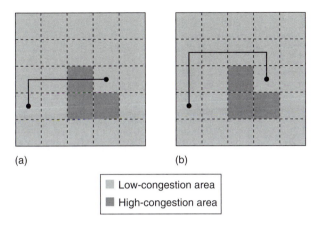

(a)   (b)

Low-congestion area
High-congestion area

FIGURE 23.8 Two possible configurations for a routing segment: (a) minimum wirelength, increased congestion and (b) increased wirelength, minimum congestion.

23.4.4 TIMING

Timing optimization can be another important metric for high-speed designs. Typically, the critical nets are identified, and certain timing bounds are imposed on critical connections. These connections are then prioritized so that they can use faster resources, and scarce resources in the congested areas. Furthermore, some restrictions can be imposed on the maximum detours introduced while routing the critical connections.

23.4.5 COUPLING

Because of the scaling down of device geometry and increasing clock frequencies, detrimental effects of coupling capacitances are becoming more significant. Coupling capacitance between two wires is proportional to the amount of parallel overlap between them, and inversely proportional to the distance between them. Avoiding coupling during global routing can be important for coupling management in general. Figure 23.9 [22] illustrates two configurations of a set of connections with and without coupling. Zhou and Wong [30] propose a Lagrangian relaxation-based methodology to minimize coupling during global routing.

23.5 SINGLE NET ROUTING

In this section, we focus on the problem of global routing of a single net. Given a global routing grid with possible blockages, the objective is to find the best routing solution for one net. In Section 23.5.1,

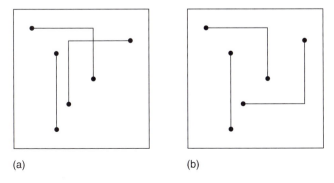

(a)   (b)

FIGURE 23.9 (a) Layout with coupling owing to long parallel wires and (b) layout with no coupling.

we start with a description of the classical maze routing algorithm [31], which is one of the earliest algorithms on automated wire-routing problem. Because this algorithm can be too expensive for large designs, several enhancements have been proposed in the literature, as discussed in Section 23.5.2. Inherently, maze routing algorithms are based on searching a path as a sequence of grid points. Another class of routing algorithms represent the paths as a sequence of line segments for the purpose of efficient execution. These line-search algorithms are described in Section 23.5.3. Another class of algorithms simplify the routing solution space to certain patterns such as I-, L-, and Z-shaped routes for the purpose of further speedup, as discussed in Section 23.5.4. For simplicity of the presentation, these algorithms are described in the context of nets with two terminals. In Section 23.5.5, we outline typical approaches to handle nets with multiple terminals.

23.5.1 LEE'S MAZE ROUTING ALGORITHM

Lee's algorithm [31] is one of the earliest routing algorithms proposed for automated wire routing. It is basically an extension of Moore's shortest path algorithm [32] to a uniform grid structure. The basic algorithm operates on a single two-terminal net n, and a uniform grid G, which can have some of its cells specified as blockages. It is guaranteed to find a path between the terminals of the nets, and this path is guaranteed to be the shortest possible.

The algorithm consists of two main phases. In the first phase, a wavefront is expanded from one of the terminals, as illustrated in Figure 23.10a. As the first step, the immediate neighboring cells of the terminal are marked with label 1. Then, at every step $i(i > 1)$, the unmarked neighbors of the cells that were marked with label L at step $i - 1$ are marked with label $L + 1$. This process continues until the wavefront reaches the target terminal. Once the target terminal is found, the shortest path is constructed by backtracking in the second phase of the algorithm, as shown in Figure 23.10b. The backtracking operation starts with the target cell, and continues iteratively until the source cell

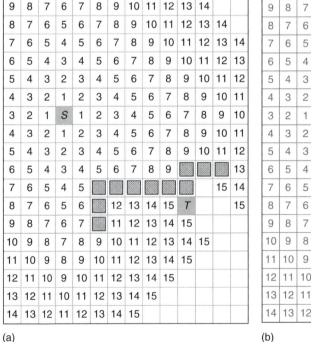

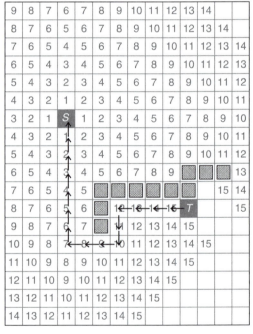

(a)   (b)

FIGURE 23.10 Two phases of maze routing algorithm are illustrated: (a) wave expansion and (b) backtracking. The source and target terminals are marked as S and T, respectively.

is reached. At one step, if the current cell c has label L, then backtracking continues with one of the neighbors of c that has label $L - 1$. If there are multiple neighbors with the same label, then a practical guideline for tie-breaking is to select the neighbor that will cause no change in the direction of the path (if any). This heuristic tends to choose the shortest paths with reduced bend counts.

23.5.2 MAZE-ROUTING ENHANCEMENTS

The worst-case time complexity of the original maze routing algorithm is $O(N \times M)$, where N and M are the height and width of the grid, respectively. Several enhancements have been proposed in the literature to reduce the practical runtime and memory requirements of this algorithm. Furthermore, some generalizations of the problem formulation have been proposed to extend its application areas.

Some straightforward speedup techniques have been proposed [33] to reduce the runtime of the original algorithm with only small modifications. One of them is the selection of the starting point of the wave propagation. If we start expanding the wavefront from the terminal that is closer to the circuit boundary, then the area of wave propagation will tend to be smaller. Another technique is to expand the wavefront from both terminals simultaneously until two wavefronts meet each other. This also reduces the number of grid points visited during wave propagation. Another heuristic is to define an artificial bounding box on the search region, and to allow wavefront expansion only within this bounding box.

For the purpose of reducing the memory requirements of maze routing, Akers [34] proposed some coding schemes for cell labeling. In the original algorithm, k bits are necessary to represent a cell label, where $k = \lg(N \times M)$, because the maximum label can be as large as $N \times M$. However, it is possible to make the following observation. During backtracking, path computation is done by iteratively visiting the predecessor of each cell, starting from the target cell. Hence, it is only necessary to distinguish two types of neighbors for each cell C: the predecessors and the successors of C. As long as the predecessors of C can be distinguished from the successors of C, we do not need to store the labels of the cells. In the coding scheme proposed by Akers, the following sequence is used to label the cells during wavefront expansion phase: $1, 1, 2, 2, 1, 1, 2, 2, \ldots$, as illustrated in Figure 23.11a. Observe that the predecessor of each cell C is labeled different from the successor of cell C. During backtracking, the same sequence is used to construct the path from target to source, as illustrated in Figure 23.11b. In this coding scheme, only two bits need to be stored for each cell, representing four states: empty, blocked, 1, and 2. This can reduce the memory requirements of the algorithm significantly especially for large circuits.

Some other heuristics involve manipulation of the direction of the wavefront propagation. Hadlock's minimum detour algorithm [35] uses a variant of A^* search algorithm [36] to reduce the size of the search space. It is straightforward to show that the length of path P between nodes A and B is equal to $M(A, B) + 2d(P)$, where $M(A, B)$ is the Manhattan distance between A and B, and $d(P)$ is the detour number for path P (i.e., the number of cells directed away from target B).

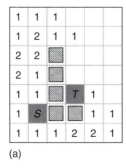

(a)

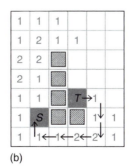

(b)

FIGURE 23.11 Coding scheme proposed by Akers is illustrated: (a) wavefront expansion and (b) backtracking.

Because the Manhattan distance between A and B is fixed for a given source–target pair, finding the path with the shortest path is equivalent to finding the path with the minimum detour number. Based on this observation, Hadlock's minimum detour algorithm uses the detour numbers as the cell labels, and the cells with smaller detour numbers are expanded before the cells with higher detour numbers. Wavefront expansion phase of this algorithm is illustrated in Figure 23.12a with an example. The worst-case time complexity of this algorithm is the same as the original maze-routing algorithm; however, it is significantly faster in practice. Also, it is guaranteed to find the shortest path if one exists.

Another algorithm that improves the runtime of the original maze-routing algorithm is Soukup's fast maze algorithm [37]. In this algorithm, search is conducted iteratively in two different phases. In the first phase, wavefront expansion is done toward the target without changing direction until an obstacle is reached. Once an obstacle is reached, the second phase begins. In this phase, the same wavefront expansion methodology as the original maze-routing algorithm is used to search around the obstacle. Once a cell in the direction of the target is found, the first phase begins again for a directed search toward the target. Basically, this algorithm combines depth-first search (first phase) and breadth-first search (second phase) as an effective heuristic for wavefront propagation. Wavefront expansion phase of this algorithm is illustrated in Figure 23.12b with an example, where the edges expanded in the first phase are highlighted. This algorithm is guaranteed to find a path from source to target if one exists; however, the path found is not guaranteed to be the shortest one. Although the worst-case running time of this algorithm is still the same as the original algorithm, significant reduction of runtimes can be obtained in practice. The reason can be observed by comparing the sizes of the search spaces in Figures 23.10 and 23.12.

Maze routing algorithms can also be generalized to multilayer problems in a straightforward way. The basic idea is to model the routing resources as a three-dimensional grid (as in Section 23.2.2),

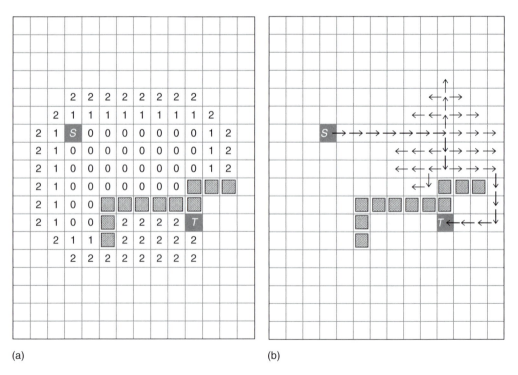

(a)   (b)

FIGURE 23.12 Wavefront expansion phases of (a) Hadlock's minimum detour algorithm and (b) Soukup's fast maze algorithm are illustrated from source S to target T.

(a)

1	1	1	1	1	1
1	1	1	1	1	1
1	1	▨	1	1	1
1	1	▨	1	1	1
1	1	▨	T	1	1
1	S	▨	▨	1	1
2	2	2	2	2	2

(b)

6	5	6	7		
5	4	5	6	7	
4	3	▨	7		
3	2	▨		11	
2	1	▨	11	10	11
1	0	▨	▨	9	10
2	2	4	6	8	10

(c)

6	5	6	7	8	9
5	4	5	6	7	8
4	3	▨	7	8	9
3	2	▨	8	9	12
2	1	▨	9	10	11
1	0	▨	▨	9	10
2	2	4	6	8	10

FIGURE 23.13 (a) Routing grid with different weights assigned to each cell, (b) wave expansion from source S reaches target T the first time with cost 11, and (c) further expansion of the wavefront reduces the cost of the target cell T from 11 to 9.

and to perform wave expansion in all three dimensions at each step. Note here that an edge in the third dimension corresponds to layer change, and can be assigned a higher cost to discourage via usage. As mentioned in Section 23.2.2, typically each layer is assigned one of the horizontal or vertical orientations for routing. For such designs, wave expansion on each layer can be limited to either horizontal or vertical orientations at each step.

It is also possible to perform weighted path computations using maze routing algorithms. As discussed in Section 23.4, some paths can be more preferable than others because of various routing metrics, such as congestion minimization. For the purpose of incorporating different routing objectives into path computations, different edges in the routing graph can be assigned different costs. For instance, an edge passing through a congested region can be assigned a higher cost. In its original form, the maze routing algorithm does not guarantee to find the path with the minimum cost, because it is possible that a longer path can have smaller total cost. An example is illustrated in Figure 23.13. In Figure 23.13a, different weights are assigned to each grid cell based on a given metric. In Figure 23.13b, the wave expanded from the source reaches the target cell the first time. Note here that, if wave expansion is stopped as soon as the target is reached, then the path found will have a total cost of 11. However, if wave expansion is allowed to continue as in Figure 23.13c, then the path found will have a total cost of 9. In the original maze-routing algorithm, each cell is labeled at most once during wave expansion. In case of weighted routing edges, cells can be labeled multiple times, and the original worst time complexity of $O(N \times M)$ is not guaranteed anymore for an $N \times M$ grid. An efficient methodology to handle this issue is to prioritize cells during wave expansion based on their labels. Typically, a priority queue is used to expand the cells with the smallest labels at each step. This approach is actually a special case of Dijsktra's shortest path algorithm [38], and its worst-case time complexity is $O[N \times M \log(N \times M)]$. In practice, the well-known A^* heuristic methodology [36] can further reduce the average runtime requirements of this algorithm.

23.5.3 LINE-SEARCH ALGORITHMS

The main idea behind the line-search algorithms is to represent the routing search space as a set of line segments instead of grid points. This feature makes it possible to reduce memory and runtime requirements, compared to the maze routing algorithms, which typically need to allocate memory for each grid point. The first line-search algorithms were independently proposed by Mikami–Tabuchi [39] and Hightower [40] with small variations.

An example illustrating Mikami–Tabuchi algorithm is given in Figure 23.14a. The algorithm starts with expanding one horizontal and one vertical line segment from each of the source and target points. After that, line expansion continues iteratively until one of the line segments originating from

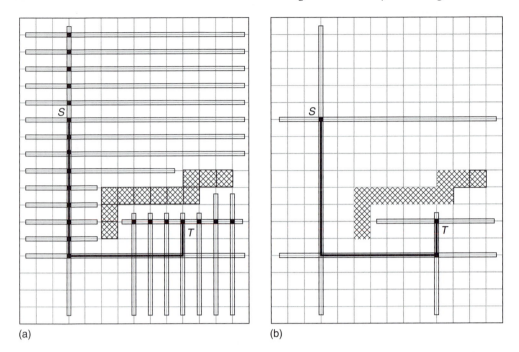

(a)   (b)

FIGURE 23.14   Illustration of the line-search algorithms proposed by (a) Mikami–Tabuchi and (b) Hightower. The dark circles represent the originating points of the line segments created. The path computed between source S and target T is highlighted.

the source point intersects with one of the line segments originating from the target point. In each iteration, potential expansion points (represented as dark circles in Figure 23.14a) are identified on the most recently expanded line segments; then perpendicular line segments are created originating from these points. Once a line segment originating from the source intersects with a line segment originating from the target, the path is constructed by backtracking from the intersection point to the source and the target points. It is shown that this algorithm is guaranteed to find a path if one exists, and the path found is guaranteed to have the minimum possible number of bends.

Observe that each grid point on a line segment created in Mikami–Tabuchi algorithm is a potential expansion point for new line segments. Hightower algorithm [40] differs from Mikami–Tabuchi algorithm in the way it chooses potential expansion points for the line segments. Instead of expanding a new line segment on each candidate point, Hightower algorithm identifies escape lines on the most recently created line segments based on the positions of the blockages. This algorithm is illustrated in Figure 23.14b. Observe that only the line segments that are extendable beyond the obstacle that blocked the previous line segment are considered as candidates in this algorithm. Compared to Mikami–Tabuchi algorithm, fewer line segments are generated. However, Hightower algorithm does not guarantee to find a path even if it exists, because the solution space is not explored completely.

Typically, line-search algorithms are effective in minimizing the number of bends, and they do not guarantee shortest paths. The main assumption behind these algorithms is that routing can be accomplished with relatively few bends (hence few line segments) so that memory and runtime requirements are small. This is especially true for problems with low congestion and few number of blockages. However, if the routing problem is complicated, line-search algorithms run slower, and typically require more memory and runtime than maze routing algorithms. Furthermore, some class of line-search algorithms (e.g., Hightower algorithm [40]) do not guarantee to find a feasible path even if one exists. Because of their nature, line-search algorithms are more preferable early in the routing process when there are relatively fewer blockages in the design.

FIGURE 23.15   Some routing patterns with 0, 1, and 2 bends are illustrated.

23.5.4   PATTERN ROUTING

As discussed in Section 23.5.3, representing the routing solution space as a set of line segments can potentially reduce memory and runtime requirements. A more aggressive approach is to restrict the solution space to routes with predefined patterns, such as I-, L-, Z-, and U-shaped patterns. In general, routing patterns can be defined based on the number of bends on them. Figure 23.15 illustrates some patterns with 0, 1, and 2 bends.

Because the objective of global routing is to generate rough routing solutions for the nets, pattern routing can be effectively used in global routing to reduce the runtime requirements. For example, in the experiments of Ref. [24], it is reported that on average about 2 percent of the nets are routed with maze routing, while the rest of the nets are routed with pattern routing. Yet, about 48 percent of the total runtime is spent on maze routing. In general, it is an effective heuristic to use pattern routing for the nets that have feasible few-bend solutions, and maze routing for the nets that require larger number of bends.

23.5.5   ROUTING NETS WITH MULTIPLE TERMINALS

In the previous subsections, we mainly focused on routing algorithms for two terminal nets. However, it is possible to use these algorithms in the context of routing nets with multiple terminals. Note that the problem of finding the optimal route for a multiterminal net is an NP-complete problem. However, there are several heuristic-based algorithms that are used frequently in practice, as will be described in more detail in Chapter 24. A typical approach to route a multiterminal net N consists of two main steps: (1) generate a Steiner topology T for the terminals of net N and (2) perform point-to-point routing between the terminals and Steiner points of topology T. This two-step approach is illustrated in Figure 23.16 with an example.

Another practical approach is to apply maze routing algorithm iteratively between terminal pairs of the net. Typically, wave expansion starts from the driver terminal T_d until a receiver terminal T_r is reached. Then, the route between T_d and T_r is implemented by backtracking, as in the original maze-routing algorithm. After that, the route between T_d and T_r is regarded as the new source of

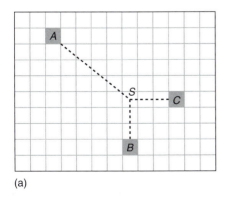
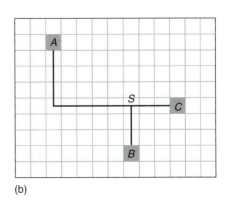

(a)   (b)

FIGURE 23.16   (a) Steiner topology is generated for a net with three terminals: A, B, and C, where S is a Steiner point and (b) final routing solution is obtained by point-to-point routing between A–S, S–B, and S–C.

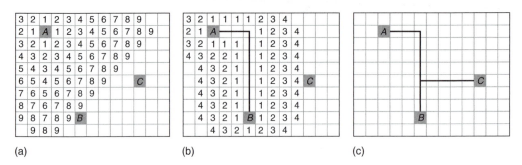

FIGURE 23.17   Maze routing is applied repeatedly to find the routing solution of a net with three terminals. (a) Wave expansion starts from terminal A, and it reaches terminal B; (b) the route between A and B is implemented, and the new wavefront is expanded from the partial route; and (c) the final routing solution obtained.

the wave expansion. In other words, the next wavefront is expanded starting from the partial route implemented. This process continues until all the terminals of the net are routed. Figure 23.17 illustrates this process with an example. Here, wave expansion starts from terminal A, and it reaches terminal B (Figure 23.17a). Then, the route between A and B is implemented by backtracking. The next wavefront is started to be expanded from this partial route (Figure 23.17b). Finally, the new wavefront reaches C, and the final solution is obtained. Note here that this approach can easily lead to suboptimal solutions because of its greedy nature. For example, if the lower L route was selected in Figure 23.17b as the route between A and B, then the wirelength of the final routing solution would be significantly larger. To avoid this problem, a biasing technique is proposed in Ref. [41] to direct the maze search toward regions where overlap with future connections of the net is more likely.

23.6   ROUTING MULTIPLE NETS

In this section, we focus on the problem of routing multiple nets together. The main difficulty here is that routing solution for one net potentially impacts the routing of other nets, because common routing resources are being used by multiple nets. We can divide the routing methodologies that deal with multiple nets into two broad categories: sequential and concurrent routing methodologies. In the following subsections, we give a brief overview of these techniques.

23.6.1   SEQUENTIAL ROUTING

The most straightforward way of routing multiple nets is to route them sequentially in a specific order. Once a net is routed, the congestion values of the global routing resources being used are updated. As a result, some of the nets to be routed in the later iterations may be forced to use overcongested routing resources. So, this approach is very sensitive to the order of nets that are being routed. Figure 23.18 illustrates an example where net ordering has an impact on the final solution. In Figure 23.18a, net C is routed after nets A and B, and its path is blocked by the other routing segments. This leads to an overcongested solution. In Figure 23.18b, net A is routed after nets C and B, and all its shortest paths are blocked by the other routing segments. This leads to a solution with suboptimal wirelength for net A. In Figure 23.18c, the best net ordering is illustrated, which leads to a congestion-free routing solution with optimal routing for each net.

Several practical considerations are taken into account while making the net ordering decision. The nets that have higher criticalities are typically routed first so that they have higher priorities while using contentious routing resources. The criticality of a net is determined by the importance of the net and the timing requirements imposed on it. For example, if a net is on the critical path of the circuit, it can be prioritized so that it uses the fastest routing resources before they are acquired by

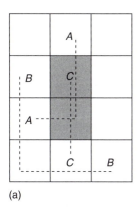 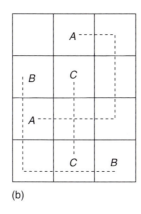 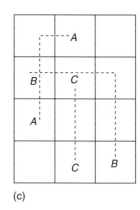

(a)   (b)   (c)

FIGURE 23.18 Net ordering problem is illustrated for three nets. The capacity of each tile is assumed to be one vertical and one horizontal track. Routing nets in the order (a) A–B–C leads to a solution with two overcongested tiles (shown as shaded rectangles), (b) C–B–A leads to a solution where A is detoured to avoid congestion, and (c) C–A–B leads to the congestion-free solution with optimal routing for each net.

other nets. Another practical consideration is routing nets with less routing alternatives before other nets. Typically, routing choices are limited for the nets of which terminals are close to each other. Similarly, if all the terminals of a net align with each other on one row or column of the routing grid (e.g., net C in Figure 23.18), then routing choices will be limited for such a net. So, it is a commonly used heuristic to determine net ordering based on increasing Manhattan distances of the terminals.

The main disadvantage of sequential routing methodologies is that the nets that are routed earlier affect the routing of the latter nets. To alleviate this problem, rip-up and reroute techniques [42,43] are used so that the nets that are routed in the earlier iterations can be rerouted based on the routing requirements of the latter nets. Typically, nets are first routed allowing congestion, and then the nets in the overcongested regions are ripped up and rerouted in the later iterations. For example in Figure 23.18a, nets are routed in the order A–B–C. Here, if net A is ripped up and rerouted, it will prefer the uncongested region, and the solution in Figure 23.18b will be obtained.

A problem with the rip-up- and reroute-based algorithms is solution oscillations. It is possible that the congestion will oscillate between two regions during the routing iterations as nets are being ripped up and rerouted. To avoid this problem, some algorithms incorporate the congestion history into the routing objective function. Pathfinder is a negotiated-congestion-based algorithm, which was proposed for FPGA routing [44–46], and extended to different aplication areas such as PCB routing [47]. Recently, global routing algorithms have been proposed that utilize congestion histories [23,25,48], and outperform other algorithms on recently released public benchmarks [49]. The main idea of congestion negotiation can be summarized as follows. First, every net is routed individually, regardless of any overuse (i.e., congestion) of routing grid edges. Then the nets are ripped up and rerouted one by one iteratively. In each iteration, the congestion cost of each edge is updated based on the current and past overuse of it. By increasing the congestion cost of an overused edge gradually, the nets with alternative routes are forced not to use this edge. Eventually, only the net that needs to use this edge most ends up using it. For example, Archer [23] uses the following cost function to compute the congestion history of edge e:

$$\text{cost}(e) = (1 + \alpha.h_e^k) \times \text{overflow}(e) \qquad (23.1)$$

Here, h_e^k represents the history cost for edge e in iteration k, and it reflects for how long edge e has been congested. It is computed as follows:

$$h_e^k = \begin{cases} h_e^{k-1} & \text{if edge } e \text{ is congestion free in iteration } k \\ h_e^{k-1} + k & \text{if edge } e \text{ has nonzero overflow in iteration } k \end{cases} \qquad (23.2)$$

Based on this formulation, if edge e is congested repeatedly for several iterations, its cost will increase significantly to discourage its usage. Aging effect is also captured by this formulation. The edges that are congested only in the earlier iterations will have less costs than the ones that are congested in the later iterations.

In Chapter 31, a more thorough survey of rip-up and reroute algorithms is provided.

23.6.2 CONCURRENT ROUTING

The sequential routing algorithms are commonly used mainly because of their simplicity and low-runtime requirements. However, they are heuristics-based, and they typically do not have any theoretical guarantee about solution quality. As discussed in the previous section, the order in which nets are routed typically affects the routing results of sequential algorithms significantly. For the purpose of avoiding this problem, another class of algorithms try to find the routing solutions of all nets concurrently. In this subsection, a brief overview of routing formulations based on multicommodity flow and integer linear programming will be given.

Global routing problem can be formulated as a multicommodity flow problem as follows. Let $G = (V, E)$ be the global routing graph with vertices V and edges E. A flow network can be modeled based on this graph G. Each edge $e \in E$ in this network will have flow capacity cap(e) (which can be set based on the techniques presented in Section 23.3), and cost cost(e) (which can be set based on the cost metrics discussed in Section 23.4). A commodity must be transported over this network corresponding to each net between the vertices corresponding to its terminals. The multicommodity flow problem is defined as finding a flow for each commodity between specified vertices while satisfying all flow capacity constraints of the edges in the network. There are two variations of this problem depending on whether fractional flow values on edges are allowed or not. While the fractional multicommodity flow problem is polynomial-time solvable, integer multicommodity flow problem is NP-complete.

Shragowitz et al. [50] present one of the earlier global routing algorithms that uses multicommodity flow formulation for two-terminal nets. Raghavan et al. [51] present an improved network flow formulation that can also handle three-terminal nets. A more recent algorithm proposed by Albrecht [18] operates on a set of given Steiner trees T_i for each net i with the objective of choosing exactly one $T \in T_i$ such that the maximum relative congestion in the circuit is minimized. The readers can refer to Chapter 32 for a more detailed survey of concurrent routing algorithms.

23.7 CONCLUSIONS

In this chapter, we have discussed the basics of global routing. As discussed before, global routing is an important step in the physical design process, and it impacts the final interconnect qualities considerably. As the circuit densities have been significantly increasing in the past several years, the routing problem for integrated circuits is becoming a more and more challenging problem. A recent global routing competition in ISPD 2007 [49] attracted renewed interest in global routing, and the results of the recently proposed algorithms [23,25,48] demonstrated that there is still significant room for routing quality improvements.

The next two chapters provide detailed discussions on net-topology optimization techniques for multiterminal nets. Although these chapters focus on single-net optimization, they can be utilized within a global routing framework to determine net topologies, as discussed in Section 23.5.5.

REFERENCES

1. G. W. Clow. A global routing algorithm for general cells. In *21st Design Automation Conference*, IEEE Press, Piscataway, NJ, pp. 45–51, 1984.
2. J. Cong and P. Madden. Performance driven global routing for standard cell design. In *International Symposium on Physical Design*, ACM, NY, pp. 73–80, 1997.

3. J. T. Mowchenko and C. S. R. Ma. A new global routing algorithm for standard cell ICs. In *International Symposium on Circuits and Systems*, pp. 27–30, 1987.
4. C. Sechen and A. Sangiovanni-Vincentelli. Timberwolf 3.2: A new standard cell placement and global routing package. In *23rd Design Automation Conference*, IEEE Computer Society Press, Los Alamitos, CA, pp. 432–439, 1986.
5. J. Cong and B. Preas. A new algorithm for standard cell global routing. *Integration: The VLSI Journal*, 14(1): 49–65, 1992. (ICCAD 1988.)
6. W. Swartz and C. Sechen. A new generalized row-based global router. *International Conference on Computer Aided Design*, IEEE Computer Society Press, Los Alamitos, CA, pp. 491–498, 1993.
7. M. Burstein and R. Pelavin. Hierarchical channel router. In *Proceedings of 20th Design Automation Conference*, ACM, NY, pp. 591–597, 1983.
8. S. C. Fang, W. S. Feng, and S. L. Lee. A new efficient approach to multilayer channel routing problem. In *Proceedings of the 29th Design Automation Conference*, IEEE Computer Society Press, Los Alamitos, CA, pp. 579–584, 1992.
9. A. Hashimoto and J. Stevens. Wire routing by optimizing channel assignment within large apertures. In *Proceedings of the 8th Design Automation Workshop*, ACM, NY, pp. 214–224, 1971.
10. M. M. Ozdal and M. D. F. Wong. Two layer bus routing for high-speed printed circuit boards. *ACM Transactions on Design Automation of Electronic Systems*, 11(1): 213–227, 2006. (ICCAD 2004.)
11. R. L. Rivest and C. M. Fiduccia. A greedy channel router. In *Proceedings of 19th Design Automation Conference*, IEEE Press, Piscataway, NJ, pp. 418–424, 1982.
12. T. Yoshimura. Efficient algorithms for channel routing. *IEEE Transactions on Computer-Aided Design*, CAD-1(1): 25–35, 1982.
13. C. Hsu. General river routing algorithm. In *Proceedings of 20th Design Automation Conference*, IEEE Press, Piscataway, NJ, pp. 578–582, 1983.
14. M. M. Ozdal and M. D. F. Wong. Algorithmic study of single-layer bus routing for high-speed boards. *IEEE Transactions on Computer-Aided Design of Integrated Circuits and Systems*, 25(3): 490–503, 2006. (ICCAD 2004.)
15. R. Y. Pinter. On routing two-point nets across a channel. In *Proceedings of 19th Design Automation Conference*, IEEE Press, Piscataway, NJ, pp. 894–902, 1982.
16. R. Y. Pinter. River routing: Methodology and analysis. In *Proceedings of 3rd Caltech Conference on VLSI*, Computer Science Press, pp. 141–163, 1983.
17. H. Zhou and M. D. F. Wong. Optimal river routing with crosstalk constraints. *ACM Transactions on Design Automation of Electronic Systems*, 3(3): 496–514, 1998.
18. C. Albrecht. Provably good global routing by a new approximation algorithm for multicommodity flow. In *International Symposium on Physical Design*, ACM, NY, pp. 19–25, 2000.
19. M. Cho and D. Z. Pan. Boxrouter: A new global router based on box expansion and progressive ilp. In *Proceedings of Design Automation Conference*, ACM, NY, pp. 373–378, 2006.
20. R. T. Hadsell and P. H. Madden. Improved global routing through congestion estimation. In *Proceedings of Design Automation Conference*, ACM, NY, pp. 28–31, 2003.
21. R. Kastner, E. Bozorgzadeh, and M. Sarrafzadeh. Predictable routing. In *Proceedings of International Conference on Computer Aided Design*, IEEE Press, Piscataway, NJ, pp. 110–114, 2000.
22. R. Kastner, E. Bozorgzadeh, and M. Sarrafzadeh. Pattern routing: Use and theory for increasing predictability and avoiding coupling. *IEEE Transactions on Computer Aided Design of Integrated Circuits and Systems*, 21(7): 777–791, 2002.
23. M. M. Ozdal and M. D. F. Wong. Archer: A history-driven global routing algorithm. In *Proceedings of International Conference on Computer Aided Design*, IEEE Press, Piscataway, NJ, pp. 488–495, 2007.
24. M. Pan and C. Chu. Fastroute: A step to integrate global routing into placement. In *Proceedings of International Conference on Computer Aided Design*, IEEE Press, Piscataway, NJ, pp. 464–471, 2006.
25. J. A. Roy and I. L. Markov. High-performance routing at the nanometer scale. In *Proceedings of International Conference on Computer Aided Design*, IEEE Press, Piscataway, NJ, pp. 496–502, 2007.
26. J. Cong, J. Fang, and K. -Y. Khoo. DUNE: A multi-layer gridless routing system. *IEEE Transactions on Computer-Aided Design of Integrated Circuits and Systems*, 20(5): 633–647, 2001. (ISPD 2000).
27. J. Cong, J. Fang, M. Xie, and Y. Zhang. MARS: A multilevel full-chip gridless routing system. *IEEE Transactions on Computer-Aided Design of Integrated Circuits and Systems*, 24(3): 382–394, 2005. (ICCAD 2002.)

28. J. Cong and P. H. Madden. Performance driven multi-layer general area routing for PCB/MCM designs. In *Proceedings of Design Automation Conference*, ACM, NY, pp. 356–361, 1998.

29. R. Linsker. An iterative-improvement penalty-function-driven wire routing system. *IBM Journal of Research and Development*, 28(5): 613–624, 1984.

30. H. Zhou and M. D. F. Wong. Global routing with crosstalk constraints. In *Proceedings of Design Automation Conference*, ACM, NY, pp. 374–377, 1998.

31. C. Y. Lee. An algorithm for path connection and its applications. *IRE Transactions on Electronic Computers*, EC-10: 346–365, 1961.

32. E. F. Moore. The shortest path through a maze. In *Proceedings of the International Symposium on the Theory of Switching*, pp. 285–292. Harvard University Press, Cambridge, 1959.

33. S. Akers. *Routing*, Vol. 1. Prentice-Hall, Englewood Cliffs, NJ, 1972.

34. S. Akers. A modification of lee's path connection algorithm. *IEEE Transactions on Electronic Computers*, EC-16(2): 97–98, 1967.

35. F. O. Hadlock. A shortest path algorithm for grid graphs. *Networks*, 7(4): 323–334, 1977.

36. P. E. Hart, N. J. Nilsson, and B. Raphael. A formal basis for the heuristic determination of minimum cost paths in graphs. *IEEE Transactions on Systems Science and Cybernetics*, SSC-4(2): 100–107, 1968.

37. J. Soukup. Fast maze router. In *Proceedings of the 15th Design Automation Conference*, IEEE Press, Piscataway, NJ, pp. 100–102, 1978.

38. E. W. Dijkstra. A note on two problems in connection with graphs. *Numerische Mathematik*, 1: 269–271, 1959.

39. K. Mikami and K. Tabuchi. A computer program for optimal routing of printed circuit connectors. In *IFIPS Proceedings*, H47: 1475–1478, 1968.

40. D. W. Hightower. A solution to line-routing problems on the continuous plane. In *Proceedings of the 6th Annual Conference on Design Automation*, ACM, NY, pp. 1–24, 1969.

41. R. F. Hentschke, J. Narasimham, M. O. Johann, and R. L. Reis. Maze routing steiner trees with effective critical sink optimization. In *Proceedings of International Symposium on Physical Design*, ACM, NY, pp. 135–142, 2007.

42. H. Bollinger. A mature DA system for PC layout. In *Proceedings of 1st International Printed Circuit Conference*, IEEE Computer Society Press, Los Alamitos, CA, pp. 85–99, 1979.

43. W. A. Dees and P. G. Karger. Automated rip-up and reroute techniques. In *Proceedings of Design Automation Conference*, IEEE Press, Piscataway, NJ, pp. 432–439, 1982.

44. V. Betz and J. Rose. Directional bias and non-uniformity in FPGA global routing architectures. In *International Conference on Computer Aided Design*, IEEE Computer Society, Washington, DC, pp. 652–659, 1996.

45. V. Betz and J. Rose. VPR: A new packing, placement and routing tool for FPGA research. In *7th International Workshop on Field-Programmable Logic*, pp. 213–222, 1997.

46. C. Ebeling, L. McMurchie, S. A. Hauck, and S. Burns. Placement and routing tools for the triptych FPGA. *IEEE Transactions on VLSI Systems*, IEEE Press, Piscataway, NJ, pp. 473–482, 1995.

47. M. M. Ozdal and M. D. F. Wong. A length-matching routing algorithm for high-performance printed circuit boards. *IEEE Transactions on Computer-Aided Design of Integrated Circuits and Systems (TCAD)*, 25: 2784–2794, 2006. (ICCAD 2003).

48. M. Cho, K. Lu, and D. Z. Pan. Boxrouter 2.0: Architecture and implementation of a hybrid and robust global router. In *Proceedings of International Conference on Computer Aided Design*, Press, Piscataway, NJ, pp. 503–508, 2007.

49. G. -J. Nam. *ISPD 2007 Global Routing Contest*, 2007. Available at: http://www.sigda.org/ispd2007/contest.html

50. E. Shragowitz and S. Keel. A global router based on a multicommodity flow model. *Integration: The VLSI Journal*, 5(1): 3–16, 1987.

51. P. Raghavan and C. D. Thompson. Multiterminal global routing: A deterministic approximation scheme. *Algorithmica*, 6: 73–82, 1991.

24 Minimum Steiner Tree Construction*

Gabriel Robins and Alexander Zelikovsky

CONTENTS

24.1 INTRODUCTION

In optimizing the area of very large scale integrated (VLSI) layouts, circuit interconnections should generally be realized with minimum total interconnect. This chapter addresses several variations of the corresponding fundamental Steiner minimal tree (SMT) problem, where a given set of pins is to be connected using minimum total wirelength. Steiner trees are important in global routing and wirelength estimation [1], as well as in various nonVLSI applications such as phylogenetic tree reconstruction in biology [2], network routing [3], and civil engineering, among many other areas [4–9].

In modern deep-submicron VLSI layout other criteria often dominate the routing objectives, such as pathlengths, skew, density, inductance, manufacturability, electromigration, reliability, noise,

---

* This work was supported by a Packard Foundation Fellowship, by National Science Foundation Young Investigator Award MIP-9457412, by a GSU Research Initiation Grant, by NSF grants CCR-9988331, CCF-0429737, CCF-0429735, and CNS-0716635, and by U.S. Civilian Research and Development Foundation grant MOM2-3049-CS-03.

power, non-Hanan topologies, signal integrity, three-dimensionality, alternate models, and various combinations and trade-offs of these Refs. [10–22]. However, large noncritical nets are still common in modern designs, and this chapter focuses on the corresponding classical objective of wirelength/area minimization (which also minimizes the total capacitance). This exposition is not an exhaustive survey on the Steiner problem, about which hundreds of papers and several entire books were written [2,4–9]. Rather, it focuses on a few selected results and approaches to Steiner tree construction. A broader overview of the field of computer-aided design of VLSI is given by several textbooks on this subject [23–27].

Given a set P of n pins (i.e., terminals of a signal net), we seek to interconnect these points using a minimual total amount of wire. This objective arises in VLSI minimum-area global routing, because VLSI minimum-spacing design rules induce an essentially linear relationship between wirelength and wiring area. When all wires are point-to-point, with no intermediate junctions other than points of P, the optimum solution is a minimum spanning tree (MST) over P, denoted as MST(P). However, we can usually introduce intermediate junctions, called Steiner points, in connecting the points of P. The SMT problem can be formulated as follows.

Steiner minimal tree problem: Given a set P of n points, determine a set S of Steiner points such that the MST cost over $P \cup S$ is minimized.

An optimal solution to this problem is referred to as a SMT (or simply Steiner tree) over P, denoted SMT(P). An edge in a tree T has cost equal to the distance between its endpoints, and the cost of T itself is the sum of its edge costs, denoted cost(T). The wiring cost between a pair of pins (x_1, y_1) and (x_2, y_2) in a VLSI layout is typically modeled by the Manhattan or rectilinear distance:[*]

$$\text{dist}\big[(x_1, y_1), (x_2, y_2)\big] = (\Delta x) + (\Delta y) = |x_1 - x_2| + |y_1 - y_2|$$

We will focus on the rectilinear SMT problem, where every edge is embedded in the plane using a path of one or more alternating horizontal and vertical segments between its endpoints. Figure 24.1 depicts an MST and an SMT for the same pointset in the Manhattan plane. The bounding box of a pointset P denotes the smallest rectangle,[†] which contains all points of P and whose sides are oriented parallel to the coordinate axes. If an edge between two points is embedded with minimum possible wirelength, its routing segments will remain within the bounding box induced by its endpoints.

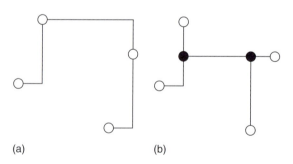

(a)   (b)

FIGURE 24.1   (a) MST and (b) SMT in the rectilinear plane. Hollow dots represent the original pointset P, and solid dots represent Steiner points.

---

[*] More recently, non-Manhattan interconnect architectures such as preferred direction routing and λ-geometries, have been gaining popularity [4,28–36]. However, most of the methods described in this chapter can be generalized to these other geometries and metrics, as well as to higher dimensions.

[†] Bounding boxes in non-Manhattan metrics/geometries have corresponding nonrectangular shapes, induced by the underlying metric/geometry [4].

24.2 HISTORICAL PERSPECTIVES

The Steiner problem is named after the Swiss mathematician Jacob Steiner (1796–1863), who solved and popularized the problem of joining three villages by a system of roads having minimum total length [37] (he also addressed the general case of this problem, and made many fundamental contributions to projective geometry). However, while Jacob Steiner's work on this problem was independent of its predecessors, about two centuries earlier Pierre de Fermat (1601–1665) proposed this problem to Evangelista Torricelli (1608–1647), who solved it and passed it along to his student Vincenzo Viviani (1622–1703), who in turn published his own solution as well as Torricelli's in 1659 [38]. An even earlier (and presumably independent) published discussion of this problem is found in a 1647 book by the Italian mathematician Bonaventura Francesco Cavalieri (1598–1647) [39]. Luckily, today we refer to this problem simply as the Steiner problem, instead of the more accurate but considerably less wieldy title the Fermat–Torricelli–Viviani–Cavalieri–Steiner problem.

More recent research progress on the SMT problem has been historically driven by several main results.

1. In 1966, Hanan [40] showed that for a pointset P there exists an SMT whose Steiner points S are all chosen from the Hanan grid, namely the intersections of all the horizontal and vertical lines passing through every point of P (Figure 24.2). Snyder [41] generalized Hanan's theorem to all higher dimensional Manhattan geometries; on the other hand, extensions of Hanan's theorem to λ-geometries are less straightforward [42].

2. In 1977, Garey and Johnson showed that despite restricting the Steiner points to lie on the Hanan grid, the rectilinear SMT problem is NP-complete [43]. Only a very few special cases have been solved optimally (e.g., a linear-time solution exists when all points of P lie on the boundary of a rectangle [44]). Many heuristics have been proposed for the general problem, as surveyed in Refs. [2,5–8].

3. In 1976, Hwang [45] showed that the MST over P is a good approximation to the SMT, having performance ratio* $\frac{\text{cost}[\text{MST}(P)]}{\text{cost}[\text{SMT}(P)]} \leq \frac{3}{2}$ for any pointset P in the rectilinear plane. In attacking intractable problems, a standard goal is to achieve a provably good heuristic having a constant-factor performance ratio (i.e., asymptotic worst-case error bounded with respect to the optimal solution). In light of the intractability of the rectilinear SMT problem, Hwang's result implies that any Steiner approximation approach that improves upon an initial MST solution will have performance ratio at most $\frac{3}{2}$. Thus, many SMT heuristics in the literature are MST-improvement strategies, i.e., they resemble classic MST constructions (e.g., Refs. [46,47]).

   For over 15 years after the publication of Ref. [45], the fundamental open problem was to find a heuristic with (worst-case) performance ratio strictly less than $\frac{3}{2}$. A complementary

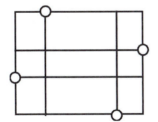 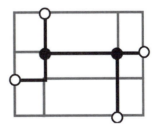

FIGURE 24.2   Hanan's theorem: There exists an SMT with Steiner points chosen from the Hanan grid, i.e., intersection points of all horizontal and vertical lines drawn through the points.

---

* The performance ratio of a heuristic is an upper bound on the heuristic solution cost divided by the optimal solution cost, over all possible problem instances $\left(\text{i.e., the worst-case of } \frac{\text{cost(APPROX)}}{\text{cost(OPT)}}\right)$.

research goal has been to find new practical heuristics with improved average-case solution quality. In practice, most SMT heuristics, including MST-based strategies, exhibited very similar average performance. On uniformly distributed random instances (the typical benchmark), heuristic Steiner tree costs averaged between 7 and 9 percent improvement over the corresponding MST costs [2].

4. In 1990, Kahng and Robins have shown [19,48–50] that any Steiner tree heuristic in a general class of greedy MST-based methods has worst-case performance ratio arbitrarily close to $\frac{3}{2}$, i.e., the MST for certain classes of pointsets is unimprovable. Thus, the $\frac{3}{2}$ bound is tight for a wide range of MST-based strategies in the rectilinear plane [49], which resolved the performance ratios for a number of heuristics in the literature with previously unknown worst-case behavior. Moreover, this established that in general, MST-based Steiner heuristics (e.g., where MST edges are flipped within their bounding boxes) are unlikely to achieve performance ratio better than $\frac{3}{2}$. Analogous constructions in higher d-dimensional Manhattan geometry showed that all of these heuristics have performance ratio of at least $\frac{2d-1}{d}$, which is bounded from above by 2 as the dimension grows [19,49].

5. In 1992, Zelikovsky developed a rectilinear Steiner tree algorithm with a performance ratio of $\frac{11}{8}$ times optimal [51], the first heuristic provably better than the MST. His techniques yield a general graph Steiner tree algorithm with a $\frac{11}{6}$ performance ratio [52], the first graph Steiner approximation proven to beat the MST-based graph Steiner heuristic of Kou et al. [53]. This settled in the affirmative longstanding open question of whether there exists a polynomial-time rectilinear Steiner tree heuristic with performance ratio $<\frac{3}{2}$, and whether there exists a polynomial-time graph Steiner tree heuristic with performance ratio <2.

In light of this sequence of developments, research on Steiner tree approximation has turned away from MST-improvement heuristics. One of the earliest and most effective Steiner tree approximation schemes to break away from the herd of MST-improvement shemes is the iterated 1-Steiner (I1S) approach of Kahng and Robins [19,48,50,54]. The I1S heuristic is simple, easy to implement, generalizes naturally to any dimension and metric (including arbitrary weighted graphs), and significantly outperforms previous approaches, as detailed below. The I1S algorithm was subsequently proven to be the earliest published Steiner approximation method to have a nontrivial performance ratio (of 1.5 times optimal) in quasi-bipartite graphs [55,56].

24.3 ITERATED 1-STEINER APPROACH

This section outlines the I1S heuristic [19,54], which repeatedly finds optimum single Steiner points for inclusion into the pointset. Given two pointsets A and B, we define the MST savings of B with respect to A as

$$\Delta \mathrm{MST}(A, B) = \mathrm{cost}\,[\mathrm{MST}(A)] - \mathrm{cost}\,[\mathrm{MST}(A \cup B)]$$

Let $H(P)$ denote the Steiner candidate set, i.e., the intersection points of all horizontal and vertical lines passing through points of P (as defined by Hanan's theorem [40], see Figure 24.2). For any pointset P, a 1-Steiner point with respect to P is a point $x \in H(P)$ that maximizes $\Delta \mathrm{MST}(P, \{x\}) > 0$. Starting with a pointset P and a set $S = \emptyset$ of Steiner points, the I1S method repeatedly finds a 1-Steiner point x for $P \cup S$ and sets $S \leftarrow S \cup \{x\}$. The cost of $\mathrm{MST}(P \cup S)$ will decrease with each added point, and the construction terminates when there no longer exists any point x with $\Delta \mathrm{MST}(P \cup S, \{x\}) > 0$.

An optimal Steiner tree over n points has at most $n - 2$ Steiner points of degree at least 3 (this follows from simple degree arguments [57]). However, the I1S method can (on rare occasions) add more than $n - 2$ Steiner points. Therefore, at each iteration we eliminate any extraneous Steiner points that have degree ≤ 2 in the MST over $P \cup S$ (because such points cannot contribute to the tree cost savings). Figure 24.3 formally describes the algorithm, and Figure 24.4 illustrates a sample execution.

```
Iterated 1-Steiner (I1S) heuristic
Input: Set P of n points
Output: Rectilinear Steiner tree spanning P
S = ∅
While Candidate _ Set = {x∈H(P∪S)|ΔMST(P∪S,{x}) > 0}≠ ∅ Do
    Find x∈ Candidate_Set which maximizes ΔMST(P∪S,{x})
    S = S∪{x}
    Remove points in S which have degree ≤2 in MST(P∪S)
Output MST(P∪S)
```

FIGURE 24.3 I1S method. (From Kahng, A. B. and Robins, G., *On Optimal Interconnections for VLSI*, Kluwer Academic Publishers, Boston, MA, 1995; Kahng, A. B. and Robins, G., *IEEE Trans. Computer-Aided Design*, 11, 893, 1992; Griffith, J. Robins, G., Salowe, J. S., and Zhang, T., *IEEE Trans. Computer-Aided Design* 13, 1351, 1994.)

To find a 1-Steiner point in the Manhattan plane, it suffices to construct an MST over $|P \cup S| + 1$ points for each of the $O(n^2)$ members of the Steiner candidate set (i.e., Hanan grid points), and then pick a candidate that minimizes the overall MST cost. Each MST computation can be performed in $O(n \log n)$ time [59], yielding an $O(n^3 \log n)$ time method to find a single 1-Steiner point. A more efficient algorithm based on Ref. [60] can find a new 1-Steiner point within $O(n^2)$ time [19]. A linear number of Steiner points can therefore be found in $O(n^3)$ time, and trees with a bounded number of k Steiner points require $O(kn^2)$ time. Because the MSTs between trying one candidate Steiner point and the next change very little (by only a constant number of tree edges), incremental/dynamic MST updating schemes can be employed, resulting in further asymptotic time-complexity improvements [19,58].

In practice, the number of iterations performed by I1S averages less than $\frac{n}{2}$ for uniformly distributed random pointsets [19]. Furthermore, the I1S heuristic is provably optimal for four or less points [19]; this is not a trivial observation, because many earlier heuristics were not optimal even for four points. On the other hand, the worst-case performance ratio of I1S over small pointsets is at least $\frac{7}{6}$ and $\frac{13}{11}$ for five and nine points, respectively [19,54], and is at least 1.3 in general [61]. The

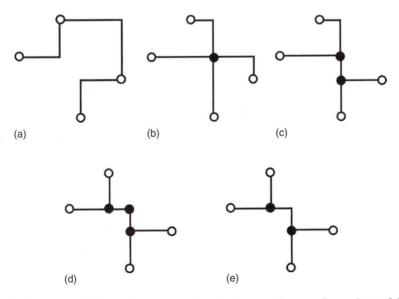

(a)   (b)   (c)

(d)   (e)

FIGURE 24.4 Execution of I1S on a four-pin net. Note that in step (d) a superfluous degree-2 Steiner point forms, and is then eliminated from the topology in step (e).

next subsection discusses a batched variant of the I1S approach, which offers runtime improvements in practice.

24.3.1 BATCHED 1-STEINER VARIANT

Although a single 1-Steiner point may be found in $O(n^2)$ time, the required computational geometry techniques are complicated and not easy to implement. To address these issues, a batched variant of I1S was developed [19,54], which amortizes the computational expense of finding 1-Steiner points by adding as many independent 1-Steiner points as possible in every round.

The batched 1-Steiner (B1S) variant computes $\Delta MST(P, \{x\})$ for each candidate Steiner point $x \in H(P)$ (i.e., the Hanan grid candidate points). Two candidate Steiner points x and y are independent if

$$\Delta MST(P, \{x\}) + \Delta MST(P, \{y\}) \leq \Delta MST(P, \{x, y\})$$

that is, introducing each of the two 1-Steiner points does not reduce the potential gain in MST cost relative of the other 1-Steiner point. Given pointset P and a set of Steiner points S, each round of B1S greedily adds into S a maximal set of independent 1-Steiner points. Termination occurs when a round fails to add any new Steiner points (Figure 24.5). The total time required for each round is $O(n^2 \log n)$.

In three dimensions, I1S exploits a generalization of Hanan's theorem to higher dimensions [41], namely that there always exists an optimal Steiner tree whose Steiner points are selected from the $O(n^3)$ intersections of all axis-orthogonal planes passing through points of P. The three-dimensional analog of Hwang's result suggests that the Steiner ratio, i.e., the maximum $\frac{cost(MST)}{cost(SMT)}$ ratio for three dimensions is at most $\frac{5}{3}$; however, this is only a conjecture and generalizing Hwang's theorem to dimensions three and higher is still an open problem. An example consisting of six points located in the middle of the faces of a rectilinear cube establishes that $\frac{5}{3}$ is a lower bound for the Steiner ratio in three dimensions.

The I1S and B1S algorithms are highly parallelizable because each processor can independently compute the MST savings of different candidate Steiner points. The iterated Steiner approach is therefore very amenable to parallel implementation on grid computers [19,58]. As with I1S, the time complexity and practical runtime of B1S can be further improved using incremental/dynamic MST update techniques [62]. Moreover, by exploiting tighter bounds on the maximum MST degree in the rectilinear metric,[*] further runtime improvements can be obtained [19,58,63].

> **Batched 1-Steiner (B1S) heuristic**
> **Input:** Set P of n points
> **Output:** Rectilinear Steiner tree spanning P
> **While** $T = \{x \in H(P) | \Delta MST(P, \{x\}) > 0\} \neq \emptyset$ **Do**
> $\quad S = \emptyset$
> $\quad$ **For** $x \in \{T$ in order of non-increasing $\Delta MST\}$ **Do**
> $\quad\quad$ **If** $\Delta MST(P \cup S, \{x\}) \geq \Delta MST(P, \{x\})$ **Then** $S = S \cup \{x\}$
> $\quad P = P \cup S$
> $\quad$ **Remove** from P Steiner points with degree ≤ 2 in MST(P)
> **Output** MST(P)

FIGURE 24.5 The B1S algorithm. (From Kahng, A. B. and Robins, G., *On Optimal Interconnections for VLSI*, Kluwer Academic Publishers, Boston, MA, 1995 and Kahng, A. B. and Robins, G., *IEEE Trans. Computer-Aided Design*, 11, 893, 1992.)

---

[*] In Refs. [58,63] it was proven that the maximum rectilinear MST degree in two dimensions does not have to exceed 4, and that the maximum rectilinear MST degree in three dimensions does not have to exceed 14, settling these long-standing open questions.

24.3.2   EMPIRICAL PERFORMANCE OF ITERATED 1-STEINER

In benchmark tests, I1S and B1S compare very favorably with optimal Steiner tree algorithms, such as those of Salowe and Warme [64,65] on random uniformly distributed pointsets (i.e., the standard testbed for Steiner tree heuristics [2]). Both I1S and B1S exhibit very similar average performance in terms of solution quality, approaching 11 percent average improvement over MST cost, which is on average less than half a percent from optimal. Moreover, I1S and B1S produce optimal solutions on 90 percent of all random eight-point instances (and on more than half of all random 15-point instances). For $n = 30$ points, I1S and B1S are on average only about 0.3 percent away from optimal, and yield optimal solutions in about one quarter of the cases [19,58]. I1S and B1S also perform similarly well in three dimensions and in other L_k norms [19,58].

Empirical experiments also indicate that the number of rounds required by B1S grows very slowly (i.e., apparently logarithmically) with the number of points [19,58]. For example, on sets of 300 points the average number of B1S rounds is only 2.5, and was never observed to be more than 5 on any instance. As expected, over 95 percent of the total tree-cost improvement occurs in the first B1S round, and over 99 percent of the total improvement occurs in the first two rounds [19,58]. The average number of Steiner points generated by B1S grows linearly with the number of points (and is typically less than half the number of input points) [19,58]. An example of the output of B1S on a random set of 300 points is shown in Figure 24.6.

Experimental data also indicates that only a small fraction of the Hanan candidates yield positive MST savings in a given B1S round, and that such positive-gain candidates are more likely to produce positive MST savings in subsequent rounds [19,54]. Therefore, rather than examining the

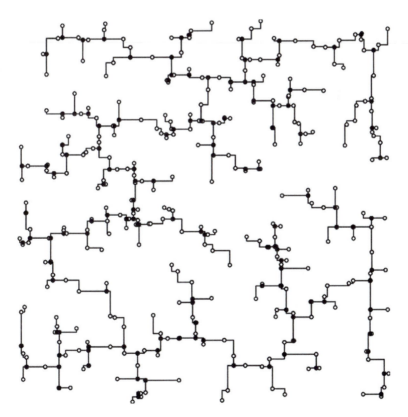

FIGURE 24.6   Example of the output of B1S on a random set of 300 points (hollow dots). The Steiner points produced by B1S are denoted by solid dots.

MST savings of all Hanan candidates in a given round, subsequent rounds may consider only the candidates that produced positive savings in the previous round. In practice, this strategy significantly contributes to reduction in the time spent during each round, without affecting the solution quality.

24.3.3 Generalization of I1S to Steiner Arborescences

The I1S algorithmic template also generalizes to produce Steiner arborescences, i.e., shortest path trees with minimum wirelength, which are known to yield high-performance critical net routings [15]. The iterated dominance (IDOM) graph arborescence heuristic of Ref. [66] recapitulates the I1S strategy, by greedily iterating over a given spanning arborescence construction. To construct a Steiner arborescence, the IDOM heuristic repeatedly finds Steiner candidates that reduce the overall spanning arborescence cost by the greatest amount, and includes them into the growing set of Steiner nodes. The reason that a spanning arborescence criterion is used to drive the Steiner arborescence construction is that the former is easy to compute [66], while the latter is NP-complete [67]. Arborescence constructions are described in greater detail in Chapter 25.

24.4 STEINER TREES IN GRAPHS

A more general version of the Steiner problem arises when interpoint distances can be arbitrary, rather than induced by an underlying metric or a particular geometry. This topological, or graph-based version of the Steiner problem, occurs in practice when we wish to route a signal net in the presence of obstacles, congestion, or variable-cost routing resources, such as in field-programmable gate arrays [66]. More formally, given an arbitrary weighted graph with a distinguished vertex subset, the graph Steiner tree problem seeks a minimum-cost subtree spanning the distinguished vertices.

Graph Steiner minimal tree (GSMT) problem: Given a weighted graph $G = (V, E)$, and a distinguished set of nodes $N \subseteq V$, find a minimum-cost spanning tree $T = (V', E')$ with $N \subseteq V' \subseteq V$ and $E' \subseteq E$.

In particular, any node in $V - N$ can serve as a potential Steiner point. As usual, each graph edge $e_{ij} \in E$ has a real-valued weight w_{ij}, and the cost of a tree (or any subgraph) is the sum of the weights of its edges. The GSMT problem is NP-complete, even in the Euclidean or rectilinear metrics [43], because the geometric SMT problems are special cases of the general graph SMT problem. The method of Kou, Markowsky, and Berman (KMB) [53] was the first provably-good heuristic to solve the GSMT problem in polynomial time with approximation ratio of twice the optimal.

24.4.1 Graph Generalization of Iterated 1-Steiner

The I1S approach generalizes to solve the Steiner problem in arbitrary weighted graphs, by combining the geometric I1S heuristic with the KMB [53] graph Steiner algorithm [19,66]. The resulting hybrid method inherits the good average-case performance of the I1S method, while also enjoying the error-bounded performance of the KMB algorithm. We refer to this hybrid method as the graph iterated 1-Steiner (GI1S) algorithm. The GI1S method is essentially an adaptation of I1S to graphs, where the MST in the inner loop is replaced with the KMB construction. That is, instead of using an MST subroutine to determine the savings of a candidate Steiner point/node, we use the KMB (or any other) approximation algorithm for this purpose. Thus, given a graph $G = (V, E)$, a set $N \subseteq V$, and a set S of potential Steiner points, we define the following:

$$\Delta\text{KMB}(N, S) = \text{cost}[\text{KMB}(N)] - \text{cost}[\text{KMB}(N \cup S)]$$

Thus, the GI1S template (Figure 24.7) repeatedly finds Steiner node candidates that reduce the overall KMB cost and includes them into the growing set of Steiner nodes S. The cost of the KMB tree over $N \cup S$ will decrease with each added Steiner node, and the construction terminates when there is no $x \in V$ with $\Delta\text{KMB}(N \cup S, \{x\}) > 0$.

```
Graph iterated 1-Steiner (GI1S) heuristic
Input: Weighted graph G = (V, E) and a set N ⊆ V
Output: Low-cost tree T' = (V', E') spanning N (i.e., N ⊆ V' ⊆ V and E' ⊆ E)
S = ∅
While T = {x ∈ V−N | ΔKMB(N ∪ S, {x}) > 0} ≠ ∅ Do
    Find x ∈ T with maximum ΔKMB(N ∪ S, {x})
    S = S ∪ {x}
Return KMB(N ∪ S)
```

FIGURE 24.7 GI1S algorithm. (From Kahng, A. B. and Robins, G., *On Optimal Interconnections for VLSI*, Kluwer Academic Publishers, Boston, MA, 1995 and Alexander, M. J. and Robins, G., *IEEE Trans. Computer-Aided Design*, 15, 1505, 1996.)

The approximation ratio for GI1S is $2 \cdot \left(1 - \frac{1}{L}\right) \leq 2$ times optimal, where L is the number of leaves in the resulting tree. This follows from the KMB bound and from the fact that the cost of the GI1S construction cannot exceed that of the KMB construction [19,66]. If $|N| \leq 3$ (e.g., a VLSI signal net with three or fewer terminals—a very common occurrence in VLSI layouts), GI1S is guaranteed to find an optimal solution. Although the worst-case performance ratio of GI1S is the same as that of KMB, in practice GI1S significantly outperforms KMB in terms of solution quality [66]. Given a faster implementation of the KMB method [68], the GI1S algorithm can be implemented within time $O(|N| \cdot |G| + |N|^4 \log |N|)$, where $|N| \leq |V|$ is the number of nodes to be spanned and $|G| = |V| + |E|$ is the size of the graph. Moreover, like with I1S, the GI1S approach can be batched, and incremental/dynamic MST computations [62] can be exploited, resulting in further runtime improvements.

Note that the GI1S template above can be viewed as an iterated KMB (IKMB) construction, and that KMB inside the inner loop may be replaced with any other graph Steiner approximation heuristic, such as that of Zelikovsky (ZEL) [52], yielding an iterated Zelikovsky (IZEL) heuristic. IZEL has the same theoretical performance bound as ZEL, namely $\frac{11}{6}$, but provides improved solutions in practice. Experiments have shown that these heuristics of increasing average solution quality are KMB < ZEL < IKMB < IZEL [66]. In general, iterating a given Steiner approximation heuristic greedily is an effective general mechanism to improve empirical performance without sacrificing the theoretical performance bounds.

24.4.2 Loss-Contracting Approach

For arbitrary weighted graphs, the best Steiner approximation ratio achievable within polynomial time was steadily improved from 2 down to 1.5493 in a series of papers [52,53,55,69–73]. On the negative side, it is known that unless $P = NP$, the Steiner tree problem in general graphs cannot be approximated within a factor of $1 + \epsilon$ for sufficiently small $\epsilon > 0$ [74]. More recently, an improved nonapproximability lower bound of $\frac{96}{95}$ for the graph Steiner problem was proved in Ref. [75].

The graph Steiner tree heuristic with the best-known performance ratio, approaching $1 + \frac{\ln 3}{2} \approx 1.5493$, was given by Robins and Zelikovsky [55,56]. This approach, called the loss-contracting algorithm (LCA), proceeds by adding full components to a growing solution, based on their relative cost savings. A full component is a Steiner tree over a terminal subset in which all of the terminals are leaves (Figure 24.8a). Any Steiner tree can be decomposed into full components by splitting all the nonleaf terminals (we assume that any full component has its own copy of each Steiner point, so that full components chosen by the algorithm do not share Steiner points). A Steiner tree that does not contain any Steiner points (i.e., where each full component consists of a single edge) is called a terminal-spanning tree. The LCA algorithm computes relative cost savings with respect to a shrinking terminal-spanning tree.

All previous graph Steiner heuristics (except Ref. [70]) with provably good approximation ratios repeatedly choose appropriate full components and then contract them to form the overall solution.

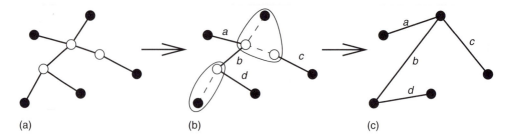

FIGURE 24.8 LCA idea: (a) full component K, where filled circles denote terminals and hollow circles denote Steiner points; (b) connected components of Loss(K) to be collapsed, with dashed edges belong to Loss(K); and (c) the corresponding terminal-spanning tree with the contracted Loss(K).

However, this strategy does not allow the discarding of an already-accepted full component, even if it turns out later that a better full component conflicts with a previously accepted component (two components conflict if they share at least two terminals).

The intuition behind the LCA method is to contract as little as possible so that a chosen full component may still participate in the overall solution, but not many other full components would be rejected. The LCA approach iteratively modifies a terminal-spanning tree T, which is initially MST(G_S), by incorporating into T loss-contracted full components greedily chosen from G. Each such component has positive gain, and therefore contains at least three terminals and has nonzero loss (see Refs. [55,56] for more details).

The loss-contracting approach also solves the Steiner tree problem in quasi-bipartite graphs (i.e., where no two nonterminals are adjacent), achieving an approximation ratio of ≈ 1.28 times optimal within time $O(mn^2)$, where m and n are the numbers of terminals and nonterminals in the graph, respectively. This improves a previous primal-dual algorithm for Steiner trees in quasi-bipartite graphs [76] whose bound exceeds 1.5 times optimal.

Similar techniques were also used to show that the graph version of the I1S heuristic described above [19,49] achieves an approximation ratio of 1.5 in quasi-bipartite graphs [55,56]. Along similar lines, the approximation ratio achievable for the Steiner tree problem in complete graphs with edge weights 1 and 2 was recently improved from the best previously known bound of $\frac{4}{3}$ times optimal [74] to less than 1.28 times optimal [55,56].

24.5 GROUP STEINER TREES

Most papers on VLSI routing assume either implicitly or explicitly that each terminal consists of a single port. However, in actual layouts (e.g., in a gridded routing regime), a terminal to which a wire is to be routed can consist of a large collection of distinct, electrically equivalent ports [77–79]. Even though a wire may connect to any one of these ports, this degree of freedom is often not fully exploited in routing or in wiring estimation. This section addresses the general problem of minimum-cost Steiner tree construction in the presence of multiport terminals, where rather than spanning a set of nodes, the objective is to connect groups of nodes. This is also known as the group Steiner problem (Figure 24.9), formulated as follows.

Group Steiner problem [2,80]: Given a weighted graph $G = (V, E)$ and a family $N = \{N_1, \ldots, N_k\}$ of k disjoint groups of nodes $N_i \subseteq V$, find a minimum-cost spanning tree in G containing at least one node from each group N_i.

As in the classical Steiner problem, we are allowed to include optional Steiner nodes to reduce the cost of the tree interconnecting the groups of N. The problem of interconnecting a net with multiport terminals is a direct generalization of the NP-complete Steiner problem (i.e., in the classical Steiner problem each terminal contains exactly one port), and is therefore itself NP-complete.

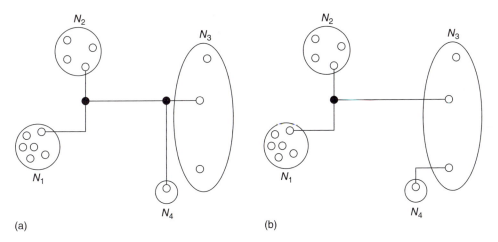

(a)   (b)

FIGURE 24.9 (a) Solution to the same group Steiner problem instance under the weak-connectivity assumption and (b) a feasible solution for the strong-connectivity version of the group Steiner problem. Ovals represent multiport terminals (i.e., groups), hollow dots represent ports within a terminal, and solid dots represent Steiner nodes.

One version of the group Steiner problem, known as the strong-connectivity version, allows multiple connections to attach to different nodes in the same group (i.e., all the nodes of a group are implicitly connected to each other, which allows the solution to the group Steiner problem to be a forest—see Figure 24.9b). The version of the group Steiner problem described below involves weak connectivity: the solution must be strictly a tree, and intragroup edges must be represented explicitly in the solution (see Figure 24.9a).

24.5.1 APPLICATIONS OF GROUP STEINER TREES

The group Steiner problem models several practical scenarios in VLSI layout design [78]:

- Rotating and flipping a module can induce multiple locations for the given port, even in single-port-per-terminal instances. For a general module, there are up to eight possible orientations [80] (Figure 24.10a), and a given terminal can induce a group of up to eight nodes in the group Steiner problem (Figure 24.10b). The weak-connectivity model applies here, because the use of virtual ports is mutually exclusive.

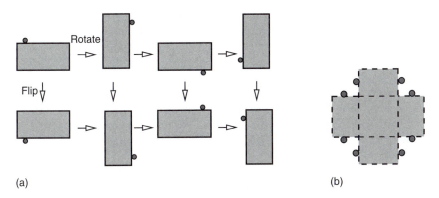

(a)   (b)

FIGURE 24.10 (a) Module is rotated and flipped to induce a group of eight terminal positions, as shown in (b).

- Complicated terminal geometry can easily have many ports located on multiple fabrication layers in grid-based maze routing regimes. These ports form a group in a strong-connectivity version of the group Steiner problem, because the ports are electrically equivalent, and a routing tree may connect to multiple ports of a given terminal.
- Pin assignment problem [81] seeks to optimally determine pin locations on module boundaries. This can be modeled by the weak-connectivity version of the group Steiner problem, where exactly one pin is assigned to each module [78].
- Multiple ports on a block boundary may be connected inside the block and thus be electrically equivalent. These sets of ports form groups in the weak-connectivity group Steiner problem.
- Instances of the group Steiner problem can also occur in hierarchical design methodologies, where some global nets are partially prerouted. Here, each connected component of a partially routed net can be modeled as a multiport terminal in a *weak-connectivity* version of the group Steiner problem.

Despite these numerous applications, surprisingly few routing papers address or exploit the freedom to connect to any of multiple port locations. The first provably good approximation algorithms for the weak-group Steiner problem produced solutions $k - 1$ times worse than optimal, where k is the number of groups [82]. In contrast, the strong-connectivity version, though also NP-hard, is somewhat more tractable than the weak-connectivity version: by converting an instance of the strong-connectivity version into an instance of the graph Steiner problem, then setting to zero the weight of every intragroup edge, we can efficiently solve the strong-group Steiner problem to within a factor of 2 times optimal or better, using any of the existing graph Steiner tree algorithms such as Refs. [52,53,56,83].

The following section describes a group Steiner heuristic with an improved sublinear approximation ratio of $2 \cdot (2 + \ln \frac{k}{2}) \cdot \sqrt{k}$ times optimal, where k is the number of groups [77,78]. This algorithm is general and applies to arbitrarily weighted graphs. On the negative side, it is also known that the group Steiner problem is NP-hard to approximate to a sublogarithmic performance bound [77–79,84].

24.5.2 Depth-Bounded Group Steiner Tree Approach

The group Steiner algorithm relies on depth-bounded* trees. The motivation for using depth-bounded trees is twofold: (1) optimal depth-2-bounded trees can be used to approximate optimal group Steiner trees to within a factor of $2 \cdot \sqrt{k}$, and (2) optimal depth-2-bounded trees in turn can be approximated efficiently, as discussed below. The overall Depth-Bounded Star (DBS) group Steiner algorithm [78,79] composes these two approximations, and therefore enjoys a performance bound that is the product of the two corresponding bounds.

A given graph G may in general violate the triangle inequality, i.e., there may be edges (u, v) in G whose cost is greater than the cost of the minimum u–v path in G. An optimal group Steiner tree contains no such edges, because replacing such an edge with the corresponding shortest path will decrease the total tree cost, a contradiction to minimality. Therefore, without loss of generality, we replace G by its metric closure, defined as a complete graph where the cost of each edge (u, v) is equal to the cost of the minimum u–v path in G.

Let a d-star be a rooted tree of depth of at most d (Figure 24.11a and b). It can be shown that for any arbitrary rooted tree T, there exists a low-cost 2-star spanning the leaves of T. This will imply that an optimal group Steiner tree can be approximated by a low-cost group Steiner 2-star (defined as a 2-star that spans all of the groups), which is exactly how the DBS group Steiner algorithm operates (Figures 24.12 and 24.13).

The overall strategy in deriving a performance bound for the DBS group Steiner algorithm is based on bounding the total cost of 2-stars. Analyzing the edge reuse with respect to an appropriately

---

* The depth of a rooted tree is defined as the maximum number of edges in any root-to-leaf path.

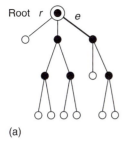
(a)

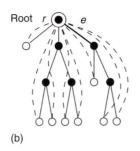
(b)

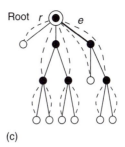
(c)

FIGURE 24.11 DBS group Steiner algorithm: (a) tree T rooted at r may have an arbitrary depth; (b) 1-star and (c) 2-star are represented by dashed lines, which connect the root r to all leaves. To derive the performance bound of the DBS algorithm we sum the edge reuse; e.g., here the edge e is reused three times by edges of the 1-star in (b) and twice by edges of the 2-star in (c).

selected set of intermediate nodes yields an upper bound of $2 \cdot \sqrt{k}$ times optimal on the cost of 2-stars, where k is the number of groups (similarly, the cost of an optimal Steiner 1-star is at most $\frac{k}{2}$ times optimal) [77,78]. However, while an optimal Steiner 2-star is a reasonable approximation of an optimal group Steiner tree, it is known that the problem of even approximating an optimal Steiner d-star is as difficult as approximating a minimum set cover. In particular, unless NP $\subseteq$ DTIME[$n^{\log \log n}$], a depth-2 group Steiner tree cannot be approximated to a factor of better than $[1 - o(1)]$. ln k times optimal, where k is the number of groups [84].

Nevertheless, it is possible to approximate a Steiner 2-star within a factor of $2 + \ln \frac{k}{2} \approx 1.307 +$ ln k times optimal [77–79]. Therefore, the overall performance bound for the DBS group Steiner heuristic will be the product of these two factors, namely the approximation bound of 2-stars with respect to optimal, times the bound with which 2-stars can themselves be approximated. The DBS group Steiner heuristic (Figures 24.12 and 24.13) therefore solves the group Steiner minimal tree problem with performance ratio $2 \cdot (2 + \ln \frac{k}{2}) \cdot \sqrt{k}$, where k is the number of groups.

24.5.3 TIME COMPLEXITY OF THE DBS GROUP STEINER ALGORITHM

The time complexity of computing minimum-norm partial stars (a subroutine in the DBS algorithm) is $O(|V| \cdot k \cdot \log k)$, where k is the number of groups. Approximating rooted 2-stars requires $O(|V| \cdot k^2 \cdot \log k)$ time. The total runtime of the overall DBS group Steiner heuristic (Figures 24.12 and 24.13) is therefore $O(\tau + |V|^2 \cdot k^2 \cdot \log k)$, where k is the number of groups, and τ is the time complexity of computing all-pairs graph shortest paths.

```
Depth-bounded star (DBS) group Steiner algorithm
Input: Weighted graph G = (V, E), a family N
       of k disjoint groups N₁,...,Nₖ ⊆ V
Output: A low-cost tree Approx spanning
        at least one vertex from each group Nᵢ
For each node r ∈ V do
    Find a low-Cost 2-star Approx₂(r) rooted at r
        intersecting each group Nᵢ, i = 1,...,k
    Output the least-cost 2-star Approx,
        i.e., cost(Approx) = min_{rev} cost(Approx₂(r))
```

FIGURE 24.12 DBS approximation algorithm for the group Steiner problem on arbitrary weighted graphs produces a low-cost Steiner 2-star. (From Bateman, C. D., Helvig, C. S., Robins, G., and Zelikovasky, A., Proceedings of the International Symposium on Physical Design, pp. 96–102, Napa Valley, CA, 1997 and Helvig, C. S., Robins, G. and Zelikovsky, A., *Networks*, 37, 8, 2001.)

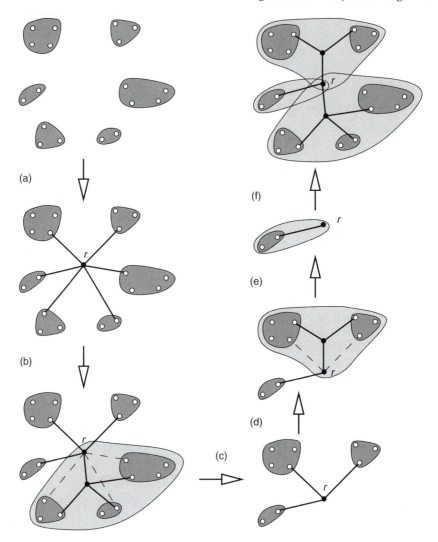

FIGURE 24.13 Given an instance of the group Steiner problem, for each possible root r, the DBS heuristic: (a) finds the optimal 1-star, (b) finds the minimum-norm partial star (shaded region), (c) stores this star in the solution and removes its groups from future consideration, (d) finds the next minimum-norm partial star (shaded region), (e) repeats step (c) for the new partial star, and finally (f) finds the last minimum-norm partial star and outputs the union of all stored partial stars.

A practical enhancement to the runtime of the DBS algorithm entails computing a group MST instead of a group SMT (i.e., computing a MST for a set of nodes containing exactly one port from each group). It can be shown that the optimal group MST is at most twice as long as the optimal group SMT. Thus, in approximating the group SMT by a group MST, only a factor of 2 is lost, which does not asymptotically increase the overall solution quality bound of $2 \cdot (2 + \ln \frac{k}{2}) \cdot \sqrt{k}$ times optimal, yet yields substantial savings in runtime.

24.5.4 DEGENERATE GROUP STEINER INSTANCES

While solving the group Steiner problem, optimizing degenerate groups (i.e., groups of size 1) as a special case can yield substantial improvements in solution quality as well as in runtime. The degenerate groups by themselves induce an instance of the classic Steiner problem, and such an

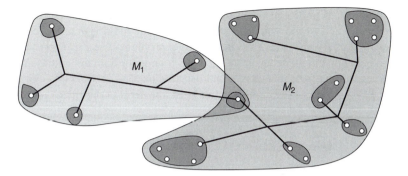

FIGURE 24.14   Group degeneracy can be exploited in solving the group Steiner problem. The set of degenerate groups (M_1) is spanned with a classical approximate Steiner tree (left). Then, all the nondegenerate groups (M_2) are spanned, together with an arbitrary degenerate group, using a group Steiner tree algorithm such as DBS (right). The combination of these two resulting trees spans the original instance of the group Steiner quite effectively, with an overall performance ratio equal to the sum of the two individual bounds.

instance can be approximated efficiently with a constant performance ratio. Thus, to solve the SMT problem for degenerate groups, we may choose a provably good heuristic from among the numerous existing ones [19,52–56,58,85]. For example, in time $O(|V|^3)$ we may find a Steiner tree that is at most $\frac{11}{6}$ times optimal [83]. All that remains now is connecting the SMT over the degenerate groups with a tree spanning the other, nondegenerate groups, without degrading the overall performance ratio.

To achieve this goal, we partition the set of all groups $N = M_1 \cup M_2$ into two subsets: the degenerate groups containing one terminal (M_1) and the nondegenerate groups containing two or more terminals (M_2). The combined DBS group Steiner heuristic is modified to work as follows: first, it computes the usual Steiner tree Approx_1 for the terminals M_1 using the algorithm from say Ref. [83]. Next, using the group Steiner heuristic (Figure 24.12), it finds the group Steiner tree Approx_2 for the family of groups that includes all of M_2 as well as a single arbitrary degenerate group from M_1. Finally, it outputs a minimum spanning tree over the union $\text{Approx}_1 \cup \text{Approx}_2$ (Figure 24.14).

If the number of degenerate groups is large, then the combined group Steiner heuristic will enjoy considerable runtime savings as compared to the basic DBS group Steiner heuristic (of Figures 24.12 and 24.13). Moreover, the heuristic also enjoys an improved overall performance bound of at most

$$\frac{11}{6} + 2 \cdot \left(2 + \ln \frac{|M_2| + 1}{2} \right) \cdot \sqrt{|M_2| + 1}$$

where M_2 is the set of degenerate groups of size 2 or more. In particular, if the number of nondegenerate groups is bounded by a constant independently of the total number of nodes in the graph (i.e., $|M_2| = O(1)$), then the above hybrid DBS algorithm will solve such instances of the group Steiner problem within a constant factor of optimal.

24.5.5   BOUNDED-RADIUS GROUP STEINER TREES

The objective of delay minimization can induce wiring geometries that are substantially different from those dictated by an optimal-area objective, particularly in deep submicron regimes. This has motivated a number of bounded-radius* routing constructions [19,86,87]. The basic group Steiner tree approach can be easily extended to a bounded-radius construction, thereby yielding routing trees with source-to-sink pathlengths bounded by a user-specified parameter.

---

* The radius of a graph is defined as the maximum pathlength of any shortest source–sink path. Note that 2-stars implicitly have a radius bound of $2 \cdot \text{OPT}$, although an MST postprocessing step does not preserve this bound.

For example, the tree produced by the DBS group Steiner algorithm above (Figures 24.12 and 24.13) can be utilized as the starting point in the bounded-radius bounded-cost construction of Ref. [87]. For an arbitrary instance of the group Steiner problem (with k groups), this combination yields a routing tree with simultaneous provably good bounds for both tree radius and tree cost. In particular, the tree resulting from this merger will have radius $(1 + \epsilon)$ times the optimal radius, and total cost $(1+\frac{2}{\epsilon}) \cdot 2 \cdot (2+\ln\frac{k}{2}) \cdot \sqrt{k}$ times the optimal cost, for any user-specified radius-cost trade-off parameter $\epsilon > 0$.

24.5.6 EMPIRICAL PERFORMANCE OF THE GROUP STEINER HEURISTIC

The group Steiner heuristic above compares favorably with the RW heuristic proposed by Reich and Widmayer [80]. The RW group Steiner heuristic begins by first finding the MST T for the entire set of nodes of all the groups. If a leaf node is not the last member of its group in the tree T, then it may be removed. The RW heuristic then repeatedly deletes such a leaf node that is incident to the longest edge among all such nodes. On random uniformly distributed pointsets with varying predetermined group areas, the DBS group Steiner algorithm described above significantly outperforms the RW algorithm, especially as the group sizes and the group areas increase [78,79].

24.6 OTHER STEINER TREE METHODS

Once it became known [48,49] that MST-improvement-based Steiner heuristics having worst-case performance bounds no better than the MST itself (i.e., $\frac{3}{2}$ in the rectilinear plane), other rectilinear Steiner heuristics with average performance approaching that of I1S were subsequently proposed [88–94]. While it is generally difficult to analytically quantify the solution quality of heuristics, the I1S method was later proven to be the earliest Steiner approximation with a nontrivial performance ratio in quasi-bipartite graphs [55,56].

In 2003, Kahng et al. developed a highly scalable heuristic for computing near-optimal Steiner trees, based on the B1S approach [95]. This batched greedy algorithm (BGA) achieves its speed by combining greedy triple contraction [52,95] with a new linear size data structure for finding bottleneck edges [97]. The BGA can route in graph-based uniform orientation geometries, in the presence of obstacles, and under varying via costs, requiring only $O(n)$ space and $O(n \log^2 n)$ time for n terminals. BGA can route noncritical nets with thousands of terminals within seconds of CPU time while maintaining high-solution quality (i.e., on par with that of B1S, about 11 percent improvement over MST cost for random instances). More recently, Ref. [98] developed an $O(n \log n)$-time octilinear Steiner tree heuristic based on spanning graphs, with performance and runtime similar to that of BGA.

On another front, exact Steiner tree algorithms have also evolved rapidly in recent years [32,65], enabling exact solutions of large instances (up to several thousand points) within reasonable runtimes. However, the faster exact methods typically work only in two-dimensional geometric versions of the Steiner problem, where the underlying geometry can be carefully analyzed and heavily exploited to reduce the size of the search space. Nevertheless, exact Steiner algorithms for the rectilinear plane have been optimized to the point of actually becoming practical for use on small pointsets in commercial applications.

24.7 IMPROVING THE THEORETICAL BOUNDS

Berman and Ramaiyer [70] and Zelikovsky et al. [51,61,96] have developed several SMT heuristics similar to I1S, with approximation ratios substantially less than $\frac{3}{2}$. These methods were derived from the pioneering technique developed by Zelikovsky for the Steiner problem in graphs [52]. In particular, an algorithm with an approximation ratio of $\frac{11}{8}$ in the rectilinear plane was given in Ref. [51]. These series of results have settled in the affirmative the longstanding open question of whether there exists a polynomial-time rectilinear Steiner heuristic with approximation ratio better than $\frac{3}{2}$.

Subsequent work by Fößmeier et al. [96] has improved on the $O(n^{3.5})$ time complexity and $\frac{11}{8}$ approximation bound of Ref. [51], with an $O(n^{1.5})$ implementation, where only a linear number of triples needs to be considered. The authors of Ref. [61] have shown that Zelikovsky's algorithm has performance ratio between 1.3 and 1.3125, and that Berman and Ramaiyer's algorithm has performance ratio at most 1.271; the latter algorithm can also be implemented to run in $O(n \log^2 n)$ time. A subsequent algorithm achieved a rectilinear performance ratio of 1.267 time optimal within $O(n \log^2 n)$ time [72].

In a 1996 landmark result, Arora has established that Euclidean and rectilinear minimum-cost Steiner trees can be approximated arbitrarily close to optimal within polynomial time [99], settling the longstanding open question whether this is indeed possible. Arora's methods also yield polynomial-time approximation schemes arbitrarily close to optimal for other combinatorial optimization problems, such as the Euclidean traveling salesman problem. Arora's techniques were also used to achieve a polynomial-time approximation scheme for the rectilinear arborescence problem, with a performance bound arbitrarily close to optimal [100].

The performance bound of the group Steiner algorithm described above [78] was significantly improved in Ref. [79]. This was achieved by using d-stars rather than 2-stars, which improves the $\sqrt{k}$ factors in all the bounds of Section 24.5 to $d \cdot \sqrt[d]{k}$. Thus, the performance ratio of the DBS group Steiner algorithm (Figures 24.12 and 24.13) improved to $O(k^\epsilon)$ for arbitrarily small $\epsilon > 0$. In particular, a group Steiner tree with cost at most $2d \cdot [2 + \ln(2k)]^{d-1} \cdot \sqrt[d]{k}$ time optimal is computed by this more general d-star-based group Steiner algorithm within $O[\tau + (|V| \cdot k)^d]$ time, where τ is the time complexity of computing all-pairs shortest paths [79], k is the number of groups, and d is a user-selectable parameter that trades-off runtime against solution quality. A group Steiner heuristic with a polylogarithmic performance bound was more recently given in Ref. [101].

24.8   STEINER TREE HEURISTICS IN PRACTICE

While Steiner heuristics such as the I1S approach [19,58] yield highly accurate (i.e., near-optimal) solutions, industrial CAD applications sometime demand high runtime speed over solution quality. This is especially true, e.g., inside the inner loop of modern placement tools, where fast wirelength estimators are repeatedly invoked during the construction of timing-driven placements. In such scenarios therefore, more accurate heuristics (e.g., the I1S approach) may be useful when the number of pins in a net is small (say, less than ten). On the other hand, when the number of pins grows into dozens or hundreds, more efficient heuristics such as those of Ref. [11] or [89] are more likely to deliver faster execution speeds. This motivated the recent development of progressively faster wirelength estimators such as the FLUTE algorithm of Ref. [102], whose speed derives from precomputed table lookup. However, faster execution speeds typically come at a price, such as degraded solution quality, limitations on net sizes, restriction to specific metrics, etc. Careful empirical testing can determine which Steiner heuristics best suit a particular practical scenario and design regime.

24.9   FUTURE DIRECTIONS FOR THE STEINER PROBLEM

Chief among future research directions for the Steiner problem is finding general graph Steiner heuristics with improved performance bounds, i.e., smaller than the currently best-known bound of $1 + \frac{\ln 3}{2} \approx 1.5493$ times optimal of the loss-contracting algorithm (LCA) [55,56]. Steady improvements in this upper bound over the last 25 years progressed at an average rate of about 2 percent per year. Other special cases of the Steiner problem for special metrics, specific cost functions, and particular graph types may be explored separately, where it may be possible to exploit the underlying geometry to further improve the performance bounds.

Interestingly, the LCA algorithm is the first (and so far only) heuristic that works provably well for all of the special graph types discussed above. It would also be of interest to find a minimum α, such that for any $\beta > \alpha$, there exists polynomial-time β-approximation of the general graph Steiner problem, as well as to improve the nonapproximability lower bounds, the best of which is currently $\frac{96}{95}$ for general weighted graphs [75]. Group Steiner heuristics with improved approximation ratio are also of significant interest.

It would be interesting to generalize Hwang's theorem to higher rectilinear dimensions [6]. It is known that Hwang's ratio in any rectilinear dimension d is bounded from below by $2 - \frac{1}{d}$ [49], and is also bounded from above by 2 for arbitrary metrics (including all rectilinear d dimensions). This leaves an open gap of size $\frac{1}{d}$ for Hwang's spanning-to-Steiner ratio in rectilinear d dimensions. Generalizing Hanan's theorem to λ-geometries seems to be more difficult than for the rectilinear metric [42]. Moreover, relatively little is known regarding generalizations of Hwang's theorem to arbitrary λ-geometries (one unusual result along these lines is that the Steiner ratio in λ-geometries is not monotonic in the parameter λ [6]). More research is also needed to tighten both the upper and lower bounds for minimum-cost arborescences in graphs. Similarly, almost nothing is known about arborescences in three-dimensional rectilinear space (or in any higher dimensions or alternative geometries).

From a practical perspective, for any given fixed performance bound it would be useful to minimize the running times of the associated heuristics, and to quantify and explore various trade-offs between runtimes and solution quality. That a heuristic has a provably good performance bound does not automatically imply that its solutions are necessarily superior to those of a heuristic with a worse (or no) bound (because in practice, actual solutions of the various heuristics are rarely as bad as the theoretical bound would suggest; in fact, solutions produced by most reasonable Steiner heuristics are on average within a few percent of optimal for most random instances). Thus, it would be very useful to undertake research that would bring theory into closer alignment with practice.

Along similar lines, additional research is needed to implement various heuristics (e.g., Arora's algorithm [99]) and benchmark their practical runtime and empirical solution quality. The fast-Steiner code for the BGA scalable implementation of the provably good heuristic of Ref. [61] is freely available from the authors of Refs. [95,97]; it would be interesting to see how future heuristics fare against this method. Various Steiner heuristics should be compared side-by-side on numerous realistic classes and sizes of inputs, including benchmarking on actual commercial VLSI designs, whenever possible. Creating more realistic and robust standard benchmarks for testing the various kinds of Steiner heuristics would also be highly beneficial.

Finally, modern VLSI layout seeks to optimize not only wirelength, but must also take into consideration many other technological issues and criteria, such as timing, skew, density, manufacturability, yield, reliability, power, noise, and various combinations of these. While recent routing formulations strive to achieve some of these objectives [11–13,15,17–20], much interesting research remains to be done in these areas.

REFERENCES

1. A. Caldwell, A. B. Kahng, S. Mantik, I. Markov, and A. Zelikovsky. On wirelength estimations for row-based placement. In *Proceedings of the International Symposium on Physical Design*, pp. 4–11, Monterey, CA, April 1998.
2. F. K. Hwang, D. S. Richards, and P. Winter. *The Steiner Tree Problem*. Annals of Discrete Mathematics, Vol. 53, North-Holland, The Netherlands, 1992.
3. B. Korte, H. J. Promel, and A. Steger. *Steiner Trees in VLSI-Layouts, in Paths, Flows and VLSI-Layout*. Springer-Verlag, New York, 1990.
4. X. Cheng and D. -Z. Du. *Steiner Trees in Industry*. Kluwer Academic Publishers, Dordrecht, The Netherlands, 2001.
5. D. Cieslik. *Steiner Minimal Trees*. Kluwer Academic Publishers, Dordrecht, The Netherlands, 1998.
6. D. Cieslik. *The Steiner Ratio*. Kluwer Academic Publishers, Dordrecht, The Netherlands, 2001.

7. D. -Z. Du, J. M. Smith, and J. H. Rubinstein. *Advances in Steiner Trees*. Kluwer Academic Publishers, Dordrecht, The Netherlands, 2000.
8. A. O. Ivanov and A. A. Tuzhilin. *Minimal Networks: The Steiner Problem and Its Generalizations*. CRC Press, Boca Raton, FL, 1994.
9. H. J. Promel and A. Steger. *The Steiner Tree Problem: A Tour Through Graphs, Algorithms, and Complexity*. Friedrich Vieweg and Son, Braunschweig, Germany, 2002.
10. C. J. Alpert, G. Gandham, M. Hrkic, J. Hu, A. B. Kahng, J. Lillis, B. Liu, S. T. Quay, S. S. Sapatnekar, and A. J. Sullivan. Buffered steiner trees for difficult instances. *IEEE Transactions Computer-Aided Design*, 21(1): 3–14, January 2002.
11. C. J. Alpert, A. B. Kahng, C. N. Sze, and Q. Wang. Timing-driven steiner trees are (practically) free. In *Proceedings of the ACM/IEEE Design Automation Conference*, pp. 389–392, San Francisco, CA, 2006.
12. K. D. Boese, A. B. Kahng, B. A. McCoy, and G. Robins. Near-optimal critical sink routing tree constructions. *IEEE Transactions Computer-Aided Design*, 14(12): 1417–1436, December 1995.
13. J. Cong, A. B. Kahng, C. K. Koh, and C. -W. A. Tsao. Bounded-skew clock and steiner routing. *ACM Transactions on Design Automation of Electronic Systems*, 3: 341–388, October 1999.
14. J. Hu and S. S. Sapatnekar. Algorithms for non-hanan-based optimization for VLSI interconnect under a higher order awe model. *IEEE Transactions Computer-Aided Design*, 19(4): 446–458, April 2000.
15. J. Hu and S. S. Sapatnekar. A survey on multi-net global routing for integrated circuits. *Integration: The VLSI Journal*, 11: 1–49, 2001.
16. J. Hu and S. S. Sapatnekar. A timing-constrained simultaneous global routing algorithm. *IEEE Transactions Computer-Aided Design*, 21(9): 1025–1036, September 2002.
17. Y. I. Ismail and E. G. Friedman. *On-Chip Inductance in High-Speed Integrated Circuits*. Kluwer Academic Publishers, Boston, MA, 2001.
18. A. B. Kahng, S. Mantik, and D. Stroobandt. Towards accurate models of achievable routing. *IEEE Transactions Computer-Aided Design*, 20: 648–659, May 2001.
19. A. B. Kahng and G. Robins. *On Optimal Interconnections for VLSI*. Kluwer Academic Publishers, Boston, MA, 1995.
20. B. A. McCoy and G. Robins. Non-tree routing. *IEEE Transactions Computer-Aided Design*, 14(6): 790–784, June 1995.
21. S. Peyer, M. Zachariasen, and D. J. Grove. Delay-related secondary objectives for rectilinear steiner minimum trees. *Discrete and Applied Mathematics*, 136(2): 271–298, February 2004.
22. N. Sherwani, S. Bhingarde, and A. Panyam. *Routing in the Third Dimension*. IEEE Press, New York, 1995.
23. S. H. Gerez. *Algorithms for VLSI Design Automation*. John Wiley and Sons, Chichester, United Kingdom, 1998.
24. B. T. Preas and M. J. Lorenzetti. *Physical Design Automation of VLSI Systems*. Benjamin/Cummings, Menlo Park, CA, 1988.
25. S. M. Sait and N. Youssef. *VLSI Physical Design Automation—Theory and Practice*. World Scientific Publishing Company, Singapore, 1999.
26. M. Sarrafzadeh and C. K. Wong. *An Introduction to VLSI Physical Design*. McGraw Hill, New York, 1996.
27. N. Sherwani. *Algorithms for VLSI Physical Design Automation*, Third Edition. Kluwer Academic Publishers, Boston, MA, 1998.
28. H. Chen, C. -K. Cheng, A. B. Kahng, I. Măndoiu, and Q. Wang. Estimation of wirelength reduction for λ-geometry vs. manhattan placement and routing. In *Proceedings of the ACM International Workshop on System-Level Interconnect Prediction*, Monterey, CA, pp. 71–76, 2003.
29. H. Chen, C. -K. Cheng, A. B. Kahng, I. I. Măndoiu, Q. Wang, and B. Yao. The y-architecture for on-chip interconnect: Analysis and methodology. *IEEE Transactions Computer-Aided Design*, 24(4): 588–599, April 2005.
30. C. -K. Koh and P. H. Madden. Manhattan or non-Manhattan?: A study of alternative VLSI routing architectures. In *Proceedings of the Great Lakes Symposium VLSI*, pp. 47–52, Chicago, IL, 2000.
31. Y. Y. Li, S. K. Cheung, K. S. Leung, and C. K. Wong. Steiner tree construction in λ_3-metric. *IEEE Transactions Circuits and Systems-II: Analog and Digital Signal Processing*, 45(5): 563–574, May 1998.
32. B. K. Nielsen, P. Winter, and M. Zachariasen. An exact algorithm for the uniformly-oriented steiner tree problem. In *Proceedings of the European Symposium on Algorithms*, Springer Verlag Lecture Notes in Computer Science, Vol. 2461. Springer-Verlag, Rome, Italy, 2002 pp. 760–771.

33. M. Sarrafzadeh and C. K. Wong. Hierarchical Steiner tree construction in uniform orientations. *IEEE Transactions Computer-Aided Design*, 11(9): 1095–1103, September 1992.

34. S. Teig. The x architecture: Not your father's diagonal wiring. In *Proceedings of the ACM International Workshop on System-Level Interconnect Prediction*, San Diego, CA, pp. 33–37, 2002.

35. The X Initiative, 2006. Available at http://www.xinitiative.org.

36. M. C. Yildiz and P. H. Madden. Preferred direction steiner trees. In *Proceedings of the Great Lakes Symposium VLSI*, pp. 56–61, West Lafayette, IN, 2001.

37. S. Gueron and R. Tessler. The Fermat–Steiner problem. *The American Mathemtical Monthly*, 109(5): 443–451, 2002.

38. V. Viviani. *Treatise De Maximis et Minimis*. Appendix, pp. 144–150, Italy, 1659.

39. B. Cavalieri. *Exercitationes Geometriae Sex*. Bologna, Italy, 1647.

40. M. Hanan. On Steiner's problem with rectilinear distance. *SIAM Journal of Applied Mathematics*, 14: 255–265, 1966.

41. T. L. Snyder. On the exact location of Steiner points in general dimension. *SIAM Journal on Computing*, 21(1): 163–180, 1992.

42. G. Y. Yan, A. A. Albrecht, G. H. F. Young, and C. -K. Wong. The Steiner tree problem in orientation metrics. *Journal of Computer and System Sciences*, 55(3): 529–546, 1997.

43. M. Garey and D. S. Johnson. The rectilinear Steiner problem is NP-complete. *SIAM Journal of Applied Mathematics*, 32(4): 826–834, 1977.

44. P. K. Agarwal and M. T. Shing. Algorithms for special cases of rectilinear Steiner trees: Points on the boundary of a rectilinear rectangle. *Networks*, 20(4): 453–485, 1990.

45. F. K. Hwang. On Steiner minimal trees with rectilinear distance. *SIAM Journal of Applied Mathematics*, 30(1): 104–114, 1976.

46. N. Hasan, G. Vijayan, and C. K. Wong. A neighborhood improvement algorithm for rectilinear Steiner trees. In *Proceedings of the IEEE International Symposium Circuits and Systems*, New Orleans, LA, pp. 2869–2872, 1990.

47. J. M. Ho, G. Vijayan, and C. K. Wong. New algorithms for the rectilinear Steiner tree problem. *IEEE Transactions Computer-Aided Design*, 9(2): 185–193, 1990.

48. A. B. Kahng and G. Robins. A new family of Steiner tree heuristics with good performance: The iterated 1-steiner approach. In *Proceedings of the IEEE International Conference Computer-Aided Design*, pp. 428–431, Santa Clara, CA, November 1990.

49. A. B. Kahng and G. Robins. On performance bounds for a class of rectilinear Steiner tree heuristics in arbitrary dimension. *IEEE Transactions Computer-Aided Design*, 11(11): 1462–1465, November 1992.

50. G. Robins. *On Optimal Interconnections*. PhD thesis, Department of Computer Science, UCLA, Los Angeles, CA, CSD-TR-920024, 1992.

51. A. Z. Zelikovsky. An 11/8-approximation algorithm for the steiner problem on networks with rectilinear distance. In *Janos Bolyai Mathematica Societatis Conference: Sets, Graphs, and Numbers*, Amsterdam, The Netherlands, pp. 733–745, January 1992.

52. A. Z. Zelikovsky. An 11/6 approximation algorithm for the network steiner problem. *Algorithmica*, 9: 463–470, 1993.

53. L. Kou, G. Markowsky, and L. Berman. A fast algorithm for steiner trees. *Acta Informatica*, 15: 141–145, 1981.

54. A. B. Kahng and G. Robins. A new class of iterative steiner tree heuristics with good performance. *IEEE Transactions Computer-Aided Design*, 11(7): 893–902, July 1992.

55. G. Robins and A. Zelikovsky. Improved steiner tree approximation in graphs. In *Proceedings of the ACM/SIAM Symposium Discrete Algorithms*, pp. 770–779, San Francisco, CA, January 2000.

56. G. Robins and A. Zelikovsky. Tighter bounds for graph steiner tree approximation. *SIAM Journal on Discrete Mathematics*, 19(1): 122–134, 2005.

57. E. N. Gilbert and H. O. Pollak. Steiner minimal trees. *SIAM Journal of Applied Mathematics*, 16: 1–29, 1968.

58. J. Griffith, G. Robins, J. S. Salowe, and T. Zhang. Closing the gap: Near-optimal steiner trees in polynomial time. *IEEE Transactions Computer-Aided Design*, 13(11): 1351–1365, November 1994.

59. F. P. Preparata and M. I. Shamos. *Computational Geometry: An Introduction*. Springer-Verlag, New York, 1985.

60. G. Georgakopoulos and C. H. Papadimitriou. The 1-Steiner tree problem. *Journal of Algorithms*, 8: 122–130, 1987.
61. P. Berman, U. Fößmeier, M. Karpinski, M. Kaufmann, and A. Z. Zelikovsky. Approaching the 5/4— approximation for rectilinear Steiner trees. In *Proceedings of the European Symposium on Algorithms*, Utrecht, The Netherlands, pp. 533–542, 1994.
62. G. Cattaneo, P. Faruolo, U. F. Petrillo, and G. F. Italiano. Maintaining dynamic minimum spanning trees: An experimental study. In *Proceedings of the International Workshop on Algorithm Engineering and Experiments (ALENEX)*, Lecture Notes in Computer Science, Vol. 2409, D. M. Mount and C. Stein (Eds.). Springer Verlag, Utrecht, The Netherlands, 2002, pp. 111–125.
63. G. Robins and J. S. Salowe. Low-degree minimum spanning trees. *Discrete and Computational Geometry*, 14: 151–165, September 1995.
64. J. S. Salowe and D. M. Warme. An exact rectilinear Steiner tree algorithm. In *Proceedings of the IEEE International Conference Computer Design*, pp. 472–475, Cambridge, MA, October 1993.
65. D. M. Warme, P. Winter, and M. Zachariasen. Exact algorithms for plane Steiner tree problems: A computational study. In *Advances in Steiner Trees*, D. Z. Du, J. M. Smith, and J. H. Rubinstein (Eds.). Kluwer Academic Publishers, Dordrecht, The Netherlands, 2000.
66. M. J. Alexander and G. Robins. New performance-driven FPGA routing algorithms. *IEEE Transactions Computer-Aided Design*, 15(12): 1505–1517, December 1996.
67. W. Shi and C. Su. The rectilinear Steiner arborescence problem is NP-complete. *SIAM Journal on Computing*, 35(3): 729–740, 2006.
68. Y. F. Wu, P. Widmayer, and C. K. Wong. A faster approximation algorithm for the Steiner problem in graphs. *Acta Informatica*, 23(2): 223–229, 1986.
69. H. Takahashi and A. Matsuyama. An approximate solution for the Steiner problem in graphs. *Mathematica Japonica*, 24(6): 573–577, 1980.
70. P. Berman and V. Ramaiyer. Improved approximations for the Steiner tree problem. *Journal of Algorithms*, 17: 381–408, 1994.
71. H. J. Promel and A. Steger. Rnc-approximation algorithms for the Steiner problem. In *Proceedings of the ACM Symposium the Theory of Computing*, pp. 559–570, 1997.
72. M. Karpinski and A. Zelikovsky. New approximation algorithms for the Steiner tree problems. *Journal of Combinatorial Optimization*, 1(1): 47–65, March 1997.
73. S. Hougardy and H. J. Promel. A 1.598 approximation algorithm for the Steiner problem in graphs. In *Proceedings of the ACM/SIAM Symposium Discrete Algorithms*, Baltimore, Maryland, pp. 448–453, January 1999.
74. M. Bern and P. Plassmann. The Steiner tree problem with edge lengths 1 and 2. *Information Processing Letters*, 32(4): 171–176, September 1989.
75. M. Chlebik and J. Chlebikova. Approximation hardness of the Steiner tree problem on graphs. In *Scandinavian Workshop on Algorithm Theory*, Lecture Notes in Computer Science, Vol. 2368. Springer-Verlag, Turku, Finland, 2002, pp. 170–179.
76. S. Rajagopalan and V. V. Vazirani. On the bidirected cut relaxation for the metric Steiner tree problem. In *Proceedings of the ACM/SIAM Symposium Discrete Algorithms*, Baltimore, Maryland, pp. 742–751, January 1999.
77. C. D. Bateman, C. S. Helvig, G. Robins, and A. Zelikovsky. Provably-good routing tree construction with multi-port terminals. In *Proceedings of the International Symposium on Physical Design*, pp. 96–102, Napa Valley, CA, April 1997.
78. C. S. Helvig, G. Robins, and A. Zelikovsky. New approximation algorithms for routing with multi-port terminals. *IEEE Transactions Computer-Aided Design*, 19(10): 1118–1128, 2000.
79. C. S. Helvig, G. Robins, and A. Zelikovsky. An improved approximation scheme for the group Steiner problem. *Networks*, 37(1): 8–20, January 2001.
80. G. Reich and P. Widmayer. Beyond Steiner's problem: A VLSI oriented generalization. In *Proceedings of the 15th International Workshop on Graph-Theoretic Concepts in Computer Science*, Lecture Notes in Computer Science, Vol. 411, Castle Rolduc, The Netherlands, pp. 196–211, 1989.
81. N. L. Koren. Pin assignment in automated printed circuit board design. In *Proceedings of the Design Automation Workshop*, Dallas, TX, pp. 72–79, June 1972.

82. E. Ihler. Bounds on the quality of approximate solutions to the group Steiner problem. In *Proceedings of the 16th International Workshop on Graph-Theoretic Concepts in Computer Science*, Lecture Notes in Computer Science, Vol. 484, Berlin, Germany, 1991, pp. 109–118.

83. A. Z. Zelikovsky. A faster approximation algorithm for the Steiner tree problem in graphs. *Information Processing Letters*, 46(2): 79–83, May 1993.

84. U. Feige. A threshold of ln n for approximating set cover. In *Proceedings of the ACM Symposium the Theory of Computing*, Philadelphia, Pennsylvania, pp. 314–318, May 1996.

85. P. Berman and V. Ramaiyer. Improved approximations for the Steiner tree problem. In *Proceedings of the ACM/SIAM Symposium Discrete Algorithms*, pp. 325–334, San Francisco, CA, January 1992.

86. C. J. Alpert, T. C. Hu, J. H. Huang, A. B. Kahng, and D. Karger. Prim–Dijkstra tradeoffs for improved performance-driven routing tree design. *IEEE Transactions Computer-Aided Design*, 14(7): 890–896, 1995.

87. J. Cong, A. B. Kahng, G. Robins, M. Sarrafzadeh, and C. K. Wong. Provably good performance-driven global routing. *IEEE Transactions Computer-Aided Design*, 11(6): 739–752, 1992.

88. M. Borah, R. M. Owens, and M. J. Irwin. An edge-based heuristic for Steiner routing. *IEEE Transactions Computer-Aided Design*, 13: 1563–1568, 1994.

89. M. Borah, R. M. Owens, and M. J. Irwin. A fast and simple Steiner routing heuristic. *Discrete and Applied Mathematics*, 90(1–3): 51–67, 1999.

90. T. H. Chao and Y. C. Hsu. Rectilinear Steiner tree construction by local and global refinement. *IEEE Transactions Computer-Aided Design*, 13(3): 303–309, March 1994.

91. C. Chu and Y. -C. Wong. Fast and accurate rectilinear Steiner minimal tree algorithm for VLSI design. In *Proceedings of the International Symposium on Physical Design*, pp. 28–25, San Francisco, CA, 2005.

92. F. D. Lewis, W. C. Pong, and N. VanCleave. Local improvement in Steiner trees. In *Proceedings of the Great Lakes Symposium VLSI*, pp. 105–106, Kalamazoo, MI, March 1993.

93. I. I. Mandoiu, V. V. Vazirani, and J. L. Ganley. A new heuristic for rectilinear Steiner trees. *IEEE Transactions Computer-Aided Design*, 19: 1129–1139, October 2000.

94. H. Zhou. Efficient Steiner tree construction based on spanning graphs. *IEEE Transactions Computer-Aided Design*, 23: 704–710, May 2004.

95. A. B. Kahng, I. I. Măndoiu, and A. Z. Zelikovsky. Highly scalable algorithms for rectilinear and octilinear Steiner trees. In *Proceedings of the Asia and South Pacific Design Automation Conference*, Yokohama, Japan, pp. 827–833, 2000.

96. U. Fößmeier, M. Kaufmann, and A. Zelikovsky. Faster approximation algorithms for the rectilinear Steiner tree problem. *Discrete and Computational Geometry*, 18: 93–109, 1997.

97. A. B. Kahng, I. I. Măndoiu, and A. Z. Zelikovsky. Practical approximations of Steiner trees in uniform orientation metrics. In *Handbook of Approximation Algorithms and Metaheuristics*, T. E. Gonzalez, (Ed.). CRC Press, Boca Raton, FL, 2006.

98. Q. Zhu, H. Zhou, T. Jing, X. -L. Hong, and Y. Yang. Spanning graph based non-rectilinear Steiner tree algorithms. *IEEE Transactions Computer-Aided Design*, 24(7): 1066–1075, July 2005.

99. S. Arora. Polynomial time approximation schemes for Euclidean tsp and other geometric problems. *Journal of the Association for Computing Machinery*, 45(5): 753–782, September 1998.

100. B. Lu and L. Ruan. Polynomial time approximation scheme for the rectilinear Steiner arborescence problem. *Journal of Combinatorial Optimization*, 4(3): 357–363, September 2000.

101. L. Zosin and S. Khuller. On directed Steiner trees. In *Proceedings of the ACM/SIAM Symposium Discrete Algorithms*, San Francisco, CA, pp. 59–63, 2002.

102. C. Chu and Y. -C. Wong. Fast and accurate rectilinear Steiner minimal tree algorithm for VLSI design. In *Proceedings of the International Symposium on Physical Design*. ACM Press, New York, 2005, pp. 28–35.

25 Timing-Driven Interconnect Synthesis

Jiang Hu, Gabriel Robins, and Cliff C. N. Sze

CONTENTS

25.1 INTRODUCTION

In this chapter, we address performance-driven interconnect synthesis, which seeks to optimize circuit performance by minimizing signal delays to critical sinks. Timing-driven wiring geometries are in general quite different from optimal-area (i.e., Steiner) interconnect trees, especially as die sizes continue to grow while feature dimensions steadily shrink.* The exposition below focuses on selected approaches to performance-driven routing, and details key historical research developments that helped usher in the era of high-performance interconnect synthesis. For extensive surveys on this subject, see Refs. [19,20]. For a general overview of computer-aided design (CAD) of very large scale integrated (VLSI) circuits, see some of the classical textbooks [21–25].

As transistor sizes continued to dramatically shrink while their switching speeds have increased into the multigigahertz range, the circuit performance bottlenecks migrated from the devices themselves to the wires that interconnect them. Indeed, it was observed in the late 1980s that given the VLSI scaling trends at that time, interconnection delay was already contributing up to 70 percent of the clock cycle in circuits [26–28]. Performance-driven layout design thus started to receive much research attention, especially timing-driven placement, which has a particularly significant effect on signal delays [27–32]. However, during that early era in the evolution of VLSI CAD, routing solutions were typically not available during the placement phase. Performance-driven methods of

---

This work was supported by a Packard Foundation Fellowship, by National Science Foundation Young Investigator Award MIP-9457412, and by NSF grants CCR-9988331, CCF-0429737, and CNS-0716635.

* In routing noncritical nets (or sinks), rather than optimize delay we instead seek to minimize overall wirelength, an objective that gives rise to variants of the classical Steiner problem [1–10]. On the other hand, modern ultra-deep-submicron VLSI CAD seeks to optimize and trade-off various combinations of objectives and criteria, such as delay, skew, area, density, manufacturability, reliability, power, electromigration, parasitics, noise, and signal integrity [11–18].

the early 1990s therefore used simple (e.g., geometric or linear) estimates of interconnection delay to drive the placement process, sacrificing modeling accuracy in favor of computational tractability.

For a given timing-driven placement, a corresponding timing-driven routing seeks to minimize source-to-sink signal delays. To optimize circuit performance, early timing-driven routing methods relied on, e.g., net priorities [22], static timing analysis [33], hierarchical approaches [34], and A* search [35]. Since the early 1990s, there has been a steady shift from technology-independent routing methodologies to technology-dependent interconnect synthesis. Analyses of the Elmore delay formula [36] for distributed RC trees [37–39] motivated cost-radius trade-offs that depended on the underlying technology [40–44]. Thus, routing tree constructions that were based on various technology parameters, net criticalities, and other timing or performance issues provided improvements over the previous static, technology-oblivious methods [16].

Several early works abandoned the algorithmic convenience and analytic simplicity of classical geometric objectives, and began to address the less tractable but more realistic actual delay. For example, an early sequence of papers by Boese et al. [12,45–47] proposed new classes of delay objectives, along with improved-performance routing algorithms that directly optimized, e.g., the Elmore delay. These works also established the fidelity of Elmore-based constructions relative to accurate delay simulators (e.g., SPICE) [16]. That is, it was observed that optimizing the Elmore delay tends to also minimize real delay.

In parallel with these advances, sink-dependent delay objectives were recognized as more critical than net-dependent delay minimization. Because the timing-driven placement and routing design loop usually iterated tightly with static timing estimation, critical-path information was often available during routing. Thus, formulations that optimized delays with respect to a set of critical sinks proved more effective than formulations that optimized delays in individual nets while ignoring the critical sinks [16]. The near-optimality of minimum-delay routing heuristics was also quantified empirically, showing, e.g., that certain simple heuristics achieved almost optimal critical sink delays [12,16, 47,48]. Other advances in timing-driven interconnect synthesis for improving circuit performance included various approaches to wire sizing, non-Hanan routing, nontree topologies, and arborescence trees. The remainder of this chapter discusses some of these topics and techniques in greater detail.

25.2 WIRELENGTH-RADIUS TRADE-OFFS

Researchers in interconnect synthesis observed that while low-wirelength routing trees have smaller capacitance-related delays, low-radius interconnects have shorter pathlength-related signal propagation delays [16].* However, there exists an inherent conflict between these two objectives (i.e., minimizing overall tree cost versus minimizing source-to-sink pathlengths), and when one of these two objectives is optimized, the other objective typically suffers (Figure 25.1). Indeed, shortest paths trees (i.e., those produced by Dijkstra's classical algorithm [57]) have the best possible source-to-sink pathlengths but usually induce high overall tree cost (Figure 25.1a). On the other hand, minimum spanning trees (i.e., those produced by Prim's classical algorithm [58]) have optimal tree cost but produce potentially high source-to-sink pathlengths (Figure 25.1b).

To simultaneously optimize both the routing tree radius as well as its cost, the following formulation was proposed [59]:

The Bounded-Radius Minimum Routing Tree Problem: Given a parameter $\epsilon \geq 0$ and a signal net with radius R, find a minimum-cost routing tree T with radius$(T) \leq (1 + \epsilon) \cdot R$.

---

* We define the radius of a routing tree/topology to be its maximum source-to-sink pathlength, and its cost to be its total wirelength. Similarly, the radius of a net is defined as its farthest source-to-sink distance. Distances and wirelengths are usually measured using the Manhattan/Rectilinear norm, although alternative interconnect architectures with more complicated underlying metrics have recently become popular, such as preferred direction routing and λ-geometries [2,49–56].

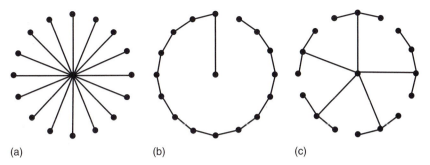

FIGURE 25.1   Candidate interconnection trees for the same net, where the signal source pin is located at the center and the sinks are located on the circumference of a circle: (a) shortest paths tree, (b) minimum spanning tree, and (c) low-cost low-radius trade-off hybrid tree.

The user-specified parameter ϵ controls the trade-off between the competing minimum-radius and minimum-cost objectives. Setting $\epsilon = 0$ induces a minimum-radius (i.e., shortest paths) tree, while increasing ϵ loosens the radius restriction, thus allowing further tree cost optimization. At the other extreme, setting $\epsilon = \infty$ results in a minimum-cost spanning tree. Note that these definitions and formulations easily generalize from spanning trees to Steiner trees (i.e., where new points/vias may be added to further optimize total wirelength). However, in performance-driven layout, where a fast delay estimator is employed in a tight iterative design loop, spanning trees are typically easier to compute than Steiner trees. Moreover, a spanning tree can usually be easily converted into a corresponding Steiner solution (e.g., by edge-overlapping), without disimproving its original radius.

The earliest heuristic to solve the Bounded-Radius Minimum Routing Tree (BRMRT) problem was the bounded-Prim (BPRIM) approach of Refs. [43,59], which follows the general structure of Prim's minimum spanning tree (MST) algorithm [58]. Although simple to implement and effective in practice over typical inputs, this approach can produce trees with cost arbitrarily larger than optimal in the worst case. Shallow-light tree constructions avoid such worst-case scenarios by simultaneously bounding both the worst-case radius and the worst-case cost of the resulting routing tree [41–44].

The basic approach of algorithms such as the bounded-radius bounded-cost (BRBC) method [43] is as follows: (1) traverse a minimum spanning tree in depth-first order, (2) insert additional edges whenever the prescribed radius bound is violated, and (3) return the shortest paths tree over the resulting graph (Figure 25.2). The BRBC algorithm produces a tree with radius at most $(1 + \epsilon)$ times optimal, and cost at most $(1 + \frac{2}{\epsilon})$ times optimal [16,43].

The BRMRT problem formulation and the BRBC algorithm generalize to regimes where we seek a low-radius tree that spans a vertex subset in an underlying graph, while using the remaining graph vertices as potential Steiner points to minimize the overall interconnection cost. Note that when $\epsilon = \infty$, the classical graph Steiner problem is a special case of this generalization. A BRBC Steiner analogue first constructs an approximate minimum-cost Steiner tree T that spans the target vertex subset, and then proceeds with the remaining radius-minimization optimization as before. This will yield a routing tree with radius bounded by $(1 + \epsilon)$ times optimal, and cost bounded by $(1 + \frac{2}{\epsilon})$ times the cost of T.

Note that the cost of the heuristic Steiner tree T can itself be bounded by a constant times optimal. For example, if we use the best-known general graph Steiner heuristic of Robins and Zelikovsky [10,60] that has an approximation bound of $1 + \frac{\ln 3}{2} \approx 1.5493$ times optimal for arbitrary weighted graphs, then the resulting Steiner-BRBC tree cost bound will be $(1 + \frac{\ln 3}{2}) \cdot (1 + \frac{2}{\epsilon})$ times optimal for general graphs. The underlying geometry can be exploited to further improve the cost bound of Steiner-BRBC to $2 \cdot (1 + \frac{1}{\epsilon})$ times optimal for any metric. In particular, for the Manhattan and Euclidean geometries, this general bound can be further improved to $\frac{3}{2} \cdot (1 + \frac{1}{\epsilon})$ times optimal

BRBC algorithm
Input: Graph $G = (V, E)$ (with radius R, source $s_0 \in V$), $\epsilon \geq 0$
Output: Spanning tree T_{BRBC} with $r(T_{\text{BRBC}}) \leq (1 + \epsilon) \cdot R$
         and $cost(T_{\text{BRBC}}) \leq (1 + \frac{2}{\epsilon}) \cdot cost(T_M)$
$Q = T_M$
$L =$ depth-first tour of T_M
$Sum = 0$
For $i = 1$ to $|L| - 1$
   $Sum = Sum + dist(L_i, L_{i+1})$
   If $Sum \geq \epsilon \cdot dist_G(s_0, L_{i+1})$ **Then**
      $Q = Q \cup \{$edges in $minpath_G(s_0, L_{i+1})\}$
      $Sum = 0$
Output $T_{\text{BRBC}} =$ shortest paths tree of Q

FIGURE 25.2   BRBC spanning tree algorithm produces a tree T_{BRBC} with radius at most $(1 + \epsilon) \cdot R$ and cost at most $(1 + \frac{2}{\epsilon}) \cdot cost(T_M)$. (From Cong, J., Kahng, A. B., Robins, G., Sarrafzadeh, M., and Wong, C. K., *IEEE Trans. Comput. Aided Des.*, 11, 739, 1992; Kahng, A. B. and Robins, G., *On Optimal Interconnections for VLSI*, Kluwer Academic Publishers, Boston, MA, 1995.)

and $\frac{2}{\sqrt{3}} \cdot (1 + \frac{1}{\epsilon})$ times optimal, respectively. For λ-geometries (which allow wiring angles of $\frac{i\pi}{\lambda}$ [54]), a cost bound of $(\frac{2}{\sqrt{3}} \cos \frac{\pi}{\lambda}) \cdot (1 + \frac{1}{\epsilon})$ times optimal can be shown for BRBC [16].

Experimental benchmarks indicate that both the BPRIM and BRBC algorithms run quickly and indeed yield a smooth trade-off between tree cost and tree radius [16,43]. In fact, on typical nets, the cost-radius trade-off is on average significantly more favorable than suggested by the theoretical bounds. For example, for ten pins and $\epsilon = 1$, BRBC offers an average of 21 percent savings in tree radius over optimal, at the expense of only 13 percent average rise in tree cost over optimal. Moreover, the interconnects produced by BPRIM and BRBC have significantly better delay characteristics than classical Steiner trees, as verified by accurate timing simulators (e.g., SPICE) [16,43].

An alternative approach to the wirelength-radius trade-offs is the AHHK algorithm [40], which integrates Prim's minimum spanning tree algorithm [58] and Dijkstra's shortest path tree algorithm [57]. Prim's algorithm minimizes the total wirelength, while Dijkstra's algorithm minimizes the tree radius (i.e., the source-to-sink pathlengths). Thus, these two classic algorithms address, albeit separately, two major concerns in performance-driven interconnect synthesis. On the other hand, these two algorithms can be implemented similarly, by starting from the source node and adding one edge at a time until all the specified vertices in V are spanned.

The main difference between these two algorithms is the criterion for selecting which edge to be added at each iteration. Prim's algorithm [58] selects the edge with the minimum length. In particular, Prim's algorithm iteratively adds to the growing tree T a new node v_j and edge e_{ij}, where $v_i \in T$ and $v_j \in V - T$ are chosen to minimize the edge length $|e_{ij}|$. In contrast, Dijkstra's algorithm [57] attempts to minimize the pathlength from the source node when selecting an edge. Specifically, Dijkstra's algorithm iteratively adds to the growing tree T a new node v_j and edge e_{ij}, where $v_i \in T$ and $v_j \in V - T$ are chosen to minimize the the sum of the edge length $|e_{ij}|$ and the pathlength l_i from the source node to vertex v_i in T.

Generalizing this similarity between the two traditional methods of Prim and Dijkstra, the AHHK algorithm iteratively adds to the growing tree T a new node v_j and edge e_{ij}, where $v_i \in T$ and $v_j \in V - T$ are chosen to minimize the sum of the edge length $|e_{ij}|$ and the pathlength l_i from the source node to vertex v_i in T times a fixed constant c. In this hybrid scheme, the chosen constant $0 \leq c \leq 1$ serves to smoothly trade-off total wirelength against tree radius (i.e., source-to-sink pathlengths). In particular, when $c = 0$, the resulting AHHK tree is identical to Prim's minimum spanning tree, and when $c = 1$, the resulting AHHK tree is the same as Dijkstra's shortest paths tree. Varying the value

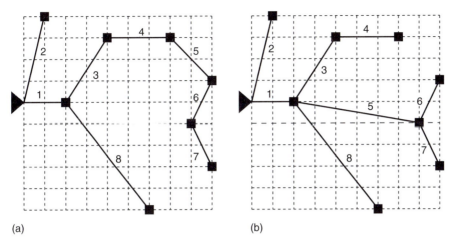

(a)   (b)

FIGURE 25.3   Examples of AHHK tree in the Euclidean plane, with (a) $c = \frac{1}{3}$ (radius 15.9 and cost 26.4) and (b) $c = \frac{2}{3}$ (radius 10.3 and cost 29.7). The edge labels indicate the order of adding the edges in the algorithm. (From Alpert, C. J., Hu, T. C., Huang, J. H., Kahng, A. B., and Karger, D., *IEEE Trans. Comput. Aided Des. Integrated Circuits Syst.*, 14, 890, 1995. With permission.)

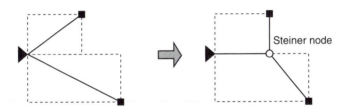

FIGURE 25.4   Examples of converting a spanning tree into a rectilinear Steiner tree through edge overlapping.

of c between 0 and 1 results in intermediate trade-off trees between the two extremes of Prim's and Dijkstra's constructions. Figure 25.3 gives examples of AHHK trees for different values of the trade-off parameter c.

Once an AHHK spanning tree is obtained, it can be converted to a rectilinear Steiner tree using edge overlapping. That is, if the bounding boxes of two tree edges overlap, the overlapping portions can form a new edge with one end being a Steiner node, as illustrated in Figure 25.4. Such edge overlappings can usually reduce wirelength with respect to the original spanning tree.* If there are multiple options for edge overlapping at a given step, we can break ties by giving priority to overlapping edges that yield the greatest wirelength reduction.

25.3   STEINER ARBORESCENCES

Historically, the primary application of rectilinear Steiner minimum trees in VLSI CAD has been in global routing, because older physical design paradigms did not require the modeling of wires in the placement and floorplanning stages. However, the last several generations of technology have made it necessary to model the impact of wiring much earlier in the design process. For example, during placement, physical synthesis, and even floorplanning, we commonly wish to perform static timing

---

* While edge overlapping is a practical technique that reduces wirelength in typical scenarios, there are known pathological pointset instances where edge overlapping over any minimum spanning tree does not yield any wirelength savings whatsoever [61], whereas other Steiner-point inducing methods can still yield substantial savings [62,63].

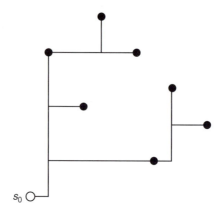

FIGURE 25.5 Minimum-cost RSA.

analysis to evaluate the performance of the current design iteration. To predict this with reasonable accuracy, a model of the wiring of each net must be available. Because blocks and cells may move quite often during these earlier phases of the physical design process, it is imperative to be able to efficiently and accurately estimate wiring delays.

Such interconnect estimation was traditionally formulated as the Steiner problem. However, given the scaling trends in VLSI technology, a Steiner tree often results in inaccurate timing estimates, which may in turn misguide the floorplanning, placement, and physical synthesis design phases. On the other hand, Elmore delay analyses and cost-radius trade-offs have motivated research into routing constructions that simultaneously optimize interconnect length, source–sink paths, and a quadratic objective that optimizes the sum of source–sink pathlengths [16]. In particular, it was discovered that a minimum-cost rectilinear Steiner arborescence (RSA) heuristically addresses all of these objectives reasonably well [64], and thus provides highly accurate (as well as efficient) timing estimates.

The Rectilinear Steiner Arborescence Problem: Given a signal net S in the Manhattan plane with source pin s_0, find a minimum-cost Steiner tree T that spans S, where the pathlengths in the tree T from s_0 to every sink are equal to the corresponding Manhattan distances.

The RSA problem seeks a minimum-cost shortest paths Steiner tree (Figure 25.5), and is thus a special case of the Steiner version of the BRMRT problem discussed above (where $\epsilon = 0$). The RSA problem originated with early works such as Refs. [65,66]. Efforts were made to find a polynomial-time optimal arborescence algorithm, resulting in a proliferation of RSA heuristics [64,67–70], until it was finally proven that the RSA problem is NP-complete [71].

The first well-known effective RSA heuristic was proposed in Ref. [69]. Given a signal net in the Manhattan plane, the heuristic of Ref. [69] maintains a set of points, originally being all of the pins of the net, and repeatedly merges (i.e., connects) in this set a pair of points/pins whose bounding box is farthest from the source pin. This process terminates when the resulting arborescence spans the entire net. Choosing a new merge point that is dominated by two existing points allows the greatest flexibility for subsequent merges to optimize wirelength while always maintaining the shortest paths property of partial solutions. Figure 25.6 describes this heuristic more formally, while Figure 25.7 gives an illustrative execution example. The running time of this method is $O(n \log n)$.

Empirical studies indicate that for typical nets, the RSA heuristic of Ref. [69] as well as the A-tree construction of Ref. [64], both yield solutions with average cost within 4 percent of the optimal RSA cost. On the theoretical side, both of these approaches have been proven to produce rectilinear arborescence trees that are never worse than twice the optimal [69], and pathological examples were found where both methods meet this twice-optimal worst-case bound [16]. Whereas, previous approaches typically handle cases where the sinks lie in the first quadrant (with respect to

```
Algorithm: Rectilinear Steiner arborescence (RSA)
Input: A set of sink vertices {v₁,v₂,...,vₙ} in the first quadrant
Output: A rectilinear Steiner arborescence rooted at (0,0)
Let Γ be the set of subtrees (Initially Γ = ∅)
For each sink vᵢ at location (xᵢ,yᵢ)
    Insert into Γ a subtree Tᵢ rooted at (xᵢ,yᵢ) which contains only vᵢ
While |Γ| > 1 Do
    Find two subtrees Tⱼ and Tₖ in Γ such that xᵣ+yᵣ is maximum,
        where xᵣ=min(xⱼ,xₖ) and yᵣ=min(yⱼ,yₖ)
    Create a new subtree Tᵣ by creating a new root at (xᵣ,yᵣ)
    Connect the new root to (xⱼ,yⱼ) and (xₖ,yₖ) by a horizontal and/or
    a vertical edge
    Remove Tⱼ and Tₖ from Γ
    Insert Tᵣ into Γ
Construct a tree T by connecting (0,0) to (xᵣ,yᵣ) by a horizontal
and/or a vertical edge
Return T
```

FIGURE 25.6 The RSA algorithm of Ref [69].

a net's source pin), an extension to all four quadrants, with running time $O(n \log n)$, was given in Ref. [72].

The RSA problem was generalized to arbitrary graphs as follows [73]. For an arbitrary weighted graph $G = (V, E)$ and two nodes u, $v \in V$, let minpath$_G(u, v)$ denote the cost of a shortest path between u and v in G. The graph Steiner arborescence (GSA) problem can now be defined.

The Graph Steiner Arborescence Problem: Given a weighted graph $G = (V, E)$, and a specified net $N \subseteq V$ with source pin/node $n_0 \in N$ to be interconnected in G, construct a least-cost spanning tree $T = (V', E')$ with $N \subseteq V' \subseteq V$ and $E' \subseteq E$ such that minpath$_T(n_0, n_i) = $ minpath$_G(n_0, n_i)$ for all $n_i \in N$.

As with the rectilinear arborescence problem, the GSA problem is NP-complete [73]. Constructing an arborescence can be viewed as folding or overlapping paths within a shortest paths tree, so as to induce the maximum wirelength savings while maintaining shortest paths. Indeed, this is the operational principle of the RSA heuristic of Ref. [69], among others. To generalize this strategy to arbitrary graphs, we define dominance in weighted graphs as follows [73].

Definition 1   *Given a weighted graph $G = (V, E)$, and nodes $\{n_0, p, s\} \subseteq V$, we say that p dominates s if minpath$_G(n_0, p) = $ minpath$_G(n_0, s) + $ minpath$_G(s, p)$.*

Thus, a node p dominates a node s if there exists a shortest path from the source n_0 to p that also passes through s (Figure 25.8a). Keeping in mind that the shortest path between a pair of nodes in a graph may not be unique, MaxDom(p, q) is defined as a node in V dominated by both p and q, which maximizes the distance minpath$_G[n_0, \text{MaxDom}(p, q)]$ to the source node n_0 (Figure 25.8b). The dominated vertex MaxDom is chosen to be as far from the source node as possible, so as to yield the greatest possible wirelength overlap between the two paths, while still maintaining the shortest paths property with respect to the two target nodes.

The above definitions enable the following path-folding arborescence (PFA) heuristic [73], as follows. Starting with the set of nodes N that initially contains the net (i.e., the source and all the sinks), we find a pair of nodes p and q in N such that $m = $ MaxDom(p, q) in G is farthest away from the source node n_0 among all such pairs. We then replace p and q in N with m, and iterate until only the source remains in N. The overall GSA solution is formed by using shortest paths

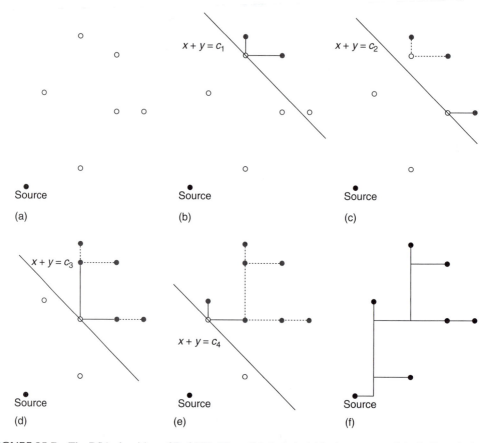

FIGURE 25.7 The RSA algorithm of Ref [69]. The solid circle in (a) is the source and the hollow circles are sinks. The first four iterations are shown in (b–e). At the beginning (a), there are seven (one node) subtrees, one per sink, plus the source itself. In (b) a pair of (distant-from-the-source) subtrees is merged to form a new subtree, resulting in five remaining subtrees. Trees continue to merge during subsequent iterations, resulting in the final RSA shown in (f).

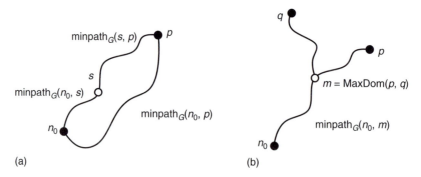

FIGURE 25.8 Defining dominance in graphs: (a) Graph node p dominates node s when $\text{minpath}_G(n_0, p) = \text{minpath}_G(n_0, s) + \text{minpath}_G(s, p)$ and (b) shows $\text{MaxDom}(p, q)$ with respect to p and q. To maximize the wirelength savings, we seek the farthest point $m = \text{MaxDom}(p, q)$ from the source n_0, where p and q both dominate m.

```
Path-folding arborescence (PFA) algorithm
Input: Weighted graph G = (V, E) and net N ⊆ V with source n₀ ∈ N
Output: A low-cost shortest-paths tree spanning N in G
M = N
While N ≠ {n₀} Do
   Find a pair {p, q} ⊆ N such that m = MaxDom(p, q)
      has maximum minpath(n₀, m) over all {p, q} ⊆ N
   N = {N−{p, q}} ∪ {m}
   M = M ∪ {m}
Output the tree formed by connecting each node p ∈ M
      (using a shortest path in G) to the nearest node in M that p
      dominates
```

FIGURE 25.9 The graph-based PFA heuristic. M initially holds all the nodes to be spanned, and is then augmented with the MaxDom Steiner points found during each iteration. (From Alexander, M. J. and Robins, G., *IEEE Trans. Comput. Aided Des.*, 15, 1505, 1996.)

in G to connect each MaxDom(p, q) to p and to q (Figure 25.9). Empirical experiments indicate that the PFA method is effective in producing shortest paths trees with low wirelength (i.e., PFA's average wirelength is close to that of the best existing graph Steiner heuristics) [73]. This observation was reconfirmed in Ref. [11], where it was demonstrated that using rectilinear arborescences during physical synthesis only induces an average of 2–4 percent wirelength penalty over rectilinear Steiner trees, while offering substantial accuracy gains in performance estimation.

A different approach to the GSA problem generalizes the Iterated 1-Steiner (I1S) approach of Kahng and Robins [16,63] to yield an effective iterated-dominance (IDOM) arborescence methodology for arbitrary weighted graphs [73]. The IDOM heuristic iteratively selects a single Steiner point that minimizes the cost of the spanning arborescence over all the sinks and Steiner points selected thus far. The reason that we iterate a spanning arborescence construction to produce a Steiner arborescence tree is that the former is easy to compute,* while the latter is NP-complete. The IDOM heuristic thus repeatedly (and greedily) finds Steiner candidates that reduce the overall spanning arborescence cost, and includes them into the growing set of Steiner nodes (Figure 25.10).

To achieve an improved runtime for the IDOM approach, Alexander and Robins [73] defined the DOM heuristic, which is a restricted version of the PFA heuristic (Figure 25.9), except where MaxDom(p, q) is selected only from N instead of allowed to be an arbitrary node in V. This substantially speeds up the search for MaxDom(p, q) at each iteration, because N is typically much smaller than V. The DOM subroutine constructs an arborescence by using a shortest path to connect each sink in N to the closest sink/source in N that it dominates, and then computes a shortest paths tree over the graph formed by the union of these paths.

Given a set of Steiner candidate node $S \subseteq V - N$, the cost savings of S with respect to DOM is defined as ΔDOM$(G, N, S) = \text{cost}[\text{DOM}(G, N)] - \text{cost}[\text{DOM}(G, N \cup S)]$. The IDOM approach starts with an initially empty set of Steiner candidates $S = \emptyset$. It then finds a node $t \in V - N$ that maximizes ΔDOM$(G, N, S \cup \{t\}) > 0$, and repeats this procedure with $S \leftarrow S \cup \{t\}$. The wirelength required by DOM to span $N \cup S$ will decrease with each added node t, and the overall construction terminates when there is no $t \in V - (N \cup S)$ such that ΔDOM$(G, N, S \cup \{t\}) > 0$. The final overall solution is DOM$(G, N \cup S)$. This method is described in Figure 25.11, and a sample execution is given in Figure 25.12.

---

* Recall that a node p dominates a node s if there exists a shortest path from the root to p passing through s. An optimal spanning arborescences can be computed efficiently by using a shortest path to connect each sink to the closest sink/source that it dominates, and then computing Dijkstra's [57] shortest paths tree over the graph formed by the union of these paths.

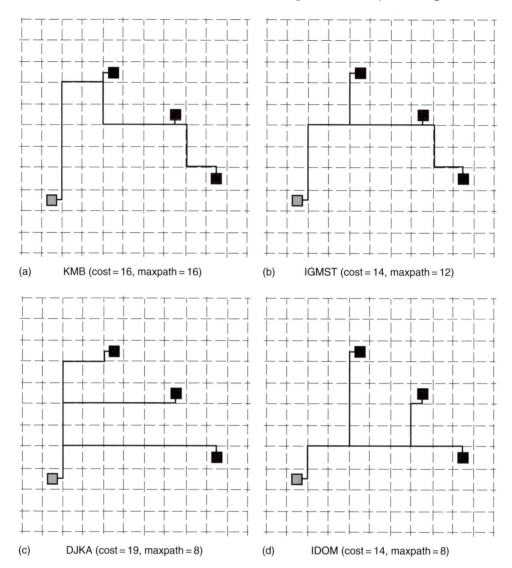

(a)   KMB (cost = 16, maxpath = 16)   (b)   IGMST (cost = 14, maxpath = 12)

(c)   DJKA (cost = 19, maxpath = 8)   (d)   IDOM (cost = 14, maxpath = 8)

FIGURE 25.10 Four routing solutions for the same four-pin net (the signal source is the gray-shaded square and the solid squares are sinks): (a) the solution produced by the KMB graph Steiner heuristic of Ref. [74]; (b) the optimal Steiner tree, which is also the solution produced by the graph I1S algorithm of Refs. [16,62]; (c) Dijkstra's shortest paths tree of Ref. [57]; and (d) the optimal Steiner arborescence, which is also the solution produced by the IDOM algorithm of Ref. [73]. Note that the IDOM solution in (d) is optimal in terms of both total wirelength as well as maximum pathlength (although this double-optimal outcome is unusual).

The IDOM approach is a general template for producing arborescences for designated subgraphs (i.e., nets) in arbitrary weighted graphs (i.e., underlying routing grids) [73]. Moreover, the IDOM heuristic escapes the known twice-optimal worst-case examples of previous arborescence heuristics, both in the rectilinear plane as well as in arbitrary weighted graphs.* The IDOM approach outperforms the previous heuristics on empirical benchmarks [73], including in field-programmable gate

---

* There exist very rare worst-case graphs that force IDOM to produce a tree with cost logarithmic factor times optimal, matching the best-known nonapproximability results for the GSA problem [73].

```
Iterated dominance (IDOM) algorithm
Input: A weighted graph G = (V, E), a net N ⊆ V with n₀ ∈ N
Output: A low-cost arborescence T' = (V', E') spanning N,
        where N ⊆ V' ⊆ V and E' ⊆ E
S = ∅
Do Forever
    T = {t ∈ V−N|ΔDOM(G, N, S∪{t}) > 0}
    If T = ∅ Then Return DOM(G, N∪S)
    Find t ∈ T with maximum ΔDOM(G, N, S∪{t})
    S = S∪{t}
```

FIGURE 25.11 IDOM algorithm for producing arborescences in arbitrary weighted graphs. (From Alexander, M. J. and Robins, G., *IEEE Trans. Comput. Aided Des.*, 15, 1505, 1996.)

array (FPGA) routing, which is inherently a graph-based regime. Subsequent graph arborescence algorithms, including fast polynomial-time heuristics as well as exponential-time optimal algorithms were introduced in Ref. [75].

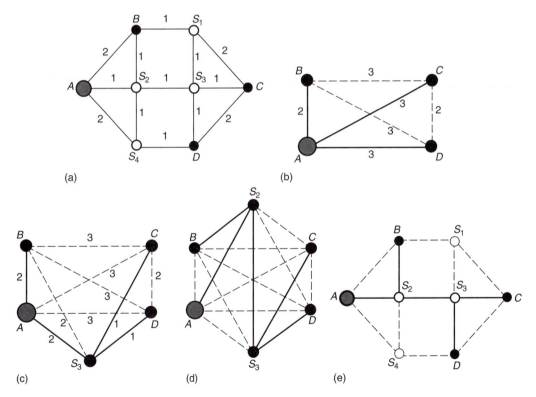

FIGURE 25.12 Execution example for the IDOM algorithm: (a) GSA problem instance with source node A (gray), sink nodes $\{B, C, D\}$ (solid), and graph edge weights shown; (b) initial DOM solution over the contracted pathlengths distance graph (over the net $N = \{A, B, C, D\}$) having cost $= 8$; (c) Steiner candidate S_3 produces a savings of $\Delta\text{DOM} = 2$, which reduces the overall tree cost from 8 to 6; thus S_3 is retained as a Steiner point; (d) Steiner candidate S_2 is the final Steiner point with positive ΔDOM, and further reduces the solution cost from 6 to 5; and (e) the final IDOM solution (having cost $= 5$), with paths reexpanded relative to the original input graph.

25.4 ELMORE DELAY-BASED ROUTING CONSTRUCTIONS

Objectives such as minimum tree cost, bounded radius, cost-radius trade-offs, and even arborescences were all motivated by analyses of the Elmore delay approximation [36–39]. However, these objectives are merely abstractions that do not directly optimize delay. This section describes approaches that optimize Elmore delay directly while synthesizing a routing tree.

The earliest Elmore-based routing approach is the Elmore routing tree (ERT) spanning construction of Boese et al. [16,47,76] (Figure 25.13). Similar to Prim's MST algorithm [58], the ERT heuristic starts with a tree $T = (V, E)$ initially containing only the source s_0, and then repeatedly finds a terminal $s_i \in V$ and a sink $s_j \in S - V$ so that adding edge (s_i, s_j) to T minimizes the maximum Elmore delay to any sink in the growing tree. The greedy approach implicit in the ERT algorithm easily generalizes to any delay model by using the corresponding delay estimator in the inner loop of Figure 25.13. For example, Ref. [77] proposed the use of a two-pole simulator within a similar greedy construction, and Ref. [78] used this strategy for multi-chip module (MCM) routing under a second-order delay model.

The ERT algorithm template can produce a timing-driven Steiner Elmore routing tree (SERT) when new sinks are allowed to connect anywhere along an edge in the growing tree, inducing a Steiner node at that connection point [12]. Following the ERT approach, the SERT variant greedily minimizes the maximum source-to-sink Elmore delay at each tree-growing step. To allow additional optimization leeway, embeddings of L-shaped edges can remain indeterminate (within their bounding boxes) for as long as possible during the execution. The SERT variant produces a Steiner topology with low source-to-sink Elmore delays. Figure 25.14 depicts the execution of the SERT heuristic on a sample eight-sink net.

In performance-driven layout, timing-critical paths are determined using timing analysis, and then cells along these paths are placed closer together [27–32]. Timing analysis thus iteratively drives changes within the placement as well as global routing phases. To avoid the "placement-routing mismatch" where inherently net-dependent methods fail to exploit the critical-path information available during iterative performance-driven layout, Boese et al. [47] proposed formulations that extend the basic (S)ERT scheme to accommodate critical sinks. They proved the NP-completeness of the critical-sink routing tree problem (CSRT) [46], and provided efficient heuristics that combine Steiner construction, delay estimation, and global slack removal [47].

To address the CSRT formulation, Boese et al. generalized their SERT method to produce a Steiner Elmore Routing Tree with identified critical sink (SERT-C) [47]. The SERT-C heuristic begins with a tree containing a direct connection (s_0, s_c) between the source and the specified critical sink, and then grows the routing tree around it while minimizing the Elmore delay (or an alternate delay model) from the source to the critical sink (Figure 25.15). Figure 25.16 illustrates the

---

Elmore routing tree (ERT) algorithm
Input: Signal net S with source $s_0 \in S$
Output: Routing tree T over S
1. $T = (V, E) = (\{s_0\}, \emptyset)$
2. **While** $|V| < |S|$ **do**
3.   **Find** $s_i \in V$ and $s_j \in S - V$ that minimize the maximum Elmore
        delay from s_0 to any sink in the tree $(V \cup \{s_j\}, E \cup \{(s_i, s_j)\})$
4. $V = V \cup \{s_j\}$
5. $E = E \cup \{(s_i, s_j)\}$
6. **Output** resulting spanning tree $T = (V, E)$

FIGURE 25.13 ERT algorithm directly uses the Elmore delay formula in a greedy routing tree construction. (From Boese, K. D., Kahng, A. B., and Robins, G., *Proc. ACM/IEEE Design Automation Conference*, Dallas, TX, 1993. With permission.)

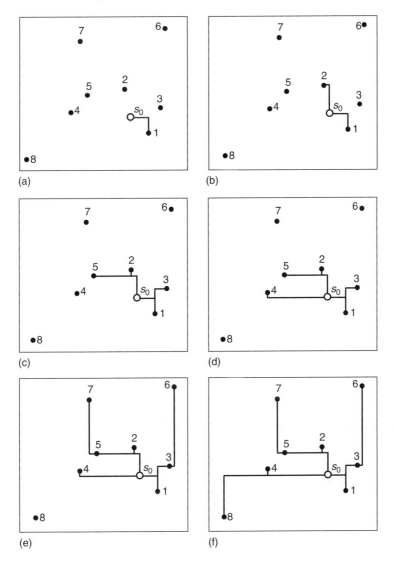

FIGURE 25.14 Execution of the SERT Steiner tree construction for an eight-sink net. The source terminal is labeled 1, and the remaining sinks are numbered in the order of their distance from the source. (From Boes, K. D., Kahng, A. B., McCoy, B. A., and Robins, G., *IEEE Transactions Computer-Aided Design*, 14, 1417, 1995. With permission.)

execution of SERT-C for various choices of the critical sink (using the same eight-sink signal net as in Figure 25.14). The SERT-C algorithm can be implemented to run within time $O(n^2 \log n)$ for n-pin nets. Similar to the ERT and SERT approaches, SERT-C's direct optimization of the Elmore delay allows considerable flexibility with respect to the underlying technology parameters, delay model, and specific input instance.

The methods described above easily extend to higher dimensions and alternate metrics and geometries, including to non-Manhattan interconnect architectures such as preferred-direction routing and λ-geometries [49–56]. The Elmore-based routing tree construction methods of [12] influenced followup works on performance-driven routing trees, addressing additional issues such as buffer insertion, wirelength estimation, alternative delay models, timing constraints, and antenna effects [79–85].

```
SERT-C algorithm
Input: A signal net S with source s₀ ∈ S and critical sink s_c ∈ S
Output: A critical-sink routing tree T over S
1. T = (V, E) = ({s₀, s_c}, {(s₀, s_c)})
2. While |V| < |S| do
3.    Find s_j ∈ S-V and (v, v') ∈ E such that connecting s_j
         to a point x on (v, v') minimizes the Elmore delay to s_c
         in the tree (V∪{s_j, x}, E∪{(v, x), (v', x), (x, s_j)} - {(v, v')})
4.    V = V∪{s_j, x}
5.    E = E∪{(v, x), (v', x), (x, s_j)} - {(v, v')}
6. Output resulting Steiner tree T = (V, E)
```

FIGURE 25.15   The SERT-C algorithm directly incorporates the Elmore delay formula into a greedy critical-sink routing tree construction. (From Boese, K. D., Kahng, A. B., and Robins, G., *Proceedings of the ACM/IEEE Design Automation Conference*, Dallas, 1993.)

25.5 NON-HANAN INTERCONNECT SYNTHESIS

In older (pre-1990s) VLSI regimes, where interconnect delay was mostly capacitive, resistance-related delay components were negligible, and the objective of delay optimization therefore coincided with minimizing the total interconnect length. However, as discussed above, in more modern VLSI technologies, interconnect resistance began to dominate circuit performance, causing optimized performance-driven interconnect to resemble minimum wirelength topologies less and less. Another modern deviation from classical constructions involves the Hanan grid, which is obtained by drawing horizontal and vertical lines through all the pins of a given net [86] (Figure 25.17). Hanan's theorem states that there always exists a rectilinear minimum Steiner tree embedded in the Hanan grid [86,87].

Boese et al. [12] proved that only points from the Hanan grid need be considered in minimizing the weighted sum of critical-sink delays. On the other hand, for the minmax objective of minimizing the maximum sink delay, better routing solutions are possible when considering points that lie off the Hanan grid [12]. For example, in Figure 25.18 a non-Hanan point is required to minimize the maximum source–sink delay during tree construction. Such examples illustrate that the timing requirements at different sinks are often mutually competing, and therefore good approaches must consider all the sinks simultaneously, and utilize every available degree of optimization to produce improved timing-driven interconnect solutions. In particular, the observation that restricting Steiner nodes to be Hanan grid points is suboptimal motivates the problem of non-Hanan interconnect synthesis.

Below we outline a general interconnect synthesis methodology that uses non-Hanan optimization to yield better-performing interconnect topologies [82]. In particular, we address two problem variants: (1) the minmax problem of minimizing the maximum source-to-sink delay and (2) the critical-sink problem that seeks a specified delay at each sink. The later problem can be transformed into a variant of the former problem, and optimal solutions may lie off the Hanan grid in either variant. We next describe a procedure for constructing low-cost routing trees that satisfy prescribed delay constraints at each sink.

The delay violation at each sink is defined as its delay minus its required arrival time (RAT). A positive delay violation value therefore implies that the corresponding delay constraint was not met. On the other hand, a negative delay violation value indicates timing slack, and enables the possibility of further optimizing the routing tree cost by reducing the timing slacks. This trade-off motivates the maximum delay-violation Elmore routing tree (MVERT) problem formulation, as follows.

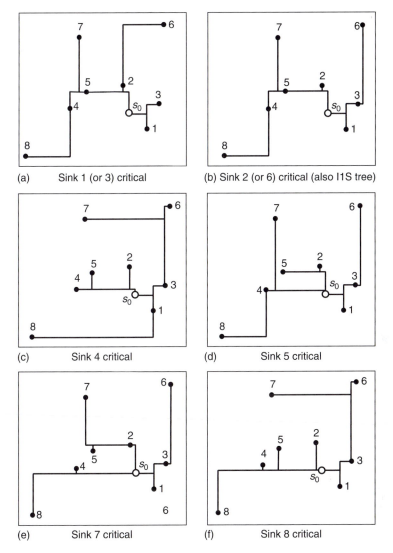

FIGURE 25.16 The SERT-C critical-sink routing tree construction for an eight-sink net, showing solutions for different choices of critical sink. The tree constructed when the source s_c is node 2 or node 6 is also the I1S solution, and the tree constructed when s_c is node 7 is also the generic SERT result.

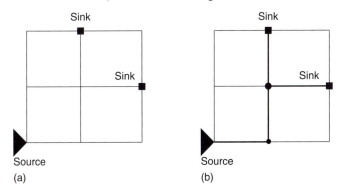

FIGURE 25.17 Example of (a) a Hanan grid induced by a net and (b) a minimum Steiner tree embedded in the Hanan grid.

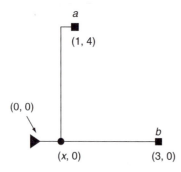

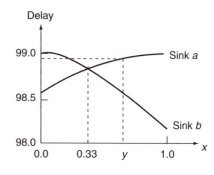

FIGURE 25.18 Example illustrating the efficacy of non-Hanan routing. We assume unit resistance and unit capacitance per unit wirelength. The driver has a source resistance of 6, and the sinks a and b have load capacitances of 1 and 4.5 units, respectively. The variation in the Elmore delay at each sink as the Steiner point x is moved from $(0, 0)$ to $(1, 0)$ is plotted on the right. The maximum sink delay for the tree is minimized at the non-Hanan point $x = 0.33$. The analyses of Ref. [12] can be used to show that a Steiner point to the right of $(1, 0)$ is suboptimal. Even more dramatic discrepancies between Hanan and non-Hanan routings are achievable in larger examples.

The Maximum Delay Violation Elmore Routing Tree Problem: Given a signal net N with source v_0 and a set of sinks $V_{\text{sink}} = \{v_1, v_2, \ldots, v_n\}$, construct a Steiner routing tree with minimum total wirelength, so that the delay violation at each sink is nonpositive (i.e., meets the corresponding timing constraints).

Because the routing-tree topology is no longer restricted to the Hanan grid, the set of candidate Steiner points is unbounded (as opposed to corresponding to the set of Hanan points as in classical formulations). We must therefore find an efficient method for identifying the best (non-Hanan) Steiner points that produce a good routing tree. We now describe a framework that utilizes properties of the delay function to develop a simple and efficient algorithm to address this challenge.

Following Ref. [12], define a maximal segment to be a set of contiguous edges, being either all vertical or all horizontal. The work of Ref. [12] shows that the Elmore delay at each sink is a concave function with respect to the location of a Steiner node moving along a maximal segment. This property also holds for a soft edge that is an edge connecting two nodes $v_i, v_j \in V$, $v_i = (x_i, y_i)$, $v_j = (x_j, y_j)$, such that (1) $x_i \neq x_j$ and $y_i \neq y_j$ and (2) the precise edge route between v_i and v_j is not yet determined. The length l_{ij} of edge (v_i, v_j) is the Manhattan distance $|x_i - x_j| + |y_i - y_j|$. The use of soft edges avoids premature commitment to a specific geometric embedding of a wire in rectilinear space, which enables further wirelength optimization later on [82].

For a general routing-tree topology (Figure 25.19), consider the process of determining an optimal connection between a new node v_k to be attached to an existing edge e_{ij}. The dashed lines in Figure 25.19 denote other nodes and edges of the existing routing tree, and CC represents the closest connection point between node v_k and edge e_{ij}. It can be shown that any connection downstream of CC cannot yield an optimal solution [12]. Specifically, we seek an optimal connection point within the bounding box defined by v_i and CC. Suppose we connect v_k to e_{ij} at point $v' = (x', y')$. Let $z = |x' - x_i| + |y' - y_i|$ be the Manhattan distance from v' to v_i. For convenience, we overload the term CC to also denote its Manhattan distance to v_i.

Following the work of Ref. [12], a delay function with respect to the connection locations for soft edges under the Elmore delay model can be derived as follows. If a node is not downstream from node v_i, its Elmore delay from the source is

$$f_1 = R_d(C_t - cz) + \lambda_0 + \lambda_1(l_{ik} - z) \tag{25.1}$$

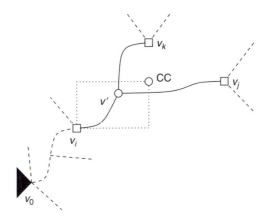

FIGURE 25.19 General routing topology where a new node v_k is to be connected to an existing edge e_{ij}.

where
    λ_0 and λ_1 are constants
    C_t denotes the total capacitive load that would be seen from the last stage of the driver if v_k was connected to v_i

The Elmore delay from v_i to v' is given by

$$f' = rcz \left(\frac{z}{2} + l_{ij} - z + l_{ik} - z \right) + rz \left(C_j + C_k \right) \tag{25.2}$$

The delay from v' to any node in the subtree T_j rooted at v_j can be calculated as

$$f_2 = r \left(l_{ij} - z \right) \left[\frac{c \left(l_{ij} - z \right)}{2} + C_j \right] + \lambda_2 \tag{25.3}$$

Similarly, the delay from v' to any node in subtree T_k is

$$f_3 = r \left(l_{ik} - z \right) \left[\frac{c \left(l_{ik} - z \right)}{2} + C_k \right] + \lambda_3 \tag{25.4}$$

where λ_2 and λ_3 are constants. The Elmore delay of a sink in T_j is given by the sum of f_1, f', and f_2. The Elmore delay of a sink in T_k is the sum of f_1, f', and f_3. The Elmore delay of a sink, not downstream of v_i, is simply f_1. In all these cases, the delay is either a linear or a quadratic function of the Manhattan distance z with nonpositive coefficient for the second-order term. We can therefore conclude that the delay for any sink is a concave function with respect to z, as follows.

Theorem 1   *Under the Elmore delay model, the delay at any sink in the routing tree is a concave function with respect to the Manhattan distance* [82].

    Rewriting the constraints on the routing tree into the form $t(v_i) - q(v_i) \le 0$ for all sinks $v_i \in V_{\text{sink}}$, we see that the maximum delay violation must always be nonpositive. As per Theorem 1, each of the $t(v_i)$'s is a concave function of the connection point z, and because any concave function shifted by a constant is a concave function, this implies that we must find a reconnection point z such that the maximum of the set of concave functions is nonpositive. This is pictorially shown in Figure 25.20 for a net with four sinks u, v, w, and y, all of which have the same timing specification q. The maximum

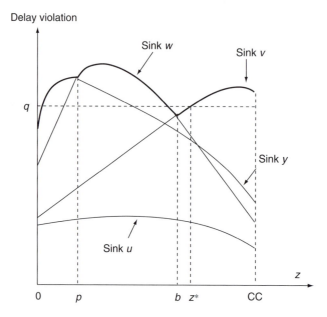

FIGURE 25.20   Finding the optimal value of z that satisfies all the timing constraints.

violation function (depicted by a thicker line) is a piecewise concave function composed of three concave pieces. Note that the graph shows that sink u is never critical in this case, for any value of z. The delay violation at each sink as a function of z is a concave function and the objective is to find a value of z closest to CC (corresponding to a minimal increase in the netlength) that satisfies all the timing constraints. In Figure 25.20, this point is found to be z^*, and in general this point will be a non-Hanan point.

In searching for the point z^*, we observe that it is possible to perform a search on the value of z from 0 to CC, while taking advantage of the fact that the value on each concave piece is minimized at its intersection with the concave piece on either side (if such a piece exists), or at 0 or CC otherwise. In Figure 25.20, this translates to the fact that for the minmax problem, the only candidate solutions are $0, p, b$, and CC. This permits a dramatic reduction of the search space from the infinity of possible intermediate points between 0 and CC.

For the problem of meeting the timing constraints at each sink, several pruning strategies are possible during the search. Consider a binary search on a concave segment with endpoints x_1 and x_2 ($x_1 < x_2$) where the function values are $f(x_1)$ and $f(x_2)$, respectively. If $f(x_1) < T_{spec} < f(x_2)$ and $T_{spec} < f(\frac{x_1+x_2}{2})$, as illustrated in Figure 25.21, then the search can completely eliminate the interval $\left[\frac{x_1+x_2}{2}, x_2\right]$. This follows from the fact that any concave function over an interval is concave over any continuous subinterval. By a symmetric argument, if $T_{spec} \geq f(\frac{x_1+x_2}{2})$, then the search can be confined to the interval $\left[\frac{x_1+x_2}{2}, x_2\right]$.

The pseudocode corresponding to this search is shown in Figure 25.22. The routing tree without subtree T_k is denoted by $T\backslash T_k$. The efficiency of the search can be greatly enhanced by taking advantage of the piecewise-concave nature of the delay function. The search for z^* occurs between 0 and CC in a binary search fashion, and begins at CC. If the value of the delay violation at CC is negative, then we are done; otherwise, we need to test the delay violation at 0. We use CS to represent the critical sink that has the maximum delay violation $\Delta_{max} = \max\{t(v_i) - q(v_i), \forall\ v_i \in V_{sink}\}$. If Δ_{max} is positive at both 0 and CC, and the critical sink at 0 is the same as at CC, then there is no solution satisfying the timing constraints. In this case, we choose the solution that yields the least delay violation between 0 and CC.

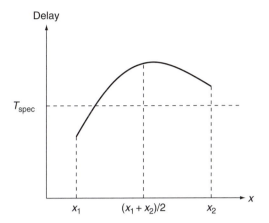

FIGURE 25.21   Using piecewise concavity to speed up the optimization procedure.

A more complicated situation occurs when Δ_{max} at 0 is negative, or Δ_{max} is positive at 0, but the corresponding critical sink is different from that at CC. Then, the search proceeds as a quasi-binary search, as encoded in the function Search(S_{lft}, S_{rit}) in Figure 25.22. The variable S denotes a solution that is triple of the form (connection node, Δ_{max}, critical sink), and S_{lft} and S_{rit} denote the solutions

```
Optimal connection algorithm
Input: Subtree T_k rooted at sink v_k,
        Partial routing tree T\T_k, edge e_ij ∈ T\T_k
Output: Optimal connection between v_k and e_ij
1. Tentatively join v_k to CC, Δ_rit ← Δ_max,
    CS_rit ← sink with Δ_max, S_rit ← (CC, Δ_rit, CS_rit)
2. If Δ_rit ≤ 0, Return CC
3. Tentatively join v_k to v_i
    CS_lft ← sink with Δ_max, S_lft ← (v_i, Δ_max, CS_lft)
4. Return Search(S_lft, S_rit)

Function: Search(S_lft, S_rit)

5. If Δ_rit ≤ 0, Return S_rit
6. If (Δ_lft > 0 and CS_lft == CS_rit) or dist(v_lft, v_rit) < resolution
7.    If Δ_lft < Δ_rit, Return S_lft
8.    Else Return S_rit
9. v_mid ← ((x_lft + x_rit)/2, (y_lft + y_rit)/2)
10. Join v_k to e_ij at v_mid, Δ_mid ← Δ_max
    CS_mid ← sink with Δ_max, S_mid ← (v_mid, Δ_mid, CS_mid)
11. If Δ_mid ≤ 0, Return Search(S_mid, S_rit)
12. S_r ← Search(S_mid, S_rit)
13. If Δ_r ≤ 0, Return S_r
14. S_l ← Search(S_lft, S_mid)
15. If Δ_l < Δ_r, Return S_l
16. Else Return S_r
```

FIGURE 25.22   Algorithm for finding an optimal connection point between a sink and an edge. (From Hu, J. and Sapatnekar, S. S., *IEEE Trans. Comput. Aided Des.*, 19, 446, 2000.)

at the left and right end of the search interval, respectively. If the size of the interval is less than a user-specified resolution, then the search terminates (lines 6–10 in Figure 25.22). On the other hand, if the connection at the middle point of the interval yields a nonnegative Δ_{max}, then the search continues only on the right half of the interval (line 11 in Figure 25.22); otherwise, the left half of the interval may be searched as well (lines 12–16 in Figure 25.22).

The MVERT algorithm [82] operates in two phases: (1) initial tree construction phase, where an initial tree is heuristically built to minimize delay and (2) cost-improvement phase, where the tree is iteratively refined to reduce its cost while ensuring that it still meets all the timing constraints. The tree construction in Phase 1 is similar to the SERT construction procedure proposed in Ref. [12] (described above). Recall that the essential idea of the SERT method is based on greedily building a Steiner tree using a Prim-like method. Starting with a trivial tree T consisting of only the source v_0, the tree is iteratively built by joining a sink v_k outside the tree to an edge (or the source) already in the tree, so as to yield a resulting new tree with minimum Elmore delay. This process iterates until all the sinks are included in the tree.

The initial tree construction procedure above considers only Hanan grid points as candidate Steiner points. It therefore attempts to connect each point to either the closest connection (CC), the upstream end of a tree edge, or directly to the source node. If the delay associated with a CC connection is larger than the delay associated with a connection to the upstream edge endpoint, then the algorithm will not choose the connection at CC. However, because of the interactions between paths, MVERT solutions may lie at different (and possibly non-Hanan) points, and a connection to the upstream end of an edge may result in a larger net length than is necessary. We therefore examine the tree constructed in Phase 1 and move node connections from the upstream end of an edge toward CC to reduce the tree length while still satisfying all the timing constraints. The idea is illustrated in the example of Figure 25.18 for the constraint of 98.8 units, where a connection to $(y, 0)$ is preferable over a connection to $(0.33, 0)$.

This non-Hanan interconnect synthesis algorithm (shown in Figure 25.23) can be implemented as follows [82]. We first sort all the sinks in descending order of distance from the source. We then disconnect each sink v_k (along with its downstream subtree T_k) and reconnect it back to the tree at a better reconnection point, if possible (as determined by the subroutine of Figure 25.22). Thus, at each iteration, we choose an edge that provides the largest wirelength improvement while still respecting the timing constraints. The computational complexity of the MVERT algorithm is $O(n^4)$, where n is the number of sinks. The experimental results in Ref. [88] show that non-Hanan optimization can in some instances provide considerable wirelength reduction as compared to other timing-driven routing methods.

```
Non-Hanan optimization algorithm
Input: Routing tree T(V, E)
Output: Optimized routing tree T'
1. T' = T
2. Sort all the sinks in descending order of distance to source
3. For each v_k ∈ V_sink
4.   Disjoin v_k and its subtree T_k from T
5.   For each edge e_ij ∈ T\T_k
6.     Reconnect v_k to e_ij at FindOptimalConnection(T_k, T\T_k, e_ij)
7.     If ∃ improvement compared to T', Then T' = T
8. Return T'
```

FIGURE 25.23 Non-Hanan optimization algorithm. (From Hu, J. and Sapatnekar, S. S., *IEEE Trans. Comput. Aided Des.*, 19, 446, 2000.)

25.6 WIRE SIZING

The fundamental trade-offs between interconnect capacitance and resistance in modern VLSI technology suggests that to maximize performance, some wire segments should be made wider than others. This motivates the technique of wire sizing, where every wire segment may have a different width, independently of all the other wires. This degree of freedom afforded by wire sizing can be leveraged throughout every phase of the performance-driven physical layout process. Historically, although early works wire sized mainly clock trees [89–92] and power distribution networks [93], the wire sizing of general interconnect became viable in the early 1990s [64,94–96] because of the confluence of VLSI scaling trends and algorithmic advances. Wire sizing considerations can be easily incorporated into all the routing constructions discussed above [16], and can even drive the routing process itself [95], as well as other layout phases higher in the design hierarchy. A more detailed discussion of wire sizing techniques can be found in Chapter 29.

25.7 NONTREE ROUTING

Historically, routing methodologies implicitly assumed that interconnections must have tree topologies. In retrospect, this was a natural constraint because a tree achieves electrical connectivity using minimum wire, and the VLSI technology trends of the 1980s were heavily skewed toward wirelength and area minimization as the primary objective. However, as feature sizes shrank dramatically and interconnect delays began to dominate circuit performance, researchers began to investigate nontree (i.e., general graphs) routing topologies. Aside from improving performance, nontree routing topologies offer other advantages, including the management of signal reflections, increased reliability, and reduced skew in sink delays. Thus, nontree topologies were used for power/ground distribution, where general graph topologies enhance reliability by lowering current densities and electromigration damage [93,97,98], as well as for clock distribution, where nontree topologies can reduce skew and minimize the impact of manufacturing variation [99].

Adding extra wires to an existing routing tree can improve certain source–sink delays. Although additional wires will always increase the total tree capacitance, the creation of multiple source–sink paths can substantially lower certain internode resistance. Thus, as VLSI interconnect becomes thinner and more resistive, nontree routing topologies become increasingly attractive. McCoy and Robins [17] have studied the following optimal routing graph (ORG) problem, which is a generalization of some of the routing problems discussed above.

The Optimal Routing Graph Problem: Given a signal net $S = \{s_0, s_1, \ldots, s_n\}$ with source s_0, find a set N of Steiner points and routing graph $G = (S \cup N, E)$ such that G spans S and minimizes $t(G) = \max_{i=1}^{n} t(s_i)$.

The ORG problem extends to critical-sink formulations as well as lumped RC and Elmore delay models, which can be computed efficiently for general RC graph topologies [100,101]. The ORG problem is addressed algorithmically in Ref. [17] by starting with a reasonable initial topology (e.g., a heuristic Steiner or spanning tree), and greedily adding new edges to this topology so as to keep improving the specified delay objectives in the growing routing graph. Steiner points may also be introduced during this process to further optimize both delay and wirelength. Using a fast delay estimator to drive this process yields an efficient technique for synthesizing nontree routing topologies with significantly improved performance characteristics (in terms of skew as well as delay), as compared with the corresponding initial trees [16,17]. Nontree routing topologies can also be combined with wire sizing optimizations, as discussed above. More recently, nontree routings were used for manufacturing yield improvement [102] and robust performance [103].

25.8 DISCUSSION AND FUTURE RESEARCH DIRECTIONS

Given the numerous existing algorithms for performance-driven Steiner tree construction, CAD practitioners are often faced with the question of which algorithm to choose for particular applications. In Ref. [11], a comparative study is performed for several Steiner tree algorithms [12,40,75,104,105]. One important result from Ref. [11] is that the wirelength of (minimum rectilinear Steiner arborescence (MRSA)) is not prohibitively large, even though MRSA constructions provide shortest paths from the source to all sinks. Experiments with several industrial designs show that the average wirelengths of heuristic RSAs are only around 2–4 percent larger than those of rectilinear Steiner minimum trees. Arborescence constructions (e.g., AHHK-based Steiner trees with $c = 1$) are therefore a good option for acheiving minimum tree radii with relatively small wirelength overhead.

As ultra-deep-submicron VLSI technology continues to evolve, new efficiently computable models are needed to accurately capture the relationships and trade-offs between high-performance routing and actual delays, parasitics, noise, signal integrity, reliability, power, manufacturability, and yield. The techniques described in this chapter can be generalized to alternate metrics, geometries, and novel interconnect architectures such as preferred-direction routing and λ-geometries. As VLSI engineering tolerances shrink, issues such as buffer insertion, wirelength estimation, and antenna effects will have to be revisited. In particular, extensive application of buffers [106] for performance improvement may drastically alter the landscape for interconnect topology construction. When buffers are inserted, the fanout size of subtrees between buffers are usually smaller than that of unbuffered nets. Moreover, the construction of global topology connecting the subtrees should be aware of the concerns in buffering algorithms [79,107]. As always, tighter and more effective integration between timing-driven routing and other design phases will enable additional optimizations of various combinations of objectives and criteria. Finally, when feature sizes become small enough, entirely new issues such as quantum effects will have to be considered during interconnect synthesis, as well as elsewhere in the design process.

ACKNOWLEDGMENT

Part of Section 25.2 has been published in *IEEE Transactions on Computer-Aided Design of Integrated Circuits and Systems*, by Alpert, C. J., Hu, T. C., Huang, J. H., Kahng, A. B., and Karger, D., Vol 14, pages 890–896, 1995 and all of Section 25.5 has been published in *Layout Optimization in VLSI Design*, authored by Hu, J. and Sapatnekar, S. (edited by Lu, B., Du, D.-Zu, and Sapatnekar S.), Kluwer Academic Publisher, 2001, pp. 95–104. Used with kind permission.

REFERENCES

1. Caldwell, A., Kahng, A. B., Mantik, S., Markov, I., and Zelikovsky, A. On wirelength estimations for row-based placement. In *Proceedings of the International Symposium on Physical Design*, Monterey, CA, April 1998, pp. 4–11.
2. Cheng, X. and Du, D. -Z. *Steiner Trees in Industry*. Kluwer Academic Publishers, the Netherlands, Dordrecht 2001.
3. Cieslik, D. *Steiner Minimal Trees*. Kluwer Academic Publishers, the Netherlands, Dordrecht 1998.
4. Cieslik, D. *The Steiner Ratio*. Kluwer Academic Publishers, the Netherlands, Dordrecht 2001.
5. Du, D. -Z., Smith, J. M., and Rubinstein, J. H. *Advances in Steiner Trees*. Kluwer Academic Publishers, the Netherlands, Dordrecht 2000.
6. Hwang, F. K., Richards, D. S., and Winter, P. The Steiner tree problem. *Annals of Discrete Mathematics* 53, North-Holland, the Netherlands, 1992.
7. Ivanov, A. O. and Tuzhilin, A. A. *Minimal Networks: The Steiner Problem and Its Generalizations*. CRC Press, Boca Raton, FL, 1994.
8. Korte, B., Promel, H. J., and Steger, A. *Steiner Trees in VLSI-Layouts, in Paths, Flows and VLSI-Layout*. Springer-Verlag, New York, 1990.

9. Promel, H. J. and Steger, A. *The Steiner Tree Problem: A Tour Through Graphs, Algorithms, and Complexity*. Friedrich Vieweg and Son, Braunschweig, Germany, 2002.

10. Robins, G. and Zelikovsky, A. Tighter bounds for graph Steiner tree approximation. *SIAM Journal on Discrete Mathematics* 19(1): 122–134, 2005.

11. Alpert, C. J., Kahng, A. B., Sze, C. N., and Wang, Q. Timing-driven Steiner trees are (practically) free. In *Proceedings of the ACM/IEEE Design Automation Conference*, San Francisco, CA, 2006, pp. 389–392.

12. Boese, K. D., Kahng, A. B., McCoy, B. A., and Robins, G. Near-optimal critical sink routing tree constructions. *IEEE Transactions Computer-Aided Design* 14(12): 1417–1436, December 1995.

13. Cong, J., Kahng, A. B., Koh, C. K., and Tsao, C. -W. A. Bounded-skew clock and Steiner routing. *ACM Transactions on Design Automation of Electronic Systems* 3: 341–388, October 1999.

14. Ismail, Y. I. and Friedman, E. G. *On-Chip Inductance in High-Speed Integrated Circuits*. Kluwer Academic Publishers, Boston, MA, 2001.

15. Kahng, A. B., Mantik, S., and Stroobandt, D. Towards accurate models of achievable routing. *IEEE Transactions Computer-Aided Design* 20: 648–659, May 2001.

16. Kahng, A. B. and Robins, G. *On Optimal Interconnections for VLSI*. Kluwer Academic Publishers, Boston, MA, 1995.

17. McCoy, B. A. and Robins, G. Non-tree routing. *IEEE Transactions Computer-Aided Design* 14(14): 790–784, June 1995.

18. Sherwani, N., Bhingarde, S., and Panyam, A. *Routing in the Third Dimension*. IEEE Press, New York, 1995.

19. Cong, J., He, L., Koh, C. -K., and Madden, P. H. Performance optimization of VLSI interconnect layout. *Integration: The VLSI Journal* 21: 1–94, November 1996.

20. Hu, J. and Sapatnekar, S. S. A survey on multi-net global routing for integrated circuits. *Integration: The VLSI Journal* 11: 1–49, 2001.

21. Gerez, S. H. *Algorithms for VLSI Design Automation*. John Wiley and Sons, Chichester, United Kingdom, 1998.

22. Preas, B. T. and Lorenzetti, M. J. *Physical Design Automation of VLSI Systems*. Benjamin/Cummings, Menlo Park, CA, 1988.

23. Sait, S. M. and Youssef, N. *VLSI Physical Design Automation—Theory and Practice*. World Scientific Publishing Company, Singapore, 1999.

24. Sarrafzadeh, M. and Wong, C. K. *An Introduction to VLSI Physical Design*. McGraw Hill, New York, 1996.

25. Sherwani, N. *Algorithms for VLSI Physical Design Automation*, Third edition. Kluwer Academic Publishers, Boston, MA, 1998.

26. Bakoglu, H. *Circuits, Interconnections and Packaging for VLSI*. Addison-Wesley, Reading, MA, 1990.

27. Donath, W. E., Norman, R. J., Agrawal, B. K., Bello, S. E., Han, S. Y., Kurtzberg, J. M., Lowy, P., and McMillan, R. I. Timing driven placement using complete path delays. In *Proceedings of the ACM/IEEE Design Automation Conference*, Orlando, FL, 1990, pp. 84–89.

28. Sutanthavibul, S. and Shragowitz, E. An adaptive timing-driven layout for high speed VLSI. In *Proceedings of the ACM/IEEE Design Automation Conference*, Orlando, FL, 1990, pp. 90–95.

29. Hauge, P. S., Nair, R., and Yoffa, E. J. Circuit placement for predictable performance. In *Proceedings of the IEEE International Conference Computer-Aided Design*, Santa Clara, CA, November 1987, pp. 88–91.

30. Jackson, M. A. B. and Kuh, E. S. Performance-driven placement of cell-based ICs. In *Proceedings of the ACM/IEEE Design Automation Conference*, Las Vegas, NV, 1989, pp. 370–375.

31. Lin, I. and Du, D. H. C. Performance-driven constructive placement. In *Proceedings of the ACM/IEEE Design Automation Conference*, Orlando, FL, 1990, pp. 103–106.

32. Marek-Sadowska, M. and Lin, S. P. Timing driven placement. In *Proceedings of the IEEE International Conference Computer-Aided Design*, Santa Clara, CA, November 1989, pp. 94–97.

33. Dunlop, A. E., Agrawal, V. D., Deutsch, D., Jukl, M. F., Kozak, P., and Wiesel, M. Chip layout optimization using critical path weighting. In *Proceedings of the ACM/IEEE Design Automation Conference*, 1984, pp. 133–136.

34. Jackson, M. A. B., Kuh, E. S., and Marek-Sadowska, M. Timing-driven routing for building block layout. In *Proceedings of the IEEE International Symposium Circuits and Systems*, Miami Beach, FL, 1987, pp. 518–519.

35. Prasitjutrakul, S. and Kubitz, W. J. A timing-driven global router for custom chip design. In *Proceedings of the IEEE International Conference Computer-Aided Design*, Santa Clara, CA, November 1990, pp. 48–51.

36. Elmore, W. C. The transient response of damped linear networks with particular regard to wide-band amplifiers. *Journal of Applied Physics* 19(1): 55–63, 1948.
37. Lin, T. M. and Mead, C. A. Signal delay in general RC-networks. *IEEE Transactions Computer-Aided Design* CAD-3(4): 331–349, October 1984.
38. Rubinstein, J., Penfield, P., and Horowitz, M. A. Signal delay in RC tree networks. *IEEE Transactions Computer-Aided Design* 2(3): 202–211, 1983.
39. Tsay, R. S. Exact zero skew. In *Proceedings of the IEEE International Conference Computer-Aided Design*, Santa Clara, CA, November 1991, pp. 336–339.
40. Alpert, C. J., Hu, T. C., Huang, J. H., Kahng, A. B., and Karger, D. Prim-Dijkstra tradeoffs for improved performance-driven routing tree design. *IEEE Transactions Computer-Aided Design* 14(7): 890–896, July 1995. (ISCAS 1993).
41. Awerbuch, B., Baratz, A., and Peleg, D. Cost-sensitive analysis of communication protocols. In *Proceedings of the ACM Symposium Principles of Distributed Computing*, Quebec City, Quebec, Canada, 1990, pp. 177–187.
42. Cong, J., Kahng, A. B., Robins, G., Sarrafzadeh, M., and Wong, C. K. Provably good algorithms for performance-driven global routing. In *Proceedings of the IEEE International Symposium Circuits and Systems*, San Diego, CA, May 1992, pp. 2240–2243.
43. Cong, J., Kahng, A. B., Robins, G., Sarrafzadeh, M., and Wong, C. K. Provably good performance-driven global routing. *IEEE Transactions Computer-Aided Design* 11(6): 739–752, 1992.
44. Khuller, S., Raghavachari, B., and Young, N. Balancing minimum spanning and shortest path trees. In *Proceedings of the ACM/SIAM Symposium Discrete Algorithms*, Austin, TX, January 1993, pp. 243–250.
45. Boese, K. D., Kahng, A. B., McCoy, B. A., and Robins, G. Fidelity and near-optimality of Elmore-based routing constructions. In *Proceedings of the IEEE International Conference Computer Design*, Cambridge, MA, October 1993, pp. 81–84.
46. Boese, K. D., Kahng, A. B., McCoy, B. A., and Robins, G. Rectilinear Steiner trees with minimum Elmore delay. In *Proceedings of the ACM/IEEE Design Automation Conference*, San Diego, CA, June 1994, pp. 381–386.
47. Boese, K. D., Kahng, A. B., and Robins, G. High-performance routing trees with identified critical sinks. In *Proceedings of the ACM/IEEE Design Automation Conference*, Dallas, TX, June 1993, pp. 182–187.
48. Lillis, J., Cheng, C. K., Lin, T. -T. Y., and Ho, C. -Y. New performance driven routing techniques with explicit area/delay tradeoff and simultaneous wire sizing. In *Proceedings of the ACM/IEEE Design Automation Conference*, Las Vegas, NV, 1996, pp. 395–400.
49. Chen, H., Cheng, C. -K., Kahng, A., Măndoiu, I. I., Wang, Q., and Yao., B. The y-architecture for on-chip interconnect: Analysis and methodology. *IEEE Transactions Computer-Aided Design* 24(4): 588–599, April 2005.
50. Chen, H., Cheng, C. -K., Kahng, A. B., Măndoiu, I., and Wang, Q. Estimation of wirelength reduction for λ-geometry vs. Manhattan placement and routing. In *Proceedings of the ACM International Workshop on System-Level Interconnect Prediction*, Monterey, CA, 2003, pp. 71–76.
51. Koh, C. -K. and Madden, P. H. Manhattan or non-Manhattan?: A study of alternative VLSI routing architectures. In *Proceedings of the Great Lakes Symposium VLSI*, Chicago, IL, 2000, pp. 47–52.
52. Li, Y. Y., Cheung, S. K., Leung, K. S., and Wong, C. K. Steiner tree construction in λ_3-metric. *IEEE Transactions Circuits and Systems-II: Analog and Digital Signal Processing* 45(5): 563–574, May 1998.
53. Nielsen, B. K., Winter, P., and Zachariasen, M. An exact algorithm for the uniformly-oriented Steiner tree problem. In *Proceedings of the European Symposium on Algorithms*, Lecture Notes in Computer Science 2461. Springer-Verlag, Rome, Italy, 2002, pp. 760–771.
54. Sarrafzadeh, M. and Wong, C. K. Hierarchical Steiner tree construction in uniform orientations. *IEEE Transactions Computer-Aided Design* 11(9): 1095–1103, September 1992.
55. Teig, S. The x architecture: Not your father's diagonal wiring. In *Proceedings of the ACM International Workshop on System-Level Interconnect Prediction*, San Diego, CA, 2002, pp. 33–37.
56. Yildiz, M. C. and Madden, P. H. Preferred direction Steiner trees. In *Proceedings of the Great Lakes Symposium VLSI*, West Lafayette, IN, 2001, pp. 56–61.
57. Dijkstra, E. W. A note on two problems in connection with graphs. *Numerische Mathematik* 1: 269–271, 1959.
58. Prim, A. Shortest connecting networks and some generalizations. *Bell System Technical Journal* 36: 1389–1401, 1957.

59. Cong, J., Kahng, A. B., Robins, G., Sarrafzadeh, M., and Wong, C. K. Performance-driven global routing for cell based ICs. In *Proceedings of the IEEE International Conference Computer Design*, Cambridge, MA, October 1991, pp. 170–173.

60. Robins, G. and Zelikovsky, A. Improved Steiner tree approximation in graphs. In *Proceedings of the ACM/SIAM Symposium Discrete Algorithms*, San Francisco, CA, January 2000, pp. 770–779.

61. Kahng, A. B. and Robins, G. On performance bounds for a class of rectilinear Steiner tree heuristics in arbitrary dimension. *IEEE Transactions Computer-Aided Design* 11(11): 1462–1465, November 1992.

62. Griffith, J., Robins, G., Salowe, J. S., and Zhang, T. Closing the gap: Near-optimal Steiner trees in polynomial time. *IEEE Transactions Computer-Aided Design* 13(11): 1351–1365, November 1994.

63. Kahng, A. B. and Robins, G. A new class of iterative Steiner tree heuristics with good performance. *IEEE Transactions Computer-Aided Design* 11(7): 893–902, July 1992.

64. Cong, J., Leung, K. S., and Zhou, D. Performance-driven interconnect design based on distributed RC delay model. In *Proceedings of the ACM/IEEE Design Automation Conference*, Dallas, June 1993, pp. 606–611.

65. Nastansky, L., Selkow, S. M., and Stewart, N. F. Cost-minima trees in directed acyclic graphs. *Zeitschrift for Operations Research* 18: 59–67, 1974.

66. de Matos, R. R. L. A Rectilinear Arborescence Problem. PhD thesis, University of Alabama, Tuscaloosa, Alabama, 1979.

67. Ho, J. M., Ko, M. T., Ma, T. H., and Sung, T. Y. Algorithms for rectilinear optimal multicast tree problem. In *Proceedings of the International Symposium on Algorithms and Computation*, Nagoya, Japan, June 1992, pp. 106–15.

68. Leung, K. -S. and Cong, J. Fast optimal algorithms for the minimum rectilinear Steiner arborescence problem. In *Proceedings of the IEEE International Symposium Circuits and Systems*, Vol. 3, Hong Kong, 1997, pp. 1568–1571.

69. Rao, S. K., Sadayappan, P., Hwang, F. K., and Shor, P. W. The rectilinear Steiner arborescence problem. *Algorithmica* 7(1): 277–288, 1992.

70. Trubin, V. A. Subclass of the Steiner problems on a plane with rectilinear metric. *Cybernetics and Systems Analysis* 21(3): 320–322, 1985.

71. Shi, W. and Su, C. The rectilinear Steiner arborescence problem is np-complete. *SIAM Journal of Computation* 35(3): 729–740, 2006.

72. Cordova, J. and Lee, Y. H. A heuristic algorithm for the rectilinear Steiner arborescence problem. Technical Report TR-94-025, University of Florida, Gainesville, FL, 1994.

73. Alexander, M. J. and Robins, G. New performance-driven FPGA routing algorithms. *IEEE Transactions Computer-Aided Design* 15(12): 1505–1517, December 1996.

74. Kou, L., Markowsky, G., and Berman, L. A fast algorithm for Steiner trees. *Acta Informatica* 15: 141–145, 1981.

75. Cong, J., Kahng, A. B., and Leung, K. -S. Efficient algorithms for the minimum shortest path Steiner arborescence problem with applications to VLSI physical design. *IEEE Transactions Computer-Aided Design* 17(1): 24–39, January 1998.

76. Robins, G. On Optimal Interconnections. PhD thesis, Department of Computer Science, UCLA, CSD-TR-920024, Los Angeles, CA, 1992.

77. Zhou, D., Tsui, F., and Gao, D. S. High performance multichip interconnection design. In *Proceedings of the ACM/SIGDA Physical Design Workshop*, Lake Arrowhead, CA, April 1993, pp. 32–43.

78. Sriram, M. and Kang, S. M. Performance driven MCM routing using a second order RLC tree delay model. In *IEEE International Conference on Wafer Scale Integration*, San Francisco, CA, January 1993, pp. 262–267.

79. Alpert, C. J., Gandham, G., Hrkic, M., Hu, J., Kahng, A. B., Lillis, J., Liu, B., Quay, S. T., Sapatnekar, S. S., and Sullivan, A. J. Buffered Steiner trees for difficult instances. *IEEE Transactions Computer-Aided Design* 21(1): 3–14, January 2002.

80. Ganley, J. L. Accuracy and fidelity of fast net length estimates. *Integration: The VLSI Journal* 23(2): 151–155, 1997.

81. Hong, X., Xue, T., Kuh, E. S., Cheng, C. K., and Huang, J. Performance-driven Steiner tree algorithms for global routing. In *Proceedings of the ACM/IEEE Design Automation Conference*, Dallas, TX, June 1993, pp. 177–181.

82. Hu, J. and Sapatnekar, S. S. Algorithms for non-Hanan-based optimization for VLSI interconnect under a higher order awe model. *IEEE Transactions Computer-Aided Design* 19(4): 446–458, April 2000.

83. Hu, J. and Sapatnekar, S. S. A timing-constrained simultaneous global routing algorithm. *IEEE Transactions Computer-Aided Design* 21(9): 1025–1036, September 2002.

84. Peyer, S., Zachariasen, M., and Grove, D. J. Delay-related secondary objectives for rectilinear Steiner minimum trees. *Discrete and Applied Mathematics* 136(2): 271–298, February 2004.

85. Wu, D., Hu, J., and Mahapatra, R. Coupling aware timing optimization and antenna avoidance in layer assignment. In *Proceedings of the International Symposium on Physical Design*. ACM Press, New York, 2005, pp. 20–27.

86. Hanan, M. On Steiner's problem with rectilinear distance. *SIAM Journal of Applied Mathematics* 14: 255–265, 1966.

87. Zachariasen, M. A catalog of Hanan grid problems. *Networks—An International Journal* 38(2): 76–83, 2001.

88. Hou, H., Hu, J., and Sapatnekar, S. S. Non-Hanan routing. *IEEE Transactions Computer-Aided Design* 18(4): 436–444, April 1999.

89. Fisher, A. L. and Kung, H. T. Synchronizing large systolic arrays. In *Proceedings of SPIE*, Arlington, VA, May 1982, pp. 44–52.

90. Friedman, E. G. Clock distribution design in VLSI circuits—an overview. In *Proceedings of the IEEE International Symposium Circuits and Systems*, Chicago, IL, May 1993, pp. 1475–1478.

91. Pullela, S., Menezes, N., and Pillage, L. T. Reliable non-zero skew clock trees using wire width optimization. In *Proceedings of the ACM/IEEE Design Automation Conference*, San Diego, CA, 1993, pp. 165–170.

92. Zhu, Q., Dai, W. W. M., and Xi, J. G. Optimal sizing of high-speed clock networks based on distributed RC and lossy transmission line models. In *Proceedings of the IEEE International Conference Computer-Aided Design*, 1993, pp. 628–633.

93. Dutta, R. and Marek-Sadowska, M. Algorithm for wire sizing of power and ground networks in VLSI designs. *Journal of Circuits, Systems and Computers* 2: 141–157, June 1992.

94. Cong, J., and Leung, K. S. Optimal wiresizing under the distributed Elmore delay model. In *Proceedings of the IEEE International Conference Computer-Aided Design*, 1993, pp. 634–639.

95. Hodes, T. D., McCoy, B. A., and Robins, G. Dynamically-wiresized Elmore-based routing constructions. In *Proceedings of the IEEE International Symposium Circuits and Systems*, Vol. I, London, United Kingdom, May 1994, pp. 463–466.

96. Sapetnekar, S. RC interconnect optimization under the Elmore delay model. In *Proceedings of the ACM/IEEE Design Automation Conference*, San Diego, CA, June 1994, pp. 387–391.

97. Erhard, K. H. and Johannes, F. M. Power/ground networks in VLSI: Are general graphs better than trees? *Integration: The VLSI Journal* 14(1): 91–109, November 1992.

98. Erhard, K. H., Johannes, F. M., and Dachauer, R. Topology optimization techniques for power/ground networks in VLSI. In *Proceedings of the European Design Automation Conference*, Hamburg, Germany, September 1992, pp. 362–367.

99. Lin, S. and Wong, C. K. Process-variation-tolerant clock skew minimization. In *Proceedings of the IEEE International Conference Computer-Aided Design*, San Jose, CA, November 1994, pp. 284–288.

100. Chan, P. K. and Karplus, K. Computing signal delay in general RC networks by tree/link partitioning. *IEEE Transactions Computer-Aided Design* 9(8): 898–902, August 1990.

101. Martin, D. and Rumin, N. C. Delay prediction from resistance-capacitance models of general MOS circuits. *IEEE Transactions Computer-Aided Design* 12(7): 997–1003, July 1993.

102. Kahng, A. B., Liu, B., and Mandoiu, I. I. Non-tree routing for reliability and yield improvement. *IEEE Transactions Computer-Aided Design* 23(1): 148–156, 2004.

103. Hu, S., Li, Q., Hu, J., and Li, P. Steiner network construction for timing critical nets. In *Proceedings of the ACM/IEEE Design Automation Conference*, 2006, pp. 379–384.

104. Borah, M., Owens, R. M., and Irwin, M. J. An edge-based heuristic for Steiner routing. *IEEE Transactions Computer-Aided Design* 13: 1563–1568, 1994.

105. Qiu, W. and Shi, W. Minimum moment Steiner trees. In *Proceedings of the ACM/SIAM Symposium Discrete Algorithms*, 2004, pp. 488–495.

106. Saxena, P., Menezes, N., Cocchini, P., and Kirkpatrick, D. A. Repeater scaling and its impact on CAD. *IEEE Transactions Computer-Aided Design* 23(4): 451–463, April 2004.

107. Hrkic, M. and Lillis, J. Buffer tree synthesis with consideration of temporal locality, sink polarity requirements, solution cost, congestion and blockages. *IEEE Transactions Computer-Aided Design* 22(4): 481–491, April 2003.

26 Buffer Insertion Basics

Jiang Hu, Zhuo Li, and Shiyan Hu

CONTENTS

26.1 MOTIVATION

When the VLSI technology scales, gate delay and wire delay change in opposite directions. Smaller devices imply less gate-switching delay. In contrast, thinner wire size leads to increased wire resistance and greater signal propagation delay along wires. As a result, wire delay has become a dominating factor for VLSI circuit performance. Further, it is becoming a limiting factor to the progress of VLSI technology. This is the well-known interconnect challenge [1–3]. Among many techniques addressing this challenge [4,5], buffer (or repeater) insertion is such an effective technique that it is an indispensable necessity for timing closure in submicron technology and beyond. Buffers can reduce wire delay by restoring signal strength, in particular, for long wires. Moreover, buffers can be applied to shield capacitive load from timing-critical paths such that the interconnect delay along critical paths are reduced.

As the ratio of wire delay to gate delay increases from one technology to the next, more and more buffers are required to achieve performance goals. The buffer scaling is studied by Intel and the results are reported in Ref. [6]. One metric that reveals the scaling is critical buffer length, the minimum distance beyond which inserting an optimally placed and sized buffer makes the interconnect delay less than that of the corresponding unbuffered wire. When wire delay increases because of the technology scaling, the critical buffer length becomes shorter, i.e., the distance that a buffer can comfortably drive shrinks. According to Ref. [6], the critical buffer length decreases by 68 percent when the VLSI technology migrates from 90 to 45 nm (for two generations). Please note that the critical buffer-length scaling significantly outpaces the VLSI technology scaling, which is roughly $0.5\times$ for every two generations. If we look at the percentage of block level nets requiring buffers, it grows from 5.8 percent in 90-nm technology to 19.6 percent in 45-nm technology [6]. Perhaps the most alarming result is the scaling of buffer count [6], which predicts that 35 percent of cells will be buffers in 45-nm technology as opposed to only 6 percent in 90-nm technology.

The dramatic buffer scaling undoubtedly generates large and profound impact to VLSI circuit design. With millions of buffers required per chip, almost nobody can afford to neglect the importance of buffer insertion as compared to a decade ago when only a few thousands of buffers are needed for a chip [7]. Because of this importance, buffer insertion algorithms and methodologies need to be deeply studied on various aspects. First, a buffer insertion algorithm should deliver solutions of high quality because interconnect and circuit performance largely depend on the way that buffers are placed. Second, a buffer insertion algorithm needs to be sufficiently fast so that millions of nets can be optimized in reasonable time. Third, accurate delay models are necessary to ensure that buffer insertion solutions are reliable. Fourth, buffer insertion techniques are expected to simultaneously handle multiple objectives, such as timing, power, and signal integrity, and their trade-offs. Last but not the least, buffer insertion should interact with other layout steps, such as placement and routing, as the sheer number of buffers has already altered the landscape of circuit layout design. Many of these issues will be discussed in subsequent sections and other chapters.

26.2 OPTIMIZATION OF TWO-PIN NETS

For buffer insertion, perhaps the most simple case is a two-pin net, which is a wire segment with a driver (source) at one end and a sink at the other end. The simplicity allows closed form solutions to buffer insertion in two-pin nets.

If the delay of a two-pin net is to be minimized by using a single buffer type b, one needs to decide the number of buffers k and the spacing between the buffers, the source and the sink. First, let us look at a very simple case to attain an intuitive understanding of the problem. In this case, the length of the two-pin net is l and the wire resistance and capacitance per unit length are r and c, respectively. The number of buffers k has been given and is fixed. The driver resistance is the same as the buffer output resistance R_b. The load capacitance of the sink is identical to buffer input capacitance C_b. The buffer has an intrinsic delay of t_b. The k buffers separates the net into $k + 1$ segments, with length of $\vec{l} = (l_0, l_1, \ldots, l_k)^T$ (Figure 26.1). Then, the Elmore delay of this net can be expressed as

$$t(\vec{l}) = \sum_{i=0}^{k} \left(\alpha l_i^2 + \beta l_i + \gamma \right) \tag{26.1}$$

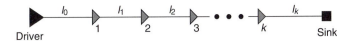

FIGURE 26.1   Buffer insertion in a two-pin net.

where $\alpha = \frac{1}{2}rc$, $\beta = R_b c + r C_b$, and $\gamma = R_b C_b + t_b$. A formal problem formulation is

$$\text{minimize} \quad t(\vec{l}) \tag{26.2}$$

$$\text{subject to} \quad g(\vec{l}) = l - \sum_{i=0}^{k} l_i = 0 \tag{26.3}$$

According to the Kuhn–Tucker condition [8], the following equation is the necessary condition for the optimal solution.

$$\vec{\nabla} t(\vec{l}) + \lambda \vec{\nabla} g(\vec{l}) = 0 \tag{26.4}$$

where λ is the Lagrangian multiplier. According to the above condition, it can be easily derived that

$$l_i = \frac{\beta}{\lambda - 2\alpha}, \quad i = 0, 1, \ldots, k \tag{26.5}$$

Because α, β, and λ are all constants, it can be seen that the buffers need to be equally spaced to minimize the delay. This is an important conclusion that can be treated as a rule of thumb. The value of the Lagrangian multiplier λ can be found by plugging Equation 26.5 into Equation 26.3.

In more general cases, the driver resistance R_d may be different from that of buffer output resistance and so is the sink capacitance C_L. For such cases, the optimum number of buffers minimizing the delay is given by Ref. [9]

$$k = \left\lfloor -\frac{1}{2} + \sqrt{1 + \frac{2[rcl + r(C_b - C_L) - c(R_b - R_d)]^2}{rc\,(R_b C_b + t_b)}} \right\rfloor \tag{26.6}$$

The length of each segment can be obtained through [9]

$$l_0 = \frac{1}{k+1}\left[l + \frac{k\,(R_b - R_d)}{r} + \frac{C_L - C_b}{c} \right]$$

$$l_1 = \ldots = l_{k-1} = \frac{1}{k+1}\left[l - \frac{R_b - R_d}{r} + \frac{C_L - C_b}{c} \right] \tag{26.7}$$

$$l_k = \frac{1}{k+1}\left[l - \frac{R_b - R_d}{r} - \frac{k\,(C_L - C_b)}{c} \right]$$

A closed form solution to simultaneous buffer insertion/sizing and wire sizing is reported in Ref. [10]. Figure 26.2 shows an example of this simultaneous optimization. The wire is segmented into m pieces. The length l_i and width h_i of each wire piece i are the variables to be optimized. There are k buffers inserted between these pieces. The size b_i of each buffer i is also a decision variable. A buffer location is indicated by its surrounding wire pieces. For example, if the set of wire pieces between buffer $i - 1$ and i is $\mathcal{P}_{i-1}$, the distance between the two buffers is equal to $\sum_{j \in \mathcal{P}_{i-1}} l_j$. There are two important conclusions [10] for the optimal solution that minimizes the delay. First, all wire pieces have the same length, i.e., $l_i = \frac{l}{m}, i = 1, 2, \ldots, m$. Second, for wire pieces $\mathcal{P}_{i-1} = \{p_{i-1,1}, p_{i-1,2}, \ldots, p_{i-1,m_{i-1}}\}$ between buffer $i - 1$ and i, their widths satisfy $h_{i-1,1} > h_{i-1,2} > \ldots > h_{i-1,m_{i-1}}$ and form a geometric progression.

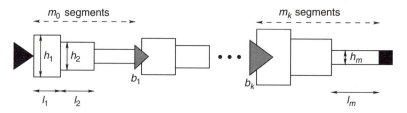

FIGURE 26.2 Example of simultaneous buffer insertion/sizing and wire sizing.

26.3 VAN GINNEKEN'S ALGORITHM

For a general case of signal nets, which may have multiple sinks, van Ginneken's algorithm [11] is perhaps the first systematic approach on buffer insertion. For a fixed signal routing tree and given candidate buffer locations, van Ginneken's algorithm can find the optimal buffering solution that maximizes timing slack according to the Elmore delay model. If there are n candidate buffer locations, its computation complexity is $O(n^2)$. Based on van Ginneken's algorithm, numerous extensions have been made, such as handling of multiple buffer types, trade-off with power and cost, addressing slew rate and crosstalk noise, and using accurate delay models and speedup techniques. These extensions will be covered in subsequent sections.

At a high level, van Ginneken's algorithm [11] proceeds bottom-up from the leaf nodes toward the driver along a given routing tree. A set of candidate solutions keep updated during the process, where three operations adding wire, inserting buffers, and branch merging may be performed. Meanwhile, the inferior solutions are pruned to accelerate the algorithm. After a set of candidate solutions are propagated to the source, the solution with the maximum required arrival time is selected as the final solution. For a routing tree with n buffer positions, the algorithm computes the optimal buffering solution in $O(n^2)$ time.

A net is given as a binary routing tree $T = (V, E)$, where $V = \{s_0\} \cup V_s \cup V_n$, and $E \subseteq V \times V$. Vertex s_0 is the source vertex and also the root of T, V_s is the set of sink vertices, and V_n is the set of internal vertices. In the existing literatures, s_0 is also referred as driver. Denote by $T(v)$ the subtree of T rooted at v. Each sink vertex $s \in V_s$ is associated with a sink capacitance $C(s)$ and a required arrival time (RAT). Each edge $e \in E$ is associated with lumped resistance $R(e)$ and capacitance $C(e)$. A buffer library B containing all the possible buffer types that can be assigned to a buffer position is also given. In this section, B contains only one buffer type. Delay estimation is obtained using the Elmore delay model, which is described in Chapter 3. A buffer assignment γ is a mapping $\gamma : V_n \to B \cup \{\bar{b}\}$ where $\bar{b}$ denotes that no buffer is inserted. The timing buffering problem is defined as follows.

Timing-driven buffer insertion problem: Given a binary routing tree $T = (V, E)$, possible buffer positions, and a buffer library B, compute a buffer assignment γ such that the RAT at driver is maximized.

26.3.1 CONCEPT OF CANDIDATE SOLUTION

A buffer assignment γ is also called a candidate solution for the timing buffering problem. A partial solution, denoted by γ_v, refers to an incomplete solution where the buffer assignment in $T(v)$ has been determined.

The Elmore delay from v to any sink s in $T(v)$ under γ_v is computed by

$$D(s, \gamma_v) = \sum_{e=(v_i, v_j)} [D(v_i) + D(e)]$$

where the sum is taken over all edges along the path from v to s. The slack of vertex v under γ_v is defined as

$$Q(\gamma_v) = \min_{s \in T(v)} \{\text{RAT}(s) - D(s, \gamma_v)\}$$

At any vertex v, the effect of a partial solution γ_v to its upstream part is characterized by a $(Q(\gamma_v), C(\gamma_v))$ pair, where Q is the slack at v under γ_v and C is the downstream capacitance viewing at v under γ_v.

26.3.2 GENERATING CANDIDATE SOLUTIONS

van Ginneken's algorithm proceeds bottom-up from the leaf nodes toward the driver along T. A set of candidate solutions, denoted by Γ, are kept updated during this process. There are three operations through solution propagation, namely, wire insertion, buffer insertion, and branch merging (Figure 26.3). We are to describe them in turn.

26.3.2.1 Wire Insertion

Suppose that a partial solution γ_v at position v propagates to an upstream position u and there is no branching point in between. If no buffer is placed at u, then only wire delay needs to be considered. Therefore, the new solution γ_u can be computed as

$$Q(\gamma_u) = Q(\gamma_v) - D(e)$$
$$C(\gamma_u) = C(\gamma_v) + C(e)$$

(26.8)

where $e = (u, v)$ and $D(e) = R(e)\left[\frac{C(e)}{2} + C(\gamma_v)\right]$.

26.3.2.2 Buffer Insertion

Suppose that we add a buffer b at u. Denote by $R(b)$, $K(b)$ the driving resistance and the intrinsic delay of buffer b, respectively. γ_u is then updated to γ_u' where

$$Q(\gamma_u') = Q(\gamma_u) - \left[R(b) \cdot C(\gamma_u) + K(b)\right]$$
$$C(\gamma_u') = C(b)$$

(26.9)

26.3.2.3 Branch Merging

When two branches T_l and T_r meet at a branching point v, Γ_l and Γ_r, which correspond to T_l and T_r, respectively, are to be merged. The merging process is performed as follows. For each solution $\gamma_l \in \Gamma_l$ and each solution $\gamma_r \in \Gamma_r$, generate a new solution γ' according to

$$C(\gamma') = C(\gamma_l) + C(\gamma_r)$$
$$Q(\gamma') = \min\{Q(\gamma_l), Q(\gamma_r)\}$$

(26.10)

The smaller Q is picked since the worst-case circuit performance needs to be considered.

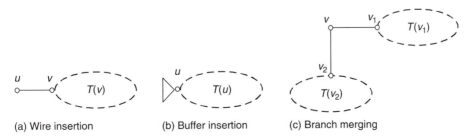

(a) Wire insertion   (b) Buffer insertion   (c) Branch merging

FIGURE 26.3 Operations in van Ginneken's algorithm.

26.3.3 INFERIORITY AND PRUNING IDENTIFICATION

Simply propagating all solutions by the above three operations makes the solution set grow exponentially in the number of buffer positions processed. An effective and efficient pruning technique is necessary to reduce the size of the solution set. This motivates an important concept—inferior solution—in van Ginneken's algorithm. For any two partial solutions γ_1 and γ_2 at the same vertex v, γ_2 is inferior to γ_1 if $C(\gamma_1) \leq C(\gamma_2)$ and $Q(\gamma_1) \geq Q(\gamma_2)$. Whenever a solution becomes inferior, it is pruned from the solution set. Therefore, only solutions that excel in at least one aspect of downstream capacitance and slack can survive.

For an efficient pruning implementation and thus an efficient buffering algorithm, a sorted list is used to maintain the solution set. The solution set Γ is increasingly sorted according to C, and thus Q is also increasingly sorted if Γ does not contain any inferior solutions.

By a straightforward implementation, when adding a wire, the number of candidate solutions will not change; when inserting a buffer, only one new candidate solution will be introduced. More efforts are needed to merge two branches T_1 and T_r at v. For each partial solution in Γ_1, find the first solution with larger Q value in Γ_r. If such a solution does not exist, the last solution in Γ_r will be taken. Because Γ_1 and Γ_r are sorted, we only need to traverse them once. Partial solutions in Γ_r are similarly treated. It is easy to see that after merging, the number of solutions is at most $|\Gamma_1| + |\Gamma_r|$. As such, given n buffer positions, at most n solutions can be generated at any time. Consequently, the pruning procedure at any vertex in T runs in $O(n)$ time.

26.3.4 PSEUDOCODE

In van Ginneken's algorithm, a set of candidate solutions are propagated from sinks to driver. Along a branch, after a candidate buffer location v is processed, all solutions are propagated to its upstream buffer location u through wire insertion. A buffer is then inserted to each solution to obtain a new solution. Meanwhile, inferior solutions are pruned. At a branching point, solution sets from all branches are merged by merging process. In this way, the algorithm proceeds in the bottom-up fashion and the solution with maximum required arrival time at driver is returned. Given n buffer positions in T, van Ginneken's algorithm can compute a buffer assignment with maximum slack at driver in $O(n^2)$ time, because any operation at any node can be performed in $O(n)$ time. Refer to Figure 26.4 for the pseudocode of van Ginneken's algorithm.

26.3.5 EXAMPLE

Let us look at a simple example to illustrate the work flow of van Ginneken's algorithm. Refer to Figure 26.5. Assume that there are three nondominated solutions at v_3 whose (Q, C) pairs are

$$(200, 10), (300, 30), \text{ and } (500, 50)$$

and there are two nondominated solutions at v_2 whose (Q, C) pairs are

$$(290, 5) \text{ and } (350, 20)$$

We first propagate them to v_1 through wire insertion. Assume that $R(v_1, v_3) = 3$ and $C(v_1, v_3) = 2$. Solution (200, 10) at v_3 becomes $(200 - 3 \cdot (2/2 + 10), 10 + 2) = (167, 12)$ at v_1. Similarly, the other two solutions become (207, 32) and (347, 52). Assume that $R(v_2, v_3) = 2$ and $C(v_2, v_3) = 2$, solutions at v_2 become (278, 7) and (308, 22) at v_1.

We are now to merge these solutions at v_1. Denote by Γ_1 the solutions propagated from v_3 and by Γ_r the solutions propagated from v_2. Before merging, partial solutions in Γ_1 are

$$(167, 12), (207, 32), \text{ and } (347, 52)$$

Algorithm: van Ginneken's algorithm
Input: T: routing tree, B: buffer library
Output: γ which maximizes slack at driver
1. for each sink s, build a solution set $\{\gamma_s\}$, where $Q(\gamma_s) = RAT(s)$
   and $C(\gamma_s) = C(s)$
2. for each branching point/driver v_t in the order given by a
   postorder traversal of T, let T' be each of the branches T_1, T_2 of v_t
   and Γ' be the solution set corresponding to T', do
3.   for each wire e in T', in a bottom-up order, do
4.   for each $\gamma \in \Gamma'$, do
5. $C(\gamma) = C(\gamma) + C(e)$
6. $Q(\gamma) = Q(\gamma) - D(e)$
7.   prune inferior solutions in Γ'
8.   if the current position allows buffer insertion, then
9.   for each $\gamma \in \Gamma'$, generate a new solution γ'
10.   set $C(\gamma') = C(b)$
11.   set $Q(\gamma') = Q(\gamma) - R(b) \cdot C(\gamma) - K(b)$
12. $\Gamma' = \Gamma' \bigcup \{\gamma'\}$ and prune inferior solutions
13.   // merge Γ_1 and Γ_2 to Γ_{v_t}
14.   set $\Gamma_{v_t} = \emptyset$
15.   for each $\gamma_1 \in \Gamma_1$ and $\gamma_2 \in \Gamma_2$, generate a new solution γ'
16.   set $C(\gamma') = C(\gamma_1) + C(\gamma_2)$
17.   set $Q(\gamma') = \min\{Q(\gamma_1), Q(\gamma_2)\}$
18. $\Gamma_{v_t} = \Gamma_{v_t} \bigcup \{\gamma'\}$ and prune inferior solutions
19. return γ with the largest slack

FIGURE 26.4   van Ginneken's algorithm.

and partial solutions in Γ_r are

$$(278, 7) \text{ and } (308, 22)$$

After branch merging, the new candidate partial solutions whose Q are dictated by solutions in Γ_1 are

$$(167, 19), (207, 39), \text{ and } (308, 74)$$

and those dictated by solutions in Γ_r are

$$(278, 59) \text{ and } (308, 74)$$

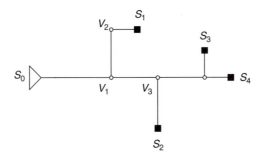

FIGURE 26.5   Example for performing van Ginneken's algorithm.

After pruning inferior solutions, the solution set at v_1 is

$$\{(167, 19), (207, 39), (278, 59), (308, 74)\}$$

26.4 VAN GINNEKEN EXTENSIONS

26.4.1 HANDLING LIBRARY WITH MULTIPLE BUFFERS

We extend the standard van Ginneken's algorithm to handle multiple buffers and buffer cost [12]. The buffer library B now contains various types of buffers. Each buffer b in the buffer library has a cost $W(b)$, which can be measured by area or any other metric, depending on the optimization objective. A function $f\colon V_n \to 2^B$ specifies the types of buffers allowed at each internal vertex in T. The cost of a solution γ, denoted by $W(\gamma)$, is defined as $W(\gamma) = \Sigma_{b\in\gamma}\, W_b$. With the above notations, our new problem can be formulated as follows.

Minimum-cost timing-constrained buffer insertion problem: Given a binary routing tree $T = (V, E)$, possible buffer positions defined using f, and a buffer library B, compute a minimal-cost buffer assignment γ such that the RAT at driver is smaller than a timing constraint α.

In contrast to the single buffer type case, W is introduced into the (Q, C) pair to handle buffer cost, i.e., each solution is now associated with a (Q, C, W) triple. As such, during the process of bottom-up computation, additional efforts need to be made in updating W: if γ' is generated by inserting a wire into γ, then $W(\gamma') = W(\gamma)$; if γ' is generated by inserting a buffer b into γ, then $W(\gamma') = W(\gamma) + W(b)$; if γ' is generated by merging γ_l with γ_r, then $W(\gamma') = W(\gamma_l) + W(\gamma_r)$.

The definition of inferior solutions needs to be revised as well. For any two solutions γ_1 and γ_2 at the same node, γ_1 dominates γ_2 if $C(\gamma_1) \le C(\gamma_2)$, $W(\gamma_1) \le W(\gamma_2)$, and $Q(\gamma_1) \ge Q(\gamma_2)$. Whenever a solution becomes dominated, it is pruned from the solution set. Therefore, only solutions that excel in at least one aspect of downstream capacitance, buffer cost, and RAT can survive.

With the above modification, van Ginneken's algorithm can easily adapt to the new problem setup. However, because the domination is defined on a (Q, C, W) triple rather than a (Q, C) pair, more efficient pruning technique is necessary to maintain the efficiency of the algorithm. As such, range search tree technique is incorporated [12]. It can be simply implemented as follows. A list of binary search trees are maintained where a tree corresponds to a W. Each binary search tree is keyed by C and each node in the tree also stores the largest Q at the node or in its left subtree [12].

26.4.2 LIBRARY WITH INVERTERS

So far, all buffers in the buffer library are noninverting buffers. There can also have inverting buffers, or simply inverters. In terms of buffer cost and delay, inverter would provide cheaper buffer assignment and better delay over noninverting buffers. As regard to algorithmic design, it is worth noting that introducing inverters into the buffer library brings the polarity issue to the problem, as the output polarity of a buffer will be negated after inserting an inverter.

26.4.3 POLARITY CONSTRAINTS

When output polarity for driver is required to be positive or negative, we impose a polarity constraint to the buffering problem. To handle polarity constraints, during the bottom-up computation, the algorithm maintains two solution sets, one for positive and one for negative buffer input polarity. After choosing the best solution at driver, the buffer assignment can be then determined by a top-down traversal. The details of the new algorithm are elaborated as follows.

Denote the two solution sets at vertex v by Γ_v^+ and Γ_v^- corresponding to positive polarity and negative polarity, respectively. Supposed that an inverter b^- is inserted to a solution $\gamma_v^+ \in \Gamma_v^+$, a new solution γ_v' is generated in the same way as before except that it will be placed into Γ_v^-. Similarly, the new solution generated by inserting b^- to a solution $\gamma_v^- \in \Gamma_v^-$ will be placed into Γ_v^+. For inserting a noninverting buffer, the new solution is placed in the same set as its origin.

The other operations are easier to handle. The wire insertion goes the same as before and two solution sets are handled separately. Merging is carried out only among the solutions with the same polarity, e.g., the positive-polarity solution set of left branch is merged with that of the right branch. For inferiority check and solution pruning, only the solutions in the same set can be compared.

26.4.4 SLEW AND CAPACITANCE CONSTRAINTS

The slew rate of a signal refers to the rising or falling time of a signal switching. Sometimes, the slew rate is referred as signal transition time. The slew rate of almost every signal has to be sufficiently small because a large slew rate implies large delay, large short-circuit power dissipation, and large vunlerability to crosstalk noise. In practice, a maximal slew rate constraint is required at the input of each gate/buffer. Therefore, this constraint needs to be obeyed in a buffering algorithm [12–15].

A simple slew model is essentially equivalent to the Elmore model for delay. It can be explained using a generic example, which is a path p from node v_i (upstream) to v_j (downstream) in a buffered tree. There is a buffer (or the driver) b_u at v_i, and there is no buffer between v_i and v_j. The slew rate $S(v_j)$ at v_j depends on both the output slew $S_{b_u,out}(v_i)$ at buffer b_u and the slew degradation $S_w(p)$ along path p (or wire slew), and is given by [16]

$$S(v_j) = \sqrt{S_{b_u,out}(v_i)^2 + S_w(p)^2} \qquad (26.11)$$

The slew degradation $S_w(p)$ can be computed with Bakoglu's metric [17] as

$$S_w(p) = \ln 9 \cdot D(p) \qquad (26.12)$$

where $D(p)$ is the Elmore delay from v_i to v_j.

The output slew of a buffer, such as b_u at v_i, depends on the input slew at this buffer and the load capacitance seen from the output of the buffer. Usually, the dependence is described as a two-dimensional lookup table. As a simplified alternative, one can assume a fixed input slew at each gate/buffer. This fixed slew is equal to the maximum slew constraint and therefore is always satisfied, but is a conservative estimation. For fixed input slew, the output slew of buffer b at vertex v is then given by

$$S_{b,out}(v) = R_b \cdot C(v) + K_b \qquad (26.13)$$

where
$C(v)$ is the downstream capacitance at v
R_b and K_b are empirical fitting parameters

This is similar to empirically derived K-factor equations [18]. We call R_b the slew resistance and K_b the intrinsic slew of buffer b.

In a van Ginneken style buffering algorithm, if a candidate solution has a slew rate greater than given slew constraint, it is pruned out and will not be propagated any more. Similar as the slew constraint, circuit designs also limit the maximum capacitive load a gate/buffer can drive [15]. For timing noncritical nets, buffer insertion is still necessary for the sake of satisfying the slew and capacitance constraints. For this case, fast slew buffering techniques are introduced in Ref. [19].

26.4.5 INTEGRATION WITH WIRE SIZING

In addition to buffer insertion, wire sizing is an effective technique for improving interconnect performance [20–24]. If wire size can take only discrete options, which is often the case in practice, wire sizing can be directly integrated with van Ginneken style buffer insertion algorithm [12]. In

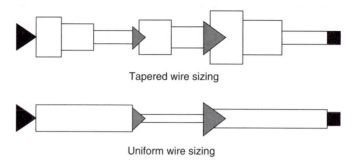

Tapered wire sizing

Uniform wire sizing

FIGURE 26.6   Wire sizing with tapering and uniform wire sizing.

the bottom-up dynamic programming procedure, multiple wire width options need to be considered when a wire is added (see Section 26.3.2.1). If there are k options of wire size, then k new candidate solutions are generated, one corresponding each wire size. However, including the wire sizing in van Ginneken's algorithm makes the complexity pseudopolynomial [12].

In Ref. [25], layer assignment and wire spacing are considered in conjunction with wire sizing. A combination of layer, width, and spacing is called a wire code. All wires in a net have to use an identical wire code. If each wire code is treated as a polarity, the wire code assignment can be integrated with buffer insertion in the same way as handling polarity constraint (see Section 26.4.3). In contrast to simultaneous wire sizing and buffer insertion [12], the algorithm complexity stays polynomial after integrating wire-code assignment [25] with van Ginneken's algorithm.

Another important conclusion in Ref. [25] is about wire tapering. Wire tapering means that a wire segment is divided into multiple pieces and each piece can be sized individually. In contrast, uniform wire sizing does not make such division and maintain the same wire width for the entire segment. These two cases are illustrated in Figure 26.6. It is shown in Ref. [25] that the benefit of wire tapering versus uniform wire sizing is very limited when combined with buffer insertion. It is theoretically proved [25] that the signal velocity from simultaneous buffering with wire tapering is at most 1.0354 times of that from buffering and uniform wire sizing. In short, wire tapering improves signal speed by at most 3.54 percent over uniform wire sizing.

26.4.6   NOISE CONSTRAINTS WITH DEVGAN METRIC

The shrinking of minimum distance between adjacent wires has caused an increase in the coupling capacitance of a net to its neighbors. A large coupling capacitance can cause a switching net to induce significant noise onto a neighboring net, resulting in an incorrect functional response. Therefore, noise avoidance techniques must become an integral part of the performance optimization environment.

The amount of coupling capacitance from one net to another is proportional to the distance that the two nets run parallel to each other. The coupling capacitance may cause an input signal on the aggressor net to induce a noise pulse on the victim net. If the resulting noise is greater than the tolerable noise margin (NM) of the sink, then an electrical fault results. Inserting buffers in the victim net can separate the capacitive coupling into several independent and smaller portions, resulting in smaller noise pulse on the sink and on the input of the inserted buffers.

Before describing the noise-aware buffering algorithms, we first introduce the coupling noise metric as follows.

26.4.6.1   Devgan's Coupling Noise Metric

Among many coupling noise models, Devgan's metric [26] is particularly amenable for noise avoidance in buffer insertion, because its computational complexity, structure, and incremental nature is the same as the famous Elmore delay metric. Further, like the Elmore delay model, the noise metric

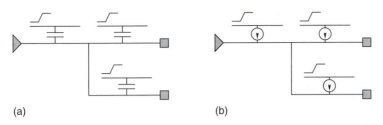

FIGURE 26.7 Illustration of noise model. (a) A net is a victim of the crosstalk noise induced by its neighboring nets. (b) The crosstalk noise can be modeled as current sources. (Modified at http://dropzone.tamu.edu/~jhu/noise.eps)

is a provable upper bound on coupled noise. Other advantages of the noise metric include the ability to incorporate multiple aggressor nets and handle general victim and aggressor net topologies. A disadvantage of the Devgan metric is that it becomes more pessimistic as the ratio of the aggressor net's transition time (at the output of the driver) to its delay decreases. However, cases in which this ratio becomes very small are rare because a long net delay generally corresponds to a large load on the driver, which in turn causes a slower transition time. The metric does not consider the duration of the noise pulse either. In general, the NM of a gate is dependent on both the peak noise amplitude and the noise pulse width. However, when considering failure at a gate, peak amplitude dominates pulse width.

If a wire segment e in the victim net is adjacent with t aggressor nets, let $\lambda_1, \ldots, \lambda_t$ be the ratios of coupling to wire capacitance from each aggressor net to e, and let $\mu_1, \ldots, \mu_t$ be the slopes of the aggressor signals. The impact of a coupling from aggressor j can be treated as a current source $I_{e,j} = C_e \cdot \lambda_j \cdot \mu_j$ where C_e is the wire capacitance of wire segment e. This is illustrated in Figure 26.7. The total current induced by the aggressors on e is

$$I_e = C_e \sum_{j=1}^{t} (\lambda_j \cdot \mu_j) \tag{26.14}$$

Often, information about neighboring aggressor nets is unavailable, especially if buffer insertion is performed before routing. In this case, a designer may wish to perform buffer insertion to improve performance while also avoiding future potential noise problems. When performing buffer insertion in estimation mode, one might assume that (1) there is a single aggressor net that couples with each wire in the routing tree, (2) the slope of all aggressors is μ, and (3) some fixed ratio λ of the total capacitance of each wire is due to coupling capacitance.

Let $I_{T(v)}$ be defined as the total downstream current see at node v, i.e.,

$$I_{T(v)} = \sum_{e \in E_{T(v)}} I_e$$

where $E_{T(v)}$ is the set of wire edges downstream of node v. Each wire adds to the noise induced on the victim net. The amount of additional noise induced from a wire $e = (u, v)$ is given by

$$\text{Noise}(e) = R_e \left[\frac{I_e}{2} + I_{T(v)} \right] \tag{26.15}$$

where R_e is the wire resistance. The total noise seen at sink si starting at some upstream node v is

$$\text{Noise}(v - \text{si}) = R_v I_{T(v)} + \sum_{e \in \text{path}(v-\text{si})} \text{Noise}(e) \tag{26.16}$$

where gate driving resistance $R_v = 0$ if there is no gate at node v. The path from v to si has no intermediate buffers.

Each node v has a predetermined noise margin NM(v). If the circuit is to have no electrical faults, the total noise propagated from each driver/buffer to each its sink si must be less than the NM for si. We define the noise slack for every node v as

$$NS(v) = \min_{si \in SI_{T(v)}} NM(si) - Noise(v - si) \tag{26.17}$$

where $SI_{T(v)}$ is the set of sink nodes for the subtree rooted at node v. Observe that NS(si) = NM(si) for each sink si.

26.4.6.2 Algorithm of Buffer Insertion with Noise Avoidance

We begin with the simplest case of a single wire with uniform width and neighboring coupling capacitance. Let us consider a wire $e = (u, v)$. First, we need to ensure $NS(v) \geq R_b I_{T(v)}$ where R_b is the buffer output resistance. If this condition is not satisfied, inserting a buffer even at node v cannot satisfy the constraint of NM, i.e., buffer insertion is needed within subtree $T(v)$. If $NS(v) \geq R_b I_{T(v)}$, we next search for the maximum wirelength $l_{e,\max}$ of e such that inserting a buffer at u always satisfies noise constraints. The value of $l_{e,\max}$ tells us the maximum unbuffered length or the minimum buffer usage for satisfying noise constraints. Let $R = R_e/l_e$ be the wire resistance per unit length and $I = I_e/l_e$ be the current per unit length. According to Ref. [27], this value can be determined by

$$l_{e,\max} = -\frac{R_b}{R} - \frac{I_{T(v)}}{I} + \sqrt{\left(\frac{R_b}{R}\right)^2 + \left(\frac{I_{T(v)}}{I}\right)^2 + \frac{2NS(v)}{I \cdot R}} \tag{26.18}$$

Depending on the timing criticality of the net, the noise-aware buffer insertion problem can be formulated in two different ways: (1) minimize total buffer cost subject to noise constraints and (2) maximize timing slack subject to noise constraints.

The algorithm for the former is a bottom-up dynamic programming procedure, which inserts buffers greedily as far apart as possible [27]. Each partial solution at node v is characterized by a three-tuple of downstream noise current $I_{T(v)}$, noise slack NS(v), and buffer assignment M. In the solution propagation, the noise current is accumulated in the same way as the downstream capacitance in van Ginneken's algorithm. Likewise, noise slack is treated like the timing slack (or RAT). This algorithm can return an optimal solution for a multisink tree $T = (V, E)$ in $O(|V|^2)$ time.

The core algorithm of noise-constrained timing slack maximization is similar as van Ginneken's algorithm except that the noise constraint is considered. Each candidate solution at node v is represented by a five-tuple of downstream capacitance C_v, RAT $q(v)$, downstream noise current $I_{T(v)}$, noise slack NS(v), and buffer assignment M. In addition to pruning inferior solutions according to the (C, q) pair, the algorithm eliminates candidate solutions that violate the noise constraint. At the source, the buffering solution not only has optimized timing performance but also satisfies the noise constraint.

26.4.7 HIGHER ORDER DELAY MODELING

Many buffer insertion methods [11,12,28] are based on the Elmore wire delay model [29] and a linear gate delay model for the sake of simplicity. However, the Elmore delay model often overestimates interconnect delay. It is observed in Ref. [30] that Elmore delay sometimes has over 100 percent overestimation error when compared to SPICE. A critical reason of the overestimation is due to the neglection of the resistive shielding effect. In the example of Figure 26.8, the Elmore delay from node A to B is equal to $R_1(C_1 + C_2)$ assuming that R_1 can see the entire capacitance of C_2 despite the fact that C_2 is somewhat shielded by R_2. Consider an extreme scenario where $R_2 = \infty$ or there

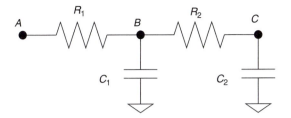

FIGURE 26.8 Example of resistive shielding effect.

is open circuit between node B and C. Obviously, the delay from A to B should be R_1C_1 instead of the Elmore delay $R_1(C_1 + C_2)$. The linear gate delay model is inaccurate owing to its neglection of nonlinear behavior of gate delay in addition to resistive shielding effect. In other words, a gate delay is not a strictly linear function of load capacitance.

The simple and relatively inaccurate delay models are suitable only for early design stages such as buffer planning. In postplacement stages, more accurate models are needed because (1) optimal buffering solutions based on simple models may be inferior, because actual delay is not being optimized and (2) simplified delay modeling can cause a poor evaluation of the trade-off between total buffer cost and timing improvement. In more accurate delay models, the resistive shielding effect is considered by replacing lumped load capacitance with higher order load admittance estimation. The accuracy of wire delay can be improved by including higher order moments of transfer function. An accurate and popular gate delay model is usually a lookup table employed together with effective capacitance [31,32], which is obtained based on the higher order load admittance. These techniques will be described in more details as follows.

26.4.7.1 Higher Order Point Admittance Model

For an RC tree, which is a typical circuit topology in buffer insertion, the frequency-domain point admittance at a node v is denoted as $Y_v(s)$. It can be approximated by the third-order Taylor expansion

$$Y_v(s) = y_{v,0} + y_{v,1}s + y_{v,2}s^2 + y_{v,3}s^3 + O(s^4)$$

where $y_{v,0}$, $y_{v,1}$, $y_{v,2}$, and $y_{v,3}$ are expansion coefficients. The third-order approximation usually provides satisfactory accuracy in practice. Its computation is a bottom-up procedure starting from the leaf nodes of an RC tree, or the ground capacitors. For a capacitance C connected to ground, the admittance at its upstream end is simply Cs. Please note that the zeroth order coefficient is equal to 0 in an RC tree because there is no DC path connected to ground. Therefore, we only need to propagate y_1, y_2, and y_3 in the bottom-up computation. There are two cases we need to consider:

- Case 1: For a resistance R, given the admittance $Y_d(s)$ of its downstream node, compute the admittance $Y_u(s)$ of its upstream node (Figure 26.9a).

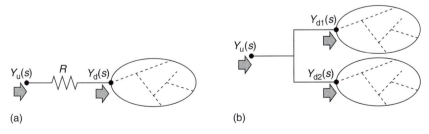

(a)   (b)

FIGURE 26.9 Two scenarios of admittance propagation.

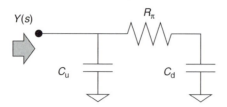

FIGURE 26.10   Illustration of π-model.

$$y_{u,1} = y_{d,1} \qquad y_{u,2} = y_{d,2} - Ry_{d,1}^2 \qquad y_{u,3} = y_{d,3} - 2Ry_{d,1}y_{d,2} + R^2y_{d,1}^3 \qquad (26.19)$$

- Case 2: Given admittance $Y_{d1}(s)$ and $Y_{d2}(s)$ corresponding to two branches, compute the admittance $Y_u(s)$ after merging them (Figure 26.9b).

$$y_{u,1} = y_{d1,1} + y_{d2,1} \qquad y_{u,2} = y_{d1,2} + y_{d2,2} \qquad y_{u,3} = y_{d1,3} + y_{d2,3} \qquad (26.20)$$

The third-order approximation (y_1, y_2, y_3) of an admittance can be realized as an RC π-model (C_u, R_π, C_d) (Figure 26.10) where

$$C_u = y_1 - \frac{y_2^2}{y_3} \qquad R_\pi = -\frac{y_3^2}{y_2^3} \qquad C_d = \frac{y_2^2}{y_3} \qquad (26.21)$$

26.4.7.2   Higher Order Wire Delay Model

While the Elmore delay is equal to the first-order moment of transfer function, the accuracy of delay estimation can be remarkably improved by including higher order moments. For example, the wire delay model [33] based on the first three moments and the closed-form model [34] using the first two moments.

Because van Ginneken style buffering algorithms proceed in a bottom-up manner, bottom-up moment computations are required. Figure 26.11a shows a wire e connected to a subtree rooted at node B. Assume that the first k moments $m_{BC}^{(1)}, m_{BC}^{(2)}, \ldots, m_{BC}^{(k)}$ have already been computed for the path from B to C. We wish to compute the moments $m_{AC}^{(1)}, m_{AC}^{(2)}, \ldots, m_{AC}^{(k)}$ so that the $A \rightsquigarrow C$ delay can be derived.

The techniques in Section 26.4.7.1 are used to reduce the subtree at B to a π-model (C_j, R_π, C_f) (Figure 26.11b). Node D just denotes the point on the far side of the resistor connected to B and is not an actual physical location. The RC tree can be further simplified to the network shown in Figure 26.11c. The capacitance C_j and $C_e/2$ at B are merged to form a capacitor with value C_n. The moments from A to B can be recursively computed by the equation

$$m_{AB}^{(i)} = -R_e \left[m_{AB}^{(i-1)} + m_{AD}^{(i-1)} C_f \right] \qquad (26.22)$$

(a)

(b)

(c)

FIGURE 26.11   Illustration of bottom-up moment computation.

where the moments from A to D are given by

$$m_{AD}^{(i)} = m_{AB}^{(i)} - m_{AD}^{(i-1)}R_\pi C_f \tag{26.23}$$

and $m_{AB}^{(0)} = m_{AD}^{(0)} = 1$. Now the moments from A to C can be computed via moment multiplication as follows:

$$m_{AC}^{(i)} = \sum_{j=0}^{i} \left[m_{AB}^{(j)} \cdot m_{BC}^{(i-j)} \right] \tag{26.24}$$

One property of Elmore delay that makes it attractive for timing optimization is that the delays are additive. This property does not hold for higher order delay models. Consequently, a noncritical sink in a subtree may become a critical sink depending on the value of upstream resistance [35]. Therefore, one must store the moments for all the paths to downstream sinks during the bottom-up candidate solution propagation.

26.4.7.3   Accurate Gate Delay

A popular gate-delay model with decent accuracy consists of the following three steps:

1. Compute a π-model of the driving point admittance for the RC interconnect using the techniques introduced in Section 26.4.7.1.
2. Given the π-model and the characteristics of the driver, compute an effective capacitance C_{eff} [31,32].
3. Based on C_{eff}, compute the gate delay using k-factor equations or lookup table [36].

26.4.8   FLIP-FLOP INSERTION

The technology scaling leads to decreasing clock period, increasing wire delay, and growing chip size. Consequently, it often takes multiple clock cycles for signals to reach their destinations along global wires. Traditional interconnect optimization techniques such as buffer insertion are inadequate in handling this scenario and flip-flop/latch insertion (or interconnect pipelining) becomes a necessity.

In pipelined interconnect design, flip-flops and buffers are inserted simultaneously in a given Steiner tree $T = (V, E)$ [37,38]. The simultaneous insertion algorithm is similar to van Ginneken's dynamic programming method except that a new criterion, latency, needs to be considered. The latency from the signal source to a sink is the number of flip-flops in-between. Therefore, a candidate solution at node $v \in V$ is characterized by a 4-tuple $(c_v, q_v, \lambda_v, a_v)$, where c_v is the downstream capacitance, q_v is the required arrival time, λ_v is the latency and a_v is the buffer assignment at v. Obviously, a small latency is preferred.

The inclusion of flip-flop and latency also requests other changes in a van Ginneken style algorithm. When a flip-flop is inserted in the bottom-up candidate propagation, the RAT at the input of this flip-flop is reset to clock period time T_ϕ. The latency of corresponding candidate solution is also increased by 1. For the ease of presentation, clock skew and setup/hold time are neglected without loss of generality. Then, the delay between two adjacent flip-flops cannot be greater than the clock period time T_ϕ, i.e., the RAT cannot be negative. During the candidate solution propagation, if a candidate solution has negative RAT, it should be pruned without further propagation. When two candidate solutions from two child branches are merged, the latency of the merged solution is the maximum of the two branch solutions.

There are two formulations for the simultaneous flip-flop and buffer insertion problem: MiLa, which finds the minimum latency that can be obtained, and GiLa, which finds a flip-flop/buffer insertion implementation that satisfies given latency constraint. MiLa can be used for the estimation of interconnect latency at the microarchitectural level. After the microarchitecture design is completed, all interconnect must be designed so as to abide to given latency requirements by using GiLa.

```
Algorithm: MiLa(T_u)/MiLa(T_{u,v})
Input: Subtree rooted at node u or edge (u,v)
Output: A set of candidate solutions Γ_u
Global: Routing tree T and buffer library B
1.      if u is a leaf, Γ_u = (C_u, q_u, 0, 0) // q is required arrival time
2.      else if u has one child node v or the input is T_{u,v}
2.1        Γ_v = MiLa(v)
2.2        Γ_u = U_{γ∈Γ_v}(addWire((u,v),γ))
2.3        Γ_b = ∅
2.4        for each b in B
2.4.1         Γ = U_{γ∈Γ_u}(addBuffer(γ,b))
2.4.2         prune Γ
2.4.3         Γ_b = Γ_b ∪ Γ
2.5        Γ_u = Γ_u ∪ Γ_b
3.      else if u has two child edges (u,v) and (u,z)
3.1        Γ_{u,v} = MiLa(T_{u,v}), Γ_{u,z} = MiLa(T_{u,z})
3.2        Γ_u = Γ_u ∪ merge(Γ_{u,v}, Γ_{u,z})
4.      prune Γ_u
5.      return Γ_u
```

FIGURE 26.12 MiLa algorithm.

The algorithm of MiLa [38] and GiLa [38] are shown in Figures 26.12 and 26.13, respectively. In GiLa, the λ_u for a leaf node u is the latency constraint at that node. Usually, λ_u at a leaf is a nonpositive number. For example, $\lambda_u = -3$ requires that the latency from the source to node u is 3. During the bottom-up solution propagation, λ is increased by 1 if a flip-flop is inserted. Therefore, $\lambda = 0$ at the source implies that the latency constraint is satisfied. If the latency at the source is greater than zero, then the corresponding solution is not feasible (line 2.6.1 of Figure 26.13). If the latency at the source is less than zero, the latency constraint can be satisfied by padding extra flip-flops in the corresponding solution (line 2.6.2.1 of Figure 26.13). The padding procedure is called ReFlop(T_u, k), which inserts k flip-flops in the root path of T_u. The root path is from u to either a leaf node or a branch node v and there is no other branch node in-between. The flip-flops previously inserted on the root path and the newly inserted k flip-flops are redistributed evenly along the path. When solutions from two branches in GiLa are merged, ReFlop is performed (line 3.3–3.4.1 of Figure 26.13) for the solutions with smaller latency to ensure that there is at least one merged solution matching the latency of both branches.

26.5   SPEEDUP TECHNIQUES

Because of dramatically increasing number of buffers inserted in the circuits, algorithms that can efficiently insert buffers are essential for the design automation tools. In this chapter, several recent proposed speedup results are introduced and the key techniques are described.

26.5.1   RECENT SPEEDUP RESULTS

This chapter studies buffer insertion in interconnect with a set of possible buffer positions and a discrete buffer library. In 1990, van Ginneken [11] proposed an $O(n^2)$ time dynamic programming algorithm for buffer insertion with one buffer type, where n is the number of possible buffer positions. His algorithm finds a buffer insertion solution that maximizes the slack at the source. In 1996, Lillis et al. [12] extended van Ginneken's algorithm to allow b buffer types in time $O(b^2n^2)$.

```
Algorithm: GiLa(T_u)/GiLa(T_{u,v})
Input: Subtree T_u rooted at node u or edge (u, v)
Output: A set of candidate solutions Γ_u
Global: Routing tree T and buffer library B
1.          if u is a leaf, Γ_u = (C_u, q_u, λ_u, 0)
2.          else if node u has one child node v or the input is T_{u,v}
2.1             Γ_v = GiLa(T_v)
2.2             Γ_u = U_{γ∈Γ_v}(addWire((u, v), γ))
2.3             Γ_b = ∅
2.4             for each b in B
2.4.1               Γ = U_{γ∈Γ_u}(addBuffer(γ, b))
2.4.2               prune Γ
2.4.3               Γ_b = Γ_b ∪ Γ
2.5             Γ_u = Γ_u ∪ Γ_b
                // Γ_u ≡ {Γ^x, ..., Γ^y}, x, y indicate latency
2.6             if u is source
2.6.1               if x > 0, exit: the net is not feasible
2.6.2               if y < 0, // insert −y more flops in Γ_u
2.6.2.1                 Γ_u = ReFlop(T_u, − y)
3.          else if u has two child edges (u, v) and (u, z)
3.1             Γ_{u,v} = GiLa(T_{u,v}), Γ_{u,z} = GiLa(T_{u,z})
3.2             //Γ_{u,v} ≡ {Γ^x, ..., Γ^y}, Γ_{u,z} ≡ {Γ^m, ..., Γ^n}
3.3             if y < m // insert m − y more flops in Γ_{u,v}
3.3.1               Γ_{u,v} = ReFlop(T_{u,v}, m − y)
3.4             if n < x // insert x − n more flops in Γ_{u,z}
3.4.1               Γ_{u,z} = ReFlop(T_{u,z}, x − n)
3.5             Γ_u = Γ_u ∪ merge(Γ_{u,v}, Γ_{u,z})
4.          prune Γ_u
5.          return Γ_u
```

FIGURE 26.13 GiLa algorithm.

Recently, many efforts are taken to speedup the van Ginneken's algorithm and its extensions. Shi and Li [39] improved the time complexity of van Ginneken's algorithm to $O(b^2 n \log n)$ for two-pin nets, and $O(b^2 n \log^2 n)$ for multipin nets. The speedup is achieved by four novel techniques: predictive pruning, candidate tree, fast redundancy check, and fast merging. To reduce the quadratic effect of b, Li and Shi [40] proposed an algorithm with time complexity $O(bn^2)$. The speedup is achieved by the observation that the best candidate to be associated with any buffer must lie on the convex hull of the (Q,C) plane and convex pruning. To utilize the fact that in real applications most nets have small number of pins and large number of buffer positions, Li and Shi [41] proposed a simple $O(mn)$ algorithms for m-pin nets. The speedup is achieved by the property explored in Ref. [40], convex pruning, a clever bookkeeping method, and an innovative linked list that allow $O(1)$ time update for adding a wire or a candidate.

In the following subsections, new pruning techniques, an efficient way to find the best candidates when adding a buffer, and implicit data representations are presented. They are the basic components of many recent speedup algorithms.

26.5.2 PREDICTIVE PRUNING

During the van Ginneken's algorithm, a candidate is pruned out only if there is another candidate that is superior in terms of capacitance and slack. This pruning is based on the information at the current

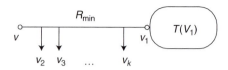

FIGURE 26.14 If α_1 and α_2 satisfy the condition in Definition 1 at v_1, α_2 is redundant. (From Shi, W. and Li, Z., *IEEE Trans Computer-Aided Design*, 24, 879, 2005. With permission.)

node being processed. However, all candidates at this node must be propagated further upstream toward the source. This means the load seen at this node must be driven by some minimal amount of upstream wire or gate resistance. By anticipating the upstream resistance ahead of time, one can prune out more potentially inferior candidates earlier rather than later, which reduces the total number of candidates generated. More specifically, assume that each candidate must be driven by an upstream resistance of at least R_{min}. The pruning based on anticipated upstream resistance is called predictive pruning.

Definition 1 Predictive Pruning. *Let α_1 and α_2 be two nonredundant candidates of $T(v)$ such that $C(\alpha_1) < C(\alpha_2)$ and $Q(\alpha_1) < Q(\alpha_2)$. If $Q(\alpha_2) - R_{min} \cdot C(\alpha_2) \leq Q(\alpha_1) - R_{min} \cdot C(\alpha_1)$, then α_2 is pruned.*

Predictive pruning preserves optimality. The general situation is shown in Figure 26.14. Let α_1 and α_2 be candidates of $T(v_1)$ that satisfy the condition in Definition 1. Using α_1 instead of α_2 will not increase delay from v to sinks in $v_2,\ldots,v_k$. It is easy to see $C(v,\alpha_1) < C(v,\alpha_2)$. If Q at v is determined by $T(v_1)$, we have

$$Q(v,\alpha_1) - Q(v,\alpha_2) = Q(v_1,\alpha_1) - Q(v_1,\alpha_2) - R_{min} \cdot [C(v_1,\alpha_1) - C(v_1,\alpha_2)] \geq 0$$

Therefore, α_2 is redundant.

Predictive pruning technique prunes more redundant solutions while guarantees optimality. It is one of four key techniques of fast algorithms proposed in Ref. [39]. In Ref. [42], significant speedup is achieved by simply extending predictive pruning technique to buffer cost. Aggressive predictive pruning technique, which uses a resistance larger than R_{min} to prune candidates, is proposed in Ref. [43] to achieve further speedup with a little degradation of solution quality.

26.5.3 CONVEX PRUNING

The basic data structure of van Ginneken's algorithms is a sorted list of nondominated candidates. Both the pruning in van Ginneken's algorithm and the predictive pruning are performed by comparing two neighboring candidates a time. However, more potentially inferior candidates can be pruned out by comparing three neighboring candidate solutions simultaneously. For three solutions in the sorted list, the middle one may be pruned according to convex pruning.

Definition 2 Convex Pruning. *Let α_1, α_2 and, α_3 be three nonredundant candidates of $T(v)$ such that $C(\alpha_1) < C(\alpha_2) < C(\alpha_3)$ and $Q(\alpha_1) < Q(\alpha_2) < Q(\alpha_3)$. If*

$$\frac{Q(\alpha_2) - Q(\alpha_1)}{C(\alpha_2) - C(\alpha_1)} < \frac{Q(\alpha_3) - Q(\alpha_2)}{C(\alpha_3) - C(\alpha_2)} \qquad (26.25)$$

then we call α_2 nonconvex, and prune it.

Convex pruning can be explained by Figure 26.15. Consider Q as the Y-axis and C as the X-axis. Then candidates are points in the two-dimensional plane. It is easy to see that the set of nonredundant

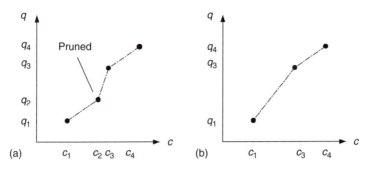

FIGURE 26.15 (a) Nonredundant candidates $N(v)$ and (b) nonredundant candidates $M(v)$ after convex pruning. (From Li, Z. and Shi, W., *IEEE Trans Computer-Aided Design*, 25, 484, 2006. With permission.)

candidates $N(v)$ is a monotonically increasing sequence. Candidate $\alpha_2 = (Q_2, C_2)$ in the above definition is shown in Figure 26.15a, and is pruned in Figure 26.15b. The set of nonredundant candidates after convex pruning $M(v)$ is a convex hull.

For two-pin nets, convex pruning preserves optimality. Let α_1, α_2, and α_3 be candidates of $T(v)$ that satisfy the condition in Definition 2. In Figure 26.15, let the slope between α_1 and α_2 (α_2 and α_3) be $\rho_{1,2}$ ($\rho_{2,3}$). If candidate α_2 is not on the convex hull of the solution set, then $\rho_{1,2} < \rho_{2,3}$. These candidates must have certain upstream resistance R including wire resistance and buffer/driver resistance. If $R < \rho_{2,3}$, α_2 must become inferior to α_3 when both candidates are propagated to the upstream node. Otherwise, $R > \rho_{2,3}$ which implies $R > \rho_{1,2}$, and therefore α_2 must become inferior to α_1. In other words, if a candidate is not on the convex hull, it will be pruned either by the solution ahead of it or the solution behind it. Please note that this conclusion only applies to two-pin nets. For multipin nets, when the upstream could be a merging vertex, nonredundant candidates that are pruned by convex pruning could still be useful.

Convex pruning of a list of nonredundant candidates sorted in increasing (Q,C) order can be performed in linear time by Graham's scan. Furthermore, when a new candidate is inserted to the list, we only need to check its neighbors to decide if any candidate should be pruned under convex pruning. The time is $O(1)$, amortized over all candidates.

In Refs. [40,41], the convex pruning is used to form the convex hull of nonredundant candidates, which is the key component of the $O(bn^2)$ algorithm and $O(mn)$ algorithm. In Ref. [43], convex pruning (called squeeze pruning) is performed on both two-pin and multipin nets to prune more solutions with a little degradation of solution quality.

26.5.4 Efficient Way to Find Best Candidates

Assume v is a buffer position, and we have computed the set of nonredundant candidates $N'(v)$ for $T(v)$, where $N'(v)$ does not include candidates with buffers inserted at v. Now we want to insert buffers at v and compute $N(v)$. Define $P_i(v, \alpha)$ as the slack at v if we add a buffer of type B_i for any candidate α:

$$P_i(v, \alpha) = Q(v, \alpha) - R(B_i) \cdot C(v, \alpha) - K(B_i) \tag{26.26}$$

If we do not insert any buffer, then every candidate in $N'(v)$ is a candidate in $N(v)$. If we insert a buffer, then for every buffer type B_i, $i = 1, 2, \ldots, b$, there will be a new candidate β_i:

$$Q(v, \beta_i) = \max_{\alpha \in N'(v)} \{P_i(v, \alpha)\}$$

$$C(v, \beta_i) = C(B_i)$$

Define the best candidate for B_i as the candidate $\alpha \in N'(v)$ such that α maximizes $P_i(v, \alpha)$ among all candidates in $N'(v)$. If there are multiple α's that maximize $P_i(v, \alpha)$, choose the one with minimum C. In van Ginneken's algorithm, it takes $O(bn)$ to find one best candidate at each buffer position.

According to convex pruning, it is easy to see that all best candidates are on the convex hull. The following lemma says that if we sort candidates in increasing Q and C order from left to right, then as we add wires to the candidates, we always move to the left to find the best candidates.

Lemma 1 *For any T(v), let nonredundant candidates after convex pruning be $\alpha_1, \alpha_2, \ldots, \alpha_k$, in increasing Q and C order. Now add wire e to each candidate α_j and denote it as $\alpha_j + e$. For any buffer type B_i, if α_j gives the maximum $P_i(\alpha_j)$ and α_k gives the maximum $P_i(\alpha_k + e)$, then $k \leq j$.*

The following lemma says the best candidate can be found by local search, if all candidates are convex.

Lemma 2 *For any T(v), let nonredundant candidates after convex pruning be $\alpha_1, \alpha_2, \ldots, \alpha_k$, in increasing Q and C order. If $P_i(\alpha_{j-1}) \leq P_i(\alpha_j)$, $P_i(\alpha_j) \geq P_i(\alpha_{j+1})$, then α_j is the best candidate for buffer type B_i and*

$$P_i(\alpha_1) \leq \cdots \leq P_i(\alpha_{j-1}) \leq P_i(\alpha_j)$$
$$P_i(\alpha_j) \geq P_i(\alpha_{j+1}) \geq \cdots \geq P_i(\alpha_k)$$

With the above two lemmas and convex pruning, one best candidate is found in amortized $O(n)$ time in Ref. [40] and $O(b)$ time in Ref. [41],[*] which are more efficient than van Ginneken's algorithm.

26.5.5 IMPLICIT REPRESENTATION

Van Ginnken's algorithm uses explicit representation to store slack and capacitance values, and therefore it takes $O(bn)$ time when adding a wire. It is possible to use implicit representation to avoid explicit updating of candidates.

In the implicit representation, $C(v, \alpha)$ and $Q(v, \alpha)$ are not explicitly stored for each candidate. Instead, each candidate contains five fields: q, c, qa, ca, and ra.[†] When qa, ca and, ra are all 0, q and c give $Q(v, \alpha)$ and $C(v, \alpha)$, respectively. When a wire is added, only qa, ca, and ra in the root of the tree [39] or as global variables themselves [41] are updated. Intuitively, qa represents extra wire delay, ca represents extra wire capacitance, and ra represents extra wire resistance.

It takes only $O(1)$ time to add a wire with the implicit representation [39,41]. For example, in Ref. [41], when we reach an edge e with resistance $R(e)$ and $C(e)$, qa, ra, and ca are updated to reflect new values of Q and C of all previous candidates in $O(1)$ time, without actually touching any candidate:

$$qa = qa + R(e) \cdot C(e)/2 + R(e) \cdot ca$$
$$ca = ca + C(e)$$
$$ra = ra + R(e)$$

---

[*] In Ref. [40], Lemma 1 is presented differently. It says if all buffers are sorted decreasingly according to driving resistance, then the best candidates for each buffer type in such order is from left to right.

[†] In Ref. [41], only two fields, q and c, are necessary for each candidate. qa, ca, and ra are global variables for each two-pin segment.

The actual value of Q and C of each candidate α are decided as follows:

$$Q(\alpha) = q - qa - ra \cdot c$$
$$C(\alpha) = c + ca \tag{26.27}$$

Implicit representation is applied on balance tree in Ref. [39], where the operation of adding a wire takes $O(b \log n)$ time. It is applied on a sorted linked list in Ref. [41], where the operation of adding a wire takes $O(1)$ time.

REFERENCES

1. J. Cong. An interconnect-centric design flow for nanometer technologies. *Proceedings of IEEE*, 89(4): 505–528, April 2001.
2. J. A. Davis, R. Venkatesan, A. Kaloyeros, M. Beylansky, S. J. Souri, K. Banerjee, K. C. Saraswat, A. Rahman, R. Reif, and J. D. Meindl. Interconnect limits on gigascale integration (GSI) in the 21st century. *Proceedings of IEEE*, 89(3): 305–324, March 2001.
3. R. Ho, K. W. Mai, and M. A. Horowitz. The future of wires. *Proceedings of IEEE*, 89(4): 490–504, April 2001.
4. A. B. Kahng and G. Robins. *On Optimal Interconnections for VLSI*. Kluwer Academic Publishers, Boston, MA, 1995.
5. J. Cong, L. He, C. -K. Koh, and P. H. Madden. Performance optimization of VLSI interconnect layout. *Integration: The VLSI Journal*, 21: 1–94, 1996.
6. P. Saxena, N. Menezes, P. Cocchini, and D. A. Kirkpatrick. Repeater scaling and its impact on CAD. *IEEE Transactions on Computer-Aided Design*, 23(4): 451–463, April 2004.
7. J. Cong. Challenges and opportunities for design innovations in nanometer technologies. *SRC Design Sciences Concept Paper*, 1997.
8. M. S. Bazaraa, H. D. Sherali, and C. M. Shetty. *Nonlinear Programming: Theory and Algorithms*. John Wiley & Sons, NY, 1993.
9. C. J. Alpert and A. Devgan. Wire segmenting for improved buffer insertion. In *Proceedings of the ACM/IEEE Design Automation Conference*, Anaheim, CA, pp. 588–593, 1997.
10. C. C. N. Chu and D. F. Wong. Closed form solution to simultaneous buffer insertion/sizing and wire sizing. *ACM Transactions on Design Automation of Electronic Systems*, 6(3): 343–371, July 2001.
11. L. P. P. P. van Ginneken. Buffer placement in distributed RC-tree networks for minimal Elmore delay. In *Proceedings of the IEEE International Symposium on Circuits and Systems*, New Orleans, LA, pp. 865–868, 1990.
12. J. Lillis, C. K. Cheng, and T. Y. Lin. Optimal wire sizing and buffer insertion for low power and a generalized delay model. *IEEE Journal of Solid-State Circuits*, 31(3): 437–447, March 1996.
13. N. Menezes and C. -P. Chen. Spec-based repeater insertion and wire sizing for on-chip interconnect. In *Proceedings of the International Conference on VLSI Design*, Goa, India, pp. 476–483, 1999.
14. L. -D. Huang, M. Lai, D. F. Wong, and Y. Gao. Maze routing with buffer insertion under transition time constraints. *IEEE Transactions on Computer-Aided Design*, 22(1): 91–95, January 2003.
15. C. J. Alpert, A. B. Kahng, B. Liu, I. I. Mandoiu, and A. Z. Zelikovsky. Minimum buffered routing with bounded capacitive load for slew rate and reliability control. *IEEE Transactions on Computer-Aided Design*, 22(3): 241–253, March 2003.
16. C. Kashyap, C. J. Alpert, F. Liu, and A. Devgan. Closed form expressions for extending step delay and slew metrics to ramp inputs. In *Proceedings of the ACM International Symposium on Physical Design*, Monterey, CA, pp. 24–31, 2003.
17. H. B. Bakoglu. *Circuits, Interconnections and Packaging for VLSI*. Addison-Wesley, Reading, MA, 1990.
18. N. H. E. Weste and K. Eshraghian. *Principles of CMOS VLSI Design: A System Perspective*. Addison-Wesley Publishing Company, Reading, MA, 1993.
19. S. Hu, C. J. Alpert, J. Hu, S. Karandikar, Z. Li, W. Shi, and C. -N. Sze. Fast algorithms for slew constrained minimum cost buffering. In *Proceedings of the ACM/IEEE Design Automation Conference*, San Francisco, CA, pp. 308–313, 2006.

20. J. Cong and C. K. Koh. Simultaneous driver and wire sizing for performance and power optimization. *IEEE Transactions on VLSI Systems*, 2(4): 408–425, December 1994.

21. S. S. Sapatnekar. RC interconnect optimization under the Elmore delay model. In *Proceedings of the ACM/IEEE Design Automation Conference*, San Diego, CA, pp. 392–396, 1994.

22. J. Cong and K. -S. Leung. Optimal wiresizing under the distributed Elmore delay model. *IEEE Transactions on Computer-Aided Design*, 14(3): 321–336, March 1995.

23. J. P. Fishburn and C. A. Schevon. Shaping a distributed RC line to minimize Elmore delay. *IEEE Transactions on Circuits and Systems*, 42(12): 1020–1022, December 1995.

24. C. P. Chen, Y. P. Chen, and D. F. Wong. Optimal wire-sizing formula under the Elmore delay model. In *Proceedings of the ACM/IEEE Design Automation Conference*, Las Vegas, NV, pp. 487–490, 1996.

25. C. J. Alpert, A. Devgan, J. P. Fishburn, and S. T. Quay. Interconnect synthesis without wire tapering. *IEEE Transactions on Computer-Aided Design*, 20(1): 90–104, January 2001.

26. A. Devgan. Efficient coupled noise estimation for on-chip interconnects. In *Proceedings of the IEEE/ACM International Conference on Computer-Aided Design*, San Jose, CA, pp. 147–151, 1997.

27. C. J. Alpert, A. Devgan, and S. T. Quay. Buffer insertion for noise and delay optimization. *IEEE Transactions on Computer-Aided Design*, 18(11): 1633–1645, November 1999.

28. C. C. N. Chu and D. F. Wong. A new approach to simultaneous buffer insertion and wire sizing. In *Proceedings of the IEEE/ACM International Conference on Computer-Aided Design*, San Jose, CA, pp. 614–621, 1997.

29. W. C. Elmore. The transient response of damped linear networks with particular regard to wideband amplifiers. *Journal of Applied Physics*, 19: 55–63, January 1948.

30. F. J. Liu, J. Lillis, and C. K. Cheng. Design and implementation of a global router based on a new layout-driven timing model with three poles. In *Proceedings of the IEEE International Symposium on Circuits and Systems*, Hong Kong, China, pp. 1548–1551, 1997.

31. J. Qian, S. Pullela, and L. T. Pillage. Modeling the effective capacitance for the RC interconnect of CMOS gates. *IEEE Transactions on Computer-Aided Design*, 13(12): 1526–1535, December 1994.

32. S. R. Nassif and Z. Li. A more effective C_{eff}. In *Proceedings of the IEEE International Symposium on Quality Electronic Design*, San Jose, CA, pp. 648–653, 2005.

33. B. Tutuianu, F. Dartu, and L. Pileggi. Explicit RC-circuit delay approximation based on the first three moments of the impulse response. In *Proceedings of the ACM/IEEE Design Automation Conference*, Las Vegas, NV, pp. 611–616, 1996.

34. C. J. Alpert, F. Liu, C. V. Kashyap, and A. Devgan. Closed-form delay and slew metrics made easy. *IEEE Transactions on Computer-Aided Design*, 23(12): 1661–1669, December 2004.

35. C. J. Alpert, A. Devgan, and S. T. Quay. Buffer insertion with accurate gate and interconnect delay computation. In *Proceedings of the ACM/IEEE Design Automation Conference*, New Orleans, LA, pp. 479–484, 1999.

36. C. -K. Cheng, J. Lillis, S. Lin, and N. Chang. *Interconnect Analysis and Synthesis*. Wiley Interscience, New York, 2000.

37. S. Hassoun, C. J. Alpert, and M. Thiagarajan. Optimal buffered routing path constructions for single and multiple clock domain systems. In *Proceedings of the IEEE/ACM International Conference on Computer-Aided Design*, San Jose, CA, pp. 247–253, 2002.

38. P. Cocchini. A methodology for optimal repeater insertion in pipelined interconnects. *IEEE Transactions on Computer-Aided Design*, 22(12): 1613–1624, December 2003.

39. W. Shi and Z. Li. A fast algorithm for optimal buffer insertion. *IEEE Transactions on Computer-Aided Design*, 24(6): 879–891, June 2005.

40. Z. Li and W. Shi. An $O(bn^2)$ time algorithm for buffer insertion with b buffer types. *IEEE Transactions on Computer-Aided Design*, 25(3): 484–489, March 2006.

41. Z. Li and W. Shi. An $O(mn)$ time algorithm for optimal buffer insertion of nets with m sinks. In *Proceedings of Asia and South Pacific Design Automation Conference*, Yokohama, Japan, pp. 320–325, 2006.

42. W. Shi, Z. Li, and C. J. Alpert. Complexity analysis and speedup techniques for optimal buffer insertion with minimum cost. In *Proceedings of Asia and South Pacific Design Automation Conference*, Yokohama, Japan, pp. 609–614, 2004.

43. Z. Li, C. N. Sze, C. J. Alpert, J. Hu, and W. Shi. Making fast buffer insertion even faster via approximation techniques. In *Proceedings of Asia and South Pacific Design Automation Conference*, Shanghai, China, pp. 13–18, 2005.

27 Generalized Buffer Insertion

Miloš Hrkić and John Lillis

CONTENTS

27.1 INTRODUCTION

It has been widely recognized that interconnect is a dominating factor in modern very large scale integration (VLSI) circuit designs. Chapter 26 gave an overview of challenges that interconnect faces and introduced a technique called repeater insertion that has proven to be very efficient in addressing emerging interconnect issues.

Early work on repeater insertion focused mainly on improving interconnect timing performance. The most influential work is van Ginneken's dynamic programming algorithm [1]. The algorithm performs buffer insertion on a fixed and embedded tree (e.g., as given by a global router) and produces an optimal timing solution under Elmore delay model [2]. Various generalizations of van Ginneken's algorithm have appeared in the literature taking into account issues of practical importance such as buffer libraries with inverting and noninverting buffers, simultaneous wire sizing, and slew-based delay models. Additionally, generalizations that address natural constrained optimization variants of the problem (e.g., minimization of area or power consumption subject to timing constraints) have also appeared. Progress has also been made in improving computational complexity as well as practical runtime. Many of these results are presented in Chapter 26.

A significant limitation of van Ginneken's approach is that it requires a fixed and embedded tree that has to be provided in advance. This constraint forces the final buffered solution quality to depend on the input tree. Even though the algorithm provides an optimal timing solution for a given tree, it will produce a poor solution when given a poor tree. A few example scenarios that are very common in practice can be used to illustrate this limitation.

As noted earlier, one of the basic interconnect optimization tasks is delay minimization. Given that sinks may have very different required signal arrival time constraints, a routing solution that focuses only on, for example, minimizing wirelength may not be good enough. In Figure 27.1, sinks F and G are timing critical while the others are not. Configuration in Figure 27.1a has better wirelength, but the buffering cost is very high. On the other hand, configuration in Figure 27.1b can achieve better timing results with slightly more wirelength but many fewer buffers.

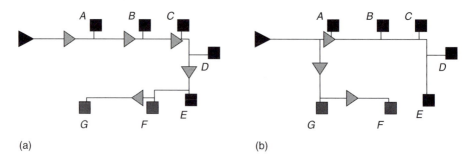

FIGURE 27.1 Buffering example: Sinks F and G are assumed to be critical; tree (a) has slightly smaller wirelength but requires more buffers (and may prevent timing constraints on F and G from being met) than the tree (b).

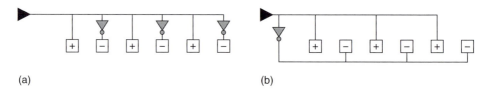

FIGURE 27.2 Buffering example: To meet signal polarity requirements, the number of buffers that is required varies significantly from one topology to another.

In some cases, certain sinks of a net require input signals of inverted polarity. Choices made during route construction can have a large impact on the cost of buffering solutions, as we can see in Figure 27.2. The two solutions Figure 27.2 have very different buffer and wiring costs.

Figure 27.3 shows a simple example illustrating the issues raised during buffering and routing in the presence of blockages. In configuration of Figure 27.3a, the route goes over the blockage and cannot be buffered (thus, possibly violating timing, load, or slew constraints). If the route completely avoids the blockage, the resulting solution is expensive in terms of wire and buffer costs (Figure 27.3b). Finally, by being aware of different types of blockages, configuration in Figure 27.3c dominates both in delay and resource usages/costs.

Recently, some designs have reserved internal areas of macroobjects for buffering of external nets (e.g., the whitespace in macros as in Figure 27.4). Any buffer insertion algorithm that has to work on a route that is not aware of the layout specifics will have limited chances of success. Referring to Figure 27.4, assuming that sink A is critical and the others are not, the two solutions in Figure 27.4 can have significant quality difference (e.g., cost or timing characteristics).

In other practical formulations, routing or buffering feasibility is not considered a zero or one property (blocked or free). Instead, a complex cost function based on the local and global design densities and congestions should drive routing and buffering algorithms; such formulations can prevent overconstraining the design space, but require incremental interaction with placers and routers. Even more, the overall design closure can suffer because irresponsible use of buffering resources on nets (or portions of nets) that are not critical can prevent other critical nets from meeting their constraints.*

Given the examples above, routing and buffering algorithms should be able to account for the cost/performance trade-off of the solutions that they produce. Generating the fastest buffering solution

---

* Some of the approaches that are specifically designed to target blockages (routing or placement) as well as design density and congestion are presented in more detail in Chapter 28. However, some of the ideas will be reviewed in this chapter because they are among the core components of some tree synthesis and buffering algorithms.

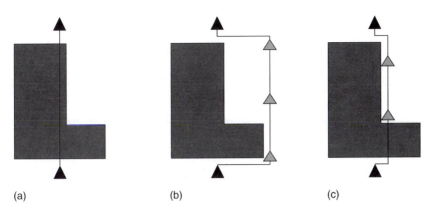

FIGURE 27.3 Buffering example: Depending on the interaction between routes and blockages, buffered solution can be (a) infeasible, (b) expensive, (c) or not bad at all.

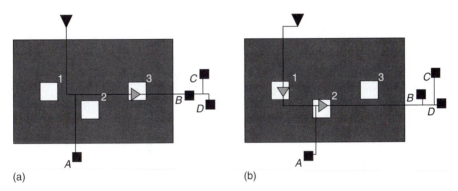

FIGURE 27.4 Buffering example: With increasing complexity of constraints, ability of buffering algorithms to handle such constraints is becoming more important. Assuming that sink A in critical, solutions (a) and (b) can have significant quality difference.

may be necessary for some nets, but if applied to all nets, the design would quickly become too expensive (e.g., in area and power usage), or even become impossible to manufacture. In addition, algorithm complexity and runtime is a very important practical factor given that hundreds of thousands of nets may need to be buffered within a given CPU time budget.

In the following sections, we give an overview of recent research that addresses one or more of the problems mentioned above. This area of research is still very active and our summary presents only a snapshot of the past and current research.

The majority of techniques that address problems mentioned above can be placed in one of the two categories. Several works propose a two-stage sequential method where a buffer-aware tree is constructed first, followed by van Ginneken style buffer insertion as in Refs. [3–6]. These techniques have small execution time with some sacrifice in solution quality and predictability. In Section 27.2, we describe techniques from Refs. [3,6] in more detail.

A more robust and predictable approach proposes simultaneous route construction while performing buffer insertion. An example is the buffered P-Tree class of algorithms [7], which integrates buffer insertion into the P-Tree Steiner tree construction algorithm [8]. The P-Tree algorithm introduced a paradigm of finding an optimal solution in a constrained, but very large, space including topological, embedding, and buffering degrees of freedom, as opposed to applying ad hoc heuristics. Section 27.3 presents methods for simultaneous routing tree construction and buffer insertion from Refs. [7–12].

27.2 TWO-PHASE APPROACH AND BUFFER-AWARE TREE CONSTRUCTION

27.2.1 C-TREE ALGORITHM

The work in Ref. [3] addresses the problem of buffering under timing and polarity constraints. Given a net with placed pins, timing and polarity requirements at sinks, driver properties, a buffer library, and the technology's interconnect parasitics, the goal is to find a Steiner tree that, after buffer insertion, meets timing constraints while minimizing solution cost (i.e., wire and buffer usage).

A two-phase flow is proposed: a buffer-aware Steiner tree construction called C-Tree is followed by a van Ginneken style buffer insertion. It is argued that an optimal buffer insertion on a fixed and routed tree can produce good/optimal results as long as it is given the right Steiner tree. However, in practice, instead of finding the right tree (which is very difficult because the tree construction algorithm is not optimizing the true objective) one can construct a buffer-aware Steiner tree, which tries to anticipate potential buffer locations.

The main idea in C-Tree (clustered tree) is to construct a tree in two stages. First, sinks are clustered based on a distance metrics (timing criticality, polarity requirements, physical distance). Then, lower level trees are constructed on each cluster. After determining tapping points for each cluster, the top-level timing-driven tree is constructed, connecting the driver with cluster tapping points. Merging the top-level tree with cluster trees yields a final tree for the entire net.

Sink properties used for clustering are spatial (physical location coordinates), temporal (required arrival times), and polarity. The distance metrics incorporate all three elements. They are defined separately and then combined using scaling factors into a single distance metric. The spatial distance is given by $sDist(s_i, s_j) = |x(s_i) - x(s_j)| + |y(s_i) - y(s_j)|$. Polarity distance is defined as $pDist(s_i, s_j) = |pol(s_i) - pol(s_j)|$. As for the temporal distance, Ref. [3] argues that required arrival time is not the only indicator of sink criticality. For example, if two sinks s_1 and s_2 have the same required arrival time, and s_1 is further away from the driver, then s_1 is more critical because it is harder to achieve the same required arrival time over the longer distance. Thus, an estimate of the achievable delay is used to adjust required arrival time and obtain achievable slack. It is further argued that the difference in achievable slacks (AS) may not yet be good enough. For example, if $AS(s_1) = -1$ ns, $AS(s_2) = 1$ ns, and $AS(s_3) = 10$ ns, sinks s_1 and s_2 seem closer although in practice s_1 is the only critical sink because s_2 and s_3 have high-positive AS. Thus, the sink criticality is defined as $crit(s_i) = e^{\alpha[mAS - AS(s_i)]/(aAS - mAS)}$, where mAS and aAS are the minimum and average AS values over all sinks and $\alpha > 0$ is a user parameter. The criticality is a value between 0 and 1, where 1 is the most critical (the average sink criticality by this formula is closer to noncritical). The temporal distance $tDist(s_i, s_j)$ is now defined as the difference in sink criticality. Finally, the distance metric is a linear combination of spatial, temporal, and polarity distances (noting that spatial distance is normalized by spatial diameter $sDiam(N)$ defined as the maximum distance between the sinks):

$$\beta[s\,Dist(s_i, s_j)/s\,Diam(N)] + (1 - \beta)t\,Dist(s_i, s_j) + p\,Dist(s_i, s_j).$$

The clustering itself is done using K-center heuristics. It is an iterative approach, which identifies sinks that are furthest away and labels them as cluster seeds. The remaining sinks are then clustered around the closest seed. More details can be found in Ref. [3].

Once the clusters are determined, timing-driven Steiner trees are constructed on each cluster and one on the top level using the Prim–Dijkstra algorithm from Ref. [13].

The experimental results show that this technique often exhibits a good trade-off between runtime and the quality of results (i.e., providing good solutions on the average in terms of both the cost and the delay while keeping low runtime). In addition, this method is not very complicated to implement. One should be aware of the fact that this algorithm is not designed to handle obstacles and design congestion in general, so results may not be very predictable in those scenarios.

27.2.2 BUFFER TREE TOPOLOGY GENERATION

A more recent work [6] also recognizes the problem of buffering fixed trees, together with the growing problem of design size, where millions of nets have to be optimized in a reasonable amount of time. This work presents a new algorithm for generation of tree topologies that are buffer-friendly. The algorithm balances achieving the signal required arrival time constraints and minimizing wirelength.

Let us first explain the notion of the tree topology in this work (we will refer to it as a partially embedded tree topology). Figure 27.5a shows a partially embedded tree topology. It is a directed tree structure where each node except the root has only one input edge, each internal node has exactly two output edges, while the root has only one output edge. In addition, each node has an assigned placement location (placement overlap is allowed). However, the embeddings of the edges (i.e., routes) as well as the number of buffers and buffer placements are not specified. An example of a completely embedded and buffered tree topology is given in Figure 27.5b.

Once the partially embedded topology tree is constructed, many of the known techniques can be used to perform two-pin routing and buffer insertion between the tree nodes (i.e., Refs. [14–16]). As opposed to the approach in Ref. [3], subtree parities (i.e., signal polarities) are resolved locally because inverters are being used for buffering.

The algorithm proceeds in the following manner. First, sinks are ordered based on criticality (the most critical first). In a manner similar to Ref. [3], criticality estimation is based on estimated slack rather than only relying on sink required arrival time. To estimate the delay from the driver to sinks, a linear delay model is used (similar to Ref. [5]) augmented by estimated buffer intrinsic delays and loads. The assumption is that these paths are going to be buffered eventually so the algorithm accounts for the delay that the path is going to have after buffering. In Ref. [6], some additional experiments are performed to justify this assumption and results show good correlation between estimates and final results.

When the ordering is complete, sinks are added to the topology one at a time (the initial topology consists of the driver and the most critical sink only). A single sink insertion is performed by examining all edges in the current topology and finding the closest tapping point within the bounding box of the edge terminals (note that the topology is partially embedded and all nodes have fixed placement locations). The edge for which the overall slack has the best value is chosen and sink insertion is performed by breaking that edge and inserting a new internal node to the tree. The parent of the new node is the source of the chosen edge and the children are the newly inserted sink and the destination node of the chosen edge. By keeping the arrival times at each topology node, a single sink insertion can be performed in linear time, giving the overall quadratic algorithm complexity (note that each operation is fairly simple, which leads to a very small execution time).

In addition, Ref. [6] proves theoretical lower bounds on slack and wirelength in two extreme cases: sinks close to the driver and sinks having large noncritical required arrival times. Among the

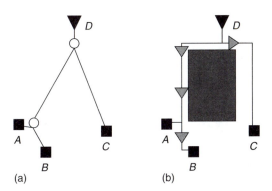

(a) (b)

FIGURE 27.5 (a) Partially embedded routing tree topology and (b) completely embedded and buffered tree.

algorithm enhancements, it is shown how to choose technology constants, how to trade off wirelength and slack, and how to deal with blockages, congestion, and high fanout nets. Experimental results demonstrate that generated trees are of good quality and that the algorithm execution time is extremely small (one million trees are computed in less than a minute; note that if a robust buffer insertion is needed, additional CPU time may be required for postprocess buffering).

27.3 SIMULTANEOUS TREE CONSTRUCTION AND BUFFER INSERTION

In this section, some of the methods that combine buffer insertion and topology construction are presented. Most of them belong to the P-Tree class of algorithms. The work started with the first version of the P-Tree algorithm [8] that was designed to construct timing-driven routing tree and it has seen a decade long evolution of various improvements and extensions that were building on the original ideas. These algorithms are designed to handle a variety of challenges seen in modern designs. Simultaneous tree construction and repeater insertion (with multiple buffers and inverters in the library) while being able to optimize multiple objectives, again, simultaneously (delay, cost, congestion, wirelength) are achieved through the core optimization engine. Practical issues such as obstacles (i.e., placement and routing blockages), multilayer routing and vias, and nonorthogonal routing are handled by the capability of the algorithms to work on general graph models as routing targets. Spatial, temporal, and polarity localities (all of them independently) are captured and exploited by implicit specification of the set of tree topologies that will be searched. In the following subsections, we give an overview of the mentioned contributions in chronological order.

27.3.1 P-TREE ALGORITHM

The work in Ref. [8] presents an algorithm that constructs rectilinear Steiner trees while explicitly optimizing both delay and wire area. Contrary to the methods presented in the previous section, it introduces the paradigm of finding an optimal solution in the constrained solution space; in other words, the solution search space is defined in advance, and then the algorithm finds an optimal solution in this constrained space.

The P-Tree algorithm simultaneously optimizes over topologies and their embeddings. To illustrate the degrees of freedom in embedding a particular topology consider Figure 27.6. The driver is the root, leaves represent sinks, and internal nodes represent Steiner or branching points. However, the branching points do not have defined placement locations. As an example, topology in Figure 27.6a can yield very different embedded solutions as shown in Figure 27.6b and c. Notice that sinks A and B when the topology is embedded (Figure 27.6b and c) are always in the same subtree, as specified by the topology (Figure 27.6a).

Thus, how one embeds a particular topology can be of great importance. But what about the topology itself? The P-Tree algorithm does not limit itself to a single topology. Instead, it optimizes

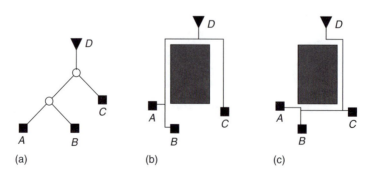

FIGURE 27.6   Routing tree topology (a) can have different embedded solutions (b) and (c).

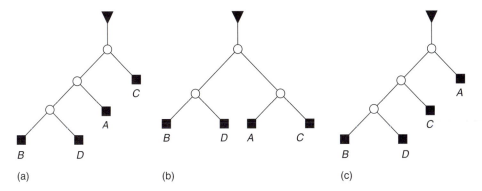

FIGURE 27.7 Topologies (a) and (b) satisfy permutation $BDAC$ while topology (c) does not.

over all topologies induced by a sink permutation (a set exponential in size). These topology trees are simultaneously explored and embedded to the routing domain.

The routing topologies that are produced are permutation-constrained routing trees (giving rise to the name P-Tree). Given an ordering of sinks (i.e., permutation) a topology satisfies the permutation constraint if some depth-first traversal of the topology tree produces the same sink ordering. As an example, given the permutation $BDAC$, trees in Figure 27.7a and b satisfy the permutation while the one in Figure 27.7c does not.

The method proposed to find a high-quality permutation consists of three steps. The first step constructs a minimum spanning tree (MST) on all pins (both driver and sinks). The next step converts the MST into topology by reorienting MST such that the driver is at the root and binarizing it such that each internal node has exactly two outgoing edges. The last step is to apply the dynamic programming algorithm to optimize the induced permutation further. The proposed approach is to optimize the tour length of the permutation (in the sense of a traveling salesman problem (TSP)). The intuition is that TSP provides good clustering information (i.e., sinks that are close in the placement should be close in the topology as well). In addition, because the permutation is consistent with the MST, it guarantees that the minimum area solution induced by this permutation can be at most 50 percent larger than the optimal Steiner tree. A more detailed description of the algorithm can be also found in Ref. [17].

Once the permutation is obtained, thus defining all topologies to be explored, the algorithm proceeds to topology embedding. The routing target is specified by a Hanan grid (note that in Ref. [10] this step of the flow is redesigned to handle general graph model, giving the capability to account for blockages and congestion). Instead of embedding topologies one at a time, algorithm exploits the structure of permutation constrained topologies and achieves polynomial computational complexity while exploring an exponential search space. For example, topologies in Figure 27.7a and b have identical subtree containing sinks B and D, and there is no need to compute solution for this subtree more than once.

The dynamic programming approach proceeds in a bottom-up fashion computing the following solution sets: $S(v, i, j)$ contains signatures* of the solutions over all permutation-induced topologies driving sinks from i to j in the permutation that are rooted at the vertex v in the target routing graph. Set $S_b(v, i, j)$ contains signatures of the solutions over all permutation-induced topologies driving sinks from i to j in the permutation that are rooted at the vertex v with a constraint that vertex v is also a branching point. The top-level view of the P-Tree algorithm is given in Figure 27.8.

Depending on the solution signature, the algorithm can optimize many objectives. In the $P-Tree_A$ mode, solution signature contains only one parameter: total wire capacitance c. This mode is used to optimize wire area. In the $P-Tree_{AT}$ mode, both timing and area are optimized simultaneously.

---

* Solution signature is described in the following paragraph.

```
P-Tree Algorithm
a1    Compute S(v, i, i)
a2    for I = 1 to n - 2 do
a3      for i = 1 to n - 1 - I do
a4        j = i + I
a5          Compute Sₑ(v, i, j)
a6          Compute S(v, i, j)
a7      endfor
a8    endfor
a9    return S(vₑ, 1, n - 1)
```

FIGURE 27.8   P-Tree algorithmic framework.

Instead of one single final solution, algorithm produces a family of nondominated solutions with area/delay trade-off. In this mode, solution signature is specified by an ordered pair (c, q), where c represents total downstream capacitance, while q represents signal required arrival time. Under the Elmore delay model [2], managing these primitives is done in a way similar to Ref. [1], as explained in Chapter 26. Just as a reminder the primitives include joining, augmenting, merging, and pruning solutions. In the followup work, $P - Tree_A$ and $P - Tree_{AT}$ modes are referred to as one-dimensional (1D) and two-dimensional (2D) modes because the algorithm optimizes only one parameter in the 1D mode, and simultaneously optimizes two parameters in the 2D mode. Details about computing S and S_b sets can be found in Ref. [8]. As a side note, computation of the set S is done by performing four sweeps of the routing grid (once in each direction). This step is very efficient under assumption that the routing target is a Hanan grid, but it cannot handle obstacles.

Once the set S is computed at the top level $S(v_d, 1, n - 1)$, the actual topology embeddings can be obtained by backtracking through the data structure containing these solution signatures.

In Ref. [7], the original algorithm is extended to perform simultaneous route construction and buffer insertion. The general flow of the algorithm is almost identical to Ref. [8], except that each internal vertex in the topology is also considered as a buffer insertion candidate location. However, some adjustments had to be made to the solution signature and, because of that, to all primitives that operate on them as well. Because inserting a buffer decouples downstream load, and effectively resets the load visible from the parent vertex to the input capacitance of the inserted buffer, the load value cannot be used for cost estimation (but remains necessary for delay estimation). Thus, a third parameter that represents solution cost (e.g., area, power, congestion, or any composite function of those) is added to the solutions signature. The solution signature now becomes a triple (p, c, q). More details about the three-dimensional (3D) (simultaneously optimizing three parameters) version of the primitives can be found in Ref. [12]. Also, methods from Ref. [12] can be applied here to extend the algorithm to support multiple buffers and inverters in the library.

Although the algorithm's computational complexity is $O(n^5)$ in the 1D mode, and pseudopoly-nomially bounded in the 2D mode, it produces solutions of very high quality in terms of both cost and delay. The algorithm may not be suitable for optimizing every single net in the design, but using this approach to optimize a smaller number of highly critical nets can be very beneficial, especially when one considers that the algorithm produces a family of solutions with delay/cost trade-off giving more choices in the overall design optimization process. Experimental results support these claims. A detailed description of the algorithm and its extensions that were summarized above can be also found in Ref. [17].

27.3.2   S-TREE ALGORITHM

The work in Ref. [11] adopts the overall philosophy of P-Tree while improving runtime and scalabil-ity, introducing a general strategy (stitching) for incorporating multiple measures of locality between sinks and subtrees (e.g., temporal, polarity), and finally adopting a general graph model as the routing target enabling natural solutions for obstacles, multilayer routing, etc.

Although the P-Tree topology space is very large and has a very good ability to capture spatial sink locality, it may create solutions of higher cost in certain scenarios that include, for example, highly critical sinks physically located among noncritical sinks. To address this issue, the S-Tree defines its topology search set using a topology tree and a sink partition. Sink partition specifies which sinks can break the original topology tree and be stitched to any other part of the topology while maintaining the order within its own partition set. The topology set is then composed of all valid stitching trees (thus, giving the name S-Tree). In Figure 27.9, given the topology on the left and a sink partition {{A, C, D, F}, {B, E}}, one can find all possible topologies that satisfy the stitching requirement. Assuming that sinks B and E are critical, note how they are allowed to break away from noncritical sinks and climb toward the root. The fact that these topologies are in the solution space guarantees only that they will be explored but whether they will be chosen at the end depends on the cost and quality of the embedded trees.

In the extreme cases, if all sinks belong to a single partition, S-Tree is equivalent to a single topology tree embedding. The other extreme case is if each sink belongs to its own partition, which explores all possible tree topologies in a way similar to Ref. [9].

The initial topology is obtained as in P-Tree, using the first two steps only: construct an MST and convert it to a topology tree by reorientation and binarization. The sink partitions can be determined based on estimated timing criticality, input signal polarity requirements, or any other criteria. Once the topology set is defined, the algorithm proceeds with the dynamic programming algorithm that performs topology set embedding. In the embedding process, no sink (nor a group of sinks) receives any special treatment.

Modifications to the topology embedding algorithm include support of a general graph model for a routing target. Propagation of candidate solutions through the routing graph is performed using timing-driven maze routing approach with simultaneous buffer insertion as in Ref. [14]. Note that solution quality depends a lot on the routing target graph. Careful graph construction is a key to

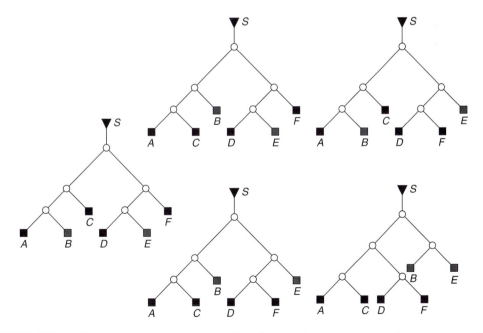

FIGURE 27.9 S-Tree topology space example. The initial topology tree on the left and a sink partition {{A, C, D, F}, {B, E}} define a set of five different topologies that will be explored simultaneously.

the high-quality solution, but one should have in mind that the size of the graph has a large impact on the execution time. Some suggestions how to construct the routing target graph can be found in Refs. [9–11,14]; however, the algorithm itself is designed to work on general graph model, thus, the routing target graph may be constructed by any other means.

Optimization modes include all three modes seen in the P-Tree algorithm (1D, 2D, and 3D). Experimental results demonstrate the effectiveness of the approach in identifying solutions with very good timing and low cost. Also, the algorithm has very good predictability characteristics.

27.3.3 SP-Tree Algorithm

The SP-Tree algorithm [10], as the name suggests (the stitching permutation constrained trees), combines the topology tree spaces of P-Tree and S-Tree. After obtaining the sink permutation and constructing a set of topology trees, sink partitions are specified and the entire set of topology trees is expanded by the stitching operation, producing a new larger set of tree topologies. The SP-Tree topology set contains both the P-Tree and the S-Tree topologies in addition to some new topologies that are not contained in either P-Tree or S-Tree.

The topology set embedding algorithm is identical to that of the S-Tree with the main difference in the construction of the topology tree set that is provided as an input to the embedder. More details about both algorithms can be found in Ref. [18], while executable solvers and examples can be found at Ref. [19].

Algorithms like buffered P-Tree, S-Tree, and SP-Tree, based on a general graph model as a routing target, provide high-quality solutions and have large flexibility with different optimization objectives. As expected, experimental results demonstrate that SP-Tree flow produces solutions that are always better or equal to those of both S-Tree and P-Tree, usually with a smaller cost, but at a runtime penalty.

27.3.4 Complete Tree Topology Exploration

For the experimental purposes, one can construct a tree topology set that contains all possible tree topologies. This is similar to topology decomposition from Ref. [20]. One can achieve that either by using the S-Tree and requesting that each sink belongs to its own partition, or by using a specific approach as in Ref. [9]. Embedded routing trees obtained in this fashion are indeed optimal, but the computational complexity prevents any practical applications, although they are valuable for research purposes and evaluation of other heuristic approaches.

REFERENCES

1. L. P. P. P. van Ginneken, Buffer placement in distributed RC-Tree networks for minimal elmore delay, in *Proceedings of the IEEE International Symposium on Circuits and Systems*, New Orleans, LA, May 1990, pp. 865–868.
2. W. C. Elmore, The transient response of damped linear networks with particular regard to wideband amplifiers, *Journal of Applied Physics*, 19: 55–63, Jan. 1948.
3. C. J. Alpert, G. Gandham, M. Hrkić, J. Hu, A. B. Kahng, J. Lillis, B. Liu, S. T. Quay, S. S. Sapatnekar, and A. J. Sullivan, Buffered Steiner trees for difficult instances, *IEEE Transactions on Computer-Aided Design of Integrated Circuits and Systems*, 21(1): 3–14, Jan. 2002.
4. C. J. Alpert, G. Gandham, M. Hrkić, J. Hu, and S. T. Quay, Porosity aware buffered Steiner tree construction, in *Proceedings of the ACM International Symposium on Physical Design*, Monterey, CA, Apr. 2003, pp. 158–165.
5. C. J. Alpert, M. Hrkić, J. Hu, and S. T. Quay, Fast and flexible buffer trees that navigate the physical layout environment, in *Proceedings of the 41st Design Automation Conference*, San Diego, CA, Jun. 2004, pp. 24–29.
6. C. Bartoschek, S. Held, D. Rautenbach, and J. Vygen, Efficient generation of short and fast repeater tree topologies, in *Proceedings of the ACM International Symposium on Physical Design*, San Jose, CA, Apr. 2006, pp. 120–127.

7. J. Lillis, C. K. Cheng, and T. T. Y. Lin, Simultaneous routing and buffer insertion for high performance interconnect, in *Proceedings of the 6th IEEE Great Lakes Symposium on VLSI*, Ames, IA, Mar. 1996, pp. 148–153.

8. J. Lillis, C. K. Cheng, T. T. Y. Lin, and C. Y. Ho, New performance driven routing techniques with explicit area/delay tradeoff and simultaneous wire sizing, in *Proceedings of the 33rd Design Automation Conference*, Las Vegas, NV, Jun. 1996, pp. 395–400.

9. J. Cong and X. Yuan, Routing tree construction under fixed buffer locations, in *Proceedings of the 37th Design Automation Conference*, Los Angeles, CA, Jun. 2000, pp. 379–384.

10. M. Hrkić and J. Lillis, Buffer tree synthesis with consideration of temporal locality, sink polarity requirements, solution cost and blockages, in *Proceedings of the ACM International Symposium on Physical Design*, Del Mar, CA, Apr. 2002, pp. 98–103.

11. M. Hrkić and J. Lillis, S-Tree: A technique for buffered routing tree synthesis, in *Proceedings of the 39th Design Automation Conference*, New Orleans, LA, Jun. 2002, pp. 578–583.

12. J. Lillis, C. K. Cheng, and T. T. Y. Lin, Optimal wire sizing and buffer insertion for low power and a generalized delay model, *IEEE Journal of Solid-State Circuits*, 31(3): 437–447, Mar. 1996.

13. C. J. Alpert, T. C. Hu, J. H. Huang, A. B. Kahng, and D. Karger, Prim-Dijkstra tradeoffs for improved performance-driven routing tree design, *IEEE Transactions on Computer-Aided Design of Integrated Circuits and Systems*, 14(7): 890–898, Jul. 1995.

14. S. W. Hur, A. Jagannathan, and J. Lillis, Timing-driven maze routing, *IEEE Transactions on Computer-Aided Design of Integrated Circuits and Systems*, 19(2): 234–241, Feb. 2000.

15. A. Jagannathan, S. -W. Hur, and J. Lillis, A fast algorithm for context-aware buffer insertion, in *Proceedings of the 37th Design Automation Conference*, Los Angeles, CA, Jun. 2000, pp. 368–373.

16. H. Zhou, D. F. Wong, I. M. Liu, and A. Aziz, Simultaneous routing and buffer insertion with restrictions on buffer locations, in *Proceedings of the 36th Design Automation Conference*, New Orleans, LA, Jun. 1999, pp. 96–99.

17. J. Lillis, Algorithms for Performance Driven Design of Integrated Circuits, 1996. Available at http://www.cs.uic.edu/~jlillis/papers/thesis.ps.

18. M. Hrkić and J. Lillis, Buffer tree synthesis with consideration of temporal locality, sink polarity requirements, solution cost, congestion and blockages, *IEEE Transactions on Computer-Aided Design of Integrated Circuits and Systems*, 22(4): 481–491, Apr. 2003.

19. M. Hrkić and J. Lillis, GSRC Single Interconnect Tree Synthesis Web Page. Available at http://eda.cs.uic.edu/software/interconnect/gsrc.html.

20. S. E. Dreyfus and R. A. Wagner, The Steiner problem in graphs, *Networks*, 1: 195–208, 1972.

28 Buffering in the Layout Environment

Jiang Hu and Cliff C. N. Sze

CONTENTS

28.1 INTRODUCTION

Chapters 26 and 27 presented buffering algorithms where the buffering problem was isolated from the general problem of timing closure. The main problem with this extraction is that there are no necessarily resources available to put the buffers or wires in their desired locations. One way to manage this flow is to put the buffers in their ideal locations and allow a legalization procedure to move them to actual locations. The problem with this approach is that buffers may be moved quite far from their ideal locations, which could completely corrupt the quality of the solution. It is much better to place the buffers in regions where there appear to be sufficient space, so that legalization would move the buffers by at most 10–20 routing tracks, which would preserve the original solution. To do this, one must certainly take into account the blockages and preferably local placement and routing congestion. In this chapter, we explore techniques that consider these factors.

28.2 PLACEMENT AND ROUTING BLOCKAGES

In realistic chip designs, some regions may be occupied by IP blocks, memory arrays, and macros. Such regions allow wires to pass through but have no room for buffer insertion. Therefore, buffer insertion has to be performed with consideration of these buffer blockages. If a wire path has large

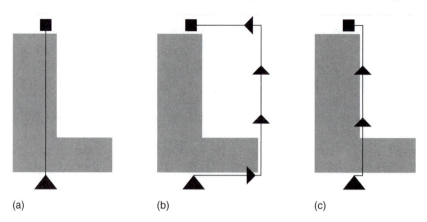

(a)   (b)   (c)

FIGURE 28.1   (a) The wire path has large overlap with the buffer blockage, which is the shaded region, and there is no feasible buffering solution. (b) Rerouting the wire to completely avoid the blockage may result in large wire detour. (c) Ideally, the wire path should largely avoid the blockage with limited detour.

overlap with blockages as in Figure 28.1a, no feasible buffering solution can be found. However, avoiding buffer blockages completely as Figure 28.1b may cause unnecessary wire detour as well as delay degradation. Hence, it is important to have algorithmic techniques that can find a proper routing topology (as Figure 28.1c) together with the buffer insertion solution. Another more intuitive example was previously described in Figure 27.4. To find the best buffered interconnect solution, the routing must consider feasible buffer insertion locations.

A similar problem is buffer insertion considering placement and routing congestions. If a buffer is inserted in a crowded place as in Figure 28.2a, it might be moved far away later during cell placement legalization. Thus, such insertion is not favorable although it is feasible, i.e., buffers are preferred to be inserted in relatively sparse regions like Figure 28.2b. Similarly, buffer insertion in a routing congested region may intensify the wire routability problem. Hence, buffer insertion algorithms need to be aware of layout environment and be able to handle the trade off between timing performance and congestion avoidance.

Section 28.3 introduces algorithms on blockage avoidance for two-pin nets, i.e., buffered paths. Blockage buffered Steiner tree methods for multipin nets are described in Section 28.4. In Section 28.5, techniques for handling congestions are discussed.

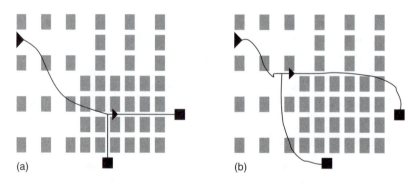

(a)   (b)

FIGURE 28.2   (a) If a buffer is placed in a crowded region, it may be moved by placement legalizer far away from its preferred location. (b) If the buffer is placed in a sparse region, its location will not be significantly changed by placement legalization.

28.3 BUFFERED PATH WITH BLOCKAGE AVOIDANCE

For two-pin nets, the problem is to find a buffered path with the minimum delay under the blockage constraints. In the literature, there exists two major approaches: (1) dynamic programming and (2) graph-based algorithm. Both are based on the Elmore delay model. It has not been showed that these approaches are fast enough to be practical for general optimization cases, but they can be very useful to a handful of the most critical nets.

28.3.1 DYNAMIC PROGRAMMING-BASED METHOD

The dynamic programming-based method [1,2] propagates partial solutions from the sink node t through a routing graph $G = (V, E)$ and picks the optimal solution at the source node s. The routing graph can be either a uniform grid reflecting routing tracks (Figure 28.3a) or an extended Hanan grid, which is obtained by drawing vertical and horizontal lines through the given pins and blockage boundaries (Figure 28.3b). For each edge $(u, v) \in E$, $R(u, v)$ and $C(u, v)$ are the edge resistance and capacitance, respectively. For each node $v \in V$, there is a label $p(v) \in \{0, 1\}$ which is equal to 0 if it overlaps with a buffer blockage and equal to 1, otherwise. Besides the routing graph, the driver resistance R_d, sink capacitance C_t, and a buffer library B are assumed to be given. Each buffer type $b \in B$ is modeled by its input capacitance $C(b)$, intrinsic delay $K(b)$, and output resistance $R(b)$.

A partial solution at a node v is characterized by a quadruple $\alpha = (c, d, m, v)$, where c is the current input capacitance seen at v, d is the delay from v to the sink t, and m is a labeling for the buffered path from v to t. The label of $m(v) = b$ indicates that buffer $b \in B$ is inserted at node v and $m(v) = 0$ implies that no buffer is inserted there. The solution $\alpha_1 = (c_1, d_1, m_1, v)$ is inferior to solution $\alpha_2 = (c_2, d_2, m_2, v)$ if $c_1 \geq c_2$ and $d_1 \geq d_2$.

The partial solutions are maintained in a priority queue Q initialized with the solution $(C_t, 0, 0, t)$ at the sink t. Each time, the top solution in Q, which has the minimum delay, is extracted for expansion. A solution (c, d, m, u) is expanded to its neighbor node v if there is an edge $(u, v) \in E$. The expanded solution is $(c + C(u, v), d + R(u, v) \cdot (c + C(u, v)/2), m, v)$ where the delay increase is based on the Elmore delay model. If a solution (c, d, m, v) is at node v where $m(v) = 0$ and $p(v) = 1$, buffers of each type are inserted there to generate new partial solutions. If the buffer type is $b \in B$, its corresponding buffered solution is $(C(b), d + R(b) \cdot c + K(b), m, v)$

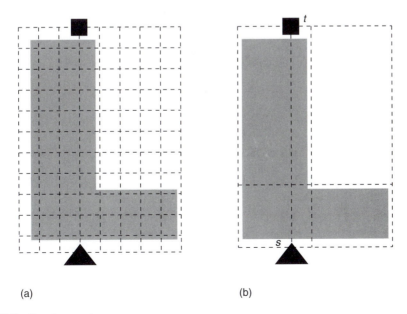

(a)   (b)

FIGURE 28.3 Routing graph.

```
Algorithm: Buffered_Path(G, B, s, t)
Input: Routing graph G = (V, E), Buffer library B
       Source node s ∈ V and sink node t ∈ V
Output: Buffered path labeling m
1. Q ← {(C, 0, 0, t)}
2. while Q ≠ Ø do
3.     (c, d, m, u) ← extract_min(Q)
4.     if c = 0, return m
5.     if u = s,
           push (0, d + R_d · c, m, s) into Q and prune continue
6.     for each (u, v) ∈ E do
           d' ← d + R(u, v) · (c + C(u, v)/2)
           push (c + C(u, v), d', m, v) into Q and prune
7.     if p(u) = 1 and m(u) = 0
8.        for each b ∈ B do
              d' ← d + R(b) · c + K(b)
              m(u) = b
              push (C(b), d', m, u) into Q and prune
```

FIGURE 28.4 Pseudocode of the dynamic programming-based buffered path algorithm.

with $m(v) = b$. If a solution reaches the source node as (c, d, m, s), the driver is added by updating the solution as $(0, d + R_d \cdot c, m, s)$. When a solution with the driver is at the top of the Q, it is the minimum delay solution.

The pseudocode of this algorithm is given in Figure 28.4. Please note that pruning is performed in many steps to remove inferior solutions so that the runtime can be improved. The complexity of this algorithm is $O(|B||V|(|E| + |B||V|) \log |B||V|)$ [1].

28.3.2 GRAPH-BASED APPROACH

The graph-based approaches [3,4] first transform the routing graph $G = (V, E)$ into a buffer graph $G_B = (V_B, E_B)$ and then obtain the minimum delay buffered path by the Dijkstra's shortest path algorithm.

The node set V_B of the buffer graph is composed of the source node, sink nodes, and a set of buffer nodes. A buffer node always has a buffer inserted and therefore it has to be out of any buffer blockage. An edge $e \in E_B$ is usually directed from the source or a buffer node to a buffer node or the sink node (Figure 28.5a). There is a delay associated with each edge. If the Elmore delay model is employed, the delay $d(u, v)$ for edge (u, v) is equal to $R(u) \cdot (C(u, v) + C(v)) + R(u, v) \cdot (C(u, v)/2 + C(v))$ where

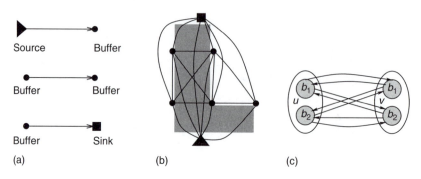

(a)   (b)   (c)

FIGURE 28.5 Buffer graph.

$R(u)$ is the driving resistance at u, $R(u, v)$ is the edge resistance, $C(u, v)$ is the edge capacitance, and $C(v)$ is the input capacitance at v. Unlike the routing graph introduced in Section 28.3.1, the two end nodes of an edge in the buffer graph do not have to be geometrical neighbors. An example of buffer graph is shown in Figure 28.5b. If the edge delay is treated as edge weight, the minimum buffered path is equivalent to the shortest path on this buffer graph. Thus, the optimal solution can be found easily by applying Dijkstra's shortest path algorithm on the buffer graph.

The graph-based approach can be easily extended to handle multiple buffer types and wire sizing. If there are k buffer types, each buffer node is split into k copies each of which corresponds to one type. Edges are inserted among these copies of nodes. In Figure 28.5c, an example of two buffer types is shown. Similarly, if there are multiple wire widths, the edge weight is chosen as the minimum edge delay among all options of wire widths [4]. Then, discrete wire sizing is naturally handled in the same framework.

Besides minimizing the path delay, the problem can be formulated [3] as maximizing delay reduction to cost ratio $\frac{D_{ref}-d(p)}{g(p)}$ where D_{ref} is a reference delay, $d(p)$ is the path delay of path p, and $g(p)$ is the path cost. The path cost is simply the total edge cost along the path. The edge cost can be defined in many different ways. For example, it can be the summation of wire capacitance and buffer/sink capacitance of its downstream end. Let R_{max} represent the maximum ratio can be obtained. Then

$$R_{max} = \frac{D_{ref} - \sum_{e \in p} d(e)}{\sum_{e \in p} g(e)}$$

or equivalently

$$R_{max} \sum_{e \in p} g(e) + \sum_{e \in p} d(e) = D_{ref}$$

If the weight of each edge e is set to $R_{max}g(e) + d(e)$, the total path weight is equal to D_{ref}. The value of R_{max} can be obtained by probing different values in a binary search manner. For a guess I of R_{max}, the shortest path weight is obtained when each edge weight is labeled as $I \cdot g(e) + d(e)$. If the result is greater (smaller) than D_{ref}, the value of I is increased (decreased). When the path weight is sufficiently close to D_{ref}, its corresponding value of I can be treated as R_{max}.

As the value of D_{ref} decreases, the cost of the corresponding maximum ratio path increases [3]. There exists a D_{ref} for which a (g, d) path is optimal if and only if (g, d) lies on the lower convex hull of the trade-off curve between cost g and delay d [3]. The solutions on a lower convex hull is illustrated in Figure 28.6.

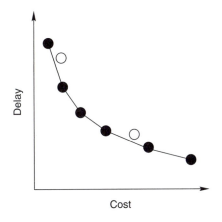

FIGURE 28.6 All circles represent the set of noninferior solutions. The dark circles lie on the lower convex hull.

28.4 BUFFERED TREE WITH BLOCKAGE AVOIDANCE

The situation of multipin nets is much more difficult than that of two-pin nets as Steiner tree construction itself is a hard problem. There are two categories of approaches: (1) constructing a Steiner tree regardless of buffer blockages and then adjusting the tree to avoid blockages and (2) simultaneous Steiner tree construction and buffer insertion with awareness of blockages.

28.4.1 TREE ADJUSTMENT TECHNIQUE

As a relatively easy method, one can start with a Steiner tree regardless of blockages and modify the tree to avoid blockages [5]. This can be performed in a fashion similar to the rip-up and reroute in congestion avoidance of global routing. In other words, if a path in the tree has large overlap with blockages, it is ripped up and reconnected back to the tree with a path having less overlap with blockages. This is illustrated in Figure 28.7.

In each iteration, the path with the largest overlap with blockages is chosen for rerouting. The reconnection procedure is done by running Dijkstra's algorithm on the extended Hanan grid graph indicated by the dashed lines in Figure 28.7. In this graph, the weight of an edge is its length if it does not overlap with any blockage. If an edge overlaps with a blockage, its weight is its length times α, where $\alpha > 1$ is a penalty coefficient. The value of α decides the trade-off between blockage avoidance and wire increase due to detour. After the tree modification, the chance of feasible buffering solutions is increased. Because the rerouting has no knowledge if buffers are needed on a path, it may cause some unnecessary wire detours.

Another technique is to integrate the tree adjustment with buffer insertion [6] so that wire detour is incurred only when it is necessary for buffer insertion. The classic van Ginneken's buffer insertion algorithm [7] propagates a set of candidate solutions from the sink nodes toward the source and picks the optimal one at the source. The adaptive tree adjustment technique generates a candidate solution with an alternative Steiner node if the original Steiner node is inside a blockage. This adjustment is a part of a candidate solution, which is propagated toward the source. This adjustment is adopted only when its corresponding candidate solution is selected at the source. In other words, the tree adjustment is made according to the need of buffer insertion. In Figure 28.8, an example is depicted to demonstrate this technique.

28.4.2 SIMULTANEOUS TREE CONSTRUCTION AND BUFFER INSERTION

The problem of whether or not to avoid a blockage and how to avoid can be solved by simultaneously constructing Steiner tree and inserting buffers [8–10]. Compared to the tree adjustment techniques, the simultaneous approach can lead to improved solution quality with increased computation cost. There are two major methods of the simultaneous approach: dynamic programming [8] and graph based [9].

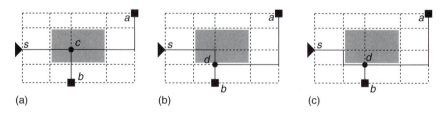

(a)   (b)   (c)

FIGURE 28.7   Rip-up and reroute to avoid blockages.

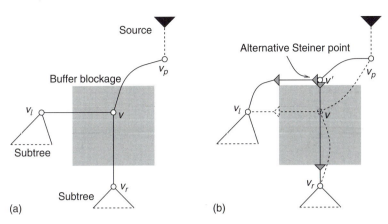

FIGURE 28.8 For a Steiner node v within a buffer blockage as in (a), an alternative Steiner node v' is generated as another candidate solution allowing buffer insertion as in (b). (From Figure 2 of Hu, J., Alpert, C. J., Quay, S. T., and Gandham, G., *IEEE Trans. Comput. Aided Des. Integrated Circuits Syst.*, 22, 494, 2003. With permission.)

28.4.2.1 Dynamic Programming-Based Method

The dynamic programming-based method, called RMP (recursive merging and pruning) is performed on a routing graph like Figure 28.3. Similar to the fast path algorithm [1], it propagates candidate solutions over the graph. The difference is that RMP considers merging solutions to form subtrees. Each candidate solution is characterized by (c, q, RE, buf, v) where c is the downstream load capacitance, q is the required arrival time, RE is the reachable sink set in the subtree, and v is the root of the subtree. The label buf $= 1$ if a buffer is inserted at the node, buf $= 0$ otherwise. The candidate solutions are maintained in a priority queue with the maximum-q solution on the top.

When merging two solutions at a node, one need to ensure that the reachable sink sets of the two solutions are disjoint. If a sink appears in both of the solutions, then the merging implies nontree topology. If solution $(c_1, q_1, RE_1, buf1, v)$ and $(c_2, q_2, RE_2, buf2, v)$ are merged, the merged solution is $(c_1 + c_2, \min(q_1, q_2), RE_1 \cup RE_2, 0, v)$. For solutions at the same node of the routing graph, a pruning can be performed among them if they all have the same reachable sink set. The pruning is same as that described in Section 28.3.1. The RMP algorithm can reach the optimal solution in exponential time. To reduce runtime, one can perform an aggressive pruning that keeps only the minimum-c solution for each reachable sink set [8]. This technique can improve runtime significantly with very limited sacrifice on solution quality.

28.4.2.2 Graph-Based Technique

The graph-based method [9] starts with constructing a look-up table storing precomputed tree components. Then, an abstraction graph is generated with each edge corresponding a tree component that can be obtained from the look-up table. The buffered tree with minimized maximum sink delay is obtained by applying Dijkstra's shortest path algorithm on the abstraction graph.

The tree components include

- Wire path: a path connecting two nodes in the routing graph by properly sized wires but no buffers are between them
- Buffered path: a path connecting two nodes in the routing graph with buffers inserted between
- Buffer combination: a tree component connecting three or more nodes in the routing graph without internal buffers
- BC-subtree: a subtree rooted with a buffer combination

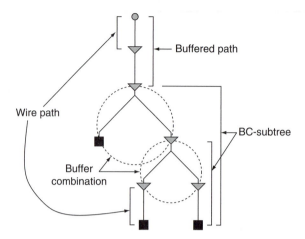

FIGURE 28.9 Notations for graph-based simultaneous tree construction and buffer insertion. (From Figure 4 of Tang, X., Tian, R., Xiang, H., and Wong, D. F., *Proc. IEEE/ACM Inter. Con. Comput. Aided Des.*, pages 51 and 52, 2001. With permission.)

These components are illustrated in Figure 28.9. The minimum delay buffered path can be obtained by the method in Refs. [3,4], which is introduced in Section 28.3.2. A buffer combination can be treated as an unbuffered Steiner tree. Its delay is specified as the maximum root-leaf delay. If the number of nodes is restricted, the minimum delay buffer combination can be obtained by enumeration. Both the minimum delay buffered paths and the minimum delay buffer combinations are saved in look-up tables for future query.

On the basis of buffer combinations, BC-subtrees, which are subtrees rooted at a buffer combination, can be constructed to drive a set of sinks. A few examples of BC-subtrees are shown in Figure 28.10.

A buffered Steiner tree (or subtree) is composed of a set of buffered paths and BC-subtrees in general. Therefore, a general problem is how to construct a buffered tree (or subtree) that drives a certain set of sinks $\Gamma = \{s_1, s_2, \ldots\}$. This is achieved by using an abstraction graph G_Γ illustrated in Figure 28.11. This graph consists of a source node, which is the set of sinks Γ, and a set of possible buffer nodes. An edge (Γ, v) represents the optimal BC-subtree rooted at v, and its weight is the maximum delay of the BC-tree. The edge (u, v), where $u, v \notin \Gamma$, represents the optimal buffered path between u and v, which can be found in the look-up table. Then, the shortest path from Γ to each other node v corresponds to the optimal subtree connecting to the sink set Γ. The algorithm proceeds to creates subtrees by increasingly considering more sinks.

This algorithm can minimize the maximum source–sink delay, but not the timing slack. In fact, it can reach the optimal solution in exponential time.

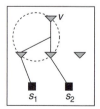 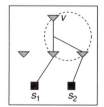 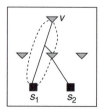 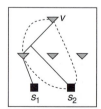

FIGURE 28.10 Example of different BC-subtrees. (From Figure 8 of Tang, X., Tian, R., Xiang, H., and Wong, D. F., *Proc. IEEE/ACM Inter. Con. Comput. Aided Des.*, pages 51 and 52, 2001. With permission.)

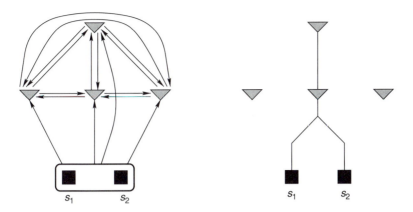

FIGURE 28.11 Graph for generating optimal subtree. (From Figure 9 of Tang, X., Tian, R., Xiang, H., and Wong, D. F., *Proc. IEEE/ACM Inter. Con. Comput. Aided Des.*, pages 51 and 52, 2001. With permission.)

28.5 LAYOUT ENVIRONMENT AWARE BUFFERED STEINER TREE

The previous sections presented different algorithms for buffer insertion and buffered tree construction avoiding buffer placement blockages. Practically, it is essential that buffer insertion algorithms consider layout environment such as the placement and routing congestion, which obviously leads to a more complicated problem. In this section, we start with the congestion assessment and then introduce several related algorithms.

28.5.1 MEASUREMENT OF PLACEMENT AND ROUTING CONGESTION

To evaluate the placement and routing congestion of a buffered net, a tile graph is usually used to capture the congestion information and at the same time reduce the problem complexity. The tile graph is represented as $G = (V_G, E_G)$ such that $V_G = \{g_1, g_2, \ldots\}$ is a set of tiles and E_G is a set of boundaries each (g_i, g_j) of which is between two adjacent tiles g_i and g_j. An example of the tile graph is shown in Figure 28.12. If a tile $g_i \in V_G$ has an area of $A(g_i)$ and its area occupied by placed cells

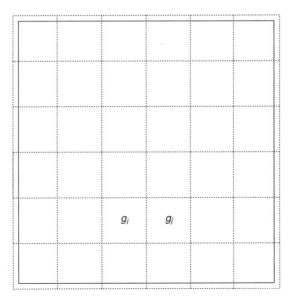

FIGURE 28.12 Example of tile graph.

are $a(g_i)$, the placement density is defined as $d(g_i) = \frac{a(g_i)}{A(g_i)}$. Let $W(g_i, g_j)$ be the maximum number of wire tracks that can be routed across the tile boundary (g_i, g_j) and $w(g_i, g_j)$ be the number of used tracks crossing (g_i, g_j). Similarly, the boundary density is $d(g_i, g_j) = \frac{w(g_i, g_j)}{W(g_i, g_j)}$. To increase the penalty of using a congested tile (similarly for a tile boundary), using square cost (i.e., $d(g_i)^2$) ensures that the cost increases more rapidly as a tile is closer to becoming full. For example, the cost of using two tiles with densities of 0.1 and 0.9 is 0.82, while the cost of using two tiles with densities of 0.5 is 0.5. When considering both the placement and routing congestion cost for a net, the total cost incurred can be a linear expression of squares of both the tile densities and boundary densities.

28.5.2 PLATE-BASED TREE ADJUSTMENT

When we consider both placement and routing congestions at the same time, applying simultaneous Steiner tree construction and buffer insertion seems to be computationally prohibitive for practical circuit designs. In the following, sequential approaches [11,12] are introduced to solve the problems. A good way to handle the placement and routing congestion is through the following four stages: (1) timing-driven Steiner tree construction, (2) plate-based adjustment for congestion mitigation, (3) local blockage avoidance (refer to Section 28.2.1), and (4) van Ginneken style buffer insertion. Because stages 1, 3, and 4 have been described in previous sections, the rest of the discussion focuses on the stage of plate-based tree adjustment.

28.5.2.1 Dynamic Programming-Based Adjustment

The basic idea for the plate-based adjustment [13] is to perform a simplified simultaneous buffer insertion and local tree adjustment so that the Steiner nodes and wiring paths can be moved to less congested regions without significant disturbance on the timing performance obtained in stage 1. The plate-based adjustment traverses the given Steiner topology in a bottom-up fashion by the dynamic programming algorithm. During this process, Steiner nodes and wiring paths may be adjusted together with buffer insertion to generate multiple candidate solutions. We only use buffer insertion to estimate the placement congestion of the buffered tree and to guide the tree adjustment. Hence, the output of this stage is still an unbuffered net, only with changes in the Steiner tree routing. Besides, because buffer insertion is merely a mean of placement congestion estimation, a single typical buffer type can be used to simplify the calculation, while the Elmore delay model can be used for interconnect and a switch level RC gate delay model is adopted.

For a Steiner node v_i which is located in a tile g_k, a *plate* $P(v_i)$ for v_i is a set of tiles in the neighborhood of g_k including g_k itself. During the plate-based adjustment, we confine the location change for each Steiner node within its corresponding plate. If v_i is a sink or the source node we set $P(v_i) = \{g_k\}$. The shaded box in Figure 28.13a gives an example of the plate corresponding to Steiner node v_4. The plate indicates any of the possible locations which the Steiner node may be moved to.

The search for alternative wiring paths is limited to the minimum bounding box covering the plates of two end nodes. In Figure 28.13, such bounding boxes are indicated by the thickened dashed lines. Therefore, the size of plates define the search range for both Steiner nodes and wiring paths. As a result, the size of the plate controls the quality of solution/runtime trade-off desired by the user. With different plate sizes, we can obtain the ability to modify the topology to move Steiner points into low-congestion regions while also capping the runtime penalty. An example of how a new Steiner topology might be constructed from an existing topology is demonstrated in Figure 28.13a through c.

It is suggested in Ref. [14] that buffer insertion can be performed in a simple nontiming-driven way by following a rule of thumb: the maximal interval between two neighboring buffers is no greater than certain upper bound. Similarly, we restrict the maximum load capacitance U a buffer/driver may

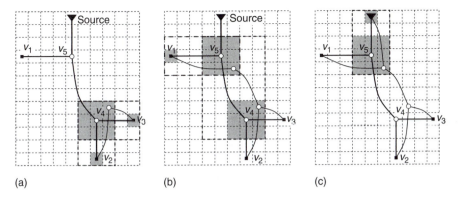

FIGURE 28.13 (a) Candidate solutions are generated from v_2 and v_3 and propagated to every tile, which is shaded, in the plate for v_4. Solution search is limited to the bounding boxes indicated by the thickened dashed lines. (b) Solutions from v_1 and every tile in the plate for v_4 are propagated to the plate for v_5. (c) Solutions from plate of v_5 are propagated to the source and the thin solid lines indicate one of the alternative trees that may result from this process. (From figure 3 of Alpert, C. J., Gandham, G., Mrkic, M., Hu, J., Quay, S. T., and Sze, C. -N., *IEEE Trans. Comput. Aided Des. Integrated Circuits Syst.*, 23, 519, 2004. With permission.)

drive, so that sink/buffer capacitance can be incorporated. To keep the succinctness of the tile-based interval metric in Ref. [14], we discretize the load capacitance in units equivalent to the capacitance of wire with average tile size. Thus, we can prune out all intermediate solutions with load capacitance greater than U.

During the bottom-up process, each intermediate solution is characterized by a 3-tuple $s(v_i, c, w)$ in which v_i is the root of the subtree, c is the discretized load capacitance seen from v_i, and w is the accumulated congestion cost. A solution can be pruned if both its c and w are no better than another one in the solution set associated with the same node v_i.

Starting from the leaf nodes, candidate solutions are generated and propagated toward the source in a bottom-up manner. Before we propagate candidate solutions from node v_i to its parent node v_j, we first find both plate $P(v_i)$ and plate $P(v_j)$ and define a bounding box that is the minimum-sized array of tiles covering both $P(v_i)$ and $P(v_j)$. Then we propagate all the candidate solutions from each tile of $P(v_i)$ to each tile of $P(v_j)$ within this bounding box. Because the Steiner nodes are more likely to be buffer sites due to the demand on decoupling noncritical branch load from the critical path, allowing Steiner nodes to be moved to less congested area is especially important. Moreover, such move is a part of a candidate solution, and therefore the move will be committed only when its corresponding candidate solution is finally selected at the driver. Thus, the tree adjustment is dynamically generated and selected according to the request of the final minimal congestion cost solution.

28.5.2.2 Hybrid Approach for Tree Adjustment

Although the stage of plate-based tree adjustment effectively improve the layout congestion issue, there are several techniques [12] to improve the computational efficiency. Actually, the runtime bottleneck is due to the fact that buffering solution has to be searched along with node-to-node* paths in a two-dimensional plane because low congestion paths have to be found at where the buffers are needed.

If we can predict where buffers are needed in advance, then we can merely focus on searching low congestion paths and the number of factors to be considered can be further reduced to one. If we

---

* The node may be the source node, a sink node, or a Steiner node of degree greater than two. Thus, degree-2 Steiner nodes are not included here.

diagnose the mechanism on how buffer insertion improves interconnect timing performance, it can be broken down into two parts: (1) regenerating signal level to increase driving capability for long wires and (2) shielding capacitive load at noncritical branches from the timing critical path. In a Steiner tree, buffers that play the first role are along a node-to-node path while buffers for the second purpose are normally close to a branching Steiner node. The majority of buffer insertion algorithms such as van Ginneken's algorithm are dynamic programming based and have been proved to be very effective for both purposes. However, optimal buffer solutions along a node-to-node path can be found analytically [15,16]. This fact suggests that we may have a hybrid approach in which buffers along paths are placed according to the closed form solutions while the buffers at Steiner nodes are still solved by dynamic programming, i.e., analytical buffered path solutions replace both the wire segmenting [15] and candidate solution generations at segmenting points in the bottom-up dynamic programming framework. Computing candidate buffered paths analytically is faster than applying dynamic programming, which makes this hybrid approach more efficient than the purely dynamic programming scheme.

It is also suggested in Ref. [12] that the plate should be selected as a set of nearby tiles with the least congestion because only the nearby tiles with relatively low buffer placement or routing congestion cost worth considering to be the alternative Steiner node. In fact, if there exists a tile with high congestion cost in the plate, it will never be used as the new Steiner node.

Instead of using a length-based buffer insertion, the algorithm uses analytical formula for buffer insertion, which is separated from the minimum congestion cost path search process. If given the driver resistance, sink loading capacitance, and buffer resistance/capacitance/intrinsic delay, the optimal number of buffers and corresponding placement locations can be found with the equations [15], which are previously described in Section 26.2.1.

We explain our buffered path routing technique by an example. For the thickened path in Figure 28.14a, if we know the driving resistance at v_1 and load capacitance at v_4, we may obtain the optimal buffer positions at v_2 and v_3. However, if we connect v_1 and v_4 in a two-dimensional plane, there are many alternative paths between them and the optimal buffer locations form rows along diagonal directions. The tiles for the optimal buffer locations are shaded in Figure 28.14a. Therefore, if we connect v_1 and v_4 with any monotone path and insert a buffer whenever this path passes through a shaded tile, the resulting buffered path should have the same minimum delay. The thin solid curve in Figure 28.14a is an example of an alternative minimum delay buffered path. Certainly, different buffer paths may have different congestion costs. Then the minimum congestion cost buffered path can be found by performing the Dijkstra's algorithm on the tile graph, which is demonstrated in Figure 28.14b. In Figure 28.14b, each solid edge corresponds to a tile boundary and its edge cost is the corresponding wiring congestion cost. There are two types of nodes, the empty circle nodes that have zero cost and filled circle nodes that have cost equal to the placement congestion cost in

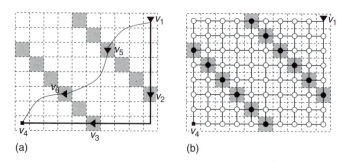

(a)   (b)

FIGURE 28.14 Find low congestion path with known buffer positions indicated by the shaded tiles. (From figure 5 of Sze, C. -N., Hu, J., and Alpert, C. J., *Proc. IEEE/ACM Asia and South Pacific Design Automation Conference*, 358, 2004. With permission.)

corresponding tile. In conclusion, the shortest path obtained in this way produces a buffered path with both good timing and low congestion cost.

One of the issue related to the use of analytical formula is that the upstream resistance is unknown in the bottom-up solution propagation process. However, the lower bound on the upstream resistance is $\underline{R} = \min(R_d, R_b)$ and the upper bound $\overline{R}$ is $\max(R_d, R_b)$ plus the upstream wire resistance.[*] R_d is the driver resistance and R_b is the buffer output resistance. Then, we can sample a few values between $\underline{R}$ and $\overline{R}$, and find the minimum cost buffered path for each value. Because the timing result is not sensitive to the upstream resistance, normally the sampling size is very limited.

28.5.3   LAYOUT NAVIGATION

To estimate the congestion efficiently, the solution quality of plate-based tree adjustment algorithms is restricted by the size of tile graph and the plate size. Because the complexity of the algorithm in Ref. [13] (described in Section 28.5.2.1) increases quadratically with plate size, using a fine tiling and a large plate size would be computationally prohibitive. More importantly, distinctions between critical and noncritical nets are missing in the algorithm. Practically, we may need to generate different solutions for critical and noncritical nets.

To speed up the tree adjustment process, at most one candidate per tile is allowed, which results in a maze routing based algorithm [17]. The right cost function is paramount so as to maintain the quality. Moreover, instead of performing plate-to-plate routing of a sequence of tile-to-tile routes, the entire optimization is performed in a single pass. This allows one to use as large a plate as necessary, for almost no runtime penalty. During the maze routing-like process, an immediate solution only contains the cost information of the subtree.

By parameterizing the cost function to trade off critical and noncritical nets, which leads to the algorithm in Ref. [18], we construct the cost function as follows, according to the criticality of the nets.

For noncritical nets, some nets require buffering to fix electrical violations (such as slew, capacitance, or noise). Some other want the net to avoid highly dense areas or routing congestion. However, one still wants to minimize wirelength to some degree. So we set the cost to be $1 + e(g_i)$ and assume that the total tile congestion cost[†] $e(g_i)$ is between 0 and 1, i.e., $0 \le e(g_i) \le 1$. This implies that a tile blocked for routing or density has cost twice that of a tile that uses no resources. The constant of one can be viewed as a delay component. A tile that corresponds to a Steiner point must merge the costs of the children into a single cost, by simply adding up the cost functions of all the children. Because these are noncritical nets, all sinks are treated equally by having initial cost zero.

For critical nets, the cost impact of the environment is immaterial. We seek the absolutely best possible slack. When a net is optimally buffered (assuming no obstacles), its delay is a linear function of its length [19]. Hence, to minimize delay, we simply minimize the number of tiles to the most critical sink, which results in a unit cost defined for each tile. When merging the branches, we pick the branch with worst slack, so the merged cost is the maximum of both costs. The costs at sinks are initialized based on the sink criticality. The more critical a sink, the higher its initial cost. Finally, the objective is to minimize cost at the source.

The algorithm is able to the trade off between the critical and noncritical cost functions during the maze routing procedure. Let $0 \le K \le 1$ be the trade-off parameter, where $K = 1$ corresponds to a noncritical net and $K = 0$ corresponds to a critical net. On the basis of the previously defined cost functions for noncritical and critical nets, the cost function for a tile g_i is then $1 + K \cdot e(g_i)$. For critical nets, merging branches is a maximization function, while it is an additive function for noncritical nets. These ideas can be combined while the merging cost of two children g_i and g_j becomes $\max[\mathrm{cost}(g_i),\ \mathrm{cost}(g_j)] + K \cdot \min[\mathrm{cost}(g_i),\ \mathrm{cost}(g_j)]$.

---

[*] The maximum upstream wire resistance can be derived from the length of maximum buffer-to-buffer interval. This is also mentioned in Ref. [14].

[†] The total congestion cost of a tile can be a linear expression of the squares of tile density and all its boundary densities.

It has been demonstrated that K can be used to trade off the cost function, the merging operation, and even sink initialization. In practice, we can first optimize all nets that need buffering with $K = 1$, which limits the use of scarce resources. After performing a timing analysis, those nets that still have negative slack can be reoptimized with a smaller value of K, e.g., 0.7. This process of reoptimizing and gradually reducing can continue until, say, $K = 0.1$.

28.5.4   RELATING BUFFERING CANDIDATE LOCATIONS TO LAYOUT ENVIRONMENT

While the previous algorithms are considering the routing tree adjustment, the following algorithm focuses on buffer insertion candidate selection for congestion reduction.

Van Ginneken style algorithm assumes that a set of buffer insertion candidate locations are predetermined for the given topology. The most common method for selecting insertion points is to choose them at regular intervals. Alpert and Devgan [15] show how the quality of results is affected by the degree of wire segmenting that is performed on the topology. For example, Figure 28.15a shows uniform segmenting for a Steiner tree with three sinks and a single blockage. For these regions for which buffer insertion is forbidden, one simply avoids inserting buffer candidate locations on top of the blockage. In Figure 28.15b, one can find the same uniform segmenting scheme, but with finer spacing. The additional buffer insertion locations could potentially improve the timing for the buffered net, for additional runtime cost. In Figure 28.15c, one can use roughly the same number of buffer insertion candidates as in uniform segmenting, but spacing them asymmetrically. The purpose is not to improve timing performance but rather to bias van Ginneken style algorithm to insert buffers in regions of the design that are more favorable, such as areas with lower congestion cost.

To accomplish this buffer candidate selection, Ref. [18] applies a linear time and linear memory shortest path algorithm. The algorithm constructs a directed acyclic graph (DAG) over the set of potential candidate locations and chooses a subset by constructing a shortest path via a topological sort.

Let L be the maximum allowable tiles in the tile graph (described in Section 28.4.1) between consecutive buffers, which could be determined by a maximum allowable slew constraint. If buffers are placed at a distance greater than L tiles away, then an electrical violation results or performance is significantly sacrificed. On the basis of L, edges are created by connecting the tiles which are no greater than L tiles away from each other. The edge represents a pair of consecutive buffer candidates on the fixed routing tree.

Moreover, we define S to be the desired number of tiles between consecutive buffer insertion candidates, which is chosen by the user to obtain the desired timing performance/CPU trade-off. For example, Figure 28.15a has a value that is twice that of Figure 28.15b. For asymmetric spacing, a penalty is associated for spacing tiles either closer to or further from the desired spacing S. We define a function $\mathrm{pen}(x, S, L) = \frac{(x-S)^2}{(L-S)^2}$ that assigns a penalty cost on an edge when the distance x

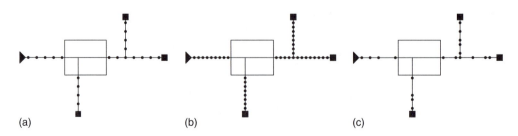

(a)   (b)   (c)

FIGURE 28.15   Given a fixed topology, one can segment wires uniformly via either (a) coarse or (b) finer spacing. Reference [18] uses asymmetric segmenting (c) based on the design characteristics.

between tiles is not equal to S. Together with the congestion consideration, the total cost of a path is the summation over the penalty cost of all edges and the congestion cost of all tiles on the path. Hence, the problem can be solved by a topological sort, which finds the minimum cost path from the source to all sinks. By the application of this preprocessing technique, buffers finally inserted significantly improve the overall design congestion with virtually no impact on either computation time or buffered net delays. In fact, because the preprocessing is more selective of the potential buffer insertion candidates, the final buffer insertion process can be speed up dramatically.

REFERENCES

1. H. Zhou, D. F. Wong, I. -M. Liu, and A. Aziz. Simultaneous routing and buffer insertion with restrictions on buffer locations. *IEEE Transactions on Computer-Aided Design*, 19(7):819–824, July 2000 (ICCD 2001).
2. S. -W. Hur, A. Jagannathan, and J. Lillis. Timing driven maze routing. In *Proceedings of the ACM International Symposium on Physical Design*, Monterey, CA, pp. 208–213, 1999.
3. A. Jagannathan, S. -W. Hur, and J. Lillis. A fast algorithm for context-aware buffer insertion. In *Proceedings of the ACM/IEEE Design Automation Conference*, Los Angeles, CA, pp. 368–373, 2000.
4. M. Lai and D. F. Wong. Maze routing with buffer insertion and wiresizing. In *Proceedings of the ACM/IEEE Design Automation Conference*, Los Angeles, CA, pp. 374–378, 2000.
5. C. J. Alpert, G. Gandham, J. Hu, J. L. Neves, S. T. Quay, and S. S. Sapatnekar. A Steiner tree construction for buffers, blockages, and bays. *IEEE Transactions on Computer-Aided Design*, 20(4):556–562, April 2001.
6. J. Hu, C. J. Alpert, S. T. Quay, and G. Gandham. Buffer insertion with adaptive blockage avoidance. *IEEE Transactions on Computer-Aided Design*, 22(4):492–498, April 2003.
7. L. P. P. P. van Ginneken. Buffer placement in distributed RC-tree networks for minimal Elmore delay. In *Proceedings of the IEEE International Symposium on Circuits and Systems*, New Orleans, LA, pp. 865–868, 1990.
8. J. Cong and X. Yuan. Routing tree construction under fixed buffer locations. In *Proceedings of the ACM/IEEE Design Automation Conference*, Los Angeles, CA, pp. 379–384, 2000.
9. X. Tang, R. Tian, H. Xiang, and D. F. Wong. A new algorithm for routing tree construction with buffer insertion and wire sizing under obstacle constraints. In *Proceedings of the IEEE/ACM International Conference on Computer-Aided Design*, San Jose, CA, pp. 49–56, 2001.
10. S. Dechu, Z. C. Shen, and C. C. N. Chu. An efficient routing tree construction algorithm with buffer insertion, wire sizing and obstacle considerations. *IEEE Transactions on Computer-Aided Design*, 24(4):600–608, April 2005.
11. C. J. Alpert, G. Gandham, M. Hrkic, J. Hu, S. T. Quay, and C. N. Sze. Porosity-aware buffered Steiner tree construction. *IEEE Transactions on CAD of Integrated Circuits and Systems*, 23(4):517–526, 2004 (ISPD 2003).
12. C. N. Sze, J. Hu, and C. J. Alpert. A place and route aware buffered Steiner tree construction. In *Proceedings of Asia and South Pacific Design Automation Conference*, Yokohama, Japan, pp. 355–360, 2004.
13. C. J. Alpert, C. Chu, G. Gandham, M. Hrkic, J. Hu, C. Kashyap, and S. T. Quay. Simultaneous driver sizing and buffer insertion using delay penalty estimation technique. *IEEE Transactions on Computer-Aided Design*, 23(1):136–141, January 2004.
14. C. J. Alpert, J. Hu, S. S. Sapatnekar, and P. G. Villarrubia. A practical methodology for early buffer and wire resource allocation. In *Proceedings of the ACM/IEEE Design Automation Conference*, Las Vegas, NV, pp. 189–194, 2001.
15. C. J. Alpert and A. Devgan. Wire segmenting for improved buffer insertion. In *Proceedings of the ACM/IEEE Design Automation Conference*, Anaheim, CA, pp. 588–593, 1997.
16. C. C. N. Chu and D. F. Wong. Closed form solution to simultaneous buffer insertion/sizing and wire sizing. In *Proceedings of the ACM International Symposium on Physical Design*, Napa Valley, CA, pp. 192–197, 1997.
17. C. J. Alpert, M. Hrkic, J. Hu, and S. T. Quay. Fast and flexible buffer trees that navigate the physical layout environment. In *Proceedings of the ACM/IEEE Design Automation Conference*, San Diego, CA, pp. 24–29, 2004.

18. C. J. Alpert, M. Hrkic, and S. T. Quay. A fast algorithm for identifying good buffer insertion candidate locations. In *Proceedings of the ACM International Symposium on Physical Design*, Phoenix, AZ, pp. 47–51, 2004.
19. C. J. Alpert, J. Hu, S. S. Sapatnekar, and C. -N. Sze. Accurate estimation of global buffer delay within a floorplan. In *Proceedings of the IEEE/ACM International Conference on Computer-Aided Design*, San Jose, CA, pp. 706–711, 2004.

29 Wire Sizing

Sanghamitra Roy and Charlie Chung-Ping Chen

CONTENTS

With the rapid shrinking of technology feature size, the interconnect delay occupies a significant portion of the circuit delay. The improvement of interconnect delay has become an important task. Without increasing chip transistors, wire sizing has been shown as an effective way to reduce interconnect delay. In this chapter, we introduce several effective techniques of wire sizing.

29.1 WIRE-SIZING BASICS

With technology scaling and decrease in feature size, interconnect delay has become a dominant factor in determining system performance. With higher level of integration, the interconnect modeling becomes more complicated as the total on-chip interconnect length increases and there are multilayered interconnect structures embedded in multiple dielectrics. The resistance per unit length of the interconnect increases with scaling; supply voltages are also scaled down resulting in slower global interconnects. Gate delay decreases with the shrink in feature size, whereas interconnect delay increases. It has been predicted that the interconnect delay can account for over 50 percent of the total path delay in a circuit. For large high-performance designs, numerous buffers are inserted resulting in smaller distance between buffers. Buffer insertion in large numbers increases power consumption dramatically. Because the interconnect delay depends on the wire width, length, and the buffer sizes and placement, optimally sizing the wires and buffers can help in minimizing the interconnect delay as well as power consumption.

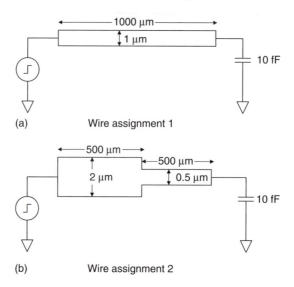

(a)   Wire assignment 1

(b)   Wire assignment 2

FIGURE 29.1   Wire-sizing result comparison.

Now we use an example to explain the effectiveness of wire sizing. As shown in Figure 29.1, the first wire with length $1000\,\mu m$, and width $1\,\mu m$ with $10\,fF$ load while the second wire with same wirelength and width $2\,\mu m$ in the first $500\,\mu m$ and $0.5\,\mu m$ in the second half. We assume the unit resistance, unit capacitance, and thickness of the wires are $0.008\,\Omega$, $0.06\,fF/\mu^2$, and $1\,\mu m$, respectively. The Elmore delay of the two wires are $0.56\,ps$ and $0.42\,ps$, respectively. A 25 percent delay reduction can be immediately obtained.

Hence modeling and optimization of interconnects is a critical component of the design of deep submicron very-large-scale integration (VLSI) circuits. Now we present an overview of interconnect and parasitics modeling.

29.1.1   DELAY AND CROSS-TALK MODELING

The Elmore delay model is easy to use and captures the distributed nature of the circuit. However, as technology scales down to deep submicron levels, the Elmore model becomes inaccurate in signal modeling, as it cannot incorporate the effects of cross talk and inductance in the circuit. The Elmore delay only uses the first moment of $h(t)$ to approximate the circuit response to a step input. For further accuracy, higher moments of $h(t)$ are used, and these are called moment matching techniques.

The asymptotic waveform evaluation [Pillage 1990] technique uses explicit moment matching for approximation of the transient response waveform of RLC (consisting of resistor R, an inductor L, and a capacitor C) circuits with nonequilibrium initial conditions. It approximates the transfer function $H(s)$ by a transfer function with q poles of the form

$$\hat{H}(s) = \sum_{i=1}^{q} \frac{k_i}{s - p_i}$$

where p_i are poles and k_i are residues to be determined. The time domain impulse response is

$$\hat{h}(t) = \sum_{i=1}^{q} k_i e^{p_i t}$$

The $2q - 1$ moments of $H(s)$ can be matched with those of $\hat{H}(s)$ to determine the poles and residues in $\hat{H}(s)$.

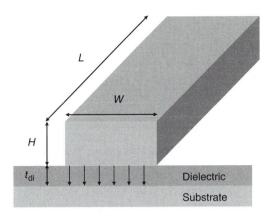

FIGURE 29.2 Interconnects.

Passive reduced–order interconnect macromodeling algorithm (PRIMA) [Odabasioglu 1998] is a moment matching technique for RLC circuits that also preserves the passivity of the system to maintain stability. The moment-based models have a higher degree of accuracy than the Elmore delay model, but their computation is more difficult and expensive.

29.1.2 PARASITICS MODELING: RESISTANCE, CAPACITANCE, AND INDUCTANCE

The resistance of a wire can be estimated using the formula

$$R = \frac{\rho L}{A} = \frac{\rho L}{HW}$$

where as shown in Figure 29.2
  ρ is the resistivity
  L is the length
  W is the width
  H is the thickness of the wire

The wire over the substrate can be modeled as a conductor over the ground plane. The parallel plate capacitance can hence be calculated as

$$C_{pp} = \frac{\varepsilon_{di}}{t_{di}} WL$$

where
  t_{di} is the distance to the substrate
  ε_{di} is the dielectric constant

The other component of the capacitance is the fringing capacitance which is more difficult to compute. The total capacitance is the sum of a parallel plate capacitor of width $W - \frac{H}{2}$ and a cylindrical capacitor of radius $H/2$. The interconnect inductance can be estimated using the definition $v = L\frac{di}{dt}$. The inductance L_{in} of a conductor can be approximately given by

$$L_{in} = L\frac{\mu_0}{2\pi} \ln\left(\frac{8t_{di}}{W} + \frac{W}{4t_{di}}\right)$$

where μ_0 is the permeability of free space. Inductive effects in interconnects can be ignored if the resistance is substantial or if the rise and fall times of the applied signals are slow.

29.2 WIRE-SIZING OPTIMIZATION: PROBLEM FORMULATION

Wire-sizing optimization tries to determine the optimal wire widths for each wire segment in an interconnect tree to minimize an objective function, which may be the interconnect delay, power, or a combination of both [Lillis 1995, Chu 1999a, Gao 1999, Tsai 2004, Zhang 2004]. We now discuss various different types of objectives in the wire-sizing problem and the different kinds of wire-sizing problems.

29.2.1 WEIGHTED DELAY, TIMING CONSTRAINTS, AND POWER CONSIDERATION

The delay in an interconnect tree consisting of multiple sinks and a single source can be minimized by using a weighted sum of delays from the source to each sink, as an objective function. In case of multiple source nets, we can minimize the weighted sum of delays between multiple source–sink pairs. Another option is to minimize the maximum delay of the tree. Also with technology scaling, power consumption has become a major design constraint in current designs. Thus an objective function consisting of the weighted sum of power and delay can also be minimized in the wire-sizing problem [Cong 1994, Cong 1996b]. Alternately, instead of minimizing the delay, the wire sizes can be minimized under maximum delay constraints. Later in the chapter, several approaches illustrate these different objectives in wire sizing.

29.2.2 DISCRETE VERSUS CONTINUOUS, UNIFORM VERSUS NONUNIFORM

Wire-sizing optimization may be continuous or discrete. In continuous wire sizing, the wire width h can take any values between the upper and lower bounds as shown in Figure 29.3a. In discrete wire sizing on the other hand, the wire width must be taken from a discrete set of values as shown in Figure 29.3b.

In uniform wire sizing, the wire segment is supposed to have a constant width throughout its length as in Figure 29.3, while in nonuniform wire sizing [Chen 1996], the width of the wire segment varies along its length as shown in Figure 29.4. Nonuniform wire sizing is discussed later in this chapter.

29.3 OPTIMIZATION ALGORITHMS

We now describe the different optimization algorithms used in solving the wire-sizing problem.

29.3.1 DISCRETE OPTIMIZATION ALGORITHM

Figure 29.5 shows a routing tree T for a signal net with source $N+$ and sinks $\{N_1, N_2, N_3\}$. The tree consists of segments $\{E1, E2, E3, E4, E5\}$. sink(T) denotes the set of sinks in T, W is a wire sizing solution (consisting of wire widths for every segment of T), and $t_i(W)$ is the delay from source to sink s_i under width assignment W. T_v denotes a subtree rooted at v. For a given edge E, Des(E) denotes the set of edges in the subtree rooted at E and Ans(E) denotes the set of edges $\{E'|E \in \text{Des}(E')\}$,

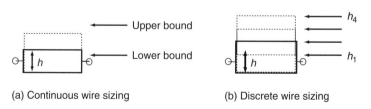

(a) Continuous wire sizing   (b) Discrete wire sizing

FIGURE 29.3 Continuous versus discrete sizing.

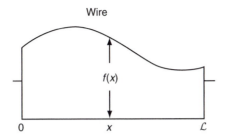

FIGURE 29.4   Nonuniform wire.

both excluding E. We now describe three important properties [Cong 1993] of optimal wire-sizing solutions that are used in designing wire-sizing algorithms.

- Monotone property: Given a routing tree T, a wire sizing solution W on T is a monotone assignment if $W_E \geq W_{E'}$ for any pair of segments E, E' such that $E \in \mathrm{Ans}(E')$.
- Separability: If the width assignment of the path from the source to a segment E is given, the optimal width assignment of each subtree branching from E can be carried out independently.
- Dominance property: A wire size assignment W dominates a wire-size assignment W' if every segment width in W is greater than or equal to the corresponding segment width in W'. For a given wire-sizing solution W for the routing tree, and one particular segment $E \in T$, the local refinement on E is the operation to optimize the width of E while keeping the widths of the other segments constant. If W^* is an optimal wire-sizing solution, and if W dominates W^*, then any local refinement of W will also dominate W^*.

The discrete wire-sizing problem [Cong 1993] can be formulated as follows:

Given	A set of discrete wire widths $\{W_1, W_2, \ldots, W_r\}$
Find	An optimal wire width assignment W
To minimize	$t(W) = \sum_{N_i \in \mathrm{sink}(T)} \lambda_i \cdot t_i(W)$

where λ_i is a weight. This algorithm minimizes a weighted sum of sink delays. The dominance property can be used to eliminate suboptimal solutions and hence solve this wire-sizing problem.

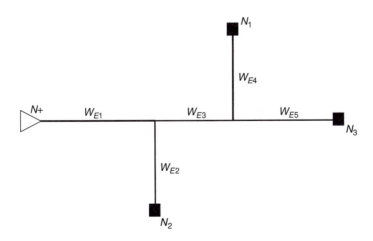

FIGURE 29.5   Interconnect tree.

29.3.2 CONVEX PROGRAMMING ALGORITHM

The Elmore delay of an RC tree is a posynomial function of the sizes of wires in the tree. A posynomial is a function almost like a polynomial but with positive coefficients and real exponents. It can be described by the general expression $t(W) = \sum_{j=1}^{k} c_j \prod_{i=1}^{n} W_i^{\alpha_{ij}}$, where c_j, $j = 1 \ldots k$ are positive real numbers, and α_{ij} are real numbers. The transformation $e^{x_i} = W_i$ transforms any posynomial function of W_i's to a convex function of x_i's.

The continuous wire-sizing problem for minimizing delay under maximum width constraints can be formulated as given below:

$$\begin{aligned} \text{minimize} \quad & \max_{N_i \in \text{sink}(T)} t_i(W) \\ \text{subject to} \quad & W_{Ej} < W_{Ej,\text{spec}} \quad \forall j \in T \end{aligned}$$

Also, the problem for minimizing the segment widths subject to maximum delay (D_{spec}) constraints can be formulated as

$$\begin{aligned} \text{minimize} \quad & \sum_{i \in T} W_{Ei} \\ \text{subject to} \quad & t_i(W) < D_{\text{spec}} \text{ and } W_{Ej} < W_{Ej,\text{spec}} \forall N_i \in \text{sink}(T) \quad \forall j \in T \end{aligned}$$

Under the Elmore delay model, the objective function as well as constraints in both of the above problems can be transformed to convex functions [Sapatnekar 1996]. Hence both the problems are unimodal, or in other words any local minimum of these optimization problems is also a global minimum. Such a problem can be solved by using convex optimization techniques, some of which are discussed in the following sections. Note that no comments can be made about the discrete wire-sizing problem. However, the solution to the continuous sizing problem gives a lower bound to the solution to the discrete problem.

29.3.3 LAGRANGIAN RELAXATION-BASED ALGORITHM

Similar to the wire-sizing problem, the simultaneous gate and wire-sizing problem can also be formulated as a convex optimization problem as the gate delay can be modeled as a posynomial function as well. Lagrangian relaxation is a technique for optimally solving these problems. We now illustrate the Lagrangian relaxation technique in the context of the gate and wire-sizing problem for combinational circuits. Figure 29.6 shows a combinational circuit with n gates or wire segments. Two virtual components, the input component (index m) and the output component (index 0) are introduced in the circuit as shown in the figure. Input(i) refers to the set of indices of components directly connected to the inputs of component i, and output(i) refers to the set of indices of components

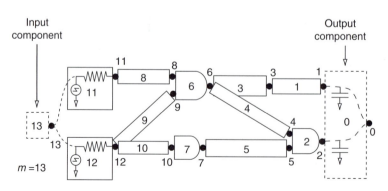

FIGURE 29.6   Combinational circuit.

directly connected to the outputs of component i. G, WS, and ID represent the set of component indices of gates, wire segments and input drivers in the circuit. Let W_i, $i \in G \cup$ WS be the gate or wire sizes. Also let L_i and U_i be the lower and upper bounds of W_i. t_i represents the arrival time or delay at node i and D_j represents the internal delay of the jth gate. Thus the problem of minimizing the total area of a combinational circuit subject to maximum delay bound T_0 can be formulated as given below [Chen 1998]. We call this formulation the primal problem PP.

$$
\begin{aligned}
\text{PP minimize} \quad & \sum_{i=1}^{n} \alpha_i W_i \\
\text{subject to} \quad & t_j \le T_0 & & j \in \text{input}(0) \\
& t_j + D_i \le t_i & & i \in G \cup \text{WS} \wedge \quad \forall j \in \text{input}(i) \\
& D_i \le t_i & & i \in \text{ID} \\
& L_i \le W_i \le U_i & & i \in G \cup \text{WS}
\end{aligned}
$$

where α_i are constants used to represent the total area in terms of the gate and wire sizes. Now we introduce nonnegative Lagrange multipliers for each constraint on arrival time. Thus the Lagrangian $L_\lambda(W, t)$ can be written as:

$$
\begin{aligned}
L_\lambda = & \sum_{i=1}^{n} \alpha_i W_i \\
& + \sum_{j \in \text{input}(0)} \lambda_{j0}(t_j - T_0) \\
& + \sum_{i \in G \cup \text{WS}} \sum_{j \in \text{input}(i)} \lambda_{ji}(t_j + D_i - t_i) \\
& + \sum_{i \in \text{ID}} \lambda_{\text{mi}}(D_i - t_i)
\end{aligned}
$$

The troublesome constraints are relaxed and incorporated into the objective function after multiplying them with nonnegative Lagrange multipliers. Thus, the Lagrangian relaxation subproblem LRS/λ associated with the multipliers λ will be

$$
\begin{aligned}
\text{LRS}/\lambda: \quad & \text{minimize} \quad L_\lambda(W, t) \\
& \text{subject to} \quad L_i \le W_i \le U_i \ i \in G \cup \text{WS}
\end{aligned}
$$

It can be shown that there exists a vector λ such that the optimal solution of LRS/λ is also the optimal solution of the original problem PP.

29.3.4 ENSURING THE CONVEXITY OF GATE DELAY MODELS BY SEMIDEFINITE PROGRAMMING

To formulate the simultaneous gate and wire-sizing problem as a convex optimization, we need convex models for both gate and wire delays. However, as technology scales down to deep submicron levels, the Elmore model becomes inaccurate in delay modeling, as it cannot incorporate the effects of cross talk and inductance in the circuit. Thus, we need techniques to model the delay accurately and also in convex form. The gate delays for standard cell libraries are available in the form of look-up tables. One option is to perform curve fitting on the table data to fit it to a general posynomial form and then use the fitted posynomials in the simultaneous gate and wire-sizing problems. But fitting the tables into posynomials may suffer from large fitting errors as the fitting problem is nonconvex with no known optimal solution.

Another method to generate convex gate delay models is to directly adjust the look-up table values into a numerically convex look-up table without any explicit analytical form. Numerically convexifying the look-up table data with minimum perturbation can be formulated as a convex semidefinite optimization [Roy 2005] problem and hence optimality can be reached in polynomial time. Thus, given a numerical function $g(\mathbf{x})$ for the original delay, let $f(\mathbf{x}) = g(\mathbf{x}) + \delta(\mathbf{x})$. $\delta(\mathbf{x})$ is the perturbation of $g(\mathbf{x})$, and $f(\mathbf{x})$ is the transformed function. Any function $\phi(\mathbf{x})$ is convex if and only if the Hessian matrix $\nabla^2 \phi(\mathbf{x}) \succeq 0$ for all $\mathbf{x} \in \mathrm{DOM}\phi$. ($\nabla^2 \phi(\mathbf{x}) \succeq 0$ means the Hessian of $\phi(\mathbf{x})$ is positive semidefinite, i.e., all the eigenvalues of the Hessian are greater than or equal to zero.) Thus, the fitting problem is to minimize $\delta(\mathbf{x})$ to make the Hessian of $f(\mathbf{x})$ positive semidefinite. The problem is defined as follows:

$$
\begin{aligned}
\text{minimize} \quad & \sum_{x \in \mathrm{DOM}g} |\delta(\mathbf{x})| \\
\text{subject to} \quad & \nabla^2(g(\mathbf{x} + \delta(\mathbf{x}))) \geq 0, \\
& \mathbf{x} \in \mathrm{DOM}_g
\end{aligned}
$$

29.3.5 SEQUENTIAL QUADRATIC PROGRAMMING ALGORITHM

The convex optimization problem of concurrent gate and wire sizing can also be solved using the sequential quadratic programming (SQP) method [Menezes 1997, Chu 1999b]. SQP reduces a nonlinear optimization to a sequence of quadratic programming (QP) subproblems. A general convex quadratic program can be represented as

$$
\begin{aligned}
\text{minimize} \quad & \tfrac{1}{2}X^{\mathrm{T}}QX + X^{\mathrm{T}}C \\
\text{subject to} \quad & A_i^{\mathrm{T}}X \leq b_i, \quad i \in I
\end{aligned}
$$

where
   Q is a symmetric positive semidefinite matrix
   I is the set of inequalities

Now if we want to minimize a function $F(X)$ subject to the constraints $h_i(X) \leq 0$, $i = 1 \ldots m$, then we can express the Lagrangian of $F(x)$ as

$$
L(X, \lambda) = F(X) + \sum_{i=1}^{m} \lambda_i h_i(X) \tag{29.1}
$$

where λ_i is the Lagrange multiplier associated with the ith constraint. Now, if $G(X) = \nabla F(x)$ be the gradient of the objective function, the original optimization problem can be solved by solving a sequence of QP subproblems as shown below:

$$
\begin{aligned}
\text{minimize} \quad & \tfrac{1}{2}(X - X_0)^{\mathrm{T}}B(X_0)(X - X_0) + (X - X_0)^{T} G(X_0) \\
\text{subject to} \quad & (X - X_0)^{\mathrm{T}}\nabla h_i(X_0) + h_i(X_0) \leq 0, \quad i = 1 \ldots m
\end{aligned}
$$

where
   X_0 is the solution of the previous QP iteration
   $B(X_0)$ is the approximation of the Hessian of the Lagrangian

29.3.6 VARIATIONAL CALCULUS-BASED NONUNIFORM SIZING ALGORITHM

All the wire-sizing techniques presented so far are uniform wire-sizing techniques. Now we illustrate a case of nonuniform wire sizing. Figure 29.7 shows a nonuniform wire segment W of length L, with source driver resistance R_d, and sink load capacitance C_L.

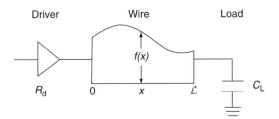

FIGURE 29.7   Nonuniform wire sizing function.

For each $x \in [0, L]$, let $f(x)$ be the wire width of W at position x. Let the wire resistance and capacitance per unit square be r_0 and c_0, respectively. Let t be the Elmore delay from the source to the sink of W. Then the optimal wire-sizing function f that minimizes t is given by $f(x) = ae^{-bx}$. $a > 0$ and $b > 0$ are constants given by $a = \frac{r_0}{bR_d}$, $b\sqrt{\frac{R_d C_L}{r_0 c_0}} - e^{(-bL)/2} = 0$. This can be proved by using variational calculus [Lee 2002]. In case of constrained wire sizing, where the wire widths are bounded by $L \le f(x) \le U$, $0 \le x \le L$, the wire sizing solution will be a truncated version of ae^{-bx} as shown in Figure 29.8. This formula can be iteratively applied to optimally size the wire segments in a routing tree.

29.3.7   OPTIMAL PROPAGATION SPEED WITH WIRES

Nonuniform wire sizing is not used widely because routing such wires is nontrivial, and it can also lead to poor track utilization. If we get a reasonably good solution by uniform wire sizing, buffer insertion, and gate sizing, it may not be worthwhile to spend a high effort in routing nonuniform wires if the delay improvement is marginal. Figure 29.9 shows two wire-sizing solutions Figure 29.9a showing optimal uniform wire sizing with buffering and Figure 29.9b showing optimal nonuniform wire-sizing solution with buffering. It has been shown that the ratio of maximum attainable signal velocities of the optimal nonuniform wire-sizing configuration to the optimal uniform wire-sizing configuration is 1.0354 with full buffering [Alpert 2001]. This means that theoretically, tapering in the best case only gives an improvement of 3.54 percent over uniform wire sizing, and this ratio is independent of technology parameters. Hence tapering only gives a small performance gain in the best case.

29.3.8   HIGH-ORDER MOMENT-BASED ALGORITHM

EWA [Kay 1998] or efficient wire-sizing algorithm is an example of an algorithm heuristic for minimizing the total wiring area of an interconnect tree, subject to hard constraints on the Elmore delay. This algorithm can use the Elmore delay model or can be extended to use higher order delay models.

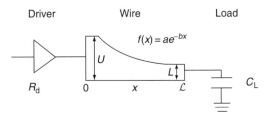

FIGURE 29.8   Optimal wire sizing.

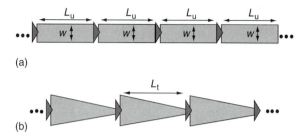

(a)

(b)

FIGURE 29.9 Optimal propagation speed.

29.4 SIGNAL INTEGRITY OPTIMIZATION ALGORITHM

Some other advances in interconnect optimization include noise-aware repeater insertion and wire sizing. In the following section we describe an algorithm for noise-aware optimization.

29.4.1 NOISE AWARE OPTIMIZATION

Noise aware optimization is a hierarchical and accurate noise estimation algorithm [Chen 1999] which can handle arbitrarily shifted attacking noise waveforms. Moment-matching techniques are used for accurate RC delay estimation. The transfer functions between nodes i and j, and nodes j and k in Figure 29.10 are computed hierarchically. The delay t_{ik} is computed by convolution of the input signal with the composite transfer function up to node k.

During backward propagation of a pair at node j, the transfer function $H_{ik}(s)$ is computed. The electrical models for computation of $H_{jk}(s)$ and $Y_i(s)$ are shown in Figure 29.10b. They are calculated as follows:

$$H_{ij}(s) = \frac{1}{R(Cs + Y_j(s)) + 1}$$

$$Y_i(s) = Cs + \frac{Cs + Y_j(s)}{R(Cs + Y_j(s)) + 1}$$

where $R = R_i$ and $C = C_i/2$. The RC delay is computed by the convolution of the waveform at i and $H_{ik}(s)$. The moments are then stored in the pair at node i.

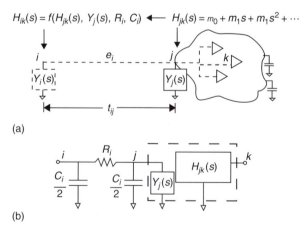

(a)

(b)

FIGURE 29.10 Hierarchical moment computation.

The hierarchical moment generation for the transfer function and input admittance always starts from either a receiver or a repeater. For this base case, if c represents the receiver/repeater input capacitance, the moment representation of the transfer function and admittance is given by $H(s) = 1$, and $Y(s) = cs$. Wire sizing can be handled during this step by backward propagation of the pairs from node j to node i for different wire widths of segment e_i. R_i and C_i are functions of the wire width.

REFERENCES

[Alpert 2001]   C.J. Alpert, A. Devgan, J.P. Fishburn, and S.T. Quay, Interconnect synthesis without wire tapering, *IEEE Transactions on Computer Aided Design of Intergrated Circuits and Systems*, 20(1), 90–104, January 2001.

[Chen 1998]   C.P. Chen, C.C.N. Chu, and D.F. Wong, Fast and exact simultaneous gate and wire sizing by Lagrangian relaxation, in *IEEE/ACM International Conference on Computer-Aided Design*, San Jose, CA, November 1998, pp. 617–624.

[Chen 1999]   C.P. Chen and N. Menezes, Noise-aware repeater insertion and wire sizing for on-chip interconnect using hierarchical moment-matching, in *Proceedings of the 36th Design Automation Conference*, New Orleans, LA, June 1999, pp. 502–506.

[Chen 1997]   C.P. Chen and D.F. Wong, Optimal wire-sizing function with fringing capacitance consideration, in *Proceedings of the 34th Design Automation Conference*, Anaheim, CA, June 1997, pp. 604–607.

[Chen 1996]   C.P. Chen, H. Zhou, and D.F. Wong, Optimal non-uniform wire-sizing under the Elmore delay model, in *IEEE/ACM International Conference on Computer-Aided Design*, San Jose, CA, November 1996, pp. 38–43.

[Chu 1999a]   C.C.N. Chu and M.D.F Wong, Greedy wire-sizing is linear time, *IEEE Transactions on Computer-Aided Design of Integrated Circuits and Systems*, 18(4), 398–405, April 1999.

[Chu 1999b]   C.C.N. Chu and D.F. Wong, A quadratic programming approach to simultaneous buffer insertion/sizing and wire sizing, *IEEE Transactions on Computer-Aided Design of Integrated Circuits and Systems*, 18(6), 787–798, June 1999.

[Cong 1996a]   J. Cong, L. He, C.K. Koh, and P.H. Madden, Performance optimization of VLSI interconnect layout, *Integration, the VLSI Journal*, 21(1–2), 1–94, November 1996.

[Cong 1994]   J. Cong and C.K. Koh, Simultaneous driver and wire sizing for performance and power optimization, in *Proceedings of the IEEE/ACM International Conference on Computer-Aided Design*, San Jose, CA, November 1994, pp. 206–212.

[Cong 1996b]   J. Cong, C.K. Koh, and K.S. Leung, Simultaneous buffer and wire sizing for performance and power optimization, in *International Symposium on Low Power Electronics and Design*, Monterey, CA, August 1996, pp. 271–276.

[Cong 1993]   J. Cong and K.S. Leung, Optimal wiresizing under the distributed Elmore delay model, in *Proceedings of the IEEE/ACM International Conference on Computer Aided Design*, Santa Clara, CA, 1993, pp. 634–639.

[Gao 1999]   Y. Gao and D.F. Wong, Wire-sizing optimization with inductance consideration using transmission-line model, *IEEE Transactions on Computer-Aided Design of Integrated Circuits and Systems*, 18(12), 1759–1767, December 1999.

[Kay 1998]   R. Kay and L.T. Pileggi, EWA: Efficient wiring-sizing algorithm for signal nets and clock nets, *IEEE Transactions on Computer-Aided Design of Integrated Circuits and Systems*, 17(1), 40–49, January 1998.

[Lee 2002]   Y. Lee, C.C.P. Chen, and D.F. Wong, Optimal wire-sizing function under the Elmore delay model with bounded wire sizes, in *IEEE Transactions on Circuits and Systems-I*, 49(11), 1671–1677, November 2002.

[Lillis 1995]   J. Lillis, C.K. Cheng, and T.T.Y. Lin, Optimal and efficient buffer insertion and wire sizing, in *Proceedings of the IEEE Custom Integrated Circuits Conference*, Santa Clara, CA, May 1995, pp. 259–262.

[Menezes 1997]   N. Menezes, R. Baldick, and L.T. Pileggi, A sequential quadratic programming approach to concurrent gate and wire sizing, *IEEE Transactions on Computer-Aided Design of Integrated Circuits and Systems*, 16(8), 867–881, August 1997.

[Odabasioglu 1998]   A. Odabasioglu, M. Celik, and L.T. Pileggi, PRIMA: Passive reduced-order interconnect macromodeling algorithm, *IEEE Transactions on Computer Aided Design of Intergrated Circuits and Systems*, 17(8), 645–654, August 1998.

[Pillage 1990]   L.T. Pillage and R.A. Rohrer, Asymptotic waveform evaluation for timing analysis, *IEEE Transactions on Computer Aided Design*, 9(4), 352–366, April 1990.

[Roy 2005]   S. Roy, W. Chen, and C.C.P. Chen, ConvexFit: An optimal minimum-error convex fitting and smoothing algorithm with application to gate sizing, in *Proceedings of the International Conference on Computer Aided Design*, San Jose, CA, November 2005 pp. 196–203.

[Sapatnekar 1996]   S.S. Sapatnekar, Wire sizing as a convex optimization problem: Exploring the area-delay tradeoff, *IEEE Transactions on Computer-Aided Design of Integrated Circuits and Systems*, 15(8), 1001–1011, August 1996.

[Tsai 2004]   J.L. Tsai, T.H. Chen, and C.C.P. Chen, Zero skew clock-tree optimization with buffer insertion/sizing and wire sizing, *IEEE Transactions on Computer-Aided Design of Integrated Circuits and Systems*, 23(4), 565–572, April 2004.

[Zhang 2004]   L. Zhang, Z. Luo, X. Hong, Y. Cai, S.X.D Tan, and J. Fu, Optimal wire sizing in early-stage design of on-chip power/ground (P/G) networks, in *Proceedings of the 7th International Conference on Solid-State and Integrated Circuits Technology*, 3, 1936–1939, October 2004.

Part VI

Routing Multiple Signal Nets

30 Estimation of Routing Congestion

Rupesh S. Shelar and Prashant Saxena

CONTENTS

30.1 INTRODUCTION

A design is said to exhibit routing congestion if the demand for the routing resources in some region within its layout exceeds their supply. Congestion is undesirable because it can degrade the performance and the yield of a design, and can add uncertainty to its convergence. With wire delays no longer being insignificant in modern process technologies, an unexpected increase in the delay of a net that lies on a critical path can cause a design to miss its frequency target. The routing of a net passing through a congested region may be detoured significantly, or forced to use the more resistive metal layers. Consequently, the delay estimates for nets that pass through congested regions are often erroneous. These estimates may mislead the design optimization trajectory by failing to correctly identify the truly critical paths, thus aggravating the design convergence problem. A densely congested design is also likely to result in a lower manufacturing yield than a similar uncongested design. Congestion typically results in an increased number of vias in the routes, which can affect the yield. Additionally, congested layouts tend to have larger critical areas for the creation of shorts and opens because of random defects.

Furthermore, it can be shown using first-order scaling models that the congestion problem is likely to worsen in the future, as design sizes increase and process geometries shrink [SSS07]. As a result, it is desirable to minimize the routing congestion in a design. Congestion can be measured accurately only after the routing has been completed. However, if the design exhibits congestion problems at that stage, mere rerouting of the nets may not be able to resolve these problems. This may necessitate a new design iteration with changes being made to the placement or to the netlist. However, one has to be able to measure routing congestion before one can optimize it. This chapter describes the measurement of congestion at all levels of abstraction, from a routed layout up to a multilevel Boolean network.

The rest of this chapter is organized as follows. Section 30.2 describes the postrouting metrics for congestion, and Section 30.3 discusses placement-level congestion estimation. Congestion metrics at the technology mapping level are covered in Section 30.4, whereas those that serve as proxies for congestion during logic synthesis are presented in Section 30.5. Finally, some closing remarks are presented in Section 30.6.

30.2 POSTROUTING CONGESTION METRICS

Before discussing the metrics used to measure postrouting congestion, it is useful to describe the underlying routing model. As was discussed in Section 23.2.2, the entire routing space is usually tessellated into a grid array. The small subregions created by this tessellation of the routing region have variously been referred to as grid cells, global routing cells, or bins. The bins are usually gridded employing horizontal and vertical gridlines, referred to as routing tracks, along which wires can be created. The dual graph of the tessellation is the routing graph. In this graph, each vertex represents a bin and each edge denotes the boundary between the bins corresponding to its vertices. Routing graphs used for congestion estimation may bundle the horizontal (vertical) routing tracks on all the layers, or they may distinguish individual metal layers to identify the congestion on each layer. The number of tracks available in a bin denotes the supply of routing resources for that bin; this number is also known as the capacity of the bin. Similarly, the number of tracks crossing a bin boundary is referred to as the supply or the capacity of the routing graph edge corresponding to that boundary. A route passing through a bin (or crossing a bin boundary) requires a track in either the horizontal or the vertical direction. Thus, each such route contributes to the routing demand for that bin (or edge). Further details on capacity computation may be obtained in Section 23.3.

One of the metrics commonly used to gauge the severity of routing congestion is the track overflow that measures the number of extra tracks required to route the wires in a bin. It can be defined formally* as follows:

Definition 1   *The* horizontal (vertical) track overflow T_x^v (T_y^v) *for a given bin v is defined as the difference between the number of horizontal (vertical) tracks required to route the nets through the bin and the available number of horizontal (vertical) tracks when this difference is positive, and zero otherwise.*

In other words, $T^v = \max\{[\text{demand}(v) - \text{supply}(v)], 0\}$.

The formal definition of the *congestion* metric is as follows:

Definition 2   *The* horizontal (vertical) congestion C_x^v (C_y^v) *for a given bin v is the ratio of the number of horizontal (vertical) tracks required to route the nets assigned to that bin to the number of horizontal (vertical) tracks available.*

Thus, the congestion in a given bin is simply the ratio of the demand of the tracks to their supply in that bin, and can be written as $C^v = \frac{\text{demand}(v)}{\text{supply}(v)}$. The overflow and congestion metrics can be defined similarly for the bin boundaries (or equivalently, for the routing graph edges). These definitions can also be extended to consider each routing layer individually.

The notion of a congestion map is often used to obtain the complete picture of routing congestion over the entire routing area. The congestion map is a three-dimensional array of congestion two-tuples indexed by bin locations and can be visualized by plotting congestion on the z-axis while

---

* Throughout this chapter, whenever the routing direction is left unspecified in some equation or discussion, it is implied that the equation or discussion is equally applicable to both the horizontal and the vertical directions. Thus, for instance, the notation T^v in a statement implies that the statement is equally applicable to both T_x^v and T_y^v. Similarly, if the bin to which a congestion metric pertains is clear from the context, it may be dropped from the notation.

denoting bins on the xy-plane. Such a visualization helps designers easily identify densely congested areas (that correspond to peaks in the congestion map).

Some other commonly used metrics that capture the overall routability of the design rely on scalar values (in contrast to three-dimensional congestion map vectors). These metrics include the total track overflow, maximum congestion, and the number of congested bins. The total track overflow is defined as the sum of the individual track overflows in all the bins. The maximum congestion is defined as the maximum of the congestion values over all the bins. The number of congested bins is defined as the number of bins whose congestion is greater than some specified threshold C_{th}.

30.3   PLACEMENT-LEVEL CONGESTION ESTIMATION

Most industrial congestion-aware physical synthesis flows rely on improving the routability of a design during the placement stage itself. However, for a placement algorithm to be congestion aware, it must first be able to evaluate whether a given placement configuration is likely to be congested after routing, as well as discriminate between any two placement configurations based on their expected congestion. Different congestion metrics involve different trade-offs between the computational overhead required for their estimation and the accuracy that they can provide. They range from quick-and-dirty proxies for congestion, such as the total wirelength, to expensive but accurate congestion prediction techniques such as probabilistic estimation or fast global routing. The quick-and-dirty metrics are often employed during the early stages of placement, whereas the expensive but accurate ones are better suited to the later stages, when the the placement is relatively stable.

30.3.1   FAST METRICS FOR ROUTING CONGESTION

The fast placement-level metrics for congestion include the total wirelength, the pin density, and the perimeter degree. They are best used by fast congestion analyzers embedded within optimizers during the early stages of global placement. During these applications, their fidelity to the actual congestion can help choose between alternative optimization moves based on their expected congestion impact, without incurring a significant runtime overhead.

Traditionally, placers have targeted the minimization of cost functions involving wirelength in the belief that the optimization of the wirelength also leads to a reduction in the average congestion. The length of a net can be estimated using metrics such as the half-rectangle perimeter (HRPM) of its bounding box or the length of a minimum spanning tree (MST) for the net. However, this metric does not capture the spatial aspects (i.e., the locality) of the congested regions. A design can easily have low average congestion and yet have a few densely congested bins that may be very difficult to route successfully. Moreover, the predicted netlength of a given net can be quite erroneous because it ignores congestion-caused detours and uses simplistic topology generation, and because the placement itself may change during the remainder of the physical synthesis flow. Consequently, the HRPM metric is often preferred to the slightly more accurate but slower MST scheme. Indeed, the accuracy of the HRPM metric can be improved by the use of an empirical multiplicative factor depending on the pin count for the net, to compensate for its tendency to underestimate the netlength for multipin nets [Che94].

Two other fast metrics that have been used for congestion optimization during placement are the pin density and the perimeter degree. Unlike the total wirelength, which is a scalar that characterizes the entire design, these metrics are good at identifying the specific bins that are likely to be congested. The pin density metric is defined for a bin as the ratio of the number of pins in the bin to the area of the bin [HM02]. This metric captures the contributions of the intrabin nets and those interbin nets that have at least one pin within the bin. It, however, ignores the global wires that are routed through the bin but do not connect to any pins inside the bin, even though they consume routing resources within the bin. The perimeter degree of a bin is defined as the ratio of the number of interbin nets that have at least one pin inside a bin, to the perimeter of the bin [SPK03]. This metric ignores the routing demand for all intrabin nets as well as the global wires routed through the bin that do not connect to any pin inside the bin. It captures the expected congestion at the boundary of the bin rather than that within the bin, in contrast to the pin density metric. However, this metric lends itself to very efficient approximation using Rent's rule [LR71].

30.3.2 PROBABILISTIC ESTIMATION METHODS

Probabilistic estimation methods (also referred to as stochastic methods) have been developed as a fast way to approximate the behavior of global routers. Instead of attempting to find a unique route for each net, probabilistic estimation methods assume that all reasonable routes for a net are equally likely, and consider all these routes while computing the congestion contribution of a net to the bins that it may be routed through. Different flavors of probabilistic congestion maps use different notions for what constitutes a reasonable route.

Because probabilistic estimation techniques avoid choosing between the different routes possible for a given net or even enumerating these routes, they also avoid the combinatorial optimization problem that a global router attempts to solve while routing the nets. In particular, probabilistic estimation is independent of the order in which the nets are considered. As a result, these techniques are considerably faster than global routing. However, this computational efficiency is obtained at the cost of accuracy; real-world global routers can diverge significantly from the simple routing behavior that these techniques model. Yet, in spite of all the inaccuracies in probabilistic congestion map estimation, these techniques are good candidates for use during the later stages of placement.

To model the behavior of routers, probabilistic estimation techniques consider shortest path routes, because routers typically try to minimize netlengths. Furthermore, these techniques simplify topology generation by decomposing each multipin net into two-pin segments using simple heuristic models such as cliques or MSTs. In the same vein, the layer assignment of the routes can be ignored or approximated by a length-layer table, which specifies the layer for a net based on its length. For any given net, a probabilistic estimation technique considers all its valid routes that satisfy the modeling assumptions for that technique. The congestion contribution of each such route to every bin that it passes through is then weighted by the probability of that route being selected, based on some specified probability distribution (e.g., a uniform distribution).

Although several probabilistic estimation models have been explored, the two that have received the most attention are distinguished by the number of bends that they allow in their routings. The more general model of the two permits an arbitrary number of bends [LTK+02], in contrast to the other model that considers only those routes that have at most two bends [CZY+99,WBG04]. Routes that involve just a single bend are said to be L-shaped, whereas those with two bends are said to be Z-shaped. Given a choice of two routes having the same wirelength but different numbers of vias, most routers will select the one with the fewer vias (and consequently, fewer bends). Therefore, the probabilistic estimation model that restricts its routes to those with at most two bends usually does a better job of modeling actual router behavior than the one that considers routes with arbitrarily many bends.

Given a two-pin net and a bin, the general procedure for probabilistic congestion map generation attempts to obtain an expression for the expected routing demand (also called the utilization) of the net in that bin. This is achieved by weighting the track usage for each valid route of the net that passes through the bin by the probability of the route being selected. All the weighted track usages are then summed up over all the routes of the net to obtain the routing demand of the net in the bin. We illustrate this computation for an interbin net considering only L-shaped and Z-shaped routes as follows.

For the computation of the routing demand, let the bins created by the tessellation of the layout area be indexed by their column and row indices, with the bin $(1, 1)$ lying in the lower left corner of the layout. Without loss of generality, assume that the net whose routing demand is being computed has its pins in the bins $(1, 1)$ and (m, k). Let the utilization of the net in some bin (i, j) (which lies in the ith column and the jth row) be denoted by $U^{(i,j)}$ (with $U_x^{(i,j)}$ and $U_y^{(i,j)}$ referring to routing demands in the horizontal and vertical directions, respectively). Moreover, let $U^{p(i,j)}$ denote the utilization owing to only the p-bend routes for the net. For the sake of simplicity, assume that all bins have the same width and height, denoted by W and H, respectively. Furthermore, assume that the two pins of the net are denoted by a and b, with coordinates (x_a, y_a) and (x_b, y_b), respectively. Let the horizontal (vertical) distance of pin a from the right (upper) boundary of the bin $(1, 1)$ that contains it be denoted by d_x^a (d_y^a), and the horizontal (vertical) distance of pin b from the left (lower) boundary of the bin (m, k) that contains it be denoted by d_x^b (d_y^b), as illustrated in Figure 30.1.

For this net with pins $a(x_a, y_a)$ in bin $(1, 1)$ and $b(x_b, y_b)$ in bin (m, k), there are two possible single bend routes, whereas the number of double bend routes is $(m + k - 4)$ (assuming $m, k > 1$). These routes lead to different routing demands in different bins lying within the bounding box of the net. The computation of the routing demand in all these bins can be covered by the analysis of nine different cases, based on the location of the bin relative to the pins of the net. These cases include the four bins located at the corners of the bounding box, bins located along the four sides of the bounding box but not at its corners, and the bins located in the interior of the bounding box.

Let us first consider the bin $(1, 1)$, located at the lower left corner of the bounding box of the net. In this case, all the routes to the destination bin (m, k) leave either horizontally or vertically from

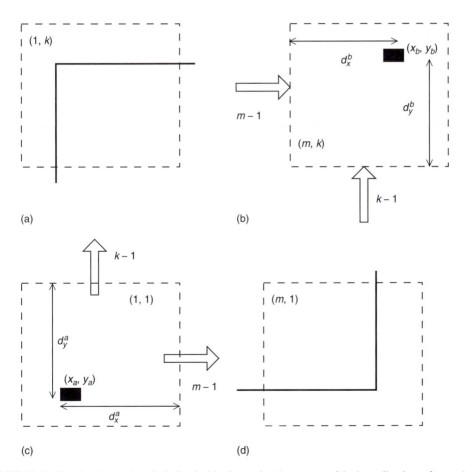

(a)

(b)

(c)

(d)

FIGURE 30.1 Routing demand analysis for the bins located at the corners of the bounding box of a net: (a) bin $(1, k)$ at the upper left corner, (b) bin (m, k) at the upper right corner, (c) bin $(1, 1)$ at the lower left corner, and (d) bin $(m, 1)$ at the lower right corner. (From Shelar, R., Saxena, P., and Sapatnekar, S., *IEEE Trans. Comput. Aided Des. Integrated Circuits Syst.*, 25, 625, 2006. With permission.)

this bin. The numbers of routes leaving this bin horizontally and vertically are $(m-1)$ and $(k-1)$, respectively, as shown in Figure 30.1c. Of these routes, one route in either direction is L-shaped; these two single bend routes pass through the bins lying along the edge of the bounding box. The remaining $(m+k-4)$ routes are Z-shaped and pass through the interior of the bounding box. One can observe that the routes leaving the bin horizontally require a horizontal track of length d_x^a, whereas routes departing vertically use a vertical track of length d_y^a. Therefore, the contribution to the routing utilization owing to the L-shaped paths is given by $U_x^{1,(1,1)} = \frac{d_x^a}{2W}$ and $U_y^{1,(1,1)} = \frac{d_y^a}{2H}$. Similarly, the contribution owing to Z-shaped paths is given by $U_x^{2,(1,1)} = \frac{m-2}{m+k-4} \times \frac{d_x^a}{W}$, and $U_y^{2,(1,1)} = \frac{k-2}{m+k-4} \times \frac{d_y^a}{H}$. These expressions can be combined to yield the overall routing demand in bin $(1, 1)$, given by $U_x^{(1,1)} = \alpha_1 U_x^{1,(1,1)} + \alpha_2 U_x^{2,(1,1)}$ and $U_y^{(1,1)} = \alpha_1 U_y^{1,(1,1)} + \alpha_2 U_y^{2,(1,1)}$, where α_1 and α_2 are empirically chosen weights indicating the relative preferences for single and double bend routes, respectively. Typically, $\alpha_1 \geq \alpha_2$, $\alpha_1 + \alpha_2 = 1$, and α_1, $\alpha_2 \geq 0$. This allows α_1 and α_2 to be interpreted as probabilities, with L-shaped routes preferred over Z-shaped ones. The analysis of the routing demand for bin (m, k), located in the top right corner of the bounding box and illustrated in Figure 30.1b, is similar.

The only routes that pass through the bins located in the upper left and lower right corners of the bounding box (illustrated in Figure 30.1a and d) are the single bend routes. Therefore, the utilization for the bin in the upper left corner can easily be shown to be $U_x^{(1,k)} = \alpha_1 \frac{d_x^a}{2W}$ and $U_y^{(1,k)} = \alpha_1 \frac{d_y^b}{2H}$. Similarly, the utilization for bin $(m, 1)$, in the lower right corner, can be derived as $U_x^{(m,1)} = \alpha_1 \frac{d_x^b}{2W}$ and $U_y^{(m,1)} = \alpha_1 \frac{d_y^a}{2H}$.

Next, let us analyze the utilization in a bin (i, j) (with $1 < i < m$ and $1 < j < k$) that lies in the interior of the bounding box of the net. Two Z-shaped routes pass through the bin, one entering horizontally and the other vertically. These two routes leave without any bends, using up one horizontal and one vertical track in the process. Therefore, the horizontal and vertical routing demand in the bin is given by $U_x^{(i,j)} = \frac{\alpha_2}{m+k-4}$ and $U_y^{(i,j)} = \frac{\alpha_2}{m+k-4}$.

Now, consider the noncorner bins located in the leftmost column of the bounding box of the net, that is, a bin $(1, j)$ with $1 < j < k$, as shown in Figure 30.2a. One of the two L-shaped routes passes through this bin, entering and exiting vertically. Of the $(k-2)$ Z-shaped routes whose middle segments are horizontal, $(k-j)$ routes enter this bin, across its lower boundary. One of these Z-shaped routes turns right and exits the bin horizontally, whereas the remaining $(k-j-1)$ routes continue vertically (to turn right at some bin $(1, j')$ with $j < j' < k$). The Z-shaped route that leaves the bin horizontally requires half of a vertical track and a horizontal track of length d_x^a. The remaining routes passing through this bin use up one full vertical track each. Therefore, the horizontal routing demand is given by $U_x^{(1,j)} = \alpha_2 \frac{d_x^a}{(m+k-4)W}$. The vertical routing demand because of the L-shaped route passing through the bin is given by $U_y^{1,(1,j)} = \frac{1}{2}$, whereas that because of the Z-shaped routes is given by $U_y^{2,(1,j)} = \frac{1}{2(m+k-4)} + \frac{k-j-1}{m+k-4}$. Therefore, the total vertical routing utilization in the bin is given by $U_y^{(1,j)} = \frac{\alpha_1}{2} + \alpha_2 \frac{2(k-j-1)+1}{2(m+k-4)}$. The analysis of the utilization in the noncorner bins located along the remaining three edges of the bounding box of the net is analogous.

The method discussed in the previous section for single and double bend routes can be extended to consider all minimum length multibend routes also [LTK+02]. Because the routing model that considers multibend routes explores a larger space than one that considers single and double bend routes only, it leads to a different distribution of the routing demands.

The modeling of routing blockages is one of the most challenging issues faced by probabilistic estimation methods. Because a router cannot use any tracks in a blocked bin, any probabilistic utilization within such a bin should also be zero. For nets some of whose minimum length routes pass through blocked bins, it is reasonable to assume that a router will try to find a minimum length route through neighboring unblocked bins if such a path exists. Therefore, for a net whose bounding box includes blocked bins but that also has some minimum length route passing only through unblocked bins, the routing demand in the blocked bins can be distributed to their neighboring bins to reflect the expected behavior of the router. However, this simple heuristic can often result in significant errors.

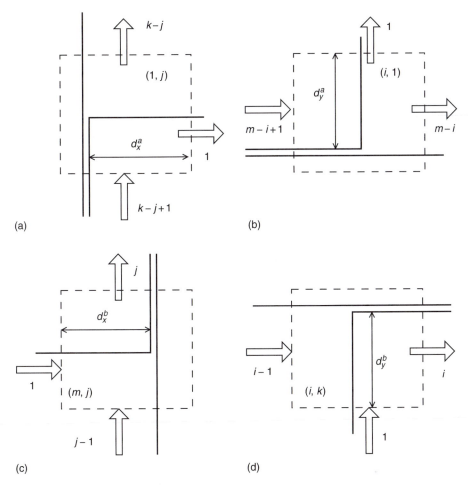

FIGURE 30.2 Routing demand analysis for the noncorner bins along the edges of the bounding box: (a) bin $(1, j)$ in the leftmost column, (b) bin $(i, 1)$ in the bottom row, (c) bin (m, j) in the rightmost column, and (d) bin (i, k) in the top row.

Furthermore, if no minimum length route for a net can avoid blocked bins, the router will usually try to complete the routing of the net with the shortest possible detour. Depending on the complexity of the blockage, the detour can be modeled during probabilistic estimation either by creating pseudopins on the net or by performing explicit routing. In general, heuristics for modeling routing blockages allow reasonably accurate congestion estimates without excessive computation overhead only when the blockages are simple. However, in the presence of a large number of complicated blockages, probabilistic estimation methods are highly inaccurate. Partial wiring blockages are somewhat easier to handle, an example being a recent work [LAQ+07] that extends the probabilistic estimation scheme of Ref. [WBG04] to handle partial blockages.

The price that probabilistic methods pay for efficiency when compared to routing-based conges-tion estimation methods is an inability to capture the behavior of routers on nets that are difficult to route. This includes approximations in the handling of blockages, limited or nonexistent modeling of detours, layer assignment, and via stack blockages, as well as approximations in topology generation for multipin nets.

Another significant source of error is the failure of these schemes to model the response of a router to existing congestion. As a result, probabilistic estimates can be pessimistic in densely congested regions. This pessimism in the probabilistic congestion maps can be reduced to some extent by applying postprocessing techniques that redistribute the routing demand from the densely congested bins to sparsely congested bins [KX03,SY05].

If the maximum number of pins in a net is assumed to be a constant (as is often the case because of fanout constraints during circuit optimization), and b and n are the number of bins in layout and the number of nets in the design, respectively, then the overall complexity of probabilistic congestion estimation is $O(nb)$ (because these methods require $O(b)$ time for a two-pin net). Thus, in the presence of a few, relatively simple blockages, this complexity is linear in the number of nets. However, if many complicated blockages are present and many nets require routing to compute the utilization, the overall time complexity for probabilistic estimation may trend toward that for global routing.

30.3.3 Estimation Based on Fast Global Routing

As discussed above, probabilistic congestion estimation suffers from several significant sources of errors. For instance, the only viable alternative to deal with complicated blockages is to carry out routing in their vicinity. It is natural to investigate whether even more extensive use of routing can help improve the accuracy of the predicted congestion maps. Of course, runtime considerations make it impractical to invoke a full-fledged global router inside a placement optimization loop. However, if the global routing can be carried out in a low-effort mode, it may yield a congestion map prediction that is more accurate than one generated employing probabilistic estimation. This has motivated the recent development of fast global routing techniques such as Refs. [WBG05,PC06] that are targeted primarily toward congestion estimation. When global routing is used for congestion estimation, some inaccuracy in the predicted routes for the nets (as compared to their actual routes) can be tolerated, especially if it improves the runtime significantly. Therefore, efforts to use global routing for congestion estimation have focused primarily on two strategies: (1) the reduction of the search space through coarsening of the routing graph and (2) the extensive use of fast search algorithms.

The availability of a growing number of routing layers causes the routing graph to be large. Its size can be reduced significantly by collapsing all the horizontal layers and all the vertical layers into two orthogonal layers. The horizontal (vertical) track supplies for a bin in this collapsed routing graph are obtained by adding the respective contributions because of each horizontal (vertical) layer. Another technique for reducing the size of the routing graph is to impose a coarser tessellation on the layout area than the one employed to generate the bins for the actual global routing. Although this reduces the spatial resolution of the congestion map, the loss of resolution may be a small price to pay for a significant speedup in the global routing when used for congestion estimation.

Given a routing graph, the routing of a net involves the generation of a topology for it, followed by the embedding of each of the two-pin segments in that topology into the routing graph. Unlike the actual global routing process, the congestion estimation mode can use simple and fast topology generation algorithms, even if it results in topologies with poor wirelengths. Furthermore, there are at least three basic techniques that have been used to speed up the routing of the two-pin segments during congestion estimation: (1) a significantly reduced application of rip-up and reroute heuristics, (2) the use of fast routers that do not guarantee shortest routes, and (3) the application of fast search algorithms that guarantee shortest routes.

Most industrial global routers rely heavily on finely tuned rip-up and reroute heuristics for route completion. However, the repeated rip-up and rerouting of a net can add significantly to the runtime of the router. When used for congestion estimation, these heuristics are used much more sparingly in a low-effort mode of the router. As a consequence, although the runtime of the router is improved significantly, the quality of the routing, as measured by the minimization of routing overflows in the bins, degrades significantly, becoming much more dependent on the order in which the nets have been routed.

Unlike global routing that relies heavily on search algorithms that guarantee shortest paths, one can also use the faster but often suboptimal line probe search [Hig69] to route the nets during the

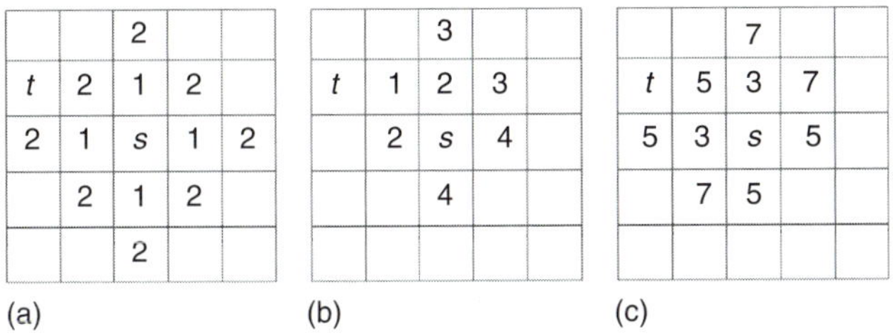

		2		
t	2	1	2	
2	1	s	1	2
	2	1	2	
		2		

(a)

		3	
t	1	2	3
2	s	4	
	4		

(b)

		7	
t	5	3	7
5	3	s	5
	7	5	

(c)

FIGURE 30.3 Wavefront expansion using (a) breadth-first, (b) best-first, and (c) A* search, where s and t denote the source and destination bins, respectively. The numbers in the bins indicate the distance traversed from s in (a), the remaining distance to t in (b), and the sum of the cost traversed from s and the remaining distance to t in (c).

congestion estimation mode. Although these algorithms are much faster than the usual breadth-first search used for routing and are often close to optimal in sparsely congested regions that have at most a few blockages, they can perform poorly in congested regions or regions that are fragmented by numerous complicated blockages. In such regions, they may fail to find a route even if it exists, or find one with a poor wirelength, requiring a fallback to a maze routing mode.

The standard breadth-first search used in global routers is based on Dijkstra's shortest path algorithm. This algorithm can be sped up significantly during the congestion estimation mode by applying fast search techniques such as best-first search and A* search [HNR68]. These techniques rely on being able to estimate the distance to the destination, and are therefore not always easily applicable during the regular global routing process (because it may be difficult to estimate the cost of the unexplored portion of a route if the cost function includes components for delay or congestion). In contrast, the cost function used for routing during the congestion estimation mode is almost always the wirelength, which can be approximated at any arbitrary bin by the Manhattan distance between that bin and the destination bin. The difference between the A* search and best-first search techniques is that A* considers the cost from the source as well as distance to the destination while expanding the search wavefront, in contrast to best-first search, which expands at a bin that is closest to the destination. Although the asymptotic time complexity of both best-first search and A* search is same as that of breadth-first search, they offer significant speed-up in practice, because they usually visit fewer nodes while finding a route. For example, as shown in Figure 30.3, breadth-first search visits twelve nodes while finding a route from bin s to bin t, whereas best-first search and A* search can do so by visiting only seven and nine bins, respectively.

Of course, the consequence of all these approximations is that the predicted route for a net as obtained during the congestion estimation mode may be quite different from its actual route generated during the routing stage.

30.3.3.1 Comparison of Fast Global Routing with Probabilistic Methods

Fast global routing techniques can predict the congestion more accurately than probabilistic methods, but tend to be somewhat slower [WBG05]. Typically, the probabilistic congestion estimation method based on the assumption of single and double bend routes is two to three times faster than the fast global routing technique. In addition to being faster, the use of only single and double bend routes is also a better approximation of the behavior of real routers than multibend routes, at least on designs that are not very congested.

Probabilistic congestion estimation is known to be pessimistic, especially when it does not include postprocessing to consider detours or to model rip-up and reroute, as it is not congestion aware. As a result, the maximum congestion, total track overflows, or the number of congested bins predicted by probabilistic estimation overestimate the corresponding postrouting metrics, and may cause a circuit to be deemed unroutable, even if it can be routed successfully. On the other hand, fast global routing tends to overestimate the congestion to a much lesser degree, because it finds routes that avoid congested bins. Consequently, it distributes the congestion evenly in a manner similar to the behavior of real routers. Although probabilistic congestion maps can be postprocessed to reduce the pessimism in their prediction, this reduction comes at the cost of additional runtime. Design blockages too are handled more naturally in fast global routing techniques than in probabilistic methods, because fast routers simply try to find a route around them just like real routers. In the same vein, fast global-routing-based methods automatically handle detoured routes in congested regions in the process of routing the nets, whereas probabilistic methods usually do not model detours and require postprocessing for the same.

30.4 CONGESTION METRICS FOR TECHNOLOGY MAPPING

Even with the best possible placement, it may not be always possible to route the area- or delay-optimized mapped netlist successfully. This observation has motivated research on congestion optimization during the preplacement stages of typical design flows. The technology mapping stage maps a subject graph, which is a network comprising only of primitive gates such as two-input NANDs, on to cells in some library. This stage has a large impact on routing congestion, because it decides the wires in the netlist. Several congestion estimation metrics have been proposed for use during this stage. They include metrics that rely on some placement information, such as the netlength and predictive and constructive congestion maps, as well as structural metrics such as mutual contraction.

The netlength for a mapping solution is computed based on the placement of the subject graph. It can then be linearly combined with traditional cost functions such as area or delay, so that the solution is biased toward wirelength reduction (and consequently, reduced average congestion) [PPS03,SK01]. The netlength metric when used at the mapping stage suffers from the same limitations (for instance, an insensitivity to the spatial aspects of congestion) as when used at the placement stage. Although its use does not impact the time complexity of the mapping algorithm (because the netlength for a two-pin net can be computed as a Manhattan distance in constant time), the placement of the subject graph affects the overall runtime of the flow, because this graph is considerably larger than the mapped netlist. However, the subject graph placement need not be legalized, thus reducing the runtime overhead. Moreover, many modern physical synthesis flows anyway place either the subject graph or early versions of the mapped netlist, to estimate the net delays accurately during technology mapping [Dai01,SK01]. Alternatively, this placement can be derived from a previous iteration of mapping and mapped netlist placement [LJC03].

The predictive congestion map [SSS+05] is a probabilistic congestion map based on the connectivity and placement of the subject graph. Because it can differentiate between regions of high and low routing demand, this metric has been employed during technology mapping to select area- or delay-optimal matches in sparsely congested portions of the circuit and to choose congestion-optimal matches in densely congested, noncritical regions. This allows the mapper to avoid the large area and delay penalties that are likely with metrics such as the netlength that weight the routing demand uniformly across the entire design. The runtime for technology mapping using a predictive congestion map is higher than that with netlength, because the computations of the predictive map and of the congestion cost during the mapping require $O(bn)$ and $O(b)$ time, respectively, where b is the number of bins in the layout and n is the number of nets in the subject graph.

Constructive congestion maps [SSS06] are created dynamically, employing either probabilistic estimation or fast global routing, during the technology mapping process. These maps can be explained using the example shown in Figure 30.4 (which depicts only the horizontal routing demands for the sake of simplicity). Figure 30.4a shows a subject graph in which a match M_1 (namely, a two-input NAND gate) is being considered for a node N_1. The matching phase of the technology mapping algorithm, which creates solution candidates at each node, proceeds in topological order, whereas

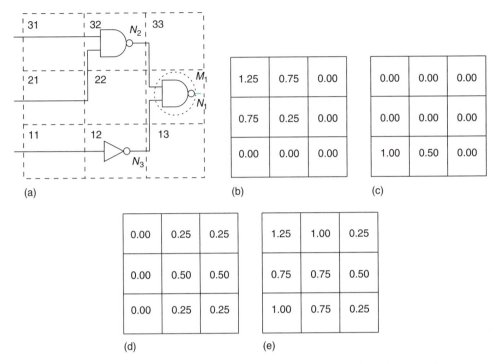

(a)

1.25	0.75	0.00
0.75	0.25	0.00
0.00	0.00	0.00

(b)

0.00	0.00	0.00
0.00	0.00	0.00
1.00	0.50	0.00

(c)

0.00	0.25	0.25
0.00	0.50	0.50
0.00	0.25	0.25

(d)

1.25	1.00	0.25
0.75	0.75	0.50
1.00	0.75	0.25

(e)

FIGURE 30.4 Constructive congestion map generation: (a) subject graph during matching process in technology mapping with match M_1 at node N_1, (b) horizontal track demand because of the solution at N_2, (c) horizontal track demand because of the solution at N_3, (d) horizontal track demand because of the fanin nets to the match M_1, (e) overall horizontal track demand owing to the mapping solution because of M_1. (Reprinted from Shelar, R., Saxena, P., and Sapatnekar, S., *IEEE Trans. Comput. Aided Des. Integr. Circuits Syst.*, 25, 625, 2006.)

the subsequent covering phase, which selects among the solutions generated during the matching phase, is carried out in reverse topological order. Therefore, when the matching phase is evaluating the solution for N_1 using match M_1, the (partial) congestion maps because of the best solutions at nodes N_2 and N_3 are already known. Let these maps be as shown in Figure 30.4b and c, respectively. Figure 30.4d shows the congestion map associated with the circled match M_1 at node N_1, accounting for the nets at the two fanins of the match. Finally, Figure 30.4e shows the congestion map representing the mapping solution because of the match M_1 at N_1. It is obtained by the binwise addition of the congestion maps in Figure 30.4b through d.

The congestion map for the mapping solution because of a match is propagated across a multifanout point by distributing the congestion equally among all the fanouts. The matching process continues in topological order, so that the congestion maps because of all the wires in the mapping solutions are available at the primary outputs when the process finishes.

As with predictive congestion maps, the constructive maps also require the subject graph to be placed before the technology mapping. Note that different mapping solutions represent different set of wires in the design, and result in different constructive congestion maps. Unlike predictive congestion maps that are static regardless of the chosen matches, constructive maps capture the congestion impact of different matches dynamically. As with predictive maps, the time complexity for the computation of the constructive congestion map for a two-pin net is $O(b)$, where b is the total number of bins. However, constructive maps require more memory than predictive maps, because different (partial) congestion maps owing to selected matches at different primary outputs may be required to create the map for the final mapping solution. There are several heuristics suggested in Ref. [SSS06] that can help reduce this memory overhead substantially.

The mutual contraction metric was previously discussed in Chapter 7. Unlike the metrics discussed so far, this metric does not depend on placement information, capturing congestion using structural properties of the netlist instead. It is defined for nets, and measures the tendency of the endpoints of a net to resist being pulled apart because of their connectivity to other cells. For the purpose of this metric, multipin nets are modeled as cliques. Thus, a net connecting n cells is modeled using $n(n-1)/2$ edges corresponding to all possible pairs among the n pins of the net. The weight of a net is distributed equally among all the edges that are used to model that net. Thus, the contribution of an edge $e(u, v)$ from a clique denoting a unit weight net connecting n vertices that includes u and v to the weight $w(u, v)$ is given by $2/[n(n-1)]$. Note that an edge $e(u, v)$ can simultaneously belong to several different cliques (corresponding to different multipin nets that share two or more pins). In such a case, the total weight of an edge is the sum of the contributions from each of the cliques that contain that edge. The relative weight $w_r(u, v)$ of the edge $e(u, v)$ is defined as the ratio of the weight $w(u, v)$ to the sum of the weights of all the edges incident on u. Observe that although $w(u, v) = w(v, u)$ for any edge $e(u, v) \in E$, the relative weights $w_r(u, v)$ and $w_r(v, u)$ may not be the same. The mutual contraction of an edge $e(u, v)$ is defined as the product of relative weights $w_r(u, v)$ and $w_r(v, u)$. In other words, the mutual contraction $mc[e(u, v)]$ for edge $e(u, v)$ is given by

$$mc[e(u, v)] = \frac{[w(u, v)]^2}{\sum_{z:e(z,u)\in E} w(z, u) \sum_{z:e(z,v)\in E} w(z, v)}$$

As with all metrics that ignore placement information, mutual contraction is not very effective at predicting the netlengths for individual nets accurately. However, Ref. [HM02] empirically demonstrates a good negative correlation between the mutual contraction and the average netlength for nets at the placement level, with large mutual contraction values corresponding to short netlengths. Because the total netlength is a measure of the average congestion, the selection of mapping choices with higher mutual contraction is likely to lead to a netlist that has a shorter total netlength. The use of this metric suffers from the same problems as the use of the total netlength to measure congestion, in addition to the inaccuracies inherent in the use of any placement-oblivious structural netlength prediction metric. Furthermore, the mutual contraction metric is not very effective at predicting the netlength for multipin nets. Therefore, technology mapping based on mutual contraction [LM05] also uses additional metrics such as the net range (discussed in Section 30.5). The computation of the mutual contraction of an edge $e(u, v)$ requires $O[\deg(u) + \deg(v)]$ time, where $\deg(x)$ represents the degree of node x. However, although mutual contraction is asymptotically more expensive than netlength computations, it is usually faster in practice because its use in technology mapping does not require the runtime intensive step of subject graph placement.

30.5   CONGESTION METRICS FOR LOGIC SYNTHESIS

Transformations carried out during (technology independent) logic synthesis have a large impact on the structure of a Boolean network and, therefore, on the eventual routing congestion. However, the perturbation because of the subsequent mapping and placement stages is often too large to maintain consistency with a congestion map obtained using a placement of the nodes of the Boolean network during logic synthesis. As a result, the congestion metrics at this level of abstraction often rely on structural properties. These metrics include the literal count, adhesion, fanout range and net range, and neighborhood population.

The literal count has been traditionally used as an area metric during logic synthesis. It has recently also been shown to correlate with the peak congestion when a Boolean network is mapped on to a trivial library containing two-input NANDs and inverters [KSD03]; however, the correlation in the case of realistic libraries containing complex gates is unknown. Intuitively, the literal count correlates to congestion because it represents the number of nets in the Boolean network. However, many of these nets are subsumed during the subsequent technology mapping. Moreover, the number of nets is a weak proxy for the total netlength, which in turn is merely an approximation for the average congestion.

Congestion is impacted not only by the number of nets, but also by the complexity of their connectivity. Entangled, nonplanar circuit graphs typically lead to more congestion than planar circuit graphs. The adhesion metric, defined as the sum of the mincuts between all pairs of nodes in a network [KSD03], tries to capture this interconnection complexity. Adhesion has been shown to correlate well with peak congestion for networks mapped on to the trivial library. The correlation improves further when adhesion is combined with additional metrics such as the literal count. However, the computation of adhesion is expensive, being cubic in the number of nodes in the network. Even approximation algorithms for adhesion require time that is linear in the size of the network.

The fanout range and net range metrics attempt to capture the length of a net in a graph theoretic sense. The fanout range of a node is defined as the range of topological levels spanned by all fanout pins of the node, whereas the net range is defined as the range of topological levels spanned by all the pins of the net. Thus, the net range is more discriminatory than the fanout range; as an example, the fanout range of a two-pin net is always zero, whereas the net range for such a net can vary. Although a longer fanout range or net range is likely to result in a larger wirelength, this correlation may not always hold after the actual placement. The fanout range has been used to guide fast extraction during logic synthesis [VP95], whereas the net range has been employed during fanout optimization [LM05]. Neither of these metrics is too expensive to compute, requiring time linear in the net degree.

The neighborhood population metric [PP89] tries to measure the local congestion caused by the cells that are topologically close to a given cell. It employs a notion of distance that is defined as the number of nodes on a shortest path between two nodes in the undirected graph underlying a given Boolean network. The neighborhood population at a specified distance for a given node is the number of nodes lying at that distance from the node; the definition can be extended to total (average) neighborhood populations by summing (averaging) the populations over all the nodes in the network. Intuitively, a high-neighborhood population for a given node at short distances implies strong local connectivity, and therefore a possible local congestion hot spot. Several conventional logic synthesis transformations such as substitution, fast extraction, and speed-up have been extended to consider neighborhood populations, so that the routing demand is spread uniformly, avoiding locally congested hot spots [KK03]. However, the subsequent technology mapping stage also affects the neighborhood population significantly, potentially causing much of the predicted congestion gains to be lost. The neighborhood population metric is more expensive than the fanout range or net range, as its computation requires visiting all the nodes within a specified distance (and not just the fanout nodes).

Several other graph theoretic metrics have been proposed in the context of placement or partitioning, in an effort to capture the tendency of the tightly connected nodes to be placed together. These include edge separability [CL00], connectivity [HB97], closeness [SK93], and the intrinsic shortest path length [KR05]. Although they have not yet been employed to guide logic synthesis transformations, they are candidates for such an application.

30.6   FINAL REMARKS

Although routing congestion manifests itself only at the very end of the typical design flow, it is often too late to resolve all such problems at that stage. However, any congestion mitigation during earlier stages of the design flow requires metrics that can be used for the prediction of postrouting congestion. In this chapter, we reviewed several such metrics applicable at different stages of the design flow. These metrics differ in their accuracy, fidelity, computation time, and scope of application. Congestion maps allow the identification of routing hot spots, whereas scalar metrics such as the total netlength can serve as fast discriminants between different implementation choices. Some metrics are derived from the placement of the preliminary or final versions of the netlist, whereas others such as mutual contraction and adhesion rely on the structural, graph theoretic properties of the circuit graph.

In general, the accuracy of placement-based metrics decreases as the level of abstraction of the netlist increases. Indeed, almost all the metrics proposed for use during logic synthesis to date are graph theoretic in nature. With the problem of routing congestion getting worse because of the scaling of design sizes and process technologies, a comprehensive congestion management strategy must target congestion through the entire design flow, relying on the appropriate congestion estimators at each stage.

The interested reader can find further details on all the metrics discussed in this chapter in the corresponding papers, or in Ref. [SSS07].

REFERENCES

[CZY+99] Chen, H. -M., Zhou, H., Young, F. Y., Wong, D. F., Yang, H. H., and Sherwani, N., Integrated floorplanning and interconnect planning, *Proceedings of the International Conference on Computer-Aided Design*, San Jose, CA, pp. 354–357, 1999.

[Che94] Cheng, C. -L. E., RISA: Accurate and efficient placement routability modeling, *Proceedings of the International Conference on Computer-Aided Design*, San Jose, CA, pp. 690–695, 1994.

[CL00] Cong J. and Lim, S., Edge separability based circuit clustering with application to circuit partitioning, *Proceedings of the Asia and South Pacific Design Automation Conference*, Yokohama, Japan, pp. 429–434, 2000.

[Dai01] Dai, W., Hierarchial physical design methodology for multi-million gate chips, *Proceedings of the International Symposium on Physical Design*, Sonoma, CA, pp. 179–181, 2001.

[HNR68] Hart, P. E., Nilsson, N. J., and Raphael, B., A formal basis for the heuristic determination of minimum cost paths, *IEEE Transactions on System Science and Cybernetics SSC-4*, pp. 100–107, 1968.

[HB97] Hauck, S. and Borriello, G., An evaluation of bipartitioning techniques, *IEEE Transactions on Computer-Aided Design of Integrated Circuits and Systems* 16(8): 849–866, August 1997. (ARVLSI 1995).

[Hig69] Hightower, D. W., A solution to line routing problems on the continuous plane, *Proceedings of the Design Automation Workshop*, NY, pp. 1–24, 1969.

[HM02] Hu, B. and Marek-Sadowska, M., Congestion minimization during placement without estimation, *Proceedings of the International Conference on Computer-Aided Design*, San Jose, CA, pp. 739–745, 2002.

[KR05] Kahng, A. B. and Reda, S., Intrinsic shortest path length: A new, accurate a priori wirelength estimator, *Proceedings of the International Conference on Computer-Aided Design*, San Jose, CA, pp. 173–180, 2005.

[KX03] Kahng, A. B. and Xu, X., Accurate pseudo-constructive wirelength and congestion estimation, *Proceedings of the International Workshop on System-Level Interconnect Prediction*, Monterey, CA, pp. 61–68, 2003.

[KK03] Kravets, V. and Kudva, P., Understanding metrics in logic synthesis for routability enhancement, *Proceedings of the International Workshop on System-Level Interconnect Prediction*, Monterey, CA, pp. 3–5, 2003.

[KSD03] Kudva, P., Sullivan, A., and Dougherty, W., Measurements for structural logic synthesis optimizations, *IEEE Transactions on Computer-Aided Design of Integrated Circuits and Systems* 22(6): 665–674, June 2003. (ICCAD 2002).

[LR71] Landman, B. S. and Russo, R. L., On a pin versus block relationship for partitions of logic graphs, *IEEE Transactions on Computers* C-20(12): 1469–1479, December 1971.

[LAQ+07] Li, Z., Alpert, C. J., Quay, S. T., Sapatnekar, S., and Shi, W., Probabilistic congestion prediction with partial blockages, *Proceedings of the International Symposium on Quality Electronic Design*, San Jose, CA, pp. 841–846, 2007.

[LJC03] Lin, J., Jagannathan, A., and Cong, J., Placement-driven technology mapping for LUT-based FPGAs, *Proceedings of the International Symposium on Field Programmable Gate Arrays*, Monterey, CA, pp. 121–126, 2003.

[LM05] Liu, Q. and Marek-Sadowska, M., Wire length prediction-based technology mapping and fanout optimization, *Proceedings of the International Symposium on Physical Design*, San Francisco, CA, pp. 145–151, 2005.

[LTK+02]   Lou, J., Thakur, S., Krishnamoorthy, S., and Sheng, H. S., Estimating routing congestion using probabilistic analysis, *IEEE Transactions on Computer-Aided Design of Integrated Circuits and Systems* 21(1): pp. 32–41, January 2002. (ISPD 2001).

[PC06]   Pan, M. and Chu, C., FastRoute: A step to integrate global routing into placement, *Proceedings of the International Conference on Computer-Aided Design*, San Jose, CA, pp. 464–471, 2006.

[PPS03]   Pandini, D., Pileggi, L. T., and Strojwas, A. J., Global and local congestion optimization in technology mapping, *IEEE Transactions on Computer-Aided Design of Integrated Circuits and Systems* 22(4): 498–505, April 2003. (ISPD 2002).

[PP89]   Pedram, M. and Preas, B., Interconnection length estimation for optimized standard cell layouts, *Proceedings of the International Conference on Computer-Aided Design*, Santa Clara, CA, pp. 390–393, 1989.

[SSS07]   Saxena, P., Shelar, R. S., and Sapatnekar, S. S., *Routing Congestion in VLSI Circuits: Estimation and Optimization*, New York: Springer, 2007.

[SPK03]   Selvakkumaran, N., Parakh, P. N., and Karypis, G., Perimeter-degree: A priori metric for directly measuring and homogenizing interconnection complexity in multi-level placement, *Proceedings of the International Workshop on System-level Interconnect Prediction*, Monterey, CA, pp. 53–59, 2003.

[SY05]   Sham, C. and Young, E. F. Y., Congestion prediction in early stages, *Proceedings of the International Workshop on System-level Interconnect Prediction*, San Francisco, CA, pp. 91–98, 2005.

[SSS+05]   Shelar, R., Sapatnekar, S., Saxena, P., and Wang, X., A predictive distributed congestion metric with application to technology mapping, *IEEE Transactions on Computer-Aided Design of Integrated Circuits and Systems* 24(5): 696–710, May 2005. (ISPD 2004).

[SSS06]   Shelar, R., Saxena, P., and Sapatnekar, S., Technology mapping algorithm targeting routing congestion under delay constraints, *IEEE Transactions on Computer-Aided Design of Integrated Circuits and Systems* 25(4): 625–636, April 2006. (ISPD 2005).

[SK93]   Shin, H. and Kim, C., A simple yet effective technique for partitioning, *IEEE Transactions on Very Large Scale Integration Systems* 1(3): 380–386, September 1993.

[SK01]   Stok, L. and Kutzschebauch, T., Congestion aware layout driven logic synthesis, *Proceedings of the International Conference on Computer-Aided Design*, San Jose, CA, pp. 216–223, 2001.

[VP95]   Vaishnav, H. and Pedram, M., Minimizing the routing cost during logic extraction, *Proceedings of the Design Automation Conference*, San Francisco, CA, pp. 70–75, 1995.

[WBG04]   Westra, J., Bartels, C., and Groeneveld, P., Probabilistic congestion prediction, *Proceedings of the International Symposium on Physical Design*, Phoenix, AZ, pp. 204–209, 2004.

[WBG05]   Westra, J., Bartels, C., and Groeneveld, P., Is probabilistic congestion estimation worthwhile?, *Proceedings of the International Workshop on System-Level Interconnect Prediction*, San Francisco, CA, pp. 99–106, 2005.

31 Rip-Up and Reroute

Jeffrey S. Salowe

CONTENTS

31.1 OVERVIEW

In this chapter, we explain some of the intricacies of rip-up and reroute by focusing on one common routing formulation. With respect to this routing formulation, we examine two rip-up-and-reroute schemas, which are basic techniques. After examining the schemas and assessing their strengths and weaknesses, we show how strategies that combine the different schemas can be constructed. The strategies attempt to counter the weaknesses of the schemas themselves. These concepts are illustrated with some of the seminal papers in the field. Rip-up and reroute has been successfully applied during all phases of routing, including global routing, detailed routing, track assignment, and layer assignment.

31.1.1 DEFINITION

Rip-up and reroute is an iterative technique whose basic step is to remove one or more connections and replace them with new connections. This idea can be applied in many ways. For instance, suppose as depicted in Figure 31.1a that connection $r1$ has been added, but connection $r2$ cannot be added without a violation because connection $r1$ uses a resource that $r2$ needs. One can remove all or part of $r1$, add connection $r2$, and then make a new connection for $r1$ as depicted in Figure 31.1b through d, respectively. Another possibility is to shift connection $r1$ away from the critical resource, and then to add $r2$. Yet another possibility is to place a tax, or congestion cost, on the common resource, hoping that connection r1 or connection r2 will avoid the taxed region.

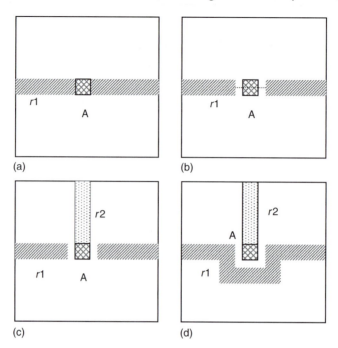

FIGURE 31.1   (a) Wire $r1$ blocks pin access to A. A is on metal 1, A is surrounded by blockages (not depicted), and $r1$ is on metal 2. (b) A portion of wire $r1$ is removed to allow access to A. (c) Wire $r2$ on metal 3 can access pin A using a via stack from metal 3 to metal 1. (d) Wire $r1$ is rerouted on metal 2.

31.2   ROUTING FORMULATION

To illustrate rip-up and reroute, we simplify the routing problem using Lagrangian relaxation, ultimately transforming the problem into successive shortest-path problems. This basic framework was outlined by Linsker (1984). Once the basic framework is established, we examine different rerouting strategies, pointing out their strengths and weaknesses.

31.2.1   LAGRANGIAN RELAXATION

A routing problem is an optimization problem of the form

minimize $f(X)$

$$\text{subject to} \qquad g_i(X) \le 0, 1 \le i \le n$$

We separate the constraints into two classes, network constraints $n_i(X) \le 0,\ 1 \le i \le N$, and design constraints $d_i(X) \le 0,\ 1 \le i \le D$.

minimize $f(X)$

$$\text{subject to} \qquad n_i(X) \le 0, 1 \le i \le N$$
$$d_i(X) \le 0, 1 \le i \le D$$

Network constraints state that the network topology must satisfy certain requirements, such as the network must connect all the pins without forming loops. Except for special nets, the network constraints state that a Steiner tree implements each net. Design constraints state that the network is designed in a legal way, such as no two routes occupy the same spot, or no two shapes are too close together.

The global routing design constraints state that no area contains too many routing shapes. If an area contains too many global routing shapes, it may not be possible to detail route the area without violating the detail routing design constraints.

A routing problem is feasible if there is any solution that satisfies the constraints. For any interesting routing problem, it is NP-hard to determine if there is a feasible solution.

Chip designers, however, are not interested in abstract complexity issues: they typically try to make chips that have feasible routing (based on earlier experience) and then adjust the constraints to achieve their objectives. The typical input is therefore likely to have a feasible solution. Furthermore, some design constraints are soft, such as those given to a global router. It may be possible to overcongest a few areas and still solve the resulting detailed routing problem. This means that even if the result is infeasible for the original problem, it may still be useful.

A general and powerful technique to solve hard optimizations problems is to apply Lagrangian relaxation (Ahuja et al. 1993). In Lagrangian relaxation, one or more constraints are added to the objective function using Lagrangian multipliers λ_i. Under appropriate conditions, Lagrangian relaxation can be used to solve optimization problems exactly; conditions for convergence are discussed in Ahuja et al. (1993). In other cases, however, Lagrangian relaxation is used to simplify complicating constraints. Routing falls into the second category: one applies Lagrangian multipliers to the design constraints, resulting in an optimization problem:

$$\text{minimize } f(X) + \lambda_i^* d_i(X)$$

$$\text{subject to} \quad n_i(X) \leq 0$$
$$\lambda_i \geq 0$$

In the Lagrangian relaxation of a routing problem, only the network constraints need to be satisfied. This means that any set of Steiner trees is a feasible solution, which is a considerable simplification. The design constraints are "taxed" by the Lagrangian multiplier. The penalty for violating a design constraint is proportional to the Lagrangian tax.

Global routing problems have some soft constraints, so the Lagrangian relaxation technique is natural. Detailed routing problems can be phrased in exactly the same way, but the Lagrangian taxes are high because a violated design constraint may cause a chip to fail. Sometimes, though, there are soft constraints in detailed routing, where a violation is unwelcome but not prohibited. An example is a wide spacing rule to minimize cross talk that can be violated in a congested region.

31.2.2 STEINER TREE CONSTRUCTION

A Steiner minimal tree is a shortest connection of a set of points. Finding a Steiner minimal tree in the plane or in a graph is NP-hard, even if there are no obstructions. To make matters even more complicated, there are usually several routing layers, routing obstructions, and congestion.

Lagrangian relaxation simplifies the routing problem into simultaneous Steiner tree construction of a set of nets. Although the Steiner tree problem is itself hard, one may not need the absolutely shortest tree, and there are special cases that are solvable in polynomial time. For instance, a Steiner minimal tree for a two-pin net is a shortest-path problem, which can be found efficiently. Furthermore, a properly embedded minimum spanning tree is an excellent heuristic for a Steiner minimal tree (Hwang et al. 1992). The basic step in Prim's minimum spanning tree is to find a vertex that is closest to the tree. It is therefore reasonable to assume that the shortest-path problem is an important component in a routing problem.

31.2.3 A* MAZE SEARCH

The Lee–Moore algorithm is described in Section 23.5. There are one or more sources and one or more targets; initially, the weight of a source is zero and the weight of a target is infinite. Vertices are considered in order of weight from the source; when a vertex u is visited, the graph edges (u, v) incident to u are examined to see if they improve the smallest weight to v. The search stops when a target is to be considered.

One can decrease the number of vertices visited in the search if one has a conservative estimate of the distance from each node to the targets. This value, the lower bound, reflects how close each

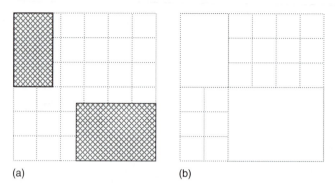

(a)   (b)

FIGURE 31.2   (a) Blockages on a routing grid graph and (b) pruned routing grid graph.

vertex is to a target. In the A^* technique, invented by Nilsson (Hart et al. 1968), the weight of the path to u plus the estimated distance to a closest target form a new measure, the estimated weight of a shortest path using the vertex u. Instead of considering vertices in order of weight from the source, A^* considers them in order of estimated shortest-path weight.

The A^* technique can speed up the path search enormously if the estimated path length is close to the actual path length. Unfortunately, A^* becomes less effective when the lower bound is overly conservative. This happens when obstructions are not accounted for in the lower bound, and it happens when congestion is present but not reflected in the lower bound. Nevertheless, A^* has proven to be of great practical use. In our formulation, the general routing problem is transformed into a set of path problems in a weighted graph that are solved using A^* maze search.

31.2.4 COST FUNCTIONS AND CONSTRAINTS

Using Lagrangian relaxation, the routing problem becomes a problem of finding shortest paths in a weighted graph because the Lagrangian taxes are a cost function on the vertices and edges. An alternative to a very high cost function on a vertex or edge is to remove that vertex or edge from the graph. For instance, spacing rules in a gridded detailed routing problem can be handled by removing grid points that are in violation with existing objects. This places a constraint on the graph, and it ensures that the vertex or edge is not used; it may speed up a graph search because the expensive edges or vertices need not be visited. (Figure 31.2) The main factor in deciding how to represent the constraint is the complexity of the resulting subproblem. If one uses A^* in a weighted graph, the removal of a graph vertex or edge does not substantially alter the strategy, though it may affect the running time.

It is also possible to further constrain the path; for instance, one can prune paths that do not satisfy certain criteria, such as the number of bends in the path (this is done, for instance, in Shin and Sangiovanni-Vincentelli [1987]). Note that some pruning options are not compatible with an A^* search.

31.3 RIP-UP-AND-REROUTE SCHEMAS

Now that the general formulation is in place, we can examine different rip-up-and-reroute schemas. A schema reflects a basic methodology, though the actual implementation details may differ from one author to another. Schemas can be separated based on

1. Identification of rip-up-and-reroute subproblems
2. Selection of routes that are removed when a subproblem is considered
3. Method used to solve these subproblems

We describe two important schemas, the progressive rerouting schema and the iterative improvement schema. They appear in two key papers in the field, and their concepts have interesting parallels in network optimization. They form a foundation for powerful routing strategies.

31.3.1 Progressive Rerouting Schema

An important rip-up-and-reroute schema can be illustrated with the global routing algorithm invented by R. Nair (1987). In Nair's schema, each net forms a subproblem, and only that net is removed when the subproblem is considered.

```
1. For pass = 1 to k
2. For each net n
3. For each connection r in n
   a. Remove r
   b. Reroute r
```

Nair tessellated the chip using vertical and horizontal lines into a two-dimensional "gcell grid" as described in Section 23.2.2. A gcell is defined as a smallest rectangle formed by the horizontal and vertical lines. Nair's routing graph is the dual of the grid graph: each gcell is a vertex, and an edge is present between each pair of adjacent gcells.

Nair placed a constraint on each line segment in the grid graph that reflected the number of wires that could cross that line segment. These represent the design constraints in that area. Using Lagrangian relaxation, the constraints became costs on the routing graph edges.

Two-pin nets are routed using an A* search. Multipin nets are routed by successive A* searches, where the source consists of all gcells that intersect the partially constructed net, and the targets are all pins that are not yet connected in the net.

Nair's key contribution was the overall routing strategy. In the first pass, each net is routed subject to the congestion costs incurred from the nets already visited. In each subsequent pass, a net is removed and completely rerouted. Note that after the first pass, each net will see the congestion from all the other nets.

Nair justified his method, progressive rerouting, with the intuition that the second pass is better informed about congestion than the first pass because the second pass sees all the congestion, while the first pass only sees what was routed so far. He discovered that the overall solution cost generated by the rerouting process converged to equilibrium after several passes; in his case, he stated that fewer than five passes sufficed.

Although it was not suggested in Nair's paper, his algorithm can be understood in the context of noncooperative games. In a noncooperative game, each "agent" acts selfishly on its own behalf, without regard to the effect on the other agents. An important notion in the theory of noncooperative games is the concept of a Nash equilibrium. In a Nash equilibrium, no agent can change its behavior to improve its own state. In time, noncooperative games converge to a Nash equilibrium. It is known, however, that a Nash equilibrium may not be a global optimum.

Progressive routing can be seen to be a noncooperative game among the different nets. Each net is routed in a greedy fashion to minimize its own latency. Progressive rerouting bears a remarkable similarity to the problem of making traffic assignments. Recent results in traffic assignment theory shed some light on the efficacy of Nair's technique. The ratio of the cost of a Nash equilibrium to the overall minimum cost is called the price of anarchy. Roughgarden and Tardos (2002) showed that for single commodity flows where the latency function is a linear function of the congestion, any Nash equilibrium has latency at most 4/3 times the minimum possible total latency. Global routing, on the other hand, is a multicommodity flow where the commodity cannot be split; for general multicommodity flows, the price of anarchy can be exponential in the polynomial degree of the latency function (Lin et al. 2005).

It is not clear that these negative results are immediately applicable to global routing. Global routing problems are often well behaved; designers are interested in making chips, not confounding routers. Perhaps one can show a positive result on the price of anarchy of a well-behaved global routing problem.

Nair's algorithm also has an interesting parallel to the multicommodity flow approximation technique described in Chapter 32 (Albrecht 2001). The multicommodity flow approximation technique proceeds in a series of passes. In each pass, a Steiner minimal tree is found for each net with respect to a weighted graph. The graph weights are successively modified due to the placement of the trees. At the end, a rounding technique is used to select the actual implementation of the net. This can be seen as identical to the structure of Nair's algorithm; the main difference is in the choice of the graph weights and in the selection of the Steiner tree implementation. In Nair's approach, there is exactly one Steiner tree representation. Steiner trees from prior passes are forgotten, except by how they affect the graph weights.

31.3.1.1 Issues

The strength of progressive rerouting is simplicity of design. The basic component is A* search; it is repeated over several passes. The schema converges rapidly to a reasonable equilibrium state (Nair 1987). However, it has several weaknesses, some of which are given below.

31.3.1.1.1 Detouring
The key problem with successive rerouting is detouring. This is where the length of the routed connection is much longer than the length of a connection if congestion is not considered. The price of anarchy refers to the total path length; a single connection, however, can have an arbitrarily long detour. This is particularly undesirable when timing issues are considered. A net with a weak driver cannot be detoured, so nets on timing-critical paths must be carefully constructed.

31.3.1.1.2 Initialization
A second issue is establishing a good starting point. At the time of the first pass, no nets are routed, so these initial nets receive preferential treatment. The nets routed at the end of the first pass will see the congestion of the preceding nets, and they may detour unnecessarily as a result. Hadsell and Madden (2003) suggest that this initial routing phase can be seeded with a congestion estimation. The congestion estimation affects the cost function by applying a tax to high-demand areas.

31.3.1.1.3 Net Ordering
Refer to Figure 31.3. Assume that two wires each need to pass through one of two bottlenecks. Wire *a* is wide, and wire *b* is narrow; gap *A* can accommodate either wire *a* and wire *b* but not both, but gap *B* can only accommodate wire *b*. If wire *b* is assigned to gap *A*, it has no incentive to relinquish its position unless wire *a* is also assigned to gap *A*. If the cost of putting wire *a* in gap *A* is less than the cost of putting wire *a* in gap *B*, wire *b* prevents an optimal assignment of wires to gaps.

This issue is typically dealt with using net ordering. If the connection containing wire *a* is routed first, wire *a* will be placed in gap *A* rather than gap *B* because it does not fit in gap *B*. The connection containing wire *b* will then be assigned to gap *B*. Net ordering is an imperfect attempt to add centralized control to the progressive rerouting process. The task of assigning wires to bottleneck gaps is a packing problem; such a problem is NP-complete, and heuristics with good performance can be sophisticated.

31.3.1.1.4 Determining Good Lagrangian Multipliers
Though there are some general techniques to find Lagrangian multipliers (Ahuja et al. 1993), ad hoc techniques are often used in practice. Users want fast convergence and few detours. Also note that A* performs better when lower bounds and upper bounds match, so the use of a Lagrangian multiplier when the design is uncongested may slow down the algorithm, even if it is the theoretically correct

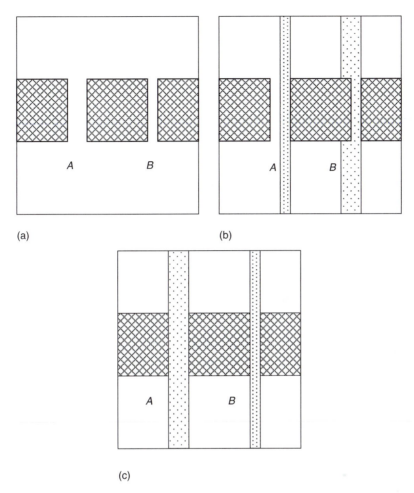

FIGURE 31.3 (a) Bottleneck gaps A and B. Thin wire b can fit through either. Thick wire a can only fit through gap A. (b) If wire b is routed first, it may take gap A or gap B. If thin wire b takes a resource A that thick wire a needs, a cannot fit through. (c) If wire a is routed first, it takes gap A. Wire b can make it through gap b.

thing to do. Several authors have investigated this issue. Note that the multipliers may be affected by how congestion is modeled and by the routing objectives.

31.3.1.1.5 Divergence

Worse than detouring is divergence, where the design may be so congested that almost all connections detour. In each successive pass, rerouted connections detour even more to avoid congestion, thereby increasing wirelength dramatically and inducing more congestion. Although successive rerouting will converge to a Nash equilibrium, there is neither a statement that it must converge in a small number of passes (it diverges during these passes) nor is there a bound on the total wirelength increase per pass. Divergence commonly happens when a design is infeasible.

31.3.2 ITERATIVE IMPROVEMENT SCHEMA

This is the second major schema illustrated. Suppose we have a routing solution that satisfies the network constraints but not the design constraints. Suppose we select one violated design constraint and then attempt to resolve it by rip-up and reroute. If no additional design constraints are violated, the resulting routing solution is deemed to be superior to the original one and therefore closer to the overall solution. This schema represents an iterative optimization technique; i.e., a pivot is made by tightening some violated constraint and then solving the resulting problem.

1. Route nets
2. Identify areas where the design constraints are violated
3. Identify nets/connections r to
   a. Remove r
   b. Reroute r

This schema was proposed in the earliest papers on rip-up and reroute. An early, sophisticated discussion is in Ting and Tien (1983). They define a loop as a closed, nonintersecting sequence of boundaries in the grid graph. The loop constraint states that the number of times that connections cross a loop must be no greater than the maximum number of crossings allowed on the loop. For each connection, define its crossing count to be the number of times the connection intersects the loop. The crossing count of a net is the sum of the crossing counts of its connections. A net is said to violate the loop constraint if there exists a Steiner tree that can decrease the crossing count. As a specific example, suppose a net contains two pins that are outside the loop, but the routed connection for these two pins crosses the loop (Figure 31.4). This connection violates the loop constraint because there must be a Steiner tree that lies entirely outside the loop.

Ting and Tien consider several loops simultaneously. Given a set of loops and a set of violating nets, they form a bipartite graph. One set of vertices are the violating nets, the other set are the loops, and there is an edge between a net and a loop if the net violates the corresponding loop constraint. Using this bipartite graph, Ting and Tien attempt to find an intelligent subset of nets to rip-up and reroute. They select a minimal set of nets such that, if removed, no loop constraint will be violated. (By minimal, this means that if any net was removed from the set, some loop constraint would be violated.) The smallest such set is called a set cover, which is also an NP-complete problem, so a suitable approximation is used.

After the set of nets to reroute is obtained, Ting and Tien (1983) use a greedy strategy to obtain a net ordering, and then reroute the connections in that order. They note that their sequence may not remove all congestion, even if an uncongested solution can be found by another sequence. Such an issue is endemic to the iterative rip-up-and-reroute schema.

31.3.2.1 Issues

The strength of iterative improvement is its consistent progress. Design constraint violations are found and resolved if possible. If the routing problem is feasible and the initial solution is of reasonable quality, the number of violations will be a small fraction of the design. If the probability of a successful rip-up and reroute is sufficiently high, the iterative improvement methodology will converge rapidly (see Dees and Smith [1981] for a probabilistic justification).

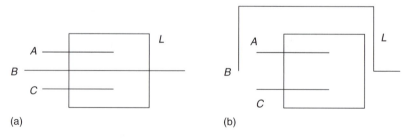

(a)   (b)

FIGURE 31.4   (a) Loop L has four crossings, but it can only support two. (b) Net B is rerouted to avoid loop L.

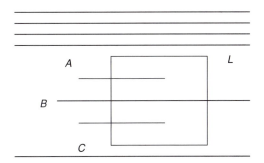

FIGURE 31.5   Region *R* is the area outside of *L*. Routing in *R* prevents *B* from being successfully rerouted.

The weakness of iterative improvement depends on the exact method used. Here are some issues that can arise.

31.3.2.1.1   Insufficient Rip-Up

Ting and Tien take a direct approach; they remove violating routes. However, it is also possible that nets that are not in violation may need to be ripped up as well. (Figure 31.5) A net that is nearby a violation may control a resource that is needed to remove the violation. For instance, suppose that wire *a* avoids closed region *R*, but it must pass through *R* in an optimal solution. There is no incentive to reroute wire *a* when considering *R* because it does not cross *R*.

Another example is if wire *a* is placed in the middle of a two-track gap (Figure 31.6). Near the gap, wires *b* and *c* cross. If the rip-up-and-reroute region is at the spot where *b* and *c* cross, and wire *a* is not in the region, wire *a* would not be considered. If, however, wire *a* is moved to make room for wire *b*, then the violation would be removed.

31.3.2.1.2   Net Ordering

Ting and Tien noted that their net ordering strategy may not produce a global minimum. This is always the case with iterative optimization techniques. Many authors have noted this issue; the net ordering problem is dealt with using heuristics, Lagrangian weights, and randomization (Dees and Karger 1982).

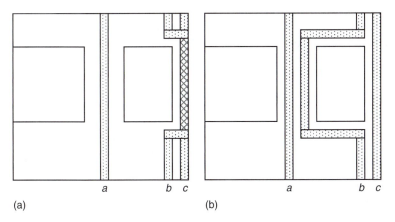

(a)   (b)

FIGURE 31.6   (a) Wires *b* and *c* cross. Assume the rip-up region is the cross-hatched area. Wire *a* is not moved. (b) If the rip-up region is enlarged to contain wire *a*, then the rip-up and reroute is successful.

31.3.2.1.3   Lack of Progress

Suppose that the rip-up and reroute of a region does not reduce the total cost. Such an issue is called a lack of progress. A lack of progress always occurs if a design constraint cannot be removed, but it may occur because of insufficient rip-up, for instance.

31.3.2.1.4   Oscillation

Oscillation is a phenomenon where a sequence of rip-up-and-reroute operations results in a return to the original configuration. For instance, a reroute may move wire *a* out of a region, and then a successive reroute may place the route back in its original configuration. Oscillation may occur if a lack or progress is permitted. If oscillations do occur, there is the possibility of an infinite loop in the routing strategy.

A special type of oscillation occurs when no change takes place during the rip-up and reroute of a connection.

31.4   RIP-UP-AND-REROUTE STRATEGIES

The two schemas presented have strengths and weaknesses. For some routing problems, the strengths may suffice. However, the most successful routers use combinations of these schemas that form a strategy.

A good example of the strategic development of a router is the router Mighty, developed by Shin and Sangiovanni-Vincentelli (1987), which mixes progressive rerouting and iterative improvement in a sophisticated way. The first pass of Mighty routes all the connections, but it does not commit them. The information is used to order the connections for the second pass. Specifically, connections are placed on a priority queue that is ordered by length. In the second pass, connections are either implemented if no network constraint is violated, or they are rerouted. Connections are rerouted so that they avoid conflicts, and the resulting connection is tested for quality. Connections that pass the quality test are placed on the priority queue. Connections that fail the quality test cause a sequence of modifications to the implemented connections. These modifications are either localized moves such as shifting the location of the wire (weak modifications) or more drastic moves that involve the rip-up of the conflicting connections (strong modifications). In the strong modification stage, connections are routed so that they are allowed to conflict with existing objects. During this stage, conflicts are taxed, and a minimum-weight path is used to identify the connections to remove.

Mighty demonstrates the power of strategy. It deals with the schema issues in the following way. With respect to progressive reroute, the initialization problem is resolved by routing all connections independently of each other. They use a strategy for net ordering where certain simple connections are done first. There are two routing phases; in one phase, violations are not allowed, so Lagrangian weights are not an issue. In the second phase, violations are allowed, and Lagrangian weights are needed, though it is expected that the first phase will succeed most of the time. With respect to iterative improvement, there are two types of rip-up techniques. When using weak modifications, a history is stored to avoid oscillation. Lack of progress is dealt with using a sequence of more powerful (and extensive) rip-up-and-reroute operations.

31.5   HISTORY

Rip-up and reroute was mentioned in early papers on printed circuit boards (PCBs) in the late 1960s. The earliest reference appears to be Dunne (1967). A slightly later work in a more visible publication is by Lass (1969). In that paper, Lass described a rip-up-and-reroute technique where the changes were localized to a small window. Further work on PCBs was given by Rubin (1974).

For IC design, IBM played a particularly important role in developing area routers (Darringer et al. 2000) and in the use of rip-up and reroute to solve these problems. The central concepts were established by the mid-1980s. The schemas described here were also established in the early-to-mid 1980s.

A good short survey of rip-up-and-reroute techniques for global routing appears in Hu and Sapatenekar (2001). One interesting rip-up-and-reroute algorithm that does not use path search as its main component appears in Meixner and Lauther (1990). Rip-up-and-reroute concepts appear in some recent work as well, such as Hu and Sapatnekar (2002), Liu and Sechen (1999), and Tseng and Sechen (1997). We note that much of the commercial work on rip-up and reroute is folklore. Key developers of proprietary routing software have not published all of their discoveries.

31.6 ENGINEERING PRACTICALITY

Rip-up-and-reroute strategies are used in many commercial routers and are mentioned in recent technical papers. There are many reasons why rip-up and reroute is so common.

First of all, rip-up-and-reroute algorithms always satisfy the network constraints. After the reroute step, one can perform an analysis such as a timing analysis or a process antenna check. Because the network constraints are satisfied, only a single routing representation is needed; intermediate results are lost.

Rip-up-and-reroute algorithms typically allow individual control over a net. For instance, if a net is involved in a timing violation because it has too much cross capacitance, only that net and nearby affected nets need to be rerouted.

Many of the rip-up-and-reroute schemas are easy to implement. If one implements the basic components of the routing algorithm, then the rip-up step consists of deleting routes and remarking the routing grid. For example, only an A^* routing engine is needed in progressive rerouting. This represents a significant simplification from the standpoint of software engineering—there is only one place that would need to be updated or fixed when an enhancement is needed.

Rip-up-and-reroute algorithms typically represent only one physical realization of a connection at a time. The routing representation is a significant memory consumer, so care must be taken to ensure that the memory footprint is small. In rip-up and reroute, the memory footprint is as efficient as possible because alternate solutions are not represented.

Through the use of strategies, a variety of rip-up-and-reroute techniques can be used to solve difficult problems. In this sense, some different techniques dovetail in the same way as optimizing compiler techniques dovetail: each additional strategic tool improves router quality without affecting the quality of the other tools.

Finally, rip-up-and-reroute algorithms have been used successfully in many practical applications. From the commercial risk–reward standpoint, there is little risk to implement an improved rip-up-and-reroute algorithm, and there is little reward if the underlying routing algorithm worked as well as the competition but took longer to develop.

REFERENCES

R. K. Ahuja, T. L. Magnanti, and J. B. Orlin. *Network Flows: Theory, Algorithms, and Applications*. Prentice Hall, New Jersey, 1993.

C. Albrecht. Global routing by new approximation algorithms for multicommodity flow. *IEEE Transactions on CAD*, 20(5), 2001, 622–632.

J. Darringer et al. EDA in IBM: Past, present, and future. *IEEE Transactions on CAD*, 19(12), 2000, 1476–1497.

W. A. Dees, Jr. and P. G. Karger. Automated rip-up and reroute techniques. *19th Design Automation Conference*, Annual ACM IEEE Design Automation Conference, IEEE Press, Piscataway, NJ, 1982, pp. 432–439.

W. A. Dees, Jr. and R. J. Smith, II. Performance of interconnection rip-up and reroute strategies. Proceedings of the *18th Design Automation Conference*, Nashville, TN, Annual ACM ICEEE Design Automation Conference, IEEE Press, Piscataway, NJ, 1981, pp. 382–390.

G. V. Dunne. The design of printed circuit layouts by computer. *Proceedings of Australian Computer Conference* 3, 1967, pp. 419–423.

R. T. Hadsell and P. H. Madden. Improved global routing through congestion estimation. *DAC*, Anaheim, CA. ACM, NY, 2003, pp. 28–31.

P. E. Hart, N. J. Nilsson, and B. Rafael. A formal basis for the heuristic determination of minimum cost paths. *IEEE Transactions on Systems Science and Cybernetics*, 4, 1968, 100–107.

J. Hu and S. S. Sapatenekar. A survey on multi-net global routing for integrated circuits. *Integeration: The VLSI Journal*, 31(1), 2001, 1–49.

J. Hu and S. S. Sapatnekar. A timing-constrained simultaneous global routing algorithm. *IEEE Transactions on CAD*, 21(9), 2002, 1025–1036.

F. K. Hwang, D. S. Richards, and P. Winter. *The Steiner Tree Problem*. Annals of Discrete Mathematics, 53, Amsterdam, The Netherlands, 1992.

S. E. Lass. Automated printed circuit routing with a stepping aperture. *CACM*, 12(5), 1969, 262–265.

H. Lin, T. Roughgarden, E. Tardos, and A. Walkover. Braess's paradox, Fibonacci numbers, and exponential inapproximability, ICALP, Lisbon, Portugal, 2005, pp. 497–512.

R. Linsker. An iterative-improvement penalty-function-driven wire routing system. *IBM Journal of Research and Development*, 28(5), 1984, 613–624.

L. E. Liu and C. Sechen. Multilayer chip-level global routing using an efficient graph-based Steiner tree heuristic. *IEEE Transactions on CAD*, 18(10), 1999, 1442–1451.

G. Meixner and U. Lauther. A new global router based on a flow model and linear assignment. *Proceedings of the IEEE/ACM International Conference on Computer-Aided Design*, Santa Clara, CA, 1990, pp. 44–47.

R. Nair. A simple yet effective technique for global wiring. *IEEE Transactions on CAD*, 6(2), 1987, 165–172.

T. Roughgarden and E. Tardos. How bad is selfish routing? *Journal of the ACM*, 49(2), 2002, 236–259.

F. Rubin. An iterative technique for printed wire routing. *11th Design Automation Workshop*, Annual ACM IEEE Design Automation Conference, IEEE Press, Piscataway, NJ, 1974, pp. 308–313.

H. Shin and A. Sangiovanni-Vincentelli. A detailed router based on incremental routing modifications: Mighty. *IEEE Transactions on CAD*, 6(6), 1987, 942–955.

B. S. Ting and B. N. Tien. Routing techniques for gate array. *IEEE Transactions on CAD*, 2(4), 1983, 301–312.

H. -P. Tseng and C. Sechen. Multi-layer over-the-cell routing with obstacles. *IEEE Custom Integrated Circuits Conference*, Santa Clara, CA, 1997, pp. 565–568.

32 Optimization Techniques in Routing

Christoph Albrecht

CONTENTS

32.1 INTRODUCTION

Today's routing instances are of enormous complexity. Millions of nets need to be routed on chip images that have tens of thousands routing channels in x- and y-direction and up to eight routing planes. Because of this complexity, routing is usually split up into two subtasks: global routing, which gives the approximate area for the Steiner tree of each net, and detailed routing, which performs a path search in this area and determines the actual tracks and vias for the nets. Global routing also provides a fast method to determine if a routing instance is feasible or not, or feasible only with long detours that may not be acceptable. If the global routing does not have a solution, it is necessary to change the placement. This chapter focuses on the global routing problem.

Many global routers are based on an initial route of all nets followed by a rip-up and reroute procedure, which tries to reduce the congestion of the edges by rerouting segments of nets on overloaded edges as described in Chapter 31. For difficult instances, these algorithms may run forever and not come up with a solution, even though a solution exists.

In this chapter, we discuss routing techniques that are based on the linear relaxation of an integer programming formulation of the global routing problem. If the linear program does not have a solution, by linear programming duality the dual linear program provides a proof, and this is a certificate that also the given global routing instance does not have a solution.

The linear relaxation of the global routing problem allows multiple Steiner trees (or routes) for a single net, each Steiner tree having a nonnegative weight. The weights of the Steiner trees for each net sum up to 1. In the end, we would like to have an integer solution that has only on single Steiner tree for each net. This is achieved by randomized rounding as introduced by Raghavan and Thompson in 1987 [1,2].

Solving the linear programming relaxation was (and still is) the computationally most expensive part in this approach and this was the reason why the approach was used only very limitedly in practice. This changed with new developments of approximation algorithms for the multicommodity flow problem and the fractional packing problem [3–8]. These problems are related to the linear relaxation of the global routing problem, the fractional global routing problem. We present an approximation scheme for the linear relaxation of the global routing problem, which is based on the approximation algorithms by Garg and Könemann [6] and Fleischer [7]. In the year 2000, it was possible to route the latest IBM application specific integrated circuit (ASIC) and microprocessor designs with up to 1,000,000 nets with this approximation scheme [9]. Subsequently, the algorithm was also used in commercial electronic design automation (EDA) tools for the X-architecture as discussed in Chapter 40.

This chapter is organized as follows. In the next section, Section 32.2, we formulate the global routing problem. Then in Section 32.3, we discuss the linear relaxation and the dual linear program. In Section 32.4, we present early work on linear programming for global routing, in particular the simplex method with column generation. In Section 32.5, we describe the multicommodity flow problem and the fractional packing problem and show the relationship to the fractional global routing problem. In Section 32.6, we present a fully polynomial approximation scheme for the fractional global routing problem based on the multicommodity flow approximation schemes and prove the approximation ratio. In Section 32.7, we present randomized rounding as introduced by Raghavan and Thompson [1,2], which is used to achieve the final integer solution. In the last section, we discuss extensions of the approach.

32.2 GLOBAL ROUTING PROBLEM FORMULATION

In global routing, an undirected grid graph $G = (V, E)$ is constructed. A two-dimensional grid is placed over the chip. For each tile, there is a vertex $v \in V$ and two vertices corresponding to adjacent tiles are connected by an edge. It is possible that the grid graph G consists of different layers such that via-capacities as well as capacities for different layers can be considered. Figure 32.1 shows a global routing graph with two layers, one for wiring in x-direction, the other for wiring in y-direction, and via edges in between.

The number of edges in G is denoted by m, that is $m = |E|$. For global routing, only nets with pins in different tiles are considered. Let k be the total number of these nets and for each net $i, i = 1, \ldots, k$, let $N_i \subseteq V$ be the set of vertices for which there exists a pin of the net in the corresponding tile. The vertices of N_i are called the terminals of net i.

For a given net i, let $\mathcal{T}_i$ be the set of all possible Steiner trees. This set might be restricted such that it contains only a subset of all possible Steiner trees—for example, for timing critical nets, the set may contain only the Steiner trees with minimum L_1-length.

For the algorithms presented in this chapter, we assume that given any nonnegative lengths for the edges, a subroutine can be queried to compute a Steiner tree $T \in \mathcal{T}_i$ of minimum length with respect to these edge lengths. In practice, a heuristic that does not necessarily return the optimum Steiner tree is often good enough.

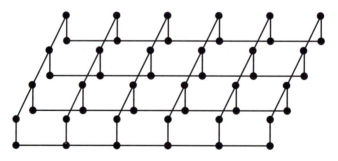

FIGURE 32.1   Global routing graph with two layers and via edges.

For each edge $e = \{u, v\}$, a capacity $c(e)$ is computed according to the number of free channels between the two tiles corresponding to u and v, taking into account the entanglement of the nets that have all pins either in u or in v.

Global routing asks for a Steiner tree T_i for each net i. Given these Steiner trees, the relative congestion of an edge e is defined as $\lambda(e) := |\{i | e \in T_i\}|/c(e)$, and the maximum relative congestion is $\lambda := \max_{e \in E} \lambda(e)$.

Several versions of the global routing problem have been studied. As a first approach, we will consider the task to find for each net i a Steiner tree T_i such that the maximum relative congestion is minimized. Later, in Section 32.6.2, we consider another version of the global routing problem: Find Steiner trees such that the maximum relative congestion is at most 1 and the total weighted netlength is minimized.

With the notation above, the global routing problem for minimizing the maximum relative congestion can be formulated as a mixed integer linear program:

$$\min \lambda$$

subject to

$$\sum_{i,T:e \in T \in \mathcal{T}_i} x_{i,T} \leq \lambda\, c(e) \quad \text{for} \quad e \in E$$

$$\sum_{T \in \mathcal{T}_i} x_{i,T} = 1 \quad \text{for} \quad i = 1, \ldots, k \qquad (32.1)$$

$$x_{i,T} \in \{0, 1\} \quad \text{for} \quad i = 1, \ldots, k;\ T \in \mathcal{T}_i$$

In this mixed integer linear program, the variable $x_{i,T}$ is 1, if and only if for net i the Steiner tree T is part of the solution.

The global routing problem is NP-complete as was shown by Kramer and van Leeuwen [10]. It is even NP-complete for the special case that all nets have only two terminals and the capacities are $c(e) = 1$ for all edges (edge-disjoint path problem), see Ref. [11].

The problem presented here is simplified compared to previous problem formulations. For example, it is possible to consider different wire widths for the nets and if the global routing graph models different layers, these wire widths may depend not only on the net but also on the edge. It is straight forward to adjust the algorithms presented here to incorporate additional factors that represent the wire width [9].

32.3 FRACTIONAL GLOBAL ROUTING AND LINEAR PROGRAMMING DUALITY

In this section, we consider the linear relaxation of the global routing problem introduced in the previous section. We then analyze and discuss the dual linear program.

The linear programming relaxation of the mixed integer linear program (Equation 32.1) is the following:

$$\min \lambda$$

subject to

$$\sum_{i,T:e \in T \in \mathcal{T}_i} x_{i,T} \leq \lambda c(e) \quad \text{for} \quad e \in E$$

$$\sum_{T \in \mathcal{T}_i} x_{i,T} = 1 \quad \text{for} \quad i = 1, \ldots, k \qquad (32.2)$$

$$x_{i,T} \geq 0 \quad \text{for} \quad i = 1, \ldots, k;\ T \in \mathcal{T}_i$$

We call the problem of solving this linear program the fractional global routing problem and denote the value of the optimum solution by λ^*. For any feasible solution of this linear program, the relative congestion of an edge e is given by $\lambda(e) := \sum_{i,T:e \in T \in \mathcal{T}_i} x_{i,T}/c(e)$. We will sometimes write a solution $(x_{i,T})_{i=1,\ldots,k;T \in \mathcal{T}_i}$ for the fractional global routing problem simply as a vector x.

The dual linear program of the linear program (Equation 32.2) is given by

$$\max \sum_{i=1}^{k} z_i$$

subject to

$$\sum_{e \in E} c(e) y_e = 1$$

$$\sum_{e \in T} y_e \geq z_i \quad \text{for} \quad i = 1, \ldots, k; T \in \mathcal{T}_i \tag{32.3}$$

$$y_e \geq 0 \quad \text{for} \quad e \in E$$

By linear programming duality (a comprehensive overview about linear programming can be found in the books by Chvátal [12] and Schrijver [13]), any feasible solution of the dual linear program provides a lower bound on the optimum solution for the primal linear program, and for the optimum solutions equality holds.

According to the second inequality in Equation 32.3, the value of z_i has to be smaller than the minimum length of all Steiner trees $T \in \mathcal{T}_i$ with respect to the length y_e for edge e. As $\sum_{i=1}^{k} z_i$ is maximized, z_i can be substituted by this minimum value, and by rescaling all lengths $y_e, e \in E$ by $1/\sum_{e \in E} c(e) y_e$ such that the first inequality in Equation 32.3 holds, we get the following theorem:

Theorem 1 *Given any nonnegative values y_e for the edges $e \in E$, the expression*

$$\frac{\sum_{i=1}^{k} \min_{T \in \mathcal{T}_i} \sum_{e \in T} y_e}{\sum_{e \in E} c(e) y_e}$$

provides a lower bound on the optimum value of the fractional global routing problem.

Moreover, there exist nonnegative values $y_e, e \in E$, such that the expression above is equal to the optimum value of the fractional global routing problem.

We briefly prove the weak duality, that the expression in Theorem 1 provides a lower bound on the minimum relative congestion. Let $\lambda, x_{i,T}$ for $i = 1, \ldots, k; T \in \mathcal{T}_i$ be a feasible solution of Equation 32.2 and $y_e, e \in E, z_i, i = 1, \ldots, k$ of Equation 32.3. Then, we get

$$\lambda \sum_{e \in E} c(e) y_e \geq \sum_{e \in E} \left(\sum_{i,T:e \in T \in \mathcal{T}_i} x_{i,T} \right) y_e = \sum_{i=1}^{k} \sum_{T \in \mathcal{T}_i} x_{i,T} \sum_{e \in T} y_e \geq \sum_{i=1}^{k} \min_{T \in \mathcal{T}_i} \sum_{e \in T} y_e \geq \sum_{i=1}^{k} z_i$$

These inequalities show that for any optimal solution of Equations 32.2 and 32.3 the following holds: First, an edge e can have a positive length $y_e > 0$ only if it has the maximum relative congestion, that is, $\lambda c(e) = \sum_{i,T:e \in T \in \mathcal{T}_i} x_{i,T}$. Second, every Steiner tree with positive $x_{i,T}$ has to be minimal with respect to the dual lengths y_e, that is, $\sum_{e \in T} y_e = \min_{T \in \mathcal{T}_i} \sum_{e \in T} y_e$.

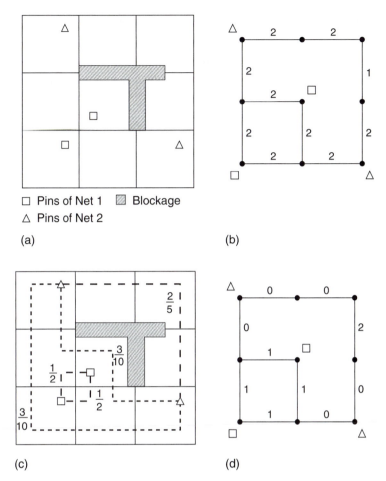

FIGURE 32.2 Example for fractional global routing with the dual solution: (a) the chip with some blockages and the pins for two nets, (b) the global routing graph with the capacitances $c(e)$, $e \in E$, (c) a fractional solution for the global routing problem minimizing the maximum relative congestion, and (d) an optimal dual solution y_e, $e \in E$ (without scaling).

Figure 32.2 shows an example for the fractional global routing problem with an optimal fractional global routing for the primal problem in Figure 32.2c in which the fractional numbers specify the values for the variables $x_{i,T}$, and an optimal solution for the dual problem in Figure 32.2d. We can verify Theorem 1: The maximum relative congestion is $\frac{2}{5}$ and five edges have a congestion equal to the maximum relative congestion. For the dual solution, the value of the expression $\sum_{e \in E} c(e) y_e$, which can be considered (speaking of flows) as the total volume available, is 10, and the value of the expression $\sum_{i=1}^{k} \min_{T \in T_i} \sum_{e \in T} y_e$, the total volume needed, is 4. Hence, the value of the lower bound in Theorem 1 is $\frac{2}{5}$ and the primal and dual solutions are optimal.

In this example, the length of one edge in the dual solution has to be twice as high as the length of all other edges that have a positive length. In most cases, the dual solution just consists of a solution in which the edges with positive length form a cut and all edges in the cut have the same positive length. It is possible to extend this example such that in any optimal dual solution the length of one edge is required to be an arbitrary multiple of any other length [14].

32.4 SIMPLEX ALGORITHM WITH COLUMN GENERATION

The first algorithm to solve the fractional global routing problem (Equation 32.2) by Hu and Shing in 1985 [15] used the simplex algorithm by Dantzig in 1951 [16] with column generation. This method finds an optimal solution even though it does not explicitly enumerate all the possible Steiner trees, nor has variables for all Steiner trees in memory. The method is limited in the size of the problem instances, and hence Hu and Shing propose a decomposition and cut-and-paste approach.

In this section, we show how the simplex algorithm with column generation is applied to the fractional global routing problem. The simplex method goes from vertex to vertex along edges of the polyhedron underlying the linear program until an optimal vertex is reached. For a complete description of the simplex method, we refer the reader to Refs. [12,13,17]. Interesting is that this method requires a subroutine that computes minimal Steiner trees for nets with respect to a nonnegative length function on the edges, a subroutine that is also required by the approximation schemes is presented later.

The linear program of the fractional global routing problem (Equation 32.2) can be rewritten with matrices as follows in a standard form for linear programs:

$$\min \left\{ \lambda : \begin{pmatrix} M & -c & I \\ N & 0 & 0 \end{pmatrix} \begin{pmatrix} x \\ \lambda \\ v \end{pmatrix} = \begin{pmatrix} 0 \\ 1 \end{pmatrix}, x, \lambda, v \geq 0 \right\} \tag{32.4}$$

In this linear program, the first constraint $\begin{pmatrix} M & -c & I \end{pmatrix} \begin{pmatrix} x \\ \lambda \\ v \end{pmatrix} = 0$ corresponds to the capacity constraints on the edges, the first inequality in Equation 32.2. Each row corresponds to an edge and each column of the matrix M corresponds to a Steiner tree T for a net i and is the incidence vector for the edges of the corresponding Steiner tree. The vector v contains slack variables for the equality constrains.

The second constraint $\begin{pmatrix} N & 0 & 0 \end{pmatrix} \begin{pmatrix} x \\ \lambda \\ v \end{pmatrix} = 1$ of the linear program ensures that the weights $x_{i,T}$ for each net i and all Steiner trees T for the net sum up to 1, the second inequality in Equation 32.2. The matrix N has one row for each net and each row is the incidence vector for all the Steiner trees of the corresponding net.

The dual of this linear program is as follows:

$$\max\{1z : zN \leq yM, yc \leq 1, y \geq 0\} \tag{32.5}$$

The simplex method requires an initial vertex of the polyhedron as a starting point and basis of the matrix $A = \begin{pmatrix} M & -c & I \\ N & 0 & 0 \end{pmatrix}$: for each net i, pick one Steiner tree T arbitrarily, set $x_{i,T} = 1$, and the corresponding column of $\begin{pmatrix} M \\ N \end{pmatrix}_{i,T}$ becomes part of the basis. Next, $\begin{pmatrix} -c \\ 0 \end{pmatrix}$ is part of the basis. We can assume that this column is always part of the basis, because λ does not become 0. Finally, for all edges that do not have the maximum relative congestion, the corresponding columns $\begin{pmatrix} I \\ 0 \end{pmatrix}_e$ are part of the basis. In case several edges have the maximum relative congestion, additional columns $\begin{pmatrix} I \\ 0 \end{pmatrix}_e$ are chosen until the basis has $|E| + k$ columns. We denote by $\left[\begin{pmatrix} M \\ N \end{pmatrix}_{\mathcal{B}_1} \begin{pmatrix} -c \\ 0 \end{pmatrix} \begin{pmatrix} 1 \\ 0 \end{pmatrix}_{\mathcal{B}_2} \right]$ the matrix that has all the columns for the basis. This matrix has the full rank and can be inverted. The simplex algorithm computes a dual solution as follows:

$$
(-y, z) = \left[\begin{pmatrix} M \\ N \end{pmatrix}_{B_1} \begin{pmatrix} -c \\ 0 \end{pmatrix} \begin{pmatrix} I \\ 0 \end{pmatrix}_{B_2} \right]^{-1} \begin{pmatrix} 0 \\ 1 \\ 0 \end{pmatrix}
$$

The algorithm checks if this is a feasible dual solution: We have $yc = 1$ because $\begin{pmatrix} -c \\ 0 \end{pmatrix}$ is part of the basis. Checking $y \geq 0$ is straight forward. The inequality $zN \leq yM$ is checked by computing a minimal Steiner tree for each net i with respect to the length function $y_e, e \in E$ and comparing this length with z_i. We will later see that the approximation algorithms require the same subroutine.

If (y, c) is a feasible dual solution, the vertex for the primal linear program is an optimal solution. Otherwise a column corresponding to a violated constraint becomes part of the basis, another column leaves the basis, and if the vertex was not degenerate, a new vertex is computed. The simplex algorithm terminates in the worst case, after exponentially many steps; however, in practice, it is reasonably fast for most applications.

We conclude this section by mentioning another linear programming approach for the global routing problem by Vannelli from 1989 [18]. In a first step, Vannelli reduces the complexity and size of the linear program by restricting the set of Steiner trees to only the minimal or near-minimal Steiner trees using also the result by Hanan, that a shortest rectilinear Steiner tree can be found in the grid induced by the terminals [19]. This restriction of the solution space may of course result in a suboptimal solution of the fractional global routing problem. Then he uses the Karmarkar algorithm [20], an interior point algorithm, which moves through the interior of the feasible region and reaches the optimal solution asymptotically. The runtime of the Karmarkar algorithm is polynomial, but it has the disadvantage compared to the simplex algorithm that it requires the complete linear program as input.

32.5 MULTICOMMODITY FLOW AND FRACTIONAL PACKING PROBLEMS

In this section, we give an overview about multicommodity flow and fractional packing problems. These problems are similar to the fractional global routing problem. In fact, the fractional packing problem is a generalization of the fractional global routing problem. There have been many advances in the field of approximation algorithms for multicommodity flow and fractional packing problems and we will apply these to the fractional global routing problem in the next section.

For this section, let $G = (V, E)$ be a directed graph with an edge utilization (or capacity) function $c : E \to \mathbf{R}_+$. For a vertex $v \in V$ we denote by $\delta^+(v)$ all outgoing edges of v and by $\delta^-(v)$ all incoming edges of v. Let s (the source) and t (the sink) be two specified vertices. An s–t flow is a function $f : E \to \mathbf{R}_+$, which fulfills the flow conservation rule $\sum_{e \in \delta^-(v)} f(e) = \sum_{e \in \delta^+(v)} f(e)$ for all $v \in V \setminus \{s, t\}$ and the capacity constraints $f(e) \leq c(e)$ for all $e \in E$. The value of an s–t flow f is defined as $\text{value}(f) := \sum_{e \in \delta^-(s)} f(e) - \sum_{e \in \delta^+(s)} f(e)$.

It is possible to decompose an s–t flow into at most $m = |E|$ flows along s–t paths: Given an s–t flow f of nonzero value, we find an s–t path P with $f(e) > 0$ for all $e \in P$. If we set $x := \min\{f(e) | e \in P\}$, the function $f' : E \to \mathbf{R}_+$ with $f'(e) = f(e) - x$ if $e \in P$ and $f'(e) = f(e)$ otherwise is again an s–t flow, but it has at least one edge e with $f(e) > 0$ less. Repeating this procedure until the value of the flow is 0 (flow along cycles may remain), we find $x_1, \dots, x_t$ and $P_1, \dots, P_t$ such that $\sum_{i:e \in P_i} x_i \leq f(e)$ for all $e \in E$.

For the multicommodity flow problem, several commodities are given. Each commodity i has a source s_i, a sink t_i, and a demand d_i. Let k be the number of commodities. The task of the maximum-concurrent multicommodity flow problem is to find an s_i–t_i flow f_i for each commodity i subject to the capacity constraints $\sum_{i=1}^k f_i(e) \leq c(e)$ for all $e \in E$ such that the total throughput μ is maximized. The value of each flow f_i is at least $\mu\, d_i$.

Other version of the multicommodity flow problem are the maximum multicommodity flow problem for which no demands are given and just the sum of the flows is maximized and the minimum-cost multicommodity flow problem for which a cost function for the edges is given in addition to the capacitances and the task is to minimize the total cost of all the flows.

It is possible to formulate the maximum concurrent flow problem as a linear program in which the variables are the flow values for the edges $f_i(e)$. The size of this linear program is polynomial in the size of the input, hence we can find an optimal solution in polynomial time using the ellipsoid method [21]. However, for large problem instances, it is computationally impossible to solve the linear program optimally.

Let $\mathcal{P}_i$ be the set of all $s_i - t_i$ paths. The following linear programming formulation makes use of the decomposition of flows into paths.

$$\max \mu$$

subject to

$$\sum_{i,P:e\in P\in\mathcal{P}_i} x_{i,P} \leq c(e) \quad \text{for} \quad e \in E$$

$$\sum_{P\in\mathcal{P}_i} x_{i,P} = \mu d_i \quad \text{for} \quad i = 1,\dots,k \tag{32.6}$$

$$x_{i,P} \geq 0 \quad \text{for} \quad i = 1,\dots,k; \ P \in \mathcal{P}_i$$

This linear program has exponentially many variables. Nevertheless, it is possible to compute an ϵ-approximate solution in polynomial time using this formulation implicitly as most of the variables $x_{i,P}$ can be 0.

There has been a series of papers about fully polynomial-time approximation schemes (FPTAS) for multicommodity flow problems in the last decade. An approximation scheme is a family of algorithms that compute a solution within a factor $(1 - \epsilon)$ of the optimal for any constant ϵ. If the running time can be bounded by a polynomial depending on the input size and $1/\epsilon$, then the scheme is called fully polynomial time.

All approximation algorithms maintain a flow and then iteratively improve it by computing single commodity flows or single commodity flows restricted to paths with respect to a cost function depending on the congestion.

The fractional packing problem is a generalization of the multicommodity flow problem. Given a convex set $P \subseteq \mathbf{R}^n$, a matrix $A \in \mathbf{R}_+^{m\times n}$, and a vector $b \in \mathbf{R}^m$, the task is to find an $x \in P$ with $Ax \leq b$. The approximation scheme, as for example by Plotkin et al. [4], requires a subroutine, which finds for a vector $c \in \mathbf{R}_+^n$, a vector $x \in P$ that minimizes $c^T x$.

The fractional global routing problem is a special case of the fractional packing problem: The convex set P is given by the constraints $\sum_{T\in\mathcal{T}_i} x_{i,T} = 1$ for $i = 1,\dots,k$ and $x_{i,T} \geq 0$ for $i = 1,\dots,k, T \in \mathcal{T}_i$ and the constraints $Ax \leq b$ represent the constraints $\sum_{i,T:e\in T\in\mathcal{T}_i} x_{i,T} \leq \lambda c(e)$ for $e \in E$. The subroutine needs to find a Steiner tree for each net minimizing a cost function and this cost function is the sum of some nonnegative cost of the edges of the Steiner tree.

32.6 FULLY POLYNOMIAL-TIME APPROXIMATION SCHEME FOR FRACTIONAL GLOBAL ROUTING

In this section, we present and describe a fully polynomial-time approximation scheme for the fractional global routing problem. Carden et al. in 1996 [22] were the first to apply a multicommodity flow approximation algorithm to global routing. They use the approximation algorithm by Shahrokhi and Matula [3]. The approximation scheme presented here, first published in Ref. [9], is based on the approximation scheme by Garg and Könemann [6], but also use ideas from Fleischer [7]. The approximation scheme iteratively finds Steiner trees with respect to dual lengths y_e, then adjusts the dual lengths just for the Steiner tree found.

32.6.1 APPROXIMATION SCHEME MINIMIZING THE RELATIVE CONGESTION

The approximation scheme that solves the fractional global routing problem for any given approximation ratio $1 + \epsilon_0$ is shown in Figure 32.3.

The variables are initialized in lines 1 and 2. The algorithm is called with the parameters ϵ and M. The proof of the theorem in this section will show which value to choose for these parameters to get the desired approximation ratio.

The algorithm runs through several phases. A phase starts in line 4 and ends in line 11. For each net i, a minimal Steiner tree $T \in \mathcal{T}_i$ with respect to lengths y_e, $e \in E$ is computed (line 7). For this Steiner tree, the variable $x_{i,T}$ is increased by 1 (line 8). To achieve that for each net i, the variables $x_{i,T}$, $T \in \mathcal{T}_i$, sum up to 1, all variables $x_{i,T}$ are divided by the total number of phases at the end of the algorithm. Finally, the dual variables y_e are increased for all edges used by the Steiner tree T (line 9). The variables are increased more if the net uses a greater fraction of the capacity of the edge.

Theorem 2 *If there exists a solution for the fractional global routing problem with maximum relative congestion at most 1, the algorithm finds a $(1 + \epsilon_0)$-approximation in*

$$O\left(\frac{1}{\epsilon_0^2 \lambda^*} \ln m\right)$$

phases, if $\epsilon := \min\left\{1, \frac{1}{4}\left[1 - \left(\frac{1}{1+\epsilon_0}\right)^{\frac{1}{3}}\right]\right\}$ and $M := \left(\frac{m}{1-\epsilon'}\right)^{\frac{1}{\epsilon'}}$ with $\epsilon' := \epsilon(1 + \epsilon)$.

Moreover, the variables $y_e, e \in E$, provide at some time during the algorithm a $(1 + \epsilon_0)$-approximation for the dual linear program.

The total number of phases of the algorithm depends on λ^*, but usually in the application of global routing λ^* is not arbitrarily small, for example, we can assume $\lambda^* \geq \frac{1}{2}$.

To prove this theorem, we follow the proof by Garg and Könemann [6], but also use parts from the proof by Fleischer [7] because we have a modified update rule for y_e.

Proof Let t be the total number of phases executed by the algorithm. We will prove that if the algorithm had stopped one phase before the last one, namely after $t - 1$ phases, the solution would have had the desired approximation ratio.

```
(1)   Set y_e := 1/c(e) for all e ∈ E.
(2)   Set x_{i,T} := 0 for i = 1, ..., k; T ∈ T_i.
(3)   While (∑_{e∈E} c(e) y_e < M)
(4)   begin
(5)     For i := 1 to k
(6)     begin
(7)       Find a minimal Steiner tree T ∈ T_i for net i
          with respect to length y_e, e ∈ E.
(8)       Set x_{i,T} := x_{i,T} + 1.
(9)       Set y_e := y_e e^{ε 1/c(e)} for all e ∈ T.
(10)    end
(11)  end
```

FIGURE 32.3 Approximation scheme for fractional global routing.

Let $y_e^{(p,i)}$ be the value of variable y_e, after net i has been considered in phase p and y_e has been increased in line 9, $y_e^{(0,0)} = \frac{1}{c(e)}$ and let $y_e^{(p)} := y_e^{(p,k)}$ be the value at the end of phase p. So we compute the minimal Steiner tree in phase p and iteration i with $y_e^{(p,i-1)}$ as edge lengths. At the beginning, we have

$$\sum_{e \in E} c(e) y_e^{(0)} = \sum_{e \in E} c(e) \frac{1}{c(e)} = m \tag{32.7}$$

When the dual variables y_e are increased in line 9 after a Steiner tree T has been found, the expression $\sum_{e \in E} c(e) y_e$ increases, and we have

$$\sum_{e \in E} c(e) y_e^{(p,i)} = \sum_{e \notin T} c(e) y_e^{(p,i-1)} + \sum_{e \in T} c(e) y_e^{(p,i-1)} e^{\epsilon \frac{1}{c(e)}}$$

$$\leq \sum_{e \notin T} c(e) y_e^{(p,i-1)} + \sum_{e \in T} c(e) y_e^{(p,i-1)} \left\{ 1 + \epsilon \frac{1}{c(e)} + \epsilon^2 \left[\frac{1}{c(e)} \right]^2 \right\}$$

For the last inequality, we used $e^x \leq 1 + x + x^2$ for $0 \leq x \leq 1$. We can assume $c(e) \geq 1$ and because $\epsilon \leq 1$ we have $x = \epsilon \frac{1}{c(e)} \leq 1$. Hence,

$$\sum_{e \in E} c(e) y_e^{(p,i)} \leq \sum_{e \notin T} c(e) y_e^{(p,i-1)} + \sum_{e \in T} c(e) y_e^{(p,i-1)} \left[1 + \epsilon(1+\epsilon) \frac{1}{c(e)} \right]$$

$$= \sum_{e \in E} c(e) y_e^{(p,i-1)} + \epsilon(1+\epsilon) \sum_{e \in T} y_e^{(p,i-1)}$$

Because y_e increases only during the algorithm, for the Steiner tree T found in line 7, we have

$$\sum_{e \in T} y_e^{(p,i-1)} \leq \min_{T \in T_i} \sum_{e \in T} y_e^{(p)}$$

which means that at the end of phase p, we get

$$\sum_{e \in E} c(e) y_e^{(p)} \leq \sum_{e \in E} c(e) y_e^{(p-1)} + \epsilon' \sum_{i=1}^{k} \min_{T \in T_i} \sum_{e \in T} y_e^{(p)} \tag{32.8}$$

where $\epsilon' := \epsilon(1+\epsilon)$. By linear programming duality (Theorem 1), the expression

$$\lambda_{lb}^{(p)} := \frac{\sum_{i=1}^{k} \min_{T \in T_i} \sum_{e \in T} y_e^{(p)}}{\sum_{e \in E} c(e) y_e^{(p)}}$$

is a lower bound on the maximum relative congestion, that is, $\lambda_{lb}^{(p)} \leq \lambda^*$.

With this, inequality (Equation 32.8) can be rewritten as

$$\sum_{e \in E} c(e) y_e^{(p)} \leq \sum_{e \in E} c(e) y_e^{(p-1)} + \epsilon' \lambda_{lb}^{(p)} \sum_{e \in E} c(e) y_e^{(p)}$$

which can be transformed to

$$\sum_{e \in E} c(e) y_e^{(p)} \leq \frac{1}{1 - \epsilon' \lambda_{lb}^{(p)}} \sum_{e \in E} c(e) y_e^{(p-1)}$$

If we set $\lambda_{\text{lb}} := \max_{p=1,\dots,t} \lambda_{\text{lb}}^{(p)}$, we get with Equation 32.7

$$
\begin{aligned}
\sum_{e \in E} c(e) y_e^{(p)} &\leq \frac{m}{(1 - \epsilon' \lambda_{\text{lb}})^p} \\
&= \frac{m}{(1 - \epsilon' \lambda_{\text{lb}})} \left(1 + \frac{\epsilon' \lambda_{\text{lb}}}{1 - \epsilon' \lambda_{\text{lb}}} \right)^{p-1} \\
&\leq \frac{m}{(1 - \epsilon')} \left(1 + \frac{\epsilon' \lambda_{\text{lb}}}{1 - \epsilon'} \right)^{p-1} \\
&\leq \frac{m}{(1 - \epsilon')} e^{\frac{\epsilon' \lambda_{\text{lb}} (p-1)}{1 - \epsilon'}}
\end{aligned}
\tag{32.9}
$$

For the last inequality, $1 + x \leq e^x$ for $x \geq 0$ is used.

An upper bound on the relative congestion of an edge e can now be derived: Suppose edge e is used s times by some tree during the first $t - 1$ phases, and let the jth increment in the relative congestion of edge e be $a_j := \frac{1}{c(e)}$ for the appropriate i. After rescaling the variables $x_{i,T}$, the relative congestion of edge e is $\lambda(e) = \sum_{j=1}^{s} a_j/(t - 1)$. Because $y_e^{(0)} = \frac{1}{c(e)}$ and $y_e^{(t-1)} < \frac{M}{c(e)}$ (because the condition in line 4 still holds before the last phase is executed) and because

$$
y_e^{(t-1)} = \frac{1}{c(e)} \prod_{j=1}^{s} e^{\epsilon a_j}
$$

we get

$$
\frac{1}{c(e)} \prod_{j=1}^{s} e^{\epsilon a_j} \leq \frac{M}{c(e)}
$$

It follows that

$$
e^{\epsilon \sum_{j=1}^{s} a_j} \leq M
$$

and hence

$$
\lambda(e) = \frac{\sum_{j=1}^{s} a_j}{t - 1} \leq \frac{\ln M}{\epsilon(t - 1)}
\tag{32.10}
$$

Because $\sum_{e \in E} c(e) y_e^{(t)} \geq M$, solving inequality (Equation 32.9) with $p = t$ for λ_{lb} gives a lower bound on the optimum solution value:

$$
\lambda_{\text{lb}} \geq \frac{1 - \epsilon'}{\epsilon'(t - 1)} \ln \left[\frac{M}{m} (1 - \epsilon') \right]
$$

from which together with Equation 32.10, we get an upper bound on the approximation ratio ρ:

$$
\frac{\max_{e \in E} \lambda(e)}{\lambda_{\text{lb}}} \leq \frac{\frac{\ln M}{\epsilon(t-1)}}{\frac{1-\epsilon'}{\epsilon'(t-1)} \ln \left[\frac{M}{m} (1 - \epsilon') \right]} = \frac{\epsilon'}{(1 - \epsilon') \epsilon} \frac{\ln M}{\ln \left[\frac{M}{m} (1 - \epsilon') \right]}
$$

If M is now chosen to be $M := \left(\frac{m}{1 - \epsilon'} \right)^{\frac{1}{\epsilon'}}$, we get

$$
\frac{\ln M}{\ln \left[\frac{M}{m} (1 - \epsilon') \right]} = \frac{1}{1 - \epsilon'}
$$

such that

$$\rho \leq \frac{\epsilon'}{(1 - \epsilon')^2 \epsilon} = \frac{\epsilon(1 + \epsilon)}{[1 - \epsilon(1 + \epsilon)]^2 \epsilon} = \frac{(1 + \epsilon)}{[1 - \epsilon(1 + \epsilon)]^2}$$

If $\epsilon \leq 1, 1 + \epsilon \leq 2$, we get

$$\rho \leq \frac{(1 + \epsilon)}{(1 - 4\epsilon)^2} \leq \frac{1}{(1 - 4\epsilon)^3} \quad \left(\begin{array}{l} \text{because} \\ 1 + \epsilon \leq \frac{1}{1-\epsilon} \leq \frac{1}{1-4\epsilon} \end{array} \right)$$

If ϵ is chosen such that $\frac{1}{(1-4\epsilon)^3} \leq 1 + \epsilon_0$, so we choose

$$\epsilon = \min\left\{ 1, \frac{1}{4}\left[1 - \left(\frac{1}{1+\epsilon_0}\right)^{\frac{1}{4}}\right] \right\}$$

we get $\rho \leq 1 + \epsilon_0$. After all, we have $\epsilon = O(\epsilon_0)$ and also $\epsilon' = O(\epsilon_0)$.
Because $\max_{e \in E} \lambda(e) \geq \lambda^*$, we get from Equation 32.10 that

$$\lambda^* \leq \frac{\ln M}{\epsilon(t - 1)}$$

which means that the maximum number of phases is bounded by

$$t \leq 1 + \frac{\ln M}{\lambda^* \epsilon} = 1 + \frac{1}{\epsilon \epsilon' \lambda^*} \ln\left(\frac{m}{1 - \epsilon'}\right)$$

The last expression can be bounded by $O(\frac{1}{\epsilon_0^2 \lambda^*} \ln m)$.

It is important that the actual implementation does not have one single variable $x_{i,T}$ for every possible Steiner tree, because there are exponentially many. A variable is only needed for a Steiner tree that was at some point during the algorithm the minimal Steiner tree and found by the algorithm in line 7 and for which the variable $x_{i,T}$ is greater than 0.

To simplify the presentation of the algorithm and the proof we have omitted one idea that gives additional runtime improvements. The algorithm in Figure 32.3 computes a Steiner tree for all the nets in every phase. However, this is not necessary. The length (with respect to y_e) of a newly computed Steiner tree is stored and then in the following phases a new Steiner tree is computed for the net only if the length of the Steiner tree has increased by more than a certain factor (depending on ϵ). It can be shown that still any approximation ratio can be achieved [9]. This idea was used by Fleischer [7] to reduce the theoretical runtime of the maximum multicommodity flow problem.

Another practical speedup can be achieved with the Newton method as used in Refs. [5,9]: After p phases, the last Steiner tree computed has a weight of $\frac{1}{p}$ in the current solution where all previously computed Steiner trees have a total weight of $\frac{p-1}{p}$. After each Steiner tree is computed, the Newton method is used to compute a new weight for the new Steiner tree with respect to the other Steiner trees minimizing an expression similar to $\psi = \sum_{e \in E} e^{\alpha \lambda(e)}$.

Another advantage of this approximation algorithm (compared to some rip-up and reroute algorithms) is that not only the maximum relative congestion is minimized, but also that the congestion of the edges is distributed and that the algorithm works toward a solution that is optimal in a well-defined sense—the vector of the relative congestion of the edges sorted in nonincreasing order is minimal by lexicographic order [9]. Reducing the congestion beyond the maximum relative congestion on some edges can speed up the local router and also improves the signal integrity.

32.6.2 APPROXIMATION SCHEME MINIMIZING THE TOTAL WEIGHTED NETLENGTH

The approximation scheme described in Section 32.6.1 can be modified such that the total weighted netlength is considered and minimized subject to the condition that the maximum relative congestion of the edges is at most 1. We follow the approach by Garg and Könemann [6] for the minimum-cost multicommodity flow problem.

In addition to the capacity for each edge $e = \{u, v\}$, the L_1-length $l(e)$ is given, that is, for an edge in x- or y-direction as the distance between the midpoints of the tiles corresponding to u and v. For each net i, a weight $g_i \in \mathbf{R}_+$ is given. We would like to minimize the total weighted netlength, which is given by the expression $\sum_{i=1}^{k} g_i \sum_{T \in T_i} \left[\sum_{e \in T} l(e) \right] x_{i,T}$.

Let L be a target for the total weighted netlength. Then the constraint

$$\sum_{i=1}^{k} g_i \sum_{T \in T_i} \left[\sum_{e \in T} l(e) \right] x_{i,T} \leq \lambda L \qquad (32.11)$$

is added to the linear program (Equation 32.2) of the fractional global routing problem. This constraint is very similar to the capacity constraints for the edges, the first constraint in (Equation 32.2), and the algorithm can be modified to treat this new constraint in the same way as the capacity constraints. To minimize the total weighted netlength, we want L to be as small as possible such that λ, the maximum relative congestion, is at most 1. This is achieved by binary search over L. In practice, the netlength in the final solution is only slightly higher compared to the minimum netlength if each Steiner tree is as short as possible ignoring capacities. This gives a good estimate for L.

For the dual of the linear program, an additional dual variable y_L for the constraint in Equation 32.11 is needed. The dual linear program is given by

$$\max \sum_{i=1}^{k} z_i$$

subject to

$$\sum_{e \in E} c(e) y_e + L y_L = 1$$

$$\sum_{e \in T} [y_e + g_i l(e) y_L] \geq z_i \quad \text{for} \quad i = 1, \ldots, k; \ T \in T_i$$

$$y_e \geq 0 \quad \text{for} \quad e \in E$$

$$y_L \geq 0$$

Figure 32.4 shows the modified approximation scheme. During the algorithm, minimal Steiner trees are computed with respect to the length $y_e + g_i l(e) y_L$ for net i and edge $e \in E$ (line 7). The length of an edge e is the sum of the congestion cost y_e and the wirelength cost $g_i l(e) y_L$ of the edge.

With the assumption that $g_i \sum_{e \in T} l(e) \leq L$ for each Steiner tree T found in line 7 (which usually holds for the global routing problem), the proof in Section 32.6.1 can be extended to show that a $(1 + \epsilon_0)$–approximation for the fractional global routing problem with the constraint in Equation 32.11 is found by the algorithm in Figure 32.4 in $O\left(\frac{1}{\epsilon_0^2 \lambda^*} \ln m \right)$ phases. If for some Steiner tree T we have

(1)   Set $y_e := \frac{1}{c(e)}$ for all $e \in E$ and $y_L := \frac{1}{L}$.
(2)   Set $x_{i,T} := 0$ for $i = 1, \ldots, k$; $T \in T_i$.
(3)   While $\left(\sum_{e \in E} c(e) y_e + L y_L < M \right)$
(4)   **begin**
(5)   For $i := 1$ to k
(6)   **begin**
(7)   Find a minimal Steiner tree $T \in T_i$ for net i
          with respect to lengths $(y_e + g_i l(e) y_L)$, $e \in E$.
(8)   Set $x_{i,T} := x_{i,T} + 1$.
(9)   Set $y_e := y_e e^{\epsilon \frac{1}{c(e)}}$ for all $e \in T$.
        Set $Y_L := y_L e^{\epsilon \frac{g_i \sum_{e \in T} l(e)}{L}}$
(10)   **end**
(11) **end**

FIGURE 32.4   Approximation scheme for fractional global routing optimizing the total weighted netlength.

$g_i \sum_{e \in T} l(e) > L$, variable $x_{i,T}$ in line 9 is increased only by $L / [g_i \sum_{e \in T} l(e)]$, and another Steiner tree has to be found for the same net until the total increment of $\sum_{T \in T_i} x_{i,T}$ is 1 (for details see Ref. [6]).

32.7   RANDOMIZED ROUNDING

So far we have focused on solving the linear relaxation of the global routing problem. To come from a fractional solution of the global routing problem to an integer solution it is necessary to choose one Steiner tree for each net. This is done by randomized rounding, a technique developed by Raghavan and Thompson [1,2], which we present in this section.

The technique of randomized rounding can be summarized as follows:

RULE 32.1   *Independently for each net i choose randomly one Steiner tree out of the set T_i. The probability to choose Steiner tree T is $x_{i,T}$.*

The expected value for the relative congestion of an edge or of the maximum relative congestion after randomized rounding is equal to the relative congestion of the fractional solution.

Randomized rounding may increase the relative congestion of some edges. However, it is possible to prove that there is a positive probability that the relative congestion does not increase by more than by a certain factor, and this factor decreases with increasing capacity of the edges. We will present these results with the proofs.

In the following, we denote the probability of an event by $P[\cdot]$ and the expectation of a random variable X by $E[X]$. The following lemma was proved in this version by Raghavan and Spencer [23], and gives a variation of Chernoff's bound [24]. The lemma bounds the tail of the distribution of the sum of independent random variable in $[0,1]$. To simplify the notation, we use $b(\epsilon) := (1 + \epsilon) \ln(1 + \epsilon) - \epsilon$. For small values of ϵ, $b(\epsilon)$ is approximately $\frac{1}{2} \epsilon^2$.

Lemma 1   *Let $X_1, \ldots, X_t$ be independent random variables in $[0, 1]$. Let $X := \sum_{p=1}^{t} X_p$, $\mu > \sum_{p=1}^{t} E[X_p]$ and $\epsilon > 0$. Then*

$$P[X \geq (1 + \epsilon)\mu] \leq \frac{1}{e^{b(\epsilon)\mu}}$$

Proof   We first consider the case $\mu = \sum_{p=1}^{t} E[X_p]$. Using (1) the Markov inequality, (2) the independence of the random variables $X_1, \ldots, X_t$, (3) $(1 + \epsilon)^x \leq 1 + \epsilon x$ for $0 \leq x \leq 1$, and (4) $1 + x \leq e^x$, we compute

$$P[X \geq (1+\epsilon)\mu] = P[(1+\epsilon)^X \geq (1+\epsilon)^{(1+\epsilon)\mu}]$$

$$= P\left[(1+\epsilon)^{\sum_{p=1}^{t} X_p} \geq (1+\epsilon)^{(1+\epsilon)\mu}\right]$$

$$= P\left[\frac{\Pi_{p=1}^{t}(1+\epsilon)^{X_p}}{(1+\epsilon)^{(1+\epsilon)\mu}} \geq 1\right] \overset{(1)}{\leq} E\left[\frac{\Pi_{p=1}^{t}(1+\epsilon)^{X_p}}{(1+\epsilon)^{(1+\epsilon)\mu}}\right] \overset{(2)}{=} \frac{\Pi_{p=1}^{t}(1+\epsilon)^{E[X_p]}}{(1+\epsilon)^{(1+\epsilon)\mu}}$$

$$\overset{(3)}{\leq} \frac{\Pi_{p=1}^{t}(1+\epsilon E[X_p])}{(1+\epsilon)^{(1+\epsilon)\mu}} \overset{(4)}{\leq} \frac{\Pi_{p=1}^{t} e^{\epsilon E[X_p]}}{(1+\epsilon)^{(1+\epsilon)\mu}}$$

$$= \frac{e^{\epsilon \sum_{p=1}^{t} E[X_p]}}{(1+\epsilon)^{(1+\epsilon)\mu}} = \frac{e^{\epsilon\mu}}{(1+\epsilon)^{(1+\epsilon)\mu}} = \frac{1}{e^{b(\epsilon)\mu}}$$

The lemma also holds if $\mu > E[X]$. We add additional independent random variables in $[0,1]$ to X until $\mu = E[X]$. This only increases $P[X \geq (1+\epsilon)\mu]$.

For an edge $e \in E$, we denote the relative congestion after randomized rounding with respect to Rule 32.1 by $\hat{\lambda}(e)$. The probability that the relative congestion of one edge increases by at least a factor of $(1+\epsilon)$ can be bounded as follows:

Lemma 2 $P[\hat{\lambda}(e) \geq (1+\epsilon)\lambda] \leq \frac{1}{e^{b(\epsilon)c(e)\lambda}}$

Proof   We apply Lemma 1: for $i = 1, \ldots, k$, let the random variable X_i be 1 if for net i a Steiner tree is chosen that uses edge e, and zero otherwise. The variables $X_1, \ldots, X_k$ are independent random variables in $[0,1]$ and with $X := \sum_{i=1}^{k} X_p$, we have $E[X] = c(e)\lambda$. Then, we have $P[\hat{\lambda}(e) \geq (1+\epsilon)\lambda] = P[X \geq (1+\epsilon)c(e)\lambda] \leq \frac{1}{e^{b(\epsilon)c(e)\lambda}}$.

Finally, the probability of the overall failure, that is, the probability that any one edge has a relative congestion of at least $(1+\epsilon)\lambda$ can now be bounded. Let $\hat{\lambda} := \max_{e \in E} \hat{\lambda}(e)$ be the maximum relative congestion after randomized rounding and $C := \min_{e \in E} c(e)$.

Theorem 3

$$P[\hat{\lambda} \geq (1+\epsilon)\lambda] \leq \sum_{e \in E} \frac{1}{e^{b(\epsilon)c(e)\lambda}} \leq \frac{m}{e^{b(\epsilon)C\lambda}}$$

If ϵ is chosen so large that the expression $\frac{m}{e^{b(\epsilon)C\lambda}}$ is smaller than 1, then the probability of success, $\hat{\lambda} < (1+\epsilon)\lambda$, is positive. Repeating the randomized rounding experiment increases the probability that one of the experiments is successful.

It is possible to derandomize this random experiment. Assuming that for some nets a Steiner tree has already been chosen and that for each remaining net a Steiner tree is chosen according to Rule 32.1, the probability of failure is computed. This is a pessimistic estimator. It is then possible to choose one Steiner tree for the next net such that the probability of failure does not increase. Because the total probability was smaller than 1 at the beginning, in the end this probability is also smaller than 1, and because the Steiner trees for all nets are chosen, the final solution has to be a success.

32.8   EXTENSIONS

The approach of solving a fractional global routing problem and then applying randomized rounding has been used successfully in practice and has been extended to consider additional tasks and objectives.

Albrecht et al. [25] consider the problem of finding global routes that need to buffered. In addition, the sizes of the buffers and the widths of the wires are optimized. Some areas on the chip may be partially or completely blocked and buffers cannot be placed in these areas. As the capacity constraints for the edges in the global routing graph ensure that not too many wires cross the boundaries between two adjacent global routing tiles, similar constraints ensure that not too many buffers are placed in one global routing tile.

Vygen [26] considers the coupling capacitance and minimizes the total power consumption while ensuring the timing constraints for individual nets and certain paths. A Steiner tree for a net is characterized not only by the edges of the global routing graph, but also each edge of the Steiner tree has a continuous parameter specifying the spacing to each side of the final route. It is assumed that the coupling capacitance decreases linearly with the spacing. The timing constraints are ensured by bounding the weighted capacitance for subsets of the nets, a constraint similar to the constraint that bounds the total weighted wirelength. While more space decreases the coupling capacitance also more routing resources are used. The problem can be formulated as a fractional packing problem of infinitely many Steiner trees, infinitely many because of the continuous spacing parameters. Because the capacitance depends linearly on the spacing, every edge of the Steiner tree that minimizes the cost function with respect to the dual variables either has the maximum or minimum spacing. The task of the subroutine is still to find a Steiner minimal tree in the grid graph with respect to a nonuniform length function.

Müller [27] describes a parallel multithreaded implementation of the approximation scheme. He shows that it is possible to update the dual variables at the end of each phase for all nets instead of updating them immediately after a Steiner tree is found. The set of nets is split into subsets and each thread computes the minimal Steiner trees for one subset in the global routing graph.

32.9 CONCLUSION

This chapter is about the global routing problem, and specifically about algorithms solving the linear programming relaxation. The complexity of the linear program is enormous and hence it is not possible to solve the linear program optimally. The linear programming relaxation for global routing is a special case of a fractional packing problem and is similar to the multicommodity flow problem. We showed that the approximation algorithm for the multicommodity flow problem can be applied to the fractional global routing problem. A final integer solution is derived by randomized rounding. This approach has been used successfully in practice and has been extended to consider additional constraints and objectives.

The approach of the linear relaxation and randomized rounding is general and it may be possible to apply it to other combinatorial optimization problems in physical design. For global routing, the approach works well because the capacities of the edges are relatively large and hence randomized rounding does not disturb the solution much.

REFERENCES

1. P. Raghavan and C. D. Thompson, Randomized rounding: A technique for provably good algorithms and algorithmic proofs, *Combinatorica*, 7(4): 365–374, 1987.
2. P. Raghavan and C. D. Thompson, Multiterminal global routing: A deterministic approximation, *Algorithmica*, 6: 73–82, 1991.
3. F. Shahrokhi and D. W. Matula, The maximum concurrent flow problem, *Journal of the Association for Computing Machinery*, 37: 24–31, 1990.
4. S. Plotkin, D. Shmoys, and E. Tardos, Fast approximation algorithms for fractional packing and covering problems, *Mathematics of Operations Research*, 20: 257–301, 1995.
5. A. V. Goldberg, J. D. Oldham, S. Plotkin, and C. Stein, An implementation of a combinatorial approximation algorithm for minimum-cost multicommodity flow, in *Integer Programming and Combinatorial Optimization (6th International IPCO Conference)*, Houston, TX, pp. 338–352, 1998.
6. N. Garg and J. Könemann, Faster and simpler algorithms for multicommodity flow and other fractional packing problems, in *Proceedings of the 39th Annual Symposium on Foundations of Computer Science*, Palo Alto, CA, pp. 300–309, 1998.

7. L. K. Fleischer, Approximating fractional multicommodity flow independent of the number of commodities, *SIAM Journal on Discrete Mathematics*, 13(4): 505–520, 2000. (FOCS 1999).
8. G. Karakostas, Faster approximation schemes for fractional multicommodity flow problems, in *Proceedings of the 13th Annual ACM-SIAM Symposium on Discrete Algorithms*, San Francisco, CA, pp. 166–173, 2002.
9. C. Albrecht, Global routing by new approximation algorithms for multicommodity flow, *IEEE Transactions on Computer-Aided Design of Integrated Circuits and Systems*, 20: 622–632, May 2001. (ISPD 2000).
10. M. R. Kramer and J. van Leeuwen, The complexity of wire routing and finding minimum area layouts for arbitrary VLSI circuits, in *Advances in Computing Research, Vol. 2: VLSI Theory*, F. P. Preparata (Eds), JAI Press, Greenwhich, CT, pp. 192–146, 1984.
11. J. Vygen, Disjoint paths, Technical Report 94816, Research Institute for Discrete Mathematics, University of Bonn, Bonn, Germany, 1994.
12. V. Chvátal, *Linear Programming*. New York: Freeman, 1983.
13. A. Schrijver, *Theory of Linear and Integer Programming*. Chichester, United Kingdom: Wiley, 1986.
14. J. Werber, *Das Multicommodity-Flow-Problem und seine Anwendung im Global Routing*. Diplomarbeit, Universität Bonn, Bonn, Germany, 2000.
15. T. C. Hu and M. T. Shing, A decomposition algorithm for circuit routing, in *VLSI Circuit Layout: Theory and Design*, T. C. Hu and E. S. Kuh (Eds), IEEE Press, pp. 144–152, 1985.
16. G. B. Dantzig, Maximization of a linear function of variables subject to linear inequalities, in *Activity Analysis of Production and Allocation*, Tj. C. Koopmans (Eds), Wiley, NY, pp. 399–347, 1951.
17. H. T. Jongen, K. Meer, and E. Triesch, *Optimization Theory*. Norwell, MA: Kluwer Academic Publishers, 2004.
18. A. Vannelli, An adaptation of the interior point method for solving the global routing problem, *IEEE Transactions on Computer-Aided Design of Integrated Circuits and Systems*, 10: pp. 193–203, February 1991. (CICCC 1989).
19. M. Hanan, On Steiner's problem with rectilinear distance, *Soviet Mathematics Doklady*, 14(2): 255–265, 1966.
20. N. Karmarkar, A new polynomial-time algorithm for linear programming, *Combinatorica*, 4: 373–395, 1984.
21. L. G. Khachiyan, A polynomial-time algorithm in linear programming, *Soviet Mathematics Doklady*, 20: 191–194, 1979.
22. R. C. Carden IV, J. Li, and C. -K. Cheng, A global router with a theoretical bound on the optimum solution, *IEEE Transactions on Computer-Aided Design of Integrated Circuits and Systems*, 15: 208–216, February 1996.
23. P. Raghavan, Probabilistic construction of deterministic algorithms: Approximating packing integer programs, *Journal of Computer and System Sciences*, 37: 130–143, 1988.
24. H. Chernoff, A measure of asymptotic efficiency for tests based on the sum of observations, *Annals of Mathematical Statistics*, 23: 493–509, 1952.
25. C. Albrecht, A. Kahng, I. Măndoiu, and A. Zelikovsky, Multicommodity flow algorithms for buffered global routing, in *Handbook of Approximation Algorithms and Metaheuristics*, T. F. Gonzales (Ed.), Boca Raton, FL: Chapman & Hall/CRC, pp. 80.1–80.18, 2007. (ASPDAC 2002).
26. J. Vygen, Near-optimum global routing with coupling, delay bounds, and power consumption, in *Integer Programming and Combinatorial Optimization (10th International IPCO Conference)*, LNCS 3064, G. Nemhauser and D. Bienstock (Eds.). Berlin, Germany: Springer, pp. 308–324, 2004.
27. D. Müller, Optimizing yield in global routing, in *Digest of Technical Papers of the IEEE/ACM International Conference on Computer-Aided Design*. San Jose, CA, November 2006.

33 Global Interconnect Planning

Cheng-Kok Koh, Evangeline F.Y. Young,
and Yao-Wen Chang

CONTENTS

With the growing dominance of global interconnects on circuit performance, it is desirable to optimize interconnects as early as possible. Recall from Chapter 26 that buffer insertion is generally considered the most effective and popular technique to reduce interconnect delay, especially for global signals. A buffer is composed of two inverters while a repeater is referred to as a buffer or an inverter. To simplify the discussions, we shall use buffer and repeater interchangeably throughout this chapter.

As hundreds of thousands of buffers may be inserted for modern high-performance VLSI designs, it is imperative to plan for the buffer positions as early as possible to ensure timing closure and design convergence. In this chapter, we shall first present the enabling concept of buffer planning, namely, the feasible region in which a buffer can be inserted such that the timing constraint is met. Following a description of two fundamental approaches to buffer planning, taking into account only timing constraints, we address also other important design issues such as noise constraints and routability in buffer planning. When buffer insertion fails to meet the timing constraints, pipelining of global interconnects with flip-flops becomes necessary. We devote a section on flip-flop and buffer planning to deal with the challenges that arise from the additional latency introduced by interconnect pipelining.

33.1 BUFFER PLANNING BASICS

Some VLSI designs may not allow buffers to be inserted inside a circuit block as they consume silicon resource and require connections to the power/ground network. Consequently, buffers are placed in channels and dead spaces of a floorplan, and they are often clustered to form buffer blocks between existing circuit blocks of the floorplan, which inevitably increases the chip area [1]. It is thus desirable to carefully plan for the buffer blocks during/after floorplanning to minimize the area overhead and facilitate routing. This is known as buffer block planning.

However, the existence of buffer blocks imposes more design constraints. Because buffers connect global nets, the routing regions where buffer blocks are located might be congested. Furthermore, buffers might be placed in poor locations because buffers are clustered into blocks and thus the best location for a buffer is forbidden. A remedy to this deficiency is to distribute buffers more uniformly in a chip, so as to naturally spread out global nets. This approach looks promising in handling the aforementioned problems with wire congestion and buffer blockages. In contrast to the buffer block planning methodology, Alpert et al. [2] proposed the buffer site methodology. The methodology allocates a buffering resource within a block by inserting a buffer site that can accommodate buffers (or other logic gates if the buffer site is not used for buffering). For buffer site planning, we shall plan for the buffers during/after floorplanning such that the given buffer sites can accommodate buffers and the routing timing and congestion constraints are satisfied.

To determine the optimal location for buffer insertion, we shall first consider the feasible region (FR) for a buffer, which is referred to as the region where the buffer can be placed to satisfy the timing constraint. Figure 33.1 shows respective FRs for inserting (a) one buffer and (b) multiple buffers into a net between a source and a sink, where the FRs are shaded.

The concepts of the feasible region come in two forms. Cong, Kong, and Pan first defined in Ref. [1] the feasible region for buffer insertion to be the region where a buffer could be placed to satisfy a target timing constraint, assuming that all the remaining buffers were placed in their optimal positions. In contrast, Sarkar and Koh [3] introduced the idea of independent feasible region (IFR) for buffer insertion, which was defined as the region where a buffer could be placed such that the timing constraint of the net was satisfied, assuming that the other buffers were also placed within their respective independent feasible regions.

Before presenting the analytical formulas for computing the feasible regions, we shall first introduce the notation and delay model that will be used throughout this chapter. Each driver/buffer is modeled as a switch-level RC circuit [4] and each wire is modeled as a π-type circuit, as shown in Figure 33.2. We use the Elmore delay model [5] covered in Chapter 3 for delay computation. The notation for the physical parameters of wire and buffer is listed in Table 33.1.

Given a wire segment of length l with driver output resistance R and sink capacitance C, the Elmore delay of this segment is given by

$$D(R, C, l) = \left(\frac{rc}{2}\right) l^2 + (Rc + rC)l + RC.$$

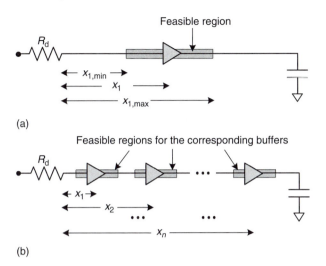

FIGURE 33.1 Feasible regions for buffer insertion. (a) Single-buffer insertion and (b) multiple-buffer insertion. (From Cong, J., Kong, T., and Pan, Z., *IEEE Trans. VLSI Sys.*, 9, 929, 2001 (ICCAD 1999).)

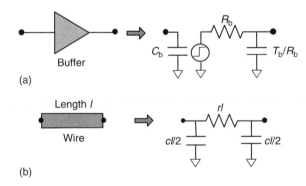

FIGURE 33.2 Buffer and wire model. (a) Switch-level buffer model and (b) wire model.

Using the preceding expression, the Elmore delay of a single-source, single-sink net (i.e., two-pin net) N of length L with n buffers can be computed as

$$D^N(x_1, x_2, \ldots x_n, L) = D(R_d, C_b, x_1) + D(R_b, C_s, L - x_n) + \sum_{i=1}^{n-1} D(R_b, C_b, x_{i+1} - x_i) + nT_b,$$

where
  R_d is the driver resistance
  C_s is the sink capacitance
  x_i is the location of the ith buffer

For convenience, we reexpress the optimal locations of the n buffers for the delay minimization of a net [6], presented in Chapter 26, as follows:

$$x_i^* = (i - 1)y_L^* + x_L^* \quad i \in \{1, 2, \ldots n\},$$

TABLE 33.1

Parameters of Wire and Buffer

Parameter	Description
r	Wire resistance per unit length
c	Wire capacitance per unit length
T_b	Intrinsic buffer delay
C_b	Buffer input capacitance
R_b	Buffer output resistance

where

$$x_L^* = \frac{1}{n+1}\left(L + \frac{n(R_b - R_d)}{r} + \frac{(C_s - C_b)}{c}\right) \quad \text{and} \quad y_L^* = \frac{1}{n+1}\left(L - \frac{(R_b - R_d)}{r} + \frac{(C_s - C_b)}{c}\right).$$

We denote the optimal delay for the net **N**, of length L, with n buffers by

$$D_{\text{opt}}^{\mathbf{N}}(n, L) = D^{\mathbf{N}}(x_1^*, x_2^*, \ldots\ldots, x_n^*, L).$$

In the following subsections, we first discuss the computation of the feasible region and the independent feasible region of a buffer on a one-dimensional line segment, and then extend the idea to a two-dimensional chip plane.

33.1.1 FEASIBLE REGIONS

For n buffers inserted in a two-pin net **N** as shown in Figure 33.1b, their feasible regions can be computed as follows [1].

Theorem 1 *For a two-pin net* **N** *of length L and with n buffers inserted and a given timing bound $D_{\text{tgt}}^{\mathbf{N}}$, the feasible region for the ith buffer ($i \leq n$) is $x_i \in [x_{i,\min}, x_{i,\max}]$ with*

$$x_{i,\min} = \max\left\{0, \frac{K_2 - \sqrt{K_2^2 - 4K_1 K_3}}{2K_1}\right\},$$

and

$$x_{i,\max} = \min\left\{L, \frac{K_2 - \sqrt{K_2^2 + 4K_1 K_3}}{2K_1}\right\},$$

where
$$K_1 = \frac{(n+1)rc}{2i(n-i+1)},$$

$$K_2 = \frac{(R_b - R_d)c}{i} + \frac{(C_s - C_b)r + rcL}{n-i+1}, \text{ and}$$

$$K_3 = nT_b - D_{\text{tgt}}^{\mathbf{N}} + \left(R_d + (i-1)R_b + \frac{(n-i)rL}{n-i+1}\right)C_b + R_b((n-1)C_b + C_s + cL) + \frac{rcL^2}{2(n-i+1)}$$

$$+ rLC_s - \frac{(i-1)c(R_b - R_d)^2}{2ir} - \frac{(n-i)r(C_b - C_s)^2}{2(n-i+1)c}.$$

We denote the width of the feasible region for a given buffer by W_{FR}. Cong, Kong, and Pan gave an analytical expression for W_{FR} in Ref. [1]. Sarkar and Koh presented an equivalent analytical expression in Ref. [3], as given below.

Theorem 2   *For $D_{\text{tgt}}^N \geq D_{\text{opt}}^N(n, L)$, the width of the feasible region for the ith buffer $(i \leq n)$ of the net* **N** *is*

$$W_{FR} = 2 \cdot \sqrt{\frac{2(D_{\text{tgt}}^N - D_{\text{opt}}^N(n, L))(n - i + 1)(i)}{rc(n + 1)}}.$$

33.1.2   INDEPENDENT FEASIBLE REGIONS

In contrast to the definition of feasible region, the IFR of a buffer is the region where it can be placed to satisfy the timing constraints of the net, assuming that the other buffers are placed within their respective IFRs [3]. To provide every buffer in the net with an equal degree of freedom to move within its IFR, the IFRs are chosen to have the same width, denoted by W_{IFR}. Hence, the IFR for the *i*th buffer of a net **N** with a corresponding target delay D_{tgt}^N is given by

$$\text{IFR}_i = (x_i^* - W_{IFR}/2, x_i^* + W_{IFR}/2) \cap (0, L),$$

such that $\forall\, (x_1, x_2, \ldots, x_i, \ldots, x_n) \in \text{IFR}_1 \times \text{IFR}_2 \times \ldots \times \text{IFR}_n$ and $D^N(x_1, x_2, \ldots, x_n, L) \leq D_{\text{tgt}}^N$. The following theorem gives an analytical expression for W_{IFR}.

Theorem 3   *For $D_{\text{tgt}}^N \geq D_{\text{opt}}^N(n, L)$, the width of the independent feasible region for the ith buffer $(i \leq n)$ of the net* **N** *is*

$$W_{IFR} = 2\sqrt{\frac{D_{\text{tgt}}^N - D_{\text{opt}}^N(n, L)}{rc(2n - 1)}}.$$

33.1.3   TWO-DIMENSIONAL FEASIBLE REGION

Implicit in the preceding discussions are the assumptions that a routing from source to sink exists, which is not true for buffer planning during floorplanning, and that buffer insertion occurs only along an one-dimensional line. For buffer planning, we typically assume that the two terminals of a net are connected with a shortest path within the bounding box of the net. The union of the one-dimensional FRs (or one-dimensional IFRs) of a buffer on all monotonic Manhattan routes between source and sink forms the two-dimensional FR (or two-dimensional IFR) of that buffer (see Figure 33.3).

The feasible region of a buffer may be reduced by circuit blocks. Moreover, 2D IFRs of buffers of the same net are not entirely independent of each other. As the widths and locations of a 2D IFR are determined under the assumption of a monotonic Manhattan route between the source and the sink, an assignment of buffers to locations within their respective 2D IFRs is legal only if the buffers lie along a monotone source-to-sink path. Figure 33.3 shows a nonmonotonic buffer assignment, which may not meet the timing constraint, even though the buffers are all within their respective 2D IFRs. Therefore, when we have committed a buffer to a location in its 2D IFR, it may be necessary to update the 2D IFRs of all other buffers in the net.

33.2   BUFFER BLOCKS AND SITES

There are two approaches to buffer planning: buffer block planning and buffer site planning. For buffer block planning, top-level macroblocks with only buffers, or buffer blocks, are inserted into the floorplan [1,3,7–9]. The underlying idea to this methodology is that when one moves a buffer considerably from its optimal location, only a small delay penalty is incurred. As a result, buffers can

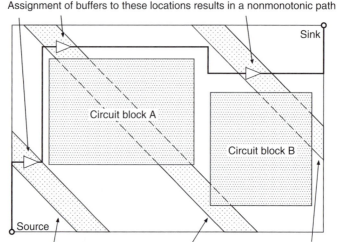

Assignment of buffers to these locations results in a nonmonotonic path

Feasible regions of three buffers, two of which have their areas reduced by
circuit blocks

FIGURE 33.3   2D feasible regions and their implications on buffer assignment.

be relocated within their respective feasible regions or independent feasible regions such that they
can be clustered together to form buffer blocks. The buffer site methodology puts the onus on block
designers to allocate a buffering resource within a block by inserting a buffer site. The allocation
of buffer sites within blocks may not be uniform; a low-performance block may accommodate more
buffer sites than a high-performance one, and some blocks, such as a cache, may not have any buffer
sites. A preallocated buffer site may remain unassigned to a net after planning. In that case, unused
buffer sites can be used to accommodate other useful circuit elements, such as decoupling capacitors.

To facilitate buffer planning, a chip is typically divided into tiles first. Figure 33.4 shows a tiled
chip layout with channel regions, hard blocks, and soft blocks. The capacity of each tile for buffer
insertion depends on whether the tile overlaps with channel regions, dead areas, or hard blocks.
Channel regions and dead areas of the floorplan have high capacity for buffer insertion. In contrast,
hard blocks have very low capacity for buffer insertion unless some buffer sites have been inserted
intentionally [2]. As the exact layout of each soft block is yet to be determined, it is typically
assumed that as long as the total area of functional units and buffers in a soft block is not larger than
its preallocated space, the layout of this block can be completed in the placement stage. For ease
of problem formulation, all the tiles in a soft block may be merged together, as in Figure 33.4. The
buffer capacity of this merged block tile is the total area less the area consumed by its functional
units. It is the responsibility of the placement tool to ensure that buffers are placed at appropriate
locations in the physical realization of a soft block.

Let V_T denote the set of tiles obtained as described in the preceding paragraph. We can construct
a tile graph $G_T(V_T, E_T)$, where every two neighboring tiles u and v in V_T are connected by an edge $e_{u,v}$
in E_T. For a tile v, let $B(v)$ be the number of buffer sites within v and $b(v)$ be the number of buffers
assigned to v. Let $W(e_{u,v})$ be the wire capacity of the edge $e_{u,v}$, and $w(e_{u,v})$ denote the actual wire
usage of $e_{u,v}$. It is clear that a buffer planning solution is feasible only if $b(v) \leq B(v)$ for all $v \in V_T$
and $w(e) \leq W(e)$ for all $e \in E_T$.

33.2.1   BUFFER BLOCK PLANNING

The buffer block planning problem can be informally stated as follows: Given a set of circuit blocks
and a set of connections with feasible regions for buffer insertion to satisfy the design constraints (e.g.,
timing, noise), plan the locations of buffer blocks within the available free space (e.g., dead spaces

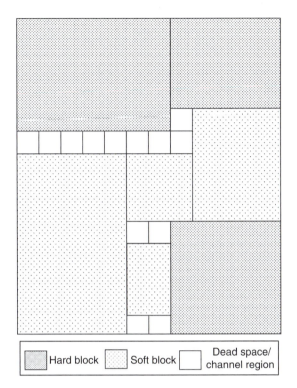

Hard block   Soft block   Dead space/ channel region

FIGURE 33.4   Tile graph for buffer planning.

and channels) so as to route a maximum number of connections. Buffer blocks can be planned after floorplanning [1,3,7,9] or during floorplanning [10–13]. Postfloorplanning buffer block planning is more efficient, but is often limited by the quality of a given floorplan because the location and size of the space for buffer insertion are fixed. Furthermore, as the dead spaces are often treated as undesired cost during floorplanning, they are usually avoided or minimized. As a result, the size and location of dead spaces may not be suitable for postfloorplanning buffer insertion. Therefore, there are also efforts that integrate buffer block planning into floorplanning to fully utilize useful dead spaces for performance optimization. This approach typically enjoys higher design flexibility, but inevitably incurs higher time complexity.

Cong, Kong, and Pan first considered postfloorplanning buffer block planning in Ref. [1]; they derived feasible region formulas to determine where to insert buffers to meet timing constraints and proposed a greedy algorithm to plan buffer blocks in a slicing floorplan. Sarkar and Koh also considered routability and addressed the concept of independent feasible regions in Ref. [3]. Moreover, both approaches in Refs. [1,3] expand channels to provide more buffers if necessary. On the basis of a network-flow formulation, Tang and Wong in Ref. [9] optimally planned as many buffers into buffer blocks as possible for all nets, each with at most one buffer. Given an existing buffer block plan, Dragan et al. in Ref. [7] performed buffering of global nets. Nets are routed using available buffer blocks such that required upper and lower bounds on buffer intervals and the wirelength upper bounds per connection are satisfied.

We describe the generic approach for postfloorplanning buffer block planning as presented in Ref. [1]. First, we construct a directed horizontal constraint graph and a vertical constraint graph for a given floorplan, denoted by G_H and G_V, respectively. Each vertex v in G_H models a vertical routing channel, and an edge $e = (v_1, v_2)$ denotes a circuit block whose respective left and right boundaries are adjacent to the routing channels v_1 and v_2. The weight of a vertex v, $w(v)$, denotes the corresponding channel width while the weight of an edge e, $w(e)$, represents the corresponding block width. The graph G_V is constructed similarly. The respective width W_c and height H_c of the chip can be computed by applying a longest-path algorithm on G_H and G_V.

Then, the algorithm divides the dead spaces and routing channels into tiles to facilitate buffer block planning. For each tile, its area slack is computed from the longest paths in G_H and G_V. For dead spaces and routing channels that are not on the critical paths of the constraint graph $G_H(G_V)$, they will each have a positive area slack in width (height). If there are buffers required to be inserted to meet timing constraints, the algorithm picks a tile that can accommodate the most number of these buffers and then inserts appropriate buffers into this tile. If there are no tiles with positive area slack, we have to shift some circuit blocks for the buffer insertion, thereby increasing the overall chip area. This block shifting might make rooms for other tiles, resulting in new positive slacks for these tiles. We pick the dead space or the routing channel with the maximum buffer-insertion demand, and then select one tile in it. For the selected tile, we insert appropriate buffers into the tile. If there is not sufficient space in the tile for buffer insertion, the associated routing channel will be expanded to make room for the buffers. After inserting buffers into the selected tile, the information of the constraint graphs, feasible regions, and the chip dimension is updated and the buffer insertion/clustering process is repeated until all buffers are placed.

More recently, there have been attempts to perform simultaneous buffer block planning and floorplanning to fully utilize useful dead spaces for performance optimization [10–13]. Jiang et al. provided a generic paradigm along this direction in Ref. [11]. The algorithm presented in Ref. [11] simultaneously considers floorplanning and buffer block planning for a general floorplan. The method adopts simulated annealing to refine the floorplan so that buffers can be inserted more effectively. In each iteration, it constructs a routing tree for each net and calculate the longest path from the source to the sink in each routing tree. On the basis of the aforementioned formulas presented in preceding sections, it computes the number of buffers needed for the longest path, the optimal distance from the source terminal to each buffer, and the width of independent feasible regions. After allocating buffers for all nets, it inserts buffer blocks as soft circuit blocks into the constraint graphs. These buffer blocks may occupy dead spaces or be inserted into routing channels. After all buffers for all nets are allocated, the area of each buffer block is determined as the bounding area of inserted buffers. It then reshapes the floorplan by Lagrangian relaxation. Unlike the work for buffer block planning after floorplanning that generates buffer blocks before buffer assignment, this work generates buffer blocks after buffer assignment. Consequently, the area of buffer blocks can be properly controlled, especially for the buffer blocks in routing channels.

33.2.2 BUFFER SITE PLANNING

In general, buffer block planning algorithms assume that routing has not been performed. In contrast, the first two steps of the buffer site planning algorithm proposed in Ref. [2] are Steiner tree construction and wire congestion reduction. The purpose is to establish the global routing so that accurate estimation of delay of global interconnects in subsequent steps can be obtained. Any timing-driven and congestion-aware global router can be used for these two steps.

The third step, buffer assignment, is the heart of the planning algorithm. Buffer assignment is performed net-by-net in decreasing order of net delay. For a general multiple-terminal net N_i, let L_i be the maximum number of tiles that can be driven by either the source or an inserted buffer. If net N_i crosses tile v, the probability of net N_i using a buffer site in v is $1/L_i$. With $p(v)$ denoting the sum of these probabilities for tile v over all unprocessed nets, $B(v)$ the number of buffer sites within v, and $b(v)$ the number of buffers assigned to v, the cost of using a buffer site in v is defined as

$$q(v) = \begin{cases} \frac{b(v)+p(v)+1}{B(v)-b(v)} & \text{if } \frac{b(v)}{B(v)} < 1, \\ \infty & \text{otherwise.} \end{cases}$$

A minimum cost buffering solution can be computed using a van Ginneken-style dynamic pro-gramming algorithm [14] as follows. First, we describe the computation of a minimum cost buffering solution for a two-pin net with source s and sink t. Let $\gamma = (c, l)$ denote a solution at v, where c is the cost of the solution and and l is the number of un-buffered tiles seen at v. Let u be the parent tile of v in the route. If $l < L_i$, there are two solutions at u that can be derived from γ: an un-buffered solution $(c, l+1)$ and a buffered solution $(c + q(u), 0)$. As in any van Ginneken-style dynamic pro-gramming approach, pruning of inferior solutions is crucial for achieving runtime efficiency. Given two solutions $\gamma = (c, l)$ and $\gamma' = (c', l')$, we say that γ is inferior and can be pruned if $c > c'$ and $l \geq l'$. Consequently, there are no more than L_i noninferior solutions at each tile along the route. The algorithm in Ref. [2] can generate the noninferior solutions at each tile in $O(L_i)$ time and compute the optimal solution of the net in $O(nL_i)$ time, where n is the number of tiles the net crosses.

For a multiple-pin net, it is necessary to consider the case where a parent tile u drives multiple child tiles. For simplicity, we assume that u has only two child tiles v and w. Given the sets of noninferior solutions at v and w, denoted respectively as C_v and C_w, we compute two sets of noninferior solutions at u, denoted as C_{uv} and C_{uw}, derived respectively from C_v and C_w, using the procedure outlined in the preceding paragraph. Let $\gamma = (c, l)$ and $\gamma' = (c', l')$ be solutions in C_{uv} and C_{uw}, respectively. If $l + l' \leq L_i$, there are two solutions in C_u that can be constructed from γ and γ': (1)$(c + c' + q(u), 0)$ is a solution if a buffer is inserted at u to drive γ and γ', and (2)$(c + c', l + l')$ is an un-buffered solution. If we assume as in Ref. [2] that a net can only be assigned one buffer in a tile, the solution in (1) is feasible only if both γ and γ' have no buffers at u, and the solution in (2) is feasible only if there is at most one buffer at u in γ and γ'. The time complexity of the algorithm is $O(nL_i^2)$ for a multiple-pin net that spans n tiles.

A final postprocessing step, which involves ripping up and rerouting nets, is then applied to reduce buffer and wire congestion, as well as the number of nets that fail to meet their length constraints.

33.3 INTERCONNECT PLANNING AND BUFFER PLANNING

Routability is a critical issue in modern VLSI design flow due to the dominance of system performance by today's interconnects. Interconnect planning must be done early to ensure an achievable routing solution. The locations of buffer blocks/sites are places where signals get in and out and it is thus essential to consider routability and buffer planning simultaneously. Early planning of buffer and wiring resources is a critical component of high-performance VLSI design methodologies. Such planning is required to evaluate the quality of RT-level partitioning, floorplanning, placement and pin assignment, etc. In this section, the topic of performing interconnect planning with buffer planning is explored.

33.3.1 ROUTABILITY-DRIVEN BUFFER PLANNING

In Ref. [3], one of the earliest works that consider congestion in the buffer block planning step, a two-level tile structure (Figure 33.5) is used. The coarser tile structure is used for estimating routing congestion, and the finer one is used for defining the candidate buffer block (CBB) locations. For each buffer b to be inserted, let S_b denote the set of CBBs in which b can be placed in order to satisfy the timing constraint. S_b contains all the finer tiles that overlap with the FR or IFR of b. The objective of buffer block planning is to assign each buffer to one CBB such that the congestion cost is minimized. A congestion-driven iterative deletion algorithm is used to obtain such an assignment.

In each iteration of the congestion-driven iterative deletion algorithm, the candidate set of each buffer is first generated. A bipartite graph $G_a = (V_a, E_a)$ that represents the set of all possible buffer assignments is then constructed. The edge set in G_a is defined as $E_a = \{(b, c)|b \in B, c \in S_b\}$ where B is the set of buffers needed to be inserted. The iterative deletion algorithm starts with all possible assignments of the buffers to their CBBs. The edges in G_a are weighted according to the compatibility of the corresponding buffer assignment. An incompatible buffer assignment (an edge

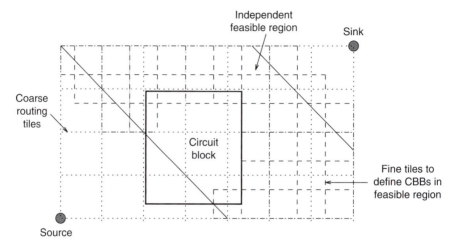

FIGURE 33.5   Two-level tile structure.

of large weight), corresponding to an assignment that may result in high-routing congestion or too many buffer blocks, will be deleted one at a time until only one assignment is left for each buffer. The weight of each edge $e = (b, c)$ is a composite function of the routing congestion cost $C_1(e)$ and the buffer block cost $C_2(e)$, assuming that all the other buffers have equal probability of being assigned to their CBBs. The congestion cost of a routing tile in the two-level tile structure is estimated by the traditional 2D grid based probabilistic map assuming two-bend shortest Manhattan route for each wire segment (a wire segment can be from the source to a buffer, from a buffer to another buffer, or from a buffer to the sink). The routing congestion cost $C_1(e)$ of an edge e is then defined as the maximum congestion cost among all the routing tiles in a one-bend routing path of the net segment represented by the edge. The buffer block cost $C_2(e)$ is computed according to the number of buffers already assigned to the CBB c and the maximum number of buffers allowed in a CBB. This iterative deletion process will remove the highest cost redundant assignment at each step, and the bipartite graph and its associated edge costs are needed to be updated dynamically.

33.3.1.1   Routability-Driven Buffer Planning with Dead Space Redistribution

Dead spaces in a floorplan or placement can be redistributed by moving some circuit blocks within their rooms to achieve better buffer insertion result. Chen et al. [15,16] considered this problem of congestion-driven buffer block planning with dead space redistribution. Dead spaces can be classified into two types, detached dead-space (DDS) and attached dead-space (ADS). A DDS is generated because of the existence of an empty room, while an ADS is generated because a room is not entirely occupied by a circuit block. The ADSs can be redistributed while keeping the topology and the total area unchanged. Each ADS or DDS is associated with a circuit block or a dummy block, which can be found efficiently from a floorplan. In order to find a good dead space distribution to insert as many buffers as possible such that the number of nets meeting their timing constraints without considering congestion is maximized [15], a bipartite graph can first be constructed to represent all possible assignments of buffers to tiles (each dead space is divided into small tiles). An s–t graph can then be constructed based on this bipartite graph to find a maximum cardinality matching in it.

   To consider congestion, a preprocessing step, presented in Ref. [16], first inserts some vertical and horizontal channels into the boundaries of the circuit blocks, based on an estimation of the buffer distribution. Instead of performing a maximum cardinality matching, a more sophisticated congestion-driven buffer planning algorithm is employed. The traditional 2D grid based probabilistic map assuming two-bend shortest Manhattan routes is used to estimate congestion. At the beginning, the congestion estimations are initialized without considering buffers. Then buffer planning and congestion updates are performed net by net. For each net i, a single-source-single-sink shortest-path problem is set up and solved to insert buffers to minimize the sum of the congestion levels at the most congested grid in each wire segment of i. The congestion information at each grid is then updated by erasing the original congestion contribution of net i and adding back the new contribution by its wire segments. The whole process is repeated until all the nets are routed and buffered. It is possible that a net cannot be buffered successfully, when there is no more dead spaces for buffer insertion, or when all the possible routing paths constrained by the buffer locations are nonmonotonic. A local search is performed to explore different ways to redistribute the ADSs. A new redistribution can be generated by randomly selecting an ADS and moving its associated block to change the dead space distribution around it. The cost function to evaluate a floorplan with different dead space redistribution is a composite function of the number of nets that fail to satisfy their delay constraints and the average congestion of the top 5 percent most congested grids.

33.3.1.2 Interconnect Planning with Fixed Interval Buffer Insertion Constraint

In fixed interval buffer insertion constraint, buffers are constrained to be inserted such that the distance between adjacent buffers is within a range [low, up] given by the user. Sham and Young [17] introduced this concept and performed interconnect planning and buffer planning based on this assumption. In their approach, wires are routed over-the-cell with multibend shortest Manhattan distance and buffers are inserted in the dead space area. A floorplan is first divided into a 2D array of grids and the size of the dead space in each grid is computed for estimating the amount of buffer resources in that grid $b_{space}()$. The probability of successful buffer insertion $b_{success}(x, y)$ at a grid (x, y) can be estimated from the amount of dead space $b_{space}(x, y)$ at (x, y) and the number of possible buffer insertions $b_{usage}(x, y)$ at (x, y) according to the formula:

$$b_{success}(x, y) = \min\{1, b_{space}(x, y)/b_{usage}(x, y)\},$$

where $b_{usage}(x, y)$ is obtained by considering all the nets and all their possible multibend shortest Manhattan distance routes satisfying the fixed interval buffer insertion constraint, assuming that every possible route of a net and every feasible way of buffer insertion is equally likely to occur. These $b_{usage}()$ values can be computed efficiently by dynamic programming, and then saved and reused. After estimating the probability of successful buffer insertion at each grid, the congestion information is computed and interconnect planning is performed accordingly, taking into account the fact that the probability of occurrence of a route will be higher if it passes through those grids with larger $b_{success}()$, that is, with a higher chance of successful buffer insertion. All these computations can be done efficiently by dynamic programming and by making use of some table look-up techniques.

Wong and Young [18] have also assumed the fixed interval buffer insertion constraint in their interconnect planning. Similar to the work in Ref. [17], all multipin nets are first broken down into a set of two-pin nets by the MST approach. For each two-pin subnet, a simple dynamic programming approach is employed to find a path from the source to the destination with buffer insertion satisfying the fixed interval buffer insertion constraint and minimizing a cost function that is the sum of the costs at the grids with buffer insertion, where the cost at a grid is a composite function of the congestion cost and the buffer insertion cost. The buffer insertion cost is computed as a ratio between the number of buffers already inserted and the largest number of buffers allowed while the congestion cost is computed by the traditional 2D grid based probabilistic map assuming multibend shortest Manhattan route for each wire segment. The wire segments of each two-pin subnet are processed one after another and the congestion cost is updated accordingly for further buffer insertions.

33.3.1.3 Methodology for Interconnect Planning in Buffer Site

The buffer site methodology was first proposed by Alpert et al. [2]. Details of their approach have been described in Section 33.2. Albrecht et al. [19] studied a similar problem of performing timing-driven buffered routing given a buffer site map. The constraints are on wire loading (maximum number of tiles driven by either the source or an inserted buffer), buffer site capacity, wire congestion, and individual sink delay, and the objective is to minimize the routing area, that is, the total wirelength and the total number of buffers. Unlike many previous works that solves each net optimally one after another, the problem of buffering all the nets simultaneously is formulated as an integer linear program (ILP). However, as solving ILP exactly is NP-hard, the approach taken in Ref. [19] is to first solve the corresponding fractional relaxed linear program and then obtain a near-optimal integral solution by randomized rounding. Their approximation algorithm can be extended to find paths with bounded delay and handle multiple buffer and wire width libraries.

33.3.1.4 Other Routability-Driven Buffer Planning Approaches

Ma et al. [20] also developed an efficient algorithm to perform congestion-driven buffer planning that could be budgeted into the floorplanning process to give better timing performance and chip area. In their approach, the dead spaces are first partitioned into rectangular empty space (ES) blocks. The ES blocks in a floorplan can be obtained efficiently based on the CBL representation, and it is proved that all the dead spaces in a packing can be partitioned into no more than $2n$ ES blocks without overlapping, where n is the total number of circuit blocks. Intersection between the feasible region (FR) of a buffer and a ES block will be a regular hexagon (with possibly some degenerations) of which two edges are parallel to the x-axis, two edges are parallel to the y-axis, and the other two edges have a slope of $+1$ or -1. To facilitate data manipulation, the ES blocks are further partitioned into grids and each grid contains buffer sites for buffer insertion. The whole process of computing the intersection between the FR of a buffer and the ES blocks is divided into two steps. The first step computes the intersection between the ES blocks and the bounding box of the net, and the second step computes the overlapping between the rectangular regions obtained from step one and the two parallel slanted lines of the FR. The grids in a ES block are ordered in parallel to these slanted lines with slope $+1$ or -1, so that the overlapping obtained from step two will just be two indices specifying the range of grids where a buffer can be inserted. Because it is only needed to compute the first and the last grid number in the range, the complexity is linear and independent of the grid size. Assuming that the probabilities of buffer insertion are equal at each possible buffer insertion site, the probability of a buffer b being inserted into a grid g is computed as $1/NFR_b$ where NFR_b is the total number of grids in some ES blocks overlapping with the FR of b. This number can be easily obtained from step two above by knowing the range of grids in each ES block overlapping with the FR of b. By summing up these probabilities for all the buffers, the expected number of buffers to be inserted in each grid can be obtained.

These probabilities of successful buffer insertion are then used for buffer allocation with consideration of routing congestion. The congestion model used is essentially the traditional 2D grid based probabilistic map assuming multibend shortest Manhattan route for each wire segment. Because the probabilities of successful buffer insertion are different at different routing tiles, the chance of the occurrence of a route will be higher if it runs through those tiles with high probabilities of successful buffer insertion. Consider the route of a net i passing through a set of tiles $\{T_1, T_2, \ldots, T_k\}$. Suppose that a buffer b of this net is to be inserted in one of these tiles T_j where $1 \geq j \geq k$. The size of the overlapping area between the feasible region of buffer b and the dead spaces in tile T_j will affect the probability of the occurrence of a route. This fact is taken into account in their congestion model. The nets are then considered one after another for buffer allocation. For each net, all its feasible routes are processed in a nondescending order of their sums of congestion levels of all the tiles it goes through. A route will be taken if all of its required buffers can be inserted successfully when it is being processed.

33.3.2 PIN ASSIGNMENT WITH BUFFER PLANNING

It is beneficial to perform pin assignment and buffer planning simultaneously to achieve better timing performance. Given a placement of macroblocks and buffer blocks, the objective is to assign pins and insert buffers for a given set of nets to minimize a weighted sum of the total wirelength, W, and the total number of buffers inserted, R:

$$C = \alpha W + \beta R.$$

Xiang, Tang, and Wong [21] presented a polynomial time algorithm to perform simultaneous pin assignment and buffer planning optimally for all two-pin nets from one particular macroblock to all the other blocks. The algorithm minimizes the cost C for any given positive constants α and β while enforcing the lower and upper bound constraints on wire segment length for each net. By applying this algorithm iteratively (picking one source block each time), pin assignment and buffer planning can be done for all the nets. The subproblem of performing simultaneous pin assignment and buffer planning from one source block to all the other blocks can be formulated as a min-cost max-flow problem. In the example shown in Figure 33.6, the source block is b_s, and it has two nets connecting to block b_1 and b_2, and each block b_i has a set of available pin locations P_i. There are two buffer blocks r_1 and r_2, and each buffer block r_i is associated with a capacity c_i denoting the maximum number of buffers r_i can hold. A network flow problem can be set up as shown in Figure 33.6b. In the constructed flow network, a directed edge from a pin $p \in P_s$ to a buffer block r_j (or from a buffer block r_j to a pin $p \in P_i$ where b_i is not the source block) exists if and only if the shortest Manhattan distance between p and r_j satisfies the lower and upper bound constraints on wire segment length. Similar conditions hold for other edges between two pins or between two buffers. Then a source node s, which is connected to all the pins in the source block b_s with capacity one and zero cost, is added. An intermediate sink node t_i is added for each block b_i other than the source block and is connected from every pin $p \in P_i$ with capacity one and zero cost. Each of these intermediate sink nodes t_i is then connected to the final sink node t with zero cost and capacity $|N_i|$ where N_i is the set of nets from b_s to b_i. For all the remaining edges, the capacities are one and the costs are $\alpha \times d$ where d is the shortest Manhattan length of the edge. For each buffer node r_i, there will be a cost of β and a capacity of c_i. For all the remaining nodes, the capacity is one and the cost is zero.

It is not difficult to see that a min-cost max-flow solution f in the flow network constructed as described above can give an optimal solution that minimizes the cost and maximizes the number

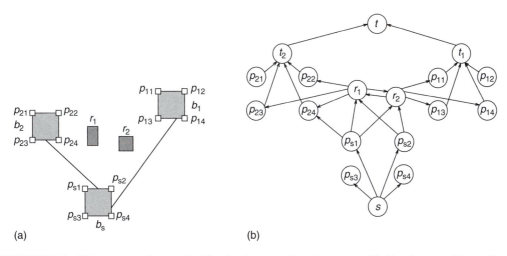

(a)   (b)

FIGURE 33.6 Min-cost max-flow method for simultaneous pin assignment and buffer planning: (a) a problem instance and (b) the corresponding flow network.

of connections made. If the flow $|f|$ is equal to $|N|$ where $N = \cup_i N_i$, a feasible solution of pin assignment and buffer planning for all the nets in N is found. However, if $|f| < |N|$, there is no way to make all the connections and have the constraints satisfied. Every flow solution can be mapped to a pin assignment and buffer planning solution of the given set of nets. However, this min-cost max-flow approach can only consider nets connecting between one source block and all the other blocks. To route all the nets between all the macroblocks, each macroblock is treated as the source block once and the min-cost max-flow algorithm is invoked; a solution for all the nets between multiple macroblocks can be obtained at the end. To reduce the complexity of this approach, neighboring pins are grouped together at the beginning. Once several nodes are grouped together, the average coordinate is used as the location of the new super-node. After getting a solution with the super-nodes, the flow solution is mapped back to the original problem, that is, distributing the flow from one super-node to its pin nodes. This subproblem can also be solved by the min-cost max-flow method.

33.3.3 NOISE-AWARE BUFFER PLANNING

The aforementioned buffer block planning is done for delay or routability optimization. It is also of crucial importance to consider the signal integrity, for example, maintain fast transition time (the inverse of slew rate) of the signal at the receiver and along the net and minimize the crosstalk-induced noise during buffer planning. Otherwise, a slow transition on a net may be highly susceptible to coupling noise injection from faster switching signal lines in its vicinity. Furthermore, if the length of the net between two successive buffers is too long, the interconnect resistance becomes comparable to the driver resistance. This effectively decouples the receiver from the driver and makes the receiver highly susceptible to any attacking signals. Another reason for concern is that a slow transition on the input causes higher short-circuit power consumption.

To avoid such signal integrity problems and higher power consumption, guidelines on most modern large-circuit designs require signal transition times to be no slower than a specified value. As a rule of thumb, the allowed signal transition time is between 10 and 15 percent of the clock cycle time for modern circuit design. Without considering the signal transition time constraint for buffer planning, as pointed out in Ref. [3], the buffer insertion solution may not maintain the required signal transition rate even though the target delay (as defined by 50 percent input to 50 percent output) on a net may be satisfied. Therefore, it is desirable to consider the problem of buffer block planning under delay, rise/fall time, and crosstalk-induced noise constraints for interconnect-centric floorplanning.

In the following subsections, we describe the independent feasible regions defined by the transition time and delay constraints presented in Ref. [22], as well as the crosstalk-induced noise constraint introduced in Ref. [23].

33.3.3.1 Independent Feasible Regions with Transition Time Constraints

In addition to inserting buffers to improve signal delay, it is also popular to insert buffers at regular intervals to ensure a proper slew rate (or transition time) at the input to all gates. Let R be the driver output resistance, C be the sink capacitance, and $L(R, C, R_{tgt})$ be the maximum length of a net such that the signal transition time at the sink is no more than R_{tgt} (it can be assumed that the input signal transition time is also R_{tgt}).

The independent feasible region under the signal transition time constraint for the ith buffer of a net $\mathbf{N}$ is given by

$$\text{IFR}(R)_i = \left(x_i^{\otimes} - W_{\text{IFR}(R)}/2, x_i^{\otimes} + W_{\text{IFR}(R)}/2\right) \cap (0, l),$$

such that $\forall (x_1, x_2, \ldots, x_i, \ldots, x_n) \in \text{IFR}(R)_1 \times \text{IFR}(R)_2 \times \ldots \times \text{IFR}(R)_n$ and the input transition times for all buffers and the sink satisfy the signal transition time constraint. Here, $W_{\text{IFR}(R)}$ denotes the width of independent feasible region $\text{IFR}(R)_i$, and $x_i^{\otimes}$ the center of $\text{IFR}(R)$ for the ith buffer.

For all segments of the net **N** to satisfy the signal transition time constraint, the following inequalities must hold:

$$x_1^\otimes + W_{IFR(R)}/2 \le l_1,$$
$$x_{i+1}^\otimes - x_i^\otimes + W_{IFR(R)} \le l_2 \quad \text{for} \quad 1 \le i \le n-1, \quad \text{and}$$
$$l - x_n^\otimes + W_{IFR(R)}/2 \le l_3,$$

where

$$l_1 = L\left(R_D, C_B, R_{tgt}^N\right)$$
$$l_2 = L\left(R_B, C_B, R_{tgt}^N\right)$$
$$l_3 = L\left(R_B, C_S, R_{tgt}^N\right)$$

Here, R_{tgt}^N denotes the target signal transition time for the net **N**. Summing up the preceding $n+1$ inequalities and making the IFR(R) intervals of equal width, we get

$$W_{IFR(R)} = \frac{l_1 + (n-1)l_2 + l_3 - l}{n}.$$

For this $W_{IFR(R)}$, the centers of the feasible regions are determined by the following equalities:

$$x_1^\otimes = l_1 - W_{IFR(R)}/2,$$
$$x_{i+1}^\otimes - x_i^\otimes = l_2 - W_{IFR(R)} \quad \text{for} \quad 1 \le i \le n-1, \quad \text{and}$$
$$x_n^\otimes = l - l_3 + W_{IFR(R)}/2.$$

To find the IFR of the ith buffer considering both delay and signal transition time constraints for a given number of inserted buffers, we should find the intersection of IFR$_i$ and IFR(R)$_i$. If IFR$_i$ and IFR(R)$_i$ do not overlap, we have to insert a different number of buffers. Given l_1, l_2, and l_3, the minimum number of buffers required to satisfy the transition time constraint is given by

$$n_R^{\min} = \left\lceil \frac{l - l_1 - l_3}{l_2} + 1 \right\rceil.$$

Let $n_D^{\min}$ and $n_D^{\max}$ be the respective minimum and maximum numbers of buffers that can be inserted into a net to satisfy the delay constraints. For the delay constraint, D_{tgt}^N, $n_D^{\min}$ to $n_D^{\max}$ can be computed as follows:

$$n_D^{\min} = \max\left(0, \frac{-B - \sqrt{(B^2 - 4AC)}}{2A}\right),$$

and

$$n_D^{\max} = \frac{-B + \sqrt{(B^2 - 4AC)}}{2A},$$

where

$$A = R_b C_b + T_b$$
$$B = D_{tgt}^N + \frac{r}{c}(C_b - C_s)^2 + \frac{c}{r}(R_b - R_d)^2 - (rC_b + cR_b)l - T_b - R_d C_b - R_b C_s$$
$$C = \tfrac{1}{2}rcl^2 + (rC_s + cR_d)l - D_{tgt}^N$$

If $n_D^{Max} \leq 0$, the delay constraint on the net cannot be satisfied by inserting buffers of this type alone.

The number of buffers required to satisfy both delay and signal transition time constraints, denoted by $n_{D,R}$, is bounded by $\max\{n_R^{min}, n_D^{min}\} \leq n_{D,R} \leq n_D^{max}$. A linear search within the interval would typically find a feasible solution.

33.3.3.2 Common Independent Feasible Region

The common IFR for buffer i of net **N** under both delay and signal transition time constraints is referred to as the maximal region where the buffer can be placed such that both the constraints can be satisfied, assuming that the other buffers are placed within their respective common IFRs.

Both the constraints cannot be satisfied by buffer insertion if

$$\max\{n_R^{Min}, n_D^{Min}\} > n_D^{Max}.$$

For a fixed value of $n_{D,R}$ in the feasible range, the IFR(D,R) for the ith buffer (IFR$(D,R)(i)$) on the net is the region common to both IFR$(R)(i)$ and IFR$(D)(i)$. Let $W_{min} = \min\{W_{IFR(R)}, W_{IFR(D)}\}$, $\delta_i = |x_i^* - x_i^\otimes|$, and $\delta_w = |W_{IFR}(R) - W_{IFR(D)}|$.

The width of the common independent feasible region is given by

$$W_{IFR(D,R)}(i) = \begin{cases} W_{min} & ; \text{ if } \delta_i \leq \delta_w/2 \\ W_{min} - \delta_i + \delta_w/2 & ; \text{ if } \delta_w/2 \leq \delta_i \leq (W_{IFR(R)} + W_{IFR(D)})/2, \\ \text{undefined} & ; \text{ otherwise.} \end{cases}$$

We can observe that $\min_{1 \leq i \leq n_{D,R}}\{W_{IFR(D,R)}(i)\}$ will occur at $i = 1$ or $i = n_{D,R}$. To fix the number of buffers inserted on the net, we pick the value of $n_{D,R}$ that maximizes the minimum width of IFR$(D,R)(i)$.

33.3.3.3 Buffer Block Planning Considering Transition Time and Delay

In this section, we briefly describe the algorithm for buffer block planning considering both transition time and delay constraints. The inputs to the algorithm are the initial floorplan and the transition time and delay constraints on the global nets. The algorithm determines the locations, assignments, and sizes of buffer blocks to be inserted in a dead space or a routing channel such that the two constraints are satisfied.

Figure 33.7 summarizes the algorithm. Step 1 divides the available channel space, as performed in Section 33.2.1, into a set of buffer-block tiles to meet both constraints. Step 2 determines the type and the number of buffers to be inserted in each net to satisfy its timing constraints. The buffer type chosen for a net is the smallest size buffer, such that all the buffers on the net have a nonzero IFR(D,R) width. Furthermore, it constrains all the buffers on a net to be of the same size. The number of buffers required is then obtained by searching the common feasible range of buffer numbers for delay and transition time requirements. The chosen value of $n_{D,R}$ maximizes the minimum IFR(D,R) width, as mentioned in Section 33.3.3.2.

Steps 4–6 find the set of buffer-block tiles into which each buffer can be placed. Let **B** be the set of buffers needed to be inserted to satisfy the constraints, and the candidate buffer blocks (CBB) set of $b, S_b, b \in \mathbf{B}$, be the set of buffer-block tiles into which it can be placed. The intersection of the two-dimensional IFR(D,R) of a buffer with the buffer-block tiles defines the CBB set of the buffer.

If there exists one buffer to be placed along the monotonic Manhattan route with an empty CBB, non-monotone detour routes are considered. Steps 7–9 compute the CBB sets for buffers to be placed along the shortest detour route. Step 8 finds the shortest detour path. The optimal number of buffers

Algorithm: Buffer block planning with transition time and delay constraints
1.   Divide dead spaces and routing channels into buffer block tiles;
2.   Find type of buffers and $n_{D,R}$ for each net **N**
3.   Compute IFR(D,R) for each buffer $b \in$ **B**;
4.   **foreach** net **N**
5.   **foreach** buffer b in net **N**
6.   Obtain CBB set $\mathbf{S_b}$;
7.   **If** there exists $(\mathbf{S_b} = \emptyset)$ for a net **N**
8.   Find the shortest detour path;
9.   Obtain $\mathbf{S_b}$ along the detour path;
10. Generate the bipartite graph $\mathcal{G}$;
11. **While** there exists a buffer to be assigned **do**
12.   Delete the highest cost edge of $\mathcal{G}$;
13.   Update edge costs;
14.   Assign a buffer to a CBB if required;

FIGURE 33.7   Algorithm for buffer block planning considering both transition time and delay constraints. (From Sarkar, P. and Koh, C.-K., *Proceedings of IEEE/ACM Design, Automation and Test in Europe Conference*, IEEE Press, Piscataway, NJ, 2001.)

$(n_{D,R})$ to be inserted to satisfy the timing constraints is computed based on this path length. Then, the width of the IFR(D, R) for each buffer along this path is computed. Step 9 applies this width to compute the CBB set for the net **N**.

Each buffer could have several feasible CBBs to be assigned. A method based on the iterative deletion and bipartite graph formulation introduced in Section 33.3.1 is used to assign each buffer. Step 10 constructs the bipartite graph $\mathcal{G}$, and Steps 12–14 prune $\mathcal{G}$ by removing incompatible buffer assignments or edges in each iteration, similar to the process in Section 33.3.1. The algorithm terminates when a unique CBB is assigned to each buffer.

33.3.4   BUFFER PLANNING WITH NOISE CONSTRAINTS

Coupling noise between adjacent nets could induce unexpected circuit behavior. Figure 33.8 shows a noise model that considers coupling capacitance c_c. The coupling capacitance is proportional to the fringing capacitance (c_f) and the coupling length (l_c), and it is inversely proportional to the distance (d) between the aggressor and the victim nets, that is, $c_c \propto c_f l_c/d$. Because the detailed routing information is not available during floorplanning or postfloorplanning, we may adopt a more conservative approach and make d the minimum wire distance $d_{\min}$ specified by the design rule. Furthermore, we set the coupling length (l_c) to be twice the victim net's length (l_v), which is the

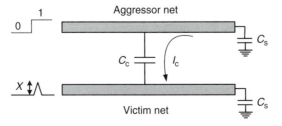

FIGURE 33.8 Noise model resulting from the coupling capacitance and crosstalk-induced current. (From Cheng, Y. -H. and Chang Y. -W., *Proceedings of IEEE/ACM Asia South Pacific Design Automation Conference*, IEEE Press, Piscataway, NJ, 2004.)

worst case when the victim net is fully coupled from both sides by two aggressor nets. Of course, more optimistic modeling, for example, based on some distribution assumption, is also applicable. Nevertheless, it will be clear that the technical conclusion, say with the distribution assumption, remains similar, and thus we should focus on the worst-case scenario for easier presentation.

With the worst-case scenario, we have

$$c_c = \frac{2l_v c_f}{d_{\min}}.$$

Furthermore, $2c_c$ is adopted in the model to account for the worst case coupling effect when all the aggressor nets have different signal transitions from that of the victim net, for which the Miller effect makes the coupling phenomenon more significant by doubling the coupling effect. Again, the technique to be presented readily applies to other models with less pessimistic estimation.

Consider a wire $e = (u, v)$, where u and v are two nodes in a buffered tree. Let the length of the wire segment e be l_e, and $T(v)$ be the subtree rooted at v. $I_T(v)$ is the total downstream current seen at v and is the current induced by aggressor nets on downstream wires of v. The current on a unit-length wire induced by aggressor nets is $i_0 = \lambda pc$ [24], where c is the unit-length wire capacitance, λ is the fixed ratio of coupling to total wire capacitance, p is the slope (i.e., power supply voltage over input rise time) of all aggressor nets' signals, and c_c is modeled as some fraction of the unit-length wire capacitance of the victim net. Let $\chi(u, v)$ be the noise on the wire segment between two neighboring buffers u and v. The resulting noise $\chi(u, v)$ induced from the coupling current is the voltage pulse coupled from aggressor nets in the victim net for a wire segment $e = (u, v)$. Using an Elmore-delay like noise metric [24] to model $\chi(u, v)$ (see Chapter 3), we can express the noise constraint as

$$\chi(u, v) = R_b I_{T(v)} + rl_e \left(\frac{i_0 l_e}{2} + I_{T(v)} \right) \le M_v, \tag{33.1}$$

where R_b is the output resistance of a minimum size buffer, and M_v is the noise margin for a buffer or a sink v, which is the maximum allowable noise without incurring any logic error.

The width $W_{\mathrm{IFR}(N)_i}$ of the independent feasible region $\mathrm{IFR}(N)_i$ for the ith buffer that satisfies the noise constraint is given by

$$W_{\mathrm{IFR}(N)_i} \le \sqrt{\left(\frac{R_b}{r} \right)^2 + \left(\frac{I_{T(v)}}{i_0} \right)^2 + \frac{2M_v}{i_0 r}} - \frac{R_b}{r} - \frac{I_{T(v)}}{i_0}. \tag{33.2}$$

For this noise model, the four factors that determine the size of a feasible region are noise margin M_v, buffer resistance R_b, unit-length wire resistance r, and crosstalk-induced unit current i_0.

The feasible region under noise constraint, denoted by $\mathrm{IFR}(N)_i$ is the maximum allowable length in each net satisfying the noise margins after buffer insertion. To estimate the feasible region under noise constraint, $\mathrm{IFR}(N)_i$, the noise formulas [11] below can be applied. The induced noise current on wire segment $e = (u, v)$ is computed by $I_e = i_0 l_e$. To satisfy the noise constraint, a buffer can be inserted at u as in Equation 33.1, where $W_{\mathrm{IFR}(N)_i}$ the width of the feasible region $\mathrm{IFR}(N)_i$ for buffers satisfying the noise constraint, is computed from Equation 33.2.

$$\chi(u, v) = R_b I_{T(u)} + rW_{\mathrm{IFR}(N)_i} \left(\frac{i_0 W_{\mathrm{IFR}(N)_i}}{2} + I_{T(v)} \right) \le M_v. \tag{33.3}$$

Given two-pin nets as inputs, the method is to scan from the sink s_i with the given M_{s_i} to the source s_0. Because the accumulated crosstalk-induced current $I_{T(v)}$ is zero for pins of two-pin nets, the noise formula is given by

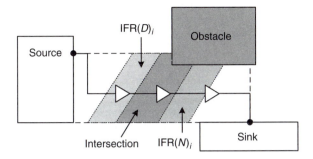

FIGURE 33.9   Respective feasible regions IFR(D)$_i$, IFR(N)$_i$, and IFR(D)$_i$ ∩ IFR(N)$_i$ for inserting a buffer that satisfy the delay, noise, and both delay and noise constraints.

$$\chi(u, v) = R_b I_{T(u)} + r W_{\text{IFR}(N)_i} \left(\frac{I_e}{2} + I_{T(v)} \right)$$

$$= R_b \left(I_e + I_{T(v)} \right) + r W_{\text{IFR}(N)_i} \left(\frac{I_e}{2} + I_{T(v)} \right)$$

$$= R_b I_e + r W_{\text{IFR}(N)_i} \frac{I_e}{2}. \tag{33.4}$$

On the basis of Equations 33.3 and 33.4, $W_{\text{IFR}(N)_i}$, can be computed by

$$W_{\text{IFR}(N)_i} \leq \sqrt{\left(\frac{R_b}{r} \right)^2 + \frac{2M_v}{i_0 r}} - \frac{R_b}{r}.$$

In the preceding equation, $W_{\text{IFR}(N)_i}$ is the maximum length from the next buffer B_{i+1} back to B_i without causing any logic error.

To handle the transition time, delay, and noise constraints simultaneously, we first compute the respective feasible regions IFR(R)$_i$, IFR(D)$_i$, and IFR(N)$_i$ for inserting buffer i to satisfy the transition time, delay, and noise constraints, and then find the intersection of IFR(R)$_i$, IFR(D)$_i$, and IFR(N)$_i$ to derive the feasible region for buffer i that meets all these constraints (see Figure 33.9 for an illustration). Furthermore, the buffer block planning algorithm presented in section 33.3.3.3 still works by additionally considering the noise constraint.

33.4   FLIP-FLOP AND BUFFER PLANNING (WIRE RETIMING)

Although buffer insertion is very effective in improving the delay performance (and noise tolerance) of interconnects, the timing constraints may be so tight that they are beyond the maximum performance deliverable by buffer insertion, making the insertion of flip-flops or latches for pipelined signal transmission necessary. In the case of modern high-performance microprocessors [13], it is not unusual for global signals to take several clock cycles to travel across the chip to reach their destinations. In fact, the wire delay can be as long as about ten clock cycles in the near future [25]. It has been shown in Ref. [26] that under an aggressive scaling scenario where the frequency of microprocessors approximately doubles and die size increases by about 25 percent in every process generation, the number of flip-flops (referred to as clocked repeaters) increases by 7 times every process generation.

As the number of flip-flops and buffers increases in an exponential fashion, the planning and design of pipelined interconnects are very important emerging problems. Several design challenges can be posed:

1. What is the minimum latency required between two communicating functional blocks of a design?
2. Given the latency constraints between two communicating functional blocks of a design, where should flip-flops and buffers be inserted to minimize, for example, the total flip-flop and buffer area?
3. How does interconnect latency affect the system behavior? Arbitrary interconnect latency may destroy the functionality of a sequential circuit. How can functional blocks and interconnects be simultaneously retimed to achieve the desired circuit performance while maintaining its functionality?
4. How can buffer planning take into consideration the retiming of logic blocks and interconnects, as well as the placement of those flip-flops relocated by retiming?

33.4.1 MINIMIZING LATENCY

In the initial stages of the design of high-performance microarchitectures, the minimum latency that can be achieved on long interconnects gives microarchitects and circuit designers an accurate prediction of the timing and routing demands required of the design. There are two approaches to the problem of latency minimization: (1) using analytical formulas [27]; and (2) using a van Ginneken-style dynamic programming approach [26].

33.4.1.1 Two-Pin Net Optimization Using Analytical Formulas

Consider a wire with length L, driver R_d, and sink C_s. On the basis of the optimal delay formula obtained when we insert n buffers into the wire [6], the optimal delay for an interconnect properly inserted with an ideal optimal number of buffers is

$$D'_{opt}(L) = \left(R_b c + r C_b + \sqrt{2rc(R_b C_b + T_b)}\right) \cdot L + (l_r + l_c) \cdot \sqrt{2rc(R_b C_b + T_b)}$$
$$+ l_r r C_b + l_c R_b c - \frac{rc}{2}(l_r^2 + l_c^2) - T_b,$$

where

$$l_r = \frac{R_d - R_b}{r}$$

$$l_c = \frac{C_s - C_b}{c}$$

Here, the ideal optimal number of buffers is defined as

$$n'_{opt}(L) = \sqrt{\frac{rc}{2(R_b C_b + T_b)}} \cdot (L + l_r + l_c) - 1,$$

which may not be an integer. Therefore, the maximum length of a wire inserted with the ideal optimal number of buffers that can meet a given delay constraint D_{tgt} is

$$L'_{max}(R_d, C_s, D_{tgt}) = \frac{D_{tgt} + T_b + \frac{rc}{2}(l_r^2 + l_c^2) - l_r r C_b - l_c R_b c - (l_r + l_c)\sqrt{2rc(R_b C_b + T_b)}}{R_b c + r C_b + \sqrt{2rc(R_b C_b + T_b)}}.$$

Although the ideal optimal number of buffers n'_{opt} may not be an integer, which is not realizable, the actual optimal number of buffers of the interconnect is either $\lfloor n'_{opt} \rfloor$ or $\lceil n'_{opt} \rceil$. Let $L_N(n)$ denote the maximal length for an interconnect $\mathbf{N}$ with n buffers under a given timing requirement D_{tgt}. ($L_N(n)$ can be obtained by solving for L in the optimal delay formula for a given n and D_{tgt}.) The maximum wire length of the interconnect inserted with buffers that can meet a given target delay D_{tgt} is

$$L_{max}(R_d, C_s, D_{tgt}) = \max\{L_N(\lfloor n'_{opt} \rfloor), L_N(\lceil n'_{opt} \rceil)\}.$$

With flip-flops inserted, we have to define target delays for the first segment, the middle segments, and the last segment of the pipelined interconnects separately. The timing constraint for any middle segment, denoted $D_{tgt,M}$, is the clock period less the setup time and the flip-flop propagation delay. The timing constraint for the first segment, denoted $D_{tgt,F}$, should ensure that the maximum delay from those source flip-flops before the driver to the first flip-flop along the pipelined interconnect is smaller than one clock period less the setup time and the flip-flop propagation delay. Similarly, the timing constraint for the last segment, denoted $D_{tgt,L}$, should ensure that the maximum delay from the last flip-flop along the pipelined interconnect to the flip-flops after the sink is smaller than one clock period less the setup time and the flip-flop propagation delay. Therefore, the minimum latency or the least number of flip-flops required to meet the delay and clock period constraints is

$$N_{FF} = \begin{cases} 0 & \text{if } L \leq L_{max}(R_d, C_s, D_{tgt}), \\ 1 & \text{if } L_{max}(R_d, C_s, D_{tgt}) < L \leq L_L + L_F, \\ \left\lceil \dfrac{L - L_F - L_L}{L_M} \right\rceil + 1 & \text{otherwise}, \end{cases}$$

where

$$L_F = L_{max}(R_d, C_F, D_{tgt}, F)$$
$$L_L = L_{max}(R_F, C_s, D_{tgt,L})$$
$$L_M = L_{max}(R_F, C_F, D_{tgt,M})$$

with R_F and C_F being respectively the output resistance and input capacitance of a flip-flop.

In the context of flip-flop and buffer planning, of greater interest is the feasible regions (or independent feasible regions) of flip-flops and buffers. Let n be the number of flip-flops inserted in an interconnect and f_i be the location of the ith ($1 \leq i \leq n$) flip-flop. With f_i^* denoting the central location of the ith flip-flop in its feasible region, and W_{FR} the uniform width of the feasible regions, we define the FR for the ith flip-flop as

$$FR_i = \left(f_i^* - W_{FR}/2, f_i^* + W_{FR}/2\right) \cap (0, L),$$

such that $(f_1, f_2, \ldots, f_i, \ldots f_n) \in FR_1 \times FR_2 \times \ldots \times FR_n, f_1 \leq L_F, f_i - f_{i-1} \leq L_M$ for $2 \leq i \leq n$, and $L - f_n \leq L_L$.

The following inequalities must hold for a flip-flop solution to be feasible:

$$f_1^* + W_{FR}/2 \leq L_F, \quad f_i^* - f_{i-1}^* + W_{FR} \leq L_M \quad \text{for} \quad 2 \leq i \leq n, \quad \text{and} \quad L - f_n^* + W_{FR}/2 \leq L_L.$$

The largest W_{FR} that satisfies these inequalities is

$$W_{FR} = (L_F + L_L + (n-1)L_M - L)/n.$$

Correspondingly, the central locations f_i^* are

$$f_i^* = L_F + (i-1)L_M - (i-1/2)W_{FR} \quad \text{for} \quad 1 \leq i \leq n.$$

The independent feasible regions of flip-flops and buffers can also be determined in a fairly straightforward fashion [27]. With the definition of feasible regions of flip-flops in place, the buffer planning algorithms outlined in preceding sections can be easily extended to handle the latency minimization problem.

33.4.1.2 Multiple-Terminal Net Optimization

In the case of two-pin net optimization (Section 33.4.1.1), the planning can be carried out without first performing routing. In the case of multiple-terminal net optimization, the assumption is that the routing solution of global nets is known. In the context of design migration, this is typically true, where the microarchitects and circuit designers would like to make minimal changes to the design. A natural algorithm to adopt would be that of van Ginneken [14].

In Ref. [26], each flip-flop and buffer insertion solution can be represented by a four-tuple $\gamma = (c, r, \lambda, a)$, where c is the capacitance seen by the upstream resistance, r is the required arrival time, λ is the maximum number of flip-flops crossed when going from this node (or edge) to its leaf nodes, and a is the flip-flop or buffer assignment at this node. For simplicity, we assume that long edges are segmented properly and that flip-flop and buffer insertion is allowed only at nodes.

At a leaf node v, the solution is $(c_v, r_v, 0, \emptyset)$, where c_v is the sink capacitance, and r_v is the required arrival time at node v. The propagation of a solution from a node to its parent edge (the edge connecting the node to its parent node) proceeds as in the dynamic programming algorithm of Ref. [14]. Let the node solution at node v be $(c_v, r_v, \lambda_v, a_v)$. The corresponding solution at the upstream node of the branch (u, v) is $(c_v + C_{u,v}, r_v - R_{u,v}(C_{u,v} + c_v), \lambda_v, \emptyset)$, where $C_{u,v}$ is the edge capacitance and $R_{u,v}$ is the edge resistance. When two downstream branches meet at a parent node, we merge two solutions $(c_u, r_u, \lambda_u, a_u)$ and $(c_v, r_v, \lambda_v, a_v)$ from the two branches to form $(c_u + c_v, \min(r_u, r_v), \max(\lambda_u, \lambda_v), a_u \cup a_v)$. When we insert a buffer g to drive a subtree with solution $(c_u, r_u, \lambda_u, a_u)$, the new solution is $(c_g, r_u - R_g c_u - t_g, \lambda_u, \{g\})$, where c_g is the gate capacitance of g, R_g is the output resistance of g, and t_g is the intrinsic delay of g. When we add a flip-flop f to drive the subtree instead, the new solution is $(c_f, T_{CP} - t_{su,f}, \lambda_u + 1, \{f\})$, where c_f is the gate capacitance of f, T_{CP} is the clock period, and $t_{su,f}$ is the setup time of f. Note that when we insert a flip-flop, we have to first verify that the pipeline stage immediately after the newly inserted flip-flop has nonnegative slack or required arrival time.

As in the van Ginneken's algorithm, it is important to perform pruning of all solutions to keep only noninferior solutions that can lead to an optimal solution at the root node. Let $\gamma = (c, r, \lambda, a)$ and $\gamma' = (c', r', \lambda', a')$ be two solutions at any node in the tree. We say that γ is inferior and can be pruned if at least one of the following is true:

- $\lambda = \lambda', c \geq c'$, and $r < r'$
- $\lambda = \lambda', c > c'$, and $r = r'$
- $\lambda = \lambda', c = c', r = r'$, and $\text{cost}(\gamma) > \text{cost}(\gamma')$, where $\text{cost}(\cdot)$ is a user-specified cost function associated with the flip-flop and buffer solution; an example of the cost function is the total area of the solution.
- $\lambda > \lambda', c \geq c'$, and $r \leq r'$

Also note that all solutions kept in the algorithm have nonnegative r.

33.4.2 Latency Constrained Optimization

Suppose the required latency at leaf node v is λ_v (assuming that the latency at the root node is zero), we can generalize the algorithm given in Section 33.4.1.2 by using $\gamma = (c_v, r_v, -\lambda_v, 0)$ at v. The algorithm in Section 33.4.1.2 can then be applied to compute an optimal solution to the latency constrained optimization problem with a minor modification: Any solution that has a latency greater than zero can be pruned [26].

As the required latency at the root node is zero, only solutions that have zero latency would be feasible. Consequently, at the root node, if a solution has a negative latency λ, more flip-flops can always be added to make the solution feasible, that is, the latency at the root node equals zero. As we search top-down to retrieve an optimal solution at all nodes, we might have to insert more flip-flops. Consider the solution $(c_u + c_v, \min(r_u, r_v), \max(\lambda_u, \lambda_v), a_u \cup a_v)$ obtained by merging solutions $(c_u, r_u, \lambda_u, a_u)$ and $(c_v, r_v, \lambda_v, a_v)$ of two downstream branches. If $\lambda_u = \max(\lambda_u, \lambda_v)$, an additional $\lambda_u - \lambda_v$ flip-flops should be inserted to the branch that contains the solution $(c_v, r_v, \lambda_v, a_v)$.

33.4.3 WIRE RETIMING

Unfortunately, long wires cannot be pipelined in isolation. It is important to consider the effect of interconnect latency on overall system behavior. Relocation of flip-flops to pipeline logic path while preserving the functionality of the circuit is known as retiming [28]. However, traditional retiming approaches ignore interconnect delay. In modern-day designs, it is imperative to consider the problem of retiming with both interconnect and gate delays [29–31].

In the context of retiming, a sequential circuit can be represented by a direct graph $G_R(V_R, E_R)$, where each node $v \in V_R$ corresponds to a combinational gate, and each directed edge $e_{uv} \in E_R$ connects the output of gate u to the input of gate v, through a nonnegative number of registers. Without loss of generality, G_R can be assumed to be strongly connected; fictitious nodes and edges can be added to make it strongly connected otherwise. Let d_u be the gate delay of node u, w_{uv} the number of flip-flops of edge e_{uv}, and d_{uv} the interconnect delay of edge e_{uv} if all the flip-flops are removed. Although it is hard to accurately model interconnect delay, it is fairly accurate to assume that the delay of a wire is linearly proportional to its length for the following reasons: When a wire is short, the linear component of the wire delay dominates the quadratic component. For a long wire, buffers inserted at appropriate locations can render the delay linear.

The retiming problem can be viewed as one of determining a labeling of the nodes $r : V_R \to Z$, where Z is the set of integers [28], such that $w_{uv} + r(v) - r(u) \geq 0$ for all edges $w_{uv} \in E_R$. The retiming label $r(v)$ of node v represents the number of flip-flops moved from its outputs to its fan-ins and $\hat{w}_{uv} = w_{uv} + r(v) - r(u)$ denotes the number of flip-flops on edge e_{uv} after retiming. Retiming can be formulated as a problem of determining a feasible retiming solution for a given clock period, that is, a solution in which the number of flip-flops on every edge is nonnegative for a given clock period. The minimum achievable clock period T^*_{CP} can then be computed by performing a binary search.

A feasible retiming solution for a given clock period T_{CP} must satisfy the following set of constraints [30]:

$$d_v \leq a(v) \quad \forall\, v \in V_R,$$

$$a(v) \leq T_{CP} \quad \forall\, v \in V_R,$$

$$w_{uv} + r(v) - r(u) \geq 0 \quad \forall\, e_{uv} \in E_R,$$

$$a(v) \geq a(u) + d_{uv} + d_v - T_{CP}[w_{uv} + r(v) - r(u)] \quad \forall\, e_{uv} \in E_R,$$

Here, $a(v)$ represents the maximum arrival time at the output of gate v from a flip-flop that directly drives the logic path containing v. The first two constraints are fairly straightforward. The third constraint is required for a feasible retiming solution. The fourth constraint ensures that sufficient flip-flops are inserted along each edge e_{uv} for the circuit to be operable at a clock period of T_{CP}. Every flip-flop along the edge e_{uv} after retiming reduces the right-hand side of the inequality by T_{CP}.

By introducing a variable $R(v)$ defined as $a(v)/T_{CP} + r(v)$ at each node v, the preceding set of constraints can be transformed into a set of difference constraints as follows [30]:

$$R(v) - r(v) \geq \frac{d(v)}{T_{CP}} \quad \forall\, v \in V_R, \tag{33.5}$$

$$R(v) - r(v) \leq 1 \quad \forall \, v \in V_R, \tag{33.6}$$

$$r(u) - r(v) \leq w_{uv} \quad \forall \, e_{uv} \in E_R, \tag{33.7}$$

$$R(v) - R(u) \geq \frac{d_{uv}}{T_{CP}} + \frac{d_v}{T_{CP}} - w_{uv} \quad \forall \, e_{uv} \in E_R, \tag{33.8}$$

These difference constraints involve $|V_R|$ real variables $R(v)$, $|V_R|$ integer variables $r(v)$, and $2|V_R| + 2|E_R|$ constraints, and can be solved in polynomial time of $O(|V_R||E_R|\log|V_R| + |V_R|^2 \log^2 |V_R|)$, using Fibonacci heap as the data structure [32].

Given a feasible retiming solution, the exact positions at which flip-flops should be inserted can be determined as follows: For each edge e_{uv} with nonzero $\hat{w}_{uv}$, the first flip-flop on this edge is inserted at a distance that corresponds to a delay of $T_{CP} - a(u)$ from the output of gate u. Other flip-flops are inserted at a distance that corresponds to a delay of T_{CP} from the previous one, until gate v is reached. All remaining flip-flops on this edge are then inserted right before v.

A fast approximation algorithm can be obtained by first replacing each gate by a wire of the same delay, and then solving optimally and efficiently the retiming problem with only interconnect delays [30]. The key to the fast approximation algorithm is the observation that for a directed graph where $d_v = 0$ for all $v \in V_R$, given $R(v)$ for all $v \in V_R$ that satisfy the constraint in Equation 33.8, the set of difference constraints can be satisfied by setting $r(v) = \lfloor R(v) \rfloor$ for all $v \in V_R$. The problem of finding $R(v)$ for all $v \in V_R$ to satisfy the constraint given in Equation 33.8 can be posed as a single-source longest-paths problem on G_R with the cost or length of each edge $e_{uv} \in E_R$ defined as $d_{uv}/T_{CP} - w_{uv}$. Any node in G_R can be the source node as the graph is strongly connected. If G_R has a positive cycle, the clock period T_{CP} is infeasible. The single-source longest-paths problem can be solved by the Bellman–Ford algorithm in $O(|V_R||E_R|)$ time complexity. With a path compaction preprocessing step to the reduce the size of G_R, the complexity can be further reduced.

Given a retiming solution for a graph with only interconnect delays, if the solution retimes some flip-flops into a wire that represents a gate, a postprocessing step is required to get back a feasible retiming solution that has both gate and interconnect delays. First, we move the flip-flops in a gate to its fan-ins or fan-outs depending on which direction has a shorter distance (delay). A linear program is then used to determine the exact positions of the flip-flops on the interconnect edges. The objective of the linear program is to minimize the clock period T_{CP} subject to constraints on the flip-flop counts and constraints on the delays between flip-flops. Let x_{uv}^k denote the delay from the kth flip-flop to the $(k+1)$st flip-flop of the wire from node u to node v in G_R, for $k = 0, 1, \ldots, \hat{w}_{uv}$. The linear program is formulated as follows:

$$\text{Minimize} \quad T_{CP}$$

$$\text{subject to} \quad \sum_{k=0}^{\hat{w}_{uv}} x_{uv}^k = d_{uv} \quad \forall \, e_{uv} \in E_R,$$

$$x_{uv}^{\hat{w}_{uv}} + d_v \leq a(v) \quad \forall \, e_{uv} \in E_R \text{ s.t. } \hat{w}_{uv} > 0,$$

$$a(u) + x_{uv}^0 \leq T_{CP} \quad \forall \, e_{uv} \in E_R \text{ s.t. } \hat{w}_{uv} > 0,$$

$$a(u) + d_{uv} \leq a(v) \quad \forall \, e_{uv} \in E_R \text{ s.t. } \hat{w}_{uv} > 0,$$

33.4.4 AREA CONSTRAINED WIRE RETIMING

To account for the area overhead incurred by wire retiming during the planning stage, a more closely related problem is that of minimum-area retiming. To render conventional minimum-area retiming applicable to interconnects, each long interconnect can be represented as a series of interconnect units, each of which has delay but performs no logic function. A natural segmentation of an interconnect can be obtained by buffer insertion, with each interconnect unit being a buffer driving an interconnect segment.

Although minimum-area retiming is optimal in terms of overall area consumption, it may not be directly applicable to interconnect retiming and planning. To minimize the total area consumption, it may relocate flip-flops from regions with a lot of empty space to overcongested regions. That may result in area constraint violations in a given floorplan, necessitating iterations of floorplanning and interconnect planning. Therefore, for interconnect retiming and planning, it is necessary to consider local area constraints such that both the timing and the impact on floorplan of the relocated flip-flops can be taken into account. In Ref. [29], a new retiming problem, called local area constrained (LAC) retiming problem, has been formulated with the following three sets of constraints, of which the first two are typical of the retiming problem [28] and the third captures the local area constraints:

1. Edge weights must be nonnegative:

$$r(v) - r(u) \geq -w(e_{u,v}), \quad \forall\, e_{u,v} \in E_R.$$

2. For any path $u \rightsquigarrow v$ whose delay (along successive combinational logic paths) is larger than the clock period T_{CP}, there should be at least one flip-flop on it after retiming:

$$r(v) - r(u) \geq -W(u,v) + 1, \forall\, u \rightsquigarrow v, D(u,v) > T_{CP},$$

where
  $W(u,v)$ defines the minimum latency for a signal to transfer from u to v before retiming
  $D(u,v)$ is the maximum delay (of successive combinational logic paths) of the logic path from u to v with the minimum latency $W(u,v)$

3. To define the local area constraints, we let F be the set of all functional units, V_T be the set of all tiles, and for any $t_i \in V_T$, $C(t_i)$ be the remaining capacity (after buffer insertion) that is available for flip-flop insertion. The function $P : F \rightarrow V_T$ maps each functional unit $v \in F$ to a tile $t_i \in V_T$ such that $P(v) = t_i$ means that functional unit or interconnect unit v is in tile t_i of the floorplan. The local area constraint of a tile requires that

$$\sum_{P(u)=t_i,\ e_{u,v}\in E_R} \left[w(e_{u,v}) + r(v) - r(u) \right] \leq C(t_i), \quad \forall\, t_i \in V_T.$$

As each local area constraint involves more than two retiming variables, the LAC-retiming problem is an integer linear programming problem, which is NP-complete. In Ref. [29], a heuristic based on minimum-area retiming was used to solve the LAC-retiming problem. In minimum-area retiming, all flip-flops are assumed to have the same area cost; thus, the minimization of total number of flip-flops is equivalent to the minimization of the total area. In LAC-retiming, the insertion of flip-flops into different tiles should take into account the differences in the tile capacities. To achieve that, the LAC-retiming problem was solved in Ref. [29] as a series of weighted minimum-area retiming problems, with the weights of flip-flops adjusted according to the congestion levels in the tiles. As different weights are assigned to flip-flops in different tiles based on the area consumption and tile capacities in the series of minimum-area retiming problems, flip-flops from overutilized tiles can be repositioned to those with low-area consumption.

33.5 CONCLUDING REMARKS

While Semiconductor process scaling has enabled integrated circuits of increasingly high performance, it has also created several new design concerns. In this chapter, we have summarized several buffer planning methodologies that tackle the design challenges brought forth by the exponential growth of buffers. Most of these methodologies address both timing and layout closure issues simultaneously by allocating sufficient silicon resources and routing resources during floorplanning or right after floorplanning. As multiple-cycle data communications become increasingly necessary, many of these buffer planning methodologies have been extended to also address the exponential growth of flip-flops (clocked repeaters). The challenge here is to account for the changes in latency introduced by additional flip-flops along global interconnects. While we have presented these planning methodologies in the context of synchronous system design, we believe that these methodologies also have an important role to play in the design of SOCs, NOCs, latency-insensitive systems, and globally asynchronous locally synchronous systems.

It is also important to recognize that the planning methodologies presented in this chapter may have fundamental limits. To a certain extent, the planning methodologies shield the downstream stages of physical synthesis from the problem of inserting a huge fraction of repeater (and clocked repeater). However, empirical studies [33] indicate that it is unlikely that incremental improvements to the physical synthesis technologies can adequately handle the exponential growth in repeater and clocked repeater counts if the scaling continues at the existing pace. Instead, a correct-by-construction design methodology that trades off optimality for predictability has been proposed in Ref. [33]. Perhaps even more alarming is a theoretical study, which is based on Rent's rule [34,35], that demonstrates the necessity of excessively long wires as the number of computing elements within a system continues to grow [36]. As large monolithic designs are unattractive, increased quality, instead of improved capacity, of CAD algorithms and tools should perhaps be the proper objective of future research [36].

REFERENCES

1. J. Cong, T. Kong, and Z. Pan. Buffer block planning for interconnect planning and prediction. *IEEE Transactions on Very Large Scale Integration (VLSI) Systems,* 9(6):929–937, 2001 (ICCAD 1999).
2. C. J. Alpert, J. Hu, S. S. Sapatnekar, and P. G. Villarrubia. A practical methodology for early buffer and wire resource allocation. *IEEE Transactions on Computer-Aided Design of Integrated Circuits and Systems,* 22(5):573–583, 2003 (DAC 2001).
3. P. Sarkar and C. -K. Koh. Routability-driven repeater block planning for interconnect-centric floorplanning. *IEEE Transactions on Computer-Aided Design of Integrated Circuits and Systems,* 20(5):660–671, 2001 (ISPD 2000).
4. J. Cong, L. He, K. -Y. Khoo, C. -K. Koh, and Z. Pan. Interconnect design for deep submicron ICs. In *Proceedings of IEEE/ACM International Conference on Computer Aided Design,* San Jose, CA, pp. 478–485, 1997.
5. W. C. Elmore. The transient response of damped linear networks with particular regard to wide-band amplifiers. *Journal of Applied Physics,* 19(1):55–63, January 1948.
6. C. J. Alpert and A. Devgan. Wire segmenting for improved buffer insertion. In *Proceedings of ACM/IEEE Design Automation Conference,* Anaheim, CA, pp. 588–593, June 1997.
7. F. F. Dragan, A. B. Kahng, I. I. Mandoiu, S. Muddu, and A. Zelikovsky. Provably good global buffering by generalized multiterminal multicommodity flow approximation. *IEEE Transactions on Computer-Aided Design of Integrated Circuits and Systems,* 21(3):263–274, 2002 (ASPDAC 2001).
8. F. F. Dragan, A. B. Kahng, S. Muddu, and A. Zelikovsky. Provably good global buffering using an available buffer block plan. In *Proceedings of IEEE/ACM International Conference on Computer Aided Design,* San Jose, CA, pp. 104–109, 2000.
9. X. Tang and D. F. Wong. Network flow based buffer planning. *Integration,* 30(2):143–155, 2001 (ISPD 2000).
10. Y. -H. Cheng and Y. -W. Chang. Integrating buffer planning with floorplanning for simultaneous multi-objective optimization. In *Proceedings of IEEE/ACM Asia South Pacific Design Automation Conference,* pp. 624–627, Piscataway, NJ, 2004. IEEE Press.

11. H. -R. Jiang, Y. -W. Chang, J. -Y. Jou, and K. -Y. Chao. Simultaneous floorplan and buffer block optimization. *IEEE Transactions on Computer-Aided Design of Integrated Circuits and Systems,* 23(5):694–703, 2004 (ASPDAC 2003).

12. Y. Ma, X. Hong, S. Dong, S. Chen, Y. Cai, C. K. Cheng, and J. Gu. Dynamic global buffer planning optimization based on detail block locating and congestion analysis. In *Proceedings of ACM/IEEE Design Automation Conference,* pp. 806–811, New York, 2003. ACM Press.

13. R. McInerney, M. Page, K. Leeper, T. Hillie, H. Chan, and B. Basaran. Methodology for repeater insertion management in the RTL, layout, floorplan, and fullchip timing databases of the Itanium microprocessor. In *Proceedings of ACM International Symposium on Physical Design,* San Diego, CA, pp. 99–104, 2000.

14. L. P. P. P. van Ginneken. Buffer placement in distributed RC-tree networks for minimal Elmore delay. In *Proceedings of IEEE International Symposium on Circuits and Systems,* New Orleans, LA, pp. 865–868, 1990.

15. S. Chen, X. Hong, S. Dong, Y. Ma, Y. Cai, C. -K. Cheng, and J. Gu. A buffer planning algorithm based on dead space redistribution. In *ASP-DAC '03: Proceedings of the 2003 Conference on Asia South Pacific Design Automation,* pp. 435–438, Piscataway, NJ, 2003. IEEE Press.

16. S. Chen, X. Hong, S. Dong, Y. Ma, Y. Cai, C. -K. Cheng, and J. Gu. A buffer planning algorithm with congestion optimization. In *Proceedings of IEEE/ACM Asia South Pacific Design Automation Conference,* pp. 615–620, Piscataway, NJ, 2004. IEEE Press.

17. C. W. Sham and E. F. Young. Routability driven floorplanner with buffer block planning. *IEEE Transactions on Computer-Aided Design of Integrated Circuits and Systems,* 22(4):470–480, 2003 (ISPD 2002).

18. K. K. Wong and E. F. Young. Fast buffer planning and congestion optimization in interconnect-driven floorplanning. In *Proceedings of IEEE/ACM Asia South Pacific Design Automation Conference,* Kitakyushu, Japan, pp. 411–416, 2003.

19. C. Albrecht, A. B. Kahng, I. Mandoiu, and A. Zelikovsky. Floorplan evaluation with timing-driven global wireplanning, pin assignment and buffer/wire sizing. In *Proceedings of IEEE/ACM Asia South Pacific Design Automation Conference,* Bangalore, India, pp. 580–591, 2002.

20. Y. Ma, X. Hong, S. Dong, S. Chen, C. -K. Cheng, and J. Gu. Buffer planning as an integral part of floorplanning with consideration of routing congestion. *IEEE Transactions on Computer-Aided Design of Integrated Circuits and Systems,* 24(4):609–621, 2005 (ISPD 2003, ASPDAC 2004).

21. H. Xiang, X. Tang, and D. F. Wong. An algorithm for integrated pin assignment and buffer planning. *ACM Transactions on Design Automation of Electronics Systems,* 10(3):561–572, 2005 (DAC 2002).

22. P. Sarkar and C. -K. Koh. Repeater block planning under simultaneous delay and transition time constraints. In *Proceedings of IEEE/ACM Design, Automation and Test in Europe Conference,* pp. 540–545, Piscataway, NJ, 2001. IEEE Press.

23. S. -M. Li, Y. -H. Cherng, and Y. -W. Chang. Noise-aware buffer planning for interconnect-driven floorplanning. In *Proceedings of IEEE/ACM Asia South Pacific Design Automation Conference,* Kitakyushu, Japan, pp. 423–426, 2003.

24. A. Devgan. Efficient coupled noise estimation for on-chip interconnects. In *Proceedings of IEEE/ACM International Conference on Computer Aided Design,* San Jose, CA, pp. 147–153, 1997.

25. D. Matzke. Will physical scalability sabotage performance gains? *IEEE Computers,* 8:37–39, September 1997.

26. P. Cocchini. A methodology for optimal repeater insertion in pipelined interconnects. *IEEE Transactions on Computer-Aided Design of Integrated Circuits and Systems,* 22(12):1613–1624, 2003 (ICCAD 2002).

27. R. Lu, G. Zhong, C. -K. Koh, and K. -Y. Chao. Flip-flop and repeater insertion for early interconnect planning. In *Proceedings of IEEE/ACM Design, Automation and Test in Europe Conference,* Paris, France, pp. 690–695, March 2002.

28. C. E. Leiserson and J. B. Saxe. Retiming synchronous circuitry. *Algorithmica,* 6:5–35,1991.

29. R. Lu and C. -K. Koh. Interconnect planning with local area constrained retiming. In *Proceedings of IEEE/ACM Design, Automation and Test in Europe Conference,* Messe Munich, Germany, pp. 442–447, March 2003.

30. C. C. Chu, E. F. Young, D. K. Tong, and S. Dechu. Retiming with interconnect delay. In *Proceedings of IEEE/ACM International Conference on Computer Aided Design,* San Jose, CA, pp. 221–226, 2003.

31. C. Lin and H. Zhou. Retiming for wire pipelining in system-on-chip. *IEEE Transactions on Computer-Aided Design of Integrated Circuits and Systems,* 23(9):1338–1345, 2004 (ICCAD 2003).

32. C. E. Leiserson and J. B. Saxe. A mixed-integer programming problem which is efficiently solvable. *Journal of Algorithms,* 9:114–128, 1988.

33. P. Saxena, N. Menezes, P. Cocchini, and D. Kirkpatrick. Repeater scaling and its impact on CAD. *IEEE Transactions on Computer-Aided Design of Integrated Circuits and Systems,* 23(4):451–463, 2004 (ISPD 2003).

34. C. E. Radke. A justification of, and an improvement on, a useful rule for predicting circuit-to-pin ratios. In *Proceedings of ACM/IEEE Design Automation Conference,* pp. 257–267, 1969.

35. B. Landman and R. Russo. On a pin versus block relationship for partitioning of logic graphs. *IEEE Transactions on Computers,* C-20:1469–1479, December 1971.

36. P. H. Madden. SuperSized VLSI: A recipe for disaster. In *Proceedings of Electronic Design Processes Workshop,* Monterey, CA, 2005.

34 Coupling Noise

Rajendran Panda, Vladimir Zolotov, and Murat Becer

CONTENTS

As a result of the scaling of physical geometries of wires and devices to ultra-deep submicron (UDSM) dimensions, signal integrity has become, in addition to area, timing, and power, an important design challenge. Although signal integrity problems can arise from many sources, such as capacitive coupling between signal wires, inductive and substrate coupling, power supply variation, degradation of devices and interconnect, and leakage current, capacitive coupling is the single major source of noise in current technologies. In UDSM technologies, its contribution has grown to be a major fraction, as much as 60–70 percent, of the total wiring capacitance. Depending on the signal levels on the coupled wires, this capacitance can speed up or slow down switching, and introduce signal-dependent variations in the delays. The domination of wire delays over gate delays in these technologies has the effect of making a significant part of the circuit delay susceptible to wide variation because of capacitive coupling. As a result, delay variation effects of coupling noise must be considered while verifying the timing of a design. In addition to delay-related failures, noise can also cause functional failures, increase power consumption, and accelerate degradation of devices. For these reasons, physical design and circuit design must seriously consider coupling noise issues.

Serious noise issues, if not caught and fixed early, may require significant design modifications at very late design stages and impact adversely the design completion schedule. Because noise analysis and repair cost significant time and resources, noise avoidance techniques should be embraced at all design stages.

In this chapter, we look at the coupling noise phenomenon, noise analysis, and some of the criteria for determining noise failures. We then present modeling and analysis techniques suitable for efficient noise analysis at the global routing, detailed routing, and postrouting stages. Techniques for reducing pessimism in noise analysis are also provided in some detail. Finally, noise avoidance, noise-aware physical and circuit design, and noise repair are discussed.

34.1 COUPLING NOISE PHENOMENON

Coupling noise can be broadly defined as distortion of a signal by other signals. The net with the distorted signal is usually called a victim net, and the nets affecting a victim net are called aggressor nets. The victim net and its aggressor nets collectively form a noise cluster. In real circuits, coupling noise is a bidirectional phenomenon: if net A injects noise into net B, then net B injects some noise into net A too. However, this symmetrical consideration of coupling noise [1] is not very popular in very large scale integration (VLSI) design, except during a full SPICE-level circuit simulation, because it complicates the analysis. Asymmetrical consideration of coupling noise significantly simplifies the analysis but may have lower accuracy.

A noise event occurs when a victim net is electrically coupled with an aggressor net. Capacitive coupling is the most important cause of coupling noise in VLSI interconnects. There are several reasons for the strong effect of capacitive coupling in UDSM technologies. Complementary metal oxide semiconductor (CMOS) transistors have a very high input gate resistance and a small gate capacitance, as compared to the coupling capacitance of interconnects. With technology scaling, the minimum spacing between wires is decreased while the ratio of thickness to width of wires is increased (to control wire resistance). The net result of this is that, in successive technology generations, the wire coupling capacitance increases relative to the wire capacitance to ground. Moreover, strict constraints on power dissipation require the use of small drivers with rather high output resistance, which accentuates the contribution of the coupling capacitance to the total delay. All these factors exacerbate coupling noise injection.

34.1.1 INTERCONNECT CAPACITANCE

The total wire capacitance consists of grounded and coupling capacitances, as shown in Figure 34.1. The grounded capacitance results from several sources. First, an important component of the grounded capacitance is wire capacitance to orthogonal wiring on upper and lower metal layers. The coupling capacitance to each of the orthogonal wires is quite small and although these wires may switch at different time moments in different directions, the total noise injected by these wires is close to zero. Therefore, the capacitance to orthogonal wires is considered as grounded capacitance. Second, if the wire is on the lowest metal layer, its grounded capacitance includes also coupling capacitance to the substrate. Third, the coupling capacitance between a wire and the power and ground distribution networks on the same or different layers contributes to the grounded capacitance. The coupling capacitance of a wire is usually the sidewall capacitance to other (nonsupply) wires in the same metal layer. This capacitance can be high compared to the capacitance to the other metal layers, because wires in modern chips are rather tall and narrow.

Although detailed capacitance extraction involves a three-dimensional field solver, for the purposes of analyzing large networks of interconnects, it is sufficient to use much simpler models. The

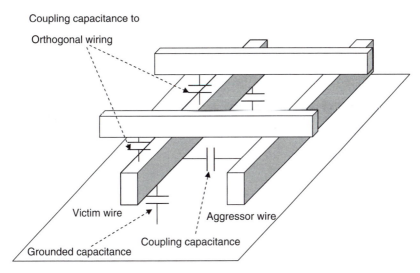

FIGURE 34.1 Coupling and grounded capacitances of interconnect wires.

coupling capacitance between two parallel wires is approximately proportional to the height of the wires and the distance that they run parallel to each other, and inversely proportional to the spacing between the wires. On the other hand, the grounded capacitance of a wire is proportional to the wire length and wire width, and inversely proportional to the thickness of the interlayer dielectric.

34.1.2 COUPLING NOISE INJECTION

The injection of capacitive coupling noise is illustrated on a simple model, as shown in Figure 34.2a. Here, the aggressor net transitions from zero voltage to Vdd during time t_a. The resistance R_h modeling the driver of the victim net is trying to hold the victim net at zero potential. The capacitance C_g is the total grounded capacitance of the victim net, and the capacitance C_c is the coupling capacitance between the victim and aggressor nets. When the aggressor transitions, it increases voltage on one terminal of the coupling capacitance C_c, which increases the voltage on the other terminal of C_c. The pair of capacitors C_c and C_g acts as a capacitive voltage divider. If the holding resistance R_h is infinitely large, the voltage on the victim net would be $V_a^* C_c/(C_g + C_c)$. The voltage on the victim

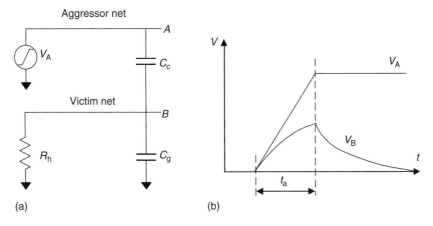

FIGURE 34.2 (a) Circuit and (b) waveforms of capacitive coupling noise injection.

net is growing during switching of the aggressor net. If the holding resistance R_h has a finite value, the current flowing through this resistance discharges the grounded capacitance C_g and charges the coupling capacitance C_c. This slows down the voltage increase on the victim and eventually makes this voltage return to zero after the aggressor completes its switching. The speed of this process and, correspondingly, the height and the widths of the noise pulse depend on the amount of current flowing through the holding resistance. The smaller the holding resistance, the higher the current it provides to the victim net and the shorter and narrower is the noise pulse. The waveforms of noise injection are shown in Figure 34.2b. A similar situation occurs if the victim is at Vdd and the aggressor net switches from Vdd to 0.

The circuit shown in Figure 34.2a can be solved analytically. A formula for the height of the noise pulse is expressed as follows [2,3]:

$$V_n = \text{Vdd} \cdot \frac{R_h C_c}{t_a} \left\{ 1 - \exp \left[\frac{-t_a}{R_h(C_g + C_c)} \right] \right\} \tag{34.1}$$

From the above formula, it is clear that noise can be reduced by the following methods:

- Slowing down the aggressor transition, i.e., increasing its transition time t_a
- Reducing the coupling capacitance C_c
- Increasing the grounded capacitance C_g
- Reducing the holding resistance R_h

These methods form the basis for the noise avoidance and repair techniques discussed in the sequel.

34.2 NOISE ANALYSIS

Depending on the victim net behavior, there are two possible types of coupling noise: functional noise and noise on delay. Functional noise occurs when the victim net is not expected to switch during noise injection. There are four types of functional noise corresponding to the combinations of undershoot and overshoot from signals that are nominally at low and high logic levels. These types of coupling noise are shown in Figure 34.3. Typically, low overshoot and high undershoot are most harmful types of noise for circuit operation. If a noise pulse on a logic low wire is high enough, it can change the state of the victim receiver gate and create a circuit logic failure. However, high overshoot and low undershoot can be problematic for some kinds of circuits, such as circuits with pass-transistors. Additionally, they affect circuit reliability by magnifying the hot electron injection (HCI) and the negative bias temperature instability (NBTI).

Noise on delay occurs when the victim net transitions from one state to the other during noise injection. The injected noise pulse affects the victim transition, making it either faster or slower, depending on whether the aggressor net switches in the same or opposite direction as the victim net. If the delay variation because of the noise pulse is too high, it may create a circuit timing failure. Figure 34.4 shows waveforms of victim and aggressor transitions for noise on delay.

34.2.1 NOISE CALCULATION

The goal of noise analysis is to identify all nets susceptible to noise that may result in circuit failure. To be useful, the noise analysis should be conservative so as not to miss any potentially dangerous noise. On the other hand, noise analysis should not be too pessimistic, or it will report too many false noise violations, which are difficult to repair and will lead to wasted power and design effort. Thus, a good noise analysis tool should be both conservative and sufficiently accurate. The simplified model shown in Figure 34.2, while useful for understanding the coupling noise phenomenon, is not accurate for computing the actual noise in VLSI interconnects.

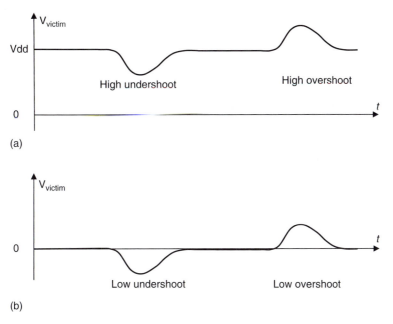

FIGURE 34.3 Types of functional noise. (a) Noise injected to high logic level and (b) noise injected to low logic level.

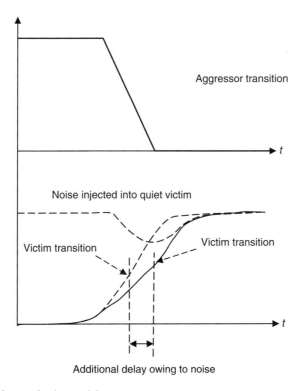

FIGURE 34.4 Waveforms of noise on delay.

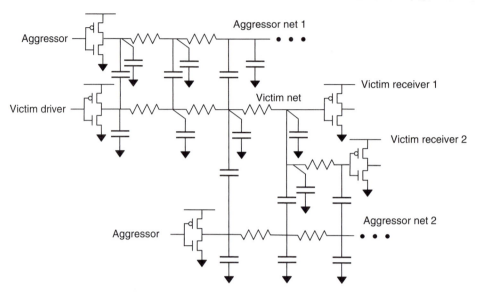

FIGURE 34.5   Example of noise cluster with capacitive coupling.

Figure 34.5 shows a more accurate model of a noise cluster. The interconnect wires are broken into segments, and each segment is modeled with its resistance, grounded capacitance and coupling capacitance. The noise is injected into the victim net along the whole length of the victim wire by multiple aggressors. The victim driver is trying to hold the victim net at the correct potential by providing the current for charging or discharging the capacitances of the victim net. This current is a nonlinear function of the voltage at the input and output of the victim driver. The injected noise pulse is propagated through the victim interconnect to the input of the victim receiver gates affecting their state and behavior.

Noise analysis requires solving two main problems: calculating the amount of injected noise and determining whether the injected noise pulse is critical for circuit operation or not. The calculation of the actual noise waveform is a difficult problem because a noise cluster is a complex nonlinear circuit. This can be solved most accurately by performing a SPICE-level transient analysis, and by solving differential equations describing the transient behavior of the noise cluster. Unfortunately, this approach is too slow for large designs because VLSI chips may have many millions of noise clusters. Moreover, the simulation-based approach with a single stimulus is not necessarily conservative enough. There can be an extremely large number of possible noise injection scenarios and we cannot guarantee that the worst of these has been chosen for simulation. The aggressors can switch at different moments in time and have various waveforms with different transition times. The actual aggressor behavior depends on many factors such as the state of the circuit, its input signals, supply voltage, temperature, and process variation. Therefore, SPICE simulation of noise clusters is resorted to only in special cases such as verifying and tuning noise analysis techniques, or in analyzing complicated situations.

To simplify the computation of an injected noise pulse, it is common to approximate the non-linear circuit of the noise cluster with a linear circuit. The approximation should be conservative enough so that the noise computed from this approximation is not less than the worst possible actual noise. The transformation of the nonlinear circuit into a linear circuit is performed by modeling the aggressor and victim drivers with linear models, as will be discussed in Section 34.3. The receivers are modeled by their input capacitances. The resulting linear circuit can be analyzed using the super-position principle, which is a key benefit of linear modeling. The noise injected by each aggressor net is computed separately assuming that all the other aggressor drivers are quiet. A model order reduction technique [4,5] is usually used for this computation. The total noise pulse is calculated by superimposing the noise pulses injected by each aggressor net. The noise pulses are aligned at their peaks to obtain the maximum possible combined noise pulse.

34.2.2 FAILURE CRITERIA

The second main problem of noise analysis is making a decision whether the injected noise is dangerous for circuit operation or not. This problem is solved differently for functional noise and noise on delay. In case of noise on delay, delay variation even from small injected noise can be harmful for correct circuit operation if the affected net is on a critical-signal propagation path. Therefore, in case of noise on delay, we must compute not only the noise pulse but compute also the delay variation due to that pulse and perform timing analysis with the delay variations obtained from noise analysis.

Accurate computation of the delay variation because of an injected noise pulse is a difficult nonlinear problem. One of the common approximate methods to solve this problem is to superimpose linearly the transition of the victim net and the injected noise pulse. According to Ref. [6], the maximum delay variation is obtained if the peak of the noise pulse is aligned with the 50 percent crossing time of the victim transition in the presence of noise. This alignment is demonstrated in Figure 34.4. However, this method maximizes the delay variation of the victim net as seen at the victim receiver's input and does not take into account the propagation of the resulting signal transition through the victim receiver gate. To improve the accuracy of delay computation, it was proposed to maximize the delay measured from the output of the victim driver to the output of the victim receiver [7]. This takes into account nonlinear and low-pass filtering properties of the victim receiver gate. However, because it is difficult to compute this delay variation without nonlinear simulation of the victim receiver gate, precharacterized multidimensional tables are used for this computation in Ref. [7]. After the noise analysis, the calculated delays are used for noise-aware timing analysis that verifies whether the circuit meets timing requirements in the presence of noise.

An alternative approach to estimating delay variation because of coupling noise is based on the observation that the noise pulse injected during victim net transition results in additional charge flowing either from or into the victim driver. From this, it was concluded that the injected noise pulse can be modeled with a change of the effective load capacitance [8,9]. The degree of the effective load capacitance variation is called the Miller coefficient. The main benefit of this approach is its simplicity and convenience for integration of the noise analysis into a timing analysis engine. The noise analysis tool simply updates values of the effective load capacitance, and then performs the timing analysis in the usual way with the updated load capacitances. Unfortunately, the accuracy of this approach is not very good because it does not take into account the fact that the waveforms in the presence of the injected noise are significantly different from the waveforms without noise, and a simple change of the victim load capacitance cannot accurately capture the effect of noise injection.

In case of functional noise, a noise pulse is injected into a victim net when it is in its stable state. If the noise pulse is large enough, it can propagate through combinational gates to memory elements (latches or flip-flops) and change their state, resulting in a circuit failure. Digital gates suppress propagation of narrow short pulses for two reasons: (1) their voltage transfer characteristic attenuates small deviations of the input voltage from the values corresponding to logic 1 and 0 and (2) CMOS gates act as low-pass filters.

There are two main classes of failure criteria for functional noise. One of them is propagation of the injected noise pulse though the circuit until memory elements [10]. The computation of the propagated noise pulse can be carried out either by precharacterized tables or by using simplified nonlinear models of gates [10,11]. The noise propagation failure criterion takes into account that the propagated noise pulse combines with noise pulses injected into the nets along the noise propagation path. Unfortunately, the noise propagation criterion requires rather complex computations. Therefore, it is more suitable for sign-off analysis.

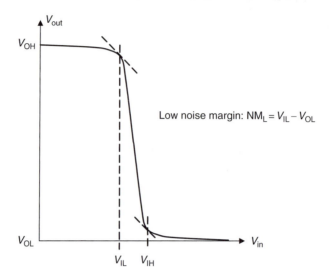

FIGURE 34.6   Inverter voltage transfer characteristic and noise margins.

The other class of noise failure criteria is based on using local noise threshold values [10–15]. Only noise signals that are higher than a specified threshold level are considered dangerous. The main difficulty with such criteria lies in the selection of the appropriate threshold. One of the common approaches is to use the static noise margin of the victim receiver gate [16] derived from the unity gain points of the transfer characteristic, as shown in Figure 34.6. This derivation is based on the consideration that, for safe operation, the differential DC amplification coefficient of the gate should be less than 1. However, this criterion does not take into account the low-pass filtering properties of CMOS gates, and therefore, it can be too pessimistic. There are several modifications of the local noise failure criteria that either directly compute a propagated noise pulse or use a noise rejection curve [12]. An example of a noise rejection curve, whose coordinates are the height and the width of the noise pulse, is shown in Figure 34.7. The points lying higher than the noise rejection curve

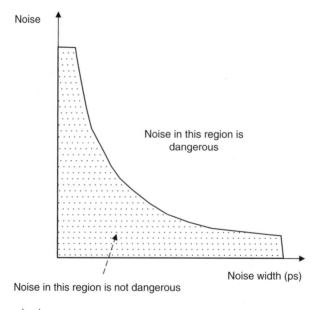

FIGURE 34.7   Noise rejection curve.

correspond to the combinations of noise height and width that are dangerous for circuit operation. To take into account the noise propagating from the input of the victim driver to its output, the local criterion can increment the injected noise by some predefined margin. In this case, the criterion checks that the noise propagated through the victim's receiver gate is less than this predefined margin. This approach is called noise budgeting, and although it is computationally efficient, the local criteria of noise failure are not very accurate because they cannot take into account how the noise pulse propagates through the circuit. However, because of their efficiency, the local noise criteria are very popular for noise avoidance, noise-aware routing, and repairing methodology.

34.3 SIMPLIFYING MODELS AND ANALYSIS

For chip-level signal-integrity verification, it is essential to analyze millions of net clusters (each cluster consisting of a victim net and its significant aggressors). Moreover, the chip-level analysis will have to be carried out several times before a complete noise sign-off, nearly as often as significant changes are made to the design layout. Design productivity requires this analysis be performed with a reasonable computational time, typically within a few hours. A fast noise analysis turnaround is made possible mainly through two simplifications discussed in this section: simplification of models and conservative filtering of nonrisky nets. These simplifications are indispensable for early noise estimation during the global and detailed routing procedures, wherein noise is to be estimated in an inner loop of routing optimization.

34.3.1 SIMPLIFICATION OF MODELS

Linear models for the victim and aggressor drivers, receivers, and the interconnection significantly speed up noise simulation while providing acceptable accuracy. Linear simulation is extremely fast compared to nonlinear simulation. Moreover, in certain situations, even analytical formulations can be used. Another key advantage of working with linear models is the ability to apply the principle of superposition, which permits simulating the victim and aggressor driver sources individually and later combining their effects. This is crucial for determining a temporal alignment between the switching of the victim and aggressors that produces conservative noise estimation. Searching for a proper alignment of source waveforms that will maximize the noise effect (i.e., glitch or delay variation at a receiver gate) is prohibitively expensive for nonlinear circuits. Using superposition, the results of independent simulations of linear aggressor and victim driver sources can be easily combined to maximize the noise effect. The construction of linear models of drivers and receivers is described in the following subsections.

34.3.1.1 Aggressor Driver Model

A simple linear model of the aggressor driver consists of a Thevenin voltage source with a series resistance, as shown in Figure 34.8. Typically, a saturated ramp is used as the voltage source, although other waveforms can also be used. Such a model is fitted by matching the salient time points (e.g., 10, 50, and 90 percent crossing points) of the output waveforms obtained with the linear model and with the actual nonlinear driver, for a given load capacitance. The model is precharacterized for a range of load capacitance values. During noise analysis, the effective capacitance [17] of the distributed parasitic elements of the interconnect wires and the driver slew are determined using either iterative or noniterative techniques.

34.3.1.2 Quiet Victim Model (for Functional Noise)

For a small noise height, the driver can be approximated by a holding resistor connected to ground or Vdd. The holding resistance can be characterized in several ways:

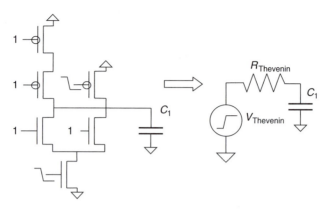

FIGURE 34.8   Aggressor driver model.

1. A small signal analysis of the gate can be performed, wherein a small noise voltage is applied at the output (over a 0 or Vdd bias as appropriate for the output state) and the output current is measured. The ratio of the output current to the applied noise voltage then characterizes the holding resistance. Note that, a conservative (larger) holding resistance value is obtained when the output is biased to the maximum expected noise level.

2. The holding resistance of the driver gate can be computed from the channel resistances of individual transistors, by traversing all the conducting paths in the gate from output node to Vdd/ground [12]. As the transistors in the conducting paths will be in the linear operating region, the transistor channel resistance in the linear region may be precharacterized as a function of transistor width. For a conservative analysis, the inputs of the gate must be asserted so as to obtain the maximum holding resistance.

34.3.1.3 Switching Victim Driver Model (for Delay Noise)

A switching event on the victim affects the load seen by the aggressors and vice versa. The change in aggressor's effective loading owing to victim's switching has only secondary effects on the noise induced on the victim (effected through the change in aggressor's output slew), and so can be ignored. For this reason, the aggressor driver model (discussed before) is created with no special consideration of the victim's switching. However, a driver model created thus cannot be used for a switching victim without incurring significant error, because the nonlinearity error is severe in the victim driver case. The change in effective loading of victim owing to aggressors' switching and its impact on victim's delay is significant. One way to compensate this error is to adjust the Thevenin resistance of the driver model to a larger resistance, called the transient holding resistance, R_{tr}, which is calculated as below and illustrated in Figure 34.9 [7].

1. Obtain the noise waveform on the victim by performing a linear simulation using an initial (uncompensated) Thevenin model with the victim source grounded. Aggressors are simulated individually and aligned appropriately to get the maximum peak noise. From the noise voltage waveform, $V_n(t)$, compute the associated noise current waveform, $I_n(t)$, using the simplified model in Figure 34.9a: $I_n = V_n/R_{th} + C_{LOAD}(\partial V_n/\partial t)$.

2. Perform nonlinear simulations of the victim driver gate with C_{LOAD}, with and without the added current source $I_n(t)$ at the output, to obtain the noiseless transition V_1 and noisy transition V_2, as shown in Figure 34.9b, and calculate the noise voltage response of the nonlinear model, V'_n, by subtracting the two nonlinear simulation results: $V'_n = V_1 - V_2$ (Figure 34.9c).

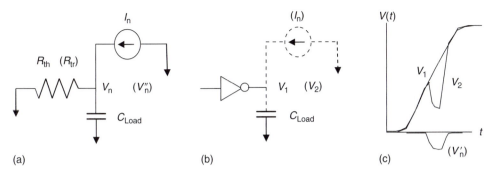

FIGURE 34.9   Characterization of transient Thevenin resistance: (a) Computation of noise current waveform using a linear driver model, (b) Computation of noisy and nonnoisy output waveforms with a nonlinear driver model, and (c) Computation of noise voltage waveform for computing transient holding resistance.

3. Finally, construct the equivalent linear model with the transient holding resistance R_{tr} by replacing $\underline{R_{th}}$ in Figure 34.9a with R_{tr}. Determine the value of R_{tr} such that the area under the resulting noise voltage waveform V''_n matches the area under V'_n. It can be shown that $R_{tr} = \int V'_n \, dt / \int I_n \, dt$.

34.3.1.4   Receiver Characterization

The loading of a receiver gate on a victim or an aggressor net is modeled as a fixed capacitance, averaged over the period of transition of its input. A receiver gate is also characterized for its noise threshold values that define a local failure, or for noise propagation. The noise threshold can be as detailed as a noise rejection table, such as the one shown in Figure 34.7, or as simple as the static noise margin. The noise propagation table, which gives the amount of output noise as a function of properties of input noise pulse (width and height), provides a very efficient mechanism for propagating noise to memory elements, without a need to perform an expensive simulation of a cascade of multiple stages of nets together. Where a noise propagation table is available, the noise threshold can be computed on the fly when a local noise check is to be performed.

The above discussed linear models do introduce some error, but their accuracy is acceptable in most situations. Situations requiring high accuracy may be simulated using accurate nonlinear models with SPICE level accuracy, using the worst-case conditions (e.g., alignment of aggressors) predicted through the linear model.

34.3.2   Conservative Filtering of Nonrisky Nets

Simulation with detailed models is unnecessary for a majority of nets as coupling noise is significant only in a small fraction of the nets. We can use extremely simplified, but conservative, models to quickly identify potentially risky nets (a very small number usually) for detailed noise analysis. It is a common practice to use initially very simple driver and interconnection models and then gradually increase the details of the models and resimulate only those net clusters that fall with the simpler model. A hierarchy of filters used by Ref. [12] is shown in Figure 34.10 and described below as an example of this approach:

1. Conservative default driver models are used for victims and aggressors. Lumped resistance-capacitance (RC) models are used for nets. The lumped grounded capacitor of the victim net is placed at the driving end of the victim net and the lumped coupling capacitance at the receiver end of the net. The resulting model is shown in Figure 34.10a. In this case, the actual driver models and the distributed RC need not be loaded, and the noise can be computed analytically.

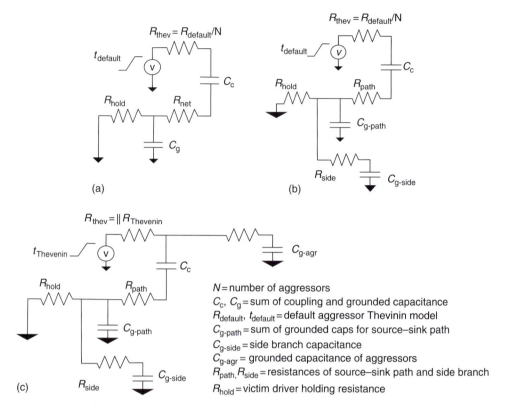

FIGURE 34.10   Hierarchy of conservative noise filters.

2. The default victim driver is now replaced by the linear model of the actual driver and the victim net model is expanded to handle the main path to receiver and the side paths differently, as shown in Figure 34.10b.
3. The default aggressor driver is now replaced by the actual aggressor linear drivers and the aggressor nets are expanded to include topology details, as shown in Figure 34.10c.

34.4   REDUCING PESSIMISM IN CROSSTALK NOISE ANALYSIS

As described in the previous sections, practical noise analysis is performed in a static way that locally creates a worst-case scenario. This results in an inherent pessimism in both functional and delay noise analyses. Crosstalk noise induced on a net greatly depends on how many aggressor nets switch and how their transitions are aligned among themselves, and in the case of delay noise, also with respect to the victim transition. An infinite number of switching scenarios is possible, depending on input signal arrival times, process variation, environment parameters, and the logical operation of the circuit. Predicting the exact worst-case noise occurrence is very difficult. Therefore, noise analysis tools compute a conservative estimate of possible induced noise. Typically, it is assumed that all aggressor nets switch in the same direction at the worst alignment time. However, many switching scenarios are prohibited in reality because of timing and logic correlations between the victim and aggressor signals. In most cases, worst-case switching scenario does not occur due to such correlations, rendering the estimated noise from a naive analysis approach very pessimistic. This pessimism, also called false noise, results in false functional and timing violations. False noise results in wastage of precious design and silicon resources, which are spent for fixing nonexisting problems.

In this section, we present an overview of approaches that utilize the timing and logical correlations to reduce false noise. Note that this section presents techniques that make use of available design data to reduce pessimism. Choosing a meaningful failure criterion during analysis, as explained in Section 34.2.2, is an orthogonal way to reduce false failures.

34.4.1 LOGIC CORRELATION

A pair of aggressor nets, which can each switch individually at a particular time point, may not be able to switch together at that time because of logic relationships in the circuit. A simple example of such a situation is shown in Figure 34.11. Aggressor 1 and Aggressor 2 can never both be at logic 0, therefore they cannot have a falling transition at the same time.

Any circuit has many logic correlations between its signals. For noise analysis, these correlations can be considered as logic constraints prohibiting circuit nets to have some combinations of signals. For false noise analysis, it is especially important to find that a group of aggressor nets are prohibited from having simultaneous rising or falling transition if the victim net is at the given voltage level. Aggressor nets $(a_1, a_2, \ldots, a_n)$ cannot switch simultaneously in the same direction if one of the two signal combinations $(a_1 = 1, a_2 = 1, \ldots, a_n = 1)$ or $(a_1 = 0, a_2 = 0, \ldots, a_n = 0)$ is prohibited when the victim net is at the given state.

In Refs. [18–21], logic constraints between the pins of a gate are represented in disjunctive form, which coincides with the gate's characteristic equation. For example, logic constraints for a two-input AND gate with logic function $x = a \cdot b$ can be written as $\overline{x} \cdot a \cdot b + x \cdot \overline{a} + x \cdot \overline{b} = 0$, which is exactly its characteristic function. Here term $\overline{x} \cdot a \cdot b$ prohibits the combination $(x = 0, a = 1, b = 1)$. In Figure 34.12, a simple circuit and some of its logic constraints are shown.

Such logic constraints are generated at gate or transistor level and propagated through the circuit with the purpose of generating nontrivial logic relations. Logic correlations can be in the form of simple pairwise relations, such as simple logic implications (SLIs) [18] and new implications can be generated by forward and backward propagation of existing ones. They can also be among multiple signals and resolution method can be used for propagation and generation of new relations [21].

In case of functional noise, after logic constraints generation, noise analysis is performed for every cluster for its respective noise type. If the generated logic constraints are made of two variable relations only, a constraint graph is formed based on generated SLIs, and then maximum weighted independent set (MWIS) problem is solved [18]. If the constraints involve many variables [21], then the constraint graph turns into a hypergraph. Therefore, instead of the constraint graph, a reduced order binary decision diagram (ROBDD) of the noise cluster constraints is constructed. Using the characteristic ROBDD of the noise cluster, the maximum noise of a given type is calculated by finding the maximum weighted set of the aggressors for which simultaneous switching of the same type is not prohibited. In Figure 34.13, examples for a constraint graph and a constraint hypergraph are given.

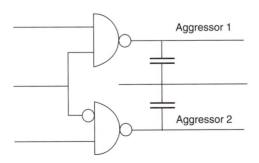

FIGURE 34.11   Example illustrating logic correlations.

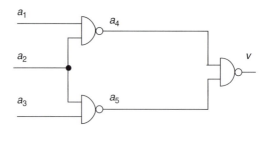

$$\overline{v} \cdot \overline{a_4}, \, \overline{v} \cdot \overline{a_5}, \, \overline{v} \cdot \overline{a_4} \cdot \overline{a_5}$$

$$\overline{a_1 \cdot a_4}, \, \overline{a_2 \cdot a_4}, \, \overline{a_2 \cdot a_5}, \, \overline{a_3} \cdot \overline{a_5}$$

$$\overline{a_1 \cdot a_2 \cdot a_4}, \, \overline{a_2 \cdot a_3 \cdot a_5}$$

FIGURE 34.12   Example circuit and its logic constraints.

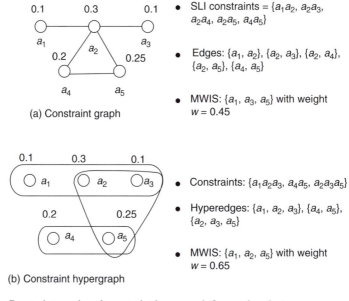

(a) Constraint graph

- SLI constraints $= \{a_1a_2, \, a_2a_3, \, a_2a_4, \, a_2a_5, \, a_4a_5\}$

- Edges: $\{a_1, a_2\}, \, \{a_2, a_3\}, \, \{a_2, a_4\}, \, \{a_2, a_5\}, \, \{a_4, a_5\}$

- MWIS: $\{a_1, a_3, a_5\}$ with weight $w = 0.45$

(b) Constraint hypergraph

- Constraints: $\{a_1a_2a_3, \, a_4a_5, \, a_2a_3a_5\}$

- Hyperedges: $\{a_1, a_2, a_3\}, \, \{a_4, a_5\}, \, \{a_2, a_3, a_5\}$

- MWIS: $\{a_1, a_2, a_5\}$ with weight $w = 0.65$

FIGURE 34.13   Constraint graph and constraint hypergraph for a noise cluster.

On the other hand, in case of delay noise analysis, a maximal set of aggressors needs to be selected such that the effect of noise is maximized globally and conservatively over several signal stages of a timing path. As a result, logical constraints must be considered among a much larger set of signals (set of victims in the timing path and all their aggressors) than is necessary for functional analysis. Because an aggressor can interact with multiple victim nets on a timing path and each interaction can contribute different amount of delay change relative to other aggressors, the problem of finding such an aggressor set becomes difficult. Despite the exponential complexity, enumerative traversal of the ROBDD of constraints is a reasonable approach for functional noise analysis, as each noise cluster is analyzed separately and a typical noise cluster consists of only about ten aggressor nets. However, to achieve maximum possible pessimism reduction in delay noise analysis, it is necessary to consider all victim nets of an analyzed path and all their aggressor nets together. As a result, one needs to compute MWIS from about 100 or more nets depending on the length of the timing path. Thus, more sophisticated techniques than direct enumeration are necessary. In Ref. [19], a branch-and-bound method as well as several heuristic techniques to address this need are provided.

34.4.2 SWITCHING (TIMING) WINDOWS

In addition to logic correlations, the victim and the aggressor nets may have restrictions in the temporal domain because of signal delays in the circuit. An activity window is defined as the interval from the earliest time to the latest time the net can switch. Typically, activity windows are obtained from static timing analysis by propagating the early and the late arrival times of the circuit inputs (or sequential element outputs) along all paths to the outputs (or sequential element inputs). In functional noise, sensitivity windows are also useful and can be generated by performing backward propagation of required times at circuit outputs or latch inputs. A sensitivity window of a victim net is defined as the interval from the earliest required time to the latest required time, in other words the period of time when the net should stay stable for a correct logic value acquisition at a sequential element.

Timing windows can be used simply to decide whether an aggressor can induce noise on a victim by checking for the existence of overlap between the aggressor net timing window and the proper timing window of the victim net (activity window in delay noise and sensitivity window in functional noise). We will use Figure 34.14 to explain some concepts in timing window usage. In case of functional noise, suppose that A_1, A_2, and A_3 are aggressor timing windows for rising transition and V is victim sensitivity window. A_1, A_3, and V overlap in region r_1. A_1, A_2, and V overlap in region r_2. In other words, A_1 and A_2 can induce noise together as well as A_1 and A_3, but not all three of them at the same time. Scan line algorithms are usually used to determine the worst-feasible aggressor set. In case of delay noise, suppose that V is victim timing window for falling transition. Same arguments apply as in functional noise analysis in determining the worst aggressor set that will impact the victim net delay the most. Note that timing windows of nets can only be compared if they are in the same synchronous clock domain, otherwise nets in asynchronous clock domains can switch at any time relative to each other.

Besides the above simple idea of using temporal relations in the circuit to reduce pessimism in crosstalk noise analysis, several ideas have been proposed to refine the usage of timing windows. In Ref. [15], instead of obtaining sensitivity windows by backward propagation of required times, noise windows (period of time when noise pulse can occur) are propagated and checked against required time window at the timing check points. Because propagated noise pulses have windows associated with them, this method allows one to see whether the propagated and injected noise can occur at the same time. In Ref. [22], a more refined definition of a timing window is used where instead of the traditional continuous timing window, a set of discontinuous timing windows are used to more accurately represent possible switching events.

In the case of delay noise, further refinement in timing window usage has been proposed by finding how much of an induced delay by an overlapping active aggressor should actually be taken

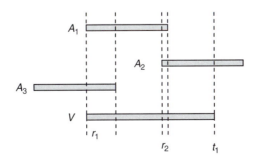

FIGURE 34.14   Timing windows for noise evaluation.

into account in the noise-aware static timing analysis traversal. For example, in Figure 34.14, although A_1 and A_3 may impact the delay of the victim net, this may not be important from a setup analysis point of view as long as the delay increase does not go beyond the latest arrival time of the victim net (t_l). In this scenario, aggressor A_2 considered to be switching around time t_l is the most likely one to impact the latest arrival time of the victim net. Because the latest arrival time is the one that is finally checked against timing constraints at a path endpoint, this is sufficient for a noise-aware timing analysis in terms of delay increase [23]. Timing windows depend on signal propagation delays and therefore depend on the injected noise. On the other hand, the injected noise depends on the timing windows. So we have a chicken and egg problem. This problem is usually resolved by iterating timing window calculations and noise analysis until convergence.

Note that the logic correlation techniques presented in the previous section are based on zero-delay implications. These logic relations are valid only when the circuit has reached a stable state, i.e., at the beginning and end of a clock cycle. However, when the circuit is in transition, it is possible that two aggressor nets can switch simultaneously even though their zero-delay logic relations would indicate that such switching is impossible. This occurs when there are glitches in the circuit. Methods to handle this have been proposed where timing and logic information are propagated together in the form of timed logic representation [2].

34.5 NOISE AVOIDANCE, NOISE-AWARE DESIGN, AND NOISE REPAIR

In previous sections, we talked about crosstalk noise phenomenon, accurate and efficient analysis techniques, as well as pessimism reduction techniques to prevent false failures. In this section, we turn to design implications of crosstalk noise and present techniques and methodology to be incorporated in the design flow with the purpose of early detection and avoidance of noise problems, as well as postroute repair approaches.

As mentioned in Section 34.2, several approaches are available to avoid and reduce crosstalk noise. In literature, fast crosstalk noise estimation methods [24,25] have been developed, which can be used as metrics to evaluate what-if scenarios as well as study the effectiveness of noise reduction approaches [26]. Also, extensive work has been carried out in noise prevention, noise-aware design, and noise repair [27–35]. In what follows, we present some widely used practical approaches.

34.5.1 NOISE PREVENTION AND NOISE-AWARE DESIGN

Modern design flows have adopted crosstalk noise prevention and noise-aware design techniques such that this issue is addressed early in the design cycle. In this section, we look at some of these methods.

34.5.1.1 Slew Control

Signal slope on a net is a good indicator of how strongly the net is driven compared to its RC loading characteristics. Strongly driven nets not only become more noise immune but also become stronger aggressors. Slew control targets to balance this throughout the design, preventing very weak victims and very strong aggressors. This is a noise avoidance technique employed early in the design cycle, during synthesis and placement. Although applying slew optimization globally results in stronger aggressor drivers, its benefit on overall noise because of the prevention of unacceptably weak victim drivers is greater [30].

In practice, a faster slew constraint produces a better design for noise, both in number of functional and delay noise violations, as well as the severity of worst-path delay slack. Balancing the slew rates throughout the design reduces the possibility of strong aggressors injecting high amounts of noise into weak victims, thus reducing functional noise failures. On the other hand, delay variation owing to crosstalk noise, in a first-order approximation, is proportional to $t_r \cdot (V_n/\text{Vdd})$, where t_r is the transition time and V_n is the injected noise height. Therefore, improving slew rate also helps to reduce crosstalk-induced delay variation. Achieving faster slew may increase the layout area and the power consumption of the design, as buffers are inserted to meet the target slew rate. It has been reported that the increase in power consumption because of the inserted buffers is minimal as a result of improved slew rates, which help reduce the short circuit power [30]. These effects should be taken into consideration as constraints during design decision process.

34.5.1.2 Congestion Minimization

Coupling capacitance is the factor that crosstalk noise is most sensitive to [26] and therefore reducing coupling is a very effective noise prevention/repair method. As crosstalk capacitance and spacing between nets are closely correlated, reducing routing congestion in a design helps reduce noise. This is an avoidance method applied during placement and routing stages of the design cycle.

34.5.1.3 Noise-Aware Routing (Spacing, Shielding, Layer Assignment)

A router can use simple crosstalk noise estimation methods as mentioned earlier to be noise-aware. Capacitances and resistances in the noise estimation model can be calculated using per unit length parasitic information and wirelength, wire width, spacing to neighbor nets, and coupling length (distance where two wires run parallel to each other). Routers can try to optimize parameters under their control (wirelengths and coupling lengths) using techniques available to them such as spacing, shielding, layer/track assignment, etc. [31–37].

34.5.2 POSTROUTE NOISE REPAIR

Noise prevention methods presented in Section 34.5.1 help with the overall crosstalk noise quality of the design. In later stages of the design cycle, i.e., after detailed routing, flexibility to make modifications is reduced and targeted actions are required to handle remaining functional and timing failures owing to crosstalk noise.

34.5.2.1 Gate Sizing, Buffer Insertion

Even after employing the prevention and noise-aware design techniques given in Section 34.5.1, some failures remain in postroute stage. It has been shown that the crosstalk noise induced functional and timing failures in a design usually have common causes and attacking functional noise problems first results in a more straightforward noise repair approach [30].

The most commonly used techniques in postroute noise repair are gate sizing, buffer insertion, net spacing, and shielding. There are benefits and drawbacks with all these approaches. To reduce crosstalk noise on a victim net, its driving gate's strength can be increased (i.e., same functionality with bigger equivalent transistor widths). However, this also causes the victim net to be a stronger aggressor on its neighbors, causing new problems to show up while fixing existing ones. Even worse, a sequence of gate sizing actions can become cyclic involving few nets and thus prevent the convergence of the repair actions. Algorithms have been developed to identify and address such cyclic effects such that the sizing is very effective and the convergence is fast [29]. Buffer insertion helps both by dividing a net into two separate nets thus reducing coupling, and by providing additional drive strength if necessary. However, buffer insertion is more intrusive in the design than gate sizing. It is a common practice to place dummy buffers in the design at early stages, which can then be used for such repair purposes. Net spacing on the other hand reduces coupling capacitance between particularly targeted nets. However, in already congested routing situations, this technique may result in dense routing regions to shift from one area of the design to another resulting in new failures. Net shielding is another effective method to address crosstalk noise issues. This method places a power (Vdd or ground) net next to a crosstalk noise problematic net, virtually eliminating its coupling capacitance. As with spacing, this technique may not be feasible depending on the availability of power grid and signal routing resources.

Hierarchical properties of the design being worked on also play a role in deciding which noise repair techniques will be most effective. Routing changes are to be preferred over sizing and buffering for fixing noise at the system-on-chip (SoC) integration stage. This assumes that all SoC blocks are timing clean, and long global nets are already buffered in the previous timing optimization phase. Although both sizing and buffering can be used for block level noise fixing, driver sizing is not to be preferred at the chip level because the drivers reside in the SoC blocks that are being integrated. However, gates in the sea of gates can be resized at the chip level, because they are legalized and routed at the chip level.

REFERENCES

1. H. Zhou, Timing analysis with crosstalk is a fixpoint on a complete lattice, *IEEE Transactions on Computer-Aided Design*, 22(9): 1261–1269, Sept. 2003.
2. P. Chen and K. Keutzer, Towards true crosstalk noise analysis, *IEEE/ACM International Conference on Computer-Aided Design*, San Jose, CA, Nov. 7–11, 1999, pp. 132–137.
3. A. Rubio, N. Itazaki, X. Zu, and K. Kinoshita, An approach to the analysis and detection of crosstalk faults in digital VLSI circuits, *IEEE Transactions on Computer-Aided Design*, 13: 387–394, Mar. 1994.
4. A. Odabasioglu, M. Celic, and L. Pileggi, PRIMA—Passive reduced order interconnect macromodeling algorithm, *IEEE/ACM International Conference on Computer-Aided Design*, San Jose, CA, Nov. 9–13, 1997, pp. 58–65.
5. P. Feldmann and R. W. Freund, Circuit noise evaluation by Pade approximation based model-reduction technique, *IEEE/ACM International Conference on Computer-Aided Design*, San Jose, CA, Nov. 9–13, 1997, pp. 132–138.
6. P. D. Gross, R. Arunachalam, K. Rajagopal, and L. T. Pileggi, Determination of worst-case aggressor alignment for delay calculation, *IEEE/ACM International Conference on Computer-Aided Design*, San Jose, CA, Nov. 8–12, 1998, pp. 212–219.
7. D. Blaauw, S. Sirichotiyakul, and C. Oh, Driver modeling and alignment for worst-case delay noise, *IEEE Transactions on Very Large Scale Integration (VLSI) Systems*, 11(2): 157–166, April 2003.
8. P. Chen, D. A. Kirkpatrick, and K. Keutzer, Miller factor for gate-level coupling delay calculation, *IEEE/ACM International Conference on Computer Aided Design*, San Jose, CA, Nov. 5–9, 2000, pp. 68–74.
9. F. Dartu and L. T. Pileggi, Calculating worst-case gate delays due to dominant capacitance coupling, *34th Design Automation Conference*, Anaheim, CA, Jun. 9–13, 1997, pp. 46–51.
10. V. Zolotov, D. Blaauw, S. Sirichotiyakul, M. Becer, C. Oh, R. Panda, A. Grinshpon, and R. Levy, Noise propagation and failure criteria for VLSI designs, *IEEE/ACM International Conference on Computer Aided Design*, San Jose, CA, Nov. 10–14, 2002, pp. 587–594.
11. I. Keller, K. Tseng, and N. Verghese, A robust cell-level crosstalk delay change analysis, *IEEE/ACM International Conference on Computer Aided Design*, San Jose, CA, Nov. 7–11, 2004, pp. 147–154.
12. R. Levy, D. Blaauw, G. Braca, A. Dasgupta, A. Grinshpon, C. Oh, B. Orshav, S. Sirichotiyakul, and V. Zolotov, ClariNet: A noise analysis tool for deep submicron design, *37th Design Automation Conference*, Los Angeles, CA, June 5–9, 2000, pp. 233-238.
13. K. L. Shepard and V. Narayanan, Noise in deep submicron digital design, *IEEE/ACM International Conference on Computer-Aided Design*, San Jose, CA, Nov. 10–14, 1996, pp. 524–531.
14. K. L. Shepard, V. Narayanan, and R. Rose, Harmony: static noise analysis of deep submicron digital integrated circuits, *IEEE Transactions on Computer-Aided Design of Integrated Circuits and Systems*, 18(8): 1132–1150, Aug. 1999.
15. K. Tseng and V. Kariat, Static noise analysis with noise windows, *Design Automation Conference*, Anaheim, CA, Jun. 2–6, 2003, pp. 864–868.
16. K. L. Shepard, Design methodologies for noise in digital integrated circuits, *Design Automation Conference*, San Francisco, CA, Jun. 15–19, 1998, pp. 94–99.
17. J. Qian, S. Pullela, and L.T. Pillage, Modeling the effective capacitance for the RC interconnect of CMOS gates, *IEEE Transactions on Computer-Aided Design*, San Jose, CA, Dec. 1994, pp. 1526–1535.

18. A. Glebov, S. Gavrilov, D. Blaauw, S. Sirichotiyakul, C. Oh, and V. Zolotov, False-noise analysis using logic implications, *IEEE/ACM International Conference on Computer Aided Design*, San Jose, CA, Nov. 4–8, 2001, pp. 515–521.

19. A. Glebov, S. Gavrilov, R. Soloviev, V. Zolotov, M. R. Becer, C. Oh, and R. Panda, Delay noise pessimism reduction by logic correlations, *IEEE/ACM International Conference on Computer Aided Design*, San Jose, CA, Nov. 7–11, 2004, pp. 160–167.

20. A. Glebov, S. Gavrilov, V. Zolotov, C. Oh, R. Panda, and M. Becer, False-noise analysis for domino circuits, *Design, Automation and Test in Europe Conference and Exhibition*, Paris, France, Feb. 16–20, 2004, pp. 784–789.

21. A. Glebov, S. Gavrilov, D. Blaauw, V. Zolotov, R. Panda, and C. Oh, False-noise analysis using resolution method, *International Symposium on Quality Electronic Design*, San Jose, CA, Mar. 18–21, 2002, pp. 437–442.

22. P. Chen, Y. Kukimoto, and K. Keutzer, Refining switching window by time slots for crosstalk noise calculation, *IEEE/ACM International Conference on Computer Aided Design*, San Jose, CA, Nov. 10–14, 2002, pp. 583–586.

23. M. Becer, V. Zolotov, R. Panda, A. Grinshpon, I. Algor, R. Levy, and C. Oh, Pessimism reduction in crosstalk noise aware STA, *International Conference on Computer Aided Design*, San Jose, CA, Nov. 2005, pp. 954–961.

24. L. Ding, D. Blaauw, and P. Mazumder, Accurate crosstalk noise modeling for early signal integrity analysis, *IEEE Transactions on Computer-Aided Design of Integrated Circuits and Systems*, 22(5): 627–634, May 2003.

25. J. Gong, D. Z. Pan, and P. V. Srinivas, Improved crosstalk modeling for noise constrained interconnect optimization, *Asia and South Pacific Design Automation Conference*, Yokohama, Japan, Jan. 30 to Feb. 2, 2001, pp. 373–378.

26. M. R. Becer, D. Blaauw, V. Zolotov, R. Panda, and I. N. Hajj, Analysis of noise avoidance techniques in DSM interconnects using a complete crosstalk noise model, *Design, Automation and Test in Europe Conference and Exhibition*, Munich, Germany, Mar. 4–8, 2002, pp. 456–463.

27. M. R. Becer, D. Blaauw, S. Sirichotiyakul, R. Levy, C. Oh, V. Zolotov, J. Zuo, and I. N. Hajj, A global driver sizing tool for functional crosstalk noise avoidance, *International Symposium on Quality Electronic Design*, San Jose, CA, Mar. 26–28, 2001, pp. 158–163.

28. M. R. Becer, D. Blaauw, R. Panda, and I. N. Hajj, Early probabilistic noise estimation for capacitively coupled interconnects, *IEEE Transactions on Computer-Aided Design of Integrated Circuits and Systems*, 22(3): 337–345, Mar. 2003.

29. M. R. Becer, D. Blaauw, I. Algor, R. Panda, C. Oh, V. Zolotov, and I. N. Hajj, Postroute gate sizing for crosstalk noise reduction, *IEEE Transactions on Computer-Aided Design of Integrated Circuits and Systems*, 23(12): 1670–1677, Dec. 2004.

30. M. Becer, R. Vaidyanathan, C. Oh, and R. Panda, Crosstalk noise control in an SoC physical design flow, *IEEE Transactions on Computer-Aided Design of Integrated Circuits and Systems*, 23(4): 488–497, Apr. 2004.

31. D. Sylvester and K. Keutzer, A global wiring paradigm for deep submicron design, *IEEE Transactions on Computer-Aided Design of Integrated Circuits and Systems*, 19(2): 242–252, Feb. 2000.

32. T. Zhang and S. S. Sapatnekar, Simultaneous shield and buffer insertion for crosstalk noise reduction in global routing, *IEEE International Conference on Computer Design: VLSI in Computers and Processors*, San Jose, CA, Oct. 11–13, 2004, pp. 93–98.

33. C. C. -P. Chen and N. Menezes, Noise-aware repeater insertion and wire sizing for on-chip interconnect using hierarchical moment-matching, *36th Design Automation Conference*, New Orleans, CA, Jun. 21–25, 1999, pp. 502–506.

34. C. J. Alpert, A. Devgan, and S. T. Quay, Buffer insertion for noise and delay optimization, *IEEE Transactions on Computer-Aided Design of Integrated Circuits and Systems*, 18(11): 1633–1645, Nov. 1999.

35. R. Kastner, E. Bozorgzadeh, and M. Sarrafzadeh, Coupling aware routing, *13th Annual IEEE International ASIC/SOC Conference*, Arlington, VA, Sept. 13–16, 2000, pp. 392–396.

36. P. Saxena and C. L. Liu, A postprocessing algorithm for crosstalk-driven wire perturbation, *IEEE Transactions on Computer-Aided Design of Integrated Circuits and Systems*, 19(6): 691–702, Jun. 2000.

37. T. Jing and X. Hong, The key technologies of performance optimization for nanometer routing, *5th International Conference on ASIC*, Beijing, China, Vol. 1, Oct. 21–24, 2003, pp. 118–123.

Part VII

Manufacturability and Detailed Routing

35 Modeling and Computational Lithography

Franklin M. Schellenberg

CONTENTS

35.1 INTRODUCTION

35.1.1 MODELING IN A DESIGN FLOW

Electronic design automation (EDA) for integrated circuits, and especially digital circuits, by and large concerns itself with computer algorithms for the arrangement and interconnection of transistors [1]. These are often fairly abstract representations of an IC Design, and their use and optimization is generally an application of algorithms in computer science. At some point, however, an IC layout must be generated and fabricated as actual structures on a silicon wafer. It is at this point where process modeling and simulation must enter the domain of EDA.

To fabricate an IC, numerous processes are employed: doping of materials, deposition of thin film layers, planarization, and etching or removing material, among others. [2–4] Most of these processes are bulk processes, carried out on an entire wafer or batches of wafers at one time, but each can leave its signature on the individual features as they are fabricated. These differences between the ideal, as-designed layout and the final as-manufactured device can be trivial and insignificant, or can cause the device to fail utterly, depending on the sensitivity to variation.

Technology CAD (TCAD) tools have existed to model aspects of certain processes and devices ever since these processes and devices came into existence [5]. TCAD tools typically set up a physics-based model of a structure or process, and are used to examine these physical structures in great detail. They have served as useful tools for research scientists and process engineers to study the relationships between different process variables and predicted device properties. They can be extremely cost effective, in that one can run a virtual experiment without incurring the expense of a complicated, multivariable experiment in a silicon clean room. These tools, however, are generally run off-line—that is, they are tools for simulating small, representative samples of layouts or devices in great detail to guide experts in process and device engineering. These are not tools for the simulation of entire layouts.

With the advent of inexpensive parallel processing for computing, simulation tools are now becoming more streamlined and their use on entire layouts can be reconsidered. A typical EDA flow [6] incorporating a process model is shown in Figure 35.1. In this flow, once the physical layout has been created in a layout format such as GDS-II [7] or OASIS [8], a model is called to transform

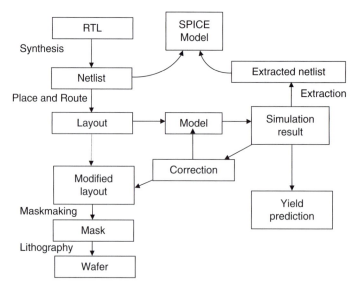

FIGURE 35.1 Example of an EDA flow with the insertion of a modeling step, in this case a model for correction of the layout for physical effects. RTL is the Register Transfer Level; SPICE stands for Simulation Program with Integrated Circuit Emphasis and is a general purpose analog circuit simulator.

this layout into a new version that represents what is expected on the wafer. Sections of a layout, discrete cells, or the entire layout can be simulated, depending on the desired outcome. The output of this model is typically represented as a set of contours, and stored as new data layers in the layout file.

Extraction tools can then be used on this modified layout, and the suitable SPICE models used to predict the expected electrical behavior of the manufactured result [9]. If the results deviate too much for the desired electrical specifications, the information is passed back into the earlier design flow in the form of new constraints or rules would prevent this specific deviation from occurring, and that the upstream tools must now consider in creating revised versions of the IC.

There are other processing steps besides lithography that can be modeled. Bulk processing steps such as plasma etching or chemical–mechanical polishing (CMP) are broadly understood, but detailed modeling behavior, especially on individual feature scale, is still an active area of research. [10–12] And, even if perfectly understood, the ability to quantify and manage statistical variation expected in these processes also affects the yield expected for a particular design [13]. Coping with variation in IC modeling and incorporating those results into EDA tools for improved IC performance and yield remains an active topic of research [14]. A number of related issues are described in Chapter 36.

On the other hand, various analysis tools such as Critical area analysis (CAA) [15–18] or various density metrics [19] can be applied once simulated results have been generated, to better estimate expectations of real wafer yield. Such analysis tools are currently run on layouts generated by EDA tools, but their use with simulated wafer results can lead to a more accurate estimation of real yield [20]. The accuracy of the overall yield model then depends on the accuracy of the underlying model used for the simulation. A more detailed discussion is provided in Chapter 37.

35.1.2 LITHOGRAPHIC PROCESSING

The most commonly used process for detailed patterning has been relatively well understood in principle for nearly a century. This process is optical lithography [21]. The processing steps for optical lithography are illustrated in Figure 35.2. To begin, a photomask, sometimes called simply a mask but more precisely referred to as a reticle, is retrieved from its storage location. The mask is a flat piece of quartz coated with an opaque layer (usually chrome) written with the layout patterns required for a particular layer (e.g., poly, contact, metal-1, etc.). This serves as the master for patterning the wafers, analogous to a negative for printing conventional photography. This photomask is mounted in a projection printer, which forms a miniaturized image of the mask (usually four times smaller) using a highly precise multielement lens system.

The lithographic process flow starts by loading wafers in the processing system (called a track) and preprocessing them. This involves an initial cleaning, to remove any particles or contaminants, coating with photosensitive polymer, called a photoresist, and sometimes a baking step, to drive

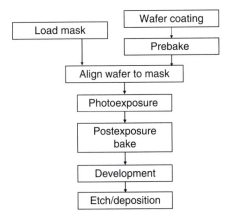

FIGURE 35.2 Typical steps in an optical lithography process.

any remaining solvent out of the photoresist. Once prepared, the wafer is then transferred into the optical projection system for exposure. The wafer is aligned precisely to the patterns on the photomask to minimize overlay errors, and a timed exposure of the image of the photomask is made onto the photosensitive polymer. With photoexposure, the polymer properties (usually the polymer solubility) change. The wafer is subsequently transferred back to the track and further processed (e.g., developed) to selectively remove the more soluble materials, leaving resist polymer in a local pattern corresponding to the patterns in the IC layout.

This wafer will then be used in the subsequent processing step. Only the uncovered regions experience the desired process action (e.g., material deposition, etching, etc.). The regions that remain covered by the polymer are protected and remain unchanged (hence the name – they resist the process) [22].

Typically, a photomask will contain the layouts for the appropriate layers (e.g., gate, contact, etc.) for only a few chips (or, for a complex microprocessor, a single chip). Repetition throughout the wafer, allowing hundreds of chips to be printed on a standard 300 mm diameter silicon wafer, occurs by moving the wafer stage under the photomask and making a succession of exposures until exposures have been made for all chips on the wafer. Projection exposure equipment is commonly called a stepper, because the wafer is stepped from exposure to exposure.

Lithographic patterning processes are superb examples of the highest precision imaging ever achieved. With contemporary processing, light with a wavelength of $\lambda = 193$ nm is being used to produce ICs with dimensions of 65 nm, and even being considered for the next generations as well, which have features as small as 45 nm or 32 nm [23]. However, certain limitations inherent in the patterning and subsequent processing steps can distort the transfer of the pattern from the desired, ideal layout. When projection optical lithography was initially introduced in the manufacture of ICs, the wavelength of the light used to form patterns was much smaller than the individual feature sizes. As a result, there was very little image distortion, and the patterns on the wafer appeared essentially as designed. The alignment and overlay of these features was a more critical concern.

As Moore's law [24] continued to push transistors to be ever smaller, in 1998 the feature size became smaller than the wavelength used for manufacturing. This is shown in Figure 35.3 [25,26].

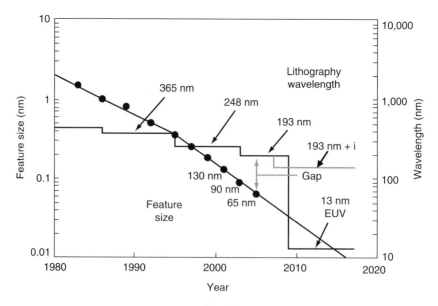

FIGURE 35.3   Evolution of lithography wavelength and IC feature size. (Data from Bohr, M., Intel's 65 nm Process Technology, Intel Developer Forum, Sept. 8, 2004. Figure adapted from Schellenberg, F. M., *EDA for IC Implementation, Circuit Design and Process, and Process Technology*, L. Scheffer, L. Lavagno, and G. Martin, Eds., CRC Press, Boca Raton, FL, 2006.)

Now, significant process distortions were routinely occurring on the wafer, and without correction, wafer yield would be impacted. Although some relief was provided by introducing lithography technology using immersion, with the shrinking of IC dimensions to be smaller than 100 nm, these distortions are significant, and unless compensated, IC yield drops to zero. Process modeling for lithography is therefore essential for the design of manufacturable ICs in this sub-wavelength world.

In this chapter, I give an overview of the requirements of lithography modeling for subwavelength EDA flows. In Section 35.2, I describe the physics of optical image formation for lithography, and the various lithographic techniques that must be modeled. This is essentially the framework in which the models must fit to describe the lithographic process. In Section 35.3, I describe some of the mathematical techniques used to compute specific results that fit into the framework of Section 35.2. Finally, in Section 35.4, I describe some of the issues encountered in the implementation of the models in contemporary EDA software.

35.2 LITHOGRAPHIC MODELING

35.2.1 INTRODUCTION

In this section, the fundamental steps of a lithographic process are described, along with the techniques used to represent lithography in models. Then, the most frequently used configurations of models needed for the implementation of various resolution enhancement techniques (RETs) are presented.

The fundamental elements of the lithographic patterning process are shown in Figure 35.4. Light from a source (typically UV light from a lamp or an excimer laser) is shaped by the illumination system to control intensity uniformity, polarization properties, and angular spectrum. This light illuminates the photomask, patterned with the layout for the particular layer to be reproduced. A very large and complex lens system then forms an image of the photomask (typically reduced in linear dimension by a factor of four) on the resist-coated silicon wafer. The wafer may actually be coated with a number of layers that complicate exposure considerably. For immersion lithography systems, the lens–wafer gap itself may be filled with a fluid (typically water) to enhance imaging fidelity [27]. Once exposed, the patterns are developed and the wafer moved on to the next process step.

35.2.2 LITHOGRAPHIC MODELING FUNDAMENTALS

Although the imaging systems are very complex, with lenses containing over 20 precision optical elements and costing several million dollars, modeling this process is actually a fairly straightforward procedure. This is due to the following:

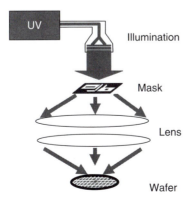

FIGURE 35.4 Elements of a typical lithographic exposure system. (After Schellenberg, F. M., *EDA for IC Implementation, Circuit Design, and Process Technology*, L. Scheffer, L. Lavagno, and G. Martin, Eds., CRC Press, Boca Raton, FL, 2006.)

1. Light in the system is an electromagnetic wave, governed by Maxwell's Equations [28].
2. Propagation through the illumination system is generally collimated, and therefore can be modeled by the approximations for far-field diffraction.
3. All optical processes in the stepper (aside from the possible generation of the initial source photons) can be represented by a linear superposition (typically of electric fields, however, under some circumstances, using field intensity).
4. Imaging for complex illumination systems and layout patterns can be modeled with a suitable linear superposition of subcomponent systems (because of (3)).

35.2.2.1 Maxwell's Equations

All electromagnetic phenomena can be described through the use of the well-known Maxwell equations [28,29]:

$$\nabla \times \vec{E} = -\mu \frac{\partial \vec{H}}{\partial t} \tag{35.1a}$$

$$\nabla \times \vec{H} = \varepsilon \frac{\partial \vec{E}}{\partial t} + \sigma \vec{E} \tag{35.1b}$$

$$\nabla \cdot \varepsilon \vec{E} = \rho \tag{35.1c}$$

$$\nabla \cdot \mu \vec{H} = 0 \tag{35.1d}$$

where
$\vec{E}$ and $\vec{H}$ represent the vector electric and magnetic fields, respectively
ε and μ the electric permittivity and magnetic permeability of the material in which the fields exist
ρ represents the electric charge density
σ the electrical conductivity

When combined, and in the absence of charges and currents, a wave equation is formed [29].

$$\nabla^2 \vec{E} - \frac{n^2}{c^2} \frac{\partial^2 \vec{E}}{\partial t^2} = 0 \tag{35.2}$$

where the refractive index n is defined relative to the permittivity ε_0 and permeability μ_0 of the vacuum by

$$n = \sqrt{\frac{\varepsilon}{\varepsilon_0} \frac{\mu}{\mu_0}} \tag{35.3}$$

and c is

$$c = \frac{1}{\sqrt{\mu_0 \varepsilon_0}} = 2.998 \times 10^8 \text{ m/s} \tag{35.4}$$

This corresponds to the speed of light in a vacuum (which has $n = 1$). The value of n, which is better known as the refractive index of the material, relates the speed v of a wave in a material to the speed of light in a vacuum.

$$v = \frac{c}{n} \tag{35.5}$$

c is related to the physical properties of wavelength (λ, λ_0 in vacuum) and frequency v of the wave through

$$v = \frac{c}{n} = \lambda v = \frac{\lambda_0 v}{n} \tag{35.6}$$

In the presence of charges and currents, the wave equation becomes

$$\nabla^2 \vec{E} - \frac{n^2}{c^2}\frac{\partial^2 \vec{E}}{\partial t^2} - \mu\sigma\frac{\partial \vec{E}}{\partial t} = 0 \tag{35.7}$$

For most situations, this simply becomes a more complex wave, in which the refractive index can be represented by a complex number

$$\hat{n} = n + i\kappa \tag{35.8}$$

where
  n represents the ratio of speeds as before
  κ (kappa) represents a loss related to electrical conductivity σ as the wave propagates through the material, and is sometimes called the extinction coefficient

35.2.2.2 Propagation

When a collimated wave propagates through a well-behaved medium, the propagation of waves from an extended source P_S at some point P a distance r_p away can be represented by an integral of spherical waves emitted from across the source:

$$E(P) = \iint_S M(P_S)\frac{e^{+i(2\pi/\lambda)r_p}}{r_p}\,dS \tag{35.9}$$

where $M(P_S)$ is a representation of the field strength (or amplitude) and phase at various points P_S in the source. This illuminating source can in turn fall on a mask, with a transmission function $M(x, y)$. The mask acts as a secondary source, and the integral of Equation 35.9 applies again, this time with the mask function describing the source. In the far field, when the light is monochromatic (λ constant), the transmission through the mask becomes a function of the patterns on the mask,

$$E(p, q) \propto -i\frac{e^{+i(2\pi/\lambda)R_0+R_p}}{R_0 R_p} \iint_M M(x, y)e^{-i(2\pi/\lambda)(xp+yq)}\,dx\,dy \tag{35.10}$$

where the R_0 and R_p factors are geometric distances from the source to the mask, and the and each point in the mask having both a transmission value (typically 0 or 1) and a phase shift ϕ. This is called the Fraunhofer diffraction formula, and it is clear that, with the exception of the phase factor in front, the far field amplitude pattern will be proportional to the 2D Fourier transform [30] of the mask function $M(x, y)$. The approximation that the mask can be represented by this infinitely thin transmission function is sometimes called the Kirchhoff boundary condition [29].

Although electromagnetic wave propagation can occur in arbitrary directions, for most optical systems, the direction of propagation is very well defined. Light falls on a mask at near normal incidence, and diffracts at relatively small angles (typically less than 20°). When a simple lens of focal length f is inserted into the optical path, the lens introduces a quadratic phase factor:

$$L(a, b) = e^{-i(2\pi/\lambda)(1/f)(a^2+b^2)} \tag{35.11}$$

where a and b are the Cartesian coordinates in the lens plane.

It can be shown that, when the diffraction pattern of Equation 35.10 is placed at exactly the focal distance in front of the lens, the field at the focal plane (a distance f behind the lens) allows this phase factor to cancel the phase factor in the Fraunhofer diffraction formula, and the field in the image plane becomes

$$E(p,q) \propto -i\frac{1}{\lambda f} \int\limits_{-\infty}^{\infty} \int\limits_{-\infty}^{\infty} M(x,y) e^{-i(2\pi/\lambda)(xp+yq)} dx\, dy \qquad (35.12)$$

This form will be recognized as a mathematical representation that corresponds to the 2D Fourier transform [30] of the mask pattern:

$$E(p,q) \propto \text{FT}[M(x,y)] \qquad (35.13)$$

To actually form the image of the mask at position (x_1, y_1), the lens aperture and behavior, represented by a pupil function designated as $P(a,b)$, are multiplied with the diffraction pattern at the focal point. This image in the focal plane is in turn transformed by a second lens at a distance f:

$$E(x_1, y_1) \propto \text{FT}\left[P(a,b) \cdot E(p \cdot q)\right] = \text{FT}\left\{P(a,b) \cdot \text{FT}\left[M(x,y)\right]\right\} \qquad (35.14)$$

where P represents the pupil function, encompassing the wavefront transforming behavior of the lens. This is illustrated in Figure 35.5.

Pupil functions can be simple mathematical structures, such as

$$P(a,b) = \begin{Bmatrix} 1, & a^2 + b^2 \le r \\ 0, & a^2 + b^2 > r \end{Bmatrix} = \begin{Bmatrix} 1, & \rho \le r \\ 0, & \rho > r \end{Bmatrix} \qquad (35.15)$$

representing the physical cutoff of the circular lens housing or radius r (shown in both Cartesian (a,b) and polar coordinates (ρ, ϕ)). However, additional phase behavior of the lens can also be included in the pupil function. Lens aberrations can be represented by an orthonormal set of polynomials called Zernike polynomials, each representing a specific aberration [29]. The Zernike polynomials are generally represented in polar coordinates, following the form

$$Z_j(\rho, \phi) = a_n^m R_n^m(\rho) Y_j^m(\phi) \qquad (35.16)$$

Table 35.1 below shows a few of the Zernike polynomials and the corresponding aberration. More detail on these functions can be found in Ref. [29].

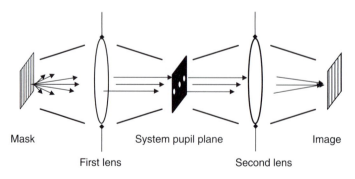

Mask   System pupil plane   Image

First lens   Second lens

FIGURE 35.5 Simplified representation of the optical system of an imaging tool. At the pupil plane, the amplitude of the field represents a two-dimensional Fourier transform of the object, multiplied with the pupil function.

TABLE 35.1

First Ten Zernike Polynomials, an Orthogonal Set of Functions
That Describe the Lens Aberrations

j	n	m	a_n^m	$R_n^m(\rho)$	$Y_n^m(\phi)$	Aberration
1	0	0	$\sqrt{1}$	1	1	Piston
2	1	1	$\sqrt{4}$	ρ	$\mathrm{Cos}\phi$	x-Tilt
3	1	1	$\sqrt{4}$	ρ	$\mathrm{Sin}\phi$	y-Tilt
4	2	0	$\sqrt{3}$	$2\rho^2 - 1$	1	Defocus
5	2	2	$\sqrt{6}$	ρ^2	$\mathrm{Sin}2\phi$	45° Astigmatism
6	2	2	$\sqrt{6}$	ρ^2	$\mathrm{Cos}(2\phi)$	90° Astigmatism
7	3	1	$\sqrt{8}$	$3\rho^3 - 2\rho$	$\mathrm{Sin}\phi$	(Balanced) y-coma
8	3	1	$\sqrt{8}$	$3\rho^3 - 2\rho$	$\mathrm{Cos}\phi$	(Balanced) x-coma
9	3	3	$\sqrt{8}$	ρ^3	$\mathrm{Sin}3\phi$	Shamrock
10	3	3	$\sqrt{8}$	ρ^3	$\mathrm{Cos}3\phi$	Shamrock

Note: More details can be found in Ref. [29].

At this point, the image can be calculated, but the representation is still in terms of the amplitude and phase of the local electric field. Photosensors, whether they be the retinas of the eye, a photoelectric cell, or the molecules of a photoresist, produce a signal in proportion to the amount of energy in the electromagnetic field. The energy is proportional to the image intensity, found by squaring the modulus of the electric field:

$$I(x, y) = E \cdot E^* \tag{35.17}$$

where * denotes the complex conjugate operation.

35.2.2.3 Linearity

Although actual imaging systems comprise more than two simple phase front transformations, a key theorem on which all lens design is based is that any complex lens can be reduced to a simple Fourier transform, a Pupil function, and an inverse Fourier transform.

This is a very powerful result, and is the basis of the entire field of Fourier optics [30]. Regardless of the exact lens structure and configuration, image simulation becomes a simple matter of designating the appropriate coordinate system, computing Fourier transforms and finding the proper representation of the pupil function P. Because Fourier transforms themselves are linear, the optical system is modeled by a linear process. This means that any arbitrary image can be assembled by creating a superposition of images from a suitable set of building blocks, each computed on its own.

The linearity of the Fourier transform allows a complex 2D pattern to be decomposed into a Fourier series expansion of different 2D spatial frequencies, each being treated in turn and the final fields summed together. Note also that a nonmonochromatic distribution of wavelengths λ can similarly be computed wavelength by wavelength, and the final results summed as appropriate. This linearity holds as long as the media can be adequately descried by a refractive index, as in Equation 35.8.

Note that for some materials, optical properties can change in the presence of strong electric fields, and the refractive index itself becomes an expansion:

$$n = n_1 + n_2 E^2 + \cdots \tag{35.18}$$

Materials in which these effects are significant are called 'nonlinear optical materials' [31]. Clearly, these nonlinearities can cause additional complications if they were to be used in imaging applications. However, values of n_2 are generally very small, even for highly nonlinear materials, and these nonlinear effects are generally only observed using lasers with extremely high power densities. In general, the assumption that a total E field can be represented by a linear superposition of E fields remains valid.

35.2.2.4 Computation by Superposition

The mathematics of Equation 35.14 represent that the imaging of any particular mask function is the multiplication of the FT of the mask with the pupil function. Because multiplication in Fourier space corresponds to convolution in position (x, y) space, image simulation reduces to the ability to do the following computational tasks in various combinations:

1. Digitize the mask function into a 2D amplitude and phase pixel array $[M(x, y)]$
2. Estimate a discrete 2D representation of the pupil function $[P(\omega_x, \omega_y)]$
3. Perform array multiplication (e.g., $[P] \bullet [M]$ in frequency space)
4. Compute discrete Fourier transforms (and inverse transforms as well)

35.2.2.4.1 Pixel Representation of the Mask
Creating a pixel representation of the mask is usually fairly straightforward. Mask layouts are generated using polygons, often exclusively with Manhattan geometries. The ability to create an accurate discrete representation of the layout then becomes a question of the resolution desired and the size of array that can be computationally managed. This selection of the address grid can impact the computation and data management properties significantly, so should be done with care. Generally, a grid around 1 nm is selected for contemporary ICs with features as small as 45 nm.

35.2.2.4.2 Pixel Representation of the Pupil
Once the pupil function is known, a similar mapping onto a grid is carried out. Here, the resolution of the pupil components need not be nearly as dense as the grid selected for the layout. However, because the transform of the mask and the pupil must be entry-wise multiplied, some care should be taken to ensure that the two grids match well. Although the simplest pupil functions are mathematically easy to represent (e.g., a circular aperture), these functions do not map to a Manhattan grid in the same way most mask functions can. In addition to this, the lens aberrations, also incorporated into the pupil, typically have circular symmetry (Table 35.1). Staircasing of these non-Manhattan functions occurs, and without a very fine grid, the results are less accurate.

35.2.2.4.3 Array Multiplication
This is one of the basic computing operations, and is typically straightforward. The matrix multiplication occurs pixel by pixel, and the entries in the corresponding matrices are therefore multiplied entrywise.

$$
\begin{bmatrix}
P_{1,1}M_{1,1} & P_{1,2}M_{1,2} & P_{1,3}M_{1,3} & P_{1,4}M_{1,4} \\
P_{2,1}M_{2,1} & P_{2,2}M_{2,2} & P_{2,3}M_{2,3} & P_{2,4}M_{2,4} \\
P_{3,1}M_{3,1} & P_{3,2}M_{3,2} & P_{3,3}M_{3,3} & P_{3,4}M_{3,4} \\
P_{4,1}M_{4,1} & P_{4,2}M_{4,2} & P_{4,3}M_{4,3} & P_{4,4}M_{4,4}
\end{bmatrix}
$$

$$
=
\begin{bmatrix}
P_{1,1} & P_{1,2} & P_{1,3} & P_{1,4} \\
P_{2,1} & P_{2,2} & P_{2,3} & P_{2,4} \\
P_{3,1} & P_{3,2} & P_{3,3} & P_{3,4} \\
P_{4,1} & P_{4,2} & P_{4,3} & P_{4,4}
\end{bmatrix}
\bullet
\begin{bmatrix}
M_{1,1} & M_{1,2} & M_{1,3} & M_{1,4} \\
M_{2,1} & M_{2,2} & M_{2,3} & M_{2,4} \\
M_{3,1} & M_{3,2} & M_{3,3} & M_{3,4} \\
M_{4,1} & M_{4,2} & M_{4,3} & M_{4,4}
\end{bmatrix}
\tag{35.19}
$$

where $M_{1,1}$ represents, for example, a pixel of the Fourier transform of $M(x, y)$,

$$M_{1,1} = FT\left[M(x, y)\right]_{\text{Pixel}(a_1, b_1)} \tag{35.20}$$

$P_{1,1}$ represents the pupil function at pixel (a_1, b_1), etc.

It is clear from this that the grids of the mask function, the pupil function, and the final image need to be matched to avoid excessive interpolation.

35.2.2.4.4 Fast Fourier Transform

The fast Fourier transform (FFT) is one of the best known and widely used computational algorithms [32–34]. Normally, a discrete Fourier transform (DFT) numerically executing the Fourier transform in a brute force manner, would require $O(N^2)$ arithmetic operations. However, when the functions to be transformed can be discretized into elements that are a multiple of 2, the DFT can be broken down into a number of smaller DFTs. The final result can be constructed to only have $O(N \log N)$ arithmetic operations. In a similar fashion, 2D discrete Fourier transforms can be broken down into a collection of 1D DFTs, each with a similar gain in computational efficiency.

Because the mask function M is well behaved (with values of either 0 or 1, depending on the coordinates) and the pupil function P is continuous, both the mask function and pupil function can be digitized into a 2D array of pixels, with the number of pixels on each side being some multiple of 2. The FFT can therefore be used for this computation, and it has become the main engine of image simulation.

35.2.3 RET TOOLS

The ability to simulate images quickly with tools such as the FFT and to compose arbitrary images based on the superposition of partial images gives rise to the possibility of EDA tools with dual, complementary capabilities: a database engine, to manage and process layout polygons, and a process simulation engine. The process engine calls on certain layers of data representing portions of the IC layout, transforms them to simulate processing behavior, and returns a representation of the transformed data to the database for further analysis. This is illustrated schematically in Figure 35.6. This combination of data management and simulation is how the entire class of 'resolution enhancement techniques (RETs) [35] are implemented in an EDA flow.

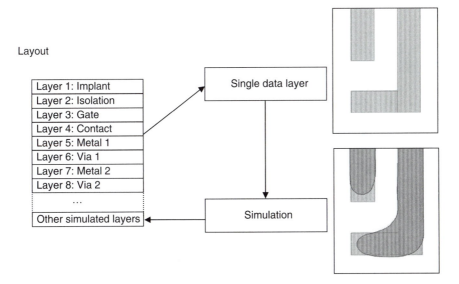

FIGURE 35.6 Lithographic simulation of a single layer of an IC layout.

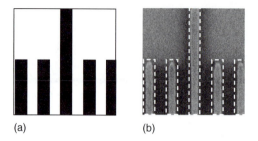

(a)   (b)

FIGURE 35.7 Iso-dense bias. (a) represents the drawn layout, while (b) illustrates the result on the wafer. For this process, the lines in the dense region are thinner than isolated lines with the same nominal dimension. (Reproduced from Schellenberg, F.M., Zhang, H., and Morrow, J., *Optical Microlithography XI, Proceedings of SPIE*, 3334, 892, 1998. With permission.)

There are three major RETs in use today: Optical and process correction (OPC), phase-shifting masks (PSM), and off-axis illumination (OAI) [35–37]. Each corresponds to control and manipulation of one of the independent variables of the optical wave at the mask: amplitude (OPC), phase (PSM), and direction (OAI). The changes required for OPC and PSM are implemented by changing the layout of the photomask, while OAI is implemented by changing the pattern of light emerging from the illuminator as it falls on the mask.

35.2.3.1 OPC

The acronym 'OPC', which is now used as a general term for changing the layout to compensate for process effects (optical and process correction), originally stood for optical proximity correction, and was used to predict and compensate for one-dimensional proximity effects. One example of a 1D effect, 'iso-dense bias' [38,39], is illustrated in Figure 35.7 [40]. Here, isolated and dense features of identical dimension on the photomask print at different dimensions on the wafer, depending on the proximity to nearby neighbors. Shown in the 'pitch curve' of Figure 35.8 is the characteristic behavior observed for 1D periodic features in a typical optical lithography process [41]. In this case, 'pitch' is the 1D sum of line and space dimensions.

Some of this can be readily understood as an interaction of the Fourier spectrum of the photomask layout and the low-pass properties of the stepper lens and process: Dense lines have a well-defined

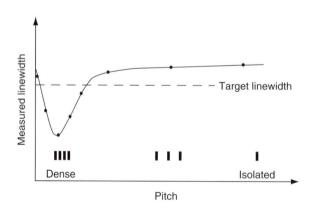

FIGURE 35.8 Iso-dense pitch curve, quantifying the linewidth changes for nominally identical features (i.e., lines all at a single target dimension) as a function of pitch. (Adapted from Cobb, N.B., Fast optical and process proximity correction algorithms for integrated circuit manufacturing, Ph.D. Dissertation, University of California, Berkeley, California, 1998. With permission.)

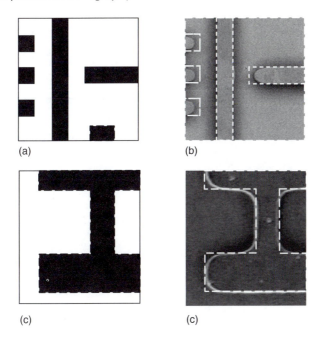

(a)   (b)

(c)   (c)

FIGURE 35.9   (a) and (b) Line-end pullback and (c) and (d) corner rounding. (Reproduced from Schellenberg, F.M., Zhang, H., and Morris, J., *Optical Microlithography XI, Proceedings of SPIE*, 3334, 892, 1998. With permission.)

pitch and therefore a narrow spectrum, which passes easily through the pupil, while isolated features with sharp edges correspond to a range of spatial frequencies, including many high frequencies that are cut off by the pupil. It is therefore not a surprise that isolated and dense features of the same nominal dimension may have different images on the wafer.

Additional effects that can impact the image are line-end pullback and 2D corner rounding, illustrated in Figure 35.9 [40]. These also are interpretable partly through the spectral analysis of the layout.

To compensate for the loss in higher spatial frequencies, the positions of the edges in the original layout can be altered and adjusted as appropriate to correct the image in the local environment. [38,42,43] This is illustrated in Figure 35.10. Additional features not present in the original layout, sometimes called 'scattering bars' or 'assist features' can also be added to the layout [44,45]. These features, with dimensions chosen so that they themselves do not print on the wafer, form a quasi-dense environment around printing features, which would otherwise be isolated. An example is illustrated in Figure 35.11. The overall effect is to make the behavior of the isolated features better match the behavior of dense features on the final wafer.

35.2.3.2   PSM

Traditional photomasks are fabricated using a lithography process to etch away portions of a layer of opaque chrome coated on a quartz mask blank [46,47]. The presence or absence of chrome forms the pattern to be reproduced on the wafer. However, the underlying quartz substrate of the mask can be etched as well. Because the refractive index of the quartz and air are different, a relative phase shift between the two neighboring regions can be created. This is illustrated in Figure 35.12.

For apertures that are close together, if the light emerging from the apertures has the same phase, the images overlap on the wafer, the fields add, and the spots blur together, as shown in Figure 35.13a. If the phase difference is 180°, as shown in Figure 35.13b, however, the wave peaks and troughs sum to zero in the overlap region, and destructive interference occurs. Therefore, for two regions in close

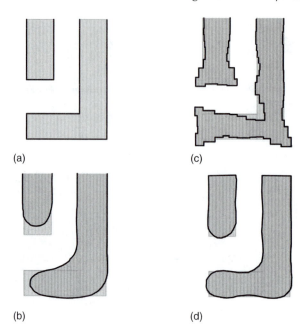

(a)

(b)

(c)

(d)

FIGURE 35.10 (a) Original layout and (b) its simulated wafer result, and (c) layout after modification with OPC and (d) its simulated wafer result. The wafer result for the corrected version is clearly a better match to the original drawn polygon. (Adapted from Maurer, W. and Schellenberg, F.M., *Handbook of Photomask Manufacturing Technology*, S. Rizvi, Eds., CRC Press, Boca Raton, Florida, 2005. With permission.)

FIGURE 35.11 Example of a contemporary layout with printing features and SRAF. (Reproduced, Courtesy Mentor Graphics.)

proximity, a dark fringe forms, allowing the images to remain distinct. [48–50] This is often called an 'alternating' PSM, because the phase alternates between apertures.

Careful assignment of the mask regions to be etched, or phase-shifted, can lead to enhanced resolution for an IC layout. This can lead to problems, however, if polygons that require phase shifting

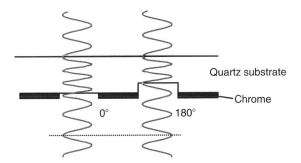

FIGURE 35.12 Cross-section view of an optical wave passing through two apertures of a photomask. Etching the mask substrate for one of the apertures can produce a phase shift of 180°.

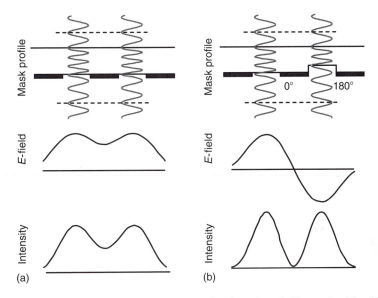

FIGURE 35.13 Amplitude and intensity for (a) a conventional mask, and (b) a mask with a 180° phase shift. Contrast for neighboring apertures is clearly enhanced for the phase-0 shifting mask. (Adapted from Maurer, W. and Schellenberg, F.M., *Handbook of Photomask Manufacturing Technology*, S. Rizvi, Ed., CRC Press, Boca Raton, Florida, 2004. With permission.)

in one area of the chip are contiguous with polygons in other regions that require the opposite phase. These topological constraints, illustrated in Figure 35.14, are called 'phase conflicts', and can place additional design rule restrictions on layouts [51–54].

Several variations on phase-shifting techniques have been adopted. The most common is a hybrid phase shifter, called an 'attenuated PSM' [55]. Here, the opaque chrome material of a conventional photomask is replaced with an attenuating but partially transmitting material (typically a MoSi film with 6 percent transmission [56]), with properties selected such that the light weakly transmitted through the film emerges with a phase shift of 180°. This improves contrast between light and dark regions, because the E-field (and therefore intensity) must be zero somewhere near the edge between the clear region and the phase shifted, darker region. However, fabrication techniques are similar to regular chrome mask processing, and no additional quartz etch step is required.

There are also several double exposure techniques, in which certain phase-shifted features are created on a first photomask, while a second mask is used to trim or otherwise adapt the exposed

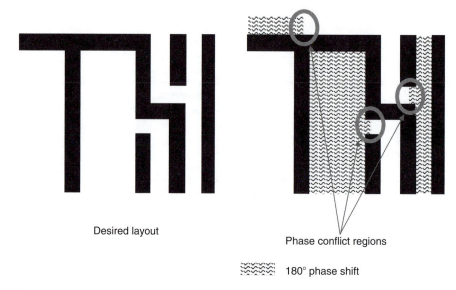

Desired layout

Phase conflict regions

:::::::::   180° phase shift

FIGURE 35.14   Examples of layouts that have phase conflicts.

region to complete the exposure. [57–60] In this way, some of the unwanted artifacts of the phase-shifting structures can be eliminated in the second exposure. More details on various PSM techniques can be found in the literature. [35,37]

35.2.3.3   OAI

For light falling at or near normal incidence to the photomask (on-axis illumination), the diffraction spectrum is straightforward to interpret. For light entering at an angle (i.e., using off-axis illumination [OAI]), the spectrum is shifted [61], as shown in Figure 35.15. Clearly, depending on the layout on the mask and the imaging properties of the lens system, the spectral content of the image can be significantly affected.

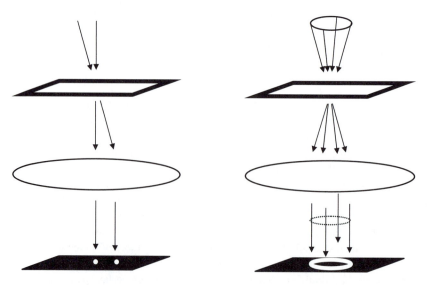

FIGURE 35.15   Spectrum for an off-axis ray (left) and spectrum for an annular cone of off-axis rays (right).

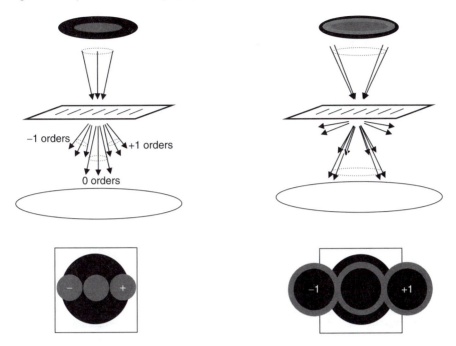

FIGURE 35.16 Spectrum for conventional illumination (left), and for off-axis annular illumination (right), in which the annulus has been chosen to coincide with the diffracted orders of the pattern on the photomask.

Typical illuminators shape the light to be uniform and to illuminate the photomask with a fairly narrow range of angles. The spectrum of illumination then corresponds to a circle. By using illumination with a specific angle of incidence, represented, for example, by the annulus in Figure 35.16, certain pitches can be emphasized and their imaging contrast enhanced, but only at the expense of lower contrast for other spatial frequencies [61,62]. For IC layouts with a large proportion of periodic patterns, such as memories, a suitable choice of illuminator pattern that matches the spatial frequencies of the layout can enhance imaging performance significantly [62]. An example of this is shown in Figure 35.17, in which a quadrupole-like illuminator was used in combination with subresolution assist features (SRAFs) to overcome certain "forbidden pitches" of low contrast [63].

More elaborate interactions between the spectrum of source angles and the photomask layout are possible. Shown in Figure 35.18 is an example of an IC cell and a source spectrum created through mask/source co-optimization. There are several methods demonstrated to achieve this goal [64–67].

35.2.3.4 RET Combinations

Although each of these techniques can enhance lithographic performance in and of itself, it is in combinations that dramatic improvements in imaging performance are achieved. For example, phase-mask images may have higher contrast, but still suffer from iso/dense bias, requiring OPC [59]. Likewise, combinations of OAI tuned for photomasks with OPC layouts can be very effective [68–70]. In some cases, all three techniques have been used together to create the best lithographic performance [35,71,72]. Success with developing processes using these combinations, with choices tuned to the unique combinations of skills present in individual companies, is a lively source of competition among IC makers.

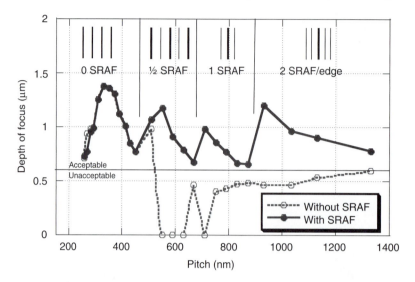

FIGURE 35.17 Pitch curve for lines and spaces under a particular OAI approach called QUASAR illumination. Without SRAFs, certain pitches do not have enough contrast, and will not print. SRAF are added to restore the contrast. (Adapted from Schellenberg, F.M., Capodieci, L., and Socha, B., Proceedings of the 38th Design Automation Conference, ACM, New York, 2001, pp. 89–92. With permission.)

35.2.3.5 Polarization

At this time, there is a fourth independent variable of the EM field that has not yet been as fully exploited as the other three: polarization [73]. For advanced steppers, which fill the gap between the last lens element and the wafer with water for the higher angle coupling it allows (water immersion

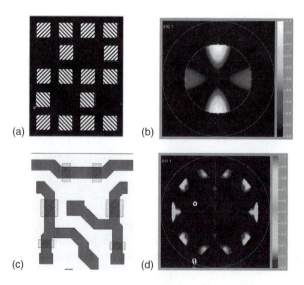

FIGURE 35.18 (a) Layout with alternating phase-shifted apertures, (black is opaque, left stripe is 0°, right stripe 180°), and (b) pupil map of an illumination pattern optimized for this layout; (c) Layout with or a memory cell (dark is opaque, clear is normal 0° mask transmission), and (d) pupil map of an illumination pattern optimized for this layout. (Adapted from Granik, Y., *J. Microlith. Microfab. Microsyst.*, 3, 509, 2004. With permission.)

steppers [26]), anticipation of and compensation for polarization properties of the light is becoming crucial [73–76]. At the time of this writing, however, although some very creative techniques exploiting polarization have been proposed [77], no definitive polarization-based RET has been demonstrated as practical. Instead, polarization is considered in each of the other RETs—source illumination, mask diffraction, and lens pupil transmission. This may change in the future as the polarization issues with advanced immersion lithography become better understood.

35.2.4 RET FLOW AND COMPUTATIONAL LITHOGRAPHY

No matter what patterning technique is used, incorporating the simulation of the corresponding effects requires some care for insertion into an EDA environment. Complete brute force image simulation of a 32 mm × 22 mm IC with resolution at the nanometer scale would require a gigantic amount of simulation and days or even weeks to complete. Some effort to therefore determine the minimum necessary set for simulation is called for.

Therefore, the initial step simulation for an EDA flow involves fragmentation of the layout. In a layout format such as GDS-II or OASIS, a polygon is defined by a sequence of vertices. These vertices are only placed where the boundary of a polygon makes a change (e.g., at the corners of rectangles). With fragmentation, additional vertices are inserted [41,78]. The rules governing fragmentation can be complex, but the intention is to basically break the longer edge segments into shorter, more manageable edge segments, with more segments (higher fragmentation) in regions of high variability and fewer segments (low fragmentation) in regions of low variability. This is illustrated in Figure 35.19.

Once fragmented, a simulation point is determined for each edge segment. This is the location at which the image simulation results will be determined, and the corresponding position of the edge as expected on the wafer determined. Each simulation point has an associated cutline, along which the various values for the image intensity and its derivatives (e.g., image slope) will be calculated. This is illustrated in Figure 35.20 [41,79,80].

At this point, the simulator is invoked to systematically simulate the image properties only along the cutline for each edge segment. Using some assumptions or a suitable algorithm, the position of the edge of the resist is determined from the computed image. Once this edge position is determined, a difference between the edge position in the desired layout and the simulated edge position is computed. This difference is called the edge placement error (EPE) [41].

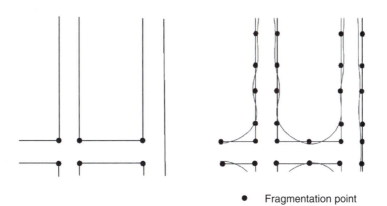

● Fragmentation point

FIGURE 35.19 Original portion of a layout with original fragmentation (left) and layout after refragmentation for OPC (right). (Adapted from Word, J. and Cobb, N., *Proc. SPIE*, 5567, 1305–1314, 2004. With permission.)

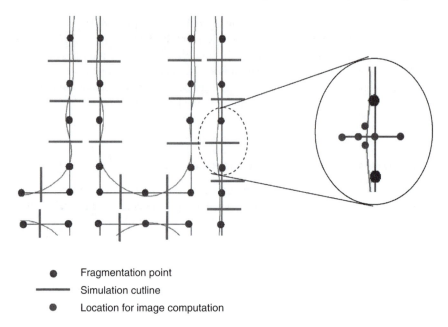

●   Fragmentation point

―――――   Simulation cutline

●   Location for image computation

FIGURE 35.20 Selection of the simulation cutlines to use with the fragmentation from Figure 35.19. (Reproduced, Courtesy Mentor Graphics.)

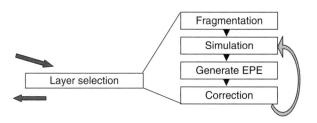

FIGURE 35.21 Sequence of operations within a typical OPC iterative loop.

For each and every edge segment there is, therefore, an EPE. For an EPE of zero, the image of the edge falls exactly on the desired location. When the EPE is nonzero, a suggested motion for the edge segment is determined from the sign and magnitude of the EPE that should reduce the EPE. The edge segment in the layout is then moved, according to this prediction. Once this happens, a new simulation and a new EPE are generated for the revised layout. The iterative process proceeds until the EPE has been reduced to be within a predetermined tolerance. This is illustrated in Figure 35.21.

Although simplistic in outline, determining fragmentation settings and suitable simulation sites while remaining optimal for the competing metrics of high accuracy, rapid convergence, and manageable data volume remains challenging. A real-world example of a layout with fragmentation selections is shown in Figure 35.22. In general, high fragmentation density leads to better accuracy, but requires more simulation and may create higher data volume. Poorly chosen simulation sites can converge rapidly, but may not accurately represent the average behavior along the entire edge fragment (and in some cases, may even lead to a motion in the wrong direction). Cutlines chosen in certain orientations (e.g., normal to the layout, not normal to the image gradient) may again produce less representative EPEs, and the iteration may require longer to converge.

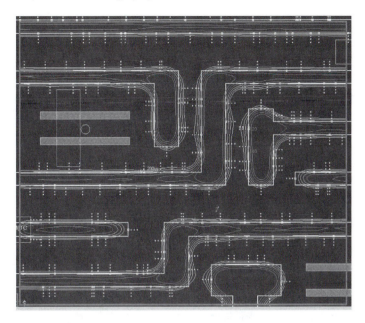

FIGURE 35.22 Example of a real-world layout, showing the target layout, simulation cutlines, and image contours. (Reproduced, Courtesy Mentor Graphics.)

35.2.5 MASK MANUFACTURING FLOW

Although originally developed for computing the relationship between the layout and the wafer image, a similar procedure can be carried out to compensate for mask manufacturing effects [81]. In this case, the model must be derived for the various processes used in mask fabrication. These typically involve exposure using an electron beam (E-beam), and because electrons are charged and repel, a significant amount of computation may be required to compensate for electron proximity effects [82]. Optical mask writers, which write masks using UV lasers and use lithography materials similar to those used for wafers [82], can also be corrected for optical proximity and processing effects.

35.2.6 CONTOUR-BASED EPE

For sparse layouts, with feature dimensions larger than the optical wavelength, selection of fragmentation settings and simulation sites can be fairly straightforward, as illustrated in Figure 35.23a. As feature dimensions become significantly smaller than the optical wavelength, however, more simulation sites can be needed, as illustrated in Figure 35.23b [83]. At some point, the advantage of a sparse simulation set is severely reduced, and the use of a uniform grid of simulation points becomes attractive again.

In this case, the simulation of the image intensity is carried out using a regular grid, as illustrated in Figure 35.24. Contours from the simulation result, using again a suitable model to predict the edge location on the wafer, are used to represent the image intensity. The EPE is then synthesized from the desired position of an edge segment and a corresponding location on the contour. Subsequent motion of the edge segments proceeds as previously described.

Representation of the contour data can present additional problems not encountered in the sparse approach. Accurate representations of contours contain far more vertices than their counterparts in the original GDS-II layout. And although storing the contours after it has been used to determine an EPE may be extremely useful, because identical regions may be encountered later and the precomputed

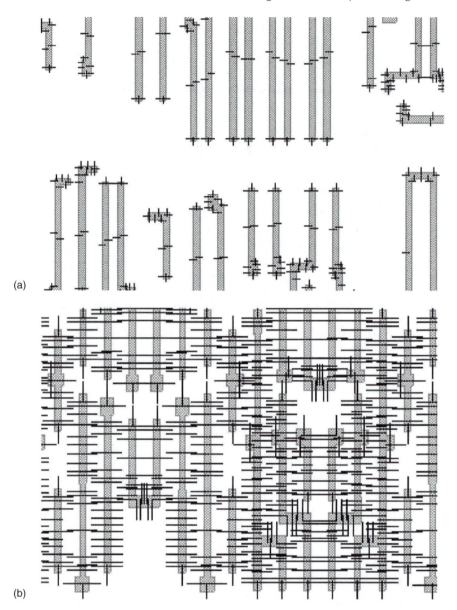

(a)

(b)

FIGURE 35.23 (a) Layout with sparse simulation plan and (b) scaled layout using sparse simulation rules when the target dimension is 65 nm and the exposure wavelength is 193 nm. At some point, sparse simulations are no longer sparse. (Adapted from Cobb, N. and Dudau, D., *Proc. SPIE*, 6154, 615401, 2006. With permission.)

solution accessed and reused, the additional data volume for storage of contours with their high vertex counts in the database can present problems. In spite of these logistical problems, however, there are some clear advantages for accuracy. With the dense approach, certain features such as the bridge shown in Figure 35.24 can be simulated and flagged; catching such a structure with a sparse number of simulation sites becomes far more problematic.

No matter what the simulation strategy, image and process simulators are invoked in these OPC flows. We now turn our attention to the simulator itself, and some of the practical approximations that are used to make a simulator functional in an EDA environment.

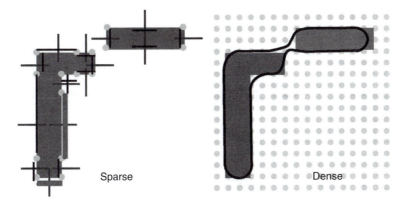

Sparse

Dense

FIGURE 35.24 Fragmentation/simulation plan for a portion of a layout using sparse rules (left), and a dense grid simulation (right). Using the contours from the dense grid, features such as the bridge between the two features can be detected. (Reproduced, Courtesy Mentor Graphics).

35.3 SIMULATION TECHNIQUES

35.3.1 INTRODUCTION

In Section 35.2, the fundamental framework for modeling lithography and various RETs were provided. In this section, computational techniques that can be used within that framework for detailed mask transmission, image propagation, and wafer process simulation are presented, and the various trade-offs in the approximations they use are discussed.

As described in Section 35.2.2.2, the imaging system can be approximated as a simple Fourier transform and its inverse, with the pupil aperture (e.g., a circle) providing a low pass cutoff for the spatial frequencies of the image.

Although abstractly true, certainly much more than a pair of FFTs are needed to provide highly accurate simulation results. The three areas that require modeling attention are the imaging system itself, the interaction with the photomask, and the interaction with the wafer.

35.3.2 IMAGING SYSTEM MODELING

A lithographic imaging system has a large number of highly polished, precision optical elements, mounted in a precision mechanical housing. The lens column can weigh over 2 t and be over 2 m tall. An example of a contemporary lens design [84] is shown in Figure 35.25. These lenses are usually designed with complex ray tracing programs that accurately represent the path that light takes through the reflective and refractive elements [85].

Because the mathematical theory of lens design is linear and well understood, the complex interactions of the lens elements can be represented as the simple, ideal Fourier lens described in Section 35.2.2.2, with all the physical properties of the lens (refraction, aberrations, etc.) lumped together into an idealized pupil function represented by Zernike polynomials. This function can be measured using precision interferometry techniques, but this is usually not easy to do for an individual stepper in the field [86].

The interaction of this pupil with the illuminator presents the essential challenge of imaging simulation. If the light falling on the lens were a single, coherent, uniform normal incidence (on-axis) plane wave, the corresponding spectrum in the pupil would be a single point at the center of the pupil. This represents coherent illumination, as shown in Figure 35.26a. In practice, however, light falls on the photomask at a range of angles, from a number of potential source points. The corresponding interactions in the lens pupil are shifted and overlapped. The degree to which the

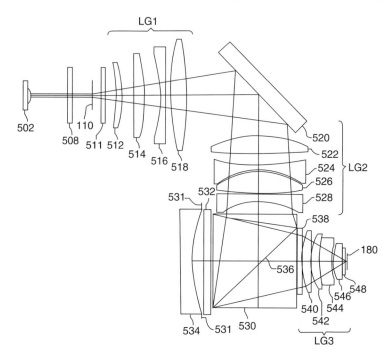

FIGURE 35.25 Example of a contemporary scanner lens design. (From Kreuzer, J., US Patent 6,836,380.)

pupil is filled is then related to the spatial coherence of the light source. For very coherent light, the pupil filling ratio is small (Figure 35.26b); for larger angles and lower coherence, the pupil filling is higher (Figure 35.26c). This ratio, also called the coherence factor, is typically designated by lithographers using the symbol σ. This should not be confused, however, with the electrical conductivity from Equation 35.1b above.

Imaging with complicated sources and pupils can be complicated to model. For coherent light, the image fields add directly both at every moment in time and in a time average, and so we can sum the various contributions individually. For incoherent light, the local fields add instantaneously, but for the time average, the correlation is lost, and so the various image intensities must be computed and added.

However, most illumination systems are partially coherent. This means that the relation between the image $I(x, y)$ from two different points in an object (x_o', y_o') and (x_o'', y_o'') (e.g., two points in a mask) do not fit either of these simple cases. Likewise, the illumination of an object by a distribution of source points follows similarly.

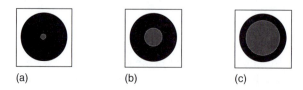

FIGURE 35.26 Pupil maps for illumination that is (a) coherent, (b) partially coherent, and (c) incoherent.

The image formulation for this situation can be computed using the mutual intensity function $J(x_o', y_o'; x_o'', y_o'')$, according to Refs. [29,87,88]

$$I(x, y) = \int\limits_{-\infty}^{\infty} \iiint J(x_o' - x_o'', y_o' - y_o'') \cdot M(x_o', y_o') \cdot M^*(x_o'', y_o'')$$

$$\times H(x_o', y_o') \cdot H^*(x_o'', y_o'') \cdot dx_o' dy_o' dx_o'' dy_o'' \qquad (35.21)$$

where

$M(x_o, y_o)$ are the points in the mask

$H(x, y, x_o, y_o)$ represents the optical system transfer function from point (x_o, y_o) to (x, y).

When the mask and the transfer function are replaced by Fourier representations,

$$M(x, y) = \int\limits_{-\infty}^{\infty} \int \hat{M}(p, q) \cdot e^{-i2\pi(px+qy)} dp\, dq \qquad (35.22a)$$

$$J(x, y) = \int\limits_{-\infty}^{\infty} \int \hat{J}(p, q) \cdot e^{-i2\pi(px+qy)} dp\, dq \qquad (35.22b)$$

the image intensity can be rewritten as

$$I(x, y) = \int\limits_{+\infty}^{+\infty} \int \iint \iint \hat{J}(p, q) \cdot \hat{H}(p+p', q+q') \hat{H}^*(p+p'', q+q'')$$

$$\times \hat{M}(p', q') \cdot \hat{M}^*(p'', q'') \cdot e^{-i2\pi[(p'-p'')x+(q'-q'')y]} dp\, dq\, dp'\, dq'\, dp''\, dq'' \qquad (35.23)$$

Changing the order of integration, the integral can be reexpressed as

$$I(x, y) = \int\limits_{+\infty}^{+\infty} \int \iint TCC(p', q', p'', q'') \cdot \hat{M}(p', q') \hat{M}^*(p'', q'') \cdot e^{-i2\pi[(p'-p'')x+(q'-q'')y]} dp'dq'dp'' \, dq''$$

$$(35.24)$$

where

$$TCC(p', q', p'', q'') = \int\limits_{+\infty}^{+\infty} \iint \hat{J}(p, q)\hat{H}(p+p', q+q')\hat{H}^*(p+p'', q+q'') dp\, dq \qquad (35.25)$$

is called the transmission cross coefficient (TCC). An illustration of this overlap integral in the pupil plane is shown in Figure 35.27.

This TCC overlap integral depends only on the illumination source and the transfer of light through the lens, which are independent of mask layout. $J(p, q)$ in Figure 35.27 is a representation of the projection of a circular source illumination. This could just as well be an annular, quadrupole, or other off-axis structure, as illustrated in Figure 35.16, or a more complex pattern, as shown in Figure 35.18. Only portions in frequency space (the pupil plane) where source light overlaps with the lens transmission (the shaded area) will contribute to the final image.

The key element here is that the interaction of the source and lens can be precomputed as TCCs and stored for later use, once the details of the mask layout $M(x, y)$ are known. This formulation for imaging was originally presented by Hopkins [88] and is often called the Hopkins approach.

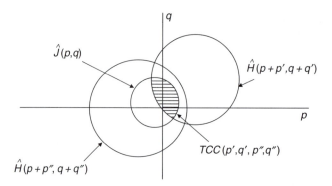

FIGURE 35.27 Diagram of the integral of overlap for the computation of images using TCCs.

One example of the utility of this approach is the simulation of defocus. Normally, the Fourier optical equations represent the image at the plane of focus. However, for propagation beyond focus, the expansion of a spherical wave from a point follows a quadratic function that is equivalent to introducing a fourth-order Zernike aberration Z_4 in the pupil plane [89] (See Table 35.1). Computation of a defocused image therefore becomes equivalent to the computation of an in-focus image with a suitable degree of fourth-order aberration. By precomputing the TCCs for a system with fourth-order aberration, defocus images for a mask pattern can therefore be calculated merely by using different sets of precalculated TCCs.

35.3.3 MASK TRANSMISSION FUNCTION

In our formulations of imaging so far, the mask transmission is a simple function, $M(x, y)$. Typically, this is a binary mask, having a value of 0 or 1 depending on the pixel coordinates. In the Kirchhoff approximation, mentioned in Section 35.2.2.2, the mask transmission is exactly this function. However, in a real photomask, with layers of chrome coated onto a substrate of quartz, the wavefronts reflect and scatter off the three-dimensional structures, and the wavefront can be a complicated function of position, amplitude, and phase.

This wavefront can still be represented as a 2D function, in which each pixel has its own transmission value and a phase factor, depending on the phase shift of the transmitted light. To derive this representation, however, a simple scalar representation of the field at the mask will not suffice. Instead, a full vector EM field computation may be required.

35.3.3.1 FDTD

A widely used first-principles method for simulating the electromagnetic field over time is the finite-difference time domain (FDTD) method [90–93]. This is illustrated in Figure 35.28. Here, a grid in time and space is established, and the initial conditions for sources (charge and current) determined and the field at the boundaries determined. Then, using Maxwell equations in a finite difference form, the time step is incremented, and the E-field recomputed, based on the previous E field and the curl of H at the previous time step. Once this is generated, the time step in incremented again, and the H field is computed, based on the previous H field and the curl of the E field. As an example, following the notation of Erdmann [93], the Maxwell equations for a transverse electric (TE) field mode can be represented for grid point i, j at time step n in finite difference form as

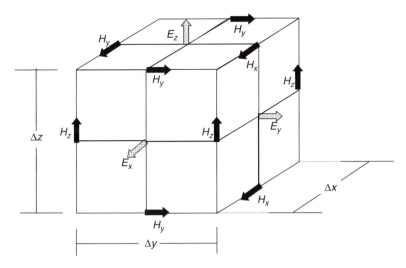

FIGURE 35.28 Illustration of the geometry used in the computation of EM fields according to the FDTD method. (Adapted from Taflove, A. and Hagness, S.C., *Computational Electrodynamics: The Finite-Difference Time-Domain Method*, Artech House, Boston, 2005. With permission. After Yee, K. S., *IEEE Trans. Antennas Propagation*, AP-14, 302, 1966, Copyright IEEE. With permission.)

$$H_x \Big|_{i,j}^{n+1/2} = H_x \Big|_{i,j}^{n-1/2} + \frac{\Delta t}{\mu \Delta x} \left(E_y \Big|_{i,j+1}^{n} - E_y \Big|_{i,j}^{n} \right) \tag{35.26a}$$

$$H_z \Big|_{i,j}^{n+1/2} = H_z \Big|_{i,j}^{n-1/2} + \frac{\Delta t}{\mu \Delta x} \left(E_y \Big|_{i,j}^{n} - E_y \Big|_{i+1,j}^{n} \right) \tag{35.26b}$$

$$E_y \Big|_{i,j}^{n+1} = C_a \Big|_{i,j} \cdot E_y \Big|_{i,j}^{n} + C_b \Big|_{i,j} \left(\cdot H_x \Big|_{i,j}^{n+1/2} - \cdot H_x \Big|_{i,j-1}^{n+1/2} + \cdot H_z \Big|_{i-1,j}^{n+1/2} - \cdot H_x \Big|_{i,j}^{n+1/2} \right) \tag{35.26c}$$

where the coefficients C_a and C_b depend on the materials properties and charge densities:

$$C_a \Big|_{i,j} = \left(1 - \frac{\sigma_{i,j} \Delta t}{2\varepsilon_{i,j}} \right) \Bigg/ \left(1 + \frac{\sigma_{i,j} \Delta t}{2\varepsilon_{i,j}} \right) \tag{35.27a}$$

$$C_b \Big|_{i,j} = \left(\frac{\Delta t}{2\varepsilon_{i,j}} \right) \Bigg/ \left(1 + \frac{\sigma_{i,j} \Delta t}{2\varepsilon_{i,j}} \right) \tag{35.27b}$$

From the initial conditions, the suitable fields are computed at half time steps throughout the spatial grid, and the revised fields are then used for the computation of the complementary fields for the next half time step. Each step, of course, could be designated as a unit time step for the algorithm. But then the entire algorithm (E generating H; H generating E) would then require two time steps to come full circle. The use of half time steps is therefore convenient so that the entire algorithm counts a single cycle in a single unit time step. This staggered computation is illustrated in Figure 35.29. The calculation proceeds through time and space until the maximum time allocated is reached.

For a steady-state source of excitation (e.g., incident electromagnetic waves), the time interval should be chosen such that the final few cycles reach a steady state, and can be time averaged to give average local fields and intensity values.

For this method to work, the optical properties of each point in the computation grid must be specified. For metals (such as the chrome photomask layer), this can be difficult, because the refractive index is less than 1 and a denser grid may be required. However, because the optical

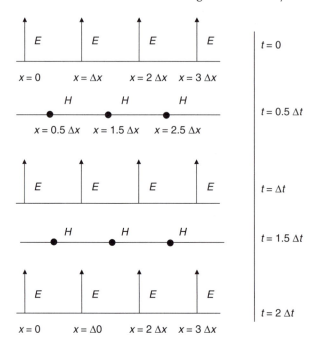

FIGURE 35.29 Illustration of the time steps used in the computation of EM fields according to the FDTD Method. (Adapted from Taflove, A. and Hagness, S.C., *Computational Electrodynamics: The Finite-Difference Time-Domain Method*, Artech House, Boston, 2005. With permission.)

properties of air, quartz, and chromium have been measured and can be found in Ref. [94], this tends to not be a practical drawback to its use.

More critical is the fact that the grid must extend throughout the space to be simulated. If a large system such as an entire lens were to be simulated point by point, the amount of computation would be gigantic. Lens propagation is well described by the approximations described previously, in Section 35.2.2.2 and using the Hopkins method of Section 35.3.2. To use the more accurate results of the FDTD simulation where it matters, at the mask and more particularly at the patterned surface of the mask, a grid can be set up to only simulate the thin region at the quartz/chrome/air interface of the photomask, using fine grids (e.g., grid spacing of 5 nm for illumination wavelength $\lambda = 193$ nm). The scattering of the mask patterning structures can then be accurately computed locally using the FDTD method, and a replacement for the mask function, a new $M'(x, y)$, can be generated from the results at the bottom of the simulation window. This $M'(x, y)$ will have the amplitude and phase information as generated by the FDTD simulator, and the angular spectrum (e.g., Fourier transform) of this complex function can be used in the established equations.

Another problem lies with the treatment of the boundary conditions. Normally, such a program would assume the edges are contiguous with another domain, periodically repeated from the grid under simulation. If this is actually the case on the photomask (e.g., with repeating cells or features), then this will be accurate, but to simulate isolated features, something must be done. The usual treatment here is to use perfectly matched layers (PMLs) [95] at the edges of the simulation domain that attenuate the incoming EM excitations. Ideally, there is no reflection at all from the PMLs, and analytically this is true. But with a discrete grid, some artificial reflection can occur, and at oblique angles, this can grow to be significant. Therefore, care must be taken when creating these black holes at the appropriate edges of the simulation regime to allow accurate simulation of local isolated layout patterns.

If a suitable grid and boundary conditions are set up, the FDTD simulator produces correct results [96,97]. However, the computation time consumed to reach steady-state result, and to then infer a function that represents a complex effective mask transmission, makes this unmanageable as an in-line simulation tool for the simulations called for in full-chip RET.

35.3.3.2 RCWA and Waveguide Techniques

Other techniques can also be used to provide a more rigorous technique for simulating the electromagnetic field without the computational intensity of the FDTD method. Rigorous coupled wave analysis (RCWA) [98] is a technique for modeling the light diffraction from gratings. The linearity of optics, as discussed above in Section 35.2, allows for the Fourier decomposition of an arbitrary pattern into a set of gratings, which can be computed individually and the final image reassembled. This technique is more commonly used for one-dimensional patterns [99].

The waveguide method (WGM) [100] assumes the object is periodic with rectangular sidewalls, and expands the fields in the object into the eigenmodes of a waveguide with a similar profile. Although these boundary conditions may be somewhat limited, they correspond to many real-world mask structures, such as certain phase-shifting masks [101], and when the boundary conditions are met, they can be several times faster than FDTD without a significant loss in accuracy [102].

35.3.3.3 DDM

An alternative approach to the in-line use of FDTD can be found in techniques such as the domain decomposition method (DDM) [103]. Here, a basis set of fundamental imaging components is determined. One possible set of basis elements is a collection of topographic edges of various dimensions, each one illuminated at particular angles and for each polarization (parallel and perpendicular). Another uses predetermined geometric regions. For each of the basis elements, the EM fields are presimulated using an accurate method, such as a FDTD simulator, and stored in a table for future use [104].

When a complex layout is encountered that requires simulation, the program decomposes the layout into a summation of the fundamental basis set elements, looks up and assembles the precomputed field contributions, and presents the resulting E fields. In this way, a fairly accurate simulation result for a complex topographic pattern can be presented without requiring a large area, time-consuming FDTD calculation.

The DDM method is illustrated in Figure 35.30. For simulating topographic mask patterns, this has been quite successful using a basis set of chrome or quartz edges of various heights and lengths, illuminated with either parallel or perpendicular polarization. It relies, however, on the linearity of the EM system and the correct choice of a basis set for its success. If certain resonant phenomena are encountered, such as the excitation of surface plasmons at a metal/dielectric interface, [105–107] the basis set must be expanded to include the fundamental resonant structures, and the decomposition must be expanded to ensure that they are recognized. If nonlinear interactions occur, the technique will not work.

35.3.4 WAFER SIMULATION

The image intensity $I(x, y)$ that is produced corresponds to the image that would be formed in free space or air (the aerial image). Defocus, as discussed above, can be introduced as equivalent to a fourth-order aberration function. To model the effect of dose in the photoresist, the behavior of the image as it coupled into the photosensitive resist must be considered [108].

Photoresists are engineered to be very high contrast materials. This means that, once the exposure dose has exceeded a certain threshold, the desired reaction (either the breaking of bonds, or the formation of crosslinks) occurs rapidly and thoroughly [22]. For this reason, an image can be evaluated for regions in which the intensity exceeds the threshold versus those where intensity does not exceed a threshold, and the final pattern defined appropriately. The simplest approach is to determine

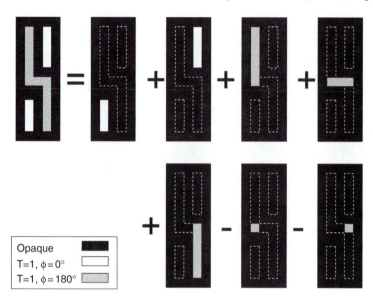

FIGURE 35.30 Illustration of the DDM (Adapted Adam, K. and Neureuther, A., *Proc. SPIE*, 4691, 107, 2002. With permission.)

a single threshold value, and apply that universally. This is called a constant threshold model for aerial image evaluation [41].

For some estimations, this works well, but results can vary with individual resists. Some modern resists for use with deep-UV exposure resists with chemical amplification operate with the creation of a catalyst through photoexposure. This catalyst then migrates through the polymer matrix, breaking bonds [22]. Depending on the density of the photocatalysts, the delivered dose can produce different effects in different regions.

One can, as above, use a first-principles method to precompute resist profiles for a basis set of structures. In this case, the actual 3D intensity profile within the resist is computed, using all the reflections at the front and back surfaces that may cause interference within the layers [109]. The refractive indices of the resist and various coating layers are needed, and their change as exposure takes place (bleaching) must also be computed. The generation of photoactive compounds and their diffusion during postexposure baking can be simulated kinetically [110], and finally, the removal of material through the development process can also be modeled [111].

These photoexposure and development processes, however, are threshold-based processes. The ability to find a suitable set of basis structures that would allow a look-up table of resist results to be assembled into an image, analogous to DDM, would require a very large look-up table.

Instead, it has been observed that the basic characteristics of resist image formation can be inferred by calibrating the actual formation of an image edge to the local aerial image parameters, such as local image maximum intensity (I_{max}), intensity slope, etc.

In a technique pioneered by Cobb [112], the variable threshold resist (VTR) method [41,112,113], creates a table of values relating image parameters (e.g., I_{max}, slope) and then determines the local threshold as a function of these imaging parameters. This is illustrated in Figure 35.31 and Figure 35.32.

Other, more complicated functions have been derived for evaluating the relationship between printed (and even etched) image and the parameters in the image. These optimizations can be level specific, and often require extensive calibration. Their use for memory ICs, which are manufactured in great volumes, provide the best return on the investment in this calibration [114].

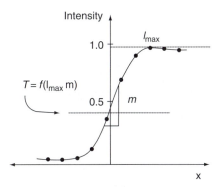

FIGURE 35.31 Intensity profile through a simulation cutline. (Adapted from Cobb, N.B., Fast optical and process proximity correction algorithms for integrated circuit manufacturing, Ph.D. Dissertation, University of California, Berkeley, California, 1998; Cobb, N.B., Zakhor, A., and Miloslavsky, E., *Optical Microlithography IX, Proceedings of SPIE*, 2726, 208, 1996. With permission.)

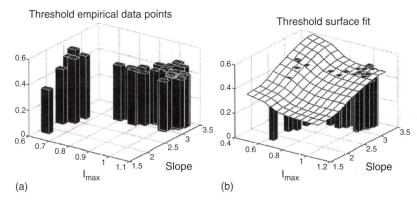

FIGURE 35.32 VTR model. (a) Empirical threshold values determined from linewidth measurements, and (b) a model surface that fits the empirical data. (Reproduced from Cobb, N.B., Fast optical and process proximity correction algorithms for integrated circuit manufacturing, Ph.D. Dissertation, University of California, Berkeley, California, 1998; Cobb, N.B., Zakhor, A., and Miloslavsky, E., *Optical Microlithography IX, Proceedings of SPIE*, 2726, 208, 1996. With permission.)

The calibration of these functions requires that a test pattern of representative features be prepared in advance and printed using the resist process in question [41,115]. Such a test pattern is illustrated in Figure 35.33. Wafer results are then measured for each of the structures, and the result compared with a aerial image simulation of the image placement and the values for the imaging parameters. From the empirical calibration of the change in line placement with image parameters, the variable threshold values can be determined.

This technique, once the test pattern calibration data has been gathered, has proven to be a very effective and fast way to generate the simulation results needed to generate EPEs and remains the fundamental methodology for most of the OPC computations in use today.

35.4 EDA RESULTS

We have shown how simulation results can be generated, and seen one case of how the use of a call to a simulator by an RET tool is used to dictate the motion of edges for process compensation.

FIGURE 35.33 Example of the layout of a test pattern used for creating empirical OPC models. (Courtesy Mentor Graphics.)

This involves the simple use of a single simulation per site, or, in more recent implementations, the comparison of a layout and a contour. There are other applications that involve more sophisticated simulations.

35.4.1 PROCESS WINDOWS

For lithographers, a typical test of a lithographic process is the focus–exposure matrix. Often called a Bossung plot, after the author of original paper proposing the technique, [116] or sometimes an ED-tree (for exposure–dose tree) [117], they are generated by making an array of exposures with a stepper, systematically changing focus and exposure dose. The resulting feature of interest is measured for each setting to form a matrix, allowing the range of settings for which the feature dimension (commonly called a CD, for critical dimension) is within a preset tolerance to be determined. The region over which acceptable feature deviation is achieved is called the process window. An example of a process window is illustrated in Figure 35.34 [60]. Typically, the acceptable region is the nominal dimension ±10 percent.

Process windows are extremely useful tools for the evaluation of, for example, a novel RET approach [60,118]. Improving the process window with the addition of assist features or by using a different illuminator design is a standard procedure. The number of simulations that must be run to accurately estimate the behavior through focus and dose can vary, and dynamic adaptation of simulation settings can lead to more computationally efficient estimations without a significant loss in accuracy [119].

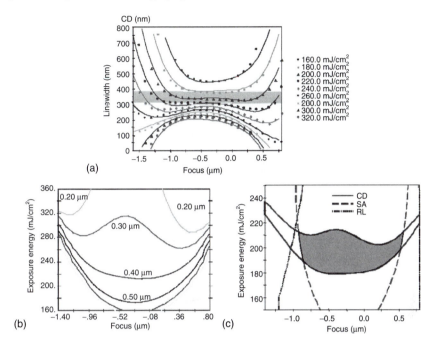

FIGURE 35.34 Determination of a process window. (a) Linewidth data as a function of defocus are plotted for various exposure doses. (b) Replotting of the data from (a) showing contours of constant linewidth and (c) determination of process conditions where the linewidth is within specification, forming a process window. (Reproduced from Mack, C., *Design, Process Integration and Characterization for Microelectronics, Proceedings of SPIE*, 4692, 454, 2002. With permission.)

Other, more complicated functions have been derived for evaluating the relationship between printed (and even etched) image and the parameters in the image. One example from a recent paper is shown in Figure 35.35 [120]. Sometimes, because resists 100 nm thick are therefore out of focus by 100 nm at the top or bottom, additional image metrics incorporating computation of defocused images can also be considered. Process window OPC is an area of increasing sophistication for modeling and calibration for OPC applications.

35.4.2 MEEF

Another use for simulation is the evaluation of the change in the image that occurs when a feature on a photomask is not accurately fabricated. The change in printed feature for a small change in the original photomask dimension is called the mask error enhancement factor (MEEF) [121,122]:

$$\text{MEEF} = M \frac{\Delta CD_{\text{wafer}}}{\Delta CD_{\text{mask}}}$$

where M (not to be confused with $M(x,y)$) is the mask magnification factor (typically $M = 4$ for modern steppers).

For large features using normal lithography, MEEF is typically 1. For smaller features, dimensions are eventually reached where these no longer print at all, as shown in Figure 35.36a. In these cases, the change in printed feature varies dramatically with the change in mask dimension, and MEEF is very large, as illustrated in Figure 35.36b [123,124].

The use of RET can be evaluated here not only by the improvement of the process window but also by the impact on MEEF [125]. For some choices of RET, this can be very advantageous. For

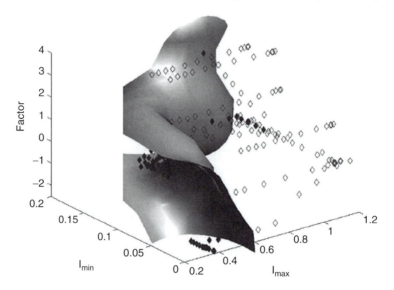

FIGURE 35.35 Contemporary illustration of the extension of the model fitting routines as illustrated in Figure 35.32, but now considering process windows. (Reproduced from Shang, S., Granik, Y., Cobb, N., Maurer, W., Cui, Y., Liebmann, L., Oberschmidt, J., Singh, R., Vampatella, B., *Optical Microlithography XVI, Proceedings of SPIE*, 5040, 431, 2003. With permission.)

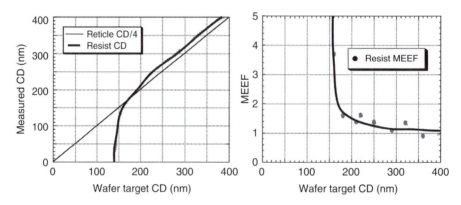

FIGURE 35.36 Measured CD versus desired CD for an isolated line (left). CD stands for critical dimension, a common metrology term to designate a linewidth. For small features, the process completely fails. Corresponding MEEF result (right). As the process fails, the MEEF clearly increases dramatically. (Adapted from Schellenberg, F.M., Boksha, V., Cobb, N., Lai, J.C., Chen, C.H., and Mack, C., *Optical Microlithography XII, Proceedings of SPIE*, 3679, 261, 1999. With permission.)

example, the image of a phase edge formed by a phase shifting mask, the dark fringe occurs no matter what the dimension of the photomask, and the MEEF approaches zero for this technique. This is illustrated in Figure 35.37 [60,126].

35.4.3 PV-BANDS

Simulation can be used to also evaluate the typical extremes of a process, and then used to generate contours representing the placement of these edges on the wafer under these extreme conditions. These contours can be converted to a sequence of vertices and stored in the layout database as

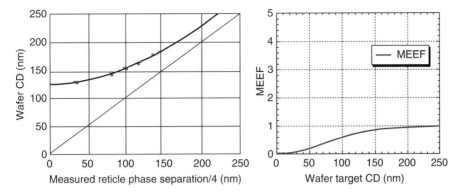

FIGURE 35.37 Measured CD versus desired CD for an isolated line fabricated using a phase-shifting mask (left). For small features, the linewidth converges to the fundamental limit formed by the narrow, dark interference fringe. The corresponding MEEF result (right). (Adapted from Schellenberg, F.M., Toublan, O., Cobb, N., Sahonria, E., Hughes, G., MacDonald, S., and West, C., *Proc. SPIE*, 4000, 1062, 2000. With permission.)

PV-bands (process variation bands) [127]. These are illustrated in Figure 35.38. These are similar to the contours generated by other image simulation techniques, and can be used in DRC and other checking operations to verify that the layout, even if distorted by manufacturing processes, can still pass.

In the past, the generation of PV-bands throughout an entire layout was too computationally intensive to be practical. Now, with the computing power typically brought to bear to generate OPC layouts, computing PV-bands for every feature in the layout becomes possible, and if the hierarchy of the original layout can be maintained for the layouts rendered as PV-bands, even practical.

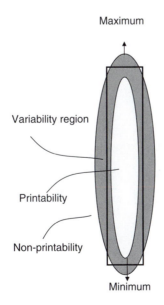

FIGURE 35.38 Illustration of a layout polygon and its corresponding process variation (PV)-bands. (Reproduced from Robles, J.A.T., Integrated circuit layout design methodology for deep sub-wavelength processes, Ph.D. Dissertation, OGI School of Science and Engineering, Beaverton, Oregon, 2005. With permission.)

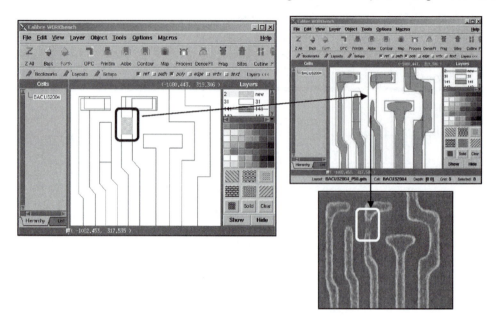

FIGURE 35.39 Portion of a layout where the PV-bands have flagged a violation (left), and (upper right) the corresponding simulated layout and (lower right) the printed wafer behavior. (After Robles, J.A.T., Integrated circuit layout design methodology for deep sub-wavelength processes, Ph.D. Dissertation, OGI School of Science and Engineering, Beaverton, Oregon, 2005. With permission.)

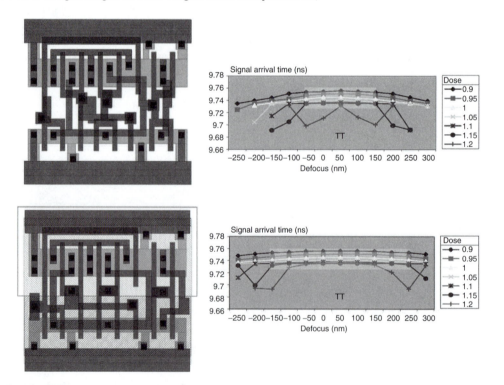

FIGURE 35.40 Standard layout (upper), with the corresponding timing information as a function of lithographic defocus. The layout (lower), modified slightly to be more uniform and to remove the possible sources of variation highlighted by the PV-bands, along with the corresponding improvement in timing with variation in defocus. (After Robles, J.A.T., Integrated circuit layout design methodology for deep sub-wavelength processes, Ph.D. Dissertation, OGI School of Science and Engineering, Beaverton, Oregon, 2005. With permission.)

35.4.4 EXTRACTION

The generation of data layers corresponding to PV-Bands opens up the possibility of linking the PV-band layout not only to a DRC tool but also to an extraction tool. By using the PV band for a circuit instead of the nominal layout (or a simulated result at perfect focus and exposure) in an extraction tool, the effect of process variations on electrical properties can now be determined [128].

An example of this is shown in Figures 35.39 and 35.40. Here, simulated results for a cell have been generated with PV-bands under various settings, and the timing behavior of the circuit determined using an extraction tool. Rather than predict the imaging fidelity using process windows (which may or may not correlate with electrically meaningful performance), this link to extraction and SPICE modeling can allow lithographic modeling to predict the electrical performance of a circuit, and its response to variation in optical parameters.

35.5 CONCLUSION

This chapter has attempted to present an overview of the interaction of an EDA layout flow using process modeling, and given details on the specific example of lithographic process modeling. Maxwell's equations and the Fourier transforms used in optics have been well known and characterized for over a century, and this has lead to a very mature algorithmic environment for introducing these computations for all features in an EDA layout.

There are other processes that can be modeled, such as (CMP) [11–13] and plasma etching [129]. The results of these models have direct consequences for the layout and design, for example, in the domain of density dummy fill patterns inserted into a layout to improve the CMP uniformity. However, these are not as well understood as lithography processes, and are often based purely on empirical characterization. The utility of these models, however, will follow the same principle as for the flow outlined in Figure 35.1.

As computing power continues to grow and become even more inexpensive, the seamless insertion of large computational modeling modules into EDA flows, as has already been done for RET, is expected to grow and make the accounting of process variability a routine part of the design process.

REFERENCES

1. L. Scheffer, L. Lavagno, and G. Martin, *Electronic Design Automation for Integrated Circuits Handbook*, CRC Press, Boca Raton, FL, 2006.
2. *Handbook of Semiconductor Manufacturing Technology*, Y. Nishi and R. Doering, Eds., Marcel Dekker, New York, 2000.
3. S. Wolf, *Microchip Manufacturing*, Lattice Press, Sunset Beach, CA, 2004.
4. S. Wolf, *Silicon Processing for the VLSI Era*, Vols. 1–4, Lattice Press, Sunset Beach, CA, 2002.
5. R. Dutton and Z. Yu, *Technology CAD—Computer Simulation of IC Processes and Devices*, Kluwer Academic Publishers, Dordrecht, Netherlands, 1993.
6. F.M. Schellenberg, Design for manufacturing in the semiconductor industry: The litho/design workshops, in *Proceedings of the 12th International Conference on VLSI Design*, R. Sipple, Ed., IEEE Computer Society Press, Los Alamitos, CA, 1999, pp. 111–119.
7. *GDSII Stream Format Manual*, Release 6.0, Documentation No. B97E060, Cadence Design Systems, Inc./Calma, San Jose, CA, Feb. 1987.
8. *SEMI P39-0304E2-OASIS—Open Artwork System Interchange Standard*, available at. www.semi.org/.
9. A. Vladimirescu, *The SPICE Book*, John Wiley, New York, 1994; and G. Roberts and A. Sedra, *SPICE*, Oxford University Press, Oxford, United Kingdom, 1997.
10. A.B. Kahng, G. Robins, A. Singh, and A. Zelikovsky, Filling algorithms and analyses for layout density control, *IEEE Transactions on Computer-Aided Design*, 18(4), 445–462, 1999.
11. Y. Chen, A.B. Kahng, G. Robins, and A. Zelikovsky, Area fill synthesis for uniform layout density, *IEEE Transactions on Computer-Aided Design*, 21(10), 1132–1147, 2002.

12. D.O. Ouma, D.S. Boning, J.E. Chung, W. Easter, V. Savene, S. Misra, and A. Crevasse, Characterization and modeling of oxide chemical-mechanical polishing using planarization length and pattern density concepts, *IEEE Transactions on Semiconductor Manufacturing*, 15(2), 232–244, 2002.

13. A. Srivastava, D. Sylvester, and D. Blaauw, *Statistical Analysis and Optimization for VLSI: Timing and Power*, Springer, New York, 2005.

14. W. Maly, Computer-aided design for VLSI circuit manufacturability, *Proceedings of IEEE*, 78(2), 356–390, Feb. 1990.

15. W. Maly and J. Deszczka, Yield estimation model for VLSI artwork evaluation, *Electronics Letters*, 19(6), 226–227, 1983.

16. A.V. Ferris-Prabhu, Role of defect size distributions in yield modelling, *IEEE Transactions on Electron Devices*, ED-32(9), 1727–1736, 1985.

17. C.H. Stapper, Modeling of integrated circuit defect sensitivities, *IBM Journal of Research and Development*, 27(6), 549–557, 1983.

18. G.A. Allan and A.J. Walton, Hierarchical critical area extraction with the EYE tool, in *Proceedings of the IEEE Workshop Defect Fault Tolerance in VLSI Systems*, pp. 28–36, Nov. 1995.

19. W. Maly, H.T. Heineken, and F. Agricola, A simple new yield model, *Semiconductor International*, pp. 148–154, July 1994.

20. I. Bubel, W. Maly, T. Waas, P.K. Nag, H. Hartmann, D. Schmitt-Landsiedel, and S. Griep, AFFCCA: A tool for critical area analysis with circular defects and lithography deformed layout, in *Proceedings of the IEEE International Workshop on Detect and Fault Tolerance in VLSI Systems*, pp. 19–27, IEEE Computer Society Press, 1995.

21. H. Levinson, *Principles of Lithography*, 2nd edn., SPIE Press, Bellingham, WA, 2005; or *Microlithography, Science and Technology*, 2nd edn. K. Suzuki and B.W. Smith, Eds., CRC Press, Boca Raton, FL, 2007.

22. C.G. Willson, Organic resist materials, *Introduction to Microlithography*, 2nd edn., L. Thompson, C.G. Willson, and M. Bowden, Eds., American Chemical Society, Washington, DC, 1994.

23. The International Technology Road Map for Semiconductors (http://www.itrs.net/).

24. G. Moore, Cramming more components onto integrated circuits, *Electronics*, 38, 114–117, 1965.

25. M. Bohr, Intel's 65 nm Process Technology, Intel Developer Forum, Sept. 8, 2004, available at http://www.intel.com/technology/silicon/65 nm_technology.htm or ftp://download.intel.com/technology/silicon/IRDS002_65 nm_logic_process_100_percent.pdf.

26. F.M. Schellenberg, Resolution enhancement techniques and mask data preparation, *EDA for IC Implementation, Circuit Design, and Process Technology*, L. Scheffer, L. Lavagno, and G. Martin, Eds., CRC Press, Boca Raton, FL, 2006.

27. B.J. Lin, Immersion lithography and its impact on semiconductor manufacturing, *Journal of Microlithography Microfabrication and Microsystems*, 3, 377–395, 2004.

28. J.D. Jackson, *Classical Electrodynamics*, 3rd edn., J. Wiley, New York, 1999.

29. A.K.K. Wong, *Optical Imaging in Projection Microlithography*, SPIE Press, Bellingham, WA, 2005.

30. R.N. Bracewell, *The Fourier Transform and Its Application*, 3rd edn., McGraw Hill, New York, 1999; or J.W. Goodman, *Introduction to Fourier Optics*, 3rd edn., Roberts & Co, Greenwood Village, CO, 2005.

31. C.L. Tang, Nonlinear optics, The *Handbook of Optics, Part II: Devices, Measurements, and Properties*, M. Bass, editor in chief, McGraw Hill, New York, 1995.

32. J.W. Cooley and J.W. Tucky, An algorithm for the machine calculation of complex Fourier series, *Mathematics of Computation*, 19(90), 297–301, April 1965.

33. E. Brigham, *The Fast Fourier Transform and Its Applications*, Prentice Hall, New York, 1988.

34. W.H. Press, S.A. Teukolsky, W.T. Vetterling, and B.P. Flannery, *Numerical Recipes in C++: The Art of Scientific Computing*, 2nd edn., Cambridge University Press, New York, Feb. 2002.

35. A.K.K. Wong, *Resolution Enhancement Techniques in Optical Lithography*, SPIE Press, Bellingham, WA, 2001.

36. M.D. Levenson, Wavefront engineering for photolithography *Physics Today*, 46(7), 28–36, 1993.

37. *Selected Papers on Resolution Enhancement Techniques in Optical Lithography*, F.M. Schellenberg, Ed., SPIE Press, Bellingham, WA, 2004.

38. O. Otto, J.G. Garofalo, K.K. Low, C.M. Yuan, R.C. Henderson, C. Pierrat, R.L. Kostelak, S. Vaidya, and P.K. Vasudev, Automated optical proximity correction: A rules-based approach, in *Optical/Laser Microlithography VII, Proceedings of SPIE*, vol. 2197, p. 278–293, 1994.

39. N. Shamma, F. Sporon-Fiedler, and E. Lin, A method for the correction of proximity effects in optical projection lithography, in *Interface 91, Proceedings of the 1991 KTI Microelectronics Seminar*, pp. 145–156 San Jose, CA, 1991.

40. F.M. Schellenberg, H. Zhang, and J. Morrow, SEMATECH J111 project: OPC validation, in *Optical Microlithography XI, Proceedings of SPIE*, vol. 3334, pp. 892–911, 1998.

41. N.B. Cobb, Fast optical and process proximity correction algorithms for integrated circuit manufacturing, Ph.D. Dissertation, University of California, Berkeley, California, 1998.

42. M. Rieger and J. Stirniman, Using behavior modeling for proximity correction, in *Optical/Laser Microlithography VII, Proceedings of SPIE*, vol. 2197, pp. 371–376, 1994.

43. W. Maurer and F.M. Schellenberg, Advanced lithographic masks, *Handbook of Photomask Manufacturing Technology*, S. Rizvi, ed., CRC Press, Boca Raton, FL 2005.

44. J. Garofalo, C. Biddick, R.L. Kostelak, and S. Vaidya, Mask assisted off-axis illumination technique for random logic *Journal of Vacuum Science and Technology B*, B11, 2651–2658, 1993.

45. J.F. Chen and J.A. Matthews, Mask for photolithography, US Patent No. 5,242,770 (filed Jan. 16, 1992; issued Sept. 7, 1993).

46. *Handbook of Photomask Manufacturing Technology*, S. Rizvi, Ed., CRC Press, Boca Raton, FL 2005.

47. B. Eynon Jr. and B. Wu, *Photomask Fabrication Technology*, McGraw Hill, New York, 2005.

48. Masato Shibuya, "透過照明用被投影原板" [Projection master for use with transmitted illumination], 公開特許公報(A) 昭 57–62052, 特許公報(B) 昭 62–50811 [Japan Patent Office Laid-open Patent Publication (A) Showa 57-62052, Patent Publication (B) Showa 62–50811] (filed Sept. 30, 1980; published Apr. 14, 1982, issued Oct. 27, 1987).

49. M.D. Levenson, N.S. Viswanathan, and R.A. Simpson, Improving resolution in photolithography with a phase-shifting mask, *IEEE Transactions Electron Devices* ED-29, 1828–1836, 1982.

50. M.D. Levenson, D.S. Goodman, S. Lindsey, P.W. Bayer, and H.A.E. Santini, The phase-shifting mask II: Imaging simulations and submicrometer resist exposures, *IEEE Transactions on Electron Devices*, ED-31, 753–763, 1984.

51. K. Ooi, S. Hara, and K. Koyama, Computer aided design software for designing phase shifting masks, *Japanese Journal of Applied Physics*, 32, 5887–5891, 1993.

52. L.W. Liebmann, G.A. Northrop, J. Culp, L. Sigal, A. Barish, and C.A. Fonseca, Layout optimization at the pinnacle of optical lithography, in *Design and Process Integration for Microelectronic Manufacturing, Proceedings of SPIE*, vol. 5042, pp. 1–14, 2003.

53. L. Liebmann, J. Lund, F.L. Heng, and I. Graur, Enabling alternating phase shifted mask designs for a full logic gate level: Design rules and design rule checking, in *Proceedings of the 38th Design Automation Conference*, pp. 79–84, ACM, New York, 2001.

54. L. Liebmann, J. Lund, F.L. Heng, and I. Graur, Enabling alternating phase shifted mask designs for a full logic gate level, *Journal of Microlithography, Microfabrication, and Microsystems*, 1, 31–42, 2002.

55. Y.-C. Ku, E.H. Anderson, M.L. Schattenburg, and H.I. Smith, Use of a pi-phase shifting x-ray mask to increase the intensity slope at feature edges, *Journal of Vacuum Science and Technology B*, B6, 150–153, 1988.

56. Y. Saito, S. Kawada, T. Yamamoto, A. Hayashi, A. Isao, and Y. Tokoro, Attenuated phase-shift mask blanks with oxide or oxinitride of Cr or MoSi absorptive shifter, in *Photomask and X-Ray Mask Technology, Proceedings of SPIE*, vol. 2254, pp. 60–63, 1994.

57. H. Jinbo and Y. Yamashita, Improvement of phase-shifter edge line mask method, *Japanese Journal of Applied Physics*, 30, 2998–3003, 1991.

58. H.Y. Liu, L. Karklin, Y.T. Wang, and Y.C. Pati, Application of alternating phase-shifting masks to 140-nm gate patterning: II. Mask design and manufacturing tolerances, in *Optical Microlithography XI, Proceedings of SPIE*, vol. 3334, pp. 2–14, 1998.

59. C. Spence, M. Plat, E. Sahouria, N. Cobb, and F. Schellenberg, Integration of optical proximity correction strategies in strong phase shifter design for poly-gate layer, in *19th Annual Symposium on Photomask Technology, Proceedings of SPIE*, vol. 3873, pp 277–287, 1999.

60. C. Mack, Characterizing the process window of a double exposure dark field alternating phase shift mask, in *Design, Process Integration and Characterization for Microelectronics, Proceedings of SPIE*, vol. 4692, pp. 454–464, 2002.

61. A.K.K. Wong (Ed.) Modified illumination, in *Resolution Enhancements Techniques in Optical Lithography*, SPIE Press, Bellingham, WA, 2001.

62. N. Shiraishi, S. Hirukawa, Y. Takeuchi, and N. Magome, New imaging technique for 64M-DRAM in *Optical/Laser Microlithography V, Proceedings of SPIE*, vol. 1674, pp. 741–752, 1992.

63. F.M. Schellenberg and L. Capodieci, and B. Socha, Adoption of OPC and the Impact on Design and Layout, *Proceedings of the 38th Design Automation Conference*, ACM, New York, 2001, pp. 89–92.

64. M. Burkhardt, A. Yen, C. Progler, and G. Wells, Illuminator design for printing regular contact patterns, *Microelectronic Engineering*, 41, 91, 1998.

65. E. Barouch, S.L. Knodle, S.A. Orszag, and M. Yeung, Illuminator optimization for projection printing, in *Optical Microlithography XII, Proceedings of SPIE*, vol. 3679, pp. 697–703, 1999.

66. A.E. Rosenbluth, S. Bukofsky, M. Hibbs, K. Lai, R.N. Singh, A.K. Wong, Optimum mask and source patterns for printing a given shape, *Journal of Microlithography, Microfabrication, and Microsystems*, 1, 13–30, 2002.

67. Y. Granik, Source optimization for image fidelity and throughput, *Journal of Microlithography, Microfabrication, and Microsystems*, 3, 509–522, 2004.

68. Y. Granik and N. Cobb, New process models for OPC at sub-90 nm nodes, in *Optical Microlithography XVI, Proceedings of SPIE*, vol. 5040, pp. 1166–1175, 2003.

69. J.F. Chen, J.S. Petersen, R. Socha, T. Laidig, K.E. Wampler, K. Nakagawa, G. Hughes, S. MacDonald, and W. Ng, Binary halftone chromeless PSM technology for $\lambda/4$ optical lithography, in *Optical Microlithography XIV, Proceedings of SPIE*, vol. 4346, pp. 515–533, 2001.

70. D.J. Van Den Broeke, J.F. Chen, T. Laidig, S. Hsu, K.E. Wampler, R.J. Socha, and J.S. Petersen, Complex two dimensional pattern lithography using chromeless phase lithography (CPL), *Journal of Microlithography, Microfabrication, and Microsystems*, 1, 229–242, 2002.

71. S.R.J. Brueck and A.M. Biswas, Extension of the 193-nm optical lithography to the 22-nm half pitch node, in *Optical Microlithography XVII, Proceedings of SPIE*, vol. 5377, pp. 1315–1322, 2004.

72. S.R.J. Brueck, There are no fundamental limits to optical lithography *International Trends in Applied Optics*, A. Guenther, Ed., SPIE Press, Bellingham, WA, 2002.

73. S. Asai, I. Hanyu, and M. Takikawa, Resolution limit for optical lithography using polarized light illumination, *Japanese Journal of Applied Physics, Part I*, 32, 5863–5866, 1993.

74. S.H. Jeon, B.D. Cho, K.W. Lee, S.M. Lee, K.H. Biak, C.N. Ahn, and D.G. Yim, Study on elliptical polarization illumination effects for microlithography, *Journal of Vacuum Science and Technology B*, B14, 4193–4198, 1996.

75. Z.M. Ma and C.A. Mack, Impact of illumination coherence and polarization on the imaging of attenuated phase shift masks, in *Optical Microlithoraphy XIV, Proceedings of SPIE*, vol. 4346, pp. 1522–1532, 2001.

76. K. Adam and W. Maurer, Polarization effects in immersion lithography, *Journal of Microlithography, Microfabrication, and Microsystems*, 4, 031106, 2005.

77. R. Wang, W. Grobman, A. Reich, and M. Thompson, Polarized phase shift mask: Concept, design, and potential advantages to photolithography process and physical design, in *21st Annual BACUS Symposium on Photomask Technology, Proceedings of SPIE*, vol. 4562, pp. 406–417, 2002.

78. M. Rieger and J. Stirniman, Using behavior modelling for proximity correction, in *Optical/Laser Microlithography VII, Proceedings of SPIE*, vol. 2197, pp. 371–376, 1994.

79. N. Cobb and Y. Granik, New concepts in OPC, in *Optical Microlithography XVII, Proceedings of SPIE*, vol. 5377, pp. 680–690, 2004.

80. J. Word and N. Cobb, Enhanced model based OPC for 65 nm and below, *24th Annual BACUS Symposium on Photomask Technology, Proceedings of SPIE*, vol. 5567, pp. 1305–1314, 2004; J. Word, J.A. Torres, and P. LaCour, Advanced layout fragmentation and simulation schemes for model based OPC, *Optical Microlithography XVIII, Proceedings of SPIE*, vol. 5754, pp. 1159–1168, 2004.

81. N.B. Cobb and W. Maurer, Flows for model-based layout correction of mask proximity effects, in *23rd Annual BACUS Symposium on Photomask Technology, Proceedings of SPIE*, vol. 5256, pp. 956–964, 2003.

82. M. Gesley, Pattern generation, *Photomask Fabrication Technology*, B. Eynor, Jr. and B. Wu, Eds., McGraw Hill, New York, 2005.

83. N. Cobb and D. Dudau, Dense OPC and verification for 45 nm, in *Optical Microlithography XIX, Proceedings of SPIE*, vol. 6154, p. 615401, 2006.

84. J. Kreuzer, US Patent 6,836,380 (filed Feb. 14, 2003; issued Dec. 28, 2004).

85. Litel Corporation (http://www.opticalres.com/).

86. Litel Corporation (http://www.litel.net).

87. K.K.H. Toh and A.R. Neureuther, Identifying and monitoring effects of lens aberrations in projection printing, in *Optical Microlithography VI, Proceedings of SPIE*, vol. 772, pp. 202–209, 1987.

88. H.H. Hopkins, On the diffraction theory of optical images, *Proceedings Royal Society London Series A*, 217, 408–432, 1953.

89. A.K.K. Wong, *Optical Imaging in Projection Microlithography*, SPIE Press, Bellingham, WA, 2005.

90. K.S. Yee, Numerical solution of initial boundary value problems involving Maxwell's equations in isotropic media, *IEEE Transactions on Antennas and Propagation*, 14, 302–307, 1966.

91. A. Taflove and S.C. Hagness, *Computaional Electrodynamics: The Finite-Difference Time-Domain Method*, 3rd edn., Artech House, Boston, MA, 2005.

92. www.fdtd.org (For more references on the FDTD method).

93. A. Erdmann, Modelling and simulation, *Handbook of Photomask Manufacturing Technology*, S. Rizvi, Ed., CRC Press, Boca Raton, FL 2005.

94. E. Palik, *Handbook of Optical Constants of Solids*, Vols. 1–4, Academic Press, San Diego, CA, 1991.

95. *Computational Electrodynamics: The Finite Difference Time-Domain Method*, 3rd edn., A. Taflove and S.C. Hagness, Eds., Artech House, Boston, MA, 2005, Chapter 7.

96. A.K.K. Wong and A.R. Neureuther, Rigorous three dimensional time-domain finite difference electromagnetic simulation, *IEEE Transactions on Semiconductor Manufacturing*, 8, 419–431, 1995.

97. T.V. Pistor, Accuracy issues in the finite difference time domain simulation of photomask scattering, in *Optical Microlithography XIV, Proceedings of SPIE*, vol. 4346, pp. 1484–1491, 2001.

98. M.G. Moharam and T.K. Gaylord, Rigorous coupled-wave analysis of planar grating diffraction, *Journal of the Optical Society of America*, 71, 811, 1981.

99. A. Estroff, Y. Fan, A. Bourov, F. Cropanese, N. Lafferty, L. Zavyalova, and B. Smith, Mask Induced polarization, in *Optical Microlithography XVII, Proceedings of SPIE*, vol. 5377, pp. 1069–1080, 2004.

100. D. Nyyssonen, The theory of optical edge detection and imaging of thick layers, *Journal of the Optical Society of America*, 72, 1425, 1982.

101. C.M. Yuan, Calculation of one-dimensional lithographic aerial images using the vector theory, *IEEE Transactions on Electron Devices*, ED-40, 1604, 1993.

102. A. Erdmann, P. Evanschitzky, G. Citarella, T. Fuehner, and P. De Bisschop, Rigorous mask modeling using waveguide and FDTD methods: An assessment for typical hyper NA imaging problems, in *Photomask and Next-Generation Lithography Mack Technology XIII, Proceedings of SPIE*, vol. 6283, 628319, pp. 1–11, 2006.

103. K. Adam and A. Neureuther, Algorithmic implementations of domain decomposition methods for the diffraction simulation of advanced photomasks, *Optimal Microlithography XV, Proceedings of SPIE*, vol 4691, pp. 107–124, 2002; and K. Adam and A.R. Neureuther, Domain decomposition methods for the rapid electromagnetic simulation of photomask scattering, *Journal of Microlithography, Microfabrication and Microsystems*, 1, 253–269, 2002.

104. K. Adam, Modeling of electromagnetic effects from mask topography at full-chip scale, in *Optical Microlithography XVIII, Proceedings of SPIE*, vol. 5754, pp. 498–505, 2004.

105. T.W. Ebbesen, H.J. Lezec, H.F. Ghaemi, T. Thio, and P.A. Wolff, Extraordinary optical transmission through sub-wavelength hole arrays, *Nature*, 391, 667–669, 1998.

106. H. Raether, *Surface Plasmons*, Springer, Berlin, Germany, 1988.

107. F.M. Schellenberg, K. Adam, J. Matteo, and L. Hesselink Electromagnetic phenomena in advanced photomasks, *Journal of Vacuum Science and Technology*, 23(6), 3106–3115, 2005.

108. A. Neureuther and C. Mack, Optical lithography modeling, *Handbook of Microlithography, Micromachining, and Microfabrication, Vol 1: Microlithopgraphy*, P. Rai-Choudhury, Ed., SPIE Optical Engineering Press, Bellingham, WA, 1997.

109. C.A. Mack, Analytical expression for the standing wave intensity in photoresist, *Applied Optics*, 25(12), 1958–1961, 1986.

110. R.A. Ferguson, C.A. Spence, E. Reichmanis, and L.F. Thompson, Investigation of the exposure and bake of a positive-acting resist with chemical amplification, in *Advances in Resist Technology and Processing VIII, Proceedings of SPIE*, vol. 1262, pp. 412–242, 1990.

111. F.H. Dill, W.P. Hornberger, P.S. Hauge, and J.M. Shaw, Characterization of positive photoresist, *IEEE Transactions on, Electron Devices*, ED-22, 456–464, 1975.

112. N. Cobb, A. Zakhor, and E. Miloslavsky, Mathematical and CAD framework for proximity correction, in *Optical Microlithography IX, Proceedings of SPIE*, vol. 2726, pp. 208–222, 1996.

113. N. Cobb, A. Zakhor, M. Reihani, F. Jahansooz, and V. Raghavan, Experimental results on optical proximity correction with variable threshold resist model, in *Optical Microlithography X, Proceedings of SPIE*, vol. 3051, pp. 458–468, 1997.

114. A Wong, R. Ferguson, S. Mansfield, A. Molles, D. Samuels, R. Schustr, and A. Thomas, Level-specific lithography optimization for 1 Gb DRAM, *IEEE Transactions on Semiconductor Manufacturing*, 13(1), 76–87, 2000.

115. J. Stirniman and M. Rieger, Optimizing proximity correction for wafer fabrication processes, in *14th Annual BACUS Symposium on Photomask Technology and Management, Proceedings of SPIE*, vol. 2322, pp. 239–246, 1994.

116. J.W. Bossung, Projection printing characterization, in *Semiconductor Microlithography II, Proceedings of SPIE*, vol. 100, pp. 80–84, 1977.

117. B.J. Lin, Partially coherent imaging in two dimensions and the theoretical limits of projection printing in microfabrication, *IEEE Transactions on Electron Devices*, ED-27, 931–938, 1980.

118. K.H. Kim, K. Ronse, A. Yen, and L. Van den Hove, Feasibility demonstration of 0 18 μm and 0.13 μm optical projection lithography based on CD control calculations, in *1996 Symposium on VLSI Technology, Digest of Technical Papers*, pp. 186–187, 1996.

119. C. Mack. Lithography simulation in semiconductor manufacturing, in *Advanced Microlithography Technologies, Proceedings of SPIE*, vol. 5645, pp. 63–83, 2005.

120. S. Shang, Y. Granik, N. Cobb, W. Maurer, Y. Cui, L. Liebmann, J. Oberschmidt, R. Singh, and B. Vampatella, Failure prediction across process window for robust OPC, in *Optical Microlithography XVI, Proceedings of SPIE*, vol. 5040, pp. 431–440, 2003.

121. W. Maurer, Mask specifications for 193-nm lithography, in *16th Annual BACUS Symposium on Photomask Technology and Management, Proceedings of SPIE*, vol. 2884, pp. 562–571, 1996.

122. C. Mack, Mask linearity and the mask error enhancement factor, *Microlithography World*, pp. 11–12, Winter 1999.

123. F.M. Schellenberg, V. Boksha, N. Cobb, J.C. Lai, C.H. Chen, and C. Mack, Impact of mask errors on full chip error budgets, in *Optical Microlithography XII, Proceedings of SPIE*, vol. 3679, pp. 261–275, 1999.

124. F.M. Schellenberg and C. Mack, MEEF in theory and practice, in *19th Annual Symposium on Photomask Technology, Proceedings of SPIE*, vol 3873, pp. 189–202, 1999.

125. N. Cobb and Y. Granik, Model-based OPC using the MEEF matrix, in *22nd Annual BACUS Symposium on Photomask Technology, Proceedings of SPIE*, vol. 4889, pp. 1281–1292, 2002.

126. F.M. Schellenberg, O. Toublan, N. Cobb, E. Sahouria, G. Hughes, S. MacDonald, C. West, OPC beyond 0.18 μm: OPC on PSM Gates, *Optical Microlithography XIII, Proceedings of SPIE*, vol. 4000, pp. 1062–1069, 2000.

127. J.A.T. Robles, Integrated circuit layout design methodology for deep sub-wavelength processes. Ph.D. Dissertation, OGI School of Science and Engineering, Beaverton, OR, July 2005.

128. Z. Ren, W. Zhang, and J. Falbo, Computation of parasitic capacitances of an IC cell in accounting for photolithography effect, in *6th International Conference on Computational Electromagnetics (CEM2006) Proceedings*, pp. 163–164, VDE Verlag, Berlin, Germany, 2006.

129. See J.A. Mucha, D.W. Hess, and E.S. Aydil, Plasma etching, *Introduction to Microlithography*, 2nd edn., L. Thompson, C.G. Willson, and M. Bowden, Eds., American Chemical Society, Washington, DC, 1994.

36 CMP Fill Synthesis: A Survey of Recent Studies

Andrew B. Kahng and Kambiz Samadi

CONTENTS

36.1 CHEMICAL–MECHANICAL POLISHING

Chemical–mechanical polishing (CMP) is the planarizing technique of choice to satisfy the local and global planarity constraints imposed by today's advanced lithography methods [36,58]. As device geometries scale, there is an inevitable need for better planarization of the multilevel interconnect structures. Older planarizing methods, such as flowing oxide layers, spin-on glass (SOG), and reverse etchback (REB) can no longer meet the lithographic and other requirements of modern multilevel metallization processes [52].

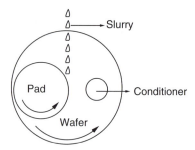

FIGURE 36.1 Thin film formation in SOG method. (Modified from Toan, N.N., Spin-on-glass materials and applications in advanced IC technologies, Ph.D. Dissertation, Universiteit Twente, Netherlands, 1999.)

SOG is a method that consists of coating the surface of a particular layer with SOG materials. These materials can be categorized into three different groups: (1) silicate-based compounds, (2) organosilicon compounds, and (3) dopant-organic compounds. In SOG, the silicon wafer must be cleaned before coating. The wafer is placed on a spinner and approximately 1 mL of SOG material is dropped on the center of the wafer. Then the carrier holding the wafer (Figure 36.1) is rotated at several thousand cycles per minute to create a thin layer of SOG material on the wafer. In most cases, a film thickness between 50 and 500 nm will result. Controlling the thickness is a matter of controlling the solution viscosity. Among the various techniques for planarization, the SOG method is advantageous because of the simplicity of the process, the good adhesion characteristics, and the low level of stress and shrinkage in the SOG material [67]. Implementation of the SOG technique requires thorough understanding of the glass and the stability of the remaining material, which leads to considerable variation in the practicality of this technique [52].

REB uses a second mask to etchback-raised areas to lower the pattern density. The etchback mask is created by shrinking all features on a given layout by a fixed amount called etchback bias. This results in removal of the majority of the raised material if the features are large. Selective reverse etchback uses customization of the etchback mask to reduce the amount material that is etched away [37]. Although the REB method is understood, it suffers from complexity and significant cost due to extra masking steps. It also requires a significant amount of monitoring to control the level of defects caused by the process [52].

Chemical–mechanical polishing uses both mechanical and chemical means to planarize the surface of the wafer. In a typical CMP tool, the wafer is held on a rotating holder as shown in Figure 36.2. The surface of the wafer being polished is pressed against the polishing pad (i.e., a resilient material), which is mounted on a rotating disk. In addition, a slurry composed of particles suspended in a chemical solution is deposited on the pad as the chemical abrasive.

The material removal mechanism of silicon dioxide (oxide) CMP is similar to the removal found in glass polishing. First, a chemical reaction softens the deposited film surface, then a mechanical surface abrasion aided by slurry particles removes the material [15,36]. The chemical reaction between the slurry and the surface of the wafer creates a -form material. The new material has weaker atomic bonds. It is therefore more easily removed during the polishing process [45]. The second step involves the removal of the weakened film surface through abrasion. The actual wear mechanism is not well understood. There is speculation that a fluid layer exerts the force necessary to remove the film surface [56]. Others speculate that the removal of the film surface is due to a complex interaction of particle, fluid, and pad [16]. In either case, the abrasion removal mechanism is a dynamic process that depends on surface characteristics of the pad and slurry particles, although the exact contributions of these factors are not known [36].

Compared with conventional planarization methods, CMP offers a more deterministic behavior and does not incur extra processing cost such as extra masking steps. However, CMP has its own drawback which is its dependence on layout pattern density. This dependency causes variations in

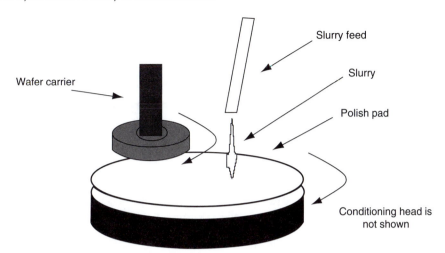

FIGURE 36.2 Typical CMP tool. (From Lee, B., Modeling for chemical–mechanical polishing for shallow trench isolation, Ph.D. Dissertation, Department of Electrical Engineering and Computer Science, MIT, Cambridge, MA, 2002)

post-CMP layout parameters (i.e., variations in interlayer dielectric [ILD] thickness, metal height, etc.), which in turn impact circuit performance. In Section 36.2, the impact of the CMP process on interconnect design is reviewed.

Major planarization defects are caused by the pattern dependency of the CMP process. Among the significant defects are metal dishing and dielectric erosion, which account for approximately 50 percent of yield loss in IC fabrication processes. In Section 36.2, these defects are introduced and their impact on interconnect design is reviewed. Section 36.3 discusses several traditional as well as recent work on oxide (dielectric), copper, and shallow trench isolation (STI) CMP characterization and modeling approaches. To increase predictability, the layout pattern density variation must be kept to a minimum. A current solution is to insert dummy metal shapes (CMP fill features) in the layout to decrease the density variation. Different density analysis methods are reviewed in Section 36.4. In Section 36.5 the problem of how to insert the required amount of CMP fill after calculating density is discussed. Section 36.6 reviews the parts of design flow that are affected by CMP fill insertion. Finally, the conclusion is presented in Section 36.7.

36.2 IMPACTS ON INTERCONNECT DESIGN AND MANUFACTURING

In the very deep-submicron VLSI regime manufacturing steps including optical exposure, resist development, and etch, and CMP have varying effects on device and interconnect features depending on local properties of the layout. Foundry economics dictate that the process window volumes be maximized, which in turn requires that device and interconnect features be fabricated as predictably and uniformly as possible. To achieve this goal, the layout must be made uniform with respect to a certain density parameter. The physics of semiconductor processing make predictable and uniform manufacturing difficult [7,18,35,55]. In particular, the quality of post-CMP depends on the pattern density of the layer beneath a given dielectric layer.

The layout pattern density is one of the dominant factors in determining the post-CMP thickness profile of the deposited film [6,9,48,63]. Pattern density can be defined as the fraction of the raised areas that affect the CMP process at a particular region on the layout. Figure 36.3 illustrates the concept of pattern density in one-dimensional and two-dimensional cases. Intuitively, the higher the pattern density the larger the contact area with the pad and the lower the pressure on raised features. High-density regions are polished more slowly than low-density regions resulting in locally planar but globally nonplanar regions [36].

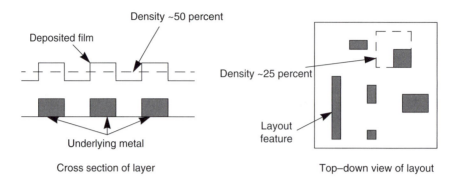

FIGURE 36.3 Pattern density in one and two dimensions. (From Lee, B., Modeling for chemical–mechanical polishing for shallow trench isolation, Ph.D. Dissertation, Department of Electrical Engineering and Computer Science, MIT, Cambridge, MA, 2002.)

In the past decade, CMP has emerged as the predominant planarization technique for multilevel metallization processes. However, significant surface topography variation can still exist for some layout patterns; this impacts depth of focus in lithography which in turn leads to variations in critical dimension (CD). Two other major defects caused by CMP are metal dishing and oxide erosion. In the copper CMP process, metal dishing is defined as the difference between the height of the oxide in the spaces and that of the metal in the trenches. Oxide erosion is defined as the difference between the oxide thickness before and after CMP [69]. In this chapter, dishing and erosion refer to metal dishing and oxide erosion, respectively. Figure 36.4 shows metal dishing and oxide erosion in copper CMP process. These two phenomena impact the performance of the circuit because variation in ILD thickness profile and interconnect height lead to variations in interconnect capacitance and resistance. This variation will increase the timing uncertainty of the circuit, hence it is crucial to minimize dishing and erosion. However, due to CMP nonidealities there will always be some amount of dishing and erosion. It is important to model the effect of these variations during parasitic extraction to obtain a more accurate estimation of the circuit performance [54].

Even though pattern density is the major cause of the CMP defects, there are other factors such as slurry flow rate and pad conditioning temperature that contribute to the amount of dishing and erosion. The slurry acts as a coolant material at the interface of the pad and wafer contact and takes away a significant part of the heat through convective heat transfer [42,59,60,72]. The dissipated heat changes the chemical kinetics and the physical properties of the polishing pad [42,59]. As the amount of dissipated heat increases, the polishing pad tends to become softer that results in an increase in

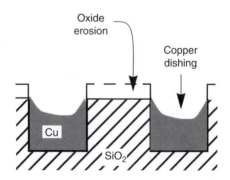

FIGURE 36.4 Dishing and erosion in copper CMP process. (From Tugbawa, T., Chip-Scale modeling of pattern dependencies in copper chemical mechanical polishing processes, Ph.D. Dissertation, Department of Electrical Engineering and Computer Science, MIT, Cambridge, MA, 2002.)

the area contact at the interface. In addition, pad conditioning has a major impact on the removal rate (RR) during the CMP process, as underconditioned pads will lose their surface roughness, which eventually leads into RR reduction [43]. For more details on effects of slurry flow rate and pad conditioning temperature on metal dishing and dielectric erosion reader is encouraged to look into Ref. [43].

To increase the fabrication process uniformity and predictability, the layout must be made uniform with respect to a certain density parameter. One solution for designers and manufacturers is to use techniques like CMP fill insertion and slotting to increase and decrease the pattern density [26]. CMP fills are dummy features that do not directly contribute to the functionality of the circuit and can either be grounded or left floating. CMP fill insertion reduces the amount of dishing and erosion by increasing the pattern density uniformity. However, it is well known that CMP fill insertion can increase the coupling and total interconnect capacitance and consequently deteriorate circuit performance [38,62]. If not modeled appropriately, this can directly affect yield and time-to-market. In the next section, characterization and modeling approaches of different CMP processes are represented.

36.3 CHARACTERIZATION AND MODELING APPROACHES

This section, first presents a number of early works on CMP modeling which have been reviewed in Ref. [45] and then introduces three recent works [36,47,68] on CMP characterization and modeling of oxide CMP, copper CMP, and STI CMP.

36.3.1 GENERAL CMP PROCESS MODELS

The combination of the chemical and mechanical aspects of CMP makes it a complex process to model based on physical principles. Typical characterization of a CMP process requires extensive experimentation that must be repeated for each particular CMP process (combination of tool, consumable, and process settings). The main objective of CMP is to remove the extraneous material from the surface of the wafer and planarize it. The process of material removal can be described by Preston's equation:

$$\frac{dT}{dt} = KP\frac{ds}{dt} \tag{36.1}$$

where

T is thickness of the wafer
P denotes the pressure caused by polishing process
s is the total distance traveled by the wafer
t is the elapsed time

The RR is proportional to the pressure exerted on the wafer as well as the speed in which the wafer is rotating. Any other physical considerations are put into the constant K, which is independent of pressure and velocity. In this subsection, a few CMP models are introduced and their advantages and disadvantages are reviewed [45].

The first model is based on works by Sivaram et al. [57]. The proposed model uses Preston's equation and considers the bending of the polishing pad. The bending of the polishing pad has a significant impact on the quality of the planarization and must be modeled in RR expression. However, this model only considers the effects of bending between two neighboring step heights on the wafer. It does not take into account the three-dimensional information of the structures, which limits its applicability.

The next model proposed by the authors of Ref. [6] depends on the degree of nonplanarity. The model has two parts: an analytical expression based on an ordinary differential equation and a more complex model which iteratively adjusts the polishing rate to the actual nonplanarity. Even though this model takes the topography of the wafer into account and adjusts the polishing rate accordingly, it does not consider the bending of the polishing pad. Neither does it consider the fluid mechanics. The model is purely empirical and does not depend on the pressure. Because of these shortcomings, it has limited use in modeling the entire CMP process.

Warnock et al. [71] propose another model that quantitatively analyzes the absolute and the relative polish rate for different sizes and pattern factors. This model defines the dependence of the polish rate on the wafer shape. In particular, it takes into account all possible geometrical cases, which makes it applicable to modeling of the entire CMP process.

Finally, a model proposed by Yu et al. [74] considers the dependence of the RR on the asperity of the polishing pad. The surface height variation for a 200 μm × 200 μm pad is reported to be 100 μm. In addition, the model divides the Preston's constant K into three different parts: (1) a constant only dependent on the pad roughness and its elasticity, (2) a factor determined by the surface chemistry, and (3) a constant that is related to the contact area. However, it is not clear how these asperities affect the global quality of planarization. A global planarization quantity of 200 Å over a distance of 0.5 cm is reported in Ref. [64]. This variation is much less than the reported polishing pad height variation (100 μm), making it unclear how the approach fits into a general CMP simulation.

36.3.2 OXIDE CMP MODELING

Pattern density is a significant contributor to oxide CMP process quality. The Preston equation shows that the material RR is a linear function of the pressure, which is affected by the pattern density at the interface between polishing pad and wafer. However, pattern density calculation is not trivial. In fact, the effective density at a particular point on the die depends on the size of the neighboring area over which density is averaged. The weighting function is also a major factor because it captures the influence of the surrounding area on the local pressure.

Modeling of CMP for oxide planarization is reduced to accurately calculating the local pressure, and hence the pattern density distribution across every die [47]. As described in the previous subsection, there are several models that have been proposed to account for pattern effects in CMP, but their applicability has been limited.

The basic model in Ref. [47] is based on the work by Stine et al. [63]. In this model, the interlayer dielectric thickness z at location (x, y) is calculated as

$$z = \begin{cases} z_0 - \left(\frac{Kt}{\rho_0(x,y)}\right) & t < (\rho_0 z_1)/K \\ z_0 - z_1 - Kt + \rho_0(x, y)z_1 & t > (\rho_0 z_1)/K \end{cases} \tag{36.2}$$

The constant K is the blanket wafer RR (i.e., where the density is 100 percent). The important element of this model is the determination of the effective initial pattern density $\rho_0(x, y)$. Figure 36.5 defines the terms used in Equation 36.2.

In Equation 36.2 when $t < (\rho_0 z_1)/K$, the local step height has not been completely removed. However, when features are planarized for a long enough time $(t > (\rho_0 z_1)/K)$, local step height is completely removed and a linear relationship between pattern density and ILD thickness exists [63].

The planarization length, which captures pad deformation during the CMP process, determines the amount in which neighboring features affect pattern density at a spatial location on the die. Thickness profile of any arbitrary mask pattern, under same process conditions, can be determined using the effective local density and an analytic thickness model. This reduces the characterization step into a single phase where only the planarization length of the process is determined. Planarization length is also a useful metric in oxide CMP process optimization because it reduces the investigation of the entire die to smaller regimes according to the planarization length [47].

Ouma [47] proposes a characterization methodology for oxide CMP processes that includes (1) the use of an elliptic pattern density weighting function that which has better correspondence to the polish pad deformation, (2) a three-step effective pattern calculation scheme that uses fast Fourier

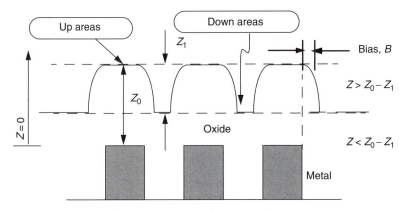

FIGURE 36.5 Dishing and erosion in copper CMP process. (From Ouma, D., Modeling of chemical–mechanical polishing for dielectric planarization, Ph.D. Dissertation, Department of Electric Engineering and Computer Science, MIT, Cambridge, 1998.)

transforms (FFTs) for computational efficiency, and (3) the use of layout masks with step densities that facilitate the determination of the characteristic length (defined as the planarization length) of the elliptic function by introducing large abrupt post-CMP thickness variations.

36.3.3 COPPER CMP MODELING

Unlike oxide CMP, which involves the removal of only oxide material, the copper CMP involves simultaneous polishing of three materials: copper, dielectric (oxide), and barrier. Barrier is a very thin layer (Tan, Ti, etc.) that prevents the copper from diffusing into the dielectric. The goal in copper CMP is to remove the excess copper (also called overburden copper) and to polish the barrier on top of the dielectric regions isolating the adjacent interconnect lines. This is required to prevent electrical connection between adjacent interconnect lines. Owing to the heterogeneous nature of copper CMP, a specific set of process parameters as well as a consumable set are required to achieve the particular RR for each corresponding material [68].

Two major defects caused by copper CMP are pattern-dependent problems of metal dishing and dielectric erosion as shown in Figure 36.6. If the height of the copper in the trench is lower than the height of the neighboring dielectric, then dishing is positive otherwise it is negative. On the other

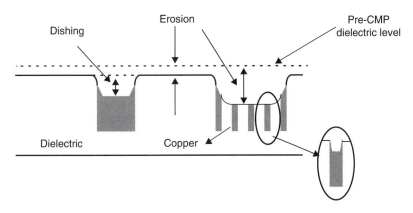

FIGURE 36.6 Dishing and erosion. (From Tugbawa, T., Chip-Scale modeling of pattern dependencies in copper chemical–mechanical polishing processes, Ph.D. Dissertation, Department of Electrical Engineering and Computer Science, MIT, Cambridge, MA, 2002.)

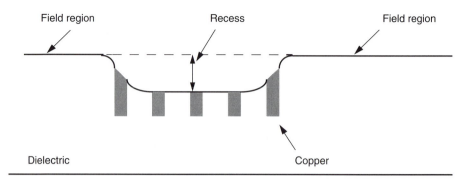

FIGURE 36.7 Definition of recess. (From Tugbawa, T., Chip-Scale modeling of pattern dependencies in copper chemical–mechanical polishing processes, Ph.D. Dissertation, Department of Electrical Engineering and Computer Science, MIT, Cambridge, MA, 2002.)

hand, dielectric erosion is always positive due to the loss of dielectric thickness during the CMP process. The sum of dishing and erosion gives the copper thickness loss (also known as the copper thinning) during CMP [68].[*]

Another pattern-dependent defect occurring during copper planarization is recess. Recess of a copper interconnect line is equivalent to the dishing of that line. However, the recess of the dielectric within an array of interconnect lines is the difference between the dielectric height at a location within the array and the height of surrounding dielectric fields as shown in Figure 36.7 [68].

The goal in copper CMP is to remove the excess copper and the unwanted barrier layer. Ideally, this process should be fast without incurring extra dishing, erosion, or other defects. Owing to heterogeneous nature of copper CMP, different materials are polished simultaneously. Initially, only overburden copper is polished followed by the polishing of both copper and barrier film. Finally, copper, barrier, and dielectric are polished at the same time. As stated in Ref. [68], to model copper CMP process three stages of polish are identified: excess copper removal, barrier film removal, and overpolish stage, as shown in Figure 36.8. In the excess copper removal stage, the evolution of the

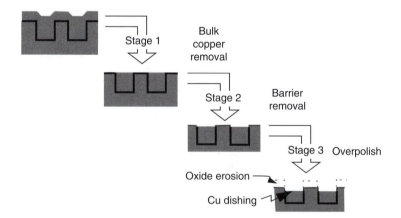

FIGURE 36.8 Three intrinsic stages in copper CMP processes. (From Tugbawa, T., Chip-Scale modeling of pattern dependencies in copper chemical–mechanical polishing processes, Ph.D. Dissertation, Department of Electrical Engineering and Computer Science, MIT, Cambridge, MA, 2002.)

---

[*] In the published literature, erosion is sometimes referenced to the height of a neighboring field dielectric region, and a separate field dielectric loss parameter is then specified. In Ref. [68], a single dielectric erosion term is used to represent dielectric loss.

copper thickness profile across the chip and the time it takes to remove the excess copper are of interest. The time to polish the overburden copper varies across the die depending on the pattern density at the location of interest.

In the second stage, copper and barrier film are polished simultaneously. The time to clear the barrier film, as well as the dishing that results when barrier is removed at any location on the die, is of interest. Due to process variation and deposited copper thickness variation across the wafer and different pattern densities across the die, the RRs of the three materials (copper, barrier, and dielectric) are different. This difference in RRs results in different polish times across the wafer for each stage. For example, by the time the excess copper and barrier are cleared at a point on the die, they might have already been cleared at another point. Hence, some points on the die are overpolished. In copper CMP, overpolishing is defined as polishing beyond the time it takes to remove the overburden copper and barrier at any spatial location. During the overpolishing stage, the dielectric is eroded [68].

In addition, the dishing that might have started during the barrier clearing stage can worsen during overpolishing. This overpolishing is identified as the third intrinsic stage in the copper CMP process. The dishing and erosion that occur during this stage are of interest. In computing the amount of dishing during the overpolish stage, the dishing that occurs during the barrier clearing stage is used as an initial condition. It is important to note that the term overpolishing is used loosely in the CMP literature, and in the CMP industry [68].*

36.3.4 STI CMP MODELING

Shallow trench isolation is the isolation technique of choice in CMOS technologies. In STI, trenches are etched in silicon substrate and filled with silicon dioxide to electrically separate active devices [31]. The previously used isolation technique, LOCOS (local oxidation of silicon), suffers from lateral growth that causes the isolation region to widen beyond the etched spaces. This lowers the integration density. It also complicates device fabrication and introduces device functionality problems such as high parasitic capacitances [47].

As described by Lee [36], the typical STI process flow initially involves growing a thin pad oxide, and then depositing a blanket nitride film on a raw silicon wafer. The isolation trenches are etched such that the desired trench depth (i.e., depth from silicon surface) is achieved. The CMP process is used to polish off the overburden dielectric down to the underlying nitride, where the nitride serves as a polishing stop layer. After CMP, the nitride layer is then removed via etch, resulting in active areas surrounded by field trenches. A typical STI process flow is shown in Figure 36.9.

Lee [36] identifies two major phases in STI CMP process. The first phase is the polish of overburden oxide. The second phase is the overpolish into the nitride layer. The second phase is due to the different pattern densities across the die, for example, CMP pad contacts the nitride layer at different locations at different times. The first phase can be further broken down into two subphases. The first subphase happens between the start of the polish and before the CMP pad contacts the down areas (i.e., areas with lower height than their surroundings). The second subphase occurs from the time CMP pad contacts the down areas until the up area overburden oxide has been completely cleared to nitride.

The first subphase has a homogeneous nature in that only one material is being polished at each moment. Reference [36] uses RR diagram to represent the polish of a single material. In this analysis, the assumption is that the initial starting point is a spatial location on the dielectric layer with a fixed step height. The feature densities for each point vary depending on the location on the die. Thus, any spatial location with a fixed effective pattern density can be expressed using a RR diagram. Figure 36.10 shows the RR diagram for phase one. For a significantly large step height, the CMP pad only contacts the up areas, and the down area RR is zero. This is the first subphase denoted as phase 1A as shown in the figure. The up areas polish at a patterned RR, K/ρ, as shown on the RR diagram.

---

* In the CMP industry, overpolishing means polishing beyond the endpoint time.

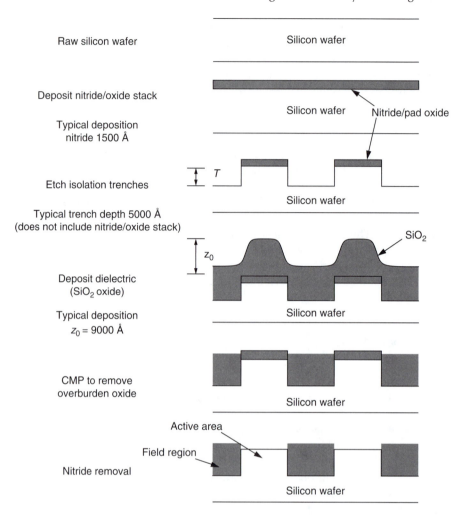

FIGURE 36.9 Typical STI process. (From Lee, B., Modeling for chemical–mechanical polishing for shallow trench isolation, Ph.D. Dissertation, Department of Electrical Engineering and Computer Science, MIT, Cambridge, MA, 2002.)

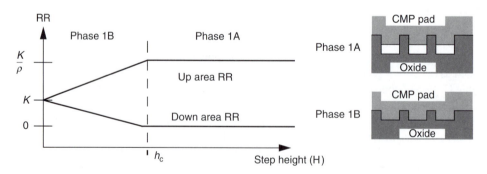

Phase 1A indicates polish before the CMP pad contacts the down areas.
Phase 1B indicates polish after down area has been initially contacted.

FIGURE 36.10 RR diagrams for STI CMP polish (oxide overburden phase). (From Lee, B., Modeling for chemical–mechanical polishing for shallow trench isolation, Ph.D. Dissertation, Department of Electrical Engineering and Computer Science, MIT, Cambridge, MA, 2002.)

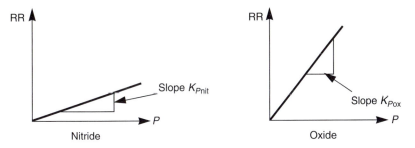

FIGURE 36.11 RR versus pressure, for oxide and nitride. (From Lee, B., Modeling for chemical–mechanical polishing for shallow trench isolation, Ph.D. Dissertation, Department of Electrical Engineering and Computer Science, MIT, Cambridge, MA, 2002.)

As CMP process progresses, the step height reduces and eventually the polishing pad contacts the down areas. This is when the second subphase starts, denoted as phase 1B in the figure. The up and down RRs linearly approach each other until the step height is zero, after which the entire oxide film is polished at the blanket oxide RR K [36].

Owing to heterogeneous nature of the second STI CMP phase, a different removal diagram is used to express the polish of the two separate materials of silicon dioxide and silicon nitride. Figure 36.11 shows the two RR versus pressure curves for nitride and oxide. Assuming a Prestonian relationship, these are linear curves [36].

Dishing and erosion equations can be derived from the amount removal equations. These equations are more useful because it is the dishing and erosion phenomenon that is of most interest in STI CMP. The dishing and erosion equations are also more useful because they isolate key model parameters, making simpler equations from which to extract out model parameters. Dishing is simply the step height as a function of time and erosion can be computed as the amount of nitride removed. Therefore, dishing and erosion can be fully specified and predicted if the phase 1 and phase 2 STI CMP model parameters are known. These model parameters are characteristic of a given CMP process (tool, consumable set, etc.), and the model equations can be used to predict dishing and erosion on wafers patterned with arbitrary layouts that are subjected to a specific characterized CMP process [36]. In Section 36.4, density analysis methods are introduced. To asses the post-CMP effect, the pattern density parameter must be computed.

36.4 DENSITY ANALYSIS METHODS

Traditionally, only foundries have performed the postprocessing needed to achieve pattern density uniformity using insertion "filling" or partial deletion "slotting" of features in the layout [26]. However, layout pattern density must be calculated before addressing the filling or slotting problem. Regions that are violating the lower and upper area density bounds are identified using density analysis methods. Kahng et al. [26] present three density analysis approaches with different time complexities all using the following density analysis problem formulation:

Extremal-density window analysis. Given a fixed window size w and a set of k disjoint rectangles in an $n \times n$ layout region, find an extremal-density $w \times w$ window in the layout.*

---

* Borrowing the terminology from Ref. [26], an extremal-density window is a window with either maximum or minimum density over all the windows throughout the layout.

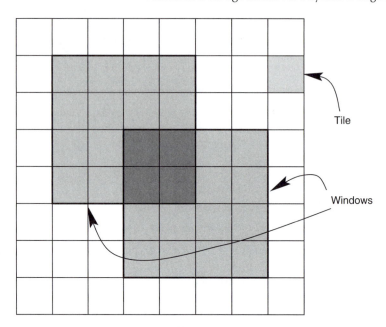

FIGURE 36.12 Layout is partitioned by $r^2(r = 4)$ fixed dissections into $\frac{nr}{w} \times \frac{nr}{w}$ *tiles. Each $w \times w$ window (light gray) consists of r^2 tiles. A pair of windows from different dissections may overlap.* (Kahng, A.B., Robins, G., Singh, A., and Zehikovsky, A., *Proceedings of IEEE International Conference on VLSI Design*, 1999.)

36.4.1 FIXED-DISSECTION REGIME

To verify (or enforce) upper and lower density bounds for $w \times w$ windows, a very practical method is to check (or enforce) these constraints only for $w \times w$ windows of a fixed dissection of the layout into $\frac{w}{r} \times \frac{w}{r}$ tiles, that is, the set of windows having top-left corners at points $(i \cdot \frac{w}{r}, j \cdot \frac{w}{r})$, for $i,j = 0, 1, \ldots, r(\frac{n}{w} - 1)$, as shown in Figure 36.12. Here r is an integer divisor of w.

To analyze all the eligible $w \times w$ windows takes a significant amount of time, while the analysis of fixed dissections can be done much faster. Simply an array of $\frac{n}{w} \times \frac{n}{w}$ counters will be associated with all the dissection windows, and then for each rectangle R the counters of windows intersecting R will be incremented by the area of intersection. In general, the above procedure must be repeated r^2 times to check all the $(r \cdot \frac{n}{w})^2$ windows [26].

36.4.2 MULTILEVEL DENSITY ANALYSIS

Even though the fixed dissection analysis can be performed quickly, it can underestimate the maximum floating-window density worst case.[*] Kahng et al. [28] propose a new multilevel density analysis approach that, as opposed to the techniques presented in Refs. [26,27], has the efficiency of the fixed dissection analysis without sacrificing the accuracy for the floating window worst-case analysis. The multilevel density analysis is based on the following simple observation.

Observation. Given a fixed r-dissection, any arbitrary floating $w \times w$ window will contain some shrunk $w(1 - 1/r) \times w(1 - 1/r)$ window of the fixed r-dissection, and will be contained in some bloated $w(1 + 1/r) \times w(1 + 1/r)$ window of the fixed r-dissection as shown in Figure 36.13.

The first implication of the above observation is that the floating window area can be upper bounded by the area of bloated windows, and lower bounded by the area of shrunk windows. A fixed

---

[*] In general, when all the eligible windows are being examined and filled, it is referred to as the floating window regime.

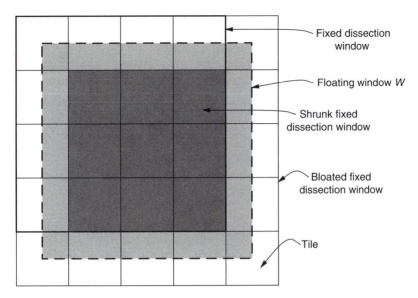

Fixed dissection window

Floating window *W*

Shrunk fixed dissection window

Bloated fixed dissection window

Tile

FIGURE 36.13 Any floating $w \times w$ window W always contains a shrunk $(r - 1) \times (r - 1)$ window of a fixed r-dissection, and is always covered by a bloated $(r + 1) \times (r + 1)$ window of the fixed r-dissection. (Kahng, A. B., Robins, G., Singh, A., and Zehikovsky, A., *Proceedings of IEEE Asia and South Pacific Design Automation Conference*, 1999.)

r-dissection regime can be recursively subdivided into smaller dissections until the number of tiles in each dissection is small. Then the floating density analysis can be applied without significant runtime complexity. In addition, the recursion can be terminated once the floating density analysis is within some user-defined criteria, say $\varepsilon = 1$ percent [28]. In this subsection, different density analysis approaches proposed by the authors of Refs. [26–28] have been presented.

36.5   CMP FILL SYNTHESIS METHODS

Layout density problem includes two stages: density analysis and fill synthesis. Having presented the different approaches proposed for the density analysis stage, in this section the techniques used in fill synthesis will be reviewed. The first fill synthesis approach proposed by Ref. [26] was basically to first sort all the wires by rows, and within each row sort them by the coordinates of their leftmost starting points. Then, for each row, from left to right, metal fill would be placed in the space between the wires as shown in Figure 36.14. This simple method is based on scanline algorithm principles and is applicable to only wiring-type layouts. Reference [26] also proposes a simple technique for slotting. However, due to the reliability issues arising from slotting (i.e., change in current density due to change in wire cross section) it was not studied further, and the main focus of research is on fill insertion approaches. In the following four subsections, in Section 36.5.1, different density-driven problem formulations are presented. In Section 36.5.2, the model-based fill synthesis approach is introduced. In Section 36.5.3 the impact of CMP fill on circuit performance is investigated. And in Section 36.5.4, a new fill insertion method to be used in STI process is discussed.

36.5.1   DENSITY-DRIVEN FILL SYNTHESIS

The following notation and definitions are used in defining the filling problem as described in Ref. [27].

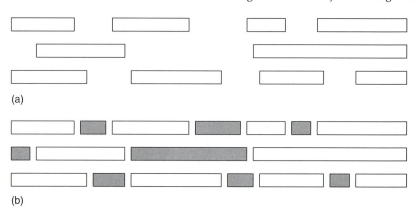

FIGURE 36.14 (a) Example of a wiring-type layout and (b) a corresponding fill solution. (Kahng, A. B., Robins, G., Singh, A., Wang, H., and Zelikovsky, A., *Proceedings of ACM/IEEE International Symposium on Physical Design*, 1998.)

- Input is a layout consisting of rectangular geometries, with all sides having length as a multiple of c (minimum feature width, spacing).
- $n \equiv$ side of the layout region. If the layout region is the entire die, n might be about $50,000 \cdot c$.
- $w \equiv$ fixed window size. The window is the moving square area over which the layout density rule applies.
- $k \equiv$ layout complexity, number of input rectangles.
- $U \equiv$ area density upper bound, expressed as a real number $0 < U < 1$. Each $w \times w$ region of the layout must contain total area of features $\leq U \cdot w^2$.
- $B \equiv$ buffer distance. Fill geometries cannot be introduced within distance B of any layout feature.
- slack $(W) \equiv$ slack of a given $w \times w$ window W. Slack (W) is the maximum amount of fill area that can be introduced into W.

Using the above notation and definition the filling problem is stated as follows [27]:

Filling problem. Given a design rule-correct layout geometry of k disjoint rectilinear rectangles in an $n \times n$ layout region, minimum feature size c, window size $w < n$, buffer distance B, and area (or perimeter) density lower bound L and upper bound U, add fill geometries to create a filled layout that satisfies the following conditions:

1. Circuit functionality and design rule-correctness are preserved.
2. No fill geometry is within distance B of any layout feature.
3. No fill is added into any window that has density $\geq U$ in the original layout.
4. For any window that has density $< U$ in the original layout, the filled layout density is $\geq L$ and $\leq U$.
5. Minimum window density in the filled layout is maximized.

Condition (5) corresponds to the so-called min-variation objective. This constraint minimizes the difference between minimum and maximum window density in the filled layout. However, adding fill will impact circuit performance by changing the total and coupling interconnect capacitances. To attack this problem, another objective called min-fill, has been added to the previous min-variation objective, which deletes as much previously inserted fill as possible, while preserving a minimum window density of no less than the lower bound L.

36.5.1.1   LP-Based and Monte-Carlo-Based Methods

Kahng et al. [27] propose the first min-variation formulation using a linear programming (LP) approach. In a fixed r-dissection regime, for any given tile $T = T_{ij}, i,j = 1, \ldots, \frac{nr}{w}$, the total feature area inside T and the maximum fill amount that can be placed within T without violating the density upper bound U in any window containing T are denoted as area (T) and slack (T), respectively. The following is the filling problem as described in Ref. [27].

Filling problem for fixed r-dissection. Suppose a fixed r-dissection of the layout with tiles of size $\frac{w}{r} \times \frac{w}{r}$, as well as an area (T) and slack (T) for each tile in the dissection. Then, for each tile T_{ij}, the total fill pattern area $p_{ij} = p(T_{ij})$ to be added to T_{ij} must satisfy

$$0 \leq p_{ij} \leq \mathrm{slack}(T_{ij})$$

and

$$\sum_{T_{ij} \in W} p_{ij} \leq \max\{U \cdot w^2 - \mathrm{area}(W), 0\} \tag{36.3}$$

for any fixed dissection $w \times w$ window W.

Then, the min-variation formulation seeks to maximize the minimum window density:

$$\mathrm{Maximize}\ \left(\min_{ij}(\mathrm{area}(T_{ij}) + p_{ij}) \right)$$

The linear programming approach seeks the optimum fill area $p(T_{ij})$ to be inserted into each tile T_{ij}. Recall that the fill area $p(T_{ij})$ cannot exceed slack (T_{ij}), which is the area available for filling inside the tile T_{ij} computed during density analysis. The first LP for the min-variation objective [27,29] is

$$\mathrm{Maximize}\quad M$$

$$\text{subject to}$$

$$0 \leq p(T_{ij}) \leq \mathrm{slack}(T_{ij})$$

$$M \leq \rho(M_{ij}) \leq U \quad i,j = 1, \ldots, \frac{nr}{w} - 1$$

An important step in the above LP approach is to determine slack values. To calculate the total area of all the possible overlapping rectangles the approach of measure of union of rectangles sweep-line-based technique [53] has been used. In a follow up work by the authors in Ref. [68], the fill placement problem was described by the following LP formulation:

$$\mathrm{Minimize}\quad \sum_{i,j} p(T_{ij})$$

$$\text{subject to}$$

$$0 \leq p(T_{ij}) \leq \mathrm{slack}(T_{ij})$$

$$L \leq \rho(M_{ij}) \leq U \quad i,j = 1, \ldots, \frac{nr}{w} - 1$$

Reference [68] also proposes a variant LP approach, that manufacturability does not require the extreme min-variation formulation, that is, given a target window density M, a variability budget ε must be minimized:

$$\text{Minimize} \quad \varepsilon$$

$$\text{subject to}$$

$$0 \leq p(T_{ij}) \leq \text{slack}(T_{ij})$$

$$M - \frac{\varepsilon}{2} \leq \rho(T_{ij}) \leq M + \frac{\varepsilon}{2} \; i,j = 1, \ldots, \frac{nr}{w} - 1$$

The above formulation is also called a ranged LP formulation where the manufacturability is guaranteed by the constraints.

In addition to the LP approaches, Ref. [14] introduces the Monte-Carlo method for min-variation objective. In the Monte-Carlo approach, a tile is chosen randomly and its content is increment with a predetermined fill amount. Tiles are chosen based on their priority, which is the probability of choosing a particular tile T_{ij}. The priority of a tile T_{ij} is zero if and only if either T_{ij} belongs to a window that has already achieved the density upper bound U, or the slack of T_{ij} is equal to the already-inserted fill area. As described in Ref. [14], the priority of a tile T_{ij} is chosen to be proportional to $U - \text{MinWin}(T_{ij})$, where $\text{MinWin}(T_{ij})$ is the minimum density over windows containing the tile T_{ij}. The only drawback of the Monte-Carlo method is that it may insert an excessive amount of total fill. A variant of the Monte-Carlo approach is the greedy algorithm. At each step, the min-variation greedy algorithm adds the maximum possible amount of fill into a tile with the highest priority, which causes the priority of that particular tile to become zero.

In the presence of two objectives, namely min-variation and min-fill, the intuitive approach would be to first find a solution that optimizes one of the objectives then modifying the solution with respect to the other objective. Min-fill objective tries to delete as much previously inserted fill as possible, while maintaining the density criteria.

To optimize the min-fill objective problem with the Monte-Carlo approach, a filling geometry from a tile randomly chosen according to a particular priority is iteratively deleted. Priorities are chosen symmetrical to the priority in the min-variation Monte-Carlo algorithm, that is, proportional to $\text{MinWin}(T_{ij}) - L$. Again, symmetrically no filling geometry can be deleted from the tile T_{ij} (i.e., T_{ij} is locked) if and only if it either has zero priority or else all fill previously inserted into T_{ij} have been deleted. Thus, the min-fill Monte-Carlo algorithm deletes fill geometries from unlocked tiles, which are randomly chosen according to the above priority scheme. Similarly, the min-fill greedy algorithm iteratively deletes a filling geometry from an unlocked tile with the current highest priority.

A variant of the Monte-Carlo approach is the deterministic greedy algorithm where at each step the greedy min-variation algorithm adds the maximum possible amount of fill into a tile with the highest priority. The runtime for this approach is slightly higher than Monte-Carlo because of finding highest-priority tile rather than random ones [12].

36.5.1.2 Iterated Monte-Carlo and Hierarchical Methods

Monte-Carlo and greedy approaches are both suboptimal for the min-variation objective resulting in a minimum window density that may be significantly lower than the optimum. Reference [12] proposes a new iterative technique alternating between the min-variation and min-fill objectives, to narrow the gap between the upper window density bound U and the minimum window density bound L. As described in Ref. [12] the iterated Monte-Carlo and greedy filling algorithms are modified as follows:

1. Interrupt the filling process as soon as the lower bound L on window density is reached, that is, when $M = L$, instead of improving the minimum window density (while possible) for the min-variation objective.
2. Continue iterating, but without changing the lower density bound $M = L$. An improved solution can typically be obtained by keeping track of the best solution oserved over all iterations.

All the filling methods mentioned above were proposed for flat designs; however, the filling problem for hierarchical layouts (standard-cell) is similar to the one for flat layouts. The constraints for the hierarchical filling problem as described by the authors in Ref. [13] are as follows:

- Filling geometries are added to master cells
- Each cell in a filled layout is a filled version of the original master cell
- Layout data volume should not exceed a given threshold

The proposed method by the authors in Ref. [13] first computes the slack value for all the master cells. Then a keep-off zone around master cells will be created to avoid overfilling the regions near master cell boundaries. Then master cells are filled using a Monte-Carlo method where master cells that are more underfilled will be assigned a higher priority. This process is continued until either all the master cells are filled above their minimum density lower bound or the slack in the underfilled master cells becomes zero.

However, due to overlaps between different instances of master cells and features or the inter-actions among the bloat regions in the vicinity of the master cells, pure hierarchical filling may result in some sparse or unfilled regions. This could result in high layout density variation. An intu-itive solution would be to apply a postprocessing phase, that is, apply a standard flat fill approach. However, this will greatly increase the resultant data volume and runtime and diminish the benefit of the hierarchical approach. Reference [13] proposes a three-phase hybrid hierarchical flat-filling approach as follows:

1. Purely hierarchical phase
2. Split-hierarchical phase, where certain master cells that were considered underfilled in phase 1 would be replicated so that distinct copies of a master cell may be filled differently than other copies of the same master cell
3. Flat-fill cleanup phase (i.e., LP, Monte-Carlo, etc.), which will fill any remaining sparse or underfilled regions that were not satisfactorily processed during the first two phases

36.5.1.3 Timing-Driven Fill Synthesis

One of the largest concerns in fill synthesis, apart from meeting the CMP design rules, is the impact of fill insertion on the interconnect capacitance. An excessive increase in wire capacitance can cause a net to violate its setup timing constraint. A large value for keep-off distance (i.e., minimum distance from fill to wire) reduces the impact but it erodes into available areas to insert fills and sometimes makes it impossible to meet the minimum density constraint. Reference [11] proposes the first formulation of the performance impact limited fill (PIL-Fill) problem with the objective of either minimizing total delay impact or maximizing the minimum slack of all nets, subject to a given predetermined amount of fill. They also developed simple capacitance models to be used in their delay calculations. The PIL-Fill synthesis formulation has two objectives:

- Minimizing layout density variation
- Minimizing the CMP fill features' impact on circuit performance (e.g., signal delay and timing slack)

Because it is difficult to satisfy both the objectives simultaneously, practical approaches tend to optimize one objective while transforming the other into constraints. Using the terminology in Ref. [11], the two problem formulations proposed are as follows (note that these formulations are for fixed-dissection regimes):

1. Given tile T, a prescribed amount of fill is to be added into T, a size for each fill feature, a set of slack sites (i.e., sites available for fill insertion) in T per the design rules for floating square fill, and the direction of current flow and the per-unit length resistance for each interconnect segment in T, insert fill features into T such that total impact on delay is minimized.
2. Given a fixed-dissection routed layout and the design rule for floating square fill features, insert a predetermined amount of fill in each tile such that the minimum slack over all nets in the layout is maximized.

The first formulation corresponds to minimum delay with fill constrained formulation while the second one is the maximum min-slack with fill constrained formulation. A weakness with the first formulation is that it minimizes the total delay impact independently for each tile. Hence, the impact due to fill features on signal delay of the complete timing path is not considered. The second formulation, therefore has been proposed to alleviate this problem by maximizing the minimum slack of all nets, subject to a constraint of inserting a predetermined amount of fill in every tile of the layout. Reference [11] proposes two integer linear programming (ILP) methods and a greedy approach for the minimum delay and maximum min-slack formulations, respectively. However, the capacitance models used in delay calculations of Ref. [10] are not accurate as they do not consider the presence of fill features on the neighboring layers. This incurs inaccuracy in the estimated capacitance values and eventually causes uncertainty in the timing analysis. Also, they do not account for signal flow direction, which causes layout nonuniformity (i.e., as fills are pushed to the receiver edge, the driver edge becomes less dense).

In addition to the timing-driven fill synthesis, recently an auxiliary objective-driven fill synthesis has been introduced by the authors in Ref. [41]. In this work, in addition to meeting the layout pattern density criteria, the IR-drop of the power distribution network is also reduced. IR-drop is an increasing challenge in 90 nm (and beyond) designs. The tolerance for IR-drop is becoming smaller as the voltage source scales. It also adds excess burden on routing resources. The work by Leung et al. [41] addresses these issues and according to their experimental results achieves an average IR-drop reduction of 62.2 percent.

36.5.2 MODEL-BASED FILL SYNTHESIS

Methods for fill insertion can be categorized into two groups: rule-based and model-based. Rule-based fill insertion is usually performed by Boolean operations considering design rule constraints such as minimum fill-to-fill spacing, and minimum fill-to-wire spacing (keep-off distance). On the other hand, the model-based fill insertion approach is based on analytical expressions that define the relationship between local pattern density and ILD thickness. Figure 36.15 shows possible rule- and model-based fill insertion approaches.

The model-based fill insertion approach, given a CMP process model, is to find the amount and the location of the fill features to be inserted in the layout so that certain electrical and physical design rules are preserved and certain post-CMP topography variation is met. Reference [65] proposes a two-step solution with consideration of both single- and multiple-layer layouts in the fixed-dissection regime. The first step uses linear programming to compute the necessary amount of fill to be inserted in each of the dissection's tiles. In the second step, the amount of fill calculated by the first step will be placed into each tile such that certain local properties (i.e., electrical, physical, etc.) are preserved. Experimental results with the single-layer formulation (i.e., the cumulative variation of underlying layers is ignored) show reduction of post-CMP topography variation from 767 to 152 Å.

36.5.3 IMPACT OF CMP FILL ON INTERCONNECT PERFORMANCE

In this subsection, the impacts of CMP fill on both interconnect resistance and capacitance have been reviewed. CMP fill insertion can change both coupling and total capacitance of interconnect. In

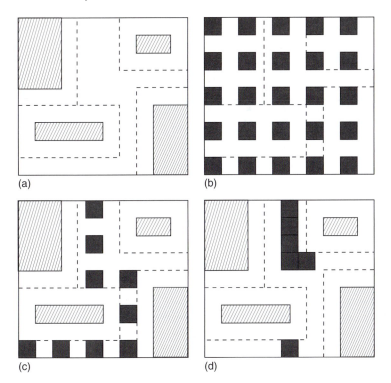

FIGURE 36.15 (a) Example layout with features lightly shaded and exclusion zone in dashed lines. (b) Twenty-five percent density fill insertion before Boolean operations. (c) Rule-based fill insertion after the application of the Boolean operations. (d) Possible model-based fill insertion. (Tian, R., Wong, D.F., and Boone, R., *Proceedings of ACM/IEEE Design Automation Conference*, 2000.)

addition, metal dishing and dielectric erosion change interconnect cross section and therefore affect interconnect resistance. He et al. [23] report an increase of more than 30 percent in interconnect resistance due to dishing and erosion, while the impact on interconnect capacitance is insignificant. Reference [24] proposes a wire sizing approach to lessen the amount of interconnect resistance variation due to the CMP process. Increased wire size compensates for the increased resistance caused by dishing and erosion and also reduces the effect of the large R_{eff} (i.e., driver output resistance) variation on delay.

36.5.3.1 Fill Patterns

CMP fill insertion, even as it contributes to layout pattern density uniformity, increases the coupling and total interconnect capacitance. Therefore, it is important to assess the impact of CMP fill on interconnect capacitance to reduce the uncertainty in circuit timing calculations. Reference [22] explores a space of different fill patterns that are equivalent from the foundry perspective (i.e., respecting all the minimum design rules, etc.) and their respective impact on interconnect capacitance. All the fill features are assumed to be rectangular, and are aligned horizontally and vertically as shown in Figure 36.16. Using the notation from Ref. [22], conductors A and B are active interconnects and the metal shapes between them are CMP fills. Each distinct fill pattern is specified by (1) the number of fill rows (M) and columns (N); (2) the series of widths $\{W_i\}_{i=1...N}$ and lengths $\{L_j\}_{j=1...M}$ of fills; and (3) the series of horizontal and vertical spacings, $\{S_{x,i}\}_{i=1...N-1}$ and $\{S_{y,j}\}_{j=1...M-1}$ between fills.

Enumeration of all the possible combinations of the above parameters is not feasible. Therefore, to restrict the space of exploration, Ref. [22] proposes a positive distribution characteristic function (DCF), denoted $f(k)$, where k is an integer variable that takes the index of the element in the series.

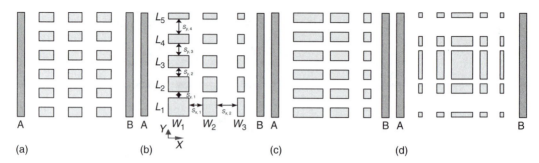

FIGURE 36.16 Examples of fill pattern. (a) Traditional fill pattern, (b) fill with different length and spacing, (c) fill with different width and spacing, and (d) fill with different length, width and spacing (L. He, Kahng, A. B., Tam, T. H., and Xiong, J., *Proceedings of International VLSI/ULSI Multilevel Interconnection Conference,* 2004.)

For example, the value of the *i*th element of the width is calculated as $W_i = f(i) + \overline{W}_l$, where $\overline{W}_l$ is the minimum width design rule. Figure 36.17 shows an example of three different DCFs for width. Reference [22] uses combinations of different DCFs for the parameters mentioned. On the basis of the results of the experiments, Ref. [22] proposes two guidelines as to what a "good" fill pattern might be among all the possible valid fill pattern combinations. The criteria for this assessment are based on the impact of the pattern on interconnect capacitance. According to these guidelines

- In a fixed length budget, the number of fill columns should be maximized
- In a fixed width budget, the number of fill rows should be minimized

In addition to the parameters covered in the previous experiments, Ref. [20] adds four more parameters in its space of exploration. These parameters are, metal width, metal height, dielectric constant, and keep-off distance. The trend of changes in interconnect capacitance were observed for the corresponding parameters. A recent work by Kahng et al. [30] systematically studies the impact of various floating fill configuration parameters, such as fill size, fill location, interconnect size, separation from interconnect edges, multiple fill columns and rows, etc., on coupling capacitance. On the basis of their studies, Ref. [30] proposes certain guidelines for fill insertion to reduce their impact on coupling capacitance while achieving the prescribed metal density. The following are the proposed guidelines in order of decreasing importance:

1. High-impact region. Fill insertion impacts the coupling capacitance most in the area between the two overlapping interconnects and in a close proximity to it.
2. Edge effects. Fill insertion should be preferred at the edges of the above region.
3. Wire spacing. Impact on coupling capacitance is smaller if spacing between the two interconnects is large. Hence, fill must be inserted where spacing is large.

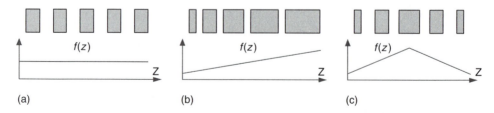

FIGURE 36.17 Examples of DCFs and their corresponding geometrical interpretation. (a) $f(z)$ is a constant, (b) $f(z)$ is nearly increasing, and (c) $f(z)$ is a triangular function. (L. He, Kahng, A. B., Tam, T. H., and Xiong, J., *Proceedings of International VLSI/ULSI Multilevel Interconnection Conference,* 2004.)

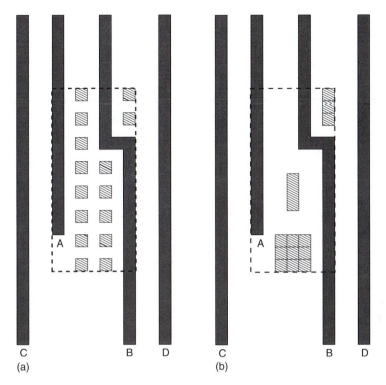

FIGURE 36.18 (a) Regular fill pattern and (b) fill insertion with guidelines.

4. Wire width. Large-width wires are more susceptible to increase in capacitance due to fill insertion. Thinner wire must be preferred as neighbors of fill.
5. Maximize columns. The number of columns should be maximized. That is, fill must be split up subject to the minimum size design rules in a column and spread evenly between the two interconnects.
6. Minimize rows. Fill rows may be merged to reduce the coupling capacitance.
7. Increase length not width. Increasing fill length must be preferred to increasing width to attain the same fill area.
8. Centralize fill. Fill or fill configurations when centered between the two interconnects have a smaller impact on the increase in coupling capacitance.

Figure 36.18 shows an application of the proposed guidelines for a represented fill/wire configuration. In this configuration Guidelines 1, 2, 3, 6, and 8 have been utilized. Increase in coupling capacitance is 27 percent and 11 percent when fill is inserted in a regular pattern and with the proposed guidelines respectively. Reference [30] reports that on average 53 percent reduction in coupling capacitance increase is achieved through applying the guidelines for fill insertion.

36.5.3.2 CMP Fill and Interconnect Capacitance

CMP fill features despite their role in uniforming layout pattern density have a significant impact on coupling and total interconnect capacitance. There is a body work that addresses different issues regarding the estimation or optimization of the capacitance impact of the CMP fill.

Reference [50] briefly described a model-library-based approach to extract floating-fill. Results demonstrating the accuracy of the approach and characterization time were, however, not presented. Reference [40] presented a methodology for full-chip extraction of total capacitance in presence of floating-fill and Ref. [39] extended their analysis. Their approach adjusts the permittivity and sidewall thickness of dielectric to account for the capacitance increase due to fill. According to Ref. [34] capacitance of a configuration is directly proportional to the charge accumulated on one of the electrodes ($Q = CV$). The charge density on an electrode depends on the electric field close to the electrode ($E = \sigma/A$). Therefore, the electric field close to an electrode determines the capacitance of a configuration. When a floating plate of thickness $t (t < d)$ and the same size as the conductor plates is inserted in the space between the conductors, the capacitance increases to $\varepsilon A/(d - t)$.

Also, Ref. [1] has proposed an extraction methodology, where fills are eliminated one by one using a graph-based random walk algorithm while updating the coupling capacitances. In this method, a network of capacitors is collapsed into the equivalent capacitance between two nets. In addition, Yu et al. [75] propose enhancements to the current field solvers by taking into account floating fills and their conditions in the direct boundary element equations. The basic idea in their approach is to add additional equations about the floating CMP fill features to generate a solvable system of linear equations. In the conventional approach, the field solver is called as many times as the number of conductors and floating fill features, whereas in the proposed method the field solver is only called as many times as the number of conductors. Hence, the proposed method has reduced the computation runtime of the field solving process compared to traditional methods. Reference [8] presents a charge-based capacitance measurement methodology to analyze the impact of fills. And finally Ref. [33] proposes three techniques of fill insertion to reduce the interconnect capacitance and the number of fills inserted. It also provides an estimation of the required number of fill geometries for each of the proposed techniques. However, it fails to report the accuracy and reliability of the methods and estimations for densities greater than 30 percent.

36.5.4 STI FILL INSERTION

Shallow trench isolation is the isolation technique of choice for IC manufacturing designs. STI is used to created trenches in silicon substrate between regions that must be isolated. Today's STI processes involve many steps of which nitride deposition, oxide deposition, and CMP are of interest. Nitride is deposited on silicon to protect the underlying regions and to act as a polish stop (i.e., in overburden oxide removal stage). In the next stage, oxide is deposited to fill in the trenches and cover the nitride regions by means of chemical vapor deposition (CVD). CMP is required to remove the overburden oxide over the nitride and in the trenches to ensure the planarity.

In STI, the oxide is polished until all the deposited oxide over the nitride regions have been removed. However, due to the pattern-dependent nature of CMP, the planarization is imperfect as shown in Figure 36.19. Depending on the underlying pattern density, different regions have different polish rates causing oxide thickness variation which results in functional and parametric yield loss.

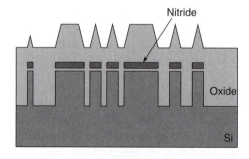

FIGURE 36.19 Cross section of silicon substrate with nitride and oxide being deposited. (From Kahng, A. B., Sharma, P., and Zelikovsky, A., *Proceedings of IEEE International Conference on Computer-Aided Design*, 2006.)

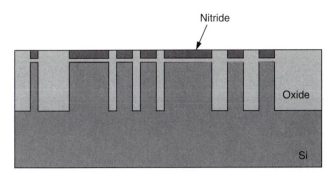

FIGURE 36.20 Desired planarization profile after CMP. (From Kahng, A. B., Sharma, P., and Zelikovsky, A., *Proceedings of IEEE International Conference on Computer-Aided Design*, 2006.)

Figure 36.20 shows an ideal planarization case after CMP process where there is no nitride erosion or oxide dishing.

In STI CMP, the planarization quality depends on pattern densities of both nitride and oxide. Because the oxide is deposited over the nitride, the oxide density is dependent on nitride pattern density. Owing to the variation in underlying nitride pattern density, three key failures may occur after STI CMP process. First, the CMP process may fail to completely remove the excess oxide. Second, even if it does remove the excess oxide completely, it may cause erosion of the underlying nitride. Third and finally, it may remove an excessive amount of oxide within the trenches causing oxide dishing [4]. If the overburden oxide is not completely removed, it will prevent the stripping of the underlying nitride resulting in a circuit failure. Nitride erosion exposes the underlying active devices and causes device failure. On the other hand, oxide dishing results in poor isolation. These failures due to the CMP process have been shown in Figure 36.21. Traditionally, CMP imperfections have been addressed by reverse etchback and fill insertion. However, the etchback process incurs extra processing cost (i.e., mask cost and others) and hence is not economically desirable. Fill insertion for STI is the other technique that involves the addition of dummy nitride features to increase the nitride (and hence oxide) density.

The postplanarization topography in STI CMP is dependent on the overburden oxide density, which is affected by the underlying nitride density. Due to the high density plasma (HDP) process, which is used widely as the oxide deposition technology, the deposited oxide exhibits an interesting property (i.e., slanted sidewalls). Hence, features on the oxide layer are a shrunk version of the nitride features [2,49,73]. For example, a square feature on the nitride layer with sides of five times will have sides of three when deposited on the oxide layer. Therefore, features with sides less than two times will not appear on the oxide layer. As mentioned earlier, the density of the oxide is dependent on the underlying nitride density. Therefore, fill is inserted in the nitride layer to control the densities of both nitride and oxide layers.

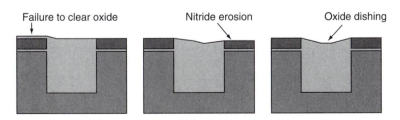

FIGURE 36.21 Three main defects caused by CMP process. (From Kahng, A. B., Sharma, P., and Zelikovsky, A., *Proceedings of IEEE International Conference on Computer-Aided Design*, 2006.)

Failure to remove the overburden oxide completely is the main cause of failure in the oxide CMP process. This phenomenon happens over the regions where oxide density is higher than average. In higher density regions, the CMP pad pressure is reduced and hence the RR is less than that of the regions with lower density [47]. Oxide dishing and nitride erosion can be significantly reduced by increasing the nitride density. In fact, because nitride is used as a polish stop, higher nitride density makes the detection of the nitride more accurate. In a recent work, Kahng et al. [31] propose a new fill insertion methodology for STI CMP processes. In the problem formulation they propose the following fill insertion objectives in the order of their priority:

- Minimize oxide density variation
- Maximize nitride density

Correspondingly, a bicriteria problem formulation was introduced by Ref. [31] as follows.
  Given:

- Set of rectilinear nitride regions contributed by the devices in the design
- Parameter α by which nitride features shrink on each side to give oxide features
- Design rules: minimum nitride width, maximum nitride width, minimum nitride space and notch, minimum nitride area, and minimum enclosed area by nitride

Find:

- Locations for fill insertion

Such that:

1. Oxide density variation is minimized
2. Nitride density is maximized

For the first objective, Ref. [31] uses the same LP formulation proposed in Ref. [29], as mentioned in Section 36.4. The fill slack in the STI method is the maximum oxide density due to fill insertion and the maximum contribution is made by maximum fill insertion on the nitride layer. Using the terminology of Ref. [31], the maximum fill region, the union of all regions where fill can be inserted subject to design rule constraints, is denoted by $Nitride_{max}$ and its density is denoted as $|Nitride_{max}|$. The proposed procedure for finding the region $Nitride_{max}$ is shown in Figure 36.22.

Maximum oxide density could be achieved by shrinking $Nitride_{max}$ by x on all sides for any polygon. To address the second objective of the bicriteria formulation, Ref. [31] introduces $|Oxide_{max}|$ to denote the oxide density due to $Nitride_{max}$, which is highest oxide density achievable by fill insertion. Experimental results show that using the proposed method, averaged over two testcases, the oxide density variation is reduced by 63 percent and minimum nitride density is increased by 79 percent compared with tiling-based fill insertion. Also, the quality of post-CMP topography is improved as the maximum final step height is reduced by 9 percent with only 17 percent increase in the planarization window [31].

36.6 DESIGN FLOWS FOR FILL SYNTHESIS

The impact of CMP-induced variations on yield and performance can be controlled by inserting CMP fill features. When it comes to CMP fill insertion, there are two different hypotheses. The first hypothesis is that the fill synthesis and timing should be closed inside the detailed router. This might sound like an intuitive solution due to the following:

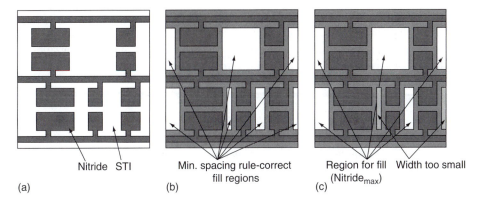

Nitride STI   Min. spacing rule-correct   Region for fill   Width too small
                                  fill regions   (Nitride$_{max}$)
(a)   (b)   (c)

FIGURE 36.22   Computation of maximum fill region (Nitride$_{max}$). (a) Unfilled layout. (b) Possible regions for fill insertion. (c) Spaces of small width and area (shown in the lightest shade of gray) are not available for fill. (From Kahng, A. B., Sharma, P., and Zelikovsky, A., *Proceedings of IEEE International Conference on Computer-Aided Design*, 2006.)

- Routers lay down geometries and close timing, and so they are the natural candidate to perform fill synthesis.
- Timing closure will be more certain for the design team before hand off to manufacturing.
- Multi-grounded fill, which reduces timing uncertainty and improves IR drop, is a natural extension of power/ground routing capability.

The other hypothesis suggests that the router should not perform the fill insertion due to the following:

- Complicated density analyses that support high-quality CMP modeling are not easily performed by the router (wrap-around, full-chip, width-distribution dependent, etc.).
- Routers cannot deliver high-quality fill without a runtime hit.
- With the possible exception of hold time slack and coupling-induced delay uncertainty issues, grounded fill is a bad idea from a performance standpoint (there are some verification and planning closure issues as well). Floating fill synthesis is preferable, but is unnatural for a router.
- Foundries want to own more and more of the RET (reticle enhancement technique), including CMP fill, because RET exposes the process. Extraction, coverage, and fill pattern rules provide a huge amount of leverage, to avoid any need for solving fill in the router.
- Better passing of design intent from design to manufacturing can reduce the need to solve the problem in the router as mentioned in Ref. [11].

36.6.1   RC EXTRACTION AND TIMING CLOSURE

CMP fill insertion must not compromise the sign-off timing and signal integrity. However, it has been shown that CMP fill insertion will adversely impact the interconnect capacitance and therefore the signal delay [22]. Gupta et al. [10,11] propose CMP fill insertion approaches aimed at minimizing the impact of the fill features on the circuit performance. Their method has two objectives, minimizing the layout density variation, and minimizing the CMP fill features' impact on circuit performance (i.e., signal delay and timing slack). Practical approaches tend to find an optimized solution for one objective and then the solution will be adjusted to satisfy the other objective while preserving the first constraint. The PIL-Fill approach discussed in Section 36.5.1.3 can reduce the negative timing slack impact of floating fill by more than 80 percent [11].

As mentioned in Section 36.2, CMP-induced metal dishing increases the line resistance. In addition, metal height can vary as a function of line width, local and global densities. It is critical to ensure the basic computational accuracy of RC extraction tools before including process variation effects. Silicon validation of parasitics helps in closing the loop between process realities and interconnect extraction [44].

36.6.2 IMPACT OF SPATIAL VARIATION

As device and interconnect dimensions continue to shrink, maintaining process uniformity is increasing in importance and difficulty [61]. The 2004 edition of the *International Technology Roadmap for Semiconductors (ITRS)* [25] lists the control of printed transistor gate length in the lithography process as falling short of expectations for the coming technology generations. Variability is happening at multiple scales in semiconductor manufacturing processes, but only the largest of these scales has been studied. Statistical metrology methods are now used to model the variation of different parameters not only across the wafer but also within the die itself. The modeling of both wafer-level and die-level spatial dependencies will become increasingly important for effective process control. The quality of planarization with CMP depends on the layout feature density uniformity. In addition, the features on each die follow a systematic within-die variation. Therefore, different devices within the wafer will exhibit similar characteristics even though they have different characteristics within the die [3]. This interaction between wafer and die variation, if not considered, leads to erroneous modeling as shown in Figure 36.23. Figure 36.23a displays a one-dimensional cross section through the wafer displaying the ILD thickness over a particular device. Although the die mean (or wafer-level trend) across the wafer shows a small curvature, the enclosing curvature of wafer and die variation is larger. A sampling of only one device on each die may erroneously assign both die and wafer variation to the wafer scale uniformity, as illustrated in Figure 36.23a. A control technique that tries to make these sampled values more uniform will be ineffective as shown in Figure 36.23b.

A method to solve this sampling problem is to intensively sample the devices within the measured die in addition to sampling them across the wafer. However, this method comes with extra cost of gathering the measurements. An alternative approach, for example, in CMP, is to measure both a sparse and a dense region of the measured die to obtain a simple estimate for die variance [3].

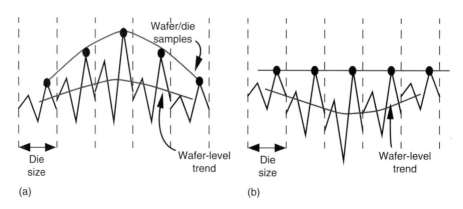

(a)   (b)

FIGURE 36.23 (a) Wafer-level trend generated by single-point sampling within each die can be very different than the mean surface. (b) Control based on sampled surface may achieve erroneous uniformity. (From Boning, D., Chung, J., Ouma, D., and Divecha, R., *Proceedings in Process Control, Diagnostics and Modeling in Semiconductor Manufacturing II*, 1997.)

36.6.3 TOPOGRAPHY-AWARE OPTICAL PROXIMITY CORRECTION

Depth of focus is the major contributor to lithographic process margin. One of the major causes of focus variation is imperfect planarization of fabrication layers. Presently, OPC (optical proximity correction) methods are oblivious to the predictable nature of focus variation arising from wafer topography. As a result, designers suffer from manufacturing yield loss, as well as loss of design quality through unnecessary guardbanding. Figure 36.24 shows how post-CMP thickness variation results in loss of CD (critical dimension) control. Figure 36.24a shows how post-CMP thickness in copper-oxide polishing will predictably change with the region pattern density. The depth-of-focus (DOF) variation corresponding to the thickness variation severely affects metal patterning of the subsequent upper layer, as shown in Figure 36.24b. In this figure, t_1 and t_2 are post-CMP thickness variations over dense and sparse regions, respectively. Hence, to minimize the impact of pattern-dependent effects of the CMP process, the OPC methods should be aware of the post-CMP topography to assign appropriate defocus value for all the features with the same topography. A recent work by Gupta et al. [21] proposes a flow and methodology to drive OPC with a topography map of the layout that is generated by CMP simulation. The experimental results showed that the proposed topography-aware OPC can yield up to 67 percent reduction in edge placement errors at the cost of little increase in mask cost.

36.6.4 INTELLIGENT CMP FILL SYNTHESIS

Current commercial CMP fill insertion tools such as Encounter from Cadence perform fill insertion after routing and before RC extraction. Upon analyzing the density and calculating the required amount of fill to be inserted, there are designated commands that set the metal fill parameters for a given metal layer, including minimum and maximum length and width of fill metal, keep-off distance, spacing between fill metal geometries, preferred and maximum metal density, and window size. In particular, to insert fill features, Encounter starts with bigger fills and makes them smaller as it goes along. It uses the maximum metal fill size specified until it is impossible to fit a piece of metal fill of that size into a particular area, then it uses successively smaller pieces of metal fill until reaching the

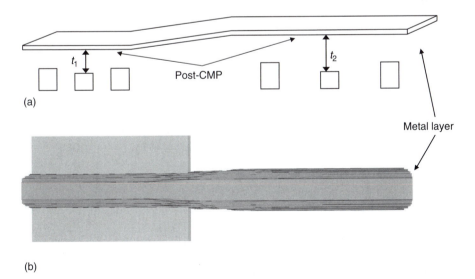

FIGURE 36.24 (a) Side view showing thickness variation over regions with dense and sparse layout. (b) Top view showing CD variation when a line is patterned over a region with uneven wafer topography, that is, under conditions of varying defocus. (From Gupta, P., Kahng, A. B., Park, C. -H., Samadi, K., and Xu, X., *Proceedings of the SPIE*, 2005.)

minimum length [32]. CMP fill insertion tools, however, do not have much flexibility in controlling the impact of the added fill features on interconnect performance (i.e., they only have a set of rules to abide). Therefore, a more sophisticated fill insertion methodology is required.

As the industry moves toward the 65 nm node and beyond, traditional fill synthesis methods reach their limits of usefulness. One indication of this is the emergence of the so-called recommended rules, for example, "it is better to have a small difference between the density values of adjacent windows," or "it is better to maximize the overlap of fill shapes on adjacent layers to enable dummy via insertion." Of course, the impact of fill synthesis on timing continues to be a key concern for the designer. It is increasingly difficult for a DRC platform to obtain an optimal, design-driven fill synthesis solution that meets all basic CMP design rules and as many recommended rules as possible, while minimizing the impact on timing. In this subsection, we sketch the anticipated features of a more sophisticated, dedicated CMP fill synthesis tool—*intelligent fill synthesis*—that can potentially reduce engineering effort while enhancing manufacturability (by increasing process and design latitudes). Hence, an intelligent fill synthesis must embody such features as the following [20].

- Multilayer density control. Post-CMP deposition of oxide in the back end is conformal; therefore, the topography variation in one layer is almost directly transferred to the upper layer, and the topography variation of the upper layer is added to that from the previous layer. Even when the density variation of one layer is small, it is possible to have large enough variation for the entire back-end stack to cause yield loss or to exceed DOF limits of lithography. Intelligent fill synthesis should perform concurrent minimization of the density variation of multiple layers, as well as that of each individual layer.
- Model-based fill synthesis. Rule-based fill synthesis is based on concepts such as density or keep-off distance rules, which are applied to wiring segments that have less than certain threshold amounts of timing slack. Model-based fill synthesis, on the other hand, would use CMP models to identify regions where planarity is important (next to heavily loaded critical segments and below critical segments). The model-based approach has implicit tight coupling to a timer, and models the impact of fill on coupling capacitance.
- Timing-driven fill synthesis. One of the largest concerns in fill synthesis, apart from meeting the CMP design rules, is the impact of fill insertion to the capacitances of the existing nets. An excessive increase in wire capacitance can cause a net to violate its setup timing constraint. A large value for keep-off distance reduces this danger but it erodes into available areas to insert fills and sometimes makes it impossible to meet the minimum density constraint. With timing-driven intelligent fill, the impact of inserting fills on timing is continually assessed, and the minimum keep-off distance for each net to meet the setup time constraint can be computed to avoid a wastefully large one-size-fits-all keep-off distance. In a more advanced, intelligent timing-driven fill flow, the impact of fill insertion on both wafer topography and timing would be analyzed and optimized concurrently. One additional advantage of timing-driven fill is that it can improve the hold-time slack of a net by deliberately and selectively introducing capacitance to that net.
- Wire sizing. Changing the width of a wire has certain impact on the parasitics of the wire such as resistance and capacitance. For example, in an organic low-k/Cu system, widening a wire may result in reduced resistance not only because the wire gains width but also because wider wire suppresses metal thickness loss. To complement the execution of timing-driven fill, it is possible to bias the wires by some small amount (<10 percent) and gain small timing slack. This will increase the operating latitude of the circuit. Alternatively, the impact of the height variation of wires can be compensated by width sizing to tighten the distribution of wire parasitics for any given drawn width.

Figure 36.25 shows a practical approach to intelligent timing-driven fill. In the following approach, after all the required fill has been inserted, the windows that are still violating the minimum density

Timing-Driven Fill

Loop:

0. Set an initial conservatism factor
1. Do (initial) RCX and STA
2. Identify timing-violating nets (TVNs) – i.e., timing-critical nets
3. Apply conservative net-protection (+keep-off distance and blocking $M + 1/M - 1$ layers) per TVN segment
4. Run (incremental) MC-Fill? target fill amount
5. PIL-FILL Synthesis:
    5.1 Greedy insert fill in fill slack columns, targeting most-needy tiles and largest-slack nets first
    5.2 After K fill shapes have been inserted, re-run (incremental) STA based on ΔC's
    5.3 Iterate until all required fill has been inserted (or, until no timing constraint looks safe) – return to step 5
6. Update Conservatism
    6.1 Analyze windows that violate *min density* constraints
    6.2 Identify nets that belong to the windows that violate the constraints
    6.3 Do (incremental) RCX and STA to change the conservatism factor of TVNs – return to Step 2

FIGURE 36.25 Timing-driven fill synthesis approach. (From Gupta, P., Kahng, A.B., Nakagawa, O.S., and Samadi, K., *Proceedings of the International VLSI/ULSI Multilevel Interconnection Conference*, 2005.)

criteria are identified. Then all the nets belonging to these windows will be selected. To meet the density criteria the conservatism factor of TVNs must be updated by allowing the fill to be inserted. This is done in accordance with the results of an incremental RCX and STA (i.e., basically to update the timing slacks of TVNs).

36.7 CONCLUSION

In this survey, an overview of CMP processes was presented. Different characterization and modeling approaches were investigated. Even though CMP is the planarizing technique of choice in silicon manufacturing processes, its effectiveness is dominated by the layout pattern density. One technique that designers and manufacturers use to uniform the layout pattern density is CMP fill insertion. CMP fill features are nonfunctional metal features that are added to the layout to make the layout pattern density uniform while not contributing to the logic of the circuits. However, before addressing the problem of filling the layout with fill features, the density of the layout must to be analyzed. Different density calculation approaches such as fixed dissection regime and multilevel density analyses have been presented. Next, different fill synthesis methods including density-driven, model-based, and auxiliary objective-driven have been introduced. Even though CMP fill features help in making the layout pattern density more uniform, they impact total and coupling interconnect capacitances. In this survey, several different fill patterning and modeling techniques that aim at accurately assessing the impact on interconnect capacitance have also been presented. Finally, the concept of intelligent fill (IF) has been introduced. IF has the capability to produce globally optimized, design-driven CMP fill that satisfies difficult fill pattern and density constraints arising in 90 nm and 65 nm technology nodes.

REFERENCES

1. S. Batterywala, R. Ananthakrishna, Y. Luo, and A. Gyure, A statistical method for fast and accurate capacitance extraction in the presence of floating dummy fills, in *Proceedings of VLSI Design*, Hyderabad, India, 2006.

2. P. Beckage, T. Brown, R. Tian, E. Travis, A. Phillips, and C. Thomas, Prediction and characterization of STI CMP within-die thickness variation on 90 nm technology, in *Proceedings of CMP-MIC Conference*, Marina Del Ray, CA, 2004, pp. 267–274.

3. D. Boning, J. Chung, D. Ouma, and R. Divecha, Spatial variation in semiconductor processes: Modeling for control, in *Proceedings in Process Control, Diagnostics and Modeling in Semiconductor Manufacturing II*, 1997.

4. D. Boning and B. Lee, Nanotopography issues in shallow trench isolation CMP, in *Materials Gateway*, 2002, pp. 761–765.

5. D. Boning, B. Lee, C. Oji, D. Ouma, T. Park, T. Smith, and T. Tugbawa, Pattern dependent modeling for CMP optimization and control, in *Proceedings of Symposium of Chemical–Mechanical Polishing*, 1999.

6. P. A. Burke, Semi-empirical modeling of SiO_2 chemical mechanical polishing planarization, in *Proceedings of International VLSI/ULSI Multilevel Interconnection Conference*, 1991, pp. 379–384.

7. L. E. Camilletti, Implementation of CMP-based design rules and patterning practices, in *Proceedings of IEEE/SEMI Advanced Semiconductor Manufacturing Conference*, Cambridge, MA, 1995, pp. 2–4.

8. Y. W. Chang, H. W. Chang, T. C. Lu, Y. King, W. Ting, J. Ku, and C. Y. Lu, A novel CBCM method free from charge injection induced errors: Investigation into the impact of floating dummy fills on interconnect capacitance, in *Proceedings of International Conference on Microelectronic Test Structures*, Leuven, Belgium, 2005, pp. 235–238.

9. E. Chang, B. Stine, T. Maung, R. Divecha, D. Boning, J. Chung, K. Chang, G. Ray, D. Bradbury, S. Oh, and D. Bartelink, Using a statistical metrology framework to identify systematic and random sources of die- and wafer-level ILD thickness variation in CMP processes, in *Proceedings of IEEE International Electron Devices Meeting*, 1995, pp. 499–502.

10. Y. Chen, P. Gupta, and A. B. Kahng, Performance-impact limited area fill synthesis, in *Proceedings of SPIE Conference on Design and Process Integration for Microelectronic Manufacturing*, 2003, pp. 75–86.

11. Y. Chen, P. Gupta, and A. B. Kahng, Performance-impact limited area fill synthesis, in *Proceedings of ACM/IEEE Design Automation Conference*, Anaheim, CA, 2003, pp. 22–27.

12. Y. Chen, A. B. Kahng, G. Robins, and A. Zelikovsky, Practical iterated fill synthesis for CMP uniformity, in *Proceedings of ACM/IEEE Design Automation Conference*, Los Angeles, CA, 2000, pp. 671–674.

13. Y. Chen, A. B. Kahng, G. Robins, and A. Zelikovsky, Hierarchical dummy fill for process uniformity, in *Proceedings of IEEE Asia and South Pacific Design Automation Conference*, Las Vegas, NY, 2001, pp. 139–144.

14. Y. Chen, A. B. Kahng, G. Robins, and A. Zelikovsky, Monte-Carlo algorithms for layout density control, in *Proceedings of IEEE Asia and South Pacific Design Automation Conference*, Yokohama, Japan, 2000, pp. 523–528.

15. L. M. Cook, Chemical processes in glass polishing, *Journal of Non-Crystalline Solids*, 520, 152–171, 1990.

16. D. Dornfeld, Mechanical aspects of CMP, in *Proceedings of International VLSI/ULSI Multilevel Interconnection Conference*, Santa Clara, CA, 2000, pp. 105–112.

17. P. Friedberg, W. Cheung, and C. J. Spanos, Spatial variability of critical dimensions, in *Proceedings of International VLSI/ULSI Multilevel Interconnection Conference*, Fremont, CA, 2005.

18. W. B. Glendinning and J. N. Helbert, *Handbook of VLSI Microlithography: Principles, Technology, and Applications*, Noyes Publications, 1991.

19. Y. Gotkis, D. Schey, S. Alamgir, J. Yang, and K. Holland, Cu CMP with orbital technology: Summary of the experience, in *Proceedings of ASMC*, 1998, pp. 364–371.

20. P. Gupta, A. B. Kahng, O. S. Nakagawa, and K. Samadi, Closing the loop in interconnect analyses and optimization: CMP fill, lithography and timing, in *Proceedings of International VLSI/ULSI Multilevel Interconnection Conference*, Fremont, CA, 2005, pp. 352–363.

21. P. Gupta, A. B. Kahng, C.-H. Park, K. Samadi, and X. Xu, Wafer topography-aware optical proximity correction for better DOF margin and CD control, in *Proceedings of the SPIE*, vol. 5853, 2005, pp. 844–854.

22. L. He, A. B. Kahng, K. H. Tam, and J. Xiong, Variability-driven considerations in the design of integrated-circuit global interconnects, in *Proceedings of International VLSI/ULSI Multilevel Interconnection Conference*, Waikoloa Beach, Hawai, 2004, pp. 214–221.

23. L. He, A. B. Kahng, K. H. Tam, and J. Xiong, Design of IC interconnects with accurate modeling of CMP, in *Proceedings of SPIE Conference on Design and Process Integration for Microelectronic Manufacturing*, 2005, pp. 109–119.

24. L. He, A. B. Kahng, K. H. Tam, and J. Xiong, Simultaneous buffer insertion and wire sizing considering systematic CMP variation and random leff variation, in *Proceedings of ACM/IEEE International Symposium on Physical Design*, San Francisco, CA, 2005, pp. 78–85.

25. *International Technology Roadmap for Semiconductors*, 2007.

26. A. B. Kahng, G. Robins, A. Singh, H. Wang, and A. Zelikovsky, Filling and slotting: Analysis and algorithms, in *Proceedings of ACM/IEEE International Symposium on Physical Design*, Monterey, CA, 1998, pp. 95–102.

27. A. B. Kahng, G. Robins, A. Singh, and A. Zelikovsky, New and excat filling algorithms for layout density control, in *Proceedings of IEEE International Conference on VLSI Design*, Goa, India, 1999, pp. 106–110.

28. A. B. Kahng, G. Robins, A. Singh, and A. Zelikovsky, New multilevel and hierarchical algorithms for layout density control, in *Proceedings of IEEE Asia and South Pacific Design Automation Conference*, Wanchai, Hong Kong, 1999, pp. 221–224.

29. A. B. Kahng, G. Robins, A. Singh, and A. Zelikovsky, Filling algorithms and analyses for layout density control, in *Proceedings of IEEE Transactions on Computer-Aided Design of Integrated Circuits and Systems*, 18(4), 445–462, 1999 (ISPD 1998).

30. A. B. Kahng, K. Samadi, and P. Sharma, Study of floating fill impact on interconnect capacitance, in *Proceedings of IEEE International Symposium on Quality Electronic Design*, San Jose, CA, 2006, pp. 691–696.

31. A. B. Kahng, P. Sharma, and A. Zelikovsky, Fill for shallow trench isolation CMP, in *Proceedings of IEEE International Conference on Computer-Aided Design*, San Jose, CA, 2006, pp. 661–668.

32. K. Kelly, Effect of grounded vs. floating fill metal on parasitic capacitance, *International Cadence Users-Group Conference*, 2004.

33. A. Kurokawa, T. Kanamoto, T. Ibe, A. Kasebe, C. W. Fong, T. Kage, Y. Inoue, and H. Masuda, Dummy filling methods for reducing interconnect capacitance and number of fills, in *Proceedings of IEEE International Symposium on Quality Electronic Design*, San Jose, CA, 2005, pp. 586–591.

34. A. Kurokawa, T. Kanamoto, A. Kasebe, Y. Inoue, and H. Masuda, Ecient capacitance extraction method for interconnects with dummy fills, in *Proceedings of CICC*, Orlando, FL, 2004, pp. 485–488.

35. H. Landis, P. Burke, W. Cote, W. Hill, C. Hoffman, C. Kaanta, C. Koburger, W. Lange, M. Leach, and S. Luce, Integration of chemical–mechanical polishing into CMOS integrated circuit manufacturing, *Thin Solid Films*, 220, 1–7, 1992.

36. B. Lee, Modeling of chemical–mechanical polishing for shallow trench isolation, Ph.D. Dissertation, Department of Electrical Engineering and Computer Science, MIT, Cambridge, MA, 2002.

37. B. Lee, D. S. Boning, D. L. Hetherington, and D. J. Stein, Using smart dummy fill and selective reverse etchback for pattern density equalization, in *Proceedings of Chemical Mechanical Polish for ULSI Multilevel Interconnection Conference*, Santa Clara, CA, 2000, pp. 255–258.

38. W. -S. Lee, K. -H. Lee, J. -K. Park, T. -K. Kim, and Y. -K. Park, Investigation of the capacitance deviation due to metal-fills and the effective interconnect geometry modeling, in *Proceedings of International Symposium on Quality Electronic Design*, San Jose, CA, 2003, pp. 354–357.

39. W. -S. Lee, K. -H. Lee, J. -K. Park, T. -K. Kim, Y. -K. Park, and J. -T. Kong, Investigation of the capacitance deviation due to metal fills and the effective interconnect geometry modeling, in *Proceedings of International Symposium on Quality Electronic Design*, San Jose, CA, 2003, pp. 373–376.

40. K. -H. Lee, J. -K. Park, Y. -N. Yoon, D. -H. Jung, J. -P. Shin, Y. -K. Park, and J. -T. Kong, Analyzing the effects of floating dummy fills: From feature scale analysis to full-chip RC extraction, in *Proceedings of IEDM*, Washington, Washington D.C., 2001, pp. 31.3.1–31.3.4.

41. K. -S. Leung, SPIDER: Simultaneous post-layout IR-drop and metal density enhancment with redundant fill, in *Proceedings of International Conference on Computer-Aided Design*, San Jose, CA, 2005, pp. 33–38.

42. Z. Li, L. Borucki, I. Koshiyama, and A. Philipossian, Effect of slurry flow rate on tribological, thermal, and removal rate attributes of copper CMP, *Journal of Electrochemical Society*, 151, G482–G487, 2004.

43. S. Mudhivarthi, N. Gitis, S. Kuiry, M. Vinogradov, and A. Kumar, Effects of slurry flow rate and pad conditioning temperature on dishing, erosion, and metal loss during copper CMP, *Journal of Electrochemical Society*, 153(5), G372–G378, 2006.

44. N.S. Nagaraj, T. Bonifield, A. Singh, C. Bittlestone, U. Narasimha, V. Le, and A. Hill, BEOL variability and impact on RC extraction, in *Proceedings of Design Automation Conference*, Anaheim, CA, 2005, pp. 758–759.

45. G. Nanz and L. E. Camilletti, Modeling of chemical–mechanical polishing, in *IEEE Transactions on Semiconductor Manufacturing*, 8(11), 382–389, 1995.
46. M. Nelson, B. Williams, C. Belisle, S. Aytes, D. Beasterfield, J. Liu, S. Donaldson, and J. Prasad, Optimizing pattern fill for planarity and parasitic capacitance, in *Proceedings of International Semiconductor Device Research Symposium*, 2003, Washington, Washington D.C., pp. 428–429.
47. D. Ouma, Modeling of chemical–mechanical polishing for dielectric planarization, Ph.D. Dissertation Department of Electrical Engineering and Computer Science, MIT, Cambridge, MA, 1998.
48. D. Ouma, B. Stine, R. Divecha, D. Boning, J. Chung, I. Ali, and M. Islamraja, Using variation decomposition analysis to determine the effects of process on wafer and dielevel uniformity in CMP, *Symposium on Chemical Mechanical Planarization (CMP) in IC Device Manufacturing, 190th Electrochemical Society Meeting*, 1996.
49. J. T. Pan, D. Ouma, P. Li, D. Boning, F. Redecker, J. Chung, and J. Whitby, Planarization and integration of shallow trench isolation, in *Proceedings of International VLSI/ULSI Multilevel Interconnection Conference*, 1998, pp. 467–472.
50. J. -K. Park, K. -H. Lee, J. -H. Lee, Y. -K. Park, and J. -T. Kong, An exhaustive method for characterizing the interconnect capacitance considering the floating dummy fills by employing an efficient field solving algorithm, in *Proceedings of SISPAD* 2000, Seattle, Washington, pp. 98–101.
51. W. J. Patrick, W. Doedel, T. Souts, and P. H. Schiable, Application of chemical–mechanical polishing to the fabrication of VLSI circuit interconnects, *Journal of Electrochemical Society*, 138(6), 1778–1784, 1991.
52. K. A. Perry, Chemical mechanical polishing: The impact of a new technology on an industry, *Proceedings of Symposium on VLSI Technology*, Honalulu, Hawaii, 1998, pp. 2–5.
53. P. F. Preparata and M. I. Shamos, *Computational Geometry: An Introduction*, Springer-Verlag, New York, 1985.
54. S. Raghvendra and P. Hurat, DFM: Linking design and manufacturing, in *Proceedings of International Conference on VLSI Design*, Kolkata, India, 2005, pp. 705–708.
55. P. Rai-Choudhury (Ed.), *Handbook of Microlithography, Micromachining, and Microfabriation, vol. 1: Microlithography*, Bellingham, SPIE Optical Engineering Press, 1997.
56. S. Runnels, M. Kim, J. Schleuter, C. Karlsrud, and M. Desai, A modeling tool for chemical–mechanical polishing design and evaluation, *IEEE Transactions on Semiconductor Manufacturing*, 11(8), 501–510, 1995.
57. S. Sivaram, H. Bath, E. Lee, R. Leggett, and R. Tolles, Measurement and modeling of pattern sensitivity during chemical–mechanical polishing of interlevel dielectrics, SEMTECH, Austin, TX, Technical Report, 1992.
58. S. Sivaram, H. Bath, R. Legegett, A. Maury, K. Monning, and R. Tolles, Planarizing interlevel dielectrics by chemical mechanical polishing, *Solid State Technology*, pp. 87–91, May 1992.
59. J. Sorooshian, D. Hetherington and A. Philipossian, Effect of process temperature on coefficient of friction during CMP, *Electrochemical Solid-State Letters*, G222–G224, 2004.
60. J. Sorooshian, D. DeNardis, L. Charns, Z. Li, F. Shadman, D. Boning, D. Hetherington and A. Philipossian, Arrhenius characterization of ILD and copper CMP process, *Journal of Electrochemical Society*, 151, G85–G88, 2004.
61. B. E. Stine, D. S. Boning, and C. E. Chung, Analysis and decomposition of spatial variation in integrated circuit processes and devices, *IEEE Transactions on Semiconductor Manufacturing*, 10(2), 24–41, 1997.
62. B. E. Stine, D. S. Boning, J. E. Chung, L. Camilletti, F. Kruppa, E. R. Equi, W. Loh, S. Prasad, M. Muthukrishnan, D. Towery, M. Berman, and A. Kapoor, The physical and electrical effects of metal-fill patterning practices for oxide chemical-mechanical polishing processes, in *IEEE Transactions on Electron Devices*, 45(3), 665–679, 1998.
63. B. Stine, D. Ouma, R. Divecha, D. Boning, J. Chung, D. L. Hetherington, I. Ali, G. Shinn, J. Clark, O. S. Nakagawa, and S. -Y. Oh, A closed-form analytic model for ILD thickness variation in CMP processes, in *Proceedings of Chemical–Mechanical Polish for ULSI Multilevel Interconnection Conference*, Santa Clara, CA, 1997, pp. 266–273.
64. M. E. Thomas, S. Sekigahama, P. Renteln, and J. M. Pierce, The mechanical planarization of interlevel dielectrics for multilevel interconnect applications, in *Proceedings of International VLSI/ULSI Multilevel Interconnection Conference*, 1990, pp. 438–440.

65. R. Tian, D. F. Wong, and R. Boone, Model-based dummy feature placement for oxide chemical–mechanical polishing manufacturability, in *Proceedings of ACM/IEEE Design Automation Conference*, Los Angeles, CA, 2000, pp. 667–670.
66. R. Tian, D. F. Wong, R. Boone, and A. Reich, Dummy feature placement for oxide chemical–mechanical polishing manufacturability, in *Technical Report*, University of Texas at Austin CS Department, 1999, pp. 9–19.
67. N. N. Toan, Spin-on glass materials and applications in advanced IC technologies, Ph.D. Dissertation, Universiteit Twente, Netherlands, 1999.
68. T. Tugbawa, Chip-scale modeling of pattern dependencies in copper chemical mechanical polishing processes, Ph.D. Dissertation, Department of Electrical Engineering and Computer Science, MIT, Cambridge, MA, 2002.
69. T. Tugbawa, T. Park, D. Boning, T. Pan, P. Li, S. Hymes, T. Brown, and L. Camilletti, A mathematical model of pattern dependence in Cu CMP process, in *Proceedings of CMP Symposium Electrochemical Society Meeting*, 1999, pp. 605–615.
70. X. Wang, C. C. Chiang, J. Kawa, and Q. Su, A min-variance iterative method for fast smart dummy feature density assignment in chemical–mechanical polishing, in *Proceedings of International Symposium on Quality Electronic Design*, San Jose, California, 2005, pp. 258–263.
71. J. Warnock, A two-dimensional process model for Ic chemimechanical polish planarization, *Journal of Electrochemical Society*, 138(8), 2398–2402, 1991.
72. D. White, J. Melrin, and D. Boning, Characterization and modeling of dynamic thermal behavior in CMP, *Journal of Electrochemical Society*, 150, G271–G278, 2003.
73. X. Xie, T. Park, D. Boning, A. Smith, P. Allard, and N. Patel, Characterizing STI CMP processes with an STI test mask having realistic geometric shapes, in *Chemical–Mechanical Polishing Symposium, MRS Spring Meeting*, 2004.
74. T. -K. Yu, C. C. Yu, and M. Orlowski, A statistical polishing pad model for chemical–mechanical polishing, in *Proceedings of IEEE International Electron Devices Meeting*, 1993, pp. 865–868.
75. W. Yu, M. Zhang, and Z. Wang, Ecient 3-D extraction of interconnect capacitance considering floating metal fills with boundary element method, *IEEE Transactions on Computer-Aided Design of Integrated Circuits and Systems*, 25(1), 12–18, 2006.

37 Yield Analysis and Optimization

Puneet Gupta and Evanthia Papadopoulou

CONTENTS

In this chapter, we discuss yield loss mechanisms, yield analysis and common physical design methods to improve yield. Yield is defined as the ratio of the number of products that can be sold to the number of products that can be manufactured. To motivate the importance of yield, it is instructive to look at the economics of chip manufacturing. The estimated typical cost of a modern 300 mm or 12 in. wafer 0.13 μm process fabrication plant is $ 2–4 billion, a typical number of processing steps for a modern integrated circuit is more than 150, a typical production cycle-time is over six weeks, and individual wafers cost multiple thousands of dollars. Given the huge investments that this entails, consistent high yield is necessary for faster time to profit.

37.1 INTRODUCTION

The total yield for an integrated circuit Y_{total} can be expressed a follows:

$$Y_{total} = Y_{line} \times Y_{batch} \qquad (37.1)$$

Here Y_{line} denotes line yield or wafer yield that is the fraction of wafers which survive through the manufacturing line, and Y_{batch} is the fraction of integrated circuits which, on each wafer, are fully functional at the end of the line. A steep yield ramp implies a quicker path to high batch yield, and hence, volume production, which in turn, means higher profitability for the semiconductor manufacturer who operates under time-to-market pressures.

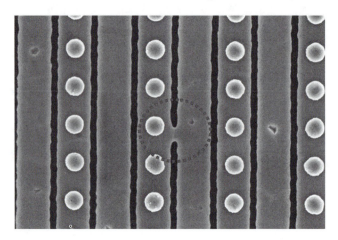

FIGURE 37.1 SEM picture showing a bridging fault on Metal 3. Note the row of vias on each metal line. (Reprinted from Song, Z.G., Neo, S.P., Loh, S.K., and Oh, C.K., *International Symposium for Testing and Failure Analysis*, 2005. With permission.)

The yield ingredient, Y_{batch} can be further classified based on either type of defect or of failure. A taxonomy of failure types is as follows:

- Catastrophic yield loss. These are functional failures such as open or short circuits that cause the part to not work at all. Extra or missing material particle defects are the primary causes for such failures. Figure 37.1 [2] shows a magnified view of a bridging fault. The yield loss due to such faults can be predicted by critical area analysis, and this is discussed later in this chapter.
- Parametric yield loss. These failures occur when the chip is functionally correct but it fails to meet some power or performance criteria. Parametric failures are caused by variations in one or set of circuit parameters, such that their specific distribution in a design causes it fall out of specifications. For example, a part may function at a certain VDD value, but not over entire required range of VDD. Another example of parametric yield loss is due to leakage in deep submicron technologies [3], where parametric failures may be caused by process variations. Some classes of integrated circuits may be speed-binned (i.e., grouped by performance): a common example of this class of designs is microprocessors, wherein lower performance parts are priced lower. Typical ASICs are an example of a class of circuits that cannot be speed-binned, because they cannot be sold if their performance is below a certain threshold (e.g., due to compliance with standards). For these circuits, there can be significant performance-limited yield loss, and therefore, they are designed with a large guardband. However, even in case of speed-binned circuits, yield loss is important because there can be significant dollar value loss even if there is little yield loss.

In addition to these, another source of yield loss is due to testing-related yield loss, as no practical testing process can detect all possible faults (and potential faults). Such yield loss is related to defect level (e.g., see Ref. [4]) and field returns (e.g., see Ref. [5]). We are not including such yield losses in our discussion as they are not related to physical design. We add that another aspect of field-returns is long-term reliability of designs (e.g., see Ref. [6]). Reliability is typically treated as a separate topic and we discuss yield loss only in terms of its most common definition: number of bad parts at the end of manufacturing line.

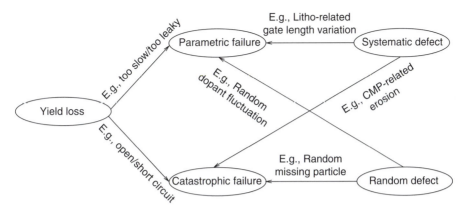

FIGURE 37.2 Sources and types of yield loss. Note that either type of failure can be caused by either type of defects.

Defect types can be classified as follows:*

- Random defects. These are randomly distributed faults due to sources such as particle contamination.
- Systematic defects. These kind of defects are predictable. Example sources include CMP (chemical mechanical polishing) and photoresist pattern collapse, which are treated elsewhere in this book.

It is important to understand that both random and systematic defects can cause parametric or catastrophic yield loss. For example, lithographic variation, which is typically systematic and pattern dependent, can cause catastrophic line-end shortening, leading to an incomplete formation of the gate (polysilicon over diffusion) of the MOS transistor, and hence a functional failure. A less drastic rendition of lithographic variation is shown by gate-length variation, causing gates on critical paths to speed up too much, leading to hold-time violations under certain voltage and temperature conditions. Various defect types and failure modes are shown in Figure 37.2. Systematic mechanism limited yield loss is projected to be the dominant source of yield loss in current and future technology generations [1].

The decision at the IC manufacturing site, of which parts are nonfunctional and should be discarded, is an important one. Though this discussion is more closely related to testing and testability, a very brief introduction is essential to understand final yield measurement at the foundry. For a more detailed discussion, see Ref. [7]. Tests are usually classified as delay tests (intended usually to test for parametric failures) and functional tests (intended usually to test for catastrophic failures). Two common examples of test are FMAX testing and IDDQ testing. FMAX tests essentially keep increasing the clock frequency until a failure is detected, and permit the determination of the maximum frequency of operation of the circuit, while IDDQ tests measure the quiescent current in the power supply after bringing the circuit to a known state. Such tests can help detect, for example, bridging faults.

Root cause analysis of failures is a necessary component of the yield improvement and process ramp-up process. Failure analysis attempts to determine both the failure mechanism and their underlying cause. Modern failure analysis laboratories have several advanced techniques at their disposal. For example, with focused ion beam (FIB), existing circuit lines can be cut and new lines inserted for mechanical or electron beam probing. In some cases, a transmission electron microscope (TEM) may be used to provide atomic resolution images of structures.

---

* A similar taxonomy is typically used for process variations as well. The terms defects and variations are used interchangeably in literature. One common distinction between the two terms is the exclusion of the particle defects from variations.

Inline process monitoring is another common way to make sure that the fabrication line is running fine, and is also used for characterization purposes (e.g., to characterize process variation). The most common way to accomplish this is to place and measure simple test structures such as ring oscillators in the scribe-line area of the wafer (i.e., the empty area on the wafer between functional chips). Such measurements are performed by wafer-level probing and do not require dicing and packaging of the structures. In addition, scanning electron microscope (SEM) measurements of critical dimension (CD)* may also provide useful diagnostics.

37.2 SOURCES OF YIELD LOSS

As mentioned earlier in the chapter, yield loss can be due to systematic as well as random defects. In this section, we focus our attention to variations; contamination-related spot defects are discussed later in the chapter. There are several ways to classify variations, depending on the axis:

- Process versus environmental. Variation occurring during circuit operation (e.g., temperature, power supply) are environmental in nature, while variations occurring during the manufacturing process (e.g., mask misalignment, stepper focus) are physical. We will focus here only on process variations.
- Systematic versus random. As discussed earlier, systematic variations (e.g., metal dishing, lithographic proximity effects) can be modeled and predicted, while random variations (e.g., material variations, dopant fluctuations) are inherently unpredictable.
- Interdie versus intradie. Depending on the spatial scale of the variation, it can be classified as die-to-die (e.g., material variations) or within-die (e.g., layout pattern dependent lithographic variation). Interdie variations correspond to variation of a parameter value across nominally identical die. Such variations may be die-to-die, wafer-to-wafer, or even lot-to-lot. Interdie variations are typically accounted for in design, by a shift in the mean of a parameter value. Intradie variations, on the other hand, correspond to parameter fluctuations across nominally identical circuit elements, such as transistors. Intradie perturbations are usually accounted in design by guardbanding and prevention. Variation compensation in design is further discussed in the next section.

An interesting point to note here is the level of abstraction for sources of variation. From the logic designer's point of view, variation may be caused by cell delay or transistor delay changes. Such modeling is evident, for example, in most statistical timing analysis tools (e.g., [8–11]). From the circuit desinger's viewpoint, the level of abstraction may go down to (say) transistor gate-length variation, which leads to cell or transistor delay variation. Going further down, a lithographer may attribute CD variation to focus variation, which may be further blamed on wafer flatness imperfections.

Variation in process conditions can manifest itself as dimensional variations or material variations. Dimensional variations include the following:

- Lateral dimension variation. Across chip linewidth variation (ACLV) is one of the largest contributors to parametric variation. In this category, important causes of parametric and functional failure include gate-length variation, line-end pullback and contact, or via overlap. Lithography and etch processes are the largest culprits for such variations. Such variations are largely systematic and layout pattern dependent.† With scaling geometries, even small variations in dimensions can be detrimental to circuit performance. For example, line edge roughness (LER) is projected to be a large concern for 32 nm device performance [12,13].

---

* CD is the commonly used term for the smallest (and hence the most critical) linewidth in the design.
† Lateral dimension variation is typically mitigated on the manufacturing side by resolution enhancement techniques (RETs) such optical proximity correction (OPC).

- Topography variation. Dielectric erosion and metal dishing caused by CMP processes is one of the largest contributors to interconnect failures. In the front end of the line, imperfect STI (shallow trench isolation) CMP process is an example cause of topographic variation. Topographic variation not only results in interconnect resistance and capacitance variation but by virtue of acting as defocus for lithographic manufacturing of subsequent layers, also results in linewidth variation [14].

Several processing steps during the manufacture of deep submicron integrated circuits can result in material parameter perturbations. Besides material purity variations, such variations can be caused, for example, by perturbations in implantation or deposition processes. An important example of material variation is discrete dopant fluctuation. Random placement of atoms at discrete locations in the channel can cause Vth variation. With the number of dopant atoms going down to a few hundred in sub-100 nm devices, random dopant fluctuation is becoming an important source of variation.

The result of these physical variations is variation in circuit metrics like performance and power. The international technology roadmap for semiconductors (ITRS) project as much as 15 percent slowdown in design sign-off delay by the year 2014. Leakage and leakage variability is an even larger problem, due to exponential dependence of leakage power on physical dimensions like gate-oxide thickness and gate length, as well material properties like dopant concentration, and a 30 times variation in leakage in microprocessors has been noted by the authors in Ref. [15]. According to ITRS projections, containing Vth variability to within 58 percent, circuit performance variability to within 57 percent, and circuit power variability to within 59 percent is a red-brick (i.e., there are no known solutions). On the BEOL (back end of the line) side, electrical parameters that see significant variation include via resistance as well as wire resistance and capacitance.

Our description in this section has only barely touched upon various sources of yield loss. A very good discussion of process variations can be found in Ref. [16].

37.3 YIELD ANALYSIS

The yield of a VLSI chip depends on its parametric as well as functional sensitivity to the various kinds of defects discussed earlier. Yield prediction requires modeling of various complicated physical and statistical phenomena. The yield analysis problem can be decomposed into the analysis of (1) parametric and (2) catastrophic failures. Yield analysis of catastrophic failures is discussed at length in Section 37.3.2. A very brief introduction to parametric yield analysis is presented next.

37.3.1 PARAMETRIC YIELD ANALYSIS

The analysis of chip failures and consequent yield loss is an active area of research, and there is little consensus on yield metrics and calculation methods in this regime. In recent years, statistical timing analysis methods, which help predict parametric yield loss due to timing failures, have received a lot of attention [8–11,17]. Other statistical methods have focused on power-limited yield as well [18–20]. Several other methods that concentrate on the systematic component of variation have also been proposed [21–24]. Statistical analysis methods can be characterized either as performance-space (directly modeling distributions of gate or interconnect delays) or parameter space (modeling distributions of sources of performance variations such as gate length, threshold voltage with performance variables modeled as functions of basic parameters) techniques. Block-based analysis tools propagate these variability distributions through circuit timing graph* to calculate arrival time and required time distributions and consequent slack distributions at all circuit nodes. Path-based methods work on a set of critical paths instead of the full design and as a result are better equipped to handle arbitrary distributions and correlations using Monte Carlo simulations. Correlations, spatial, logical, or otherwise, play an important role in such statistical timing analysis.

---

* The key operations in such propagation are sum, min, and max of random variables.

From a foundry perspective, it is very difficult to characterize the process to identify all sources of variation and their magnitude, to compute correlations between these sources, and also to find out the spatial scale to which they extend. To add to the complexity, most of these sources of variation have very systematic interactions with layout and cannot be easily split into inter- and intradie components. Nevertheless, with the magnitude and sources of variability increasing, statistical power and performance analysis, coupled with accurate modeling of systematic variations, will lead to a stage where parametric yield analysis is a part of standard design sign-off.

37.3.2 RANDOM DEFECT YIELD MODELING AND CRITICAL AREA COMPUTATION

A number of models for the prediction of yield of a semiconductor device due to random manufacturing defects have been proposed over the years. The common focus of all models is a measure called the critical area that represents the sensitivity yield of a VLSI design to random defects during the manufacturing process that result in catastrophic failures.

A majority of random defects is introduced into the IC layer by the lithography process. These are spot defects caused by various contamination particles. Spot defects may result in circuit failure, depending on their size and location, They are classified into extra-material defects (also referred to as bridges or protrusion defects) and missing-material defects (also called voids, notches, or intrusion defects). Extra-material defects result in shorts between different conducting regions, while missing-material defects result in open circuits. Missing-material defects that result in broken (open) conducting paths or destroyed contacting regions are called opens or breaks. Missing-material defects on contact and via layers that destroy contacts and vias are called via blocks. Another class of defects, known as pinholes, occur in dielectric insulators. Pinholes are tiny defects that may cause shorts if located in the overlap region between patterns at different photolithographic levels (see e.g., Ref. [25]). Shorts, opens (breaks), and via blocks are the main types of random manufacturing defects resulting in circuit failure.

The yield of a chip considering random manufacturing defects is computed as

$$Y = \prod_{i=1}^{m} Y_i$$

where Y_i is the random defect yield associated with the ith step of he manufacturing process (see, e.g., Refs. [26–28]). For convenience, the subscript is omitted, and Y is referred as the yield of a single processing step. There are a number of models to compute random defect yield such as Seed's model, the Poisson model, the negative binomial model, and Murphy's model(see, e.g., Ref. [29]). The main difference between the various yield models is in the choice of statistics that are assumed to govern the spatial distribution of defects. For example, choosing negative binomial statistics results in the widespread negative binomial yield model shown and is given by the following equation for a single processing step:

$$Y = \left(1 + \frac{dA_c}{\alpha}\right)^{-\alpha}$$

where
    d denotes the average number of defects per unit of area
    α is a clustering parameter
    A_c denotes the critical area

All yield models, independent of the statistics used, result in yield equations that are functional forms of the same quantity, termed the critical area. The critical area is a measure reflecting the sensitivity of the design to random manufacturing defects, and is defined as follows:

$$A_c = \int_0^\infty A(r)D(r)\mathrm{d}r$$

where

A(r) denotes the area in which the center of a defect of radius r must fall to cause circuit failure

$D(r)$ is the density function of the defect size

$A(r)$ is referred to as the critical area for defect size r

The total critical area integral A_c for all defect sizes is also referred to as the weighted critical area. The defect density function has been estimated as follows [25,26,29,30,68,75]:

$$D(r) = \begin{cases} \frac{Cr^q}{r_0^{q+1}}, & 0 \le r \le r_0 \\ \frac{Cr_0^{p-1}}{r^p}, & r_0 \le r \le \infty \end{cases} \tag{37.2}$$

where

p, q are real numbers (typically $p = 3, q = 1$)

$c = (q+1)(p-1)/(q+p)$

r_0 is some minimum optically resolvable size

Figure 37.3 illustrates $A(r)$, the critical area for shorts for the given defect size r. Note that the illustrated defect causes a short if and only if its center falls anywhere within the shaded area $A(r)$. The extraction of critical area requires further the computation of the total critical area integral for all defect sizes given the defect size distribution $D(r)$.

The extraction of critical area for various types of faults poses the major computational bottleneck in VLSI random yield prediction. In the following, we review the main computational paradigms proposed in the literature for the extraction of critical area and focus on their algorithmic aspects. Pinhole defects are ignored because extracting their critical area is straightforward. Pinhole defects are modeled as points of no area and their critical area is simply the area of overlap between patterns at different photolithographic levels (see, e.g., Ref. [25]). We first give some mathematical insight on various defect models.

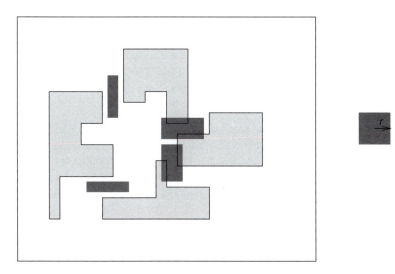

FIGURE 37.3   Critical area $A(r)$ for a given defect of size r.

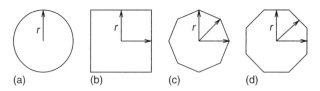

FIGURE 37.4 Common defect shapes of size r.

37.3.2.1 Defect Models

Random manufacturing defects are typically modeled as circular disks with a size distribution. In particular, a defect of size r is modeled as a circle of radius (or diagonal) r. The radius r is a random variable with a known probability density function $D(r)$ as given above. When calculating critical area, it has been a normal practice to approximate the circular defect by shapes that are computationally easier to deal with such as squares or regular k-gons for an even k, usually $k = 8$. Figure 37.4b through d depicts defect shapes commonly used in practice instead of the ordinary circular defect depicted in Figure 37.4a. This common practice has a mathematical interpretation that can facilitate the derivation of error bounds.

Modeling defects by any convex shape corresponds to measuring distance for critical area under a corresponding convex distance function. For example, the circular defect corresponds to measuring distance in the ordinary Euclidean way, where the Euclidean distance between two points $p = (x_p, y_p)$ and $q = (x_q, y_q)$ is $d_e(p, q) = \sqrt{(x_q - x_p)^2 + (y_q - y_p)^2}$. The square defect model corresponds to computing distances in the L_∞ metric, where the L_∞ distance between two points $p = (x_p, y_p)$ and $q = (x_q, y_q)$ is $d_\infty(p, q) = \max\{|x_p - x_q|, |y_p - y_q|\}$. Computing distances in the L_1 (Manhattan) metric, where $d_1(p, q) = |x_p - x_q| + |y_p - y_q|$, corresponds to a square diamond defect (a square rotated by 45°). The *k-gon distance* between two points p, q is the size of the smallest k-gon P touching p and q, where the size can be naturally defined either in terms of the diameter* or the width† of P. Depending on whether the diameter or the width of the k-gon is used to define size, the k-gon metric can be regarded as a generalization of the L_1 or the L_∞ metric respectively in $k/2$ directions. For example, the distance functions implied by Figure 37.4c and d can be defined as generalizations of the L_1 and the L_∞ metric, respectively.

The critical area computed under these metrics can serve as an upper bound to the Euclidean critical area of circular defects, for example, the L_∞ metric or the metric of Figure 37.4d, or as a lower bound, for example, the L_1 metric and the metric of Figure 37.4c. A worst-case bound of 2 for critical area between square and circular defects is given in Ref. [31]. Often in practice, the purpose of critical area computation is the prediction of relative yield. That is, predict how a new design will yield in comparison to existing designs by comparing their critical areas. In this respect, the consistency of the defect model is far more important than the actual numerical values. In the following, we review the main computational paradigms that have been proposed for the extraction of critical area.

37.3.2.1.1 Statistical Methods

There have been two types of statistical methods proposed for critical area estimation at the chip level: Monte Carlo simulation [32,33] and layout sampling [34]. Monte Carlo simulation has been the oldest and the most widely implemented technique. The method is as follows: Draw a large number of defects with their radii distributed according to $D(r)$, check for each defect if it causes a fault, and divide the number of defects causing faults with the total number of defects. The main advantage of the Monte Carlo method is simplicity and the ease to conceptualize the procedure necessary to detect almost any type of failure mechanism. A tool can potentially be constructed upon most design rule checking (DRC) platforms. The method is computationally intensive. A naive implementation could

---

* The radius of the regular k-gon P is the distance from the center of P to any of its vertices. The diameter is twice the radius.
† The width of a regular k-gon, for an even k, is the distance between two parallel edges of P.

result in prohibitively long runtimes. However, adaptive sampling and adaptive integration techniques can greatly benefit the basic method. Distributed processing can significantly improve performance further as reported in Ref. [35]. Despite potential inefficiencies, the Monte Carlo simulation method is widely accepted and it provides a good standard for comparison.

Layout sampling, in combination with a deterministic method to compute critical area over a layout window, can give an alternative statistical technique to estimate the critical area of an entire chip. Layout random sampling in combination with standard shape-shifting techniques to compute critical area were introduced in Ref. [34]. The method works as follows: Randomly sample the layout to obtain random sample windows, compute critical area in every sample using a deterministic method, and combine results on sample windows to obtain a critical area estimate for the entire chip. Stratified sampling can increase the accuracy of the prediction by dividing the layout area into a number of regions (strata) for which critical area is estimated using sampling techniques. The performance as well as the accuracy of the sampling methodology depends heavily on the method to generate samples as well as on the method to compute critical area in a selected sample. Details of the method as implemented in the EYES system combining stratified random sampling and shape-shifting techniques are given in Ref. [34].

37.3.2.1.2 Deterministic Iterative Methods

Critical area estimation methods in this category iteratively compute $A(r)$, the critical area for a specific defect size r, for several different values or r. Those values are then interpolated with the defect density function $D(r)$ to approximate the total critical area integral. The majority of these methods are based on shape-shifting techniques (see, e.g., Refs. [36–38]). For shorts, the typical shape-shifting method to compute $A(r)$ can be described as follows:

1. Expand each geometry shape by $r/2$
2. Compute the region of overlap among two or more shapes in different nets
3. Let the area of the resulting region be $A(r)$

The main advantage of the shape-shifting methods is the ease of implementation using widely available shape-manipulation functions through most DRC platforms. The disadvantage is that step 2 can be expensive demonstrating quadratic behavior even for smart scanline type of implementations. The reason is that the number of intersections between the expanded polygons, denoted as I, can be $\Omega(n^2)$, where n is the number of edges of the original shapes, especially for medium- or large-defect radii r. Even in the case where $O(N \log N)$ type of efficient scanline algorithms are used to compute the area of overlap (see, e.g., Refs. [36,37]), N has a quadratic flavor because $N = \Omega(I + n)$ and $I = \Omega(n^2)$. As a result, shape-shifting methods work well for small to medium values of r; however, they break down when trying to compute the entire critical area integral for a sizable layout because of the quadratic time required to compute $A(r)$ for medium or large values of r. The layout hierarchy can substantially speed up the computation of $A(r)$ (see, e.g., Ref. [39]) for regular designs up to medium values of r. Hierarchical processing, however, becomes less useful as the value of the defect radius r increases providing no benefit beyond a certain threshold.

For Manhattan layouts (i.e., layouts consisting of axis parallel shapes only) and square defects there are additional more efficient methods in this category that require an initial decomposition of shapes into rectangles [40,41]. Reference [41] is a scanline approach that first computes susceptible sites (rectangular regions defined by the original layout shapes that provide defect susceptibility information), then manipulates (shrink/expand) those susceptible sites to compute critical regions for a given defect size r, and finally computes $A(r)$ as the total area of those critical regions (each critical region is a rectangle). The method in Ref. [40] can be regarded as a reverse shape-shifting method that first computes $A(r_{max})$ for the maximum defect size r_{max} and then iteratively determines $A(r)$ for smaller radii r. The method can be summarized as follows: (1) Compute all maximum-critical-area rectangles (called Max-CARs) by expanding all layer rectangles by r_{max} and determining all overlapping pairs of rectangles such that the two rectangles belong to different nets. Max-CARs are collected into buckets, one bucket per net pair. (2) Given a defect radius r, the critical-area rectangles for r (called CARs) in each bucket are readily available by shrinking the Max-CARs by $\Delta r = r_{\max} - r$. (3) Let $A(r)$ be the total area of all computed CARs for defect of radius r. Computing the Max-CARs of step 1 is a rather expensive operation performed only once. The area of N rectangles can be efficiently computed in $O(N \log N)$ time using interval trees (see, e.g., Ref. [42]) and thus, once the Max-CARs are available, $A(r)$ can be computed efficiently for a number of radii r. The number N however, of Max-CARs or CARs can be large, that is $\Omega(n^2)$, where n is the number of layout edges. Clearly the number of CARs reduces as the defect radius r decreases and thus performance depends on the size of $r_{\max}$.

Most of the investigation on critical area extraction in this category has been done for shorts. Opens have been studied less and are often approximated as a dual problem, substituting shape-expansion by shape-shrinking enhanced with other shape manipulation operations to derive critical regions. The reader is referred to Ref. [43] for details on such a treatment of opens based on DRC operations. Via blocks are also treated in Ref. [43] for a simplified definition where a defect is considered a fault if it simply overlaps any portion of a contact or via. For a discussion on the sensitivity of via chains to metal opens and via opens see Ref. [44].

37.3.2.1.3 Voronoi (Noniterative) Deterministic Method

This method, originally proposed in Refs. [31,45], computes the entire critical area integral in $O(n \log n)$ time, where n is the number of layout edges, in a single pass of the layout. It is based on the following concept: Divide the area of the layout into small regions such that critical area within each region is easy to compute. The total critical area integral can be derived as the summation of all partial critical areas obtained within each region. Assuming that within each layout region the critical area integral can be computed accurately, the total critical area of the layout can be easily extracted once the appropriate layout subdivision is available. The well-known concept of a Voronoi diagram can help obtain the appropriate layout subdivision needed for each type of fault.

The Voronoi diagram of a set of polygonal sites is a partitioning of the plane into regions, one for each site, called Voronoi regions, such that the Voronoi region of a site s is the locus of points closer to s than to any other site. The Voronoi region of s is denoted as reg (s) where s is the owner of reg (s). The boundary that borders two Voronoi cells is called a Voronoi edge, and consists of portions of bisectors between the owners of the neighboring cells. The bisector of two polygonal objects (such as points or segments) is the locus of points equidistant from the two objects. The point where three or more Voronoi edges meet is called a Voronoi vertex. Figure 37.5 illustrates the Voronoi diagram of polygons under the L_∞ distance metric. The Voronoi diagram can be regarded as an encoding of nearest neighbor information. The combinatorial complexity of the Voronoi diagram is linear in the number of the original sites.

The critical radius of a layout point t, denoted $r_c(t)$, is the radius of the smallest defect centered at t causing a circuit fault. Given a layer of interest C, and a fault type, the Voronoi method subdivides C into regions such that for any point t the critical radius is easy to compute. In particular, $r_c(t)$ is given by the distance of t from the layout element owning the region where t belongs. In the L_∞ metric (similarly for L_1 and the octagon metric), $r_c(t)$ becomes a simple linear function allowing for simple critical area integration. In the following we indicate the Voronoi diagram for shorts and refer the reader to Refs. [31,46] for the case of opens and via-blocks. The L_∞ metric is assumed throughout the section. The concepts are easily extendible to the octagon metric with some penalty in the complexity of the Voronoi diagram construction (see, e.g., Ref. [47] for k-gons). For circular defects no analytical formulation for critical area integration is known.

37.3.2.1.3.1 Voronoi Diagram for Shorts

A short at a layout point t is a defect centered at t overlapping with at least two shapes in two different nets. Let P to be the polygon nearest to t. The critical radius of t is determined by the second nearest polygon to t, say Q, such that Q is in a different net than P, and $r_c(t) = d(t, Q)$. Thus,

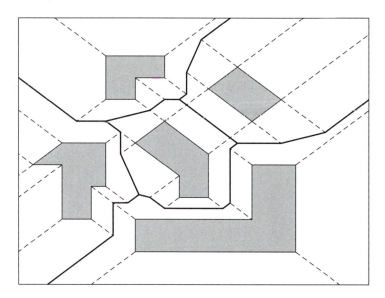

FIGURE 37.5 L_∞ Voronoi diagram of polygons. (Reproduced from Papadopoulou, E. and Lee, D.T., *IEEE Trans. Comput. Aided Des. Integr. Circuits Syst.*, 18, 463, 1999.)

second nearest neighbor information is needed, which can easily be obtained by the second-order Voronoi diagram on the layer of interest defined as follows: For every polygon P partition, the interior of reg(P) by the Voronoi diagram of all polygons other than P. In Figure 37.6, the thick lines illustrate the second-order subdivision of reg(P), where P is shown in dotted lines. Note that only Voronoi neighbors of reg(P) can contribute to the second-order subdivision of reg(P). More formally, given a layer C, the second-order Voronoi region of an element $s \in C - P$ within the Voronoi cell of P is defined as $\text{reg}_P(s) = \{x \mid d(s,x) \leq d(t,x), \forall t \in C - P\}$. For any point $t \in \text{reg}_P(s)$, $r_c(t) = d(t,s)$. To avoid counting shorts between disjoint polygons of the same net, any neighboring Voronoi regions of the same net can be united before the second-order Voronoi computation.

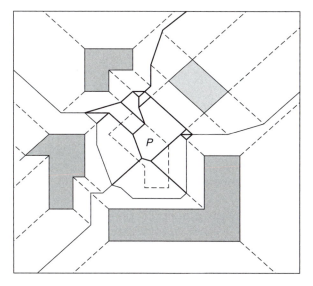

FIGURE 37.6 Second-order L_∞ Voronoi diagram in reg(P). (Reproduced from Papadopoulou, E. and Lee, D.T., *IEEE Trans. Comput. Aided Des. Integr. Circuits Syst.*, 18, 463, 1999.)

37.3.2.1.3.2   Critical Area Integration

Let us assume that the appropriate Voronoi subdivision of a layer for a fault type is available. Each Voronoi region can be partitioned into simple subregions such as rectangles and triangles (assuming the L_∞, L_1, or octagon metric), where the critical area integral can be computed analytically given the defect size distribution $D(r)$. Once analytic formulas are established for each type of simple region, the total critical area integral can be derived as a simple summation of those formulas. As formulas are analytic, there is no integration error. In Refs. [45,48] analytic formulas were derived for the widely used defect size distribution $D(r) = 1/r^3$ assuming the L_∞ metric and were shown to simplify into terms derived directly from Voronoi edges. As a result, critical area extraction becomes trivial once the appropriate Voronoi diagram is computed. In case $A(r)$, the critical area for a given specific defect size r, is also needed, it can be easily derived in linear time from the same Voronoi subdivision of the layout.

37.3.2.1.3.3   Scanline Construction of the Voronoi Diagram

The Voronoi diagram of a layout can be constructed by a scanline approach as described in Refs. [45,48] for the L_∞ metric. The main advantage of the scanline construction is the low memory requirement for critical area computation. For critical area extraction, there is never any need to keep the Voronoi diagram of the entire layout in memory. Instead, only a portion of the Voronoi diagram near the scanline is maintained. As soon as the Voronoi cell of a polygon or a net is computed, second-order computation and critical area computation within that cell can be performed and the Voronoi cell can be immediately discarded. As a result, the layout can remain in a compact hierarchical form while the scanline incrementally flattens keeping only a small neighborhood of the design flat at a time near the scanline. The time complexity of the scanline algorithm to compute the L_∞ Voronoi diagram is $O(n \log n)$, where n is the number of input layout edges, that is, the size of the layout. The second-order Voronoi diagram within the Voronoi cell of a polygon is computed in the same way maintaining the same time complexity. Critical area integration is then easily done in linear time. Thus, the entire critical area integral can be computed accurately in one scanline pass of the layout in $O(n \log n)$ time.

Results on the wide use of the Voronoi method to compute critical area and predict yield by IBM Microelectronics are given in Ref. [49].

37.3.2.1.3.4   Other Noniterative Approaches

The grid method of Ref. [26] assumes a fine grid over the layout and uses it to perform critical area integration. The grid resolution can provide a trade-off between accuracy and speed. The method computes the critical radius for every grid point and uses this information to compute the critical area integral. The approach is appropriate for an interactive tool and can be sped up as shown in Ref. [45].

FedEx [50] is a fault extractor for shorts. That is, instead of computing critical area, it extracts a list of all two node intralayer bridges (shorts). It also computes approximate weighted critical area for each bridge, and provides approximate fault locations. As pointed out in Ref. [50] FedEx trades accuracy for speed and memory. It assumes Manhattan layouts. FedEx starts with a hierarchical design description, incrementally flattens the layout, and writes bridging faults out in a flat manner. For circuit and fault extraction uses a scanline algorithm that first converts polygons into rectangles. Memory consumption is relatively small as only a moving window of geometry is kept, that is, approximately $O(\sqrt{n})$, where n is the size of the layout (number of rectangles). Bridge fault sites are written flat to the output file. There are several performance similarities between FedEx and the Voronoi method. Both methods start with a hierarchical design using a scanline that only locally sees the layout geometry flat. Memory consumption is relative small as only a neighborhood of the design near the scanline is kept in memory. The first-order Voronoi diagram of the layout geometry also provides information on same layer two node bridges as obtained by FedEx. FedEx outputs fast an approximate critical area for each bridge and the Voronoi method uses the second-order Voronoi diagram to obtain an accurate same layer critical area number maintaining an $O(n \log n)$ worst-case performance.

37.4 METHODS FOR YIELD OPTIMIZATION

Aggressive technology scaling has made process variation control from purely manufacturing perspective very tough. Design-related yield losses have been projected to increase [51], which implies greater cooperation between physical design and process communities is necessary. Yield optimization methods work with the measure, model, and mitigate flow. Measurements are usually done by targeted test structures, which are measured on silicon for physical parameters like linewidth and thickness as well as electrical parameters like sheet resistance and transistor saturation current. A good publication to keep track of for those interested in test-structure design and measurement is ICMTS [52]. Models of process extracted from such test-structure measurements are usually abstracted to simpler models or a set of rules for physical design and verification tools to use. In this section, we briefly discuss the evolution of yield optimization physical design techniques.

37.4.1 CRITICAL AREA AND CATASTROPHIC YIELD OPTIMIZATION METHODS

Back-end-of-the-line yield and manufacturability optimization is a complicated task. Methods for yield improvement vary ranging from critical-area-based wire spreading, metal fill, and the development of new rules and optimization for routers. We start with a review of available methods for wire spreading and critical area reduction.

Methods for critical area reduction fall into two broad categories: methods that alter the topology of the layout by attempting critical area optimization at the routing phase and methods used as a postprocessing step that keep the layout topology fixed while attempting to alleviate congestion and increase wire spacing. The two categories can be regarded complementary and both can be incorporated into the design cycle.

In the first category, the most representative method is Ref. [53], where a general routing cost function is described that takes into account critical area in conjunction with traditional routing objectives. The cost function combines most types of major defects, that is, shorts, opens, number of vias, and pinhole defects. Results verify that taking critical area into account at the routing phase can result in effective critical area reduction and therefore effective optimization for yield. In Ref. [54], channel routing is modified to reduce critical area between wire segments. Reference [54] also minimizes the number of vias as their presence increases manufacturability complexity and degrades the yield.

The methods in the second category attempt to redistribute spacing between adjacent wires without changing the layout topology. They are usually based on compaction techniques using the following observation: In a VLSI layout, distances between shapes can vary as long as the minimum value imposed by the design rules is met. Slack between two shapes is defined by the difference of the current distance between the two shapes and the minimum distance required by the design rules. Carefully redistributing the slacks can result in a layout with a better yield. Several slack redistribution techniques have been proposed, see Refs. [55–58]. In their majority, they are based on principles of layout compaction and are formulated as a one-dimensional layout optimization problem. They start with a constraint graph representation of the layout and perform layout modification for yield in one direction at the time, using in majority a one-dimensional yield objective function. The main drawback of a one-dimensional yield objective function is that, although it optimizes for critical area in one direction, it fails to take into consideration a potential critical area increases in the orthogonal direction. Figure 37.7 illustrates one such situation where movement of a layout element in one direction decreases critical area in one direction but increases critical area in the orthogonal direction. To address this problem, Ref. [57] combines the one-dimensional movement for slack redistribution with a two-dimensional yield objective.

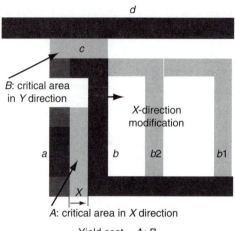

FIGURE 37.7 Movement of wire *b* in *x*-direction decreases critical area in *x*-direction but increases critical area in *y*-direction. (Reproduced from Heng, F.L. and Chen, Z., VLSI yield enhancement through layout modification, IBM T.J. Watson Research Report, 1999.)

The first compaction based algorithm to improve yield was given in Ref. [55]. A heuristic algorithm increases the spacing of layout objects through a series of spacing iterations in one direction. Only objects off the critical path are allowed to move maintaining the original layout area. The defect sensitivity of open-circuit type faults is reduced by increasing the width of certain noncritical elements in the layout. In Ref. [56] the slack redistribution problem in one direction was transformed into a network flow problem, which can be solved via the fast wirelength minimization algorithm of Ref. [59]. The layout is represented by a constraint graph where a node corresponds to a layout object and an edge links the nodes of two adjacent layout objects. The cost of each graph edge is an estimate of the fault probability between the two corresponding objects, expressed as a function of the length of the graph edge, that can be approximated by a convex piecewise linear cost function. Another one-dimensional compaction based formulation is given in Ref. [58] where first the critical area rectangles for one chosen defect size are computed. The standard compaction area optimization objective is enhanced with the additional terms of minimizing the critical area rectangles, which are reduced into functions of original layout variables. In this manner, the original compaction algorithm is upgraded with yield enhancement without introducing extra variables or constraints.

A noncompaction-based approach in this category is based on postroute optimization using a rubber-band wiring model [60]. The layout is given in a rubber-band sketch (RBS) form, which represents every layer of interconnect as a set of flexible rubber-bands with elastic properties. Wire spreading is achieved by estimating the critical area of the RBS and exploiting the flexibility of the rubber band behavior while maintaining wire connectivity. For more information see Ref. [60]. Heuristic layout changes to improve yield are described in Ref. [61] through the use of a set of local rules for contacts, metal and polysilicon layers. A system that allows the user to first evaluate layout modifications by applying them to samples only of the chip layout, rather than the entire layout, is described in Ref. [62]. The results from these samples can be used to define the modifications to be applied to the whole chip.

An effective way to reduce open faults is the introduction of redundant interconnects. Using redundant interconnects, the potential for open faults reduces at the cost of increasing the potential for shorts. By trading off, the two overall design reliability can increase. The problem was formulated in Ref. [63] as a variant of the classic 2-edge connectivity augmentation problem taking into account a wirelength increase budget, Steiner points, and routing obstacles. The formulation is as follows:

Manhattan routing tree augmentation (MRTA) problem: Given a rectilinear feasible routing region (FRR), a rectilinear Steiner routing tree T within FRR, and a wirelength budget W, find a set of augmenting paths. A within the FRR such that the total length of augmenting paths is at most W, and the total length of edges of T that ate nonbridges in $G = T \cup A$ is maximum.

An cxact algorithm based on an integer programming formulation, and a greedy heuristic algorithm that iteratively adds an augmenting path between vertices were given in Ref. [63]. Experimental results show that the greedy augmentation method achieves significant increase in reliability, as measured by the percentage of biconnected tree edges, with only small increase in wirelength.

In addition to reducing the potential for opens, redundant interconnects have also been proposed in clock networks to overcome the clock skew variation problem. In Ref. [64] cross links are inserted to a regular clock tree converting it to a nontree with lower skew variability and only a small increase in wirelength.

Redundant via insertion provides another effective way of increasing design reliability and yield. Vias have an inherently low reliability (e.g., due to stress related via voids) and thus redundant via insertion is a good solution to reduce the yield loss by via failure. Typically redundant via insertion is done postrouting on a "wherever space is available" basis but considering redundant vias in detailed routing also has been proposed [65]. Note that an increased number of vias could have a negative impact in terms of routing area and may reduce critical area for via blocks at the cost of increasing the critical area for shorts. Overall, however, making appropriate trade-offs design reliability can increase considerably.

Antenna fixes is another topic for improving design reliability. Because VLSI layers are formed one at a time during fabrication, dangling metal1 routes (e.g., nets not yet fully fabricated) connected to the polygate can cause stray charge deposition on gate damaging it. Methods to correct such situations include inserting jumpers in routes such that the maximum dangling route length is limited (see e.g., Ref. [66]). Diffusions diodes can also be inserted to provide a discharge path if space is available.

37.4.2 DESIGN RULES

The abstraction of manufacturing constraints into a set geometric of constraints or design rules, for the layout designers to follow, has traditionally been the foundry's main method to ensure a high probability of correct fabrication of integrated circuits. Typical design rules are constraints on width, spacing, or pattern density. The origins of design rules lie in the constraints imposed by various manufacturing steps such as lithography, etch, implant, and CMP. Other factors influencing design rule values include preserving scaling, area overhead, layout migratability,* and the ability of design tools and flows to handle them.

Manufacturability implications of technology scaling have led to three major trends in design rules:

- More complicated rule sets. The sheer number of design rules has been growing at a rapid pace with every technology generation. More process constraints have required new kinds of rules [67,68]. This has made physical verification, routing as well as custom layout very difficult and time-consuming tasks.
- Restrictive design rules. To cope with sub-100 nm manufacturability concerns where manufacturing equipment is not keeping pace with feature scaling, radically restraining layout options has been proposed as a viable option [69,70]. One common restriction is to enforce regularity in layout that aids printability. An example of such a rule is allowing only one or two pitches on the polysilicon layer.

---

* The automatic migration of layouts from one technology generation to next is an important concern, especially for custom layouts.

- DFM rules. Most 90 and 65 nm design rule manuals include a separate set of nonminimum design rules. These design rules if obeyed by the layout, enhance its manufacturability. For example, the minimum metal-via enclosure can be 20 nm while the corresponding DFM rule can be 30 nm. The increased enclosure can reduce chances of loss of contact between metal route and via at the cost of increased routing area.

Though design rules have served the industry well in the past as the abstraction layer, the inadequacy and suboptimality of such yes/no rules has led to a slow but steady adoption of model-based checking methods [68].

37.4.3 CORNER-BASED DESIGN ANALYSIS

Traditionally, static timing and power analysis tools have relied on two or more corners of process, voltage, and temperature or PVT. We are not going to discuss operating variations such as voltage fluctuations and temperature gradients here. Timing corners are typically specified as slow (S), typical (T), or fast (F). Thus, SS represents a process corner with slow PFET and slow NFET behavior. The common performance analysis process corners are (TT, SS, FF, SF, FS). Similarly, interconnect parasitics are extracted at multiple (usually two) corners. A more systematic approach to determine interconnect R/C corners is given in Ref. [71]. Usually, hold time violations are checked at the FF corner and setup time violations are checked at the SS corner. Similarly, interconnect parasitics can also have typical, minimum, and maximum values. The rationale for corner-based analyses lies in the fact that ensuring correct operation of the design at the PVT extrema ensures correct operation throughout the process and operation range. This assumption, though not strictly correct, usually holds well in practice. Corner-based analysis enables pessimistic but deterministic analysis and optimization of designs. Most modern physical design algorithms rely on corner-based design being acceptable. Sub-100 nm process issues (especially variability) have led to the following trends in corner-based design analysis and optimization.

- More corners. As more complicated process effects emerge and as a result of nonmonotone dependence of delay on many of the process parameters, the number of PVT corners at which a design needs to be signed off is increasing.
- On chip variation (OCV) analysis. To model within-die variation in static timing tools implicitly analyze clock paths and data paths at separate corners [72]. For example, for setup time analysis, the launching clock path may be analyzed at a slow corner while the capturing clock is analyzed at a fast corner and the data path is analyzed at the slow corner. This in essence tries to model the worst-case impact of on chip variation. Additional techniques such as common path pessimism removal (CPPR), which figures out the shared logic between launching and capturing paths to avoid pushing them to different corners, are used to reduce the inherent pessimism in OCV analysis.

Though the runtime overhead of ever-increasing number of corners, the excess pessimism in corner-based analysis and fear of missing some corners in a high process-variability regime has led to an increasing interest in statistical analysis tools, corner-based design deterministic design optimization still remains mainstay of commercial parametric yield optimization.

37.4.4 FUTURE OF PARAMETRIC YIELD OPTIMIZATION

As mentioned earlier, explicit parametric yield analysis and optimization is a relatively new field of research. Several interesting published works in the past few years have attempted to deal with the problem of manufacturing variability.

37.4.4.1 Methods for Systematic Variability

There are several pattern-dependent process effects, which are systematic in nature. These can be compensated for during physical design to aid manufacturability and hence improve yield. The largest contributors in this bucket are CMP and photolithography. Metal filling and slotting techniques for CMP are discussed elsewhere in the book. Traditionally, design rules have been the method to optimize for systematic variation. Recently, more explicit mitigation of impact of systematic variation on circuit power and performance has been studied. For instance, some methods have tried to reduce CD variability by avoiding lithography-induced forbidden pitches during detailed placement [73] or detailed routing [74,75]. Making circuit more robust to focus variations has been studied in Refs. [76,77].

37.4.4.2 Statistical Optimization

Just as statistical analyses, statistical physical design is an active area of research with very little in terms of well-accepted methods of optimization. Deterministic physical design tends to generate a wall of slack. As the number of uncorrelated critical paths increase in a design, any of them can pop up to being critical and hence be the determinant of circuit delay. As a result, a higher wall of slack can mean a slower circuit delay distribution. Intentional under-optimization by assigning a penalty to paths that are close to critical has been suggested as a simple technique to overcome this issue [78]. Another approach in same vein assigns a delay penalty to every gate proportional to its delay variability [79] and uses standard static timing analysis in optimization. Other approaches explicitly rely on a statistical timing engine in a statistical sensitivity [80,81] or nonlinear programming based optimization [82]. The largest challenge in statistical physical design besides computational complexity is accurate modeling of physical reality. For example, ignoring parametric or spatial correlations (i.e., assuming independence or perfect correlation between performance or process random variables) can undo any benefit from statistical optimization.

37.5 CONCLUSION

In this chapter, we have touched upon various sources of manufacturing yield loss in modern sub-micron processes. We have briefly described methods of yield calculation and optimization with emphasis on well-known methods related to random-defect driven yield loss. We have also discussed the emerging area of parametric yield analysis and optimization in physical design.

REFERENCES

1. International Technology Roadmap for Semiconductors: Yield Enhancement. http://public.itrs. net, 2005.
2. Z.G. Song, S.P. Neo, S.K. Loh, and C.K. Oh. Root cause analyses of metal bridging for copper damascene process. In *International Symposium for Testing and Failure Analysis*, 2005.
3. Richard Goering. 90-, 65-nm yields prey to leakage. *EE Times*. http://www.eetimes.com/news/latest/showArticle.jhtml?articleID=172303036, October 24, 2005.
4. W.-B Jone and K.S. Tsai. Confidence analysis for defect-level estimation of VLSI random testing. *ACM Transactions on Design Automation of Electronic Systems*, 3(3):389–407, July 1998.
5. S. Pateras, J. Hussain, and T. Martis. Reducing leakage-induced field returns. Whitepaper Logicvision Inc., 2005.
6. C. Constantinescu. Trends and challenges in VLSI circuit reliability. *IEEE Micro*, 23(4):14–19, July–August 2003.
7. M. Abramovici, M.A. Breuer, and A.D. Friedman. *Digital Systems Testing and Testable Design*. John Wiley & Sons, New York, 1994.
8. M. Orshansky and K. Keutzer. A general probabilistic framework for worst-case timing analysis. In *Proceedings of the ACM/IEEE Design Automation Conference*, pp. 556–561, 2002.

9. H. Chang and S.S. Sapatnekar. Statistical timing analysis considering spatial correlations using single PERT-like traversal. In *Proceedings of the IEEE/ACM International Conference on Computer-Aided Design*, pp. 621–625, 2003.

10. A. Agarwal, D. Blaauw, and V. Zolotov. Statistical timing analysis for intra-die process variations with spatial correlations. In *Proceedings of the IEEE/ACM International Conference on Computer-Aided Design*, pp. 900–907, 2003.

11. C. Visweswariah, K. Ravindran, K. Kalafala, S.G. Walker, and S. Narayan. First-order incremental block-based statistical timing analysis. In *Proceedings of the ACM/IEEE Design Automation Conference*, pp. 331–336, 2004.

12. International Technology Roadmap for Semiconductors: Front End Processes. http://public.itrs.net, 2005.

13. S.-D. Kim, H. Wada, and J.C.S. Woo. TCAD-based statistical analysis and modeling of gate line-edge roughness effect on nanoscale mos transistor performance and scaling. *IEEE Transactions on Semiconductor Manufacturing*, 17(2):192–200, May 2004.

14. P. Gupta, A.B. Kahng, C.-H. Park, K. Samadi, and X. Xu. Wafer topography-aware optical proximity correction. *IEEE Transactions on Computer-Aided Design of Integrated Circuits and Systems*, 25(12):2747–2756, December 2006.

15. S. Borkar, T. Karnik, S. Narendra, J. Tschanz, A. Keshavarzi, and V. De. Parameter variations and impact on circuits and microarchitecture. In *Proceedings of the ACM/IEEE Design Automation Conference*, pp. 338–342, 2003.

16. D. Boning and S. Nassif. Models of process variations in device and interconnect. In A. Chandrakasan, W.J. Bowhill, and F. Fox, Eds., *Design of High-Performance Microprocessor Circuits*, pp. 98–116. Wiley-IEEE Press, New York, 2000.

17. C. Visweswariah. Death, taxes and failing chips. In *Proceedings of the ACM/IEEE Design Automation Conference*, pp. 343–347, 2003.

18. R.R. Rao, A. Devgan, D. Blaauw, and D. Sylvester. Modeling and analysis of parametric yield under power and performance constraints. *IEEE Design & Test*, 22(4), 376–385, July–August 2005.

19. H. Chang and S.S. Sapatnekar. Full-chip analysis of leakage power under process variations, including spatial correlations. In *Proceedings of the ACM/IEEE Design Automation Conference*, pp. 523–528, 2005.

20. A. Srivastava, D. Sylvester, and D. Blaauw. *Statistical Analysis and Optimization for VLSI*. Springer, Boston, MA, 2005.

21. L. Chen, L. Milor, C. Ouyang, W. Maly, and Y. Peng. Analysis of the impact of proximity correction algorithms on circuit performance. *IEEE Transactions on Semiconductor Manufacturing*, 12(3):313–322, August 1999.

22. M. Orshansky, L. Milor, and C. Hu. Characterization of spatial intrafield gate CD variability, its impact on circuit performance, and spatial mask-level correction. *IEEE Transactions on Semiconductor Manufacturing*, 17(1):2–11, February 2004.

23. P. Gupta and F.-L. Heng. Toward a systematic-variation aware timing methodology. In *Proceedings of the ACM/IEEE Design Automation Conference*, pp. 321–326, 2004.

24. J. Yang, L. Capodieci, and D. Sylvester. Advanced timing analysis based on post-OPC extraction of critical dimensions. In *Proceedings of the ACM/IEEE Design Automation Conference*, pp. 359–364, 2005.

25. C.H. Stapper. Modeling of integrated circuit defect sensitivities. *IBM Journal of Research and Development*, 27(6):549–557, November 1983.

26. I.A. Wagner and I. Koren. An interactive VLSI CAD tool for yield estimation. *IEEE Transactions on Semiconductor Manufacturing*, 8(2):130–138, May 1995.

27. W. Maly. Computer-aided design for VLSI circuit manufacturability. In *Proceedings of the IEEE*, pp. 356–392, February 1990.

28. A.V. Ferris-Prahhu. *Introduction to Semiconductor Device Yield Modeling*. Artech House, Norwood, MA, 1992.

29. A.V. Ferris-Prabhu. Role of defect size distribution in yield modeling. *IEEE Transactions on Electron Devices*, 32(9):1727–1736, September 1985.

30. A.V. Ferris-Prabhu. Defect size variations and their effect on the critical area of VLSI devices. *IEEE Journal of Solid State Circuits*, 20(4):878–880, August 1985.

31. E. Papadopoulou. Critical area computation for missing material defects in VLSI circuits. *IEEE Transactions on Computer-Aided Design of Integrated Circuits and Systems*, 20(5):583–597, May 2001.

32. H. Walker and S.W. Director. VLASIC: A yield simulator for integrated circuits. *IEEE Transactions on Computer-Aided Design of Integrated Circuits and Systems*, 5(4):541–556, April 1986.

33. C.H. Stapper. Modeling of defects in integrated circuit photolithographic patterns. *IBM Journal of Research and Development*, 28(4):461–475, July 1984.

34. G.A. Allan. Yield prediction by sampling IC layout. *IEEE Transactions on Computer-Aided Design of Integrated Circuits and Systems*, 19(3):359–371, March 2000.

35. D.M.H. Walker and D.S. Nydick. DVLASIC; Catastrophic yield simulator in a distributed processing environment. *IEEE Transactions on Computer-Aided Design of Integrated Circuits and Systems*, 9(6): 655–664, June 1990.

36. G.A. Allan and A.J. Walton. Efficient extra material critical area algorithms. *IEEE Transactions on Computer-Aided Design of Integrated Circuits and Systems*, 18(10):1480–1486, October 1999.

37. I. Bubel, W. Maly, T. Wass, P. Nag, H. Hartmann, D. Schmitt-Landsiedel, and S. Griep. AFFCA: A tool for critical area analysis with circular defects and lithography deformed layout. In *Proceedings of the IEEE International Workshop on Defect and Fault Tolerance in VLSI Systems*, pp. 10–18, 1995.

38. A.L. Jee and F.J. Ferguson. CARAFE: An inductive fault analysis tool for CMOS VLSI circuit. In *Proceedings of the IEEE VLSI Test Symposium*, pp. 92–98, 1992.

39. P.K. Nag and W. Maly. Hierarchical extarction of critical area for shorts in very large ICs. In *Proceedings of the IEEE International Workshop on Defect and Fault Tolerance in VLSI Systems*, pp. 19–27, 1995.

40. S. T. Zachariah and S. Chakravarty. Algorithm to extract two-node bridges. *IEEE Transactions on VLSI Systems*, 11(4):741–744, April 2003.

41. J. Pineda de Gyvez and C. Di. IC defect sensitivity for footprint-type spot defects. *IEEE Transactions on Computer-Aided Design of Integrated Circuits and Systems*, 11(5):638–658, May 1992.

42. M. de Berg, M. van Kreveld, M. Overmars, and O. Schwarzkopf. *Computational Geometry, Algorithms and Applications*. Springer-Verlag, Berlin, Germany, 1997.

43. W.A. Pleskacz, C.H. Ouyang, and W. Maly. Extraction of critical areas for opens in large VLSI circuits. *IEEE Transactions on Computer-Aided Design of Integrated Circuits and Systems*, 18(2):151–162, 1999.

44. D.K. de Vries and P. L. C. Simon. Calibration of open interconnect yieldmodels. In *Proceedings of the IEEE Intermational Symposium on Defect and Fault Tolerance in VLSI Systems*, pp. 26–33, 2003.

45. E. Papadopoulou and D.T. Lee. Critical area computation via Voronoi diagrams. *IEEE Transactions on Computer-Aided Design of Integrated Circuits and Systems*, 18(4):463–474, April 1999.

46. E. Papadopoulou. The Hausdorff Voronoi diagram of point clusters in the plane. *Algorithmica*, 40:63–82, December 2004.

47. Z. Chen, E. Papadopoulou, and Jinhui Xu. Robustness of k-gon Voronoi diagram construction. *Information Processing Letters*, 97(4):138–145, February 2006.

48. E. Papadopoulou and D.T. Lee. The l_∞ Voronoi diagram of segments and VLSI applications. *International Journal of Computational Geometry and Applications*, 11(5):503–528, October 2001.

49. D.N. Maynard and J.D. Hibbeler. Measurement and reduction of critical area using Voronoi diagrams. In *Advanced Semiconductor Manufacturing IEEE Conference and Workshop*, 2005, pp. 243–249.

50. Z. Stanojevic and D.M.H. Walker. FedEx–A fast bridging fault extractor. In *Proceedings of the IEEE International Test Conference*, pp. 696–703, 2001.

51. K. Wu, D. Thon, and P. Mayor. Collaborative DFM critical for enabling nanometer design. FSA Fabless Forum. http://www.fsa.org/publications/forum/article.asp?article=0503/wu, March 2005.

52. IEEE International Conference on Microelectronic Test Structures.

53. E.P. Huijbregts, H. Xue, and J.A.G. Jess. Routing for reliable manufacturing. *IEEE Transactions on Semiconductor Manufacturing*, 8(2), 188–194, May 1995.

54. S.Y. Kuo. YOR: A yield optimizing routing algorithm by minimizing critical areas and vias. *IEEE Transactions on Computer-Aided Design of Integrated Circuits and Systems*, 12(9):1303–1311, September 1993.

55. V.K.R. Chiluvuri and I. Koren. Layout synthesis techniques for yield enhancement. *IEEE Transactions on Semiconductor Manufacturing*, 8(2):178–187, May 1995.

56. C. Bamji and E. Malavasi. Enhanced network flow algorithm for yield optimization. In *Proceedings of the ACM/IEEE Design Automation Conference*, pp. 746–751, 1996.

57. F.L. Heng and Z. Chen. VLSI yield enhancement through layout modification. IBM T.J. Watson Research Report, 1999.

58. Y. Bourai and C.J.R. Shi. Layout compaction for yield optimization via critical area minimization. In *Design and Test in Europe*, pp. 122–125, 2000.

59. R. Varadarajan and G. Lakhani. A wire length minimization algorithm for circuit layout compaction. In *Proceedings of the IEEE International Symposium on Circuits and Systems*, 1987, pp. 276–279.

60. J.Z. Su and W. Dai. Post route optimization for improved yield using a rubber-band wiring model. In *Proceedings of the IEEE/ACM International Conference on Computer-Aided Design*, pp. 700–706, 1997.

61. G.A. Allan and A.J. Walton. A yield improvement technique for IC layout using local design rules. *IEEE Transactions on Computer-Aided Design of Integrated Circuits and Systems*, 11(11):1355–1360, November 1992.

62. G.A. Allan. Targeted layout modifications for semiconductor yield/reliability enhancement. *IEEE Transactions on Semiconductor Manufacturing*, 17(4):573–581, November 2004.

63. A.B. Kahng, B. Liu, and I.I. Mandoiu. Non-tree routing for reliability and yield improvement. *IEEE Transactions on Computer-Aided Design of Integrated Circuits and Systems*, 23(1):148–156, January 2004.

64. A. Rajaram, J. Hu, and R. Mahapatra. Reducing clock skew variability via cross links. In *Proceedings of the ACM/IEEE Design Automation Conference*, pp. 18–23, 2004.

65. G. Xu, L. Huang, D.Z. Pan, and M.D.-F. Wong. Redundant-via enhanced maze routing for yield improvement. In *Proceedings of the Asia-South Pacific Design Automation Conference*, 2005, pp. 1148–1151.

66. B.-Y. Su, Y.-W. Chang, and J. Hu. An optimal jumper insertion algorithm for antenna avoidance/fixing on general routing trees with obstacles. In *Proceedings of the ACM International Symposium on Physical Design*, 2006, pp. 56–63.

67. A.B. Kahng. Research directions for coevolution of rules and routers. In *Proceedings of the ACM/IEEE International Symposium on Physical Design*, pp. 122–125, 2003.

68. P. Rabkin. DFM for advanced technology nodes: Fabless view. *Future Fab International*. Issue 20. http://www.future-fab.com, 2006.

69. L. Liebmann, G. Northrop, J. Culp, L. Sigal, A. Barish, and C. Fonseca. Layout optimization at the pinnacle of optical lithography. In *Proceedings of SPIE*, vol. 5042, pp. 1–14, 2003.

70. M. Lavin, F.-L. Heng, and G. Northrup. Backend cad flows for restrictive design rules. In *Proceedings of the IEEE/ACM International Conference on Computer-Aided Design*, p. 739746, 2004.

71. N. Chang, V. Kanevsky, O.S. Nakagawa, K. Rahmat, and S.-Y. Oh. Fast generation of statistically-based worst-case modeling of on-chip interconnect. In *Proceedings of the IEEE International Conference on Computer Design*, 1997, 720–725.

72. M. Weber. My head hurts, my timing stinks, and I don't love on-chip variation. In *SNUG*, Boston. http://www.siliconlogic.com/pdf/OCVstinks_MattWeber_SLE.pdf, 2002.

73. P. Gupta, A.B. Kahng, and C.-H. Park. Enhanced resist and etch CD control by design perturbation. In *Proceedings of the 25th SPIE BACUS Symposium on Photomask Technology and Management*, 2005, pp. 3P1–3P11.

74. S.C. Shi, A.K. Wong, and T.-S. Ng. Forbidden-area avoidance with spacing technique for layout optimization. In *Proceedings of SPIE Design and Process Integration for Microelectronic Manufacturing II*, Vol. 5379, pp. 67–75, 2004.

75. J. Mitra, P. Yu, and D.Z. Pan. RADAR: RET-aware detailed routing using fast lithography simulations. In *Proceedings of the ACM/IEEE Design Automation Conference*, 2005, pp. 369–372.

76. P. Gupta, A.B. Kahng, Y. Kim, and D. Sylvester. Self-compensating design for focus variation. In *Proceedings of the IEEE/ACM Design Automation Conference*, pp. 365–368, 2005.

77. A.B. Kahng, S. Muddu, and P. Sharma. Defocus-aware leakage estimation and control. In *Proceedings of the International Symposium on Low Power Electronics and Design*, pp. 263–268, 2005.

78. X. Bai, C. Visweswariah, P.N. Strenski, and D.J. Hathaway. Uncertainty-aware circuit optimization. In *Proceedings of the IEEE/ACM Design Automation Conference*, pp. 58–63, 2002.

79. S. Boyd, S.-J. Kim, D. Patil, and M. Horowitz. A heuristic method for statistical digital circuit sizing. In *Proceedings of the SPIE International Symposium on Microlithography*, 2006, pp. 08-1–08-9.

80. M.R. Guthaus, N. Venkateswaran, C. Visweswariah, and V. Zolotov. Gate sizing using incremental parameterized statistical timing. In *Proceedings of the IEEE/ACM International Conference on Computer-Aided Design*, pp. 1029–1036, 2005.

81. M. Hashimoto and H. Onodera. A performance optimization method by gate sizing using statistical static timing analysis. In *Proceedings of the ACM International Sympoium on Physical Design*, pp. 111–116, 2000.

82. E.T.A.F. Jacobs and M.R.C.M. Berkelaar. Gate sizing using a statistical delay model. In *Proceedings of Design and Test in Europe*, pp. 283–290, 2000.

38 Manufacturability-Aware Routing

Minsik Cho, Joydeep Mitra, and David Z. Pan

CONTENTS

38.1   INTRODUCTION

Nanometer very large scale integration (VLSI) design is facing increasing challenges from manufacturing limitations, arising from factors such as printability issues because of deep subwavelength lithography, topography variations because of chemical–mechanical polishing (CMP), and random defects because of missing/extra material, the via void. Thus, for nanometer designs, conventional design closure may not lead to closure in manufacturing because of yield factors. It has been shown, however, that the majority of the yield loss is strongly layout-dependent (as demonstrated in Chapters 35 through 37), and therefore, manufacturability-aware layout optimization can play a key role in the overall yield improvement of a design.

In this chapter, we focus on manufacturability-aware routing. Although manufacturability considerations may be brought to bear on earlier design stages such as logic synthesis and placement [1–3], routing is often believed to be one of the most effective stages to address the manufacturability issues because of the following reasons [4–7]: (1) the key manufacturing issues (e.g., topography variation because of CMP, random defects, lithography, and redundant vias) are tightly coupled with the distribution of interconnects, which is mainly determined by routing; (2) routing is the last major VLSI physical design step before manufacturing, and thus it has more a comprehensive and accurate picture on the expected manufacturability; (3) routing still has considerable design flexibility to find a reasonable trade-off between manufacturability and conventional design objectives (e.g., timing, noise, power). These factors have led to strong recent academic and industrial efforts in manufacturability-aware routing.

In general, routing consists of two steps: global routing and detailed routing. Global routing plans an approximate path for each net, while detailed routing finalizes the exact design rule checker (DRC)-compatible pin-to-pin connections [8]. Track routing, as an intermediate step between global and detailed routing, can expedite detailed routing by embedding major trunks from each net within a panel (a row/column of global routing cells) in DRC-friendly manner [9]. Manufacturability-aware routing can be accomplished at any stage of routing system if proper manufacturing model is available, and the approaches can be roughly classified into two groups: rule-based and model-based. The rule-based approach imposes additional manufacturability-driven design rules on a router to avoid manufacturability-unfriendly patterns. The model-based approach utilizes some models to estimate the manufacturability effects to guide router. There are pros and cons for both the rule-based and the model-based approaches, in terms of runtime, scalability, implementation, and controllability.

This chapter surveys recent practices and researches on manufacturability-aware routing. Before discussing key techniques, the major manufacturability challenges for advanced technologies is discussed in Section 38.2. Then, we compare the pros and cons of the rule-based and model-based approaches in Section 38.3. In practice, both approaches are used where the model-based approach can be used for optimization and the required rules must be satisfied, in particular, at the detailed routing stage. Section 38.4 then goes into details of various key aspects of manufacturability-aware routing optimizations, including CMP-aware routing, random defect-aware routing, lithography-aware routing, etc. Section 38.5 discusses techniques for dealing with manufacturing rules at the detailed routing stage. We will use a few examples to show how these rules are becoming more complicated (largely owing to lithography-related matters) and the key issues in addressing them. Finally, we conclude in Section 38.6.

38.2 MAJOR MANUFACTURABILITY ISSUES

In this section, we give an overview of the major manufacturing issues for 90-nm technology node and below, and analyze their causes and effects: (1) printability issues owing to subwavelength lithography systems [10,11], (2) random defects owing to missing/extra material, (3) topography variations owing to CMP, and (4) other causes such as via failure and antenna effect [12,13].

A fundamental limitation for the subwavelength optical lithography is WYSINWYG, i.e., "what you see (at design) is not what you get (at fab)." The printability issue arises between neighboring wires/vias because of subwavelength effects and process variations. As of now, the 193-nm (wavelength) optical lithography is still the dominant integrated circuit manufacturing process for 90-nm and 65-nm nodes. It is likely to remain so for 45- and 32-nm technology nodes [14] because of tremendous efforts in the domain of resolution enhancement techniques (RET). However, if the initial design is very litho-unfriendly, even aggressive RET may not be able to solve the printability problem. Thus, the routing stage should strive hard to construct only litho-friendly and printable layouts. It should noted that litho-aware routing is more general than the restrictive design rules (RDR), which, at this time, have mostly been adopted so far for the poly-layer [15–18].

The reduced feature sizes in nanometer VLSI designs make them more vulnerable to random defects, which can be further divided into open or short defect [19,20]. Both defects are at the back-end-of-line (BEOL) [21], and cause electrical opens or shorts between interconnects. Although it is generally believed that the yield loss because of systematic sources is greater than that because of random defects during the technology and process ramp-up stage, the systematic yield loss can be largely eliminated when the process becomes mature and systematic variations are extracted/compensated. On the other hand, the random defects that are inherent owing to manufacturing limitations will still be there even for mature fabrication processes. Thus, their relative importance will indeed be larger for mature process with systematic variations designed in Ref. [5]. A more detailed introduction on random defect is provided in Chapter 37.

Topography (thickness) variations owing to dishing and erosion after CMP are shown to be systematically determined by wire density distribution [22–26]. Even after CMP, intrachip topography variation can still be on the order of 20–40 percent [22,27]. Such topography variations lead to not only significant performance degradation owing to increased wire resistance and capacitances, but also acute manufacturing issues such as etching and printability owing to defocus [22,25–27]. The detailed description of their impact on design and manufacturability can be found in Chapter 36.

The main reason for CMP problems is related to the wire density distribution. Higher wire densities usually lead to copper thickness reduction owing to erosion after CMP [23,24], making wire resistances worse. Moreover, the reduced copper thickness after CMP can worsen the scattering effect, further increasing resistance [28].

A via may fail due to various reasons such as random defects, electromigration, cut misalignment, or thermal stress-induced voiding effects. Redundant vias (or double vias) can be inserted to build fault-tolerance into the interconnect. Redundant vias are known to be highly effective, leading to 10–100x lower failure rate [29]. Another reliability problem that during the fabrication process arises from charges from plasma etching can be accumulated in long floating wires. Such charges may create high current to the thin-oxide gate (Fowler–Nordheim tunneling current), and cause permanent damage to the gate. This is known as the antenna effect [13]. There are three kinds of solutions to prevent the antenna effect: protection diode embedding, diode insertion after placement and routing, and jumper insertion. Although the first two solutions need extra area for the inserted diode, jumper insertion incurs overhead in the routing system as it inserts additional vias [30].

These challenges will be the primary optimization target in manufacturability-aware routing, which our discussion in Sections 38.4 and 38.5 is mainly centered on.

38.3 RULE-BASED APPROACH VERSUS MODEL-BASED APPROACH

Techniques for manufacturability-aware routing can be categorized into the rule-based approach and the model-based approach. In this section, we discuss the pros and cons of each class of approaches, in terms of complexity and efficiency.

The rule-based approach extends the conventional design rules, i.e., a set of rules that must be observed by designers/tools, by introducing a new set of manufacturability-aware rules. These new manufacturability-aware rules can be required/hard rules, or recommended/soft rules. Because existing routing systems have been based on design rules for decades [31], the rule-based approach is friendly to the conventional design flow, which makes them seemingly easy to implement and apply. However, there can be several problems with this approach:

1. The number of such manufacturability-aware rules is increasing exponentially with each new technology node. For example, although the number of rules is only a few dozen at the 180-nm node, it reaches to several hundred at the 65-nm node. Moreover, design rules between similar objects may work differently depending on the design context.
2. The complexity of checking such rules becomes more computationally expensive, as the rules are becoming increasingly context-sensitive [10,32,33]. For example, the minimum spacing between wires may depend on the wirelengths and the wires in the neighborhood, as shown in an example in Figure 38.1. Therefore, simply checking rules by itself needs considerable amount of computing resource.
3. The rules are binary in nature, i.e., a design may either follow the rule or violate the rule, and thus the rule-based approach does not provide smooth trade-off with yield.
4. The rules themselves may be too restrictive and pessimistic, leading to a sacrifice in performance. In some cases, it may be infeasible to achieve the performance goals because of overguard banding from the rules. Furthermore, the rules may not be accurate enough to model very complicated manufacturing processes, in particular for the future deeper subwavelength lithography systems.

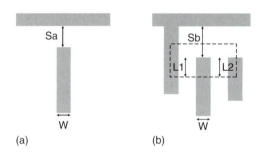

(a)   (b)

Description	Rule (μm)
Minimum spacing (*Sa*) between a metal and the end of line of the metal whose edge with (*W*) <=0.2 μm	0.12 μm
Minimum spacing (Sb) between a metal and the end of line of the metal whose edge with (*W*) <=0.2 μm, if there exist objects in the influence region on both sides with parallel overlap (L1 and L2)	0.14 μm
Otherwise, minimum spacing	0.11 μm

FIGURE 38.1 Context-dependent minimum spacing rule for 65-nm technology. Each case, (a) and (b), is described in the table. (From Cong, J., Tutorial presentation at the *IEEE/ACM International Conference on Computer-Aided Design*, San Jose, CA, 2006.)

Because of these limitations of the rule-based approach, there have been significant ongoing efforts in developing the model-based approach in both academia and industry, expecting that models will capture manufacturing effects more accurately at affordable computational overhead, when coupled with a small number of simple design rules. For example, the model-based approach may involve lithography system modeling where the light will pass through the mask and react with the chemicals on the surface of the wafer, resulting in printed structures.

The challenge with the model-based approach is in abstracting a set of reasonably accurate yet high-fidelity models at various abstraction levels to guide physical layout optimizations. A typical manufacturing system involves nonlinear optical, chemical, electrical, and mechanical processes, which could be extremely complicated to model accurately and mathematically. On the other hand, the models have to be compact and efficient to be embedded in the already time-consuming VLSI routing system. Therefore, the key technical bottleneck for model-based manufacturability-aware routing is to develop simple/compact yet effective/high-fidelity models, and apply them to existing routing flow in a seamless manner.

38.4   MANUFACTURABILITY-AWARE ROUTING OPTIMIZATION

In this section, we survey key manufacturability-aware routing optimization issues related to various aspects of manufacturability, including topography variations owing to CMP in Section 38.4.1, yield loss owing to random defects in Section 38.4.2, lithography-related printability in Section 38.4.3, and other issues such as via failure and antenna effect in Section 38.4.4. The optimization may be driven through models or some rules of thumb, depending on the nature of the optimization target.

38.4.1   CMP-Aware Routing for Topography Variation Minimization

As explained in Section 38.2, topography variation has significant impact on performance as well as printability. Widely adopted solutions to reduce the topography variation include dummy fill synthesis, where dummy features are inserted to increase copper density, and cheesing, which creates patterns of holes for fat/wide wires. The reader is referred to Chapter 36 for more details on CMP fill synthesis. However, these solutions have inherent limitations, as they are often performed after all the essential polygons are embedded, i.e., on GSDII files to mitigate the problems introduced by the upstream design stages. A more effective solution will build in intelligent CMP-awareness into the router, in particular at the global routing as CMP-induced variation is a coarse-grained variation.

CMP-aware rules include a certain maximum density rule, requiring that a density within any window of a given size should not exceed the maximum density threshold set by foundry. However, the maximum density rule does not explicitly address the topography variation problem, even though it may help to achieve more uniformness by reducing the range of density distribution.

In Ref.[6], a predictive copper (Cu) CMP model is proposed to evaluate the topography variation, and used to guide a CMP-aware global routing. Topography variation (thickness variation) after CMP is determined by the underlying metal density, contributed by both wires and dummies. As dummy fill in turn depends on wire density, the required dummy density and the Cu thickness can be predicted from a given wire density. In Figure 38.2a, the normalized Cu thickness change as a function of metal density, based on three industrial designs, is shown. For a given global routing cell v_i with a metal density m_i, the expected Cu thickness of v_i, t_i can be expressed as follows:

$$t_i = \alpha \left(1 - \frac{m_i^2}{\beta} \right) \qquad (0.2 \leq m_i \leq 0.8) \qquad (38.1)$$

where α and β are technology-dependent constants. Equation 38.1 requires the metal density m_i as an input, which is essentially the summation of the wire density w_i and the dummy density d_i in a global routing cell v_i. Figure 38.2b shows the required dummy density and the predicted Cu thickness with respect to wire density. For a given v_i, d_i can be looked up with w_i using Figure 38.2b, and then m_i can be obtained by adding w_i and d_i. Note that the metal density in real designs would neither fall below 20 percent with the aid of dummy fill nor rise above 80 percent owing to cheesing. Finally, the calculated m_i can be fed into Equation 38.1 to predict the Cu thickness t_i. This predictive model is verified with a commercial CMP simulator [34] and industry test cases. Intuitively, as copper is softer than dielectric material, a region with less copper will experience less erosion during CMP [25]. Therefore, a region with lower metal density will have higher copper thickness, and such region in turn needs more dummies to balance wire density distribution for less topography variation.

The illustration of the CMP-aware global routing is shown in Figure 38.3 where the predicted Cu thickness guides the global router for less topography variations. A unified metal density driven global router is proposed, which not only helps to reduce CMP-induced thickness variation, but also

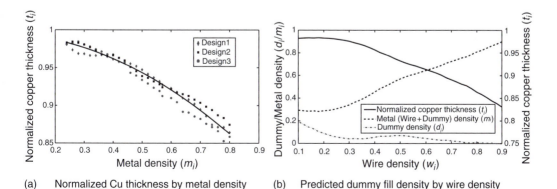

(a)   Normalized Cu thickness by metal density   (b)   Predicted dummy fill density by wire density

FIGURE 38.2 Predictive CMP model. (From Cho, M., Xiang, H., Puri, R., and Pan, D. Z., *Proceedings of the IEEE/ACM International Conference on Computer-Aided Design*, San Jose, CA, 2006, pp. 487–492. With permission.)

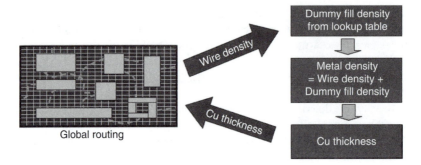

FIGURE 38.3 Illustration of CMP-aware global routing based on the predictive CMP model. (From Cho, M., Xiang, H., Puri, R., and Pan, D. Z., *Proceedings of the IEEE/ACM International Conference on Computer-Aided Design*, 2006, San Jose, CA, pp. 487–492. With permission.)

helps to improve timing. Promising experimental results are shown in Ref. [6], with 7.510 percent improvement for topography variation and timing and small runtime overhead.

38.4.2 CRITICAL-AREA-AWARE ROUTING FOR RANDOM DEFECT MINIMIZATION

Yield loss owing to random defects in general can be minimized by optimizing the critical area. As described in Section 37.3.2, the critical area is the region where, if a defect of the given size falls, a circuit will be opened or shorted [20,35]. Because of the importance of yield in semi-conductor industry, there have been considerable amount of efforts to enhance yield by reducing critical area in routing or postrouting. The probability of failure (POF) based on critical area analysis with defect size distribution is a widely used metric for yield prediction and optimization [19,20]. The defect size distribution $F(x)$ can be modeled as follows [20,36]:

$$F(x) = kx^{-r} \quad \text{for} \quad x_{min} \le x < \infty \qquad (38.2)$$

where
   x is the defect size
   x_{min} is the minimum resolvable lithographic feature size
   k is a coefficient to ensure $\int_{x_{min}}^{\infty} F(x)\mathrm{d}x = 1$
   $r \approx 3$ [37]

When the end effect is ignored [38], the critical area $A_i^o(x)$ for open defects on a wire W_i and the critical area $A_{ij}^s(x)$ for short defects between two parallel wires W_i and W_j can be approximated as follows [20,36,39]:

$$A_i^o(x) = \begin{cases} 0 & \text{for } 0 \le x < w_i \\ L_i(x - w_i) & \text{for } w_i \le x < 2w_i + S_{min} \\ L_i(w_i + S_{min}) & \text{for } 2w_i + S_{min} \le x < \infty \end{cases}$$

$$A_{ij}^s(x) = \begin{cases} 0 & \text{for } 0 \le x < s_{ij} \\ l_{ij}(x - s_{ij}) & \text{for } s_{ij} \le x < 2s_{ij} + W_{min} \\ l_{ij}(s_{ij} + W_{min}) & \text{for } 2s_{ij} + W_{min} \le x < \infty \end{cases}$$

$$(38.3)$$

where L_i, w_i, l_{ij}, and S_{ij} are the length of wire i, the width of wire i, the overlapped wirelength between wire i and j, and the spacing between wire i and j, respectively. The values of $A_i^o(x)$ and $A_{ij}^s(x)$ will saturate at defect sizes of $2s_{ij} + W_{min}$ and $2w_{iw} + S_{min}$, respectively [36]. Note that more detailed definition of critical area and various approaches to compute it are presented in Section 37.3.2. Then, the probability of failure owing to open defects on $W_i(\text{POF}_i^o)$ and owing to short defects between W_i and $W_j(\text{POF}_{ij}^s)$ on a given layer can be obtained as follows [20,36]:

$$
\begin{aligned}
\text{POF}_i^o &= \int_{x_{min}}^{\infty} F(x) \frac{A_i^o(x)}{A_{chip}} dx = \frac{kL_i}{2A_{chip}} \left(\frac{w_i + S_{min}}{2w_i^2 + S_{min}w_i} \right) \\
\text{POF}_{ij}^s &= \int_{x_{min}}^{\infty} F(x) \frac{A_{ij}^s(x)}{A_{chip}} dx = \frac{kl_{ij}}{2A_{chip}} \left(\frac{s_{ij} + S_{min}}{2s_{ij}^2 + W_{min}s_{ij}} \right)
\end{aligned}
\tag{38.4}
$$

where A_{chip} is the total chip area. As POF_i^o and POF_{ij}^s indicate the chance of having a random defect, yield can be improved by minimizing POF_i^o and POF_{ij}^s together, which can be accomplished by maximizing wire width (w_i) and wire spacing (s_{ij}), respectively. However, minimizing POF_i^o and POF_{ij}^s are two conflicting objectives, as larger w_i to decrease POF_i^o leads to smaller s_{ij} that increases POF_{ij}^s with a fixed routing area.

Yield optimization in channel routing is proposed in Refs. [40,41]. Weight interval graph is proposed [40] to facilitate the channel routing algorithm in Ref. [42] in a way that net merging in vertical constraint graph will minimize the number of channels as well as critical area. In Ref. [41], a wire segment is shifted either from top layer to bottom layer (net burying) or vice versa (net floating), like wrong way routing to reduce critical area in a greedy manner. Critical area minimization based on Equation 38.4 during global routing is proposed in Ref. [43], where a linearized critical area is one of the cost factors in multicommodity flow optimization. Redundant link insertion technique to minimize open defect is proposed in Ref. [21]. Additional wires will increase the critical area for short defect. Assumption that the POF owing to open defects of a given size is much higher than the POF owing to short defects of identical size is not always valid, as it depends on design style as well as process technology [20].

Although some level of critical area reduction is achieved, there are a few drawbacks in these early works that are mostly performed at postrouting or late-stage optimizations: (1) one single defect size is considered, rather than a defect size distribution [40,41]; (2) the trade-off between open and short defects owing to fixed routing area is ignored [21,40,41,44,45]; (3) localized/greedy optimization is performed, which may be suboptimal [21,44,46–48]; and (4) wire adjacency information is not available for accurate critical-area estimation [38,43].

In Ref. [5], the random defect issue is addressed at the track routing stage, which provides reasonable details to model random defect-induced yield loss, while also providing much more flexibility than the detailed-routing or postrouting optimization. The proposed TROY algorithm, based on mathematical programming and graph theory, attempts to find the best trade-off between open and short defects with respect to a defect size distribution through effective wire planning (wire ordering, sizing, and spacing). The mathematical formulation for the yield-driven track routing is as follows:

$$
\begin{aligned}
\text{min}: \quad & \alpha \sum_i \text{POF}_i^o + (1-\alpha) \sum_{i,j>i} \text{POF}_{ij}^s \\
\text{s.t.}: \quad & |p_i - M_i| \le d_i && \forall\, i \\
& S_{min} \le s_{ij} \le p_i - p_j - \frac{(w_i + w_j)}{2} + (1 - o_{ij})N && \forall\, i,j \\
& S_{min} \le s_{ij} \le p_j - p_i - \frac{(w_i + w_j)}{2} + o_{ij}N && \forall\, i,j \\
& o_{ij} \in \{0, 1\} && \forall\, i,j \\
& B_k + \frac{w_i}{2} \le p_i \le T_k - \frac{w_i}{2} && \forall\, i \in P_k \\
& W_{min} \le w_i \le W_{max} && \forall\, i
\end{aligned}
$$

However, this formulation is an integer nonlinear programming problem that is prohibitively expensive to solve. The key strategy in Ref. [5] is that POF_i^o and POF_{ij}^s in Equation 38.4 can be simplified into simpler convex forms as in Equation 38.5 and if the wire-ordering o_{ij} (thus, n_i as well) is known, the wire sizing and spacing problem for yield optimization can be formulated as the second-order cone programming (SOCP) shown below, which can be solved optimally and efficiently.

$$
\begin{aligned}
\min : \quad & \alpha \sum_i [\delta_i + \left(1 - \frac{b}{a}\right) d_i] + (1 - \alpha) \sum_{i,j} \gamma_{ij} \\
\text{s.t.} : \quad & |p_i - M_i| \le d_i && \forall\, i \\
& S_{\min} \le s_{ij} = p_i - p_j - \frac{w_i + w_j}{2} && \forall\, o_{ij} = 1, \forall\, j \in n_i \\
& l_{ij} W_{\min} \le s_{ij} \gamma_{ij} && \forall\, i, \forall\, j \in n_i \\
& L_i S_{\min} \le w_i \delta_i && \forall\, i \\
& B_k + \frac{w_i}{2} \le p_i \le T_k - \frac{w_i}{2} && \forall\, i \in P_k \\
& W_{\min} \le w_i \le W_{\max} && \forall\, i
\end{aligned}
$$

The wire ordering optimization is performed by finding the minimum Hamiltonian path. The experimental results are promising, with 18 percent improvement in terms of random-defects induced yield loss.

$$
\begin{aligned}
POF_i^o &\approx \frac{kL_i}{2A_{\text{chip}}} \left(a \frac{S_{\min}}{w_i} - b \right) \left(1 \le \frac{w_i}{S_{\min}} \le 40 \right) \\
POF_{ij}^s &\approx \frac{kl_{ij}}{2A_{\text{chip}}} \left(a \frac{W_{\min}}{s_{ij}} - b \right) \left(1 \le \frac{s_{ij}}{W_{\min}} \le 40 \right)
\end{aligned}
\tag{38.5}
$$

38.4.3 LITHOGRAPHY-AWARE ROUTING FOR PRINTABILITY

Optical projection systems in modern optical-lithography technology usually use partially coherent illumination. An illustration of a typical optical-lithography system is shown in Figure 38.4. Because a partially coherent system can be approximately decomposed into a small number of P fully coherent systems [4,49], the aerial image intensity $I(x, y)$ at the point (x, y) can be shown as follows by approximating Hopkins equation [50] through kernel decomposition [51]:

$$
I(x, y) = \sum_{i=0}^{P-1} \left| \sum_{j \in W_{(x,y)}} (F_j \odot K_i)(x, y) \right|^2
\tag{38.6}
$$

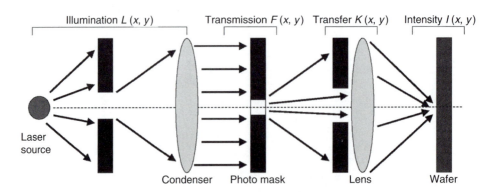

FIGURE 38.4   Illustration of optical lithography system for VLSI manufacturing.

where

K_i is the transfer function for the ith fully coherent optical subsystem

F_j is the transmission function (1 over clear regions and 0 over opaque regions) of the jth rectangle in effective window $W(x, y)$, the intensity support region of the control point at location (x, y)

The size of the $W(x, y)$ depends on the wavelength and numerical aperture of the optical system, but in general is about 1–4 µm. Based on Equation 38.6, lithography simulations can be performed to obtain aerial images and then printed silicon images.

The first attempt to address the lithography problem in routing is the optical proximity correction (OPC)-aware maze routing work in Ref. [4]. Based on aerial image simulation, it stores the expected OPC cost in a lookup table, which has the information on the interference from patterns at different length by distance. While routing a new pattern, the interferences from all existing patterns in its influence window are looked up from the table, and then summed up to evaluate the total optical interference from existing patterns. Meanwhile, the optical interference (OPC cost) on existing patterns owing to the new pattern is estimated using the maximum interference on these patterns. Figure 38.5 shows an example of optical interference lookup table. Then, a vector-weighted graph method is applied to map the grid routing model to a graph, where the edge cost is a vector consisting of the interferences from existing patterns as well as the interference of a new pattern to existing patterns. With such vector-weighted graph, OPC-aware maze routing can be casted as multiconstrained shortest path problem, which is then solved by Lagrangian relaxation. It should be noted that optical interference is not a direct lithography metric, such as the edge placement error (EPE) widely used in OPC algorithms.

Another lithography-aware maze routing algorithm is proposed in Ref. [52], where a table of EAD (electric amplitude of diffraction) is prebuilt, and the OPC error is estimated as the square of the accumulated EAD values from the patterns within process window. Then, it greedily performs maze routing such that a routed path for each net does exceed neither OPC error threshold nor path length

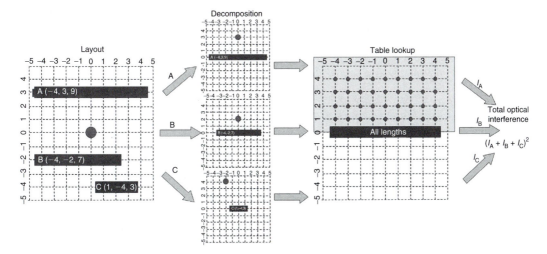

FIGURE 38.5 There patterns (A, B, and C) are within the effective window of the point (0,0) in the layout, and each effective pattern is denoted by the left most edge coordinate and its length. The layout is decomposed for each effective pattern that is further located in the center of the decomposed window. The optical interference is simulated for all lengths of patterns centered at the origin, and the interference information on every point above each pattern is kept in the lookup table. Therefore, the interferences from A, B, and C can be looked up from the table according to the length, then added up to compute the total optical interference energy. (From Huang, L. and Wong, D. F., Optimal proximity correction (OPC) friendly maze routing, in *Proceedings of the ACM/IEEE Design Automation Conference*, pp. 186–191, June 2004. With permission.)

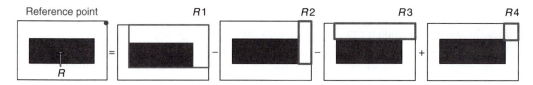

FIGURE 38.6 Convolution lookup for fast lithography simulation. (From Mitra, J., Yu, P., and Pan, D.Z., RADAR: RET-aware detailed routing using fast lithography simulations, in *Proceedings of the ACM/IEEE Design Automation*, pp. 369–372, June 2005. With permission.)

constraint. Again, it should be noted that the EAD square metric is not a direct/verified lithography measurement.

The RADAR work [7] is the first attempt to directly link a lithography simulator (using the direct EPE metric) to detailed routing. Based on fast lithography simulation techniques that are more suitable for full-chip simulations, it generates the so-called lithography hotspot maps to guide the postrouting optimization, namely wire spreading and rip-up/rerouting. As an example to measure the lithography and RET effort, the EPE metric is used. To compute EPE efficiently, Ref. [7] utilized effective kernel decomposition method and fast table-lookup techniques. In the kernel decomposition based simulation, a core computational step is the convolution term. Because of the linearity of convolution in Equation 38.6, the convolution for any arbitrary rectangle inside the effective window can be decomposed into four upper-right rectangles that can reduce the table size significantly [7], as shown in Figure 38.6. Therefore, the linear combination of the convolutions of $R1$, $R2$, $R3$, and $R4$ can be used to compute the aerial image of R. After the EPE map is obtained from fast lithography simulations, wire spreading and rip-up/rerouting can be applied to reduce the EPE hotspots and to improve printability. The fast lithography simulator is called during the routing modification if needed to make sure no new lithography hotspots occur. Figure 38.7 shows an example of RADAR for EPE hotspot reduction. The result implies that both wire spreading and rip-up/rerouting are effective in reducing EPE hotspots, but rip-up/rerouting can be more effective than wire spreading with less wirelength overhead.

Similar rip-up/rerouting approach is proposed later on in Ref. [53]. But different from Ref. [7], effective pattern searching is adopted, i.e., a set of known undesirable patterns are stored/matched to identify lithography hotspots. Then, the identified undesirable routing patterns are either removed or modified by performing rip-up/rerouting. Recently, a multilevel routing approach to minimize the number of OPC features is studied in Ref. [54]. A simple OPC cost that becomes higher for

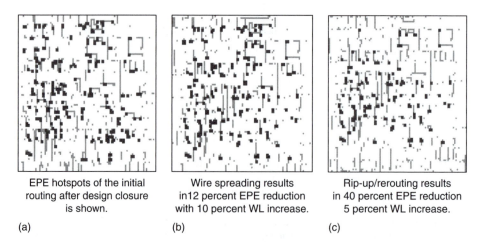

| (a) | (b) | (c) |
| EPE hotspots of the initial routing after design closure is shown. | Wire spreading results in12 percent EPE reduction with 10 percent WL increase. | Rip-up/rerouting results in 40 percent EPE reduction 5 percent WL increase. |

FIGURE 38.7 RADAR example. (From Mitra, J., Yu, P., and Pan, D. Z., *Proceedings of the ACM/IEEE Design Automation Conference*, Anaheim, CA, 2005, pp. 369–372. With permission.)

longer and wider wires is proposed, and applied as a factor in maze routing. It should be noted that the lithography-aware routing is still in its infancy, and there are many research issues to achieve a holistic understanding for it.

38.4.4 Redundant-Via- and Antenna-Effect-Aware Routings

The first redundant-via-aware routing is presented in Ref. [12]. The problem is formulated as multi-objective maze routing by assigning redundant-via cost to the routing graph, and solved by applying Lagrangian relaxation technique. In Ref. [29], the redundant via is reflected as a factor in the maze routing cost. Each original via has different number of possible redundant-via locations, namely degree of freedom (DOF). Wherever a wire occupies a possible redundant-via location during maze routing, it is inversely penalized by DOF of its corresponding original via.

In postlayout optimization, redundant-via insertion is one of the key steps for yield improvement. In Ref. [55], the redundant-via insertion problem is formulated as a maximum independent set (MIS) problem by constructing a conflict graph. Figure 38.8 shows an illustration of the approach in Ref. [55], where each original via from 1 to 5 needs one redundant via. For such original vias, there can be up to four redundant-via candidates as for via 2 in Figure 38.8a ($U2$, $R2$, $D2$, $L2$). Each redundant-via candidate will be a vertex in the conflict graph as in Figure 38.8b, unless it has electrical/rule violations with other redundant vias (no $U6$ owing to electrical violation). An edge between vertices (redundant vias) will be created, if either both belong to the same original via or two redundant vias have conflict as in Figure 38.8b. Then, finding MIS from the conflict graph in Figure 38.8b is equivalent to maximum redundant-via insertion. Because solving MIS is an NP-hard problem, a heuristic approach is adopted in Ref. [55]. Different redundant-via insertion solutions, based on geotopography information, are proposed in Ref. [56], where a redundant via is tried for each original via in a greedy manner. However, as an excessive number of vias can even worsen yield, redundant-via insertion under via-density constraint is required, which is addressed in Ref. [57] based on integer linear programming.

While via failure can occur during either fabricating or operating a chip, antenna effect occurs during manufacturing process. The first work in antenna avoidance is presented in Ref. [58] and further improved later [59] where rip-up/rerouting strategy is used. Another work on antenna avoidance during full chip-level routing is discussed in Ref. [60]. While these works try to address antenna effect during routing, there are another set of works to fix antenna issue during postlayout optimization as in redundant-via insertion. In Ref. [61], antenna avoidance is achieved by a layer assignment technique based on tree partitioning. Regarding diode and jumper insertion, the research in Ref. [62]

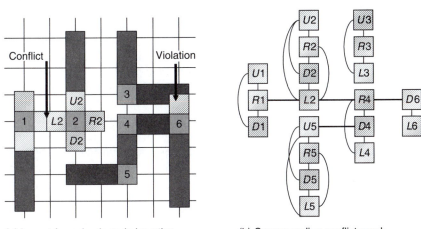

(a) Layout for redundant-via insertion   (b) Corresponding conflict graph

FIGURE 38.8   Redundant-via insertion problem in postlayout optimization can be formulated as MIS problem by constructing conflict graph.

proposes a diode insertion and routing algorithm by using minimum-cost network flow optimization, and Ref. [63] proposed an optimal algorithm for jumper insertion. However, both the diode and jumper insertion approaches only try to fix antenna problem either by diode or jumper insertion alone. The interaction between diode and jumper insertions is not taken into consideration, as diode or jumper insertion can be cheaper than one another depending on the design context. The work in Ref. [64] combines diode and jumper insertions for optimal simultaneous diode/jumper insertion, based on minimum-cost network flow optimization.

38.5   DEALING WITH MANUFACTURING RULES DURING DETAILED ROUTING

The previous section mostly focuses on manufacturability/yield optimization at various stages of routing, driven by certain manufacturing models/metrics or rules of thumb. Although their main purpose is to improve manufacturability at the global scope, the final detailed routing still has to satisfy all the required design rules set by manufactures. These rules are contracts/guarantees from manufacturers. For nanometer designs, these required rules are becoming more and more complicated. In addition to the required rules, there can be many even more complicated recommended rules for manufacturability enhancement. This is a topic with very few publications, but it is often a designer's nightmare because of the explosion in the number of design rules at the detailed routing level.

In this section, we use several representative design rules (in a progressive more complex manner), extracted from advanced technologies, and illustrate how they are becoming more complicated, and outline approaches for dealing with them at a typical grid-based detailed routing. Some complex design rules, when decomposed, each may be equivalent to several simpler rules at early technology generations, and detailed routers could handle them either during the initial route creation process or iteratively through a subsequent rip-up/reroute step. In either case, this is a tedious and time-consuming process.

As design rules become more complex with each technology node, the effort of making detailed router free of these complex design-rule violations increases exponentially. Previously, what could be achieved simply by following minimum spacing requirements by keeping routes on certain uniform pitch is no longer sufficient under complex design rules in 65 nm and below. It is necessary to monitor design-rule compliance much more frequently. As shown in Figure 38.9, for 90 nm and above, the DRC compliance check is triggered usually after the routing for the entire net, but for 65 nm and below, such check is needed during the routing of the net, e.g., for all the connected components of the net on the same layer, before going to the next layer, etc. In the worst case, such DRC checking could happen after every routing rectangle is dropped by the router. The main issue and trade-off are then how to properly select the triggering events for DRC violations. This is mainly based on the candidate shapes being dropped, such as vias that may trigger a minimum edge rule check, as to be explained soon. Moreover, routers need to select DRC correction schemes that are manufacturing friendly, as several correction alternatives may exist. For example, it may be possible to select vias that introduce the least number of vertices by selecting vias whose landing pads are aligned with the adjacent routing segments.

We will now examine three representative classes of complex rules to get a flavor of the level of complexity that the newer generation of routers have to deal with. Each class is progressively more complex than the previous one. The first class of rules is just limited to violations on the same signal net. The second class of rules limits the violations to two signal nets. The third class of rules introduces violations between three or more signal nets.

38.5.1   REPRESENTATIVE RULE 1—MINIMUM EDGE RULE

An example of the minimum edge rule is shown in Figure 38.10a [65]. This rule essentially forbids the formation of consecutive edges with length below certain minimum threshold length T. This minimum edge design rule applies to physical components of the same signal net. First, we define

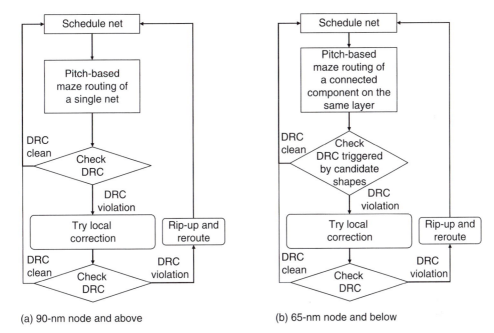

FIGURE 38.9 Typical DRC correction flow for a grid-based detailed routing system. The DRC check is more complex in 65-nm node and below than 90-nm node and above.

the concave and convex corners in Figure 38.10 as the corners with both adjacent edges less than the minimum threshold length T. There may be several variations of minimum edge rule, depending on the process technologies and routing layers where routing DRC is performed, e.g., any of the following three situations may be a minimum edge rule violation:

- Rule 1a: Formation of any concave or convex corner is a design rule violation.
- Rule 1b: The number of consecutive minimum edges (i.e., edges with length less than T) should be less than certain number (≥ 2). Otherwise, it is a design rule violation. Essentially, compared to Rule 1a, Rule 1b may allow formation of concave or convex corners up to certain point.
- Rule 1c: The same situation as in Rule 1b, but it further requires that the sum of these consecutive minimum edges is greater than another threshold for design rule violation. For example, in Figure 38.10a, there are three highlighted edges, A, B, and C, which are all minimum edges. If $A + B + C$ is larger than the threshold value, it will cause a design rule violation. Otherwise, it does not.

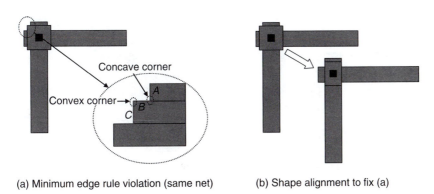

(a) Minimum edge rule violation (same net)   (b) Shape alignment to fix (a)

FIGURE 38.10 Example of the context-dependent minimum edge rules for 65-nm technology.

As can be seen from Figure 38.10a, this rule checking requires a router to perform a polygon analysis of composite shapes, to keep routes free of this design rule violation during routing construction. The challenge for a detailed router is when to trigger this analysis, as this is a rule for the same signal net and is polygon-based, whereas the routing shapes are usually rectangles. If the router is symbolic and center-line based, it needs to maintain a history of recent shapes that it has dropped to have enough information to perform this analysis. A history of only the previous shape will not suffice, because several overlapping shapes may comprise of a composite polygonal shape, which leads to this violation. Therefore, the router needs to maintain a history of at least three previous rectangles that it has dropped, to construct a composite polygon and detect the minimum edges. Moreover, the router needs to choose a proper correction method to remove any minimum-edge violations that may have been introduced. Several competing solutions may exist, such as shape alignment as shown in Figure 38.10b, via rotation, or even rerouting. The challenge would be how to select the most manufacturing-friendly one. All of the above detection and correction schemes are computationally intensive, and the router needs to have a proper trade-off between optimization during route creation or postroute correction.

38.5.2 Representative Rule 2—Width-Dependent Parallel-Length Spacing Rule

A second class of complex design rules—width-dependent parallel-run-length spacing rule—is shown in Figure 38.11a [65]. This is a spacing rule between two neighboring physical shapes on different signal nets. The spacing requirement changes depending on the context of the two physical shapes. If the width of either of the two shapes ($W1$ or $W2$) are within a certain range and the parallel run length (L) is also within a certain range, then the spacing (S) between the two shapes has to be greater than a certain threshold. There may be different spacing thresholds for various combinations of the ranges of the widths and lengths between the two shapes. In other words, this class of rules may be decomposed into two or more rules such as

- Rule 2a: If $A_1 \leq (W_1, W_2) \leq B_1$ and $C_1 \leq L \leq D_1$, then $S \geq S_1$.
- Rule 2b: If $A_2 \leq (W_1, W_2) \leq B_2$ and $C_2 \leq L \leq D_2$, then $S \geq S_2$.

The challenge for the router in this case is that this design rule involves both polygonal analysis within the connected physical components of the same signal net and area queries between different signal nets, to detect violating neighbors. Again, as in the minimal edge rule situation, a composite polygon and in particular wide wire of interest may be formed as the router may drop several overlapping shapes that trigger this rule checking/fixing. Hence, the router first needs to detect the formation of a composite wide wire and once detected, and then an area query needs to be triggered

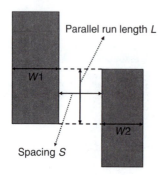

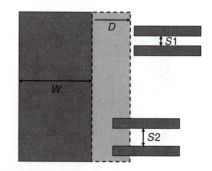

(a) Width-dependent parallel-length spacing rule   (b) Width-dependent influence spacing rule

FIGURE 38.11   Example of the context-dependent spacing rules for 65-nm technology.

to detect neighbors within the specified spacing threshold. Triggering a query based on composite wide wires while they are formed may not be sufficient, because new neighbors may be dropped later on (it should be noted that one of the two objects needs to meet the width threshold, not both). Therefore, to be safe, the router may need to either perform more frequent checks or perform a check at the end of completion of a fully connected physical component on the same layer. In this case, the only possible postroute corrections are reducing wire widths or rerouting. Hence, once again, several trade-offs between correct-by-construction routing and postrouting optimization or a hybrid approach need to be considered.

38.5.3   REPRESENTATIVE RULE 3—WIDTH-DEPENDENT INFLUENCE SPACING RULE

The third complex design rule involves with three or more nets, described as a width-dependent influence spacing rule shown in Figure 38.11b. It is more complicated than Rule 1, which involves only a single composite shape, and Rule 2, which involves the interaction between two disjoint objects/nets. Rule 3 involves the interaction of two or more shapes in the presence of a third composite wide shape. This rule has the following complex context:

- A wide wire whose width (W) is greater than some threshold
- Two or more shapes within a halo distance (D) of the above shape
- The spacing (S) between these two shapes being less than some threshold

If all of the above three situations occur simultaneously, we have an influence spacing-rule violation. Again, we first need to detect a wide-wire shape, which can be from several composite shapes. Because the rule violation has three conditions, the DRC checking may need to be triggered if any of the above three situations occur, which in the worst case could be during the dropping of any shape by the router. But doing such exhaustive checking would be too expensive. A reasonable trigger might be during the formation of a wide wire. However, as in the case of the parallel run-length rule, a neighbor within the halo distance D may appear after the wide wire has been formed. Thus, this is not a sufficient check. The router may also choose to be conservative and forbid any neighbor wires to enter the halo distance D regions from any wide wires, but this may lead to routability issues because we miss a lot of routing opportunities where this rule is not violated indeed. Therefore, the runtime and performance trade-off would be a major issue.

So far, we have discussed several representative required design rules in nanometer designs. In addition to hard constraints, nanometer designs (in 65 nm and below) have many manufacturability related recommended and soft rules for potential yield improvement, such as multicut redundant vias, vias with fatter enclosures, via and metal density requirements, etc. There are also some soft constraints for preferred versus nonpreferred routing directions. For example, routes in the nonpreferred direction or jogs are recommended to have wider widths owing to poor printability in the nonpreferred direction by specific lithographic systems. Manufacturability-aware routers attempt to follow these recommended rules, but not mandatory because there may be too many to follow, or too hard to implement them efficiently in the already highly complicated routing system.

38.6   CONCLUSION

Design for manufacturability (DFM) in nanometer integrated circuit (IC) designs has been drawing a lot of attentions from both academia and industry owing to its significant impact on manufacturing closure. This chapter surveys various key issues in manufacturability-aware routing, a crucial step in the DFM landscape, including model-based manufacturability optimization and rule-based yield improvement, as well as issues of how to deal with complex design rules. Although most current DFM solutions rely on either rule-based optimization or postlayout enhancement guided by modeling, there are tremendous ongoing research and development to capture the downstream manufacturing/process effects, and abstract them early on into the key physical design stage, through model-based manufacturability-aware routing optimization [4–7,53]. This will allow designers to perform more global optimization for manufacturability/yield in the context of other design objectives such as timing, power, area, and reliability. For rule versus model, we believe that the rule-based and model-based approaches will coexist and coevolve. Ultimately, a simple set of rules combined with powerful models would be ideal.

As manufacturability-aware routing is still at its early stage under heavy research, there are a lot of rooms to improve in terms of both process modeling/abstraction and DFM-routing algorithms/interfaces, to enable true design for manufacturing [66]. Most current optimizations for DFM are performed independently, but different DFM issues are indeed highly related with each other such as critical area, lithography, CMP, and redundant via. Improving one aspect (e.g., critical area) may make other aspects (e.g., lithography) worse, and vice versa. Therefore, holistic modeling and optimization of all key DFM effects into some global yield metric will be in great demand. This should be a future direction for manufacturability-aware routing.

ACKNOWLEDGMENTS

The author would like to thank Dr. Li-da Huang in Magma DA and Professor Martin D.F. Wong in UIUC for their help and support in making this work possible.

REFERENCES

1. A. Nardi and A. L. Sangiovanni-Vincentelli, Logic synthesis for manufacturability, in *IEEE Design and Test of Computers*, Vol. 21, pp. 192–199, May 2004.
2. P. Gupta, A. B. Kahng, and C.-H. Park, Detailed placement for improved depth of focus and CD control, in *Proceedings of the Asia and South Pacific Design Automation Conference*, Shanghai, China, pp. 343–348, Jan. 2005.
3. S. Hu and J. Hu, Pattern sensitive placement for manufacturability, in *Proceedings of the International Symposium on Physical Design*, Austin, TX, pp. 27–34, Mar. 2007.
4. L. Huang and D. F. Wong, Optical proximity correction (OPC)-friendly maze routing, in *Proceedings of the ACM/IEEE Design Automation Conference*, San Diego, CA, pp. 186–191, Jun. 2004.
5. M. Cho, H. Xiang, R. Puri, and D. Z. Pan, TROY: Track router with yield-driven wire planning, in *Proceedings of the ACM/IEEE Design Automation Conference*, San Diego, CA, pp. 55–58, Jun. 2007.
6. M. Cho, H. Xiang, R. Puri, and D. Z. Pan, Wire density driven global routing for CMP variation and timing, in *Proceedings of the IEEE/ACM International Conference on Computer-Aided Design*, San Jose, CA, pp. 487–492, Nov. 2006.
7. J. Mitra, P. Yu, and D. Z. Pan, RADAR: RET-aware detailed routing using fast lithography simulations, in *Proceedings of the ACM/IEEE Design Automation Conference*, Anaheim, CA, pp. 369–372, Jun. 2005.
8. J. Hu and S. Sapatnekar, A survey on multi-net global routing for integrated circuits, *Integration: The VLSI Journal*, 31: 1–49, Nov. 2002.
9. S. Batterywala, N. Shenoy, W. Nicholls, and H. Zhou, Track Assignment: A desirable intermediate step between global routing and detailed routing, in *Proceedings of the IEEE/ACM International Conference on Computer-Aided Design*, San Jose, CA, pp. 59–66, Nov. 2002.
10. D. Cross, E. Nequist, and L. Scheffer, A DFM aware, space based router, in *Proceedings of the International Symposium on Physical Design*, pp. 171–172, Mar. 2007.
11. D. J. Frank, R. Puri, and D. Toma, Design and CAD challenges for 45nm and beyond, in *Proceedings of the IEEE/ACM International Conference on Computer-Aided Design*, San Jose, CA, pp. 329–333, Nov. 2006.
12. G. Xu, L. Huang, D. Z. Pan, and D. F. Wong, Redundant-via enhanced maze routing for yield improvement, in *Proceedings of the Asia and South Pacific Design Automation Conference*, Shanghai, China, pp. 1148–1151, Jan. 2005.
13. W. Maly, C. Ouyang, S. Ghosh, and S. Maturi, Detection of an antenna effect in VLSI designs, in *Proceedings of the IEEE International Symposium on Defect and Fault-Tolerance in VLSI Systems*, Boston, MA, pp. 86–94, Nov. 1996.
14. International Technology Roadmap for Semiconductors (ITRS) 2007.

15. L. W. Liebmann, Resolution enhancement techniques in optical lithography: It's not just a mask problem, in *Proceedings of the SPIE*, Kanagawa, Japan, Vol. 4409, pp. 23–32, Sep. 2001.

16. A. K. Wong, Microlithography: Trends, challenges, solutions, and their impact on design, *IEEE Micro*, 23: 12–21, Mar. 2003.

17. L. W. Liebmann, Layout impact of resolution enhancement techniques: impediment or opportunity? in *Proceedings of the International Symposium on Physical Design*, Monterey, CA, pp. 110–117, Apr. 2003.

18. R. F. Pease, Lithographic technologies that haven't (yet) made it: Lessons learned (Plenary paper), in *Proceedings of the SPIE*, San Jose, CA, Vol. 5751, pp. 15–25, May 2005.

19. I. Koren, Should yield be a design objective? in *Proceedings of the International Symposium on Quality Electronic Design*, San Jose, CA, pp. 115–120, Mar. 2000.

20. P. Cristie and J. P. de Gyvez, Prelayout interconnect yield prediction, *IEEE Transactions on Very Large Scale Integration (VLSI) Systems*, 11: 55–59, Feb 2003.

21. A. B. Kahng, B. Liu, and I. I. Mandoiu, Non-tree routing for reliability and yield improvement, in *Proceedings of the IEEE/ACM International Conference on Computer-Aided Design*, San Jose, CA, pp. 260–266, Nov. 2002.

22. X. Qi, A. Gyure, Y. Luo, S. C. Lo, M. Shahram, and K. Singhal, Emerging technologies: Measurement and characterization of pattern dependent process variations of interconnect resistance, capacitance and inductance in nanometer technologies, in *Proceedings of the ACM Great Lakes Symposium on VLSI*, Philadelphia, PA, pp. 14–18, Apr. 2006.

23. P. Zarkesh-Ha, S. Lakshminarayann, K. Doniger, W. Loh, and P. Wright, Impact of interconnect pattern density information on a 90nm technology ASIC design flow, in *Proceedings of the International Symposium on Quality Electronic Design*, San Jose, CA, pp. 405–409, Nov. 2003.

24. S. Lakshminarayanan, P. J. Wright, and J. Pallinti, Electrical characterization of the copper CMP process and derivation of metal layout rules, *IEEE Transactions on Semiconductor Manufacturing*, 16: 668–676, Nov. 2003.

25. T. E. Gbondo-Tugbawa, Chip-scale modeling of pattern dependencies in copper chemical mechanical polishing process. PhD thesis, Massachusetts Institute of Technology, Cambridge, MA, 2002.

26. R. Tian, D. F. Wong, and R. Boone, Model-based dummy feature placement for oxide chemical–mechanical polishing manufacturability, *IEEE Transaction on Computer-Aided Design of Integrated Circuits and Systems*, 20: 902–910, Jul. 2001.

27. L. He, A. B. Kahng, K. Tam, and J. Xiong, Design of integrated-circuit interconnects with accurate modeling of CMP, in *Proceedings of the SPIE*, San Jose, CA, Vol. 5756, pp. 109–119, Mar. 2005.

28. S. Im, N. Srivastava, K. Banerjee, and K. E. Goodson, Scaling analysis of mulitilevel interconnect temperature for high-performance ICs, *IEEE Transactions on Electron Devices*, 52: 2710–2719, Dec 2005.

29. H. -Y. Chen, M. -F. Chiang, Y. -W. Chang, L. Chen, and B. Han, Novel full-chip gridless routing considering double-via insertion, in *Proceedings of the ACM/IEEE Design Automation Conferernce*, San Francisco, CA, pp. 755–760, Jul. 2006.

30. Z. Chen and I. Koren, Layer reassignment for antenna effect minimization in 3-layer channel routing, in *Proceedings of the Intenational Workshop on Defect and Fault-Tolerance in VLSI Systems*, Boston, MA, pp. 77–85, Nov. 1996.

31. C. Mead and L. Conway, *Introduction to VLSI Systems*. Addison-Wesley, Boston, MA, 1980.

32. H. K. -S. Leung, Advanced routing in changing technology landscape, in *Proceedings of the International Symposium on Physical Design*, Monterey, CA, pp. 118–121, Apr. 2003.

33. J. Cong, Tutorial: Advanced routing techniques for nanometer IC designs, in *Proceedings of the IEEE/ACM International Conference on Computer-Aided Design*, San Jose, CA, Nov. 2006.

34. http://www.praesagus.com/.

35. E. Papadopoulou and D. T. Lee, Critical area computation via Voronoi diagrams, *IEEE Transactions on Computer-Aided Design of Integrated Circuits and Systems*, 18: 463–474, Apr. 1999.

36. W. Maly, Modeling of lithography related yield losses for CAD of VLSI circuits, *IEEE Transactions on Computer-Aided Design of Integrated Circuits and Systems*, 4: 166–177, Jul. 1985.

37. R. Glang, Defect size distribution in VLSI chips, *IEEE Transactions on Semiconductor Manufacturing*, 4: 265–269, Nov. 1991.

38. E. P. Huijbregtz, H. Xue, and J. A. Jess, Routing for reliable manufacturing, *IEEE Transactions on Semiconductor Manufacturing*, 8: 188–194, May 1995.

39. T. Iizuka, M. Ikeda, and K. Asada, Exact wiring fault minimization via comprehensive layout synthesis for CMOS logic cells, in *Proceedings of the International Symposium on Quality Electronic Design*, San Jose, CA, pp. 377–380, Mar. 2004.

40. A. Pitaksanonku, S. Thanawastien, C. Lursinsap, and J. Gandhi, DTR: A defect-tolerant routing algorithm, in *Proceedings of the ACM/IEEE Design Automation Conference*, Las Vegas, NV, pp. 795–798, Jun. 1989.

41. S. -Y. Kuo, YOR: A yield-optimizing routing algorithm by minimizing critical areas and vias, *IEEE Transactions on Computer-Aided Design of Integrated Circuits and Systems*, 12: pp. 1303–1311, Sep. 1993.

42. T. Yoshimura and E. Kuh, Efficient algorithms for channel routing, *IEEE Transactions on Computer-Aided Design of Integrated Circuits and Systems*, 1: 25–35, Jan. 1982.

43. D. Muller, Optimizing yield in global routing, in *Proceedings of the IEEE/ACM International Conference on Computer-Aided Design*, San Jose, CA, pp. 480–486, Nov. 2006.

44. C. Bamji and E. Malavasi, Enhanced network flow algorithm for yield optimization, in *Proceedings of the ACM/IEEE Design Automation Conference*, Las Vegas, NV, pp. 746–751, Jun 1996.

45. G. A. Allan, Targeted layout modifications for semiconductor yield/reliability enhancement, *IEEE Transactions on Semiconductor Manufacturing*, 17: 573–581, Nov 2004.

46. J. Z. Su and W. Dai, Post route optimization for improved yield using a rubber-band wiring model, in *Proceedings of the IEEE/ACM International Conference on Computer-Aided Design*, San Jose, CA, pp. 700–706, Nov. 1997.

47. V. K. I. Chiluvuri and I. Koren, Layout-synthesis techniques for yield enhancement, *IEEE Transactions on Semiconductor Manufacturing*, 8: 178–187, May 1995.

48. Y. Bourai and C. -J. R. Shi, Layout compaction for yield optimization via critical area minimization, in *Proceedings of the Design, Automation and Test in Eurpoe*, pp. 122–127, Mar. 2000.

49. Y. Pati, A. Ghazanfarian, and R. Pease, Exploiting structure in fast aerial image computation for integrated circuit patterns, *IEEE Transactions on Semiconductor Manufacturing*, 10: 62–74, Feb. 1997.

50. M. Born and E. Wolf, *Principles of Optics: Electromagnetic Theory of Propagation, Interference and Diffraction of Light*, 7th edition. Cambridge University Press, NY, 1999.

51. N. B. Cobb, Fast optical and process proximity correction algorithms for integrated circuit manufacturing. PhD thesis, University of California at Berkeley, CA, 1998.

52. Y. -R. Wu, M. -C. Tsai, and T. -C. Wang, Maze routing with OPC consideration, in *Proceedings of the Asia and South Pacific Design Automation Conference*, Shanghai, China, pp. 198–203, Jan. 2005.

53. T. Kong, H. Leung, V. Raghavan, A. K. Wong, and S. Xu, Model-assisted routing for improved lithography robustness, in *Proceedings of the SPIE*, San Jose, CA, Vol. 6521, p. 65210D, Feb. 2007.

54. T. -C. Chen and Y. -W. Chang, Routability-driven and optical proximity correction-aware multilevel full-chip gridless routing, *IEEE Transactions on Computer-Aided Design of Integrated Circuits and Systems*, 26: 1041–1053, Jun. 2007.

55. K. -Y. Lee and T. -C. Wang, Post-routing redundant via insertion for yield/reliability improvement, in *Proceedings of the Asia and South Pacific Design Automation Conference*, San Francisco, CA, pp. 303–308, Jan. 2006.

56. F. Luo, Y. Jia, and W. W. -M. Dai, Yield-preferred via insertion based on novel geotopological technology, in *Proceedings of the Asia and South Pacific Design Automation Conference*, Yokohama, Japan, pp. 730–735, Jan. 2006.

57. K. -Y. Lee, T. -C. Wang, and K. -Y. Chao, Post-routing redundant via insertion and line end extension with via density consideration, in *Proceedings of the IEEE/ACM International Conference on Computer-Aided Design*, San Jose, CA, pp. 633–640, Nov. 2006.

58. H. Shirota, T. Sadakane, and M. Terai, A new rip-up and reroute algorithm for very large scale gate arrays, in *Proceedings of the IEEE Custom Integrated Circuits Conference*, San Diego, CA, pp. 171–174, May 1996.

59. H. Shirota, T. Sadakane, M. Terai, and K. Okazaki, A new router for reducing "Antenna effect" in ASIC design, in *Proceedings of the IEEE Custom Integrated Circuits Conference*, Santa Clara, CA, pp. 601–604, May 1998.

60. T. -Y. Ho, Y. -W. Chang, and S. -J. Chen, Multilevel routing with antenna avoidance, in *Proceedings of the International Symposium on Physical Design*, Phoenix, AZ, pp. 34–40, Apr. 2004.

61. D. Wu, J. Hu, and R. Mahapatra, Antenna avoidance in layer assignment, *IEEE Transactions on Computer-Aided Design of Integrated Circuits and Systems*, 25: 734–748, Apr. 2006.

62. L. -D. Huang, X. Tang, H. Xiang, M. D. F. Wong, and I. -M. Liu, A polynomial time-optimal diode insertion/routing algorithm for fixing antenna problem, *IEEE Transactions on Computer-Aided Design of Integrated Circuits and Systems*, 23: 141–147, Jan. 2004.

63. B. -Y. Su, Y. -W. Chang, and J. Hu, An optimal jumper insertion algorithm for antenna avoidance/fixing on general routing trees with obstacles, in *Proceedings of the International Symposium on Physical Design*, pp. 56–63, Nov. 2006.

64. Z. -W. Jiang and Y. -W. Chang, An optimal simultaneous diode/jumper insertion algorithm for antenna fixing, in *Proceedings of the IEEE/ACM International Conference on Computer Aided Design*, pp. 669–674, San Jose, CA, Apr. 2006.

65. *LEF/DEF Reference Manual, version 5.7.* https://www.si2.org/openeda.si2.org/projects/lefdef

66. D. Z. Pan and M. D. F. Wong, Manufacturability-aware physical layout optimizations, in *Proceedings of the International Conference on Integrated Circuit Design and Technology*, Austin, TX, pp. 149–153, May 2005.

Part VIII

Physical Synthesis

39 Placement-Driven Synthesis Design Closure Tool

Charles J. Alpert, Nathaniel Hieter, Arjen Mets,
Ruchir Puri, Lakshmi Reddy, Haoxing Ren,
and Louise Trevillyan

CONTENTS

39.1 INTRODUCTION

Much of this book has focused on the components of physical synthesis, such as global placement, detailed placement, buffering, routing, Steiner tree, and congestion estimation. Physical synthesis combines these steps as well as several others to (primarily) perform timing closure. When wire delays were relatively insignificant compared to gate delays, logic synthesis provided a sufficiently accurate picture of the timing of the design. Placement and routing did not need to focus on timing, but were exclusively wirelength driven. Of course, technology trends have transformed physical design because the physical implementation affects timing.

Today, a design that satisfies timing requirements in synthesis almost certainly will not do so once implemented physically due to wire delays. Physical synthesis is a process that modifies the design so that the impact on timing due to wiring is mitigated. It may move cells, resize logic, buffer nets, and perform local resynthesis.

Besides basic timing closure, there are many newer challenges that the physical synthesis system needs to handle [1]. Some examples include lowering power using a technology library with multiple threshold voltages (vt), fixing noise violations that show up after performing routing, and handling the timing variability and uncertainty introduced by modern design processes.

This chapter surveys IBM's physical synthesis tool, called placement-driven synthesis (PDS) or placement-driven synthesis. It builds upon a description of the basics of the tool [2] and also some innovations in turnaround time published in Ref. [3].

39.2   MAJOR PHASES OF PHYSICAL SYNTHESIS

Placement-driven synthesis has hundreds of parameter settings available to the user and can be customized by the designer to run in many ways. For example, there are different degrees of routing congestion mitigation or area recovery available. The user may want to exploit gates with low vt or allow assignment of wires to different routing planes. These choices depend on the nature of the design being closed. Although there is no single PDS algorithm to describe, the following outlines a typical invocation:

1. Netlist preparation. When PDS initializes, of course, the data model needs to be loaded with timing assertions (which encapsulate the timing constraints), user parameters, etc. There also may need to be some scrubbing of the netlist so that optimization is even viable. As examples,
   - Gates may need to be sized down so that the total area of the netlist fits within the area of the placeable region.
   - Buffers inserted during synthesis may need to be removed so that they do not badly influence placement. A placement algorithm may handle a fanout tree several levels deep, then they logically equivalent single large net.
   - If the clock tree has not yet been built, it may need to be hidden from optimization so that it is not treated as a signal net. Changes to a clocked sequential cell could otherwise cause the timing for every cell in the clock tree to be updated. Before synthesis, an ideal clock with zero skew can be assumed and later replaced with the optimized one.
   - Timing information can be extracted from either an unplaced or a previously optimized netlist to generate net weights for the placement step.
2. Global placement. This step is well-covered in Chapters 14 through 19. Besides just traditional minimum wirelength optimization, placement needs to address several other types of constraints. For example,
   - Density targets direct the placer to not pack cells in tightly in certain areas, so that physical synthesis will have the flexibility to size up cells, insert buffers, etc.
   - Designer cell movement constraints are used to enable floorplanning in a flat methodology. By restricting a set of cells to a certain rectangular region, the designer is able to plan that block, while still allowing the tool the flexibility to perform optimizations and placements of the cells within the block.
   - Routability directives can be used to improve the routability of placement, such as artificially inflating the size of cells in routing congested regions in order to force more spreading [4].
   - Clock domain constraints can be considered during placement to reduce clock tree latency and dynamic power consumption. Latches that belong to the same clock domain can be

directed to be placed close to each other by either adding special net weights or by imposing movement constraints on latches.

3. Timing analysis. At every point in the flow, timing analysis is a core component because it provides the evaluation of how well PDS is doing in terms of timing closure. It is run both stand alone and incrementally throughout the optimization. For this, IBM's static timing analysis tool, EinsTimer [5], is used.

4. Electrical correction. After placement, one will certainly find gates that drive loads above the allowed specification and long wires for which the signal exceeds the designer specified slew rate. A few bad slew rates inevitably cause terrible timing results. At this point, it makes sense to correct the design by fixing local slew and capacitance violations, typically through buffering and gate sizing, thereby getting the design into a reasonably good timing state. One can also employ a logical effort [6] type of approach to improve the global timing characteristics of the design.

5. Placement legalization. Fixing electrical violation may result in thousands of buffers being added to the design, and potentially every gate may be assigned a new gate size, which will create overlaps, causing the placement solution to become illegal. The goal of legalization is to fix these overlaps while providing minimum perturbation to the netlist (Chapter 20).

6. Critical path optimization. Once the design is legal and is in a reasonably good timing state, one can employ all kinds of techniques to try to fix the critical paths. Chapters 26 through 28 discuss powerful buffering techniques. Section 39.5 describes how other optimization or transforms can also be deployed. A transform is a change to the netlist designed to improve some aspect of the design, for example, breaking apart a complex gate into several smaller simpler ones. During this phase, incremental timing analysis and legalization may be periodically invoked to keep the design in a legal and consistent state.

7. Compression. Critical path optimization may become stuck at some point, when a certain set of the most critical paths cannot be fixed without manual design intervention (e.g., changes to the floorplan must be made). This is shown in Figure 39.1 where the original timing histogram (Figure 39.1a) is improved by critical path optimizations (Figure 39.1b) until it saturates. However, there still may be thousands of failed timing points that exist which could be fixed with lighter weight optimizations directed at the not so critical regions that still violate timing constraints. The purpose of this phase is to compress the remaining negative portion of the timing histogram to leave as little work as possible for the designer as shown in Figure 39.1c. As in critical path optimization phase, incremental timing analysis and legalization must be incorporated where appropriate.

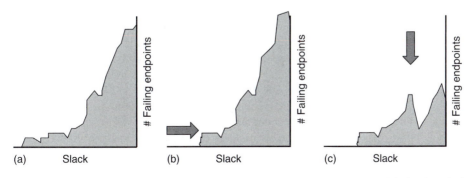

FIGURE 39.1   Timing histogram of (a) an unoptimized design can be improved by (b) critical path optimization and (c) histogram compression.

After these phases, the design may still be far from closing on the given timing constraints. At this point, a designer could intervene manually or rerun the flow to try and get a better timing-driven placement now that the real timing problems have been identified. One can run a net weighting algorithm (Chapter 21) to drive the next iteration of placement and the entire flow.

In the flow described above, one can make several assumptions to make fast optimization achievable. For example, (1) clocks can be idealized so that one assume a zero skew clock will later be inserted, (2) Steiner estimates and one-dimensional extraction can be used for interconnect delay estimation, (3) crosstalk can be ignored, etc. Making these assumptions certainly allows faster runtime than otherwise achievable. In practice, these assumptions are stripped away as the designer makes progress toward timing closure. Once the designer is reasonably happy with the design after running PDS, he or she may then perform clock insertion and perform a pass of incremental physical synthesis to fix problems resulting from actual clock skews. Similarly, once the design is routed, there could be timing problems caused by scenic routes, along with noise violations from capacitive coupling. The designer can then run incremental physical synthesis in this postrouting environment, using accurate coupling information while also modeling variability for timing.

Because several of the main components of the physical synthesis flow are covered elsewhere in the book, this chapter focuses on aspects that are not covered.

1. Optimization and placement interaction. When optimizations such as buffering or resizing need to make adjustments to the netlist, they cannot happen in a vacuum because they affect the placement. Certain regions may have blockages or be too congested to allow transforms to happen. We explain the communication mechanisms between optimization and placement.
2. Critical path optimizations. Besides buffering, there are numerous techniques one can use to improve the timing along a critical path. Section 39.4 overviews gate sizing and incremental synthesis techniques and the driver/transform model that PDS uses.
3. Recovery mechanisms. During optimization, PDS can cause damage by overfilling local regions, causing routing congestion, etc. Section 39.5 explains how one can apply specialized optimizations for repairing damage so that physical synthesis can continue effectively.
4. Specialized design styles. A typical instance for PDS is a flat ASIC, though customers also utilize it for hierarchical design and for high-performance microprocessors. Section 39.6 explains some of the issues faced by PDS and their solutions for these different types of design styles.

39.3   OPTIMIZATION AND PLACEMENT INTERACTION

During the critical-path optimization and compression, optimizations such as buffer insertion, gate sizing, box movement, and logic restructuring may need to add, delete, move, or resize boxes. To estimate benefit/cost of these transformations accurately, transforms need to generate legal or semilegal locations for these boxes on the fly. Otherwise, boxes may be moved to overcongested locations or even on top of blockages, which later need to be resolved by legalization. Legalization then may move boxes far from their intended locations and undo (at least in part) the benefits of optimization. It could even introduce new problems that need further optimization.

Of course, ideally one would like to compute the exact legal locations for such boxes during optimization, but it often can be too computationally expensive. One strategy PDS uses is to use rough legal locations during early optimization (e.g., electrical correction) when substantial changes are made. During later stages of optimization when smaller or finer changes are made, exact legal locations may be computed. Such a strategy strikes a good balance between quality of results and the runtime of the system.

39.3.1 Bin-Based Placement Model

PDS uses a synthesis–placement interface (SPI) to manage the estimation or computation of incremental placement. Before optimization, the placement image is divided into a set of regions called bins. Each placeable object in the design is assigned to a bin, and space availability is determined by examining the free space within a bin. The SPI layer manages the interface to an idealized view of the bin structure and provides a rich set of functions to access and manipulate placement data. The SPI layer uses callbacks to keep placement, optimization, and routing data consistent.

Instead of computing an exact legal location, newly created or modified logic can be placed in a bin and assigned a coarse-placement location inside the bin. A fast check is performed to make sure that there is enough free space within the bin to accommodate the logic.

The interaction between optimizations and the SPI layer works as follows. Suppose an optimization requests SPI to add or move a box to a specific (x, y) location. SPI gets the bin in which the (x, y) location falls and checks the free space. If there is enough space then optimization uses the location specified. If not, the optimization may ask SPI to find the closest bin in which there is space, in which case, SPI "spirals" through neighboring bins and returns a valid location, which the optimization can evaluate and choose to use. When a placement is actually assigned, SPI updates bin information to accurately reflect the state of the placement.

Using rough placement may result in boxes placed so they overlap each other. This is one reason why legalization needs to be called periodically (see e.g., Ref. [7]). It is important for the optimized design to remain stable, so the legalizer maintains as many pre existing locations as possible and, when a box must move, an attempt is made to disturb the timing of critical paths as little as possible.

As an example, assume the potential area of placed logic inside a bin is 1000 units and that 930 units of cells are already placed within the bin. If one tries to add a new cell of size 90, the SPI interface reports that the bin would become too full (1020) and cannot afford to allow the cell to be placed. On the other hand, a cell of size 50 can fit (total area 980) so SPI would permit the transform to place the cell in the bin.

The problem with the bin-based model is that just because the total area allows another cell to be inserted, does not mean it actually can be inserted. As a simple example, consider placing three cells of width three into two rows of width five, with height one for cell and each row. The total area of the cells is nine, while the total placeable area is ten, so it would seem like the cells could fit. However, the cells cannot be placed without exceeding the row capacity. In this sense, legalizing cells within a bin so that they all fit is like the NP-complete bin packing problem.

Consider Figure 39.2 in which Bin A and Bin B have exactly the same set of nine cells, though arranged differently. If one tries to insert a new cell into either bin, SPI would return that there is room in the bin, yet one cannot easily insert it in Bin A while one can in Bin B. It is likely that the fracturing of white space in Bin A will lead to legalization eventually moving a cell into a different bin.

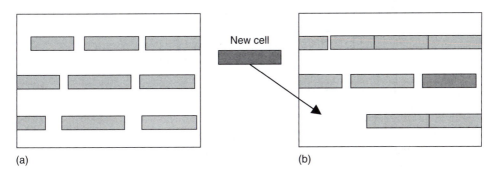

(a)   (b)

FIGURE 39.2   New cell cannot be inserted into (a) Bin A but can be in (b) Bin B even though both bins contain the same set of cells.

Because of these effects, the designer often runs with a guard band (e.g., 5 percent) to make it more likely that cells will avoid unsolvable bin packing scenarios. In our earlier example, we put the virtual bin capacity at 950. Alternatively, one can allow overfilling of bins (say by 5 percent) to allow transforms to successfully perform optimization, and then rely on powerful legalization techniques like diffusion (Chapter 20) to reduce the likelihood of legalization moving cells far away.

As physical synthesis progresses, the bins are reduced in size. This tends to limit the size of box movements that legalization must do.

39.3.2 EXACT PLACEMENT

The major problem with the bin-based model is that one can never guarantee that the cell really does fit in its bin. One could always construct test cases with cells of strange sizes that break any bin model (or force it to be ultra-conservative in preventing cells to be inserted). For example, fixed-area I/Os and decoupling capacitors can contribute to the problem. When it gets too late in the flow, PDS may not be able to recover from big legalization movements that degrade timing. During later stages of the system when the major optimizations have been completed, finding exact locations for the modified cells provides better overall quality of results with reasonable runtimes.

PDS implements exact legal locations during optimization as follows. The placement subsystem maintains an incremental bit map (imap) to track all location changes and available free space. For example, if a cell is one row high and seven tracks wide, then seven bits of the imap corresponding to the cell's location are set to one. If the two tracks next to the cell are empty, their bits are set to zero. When a new or modified box needs to be placed at a desired location, the imap capability essentially works like a hole finder. It tries to locate a hole or an empty slot (within some specified maximum distance from the desired location) large enough to place legally the newly created or modified box. As with rough locations, the optimization can evaluate and choose to use the exact locations. If this location is used then the imap data model is updated incrementally. Thus, when timing evaluates the quality of the solution, it knows exactly where the cell will end up. In this model, legalization is not necessary.

An example of one problem with the imap model occurs when a cell seven tracks wide wants to be placed in a hole that is five tracks wide. To a user, it may be obvious to simply slide the neighboring cell over by two tracks to make room. In general, small local moves like this will have minimal effect on timing and make it more likely that the cells will be placed at their desired locations. In such a case, a list of all the cells that need to be moved to make room for the new/modified box as well as their new locations is supplied to the transform. The transform can then evaluate this compound movement of a set of boxes and estimate the benefit/cost and decide to accept or reject such movement. The advantages of this approach include more successes in legally placing boxes within some specified maximum as well as obtaining legal locations that are generally closer to the desired locations. On the other hand, the transforms may get more complicated as they need to manage and evaluate the movement of, possibly unrelated, multiple cells. It may also cause more churn to the design during the later stages of optimization due to the movement of significantly larger number of boxes, which may not be directly targeted by the optimizations.

Thus, it is a bit of an art to find the right degree of placement and optimization interaction that trades off accuracy versus runtime. These models are still evolving in PDS today.

39.4 CRITICAL PATH OPTIMIZATIONS

Optimization of critical paths is at the heart of any physical synthesis system. Timing closure is clearly an important goal, but electrical correctness, placement and routing congestion, area, power, wirelength, yield, and signal integrity are also important design characteristics that must be considered and optimized when making incremental changes to the netlist.

Within PDS, there is a large menu of optimizations that can be applied to the design. The sequences of optimizations are packaged for various functions and can be enabled or disabled via system parameters. Optimizations may also be used interactively by designers. The most effective optimizations are generally buffering and gate sizing. As a secondary dimension for optimization, with buffering one can also perform wire sizing and with gate sizing one can perform assign gates to different vt. Because buffering is covered in other chapters, we turn to gate sizing.

39.4.1 GATE SIZING

Gate sizing is responsible for selecting the appropriate drive strength for a logic cell from the functionally equivalent cells available in the technology library. For example, a library may contain a set of ten inverters, each with a characteristic size, power consumption, and drive strength. Upon finding an inverter in the design, it is the task of gate sizing to assign the inverter with the appropriate drive strength to meet design objectives.

When the mapped design comes from logic synthesis, gate sizes have already been assigned based on the best information available at the time. Once the design is placed, Steiner wire estimates can be used to give a more-accurate estimation of wire loads, and many of the previous assignments will be found to be suboptimal. Likewise, gate sizes must be reevaluated after global and detailed routing, because wire delays will again have changed.

As discussed earlier, the electrical correction step performs an initial pass over the entire design. Gate sizes are assigned in a table-lookup fashion to fix capacitance and slew violations introduced by the more accurate Steiner wire models. There may be several cells in the library that meet the requirements of a logic cell, so the one with minimal area is chosen. If gate sizing is insufficient to fix the violation, buffering or box movement may be used.

Later optimizations have the option of modifying these initial gate sizes. If a cell in the design is timing critical, the library cell that results in the best path delay would be chosen, while if the cell already meets its timing requirements, area recovery will pick the cell with greatest area savings.

For critical path optimizations, gate sizing examines a size-sorted window of functional alternatives and evaluates each of them to choose the best library cell. For example, suppose that the current cell is a NAND2_D, and the library has, from smallest to largest, NAND2_A through NAND2_G cells. The program might evaluate the B, C, E, and F levels to see if they are a better fit for the optimization objectives. The size of the window is dynamic and affects both the accuracy of the choice and the runtime of the optimization. Because the design is constantly changing during optimization, it is necessary to periodically revisit the assigned gate sizes and readjust them. This allows revisiting choices, perhaps with different cell windows.

Other algorithms, such as simulated annealing, Lagrangian relaxation (see Chapter 29), or integer programming approaches [8], have been suggested for use in resizing, but they tend to be too slow, given the size of today's designs and the frequency with which this needs to be done. Further, these approaches tend to make gross assumptions about a continuous library, which then needs to be mapped to cells in a discrete library; this mapping may severely distort the quality of the optimization. Also, these methods do not account well for capacitance and slew changes resulting from new power-level assignments, and the physical placement constraints, as described above.

Gate sizing is important to nearly every facet of optimization. It is used in timing correction, area recovery, electrical correction, yield improvement, and signal-integrity optimization.

39.4.2 GATE SIZING WITH MULTIPLE-VT LIBRARIES

Besides performing timing closure, PDS also manages the total power budget. See Chapter 3 for an overview of the components of power consumption. The contribution of the static power component or leakage to the total power number is growing rapidly as geometries shrink.

To account for that, technology foundries have introduced cell libraries with multiple vt. These libraries contain separate cells with the same functionality but with different threshold. These libraries contain separate cells with the same functionality but with different vt. In the simplest form there are two different thresholds available, commonly called high-vt and low-vt, where vt stands for vt.

Cells made up with high threshold transistors are slower but leak less while cells with low threshold transistors are faster at the expense of higher leakage power and less noise immunity. In practice, there is a limit to the number of different vt in the library because each vt introduces an additional mask in the fabrication process.

Multi-vt libraries enable synthesis to select not only the appropriate gate size but also the appropriate vt for each cell. Cells on a timing critical path can be assigned a lower vt to speed up the design. Cells that are not timing critical do not need the performance of a high-leakage cell and can use the slower and less leaky versions. In general, one prefers not to use low-vt cells at all unless they are absolutely necessary to meet high-performance timing constraints.

During vt assignment, PDS simply collects all critical gates and sorts them based on their criticality. vt assignment then proceeds by lowering the vt on the cells starting with the most critical cell first. The algorithm honors designer supplied leakage limits by incrementally computing the leakage current in the design.

In general, multiple threshold libraries are designed such that the low-vt equivalent of each cell has the same area and cell image as the high-vt cell. This makes the multiple voltage threshold optimization a transformation, which does not disturb the placement of a design.

Because the input capacitance of a low-vt cell is slightly higher than that of a corresponding high-vt cell, resizing the cells after threshold optimization can yield further improvement in performance.

The impact of multiple vt optimization on the power/performance trade off depends on the distribution of slack across the logic. Designs with narrow critical regions can yield significant performance improvements with little affect on leakage power. The performance boost obtained from using low-vt cells is significant, making it one of the more powerful tools PDS has to fix critical paths.

39.4.3 INCREMENTAL SYNTHESIS

Besides buffering and gate sizing, many other techniques can be applied to improve critical paths. Techniques from logic synthesis, modified to take placement and routing into account, can at times be very effective. Even though the design comes from logic synthesis optimized for timing, the changes caused by placement, gate sizing, buffering, etc. may disrupt the original timing and may create an opportunity for these optimizations to be effective in correcting a path that may not be fixable otherwise.

- Cell movement: In general, the next most effective optimization technique is cell movement. One can move cells to not only improve timing, but also minimize wirelength, reduce placement congestion, or balance pipeline stages. For critical path optimization, a simple, yet effective approach is to find a box on a critical path and try to move it to a better location that improves timing.
- Cloning: Instead of sizing up a cell to drive a net with a fairly high load, one could copy the cell and partition the sinks of the original output nets among the copies. Figure 39.3 shows an example where four sinks are driven by two identical gates after cloning. Cloning can also improve wirelengths and wiring congestion.
- Pin swapping: Pin swapping takes advantage of cells where the input to output timings differ by pin. As an example, a 4-input NAND, with inputs A, B, C, and D and output Z. the delay from A to Z could be less than the delay from D to Z. Some cells may be architected so that the behavior is intentional. By swapping a timing critical at pin D with a noncritical signal at pin A, one can obtain timing improvement. More generally, when one has a fan-in tree as in Figure 39.4, commutative pins can also be swapped, so that the slowest net can be moved forward in the tree. Like cloning, pin swapping can also be used to improve wirelength and decrease wiring congestion.

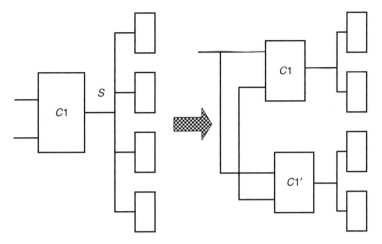

FIGURE 39.3 Cloning. (From Trevillyan, et al., *IEEE Design and Test of Computers*, pp. 14–22, 2004. With permission.)

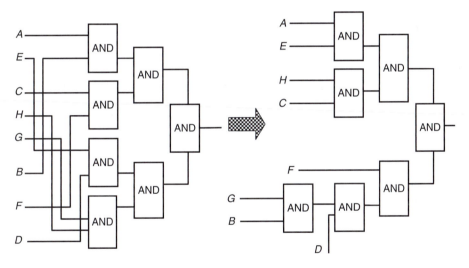

FIGURE 39.4 Pin swapping.

- Inverter processing: In a rich standard-cell library, complement and dual-complement cells are available for many functions. Timing or area can be improved by manipulating inverters. For example, Figure 39.5 shows an example of an INVERT-NAND sequence being replaced with a NOR-INVERT sequence. Other examples include changing an AND-INVERT sequence to a NAND or an AND-INVERT into and OR. Inverter processing may remove an inverter, add an inverter, or require an inverter to be moved to another sink.
- Cell expansion: The cell library may contain "complex" multilevel functions, such as AND-OR, XOR, MUX, or other less-well-defined cells. These cells normally save space, but can be slower than a breakdown into equivalent single-level cells (NAND, NOR, INVERT, etc.). Cell expansion breaks apart these cells into its components; for example, Figure 39.6 shows an XOR gate decomposed into three AND gates and two inverters.
- Off-path resizing: As discussed earlier, gate sizing is a core technique for optimization of gates on a critical path. However, one can also attempt to reduce the load driven by these gates by reducing the size of noncritical sink cells, as shown in Figure 39.7. The smaller

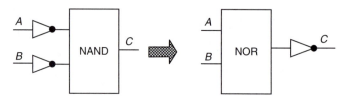

FIGURE 39.5   Inverter processing.

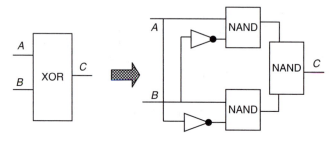

FIGURE 39.6   Cell expansion.

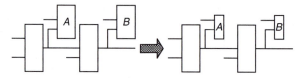

FIGURE 39.7   Off-path resizing.

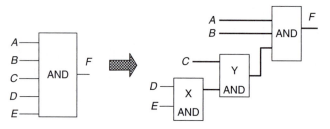

FIGURE 39.8   Shattering.

cells generally present lower pin capacitances, and so may improve the delay on a timing-critical net, though it could hurt the delay for another path. The timing analyzer and the optimization metric is the arbiter on whether the optimization suggestion is accepted by PDS. When correcting hold violations (short paths), the off-path cells can be powered up to present higher pin capacitance and slow down a path.

• Shattering: Similar to cell expansion, larger fan-in cell can be decomposed into a tree of smaller cells. This may allow the most critical path to move ahead to a faster, smaller cell. Figure 39.8 shows how the delay through pins *A* and *B* of a five-input AND gate can be reduced by shattering the gate into three NAND gates, so that *a* and *b* only need to propagate through a cell with less complexity. Merging, the opposite of shattering, can also be an effective timing optimization. A rule of thumb is that merging is good when the slacks at the inputs of a tree are similar, and shattering is good when there is a wider distribution of slacks.

Note that the optimizations are atomic actions and are synergistic. Optimizations can call other optimizations. For example, a box could be shattered, then pin-swapped, and finally resized, and the new solution could then be accepted or rejected based on the combined effect of these optimizations.

39.4.4 Advanced Synthesis Techniques

The descriptions of some of the above incremental synthesis optimizations are deceptively simple. For example, Figure 39.6 shows an XOR decomposed as two inverters and three NAND gates. It could also be implemented as two inverters, two ANDs, and an OR; two inverters, one OR, and two NANDs; or three inverters, an AND, and two NANDs; etc. An optimization like cell expansion examines several decompositions based on rules of thumb, but does not explore the expansion possibilities in any systematic way.

Another way of accomplishing cell expansion and many of the other optimizations is through logic restructuring [9], which provides a systematic way of looking at functional implementations. In this method, seed cells are chosen and a fan-in and depth-limited cone is examined for reimplementation to achieve timing or area goals. The seed box and its restricted cone of logic are represented as a Boolean decision diagram (BDD) [10]. This provides a canonical form from which different logic structures can be implicitly enumerated and evaluated. When a new structure is chosen, it is implemented based on the primitives available in the library and the new cells are placed and sized. The restructuring process can be thought of as a new technology mapping of the selected cone.

Advanced synthesis techniques can be a computationally intensive process because, for a large cone, the number of potential implementations can be huge. The fan-in and depth constraints must be chosen so as to balance design quality with runtime. However, they are quite effective and are especially useful for high-performance microprocessor blocks, which typically are small yet have very aggressive timing constraints.

39.4.5 Fixing Early Paths

Timing closure consists of correcting both long (late mode) and short (early mode) paths. The delay of long paths must be decreased because the signal is arriving at the register a cycle too late, while the delay of short paths must be increased because they are arriving a cycle too early. The strategy we use in PDS is to correct the long paths without consideration of the short paths, then do short-path correction as a postprocess in such a way as to lengthen the paths without causing a long path to be more critical. This can be tricky because it is possible that all the boxes along a short path can be intertwined with a long path.

Doing short-path correction requires that there be (at least) two timing models active: early mode timing tests are done with a slow clock and fast data, while late-mode tests are done with fast clocks and slow data. The presence of two timing models enables correction of the early mode paths while minimizing or reducing any adverse effects to the late-mode paths. In PDS, short-path correction is done very late in the process, after routing and with SPICE extraction.

The premier way of correcting short paths is by adding delay pads (similar to buffers) along the path to slow it down. In some cases, short-path nets can be reconnected to existing buffers (added for electrical violations or long-path correction) to slow down the path. This can correct the path without incurring the area overhead of a new pad. As noted above, resizing to a slower cell or powering up side-path cells can also be used for early mode correction.

39.4.6 Drivers for Multiple Objectives

The previous discussion discussed transforms primarily in the context of improving timing. However, other objectives like wirelength, routing congestion, or placement congestion can be addressed by the same set of optimizations or transforms.

To facilitate the use of transforms for multiple objectives, PDS employs a driver-transform paradigm. Programs are split into local transforms and drivers. The transforms are responsible for the actual manipulation of the logic, for example, adding a buffer, moving or resizing a cell, etc. The driver is responsible for determining the sections of logic that need to be optimized. If the optimization goal is electrical correction the driver will pick cells that violate slew or capacitance limits; if the goal is timing, it will pick cells that lie on the critical paths; if the goal is area reduction, the driver will choose cells in the noncritical region, where slack can be sacrificed for area. The transforms understand their goals (e.g., whether they should be trying so save area of time) and adjust their actions accordingly.

The drivers are also responsible for determining which transforms should be applied in what order. Given a list of available optimizations, the driver may ask for evaluations of the characteristics of applying each transform, then choose the order of application based on a cost/benefit analysis (in terms of timing, area, power, etc.). A driver may also leave it to the transform to decide when to apply, in which case the order of the transform list given to the driver becomes quite important. There are a variety of drivers available in PDS.

- The most commonly used one is the critical driver, which picks a group of pins with negative slack and sends the pins to the transforms for evaluation. Because transforms can interact, the critical driver iterates both on the current and, when no more can be done on its current list, iterates on sets of lists. To conserve runtime, it "rememebers" the transforms that have been tried and does not retry failed attempts.
- The correction driver is used to filter nets, which violate their capacitance or slew constraints, which can then be used with a transform designed to fix these violations.
- Levelized drivers that present design in "input to output" or "output to input" order, and are useful in areas like global resizing, where it is desirable to resize all of the sink cells before considering the driving cell.
- There is a randomized driver that provide pins in a random order so that an optimization that relies on the order of pins may discover alternate solution.
- The histo driver is used in the compression phase to divide all the failing paths into slack ranges and then work iteratively on each range.
- Of special important is the list driver, which simply provides a predetermined list of cells or nets for the transform to optimize. This enables the designer to selecting specific pieces of the design for optimization while in an interactive viewing session. The designer's selection is made into a list of objects for optimization to be processed by the list driver.

In summer, PDS contains a large number of atomic transformations and a variety of drivers that can invoke them. This yields a flexible and robust set of optimizations that can be included in a fixed-sequence script or can be used directly by designers.

39.5 MECHANISMS FOR RECOVERY

During the PDS flow, optimization may occur that damage the design. Local regions could become overfull, legalization could slide critical cells far away, unnecessary wiring could be introduced, etc. This is inevitable in such a complex system. Thus, a key component to PDS is its ability to gracefully recover from such conditions. We now overview a few recovery techniques.

39.5.1 AREA RECOVERY

The total area used by the design is one of the key metrics in physical synthesis. The process of reducing area is known as area recovery. The goal of area recovery is to rework the structure of the design so as to use less area without sacrificing timing quality; this contrasts with other work in area reduction, which makes more far-reaching design changes [11] or changes logic cell or IP designs to be more area efficient [12].

Aside from the obvious benefits of allowing the design to fit on the die, or of actually reducing die size, reduction in area also contributes to better routablility, lower power, and better yield. It especially useful as a recovery mechanism because it can create placement space in congested areas that other optimizations can now exploit. Recall the previously discussed SPI bin model: for a bin of size 1000, if area recovery can reduce the used call area from 930 to 800, this increases the free space available for other cell (such as buffers) from 70 to 200.

When a design comes into physical synthesis from logic synthesis, the design has normally been optimized with a simplified timing model (e.g, constant delay or wireload). Once the design is placed, routes can be modeled using Steiner estimates or actual global or detailed routes. As more accurate information is know about the real delays due to wires, logic can be restructured to reduce area without impacting timing closure or other design goals.

For example, for most designs, a plurality of the nets will be two-pin nets. A wireload model will give the same delay for every two-pin net. Obviously, this is a very gross estimate, as some such nets may be only a few tracks long, while others could span the entire chikp. Paths with shorter-than-average nets may have seemed critical during logic synthesis but, once the design is placed and routed, are noncritical, while paths with longer-than-average nets may be more critical than predicted during logic synthesis.

PDS timing optimizations can also create a need for area recovery when there are multiple intersecting critical paths. For example, in Figure 39.9, PDS will first optimize B because its slack is more critical than A. Using gate sizing, PDS may change B to larger B' and thereby improve its slack from -15 to $+20$. Net it will optimize A, improving its slack from -10 to $+10$ and also taking more area. This may improve the slack at B' to $+30$. Area reduction might then be applied to change B' to B'', reducing both area and slack.

A good strategy is to have area recovery work on the nontiming-critical paths of the design and give up delay to reduce area. Normally, the noncritical regions constitute a huge percentage—80 percent or more—of the gates in the design, so care must be taken to use very efficient algorithms in this domain. In addition to being careful about timing, area reduction optimizations must take care to not disturb other design goals, such as electrical correctness and signal integrity.

By far, the most effective method of reducing area is sizing down cells. Aside from being extremely effective, this method has the advantages of being nondestructive to placement (because

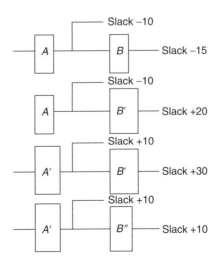

FIGURE 39.9 Physical synthesis creates opportunities for area recovery.

the new call will fit where the old one was) and minimally disruptive to wiring (the pins might move slightly). Care must be taken when reducing the size of drivers of nets so that they do not become crosstalk victims (Chapter 34). When optimizing without coupling information, noise can be captured to the first order by a slew constraint. As a rule of thumb, Ref. [13] recommends that drivers of nets in the slack range of zero to 15 percent of the clock period not have the size of their drivers reduced.

Because timing optimizations nearly always add area, a good rule of thumb for area reduction techniques is that they are the reverse of timing optimizations. So area reduction can remove buffers, inverter pairs, or hold-violation pads so long as timing and electrical correctness goals are preserved [14]. It can force the use of multilevel calls (such as XORs and AOs), which are normally smaller and slower than equivalent sigle-level implementations. If appropriate library functions are available, it can manipulate inverters to, for example, change NANDs to ANDs, ORs, or NORs, if the new configuration is smaller and maintains other design goals.

These types of optimizations may be applied locally in a pattern-matching kind of paradigm. For example, each noncritical a buffer in a design could be examined to determine whether it can be removed. Another, more general, approach would be to simultaneously apply areas-reduction techniques through re-covering a section of logic to produce a different selection of technology cells. In this context, re-covering involves a new technology mapping for the selected logic with an emphasis on area, and is more frequently used in logic synthesis, as the placement and routing aspects of physical synthesis make this technique extremely complex. Some success at re-covering small, fairly shallow (two to four levels) sections of logic has been reported [15].

A useful adjunct to area reduction is yield optimization. Overall critical-area-analysis (CAA) yield scores [16] can be reduced by considering individual CAA scores for the library cells and using this as part of the area reduction scheme. For example, suppose a transform wants to reduce the size of a particular cell. Two functionally identical cells may be of the same size and either could be used in the context of the cell to be downsized. However, one may have a better CAA score than the other (though slightly different auxiliary characteristics like delay and input capacitance), so the better scoring cell should be used. Of course, area reduction generally improves CAA scores by reducing the active area of the design.

In some cases, it is desirable to apply area reduction even in the critical-slack range. When a design, or part of a design, is placement congested, it is sometimes a good strategy to sacrifice some negative-slack paths by making them slower but smaller to create room to improve paths with even worse slack. Again, resizing is a good example. Suppose a path has a slack of -50 and it would be desirable to upsize a cell on the path, but there is no room to do so. Downsizing a cell in the neighborhood, degrading its slack from -2 to -4, may make sense as long as the loss from the downsizing is less than the gain from the upsizing. Typically, this kind of trade-off is made early in the physical synthesis process.

The effectiveness of area recovery is very dependent on the characteristics of the design, on the logic synthesis tool used to create it, and on the options used for the tool. Reductions in area of around 5 percent are typical, but reductions in excess of 20 percent have been observed.

39.5.2 ROUTING RECOVERY

Total wirelength and routing congestion can also be recovered. Damage to wirelength can be caused by legalization, buffering, or timing-driven placement. For example, when one first buffers a net, it may use a timing-driven Steiner topology (Chapter 25). Later, when one discovers that this net is not critical and meets its timing constraint, it can be rebuffered with a minimum Steiner tree (Chapter 24) to reduce the overall wirelength.

PDS has a function that rebuilds all trees with positive slack and sufficiently high windage, defined as follows. A net with $k-1$ buffers divides it into k trees. Let T_k be the sum of the minimum Steiner wirelengh of these k trees. Let T_0 be the wirelength of the minimum Steiner tree with all the buffer removed. Windage is the value of $T_k - T_0$. Nets with high windage indicate potentially good candidates for wirelength reduction through alternative buffer placement.

One can also deploy techniques to mitigate routing congestion. A buffer tree that goes through a routing congested region likely cannot be rerouted easily unless one also replaces the buffers. Smaller spacing between buffers reduces the flexibility of routing, so these problems must be handled before routing is required. PDS has a function that identifies buffer trees in routing congested regions and rebuilds them so that they avoid the routing resources using algorithms described in Chapter 28. Routing techniques can also be mitigate via spreading the placement using diffusion [17].

Of course, wiring congestion can occur independently of buffers. As noted earlier. PDS has programs that will reduce wirelength by moving boxes (also using the windage model) and by pin swapping within fan-in-trees.

39.5.3 VT RECOVERY

As explained previously, for multi-vt libraries, trade-offs among vt levels can have significant impacts on leakage power and delay. In some instances, low-vt cells may have been used to speed up the design but subsequent optimization may have made the use of low-vt unnecessary. In terms of Figure 39.9, it could be that the change from B to B' was actually a vt assignment, in which B was a high-vt cell while B' was low-vt. Once A has been changed to further improve timing, it may be possible to change B' back to a higher-vt cell to reduce power.

In fact, a reasonable strategy for timing closure is to use low-vt cells very aggressively to close on timing, even though it likely will completely explode the power budget. Then, vt recovery techniques can attempt to reduce power as much as possible while maintaining timing closure.

39.6 OTHER CONSIDERATIONS

This chapter focuses primarily on physical synthesis in the context of a typical flat ASIC design style. However, PDS is also used to drive timing closure for hierarchical designs and for designing the sub-blocks of high-performance microprocessors. We now discuss a some issues and special handling required to drive physical synthesis in these regimes.

39.6.1 HIERARCHICAL DESIGN

Engineers have been employing hierarchical design since the advent of the hardware description languages. What has changed over the years is the degree with which the hierarchy is maintained throughout the design automation flow. The global nature of optimizations like placement, buffering, and timing, means it is certainly simpler for PDS to handle a flat design. However, PDS is just one consideration for designers in terms of whether they design flat or hierarchically. Despite the simplicity of flat design, as of this writing, hierarchical design is becoming more prevalent. There are several reasons for this:

- Design size: The available memory in hardware may be insufficient to model properly the entire design. Although hardware performance may also be an issue, it can often be mitigated through various thread-parallel techniques.
- Schedule flexibility: The design begins naturally partitioned along functional boundaries. A large project, employing several engineers, will not be finished all at once. Hierarchical design allows for disparate schedules among the various partitions and design teams. This is especially true for microprocessor designs.
- Managing risk: Engineers cannot afford to generate a great deal of VHDL and then simply walk away. In some cases, the logic design process is highly interactive. The design automation tools must successfully cope with an ever-changing netlist in which logic changes may

arrive very late in the schedule. By partitioning the design, it is possible to limit the impact of these changes, protecting the large investment required to reach the current design state.

- Design reuse: It is common to see the same logic function replicated many times across the design. In a fully automated methodology, one can uniquely construct and optimize each instance of this logic. If the uses are expanded uniquely, each use can be optimized in the context in which it is used. If the physical implementation is reused, then the block must be optimized so that it works in all of its contexts simultaneously, which is a more challenging task. However, common practice shows that even the so-called fully automated methodologies require a fair amount of human intervention. Although reuse does present more complexity, there is a point (number of instances) for every design, for which the benefit of implementing the logic just once outweighs the added complexity.

After choosing and hierarchical design automation methodology, the single most important decision impacting physical synthesis is the manner in which the design is partitioned. One may work within the boundaries implied by the logic design, or instead one may completely or partially flatten the design and allow the tools to draw their own boundaries. The first choice, working within the confines of the logic design, is still the most common use of hierarchy.

Hierarchical processing based on logical partitioning involves getting a leaf set of logical partitions (perhaps using node reduction as described below) then using those partitions as physical entities, which are floorplanned. In this sense, the quality of the logical partitioning is defined by the quality of the corresponding physical and timing partitioning, which in turn directly affects difficulty of the problem presented to PDS.

But this is a source of conflict in developing the design. From a functional point of view, for example, the designer might develop a random logic block that describes the control flow for some large section of dataflow logic. This is a good functional decomposition and is probably good for simulation, but it may not be good physically because in reality one would not want the control to be segmented in a predefined area by itself, but would want it to be interspersed among the data flow block.

The distribution of function within the logical hierarchy may make it impossible to successfully execute physical synthesis. Attributes of an optimal physical partitioning include a partition placement and boundary pin assignment that construct relatively short paths between the partitions. Attributes of an optimal timing partitioning include paths that do not go in and out of several partitions before being captured by a sequential element with the signals being launched of captured logically close to the hierarchical boundaries.

An effective partitioning also include a distribution of chip resources. The first step is to reduce the number of hierarchical nodes by collapsing the design hierarchy. Collapsing the design hierarchy removes hierarchical boundaries that will constrain PDS. In practice, this node reduction is limited only by the performance of the available tools. It is possible (even probable) that some logic function get promoted all the way to the top level if it interfaces with multiple partitions. In our earlier example, the control flow logic partition would be a good candidate to promote to the top level so its logic could be distributed as needed. As noted above, one of the motivating factors for doing hierarchical design is to manage risk by limiting the impact on the design of logic changes to the logical partition. Collapsing nodes can reduce this advantage of hierarchy, so there is again a conflict between obtaining a good physical representation and maintaining the logic hierarchy for engineering changes.

The next step, floorplanning, is to assign space on the chip image to each partition while reserving some space for top level logic. These two steps, although guided by automated analysis, usually require a fair amount of human intervention.

To run PDS on a partition out of the context of the rest of the design hierarchy, sufficient detail regarding the hierarchical boundaries must be provided. The floorphanning steps specify the outline of the hierarchical boundary. What remains is the determinations determine of the location of the pins on the hierarchical boundary and their timing characteristics. These details are best determined by viewing the design hierarchy as "virtually flat" and performing placement and timing analysis.

A virtually-flat placement simultaneously places all partitions, allowing hierarchical boundary pins to float, while constraining the contents of each partition to adhere to the floorphan. The hierarchical boundary pins are then placed at the intersection of the hierarchical net route with the outline of the partition. The timing details for hierarchical boundary pins can be calculated by constructing a flat timing graph for the hierarchical design. Once the hierarchical boundary paths have been timed, the arrival and required arrival times should be adjusted by apportioning the slack.

This process of slack apportionment involves examining a timing path that crosses hierarchical boundaries and determining what portion of that path may be improved through physical synthesis. To perfectly solve this problem, the slack apportionment algorithm would have to encompass the entire knowledge base of the optimization suite. Because, this is impractical, one must rely upon simple heuristics. The elastic delay of a particular element in a hierarchical path can be modeled as a simple weight applied against the actual delay. If it is known that a portion of the design will not be changing much, one would assert a very low elasticity. In the case of an static random access memory (SRAM) or core, a zero elasticity would be used. Once the elastic delay along the hierarchical path is determined, the slack is apportioned between the partitions based upon the relative amount of elastic delay contained within each partition.

In addition to timing, capacitance and slew values are apportioned to the hierarchical pins. This results in hierarchical boundary pin placement and timing assertions allow physical synthesis to be executed on each partition individually.

Once all of the blocks have been processed out of context, all of the sequentially terminated paths within a block have been fully optimized, but there still may be some improvement needed on cross-hierarchy paths.

In Figure 39.10, consider the path between sequential elements $S1$ and $S2$. Two cells on the path are in block 1 and three cells are in block 2. There is a global net between them going from block pin 1 to block pin 2. There are timing and other assertions on BP1 and BP2 that have been developed during the apportionment phase. Out-of-content optimization on block 1 and block 2 may have made these assertions incorrect. At this point, one wants to reoptimize this path in a virtually flat way by traversing the path hierarchically and applying optimization along it with accurate (nonapportioned) timing.

Note that no additional optimization needs to be done on the logic cloud between sequentials $S0$ and $S1$ because there was no timing approximation needed during out-of-context optimization.

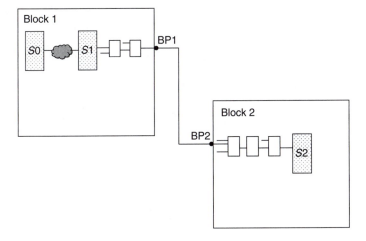

FIGURE 39.10 Hierarchical design example.

Further, when the hierarchical optimization is done on the $S1$ to $S2$ path, no timing information is needed for the logic between $S0$ and $S1$. Eliding the timing on such paths reduces CPU time and the memory footprint needed for hierarchical processing.

Again referring to Figure 39.10, top-level optimization may be performed to buffer the net from BP1 to BP2.

39.6.2 HIGH-PERFORMANCE CLOCKING

In microprocessor designs, clock frequencies are significantly higher than for ASICs and the transistor counts are large as well. Thus, the global clock distribution can contribute up to 50 percent of the total active power in high-performance multihertz designs. In a well-designed balanced clock trees, most of the power is consumed at the last level of the tree, that is , the final stage of the tree that drives the latches.

The overall clock power can be significantly reduced by constraining each latch to be as physically close as possible to the local clock buffer (LCB) that drives it. Figure 39.11 shows this clustering that latches around the LCB. One may think that constraining latches in this matter could hurt performance because latches may not be ideally placed. However, generally, there is an LCB fairly close to a latch's ideal location, which means the latch does not have to be moved too far to be placed next to an LCB. Further, there can be a positive timing effect because skew is reduced from all the latches being clustered around local clock buffers (as shown in Figure 39.12).

Savings in power are obtained as a result of the reduction in wire load being driven by the clock buffer. We have found empirically that clustering latches in this manner reduces the capacitive load on the LCB by up to 40 percent, compared to unconstrained latch placement; this directly translates into power saving for the local clock buffer.

39.6.3 POWER GATING TO REDUCE LEAKAGE POWER

Exponential increase in leakage power has been one of the most challenging issues in sub-90 nm CMOS technologies. Power gating is one of most effective techniques to reduce both subthreshold leakage and gate leakage as it cuts off the path to the supply 18, 19. Conceptually, it is a straightforward technique; however, the implementation can be quite tricky in high-performance designs where the performance trade-off is constrained to less than 2 percent of the frequency loss due to power gate

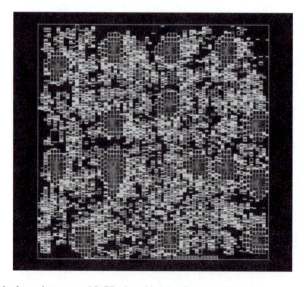

FIGURE 39.11 Latch clustering around LCBs in a high-performance block.

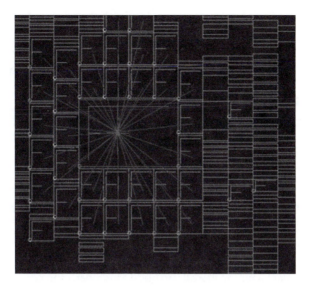

FIGURE 39.12 Cluster of latches around a single LCB.

(footer/header switch insertion). Figure 39.13 shows a simple schematic of a logic block that has been power gated by a header switch (PFET) or a footer switch (NFET). Obviously, footer switches are preferred due to the better drive capability of NFETs. Operationally, if the logic block is not active, the SLEEP signal can turn off the NFET (footer switch) and the virtual ground (drain of NFET) will float toward V_{dd} (supply voltage), thereby reducing the leakage by orders of magnitude.

Introducing a series transistor (footer/header) in the logic path results in a performance penalty. This performance penalty can be mitigated by making the size of the footer/header larger so as to reduce the series resistance. However, the leakage benefit reduces with increasing size of the power gate. Practically, in low-power applications, over 2000 times leakage saving can be obtained at the expense of 8–10 percent reduction in performance. However, in high-performance designs, this is a relatively large performance penalty. So, larger power gate sizes are chosen (approximately 6–8 percent of logic area) to achieve less than 2 percent performance penalty with over 20 times leakage reduction.

In general, power gating can be physically implemented in the designs using block-based coarse-grained power gating and intrablock fine power gating (similar to multiple-supply voltages). In a block-based implementation, the footer (or header) switches surround the boundary of the block, as shown in Figure 39.14. This physical implementation is easier because it does not disturb the internal layout of the block. However, it has a potential drawback in terms of larger IR drop on the virtual ground supply. For IP blocks, this is the preferred implementation technique for power gating.

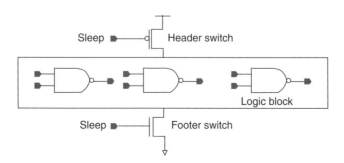

FIGURE 39.13 Power gating using header/footer switches.

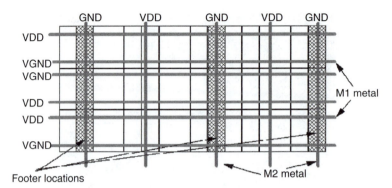

FIGURE 39.14 Coarse-grained power gating with macro/core. GND = Ground; VDD = voltage drain drain; VGND = virtual ground.

Fine-grained power gating, as shown in Figure 39.15, where the footer switches are implemented within the logic in a regular layout are more desirable in a high-performance design where the voltage drop across the power gate as well as IR and EM (electromigration) requirements are more stringent.

39.7 INTO THE FUTURE

We have summarized the current workings of IBM's physical synthesis capabilities to display the complexities of such a system. Physical synthesis requires a seamless integration of many previously separate design automation domains, such as optimization, placement, timing, extraction, and routing. However, as technology progresses toward 45 nm and beyond, more will be demanded of physical synthesis. It must be dynamic and must constantly adapt to changing technologies, design styles, and design specifications.

Timing closure will continue to evolve into the even more complex problem of design closure. Design closure requires that accurate modeling of the clock tree network and routing be incorporated earlier and earlier up the physical synthesis pipeline to take into account their effects on timing and signal integrity. Meeting global power constraints, using multithreshold voltages, voltage islands, power gating, etc. also becomes more critical. One must pay attention to how physical-design choices relate to chip fabrication, so design for manufacturability and handling of variability will become increasingly important. Optimizations must become more sophisticated to take these additional objectives into account.

Increasing chip sizes and additional requirements for physical synthesis to meet and incorporate these additional constraints also further exacerbates the ability to run efficiently, perhaps another reason why hierarchical design is becoming more prevalent.

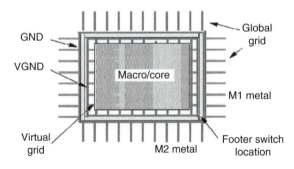

FIGURE 39.15 Fine-grained power gating within a block. GND = Ground and VGND = virtual ground.

REFERENCES

1. C. J. Alpert, C. -N. Chu, and P. G. Villarrubia. The coming of age of physical synthesis, In *IEEE/ACM ICCAD*, San Jose, CA, 2007, pp. 246–249.
2. L. Trevillyan, D. Kung, R. Puri, L. N. Reddy, and M. A. Kazda. An integrated environment for technology closure of deep-submicron IC designs. In *IEEE Design and Test of Computers*, pp. 14–22, January 2004; W. Donath, P. Kudva, L. Stok, P. Villarubia, L. Reddy, A. Sullivan, Transformational placement and synthesis, in *Proceedings of the Conference on Design, Automation and Test in Europe Exhibition*, Paris, France, 2000, pp. 194–201.
3. C. J. Alpert, S. K. Karandikar, Z. Li, G. -J. Nam, S. T. Quay, H. Ren, C. N. Sze, P. G. Villarrubia, and M. C. Yildiz. Techniques for fast physical synthesis. *Proceedings of the IEEE*, 95(3):573–599, March 2007.
4. U. Brenner and A. Rohe. An effective congestion driven placement framework. In *Proceedings of International Symposium on Physical Design*, San Jose, CA, pp. 6–11, 2002.
5. J. Darringer, E. Davidson, D. J. Hathaway, B. Koenemann, M. Lavin, J. K. Morrell, K. Rahmat, W. Roesner, E. Schanzenbach, G. Tellez, and L. Trevillyan. EDA in IBM: Past, present, and future. *IEEE Transactions on Computer-Aided Design of Integrated Circuits and Systems*, 19(12):1476–1497, December 2000.
6. I. Sutherland, R. F. Sproull, and D. Harris. *Logical Effort: Designing Fast CMOS Circuits.* Morgan Kaufmann, San Fransisco, CA, 1999.
7. L. Trevillyan, P. Kotecha, A. Drumm, and R. Puri. A Method for Incremental Cell Placement for Minimum Wire Length, U. S. patent pending.
8. E. Bozorgzadeh, S. Ghiasi, and M. Sarrafzadeh. Optimal integer delay budget assignment on directed acyclic graphs. *IEEE Transactions on CAD of ICs and Systems,* 23(8):1184–1199.
9. V. Kravets and P. Kudva. Implicit enumeration of structural changes in circuit optimization. In *Proceedings of Design Automation Conference*, San Diego, CA, pp. 439–441, June 2004.
10. R. E. Bryant. Graph-based algorithms for Boolean function maniupulation. *IEEE Transactions on Computers*, C-35(6):677–691, August 1986.
11. G. R. Chiu, D. P. Singh, V. Manohararajah, and S. D. Brown. Mapping arbitrary login functions into synchronous embedded memories for area reduction on FPGAS. In *IEEE/ACM ICCAD*, San Jose, CA, pp. 135–142, 2006.
12. B. Guan and C. Sechen. Large standard cell libraries and their impact on layout area and circuit performance. In *IEEE ICCD*, Austin, TX, pp. 378–383, 1996.
13. A. Hussain and K. Umino. Method to close timing on all corners with synopsys galaxy at and below 130 nm. In *SNUG*, San Jose, CA, 2005.
14. R. Murgai. Improved layout-driven area-constrained timing optimization by net buffering, In *18th International Conference on VLSI Design* held jointly with *4th International Conference on Embedded Systems Design* (VLSID'05), Kolkota, India, pp. 97–102, 2005.
15. V. N. Kravets. Constructive multi-level synthesis by way of functional properties. PhD Thesis, University of Michigan, Ann Arbor, MI, 2001.
16. C. Guardiani, M. Bertoletti, N. Dragone, M. Malcotti, and P. McNamara. An effective DFM strategy requires accurate process and IP pre-characterization. In *IEEE/ACM DAC*, Anaheim, CA, pp. 760–761, June 2005.
17. H. Ren, D. Z. Pan, C. J. Alpert, and P. Villarrubia. Diffusion-based placement migration. In *Proceedings of Design Automation Conference*, Anaheim, CA, pp. 515–520, 2005.
18. R. Puri, L. Stok, J. Cohn, D. Kung, D. Pan, D. Sylvester, A. Srivastava, and S. Kulkarni. Pushing ASIC performance in a power envelope. In *Proceedings of Design Automation Conference*, Anaheim, CA, p. 788, 2003.
19. H. Li, S. Bhunia, Y. Chen, T. N. Vijaykumar, and K. Roy. Deterministic clock gating for microprocessor power reduction. In *High-Performance Computer Architecture*, Anaheim, CA, pp. 113–122, 2003.

40 X Architecture Place and Route: Physical Design for the X Interconnect Architecture

Steve Teig, Asmus Hetzel, Joseph Ganley, Jon Frankle, and Aki Fujimura

CONTENTS

40.1   INTRODUCTION

For 40 years, physical design dogma has decreed that (nearly) every wire on a chip be Manhattan—either horizontal or vertical—despite the intuition that adding diagonal wires should significantly reduce the total interconnect required to implement a design. This chapter briefly provides some historical context for the ubiquity of Manhattan wiring and then introduces and explores the X interconnect architecture [IML+02,T02], which combines diagonal and Manhattan wires pervasively to improve IC layout. Realizing the theoretical benefits of X, which are substantial and surprisingly diverse, in practice has proven to be quite challenging, demanding both a careful reexamination and refinement of the manufacturing flow and a material revision of almost every tool in the physical design flow. For example, X place and route (XPR)—the X system described here—has required new methods for floorplanning, wire load estimation in synthesis, global placement, global routing, detailed placement, detailed routing, parasitic extraction, OPC, clock routing, power routing, geometric search, and even database representation. The novelty of these methods has resulted in numerous patents. Even as X has begun to see commercial use, with X chips from Toshiba and ATI, among others, many challenges remain, and X-enabled physical design techniques should become and increasingly active area of research in both academia and industry in the coming years.

40.2   HISTORY

The transistors for almost every chip are distributed across the chip's two-dimensional surface, so at least two routing directions are required for the flexible interconnection of those transistors. Until the mid-1980s, it was not practical to have more than one or two layers of metal wiring above the polysilicon, or poly, layer. Because chips are generally rectangular so that the silicon wafers on which they are manufactured can be efficiently diced, it seemed logical to make the poly layer and the one metal layer (M1) orthogonal and axis-parallel.* The second metal layer, M2, where it was used, was typically orthogonal to M1. Very short diagonal jogs were used in some channel routers and to miter the corners in the power rail through the I/O pads, but general diagonal wiring was not seriously considered. With the introduction in the late 1980s of planarization techniques to IC manufacturing, an additional layer of metal, M3, became widely available, which single-handedly precipitated the invention of modern, area-based, place-and-route methods and their rapid dominance over the row-and-channel-based techniques that preceded them. Although hexagonal wiring (i.e., $0°$, $120°$, and $240°$)—now, sometimes called the Y architecture [CCK+03]—could, in principle, have been very powerful even then, the newness of multilayer, Manhattan IC manufacturing caused the fabs to fear the added complexity of adding diagonal wires as well. So, despite a few theoretical papers (e.g., [K95] and references therein) and patents [FHM+98,SKK+96] (never reduced to practice) in the mid-1990s, there was no significant, practical exploration of diagonal wiring, either in manufacturing or in EDA, before the X effort at Simplex Solutions in the 1990s. Fortunately, the number of wiring layers increased sharply in the 1990s, which motivated a reexamination of the possible benefits of diagonal wiring and the practical hurdles involved in realizing them.

There are two apparent challenges in producing chips with diagonal wires: manufacturing and EDA. As it happens, for some diagonal interconnect architectures, such as those that add $45°$ and $135°$ wires to Manhattan wires, mainstream manufacturing flows and equipment enable reasonably straightforward fabrication. Physical design for diagonal wiring, on the other hand, is considerably more challenging than it first appears, and XPR—the first full-fledged such physical design system—required dozens of person-years of development before reaching industrial-strength maturity.

The sections that follow describe the X interconnect architecture, which uses both Manhattan and diagonal wires pervasively, and introduce some of the many EDA innovations that were required to reduce X to practice.

40.3   X INTERCONNECT ARCHITECTURE

Moore's law has been largely driven by the regularity and rapidity with which fabs have been able to shrink transistors and wires while still manufacturing them reliably. Even with the 20-fold shrink from the 5-μ (~1982) to the 0.25-μ (~1982) technology node, transistors continued to dominate area, performance, and power. But the emergence of nanometer technologies (e.g,. 180, 130, 90 nm, etc.) starting in the late 1990s so sharply increased the relative impact of wires versus transistors on area, performance, and power as to necessitate radical innovations in the interconnect. The severity of the interconnect problem at nanometer nodes is evident from the replacement of aluminum wires on chips with copper: a multibillion-dollar effort that required new chemistry, new

---

* In fact, even in the two-layer case, the total wirelength would be reduced by about 1 percent by making the two wiring directions be northeast and northwest instead, but the complexity of doing so outweighs a mere 1 percent benefit.

equipment, and revised EDA tools that collectively reduced interconnect delay by ~50 percent. Of course, changes of wiring material are not the only tools available, and other radical suggestions, such as the pervasive use of diagonal wires, reemerged as worthy of consideration. Just as with the introduction of copper wiring, though, the benefits of diagonal wires carry significant practical challenges with them.

For one, most of the equipment for the generation of masks and the manufacture of chips relies on an underlying, fine, discrete grid. All manufactured structures must have their edges on this grid, which was designed for Manhattan wiring but also directly permits 45° (*northeast* or NE) and 135° (*northwest* or NW), because a diagonal wire of length $k\sqrt{2}$, where k is a positive integer, resolves into k units in each of the horizontal and vertical directions. The apparent manufacturability of NE and NW wires suggested that an interconnect architecture with Manhattan, NE, and NW wires could provide the benefits of diagonals in a practical implementation. By contrast, the griddedness of manufacturing is a significant obstacle to the practicality of hexagonal wiring, for example, as the edges of the wires do not lie on grid. Further, at least one of the legs of a 30–60–90 right triangle must be irrational; that is the $\sqrt{3}$ term does not cancel for hexagonal wiring the way that the $\sqrt{2}$ terms do for the X architecture.

A second consideration is that lower layers of writing (e.g., M1 and M2) are typically used for the internal connections of the standard cells and IP blocks themselves. Because cells and blocks are overwhelmingly Manhattan, there was no significant benefit in adding diagonals to those wiring layers for connections between cells. On the other hand, upper layers of mental are specifically intended for connections between cells, so it is more reasonable to combine Manhattan and diagonal wires there.

An *X interconnect architecture* is one that combines the extensive use of both Manhattan wires and diagonal wires. In practice, distinct wiring layers (or, at least, regions within those wiring layers) are devoted to particular Manhattan or diagonal preferred directions. While one can construct an X architecture with each layer having wires rotated 45° with respect to the previous layer, it is improbable that such structures outperform those in which layers are stacked in orthogonal pairs. Further, the desire for backward compatibility with Manhattan-based infrastructure, such as standard cell libraries, has strongly influenced the application of diagonals in practice.

The above observations—particularly, backward compatibility—motivated the typical use in practice of X interconnect architectures in which M1–M3 are Manhattan, typically alternating between horizontal and vertical preferred directions on successive layers, M4 is diagonal (e.g., NE), and M5 is perpendicular to M4 (e.g., NW). If there are additional metal layers, such as M6 and M7, they are again Manhattan, while M8 and M9 could be diagonal. Thus,

1. Every layer is adjacent to a perpendicular layer (to facilitate efficient local wiring)
2. Every sequential quartet of layers above M1 contains a horizontal, a vertical, a NE, and a NW (to facilitate efficient, larger-scale wiring)

An interconnect architecture that satisfies these two properties makes the name "X" apparent, owing to the novel, X-shaped intersection of adjacent diagonal layers. However, the term and the techniques described in this chapter apply more generally to any interconnect architecture in which both Manhattan and diagonal wires play a significant role.

40.4   THEORETICAL BENEFITS OF X

X, both in theory and in practice, reduces chip area, wirelength, delay, coupling capacitance, and power versus Manhattan, sometimes to such as extent that a full layer of interconnect can be removed. To estimate these benefits analytically, it is easiest to begin with wirelength reduction. Most current placement algorithms minimize some approximation to the sum over all nets of the semiperimeter of each net's Manhattan bounding box.* As a result, placers optimize a correlate to wirelength, possibly weighted by timing considerations or congestion, but one might expect that they are unbiased with respect to bounding-box aspect ratios. To test this hypothesis, we examined dozens of industrial, Manhattan designs early in the X project and found that, in fact, aspect ratios are distributed uniformly.

At least 55–60 percent of nets in contemporary designs are two-pin nets even before placement, and the increasing use of buffers has sharply increased that percentage after placement. So, as a simple but reasonable estimate of the wirelength reduction versus Manhattan to expect with X, one can estimate the expected reduction in the wirelength of a two-pin net with a random aspect ratio. In the Manhattan metric, a circle (i.e., the locus of points at a fixed distance from a specified center point) is diamond-shaped; for the X metric, the circle is octagonal. Consider a connection with extent $(|\Delta x|, |\Delta y|)$. Without loss of generality, suppose that $(|\Delta x| \geq |\Delta y|)$; then, the Manhattan-to-X wirelength reduction for this connection is $1 - [|\Delta x| + |\Delta y|(\sqrt{2} - 1)]/(|\Delta x| + |\Delta y|)$. The expected value of this reduction, assuming that the source is at the center of a diamond, and the sink's location is uniformly distributed around the periphery is Ref. [T02].

$$1 - \frac{\int\limits_{0}^{1/2} \left[\left(\sqrt{2} - 2 \right) y + 1 \right] dy}{\int\limits_{0}^{1/2} dy} \cong 14.6 \text{ percent}$$

Importantly, this analysis assumes that only the router has changed, yet the real benefits of X become apparent only by making the whole system X-aware. For example, suppose that the placer is X-aware too; then, by analogy to the Manhattan system, the placer for X minimizes wirelength but is unbiased with respect to aspect ratio. To model an X placer analytically, rearrange the components that would have been placed within the Manhattan disk of radius r (i.e., filled diamond) to occupy an X disk (i.e., filled octagon) of equal area [T02]. The resulting wirelength reduction, which is one minus the ratio the octagon's radius of a diamond of equal area, is $1 - (1/2)^{1/4} \cong 15.9$ percent.†

For the significant fraction of high-end designs that are core-limited rather than pad-limited, substantial additional improvement with X is possible, though. Most designs have utilizations far below 100 percent: often as low as 70 percent or even lower for interconnect-dominated designs, such as network switches [BR02]. It is reasonable to assume that X-place-and-route systems are as good at optimizing X objective functions as Manhattan place-and-route systems are at optimizing Manhattan objectives, but reducing wirelength by 15.9 percent while leaving die size unchanged would leave the X router with a much easier problem than a Manhattan router had. Instead, an X system can exploit the wirelength reduction versus Manhattan by shrinking the die until the X routing is as dense as the Manhattan routing was in the original design. In particular, reducing wirelength by 15.9 percent would require a die size shrink of 15.9 percent to restore the wiring density of the original Manhattan layout. Of course, this die size reduction would permit an additional wirelength reduction of $1 - [1 - (1/2)^{1/4}]^{1/2} \cong 8.3$ percent, which, in turn, permits an additional die shrink of 8.3 percent, etc. The resulting infinite product converges to a wirelength and die size reduction of $(1 - 1\sqrt{2}) \cong 29.3$ percent. This reasoning demonstrates that, in general, any technique that achieves a wirelength reduction of R percent with fixed area can be used to achieve a wirelength reduction

---

* Of course, the minimization of bounding-box semiperimeters, despite its near-ubiquity in current placers, ignores the location of pins within the box and the concomitant flexibility of wiring; it is, thus, a very crude measure of placement quality.

† The analogous analysis for Euclidean (i.e., all-angle) wiring results in a wirelength reducton of $1 - \sqrt{(2/\pi)} \cong 20.2$ percent versus Manhattan.

of almost 2R percent (i.e., $R(2-R)$ percent) if area reduction is used to maintain constant layout difficulty. Particularly for wire-dominated designs such as networking chips, which typically have low utilizations with Manhattan wiring, significant die size reduction is possible with X. Although the above analysis is somewhat aggressive in assuming that all nets have only two pins, it is also conservative in that the substantial additional area reduction owing to the concomitant shrinkage of drivers and elimination of buffers is not considered. In practice, reducing the die size by 15–20 percent and the wirelength by 20–25 percent has proved straightforward in general, and the alternative of not reducing the die size but instead using X to remove a wiring layer (e.g., at ATi)—and sometimes two wiring layers—has also been achieved.

One additional, nonobvious, benefit of X is its utility for routing over IP blocks. Most IP blocks (e.g., memories) use Manhattan wiring for layers 1–3 and sometimes 4, and many have the restriction that Manhattan wiring over the block is forbidden due to capacitive coupling considerations. X, on the other hand, can cross over such such blocks diagonally with no risk of parallel runs between the over-the-block wiring and within-the-block wiring. Because more than half of a typical chip today is occupied by IP such as memory blocks, the opportunity to use the entirety of the upper wiring layers confers substantial benefit.

40.5 LIMITATIONS OF X

Although both practical experience with X and theoretical analysis demonstrate its significant benefits—to wirelength, area, delay, power, etc.—X is not a panacea. For example, the above analysis demonstrates that the wirelength reduction is nearly doubled by permitting area reduction, but for those atypical designs that have extremely high utilizations (e.g., more than 90 percent of the die is occupied by components that are not buffers), X can provide only more modest wirelength reductions. Clearly, for blocks that have highly eccentric aspect ratios (e.g., 5:1), the use of diagonals does not buy much. In practice, such narrow blocks typically abut Manhattan IP blocks, though, so over-the-IP, diagonal wiring somewhat mitigates the diminished utility of X within the eccentric block.

X requires enough wiring layers for some of them to be used for diagonals; for low-end devices for which signal routing extends only to M4, for example, X cannot be usefully applied. Finally, for designs with extensive Manhattan constraints on the upper wiring layers, diagonal wiring can be difficult to incorporate effectively. For example, if the floorplan is Manhattan-oriented, so that large horizontal buses cross an X block on M4, large-scale, diagonal wires on M4 become infeasible by construction.

In practice, though, the vast majority of designs show significant wirelength and die size reduction with X when compared to their Manhattan equivalents. Curiously, the most significant limitation of X in practice is the widespread misconception that X changes only the router and not the full layout system. Indeed, as the theoretical analysis above shows, keeping the area and the placement fixed and changing only the wiring to permit diagonals buys only 14.6 percent wirelength reduction and achieves that only for netlists with only two-pin nets. For real netlists, the improvement is somewhat lower in practice—perhaps, 10 percent (e.g., [I06])—if only the wiring is permitted to change. Using a Manhattan floorplan, and Manhattan buses on the upper layers, can make the situation even worse.

To see the benefits of X in practice, one must apply it to problems it addresses well:

- Designs for which high utilization could not be achieved in Manhattan
- Designs that are not overly eccentric in aspect ratio
- Designs with enough wiring layers to devote part of at least one to diagonals
- Designs that accommodate X by not overconstraining the upper layers with required Manhattan wires, and, most importantly
- Designs that permit the whole layout system, and just the router, to be X-aware

40.6 ROLE OF VIAS

Analyses such as the one above assume that vias between layers are free. Although the interconnect delay caused by vias is sharply reduced with copper wires, vias remain the most difficult features to manufacture reliably on an integrated circuit, and reducing the number of vias can have a significant, positive effect on yield. In addition, vias create routing obstacles on two layers, rather than one, so reducing the number of vias can significantly simplify layout.

An even more entrenched dogma than the use of Manhattan wiring is the use of preferred-direction wiring: that is, the requirement that each routing layer have a designated, preferred wiring direction (e.g., horizontal), such that virtually all of the wire length on that layer is required to be in the preferred direction. The assumption of a preferred direction for each layer significantly simplifies and accelerates routing algorithms, but it also demands a via for every change of direction and, thus, for any connection in a Manhattan layout that is not exactly vertical or horizontal. Because X can move diagonally without using a via, it has the potential to reduce the number of vias significantly. On the other hand, backward compatibility with existing, Manhattan cell libraries demands that the diagonal layers are upper layers (e.g., M4 and M5), so extra vias are required to use the diagonals, mitigating via reduction somewhat. The pronounced impact of vias on the both yield and layout thus motivates the consideration of *nonpreferred-direction* wiring: layouts in which wires in multiple orientations coexist on the same wiring layer.

Even a conservative nonpreferred-direction strategy for X, using diagonal jogs on Manhattan layers and Manhattan jogs on diagonal layers, can sharply reduce the number of vias required for layout, and XPR sees substantial via reductions in practice versus contemporary Manhattan systems. More radical than short, nonpreferred-direction jogs, though, but considerably more powerful is the complete abandonment of the *preferred-direction* requirement. Full directional freedom on all layers, called *liquid routing*, makes the fullest use of the power introduced by diagonals, but is far more challenging from an EDA point of view than preferred-direction X. In the addition, the yield benefits of a via reduction from liquid routing must be weighed against lithographic concerns about nonpreferred-direction wiring in nanometer technologies to assess its long-term practicality. From an academic point of view, though, liquid routing is almost completely unexplored territory. The problems there are particularly challenging, but the potential, practical payoff is high. The reader is encouraged to investigate the patents by Caldwell and Teig on Q* and related liquid routing ideas [TC04,TC05,TC06] as a starting point for future work.

40.7 SYSTEM FOR X PLACE AND ROUTE

In the sections that follow, we describe a few of the tools and techniques used within XPR that made X layout possible starting in 2001. Many additional X-aware tools are required, ranging from parasitic extraction to clock routing and even to visualization infrastructure, as quad and K-D trees (Section 4.3.2) are highly inefficient for region queries with both long diagonal and long Manhattan wires. We confine the presentation here to placement, global routing, detailed routing, and Steiner tree construction.

40.8 X PLACEMENT

Placement is typically performed in one of the three ways: recursive partitioning, analytical techniques, or Monte Carlo methods such as simulated annealing. Annealing, which is often used for detailed placement but rarely for global placement anymore because of its high computational expense, can be directly adapted to the X interconnect architecture by changing the objective function, but the other two placement methods require much more drastic modifications.

Another common approach to modern placement is analytical formulation. Here, the netlist's wirelength is approximated by a continuously differentiable function that is either directly minimized with a conjugate gradient-based minimizer (or other derivative-based techniques) or indirectly minimized using a linear system of equations whose solution minimizes the original wirelength formula.

An unusual and significant challenge in X placement stems from the inseparability of two-dimensional distance into independent, one-dimensional components. The Manhattan distance between $(x1, y1)$ and $(x2, y2)$ is simply $|x2 - x1| + |y2 - y1|$, so x and y can be treated independently, and reducing distance by one unit in either x or y is equally desirable, all other considerations (e.g., congestion) being equal. Distance in X, though, is $\max(|x2 - x1|, |y2 - y1|) + (\sqrt{2} - 1)^* \min(|x2 - x1|, |y2 - y1|)$. When this equation is differentiated, the resulting derivative intertwines x and y in ways for which most analytical placers and partitioners were not designed. In fact, this requirement for separability is why most analytical placers use either squared Euclidean length [KSJA91], some approximation of linear wirelength using piecewise squared length [SDJ91] or β-regularization [BKKM01], or some other approximation such as bounding-box semiperimeter [KRW05]. All of these techniques have the desirable property that the x- and y- equations are sparse and separable: that is, can be solved as two separate systems, thus greatly reducing runtime.

Typical analytical placement techniques often also require separability within the legalization step that follows, which is usually partitioning-based. For example, it is not clear that techniques such as Ref. [V97] can be made X-aware, even in principle.

Methods such as β-regularization [BKKM01] and conjugate gradient methods [KRW05] can be generalized to accommodate X, at the expense of some implementation complexity, and this would be a potentially fruitful area for future research.

By contrast, recursive partitioning methods, either standalone or as legalization methods for analytical placers, seem to be fundamentally incompatible with X. To see this, consider how a modern partitioning algorithm works. Most of these techniques are ultimately derived from the early algorithm of Kernighan and Lin [KL70], later improved by Fiducia and Mattheyses [FM82]. After the authors' names, this type of approach is typically referred to as *KLFM*.

The KLFM algorithm first divides the set of components into two roughly equal-sized subsets. It then moves or swaps individual components between these subsets heuristically to minimize the number of nets that contain components in both subsets—that is, that are cut. The KLFM algorithm itself is a fairly simple local optimization heuristic, yet it performs quite well on this problem. An enormous amount of later research builds improvements onto the basic KLFM structure (see Section 7.2).

The way that KLFM is typically used to solve the placement problem is by recursive bipartitioning, in which the two-dimensional placement problem is artificially decomposed into a sequence of one-dimensional partitioning problems. This is accomplished by specifying a vertical or horizontal cutline that roughly bisects the placement area and using KLFM to partition the set of components into two subsets that are constrained to lie on opposite sides of the cutline. Then, each partition is, in turn, bisected by a cutline, and KLFM divides the subset within the partition into two smaller subsets that are constrained to lie on opposite sides of the partition's cutline. This process continues recursively until only a few components are left in each partition. A variety of techniques have been devised for terminal propagation, which allows the algorithm to capture the influence of connected components outside the current subproblem on the placement of the components inside the subproblem to which they are connected.

Unfortunately, recursive bipartitioning of this type is poorly suited to the X interconnect architecture. The use of horizontal and vertical cutlines one at a time assumes the separability of horizontal and vertical distances in assessing placement quality just as many of the analytical placement techniques do. The inseparability of the X metric means that even the addition of diagonal cutlines to a partitioning strategy will not capture X placement quality, which depends fundamentally on the interplay between Manhattan and diagonal geometries. To modify partitioning to support X, we used two-dimensional, k-way partitioning in place of one-dimensional bipartitioning.

To exploit the benefits of the partitioning idea within an X system, we use a modified simulated annealing strategy to partition the components into an $n \times m$ grid, where n and m are both greater than 1. This approach was used by Suaris and Kedem [SK89], where $n = m = 2$, and by Bapat and Cohoon [BC93], Alexander et al. [ACGR98], and Ganley [G95], where $n = m = 3$. We refined and improved this approach for $n = m = 4$ to create the first placer for the X interconnect architecture.

The key principle behind these algorithms is to consider an approximate routing of each net, where the cell positions are rounded to the centers of the partitions in the $n \times m$ grid. The partition of a given net can then be considered to form a bit vector of length nm, in which each bit is on if a component on the net lies in the corresponding partition. The numeric value of this bit vector can then be used to index a table giving the score of that particular configuration of the net. This table is precomputed once and stored, so there is no recurring runtime cost for the computation of its values. A single, canonical value for the score can be stored and simply scaled (if necessary) to the actual size of the current grid.

The default measure used by all of the placement algorithms cited above, including ours, is the length of an optimal (in our case, octilinear) Steiner tree of the points in the $n \times m$ grid. Although Suaris and Kedem [SK89] and Huang and Kahng [HK97] report that KLFM-style partitioning works well for $n = m = 2$, it turns out to perform quite poorly for $n, m \geq 3$. The terrain of the optimization objective becomes too rough, and KLFM-style, local optimization algorithms become trapped in deep local optima that are globally poor. Our algorithm instead uses a sophisticated, multiobjective variant of simulated annealing; although this is computationally expensive, it produces substantially higher-quality solutions than KLFM or any of several other, simpler heuristics that we tried. The other objectives, aside from total Steiner tree length, enforce that both the components in each partition and the (approximate) routing congestion will fit in the partition. The increased number of partitions, and the fact that their sizes cannot be adjusted to match a particular partition, makes the balance problem harder to solve in this context as well. In particular, balancing the 16 slots alone often leads to overfilled rows or columns in the 4×4 grid. Additional terms to enforce the balance of each rows and columns are added, resulting in the overall objective function for a particular p:

$$f(p) = \sum_{\text{nets } n} \text{len}(n) + \alpha \sum_{\text{slots } s} \text{bal}(s) + \beta \sum_{\text{rows } r} \text{bal}(r) + \gamma \sum_{\text{columns } c} \text{bal}(c)$$
$$\text{bal}(s) = \max\{\text{size}(s) - \text{cap}(s), 0\}^2$$

The capacity $cap(s)$ of a slot s is calculated simply by evenly distributing the total size of the cells across the available space in the slot. The row and column are the four rows and columns of slots in the 4×4 grid. Some care must be taken in optimizing this multiobjective measure, especially because the balance terms are highly correlated with one another.

The major drawback of simulated annealing is its high running time. We alleviate this problem somewhat by using multilevel techniques [CCY03,YWES00]. The netlist is recursively clustered so that the clusters are (heuristically) loosely connected to one another and approximately the same size. The clustering recursion stops when there are a few hundred clusters. That clustered netlist is then partitioned in the 4×4 grid using annealing. One level of clusters is then resolved into its subclusters, leaving each subcluster in the same partition as its parent cluster. Annealing measures the temperature of the revised solution (in the higher-resolution optimization space) and then continues to improve it. This process is repeated until the bottom level of clustering—that is, the original netlist—is reached. Note that in this process, it is critical that the annealer accurately measure the temperature of the starting partitions; too high a temperature will destroy the quality of the partitioning solution found so far, and too low a temperature will restrict the amount of further improvement that the annealer can make.

Once a partitioning solution is found for a particular grid, the same technique is applied recursively to each of the 16 slots. This process repeats until there are few enough cells in a partition that a solution can be found by branch-and-bound, without the use of partitioning. The entire algorithm is as follows:

```
Place(Netlist N, Grid G: {

    Recursively cluster N(= N₀) to form netlists N₁,N₂, ..., Nc
    Randomly partition Nc into G
    Anneal to improve the partition of Nc in G
    Repeat for c down to 1: {
        Break the clusters that form Nc, producing netlist Nc₋₁
        Measure the temperature of Nc₋₁'s partition in G
        Continue annealing to improve the solution further
```

This technique is completely data-driven; although the default measure stored in the table is the optimal Steiner tree length, by simply swapping in a different table the algorithm can optimize different distance metrics or different measures such as low-diameter trees or cross-cut congestion.

The increased resolution of the partition matters fundamentally; just as Ganley [G95] demonstrated the superiority of a 3×3 partition over a 2×2 partition, our own work has demonstrated that the 4×4 partition is superior still to the 3×3 partition. For future work, storing the table for a 5×5 partition is probably still within reach on current hardware. It could certainly be accomplished by storing only one of each set of eight symmetric configurations, though this presents an algorithmic challenge in being able to look them up sufficiently quickly; after all, this is by far the most-executed operation in the algorithm.

To achieve the best overall results with X, the layout system must include a placement strategy that optimizes layout in an X-aware way. Accomplishing this is in many ways more difficult than in the Manhattan realm and presents challenges that require new approaches than those used historically for Manhattan placement. A few solutions to those challenges are presented here, but doubtless there is much improvement yet to be made.

40.9   X GLOBAL ROUTING

Most physical design tools start the routing process with a global router (GR), which creates a plan—that is, a set of corridors—for the detailed router to follow for each net. The basic objectives of GR are to minimize wirelength and to minimize the worst congestion, measured as (wires planned/estimated capacity) at boundaries between regions called *Gcells*.

In the X interconnect architecture, another application for GR is in determining pin placement on macros during floorplanning. Without pin assignment of the quality that an X-aware GR can provide, final X routing at both the top level and within blocks would suffer.

Global routing for the X interconnect architecture should be sensitive to problem details for which the change from a rectilinear to an octilinear distance metric makes a difference. For example, the set of pin locations of a net can be augmented up front with auxiliary Steiner points to steer the routing toward an optimal topology. Such points should be derived using octilinear Steiner tree algorithms as discussed in Section 40.11.

Another example arises in the computation of wirelength lower bounds, as in estimating distance-based future cost used to evaluate intermediate nodes in search algorithms. Given an already derived target set of wiring (e.g., wiring T in Figure 40.1), consider the subproblem of routing to it from a new point, P. A fast approximation of distance to the target set is the distance $L1$ to a minimal

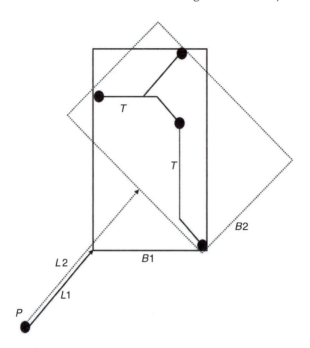

FIGURE 40.1   Use of two bounding boxes in estimating distance.

bounding box, B1, of that set. Checking the distance L2 to a second minimal bounding box B2, with sides rotated—for example, 45° with respect to the first—sometimes gives a much more useful (larger) lower bound. Although this technique springs naturally from consideration of the octilinear distance metric, it is applicable to rectilinear wiring problems as well.

The largest impact of the X interconnect architecture is that it requires fundamental rethinking of the GR problem representation. At the core of any approach is the scheme chosen to model global routes as connections between Gcells, at the boundaries of which congestion will be evaluated.

In a search algorithm, the model prescribes a routing graph: the basic *nodes* in the search space, and the available moves between nodes (*edges*). It is preferable to use three dimensions of routing nodes (x, y, layer) to allow accurate assessment of costs associated with vias, especially in areas where particular layer transition are unavailable. For octilinear routing, octagonal Gcells might seem appropriate, but they are unworkable because octagons do not tile the plane. One could consider rotating the Gcell grids on diagonal layers 45° with respect to those on Manhattan layers, but mismatched shapes complicate the modeling of layer transitions. We began with a uniform grid of square Gcells on all layers.

Planar moves are exclusively in the preferred routing direction for the given layer. But how should moves on diagonal layers be modeled? A naive approach, providing diagonal moves between Gcells that touch at their corners, would introduce two problems:

1. Routes using only diagonal layers would fall unnaturally into two disjoint sets. As with opposite-colored bishops in chess, there is no purely diagonal path between black and white squares: for example, between two Manhattan neighbors.
2. Because diagonally adjacent Gcells touch only at their corners, it is unclear where the congestion impact of a move between them would be assessed. Any detailed connection between such neighbors must also traverse one of their mutual Manhattan neighbors, but which one, is ambiguous.

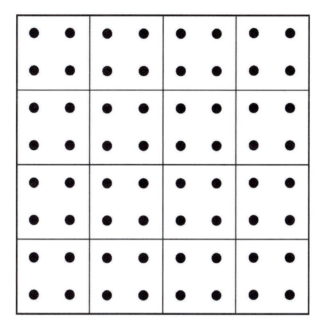

FIGURE 40.2   Gcells with routing nodes.

To address these issues, we have instead used a graph with higher-resolution moves. Each Gcell is divided into four quadrants, which serve as routing graph nodes. The Gcells with nodes are illustrated in Figure 40.2. On Manhattan layers, this doubles the steps needed to cover a given distance: half the moves are internal to a Gcell and do not pay a congestion cost.

Routes on 45° layers visit southeast (SE) and northwest (NW) quadrants alternately; routes on 135° layers visit northeast (NE) and southwest (SW) quadrants alternately. The connections for both types of diagonal layers are illustrated in Figure 40.3. Every diagonal move crosses a known Gcell boundary. Moreover, congestion is sampled at the same places (Gcell boundaries) on every layer, as

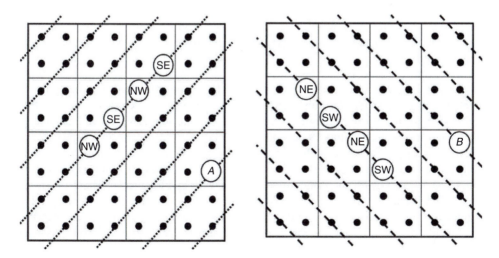

FIGURE 40.3   Alternate routing nodes on diagonal layers. The left-side illustration shows moves between quadrants in the 45° direction. The right-side illustration shows moves between quadrants in the 135° direction.

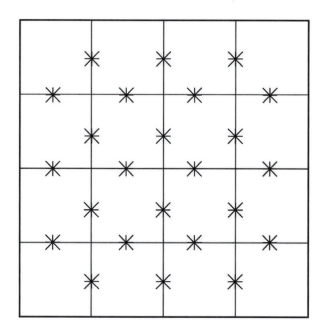

FIGURE 40.4   Congestion is measured on every layer only at Gcell boundaries.

shown in Figure 40.4. Direct moves between Gcells that touch at their corners, which suffer from ambiguous congestion effects, are eliminated.

Because in this model the different diagonal layers use disjoint sets of (x, y) nodes, special *zig* direction changes are introduced inside Gcells, providing, for example, for direct moves between a SE quadrant on a 45° layer (e.g., node A in Figure 40.3), and a NE quadrant on an adjacent 135° layer (e.g., node B in Figure 40.3).

The presence of Gcell-internal moves at which planar congestion is not assessed in unusual. Care must be taken to prevent search algorithms from abusing internal moves: for example, if NE moves across northern Gcell boundaries could be alternated with NW sequences inside Gcells, long due-north connections could be constructed in which only 45°-layer boundaries were crossed. For this reason, we allow at most one zig in a Gcell, because two successive zig moves (e.g., SE(45) to NE(135) and NE(135) to NW(45)) could form a NW sequence without incurring 135°-layer congestion.

Zig moves are awkward, and the high-resolution move grid incurs a substantial runtime penalty. We are investigating less cumbersome models. Still, the model described here has proven quite practical. The model provides the substrate for any routing algorithm chosen. Although the most popular algorithms for global routing use a rip-up-and-reroute approach, we were attracted to the multicommodity flow formulation as described by Albrecht ([A01], also in Chapter 32) for the provably optimal properties that its theoretical framework offers and because its use of multiple rounding phases reduces its dependence on routing order. This approach builds on an algorithm of Garg and Könemann [GK98] and insightful theoretical work by Fleischer [F99].

Ref. [A01] formulates a mixed integer program for GR and a linear programming relaxation that allows fractional global routes and describes cost functions in terms of edge congestion and net length with respect to which minimal Steiner trees are found for all nets in one phase and for prescribed subsets of nets in later phases. The average of solutions from the different phases is a solution to the fractional GR; selection of one route for each net from a random phase gives the GR solution. Two key strong points of this approach are that it uses a very effective exponential congestion cost function and that it provides multiple alternative routes per net.

Our work convinced us that multicommodity flow approaches to GR are more attractive than previously reported. We have found modifications of the cost function and new uses for the alternative routes, some described below, that dramatically speed up the algorithm and improve the quality of its GR solutions. A major motivation was our desire to provide tighter guidance to the detailed router by using smaller Gcells: on the order of 10–20 tracks wide versus 50–100 in Ref. [A01]. Taken together with our interest in modeling five or more layers instead of two and a fourfold increase in nodes per layer to support the routing graph discussed above, the need for performance improvement is clear.

Runtime is reduced when wirelength is considered, because length contributions to cost help rein in the very broad expansion characteristic of Dijkstra-style search when minimizing congestion cost alone. Curiously, Ref. [A01] recommends initializing the variables y_e (for congestion on each edge) and y_L (for total wirelength) so that the initial contribution to congestion cost from any move dominates its contribution to length cost by a very large factor, $L/c(e)$. (L is the total wirelength of the design, and $c(e)$ is the capacity of Gcell edge e.) If, instead, y_e and y_L are initialized to an identical value (to put length and congestion costs on an even footing), excellent congestion is still achieved with much more reasonable runtime.

Normalized to its initial value, the recommended congestion cost y_e of using an edge e during any search for a minimal Steiner tree is $\exp[\varepsilon U(e)/c(e)]$, where ε is an experimental constant, and $U(e)$ is the total capacity already used by routes passing through edge e. This cost is backward-looking in that it accounts only for earlier routes. A powerful and novel refinement is to charge a forward-looking cost equal to the increase to y_e that would result if the route being considered took the given edge, namely $\exp[\varepsilon U'(e)/c(e)] - \exp[\varepsilon U(e)/c(e)]$, where $U'(e) - U(e)$ is the incremental usage involved. Without this refinement, the cost of increasing edge usage from 0 to 3, as for a wide wire, for example, would be the same ($= \exp(0)$) whether the edge's capacity were 1 or 16.

Similarly, although a term like y_L can help optimize total wirelength, the associated cost is only linear in the length of a net during any search. Effective control of individual netlengths, as for timing-driven GR, requires a super-linear cost: for example, a term exponential in the ratio of the route length being produced to a desired length L_d. Any node n in a search can be associated with a length estimate $L_f(n) = L_g(n) + L_h(n)$, where $L_g(n)$ is the total search length along the best path found from the source to node n, and $L_h(n)$ is a lower bound on the remaining distance to the target. L_f, rather than L_g, should be consulted when optimizing route length, using a cost to step from node A to node B such as

$$\exp(\varepsilon L_f(B)/L_d) - \exp(\varepsilon L_f(A)/L_d),$$

which penalizes detouring moves but not those that move toward the target.

Assembling a GR by selecting a route for each net at random from the solutions of different phases (*randomized rounding*) is widely used and has advantages as a theoretical tool, but it is inappropriate to use only this technique to convert fractional to integer solutions in practice. Especially for problems with smaller Gcells, randomized rounding yields unreliable results because the tail of the congestion distribution is so long (i.e., has so much probability mass) that a small number of highly overcongested cells frequently results in practice with a randomized rounding strategy. A better GR can be obtained by applying heuristics to optimize the mix of solutions from different phases. Even the following simple greedy procedure is effective:

```
Input: Routes R[n][p], for nets n = 1,...,N, from phases
p = 1...P
Output: Selections s[n], defining the route to use for
each net n = 1,...,N, namely R[n][s[n]].
Procedure:

   (1) Set R[n] := 1 for n = 1,...,N.
   (2) Embed route R[n][s[n]] for n = 1,...,N, to compute
       total usages U(e) for edges e in the routing graph.
   (3) For i := 1 to k
   (4) begin
   (5)   For n := 1 to N
   (6)   begin
   (7)     Unembed the current route R[n][s[n]]
   (8)     Set cost[p] := ∑     exp(εU(e)/c(e)) for p = 1,...,P
                         e∈R[n][p]
           (where each U(e) includes the embedding of R[n][p])
   (9)     Set s[n] := the value of p (in 1...P) for which cost[p]
           is minimum.
   (10)    Embed route R[n][s[n]]
   (11)  end
   (12) end
```

The procedure admits numerous variations: for example, initial solutions other than phase 1 (line (1)), different numbers of iterations k (line 3), different net orderings (line 5), and different cost functions (line 8). Of course, more general, nongreedy heuristics are also possible. To our knowledge, the problem of optimizing the mix of results from different phases has not yet been explored—even for applications of multicommodity flow outside of global routing—which is interesting because we have observed that it can yield substantially improved solution quality compared to randomized rounding.

The X interconnect architecture requires rethinking of the basic routing graph and also encourages a fresh look at several aspects of global routing algorithms. Exponential costs new solution selection heuristics can be applied in the optimization of many criteria in a multicommodity flow approach. Although the theory of these techniques remains to be developed further, they have already proven effective in practice.

40.10   X DETAILED ROUTING

The most surprising thing about X is that the whole physical design system—not just the detailed router—must be rethought to realize its full benefit and that the full benefit goes far beyond what simple rerouting of a Manhattan design with a diagonal-aware detailed router can achieve. Perhaps the second most surprising thing about X is that the detailed router itself requires modifications, both to achieve runtimes competitive with Manhattan routers and the best possible results. The modifications can range from fairly conservative repairs of existing routing techniques all the way to radical reconceptualizations of the routing problem.

Ultimately, the complete abandonment of preferred directions—that is, liquid routing—promises the highest-quality routing, both for X and for Manhattan, with respect to wirelength, timing, and via counts. However, for reasons of both implementation simplicity and smoother adaptation of X technology (versus possible lithographic concerns with liquid routing), we opted to maintain preferred directions (except for local jogs), which still provides many of the advantages of the X interconnect architecture versus Manhattan.

X detailed routing requires changes throughout a detailed routing system, ranging from low-level functionality such as the geometry manipulation machinery up to high-level strategies for double-cut via insertion. In the following, we concentrate on two central areas of detailed routing in X: routing space modeling and path search with manufacturing constraints.

40.10.1   ROUTING SPACE MODEL AND SEARCH ALGORITHM

Today's (Manhattan) detailed routing systems vary somewhat in their specifics but are generally built on top of gridded, Dijkstra/A*/Lee maze router-based, rip-up-and-reroute strategies. For reasons of memory, runtime, and solution quality, grid-based routers are particularly common in the domain of both block-level and full-chip flat routing. Most connections are made with the minimum possible wire width and spacing: that is, at the minimum pitch at which routing segments can be placed adjacent to each other without violating design rule constraints. To model the routing space most straightforwardly, a three-dimensional rectangular grid where nodes have distance equal to the minimum pitch is a convenient and accurate data structure for representing dense packing of wires. For each layer, a preferred direction (horizontal or vertical) is given. All nodes and edges of the grid that are located on a straight line in the preferred direction are commonly referred to as a *track*. The router positions the majority of the wires onto tracks, and the remainder are connections between tracks (*jogs*). All such jogs and also all vias between the planes connect two neighboring grid nodes. Special methods are used to deal with off-grid pins, wider-than-normal wires, and other geometries, and constraints that cannot be fully modeled in the gridded approach. As described in Chapter 23, efficient search algorithms such as line search, maze routing, and, in some circumstances, track assignment methods and channel routing can be used for generating a routing on such a gridded representation.

Despite its near-ubiquity in Manhattan systems, the straightforward gridded representation is ill-suited to the X interconnect architecture. To see this, suppose the horizontal (or vertical) distance between adjacent nodes in the grid is P, as shown in Figure 40.5. Then, just adding diagonal edges between the nodes will restrict diagonal routing to diagonal pitches P' that are multiples of $P/\sqrt{2}$. Because $P' > P$, the minimum usable diagonal pitch would be $P * \sqrt{2}$, but for current manufacturing technologies, $P' \approx P$ holds. Thus, naively using the classical three-dimensional routing grid as a

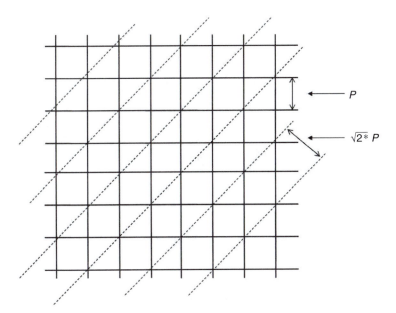

FIGURE 40.5   Gridded routing space rotation. Only every other diagonal track is usable so Manhattan pitch $P \rightarrow$ diagonal pitch $\sqrt{2} * P$.

model for diagonal routing would effectively waste more than 30 percent of all available routing resources. The seemingly reasonable notion of simply rotating Manhattan routing resources on the upper layers by 45° is not a viable approach.

A suitable model for X must provide efficient usage of the available routing space. This means that Manhattan and diagonal tracks must be available at the smallest permissible Manhattan or diagonal pitches, respectively, and grid nodes must exist at all intersections of tracks in two adjacent planes (to allow vias between these places). At the same time, the memory requirements should not be significantly higher, but this is impossible to achieve with a simple three-dimensional gridded model. Making the resolution finer to allow diagonal tracks in almost minimum pitch will necessarily bloat the grid size and also seriously affect the runtime of algorithms.

Extensions of interval-based representations as described in Ref. [H98] are much better suited for efficient detailed routing for X. Relying on the predominance of preferred-direction routing but permitting diagonals, interval-based methods model the routing space with arbitrarily high resolution in one direction per layer without impacting memory requirements.

The whole routing area is implicitly viewed as a gigantic three-dimensional grid, where the distance between two neighboring nodes is the manufacturing grid resolution M. Each plane is seen as a collection of lines with a preferred direction (horizontal, vertical, NE, or NW) within distance M, for Manhattan, or $M/\sqrt{2}$, for diagonal, planes. The lines that represent desired routing tracks (according to the minimum pitch requirements) are stored as a set of intervals. Each interval represents a maximal consecutive set of nodes on the line with the same routability status. All intervals comprising a single line are kept in an appropriate tree structure to support fast query, split, merge, and update operations. Lines not representing routing tracks are not represented at all. More details about the technique can be found in Ref. [H98].

Using this approach, tracks are modeled with manufacturing grid resolution, and at all (x, y) locations where tracks of adjacent routing layers intersect, there is a grid node on both tracks (implicitly represented by an interval on the track), as illustrated in Figure 40.6. Because the highest possible manufacturing resolution M is used for the track representation, the model preserves the flexibility of gridless routing within a superficially gridded data structure.

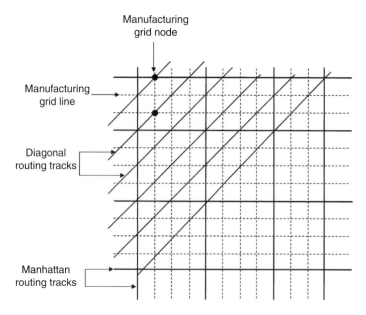

FIGURE 40.6 Efficient track-based routing space model. Dashed lines on manufacturing grid units. Solid lines represent Manhattan and diagonal routing tracks. Diagonal pitch matches almost fully the Manhattan pitch.

The memory consumption of such a data structure is determined by the complexity of the obstructions and wires in the routing layers. It does not depend on the actual grid resolution M. As the overwhelming majority of wires obey the preferred directions, this type of interval representation is very memory-efficient [SN02] . Moreover, there is no penalty for X versus Manhattan, either in terms of memory requirements or in terms of packing tracks at the minimum possible pitch.

The interval-based representation enables the efficient implementation of path search algorithms for X using extensions of the interval labeling approach in Ref. [H98]. The theoretical and practical complexity is just moderately higher than the complexity of the variant for Manhattan setups.

The best possible X routing requires full octilinear wiring in the absence of preferred direction constraints: that is, the generation of paths that make use of diagonal and Manhattan directions on the same plane. Therefore, in planes where diagonal wiring is allowed, up to three labeling operations might happen between neighboring intervals on adjacent tracks versus one in the Manhattan case. Fortunately, the runtime of a search using interval labeling is mostly determined in practice by the number of labels used to traverse between adjacent planes. Because the number of potential via locations is the same for X and Manhattan wiring, although their positions are different, the overall runtime of an interval-based router is comparable for both interconnect architectures.

40.10.2   MANUFACTURING-CONSTRAINED ROUTING

Having an efficient routing space representation and fast search algorithms as previously described makes it possible to use known sequential routing methods combined with rip-up-and-reroute strategies to do the basic routing. At nanometer technology nodes, though, the fundamental routing representation, path search machinery, and rip-up heuristics are far from sufficient for creating manufacturable X designs.

Manufacturing constraints such as OPC require metal geometries to fulfill certain spacing or length requirements and to avoid certain geometric structures completely. The space of possible geometries that an X system can produce is far richer than those generated by a Manhattan system, enabling X to produce superior solutions. On the other hand, X requires much more elaborate constraint handling to avoid creating geometries that can be difficult to manufacture. Examples include

- *Acute angles*: that is, a metal shape having two edges in a 45° outer angle. Such geometries occur when the routing process creates a path that makes a 45° or 315° bend.
- *Short edge*: that is, boundary edges of metal geometries with a length below a certain threshold. The length threshold may depend on the specific angle of the edge as well as on the angle between this edge and its neighboring edges at the corners.
- *Minimum area*: that is, a small connected piece of metal on a plane with total area below a certain threshold. Such geometries can occur if the routing process makes a very small jog on the plane between two vias.

Although acute angles cannot be created by a Manhattan system, short edges and minimum area constraints are troublesome in Manhattan routing, too. Nonetheless, there is a fundamental difference in how these constraints are handled within an X system versus its Manhattan counterparts; although it is possible to handle these constraints in mostly separate pre- and postprocessing phases for Manhattan wiring, X requires awareness of such rules in virtually all steps of the design process. The flexibility of the X approach would otherwise generate a large number of violations that could not be repaired with simple, local transformations in a postprocessor.

Short edges in Manhattan designs typically occur when complicated pin structures are accessed by wires or vias. In practice, in Manhattan systems, pin access constraints are handled by a preprocessing step in which legal pin access directions are determined. Remaining short edges aside from pin access

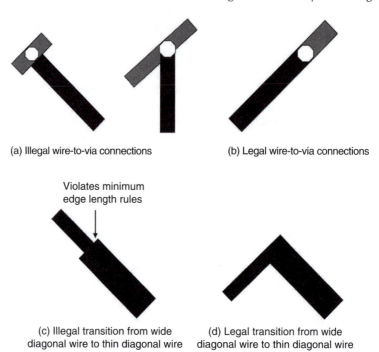

(a) Illegal wire-to-via connections   (b) Legal wire-to-via connections

(c) Illegal transition from wide   (d) Legal transition from wide
diagonal wire to thin diagonal wire   diagonal wire to thin diagonal wire

FIGURE 40.7   (a) Illegal and (b) legal access of wires to vias, (c) illegal and (d) legal pattern for a transition between a wide diagonal and a narrow diagonal wire.

are typically cleaned up after routing by a postprocessing, search-and-repair pass that performs small local routing modifications.

By contrast, X typically includes constraints that are sufficiently complex that they must be addressed in core layout steps such as path search. Manufacturers typically require diagonal geometry edges to have a significant minimum length, which leads to a menagerie of illegal patterns that must be avoided during the layout process (Figure 40.14). Vias can be accessed only at specific angles, transitions between wires of different widths must follow certain patterns, and jogging structures must obey length constraints depending on the shapes that are adjacent to both sides of the jog. Figures 40.7 and 40.8 illustrate legal and illegal geometries.

Minimum area requirements present additional challenges. Even a track-based approach such as the one described here permits via positions at arbitrary small separations because of the misalignment

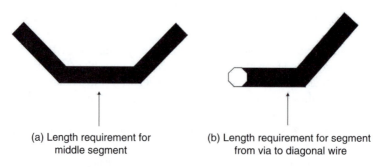

(a) Length requirement for   (b) Length requirement for segment
middle segment   from via to diagonal wire

FIGURE 40.8   (a) Diagonal U-turn structure requiring a minimum length for the middle segment and (b) via-jog-bend structure requiring a minimum length for the jog.

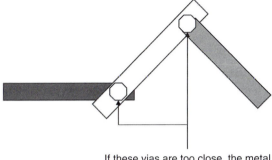

If these vias are too close, the metal
segment between them can violate
minimum area rules

FIGURE 40.9   Via positions between can be too close together thus triggering a minimum area violation.

of Manhattan and diagonal tracks. The fine resolution of the underlying representation could allow search algorithms to create paths that travel just a small distance within one plane, violating minimum area requirements. In contrast, a Manhattan setup is much more regular and prevents most such problems inherently by not having any pair of potential via locations too close together. Figure 40.9 shows a potential minimum area violation.

In practice, the entire flow of an X detailed router has to be aware of such constraints and to obey them throughout. In particular, the path search algorithms must be modified for X to address the complex design rules involved.

Path search addresses the problem of finding a minimum cost path between two points or two areas of the design such that the path geometries create a DRC-clean metal structure connecting them. Assume a found path consists of segments $S_1, S_2, \ldots, S_n$ where each S_i is either a via or a straight line. $A(S_i)$ denotes the angle of planar segments or the direction of the via (whether going downward or upward). $L(S_i)$ denotes the length of S_i if S_i is not a via. Without loss of generality, assume that all planar segments are maximally extended: that is, S_{i-1} and S_{i+1} are either vias or straight lines with an angle not equal to $A(S_i)$. The search process can be made both pattern-and length-aware as follows:

Let A be the set of all octilinear angles plus via directions (i.e., up and down), and let $R \subseteq A \times A$ be a given set of invalid patterns. Let $Q: A \times A \times A \to \Re$ be a given set of pattern length constraints. Then, the following conditions must be satisfied:

(1) $[A(S_i), A(S_{i+1})] \notin R$, for all $i = 1, \ldots, n-1$
(2) $L(S_i) \geq Q[A(S_{i-1}), A(S_i), A(S_{i+1})]$ for all planar $S_i, 1 < i < n$

R and Q can vary depending on the technology and the particular wire and via shapes involved. So, a search algorithm must provide generic support for almost arbitrary and unrelated restrictions while still maintaining a behavior similar to unconstrained Manhattan versions.

Although unusual in integrated-circuit routing, such path constraints are not uncommon in printed circuit board (PCB) routing (e.g., [TT98,MH00,SFH+91]). Because problem sizes in PCB routing are orders of magnitude smaller than in IC layout, computation- and memory-intensive search heuristics can be used in the PCB world. For an X-aware IC layout system to be compatible with traditional Manhattan flows, runtime and memory requirements cannot be arbitrarily increased.

Fortunately, constraints such as those above can be handled exactly, at least in theory, through the use of label-based path search. A traditional, node-based, Dijkstra-style, maze running algorithm can be extended to permit multiple labels per node, v, instead of just a single one. Expansion (scanning) is then done on a per-label basis rather than a per-node basis. Labels at a node v are classified by triples in $A \times \aleph \times A$, which implicitly incorporate the history of the labeling process so far that is relevant to evaluating the constraints. (A_1, d, A_2) denotes that this label has been originated from a

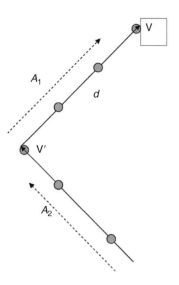

History information (A_1, d, A_2) of a label at node V

FIGURE 40.10 History information $(A1, d, A2)$ of a label at node V.

sequence of labels starting at a node v' where all of the labeling steps leading from v' to v use edges within angle A_1. v' has distance d from v, and the label at v' that was the start of these expansions has been created by a prior expansion within angle $A_2 \neq A_1$. Within each such label class, only the one with minimum cost value is kept and expanded.

This history information is sufficient to allow the algorithm to explore all paths P satisfying the constraints and to generate a shortest one: successively, the not-yet-expanded node-label pair $[v, (A_1, d, A_2)]$ with minimum cost value is retrieved and expanded toward neighboring nodes v' à la Dijkstra, as shown in Figure 40.10. The expansion operation creates a new label of class (A'_1, d', A'_2) at v'. If there already exists a label within the same class at v', the one with higher costs can be pruned while preserving the admissibility of the search algorithm.

Let $\triangle \subset A \times \aleph \times A$ be this set of label classes. For degenerate cases, P may contain self-intersections that can be addressed by separate cleanup heuristics. Conveniently, one can use integral distance values on both Manhattan and diagonal edges as distances in X are algebraic integers in $Z(\sqrt{2})$: that is, the diagonal distances can be expressed as integral multiples of $\sqrt{2}$.

Let $Q \le c, c \in \Re$. Then, for any label (A_1, d, A_2) with $d \ge c$, all short edge conditions are always honored. Therefore, there are at most $\lceil c \rceil + |c/\sqrt{2}|$ different distance values for labels that can lead to relevant short edge conditions and it is sufficient to handle at most $10 * 10 * 2 * \lceil c \rceil$ label classes. As a result, the runtime of such a generalized Dijkstra algorithm is bounded by $O[c*|V|*\log(c*|V|)]$ where V is the number of nodes in the grid,* because each pair $[v, \delta] \in V \times \triangle$ can be interpreted as a virtual node. The algorithm performs a Dijkstra search, but instead of labeling nodes $v \in V$, the virtual nodes are labeled, expanded, and stored in an appropriate priority queue.

Interval-based, Dijkstra-style searches as in Ref. [H98] can be extended in a manner directly analogous to that described for nodes above. Although only a subset of all the potential label classes is relevant in practice, and c is at most on the order of 50–80 manufacturing grid units, a rigorous implementation would still be far too high in complexity to be practical. A more runtime-efficient technique relaxes the search slightly into a heuristic that bounds the number of label classes at a node to a small value. Using heuristics to decide which label classes are most promising to find a path—for

---

* The analogously generalized A^* has linear expected time.

example, by considering which labels allow the greatest variety of bends and vias when they are expanded and by pruning away the most restricted ones—yields enormous runtime improvements without giving up significant quality.

Of course, with such a heuristic, a search may terminate unsuccessfully (even when a legal path exists) or occasionally violate the constraints to connect the source and the target. Fortunately, extensive use of such pruning heuristics on a wide variety of real-world designs has shown no significant impact on wirelength versus an optimal algorithm. In practice, failures of the heuristic to find a path are almost always caused by deadlocking close to a target area with limited access routes. In such situations, pruning can accidentally exclude the only viable path that reaches the target.

Hybrid approaches that explore only part of the solution space in noncritical areas (by considering only a few label classes per node) and automatically switch to a more exact mode in small areas with limited routing flexibility (mostly near the source and target areas) can be very powerful in an industrial setting. Because problematic areas, such as those around small pins, typically are just a few tracks in diameter, search hybrids can be tuned to have only a modest impact on runtime while achieving the last bits of solution quality in practice.

The X system uses a slightly different approach by combining pruning with bidirectional searches. Having a search process originate from both the source and the target avoids deadlocks that might otherwise occur near a target geometry. The search originating from the target still uses extensive pruning, so it is equally fast, but the likelihood of getting deadlocked near the target is much smaller, as the search starts with limited choices for expansions.

The search techniques described here generalize to a bidirectional Dijkstra or A^* setting, and deciding which partial solutions can be combined to form a fully legal path can be done efficiently during the bidirectional expansions. Suppose node v has a label L in class δ from the source–target search and a label L' in class δ' from the target–source search. Whether the two subpaths given by the labels can be combined to a path respecting all constraints depends only on the history information of the classes δ, δ'. So, provided that c is small, it is even possible to precompute all combinations out of $\triangle \times \triangle$ that allow legal stitching and to use a lookup table.

The few remaining cases where this strategy fails are handled by completing a path with a small, illegal portion and then applying powerful repair steps based on rip-up and reroute for final cleanup. This approach provides very good results in practice with only a small runtime penalty and negligible impact on wirelength and via count in the resulting layout.

It should be noted that similar constraint handling could become essential for Manhattan systems too, especially with nanometer process nodes and the increasing importance of design for manufacturability. For example, stacked vias, in which two consecutive vias have no wiring in the intermediate plane, are forbidden. This can be handled exactly within the above framework by having three label classes per node.

40.11   X STEINER TREES

The Steiner tree problem, in the context of physical design, is to find a minimum-length interconnection of a set of points in the plane. The original problem was studied in the Euclidean distance metric, in which a line may have any angle; later, because of its relevance to circuit design, the Manhattan version was considered and was dubbed the *rectilinear Steiner tree* (RST) problem [H66].

The RST problem has been well studied, and a number of excellent heuristics have been devised for finding near-optimal solutions (e.g., [KR92]) as well as a variety of algorithms for computing optimal RSTs [G99,WWZ00]. As the problem's NP-completeness would lead us to expect, these latter exact algorithms have worst-case exponential running time.

Yet a different metric is of interest in the X interconnect architecture: the octilinear metric in which each line may have an angle that is an integer multiple of 45°. Although a generalized version of the octilinear Steiner tree (OST) problem was considered before the introduction of the X interconnect architecture [SW92], the increased relevance that the X interconnect architecture provided led to a much wider examination of the problem. A number of heuristics have been devised (e.g., [CC02],[ZZJ+05]), and the GeoSteiner algorithm for the Euclidean and Manhattan problems has been generalized to the octilinear metric as well [NWZ02].

A number of characteristics make the octilinear problem more similar to the Euclidean than to the RST problem. For the rectilinear problem, Hanan [H66] proved that the grid formed by passing horizontal and vertical lines through each point contains an optimal RST. Some of the most successful RST heuristics rely on this property (e.g., [KR92]). Unfortunately, although a similar graph does exist for the octilinear problem, the number of vertices in this graph is exponential in the number of original points, thus limiting its usefulness for polynomial-time heuristics. Some heuristics and approximation algorithms use a reduced, polynomial-sized subgraph of this graph as the basis for their computations. Perhaps because of this reduction, or perhaps simply because the problem has not yet been as widely studied, OST heuristics do not seem to produce trees that are as nearly optimal as the best RST heuristics do in the Manhattan world.

Another interesting property of the OST problem is that the minimum spanning tree is a higher-quality approximation of an OST than in the Manhattan case. The Steiner ratio defines the maximum ratio of the lengths of a minimum spanning tree and an optimal Steiner tree in a given metric. The Steiner ratio in the Manhattan metric 1.5 [H76], while in the octilinear metric it is approximately 1.17 [K95].

It is also noteworthy that moving from the Manhattan to the octilinear metric achieves much of the wirelength savings that is possible in any metric. According to one computation [CCKMW03], a typical octilinear routing reduces length versus a Manhattan routing of the same set of points by 13–15 percent, and that a Euclidean routing only achieves an additional 4 percent. In other words, the wirelength savings achieved achieved by using octilinear routing is nearly as good as even Euclidean routing would be while maintaining straightforward manufacturability.

Much of the research on the OST problem has been to apply techniques from past research in other metrics to the octilinear problem. Perhaps, future work on techniques more specifically tailored to the X interconnect architecture will yield further improvements.

40.12   X MANUFACTURING CONSIDERATIONS

In the design-for-manufacturing (DFM) era, it is no longer possible to make a design innovation, particularly in physical design, without considering its manufacturing impact. Even worse, design rules today are far more arcane than the simple width and spacing rules obeyed by EDA systems of ten years ago; instead, these rules have become awkward and rather contrived approximations to the limitations imposed by optical, mechanical and chemical characteristics of manufacturing processes. As a result, in practice, contemporary design rules tend to model only existing design styles.

For example, in the case of the X interconnect architecture, the Manhattan assumption is so prevalent that the future design rules for diagonals either did not exist or were extremely conservative. When there was no practical possibility of a design with more than a tiny fraction of the wires in the non-Manhattan direction, there was no need to do the extra work required to validate diagonal design rules.

However, manufacturing permits most diagonal design rules to approximate their Manhattan analogues, and X clearly benefits from the added flexibility. To establish appropriate diagonal design rules, three changes in the electronics industry were required:

1. The design community had to validate that given the design rule changes, the benefits were substantial.
2. The manufacturing equipment community had to validate that the design rules can indeed be tighter without causing problems.
3. The fabs in IDMs and foundries had to do test chip runs to demonstrate unequivocally that the tighter design rules in manufacturable chips with good yields.

To facilitate these changes, a broad industry alliance called the X Initiative was created. It includes representatives from the entire electronics supply chain, including IDMs, foundries, fabless semiconductor companies, semiconductor IP companies, mask-making companies, mask-making equipment manufacturers, mask inspection and repair equipment manufacturers, lithography equipment manufacturers, wafer processing equipment companies, wafer inspection equipment companies, yield enhancement technologies and services companies, and EDA companies. Over 20 cofunded engineering studies, including production of test chips and test designs, were performed in the first three years of the partnership. These studies proved that, even at nanometer technology nodes, X chips with width and spacing rules for the diagonal layers roughly equivalent to those for Manhattan layers were not only manufacturable, but also that X chips actually yield better. Furthermore, these studies proved that increases in the mask cost owing to the X interconnect architecture are negligible. An image showing manufactured wires on an X chip is displayed in Figure 40.11.

Through this collaboration, we also discovered some X-specific design rules that are critical for EDA design-for-manufacturability for X. Most notably, 45° angles are forbidden, even at T-intersections, but 135° angles are permitted, as illustrated in Figure 40.12. In fact, 135° jogs are more manufacturable than 90° jogs, but 45° angles are not only hard to manufacture but also difficult to inspect adequately. Fortunately, 45° angles are unnecessary to exploit the benefits of X. In fact, by the triangle inequality, an acute angle for wiring always uses more wire than a right or obtuse angle, so one would only want an acute angle to satisfy a strange, putative design rule. Rather, even for difficult pin access and T-intersections, routes must simply exit at 90° and then turn 135°; an acute angle, if desired, must be filled to make a wider wire the outside edges of which are 90° or 135° angles. In practice, forbidding acute connections with X has had no negative impact on layout quality.

As lithography for advanced process nodes becomes increasingly difficult, light sources are becoming more and more specialized. Unidirectional or bidirectional light sources, such as dipole and quadrupole, that are more accurate for one or two directions are increasingly common. These

  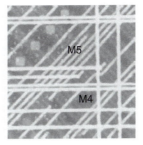

FIGURE 40.11 Images of manufactured wires on an X architecture chip.

Design rule violation   DRC clean: Notch filled   DRC clean: Jogged

FIGURE 40.12 Illegal and legal angles in the X architecture.

techniques sacrifice accuracy in nonpreferred directions to gain accuracy in the preferred directions. The appropriate design solutions for X must account for a tighter design rule in one direction per layer than in the other directions for that same layer. Fortunately, on any layer, any direction can be accommodated, whether diagonal or Manhattan.

Ever-increasing mask costs are of increasing concern in the semiconductor industry, and one might reasonably be concerned that X exacerbates an already bad situation. Fortunately, after carefully studying this question, Ken Rygler, founder of DuPont Photomasks, concludes that the degree to which X increases mask cost is negligible [X01]. Roughly half of the mask cost is associated with mask writing times, while the other half is from inspection and repair times. As evidenced by numerous studies at KLA-Tencor [X01], inspection and repair do not present any X-specific issues as long as 45° notches are never created, so the primary question is whether mask writing is significantly worsened by X.

There are two ways to write a mask, particularly for less stringent metallization layers: laser and E-beam. In laser-based mask writers, a television-like raster method is used. The write time is constant whether writing X or Manhattan (or circular for that matter) patterns. So, there is no change in mask costs because of X if laser-based systems are employed.

E-beam-based mask writing is often used when precision is important. E-beam systems expose what are called variable shaped beams (VSBs) of E-beam, one shape at a time. If these VSBs could assume only rectangular shapes, then X would take substantially longer to write than Manhattan masks because to approximate a sharp diagonal edge, many small rectangles would be needed, as shown in Figure 40.13. In practice, though, isosceles right triangles or rectangles rotated by 45° from horizontal are available as VSBs in most E-beam-based mask-masking machines. These unique capabilities enable 45° wiring (e.g., but not 60° wiring) to be precisely written on masks without a significant increase in mask write times.

In addition, metallization layers for interconnect are M2 and above. A typical implementation of the X interconnect architecture would have the predominantly diagonal layers in M4, M5, or M6. These layers are not the most data-intensive or time-consuming layers. Typical standard cell-based designs have one-quarter to one-fifth the amount of data in upper layers of metal as compared with diffusion, polysilicon, contact, or M1. Thus, slight increases in the amount of data in these upper layers of metal do not contribute noticeably to the overall mask write time or, therefore, mask cost.

Through the diligent efforts of the X Initiative, both the design and the manufacturing of X designs are now practical. Several years ago, the initial reaction to the idea of the X interconnect architecture, while acknowledging the potential benefits, included great skepticism about both the EDA technology required and the possible impact on manufacturing. In developing XPR, we learned to focus not only on the computer science and software engineering required for the EDA portion of

Fracturing with only rectangular aperture increases mask write time

Fracturing with triangular aperture reduces mask write time

Fracturing with rotated rectangular aperture minimizes mask write time

FIGURE 40.13   Effects of fracturing on mask write time.

the solution but also on the constraints and considerations imposed by customers and their vendors. Of course, customer "constraints" are often rooted in a different set of underlying physical or economic assumptions. A deep knowledge of the customer's problems can uncover opportunities that would otherwise be missed.

40.13   X IN PRACTICE

As of this writing, the X interconnect architecture has demonstrated its potential on a variety of designs and has results in several commercial chips, but it is still in the initial adoption phase. Considering the significant and diverse benefits conferred by X, though, one expects pervasive diagonal wiring to become increasingly common in future production chips.

    With a new idea such as X, one might fear that the theoretical benefits would be overshadowed by the practical inefficiencies. In practice, though, X has consistently demonstrated results that match the theoretical predictions, including the cycle of combined area and wirelength reduction predicted by the infinite series described above.

    The first production chip employing the X interconnect architecture was announced by Toshiba Corporation and Cadence Design Systems, Inc. in 2004 and is shown in Figure 40.14. The Digital TV ASSP chip went to engineering sample in 2004, and went into volume production in 2005. The X interconnect architecture portions of the chip were reduced in area by more than 10 percent.

    The first fabless production chip employing the X interconnect architecture was announced by ATI Technologies, Inc., TSMC (Taiwan Semiconductor Manufacturing Company, Ltd.), and Cadence Design Systems in 2005. The chip was manufactured at TSMC and went into volume production in 2005. Because this design was a second volume manufacturing revision of an existing PCI-Express

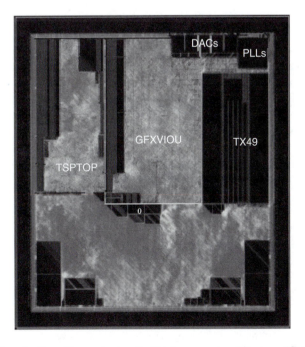

FIGURE 40.14   First production chip employing the X interconnect architecture. (Courtesy of Toshiba.)

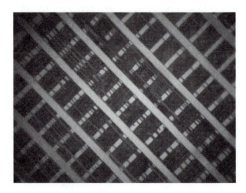

Chip micrograph of the first fabless
production chip from ATI,
manufactured at TSMC

Magnified section of the chip
micrograph of the ATI production chip
showing the diagonal power grid and
the diagonal wires in between them

FIGURE 40.15   Micrographs of the first fabless production chip from ATI.

Graphics chip, the objective was to remove a layer of metal for cost reduction. The objective was met, and the chip micrographs are shown in Figure 40.15.

40.14 SUMMARY

We have described the X interconnect architecture, which combines diagonal and Manhattan wires pervasively to improve IC layout, and portions of XPR system for X-aware placement and routing. One must consider the entire system to garner the full benefit of X; detailed routing for diagonals, while obviously crucial, is only a small part of the innovation and engineering required. Physical design for X is a surprisingly broad and rich area of inquiry, containing new challenges in floorplanning, wire load estimation in synthesis, global placement, global routing, detailed placement, detailed routing, parasitic extraction, OPC, clock routing, power routing, geometric search, and even database representation. We believe that an effective X system must be designed from scratch to incorporate X. A Manhattan-based system reworked to handle X designs as an afterthought is likely to be impractically slow and to yield poor results.

   The obvious concerns regarding X are

- Whether one can build a practical, industrially applicable layout system that is X-aware
- Whether X chips can be readily manufactured
- Whether X confers enough benefit to be worth the trouble

As this chapter shows, we have built an industrial-strength X layout system; X chips can be manufactured and are being used in production; and the benefits, both theoretical and practical, are very substantial. Even as X has begun to see commercial use, many challenges remain, and X-enabled physical design techniques should become an increasingly active area of research in both academia and industry in the coming years.

   Postscript: The XPR system has consistently won industrial benchmarks, often producing a 30 percent reduction in power over Manhattan implementations. Nonetheless, for various reasons, the XPR effort has been discontinued at Cadence, so for XPR details beyond the 2003-vintage technology described here, please refer to the numerous X-related patent applications that have now published.

REFERENCES

[A01]   C. Albrecht, Global routing by new approximation algorithms for multicommodity flow, *IEEE Transactions on Computer-Aided Design of Integrated Circuits and Systems* **20**: 622–632, May 2001.

[ACGR98]   M. J. Alexander, J. P. Cohoon, J. L. Ganley, and G. Robins, Placement and routing for performance-driven FPGAs, *VLSI Design* **7**: 97–110, 1998.

[BKKM01]   R. Baldick, A. B. Kahng, A. A. Kennings, and I. L. Markov, Efficient optimization by modifying the objective function, *IEEE Transactions on Circus and Systems* **48**: 947–957, 2001.

[BC93]   S. Bapat and J. P. Cohoon, A parallel VLSI circuit layout methodology, *Proceedings of the Sixth International Conference on VLSI Design*, pp. 236–241, 1993.

[BR02]   U. Brenner and A. Rohe, An effective congestion driven placement framework, *Proceedings of the International Symposium on Physical Design*, pp. 6–11, 2002.

[CC02]   C. Chiang and C. S. Chiang, Octilinear Steiner tree construction, *Proceedings of the 45th Midwest Symposium on Circuits and Systems*, Vol. 1, pp. 603–606, 2002.

[CCKMW03]   H. Chen, C. K. Cheng, A. B. Kahng, I. Mandoiu, and Q. Wang, Estimation of wirelength reduction for λ-geometry vs. Manhattan placement and routing, *Proceedings of the ACM International Workshop on System-Level Interconnect Prediction*, pp. 71–76, 2003.

[CCK+03]   H. Chen, C. K. Cheng, A. B. Kahng, I. I. Mandoiu, Q. Wang, and B. Yao, The Y-architecture for on-chip interconnect: Analysis and methodology, *Proceedings of the IEEE/ACM International Conference on Computer-Aided Design*, pp. 13–19, 2003.

[CCY03]   C. C. Chang, J. Cong, and X. Yuan, Multi-level placement for large-scale mixed-size IC designs, *Proceedings of the Asia-South Pacific Design Automation Conference*, pp. 325–330, 2003.

[F99]   L. K. Fleischer, Approximating fractional multicommodity flow independent of the number of commodities, *Proceedings of the 40th Symposium on Foundations of Computer Science*, pp. 24–31, 1999.

[FHM+98]   Y. Fuchida, J. Hanari, K. Matsumoto, J. Kudo, K. Yoshikara, and A. Takagi, Multilayer wiring structure, Patent No. 5,723,908, March 3, 1998, Toshiba.

[FM82]   C. M. Fiduccia and R. M. Mattheyses, A linear time heuristic for improving network partitions, *Proceedings of the ACM/IEEE Design Automation Conference*, pp. 175–181, 1982.

[G95]   J. L. Ganley, Geometric interconnection and placement algorithms, Ph.D. Dissertation, University of Virginia, Charlottesville, VA, 1995.

[G99]   J. L. Ganley, Computing optimal rectilinear Steiner trees: A survey and experimental evaluation, *Discrete Applied Mathematics* **89**: 161–171, 1999.

[GK98]   N. Garg and J. Könemann, Faster and simpler algorithms for multicommodity flow and other fractional packing problems, *Proceedings of the 39th Symposium on Foundations of Computer Science*, pp. 300–309, 1998.

[H66]   M. Hanan, On Steiner's problem with rectilinear distance, *SIAM Journal on Applied Mathematics* **14**: 255–265, 1966.

[HK97]   D. H. Huang and A. B. Kahng, Partitioning-based standard-cell global placement with an exact objective, *Proceedings of the ACM/IEEE International Symposium on Physical Design*, pp. 18–25, 1997.

[H76]   F. K. Hwang, On Steiner minimal trees with rectilinear distance, *SIAM Journal on Applied Mathematics* **30**: 104–114, 1976.

[H98]   A. Hetzel, A sequential detailed router for huge grid graphs, *Proceedings of Design and Test in Europe*, pp. 332–338, 1998.

[I06]   N. Ito, K. Hideaki, Y. Ryoichi, I. Hiroshi, S. Hiroyuki, K. Hiroaki, T. Yoshiyasu, Y. Akihiko, N. Kazuhiro, I. Kinya, A. Hiroaki, M. Yutaka, I. Yutaka, and S. Yaroku, Diagonal routing in high performance microprocessor design, *Proceedings of the Asia-South Pacific Design Automation Conference*, pp. 624–629, 2006.

[IML+02]   M. Igarashi, T. Mitsuhashi, A. Le, S. Kazi, Y. -T. Lin, A. Fujimura, and S. Teig, A diagonal-interconnect architecture and its application to RISC core design, *Proceedings of the International Solid-State Circuits Conference*, pp. 210,460, 2002.

[K95]   C. -K. Koh, Steiner problem in octilinear routing model, Master's Thesis, National University of Singapore, Singapore, 1995.

[KL70]   B. W. Kernighan and S. Lin, An efficient heuristic procedure for partitioning graphs, *Bell System Technical Journal* **49**: pp. 291–307, 1970.

[KR92]   A. B. Kahng and G. Robins, A new class of iterative Steiner tree heuristics with good performance, *IEEE Transactions on Computer-Aided Design of Integrated Circuits and Systems* **11**: 893–902, July 1992.

[KRW05]   A. B. Kahng, S. Reda, and Q. Wang, A Place: A generic analytical placement framework, *Proceedings of the International Symposium on Physical Design*, pp. 233–235, 2005.

[KSJA91]   J. M. Kleinhans, G. Sigl, F. M. Johannes, and K. J. Antreich, GORDIAN: VLSI placement by quadratic programming and slicing optimization, *IEEE Transactions on Computer-Aided Design of Integrated Circuits and Systems* **10**: 356–365, March 1991.

[MH00]   M. Murakami and N. Honda, A maze-running algorithm using fuzzy set theory for routing methods of printed circuit boards, *Proceedings of the Ninth IEEE International Conference on Fuzzy Systems*, Vol. 2, pp. 985–988, 2000.

[NWZ02]   B. K. Nielsen, P. Winter, and M. Zachariasen, An exact algorithm for the uniformly-oriented Steiner tree problem, *Proceedings of the 10th European Symposium on Algorithms (Lecture Notes in Computer Science 2461)*, pp. 760–772, 2002.

[SFH+91]   Y. Sekiyama, Y. Fujihara, T. Hayashi, M. Seki, J. Kusuhara, K. Iijima, M. Takakura, and K. Fukatani, Timing-oriented routers for PCB layout design of high-performance computers, *Proceedings of the IEEE International Conference on Computer-Aided Design*, pp. 332–335, 1991.

[SDJ91]   G. Sigl, K. Doll, and F. M. Johannes, Analytical placement: A linear or quadratic objective function? *Proceedings of the ACM/IEEE Design Automation Conference*, pp. 57–62, 1991.

[SK89]   P. R. Suaris and G. Kedem, A quadrisection-based place and route scheme for standard cells, *IEEE Transactions on Computer-Aided Design of Integrated Circuits and Systems* **8**: 234–244, March 1989.

[SKK+96]   R. Scepanovic, J. S. Koford, V. Kudryavsfev, A. Andreev, S. Aleshin, and A. Podkolzin, Microelectronic integrated circuit structure and method using three directional interconect routing based on hexagonal geometry, Patent No. 5,578,840, November 26, 1996, LSI Logic.

[SN02]   N. Shenoy and W. Nicholls, An efficient routing database, *Proceedings of the ACM/IEEE Design Automation Conference*, pp. 590–595, 2002.

[SW92]   M. Sarrafzadeh and C. K. Wong, Hierarchical Steiner tree construction in uniform orientations, *IEEE Transactions on Computer-Aided Design of Integrated Circuits and Systems* **11**: 1095–1103, September 1992.

[T02]   S. Teig, The X architecture: Not your father's diagonal wiring, *Proceedings of the International Workshop on System-level Interconnect Prediction*, 2002, pp. 33–37.

[TC04]   S. Teig and A. Caldwell, U. S. Patents 6,829,757.

[TC05]   S. Teig and A. Caldwell, U. S. Patents 6,877,146; 6,886,149; 6,889,371; 6,889,372; 6,898,773; 6,928,633; 6,931,608; 6,931,615; 6,948,144; 6,951,005; 6,951,006; 6,957,408; 6,957,409; 6,978,432.

[TC06]   S. Teig and A. Caldwell, U. S. Patents 6,986,117; 7,000,209.

[TT98]   T. Takahashi and N. Shibuya, Development of a support tool for PCB design with EMC constraint: Reflection and crosstalk noise reduction in manual design, *Proceedings of the Asia-South Pacific Design Automation Conference*, pp. 397–402, 1998.

[V97]   J. Vygen, Algorithms for large-scale flat placement, *Proceedings of the ACM/IEEE Design Automation Conference*, pp. 746–751, 1997.

[WWZ00]   D. M. Warme, P. Winter, and M. Zachariasen, Exact algorithms for plane Steiner tree problems: A computational study, in *Advances in Steiner Trees*, eds. D. Z. Du, J. M. Smith, and J. H. Rubinstein, pp. 81–116, Kluwer Academic Publishers, Boston, MA, 2000.

[X01]   www.xinitiative.org.

[YWES00]   X. Yang, M. Wang, K. Eguro, and M. Sarrafzadeh, A snap-on placement tool, *Proceedings of the International Symposium on Physical Design*, pp. 153–158, 2000.

[ZZJ+05]   Q. Zhu, H. Zhou, T. Jing, X. -L. Hong, and Y. Yang, Spanning graph-based nonrectilinear Steiner tree algorithms, *IEEE Transactions on Computer-Aided Design of Integrated Circuits and Systems* **24**: 1066–1075, July 2005.

Part IX

Designing Large Global Nets

41 Inductance Effects in Global Nets

Yehea I. Ismail

CONTENTS

41.1   HISTORICAL PERSPECTIVE

Historically, the gate parasitic impedances have been much larger than interconnect parasitic impedances because the gate geometries (the width and length) were quite large (about 5 µm was a typical minimum feature size in 1980). Thus, interconnect parasitic impedances have historically been neglected and the interconnect was modeled as a short circuit. With the scaling of the minimum gate feature size, interconnect capacitances have become comparable to the gate capacitance, requiring the interconnect to be modeled as a single lumped capacitance that is added to the gate capacitance. With this interconnect model, new design techniques emerged to drive large capacitive loads associated with long global interconnects and large interconnect trees with high fanout. Cascaded tapered buffers are used to minimize the propagation delay of CMOS gates driving these large capacitive loads (e.g., [1,2]).

With increasing device densities per unit area, the cross-sectional area of interconnects has been reduced to provide more interconnect per unit area. Also, the improved yield of CMOS fabrication processes permits manufacturing larger chips with higher reliability. Thus, the global wires connecting modules across an IC have increased in length. Both the decreased cross-sectional area and the increased wirelength have caused the global wire resistances to dramatically increase. The interconnect model now includes the resistance of the interconnect. Including resistance in the interconnect model dramatically changed the design and analysis of integrated circuits, e.g., [3–5]. With a short circuit or a capacitive interconnect model, the interconnect could be treated as a single node. However, by including the series resistance, the interconnect is composed of multiple nodes, each node having a different voltage waveform. This characteristic has greatly complicated the analysis of circuits with resistive interconnect. Completely new problems and design techniques have emerged due to the transition from a capacitive to an *RC* model such as *RC* tree analysis techniques, clock skew problems, repeater insertion techniques, power consumption estimation, model order reduction techniques, and IR drops in the power supply, to name a few. Almost every aspect of the design and analysis of integrated circuits was affected by the new interconnect model.

The rest of this chapter summarizes the importance, effects, and issues involved in a transition from an *RC* interconnect model to an *RLC* model, which includes the inductance of the interconnect. This transition has the potential to change all aspects of the design and analysis of integrated circuits in analogy to the transition from a capacitive to an *RC* interconnect model. However, unlike the transition from a capacitive to an *RC* model, which only resulted into undesirable effects, the increasing inductance effects can have several desirable consequences, which are pointed out later.

41.2 IMPORTANCE OF INDUCTANCE IN CURRENT AND FUTURE TECHNOLOGIES

On-chip inductance has currently become more important with faster on-chip rise times and wider wires. Wide wires are frequently encountered in clock distribution networks and in upper metal layers. These wires are low-resistance lines that can exhibit significant inductive effects. Furthermore, performance requirements are pushing the introduction of new materials such as copper interconnect for low-resistance interconnect and new dielectrics to reduce the interconnect capacitance. These technological advances increase the importance of inductance.

On-chip inductance can cause significant errors in current deep-submicron technologies. For example, three sets of simulation* results are presented based on IBM's 0.1-μm technology to illustrate the importance of on-chip self and mutual inductances. The first example is a four-bit coupled bus (Table 41.1). The second example is a tree coupled with two lines (Table 41.2). And the third example is a pair of lines coupled with each other (Table 41.3). In all three examples, simulations are done for three cases. In case I, self and mutual inductances are not included. That is, signal lines are considered as standard *RC* lines with coupling capacitances only. In case II, self-inductance is included, and lines are considered as *RLC* lines with coupling capacitance, but no coupling inductance. In case III, both self and mutual inductances are included and lines are considered as *RLC* lines with coupling capacitance and mutual inductance. Results show that the error owing to neglecting inductance can be more than 100 percent for the delay calculation and 70 percent in the rise time. What makes these errors even more serious is that neglecting inductance and using an *RC* model always results in underestimating the propagation delay (e.g., see Figure 41.1). Thus, VLSI circuits designed using an *RC* interconnect model may not satisfy the assigned performance targets despite a worst-case analysis being applied in the circuit design process.

In general, there are two factors controlling the error between an *RC* model and an *RLC* model. These two factors are the damping factor of an *RLC* line and the ratio between the input signal rise time to the time of flight of signals across the line [7]. The damping factor of an *RLC* line is given by

$$\xi = \frac{Rl}{2}\sqrt{\frac{C}{L}} \tag{41.1}$$

where
R, *L*, and *C* are the resistance, inductance, and capacitance per unit length of the line, respectively
l is the length of the line

The damping factor of the line represents the degree of attenuation the wave suffers as it propagates a distance equal to the length of the line. As this attenuation increases, the effects of the reflections decrease and the *RC* model becomes more accurate. Note that the damping factor is proportional to

---

* Circuit simulations in this section are either performed using HSPICE or IBM's circuit simulation tool AS/X [6].

TABLE 41.1
Circuit Simulation of a 4-Bit Bus

| Bus | All Lines Are Switching in the Same Direction | | | | |
| | Case | | | Deviation (percent) | |
	I	II	III	I–III	II–III
Delay (ps)	29.32	44.2	58.67	100	33
Rise time (ps)	84.59	25.5	26.81	68.3	5.14
Overshoot (%)	0	10.3	23.79	—	126
Time of overshoot	—	115	155.2	—	35.3

TABLE 41.2
Circuit Simulation of a Coupled Tree Network

| Tree | All Lines Are Switching in the Same Direction | | | | |
| | Case | | | Deviation (percent) | |
	I	II	III	I–III	II–III
Delay (ps)	30.46	43.59	51.98	71.5	18.5
Rise time (ps)	87.1	43.36	37.29	58.6	13.4
Overshoot (%)	0	7.2	15	—	108
Time of overshoot	—	113.4	134	—	18.2

TABLE 41.3
Circuit Simulation of a Pair of Coupled Lines

| Line | All Lines Are Switching in the Same Direction | | | | |
| | Case | | | Deviation (percent) | |
	I	II	III	I–III	II–III
Delay (ps)	63.12	74.13	83.64	32.53	12.83
Rise time (ps)	147.8	85.36	49	67	43
Overshoot (%)	0	0.74	6.2	—	737
Time of overshoot	—	269	221.5	—	17.69

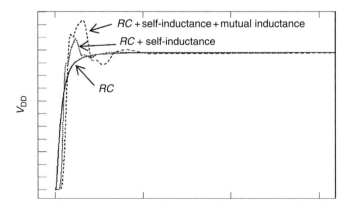

FIGURE 41.1   Signal behavior on one net of a 4-bit bus.

the length of the line and thus very long lines will exhibit less inductance effects. Alternatively, the damping factor can be expressed as

$$\xi = \frac{R_t C_t}{2\sqrt{L_t C_t}} = \frac{\tau_{RC}}{2\tau_{LC}} \tag{41.2}$$

where

    R_t, L_t, and C_t are the total resistance, inductance, and capacitance of the line, respectively

    τ_{RC} and τ_{LC} are the RC and LC time constants of the line

This relation illustrates the fight between the RC and LC time constants of the line. A reduction in the RC time constant results in a direct increase in the inductance effects exhibited by the line. Note that many of the technological advancements that have been achieved or are still in development target reducing the RC time constant. Examples are copper interconnect, dielectrics with lower ε_r, and superconductive interconnects. Also, many of the design methodologies used to reduce the delay of critical lines concentrates mainly on reducing the RC time constant of the line, such as using wider wires, wider drivers, and repeater insertion. In the limit, if the RC time constant of a line is sufficiently reduced, the line will behave as a lossless transmission line and signals can be transmitted across the line with the speed of light.

    The other factor determining inductance effects is the ratio between the input signal rise time to the time of flight of signals across the line and is given by

$$\frac{t_r}{2l\sqrt{LC}} \tag{41.3}$$

where t_r is the rise time of the input signal. As this ratio increases, the line can be more accurately modeled as an RC line. Note that in this case the relation implies that shorter lines will suffer less inductance effects mainly because the rise time of the input signal will override the LC time constant. Hence, there is a range of the length of the interconnect for which inductance effects are significant with very short and very long lines suffering no inductance effects [7]. Note that the rise times of input signals to the interconnect are becoming faster all the time with technology scaling, increasing inductance effects in future technologies. Even if some techniques can be applied today to reduce the effect of inductance allowing the use of the well-developed RC-based CAD tools, inductance effects will be very hard to suppress or ignore in future technologies and CAD tools have to be modified to include the effect of inductance.

    Equivalent figures of merit for trees were developed in Ref. [8] to characterize the importance of on-chip inductance. These expressions at node i of a tree are given by

$$\zeta_i = \frac{1}{2} \frac{\sum\limits_k C_k R_{ik}}{\sqrt{\sum\limits_k C_k L_{ik}}} \tag{41.4}$$

and

$$t_r/2 \sqrt{\sum\limits_k C_k L_{ik}} \tag{41.5}$$

respectively, where R_{ik} (L_{ik}) is the common resistance (inductance) from the input of the tree to nodes i and k and k runs over all the capacitances in the tree.

41.3 EXTRACTION AND PHYSICAL REPRESENTATIONS OF INDUCTANCE

Each interconnect line has an associated self-inductance and an associated mutual inductance to other lines in the circuit. Unlike the resistance and capacitance of interconnect lines, both self and mutual inductances are loop quantities, and they can be determined only if the whole current loop is known; i.e., the exact path in which the current returns to the source is known. The self-inductance of a loop is defined as the flux linked through the loop because of the variation in the current flowing in the loop divided by the value of the current. The current loop also has corresponding coupling inductances that couple the current loop to surrounding current loops. The coupling inductance is the flux caused by an aggressor loop linked to a given loop divided by the value of the aggressor current [9].

The current return path is frequency dependent. At low frequency, the inductive impedance (ωL) is less than the resistive impedance (R). Hence, the current tries to minimize the interconnect impedance and thus tries to minimize the interconnect resistance. This causes the current to use as many returns as possible to have parallel resistances, as shown in Figure 41.2 [9]. However, at high frequency $\omega L > R$ and the current tries to minimize interconnect impedance by minimizing the loop inductance. This causes the current to use the closest possible return path to form the smallest possible loop inductance, as shown in Figure 41.2 [9]. The current would be confined to the nearest possible return only at ultra-high frequencies (higher than 20 GHz) [10]. Therefore, at current clock frequencies, current can spread into a number of possible current return paths. This behavior makes the extraction of inductance a nontrivial task as it tremendously increases the number of surrounding interconnects that have to be considered. The distribution of the current into different wires as a function of frequency is typically referred to as proximity effects, while the confinement of current in parts of an interconnect, as shown below, is referred to as skin effect.

To limit the complexity of the problem, the inductance can be approximated [11] by assuming that the current return path is limited to the nearest power or ground line. Other approaches such as in Ref. [12] incrementally improve the accuracy by adding more ground lines to the return path until the extracted inductance is accurate enough. One way to go around the prerequisite of knowing the actual current return paths beforehand is by using the three-dimensional (3D) field solver. A common approach that is used by 3D solvers is to extract inductance by applying a finite difference or finite element method to the governing Maxwell equations in differential form. Such an approach generates a global 3D mesh for all parts of analyzed structure and for surrounding external space. This causes the number of unknowns to increase significantly, and thus a very large linear system can be generated. Solving this large linear system requires excessive memory and consumes long CPU time, which makes inductance extraction of complex 3D structures using finite element or finite difference methods impractical.

The other approach used in inductance extraction employs the partial element equivalent circuit method (PEEC) [13,14]. Using PEEC, only the volume of the conductors needs to be discretized.

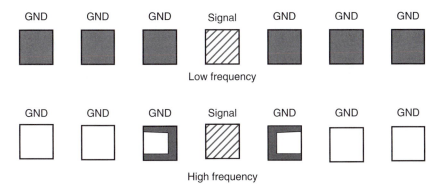

FIGURE 41.2 Frequency dependence of current distribution across signal and ground lines.

Thus, using the PEEC method produces a fewer number of unknowns than finite elements and differences. The integral formulation of the PEEC method is used in the widely known MIT inductance extraction program, FastHenry [15].

Hence, inductance extraction is a nontrivial process. However, there are two characteristics of on-chip inductance that can be exploited to simplify the extraction process of on-chip inductance. First, the sensitivity of a signal waveform to errors in the inductance values is low compared to sensitivity to errors in resistance and capacitance values, particularly the propagation delay and rise time. Second, the value of the on-chip inductance is a slow varying function of the width of the wire and the geometry of the surrounding wires [16].

The first characteristic can be explained by the fact that inductance only appears under a square root function in a waveform or timing expression characterizing a signal. The reason for this square root dependence is physical because an LC constant has the dimensions of time squared, where L and C are any inductance and capacitance values in the circuit, respectively. The square root dependence can be compared to the linear dependence of the delay expressions on the resistance because any RC constant has the dimensions of time, where R is any resistance of the circuit. For example, according to the equivalent Elmore delay for RLC trees that was introduced in Ref. [17], the 50 percent delay of the signal at node i of an RLC tree is

$$t_{\text{pdi}} = 1.047 \cdot \sqrt{\sum_k C_k L_{ik}} \cdot e^{-\frac{\zeta_i}{0.85}} + 0.695 \cdot \sum_k C_k R_{ik} \tag{41.6}$$

where ζ_i is the damping factor at node i and is

$$\zeta_i = \frac{1}{2} \frac{\sum_k C_k R_{ik}}{\sqrt{\sum_k C_k L_{ik}}} \tag{41.7}$$

Note that inductance only appears under a square root. This fact is also evident in Equations 41.8 and 41.14.

As an example, circuit [6] simulations are performed for an RLC tree with no inductance (an RC model), and with all of the inductance values increased by 10, 20, and 30 percent. These simulations are depicted in Figure 41.3. Note in the simulations that using an approximate inductance estimation

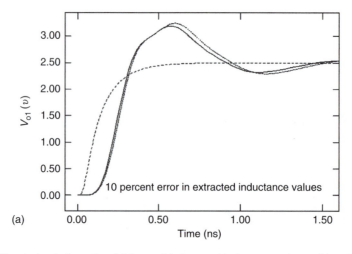

(a)

FIGURE 41.3 Circuit simulations of an RLC tree with the actual inductance values, with no inductance (an RC model), and with all of the inductance values increased by (a) 10 percent.

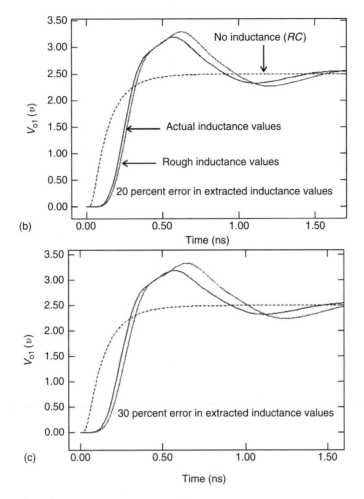

FIGURE 41.3 (continued)   (b) 20 percent, and (c) 30 percent.

greatly improves the accuracy of the waveform as compared to using an *RC* model. Even with a 30 percent error in the inductance values, the propagation delay differs by 9.4 percent from the actual value as compared to 51 percent if an *RC* model is used. The improvement in the rise time is even greater. The rise time differs from the actual value by 5.9 percent with a 30 percent error in the inductance values as compared to a 71 percent error when an *RC* model is used. The maximum error in the waveform shape occurs around the overshoots (Figure 41.3). However, estimating the overshoot requires less accuracy because the overshoot is usually evaluated to decide if the overshoot is within an acceptable limit. This high tolerance of the delay expressions to errors in the extracted inductance combined with the slow variation of extracted inductance values with changes in geometry encourage the use of simplified techniques with higher computational efficiency to extract the on-chip inductance.

41.4   EFFECTS OF INDUCTANCE

This section briefly discusses the effects of inductance on the performance of integrated circuits. The effects of inductance on signal delay and rise time, power consumption, and delay uncertainty are discussed.

41.4.1 EFFECTS OF INDUCTANCE ON DELAY AND SIGNAL RISE TIME

A general expression for the propagation delay from the input to the output of an *RLC* line of length *l* with an ideal power supply and an open circuit load is given by [18]

$$t_{pd} = \sqrt{LC} \left[e^{-2.9(\alpha_{asym}l)^{1.35}} l + 0.74\alpha_{asym}l^2 \right] \tag{41.8}$$

where

$$\alpha_{asym} = \frac{R}{2}\sqrt{\frac{C}{L}} \tag{41.9}$$

α_{asym} is the asymptotic value at high frequencies of the attenuation per unit length of the signals as the signals propagate across a lossy transmission line, as shown in Figure 41.4.

For the limiting case where $L \to 0$, Equation 41.8 reduces to $0.37RCl^2$, illustrating the square dependence on the length of an *RC* wire as aforementioned. For the other limiting case where $R \to 0$, the propagation delay is given by $\sqrt{L_tC_t} = l\sqrt{LC}$. Note the linear dependence on the length of the line. Note also that inductance always increases the delay as compared to an *RC* model; i.e., if inductance is neglected, the delay is underestimated by the incomplete *RC* model.

The rise time of signals propagating across *RLC* lines improves as the inductance effects of the line increase. This behavior can be explained by referring to Figure 41.4, which depicts the attenuation of signals as they travel across an *RLC* line as a function of frequency. Higher frequency components at the edges of a pulse suffer greater attenuation as compared to low frequency components. The shape of a signal degrades as the signal travels across a lossy transmission line because of the loss of these high-frequency components. The attenuation constant becomes less frequency dependent as inductance effects increase or as $R/\omega L$ decreases as shown in Figure 41.4. In the limiting case of a lossless line representing maximum inductance effects, the attenuation constant α is 0. Thus, as inductance effects increase, a pulse propagating across an *RLC* line maintains the high-frequency components in the edges, improving the signal rise and fall times.

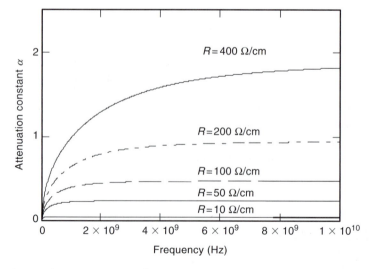

FIGURE 41.4 Attenuation constant versus frequency. $L = 10\,\text{nH/cm}$, $C = 1\,\text{pF/cm}$, and *R* is 10, 50, 100, 200, and 400 Ω/cm, respectively.

41.4.2 EFFECTS OF INDUCTANCE ON POWER DISSIPATION

Power consumption is an increasingly important design parameter with mobile systems and high performance, high-complexity circuits such as leading edge microprocessors. If the frequency of switching is f cycles per second, then the dynamic power consumption is described by the well-known formula,

$$P_{dyn} = C_t V_{DD}^2 f \tag{41.10}$$

The dynamic power depends only on the total load capacitance, the supply voltage, and the operating frequency. As discussed in Section 41.7, increasing inductance effects result in a lower number of repeaters as well as smaller repeater size. The smaller size and number of repeaters therefore significantly reduces the total capacitance of the repeaters and, consequently, reduces the total dynamic power consumption.

The short-circuit power results from the NMOS and PMOS blocks of a CMOS gate being on simultaneously during the rise and fall times of the input signal, creating a current path between the power supply and ground. As discussed in Section 41.4.1, the inductance reduces the rise time of the signals in an integrated circuit, reducing the short-circuit power. The short-circuit power consumption of a gate driven by an RLC line versus the line inductance is plotted in Figure 41.5. Note that as inductance effects increase, the short-circuit power consumption significantly decreases due to the faster input rise time. Also, the smaller repeater sizes dramatically reduces the short-circuit power consumption because the short-circuit power of a CMOS gate is super linearly dependent on the transistor widths. Finally, it has been shown in Ref. [19] that the short-circuit power consumption of a CMOS gate decreases as the inductance of the driven net becomes more significant. Intuitively, inductance is an element that does not consume any power while resistance consumes power. Hence, as the interconnect behavior becomes dominated by inductance rather than resistance, the power consumption of integrated circuits will be reduced.

41.4.3 EFFECTS OF INDUCTIVE COUPLING ON DELAY UNCERTAINTY

In a set of inductively and capacitively coupled lines, the signal propagation delay on a particular line reaches a minimum when neighbor lines are switching in the same direction. The delay on that line reaches a maximum when that particular line is switching in opposite direction to neighbor lines because of the increased effective capacitance that has to be charged or discharged. The ratio of

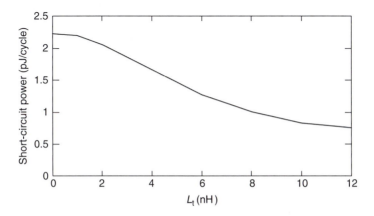

FIGURE 41.5 Short-circuit energy consumed per cycle by CMOS gate driven by an RLC line versus the inductance of the line. The total resistance and capacitance of the line are maintained constant at 100 Ω and 1 pF, respectively.

the maximum and minimum signal delays on a certain signal line can be defined as delay uncertainty (D_U) for that line, as given by

$$D_U = \frac{t_{d_{max}}}{t_{d_{min}}} \tag{41.11}$$

For *RLC* lines, the delay is given by [20]

$$t_d = 1.047 \cdot E \cdot \tau_{LC} + 1 \cdot 4 \cdot \tau_{RC} \tag{41.12}$$

where E is a term that depends on the damping factor of this line as described in Ref. [20],

$$\tau_{RC} = \sum_k \left[R_k \cdot \sum_{r,j} C_{rj} \cdot (\alpha_r - \alpha_j) \right] \tag{41.13}$$

and

$$\tau_{LC} = \sqrt{\sum_k \left[L_k \cdot \sum_{r,j} C_{rj} \cdot (\alpha_r - \alpha_j) + M_k \cdot \sum_{l,m} C_{lm} \cdot (\alpha_l - \alpha_m) \right]} \tag{41.14}$$

Each line has a switching factor associated with it and is denoted α_i for interconnect i. The switching factor takes the values 1, 0, and -1 for lines switching from low-to-high, nonswitching lines, and lines switching from high-to-low, respectively. k runs over all the branches on the path from the primary input to node i on the tree (which i belongs to), r runs over all the nodes downstream of k on that tree, and j runs over all the nodes to which r has a capacitance connected to. In the case of capacitances to ground, $j = 0$. The index l runs over all the nodes downstream of M_k on the coupled tree (which i does not belong to). The index m runs over all the nodes, which l has a capacitance connected to.

The time constants τ_{RC} and τ_{LC} depend on the switching directions of neighbor lines. As neighbor lines switch in opposite directions to the line in consideration, τ_{RC} is maximum. When neighbor lines switch in the same direction, τ_{RC} is minimum as given by Equation 41.13. On the other hand, τ_{LC} decreases when neighbor lines switch in opposite directions because of the opposite currents in neighbor lines, which causes negative mutual inductance terms to appear in Equation 41.14. When neighbor lines switch in the same direction, τ_{LC} increases because the mutual inductances add to the self-inductance as in Equation 41.14. This opposite behavior of τ_{RC} and τ_{LC} results in reducing the discrepancy between the maximum and the minimum delays of a line because of coupling with other lines.

Circuit simulation (Figure 41.6) for the signal on the middle line of three coupled lines shows that as inductance effects increase, the ratio between the maximum and the minimum delays decreases. That is, higher inductive effects lead to lower delay uncertainty and narrower switching windows. Lowering delay uncertainty is a positive effect of inductance because narrower switching windows give significant degrees of freedom in physical design to limit noise and control glitches among many other benefits.

41.5   INDUCTIVE NOISE

As discussed before, a line can inductively couple to lines that are far away unlike capacitive coupling, which only occurs between adjacent lines. The problem of inductive coupling is particularly severe in wide busses, which are commonplace in most digital integrated circuits such as DSP and microprocessor circuits. The width of busses in digital circuits is continuously increasing with technology

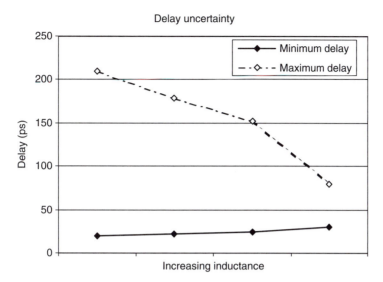

FIGURE 41.6 Delay uncertainty dependence on inductance effects. The data shown are for the delay of the middle line of three coupled parallel lines.

scaling. Hence, the problem of inductive coupling in busses will have even more significance in future technologies.

Physically, a wide bus with all the lines switching in the same direction behaves as one wide line. Such a wide line has much higher inductance effects as compared to any of the individual lines in the bus. Hence, the effective inductance of a line that is part of a bus is far larger than the self-inductance of that line. This fact can also be quantitatively understood by referring to Equation 41.14, which shows that if all the lines are switching in the same direction, the LC time constant of the line becomes much larger than the case of an individual line because of all the mutual terms adding to the self-inductance term. This increase in the LC time constant means much higher overshoots and inductive noise on any line in the bus.

To examine the impact of inductance on circuit cross talk in a high-performance 0.18-μm process, the worst-case noise generated on an 8-bit, 3000-μm long, standard data bus was simulated in Refs. [9,21]. The bus was implemented in metal 6 with all lines having a metal width of 3 μm and a metal-to-metal spacing of 1.5 μm consistent with typical high-level metal implementations of high-performance global busses. The data bus was also sandwiched between a V_{DD} line and a GND line each 15-μm wide to provide a return path for the current flowing in the buses. The drivers and receivers were implemented using simple buffers. A distributed RLC model for the interconnect was produced where FastCap [22] was used to model the interconnect capacitance, and FastHenry [15] was used to model both the resistance and the inductance of the interconnects. By applying a 5-ps rise time step signal to all the inputs except the one in the middle, SPICE simulations show a totally unacceptable voltage glitch of 1.17 V. Such a glitch could cause erroneous switching and logic failures. Note that if the inductance is neglected and not modeled, the cross-talk noise becomes only 0.59 V, which is almost half the value of the actual glitch. This shows the importance of modeling on-chip inductance for accurate detection of cross-talk voltage glitches.

In terms of substrate coupling, inductance effects increase this type of noise significantly. Overshoots and undershoots owing to inductance cause noise coupling through the common substrate, which is both difficult to measure and difficult to control. Substrate noise-conduction modes can be classified into (1) resistive coupling, (2) capacitive coupling, (3) impact ionization, and (4) body effect (Figure 41.7). All these modes involve currents running into the substrate from the drains or the sources of transistors and affecting other devices. Ideally, the p-bulk is grounded, which always

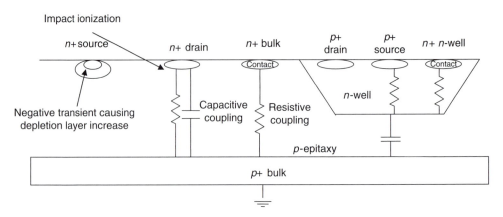

FIGURE 41.7   Mechanisms of substrate noise propagation in an integrated circuit.

reverse biases the $p - n$ junctions at the drains and sources of NMOS transistors assuming that ground is the lowest voltage that can appear at the drain or source of any transistor. Similarly, the n-well is connected to V_{DD} to reverse bias the drains and sources of PMOS transistors. However, inductance effects cause overshoots and undershoots that can forward bias these junctions resulting in currents flowing into the substrate causing substrate coupling. For that reason, substrate coupling noise is sometimes called bootstrap noise. Also, if the bulk is biased with a switching ground bus, the ground on the bulk is not perfect because switching transients will cause voltage drops across the line. Hence, the switching transients on the power supply line can couple to transistors resistively through the $p+$ bulk contacts. The parallel summation of bulk contacts and epitaxy resistances provides a very low impedance path (nearly short) to the $p+$ buried layer.

The second source of substrate noise is capacitive coupling through the MOSFET source and drain $p - n$ junctions. Each n-well on $p+$ bulk also introduces fairly large $p - n$ junctions forming a capacitance between the V_{DD} rails biasing the n-well and the V_{SS} rails biasing the bulk. The noise injected into the substrate via capacitive coupling is inversely proportional to the rise time of the signals on the drains and sources of transistors. As discussed in the previous section, inductance effects result in faster signal transition times. Another source of substrate noise is impact ionization current, generated at the pinch-off point of the NMOS transistors. Impact ionization causes a whole current in the bulk. A negative bulk transient will increase the depletion region between the source and the bulk. This depletes the channel of charge carriers and increase V_{th}. The total effect is a sporadic decrease in the I_{DS} current. In general, these transients increase with higher inductance effects owing to the higher voltage swings and overshoots.

41.6   REQUIREMENTS ON CAD TOOLS AND THEIR PERFORMANCE

The signals that occur in RLC circuits are significantly more complicated than signals in RC circuits. For example, the RLC signals shown in Figure 41.1 have overshoots, very large inertial delay, fast rise time, and are rich in harmonics. Hence, new delay models and model order reduction techniques are required to handle RLC circuits. One of the most popular approximate delay models used for the design and analysis of integrated circuits is the Elmore delay model. This first order delay model cannot be used with RLC circuits with underdamped responses, because underdamped responses involve complex poles that appear in conjugate pairs. Hence, at least a second order approximation is required for RLC circuits. One such model was developed in Ref. [17] and maintains the popular characteristics of Elmore delay.

Model order reduction techniques allow the calculation of approximations of higher orders to accurately simulate the interconnect. Asymptotic waveform evaluation (AWE) is one popular technique used successfully with RC interconnects [23]. However, AWE cannot calculate enough poles to handle complex underdamped responses because of numerical errors. Hence, a set of new model order reduction techniques have been recently developed that are capable of calculating higher order approximations necessary for simulating systems with complex responses. Examples are Pade via Lanczos (PVL) and matrix Padc via Lanczos (MPVL) [24], Arnoldi algorithms [25], block Arnoldi algorithms [26], passive reduced-order interconnect macromodeling algorithm (PRIMA) [27], and SyPVL algorithm [28]. However, these model order reduction techniques can have significantly higher computational complexity than AWE. Hence, there is a need for innovative simulation techniques for handling complex responses arising in *RLC* circuits.

Another feature that complicates the analysis and design of integrated circuits including on-chip inductance, is the far-reaching inductive coupling to other lines in the integrated circuit. Typically, a line in a wide bus couples to all the lines in the bus. As compared to capacitive coupling, which only couples a line to the immediate neighbors, inductive coupling results in larger circuits (the whole bus rather than three lines) to be analyzed, and these circuits have a significant amount of inputs.

In general, all CAD tools will run significantly slower when using an *RLC* model as compared to an *RC* model. This behavior is simply due to the more complex model used and the higher signal integrity issues involved. In addition to the lower performance of CAD tools, a very large infrastructure of *RC*-based CAD tools needs to be modified to include inductance effects.

41.7 PHYSICAL DESIGN INCLUDING INDUCTANCE EFFECTS

Currently, the industry applies a three-step design process for integrated circuits when handling inductance. First, employ design methodologies and techniques to reduce the inductance effects in the design. Second, use the well-developed *RC*-based design tools to optimize and verify the circuit. Third, pray nothing will go wrong. However, as discussed in this chapter, inductance can have useful effects such as improving the rise time of signals, reducing the power consumption, and reducing the number of inserted repeaters. Hence, by suppressing inductance effects and using *RC*-based tools, a suboptimal circuit results in terms of area, power consumption, and speed. Also, signal integrity and cross-talk issues owing to inductive coupling are neglected, which can result in undetected reliability problems. Fortunately, in recent years many researchers have started modifying design methodologies and physical design to include inductance rather than suppressing it. A sample of these works is discussed in this section.

Including inductance in interconnect routing has been dealt with in several works. An example is the work in Ref. [29]. The work mainly deals with reducing capacitive and inductive cross talk within the interconnect during full chip routing. The work shows a reduction in cross talk by a factor of 2.5 while increasing the routing area with less than 5 percent as compared to an algorithm that does not include cross talk. In wide busses, inductive cross talk can sometimes exceed capacitive coupling when all lines switch in the same direction.

Repeater insertion is another common design methodology for driving long-resistive interconnect (e.g., Refs. [3–5]). Because the *RC* time constant of a line is given by $R_t C_t = RCl^2$ and has a square dependence on the length of the line, subdividing the line into shorter sections by inserting repeaters is an effective strategy for reducing the total propagation delay. Currently, typical high-performance circuits have a significant number of repeaters inserted along global interconnect lines. These repeaters are large gates and consume a significant portion of the total circuit power.

As discussed in Section 41.2, the amount of inductance effects present in an *RLC* line depends on the ratio between the *RC* and the *LC* time constants of the line. Hence, as inductance effects increase, the *LC* time constant dominates the *RC* time constant and the delay of the line changes from a quadratic to a linear dependence on the line length [18]. As a consequence, the optimum number of repeaters for minimum propagation delay decreases as inductance effects increase. In the limit, an *LC* line requires zero repeater area to minimize the overall propagation delay.

Inserting repeaters based on an *RC* model and neglecting inductance result in a larger repeater area than necessary to achieve a minimum delay. The magnitude of the excess repeater area when

TABLE 41.4

Total Repeater Area, Total Power, and Total Maximum Path Delay of All of the Trees

Totals	Unbuffered	Savings in Delay (percent)	Buffered *RLC* Model	Savings Compared to *RC* (percent)	Buffered *RC* Model
Area (minimum inverters)	0	—	14,116	40.8	23,854
Maximum delay (ps)	6,554	42.2	3,787	6.7	4,061
Power (pJ/cycle)	—	—	1,379	15.6	1,632

The percent savings shown here represent the average savings in area, power, and maximum path delay when using an *RLC* model for repeater insertion

using an *RC* model depends upon the relative magnitude of the inductance within the *RLC* tree. The reduced number of inserted repeaters also simplifies the layout and routing constraints. Also, the reduced repeater area greatly reduces the power consumed by the repeaters in an integrated circuit. A more thorough analytical analysis of the effect of inductance on the repeater insertion process can be found in Ref. [18]. Practical data are listed in Table 41.4 for repeaters inserted in a large number of typical copper interconnects from a 0.25-μm CMOS technology [30]. Note that by using an *RLC* model rather than an *RC* model, a better delay can be achieved with significantly less repeater area and power consumption by the repeaters.

Inductance plays a central role in power and clock distribution networks [31–36]. Typically, the inductive characteristics of the clock distribution network are intimately related to the power distribution network. The return currents from the clock determine the size of the inductive loop. These currents typically return in the wide, low-resistance, power distribution network wires. The clock wires are typically wide enough to exhibit significant inductance effects. Full transmission line models are needed for these wires when sizing the clock distribution network. Several works (such as Refs. [34,35]) have dealt with these clock distribution design including inductance.

In terms of the power distribution networks, inductance does dominate the total impedance of the network [31–36]. Electromigration poses an upper limit on the current density carried by the power distribution networks. Because of the unidirectional nature of the currents carried by the power distribution network, it is crucial to upsize these wires to meet the upper bound on current density. Hence, power distribution networks typically have very wide wires that exhibit significant inductance effects. However, typically a power distribution network is designed with interleaving V_{DD} and GND lines on each layer. This design results in inductive coupling typically limited to adjacent wires with opposing currents canceling at far distances. Hence, inductance in the power grid can be easily modeled using loop inductance models rather than partial inductances. Interestingly, designers have found ways to justify ignoring inductance in power distribution networks despite its dominance. The justification is typically that currents taken from the power distribution network are DC. There is no experimental data that supports this claim. In fact, in synchronous circuits, most of the currents are drawn around the clock edges, giving rise to very large current slopes. Several works have considered inductance in the power distribution network. However, accurate estimation of the currents drawn from the power distribution network remains crucial.

REFERENCES

1. H. G. Lin and L. W. Linholm, An optimized output stage for MOS integrated circuits, *IEEE Journal of Solid-State Circuits*, SC-10(2): 106–109, April 1975.
2. B. S. Cherkauer and E. G. Friedman, Design of tapered buffers with local interconnect capacitance, *IEEE Transactions on Very Large Scale Integration (VLSI) Systems*, 3(1): 99–111, March 1995.

3. J. Cong, L. He, C. -K. Koh, and P. Madden, Performance optimization of VLSI interconnect, *Integration: The VLSI Journal*, 21: 1–94, November 1996.

4. V. Adler and E. G. Friedman, Delay and power expressions for a CMOS inverter driving a resistive-capacitive load, *Analog Integrated Circuits and Signal Processing*, 14(1/2): 29–39, September 1997.

5. S. S. Sapatnekar, RC interconnect optimization under the Elmore delay model, *Proceedings of the IEEE/ACM Design Automation Conference*, pp. 387–391, San Diego, CA, June 1994.

6. *AS/X User's Guide*, IBM Corp., 1994.

7. Y. I. Ismail, E. G. Friedman, and J. L. Neves, Figures of merit to characterize the importance of on-chip inductance, *IEEE Transactions on Very Large Scale Integration (VLSI) Systems*, 7(4): 442–449, December 1999.

8. Y. I. Ismail, E. G. Friedman, and J. L. Neves, Inductance effects in RLC trees, *Proceedings of the IEEE Great Lakes Symposium on VLSI*, pp. 56–59, Ypsilanti, MI, March 1999.

9. Y. Massoud and Y. I. Ismail, On-chip inductance in high-speed integrated circuits, *IEEE Circuits and Devices Magazine*, 17(4): 14–21, July 2001.

10. Y. Massoud and J. White, Simulation and modeling of the effect of substrate conductivity on coupling inductance, *Proceedings of the IEEE International Electron Devices Meeting*, pp. 491–494, Hong Kong, China, December 1995.

11. K. Shepard and Z. Tian, Return-limited inductances: A practical approach to on-chip inductance extraction, *IEEE Transactions on Computer-Aided Design*, 19: 425–436, April 2000.

12. B. Krauter and S. Mehrotra, Layout based frequency dependent inductance and resistance extraction for on-chip interconnect timing analysis, *Proceedings of the IEEE Design Automation Conference*, pp. 303–308, San Francisco, CA, June 1998.

13. A. E. Ruehli, Inductance calculations in a complex integrated circuit environment, *IBM Journal of Research and Development*, 16: 470–481, September 1972.

14. P. A. Brennan, N. Raver, and A. Ruehli, Three dimensional inductance computations with partial element equivalent circuits, *IBM Journal of Research and Development*, 23: 661–668, November 1979.

15. M. Kamon, M. Tsuk, and J. White, FastHenry: A mutipole-accelerated 3-D inductance extraction program, *IEEE Transactions on Microwave Theory Technology*, 42(9): 1750–1758, September 1994.

16. Y. I. Ismail and E. G. Friedman, Sensitivity of interconnect delay to on-chip inductance, *Proceedings of the IEEE International Symposium on Circuits and Systems*, pp. 403–407, Geneva, Switzerland, May 2000.

17. Y. I. Ismail, E. G. Friedman, and J. L. Neves, Equivalent Elmore delay for *RLC* trees, *IEEE Transactions on Computer-Aided Design*, 19(1): 83–97, January 2000.

18. Y. I. Ismail and E. G. Friedman, Effects of inductance on the propagation delay and repeater insertion in VLSI circuits, *IEEE Transactions on Very Large Scale Integration (VLSI) Systems*, 8(2): 195–206, April 2000.

19. Y. I. Ismail, E. G. Friedman, and J. L. Neves, Dynamic and short-circuit power of CMOS gates driving lossless transmission lines, *IEEE Transactions on Circuits and Systems 1: Fundamental Theory and Applications*, CAS-46(8): 950–961, August 1999.

20. M. Chowdhury, Y. I. Ismail, C. V. Kashyap, and B. L. Krauter, Performance analysis of deep sub micron VLSI circuits in the presence of self and mutual inductance, *Proceedings of the IEEE International Symposium on Circuits and Systems*, pp. 197–200, Scottsdale, AZ, May 2002.

21. Y. Massoud, J. Kawa, D. MacMillen, and J. White, Modeling and analysis of differential signaling for minimizing inductive cross-talk, *Proceedings of the IEEE Design Automation Conference*, pp. 804–809, Anaheim, CA, June 2001.

22. K. Nabors and J. White, Fast capacitance extraction of general three-dimensional structures, *IEEE Transanctions on Microwave Theory Technology*, 40(7): 1496–1506, June 1992.

23. L. T. Pillage and R. A. Rohrer, Asymptotic waveform evaluation for timing analysis, *IEEE Transactions on Computer-Aided Design*, CAD-9(4): 352–366, April 1990.

24. P. Feldmann and R. W. Freund, Reduced-order modeling of large linear subcircuits via block Lanczos algorithm, *Proceedings of the IEEE/ACM Design Automation Conference*, pp. 474–479, San Diego, CA, June 1995.

25. M. Silveira, M. Kamon, and J. White, Efficient reduced-order modeling of frequency-dependent coupling inductances associated with 3-D interconnect structures, *Proceedings of the IEEE/ACM Design Automation Conference*, pp. 376–380, San Diego, CA, June 1995.

26. D. L. Boley, Krylov space methods on state-space control models, *Journal of Circuits, Systems, and Signal Processing*, 13(6): 733–758, May 1994.

27. A. Odabasioglu, M. Celik, and L. T. Pillage, PRIMA: Passive reduced-order interconnect macromodeling algorithm, *IEEE Transactions on Computer-Aided Design*, CAD-17(8): 645–654, August 1998.

28. P. Feldmann and R. W. Freund, Reduced-order modeling of large passive linear circuits by means of the SyPVL algorithm, *Proceedings of the IEEE/ACM International Conference on Computer-Aided Design*, pp. 280–287, San Jose, CA, November 1996.

29. J. Xiong and L. He, Full-chip routing optimization with RLC crosstalk budgeting, *IEEE Transactions on Computer-Aided Design of Integrated Circuits and Systems*, 23(3): 366–377, March 2004.

30. Y. I. Ismail, E. G. Friedman, and J. L. Neves, Repeater insertion in tree structured inductive interconnect, *Proceedings of the ACM/IEEE International Conference on Computer-Aided Design*, pp. 420–424, San Jose, CA, November 1999.

31. H. Hu, D. Blaauw, V. Zolotov, K. Gala, M. Zhao, R. Panda, and S. Sapatnekar, Fast on-chip inductance simulation using a precorrected-FFT method, *IEEE Transactions on Computer-Aided Design of Integrated Circuits and Systems (T-CAD)*, 22(1): 49–66, January 2003.

32. H. Hu and S. S. Sapatnekar, Efficient inductance extraction using circuit-aware techniques, *IEEE Transactions on VLSI Systems*, 10(6): 746–761, December 2002.

33. G. Zhong, H. Wang, C. -K. Koh, and K. Roy, A twisted bundle layout structure for minimizing inductive coupling noise, *Proceedings of the IEEE/ACM International Conference on Computer-Aided Design*, pp. 406–411, Los Angeles, CA, June 2000.

34. M. A. El-Moursy and E. G. Friedman, Exponentially tapered H-tree clock distribution networks, *IEEE Transactions on Very Large Scale Integration (VLSI) Systems*, 13(8): 971–975, August 2005.

35. M. A. El-Moursy and E. G. Friedman, Shielding effect of on-chip interconnect inductance, *IEEE Transactions on Very Large Scale Integration (VLSI) Systems*, 13(3): 396–400, March 2005.

36. V. Mezhiba and E. G. Friedman, Inductive properties of high-performance power distribution grids, *IEEE Transactions on Very Large Scale Integration (VLSI) Systems*, 10(6): 762–776, December 2002.

42 Clock Network Design: Basics

Chris Chu and Min Pan

CONTENTS

A vast majority of VLSI chips are based on a synchronous sequential circuit design methodology. For these circuits, a clock signal is used to synchronize the operations of different components across the chip. Typically, this signal is produced by a clock generator circuit based on an external reference, and it is distributed inside the chip by a clock network. Because the timing of the entire chip is controlled by the clock signal, a poor design of the clock distribution network will limit the performance of the chip. As the clock network connects the clock generator to a huge number of clocked elements (including latches, flip-flops, memories, and dynamic gates) all over the chip and it has high switching activity, it usually consumes a significant portion of the overall routing resources and of the total chip power. Hence the clock network must be carefully designed to optimize the performance of the chip, routing resource usage, and power consumption.

This chapter discusses some basic issues in clock network design. In Section 42.1, the metrics used in designing clock networks are introduced. In Sections 42.2 and 42.3, algorithms to generate clock networks with tree structures and nontree structures are described, respectively. In Section 42.4, the clock skew scheduling technique, which makes use of intentional clock skew to optimize performance, is introduced. In Section 42.5, clock network design techniques that focus on handling variability are presented. In Chapter 43, the clock network designs of several high-performance microprocessors are presented to illustrate how the basic techniques described in this chapter are applied in practice.

42.1 METRICS FOR CLOCK NETWORK DESIGN

Unlike other signals that carry data information, the clock signal in edge-triggered circuits carry timing information by the signal transitions (i.e., edges). Therefore, the metrics used in clock network design are different from those for general signal net design, and these are discussed in the remainder of this section.

42.1.1 SKEW

Clock skew refers to the spatial variation in the arrival time of a clock transition. The clock skew between two points i and j on a chip is defined as $t_i - t_j$, where t_i and t_j are the clock arrival time to point i and point j, respectively. The clock skew of a chip is defined as the maximum clock skew between any two clocked elements on the chip. In general, clock skew forces designers to be conservative and use a longer clock period, that is, a lower clock frequency, for the design (unless both the clock network and the circuit are specially designed to take advantage of clock skew as described in Section 42.4). Therefore, clock networks with zero skew are most desirable. However, because of static mismatches in the clock paths and clock loads, clock skew is nonzero in practice, and hence skew minimization is always one of the most important objectives in clock network design. Skew can be effectively minimized in both physical design and circuit design stages. Skew minimization approaches in physical design stage are discussed in this chapter. Deskewing techniques in circuit design stage will be illustrated by several examples in Chapter 43.

Jitter is another measure of the variation in the arrival time of a clock transition. Specifically, it refers to the temporal variation of the clock period at a given point on the chip. Like skew, it is an important metric to the quality of the clock signal because it also forces designers to be conservative and use a longer clock period. The structure of the clock network has insignificant effect on jitter. Jitter is caused by delay variation in clock buffer due to power supply noise and temperature fluctuation, influence of substrate/power supply noise to the clock generator, capacitive coupling between clock and adjacent signal wires, and data-dependent nature of load capacitance of latch/register [1]. It is more effectively minimized by the design of other components like power supply network and clock generator. Therefore, it is typically not considered during clock network design.

42.1.2 TRANSITION TIME

The transition time is usually defined as the time for a signal to switch between 20 and 80 percent of the supply voltage.* This corresponds to the rise time for the rising transition, and the fall time for the falling transition. The reciprocal of the transition time is called the slew rate.[†]

Slow transitions could potentially cause large skew and jitter values in the presence of process variations or noise. Transition times also need to be substantially less than the clock period to allow the clock to achieve a rail-to-rail transition, to provide adequate noise immunity. Another motivation for sharp transition times is that they limit the short-circuit power, which is roughly proportional to input transition time [2], in the clock network. However, to reduce transition time, larger or more buffers are normally required, which would increase power consumption, layout congestion, and process variations. In practice, transition times are bounded rather than minimized in clock network design.

---

* Definitions as switching time between 10 and 90 percent, and between 30 and 70 percent are also common.
† However, in common usage, the term slew rate is often used to mean transition time rather than its reciprocal.

42.1.3 PHASE DELAY

Phase delay (or latency) is defined as the maximum delay from the clock generator to any clock terminal. It is important to realize that because the clock is a periodic signal, the absolute delay from the clock generator to a clock terminal is not important. However, it has been observed that the shorter the phase delay, the more robust the clock network will generally be [3]. Therefore, the phase delay can be used as a simple albeit indirect criterion in clock network design.

42.1.4 AREA

The clock network is a huge structure driving a large number of widely distributed terminals. It consists of a large number of wire segments, many of which are long and wide. Hence the clock network utilizes a significant wire area. For example, it consumes 3 percent of the total available metals 3 and 4 [4]. Moreover, because the clock network is sensitive to noise, it is usually shielded and hence uses even more wire resources. In addition, typically, a lot of possibly large buffers are inserted in the clock network. Those buffers could occupy a significant device area. It is important to minimize both wire area and device area in clock network design.

42.1.5 POWER

Because of battery life concern in portable electronic devices and heat dissipation problem in high-performance ICs, power consumption is a very important design consideration in recent years. The clock signal switches twice every cycle. Whenever it switches, the huge capacitance associated with the wires and devices of the clock network needs to be charged or discharged. Therefore, clock distribution is a significant component of total power consumption. The clock distribution and generation circuitry is known to consume up to 40 percent and 36 percent of the total power budget of high-performance [4] and embedded [5] microprocessors, respectively. However, a significant portion of the clock power is consumed in the input capacitance of the clocked elements [3,6]. Unless large amounts of local clock gating is done, as is typical in high-performance designs, this portion of power cannot be reduced by modifying the clock network.

42.1.6 SKEW SENSITIVITY TO PROCESS VARIATIONS

If the manufacturing process is ideal, a careful clock network design can eliminate any clock skew. However, with reductions in the feature sizes of VLSI processes, manufacturing variations are becoming increasingly significant. These variations are the major causes of clock skew in modern designs, as designers usually can keep the systematic skew under nominal process parameters low. As a design goal, it is important not only to minimize metrics such as the skew but also to minimize their sensitivity to process variations.

42.2 CLOCK NETWORKS WITH TREE STRUCTURES

A common and simple approach to distribute the clock is to use a tree structure. The most basic tree structure is the H-tree as shown in Figure 42.1, and it is obtained by recursively drawing H-shapes at the leaf nodes. With enough recursions, the H-tree can distribute a clock from the center to within an arbitrarily short distance of every point on the chip.

   If all clock terminals have the same load and are arranged in a regular array as in Figure 42.1, and if there is no process variation, the H-tree will have zero skew. However, the clock loads are almost always irregularly arranged all over the chip. To handle the irregularity, algorithms that produce generalized H-tree structures are presented in Sections 42.2.1 through 42.2.4. Wire sizing and buffer insertion in clock trees are discussed in Section 42.2.5.

   As a notational matter, we point out that Manhattan distances and rectilinear routing are assumed throughout this chapter. However, for simplicity, nonrectilinear segments are drawn in most figures

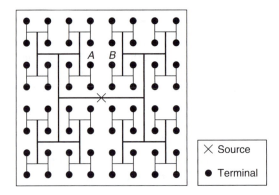

FIGURE 42.1   Clock network for 64 terminals with H-tree structure.

(e.g., Figure 42.2). Each nonrectilinear segment can be replaced by a set of two (or more) rectilinear segments in an actual implementation.

42.2.1   METHOD OF MEANS AND MEDIANS

Jackson et al. [7] proposed an algorithm called the method of means and medians (MMM) to construct a clock tree for a set of arbitrarily distributed terminals. The algorithm takes a top-down recursive approach, a recursive step of which is illustrated in Figure 42.2. In each step, the set of terminals is partitioned according to either the x- or y-coordinate into two subsets about the median coordinate of the set. Note that the number of terminals in the two subsets may be equal, if the number of nodes is even, or may differ by one otherwise. Then the center of mass (i.e., mean coordinate) of the entire set is connected to both centers of mass of the two subsets. The partitioning direction at each recursive level is determined by an one level look-ahead technique in which both x-then-y partitioning and y-then-x partitioning are attempted, and the one that minimizes skew between its current endpoints is chosen. The clock trees for the subsets are recursively constructed until there is only one terminal in each subset. The time complexity of MMM is $O(n \log n)$, where n is the number of terminals.

42.2.2   GEOMETRIC MATCHING ALGORITHM

The geometric matching algorithm (GMA) proposed by Kahng et al. [8] solves the same problem formulation as the MMM algorithm, but takes a bottom-up recursive approach. A geometric

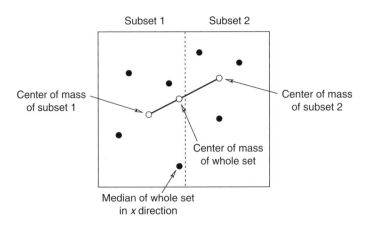

FIGURE 42.2   Recursive step of the MMM algorithm. The set is partitioned according to x-coordinate.

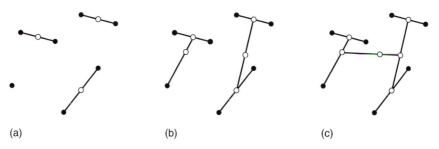

(a)   (b)   (c)

FIGURE 42.3 Recursive steps of the GMA algorithm. Seven terminals are merged into four subtrees in (a), then two subtrees in (b), and finally one subtree in (c).

matching of a set of k points is a set of $\lfloor k/2 \rfloor$ line segments connecting the points, with no two line segments connecting to the same point. The cost of the geometric matching is the sum of the lengths of its line segments. The GMA is illustrated in Figure 42.3. In each recursive step, a set of k path-length-balanced subtrees are given. (At the beginning, each terminal is a subtree by itself.) The subtrees are merged by finding a minimum-cost matching of their tapping points (i.e., roots) to form $\lfloor k/2 \rfloor$ new subtrees. The tapping point of each new subtree is chosen to be the balance point that minimizes the maximum difference in path lengths to the leaves of the subtree. The resulting set of subtrees (including the $\lfloor k/2 \rfloor$ new ones and potentially one unmatched subtree when k is odd) will be recursively matched until a single path-length-balanced tree is obtained.

In some cases, it is impossible to find a balance point such that the path lengths to all leaves are exactly the same. For example, in Figure 42.4a, if $l_1 + l < l_2$, then the best balance point is node A but the path lengths to leaves are still not completely balanced. For those cases, a H-flipping operation as shown in Figure 42.4b can be applied to reduce the skew.

If using optimal matching algorithm in planar geometry, the time complexity of GMA is $O(n^{2.5} \log n)$, where n is the number of terminals. Faster nonoptimal matching heuristics can also be used to speed up the algorithm. It was experimentally shown in Ref. [8] that the trees generated by GMA are better in wirelength and skew than those by MMM.

42.2.3 EXACT ZERO-SKEW ALGORITHM

Both the MMM algorithm and GMA assume the delay is linear to the path length, and then focus on balancing of path lengths. For high-performance designs with tight skew constraints, algorithms based on more accurate delay models are desirable. Tsay [9] presented an algorithm that produces clock trees with exact zero skew according to the Elmore delay model [10]. Like GMA, this algorithm recursively merges subtrees in a bottom-up manner. However, it assumes that a tree topology, which determines the pairing up of subtrees, is given. It addresses the problem of finding the tapping points precisely so that the merged trees have zero skew.

Suppose two zero-skew subtrees are merged by a wire of length l as shown in Figure 42.5a. The wire is divided by the tapping point into two segments of length xl and $(1 - x)l$, respectively. By representing each subtree by a lumped delay model and each segment by a π-model, we can transform the circuit into an equivalent RC tree as shown in Figure 42.5b.

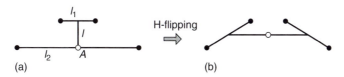

(a)   (b)

FIGURE 42.4 H-flipping operation for further skew minimization.

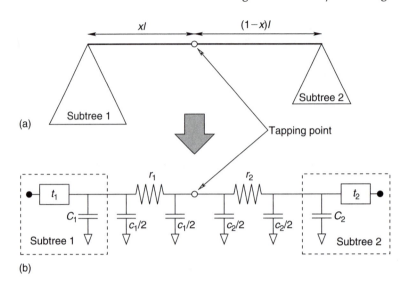

FIGURE 42.5   Zero-skew merge of two subtrees.

To ensure the delay from the tapping point to leaf nodes of both subtrees to be equal, it requires that

$$r_1 \left(c_1/2 + C_1 \right) + t_1 = r_2 \left(c_2/2 + C_2 \right) + t_2 \tag{42.1}$$

Let α be the wire resistance per unit length and β be the wire capacitance per unit length. Then, $r_1 = \alpha x l$, $r_2 = \alpha(1-x)l$, $c_1 = \beta x l$, and $c_2 = \beta(1-x)l$. Hence, after solving Equation 42.1, we find the zero-skew condition to be

$$x = \frac{(t_2 - t_1) + \alpha l \left(\beta l/2 + C_2 \right)}{\alpha l \left(\beta l + C_1 + C_2 \right)}$$

If $0 \le x \le 1$, it indicates that the delay can be balanced by setting the tapping point somewhere along the segment. On the other hand, if $x < 0$ or $x > 1$, it implies the two subtrees are too much out of balance and extra delay needs to be introduced through wire elongation, which is commonly done by snaking. Without loss of generality, consider the case $x < 0$. For this case, the tapping point has to be at the root of subtree 1 and the segment connecting subtree 1 to subtree 2 has to be elongated. Assume the length of the elongated segment is l'. To balance the delay,

$$t_1 = t_2 + \alpha l' \left(\beta l'/2 + C_2 \right)$$

or

$$l' = \frac{\sqrt{(\alpha C_2)^2 + 2\alpha \beta \left(t_1 - t_2 \right)} - \alpha C_2}{\alpha \beta}$$

Similarly, for the case $x > 1$, the tapping point should be at the root of subtree 2, and

$$l' = \frac{\sqrt{(\alpha C_1)^2 + 2\alpha \beta \left(t_2 - t_1 \right)} - \alpha C_1}{\alpha \beta}$$

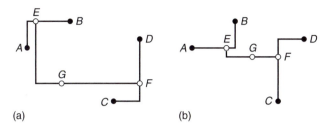

FIGURE 42.6 Two different ways to construct a zero-skew clock tree for terminals A–D. The connection EF in (b) is much shorter than the one in (a).

42.2.4 DEFERRED MERGE EMBEDDING

In the exact zero-skew algorithm in Section 42.2.3, there are many possible ways to route the connection between each pair of tapping points. As shown in Figure 42.6, the routing will determine the location of the tapping point, and hence the wirelength of the connection at the next higher level. In Ref. [9], it was suggested that a few possible wiring patterns (e.g., two one-bend connections) may be constructed and the one which gives a shorter length at the next level is picked.

In general, the problem is to embed any given connection topology to create a zero-skew clock tree while minimizing total wirelength. This problem can be solved in linear time by the deferred merge embedding (DME) method independently proposed by Edahiro [11], Chao et al. [12], and Boese and Kahng [13]. The DME algorithm consists of two phases. First, a bottom-up phase finds a line segment called the merging segment, $ms(v)$, to represent all possible placement locations for each tapping point v. Then, a top-down phase resolves the exact location for each tapping point.

We use the example in Figure 42.6 to explain how to find the merging segments in the bottom-up phase. The steps are illustrated in Figure 42.7. Consider the tapping point E. The distances d_{AE} from A to E and d_{BE} from B to E that balance the delay according to some delay model are first computed. The algorithm to compute the distances depends on the delay model used. For example, for Elmore delay model, Tsay's algorithm [9] can be applied. Then we set $ms(E)$ to be the set of all points within a distance d_{AE} from A and within a distance d_{BE} from B. $ms(F)$ can be found similarly. Next, consider the tapping point G. The least possible length of the connection between E and F is the minimum distance between any point in $ms(E)$ and any point in $ms(F)$. Based on this length, we can compute the distances d_{EG} from E to G and d_{FG} from F to G that balance the delay. Finally, we set $ms(G)$ to be the set of all points within a distance d_{EG} from some point in $ms(E)$ and within a distance d_{FG} from some point in $ms(F)$.

A Manhattan arc is defined to be a line segment, possibly of zero length, with slope $+1$ or -1. A crucial observation is that all merging segments are Manhattan arcs. To prove this observation, first

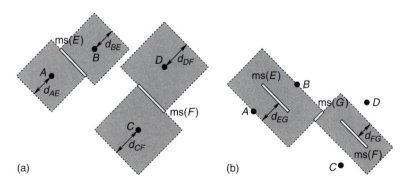

FIGURE 42.7 Construction of merging segments in the bottom-phase of DME.

notice that the merging segment of a terminal is a single point and thus a Manhattan arc. Consider the merge of two subtrees rooted at X and Y to form a tree rooted at Z such that both ms(X) and ms(Y) are Manhattan arcs. Let l be the minimum distance between any point in ms(X) and any point in ms(Y). l is the least possible length of the connection between X and Y. To balance the delay, we compute d_{XZ} and d_{YZ}. There are two possible cases. The first case is $d_{XZ} + d_{YZ} = l$. Note that both the region within a distance d_{XZ} from ms(X) and the region within a distance d_{YZ} from ms(Y) are tilted rectangles. Moreover, the two rectangles are touching each other as $d_{XZ} + d_{YZ} = l$. ms(Z) is set to the intersection of them and hence is a Manhattan arc. The second case is $d_{XZ} + d_{YZ} > l$. In this case, Z coincides with either X or Y, and wire is elongated to balance the delay. Without loss of generality, assume Z coincides with X. Then ms(Z) is set to all points in ms(X) that are also within a distance d_{YZ} from ms(Y). Hence it is also a Manhattan arc. By induction, therefore, all merging segments must be Manhattan arcs. Because of this observation, each merging segment can be found in constant time. The whole bottom-up phase requires linear time.

For the top-down phase, the locations of tapping points are fixed in a top-down manner as follows. For the root r of the whole tree, its location is set to any point in ms(r). For any other tapping point v, its location is set to any point in ms(v) that is within a distance d_{vp} (determined in bottom-up phase) from the location of v's parent p. The top-down phase also takes linear time. Therefore, DME is a linear time algorithm. It has been proved that for linear (i.e., path length) delay model, DME produces zero-skew tree with optimal wirelength. However, it has also been shown that DME is not optimal for Elmore delay model [13].

Instead of achieving zero skew, the DME algorithm can be extended to handle general skew constraints. The extended DME algorithm has applications in clock skew scheduling (Section 42.4) and process variation aware clock tree routing (Section 42.5).

42.2.5 WIRE WIDTH AND BUFFER CONSIDERATIONS IN CLOCK TREE

Wire resistance is a major concern for clock tree design in advanced process. If a clock wire is long and narrow, it will have a very significant resistance. Together with the significant capacitive load of the clock wires and terminals, this implies that the clock signal will have very long phase delay and transition time. Note that this problem cannot be resolved merely by increasing the driving strength (i.e., size) of the clock generator. Even though a strong clock generator can produce a sharp clock signal at the source, the signal degrades rapidly as it is transmitted through the lossy clock wire.

One solution is to size up the width of the clock wires as wire resistance is inversely proportional to the wire width. Such a method must require a router to handle wires of varying widths, and also requires appropriate sizing of the clock drivers to meet the delay and transition time constraints under an increased load for the stage.

Another solution is to insert buffers distributively in the clock tree: the basic concept is similar to buffer insertion for signal lines, discussed elsewhere in this book. Buffers are effective in maintaining the integrity of the clock signal by restoring degraded signals. Buffered clock trees generally use smaller clock generator and narrower wires, and hence consume less power and area [14,15]. However, buffer delay is more sensitive to process variations and power supply noise than wire delay. Hence, buffered clock trees may have more skew and jitter. Moreover, clock tree design is typically performed after placement so that clock terminals are fixed. Inserting the clock buffers into a placed circuit may be difficult.

To reduce skew and skew sensitivity to process variations in buffered clock tree design, the following guidelines are often followed:

- Buffered clock trees should have equal numbers of buffers in all source-to-sink paths
- At each buffered level, the buffers should have the same size
- At each buffered level, the buffers should have the same capacitive load and the same input transition time (potentially by adjusting the width and length of the wires)

In practice, a mixed approach of wire width adjustment and buffer insertion is typically used [16]. For example, Restle et al. [3] presented the clock network design of six microprocessor chips. In all these chips, the clock network consists of a series of buffered treelike networks driving a final set of 16–64 sector buffers. Each sector buffer drives a tree network tunable by adjusting wire widths. (The tunable trees finally drive a single clock grid, which is discussed in Section 42.3.1.)

42.3 CLOCK NETWORKS WITH NONTREE STRUCTURES

Although tree structures are relatively easy to design, a significant drawback associated with them is that, in the presence of process variations, two physically nearby points that belong to different regions of the clock tree, may have a significant skew. For example, points A and B in Figure 42.1 may experience a large skew because the two paths from source to them are distinct and may not match well with each other. This kind of local skew is particularly troublesome, because physically nearby registers are likely to be connected by a combinational path. Therefore, the significant skew can easily cause a hold time violation, which is especially costly as it cannot be fixed by slowing down the clock frequency. In the following, several nontree structures are introduced. They are more effective in reducing skew in a local region, but they consume more area and power.

42.3.1 GRID

A clock grid is a mesh of horizontal and vertical wires driven from the middle or edges. Typcially, the mesh is fine enough to deliver the clock signal to within a short distance of every clocked element. The skew minimization approach of grids is fundamentally different from that of trees. Grids try to equalize delay of different points by connecting them together, whereas trees try to balance delay of different points by carefully matching the characteristics of different paths.

As the grid connects nearby points directly, it is very effective in reducing local skew. Moreover, its design is not as sensitive to the placement details as a tree structure, which makes late design changes easier. On the other hand, for a tree-structured network, if a late design change significantly alters the locations of the clocked elements or the values of the load capacitances, an entirely new tree topology may be required. The main disadvantage of grids is that they consume a large amount of wire resources and power. In addition, grids may have significant systematic skew between the points closest to the drivers and the points furthest away. This problem can be illustrated by the clock network design of the 300 MHz Alpha 21164 processor [17], where the clock signal generated at the center of the chip is distributed to the left and right banks of final clock drivers (Figure 42.8a), which then drive a grid. It is clear from the simulation results in Figure 42.8b that the skews between points near the left and right drivers and points further away are very significant (up to 90 ps). Therefore, grids are rarely used by themselves. A balanced structure is usually employed to distribute the clock globally to various places in the grid, as discussed in Section 42.3.3.

42.3.2 SPINE

The spine structure for clock distribution is shown in Figure 42.9. A clock spine is a long and wide piece of wire running across the chip, which drives the clock signal through delay-matched serpentine wires into each small group of clocked elements. This idea was first introduced by Lin and Wong [18]. Typically, the clock signal is distributed from the clock generator to the spine by a balanced buffered tree such that it arrives at many different points of the spine simultaneously. If the load distribution induced by the serpentine wires on the spine is uniform, the spine has zero skew everywhere. If the delays of the serpentine wires are perfectly matched, then the skew at the clocked elements will also be zero.

Like grids, spines provide a stable structure that facilitates late design changes. Although this structure does not make the clock as readily available as grids so that serpentine routing is required, a serpentine is easy to design. To accommodate for late design changes, each serpentine can be tuned

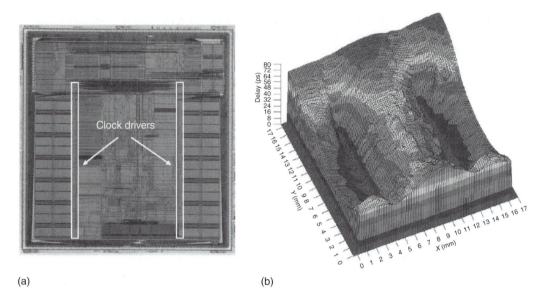

(a)   (b)

FIGURE 42.8   Clock driver locations (a) and clock delay in Alpha 21164 (b). (Courtesy of Hewlett-Packard Company.)

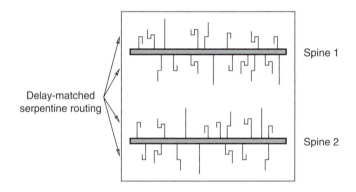

FIGURE 42.9   Clock distribution by spines with serpentine routing.

individually without affecting others. Moreover, clock gating is easy to be incorporated as each serpentine can be gated separately. However, a system with many clocked elements may require a lot of serpentine routes, which cause high area and power consumption. Like trees, spines also may have large local skews between nearby elements driven by different serpentines.

Intel has used the spine structure in its Pentium processors. Details can be found in Chapter 43.

42.3.3   HYBRID

The tree structure is good at minimizing skew globally, while the grid structure is effective in reducing skew locally. To achieve low skew at both global and local levels, tree and grid can be combined to form a hybrid structure. A practical approach is to use a balanced tree to distribute the clock signal to a large number of points across the chip, and then a grid to connect these points together. As the grid is driven in many points, the systematic skew problem of grid is resolved. Moreover, as the tree sinks are shorted by grid segments, the local skew problem of tree is eliminated. In high-performance

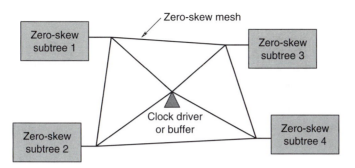

FIGURE 42.10   Clock network with a global mesh driving local trees.

design, the skew budget is too tight to be satisfied either by a pure tree or a pure grid approach. The hybrid approach is a common alternative. In addition, like a grid, the hybrid network also provides a stable structure that facilitates late design changes. The only drawback of this approach is power and area cost even higher than a pure grid approach.

Many microprocessors have used a hybrid structure for clock distribution, and several of them are discussed in Chapter 43. In particular, IBM has used the hybrid approach on a variety of microprocessors including the Power4, PowerPC, and S/390 [3]. In the IBM designs, a primary buffered H-tree drives 16–64 sector buffers arranged on the chip. Each sector buffer drives a smaller tree network. Each tree can be tuned to accommodate nonuniform load capacitance by adjusting the wire widths. Together, the tunable trees drive a global clock grid at up to 1024 points.

Su and Sapatnekar [19] proposed a different hybrid approach. In this mesh/tree approach, a global zero-skew mesh is used to drive local zero-skew trees as shown in Figure 42.10. This idea can be generalized to a multilevel structure in which each subtree sink at a certain level is driving another mesh with four subtrees at the next lower level.

To construct an one-level mesh/tree clock network, the sinks are first divided into four groups and a buffered tree is built for each group by any zero-skew tree construction algorithm (e.g., Tsay [9]). Based on the delay and downstream capacitance of the four trees, a zero-skew mesh is then constructed by adjusting the width of the eight mesh segments. Interestingly, they show that the problem of minimizing the total segment area to achieve zero skew with respect to Elmore delay (by requiring all four trees to meet a given target delay) can be formulated as a linear program of only four of the segment width variables. A heuristic procedure is presented to iteratively set the target delay and possibly elongate some segments until a feasible solution (with all segment widths within bounds) is found. As a postprocessing step, wire width optimization under an accurate higher-order delay metric is performed.

It is shown experimentally that clock networks by this hybrid mesh/tree approach are better in skew, skew sensitivity, phase delay, and transition time than trees by Tsay's algorithm. They are also better in skew, phase delay, and transition time, and similar in area when comparing to the IBM structures discussed above.

42.4   CLOCK SKEW SCHEDULING

The clock skew scheduling technique makes use of intentional nonzero clock skews to optimize the performance of synchronous systems. The basic idea is to use clock skews to balance the slack difference between combinational paths instead of achieving zero-skew clock arrival times. This idea was first proposed by Fishburn [20].

Before presenting the clock skew scheduling problem formulations, we first introduce the timing constraints on clock signals. To avoid clock hazards, setup time constraints and hold time constraints have to be satisfied by all source/destination register pairs in the system. Consider a pair of registers

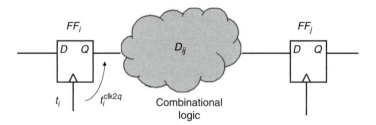

FIGURE 42.11 Clock hazards and timing constraints.

FF_i and FF_j as shown in Figure 42.11. Let t_i and t_j be the clock delays from clock source to FF_i and FF_j, respectively. Let D_{ij} be the set of all combinational path delays from FF_i to FF_j. Let t_i^{clk2q} be the clock-to-Q delay for FF_i. Let t_j^{setup} and t_j^{hold} be the setup time and hold time for FF_j, respectively. Let P be the clock period. The setup time and hold time constraints can be expressed as

$$t_i + t_i^{clk2q} + \text{MAX}\left(D_{ij}\right) + t_j^{setup} \leq t_j + P \tag{42.2}$$

$$t_i + t_i^{clk2q} + \text{MIN}\left(D_{ij}\right) \geq t_j + t_j^{hold} \tag{42.3}$$

A clock schedule is a set of delays from clock source to all registers in the synchronous system. The clock scheduling problem is to find a clock schedule $\{t_1, \ldots, t_N\}$ for all registers $FF_1, \ldots, FF_N$ to minimize the clock period P while satisfying the constraints in Equations 42.2 and 42.3. This problem can be formulated as a linear program as follows [20]:

LP_SPEED: Minimize P

subject to $t_j - t_i \geq t_j^{setup} + t_i^{clk2q} + \text{MAX}\left(D_{ij}\right) - P$ for $i,j = 1,\ldots,N$
$t_i - t_j \geq t_j^{hold} - t_i^{clk2q} - \text{MIN}\left(D_{ij}\right)$ for $i,j = 1,\ldots,N$
$t_i \geq \text{MIN\_DELAY}$ for $i = 1,\ldots,N$

Alternatively, we can find a clock schedule to maximize the minimum safety margin M for a given clock period P. This problem can be formulated as a linear program as follows:

LP_SAFETY: Maximize M

subject to $t_j - t_i \geq t_j^{setup} + t_i^{clk2q} + \text{MAX}\left(D_{ij}\right) - P + M$ for $i,j = 1,\ldots,N$
$t_i - t_j \geq t_j^{hold} - t_i^{clk2q} - \text{MIN}\left(D_{ij}\right) + M$ for $i,j = 1,\ldots,N$
$t_i \geq \text{MIN\_DELAY}$ for $i = 1,\ldots,N.$

In both formulations, $\text{MAX}(D_{ij}) = -\infty$ and $\text{MIN}(D_{ij}) = \infty$ if there is no combinational path from FF_i to FF_j.

After the clock schedule $S = \{t_1, \ldots, t_N\}$ is computed, the next step is to construct a clock network to realize the obtained schedule. The DME algorithm in Section 42.2.4 can be easily extended to handle this problem. We only need to construct the merging segments to achieve the given skews instead of zero skews in the bottom-up phase of the DME algorithm. However, the solutions of the linear programs may not be unique. Each clock delay t_i could be a range rather than a fixed value. In this case, the clock routing problem becomes the bounded-skew routing tree (BST) problem. In Ref. [21], Cong et al. proposed two algorithms, BME (boundary merging and embedding) and IME (interior merging and embedding), to handle this problem. These two algorithms extend the DME algorithm by finding a polygonal region based on the skew bounds rather than a merging segment to represent all possible locations for each tapping point.

Apart from the original formulations of clock scheduling, there are some other extensions. Neves and Friedman [22] formulated the process variation tolerant optimal clock skew scheduling problem. To better control the effects of process variations, they find the permissible range (i.e., the range of the clock skew without timing violation) for each local path, select a clock skew value that allows a maximum variation of skew within the permissible range, and finally determine the clock delay to each register. Recently, Ravindran et al. [23] discussed the multidomain clock skew scheduling problem. For a given number of clocking domains n and a maximum permissible within-domain latency δ, the multidomain range constraints require that all clock latencies must fit into n value ranges $(l(d_i), l(d_i) + \delta)$ for $i = 1, \ldots, n$. The objective of multidomain clock skew scheduling is to determine domain phase shifts $l(d_i)$ and register latencies that satisfy the clock domain constraints and minimize the clock period.

Finally, we want to have a brief discussion on two similar sequential optimization techniques, clock scheduling and retiming. They are, respectively, continuous and discrete optimizations with the same effect on minimizing the clock period [20]. The equivalence of the two techniques was studied in Ref. [24]. It is proved that there exists a retiming R to achieve clock period P if and only if there exists a clock schedule S with the same clock period. However, the practical use of retiming is limited due to two reasons. First, retiming has adverse impact on the verification methodology. Second, using retiming for maximum performance often causes a steep increase in the number of registers. Clock scheduling does not have these two limitations. Another advantage of clock scheduling is that because retiming can only move registers across discrete amounts of logic delay, the resulting system after retiming can still benefit from clock scheduling.

42.5 HANDLING VARIABILITY

In minimizing skew sensitivity to process variations, two guiding principles are that the network should be as symmetrical and as fast as possible. In a clock network designed and laid out symmetrically, chipwide process (or environmental) variations should affect all clock paths identically. An additional advantage is that any systematic skew caused by modeling errors is eliminated by symmetry. In a fast network, as the clock phase delay is small, any fractional variations in delay lead only to a modest amount of skew. In addition, a clock network with optimal delay is the most tolerant to process variations. At the optimal delay point with respect to a certain parameter, the delay sensitivity over that parameter (i.e., the slope of the delay function) should be zero. However, it is not trivial to apply these two principles in practice. Because of uneven load distribution and routing/buffer obstacles, it is usually impossible to construct a completely symmetrical network. Moreover, minimizing the network delay may be conflicting with the optimization of some other metrics (e.g., skew, area and power). Several important works on reliable clock network design under process variations are discussed below.

The concept of delay sensitivity is very useful in considering process variations. Pullela et al. [25] first made use of delay sensitivity with respect to wire width variations to improve the delay, skew and skew sensitivity of a given clock tree by wire width optimization. The Elmore delay model and the L-type RC model for each branch are used in the paper, but the concept can be generalized to other models. Let R_j be the resistance, C_j be the capacitance, and C_{d_j} be the downstream capacitance of branch j. Let $U(i)$ be the set of all branches on the path from sink i to the root. Then the Elmore delay from the root to sink i is $T_{d_i} = \sum_{j \in U(i)} R_j C_{d_j}$. Therefore, the sensitivities of Elmore delay of sink i with respect to circuit parameters C_j and R_j are

$$\frac{\partial T_{d_i}}{\partial C_j} = R_{c_{ij}} \tag{42.4}$$

$$\frac{\partial T_{d_i}}{\partial R_j} = \begin{cases} C_{d_j} & \text{if } j \in U(i) \\ 0 & \text{otherwise} \end{cases} \tag{42.5}$$

where $R_{c_{ij}}$ is the total resistance along the common path from sink i to the root and branch j to the root. R_j and C_j can be expressed as functions of width w_j of branch j as $R_j = R_0 L_j / w_j$ and $C_j = C_a L_j w_j + C_f L_j$, where R_0, C_a, and C_f are technology parameters independent of w_j, and L_j is the length of branch j. Therefore, the delay sensitivity of sink i to width w_j is

$$\frac{\partial T_{d_i}}{\partial w_j} = \frac{\partial T_{d_i}}{\partial C_j} \frac{\partial C_j}{\partial w_j} + \frac{\partial T_{d_i}}{\partial R_j} \frac{\partial R_j}{\partial w_j}$$

$$= \frac{\partial T_{d_i}}{\partial C_j} C_a L_j - \frac{\partial T_{d_i}}{\partial R_j} \frac{R_0 L_j}{w_j^2}$$

By incremental computation as described in Ref. [26], Equations 42.4 and 42.5 for all i and j can be computed in $O(n^2)$ time for a tree with n sinks.* Hence, the delay sensitivities for all sinks to all branch widths can also be found in $O(n^2)$ time.

In Ref. [25], a greedy heuristics is proposed to iteratively increase the widths to improve delay, skew, and skew sensitivity. The selection of the branch to widen in each step is based on the delay sensitivities, which give the delay change of each sink when widening a branch. In particular, they argued that wire widening is a better method for delay balancing than wire elongating as widening generally reduces skew sensitivity but elongating increases it.

Lu et al. [27] formulated the minimizing skew violation (MinSV) problem to construct a clock tree considering wire width variation due to process variations. Given the range of permissible skew for each pair of clock sinks, they tried to find a clock routing tree such that the maximum skew violation among all pairs of sinks is minimized under wire width variation. The way they construct the tree follows the framework of the DME algorithm. Because of wire width variation, the skew between a sink pair becomes a range rather than a unique value. To maximize the safety margin due to process variations, in the bottom-up stage, they chose the merging segment for the tapping point such that the center of the skew range of the most critical sink pair coincides with the center of permissible range for this sink pair. Besides improving process variation tolerance, they also proposed an algorithm to minimize wirelength when there is no skew violation under wire width variation.

Recently, Rajaram et al. [28] proposed to insert cross links in a given clock tree to improve its skew sensitivity. Like the grid and the spine structures, the cross links equalize delay of different points by connecting them together. Such an approach can tolerate both process and environmental variations. Moreover, because the cross links are selectively inserted based on the trade-off between skew sensitivity reduction and extra wire usage, this approach can achieve significant skew sensitivity reduction with little increase in wirelength. The link insertion algorithm is improved in Ref. [29].

REFERENCES

1. J. M. Rabaey, A. Chandrakasan, and B. Nikolić. *Digital Integrated Circuits: A Design Perspective*, 2nd edn. Prentice Hall, 2003.
2. H. Veendrick. Short-circuit dissipation of static CMOS circuitry and its impact on the design of buffer circuits. *IEEE Journal of Solid-State Circuits*, SC-19:468–473, August 1984.
3. P. J. Restle, T. G. McNamara, D. A. Webber, P. J. Camporese, K. F. Eng, K. A. Jenkins, D. H. Allen, M. J. Rohn, M. P. Quaranta, D. W. Boerstler, C. J. Alpert, C. A. Carter, R. N. Bailey, J. G. Petronick, B. L. Krauter, and B. D. McCredie. A clock distribution network for microprocessors. *IEEE Journal of Solid-State Circuits*, 36(5):792–799, May 2001.

---

* In [25], an $O(n^2 \log n)$ algorithm by adjoint analysis is proposed.

4. M. Gowan, L. Biro, and D. Jackson. Power considerations in the design of the Alpha 21264 microprocessor. In *Proceedings of the ACM/IEEE Design Automation Conference*, San Francisco, CA, pp. 433–439, 1998.

5. D. R. Gonzales. Micro-RISC architecture for the wireless market. *IEEE Micro*, 19(4):30–37, 1999.

6. D. E. Duarte, N. Vijaykrishnan, and M. J. Irwin. A clock power model to evaluate impact of architectural and technology optimizations. *IEEE Transactions on Very Large Scale Integration Systems*, 10(6):844–855, December 2002.

7. M. A. B. Jackson, A. Srinivasan, and E. S. Kuh. Clock routing for high-performance ICs. In *Proceedings of the ACM/IEEE Design Automation Conference*, Orlando, FL, pp. 573–579, 1990.

8. J. Cong, A. B. Kahng, and G. Robins. Matching-based methods for high-performance clock routing. *IEEE Transactions on Computer-Aided Design of Integrated Circuits and Systems*, 12(8):1157–1169, August 1993 (DAC 1991).

9. R. -S. Tsay. An exact zero-skew clock routing algorithm. *IEEE Transactions on Computer-Aided Design of Integrated Circuits and Systems*, 12(2):242–249, February 1993 (ICCAD 1991).

10. W. C. Elmore. The transient response of damped linear network with particular regard to wideband amplifiers. *Journal of Applied Physics*, 19:55–63, 1948.

11. M. Edahiro. Minimum skew and minimum path length routing in VLSI layout design. *NEC Research and Development*, 32(4): 569–575, 1991.

12. T. -H. Chao, Y. -C. Hsu, and J. -M. Ho. Zero skew clock net routing. In *Proceedings of the ACM/IEEE Design Automation Conference*, Anaheim, CA, pp. 518–523, 1992.

13. K. D. Boese and A. B. Kahng. Zero-skew clock routing trees with minimum wirelength. In *Proceedings of the IEEE International ASIC Conference*, Rochester, NY, pp. 1.1.1–1.1.5, September 1992.

14. J. G. Xi and W. W. -M. Dai. Buffer insertion and sizing under process variations for low power clock distribution. In *Proceedings of the ACM/IEEE Design Automation Conference*, San Francisco, CA, pp. 491–496, 1995.

15. A. Vittal and M. Marek-Sadowska. Low-power buffered clock tree design. *IEEE Transactions on Computer-Aided Design of Integrated Circuits and Systems*, pp. 965–975, September 1997 (DAC 1995).

16. S. Pullela, N. Menezes, J. Omar, and L. T. Pillage. Skew and delay optimization for reliable buffered clock trees. In *Proceedings of the IEEE/ACM International Conference on Computer-Aided Design*, San Jose, CA, pp. 556–562, 1993.

17. B. J. Benschneider, A. J. Black, W. J. Bowhill, S. M. Britton, D. E. Dever, D. R. Donchin, R. J. Dupcak, R. M. Fromm, M. K. Gowan, P. E. Gronowski, M. Kantrowitz, M. E. Lamere, S. Mehta, J. E. Meyer, R. O. Mueller, A. Olesin, R. P. Preston, D. A. Priore, S. Santhanam, M. J. Smith, and G. M. Wolrich. A 300-MHz 64-b quad-issue CMOS RISC microprocessor. *IEEE Journal of Solid-State Circuits*, 30(11):1203–1214, November 1995 (ISSCC 1995).

18. Shen Lin and C. K. Wong. Process-variation-tolerant clock skew minimization. In *Proceedings of the IEEE/ACM International Conference on Computer-Aided Design*, San Jose, CA, pp. 284–288, 1994.

19. H. Su and S. S. Sapatnekar. Hybrid structured clock network construction. In *Proceedings of the IEEE/ACM International Conference on Computer-Aided Design*, San Jose, CA, pp. 333–336, 2001.

20. J. P. Fishburn. Clock skew optimization. *IEEE Transactions on Computers*, 39(7):945–951, July 1990.

21. J. Cong, A. B. Kahng, C. -K. Koh, and C. -W. A. Tsao. Bounded-skew clock and Steiner routing. *ACM Transactions on Design Automation of Electronics Systems*, 3(3):341–388, 1998 (ICCAD 1995).

22. J. L. Neves and E. G. Friedman. Optimal clock skew scheduling tolerant to process variations. In *Proceedings of the ACM/IEEE Design Automation Conference*, Las Vegas, NV, pp. 623–628, 1996.

23. K. Ravindran, A. Kuehlmann, and E. Sentovich. Multi-domain clock skew scheduling. In *Proceedings of the IEEE/ACM International Conference on Computer-Aided Design*, San Jose, CA, pp. 801–808, 2003.

24. L. -F. Chao and E. H. -M. Sha. Retiming and clock skew for synchronous systems. In *Proceedings of the IEEE International Symposium on Circuits and Systems*, London, England, pp. 283–286, 1994.

25. S. Pullela, N. Menezes, and L. T. Pillage. Reliable non-zero skew clock trees using wire width optimization. In *Proceedings of the ACM/IEEE Design Automation Conference*, Dallas, TX, pp. 165–170, 1993.

26. C. -P. Chen and D. F. Wong. A fast algorithm for optimal wire-sizing under Elmore delay model. In *Proceedings of the IEEE International Symposium on Circuits and Systems*, vol. 4, Atlanta, GA, pp. 412–415, 1996.

27. B. Lu, J. Hu, G. Ellis, and H. Su. Process variation aware clock tree routing. In *Proceedings of the International Symposium on Physical Design*, Monterey, CA, pp. 174–181, 2003.

28. A. Rajaram, J. Hu, and R. Mahapatra. Reducing clock skew variability via cross links. In *Proceedings of the ACM/IEEE Design Automation Conference*, Anaheim, CA, pp. 18–23, 2004.

29. A. Rajaram, D. Z. Pan, and J. Hu. Improved algorithms for link-based non-tree clock networks for skew variability reduction. In *Proceedings of the International Symposium on Physical Design*, San Francisco, CA, pp. 55–62, 2005.

43 Practical Issues in Clock Network Design

Chris Chu and Min Pan

CONTENTS

In this chapter, we present the clock network designs of several high-performance microprocessors to illustrate how the basic techniques presented in Chapter 42 are applied in practice. We focus on the clock network design of high-performance microprocessors as the stringent slew requirements make the design most challenging. Some useful discussions on practical issues in clock network design can also be found in Bindal and Friedman [1], Zhu [2], and Rusu [3].

Section	Processor	Year/ Main Reference	Process (nm)	Clock Frequency (MHz)	Area (mm²)	Number of Transistors (M)	Clock Topology	Deskew	Skew (ps)
43.1	IBM S/390	1997 [4]	200 (L_{eff})	400	300	7.8	Tree	No	30
43.2	IBM Power4	2002 [5]	180 SOI	1300		174	Tree driving single grid	No	25
43.3	Alpha 21264	1998 [6]	350	600		15.2	Hierarchical grids	No	65
43.4	Pentium II	1997 [7]	350	300	203	7.5	1 spine	No	140
43.5	Pentium III	1999 [8]	250	650	123	9.5	2 spines	Active	15
43.6	Pentium 4	2001 [9]	180	2000	217	42	3 spines	Active	16
		2003 [10]	90	Up to 5000	109		8 spines		10
43.7	Itanium	2000 [11]	180	800		25.4	Tree driving grids	Active	28
43.8	Itanium 2	2002 [12]	180	1000	421	25	Tree driving trees	No	62
		2003 [13]	130	1500	374	410	Tree driving trees	Fuse based	24
	(dual core)	2005 [14]	90	100–2500	596	1720	Hierarchical trees	Active	10

The processors discussed in this chapter are summarized in the table above. (Some entries are left blank because the corresponding information cannot be found.)

43.1   IBM S/390

The design of a 400-MHz microprocessor for IBM S/390 Enterprise Server Generation-4 system is described in Ref. [4]. The chip is fabricated in a 0.2-μm L_{eff} CMOS technology with five layers of metal and tungsten local interconnect. The power supply is 2.5 V. The chip size is 17.35 mm $\times$ 17.30 mm with about 7.8 million transistors. The clock distribution network uses a balanced tree design, which is suitable for the relatively low clock frequency. A single-phase clock is distributed from a phase-locked loop (PLL)/central clock buffer located near the center of the chip to all the latches inside the macros in three levels of hierarchy.

The first two levels of clock distribution are in the form of balanced H-like trees, using primarily the top two metal layers. The first-level tree routes the global clock from the central clock buffer to nine sector buffers, as shown in Figure 43.1. The sector buffers repower the clock to all macros inside the sectors. There are 580 macro clock pins in the whole design.

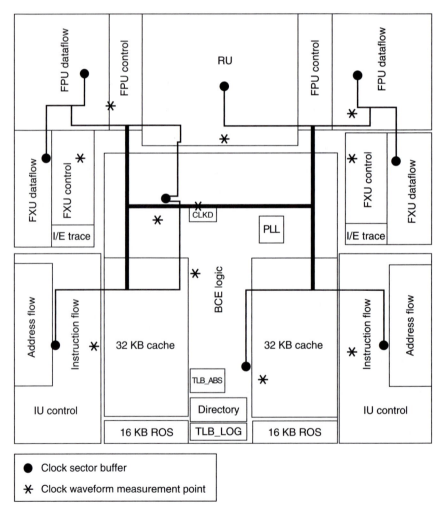

● Clock sector buffer

✳ Clock waveform measurement point

FIGURE 43.1   First-level tree of the IBM S/390 clock distribution network. (From Welb, C.F. et al., *J. Solid-State Circuits*, 32, 1665, 1997. With permission.)

The clock propagation delay along the tree is balanced against macro input capacitance and *RLC* characteristics of the tree wires. Horizontal wiring of each tree is in low-resistance Metal 5 (M5) (with 4.8-μm pitch). At various places along the tree, inductive coupling is reduced and return path is improved by using power wires for shielding. Decoupling capacitors are incorporated into central and sector buffers to reduce delta-I noise. A clock wiring methodology was developed with custom routing and timing computer-aided design (CAD) tools. The detailed routing as well as the widths of all clock wires were optimized to minimize skew, mean delay, power, wiring tracks, and sensitivity to process variations. Three-dimensional (3D) modeling was performed using a full-wave electromagnetic field solver [15], and distributed *RLC* modeling was used for virtually every wire in all the trees during the design and tuning/optimization process [16]. A number of cases were analyzed, and the results were used to generate a combination of analytic models and lookup tables containing distributed *RLC* parameters for all clock geometries used. Each wire segment was represented by an equivalent circuit consisting of up to six *RLC* π-segments. Extensive simulations and wire width tuning [17] were done to guarantee low clock skew at macro pins. Typical simulated *RLC* delay of the first-level tree is 300 ps with 20 ps skew at the sector buffers. The sector buffer delay is 230 ps. Typical simulated *RLC* delay within sectors is 210 ps with 30 ps skew at the macros.

The last level of clock distribution is local to each macro. Figure 43.2 shows the clocking scheme within macros. From the macro pin, the clocks are wired to clock blocks. The overall target skew for this wire is under 20 ps. For large area macros, multiple clock pins were used to reduce wirelength to clock blocks. The clock block generates local clocks that drive latches. The target skew for local clocks is under 50 ps.

All macrolevel wiring is done by hand for custom macros or with a place and route tool for synthesized macros. For synthesized macros that had many latches, and therefore multiple clock blocks, a clock optimization tool was used that reassigned latches to clock blocks based on cell placement. This resulted in clock blocks driving latches that were placed closest to them. Macro layouts were extracted for *R* and *C* parasitics, and the extracted netlists were used to time the macros. This means that any skew in the last level of clock distribution was captured in that macro's timing abstraction.

Figure 43.3 shows the measured waveforms of the central clock buffer output and clocks at ten points of the 580 macro pin locations (marked on Figure 43.1) driven by the second level clock tree. The measurement was performed using a novel electron-beam prober with a 20-ps time resolution on the top wiring layer. Because the chip was powered using a standard cantilever probe card in the

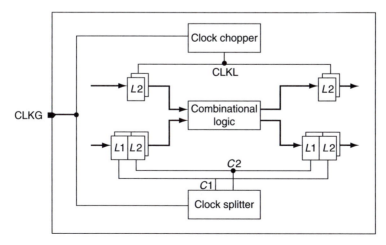

FIGURE 43.2 Last/macrolevel clock distribution of IBM S/390. (From Welb, C.F. et al., *J. Solid-State Circuits*, 32, 1665, 1997. With permission.)

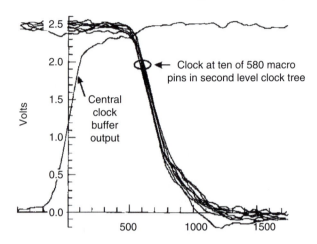

FIGURE 43.3 Electron beam measured clock waveforms at macro pin locations marked on Figure 43.1. (From Welb, C.F. et al., *J. Solid-State Circuits*, 32, 1665, 1997. With permission.)

electron-beam prober, the chip clock was run at low frequency to reduce power supply noise. Power supply noise during these measurements was measured to be less than 100 mV. The results indicate a mean delay of 740 ps and less than 30 ps skew from the central clock buffer to the macro pins.

43.2   IBM POWER4

The clock distribution of a 1.3-GHz Power4 microprocessor is described in Refs. [5,18]. The chip is fabricated in the IBM 0.18-μm CMOS 8S3 SOI (silicon-on-insulator) technology with seven levels of copper wiring. It has 174 million transistors. The power supply is 1.6 V.

The microprocessor uses a single chip-wide clock domain, with no active or programmable skew-reduction circuitry. Having multiple domains would allow active/programmable deskewing and coarse clock gating, and could result in lower skew within each small domain. Inevitably, however, with multiple domains there is increased skew and uncertainty between domains. In addition, multiple clock domains complicate early- and late-mode timings, and degrade critical paths that cross multiple domain boundaries. Extensive simulations of the Power4 chip and test-chip hardware measurements support the simplifying decision to maintain a single-domain global clock grid for the entire chip, with no programmable or active deskewing.

The global clock distribution strategy is based on a topology using a number of tuned trees driving a single full-chip clock grid [19]. This strategy is developed with the goal of being applicable to a variety of high-performance server microprocessors. It has been previously used in three S/390 chips and three PowerPC chips [19]. The trees-driving-grid topology combines many of the advantages of both trees and grids. Trees have low latency, low power, minimal wiring track usage, and the potential for very low skew. However, without the grid, trees must often be rerouted whenever the locations of clock pins change, or when the load capacitance values change significantly. The grid provides a constant structure so that the trees and the grids they are driving can be designed early to distribute the clock near every location where it may be needed. The regular grid also allows simple regular tree structures. This is important as it facilitates the design of carefully designed transmission line structures with well-controlled capacitance and inductance. The grid reduces local skew by connecting nearby points directly. The tree wires are then tuned to minimize skew over longer distances.

The global clock distribution network of the 1.3-GHz Power4 chip is illustrated in Figure 43.4 using a 3D visualization showing all wire and buffer delays. In the network, a PLL near the center of the chip drives buffered H-trees, which are designed as symmetrically as possible. The H-trees

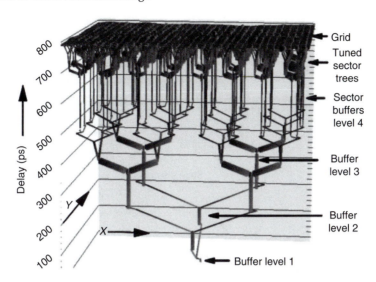

FIGURE 43.4 3D visualization of the Power4 global clock distribution. (From Restle, P.J. et al., *Proc. IEEE Intl. Solid-State Circuits Conf.*, 2002, pp. 144–145. With permission.)

drive the final set of 64 carefully placed sector buffers. Each sector buffer drives a tunable sector tree network, designed for minimum delay without length matching. These sector trees are tuned primarily by wire-width tuning. Then they all drive a single full-chip clock grid at 1024 evenly spaced points. From the global clock grid, a hierarchy of short clock routes completed the connection from the grid down to the individual local clock buffer inputs in the macros. There are 15,200 global clock pins.

It is reported in Ref. [5] that the maximum skew measured at 19 places with picoprobes is 25 ps, and the maximum skew by picosecond imaging for circuit analysis (PICA) measurements from nine sector buffers is less than 18 ps.

43.3 ALPHA 21264

The clocking design of a 600-MHz Alpha 21264 microprocessor is presented in Ref. [6]. The chip is fabricated in a 0.35-μm CMOS process with six metal layers. Four metal layers (called M1 to M4) are for signals, one (between M2 and M3) is for a V_{SS} reference plane, and one (above M4) is for a V_{DD} reference plane. It has 15.2 million transistors. This microprocessor employs a hierarchical clock distribution scheme as illustrated in Figure 43.5. At the top level, there is a global clock grid called GCLK, which covers the entire die. Next, there are six major clock grids over certain execution units. At the bottom level, local clocks are generated as needed from any clock (global clock, major clocks, or other local clocks). Previous Alpha microprocessors use a single grid to distribute the global clock signal [20,21]. The hierarchical scheme is chosen for this microprocessor because of tighter skew constraints, the importance of clock power minimization, and the need of a flexible clocking methodology to solve local timing problems. The drawback is that skew management becomes much more complicated. State elements and clocking points exist from 0 to 8 stages past GCLK. The clock distribution network needs to be carefully designed based on rigorous and thorough timing verification.

The GCLK grid is driven by a global clock distribution network as shown in Figure 43.6. The network connects a PLL located in a corner of the chip to 16 distributed global clock drivers. The arrangement of global clock drivers, which resembles four windowpanes, achieves low skew by dividing the chip into regions, thus reducing the maximum distance from the drivers to the farthest loads. A windowpane arrangement also reduces sensitivity to process variation because each grid pane is redundantly driven from four sides. In general, distributing the drivers widely across the chip

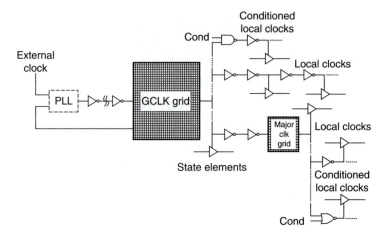

FIGURE 43.5 Alpha 21264 clock hierarchy. (From Bailey, D.W. and Behschneider, B.J., *IEEE J. Solid-State Circuits*, 33, 1627, 1998. With permission.)

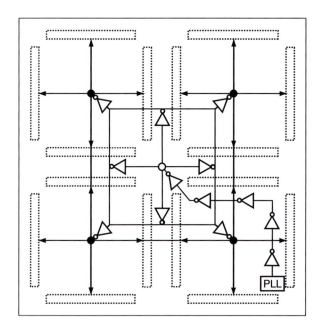

FIGURE 43.6 Global clock distribution network of Alpha 21264. (From Bailey, D.W. and Behschneider, B.J., *IEEE J. Solid-State Circuits*, 33, 1627, 1998. With permission.)

also helps power-supply and heat-dissipation problems. The GCLK grid is shown in Figure 43.7. It traverses the entire die and uses 3 percent of M3 and M4. All clock interconnect is laterally shielded with either V_{DD} or V_{SS}. All clock wires and all lateral shields are manually placed. The measured GCLK skew is 65 ps running at 0°C ambient and 2.2 V.

The six major clocks are two gain stages past GCLK with grids juxtaposed with GCLK, but shielded from it. The major clock grids are shown in Figure 43.8. Because of the wide variation of clock loads, the grid density varies widely between major clocks, and sometimes even for a single major clock. The densest areas use up to 6 percent of M3 and M4. Major clocks driven by a gridded global clock substantially reduce power because major clock drivers are localized to the clock loads and major clock grids are locally sized to meet the skew targets. A gridded global clock without major

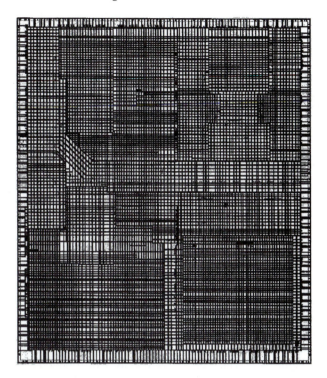

FIGURE 43.7 GCLK of Alpha 21264. (From Bailey, D.W. and Behschneider, B.J., *IEEE J. Solid-State Circuits*, 33, 1627, 1998. With permission.)

clocks would require larger drivers and a denser grid to deliver the same clock skew and edges. Major clocks are designed so that delay from GCLK is centered at 300 ps. The target specifications for skew are ±50 ps. The target specifications for 10–90 percent rise and fall times are less than 320 ps. All major clocks easily meet both sets of objectives.

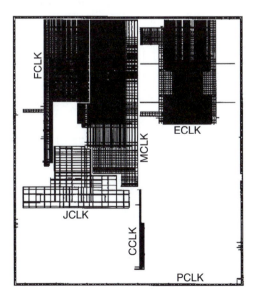

FIGURE 43.8 Six major clock grids of Alpha 21264. (From Bailey, D.W. and Behschneider, B.J., *IEEE J. Solid-State Circuits*, 33, 1627, 1998. With permission.)

Local clocks are generally neither gridded nor shielded. There are no strict limits on the number, size, or logic function of local-clock buffers, and there is no duty-cycle requirement, although timing path constraints must always be met. Local clocks have permitted ranges for clock rise and fall times, but with only this restriction there is considerable design freedom. As a result, it facilitates the implementation of clock gating to reduce power and clock skew scheduling to improve performance.

Because, rather dense grid structures are required to meet the aggressive skew targets, the clock power consumption is very significant. At 600 MHz and 2.2 V, typical power usage for the processor is 72 W. The complete distribution network that drives GCLK uses 5.8 W, and GCLK uses 10.2 W. The major clocks use 14.0 W. Local unconditional clocks use 7.6 W, and local conditional clocks use a maximum of 15.6 W, assuming they switch every cycle.

The clock distribution network design for a 1.2-GHz Alpha 21364 microprocessor can be found in Ref. [22]. We choose not to include the details here as Compaq, which acquired DEC in 1998, decided to phase out Alpha on 2001.

43.4   INTEL PENTIUM II

The clock distribution network design for a 300-MHz Intel Pentium II microprocessor is presented in Refs. [7,23]. The chip is fabricated in a 0.35-μm CMOS process with four metal layers. The power supply is 2.8 V. The chip has 7.5 million transistors and the die area is 203 mm^2. This processor uses a single spine scheme to distribute the global clock as shown in Figure 43.9. The spine is driven by a balanced tree with five levels of buffers. Global clock is distributed to all units in M4. The measured skew is also shown in Figure 43.9. The skew across M4 global distribution is 140 ps. The low skew is achieved by balancing the load of each global clock tapping and adjusting global clock track length.

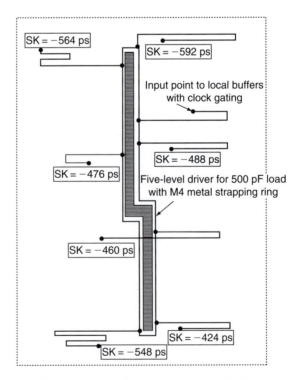

FIGURE 43.9   Global clock distribution network of Pentium II with electron beam measured skew. SK is the skew relative to feedback point from local buffer. (From Young, I.A., Mar, M.F., and Bushan, B., *Proc. IEEE Intel. Solid-State Circuits Conf.*, pp. 330–331, 1997. With permission.)

43.5 INTEL PENTIUM III

The design of an Intel Pentium III microprocessor is presented in Ref. [8]. This chip has an operating voltage of 1.4–2.2 V and is running up to 650 MHz. It is fabricated in a 0.25-μm CMOS process with five metal layers. It has 9.5 million transistors and the chip size is 10.17 mm × 12.10 mm. This processor uses a two-spine scheme for global clock distribution. A two-spine clock block diagram is shown in Figure 43.10. The two spines were shielded properly such that they would not be impacted by the fringing fields from any interconnects associated with the core as well as I/O sides. The two-spine scheme has many benefits over a single-spine approach. First, the serpentine wires can be shortened, and hence power consumption can be reduced. Second, power distribution to the clock subsystem becomes easier as the clock power demand is more spread out. Third, shielding of clock network is also easier as shields are more readily available on sides than in the center. Fourth, routing congestion can be improved because there will not be a center spine running through the center part of the chip, which is typically most congested.

Skew minimization between the two spines is a major challenge. Because of the lengthy left and right clock spines with multiple tap points, it was very difficult to match the delays with good accuracy. In addition to precision capacitance matching techniques on the global clock tree, an adaptive digital deskewing technique based on a delay-locked loop (DLL) was employed [24]. The deskewing circuit is composed of delay lines to both spines, a phase detection circuit, and a controller (Figure 43.10). The phase detection circuit determines the phase relationship between the two spines and generates an output accordingly. The controller takes the phase detection information and makes a discrete adjustment to one of the delay lines. The digital delay line is implemented with two inverters in series. Each inverter has a bank of eight capacitive loads connecting to the output. The addition or removal of the capacitive loads is controlled by the delay shift register. This allows 17 monotonic discrete steps of delay. Latency from sampling clocks to making adjustment to the delay lines is just over three cycles. Note that this DLL-based deskewing scheme compensates for not only interconnect/device mismatch but also process, voltage, and temperature variations. Adaptive deskewing helped to reduce the left-to-right clock spine skews from 100 to 15 ps.

43.6 INTEL PENTIUM 4

The clocking scheme of a 2-GHz Intel Pentium 4 microprocessor is presented in Ref. [9]. The chip is fabricated in a 0.18-μm CMOS process with six metal layers. The chip has 42 million transistors and the die area is 217 mm².

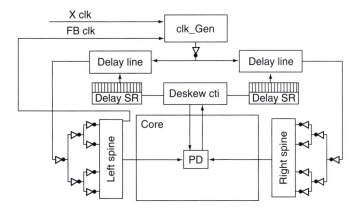

FIGURE 43.10 Block diagram for two-spine global clock distribution of Pentium III. (From Senthinathan, R., Fischer, S., Rangchi, H., and Yazdanmehr, H., *IEEE J. Solid-State Circuits*, 3, 1454, 1999. With permission.)

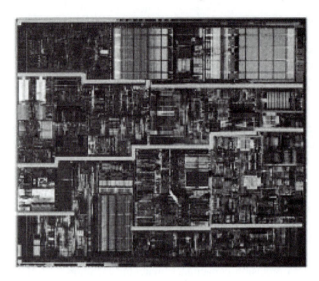

FIGURE 43.11   Three spines in a 0.18-μm Pentium 4. (From Kurd, N., Barkatullah, J., and Dizon, R., *IEEE J. Solid-State Circuits*, 36, 1647, 2001. With permission.)

To cover the large Pentium 4 die, its global clock distribution uses three spines as shown in Figure 43.11. A modified buffered binary tree is used to distribute the global clock from the clock generator to the spines. Then 47 domain buffers are driven, producing 47 independent clock domains (Figure 43.12). Domain buffers can be disabled to power down large functional units to save power. The clock distribution network includes static skew optimization capability to correct systematic skew (caused by asymmetric layout or within-die process variation) as well as provide intentional skew. Each domain buffer consists of a programmable delay stage controlled by a 5-bit domain deskew register (DDR) that determines the edge timing of the domain clock. The values of the DDRs can be set according to phase information obtained by a phase-detector network of 46 phase detectors.

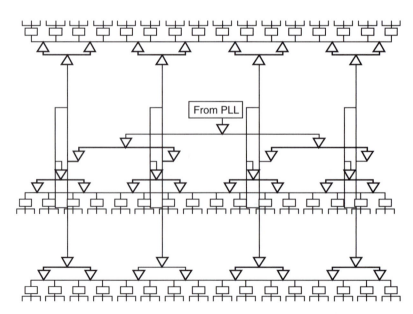

FIGURE 43.12   Global clock distribution in Pentium 4. (From Kurd, N., Barkatullah, J., and Dizon, R., *IEEE J. Solid-State Circuits*, 36, 1647, 2001. With permission.)

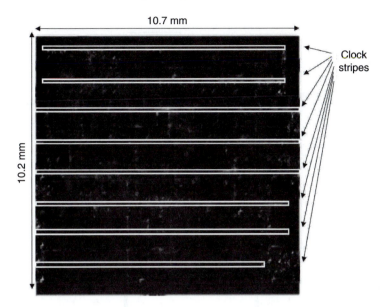

FIGURE 43.13 Eight stripes (i.e., spines) in a 90-nm Pentium 4. (From Bindal, N. et al., *Proc. IEEE Intel. Solid-State Circuits Conf.*, pp. 346–498, 2003.)

This deskewing scheme can reduce interdomain skew from 64 to about 16 ps. A major component of the clock distribution jitter is due to supply noise from logic switching. To reduce supply-noise induced jitter, an *RC*-filtered power supply is used for global clock drivers.

The clock distribution design for a next generation Pentium 4 microprocessor that scales to 5 GHz is described in Ref. [10]. The chip is implemented in a 1.2 V, 90-nm dual-Vt process with seven metal layers. The die size is 10.2 mm × 10.7 mm.

The clock network consists of a pre-global clock network (PGCN), a global clock grid (GCG), and local clocking. The PCGN comprises 12 inversion stages from the PLL to the die center, and 15 stages to the input of more than 1400 GCG drivers. It has a tree structure with strategic shorting of inputs to adjacent receivers within a stage to eliminate skew accumulation over multiple stages because of random variations. Shorting of adjacent receivers provides a very gradual clock skew gradient at the input to adjacent GCG drivers. The GCG consists of eight spines spaced roughly 1200 µm apart, as shown in Figure 43.13. The local scheme consists of two stages of gated buffering. The first stage is used for reducing power consumption through clock gating. The second stage is reserved for functional gating.

The design achieves less than 10 ps of global clock skew. The final grid stage and its driver dissipate 1.75 W/GHz in addition to 0.75 W/GHz in the PGCN. Overall die area allocation ranges from 0.25 percent for devices and lower metals, to less than 2, 3, and 5 percent for M5, M6, and M7 layers, respectively.

43.7 INTEL ITANIUM

The clock design of an 800-MHz Itanium microprocessor is presented in Ref. [11]. The microprocessor is the first implementation of Intel's IA-64 architecture. Its core contains 25.4 million transistors and is fabricated on a 0.18-µm, six layer metal CMOS process. The high level of integration requires a significant silicon real estate and high clock loading. The large die size and the small feature size result in prominent within-die process variation. Hence, the Itanium processor uses an active deskewing scheme in conjunction with a combined balanced clock tree and clock grid to distribute the clock over the die. The design also provides enough flexibility for the local clock implementation to support intentional clock skew and time borrowing.

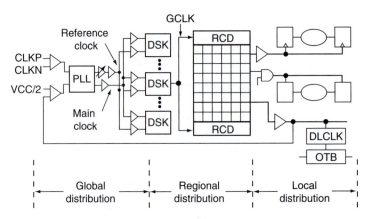

FIGURE 43.14 Clock distribution topology of the Itanium microprocessor. (From Tam, S. et al., *IEEE J. Solid-State Circuits*, 35, 1545, 2000. With permission.)

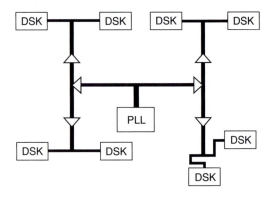

FIGURE 43.15 Global core H-tree of the Itanium microprocessor. (From Tam, S. et al., *IEEE J. Solid-State Circuits*, 35, 1545, 2000. With permission.)

The clock system architecture is shown in Figure 43.14. The clock topology is partitioned into global distribution, regional distribution, and local distribution.

In the global distribution, a core clock and a reference clock are routed from a PLL clock generator to eight deskew clusters via two identical and balanced H-trees. A schematic drawing of the global core clock tree is shown in Figure 43.15. The global clock tree is implemented exclusively in the two highest level metal layers. To reduce capacitive noise coupling and to ensure good inductive return path, the tree is fully shielded laterally with V_{DD}/V_{SS}. In addition, inductive reflections at the branch points are minimized by properly sizing the metal widths for impedance matching.

The regional clock distribution encompasses the deskew buffer, the regional clock driver (RCD), and the regional clock grid. There are 30 separate clock regions each consisting of the above three elements. The 30 regional clocks are illustrated in Figure 43.16. Each of the eight deskew clusters consists of four distinct deskew buffers. Because 32 deskew buffers are available, two of them are unused. The deskew buffer is connected to the RCDs by a binary distribution network, which uses top layer metals with complete lateral shielding. The RCDs are located at the top and bottom of the regional clock grid. The grid is implemented using M4 and M5. As with the global clock network, it contains full lateral shielding to ensure low capacitance coupling and good inductive return paths. The regional clock grid utilizes up to 3.5 percent of the available M5 and up to 4.1 percent of the available M4 routing over a region.

The deskew buffer architecture is shown in Figure 43.17. It is a digitally controlled DLL structure. A phase detector residing within the local controller of the deskew buffer analyzes the phase difference

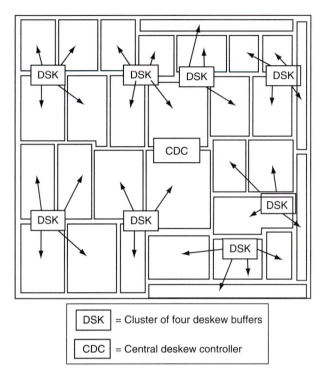

FIGURE 43.16 Thirty regional clocks of the Itanium microprocessor. (From Tam, S. et al., *IEEE J. Solid-State Circuits*, 35, 1545, 2000. With permission.)

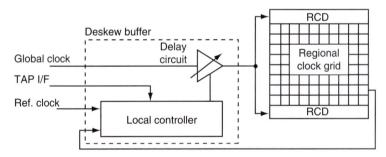

FIGURE 43.17 Deskew buffer architecture of the Itanium microprocessor. (From Tam, S. et al., *IEEE J. Solid-State Circuits*, 35, 1545, 2000. With permission.)

between the reference clock and a local feedback clock sampled from the regional clock grid. Then the core clock delay is adjusted through a digitally controlled analogue delay line. Experimental skew measurements show that the total skew is 28 ps with deskewing and is 110 ps without deskewing.

The local clock distribution consists of local clock buffers (LCBs) and local clock routings that are embedded within a functional unit. The LCBs receive the input directly from the regional clock grid and then drive the clocked sequential elements.

43.8 INTEL ITANIUM 2

The clock distribution of the 1-GHz Itanium 2 processor is described in Refs. [12,25]. The chip is fabricated on a 180-nm CMOS process with six layers of aluminum interconnects. The processor has 25 million logic transistors and 221 million total transistors. The die size is 21.6 mm × 19.5 mm.

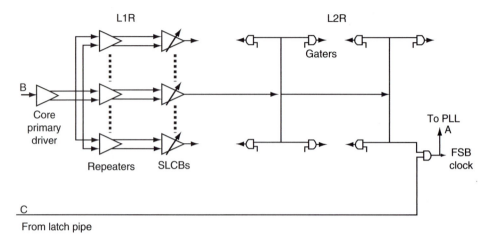

FIGURE 43.18 Clock distribution of the Itanium 2 microprocessor. (From Anderson, F.E., et al., *Proc. IEEE Intel. Solid-State Circuits Conf.*, pp. 146–147, 2002. With permission.)

The clock network of this processor is shown in Figure 43.18. Similar to that of the Itanium processor in Section 43.7, it can be partitioned into global distribution (L1R), regional distribution (L2R driven by second-level clock-buffers [SLCBs]), and local distribution (driven by gaters). However, it has three significant differences from that of Itanium. First, the global clock network, which is also implemented as a balanced H-tree, applies differential routing to reduce jitter from supply noise, injected common mode noise, and signal slew rates. It is also heavily shielded to reduce jitter because of coupled noise. Second, instead of grids, the regional distribution makes use of width and length balanced side-shielded H-trees. Third, deskewing technique is not utilized. The skew is minimized by precisely tuning the delay of the H-trees. It achieves a skew of 62 ps.

The clock distribution of a more advanced Itanium 2 processor is presented in Ref. [13]. This chip is fabricated on a 130-nm CMOS process with six layers of copper interconnects. It operates at 1.5 GHz at 1.3 V. It has a total of 410 million transistors with a die size of 374 mm².

The main difference from its 180-nm predecessor is that this design implements a fuse-based deskewing technique to address the clock skew issue and to increase the frequency of operation. There are 23 regional clocks in the core. The SLCB associated with each region contains a 5-bit register that stores the deskew setting. The register controls the delay of the SLCB. On-chip electrically programmable fuses are incorporated to set the register values. To reduce the area required for the fuses, only three of the five deskew setting bits can be addressed with fuses. When the device is under test, all five deskew bits can be accessed using SCAN for finer resolution. The fuse-based deskew can remove unintentional clock skew caused by on-die process variations and clock network design mismatches. It can also inject intentional skew to improve the critical timing paths. A fuse-based deskew scheme is selected over an active scheme because of the deterministic nature of the fuse-based algorithm and its simple implementation. The intrinsic skew without using any deskew technique is 71 ps. The skew reduces to 24 ps when operating with the 3-bit resolution fuse-based deskew. It further reduces to 7 ps when the 5-bit resolution SCAN-based deskews is applied.

The clock distribution of a dual-core Itanium 2 processor, code-named Montecito, is described in Ref. [14]. The chip is fabricated on a 90-nm CMOS process with seven layers of copper interconnect and it has 1.72 billion transistors with a die size of 21.5 mm × 27.7 mm [26]. It implements a dynamically variable-frequency clock system to support a power management scheme, which maximizes processor performance within a configured power envelop [27]. Its clock distribution delivers a variable-frequency clock from 100 MHz to 2.5 GHz over a clock network over 28-mm long.

The clock network consists of four stages as shown in Figure 43.19. The first stage is the level-0 (L0) route, which connects the PLL to 14 digital frequency dividers (DFDs). The L0 route is the only stage that does not adjust supplies and frequencies during normal operation. The L0 route is 20-mm

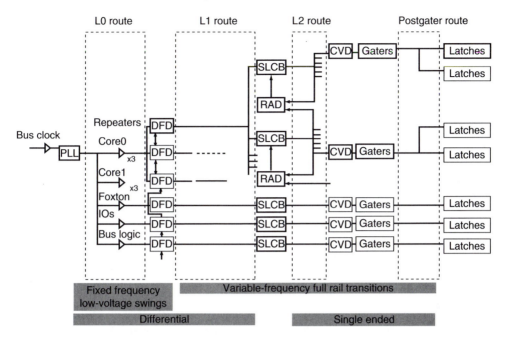

FIGURE 43.19　Clock distribution of the dual-core Itanium 2 microprocessor. (From Mahoney, P., et al., *Proc. IEEE Intel. Solid-State Circuits Conf.*, pp. 292–293, 2005. With permission.)

long consisting of four 5-mm segments that are 400-mV low-voltage swing differential routes. Each segment is resistively terminated at the receiver and is tapered to optimize *RLC* flight time and reduce power consumption. All route segments are matched in composition in both layer and length. The second stage, the level-1 (L1) route, connects the DFD to 6–10 SLCBs. The DFD output varies in frequency and it operates on a varying core supply voltage. A half-frequency distribution using differential 0° and 90° clocks is used. The third stage, the level-2 (L2) route, connects the SLCB to LCBs. A typical SLCB drives 400 LCBs at 200 different locations across 3 mm with a skew of less than 6 ps between locations. For this stage, instead of using a grid-based network as in many contemporary designs, a skew-matched *RLC* tree network technique is employed to reduce metal resources and power. An in-house tool is utilized to route the trees and to match route *RLC* delays using width and space. The resulting clock route is adaptable to changes in the design, and uses far less metal resources and power than a grid-based design while achieving skews that are nearly as low as in grid-based designs. The LCBs, called clock vernier devices, can add 70 ps of delay to any clock in 8 ps increments and are controlled via scan operations. They can facilitate postsilicon debug and remove skew not found in presilicon analysis. The fourth stage, the postgater route, is in the hands of the individual circuit designers. Clock gaters are designed by the clock team into the library in a variety of sizes. With hundreds of latches per gater, routes up to 2-mm long must be engineered for delay, shielding, and load matching.

　　Montecito implements an active deskewing system that runs continuously to null out offsets caused by process, temperature, and voltage variations across the die. The system relies on a hierarchical collection of phase comparators between the ends of different L2 routes (i.e., only the first three stages are corrected by deskewing). Each SLCB has a 128-bit delay line with 1-ps resolution. With active deskewing and scan-chain adjustments, the total clock-network skew is reduced to less than 10 ps.

REFERENCES

1. N. Bindal and E. Friedman. Challenges in clock distribution networks. In *Proc. Intl. Symp. on Phys. Des.*, Monterey, CA, p. 2, 1999.
2. Q. K. Zhu. *High-Speed Clock Network Design*. Kluwer Academic, Boston, 2003.

3. S. Rusu. Clock generation and distribution for high-performance processors. In *IEEE Intl. SOC Conf.*, Santa Clara, CA, p. 207, 2004.

4. C. F. Webb et al. A 400-MHz S/390 microprocessor. *IEEE J. Solid-State Circuits*, 32(11): 1665–1675, November 1997. (ISSCC 1997).

5. P. J. Restle et al. The clock distribution of the Power4 microprocessor. In *Proc. IEEE Intl. Solid-State Circuits Conf.*, San Francisco, CA, pp. 144–145, 2002.

6. D. W. Bailey and B. J. Benschneider. Clocking design and analysis for a 600-MHz Alpha microprocessor. *IEEE J. Solid-State Circuits*, 33(11): 1627–1633, November 1998. (ISSCC 1998).

7. I. A. Young, M. F. Mar, and B. Bhushan. A 0.35 μm CMOS 3-880MHz PLL N/2 clock multiplier and distribution network with low jitter for microprocessors. In *Proc. IEEE Intl. Solid-State Circuits Conf.*, San Francisco, CA, pp. 330–331, 1997.

8. R. Senthinathan, S. Fischer, H. Rangchi, and H. Yazdanmehr. A 650-MHz, IA-32 microprocessor with enhanced data streaming for graphics and video. *IEEE J. Solid-State Circuits*, 34(11): 1454–1465, November 1999. (Microprocessor Report 1999).

9. N. Kurd, J. Barkatullah, and R. Dizon. A multigigahertz clocking scheme for the Pentium 4 microprocessor. *IEEE J. Solid-State Circuits*, 36(11): 1647–1653, November 2001. (ISSCC 01).

10. N. Bindal et al. Scalable sub-10ps skew global clock distribution for a 90 nm multi-GHz IA microprocessor. In *Proc. IEEE Intl. Solid-State Circuits Conf.*, San Francisco, CA, pp. 346–498, 2003.

11. S. Tam et al. Clock generation and distribution for the first IA-64 microprocessor. *IEEE J. Solid-State Circuits*, 35(11): 1545–1552, 2000. (ISPD 2000).

12. F. E. Anderson, J. S. Wells, and E. Z. Berta. The core clock system on the next generation Itanium microprocessor. In *Proc. IEEE Intl. Solid-State Circuits Conf.*, San Francisco, CA, pp. 146–147, 2002.

13. S. Tam, R. D. Limaye, and U. N. Desai. Clock generation and distribution for the 130-nm Itanium 2 processor with 6-MB on-die L3 cache. *IEEE J. Solid-State Circuits*, 39(4): 636–642, April 2004. (ISSCC 2003).

14. P. Mahoney et al. Clock distribution on a dual-core, multi-threaded Itanium-family processor. In *Proc. IEEE Intl. Solid-State Circuits Conf.*, San Francisco, CA, pp. 292–293, 599, 2005.

15. B. J. Rubin and S. Daijavad. Calculations of multi-port parameters of electronic packages using general purpose electromagnetics code. In *Proc. IEEE Topical Meet. Electron. Performance Electron. Packag.*, Monterey, CA, pp. 37–39, 1993.

16. A. Deutsch et al. Modeling and characterization of long on-chip interconnections for high-performance microprocessors. *IBM J. Res. Dev.*, 39(5): 547–567, September 1995.

17. C. L. Ratzlaff and L. T. Pillage. RICE: Rapid interconnect circuit evaluation using AWE. *IEEE Trans. Comput.-Aided Des.*, 13(6): 763–776, June 1994.

18. J. D. Warnock et al. The circuit and physical design of the POWER4 microprocessor. *IBM J. Res. Dev.*, 46(1): 27–51, January 2002.

19. P. J. Restle et al. A clock distribution network for microprocessors. *IEEE J. Solid-State Circuits*, 36(5): 792–799, May 2001.

20. D. W. Dobberpuhl et al. A 200-MHz 64-b dual-issue CMOS microprocessor. *IEEE J. Solid-State Circuits*, 27(11): 1555–1567, November 1992. (ISSCC 1992).

21. W. Bowhill et al. A 300-MHz 64-b quad-issue CMOS RISC microprocessor. In *Proc. IEEE Intl. Solid-State Circuits Conf.*, San Francisco, CA, pp. 182–183, 1995.

22. T. Xanthopoulos et al. The design and analysis of the clock distribution network for a 1.2 GHz Alpha microprocessor. In *Proc. IEEE Intl. Solid-State Circuits Conf.*, San Francisco, CA, pp. 402–403, 2001.

23. M. R. Choudhury and J. S. Miller. A 300 MHz CMOS microprocessor with multi-media technology. In *Proc. IEEE Intl. Solid-State Circuits Conf.*, San Francisco, CA, pp. 170–171, 450, 1997.

24. G. Geannopoulos and X. Dai. An adaptive digital deskewing circuit for clock distribution networks. In *Proc. IEEE Intl. Solid-State Circuits Conf.*, San Francisco, CA, pp. 400–401, 1998.

25. S. Nafzigger et al. The implementation of the Itanium 2 microprocessor. *IEEE J. Solid-State Circuits*, 37(11): 1448–1459, November 2002. (ISSCC 2002).

26. S. Naffziger et al. The implementation of a 2-core, multi-threaded Itanium-family processor. *IEEE J. Solid-State Circuits*, 41(1): 197–209, January 2006. (ISSCC 05).

27. T. Fischer et al. A 90-nm variable frequency clock system for a power-managed Itanium architecture processor. *IEEE J. Solid-State Circuits*, 41(1): 218–228, January 2006. (ISSCC 05).

44 Power Grid Design

Haihua Su and Sani Nassif

CONTENTS

44.1 MOTIVATION

44.1.1 TECHNOLOGY TRENDS AND CHALLENGES

The annual report of the International Technology Roadmap (ITRS) for semiconductors [1] has shown the continued reduction of power supply voltage (V_{dd}), driven by power consumption reduction, reduced transistor channel length, and reliability of gate dielectrics. It is expected that the lowest V_{dd} target on this roadmap is 0.5 V in 2016 for low-operating power applications. The parameters and characteristics trend of microprocessor unit (MPU) (high-performance microprocessor) with on-chip static random access memory (SRAM) from the 2005 edition of ITRS is summarized in Table 44.1.

It can be seen from Table 44.1 that the trend for high-performance integrated circuits is toward higher operating frequency and lower power supply voltages. Power dissipation continues to increase, but tends to saturate at $0.64 \, \text{W/mm}^2$ from 2008 to 2020. The increased power consumption is driven by higher operating frequencies and the higher overall capacitances and resistances in larger chips that

TABLE 44.1

Trends in IC Technology Parameters

Year	Gate Length (nm)	Number of Transistors (M)	Number of Power Pads	Number of Wire Levels	f (MHz)	V_{dd} (V)	Size (mm²)	Current Per Power Pad (mA)	Average Power Density (W/mm²)
2005	32	225	2,048	15	5,204	1.1	310	74.3	0.54
2006	28	283	2,048	15	6,783	1.1	310	79.8	0.58
2007	25	357	2,048	15	9,285	1.1	310	83.9	0.61
2008	23	449	2,048	16	10,972	1.0	310	96.9	0.64
2009	20	566	2,048	16	12,369	1.0	310	96.9	0.64
2012	14	1,133	2,048	16	20,065	0.9	310	107.6	0.64
2014	11	1,798	2,048	17	28,356	0.9	310	107.6	0.64
2016	9	2,854	2,048	17	39,683	0.8	310	121.1	0.64
2018	7	4,531	2,048	18	53,207	0.7	310	138.4	0.64
2020	6	7,192	2,048	18	73,122	0.7	310	138.4	0.64

have more on-chip functions. However, such high-power consumption has to flatten out because of the single-chip package power limits, electromigration problems, and thermal impacts on reliability and performance. In addition, lowering the power supply voltage worsens switching currents and decreases noise margins. As a result, power management is recognized in Ref. [1] as one of the grand challenges in the near term and leakage power management as one of the grand challenges in the long term.

The power delivery system includes on-chip and off-chip power grid and decoupling capacitors on die, package, and board. The power grid (power distribution network) provides the V_{dd} and ground signals throughout a chip. Compared to signal wires, power wires typically have lower impedances to reduce power grid current resistance (IR) drops because of currents drawn by functional blocks. All levels of decoupling capacitors are extensively used to suppress transient noise because of the transient currents drawn by functional blocks and because of the interaction of package inductance and switching currents, also known as $L\frac{dI}{dt}$ noise or ΔI noise. The inductive components in package power grids and decoupling capacitors are the major limitation for performance at high frequency. Supply voltage variations can lead not only to problems related to spurious transitions but also to delay variations [2,3] and timing unpredictability [4]. Thus, a successful design requires careful design of all levels of the power delivery system.

In early technologies, the design of power networks was relatively easier because power wires had low resistances and transistors drew relatively low currents. Computer-aided design (CAD) techniques addressed power networks with well-designed tree topologies [5–7] that were said to be sufficient to meet the performance requirements. A typical power grid network in the early technologies consists of only thousands of nodes.

In recent deep submicron technologies (0.25 nm and below), as pointed out in Refs. [8,9], with the shrinking of feature sizes and increases in the clock frequency, the power grid noise problem has become more significant and power supply noise is among the major reasons that affect the circuit functionality. Even if a reliable supply is provided at an input pin of a chip, it can deteriorate significantly within the chip. These problems become worse with the scaling down of the voltage supply level (V_{dd}). The solutions to the above problems become even harder because of the larger size of the power distribution network. A typical power grid network size can easily exceed millions of nodes. Therefore, fast and accurate design, verification and optimization techniques are necessary to address the power grid design issue efficiently.

44.1.2 OVERVIEW OF THE CHAPTER

This chapter discusses basic concepts and techniques for deep submicron power grid design and verification in various aspects: modeling, methodology, analysis, and optimization. Section 44.2 discusses widely adopted power grid analysis and verification methodologies and modeling for every part of the power distribution system. Section 44.3 addresses four analysis techniques to handle large-scale power grid circuits with fixed and uncertain work loads. Optimization techniques including wire sizing, decoupling capacitance optimization, topology optimization, and optimal power pads/pin placement are covered in Section 44.4.

44.2 MODELING AND ANALYSIS METHODOLOGY

44.2.1 PACKAGE AND POWER GRID MODELING

The power grids in the entire power delivery system from board to die are coupled with each other, implying that the effects at one level can impact another. Because the composite board-to-die system is extremely large, analyzing the entire system can be a difficult task and a simplified model has to be applied. A typical approach is to use a simplified on-chip power grid model when package level power grid performance is analyzed. Similarly, a simplified package model is used when on-chip power grid performance is of interest, which is typically the case because it directly impacts chip timing performance and functioning.

In terms of accuracy, such macromodels that capture the major electrical properties at other levels are seen to be sufficient for the levels of accuracy desired in simulation, but ignoring these effect entirely can lead to accuracy losses. This is reinforced in Ref. [10], which motivates why a complete chip-level power grid analysis must include a package-level model that considers the effect of package inductance. An interesting comparison between a circuit under 0.25-μm technology using the flip-chip C4 package and wire-bond I/Os shows a difference of worst-case steady-state voltage drop of 0.37 V out of the 2.5 V power supply voltage.

A simplified package-level power bus model [10] is shown in Figure 44.1. The inductance dominance of the package can be clearly seen. Although there is only self-inductance in this model, mutual inductance has to be considered if the power buses are close to each other.

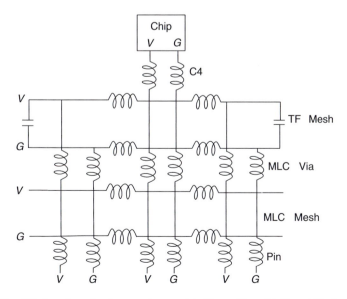

FIGURE 44.1 Simplified package-level power bus model. (From Chen, H. H. and Neely, J. S., *IEEE Trans. Component Package and Manufacturing Technology*, 21, 209, 1998. With permission.)

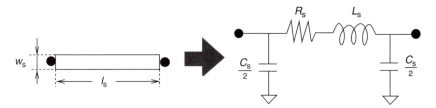

FIGURE 44.2 RLC π-model of wire segment. (From H. H. Chen and J. S. Neely, Interconnect and Circuit Modeling Techniques for Full Chip Power Supply Noise Analysis, IEEE Tran. Component Package and Manufacturing Technology, 21, 209, 1998. With permission.)

On-chip power grids in each metal layer can be accurately modeled using lumped RLC parameters. Each power wire in the power grid is represented as a set of connected segments under the π-model (Figure 44.2), with each segment modeled using lumped RLC parameters (considering self-inductances only) given by

$$R_s = \rho l_s/w_s$$
$$C_s = (\beta w_s + \alpha)\, l_s \qquad\qquad (44.1)$$
$$L_s = \gamma l_s/w_s$$

where

l_s and w_s are the length and the width of the segment

ρ, β, α, and γ are the sheet resistance per square, capacitance per square, fringing capacitance per unit length, and the self-inductance per square of the metal layer that is being used for routing the power grid

The following rules are commonly applied for most on-chip power buses:

- Grid capacitances (area and fringing capacitance) are order of magnitude less than the cell or decoupling capacitors, therefore are often ignored. However, there are some works that show that leveraging these capacitors can provide enhanced accuracy and benefit.
- Grid inductances can be ignored if they are order of magnitude smaller compared to package inductances.
- Although the inductance on the package dominates the ΔI noise, on-chip power bus inductance generally cannot be ignored for wires wider than 5 μm.

44.2.2 DECOUPLING CAPACITANCE AND CELL MODELING

The modeling of cell switching current has been an active branch of research. The difficulty of the problem lies in the complexity of determining the sets of input patterns that matter most to the power grid noise. The model must capture the worst-case, average currents or transient currents drawn by cells among all input patterns.

A typical RC model for cells and decaps was presented in Refs. [10,11]. The switching activities for each functional block can be modeled by an equivalent circuit (Figure 44.3), which consists of time-varying resistors (Ri), loading capacitors (Ci_L), and nonideal decoupling capacitor (C_{di} and R_{di}). The loading capacitance for the equivalent circuit is calculated by $Ci_L = P/V^2 f$, where P is the estimated power for the corresponding area i, V is the power supply voltage, and f is the clock frequency. When the circuit is turned on, the time-varying resistance will be set to Ri_{on}, where $Ri_{on}\, Ci_L$ is the switching time constant. Similarly, when the circuit is switched off, the time-varying resistance will be set to Ri_{off}. At the beginning of every clock cycle, a subset of the switching circuits are turned on and off, corresponding to an event list. An example showing the switching events at a node in the power network is illustrated in Figure 44.4 [12,13].

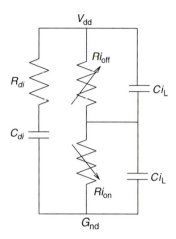

FIGURE 44.3 Equivalent switching circuit. (From H. H. Chen and J. S. Neely, Interconnect and Circuit Model-ing Techniques for Full Chip Power Supply Noise Analysis, IEEE Tran. Component Package and Manufacturing Technology, 21, 209, 1998. With permission.)

Although the above model is accurate, the simulation of the entire power grid would require analyzing a varying topology as circuit elements switch in and out of the network, complicating the simulation procedure. Therefore, a direct application of this model is not widely used.

A more convenient method is to replace the switching circuit model in Figure 44.3 with a piecewise linear current source whose waveform approximates the actual current waveform of the functional block, assuming ideal V_{dd} and G_{nd} levels. Because these current waveforms are input-pattern-dependent, algorithms for worst-case current waveform estimation are necessary. Recently published algorithms are briefly summarized below.

Algorithm 1   In Ref. [14] the circuit is divided into conbinational logic macros. The maximum current requirement for each macro is separately estimated and the input excitation at which the maximum of the transient current occurs is identified. All input-states can be enumerated using a branch-and-bound search technique. The complexity of their method is exponential, and therefore it is hard to be applied to large circuits. This work pessimistically assumes that every macro draws the maximum current simultaneously, and hence it tends to overestimate the worst-case currents.

Algorithm 2   In Ref. [15] Kriplani et al. *proposed an input-pattern-independent algorithm that estimates an upper bound for the maximum envelope current(MEC) waveform. $I_{MEC}(t)$ is defined as the maximum possible current value that could be drawn from the power grid at time t among all input patterns, given that each input can switch at any time. An accurate estimation of the MEC waveforms*

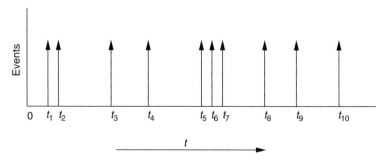

FIGURE 44.4 Switching events at a node in a P/G network. (From Shah J. C., Younis, A. A., Sapatnekar, S. S., and Hassoun, M. M., *IEEE TCAS*, 45, 1372, 1998. With permission.)

would typically require an exponential set of enumerations of all input patterns and is therefore not desirable. The algorithm proposed in this chapter has linear time performance because it ignores signal correlations. This results in a very loose upper bound for the MEC waveforms and can therefore overestimate the supply currents. The same authors extended their work in Ref. [16] to consider the signal correlations and obtained a tighter bound for the maximum instantaneous current.

Algorithm 3 *Bobba in Ref. [17] proposed a constraint-graph-based patten-independent method for maximum current estimation. This method accounts for the timing information and spatiotemporal correlations between pairs of logic gates. In this method, the maximum current value in the kth time interval is obtained as a sum of the peak current values of the gates that can switch in that time interval. Therefore, it provides an improved upper bound on the maximum current waveform.*

Algorithm 4 *In Ref. [18] a timed atomic test pattern generation (ATPG) method and a probability-based method to generate a small set of input patterns for estimating the maximum instantaneous current are presented.*

Algorithm 5 *Chaudhry and Blaauw in Ref. [19] presented a current signature compression technique, which exploits the pattern of change of individual currents, time locality, and periodicity to achieve better compression and accuracy in comparison to the single cycle compression.*

Algorithm 6 *Chen and Ling in Ref. [10] proposed a simple model to represent the switching activities for circuits with information of only the average current I_{ave} and peak current I_{peak}. Depending on the ratio of I_{peak} and I_{ave}, a triangular waveform will be generated if $I_{peak} \geq 2I_{ave}$, and a trapezoidal waveform will be generated if $I_{peak} < 2I_{ave}$.*

Algorithm 7 *In Ref. [20] Jiang et al., a genetic algorithm (GA)-based input vector generation approach was proposed, which iteratively reduces the number of patterns causing the highest power supply noise at specific blocks. The fitness value of a pattern is simply the highest power supply noise at the target chip area. Their experimental results show an average of 23 and 17 percent tighter lower and upper bounds for the benchmark circuits.*

Algorithm 8 *In Ref. [21], block currents are modeled as random variables to capture current variations. The first and second moments of the block currents, as well as the correlations between the currents are assumed to be known, because they can be obtained from simulation of the block and static timing analysis. The optimized power grids in this work show robust performance against variations in block currents.*

Three decoupling capacitor models are described in Ref. [10]: the n-well capacitor C_{nw}, the circuit capacitor C_{ckt}, and the thin-oxide capacitor C_{ox}. The n-well capacitor C_{nw} is the reverse-biased pn junction capacitor between the n-well and p-substrate. The time constant for C_{nw} is process-dependent, but usually can be characterized between 250 and 500 ps for contemporary technologies. The circuit capacitor C_{ckt} is derived from the built-in capacitance between V_{dd} and G_{nd} in nonswitching circuits. The total capacitance from nonswitching circuits is estimated to be $P/(V^2 f) * (1 - SF)/SF$, where P is the power of the circuit, V is the supply voltage, f is the frequency, and SF is the switching factor. The nonswitching capacitance are usually placed in parallel with a current source modeling of the functional block. The time constant for C_{ckt} is determined by the switching speed of the device. The thin-oxide capacitor C_{ox} uses the thin-oxide layer between n-well and polysilicon gate to provide additional decoupling capacitance needed to alleviate the switching noise.

44.2.3 LEAKAGE MODELING

As described in Chapter 3, leakage power is emerging as a key design challenge in current and future designs because of the lowering of the power supply voltage, reduction of the threshold voltage, and reduction of gate oxide thickness. It is estimated that although leakage power is only about 10 percent of total chip power for current technologies, the number is expected to rise to 50 percent for the future technologies [1].

There are two major components of leakage: subthreshold leakage I_{sub} and gate leakage I_{gate}. For a given complementary metal-oxide-semiconductor (CMOS) technology, both subthreshold and gate leakage currents have strong dependency on the environmental parameters, such as temperature and supply voltage. Based on the Berkeley short-channel IGFET model (BSIM) [22], the subthreshold leakage can be modeled as

$$I_{sub} = I_0 \cdot \exp\left[(V_{gs} - V_{th})/nV_T\right] \cdot \left[1 + \exp(-V_{ds}/V_T)\right] \tag{44.2}$$

where V_T is the thermal voltage $V_T = kT/q$. I_0 is defined as

$$I_0 = \mu_0 C_{ox} \left(W_{eff}/L_{eff}\right) \cdot V_T^2 e^{1.8} \tag{44.3}$$

From Equation 44.2, clearly the subthreshold leakage is an exponential function of V_{ds}. When the device is off, V_{ds} is proportional of supply voltage V_{dd}. Therefore, the dependency of I_{sub} on V_{dd} is also exponential:

$$\frac{\Delta I_{sub}}{\Delta V_{dd}} \sim \exp(\Delta V_{dd}) \tag{44.4}$$

Besides directly affecting the thermal voltage V_T, temperature influences the subthreshold leakage via surface potential Φ_s, which in turn affects V_{th}. Because of the short-channel effect and drain-induced barrier lowering (DIBL) effect, the equation describing V_{th} is quite complicated. It can be shown in Ref. [23] that

$$V_{th} \propto \sqrt{T} \tag{44.5}$$

Combining the above two factors, a derivation based on Equation 44.2 can show that the effect of temperature change on subthreshold leakage is about order 1.5, i.e.,

$$\frac{\Delta I_{sub}}{\Delta T} \sim (\Delta T)^{1.5} \tag{44.6}$$

The gate leakage current model used in Berkeley BSIM4 model consists of four components: gate to body (I_{gb}), gate to drain (I_{gd}), gate to source (I_{gs}), and gate to channel (I_{gc}). The last of these is then partitioned between drain and source: I_{gcd} and I_{gcs}. All four components are functions of temperature and supply voltage. The details can be found in Ref. [23]. For example, the first-order dependency of the gate-to-channel current on temperature can be shown as

$$I_{gc} = K\left(\sqrt{\Phi_s}\right) \cdot V_{aux} \tag{44.7}$$

where V_{aux} is defined as

$$V_{aux} = \text{NIGC} \cdot V_T \cdot \log\left[1 + \exp\left(\frac{V_{gse} - \text{VTH0}}{\text{NIGC} \cdot V_T}\right)\right] \tag{44.8}$$

Here V_T is the thermal voltage, V_{gse} is the equivalent gate voltage and the rest are BSIM4 parameters.

For current CMOS technologies, subthreshold leakage is much stronger than gate leakage. Therefore, when we consider the effects of temperature and V_{dd} fluctuation, subthreshold leakage is the dominate part. From Equations 44.4 and 44.6, it is clear that same amount of V_{dd} fluctuation has a stronger effect on the leakage than the temperature.

44.2.4 METHODOLOGY

Because of the modeling complexity and the large problem sizes associated with the power grid analysis problem, most of the methodologies for full-chip power grid verification proposed in the literature [10,11,24–26] simplify the nonlinear devices into linear elements (current sources and capacitors) attached to the power grid. The entire analysis is typically performed in two steps. First, the cells (nonlinear devices) are analyzed assuming perfect power and ground voltages. Static, switching, and leakage current models are generated using approaches discussed in preceding sections. Next, attaching these current sources to the power grid, DC or transient analysis for the large-scale power grid linear circuit is performed to estimate the noise or electromigration problems. In Ref. [27], one more step is added due to the nonlinear dependency of dynamic and leakage currents on V_{dd}. In this step, power grid voltages computed in step two are applied to the cells to obtain an updated static switching and leakage power. The updated power is used to reanalyze power grid noise.

The work in Ref. [10] emphasized that an integrated package-level and chip-level power bus analysis is critical. This is in comparison with traditional technologies where the resistive IR drop occurs mostly on the chip and the inductive ΔI noise only occurs on the package. Therefore, under a traditional methodology, the IR drop and ΔI noise are separately analyzed and summed up. This can become too pessimistic because of the fact that the worst-case ΔI noise and worst-case IR drop do not occur at the same time.

Realistic power grid analysis methodologies must handle cells or power grids in a hierarchical manner to manage the complexity of the problem. For example, smaller cells can be grouped into larger macros, and a global level power grid analysis can be performed by applying the current models of such macros. In addition, as indicated in Ref. [26], an important aspect to observe is the voltage distribution trends in a chip. In commercial CAD tools, a visual IR voltage drop plot is often generated to identify hot spots. Hot spot portions identified in the global level need to be investigated in detail in the next level of hierarchy.

Similarly, power bus models can also be treated hierarchically [10]. For hot spot areas roughly identified in the global level, finer grids can be generated to model the detailed power bus structure. It is pointed out that the detailed power bus of each fine grid should always be connected to the adjacent global power bus model to ensure the accuracy because of the hierarchy.

44.2.5 TOLERANCE ANALYSIS OF POWER GRIDS

To understand the tolerance analysis of power grids, we must examine two importance factors:

1. The manner in which the electrical model of the power grid is derived from the physical implementation, a process commonly referred to as circuit extraction
2. The sources of variability in a power grid model, and the impact such variability will have on the various components of the grid

Circuit extraction starts with the physical implementation of the power grid, which consists of the layout geometry of the power grid shapes and defines the power grid wires in the x and y directions, along with the semiconductor process manufacturing information that defines the thickness of the various conducting and insulating layers and that thus defines the power grid wires in the z direction. With the geometry defined, the circuit extraction process applies models for the resistance, capacitance, and inductance as a function of geometry to calculate the values of the equivalent circuit components for the various geometries defining the power grid.

For example, the resistance of a rectangular wire segment with width W and length L can be estimated using the simple formula

$$R = \rho \frac{L}{WT} \tag{44.9}$$

where

ρ is the resistivity of the metal layer in question
T is the thickness of the layer

Similar first-order equations exist for capacitance (e.g. Ref. [28]) and—to a lesser extent—for inductance. A deeper exploration of circuit extraction is, however, beyond the scope of this discussion. The important point to note is that well-established procedures exist to map the layout geometry of the power grid to equivalent circuit components.

With the above understanding in place, let us consider the sources of variability that would impact the performance of a power grid. Such sources include

1. Variations in the electrical material properties, for example, material resistivity, insulator die-electric constant, etc. Let us denote these by category A.
2. Variations in the horizontal geometry of the power grid wires, which will naturally occur in the semiconductor manufacturing process and arise primarily from the lithography and etch processes. We denote these by category B.
3. Variations in the vertical geometry of the power grid wires, which arise primarily from the chemical-mechanical polishing (CMP) process. We denote these by category C.
4. Variations in the loading of the power grid. These are caused by two possible sources: (1) lack of complete knowledge of the operational characteristics of the integrated circuit connected to the power grid (e.g., not knowing how active a certain part of the circuit is likely to be), and (2) the impact of manufacturing variations on the power dissipated by the circuit (e.g., the impact of MOSFET channel length fluctuations on the leakage current of the circuit). We denote these by category D.

Note that A, B, and C categories are the traditional sources of variations one might consider when performing a tolerance analysis, while category D has more to do without lack of knowledge of the workload. We discuss category D later in Section 44.3.3. It is important when performing such tolerance analysis to understand the relative impact of each source of variability, and to insure that no one source is over- or under-analyzed.

For resistors, we note that all three of the categories (A, B, and C) are important, and that one needs to make a careful study of the tolerances expected for each dimensions, especially for those shapes that are at the lower limits of the manufacturing process resolution limits (e.g., vias).

For capacitors, on the other hand, the distances between grid wires of different polarities are typically large enough that the small variations caused by lithography, etch, or CMP are not as important for determining the intrinsic capacitance of the power grid wires themselves. The dielectric constant, however, can play a part. Capacitance between the power grid and signal wires, which are typically interspersed between power grid wires, will vary, but such capacitance does play only a small part in the performance of the power grid compared to the decoupling capacitance presented by inactive circuits.

For inductors, the total loop inductance is primarily a function of the loop geometry and how it interacts with other loops as well as the conducting ground plane. Because the variations in geometry caused by variations B and C are small, they have minimal impact on inductance.

Therefore, in summary, the primary source of variations in a power grid is the variations in the resistive part of the power grid model. The capacitive part varies significantly, but its impact is relatively small, while the inductive part does not vary significantly.

44.3 POWER GRID NOISE ANALYSIS

44.3.1 NOISE METRICS

For static (DC) analysis, the maximum voltage drop among all power grid nodes is a general metric for the entire chip. In dynamic (transient) analysis, maximum voltage drop of a node is defined as the largest voltage drop value along the period of time for simulation. The maximum voltage drop among all nodes in the power grid circuit can indicate performance of the power grid and help identify hot spots on a chip. This measurement is widely used in most power grid noise estimation tools.

However, such a measurement is very sensitive to the accuracy of circuit analysis and does not take the timings of the voltage violations into account [29]. An efficient metric for the performance of each node in a circuit was first introduced in Ref. [29], which is the integral of voltage waveform beyond the noise margin:

$$
\begin{aligned}
z_j(p) &= \int_0^T \max\left\{\mathrm{NM_H} - v_j(t,p), 0\right\} \mathrm{d}t \\
&= \int_{t_s}^{t_e} \left\{\mathrm{NM_H} - v_j(t,p)\right\} \mathrm{d}t
\end{aligned}
\tag{44.10}
$$

where p represents the tunable circuit parameters. Su et al. in Ref. [30] initially applied this metric in transient power grid noise analysis and optimization. The transient noise in a node in the supply network is represented by the shaded area (voltage integral) in Figure 44.5.

44.3.2 FAST ANALYSIS TECHNIQUES

Because of the large scale (millions of nodes) of the power distribution network, even after separating the nonlinear devices from the linear grids and modeling them using independent current sources, the analysis of such a huge linear network in reasonable amount of time and memory is still a challenge.

The behavior of the power distribution circuit can be described by a first-order differential equation formula using modified nodal analysis (MNA) [31]:

$$
Gx(t) + C\dot{x}(t) = u(t)
\tag{44.11}
$$

where

    x is a vector of node voltages and source and inductor currents
    G is the conductance matrix
    C includes both the decoupling capacitance and package inductance terms
    $u(t)$ includes the loads and voltage sources

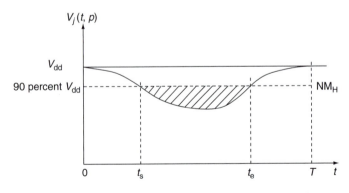

FIGURE 44.5 Illustration of the voltage drop at a given node in the V_{dd} power grid. The area of the shaded region corresponds to the integral z at that node. (From H. Su, S. S. Sapatnekar and S. R. Nassif, Optimal Decoupling Capacitor Sizing and Placement for Standard Cell Layout Designs, IEEE TCAD, 22, 428, 2003. With permission.)

By applying the backward Euler integration formula [31] to Equation 44.11, we have

$$(G + C/h) \mathbf{x}(t+h) = u(t+h) + C/h\mathbf{x}(t) \qquad (44.12)$$

where h is the time step for the transient analysis. Equation 44.12 can be shown to be formulated to consist only of node voltages and the matrix is symmetric positive definite. Typically this left-hand-side (LHS) matrix is very large and sparse. Efficient linear system solution techniques such as Cholesky factorization (direct method) and conjugate gradient (iterative method) are both good candidates. Various fast analysis techniques [12,13,32–39], etc., have been published in the literature. Ref. [39] proposed a hierarchical macromodeling approach. Even though this approach is suitable for both direct or iterative methods, direct solver is used in their work. Nassif et al. proposed a multigrid-based technique [33,34], which intended to make use of the beauties of both direct and iterative methods, i.e., it can avoid the memory limitation of direct solvers during coarse grid correction and can significantly bring down the number of iterations for the iterative solver during the fine grid relaxation or the smoothing step. While the method in Refs. [33,34] is based on geometric multigrid, the method proposed in Ref. [37] is based on the algebraic multigrid technique. Another category of analysis methods [12,13,32,38] is based on model-order reduction techniques. A random walk based [35,36] power grid analysis algorithm is presented recently and has demonstrated its success in solving large-scale power grid circuits. In the following four subsections, we discuss the above four approaches in detail.

44.3.2.1 Hierarchical Partitioning Method

In Equation 44.12, if h is kept constant, only a single initial factorization (direct method) of the matrix $G + C/h$ is required and for each successive time steps only a forward/backward solution is required. This method is very efficient for transient analysis; however, the initial Cholesky factorization is very expensive and can lead to a peak memory hit if the entire network is flatly solved. This motivates the hierarchical macromodeling technique in Ref. [39]. This approach first partitions the power grid into local and global grids: this may be achieved either by exploiting the designer-specified hierarchy or by automated partitioning. Next, macromodels for the local grids are generated, abstracting the large number of internal nodes into a port-based representation. These macromodels may be dense matrices that can be sparsified with minimal loss of accuracy: the intuition here is that if two ports are far from each other, their port-to-port resistance will be large, and may be ignored. The hierarchical approach then proceeds by passing the macromodels to the global grid and solving this reduced system. This solution yields the port voltages, which can then be used to find internal voltages within the local grids.

They first partition the whole network into macromodels, with each macromodel i described by its port currents and port voltages as follows:

$$\mathbf{I}_i = A_i \cdot \mathbf{V}_i + \mathbf{S}_i, \mathbf{I}_i \in \mathbf{R}^m, A_i \in \mathbf{R}^{m \times m}, \mathbf{V}_i \in \mathbf{R}^m, \mathbf{S}_i \in \mathbf{R}^m \qquad (44.13)$$

where
   m is the number of ports in the local grid
   A_i is the port admittance matrix
   $\mathbf{V}_i$ is the vector of voltages at the ports
   $\mathbf{I}_i$ is the current through the interface between the local and the global grids
   $\mathbf{S}_i$ is a vector of current sources connected between each port and the reference node vector

The partitioning strategy they propose is to identify a subnetwork and an interface boundary such that the number of internal nodes is much larger than the square of the number of nodes at the interface. This is to ensure that each macromodel is not too densely stamped. The authors then proposed a 0–1 integer linear programming based sparsification technique to further reduce the matrix density.

The port admittance matrix A_i and current vector $\mathbf{S}_i$ can be derived by looking at the MNA equations of the macro and by splitting the matrices into submatrices corresponding to the internal nodes and ports:

$$\begin{bmatrix} G_{11} & G_{12} \\ G_{12}^{\mathrm{T}} & G_{22} \end{bmatrix} \begin{bmatrix} \mathbf{U}_1 \\ \mathbf{V} \end{bmatrix} = \begin{bmatrix} \mathbf{J}_1 \\ \mathbf{J}_2 + \mathbf{I} \end{bmatrix} \tag{44.14}$$

and the formula for A_i and $\mathbf{S}_i$ can be derived as

$$\begin{aligned} A_i &= \left(G_{22} - G_{12}^{\mathrm{T}} G_{11}^{-1} G_{12} \right) \\ \mathbf{S}_i &= \left(\mathbf{G}_{12}^{\mathrm{T}} \mathbf{G}_{11}^{1} \mathbf{J}_1 - \mathbf{J}_2 \right) \end{aligned} \tag{44.15}$$

where

$\mathbf{V}_i$ is the vector of voltages at the ports
$\mathbf{J}_1$ and $\mathbf{J}_2$ are vectors of current sources connected at the internal nodes and ports, respectively
$\mathbf{I}_i$ is the vector of currents through the interface
G_{12} is the admittance of links between the internal nodes and the ports
G_{11} is the admittance matrix of internal nodes
G_{22} is the admittance matrix of ports.

Because the LHS matrix in Equation 44.14 is positive definite, its Cholesky factorization is

$$\begin{aligned} \begin{bmatrix} G_{11} & G_{12} \\ G_{12}^{\mathrm{T}} & G_{22} \end{bmatrix} &= \begin{bmatrix} L_{11} & 0 \\ L_{21} & L_{22} \end{bmatrix} \begin{bmatrix} L_{11}^{\mathrm{T}} & L_{21}^{\mathrm{T}} \\ 0 & L_{22}^{\mathrm{T}} \end{bmatrix} \\[2mm] &= \begin{bmatrix} L_{11}L_{11}^{\mathrm{T}} & L_{11}L_{21}^{\mathrm{T}} \\ L_{21}L_{11}^{\mathrm{T}} & L_{21}L_{21}^{\mathrm{T}} + L_{22}L_{22}^{\mathrm{T}} \end{bmatrix} \end{aligned} \tag{44.16}$$

The explicit inverse of G_{11} in Equation 44.15 can be avoided and efficiently computed by

$$\begin{aligned} A_i &= L_{22}L_{22}^{\mathrm{T}} \\ \mathbf{S}_i &= \mathbf{L}_{21}\mathbf{L}_{11}^{-1}\mathbf{J}_1 - \mathbf{J}_2 \end{aligned} \tag{44.17}$$

The nodal equation for the global power grid can be formed by feeding each macromodel in

$$\begin{bmatrix} G_{00} & G_{01} & G_{02} & \cdots & G_{0k} \\ G_{01}^{\mathrm{T}} & A_1 & G_{12} & \cdots & G_{1k} \\ G_{02}^{\mathrm{T}} & G_{12}^{\mathrm{T}} & A_2 & \cdots & G_{2k} \\ \vdots & & & & \vdots \\ G_{0k}^{\mathrm{T}} & G_{1k}^{\mathrm{T}} & G_{2k}^{\mathrm{T}} & \cdots & A_k \end{bmatrix} \begin{bmatrix} \mathbf{V}_0 \\ \mathbf{V}_1 \\ \mathbf{V}_2 \\ \vdots \\ \mathbf{V}_k \end{bmatrix} = \begin{bmatrix} \mathbf{I}_0 \\ -\mathbf{S}_1 \\ -\mathbf{S}_2 \\ \vdots \\ -\mathbf{S}_k \end{bmatrix} \tag{44.18}$$

Here, partition 0 corresponds to the global nodes, and partition $i, i > 0$, to the local grids that are represented by Equation 44.13, and G_{ij} represents the conductance links between partition and j.

44.3.2.2 Multigrid Methods

Nassif et al. first proposed to use idea of the multigrid solver for fast power grid analysis in Ref. [34] and they further expanded the idea and experiments in Ref. [33]. This method was motivated by the fact that the power grid equation system is structurally identical to that of a finite element discretization of a two-dimensional parabolic partial differential equation (PDE) because the multigrid method is very efficient in solving smooth PDEs [40].

In iterative methods, the error between the approximate solution and the exact solution can be divided into two components: high-frequency and low-frequency Fourier modes [40]. Classical iterative methods suffer from slow convergence because they are inefficient in reducing the low-frequency error components. In general, multigrid methods also consist of two complementary components [40,41]:

1. Relaxation (smoothing), which reduces the high-frequency error components using a classical iterative solver.
2. Coarse grid correction, which reduces the low-frequency error components. It involves mapping the problem to some coarser grid (Ω^{2h}), solving the mapped smaller problem using a direct solver or an iterative solver, and mapping the solution back to the original fine grid (Ω^h). A restriction operator $\mathfrak{R}_h^{2h}$ and a corresponding prolongation (interpolation) operator $\mathcal{P}_{2h}^h$ are defined for the mappings between the coarse grid and the fine grid.

Figure 44.6 illustrates a recursive V-cycle [40] of the multigrid method with three nested iterations. At the bottom level, the exact solution can be obtained from either a direct or an iterative solver.

The multigrid-like power grid analysis method is explained as follows. First, the original power grid is reduced and the interpolation operator is defined. Then, the problem is mapped to the coarser grid, solved at the coarser grid using a direct solver, and then, the solution is mapped back to the original fine grid. It is called multigrid-like because it ignores the relaxation step and therefore makes it a direct method, which has the advantage of maintaining fast speed without losing too much accuracy. Such a simiplifcation is justified by the fact that well-designed power grids are characterized by smooth voltage variation over the grid. The grid coarsening can be recursively repeated until the coarse grid is small enough to be exactly solved using a direct solver. The overall scheme consists of four passes. Initially, all voltage source nodes and corner nodes are flagged as K while other nodes are marked N. In the first pass, each K node is updated: starting from that node, we go along horizontal (vertical) direction and flag all visited nodes as H (or V). A node flagged

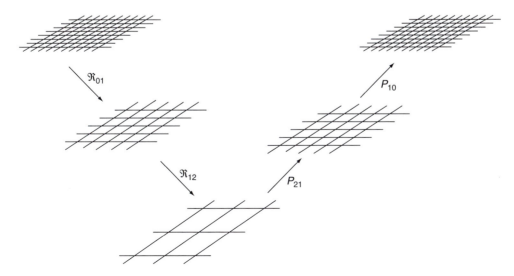

FIGURE 44.6 V-cycle of the multigrid method.

with both H and V is updated with the flag, K. In the second pass, each H (V) node is flagged as R and its neighbors along same row (column) as K. Next, in the third pass, the reduced grid is built by adding edges between the K nodes. Finally, in the fourth pass, the linear interpolation (INT()) is defined from neighboring nodes. If node m neighbors with nodes A and B, then

$$V(m) = \text{INT}(V(A), V(B)) = \alpha_0 V(A) + \alpha_1 V(B) \qquad (44.19)$$

where $\alpha_0 = \frac{g_{mA}}{g_{mA}+g_{mB}}$ and $\alpha_1 = \frac{g_{mB}}{g_{mA}+g_{mB}}$. The voltages on the fine grid can be mapped from the coarse grid using this interpolation formula.

The proposed technique is especially efficient in transient analysis. It applies a direct solver only on the reduced grid. Further more, while analyzing the reduced system matrix using fixed time step, only one initial factorization is needed and a forward/backward substitution will be performed in each following time steps. This further speedups the method because the solution for the fine grid can be obtained by linear interpolation, even though it compromises certain amount of accuracy.

The geometrical grid reduction of the above algorithm for general irregular grids can become complicated to maintain smooth reduction. A typical power grid in lower level metal layers can be as irregular (a picture of this is provided in Figure 2 of Ref. [37]). Another weakness of the above grid reduction scheme is that it geometrically builds each level of grids (from the finest to the coarsest), which requires extra memory to store the graph data structure.

To take advantage of the algebraic multigrid (AMG) technique that performs grid reduction through matrix multiplications, Ref. [37] proposes an AMG-based algorithm that constructs the restriction and interpolation matrices directly from the circuit (MNA) matrix.

In general, variables representing important boundary conditions should be preserved. In the power grid model, these variables include all ideal voltage source nodes, all nodes in the top-level metal layer that are directly connected to package/pins, all package inductance or RL-in-series branches, and all nodes in the bottom-level metal layer that are connected to critical loads. The equation for these boundary nodes/branches are put at the beginning of the original G and C matrices, which makes them easy to be preserved. For the rest of the variables, the AMG-based grid reduction algorithm can be applied to determine the coarse-level grid points.

The coarse grid has to be chosen to represent smooth errors and has to be able to interpolate these errors onto the fine grid. It is shown in Ref. [42] that smooth error varies slowly in the direction of strong connections. In power grid circuits, a strong connection between node p and node q in G means a relatively large conductance value at the off-diagonal entries (p, q) and (q, p), compared to the diagonal entries at (p, p) and (q, q). Therefore, a measure of connection between node p and q can be chosen as

$$\text{mes}_{pq} = \left(g_{pq}/G_p + g_{pq}/G_q\right)/2 \qquad (44.20)$$

where G_p and G_q are self conductance at node p and q. If $\text{mes}_{pq} > \psi$, node q is chosen in the coarse grid and p in the fine grid and will be interpolated as $x(p) = x(q)$, where ψ is a threshold chosen to control the reduction rate and accuracy. This is equivalent to shorting node p to q when the resistor connected between them is small. The corresponding restriction matrix for shorting node p to $q1$ in Figure 44.7 becomes

$$R_{5\times4} = \begin{bmatrix} 1 & & & \\ & 1 & & \\ 1 & & & \\ & & 1 & \\ & & & 1 \end{bmatrix} \begin{matrix} q1 \\ q2 \\ p \\ q3 \\ q4 \end{matrix} \qquad (44.21)$$

with column headers $q1 \quad q2 \quad q3 \quad q4$

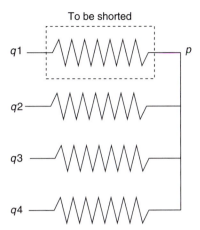

FIGURE 44.7 Shorting node p to its strongly connected neighbor $q1$.

This reduction scheme iteratively removes relatively smaller resistors in the grid, therefore the number of nonzeros in the coarse-level matrix $R^T GR$ decreases.

44.3.2.3 Model Order Reduction Methods

In model order reduction methods, the MNA equation of a linear circuit is typically described in the Laplace domain.

$$(G + sC)\,\mathbf{V}(s) = B\mathbf{u}\,(s) \tag{44.22}$$

where G and C represent the conductance and susceptance matrices. The vector $\mathbf{V}$ of the MNA variables is of dimension $N \times 1$, and includes the nodal voltages and the branch currents for voltage sources and inductors. B is the input selector matrix mapping sources to the internal states, and $\mathbf{u}$ is the vector of independent sources. One of the most popular model order reduction methods is based on Krylov subspace methods, in which the following subspace is generated:

$$\mathrm{span}\,G^{-1}B, G^{-1}CG^{-1}B, \ldots, \left(G^{-1}\right)^{n} CG^{-1}B \ldots \tag{44.23}$$

The subspace matrix is then used to project the original system (Equation 44.22) onto a smaller system that usually keeps major ports $\mathbf{u}$ of the original system:

$$\left(\tilde{G} + s\tilde{C}\right) \tilde{V}\,(s) = \tilde{B}\mathbf{u}\,(s) \tag{44.24}$$

where $\tilde{G}$, $\tilde{C}$, $\tilde{V}$, and $\tilde{B}$ are the reduced matrices/vectors.

From Equation 44.24, we can see that the number of independent source is a bottleneck of such methods. Different techniques to deal with this situation in power grid analysis have been proposed recently in Refs. [13,38].

In Refs. [13,38], instead of using piecewise linear-independent current source as the load model, a switching RC cell model is used to avoid the problem of a large number of ports. Therefore, the only independent sources in the power grid circuit are the independent voltage sources from the power pins or pads, which is significantly smaller compared to the total number of nodes in the circuit.

When a piecewise linear-independent current source model is used for each cell, because the Laplace transform of each piecewise linear (PWL) source is not a constant term, an extended Krylov subspace (EKS) [43] method or an improved EKS (IEKS) method [32] need to be used. In EKS, the contribution of source moments are considered at each step of iteration during the Krylov subspace

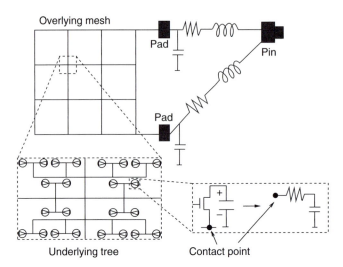

FIGURE 44.8 Hybrid mesh/tree structure with the mesh in the upper level and trees in the lower level. (From H. Su, K. H. Gala and S. S. Sapatnekar, Analysis and Optimization of Structured Power/Ground Networks, IEEE TCAD, 22, 1533, 2003. With permission.)

calculation and orthogonalization process. In addition, moment shifting has to be performed to recover the proper moments in EKS, therefore the IEKS method that no longer needs to perform moment shifting for source waveform modeling was proposed in Ref. [32].

Both works in Ref. [32] and Ref. [38] analyze the power grid circuit hierarchically. A hybrid mesh/tree topology (Figure 44.8) is proposed in Ref. [38] for fast turnaround time of design and verification of power grid. The model order reduction technique in this work is an enhanced PRIMA [44] method considering nonzero initial conditions in capacitors and inductors. The procedure contains three stages: first, each tree is reduced to an equivalent passive model. In this stage, an efficient path tracing technique [44] for trees is applied to speed up the reduced model computation. Next, the mesh along with these passive reduced tree models is further reduced using PRIMA and all nodal voltages in the mesh, i.e., mesh voltages can be obtained. Finally, these mesh voltages equivalent to voltage sources at the root of each tree are used to solve each tree individually and independently.

The HiPRIME [32] algorithm hierarchically analyzes a general power grid with the mesh structure. It first partitions the circuit into multiple blocks and then generates multiport Norton equivalent order reduced circuits using PRIMA and IEKS and then combines all the reduced order macromodels into the higher level and perform either IEKS or PRIMA for further reduction, and poles and residues in the higher grids can be obtained. Finally, internal nodes inside each partition can be computed from the reduced order model of each partition and the voltages on the ports.

44.3.2.4 Random Walk Method

In Refs. [35,36], a statistical approach based on random walks is proposed to perform power grid analysis. In this section, we only discuss in detail the DC analysis of the V_{dd} grid, given that the ground grid can be similarly analyzed and that the method can be easily extended to handle transient analysis.

For the DC analysis of a power grid, a single node x in the circuit can be illustrated in Figure 44.9. According to Kirchoff's current law, Kirchoff's voltage law, and the device equations for the conductances, we have

$$\sum_{i=1}^{degree(x)} g_i (V_i - V_x) = I_x \qquad (44.25)$$

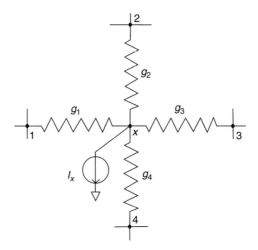

FIGURE 44.9 Representative node in the power grid. (From H. Qian, S. R. Nassif and S. S. Sapatnekar, Power Grid Analysis Using Random Walks, IEEE TCAD, 24, 1204, 2005. With permission.)

where

the nodes adjacent to x are labeled 1, 2, ..., degree(x)
V_x is the voltage at node x
V_i is the voltage at node i
g_i is the conductance between node i and node x
I_x is the current load connected to node x

Equation 44.25 can be rewritten as

$$V_x = \sum_{i=1}^{\text{degree}(x)} \frac{g_i}{\sum_{j=1}^{\text{degree}(x)} g_j} V_i - \frac{I_x}{\sum_{j=1}^{\text{degree}(x)} g_j} \tag{44.26}$$

We can see that this implies that the voltage at any node is a linear function of the voltages at its neighbors. We also observe that the sum of the linear coefficients associated with the V_i's is 1. For a power grid problem with N non-V_{dd} nodes, we have N linear equations similar to the one above, one for each node. Solving this set of equations gives the exact solution.

Now let us look at a random walk game, given a finite undirected connected graph (e.g., Figure 44.10) representing a street map. A walker starts from one of the nodes, and goes to an adjacent node i every day with probability $p_{x,i}$ for $i = 1, 2, \ldots,$ degree(x), where x is the current node, degree(x) is the number of edges connected to node x.

These probabilities satisfy the following relationship:

$$\sum_{i=1}^{\text{degree}(x)} p_{x,i} = 1 \tag{44.27}$$

The walker pays an amount m_x to a motel for lodging everyday, until he or she reaches one of the homes, which are a subset of the nodes. If the walker reaches home, he or she will stay there and be awarded a certain amount of money, m_0. We will consider the problem of calculating the expected amount of money that the walker has accumulated at the end of the walk, as a function of the starting node, assuming he or she starts with nothing. This gain function is therefore defined as

$$f(x) = E\left[\text{total money earned}|\text{walk starts at node } x\right] \tag{44.28}$$

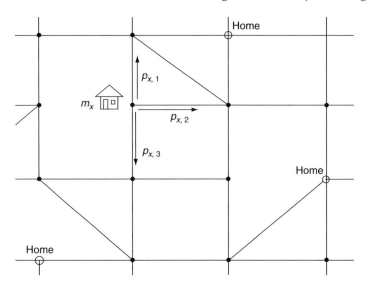

FIGURE 44.10 Instance of a random walk game. (From Qian, H., Nassif, S. R., and Sapatnekar, S. S., *IEEE TCAD*, 24, 1204, 2005. With permission.)

It is obvious that

$$f \text{ (one of the homes)} = m_0 \tag{44.29}$$

For a nonhome node x, assuming that the nodes adjacent to x are labeled $1, 2, \ldots,$ degree(x), the f variables satisfy

$$f(x) = \sum_{i=1}^{\text{degree}(x)} p_{x,i} f(i) - m_x \tag{44.30}$$

For a random-walk problem with N nonhome nodes, there are N linear equations similar to the one above, and solving this set of equations gives the exact values of f at all nodes.

It is easy to draw a parallel between this problem and power grid analysis. Equation 44.30 becomes identical to Equation 44.26, and Equation 44.29 reduces to the condition of perfect V_{dd} nodes if

$$p_{x,i} = \frac{g_i}{\sum_{j=1}^{\text{degree}(x)} g_j} \quad i = 1, 2, \ldots, \text{degree}(x)$$

$$m_x = \frac{I_x}{\sum_{j=1}^{\text{degree}(x)} g_j} \quad m_0 = V_{dd} \qquad f(x) = V_x \tag{44.31}$$

44.3.3 POWER GRID ANALYSIS WITH UNCERTAIN WORK LOADS

In Section 44.2.5, we outlined the various sources of variation that can impact power grid performance, and roughly divided them into (1) physical variations such as changes in the dimensions of power grid wires, and (2) loading variations that arise because of changes in the manner with which the integrated circuit operates.

Consider the steady-state (DC) version of the power grid system of equations first introduced in Equation 44.11, which would be

$$G\mathbf{x} = \mathbf{I} \tag{44.32}$$

where
   G and x are the same as before
   $\mathbf{I}$ is a vector of node currents representing the loading at each node of the power grid

In Refs. [45,46], it was shown that the vector $\mathbf{I}$ can be represented as

$$\mathbf{I} = A.\mathrm{diag}\,(w)\,.\mathbf{I}_b \qquad (44.33)$$

where
  A is an $n \times k$ incidence matrix with n being the number of nodes, and k being the number of circuit blocks
  diag(w) is a $k \times k$ matrix with diagonal entries being 0 for blocks that do not switch, and 1 for blocks that do
  $\mathbf{I}_b$ is a k long vector of block currents

Equations 44.11 and 44.33 describe the behavior of the power grid as the various parts of the circuit become active.

With this formulation in place, one can motivate several analyses to study the dependence of the behavior of the power grid on circuit operation. The works in Refs. [45,46] showed how an integer linear program can be set up to determine the worst-case power grid drop under various constraints, e.g., the maximum power that a design can consume.

A different approach it taken in Ref. [47] where a statistical bounding framework is developed to translate the statistical variations in leakage current, which would exhibit themselves as statistical variations in the components of the block current vector $\mathbf{I}_b$, to statistical bounds on the various node voltages.

With power dissipation increasing, and manufacturing variability increasing, this area promises to remain relevant as researchers struggle to find efficient static (i.e., not specific to a particular workload) methods to insure the performance of a power grid.

44.4 POWER GRID OPTIMIZATION

Given load current of each functional block, the goal of power distribution network optimization is to maintain voltage drop within certain threshold (typically $5 \sim 10$ percent V_{dd}) with various constraints such as wiring resource, empty space for decaps, pin and pad locations, etc. The performance of power distribution network can therefore be improved through wire sizing, decap optimization, topology optimization, and optimal placement of power pins and pads. Combination of the above techniques has also been proposed in a number of literatures, for example, Refs. [48,49] perform simultaneous wire sizing and topology optimization and Refs. [13,38] perform simultaneous wire and decap sizing.

44.4.1 WIRE SIZING

A general formulation of power wire sizing is as follows:

$$\mathrm{minimize\ area} = \sum_i l_i W_i$$
$$\mathrm{subject\ to} \quad V_g \leq V_{th}$$
$$V_p \geq V_{dd} - V_{th}$$
$$I_{i\max} \leq I_{th}$$
$$\mathrm{and} \quad w_{\min} \leq w_i \leq w_{\max}$$

where l_i represents the length of each P/G wire segment with width w_i, which subjects to the minimum and maximum wire width constraints. Each nodal voltage V_g in the ground network and V_p in the power network should be constrained within a voltage drop limit V_{th} typically chosen to be $5 \sim 10$ percent of V_{dd}. I_{th} sets a threshold corresponding to the electromigration constraint for each wire segment. Voltages and currents here can either be the DC voltages/currents or the worst-case transient voltages/currents. This is a constrained nonlinear optimization problem.

The earliest power/ground network sizing work [5,6] takes special advantage of the tree topology of the power/ground network typically used in early designs. Instead of restricting the voltage drop on every node in the P/G network, only the voltage drop from root to every leaf of the tree structure is constrained, where the root corresponds chip power pad and the leaf corresponds to the power pin of each macro. In this work, constant branch current constraints $I_{i_{max}}$ and $I_{i_{min}}$ are used to further reduce the total number of voltage and current constraints.

Chowdhury proposes to solve the general nonlinear optimization problem (Equation 44.34) on a general graph topology in Ref. [50]. In this work, both currents and voltages are treated as variables. Specifically, the entire optimization procedure consists of two optimization stages. Assuming fixed branch currents and given $w_i = \rho l_i / R_i$ and $R_i = \frac{V_{i1} - V_{i2}}{I_i}$, the first stage minimizes area, a nonlinear function of each branch voltage

$$\text{Area} = f(v) = \sum_i l_i w_i = \sum_i \frac{\alpha_i}{V_{i1} - V_{i2}} \tag{44.34}$$

where $\alpha_i = \rho I_i l_i^2$, subject to change of current direction constraints

$$\frac{V_{i1} - V_{i2}}{I_i} \geq 0 \tag{44.35}$$

the minimum width constraints,

$$\frac{V_{i1} - V_{i2}}{I_i} \leq \frac{\rho l_i}{w_{i,\min}} \tag{44.36}$$

voltage IR drop constraints, and current density constraints. This problem was converted into an unconstrained convex programming problem and was solved using the conjugate gradient method. The second stage assumes that all nodal voltages are fixed, the objective function becomes

$$\text{area} = \sum_i \beta_i I_i \tag{44.37}$$

where $\beta_i = \frac{\rho l_i^2}{V_{i1} - V_{i2}}$. Constraints include changes of current directions, minimum width constraints, and Kirchoff's current law. This is a linear programming problem.

Tan et al. [51] improves the above method by expanding the nonlinear objection function of the first-stage optimization problem using Taylor's expansion as follows:

$$g(v) = f(v^0) + \frac{\partial f(v^0)}{\partial v}(v - v^0) = \sum_i \frac{2|\alpha_i|}{v_i^0} - \sum_i \frac{|\alpha_i|}{v_i^{0^2}} v_i \tag{44.38}$$

Instead of minimizing the nonlinear objective function (Equation 44.34), they minimize Equation 44.38, which is a linear function of v. The solution is thus transformed into a sequence of linear programming problem.

Ref. [52] directly treats wire width as the optimization variable and solves the nonlinear optimization problem (Equation 44.34) using augmented Lagrangian relaxation. The following unconstrained minimization problem is formulated

$$F(v) = \text{area} + \omega \times \left(\sum_i V_{\text{drop}}^2 + \sum_j I_{\text{density}}^2 \right) \tag{44.39}$$

where

 i is every node connected to the power grid
 j is every branch in the power grid circuit
 ω is the penalty parameter

Adjoint sensitivity [53] technique is used to evaluate the sensitivity of the objective function with respect to each wire width.

The multigrid power grid analysis idea is applied to optimization in Ref. [54]. The method first reduces the original power grid to a coarse grid according to grid density in each region and maintains the total grid area. The sequence of linear program [51] algorithm is then applied to optimize the coarse grid. The optimal solution is then mapped back to a solution to the original grid.

44.4.2 Decoupling Capacitance Allocation and Sizing

Optimal decoupling capacitance allocation and placement is critical for suppressing transient power grid noise. A simple and greedy decap estimation for each module k is based on the total charge that each module will draw from the power grid:

$$Q^k = \int_0^\tau I^k(t)\, dt$$
$$C^k = Q^k / V_{\text{noise}}^{(\text{lim})} \tag{44.40}$$

where

 C^k is the upper limit of required decap for module k
 τ is the duration that the switching process lasts
 $I^k(t)$ is the switching current of module k
 $V_{\text{noise}}^{(\text{lim})}$ is the upper limit of voltage drop

As pointed out in Ref. [55], the above decap estimation is very conservative by not considering its impact on neighboring modules that draw currents from the same V_{dd} pins. An iterative process is proposed to reduce the pessimism of the above solution. The initial solution is chosen as

$$\theta = \max\left(1, \frac{V_{\text{noise}}^k}{V_{\text{noise}}^{(\text{lim})}}\right)$$
$$C^k = (1 - 1/\theta)\, Q^k / V_{\text{noise}}^{(\text{lim})} \tag{44.41}$$

Power supply noise is then verified after decap insertion. If some V_{noise}^k still go beyond V_{noise}, θ is changed to increase C^k without exceeding the upper limit (Equation 44.41). If C^k is increased to the limit and V_{noise}^k is still above the voltage limit, decap of its neighboring modules will be increased until V_{noise}^k goes below $V_{\text{noise}}^{(\text{lim})}$.

In the above work, only the worst-case voltage drop across the entire transient voltage waveform is taken into consideration. Refs. [30,56] use the integral of voltage waveform beyond the noise margin as the transient noise metric and formulates the decap sizing problem as a linearly constrained nonlinear optimization problem for row-based standard-cell designs as follows:

$$
\begin{aligned}
\text{minimize} \quad & Z(w_j) & j = 1 \cdots N_{\text{decap}} \\
\text{subject to} \quad & \sum_{k \in \text{row}_i} w_k \leq (1 - r_i) W_{\text{chip}} & i = 1 \cdots N_{\text{row}} \\
\text{and} \quad & 0 \leq w_j \leq w_{\text{max}} & j = 1 \cdots N_{\text{decap}}
\end{aligned}
$$

The scalar objective Z, defined in Equation 44.10, is a function of all of the decap widths and N_{decap} is the total number of decaps in the chip. The first constraint states that the total decap width in a row cannot exceed the total amount of empty space in that row, and W_{chip} and N_{row} denote, respectively, the width of the chip and the number of rows in the chip. The second constraint restricts the decap widths within a realistic range. An upper bound w_{max} for a cell in row i is easily seen to be $(1 - r_i)W_{chip}$, which is the largest empty space in row i; while the lower bound of each decap width is zero. Standard quadratic programming solver is applied to solve this optimization problem.

Li et al. proposes a partitioning scheme to reduce the problem size. The partition-based strategy is based on the fact that decap has a local impact on suppressing the transient noise. The partitioning task is achieved by a noise-aware graph-based multilevel minimum cut algorithm. Conjugate gradient solver is then applied for an optimal solution to each partition.

44.4.3 TOPOLOGY OPTIMIZATION

Ref. [57] presents an early work on mesh-based P/G network topology optimization for standard cell layouts. The problem was formulated into a nonlinear combinatorial optimization problem as follows:

$$
\begin{aligned}
&\text{minimize} && z = f(\mathbf{g}^x) \\
&\text{subject to} && \mathbf{g}_i^x \in N_x \\
&&& \text{voltage drop and electromigration constraints}
\end{aligned}
\tag{44.42}
$$

$$
\begin{aligned}
\text{and} \quad &\text{circuit constraints (kirchhroff's voltage law [KVL],} \\
&\text{kirchhroff's current law [KCL], and Ohm's law)}
\end{aligned}
\tag{44.43}
$$

The objective function z is the total wiring resources required by the power buses. The decision variable vector $\mathbf{g}^x$ is the conductance of every branch. $\mathbf{g}^x$ can take any discrete value between zero and $\mathbf{g}_{n_x}^x$, $n_x = |N_x|$. The problem was relaxed into a continuous optimization problem by allowing $\mathbf{g}_i^0 \leq \mathbf{g}_i^x \leq \mathbf{g}_i^X$, $i \epsilon N_x$. Starting from an initial feasible solution, the solution is improved by moving toward the direction that decreases the objective function, total wiring resources, without causing the violation of any constraint. The improvement step is iterated until no improvement is obtained. The gradient calculation was based on adjoint sensitivity technique [53]. After obtaining an approximate solution, an exact or integer solution is locally searched in a neighborhood of the approximate solution. Note that the nature of the problem formulation provides possibility of topology changes during each iteration as $\mathbf{g}^x$ may change between zero and nonzero. If $\mathbf{g}^x$ is not allowed to be zero, this work reduces to be a wire sizing technique.

Refs. [12,13,38] propose to design power grid using hybrid mesh/tree topologies. Although tree structures provide the benefits of easier to route and analyze, they can easily result in poor quality in P/G signal delivery especially in recent technologies. On the other hand, dense meshes are excellent in satisfying the quality requirements but are computationally difficult to analyze. The key idea in this work is that an approach that meets both requirements of quality and fast turnaround time of analysis would be some topology between a pure tree and a full mesh. Both Ref. [12] and Refs. [13,38] illustrate the benefit of such a hybrid power grid topology of a global mesh feeding multiple local trees by proposing a fast and accurate analysis approach and showing its efficiency of both analysis and optimization. As pointed out by Refs. [13,38], the hybrid topology can be extended to other topologies that are intermediate to the two extremes of full trees and full meshes, for example, a global mesh that feeds smaller unconnected local meshes.

Ref. [58] proposes another idea of hybrid power grid topology, which is intermediate to fully regular grids and highly irregular grids. Power grids with regularity help signal routing because power wires can be easily accounted for during routing. At global level, a regular power grid also provides well-balanced ground returns for signal lines. On the other hand, a highly irregular grid may adaptively provide excellent power delivery according to current demands at different regions of a chip. Therefore, Ref. [58] proposes a power grid topology with global irregularity and local regularity, which has the advantages for routing that is afforded by fully regular nets, while offering the flexibility in optimization and better resource utilization permitted by irregular grids.

The optimization procedure begins by abstracting the P/G network with an equivalent circuit model as described in Section 44.2. The current in each tile is assumed to be evenly distributed. The chip is then divided into k rectangular tile and an imaginary skeleton grid is superimposed on the chip area on which the actual supply grid is built, to maintain wire alignments across tile boundaries. Starting with an equal number of wires in all tiles in both horizontal and vertical directions, an initial sparse actual grid is formed on the skeleton grid. The grid is analyzed using the macromodeling technique in Ref. [39] after the required port approximations, and the most critical node x in tile i with the maximum voltage drop from V_{dd} is determined. The voltage sensitivity of the most critical node x, with respect to increase in wire area in tile i, by addition of l wires, is computed using a finite-difference based gradient calculation method. Next, the number of horizontal or vertical wires in the tile, which produces the maximum voltage sensitivity, is increased by l. The current source to internal nodes of the tile are reassigned, so that the sum of the current sources at all internal nodes is the total current drawn by the P/G buses in that tile. The analysis-sensitivity-optimization steps are repeated until the voltage of the most critical node is greater than a specified value.

44.4.4 OPTIMAL PLACEMENT OF POWER SUPPLY PADS AND PINS

For a given power supply network, Ref. [59] provides an optimal solution for placement of power pads and pins, subject to DC voltage drop constraints and maximum current constraints on each pad and pin. The problem is modeled as a mixed integer linear program using the macromodeling technique discussed in Section 44.3:

$$
\begin{aligned}
&\text{minimize} &&\text{number of pads } N \\
&\text{subject to} &&(1)\ I_i \le I_{th}, i \in \text{PC} \\
& &&(2)\ V_j \ge V_{th}, j \in \text{PC and OBS} \\
& &&(3)\ I_i \text{ and } V_j \text{ satisfy Equation 44.13}
\end{aligned}
\tag{44.44}
$$

where
  PC represents candidate pad locations
  OBS means observation nodes on ports of the macromodel
  I_{th} is the maximum current allowed through pads
  V_{th} is the worst-case voltage for each node in the power grid

Introducing 0–1 integer variables z, with $z_i = 1$ denoting that a pad is placed at pad candidate i. This will help set different voltage and port current constraints for PC nodes depending on whether a pad is connected at the candidate location or not. The constraints for PC ports can be written as

$$
V_i - V_{dd} \times z_i \ge 0
\tag{44.45}
$$

$$
V_i \le V_{dd}
\tag{44.46}
$$

$$
V_i \ge V_{th}
\tag{44.47}
$$

$$
I_{th} \times z_i - I_i \ge 0
\tag{44.48}
$$

$$
I_i \ge 0
\tag{44.49}
$$

The above formulation assumes ideal supply voltage of V_{dd} at pad locations. By further partitioning the macromodel in Equation 44.13 based on PC and OBS ports, Equation 44.13 can be rewritten as

$$
\begin{bmatrix} I_{PC} \\ I_{OBS} \end{bmatrix} = \begin{bmatrix} A_{11} & A_{12} \\ A_{21} & A_{22} \end{bmatrix} \begin{bmatrix} V_{PC} \\ V_{OBS} \end{bmatrix} + \begin{bmatrix} S_{PC} \\ S_{OBS} \end{bmatrix}
\tag{44.50}
$$

where

I_{PC} and I_{OBS} are currents through the PC and OBS ports, respectively
S_{PC} and S_{OBS} are constant current sources from these ports to the reference node

It should be noted that all elements in I_{OBS} are zero because there is no current flow into the macromodel through the observation nodes. Given $T = -A_{22}^{-1} \times A_{21}$ and $B = -A_{22}^{-1} \times S_{OBS}$, further derivation gives

$$T \times V_{PC} \geq C \tag{44.51}$$

where

$$C = \begin{bmatrix} V_{th} - B_1 \\ V_{th} - B_2 \\ \dots \\ V_{th} - B_n \end{bmatrix} \tag{44.52}$$

REFERENCES

1. SIA, ESIA, JEITA, KSIA, and TSIA. *The International Technology Roadmap for Semiconductors*. Available at http://www.itrs.net/Common/2005ITRS/Home2005.html, 2005.
2. G. Bai, S. Bobba, and T. N. Hajj. Static timing analysis including power supply noise effect on propagation delay in VLSI circuits. In *Proceedings of the Design Automation Conference*, pp. 295–300, Las Vegas, NV, June 2001.
3. L. H. Chen, M. Marek-Sadowska, and F. Brewer. Coping with buffer delay change due to power and ground noise. In *Proceedings of the Design Automation Conference*, pp. 860–865, New Orleans, LA, June 2002.
4. R. Saleh, S. Z. Hussain, S. Rochel, and D. Overhauser. Clock skew verification in the presence of IR-drop in the power distribution network. *IEEE Transactions on Computer-Aided Design of ICs and Systems*, 19(6): 635–644, June 2000.
5. S. Chowdhury. An automated design of minimum area IC power/ground nets. In *Proceedings of the Design Automation Conference*, pp. 223–229, Miami Beach, FL, June 1987.
6. S. Chowdhury and M. A. Breuter. Optimum design of IC power/ground nets subject to reliability constraints. *IEEE Transactions on Computer-Aided Design*, 7(7): 787–796, July 1988.
7. A. Vittal and M. Marek-Sadowska. Power distribution topology design. In *Proceedings of the Design Automation Conference*, pp. 503–507, San Francisco, CA, June 1995.
8. S. Bobba, T. Thorp, K. Aingaran, and D. Liu. IC power distribution challenges. In *Proceedings of the International Conference on Computer-Aided Design*, pp. 643–650, San Jose, CA, 2001.
9. K. L. Shepard and V. Narayanan. Noise in deep submicron digital design. In *Proceedings of the International Conference on Computer-Aided Design*, pp. 524–531, San Jose, CA, November 1996.
10. H. H. Chen and D. D. Ling. Power supply noise analysis methodology for deep-submicron VLSI chip design. In *Proceedings of the Design Automation Conference*, pp. 638–643, Anaheim, CA, June 1997.
11. H. H. Chen and J. S. Neely. Interconnect and circuit modeling techniques for full-chip power supply noise analysis. *IEEE Transactions on Components, Packaging, and Manufacturing Technology, Part B*, 21(3): 209–215, August 1998. (DAC 1997).
12. J. C. Shah, A. A. Younis, S. S. Sapatnekar, and M. M. Hassoun. An algorithm for simulating power/ground networks using Padé approximants and its symbolic implementation. *IEEE Transactions on Circuits and Systems I: Fundamental Theory and Applications*, 45: 1372–1382, October 1998. (ECCTD 1997).
13. H. Su, K. H. Gala, and S. S. Sapatnekar. Fast analysis and optimization of power/ground networks. In *Proceedings of the International Conference on Computer-Aided Design*, pp. 477–480, San Jose, CA, November 2000.
14. S. Chowdhury and J. S. Barkatullah. Estimation of maximum currents in MOS IC logic circuits. *IEEE Transactions on Computer-Aided Design of ICs and Systems*, 9(6): 642–654, June 1990. (ICCAD 1988).
15. H. Kriplani, F. Najm, and I. Hajj. Maximum current estimation in CMOS circuits. In *Proceedings of the Design Automation Conference*, pp. 2–7, Anaheim, CA, June 1992.

16. H. Kriplani, F. Najm, and I. Hajj. Resolving signal correlations for estimating maximum currents in CMOS combinational circuits. In *Proceedings of the Design Automation Conference*, pp. 384–388, Dallas, TX, June 1993.

17. S. Bobba and I. N. Hajj. Estimation of maximum current envelope for power bus analysis and design. In *Proceedings of the International Symposium on Physical Design*, pp. 141–146, Monterey, CA, April 2001.

18. A. Krstic and K. -T. T. Cheng. Vector generation for maximum instantaneous current through supply lines for CMOS circuits. In *Proceedings of the Design Automation Conference*, pp. 383–388, Anaheim, CA, June 1997.

19. R. Chaudhry, D. Blaauw, R. Panda, and T. Edwards. Current signature compression for IR-drop analysis. In *Proceedings of the Design Automation Conference*, pp. 162–167, Los Angeles, CA, June 2000.

20. Y. -M. Jiang, K. -T. Cheng, and A. Krstic. Estimation of maximum power and instantaneous current using a genetic algorithm. In *Proceedings of the IEEE Custom Integrated Circuits Conference*, pp. 135–138, San Diego, CA, May 1997.

21. S. Boyd, L. Vandenberghe, A. E. Gamal, and S. Yun. Design of robust global power and ground networks. In *Proceedings of the International Symposium on Physical Design*, pp. 60–65, Napa, CA, April 2001.

22. B. Sheu, D. Scharfetter, P. -K. Ko, and M. -C. Jeng. BSIM: Berkeley short-channel IGFET model for MOS transistors. *IEEE Journal of Solid-State Circuits*, 22: 558–566, August 1987.

23. University of California Berkeley. *BSIM4.2.0 Manual*, 2001. Available at http://www-device.eecs.berkeley.edu/~bsim3/bsim4.html

24. M. Benoit, S. Taylor, D. Overhauser, and S. Rochel. Power distribution in high-performance design. In *Proceedings of the International Symposium on Low Power Electronics and Design*, pp. 268–272, Monterey, CA, August 1998.

25. A. Dharchoudhury, R. Panda, D. Blaauw, and R. Vaidyanathan. Design and analysis of power distribution networks in PowerPC™ microprocessors. In *Proceedings of the Design Automation Conference*, pp. 738–743, San Francisco, CA, June 1998.

26. G. Steele, D. Overhauser, S. Rochel, and S. Z. Hussain. Full-chip verification for DSM power distribution systems. In *Proceedings of the Design Automation Conference*, pp. 744–749, San Francisco, CA, June 1998.

27. H. Su, F. Liu, A. Devgan, E. Acar, and S. R. Nassif. Full chip leakage estimation considering power supply and temperature variations. In *Proceedings of International Symposium on Low Power Electronics and Design*, pp. 78–83, Seoul, Korea, August 2003.

28. T. Sakurai and K. Tamaru. Simple formulas for two and three dimensional capacitance. *IEEE Transactions on Electronic Devices*, 30, 183–185, February 1983.

29. A. R. Conn, R. A. Haring, C. Visweswariah, and C. W. Wu. Circuit optimization via adjoint Lagrangians. In *Proceedings of the International Conference on Computer-Aided Design*, pp. 281–288, San Jose, CA, November 1997.

30. H. Su, S. S. Sapatnekar, and S. R. Nassif. An algorithm for optimal decoupling capacitor sizing and placement for standard cell layouts. In *Proceedings of the International Symposium on Physical Design*, pp. 68–73, San Diego, CA, April 2002.

31. L. T. Pillage, R. A. Rohrer, and C. Visweswariah. *Electronic and System Simulation Methods*. McGraw-Hill, New York, 1995.

32. Y. Cao, Y. Lee, T. Chen, and C. Chen. HiPRIME: Hierarchical and passivity reserved interconnect macromodeling engine for RLKC power delivery. In *Proceedings of the Design Automation Conference*, pp. 379–384, New Orleans, LA, June 2002.

33. J. N. Kozhaya, S. R. Nassif, and F. N. Najm. Multigrid-like technique for power grid analysis. In *Proceedings of the International Conference on Computer-Aided Design*, pp. 480–487, San Jose, CA, November 2001.

34. S. R. Nassif and J. N. Kozhaya. Fast power grid simulation. In *Proceedings of the Design Automation Conference*, pp. 156–161, Los Angeles, CA, June 2000.

35. H. Qian, S. R. Nassif, and S. S. Sapatnekar. Random walks in a supply network. In *Proceedings of the Design Automation Conference*, pp. 93–98, Anaheim, CA, June 2003.

36. H. Qian, S. R. Nassif, and S. S. Sapatnekar. Power grid analysis using random walks. *IEEE Transactions on Computer-Aided Design of ICs and Systems*, 24(8): 1204–1224, August 2005. (DAC 2003).

37. H. Su, E. Acar, and S. R. Nassif. Power grid reduction based on algebraic multigrid principles. In *Proceedings of the Design Automation Conference*, pp. 109–112, Anaheim, CA, June 2003.

38. H. Su, K. H. Gala, and S. S. Sapatnekar. Analysis and optimizatioin of structured power/ground networks. *IEEE Transactions on Computer-Aided Design*, 22(11): 1533–1544, November 2003. (ICCAD 2000).

39. M. Zhao, R. V. Panda, S. S. Sapatnekar, T. Edwards, R. Chaudhry, and D. Blaauw. Hierarchical analysis of power distribution networks. In *Proceedings of the Design Automation Conference*, pp. 481–486, Los Angeles, CA, June 2000.

40. W. L. Briggs, Henson, V. E., and McCormick, S., *A Multigrid Tutorial*, Available at http://computation.llml.gov/casc/people/henson/mgtut/slides.html

41. W. Hackbusch. *Multi-Grid Methods and Applications*. Springer-Verlag, Berlin, Germany, 1985.

42. J. Harris, Stocker, H., and Harris, J. W., *Handbook of Mathematics and Computational Science*, S. McCormick (Ed), Springer-Verlag, New York, 1998.

43. J. M. Wang and T. V. Nguyen. Extended Krylov subspace method for reduced order analysis of linear circuits with multiple sources. In *Proceedings of the Design Automation Conference*, pp. 247–252, Los Angeles, CA, June 2000.

44. A. Odabasioglu, M. Celik, and L. T. Pilleggi. PRIMA: Passive reduced-order interconnect macromodeling algorithm. In *Proceedings of the International Conference on Computer-Aided Design*, pp. 645–654, San Jose, CA, November 1998.

45. H. Qian, S. R. Nassif, and S. S. Sapatnekar. Early-stage power grid analysis for uncertain working modes. In *Proceedings of the International Symposium on Physical Design*, pp. 132–137, Phoenix, AZ, April 2004.

46. H. Qian, S. R. Nassif, and S. S. Sapatnekar. Early stage power grid analysis for uncertain working modes. *IEEE Transactions on Computer-Aided Design of ICs and Systems*, 24(5): 676–682, May 2005. (ISPD 2004).

47. I. A. Ferzli and F. N. Najm. Analysis and verification of power grids considering process-induced leakage current variations. *IEEE Transactions on Computer-Aided Design of ICs and Systems*, 25(1): 126–143, January 2006. (DAC 2003).

48. B. R. Stanisic, R. A. Rutenbar, and L. R. Carley. Addressing noise decoupling in mixed-signal IC's: Power distribution design and cell customization. *IEEE Journal of Solid-State Circuits*, 30: 321–326, March 1995.

49. B. R. Stanisic, N. K. Verghese, R. A. Rutenbar, L. R. Carley, and D. J. Allstot. Addressing substrate coupling in mixed-mode IC's: Simulation and power distribution synthesis. *IEEE Journal of Solid-State Circuits*, 29: 226–238, March 1994.

50. S. Chowdhury and M. A. Breuter. Minimum area design of power/ground nets having graph topologies. *IEEE Transactions on Circuits and Systems*, CAS-34(12): 1441–1451, December 1987.

51. S. X. Tan and C. R. Shi. Fast power/ground network optimization based on equivalent circuit modeling. In *Proceedings of the Design Automation Conference*, pp. 550–554, Las Vegas, NV, June 2001.

52. X. Wu, X. Hong, Y. Cai, C. K. Cheng, J. Gu, and W. Dai. Area minimization of power distribution network using efficient nonlinear programming techniques. In *Proceedings of the International Conference on Computer-Aided Design*, pp. 153–157, San Jose, CA 2001.

53. S. W. Director and R. A. Rohrer. The generalized adjoint network and network sensitivities. *IEEE Transactions on Circuit Theory*, 16(3): 318–323, August 1969.

54. K. Wang and M. Marek-Sadowska. On-chip power supply network optimization using multigrid-based technique. In *Proceedings of the Design Automation Conference*, pp. 113–118, Anaheim, CA, June 2003.

55. S. Zhao, K. Roy, and C. -K. Koh. Decoupling capacitance allocation for power supply noise suppression. In *Proceedings of the International Symposium on Physical Design*, pp. 66–71, Napa, CA, April 2001.

56. H. Su, S. S. Sapatnekar, and S. R. Nassif. Optimal decoupling capacitor sizing and placement for standard cell layout designs. *IEEE Transactions on Computer-Aided Design of ICs and Systems*, 22(4): 428–436, April 2003. (ISPD 2002).

57. T. Mitsuhashi and E. S. Kuh. Power and ground network topology optimization for cell-based VLSIs. In *Proceedings of the Design Automation Conference*, pp. 524–529, Anaheim, CA, June 1992.

58. J. Singh and S. S. Sapatnekar. Topology optimization of structured power/ground networks. In *Proceedings of the International Symposium on Physical Design*, pp. 116–123, Phoenix, AZ, April 2004.

59. M. Zhao, Y. Fu, V. Zolotov, S. Sundareswaran, and R. Panda. Optimal placement of power supply pads and pins. In *Proceedings of the Design Automation Conference*, pp. 165–170, San Diego, CA, June 2004.

Part X

Physical Design for Specialized Technologies

45 Field-Programmable Gate Array Architectures

Steven J.E. Wilton, Nathalie Chan King Choy,
Scott Y.L. Chin, and Kara K.W. Poon

CONTENTS

45.1 INTRODUCTION

Field-programmable gate arrays (FPGAs) have become the implementation medium of choice for many digital systems. FPGAs are integrated circuits that can be programmed after fabrication to implement virtually any digital circuit. This instant manufacturability reduces time-to-market as well as nonrecurring engineering costs. Most FPGAs are also reprogrammable, meaning the digital circuit implemented in the device can change as requirements or standards change or as bugs are found.

The flexibility in a FPGA is afforded through flexible logic elements connected to each other and to the I/O pads using flexible routing resources. Because the elements are prefabricated, the physical design tasks associated with mapping a circuit to an FPGA are somewhat different than those used to map a circuit to an application specific integrated circuit (ASIC). The next chapter will describe the physical design algorithms for FPGAs; this chapter sets the stage by describing the architecture of FPGAs. Section 45.2 describes several programming technologies, Section 45.3 describes logic block architectures, Section 45.4 describes routing architectures, and Sections 45.5 and 45.6 describe embedded memories and embedded computation blocks.

45.2 PROGRAMMING TECHNOLOGIES

The circuit being implemented on an FPGA is stored in the FPGA using a set of configuration bits. These bits can be constructed in various ways; this section describes static random access memory (SRAM), Flash, and antifuse-based configuration bits. These schemes are all used in contemporary commercial FPGAs; many FPGAs vendors, such as Xilinx, Altera, and Lattice, use SRAM configurable bits to control the programmable switches to configure routing and logic [Altera05,Lattice05,Xilinx05a]. Actel produces both Flash and antifuse FPGA products [Actel05a]. QuickLogic uses antifuse technology in their products [Quick05]. Table 45.1 provides a comparison among these three technologies; details on each are provided below. FPGAs based on emerging technologies have also been described [Ferrera04,Dehon05], but because they are not commercially available yet, they will not be discussed further here.

45.2.1 SRAM-Based FPGAs

The most popular scheme to implement configuration bits is to use SRAM cells. SRAM technology is fast, and allows for reprogrammability. In addition, SRAM bits can be implemented using standard complementary metal-oxide-semiconductor (CMOS) processes, meaning FPGAs using SRAMs can be implemented in leading-edge processes. Figure 45.1 shows a typical six-transistor SRAM memory cell. It uses the data bit in both the true and complement forms to achieve fast read and write time [Trimberger94]. Although a six-transistor cell is generally more stable because it is resistant to state flipping owing to crosstalk or charge sharing [Betz99], four-transistor and five-transistor SRAM cells are possible. Xilinx uses a five-transistor SRAM cell for their FPGAs [Trimberger94].

The main disadvantage of SRAM is its volatility. Data stored in SRAM cells is erased when the power is turned off. Therefore, additional off-chip memory, like electrically erasable programmable read-only memory (EEPROM), is necessary to store the configuration bits and program the FPGA at power-up. This potentially causes security concerns, because designs can be copied by capturing the external bit stream [Zeidman02]. To address this, some FPGA vendors, such as Altera and Lattice, apply on-chip Flash memory to store the configuration bits, so the SRAM-based FPGA can be programmed without external memory upon power-up. A second disadvantage of this technology is that SRAM cells are susceptible to neutron-induced errors, also known as soft-errors, which are

TABLE 45.1

Comparison among SRAM, Antifuse, and Flash

Features	SRAM	Flash	Antifuse
Volatile	Yes	No	No
In-system programmable	Yes	Yes	No
Power consumption	High	Lower	Lower
Density	High	High	High
IP security	No	Yes	Yes
Soft-error resistance	Low	High	High

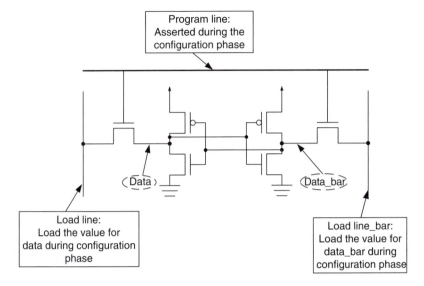

FIGURE 45.1 Six-transistor SRAM cell.

caused by neutrons, alpha particles, cosmic or terrestrial radiation. These errors are common in high-radiation environments, such as at high altitude or in space. Such errors do not permanently damage the FPGA, but they may cause instability and functional failure in the system. The main strategies to overcome these errors in SRAM-based FPGAs are triple redundancy, error-correcting or parity codes, and redundancy in time.

45.2.2 FLASH-BASED FPGAS

Flash cells provide nonvolatile programmability while retaining the ability to reprogram the FPGAs. Figure 45.2 illustrates the Flash switch used in Actel's ProASIC3. In the Flash switch, two transistors share the floating gate, which stores the programming data. The sensing transistor is used for writing and verification of the floating gate voltage while the switching transistor is employed to configure routing nets and logic. Flash-based FPGAs are more secure and consume less power than their SRAM

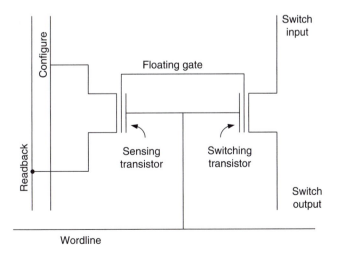

FIGURE 45.2 Flash-based switch.

counterparts [Actel05a]. However, the manufacturing process for Flash is more complicated than that of SRAM. As a result, Flash technology usually lags one to two process generations behind SRAM technologies. Testing is also lengthy owing to the nature of Flash. Therefore, Flash-based FPGAs have a slower time-to-market compared to the SRAM-based FPGAs.

45.2.3 ANTIFUSE-BASED FPGAs

Antifuses can also be used to implement configuration bits [Actel05b]. An antifuse is a thin insulating layer between conductors. The insulating layer gets mutated by applying high voltage. After the alteration, a low-resistance path is created between the conductors. Such alteration is irreversible. Like Flash, antifuse technology is nonvolatile. The major disadvantage of antifuse FPGA is its one-time programmability. However, it consumes less power and is more area-efficient than SRAM and Flash.

45.3 LOGIC BLOCK ARCHITECTURES

Programmability is provided in an FPGA in two ways. Logic is implemented in configurable logic blocks; these logic blocks are then connected to each other and to the I/O pads using a configurable routing network [Rose93,Betz99]. This section focuses on logic blocks and the next section focuses on the routing network.

45.3.1 LOOKUP-TABLES

Most FPGAs use lookup-tables (LUTs) as their basic logic element. A K-input LUT (K-LUT) is a memory with 2^K bits, K address lines, and a single output line. Each K-LUT can be configured to implement any function of K inputs by storing the truth table of the desired function in the 2^K storage bits. Figure 45.3 shows an example of a 2-input LUT implemented using SRAM cells (antifuse and Flash memory cells could also be used).

Early research has shown that $K = 4$ works well; this is used in most commercial FPGAs [Rose90,Singh92]. Later work reconfirmed that $K = 4$ is a good choice for area, but that for performance, K = 7 works well [Ahmed04]. In general, the parameter K has a significant impact on the efficiency of the architecture. If K is too large, it may not be possible to completely fill each logic block, while if K is too small, delay will suffer because more logic blocks will be needed along the critical path of a circuit. Figure 45.4 shows how a 6-input function might be implemented with two 4-LUTs; had a 6-LUT been used, only 1-LUT would be required.

Variations on the basic LUT architecture have been used. Figure 45.5 shows a logic block that employs a fracturable LUT mask (FLM) [Lewis05]. A k, m-FLM can implement a single k-input function or two functions, each with up to $k - 1$ inputs, which together use no more than $k + m$ distinct inputs. The architecture in Figure 45.5a is a 6,2-FLM. An extension of the FLM architecture, called a shared LUT mask (SLM) architecture, is shown in Figure 45.5b. A k, m-SLM can implement two identical functions of k inputs provided that the two functions share $k - m$ inputs. The SLM

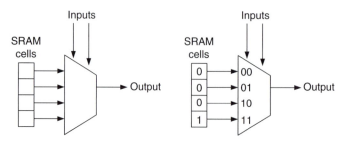

FIGURE 45.3   Two-input LUT. Unprogrammed and programmed as a two-input and gate.

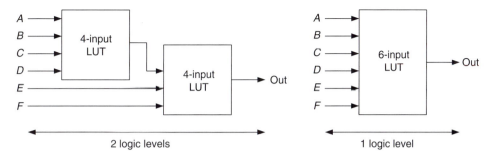

FIGURE 45.4 Implementing a 6-input function using two 4-LUTs.

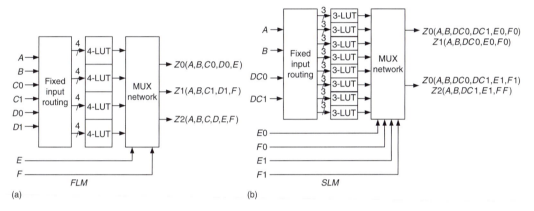

FIGURE 45.5 Advanced logic block structures.

architecture does this through the sharing of LUT masks (the set of configuration bits that indicate the function implemented by the LUT) so that both functions are the same but can have different inputs. The logic block in the Altera Stratix II FPGA is based on a 6,2-SLM [Altera05].

Lookup-tables are usually coupled with flip-flops, as shown in Figure 45.6. In this structure, a configuration bit is used to control the state of the output multiplexer. Depending on the value of this configuration bit, the output signal of the LUT can either be registered or unregistered. As in Ref. [Betz99], we refer to the LUT and flip-flop as a basic logic element (BLE).

45.3.1.1 Clusters

To increase speed and reduce area and compile time, larger logic blocks are preferred. However, LUT complexity grows exponentially with the number of inputs [Rose93]. Clusters are logic blocks of larger granularity, typically composed of multiple BLEs, internal cluster routing, and possibly specialized internal cluster connections, such as carry and arithmetic chains [Marquardt00]. Within a cluster, BLE inputs are typically connected to the cluster inputs and BLE outputs by a multiplexer-based crossbar. This internal interconnect is generally faster than the general purpose routing between

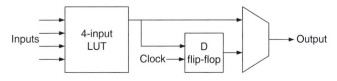

FIGURE 45.6 LUT coupled with a flip-flop (BLE).

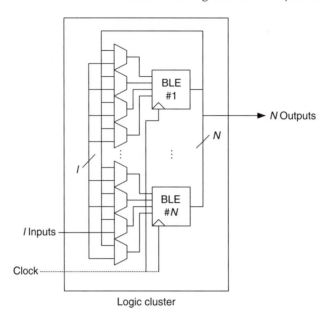

FIGURE 45.7   Basic BLE and basic cluster composed of identical BLEs.

blocks. Altera refers to clusters as logic array blocks (LABs), while Xilinx refers to clusters as configurable logic blocks (CLBs).

Figure 45.7 shows a typical cluster. The cluster architecture is described by these four parameters: (1) K, the number of inputs to a LUT, (2) N, the number of BLEs in a cluster, (3) I, the number of inputs to the cluster that connect to LUT inputs, and (4) M_{clk}, the number of clock inputs to a cluster (most studies assume this is 1).

Increasing K or N increases the functionality of the cluster. This reduces the number of blocks needed to implement circuits and the number of blocks on the critical path, but increases the size of the block and makes the local cluster interconnect slower. Research has found that $K = 4$–6 and $N = 3$–10 provide the best combined speed and area [Ahmed04].

The value of I is often smaller than $K \times N$, because BLEs often share inputs or use the outputs from BLEs within the cluster. Smaller values of I use smaller multiplexers in the crossbar, reducing area, but overly small I values make some BLEs unusable. Research has found that 98 percent utilization can be achieved when $I = [(K/2) \times (N + 1)]$ [Ahmed04].

45.3.1.2 Carry Chains

Carry chains are locally routed connections that aid in the efficient implementation of arithmetic operations. They also can be used in the efficient implementation of logical operations, such as parity and comparison. Fast carry chains are important because the critical path for these operations is often through the carry.

Each 4-LUT in a BLE can be fractured to implement two 3-LUTs; this is sufficient to implement both the sum and carry, given two input bits (a and b) and a carry input, as shown in Figure 45.8. The carry out signal from one BLE would typically be connected to the carry in of an adjacent BLE using a fast dedicated connection. The Z-input is used to break the carry chain before the first bit of an addition.

More complex carry schemes have been described. In Ref. [Hauck00], carry chains based on carry select, variable block, and Brent–Kung schemes are described; the Brent–Kung scheme is shown to be 3.8 times faster than the simple ripple carry adder in Figure 45.8. Support for carry-lookahead adders is included in the Actel Axcelerator device, the Xilinx Virtex-II, Virtex-II Pro,

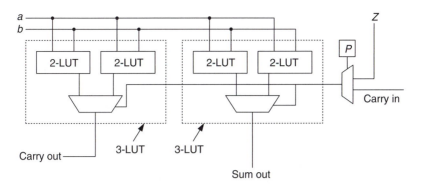

FIGURE 45.8   Carry chain connections to a 4-LUT.

and Virtex-4 devices. Carry select capabilities are included in the Altera Stratix FPGAs. The Altera Stratix-II contains two dedicated 1-bit adders in each logic block. Because high-fanin arithmetic can cause routing congestion in a small area of the device, both Xilinx and Altera parts support two independent carry chains in each cluster. This allows for narrower fanin logic, which helps reduce routing congestion around the adders.

45.3.2   NON-LUT-BASED LOGIC BLOCKS

Not all FPGAs contain logic blocks based on LUTs. The Actel ProASIC3 logic blocks contain a set of multiplexers, which allow for the implementation of 3-input combinational or sequential functions in each logic block [Actel05a]. The QuickLogic Eclipse II logic cell contains two 6-input AND gates, four 2-input AND gates, and seven two-to-one multiplexers [Quick05]. The use of universal logic modules as FPGA logic blocks has also been proposed; these blocks can implement any function of their inputs by applying input permutation and negation [Lin94]. Finally, programmable devices using more coarse-grained logic blocks exist; these logic blocks are typically arithmetic/logic units and are suitable for computationally intensive applications [Ebeling96,Goldstein00,Singh00, Mei03].

45.4   ROUTING ARCHITECTURES

Connections between logic blocks are implemented using fixed prefabricated metal tracks. These tracks are arranged in channels; channels typically run vertically and horizontally, forming a grid [Lemieux04a]. Although many academic studies have assumed that all channels contain the same number of tracks [Betz99], many commercial architectures (such as those from Altera) contain more tracks in each horizontal channel than each vertical channel. Figure 45.9 shows an FPGA with tracks arranged in horizontal and vertical channels.

45.4.1   SEGMENTATION

Tracks within a channel can span one logic block, or multiple logic blocks. Typically, not all tracks within a channel will be of the same length. Several studies have investigated the optimum segment length. In Ref. [Brown96], a heterogeneous routing architecture, in which some tracks span three logic blocks, some span two logic blocks, and some span one logic block, is found to work well. In Ref. [Betz99], it is shown that longer wires result in a more efficient architecture; they suggest a homogeneous architecture in which all tracks span either four or eight logic block gives the most efficient FPGA.

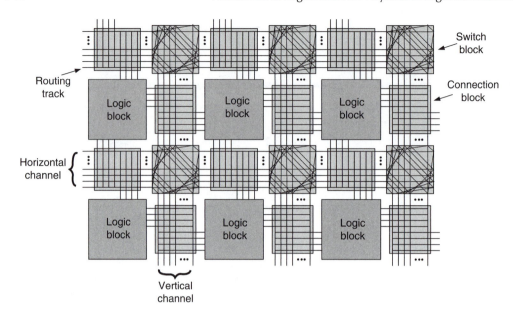

FIGURE 45.9 Overall routing architecture.

45.4.2 PROGRAMMABLE SWITCHES

The tracks are connected to each other and to the logic blocks using programmable switches. These programmable switches can be buffered or unbuffered, as shown in Figure 45.10. Switches in modern FPGAs are typically buffered, because unbuffered switches result in a quadratic increase in delay for long connections. Buffered switches can be bidirectional, as shown in Figure 45.10b or unidirectional, as shown in Figure 45.10c. Although many academic studies assume bidirectional switches [Betz99], most modern FPGAs contain unidirectional switches [Lemieux04b]; these switches allow for better delay optimization and result in a more dense routing fabric.

45.4.3 SWITCH BLOCKS AND CONNECTION BLOCKS

Tracks are connected to each other using switch blocks, and to logic blocks using connection blocks. Commercial FPGAs often contain combined switch blocks and connection blocks, however for clarity, this section will describe each separately.

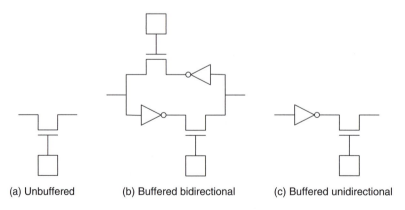

    (a) Unbuffered   (b) Buffered bidirectional   (c) Buffered unidirectional

FIGURE 45.10 Programmable switches.

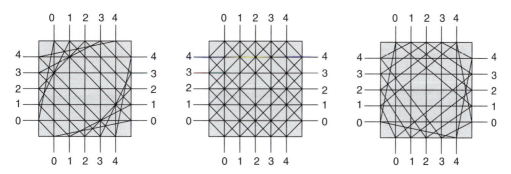

FIGURE 45.11   Switch block patterns.

A switch block lies at the intersection of each horizontal and vertical channel, and can connect each incident track to some number of other incident tracks. Academic work uses the notation F_s to describe the number of outgoing tracks to which each incoming track can be connected [Rose93]. Most physical design algorithm studies assume $F_s = 3$; in this case, each incoming track can be connected to one track on each of the other three sides of the switch block. The switch pattern determines which F_s tracks to which each incoming track can be connected. Academic work has proposed the three switch patterns in Figure 45.11. The disjoint pattern divides the routing fabric into domains; if there are W tracks in each channel, there are W domains. This simplifies the routing task, and results in an efficient layout. The universal pattern has been shown to support the largest number of simultaneous connections through each switch block [Chang96], while the Wilton block has been shown to result in good overall routability [Wilton97]. An extension of the Wilton block to architectures with different segment lengths is described in Ref. [Masud99]. In Ref. [Sivaswamy05], it is proposed that some of the connections in a switch block should be hard-wired (nonprogrammable); this gives 30 percent speedup, a slight reduction in area, and an 8 percent reduction in power.

Connection blocks are used to connect logic block pins to the routing tracks. Each logic block pin can be connected to a subset of routing tracks in the neighboring channel. The quantity F_c indicates the proportion of the tracks in each channel to which a pin can be connected. In ref. [Betz99], it is shown that $F_c = 0.25$–0.5 (depending on the type of switch block employed) works well.

45.4.4   BUS-BASED ROUTING ARCHITECTURES

FPGAs are often used to implement datapath-intensive circuits, in which many signals are part of wide buses. Because each bit of a bus is connected in the same way, it has been suggested that a datapath routing architecture, in which a single configuration bit controls multiple switches, will lead to an improvement in FPGA density. In Ref. [Ye05], the architecture in Figure 45.12 is presented. In this architecture, some of the tracks (the top four in Figure 45.12) are dedicated bus-based routing tracks, and connections to them are controlled by a bus switch; a bus switch contains one switch for each bit controlled by a single configuration cell. In this case, each bus (and each bus switch) is 4-bits wide. The lower tracks are regular bit-based routing tracks, which are connected to each other and to the logic cells using standard connection and switch blocks, as described above. In Ref. [Ye05], it is shown that a bus-width of 4 works well, and that 40–50 percent of the tracks should be buses (with the remainder being bit-based routing tracks). It is shown that this results in a density improvement of 9.6 percent compared to a conventional architecture.

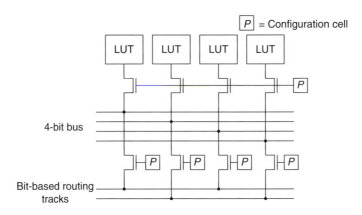

FIGURE 45.12   Bus-based routing architecture.

45.4.5   PIPELINED INTERCONNECT ARCHITECTURES

In deep-submicron technologies, the delay of long wires can limit the clock speed of the circuit implemented on an FPGA. To address this, several authors have proposed pipelined intercon-nect architectures [Singh01a,Singh01b,Weaver04]. In these architectures, some of the interconnect switches contain registers. This results in additional complexity for the router, however, because it must now balance the number of registers on each path.

45.5   MEMORIES

Today, FPGAs are often used to implement entire systems. These systems often require storage. Although it is possible to implement storage off-chip, on-chip storage has a number of advantages. On-chip storage reduces system costs, allows for a wider, faster memory interface, and reduces I/O demands on the FPGA.

There are two ways of implementing memory on FPGAs: embedded memory and distributed memory. Embedded memory solutions offer a number of relatively large fixed dedicated memory blocks on the FPGA. Distributed memory, on the other hand, uses small memories spread across the entire FPGA chip, often implemented in unused logic elements.

45.5.1   EMBEDDED MEMORY

Most FPGAs contain embedded memory blocks (EMBs). EMBs are typically arranged in columns or rows to simplify connections to logic and between other EMBs [Wilton99], as shown in Figure 45.13. Altera's Stratix and Stratix-II devices include three different sized EMBs: 512 bits, 4 Kbits, and 512 Kbits [Altera05]. Xilinx's Virtex-4, Virtex-II, and Spartan series contain 18 Kbits EMBs [Xil-inx05a]. Actel's ProASIC3 and ProASIC-Plus contain 4 Kbits and 2 Kbits EMBs, respectively [Actel05].

Each EMB has a fixed number of bits, but its aspect ratio can be configured by the user. For example, in the Stratix II architecture, a 4-Kbit EMB may be configured to act as memories with aspect ratios of $4096 \times 1, 2048 \times 2, 1024 \times 4, 512 \times 8, 256 \times 16$, or 128×32. On many devices, EMBs can be configured to act as a ROM, single-port RAM, or dual-port RAM. In addition, they typically include parity bits, various enable/reset control signals, and have synchronous inputs with synchronous or asynchronous outputs.

Of particular importance is the interface between the memory and the logic. Figure 45.14 shows one published scheme; in this architecture, each EMB connects to the logic through a memory-logic interconnect block [Wilton99]. Figure 45.15 shows the contents of one of these memory-logic

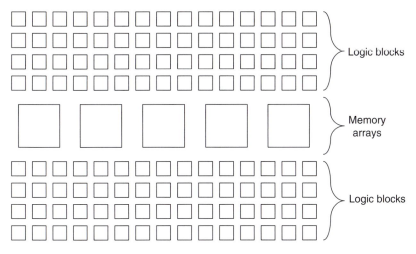

FIGURE 45.13   Logic and memory in an FPGA.

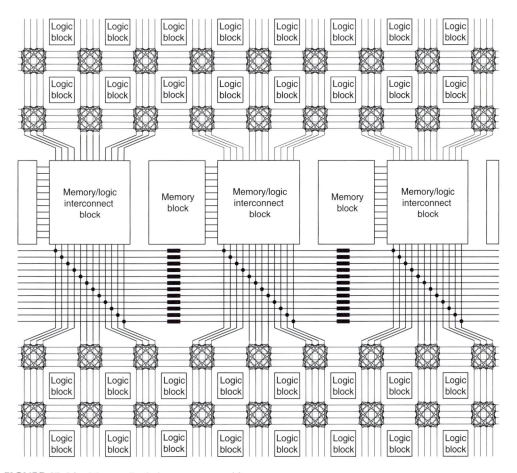

FIGURE 45.14   Memory/logic interconnect architecture.

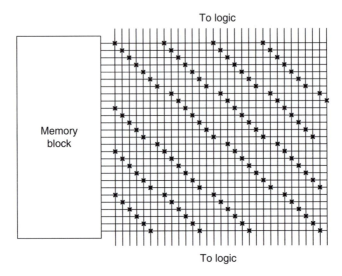

FIGURE 45.15   Memory/logic interconnect block.

interconnect blocks; crosses indicate programmable connections. The flexibility of the connection block, F_m, can be defined as the number of programmable connections available between each horizontal pin and the adjacent vertical channel. In Figure 45.14, $F_m = 4$. In Ref. [Wilton99], it is shown that a value of F_m between 4 and 7 works well. To increase routability, the architecture in Figure 45.14 includes dedicated tracks for memory-to-memory connections. These tracks are used when multiple memory arrays are cascaded together to form larger user arrays, and are more efficient for such memory-to-memory connections. EMBs can also be used to implement logic by configuring them as large ROMs [Cong98] [Wilton00].

45.5.2   DISTRIBUTED MEMORY

Commercial FPGAs such as Xilinx's Virtex-4, Virtex-II, and Spartan-3 devices allow the 4-input LUTs in their logic blocks to be configured as 16×1-bit memories [Xilinx05a]. These memories have synchronous inputs. Their outputs can be synchronous through the use of the LUTs associated register. These 16×1-bit memories can also be cascaded to implement deeper or wider memory arrays through specialized logic resources.

Another method for supporting distributed memory is proposed in Ref. [Oldridge05]. This architecture allows the configuration memory in the interconnect switch blocks to be used as user memory and is very efficient for wide, shallow memories.

45.6   EMBEDDED COMPUTATION BLOCKS

45.6.1   MULTIPLIERS AND DSP BLOCKS

To address the performance requirements of digital signal processing (DSP) applications, FPGA manufacturers typically include dedicated hardware multipliers in their devices. Altera Cyclone II and Xilinx Virtex-II/-II Pro devices include embedded 18×18-bit multipliers, which can be split into 9×9-bit multipliers [Xilinx05a]. The Virtex-II/-II Pro devices are further optimized with direct connections to the Xilinx block RAM resources for fast access to input operands. As manufacturers moved toward high-performance platform FPGAs, they began to include more complex dedicated hardware blocks, referred to as DSP blocks, which are optimized for a wider range of DSP applications. Altera's Stratix and Stratix II DSP blocks support pipelining, shift registers, and can be configured to implement

9×9-bit, 18×18-bit, or 36×36-bit multipliers that can optionally feed a dedicated adder/subtractor or accumulator [Altera05]. Xilinx Virtex-4 XtremeDSP slices contain a dedicated 18 18-bit 2's complement signed multiplier, adder logic, 48-bit accumulator, and pipeline registers. They also have dedicated connections for cascading DSP slices, with an optional wire-shift, without having to use the slower general routing fabric [Xilinx05a].

This inclusion of dedicated multipliers or DSP blocks to complement the general logic resources results in a heterogeneous FPGA architecture. Research has considered what could be gained from tuning FPGA architectures to specific application domains, in particular DSP. The work in Ref. [Leijten03] deliberately avoids creating a heterogeneous architecture because they found that DSP applications contain both arithmetic and random logic, but that a suitable ratio between arithmetic and random logic is difficult to determine. Instead they develop two mixed-grain logic blocks that are suitable for implementing both arithmetic and random logic by looking at properties of the target arithmetic operations and of the 4-LUT. Their logic blocks are coarse-grained: each block can implement up to 4-bit addition/subtraction, 4 bits of an array multiplier, 4-bit 2:1 multiplexer, or wide Boolean functions. At the same time, each logic block continues to be able to implement single-bit output random logic functions much like a normal LUT. Their architecture reduces configuration memory requirements by a factor of 4, which is good for embedded systems or those with dynamic reconfiguration, and offers higher flexibility for handling a range of proportions of datapath operations to random logic.

45.6.2 EMBEDDED PROCESSORS

The increase in the capacity of FPGAs has enabled the creation of entire systems on a chip. To support applications involving microcontrollers and microprocessors, FPGA manufacturers offer embedded processors tailored to interface with the FPGA logic fabric. There are two types of FPGA embedded processors: soft and hard.

Soft processors are intellectual property cores that have configurable features, such as caches, register file sizes, RAM/ROM blocks, and custom instructions. They are typically available as hardware description language descriptions and are implemented in the logic blocks of the FPGA. Altera and Xilinx have 32-bit reduced instruction set computer (RISC) processor cores that are optimized for their FPGAs: Nios/Nios II and PicoBlaze/MicroBlaze, respectively. Altera and Xilinx also offer development and debugging tools and other intellectual property cores that interface with their processors. The advantages of soft processors include the options to use and configure features only when they are needed, reducing area, and the ability to include multiple processors on a single chip. A Xilinx MicroBlaze requires as few as 923 LUTs [Xilinx05b] and can be used in the creation of multiprocessor systems. Because soft processors are implemented using logic resources, they are slower and consume more power than off-the-shelf processors.

Hard processors are dedicated hardware embedded on the FPGA. Altera Excalibur devices include the ARM 32-bit RISC processor and Xilinx Virtex-4 and Virtex-II Pro devices include up to two IBM PowerPC 32-bit RISC processors [Altera02,Xilinx05b].

45.7 SUMMARY

This chapter has described the essential architectural features of contemporary FPGAs. Most commercial FPGAs contain small LUTs, in which logic is implemented. These LUTs are usually arranged in clusters, often with special support for arithmetic circuits (such as carry chains). Signals are transmitted between logic blocks using fixed metal tracks, connected using programmable switches. The topology of these tracks and switches make up the device's routing architecture. In addition to logic blocks, modern FPGAs contain significant amounts of embedded memory, and dedicated arithmetic functional blocks (such as multipliers). This chapter has set the stage for the next chapter, which describes physical design algorithms that target FPGAs.

REFERENCES

[Actel05a]   Actel Corp., *ProASIC3 Flash Family FPGAs Handbook*, 2005. Available at: http://www.actel.com/documents/PA3_HB.pdf.

[Actel05b]   Actel Corp., *Actel Quality and Reliability Guide*, 2005 Available at http://www.actel.com/document/RelGuide.pdf.

[Ahmed04]   E. Ahmed and J. Rose, The effect of LUT and cluster size on deep-submicron FPGA performance and density, *IEEE Transactions on VLSI*, 12(3): 288–298, March 2004.

[Altera02]   Altera Corp., *Excalibur Device Overview*, May 2002. Available at: http://www.altera.com/literature/ds/ds_arm.pdf

[Altera05]   Altera Corp., *Stratix II Device Handbook*, 2005. Available at http://www.altera.com/literature/list_stx2.jsp

[Betz99]   V. Betz, J. Rose, and A. Marquardt, A*rchitecture and CAD for Deep-Submicron FPGAs*, Kluwer Academic Publishers, Norwell, MA, February 1999.

[Brown96]   S. Brown, M. Khellah, and G. Lemieux, Segmented routing for speed-performance and routability in field-programmable gate arrays, *Journal of VLSI Design*, 4(4): 275–291, 1996.

[Chang96]   Y. -W. Chang, D. Wong, and C. Wong, Universal switch modules for FPGA design, in *ACM Transactions on Design Automation of Electronic Systems*, Vol. 1, NY, January 1996, pp. 80–101.

[Cong98]   J. Cong and S. Xu, Technology mapping for FPGAs with embedded memory blocks, in *Proceedings of the 6th ACM/SIGDA International Symposium on Field Programmable Gate Arrays*, pp. 179–188, Monterey, CA, 1998.

[Dehon05]   A. DeHon, Design of programmable interconnect for sublithographic programmable logic arrays, in *ACM/SIGDA International Symposium on Field-Programmable Gate Arrays*, Monterey, CA, February 2005, pp. 127–137.

[Ebeling96]   C. Ebeling, D. Conquist, and P. Franklin, RaPiD—Reconfigurable pipelined datapath, in *International Conference on Field-Programmable Logic and Applications*, Darmstadt, Germany, 1996, pp. 126–135.

[Ferrera04]   S. P. Ferrera and N. Carter, A magnoelectronic macrocell employing reconfigurable threshold logic, in *ACM/SIGDA International Symposium on Field-Programmable Gate Arrays*, Monterey, CA, February 2004, pp. 143–154.

[Goldstein00] S. C. Goldstein, H. Schmit, M. Budiu, S. Cadambi, M. Moe, and R. Taylor, PipeRench: A reconfigurable architecture and compiler, *Computer*, 33(4): 70–77, 2000.

[Hauck00]   S. Hauck, M. M. Hosler, and T. W. Fry, High-performance carry chains for FPGAs, *IEEE Transactions on VLSI Systems*, 8(2): 138–147, April, 2000.

[Lattice05]   Lattice Semiconductor Corp., *LatticeXP Datasheet*, 2005. Available at http://www.latticesemi.com/lit/docs/datasheets/fpga/DS1001.pdf

[Leijten03]   K. Leijten-Nowak and J. van Meerbergen, An FPGA architecture with enhanced datapath functionality, in *ACM/SIGDA International Symposium on Field-Programmable Gate Arrays*, Monterey, CA, February 2003, pp. 195–204.

[Lemieux04a] G. Lemieux and D. Lewis, *Design of Interconnection Networks for Programmable Logic*, Kluwer Academic Publishers, Norwell, MA, November 2004.

[Lemieux04b] G. Lemieux, E. Lee, M. Tom, and A. Yu, Directional and single-driver wires in FPGA interconnect, in *IEEE International Conference on Field-Programmable Technology*, Brisbane, Australia, December 2004, pp. 41–48.

[Lewis05]   D. Lewis, E. Ahmed, G. Baeckler, V. Betz, M. Bourgeault, D. Cashman, D. Galloway, M. Hutton, C. Lane, A. Lee, P. Leventis, S. Marquardt, C. McClintock, K. Padalia, B. Pedersen, G. Powell, B. Ratchev, S. Reddy, J. Schleicher, K. Stevens, R. Yuan, R. Cliff, and J. Rose, The Stratix II logic and routing architecture, in *ACM/SIGDA International Symposium on FPGAs*, Monterey, CA, February 2005, pp 14–20.

[Lin94]   C. -C. Lin, M. Marek-Sadowska, and D. Gatlin, Universal logic gate for FPGA design, in *Proceedings of the 1994 IEEE/ACM International Conference on Computer-Aided Design*, San Jose, CA, November 1994, pp. 164–168.

[Marquardt00] A. Marquardt, V. Betz, and J. Rose, Speed and area trade-offs in cluster-based FPGA architectures, *IEEE Transactions on VLSI*, 8(1): 84–93, February 2000.

[Masud99]   M. I. Masud and S. J. E. Wilton, A new switch block for segmented FPGAs, in *International Workshop on Field Programmable Logic and Applications*, Glasgow, U.K., August 1999, pp. 274–281.

[Mei03]   B. Mei, S. Vernalde, D. Verkest, H. De Man, and R. Lauwereins, ADRES: An architecture with tightly coupled VLIW processor and coarse-grained reconfigurable matrix, in *International Conference on Field-Programmable Logic and Applications*, Lisbon, Portugal, 2003, pp. 61–70.

[Oldridge05]   S. W. Oldridge and S. J. E. Wilton, A novel FPGA architecture supporting wide, shallow memories, *IEEE Transactions on Very-Large Scale Integration (VLSI) Systems*, 13(6): 758–762, June 2005.

[Quick05]   Quicklogic, *Eclipse II Family Data Sheet*, 2005. Available at http://www.quicklogic.com/images/eclipse2_family_DS.pdf

[Rose90]   J. S. Rose, R. J. Francis, D. Lewis, and P. Chow, Architecture of field-programmable gate arrays: The effect of logic block functionality on area efficiency, *IEEE Journal of Solid-State Circuits*, 25(5): 1217–1225, October 1990.

[Rose93]   J. Rose, A. El Gamal, and A. Sangiovanni-Vincentelli, Architecture of field-programmable gate arrays, *Proceedings of the IEEE*, 81(7): 1013–1029, July 1993.

[Singh92]   S. Singh, J. Rose, P. Chow, and D. Lewis, The effect of logic block architecture on FPGA performance, *IEEE Journal of Solid-State Circuits*, 27(3): 281–287, March 1992.

[Singh00]   H. Singh, M. -H. Lee, G. Lu, F. Kurdahi, N. Bagherzadeh, and E. Chaves, MorphoSys: An integrated reconfigurable system for dataparallel and compute intensive applications, *IEEE Transactions on Computers*, 49(5): 465–481, 2000.

[Singh01a]   A. Singh, A. Mukherjee, and M. Marek-Sadowska, Interconnect pipeling in a throughput-intensive FPGA architecture, in *ACM/SIGDA International Symposium on Field-Programmable Gate Arrays*, Monterey, CA, February 2001, pp. 153–160.

[Singh01b]   D. P. Singh and S. D. Brown, The case for registered routing switches in field programmable gate arrays, in *ACM/SIGDA International Symposium on Field-Programmable Gate Arrays*, Monterey, CA, February 2001, pp. 161–172.

[Sivaswamy05] S. Sivaswamy, G. Wang, C. Ababei, K. Bazargan, R. Kastner, and E. Bozorgzadeh, HARP: Hardwired routing pattern FPGAs, in *ACM International Symposium on Filed Programmable Gate Arrays*, Monterey, CA, February 2005, pp. 21–32.

[Trimberger94] S. Trimberger, *Field-Programmable Gate Array Technology*, Kluwer Academic Publishers, Norwell, MA, 1994.

[Weaver04]   N. Weaver, J. Hauser, and J. Wawrzynek, The SFRA: A corner-turn FPGA architecture, in *ACM/SIGDA International Symposium on FPGAs*, February 2004, pp. 3–12.

[Wilton00]   S. J. E. Wilton, Hetergenous technology mapping for area reduction in FPGAs with embedded memory arrays, *IEEE Transactions on Computer-Aided Design of Integrated Circuits and Systems*, 19(1):56–68, 2000.

[Wilton97]   S. J. E. Wilton, Architecture and algorithms for field-programmable gate arrays with embedded memory, PhD thesis, University of Toronto, Toronto, Ontario, Canada, 1997.

[Wilton99]   S. J. E. Wilton, J. Rose, and Z. G. Vranesic, The memory/logic interface in FPGA's with large embedded memory arrays, *IEEE Transactions on Very-Large Scale Integration Systems*, 7(1):80–91, March 1999.

[Xilinx05a]   Xilinx Corp., *Virtex-4 Users Guide*, 2005. Available at http://www.xilinx.com/support/documentation/user_guides/ug070.pdf

[Xilinx05b]   Xilinx Corp., *Processor IP Reference Guide*, February 2005.

[Ye05]   A. G. Ye and J. Rose, Using bus-based connections to improve field-programmable gate array density for implementing datapath circuits, in *ACM/SIGDA Symposium on FPGAs*, February 2005, Monterey, CA, pp 3–13.

[Zeidman02]   B. Zeidman and R. Zeidman, *Designing with FPGAs and CPLDs*, CMP Books, Upper Saddle River, NJ, 2002.

46 FPGA Technology Mapping, Placement, and Routing

Kia Bazargan

CONTENTS

46.1 INTRODUCTION

Computer-aided design (CAD) tools for field-programmable gate arrays (FPGAs) primarily emerged as extensions of their application-specific integrated circuit (ASIC) counterparts in the 1980s because of the relative maturity of the ASIC CAD tools at that time. Traditional logic optimization techniques, simulated-annealing-based placement algorithms, and maze routing methods were common in the FPGA world. But as FPGA architecture developed distinct features both in terms of logic and routing architectures, FPGA CAD tools evolved into today's FPGA design flows that are highly optimized for specific characteristics of FPGA devices. More specialized timing models, technology mapping

---

This work is supported in part by the National Science Foundation under grant CCF-0347891.

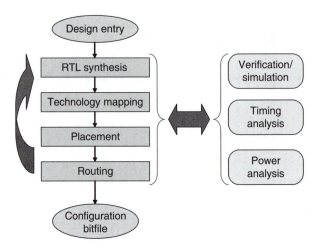

FIGURE 46.1 Typical FPGA flow.

solutions, and placement and routing strategies are needed to ensure high-quality mapping of circuits to FPGAs.

Figure 46.1 shows a common design flow for FPGA designs. The high-level description of the FPGA design is fed to a register transfer level (RTL) synthesis tool that performs technology-independent logic optimization. The synthesis tool might detect opportunities for utilizing special-purpose logic gates within the FPGA logic fabric. Examples are carry chains, high-fanin sum-of-product gates, and embedded multiplier (see Sections 45.3.1.2 and 45.3.2).

The functional gates of the technology-independent optimized design are mapped to FPGA lookup tables (LUTs) (see Section 45.3.1), a process called technology mapping. Clustering of the LUTs is performed next (see Section 45.3.2). Placement and routing steps follow clustering. Floorplanning may or may not precede placement. Each of these steps would use timing and power analysis engines to better optimize the design. Furthermore, the user might simulate or perform formal verifications at various steps of the design cycle. If timing or power constraints are not met, the design flow might backtrack to a previous step. For example, if routing fails due to high congestion, then placement might be attempted again with different parameters.

The rest of the chapter is organized into four sections. FPGA-specific technology mapping and clustering algorithms are covered in Section 46.2.1. Sections 46.3 and 46.4 cover floorplanning and placement algorithms. We conclude the chapter by discussing routing algorithms in Section 46.5.

46.2 TECHNOLOGY MAPPING AND CLUSTERING

Technology mapping converts a logic circuit into a netlist of FPGA K-LUTs and their connections. A K-LUT is usually implemented as a K-input, one output static random-access memory (SRAM) block. By writing the truth table of a Boolean function in the K-LUT, we can implement any function that has K or fewer inputs regardless of the complexity of the function. Neighboring LUTs can be clustered into local groups with dedicated fast routing resources to improve the delay of the circuit. Clustering algorithms are used to group together local LUTs to minimize connection delays. Later in the design flow, these clusters are used as input to the placement step. Some placement algorithms might never touch a cluster, but some other placement methods (such as the ones presented in Section 46.4.3) might move individual logic blocks from one cluster to another to improve timing, power, etc.

Given the fact that technology mapping considering area and delay optimization is NP-hard, Cong and Minkovich [1] synthesize benchmarks with known optimal or upper-bound technology mapping solutions and test state-of-the-art FPGA synthesis algorithms to see how far these algorithms are from producing optimal solutions (a preliminary version of their work appeared in the FPGA 2007 conference). They show that current technology mapping solutions are close to optimal (between 3 and 22 percent away, see Table III in Ref. [1]) while logic optimization methods have much room for improvement. Although some argue that the generated benchmarks are artificial and do not reflect characteristics of large industry benchmarks, nevertheless the work in Ref. [1] gives us insights into what needs to be done to improve existing CAD algorithms. Our goal in the next two sections is to introduce basic technology mapping and clustering algorithms so that the reader can better understand placement and routing algorithms for FPGAs. Many great technology mapping algorithms (such as DAOmap [2], ABC [3], and the work by Mishchenko et al. [4]) are not discussed here.

46.2.1 TECHNOLOGY MAPPING

A major breakthrough in the FPGA technology mapping came about in 1994 with the introduction of the FlowMap tool [5]. Library-based ASIC technology mapping (that maps a logic network to gates such as AND, OR, etc.) for depth minimization was known to be NP-hard, but Cong et al. proved that the K-LUT technology mapping can be done in $O(KVE)$, where V and E are the number of nodes (gates) and edges (wires) in the circuit, respectively. The FlowMap algorithm traverses the circuit graph containing simple gates and their connections in a breadth-first search fashion and determines depth-optimal mappings of the fanin cones of the nodes as it progresses toward primary outputs. The fanin cone of a node is the set of all gates from the circuit primary inputs (input pads) to the node itself.

The algorithm uses the notion of K-feasible cuts to find K-LUT mappings of a subcircuit. Figure 46.2a shows an example subgraph in which a cut separates the nodes into disjoint sets X and $\overline{X}$ where only three nodes in set X provide inputs to nodes in $\overline{X}$, that is, the nodes that are drawn using thick lines. Cut $(X, \overline{X})$ is said to be K-feasible for $K \leq 3$. All the nodes in set $\overline{X}$ can be mapped into one 3-LUT, which gets its input values from the LUTs that implement the three boundary nodes in X and their fanin cones.

The labels on the nodes in Figure 46.2a show the depth of the minimum depth K-LUT mapping of the input cone of the node. The authors prove that for a node t, the minimum depth is either the maximum label l in $\overline{X}$, or $l+1$.[*] Consider an example graph for another circuit shown in Figure 46.2b.

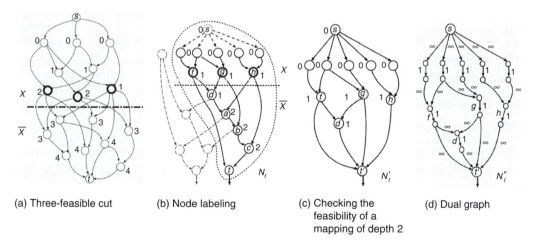

(a) Three-feasible cut   (b) Node labeling   (c) Checking the feasibility of a mapping of depth 2   (d) Dual graph

FIGURE 46.2 Flowmap mapping steps. (From Cong, J. and Ding, Y., *IEEE Trans. Comput. Aided Des. Integrated Circuits Syst.*, 13, 1, 1994. Copyright IEEE 1994. With permission.)

---

[*] If the new node t can be packed with the rest of the nodes with label l, then the depth of LUTs used in implementing the circuit up to this point would not increase. Otherwise, a new LUT with depth $l+1$ has to be allocated to house the new node t.

In a breadth-first search traversal on subgraph N_t, when we get to node t, the question is whether we can pack t with nodes a, b, c (which have the maximum depth of l) in one K-LUT.

We can create an auxiliary graph N_t' (shown in Figure 46.2c, note that nodes with labels correspond to their counterpart nodes in Figure 46.2b with the same labels), which replaces a, b, c, t with one node t' and see if t'—and possibly other nodes—can be packed in one K-LUT. Node t' can be mapped to a K-LUT if we can find a cut $(X, \overline{X})$ where $t' \in \overline{X}$ and at most K nodes in X provide input to nodes in $\overline{X}$. Network flow algorithms can be used to answer this question. We can model one LUT in the fanin cone as a flow of one unit, and look for a maximum flow of K-units at the sink node. If the maximum flow is K, it means that we have found a cut with at most K-LUTs as inputs, and anything below the cut can be packed into a K-LUT. More details are provided next. Subgraph N_t' can be transformed to a dual graph N_t'' (Figure 46.2d) in which each node y is replaced by two nodes y_i and y_o that are connected by an edge of weight 1. An edge (y, z) in N_t' corresponds to edge (y_o, z_i) in N_t'' with an infinite edge weight. If a flow of K units can be found in N_t'', then at most K nodes in X provide inputs to nodes in $\overline{X}$, which means node t in the original N_t graph can indeed be packed with other nodes with the maximum label. The authors introduce variations on the original technology mapping algorithm to minimize area as a secondary objective.

46.2.2 CLUSTERING

Today's FPGAs cluster LUTs into groups and provide fast routing resources for intracluster connections. When two LUTs are assigned to one cluster, their connections can use the fast routing resources within the cluster, and hence reduce the delay on the connection. On the other hand, if two LUTs are in two separate clusters, they have to use intracluster routing resources that are more scarce and more costly in terms of delay. Placement and routing algorithms are needed to balance the usage of intracluster routing resources (see Sections 46.4 and 46.5).

Many clustering algorithms were introduced in the past decade. Most work by first selecting a seed and then choosing LUTs to cluster with the seed. The difference between various clustering algorithms is in their criteria for choosing the seed node and the way other nodes are chosen to be absorbed by the seed. The clustering algorithm used in the popular versatile placement and routing (VPR) tool [6] is called T-VPack [7], which is an extension of the earlier packing algorithm VPack.

VPack chooses LUTs with high number of input connections as initial seeds for clusters. The criteria for packing a node B into a cluster C is the attraction of the node, defined as the number of nets that are shared between node B and nodes inside C. The more sharing there is between nodes within a cluster, the less routing demand is needed to connect clusters.

T-VPack is the timing-driven version of VPack and extends the definition of the attraction of a node to include timing criticality of nets connecting the node to those packed into the cluster. Timing criticality of a net i is defined as $1 - [\text{slack}(i)/\text{MaxSlack}]$. If two nodes have equal net criticality values connecting them to nodes packed into a cluster, then the one through which more critical paths pass is chosen to be packed into the cluster first. The results in Ref. [7] show that clusters of size 7–10 provide the best area/delay tradeoff.

Clustering algorithms such as RPack [8] and the work by Singh et al. [9] improve routability of the clustered circuit by introducing absorption costs that try to weigh nodes based on how promising they are in absorbing more nets into the cluster. The authors in Ref. [9] define connectivity factor (c) of a LUT x as $c(x) = \text{separation}(x)/\text{degree}(x)^2$, where separation of a LUT is the number of LUTs adjacent to it. Figure 46.3a shows node A with a separation value of 18, degree of 4, and connectivity of 1.125. Figure 46.3b shows node B with the same degree as A, but with a smaller separation and hence smaller connectivity. Node A cannot absorb any nets if one node from each net is clustered into the same cluster as A. On the other hand, node B can absorb all the nets shown in Figure 46.3 by including one node from each net in its cluster. The selection of the seed node in Singh et al. work is done by lexicographically sorting nodes by their (degree, −connectivity) values and choosing the ones with highest values as initial seeds (T-VPack used only the degree values).

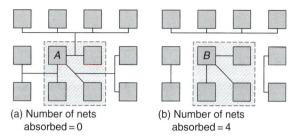

(a) Number of nets   (b) Number of nets
    absorbed = 0   absorbed = 4

FIGURE 46.3 Examples illustrating the usefulness of the connectivity factor. (Based on Singh, A. and Marek-Sadowska, M., *Proceedings of the ACM/SIGDA International Symposium on Field Programmable Gate Arrays*, 59–66, 2002. With permission.)

Nodes are greedily packed into seed clusters based on how many nets they absorb, with higher priority given to the nets with fewer terminals. To guarantee spatial uniformity of the clustered netlist, the authors limit the number of available pins to a cluster so that the number of logic blocks inside a cluster and the number of connections to the nodes within the cluster follow Rent's rule. Doing so effectively depopulates clusters to reduce overall intercluster routing demands. Such strategies are in line with what DeHon's study [10] on routing requirements of FPGA circuits suggested. Because interconnect resources (switches and buffers) consume most of the silicon area of an FPGA (80–90 percent), sometimes it is beneficial to underutilize clusters to reduce routing demand in congested regions of the FPGA array.

46.3 FLOORPLANNING

Floorplanning is used on FPGAs to speed up the placement process or to place hard macros with prespecified shapes. The traditional FPGA floorplanning problem is discussed in Section 46.3.1. Another class of floorplanning algorithms for FPGAs is the ones that deal with heterogeneous resource types. An example of this approach is the work by Cheng and Wong [11], to be covered in Section 46.3.2. A third class of floorplanning for FPGAs addresses dynamically reconfigurable systems in which modules are added or removed at runtime, requiring fast, on-the-fly modification of the floorplan. These approaches are discussed in Section 46.3.3.

46.3.1 HIERARCHICAL METHODS

Sankar and Rose [12] first use a bottom-up clustering method to build larger clusters out of logic blocks (refer to Section 46.2.2). Then they use a hierarchical simulated annealing algorithm to speed up the placement compared to a flat annealing methodology. They show trade-offs between placement runtime and quality.

While clustering the circuit into larger subcircuits, they limit the shape and size of the clusters to prespecified values. The leaves of the clustering tree are the logic blocks and the first level of the tree are nodes that combine exactly two leaves. All level-one nodes will be placed in 1×2 regions, that is, on two adjacent clusters in the same row. The next level of hierarchy clusters two level 1 clusters and will be placed as 2×2 squares. Figure 46.4 shows the clustering and placement conceptually. Such restrictions on the clustering and placement steps would limit the ability of the algorithms to search a larger solution space compared to an unrestricted version of the problem, but on the other hand relieve the algorithm designers of dealing with the sizing problem during the floorplanning process, described in Section 9.4.1.

The work by Emmert and Bhatia [13] too starts by clustering the logic elements into larger subcircuits. The input to their flow is a list of macros, each macro being either a logic block, or a set of logic blocks with a list of predefined shapes. An example of a macro is a multiplier with two shape options, one for minimum area, the other for minimum delay.

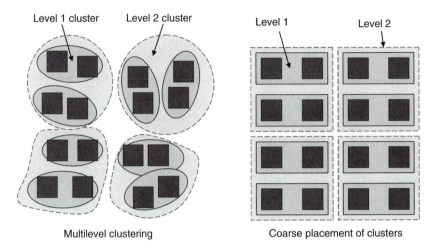

FIGURE 46.4 Multilevel clustering and placement. (Based on Sankar, Y. and Rose, J., *Proceedings of the ACM/SIGDA International Symposium on Field Programmable Gate Arrays*, 157–166, 1999. With permission.)

The flow maintains a list of clusters of macros, and a set of buckets that correspond to regions on the FPGA that have to house one cluster each. The buckets are all of the same shape, but unlike the work by Sankar and Rose [12], their shapes are not predetermined by the algorithm. Instead, the width (height) of the buckets is determined by the maximum width (height) of all macros initially, and as clustering progresses, the width might be increased so that it can fit larger clusters. For example, the algorithm could start with buckets of size 3×2, and after a clustering step merge them in pairs to get buckets of size 6×2 (it is not clear from Ref. [12] if the bucket sizes in this example could be set to 3×4 too or not, but the initial bucket shapes is determined by the maximum macro width and height). The iterative process of clustering macros and increasing the size of the buckets is repeated until the number of clusters becomes less than or equal to the number of buckets. Because the width and height requirements of clusters are calculated using an upper bound method, the buckets are guaranteed to have room for all clusters once there are at least as many buckets as there are clusters.

Once the clustering phase is done, a tabu-search* cluster placement step follows. In this step, neighboring clusters are swapped using force-directed moves, as in Chapter 18. Once a cluster is moved, it is locked and will not be swapped until a prespecified number of other moves are attempted. The force-directed moves use connections between clusters as forces pulling highly connected cluster closer together. Toward the end of the intercluster placement phase, critical edges are assigned higher weights in the force calculations, and candidate clusters for swapping are chosen based on their timing criticality rank. Hence, the intercluster placement step starts by minimizing average wirelength, and in its second phase minimizes timing-critical edges.

The intercluster placement is done in three phases: first the hard macros are placed next to each other (same Y-coordinate), then soft macros are assigned coordinates, and finally soft macro shapes might be changed to fit all macros within the bucket. Figure 46.5 shows an example intercluster placement within a bucket of size 12×9, where modules m_{16}, m_{19}, m_{27}, and m_{41} are hard macros, and the rest of the modules are soft macros. Note that the feasibility checks during clustering and bucket resizing guarantees that hard macros can be placed within their assigned buckets.

During hard macro placement, the center of gravity of the x-coordinate of all modules connected to a hard macro is calculated. Then hard macros are sorted based on the x-coordinate of the center of gravity, and placed from the right edge of the bucket to the left in decreasing order of the center of

---

* Tabu search refers to a heuristic search algorithm in which certain moves are tried and a lock is placed on a move after it is tried so that it cannot be attempted before a certain number of other moves are applied first. It is a fast solution space exploration method that tries to avoid getting stuck in local minima by locking moves.

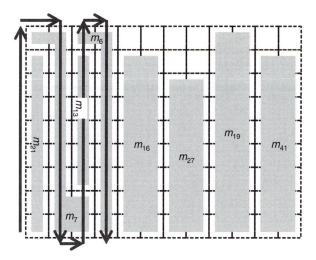

FIGURE 46.5 Intercluster placement example. (Based on Emmert, J. M. and Bhatia, D., *Proceedings of the ACM/SIGDA International Symposium on Field Programmable Gate Arrays*, 47–56, 1999. With permission.)

gravity coordinates. Soft macros are placed from left to right, filling logic block locations as shown by the arrow in Figure 46.5. A greedy method moves logic blocks to minimize wirelength.

46.3.2 FLOORPLANNING ON FPGAs WITH HETEROGENEOUS RESOURCES

Cheng and Wong [11] consider the floorplanning problem on FPGAs with heterogeneous resources such as memory blocks and embedded multipliers, described in Sections 45.5 and 45.6, respectively. The input to the problem is a set of modules with a vector of resource requirements, for example, $\phi_i = (c_i, r_i, m_i)$, where ϕ_i is the resource requirement vector of module i, and c_i, r_i, and m_i are the number of units of logic, RAM block, and embedded multiplier units that the module needs. The floorplanning problem can be formulated as assigning nonoverlapping regions to the modules such that each region satisfies resource requirements of the module that is assigned to it, all modules are assigned regions on the chip, and a given cost function such as wirelength is minimized.

Cheng and Wong [11] use slicing floorplans to explore the search space, ensuring the resource requirements are met when assigning locations and sizing the module, as in Section 9.4.1. A post-processing step follows that compacts modules by changing their shape to reduce the area of the floorplan. An example floorplan generated by this method is shown in Figure 46.6.

To ensure resource requirements are met, the authors define the irreducible realization list (IRL) for each module at any location (x, y) as a list $L(\theta, x, y) = \{r|r \in \Re_\theta, x(r) = x \wedge y(r) = y\}$, where r is defined as a rectangle $r = (x, y, w, h)$ with bottom-left coordinates (x, y) and dimensions (w, h) such that it satisfies resource requirements of the module. Another condition for the IRL of a module is that it should be the set of nondominant rectangles that satisfy resource requirements of the module (i.e., no other rectangle at location (x, y) can be found that has a smaller width and a smaller height and satisfies resource requirements of the module). Figure 46.7 shows IRLs at coordinates $(4, 1)$ and $(10, 0)$ for a module with resource requirement vector $\phi = (12, 1, 1)$. In Figure 46.7, dark modules are RAM blocks, and long white modules are multipliers.

The heterogeneous floorplanning problem discussed in Ref. [11] is different from the traditional slicing floorplanning problem described in Chapter 9. Because in the FPGA problem, the shapes a module can take depend on the location it is placed at (see the example of Figure 46.7), whereas in the traditional problem formulation, the list of the shapes a module can take is prespecified. This difference causes challenges when combining two subfloorplans. Care must be taken to ensure that the assigned shape of a subfloorplan during the bottom-up sizing process satisfies resource

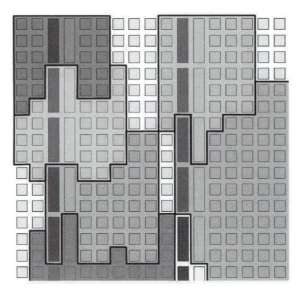

FIGURE 46.6 Floorplanning example. (Based on Cheng, L. and Wong, M. D. F., *Proceedings of the IEEE/ACM International Conference on Computer-Aided Design*, 292–299, 2004. With permission.)

requirements of the modules in the subfloorplans. The authors in Ref. [11] prove that generating the combined shape of two subfloorplans can be done in $O(l \log l)$, where $l = \max(W, H)$, in which W and H correspond to the chip width and height, respectively.

A modified slicing-tree annealing-based floorplanning algorithm is used to generate floorplans. The sizing process takes care of resource requirements as discussed above, and a cost function that includes floorplan area and wirelength as well as the sum of module aspect ratios is utilized. Because the FPGA fabric is tile-based, the authors can do a significant amount of preprocessing on each module, finding its IRL based on the (x, y) coordinate within a tile, and then utilizing the data during floorplanning. A postprocessing step follows that compacts the floorplan (Figure 46.7). Interested readers are referred to Ref. [11] for details on the compaction process.

46.3.3 DYNAMIC FLOORPLANNING

Bazargan et al. introduced a floorplanning method for dynamically reconfigurable systems in Ref. [14]. Such systems allow modules to be loaded and unloaded on-the-fly to cater to applications'

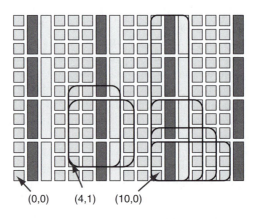

(0,0)   (4,1)   (10,0)

FIGURE 46.7 Example of an IRL. (Based on Cheng, L. and Wong, M. D. F., *Proceedings of the IEEE/ACM International Conference on Computer-Aided Design*, 292–299, 2004. With permission.)

different needs at various points in runtime. A module is unloaded to free up space for future modules to be loaded onto the system. A module corresponds to a set of datapath operations such as adders and multipliers that perform computations in a program's basic block (refer to Section 46.4.4 for a discussion on basic block modules). Limited versions of such systems have been implemented in the past [15,16].

The method in Ref. [14] divides the chip into an explicit list of rectangular empty regions, called the list of maximal empty rectangles, and when a new module is to be placed on the chip, its dimensions are compared against the empty rectangles to see if it fits in any of them. Interconnections between large modules are ignored in this work, which means the floorplanning problem can be reduced to a two-dimensional bin-packing problem.* The number of empty rectangles in an arbitrary floorplan with the ability to remove as well as add modules is quadratic in terms of the number of active modules present on the chip in the worst case [14]. As a result, the authors propose to keep a linear list of empty regions to speed up the floorplanning process at the cost of quality. If a suboptimal list is used, then there might be cases that an arriving module can fit in an empty region, but the empty region is not present in the maintained list of empty rectangles. A number of heuristics are also provided that try to choose an empty rectangle to house a new module that maximizes the chances that large enough empty regions are available to future modules.

Handa and Vemuri [17] observe that even though the number of maximal empty rectangles could be quadratic in theory, in practice the number is more likely to be linear in terms of the number of active modules on the chip. Instead of keeping an explicit list of empty rectangles, they encode the FPGA area using a smart data structure that can quickly determine if an empty region is large enough to house an incoming module.

An example floorplan is shown in Figure 46.8. A positive number at a logic block location indicates the height of the empty region above the logic block, and a negative number can be used to find the distance to the right edge of a module. These numbers are used in obtaining maximal staircases, which are data structures that help keep track of empty regions without explicitly storing the location and dimensions of every maximal empty rectangle. Such a methodology would improve runtime on average (worst-case delay is still quadratic).

Unlike Bazargan et al. [14] and Handa and Vemuri [17] who assume that the floorplanning decisions must be taken at runtime, Singhal and Bozorgzadeh [18] assume that the flow of computations

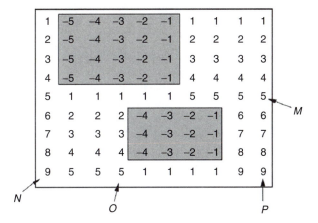

FIGURE 46.8 Encoding the area of the floorplan. (From Handa, M. and Vemuri, R., *Proceedings of the ACM/IEEE Design Automation Conference*, pp. 960–965, 2004. With permission.)

---

* In real life applications, interconnections between modules cannot be ignored. Even if modules do not communicate directly, they need to get the input data and write the results into memory resources and buffers on the FPGA. Such interactions are ignored in both Refs. [14,17].

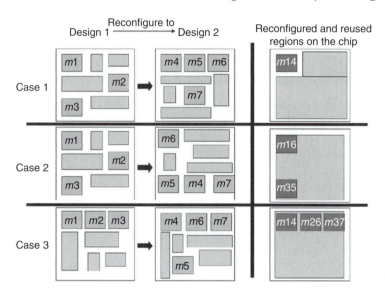

FIGURE 46.9 Reusing partial configurations. (From Singhal, L. and Bozorgzadeh, E., *Proceedings of the 2006 International Conference on Field Programmable Logic and Applications*, 2006. With permission.)

is known a priori and floorplanning for multiple configurations can be done at compile time. The goal of their approach is to floorplan multiple designs so that the number of shared modules between consecutive configurations is maximized while area is minimized and timing constraints are met. Figure 46.9 shows three floorplan examples for a two-configuration system. In Figure 46.9, design 1 is first loaded on the FPGA, followed by design 2. Assuming that modules $m1$, $m2, \ldots, m7$ are the same, case 1 in Figure 46.9 only shares the configuration of $m1$ and $m4$, while case 3 shares three modules when doing a transition from design 1 to design 2. As a result, case 3 requires the least amount of configuration time. The challenge is to share as many modules as possible between the two floorplans, but at the same time not to increase critical path delay on any of the configurations.

They propose a new floorplanning data structure called multilayer sequence pairs, which as the name suggests is an extension of the sequence pair data structure, described in Section 11.5. Consider two designs $D1$ and $D2$. Assuming that modules s_1, $s_2, \ldots, s_k$ are shared between the two designs, and $D1$ has exclusive modules m_1, m_2, $\ldots$, m_M and $D2$ has exclusive modules n_1, n_2, $\ldots$, n_N, they build one sequence pair consisting of modules $\{s_1, \ldots, s_k\} \cup \{m_1, \ldots, m_M\} \cup \{n_1, \ldots, n_N\}$. Floorplanning moves are similar to regular sequence pair moves. However, when building horizontal and vertical constraint graphs, edges are not added between exclusive modules from one design to the other. As a result, by construction, the shared modules are placed at the same location in the two designs. The cost function includes terms relating to overall area, aspect ratio, configuration length, wirelength of the two designs, and their congestions. They compare their method to a method that first floorplans one design independently of the other design, and then fixes the location of the shared modules in the floorplanning of the second design. Their approach outperforms the simplistic method because in their approach they optimize the two floorplans simultaneously. Although they showed the results on only two configurations, their approach could be extended to multiple configurations.

46.4 PLACEMENT

Early FPGA placement algorithms emerged as extensions of their ASIC counterparts. Simulated annealing was the optimization engine of choice, and still is the most common method for academic placement engines. Even though major strides have been taken in improving the quality of FPGA placement tools, there is still much room for improvement as shown in Ref. [19]. The authors first synthetically generated a number of circuits with known optimal solution, and then ran a number of FPGA placement algorithms on the circuits and showed that the length of a longest path could be from 10 to 18 percent worse than the optimal solution on the average, and between 34 and 53 percent longer in the worst case. These results are for the case in which only one path is timing-critical. If multiple critical paths are present in the circuit, then the results of existing FPGA placement algorithms are on average 23–35 percent worse than the optimal on average, and 41–48 percent worse in the worst case.

46.4.1   Island-Style FPGA Placement

There are a number of methods used in the placement of FPGAs. The dominant method is based on a simulated annealing engine, as in Chapter 16. There are also partitioning-based and hierarchical methods that we discuss later in this subsection.

Versatile placement and routing [6] is arguably the most popular FPGA placement and routing tool. It is widely used in academic and industry research projects. VPR originally was developed to help FPGA architecture designers place and route circuits with various architectural parameters (e.g., switch-block architecture, number of tracks to which the input pins of logic blocks connect [F_c], logic output F_c, etc.). Its flow reads an architectural description file along with the technology-mapped netlist.

VPR uses a simulate annealing engine to minimize wirelength and congestion. The cost function that the annealing algorithm uses is

$$\text{WiringCost} = \sum_{n=1}^{N_{\text{nets}}} q\,(n) \left[\frac{\text{bb}_x\,(n)}{C_{\text{av},x}\,(n)} + \frac{\text{bb}_y\,(n)}{C_{\text{av},y}\,(n)} \right] \tag{46.1}$$

where
   $q(n)$ is a weighting factor that adjusts the wirelength estimation as a function of a net's number of terminals
   bb_x and bb_y are the horizontal and vertical spans of a net's bounding box
   $C_{\text{av},x}$ and $C_{\text{av},y}$ are the average channel capacities in the x and y directions over the bounding box of net n

Function $q(n)$ is defined in Equation 46.2, where $T(n)$ is the number of terminals of net n. The function is equal to 1 for nets with three or fewer terminals, and gradually increases to 2.79 for nets that have at most 50 terminals, and linearly increases for nets with more than 50 terminals.

$$q\,(n) = \begin{cases} 1 & T\,(n) \leq 3 \\ \text{RISA}\,[T\,(n)] & 3 < T\,(n) \leq 50 \\ 2.79 + 0.02616\,[T\,(n) - 50] & T\,(n) > 50 \end{cases} \tag{46.2}$$

Internally, VPR uses a table RISA[] to lookup the value of q for nets that have fewer than 50 terminals. The values in the table come from the RISA routability model [20]. Essentially, RISA models the amount of routing resource sharing when the number of terminals of a net increases. Annealing parameters used in VPR automatically adjust to different circuit sizes and costs to achieve high-quality placements. Furthermore, the parameters change dynamically in response to improvements in cost.

The timing-driven version of VPR is called TVPR [21] (its placement algorithm is called T-VPlace after VPR's VPlace). TVPR optimizes for wirelength and timing simultaneously. The delay of a net is estimated using an optimistic delay model. For any bounding box that spans from coordinates (0, 0) to (x, y), the router is invoked on the FPGA architecture where all routing resources are free and a source and a sink are placed at $(0, 0)$ and (x, y), respectively. Because all routing resources are available, the best combination of wire segments and switches will be used to route the net with the smallest possible delay. The delay achieved by the router is recorded in a table at indices $[x, y]$. The process is repeated for $1 \leq x \leq W$ and $1 \leq y \leq H$, where W and H are the width and the height of the FPGA chip. The values in the table are optimistic because a net might not be routable using the best routing resources because of congestion. Furthermore, because FPGAs are built as arrays of tiles, the values in the delay table are valid for any starting point, and not just (0,0). So the table really stores the values $(\Delta x, \Delta y)$. The delay between a source node i and sink node j of a two-terminal net is therefore $d(i, j) = \text{TableLookup}(|x_i - x_j|, |y_i - y_j|)$, where x_i and x_j are the x-coordinates of nodes i and j and TableLookup is the array storing the precomputed delays. The delay values can be used as lower bound estimations for individual sinks of multiterminal nets. A multifanout net can be broken into two-terminal (source, sink) nets. Using the table on individual sinks is valid because buffers are heavily used in FPGA routing trees, effectively cutting off the branches of a route and converting it into two-terminal routes.

The timing, wirelength, and congestion costs are combined in TVPR. The timing cost is calculated as a weighted sum of delays of nets. The timing cost of a net between source i and sink j is calculated as

$$\text{NetTimingCost}(i, j) = d(i, j) \cdot \text{criticality}(i, j)^{\beta} \tag{46.3}$$

$$\text{criticality}(i, j) = 1 - \text{slack}(i, j)/D_{\max} \tag{46.4}$$

where
  slack(i, j) is calculated using static timing analysis, described in Section 3.1.1.3
  $D_{\max}$ is the critical path delay

Parameter β can be tuned by the user. The timing cost component is defined as TimingCost $= \Sigma_{i,j}$ NetTimingCost(i, j). The overall cost function in TVPR is defined as

$$\Delta \text{Cost} = \lambda \frac{\Delta \text{TimingCost}}{\text{PrevTimingCost}} + (1 - \lambda) \frac{\Delta \text{WiringCost}}{\text{PrevWiringCost}} \tag{46.5}$$

where λ can be tuned to trade off between timing and congestion. ΔCost is used during the annealing decision process to accept or reject a move based on its improvement of wiring and timing costs over the previous solution.

The timing delay table enables TVPR to balance a reasonable strike between faster runtime and acceptable lower bound estimation on the delays of all nets. However, using the lower bound during placement is bound to introduce a disconnect between what the placement engine thinks the router is going to do and what it actually does during routing. To overcome the discrepancy between the placement's notion of net delays and the actual delays after routing, Nag and Rutenbar [22] perform detailed routing at every step of the placement. The method is computationally expensive but shows that 8–15 percent improvements in delay can be achieved when using routing inside the placement loop.

Maidee et al. [23] took a different approach in their partitioning-based placement for FPGAs (PPFF) placement tool: they first placed and routed sample benchmarks and found empirical relationships between a net's wirelength bounding box, its timing-criticality at the end of the routing step, and the type of routing resources used to route it. The study would provide a better approximation of the routing behavior to be used during placement. They showed that 5 percent delay improvement can be achieved using the empirical routing models during the annealing placement phase. PPFF's main mode of operation, however, is not annealing. It uses a partitioning-based placement engine. We will cover more details of PPFF in Section 46.4.2.

46.4.2 HIERARCHICAL FPGA PLACEMENT

A clustered FPGA architecture such as the one discussed in Section 46.2.2 is an example of a hierarchical architecture with one level of hierarchy. In general, hierarchical architectures might have several tiers of hierarchies, and usually the lower levels of hierarchy can be connected to each other using faster routing resources.

The authors in Ref. [24] introduced a hierarchical placement algorithm for a hierarchical FPGA. In a hierarchical architecture, logic blocks are grouped into clusters at different levels of hierarchy. The leaf level nodes are the closest and can communicate by fast routing resources. The next level of routing would connect clusters of leaves using the second tier routing resources that are slightly slower than the first level resources. Their method can accommodate an arbitrary number of hierarchical levels, as long as a higher level hierarchy has slower routing resources than a lower level hierarchy.

For each output cone in the circuit, they compute lower and upper bounds on the number of hierarchy levels the cone has to pass through. For example, if an output cone has only four logic elements in series and the lowest hierarchy contains four logic blocks, the lower bound delay on this cone is four times the delay of the fastest routing resource. The upper bound would occur when each of the blocks on the path inside the cone are placed in different partitions at the highest level of the hierarchy. In this scenario, the delay would be four times the summation of the delays of all levels of hierarchy.

After obtaining the lower and upper bounds on the delays of all cones, they divide the cones into three categories. The first category contains paths whose lower bound delay is close to the delay constraint of the circuit. These paths are labeled critical. Paths in the second category are those whose upper bound delays violate the timing constraint, but the lower bound delays do not. The third category contains cones whose upper bound delay is smaller than the circuit's target delay. They prune out these paths in the placement process and only focus on the first two categories. As a result, they reduce the circuit size by about 50 percent.

Another partitioning-based timing-driven placement method for hierarchical FPGAs (specifically Altera's) was presented by Hutton et al. [25]. The authors perform timing-analysis at each level of the partitioning and place the netlist, trying to avoid potentially critical nets from becoming critical. The difference between this method and the one presented in Ref. [24] is that Hutton's method updates the current estimate of the criticality of the paths as the placement process progresses. Senouci's method computes crude estimates as upper and lower bound delays at the beginning and never updates these estimates.

46.4.3 PHYSICAL SYNTHESIS AND INCREMENTAL PLACEMENT METHODS

Physical synthesis refers to the process of simultaneously performing placement and logic optimization (e.g., resynthesizing a group of gates, gate duplication, retiming, etc.). Doing so has the advantage that the timing estimations available to the synthesis engine are more accurate and only synthesis optimization moves will be attempted whose benefits would sustain after placement. Timing improvements of 20–25 percent have been reported using physical synthesis [26,27] compared to a placement method that does not consider physical synthesis. In this section, we primarily focus on the placement methods used in physical synthesis approaches. Because placement and resynthesis are attempted iteratively, most of the placement methods used in physical synthesis are of an incremental nature.

Chen et al. [26] consider LUT duplication to improve timing. Timing could be improved by duplicating a LUT x that is driving two sink LUTs y and z. If we call the duplicated LUT x', then x' has to have the same inputs and the same functionality as x. Moving x' closer to y, which we assume is the more timing-critical sink, results in timing improvement because the connection (x', z) is shorter than (x, z), assuming that we do not increase the wirelength of the input wires to x' compared to the input wirelengths of x.

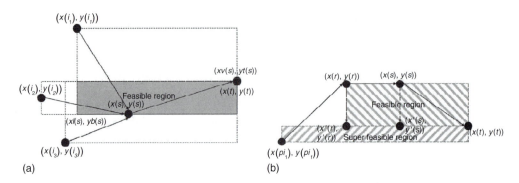

FIGURE 46.10 Feasible and super-feasible regions. (From Chen, G. and Cong, J., *Proceedings of the ACM/SIGDA International Symposium on Field Programmable Gate Arrays*, pp. 51–59, 2005. With permission.)

Placement is modified by either moving or duplicating critical gates such that critical paths become monotone. A path is defined to be monotone if the X (Y) coordinate of successive LUTs along its path increase or decrease monotonically. If a path is not monotone, it means that it is taking detours and its delay could be improved by moving LUTs (or duplicating the LUT and moving the duplicate) so that the path becomes closer to a monotone path, and hence its wirelength becomes smaller. The placement methods that Chen et al. use are (1) move a LUT or its duplicate to a location within the feasible or super-feasible region (Figure 46.10), and (2) legalize the placement immediately. Assume that node S gets its inputs from critical nodes $i_1, i_2, \ldots, i_k$ and provides an input to node T. The feasible region for node S shown in Figure 46.10a is defined to be the rectangular area in which node S can be moved without increasing the length of the path from any of its critical fanin nodes $i_1, i_2, \ldots, i_k$ to its fanout node T.

A super-feasible region shown in Figure 46.10b is a rectangular area that not only does not increase the length of the path from an immediate fanin to the fanout, but it also converts all global paths from the primary inputs in the fanin cone of a node to its fanout node into monotone paths. Moving a node to its desired destination location might result in overcrowding on the nodes, as the destination configurable logic block, which consists of LUTs and local interconnects in modern FPGAs (CLB) might already be fully utilized. Hence, there is a need for some legalization method after a placement move.

To choose a particular location in a feasible or super-feasible region to move a node to, they consider the replacement cost after legalization. The replacement cost is a linear combination of the slack improvement of the node being moved, the congestion cost of the destination, and the accumulative cost of moving other nodes to legalize the placement. The legalization procedure is an improvement over Mongrel [28]. The goal of the legalization procedure is to move nodes from overcrowded regions toward empty regions by minimally disturbing the placement. Assuming that the overcrowded CLB is at location (x, y) and the vacant CLB is at $(x + w, y + h)$, a grid graph is constructed with $w \times h$ nodes in which each node has outgoing edges to its east and north neighbors. Finding a path from the lower left to the upper right node in the grid graph determines the consecutive CLBs that LUT nodes should move through, resulting in a ripple move that transfers LUTs from overcrowded to vacant regions. The weight on an edge is determined by the amount of disturbance to a cost function (e.g., wirelength or delay) as a result of that particular move. To minimally change the current placemet, a node will only move one unit to the right or up. One of the LUTs at the newly overcrowded CLB must in turn move either to the right or up. The goal is to find a sequence of replacements from (x, y) to $(x + w, y + h)$ such that the overall cost of replacing the nodes is minimized. The authors in Ref. [26] solve this problem optimally using a longest path approach for cost functions that are linear in terms of the change in the physical location of the nodes. For example, a wirelength-based cost function can be solved optimally, but solving for minimum delay change cannot, because change in the delay of a path containing a LUT that is moved is not a linear function of the amount of dislocation of that LUT.

Another incremental placement method is presented by Singh and Brown [27]. In their approach, they define a minimally disruptive placement to be an incremental placement, which (1) is a legal placement, (2) does not increase the delay on the critical paths, and (3) does not increase routing area. Condition (1) means that the incremental placement algorithm must be flexible enough to handle many architectural constraints such as the number of inputs to a CLB, the flexibility in connections of the registers within the CLB, etc. Condition (2) above means that a node can move anywhere as long as it does not violate current timing constraints. And finally, condition (3) means that the new placement is desired to be routable.

The incremental placement algorithm starts by moving a few nodes to their preferred locations, determined by the synthesis engine. Then architectural violations are gradually removed by iteratively modifying the placement. At every placement move, a combination of three cost functions, namely cluster legality cost, timing cost, and congestion cost* is evaluated and the move is accepted greedily, that is, a move is only accepted if it reduces the overall cost. The legality cost component includes the legality of clusters based on the number of inputs, outputs, LUTs, etc. In their timing cost, they introduce a damping function that limits the range of movement of a node based on its slack: the larger the slack, the farther the node can move. This is designed to reduce fluctuations in the timing cost because of near-critical nodes becoming critical as a result of moving long distances.

The move set includes moving a candidate node to either the cluster containing one of its fanin nodes, one of its fanout nodes, a neighboring CLB, any random vacant CLB, move in the direction of critical vector, or its sibling cluster. The notion of a sibling cluster is shown in Figure 46.11. Moving in the direction of critical vector is similar to moving a node within the feasible region in the Chen and Cong work [26].

To avoid getting stuck in local minima, the authors propose a hill climbing method after a number of greedy moves fail to resolve architectural violations. The violation costs of CLBs that have not been resolved for a long time are increased compared to other CLBs, allowing LUTs to

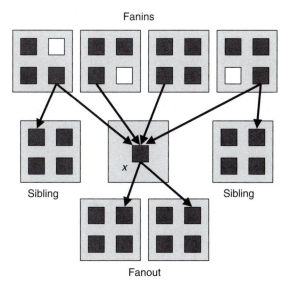

FIGURE 46.11   Fanin, fanout, and sibl4ng relationships. (Based on Singh, D. P. and Brown, S. D., *Proceedings of the IEEE/ACM International Conference on Computer-Aided Design*, pp. 752–759, 2002.)

---

* The authors call the congestion cost the wirelength cost, but they essentially evaluate congestion, not wirelength.

move to other CLBs, overcrowding them instead. This process gradually results in moving nodes from overcrowded regions to empty regions. They take care not to cause thrashing in which LUTs are moved back and forth between two clusters. Avoiding thrashing can be done by keeping a history of violations of CLBs. Hence, if thrashing has been occurring for a few moves, the relative cost of both CLBs involved in thrashing is increased, resulting in the extra LUT or register to be moved to a third CLB.

46.4.4 LINEAR DATAPATH PLACEMENT

Callahan et al. [29] presented GAMA, a linear-time simultaneous placement and mapping method for LUT-based FPGAs. They only focus on datapaths that are comprised of arrays of bitslices. The basic idea is to preserve the datapath structure so that we can reduce the problem size by primarily looking at a bitslice of the datapath. Once a bitslice is mapped and placed, other bitslices of the datapath can be mapped and placed similarly on rows above or below the initial bitslice.

One of the goals in developing GAMA was to perform mapping and placement with little computational effort. To achieve a linear time complexity, the authors limit the search space by considering only a subset of solutions, which means they might not produce an optimal solution. Because optimal mapping of directed acyclic graphs (DAGs) is NP-complete, GAMA first splits the circuit graph into a forest of trees before processing it by the mapping and placement steps. The tree covering algorithm does not directly handle cycles or nodes with multiple fanouts, and might duplicate nodes to reduce the number of trees. Each tree is compared to elements from a preexisting pattern library that contains compound modules such as the one shown in Figure 46.12. Dynamic programming is used to find the best cover in linear time. After the tree covering process, a postprocessing step is attempted to find opportunities for local optimization at the boundaries of the covered trees. Interested readers are referred to Ref. [29] for more details on the mapping process of GAMA.

Because the modules will form a bitslice datapath layout, the placement problem translates into finding a linear ordering of the modules in the datapath. Wirelength minimization is the primary goal during linear placement. The authors assume that the output of every module is available at its right boundary. A tree is placed by recursively placing its left and right subtrees, and then placing the root node to the right of the subtrees. The two subtrees are placed next to each other. Figure 46.13 shows an example of a tree placement. Because subtree $t2$ is wider, placing it to the right of subtree $t1$ will result in longer wirelength. Because the number of fanin nodes to the root of the tree is bounded, an exhaustive search for the right placement order of the subtrees is reasonable and would result in a linear-time algorithm.

In addition to the local placement algorithm, Callahan et al. also attempt some global optimizations. The linear placement algorithm arranges modules within a tree, but all trees in the circuit must also be globally placed. A greedy algorithm is used to place trees next to each other so that

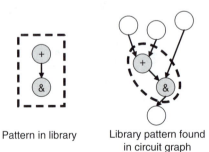

Pattern in library   Library pattern found in circuit graph

FIGURE 46.12 Example of a pattern in the tree covering library. (Based on Callahan, T. J. et al., *Proceedings of the ACM/SIGDA International Symposium on Field Programmable Gate Arrays*, 123–132, 1998. With permission.)

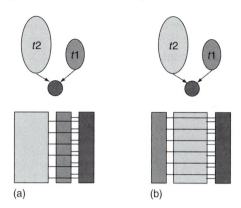

FIGURE 46.13 Tree placement example. (Based on Callahan, T. J. et al., *Proceedings of the ACM/SIGDA International Symposium on Field Programmable Gate Arrays*, 123–132, 1998. With permission.)

the length of the critical path in the circuit is minimized. Furthermore, after global and local placement is accomplished, individual modules are moved across tree boundaries to further optimize the placement.

Ababei and Bazargan [30] proposed a linear placement methodology for datapaths in a dynamically reconfigurable system in which datapaths corresponding to different basic blocks* in a program are loaded, overwritten, and possibly reloaded on linear strips of an FPGA. They assume that the FPGA chip is divided into strips as shown in Figure 46.14. An expression tree corresponding to computations in a basic block is placed entirely in one strip, getting its input values from either memory blocks on the two sides of the strip and writing the output of the expression to one of these memory blocks.

Depending on how frequently basic blocks are loaded and reloaded, three placement algorithms are developed:

1. Static placement: This case is similar to the problem considered by Callahan et al. [29], that is, each expression tree is given an empty FPGA strip to be placed on. The solution proposed by Ababei tries to minimize critical path delay, congestion, and wirelength

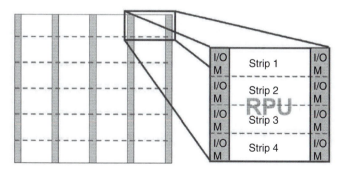

FIGURE 46.14 FPGA divided into linear strips.

---

* A basic block is a sequence of code, for example, written in the C language, with no jumps or function calls. A basic block, usually the body of a loop with many iterations, could be mapped to a coprocessor like an attached FPGA to perform computations faster. Data used by the basic block should be made accessible to the coprocessor and the output of the computations should in turn be made accessible to the processor. This could be achieved either by streaming data from the processor to the FPGA and vice versa, or by providing direct memory access to the FPGA.

using a matrix bandwidth minimization formulation. The matrix bandwidth minimization algorithm is covered in Section 47.3.2.1.

2. Dynamic placement with no module reuse: In this scenario, we assume that multiple basic blocks can be mapped to the same strip, either because a number of them run in parallel, or because there is a good chance that a mapped basic block be invoked again in the future. The goal is to place the modules of a new expression on the empty regions between the modules of previous basic blocks, leaving the previously placed modules and their connections intact. As a result, the placement of the new basic block becomes a linear, noncontiguous placement problem with blockages being the modules from previous basic blocks.

3. Dynamic placement with no module reuse: This scenario is similar to the previous one, except that we try to reuse a few modules and connections left over by previous basic blocks that are no longer active. Doing so will save in reconfiguration time and results in better usage of the FPGA real estate. Finding the largest common subgraph between the old and the new expression trees helps us maximize the reuse of the modules that are already placed.

The authors propose a greedy solution for the second problem, that is, dynamic placement without module reuse. The algorithm works directly on expression trees. Modules are rank-ordered based on parameters such as the volume (sum of module widths) of their children subtrees, and latest arrival time on the critical path. The ordering of the nodes determines the linear order in which they should be placed on the noncontiguous space.

To solve the third problem, that is, dynamic placement with module reuse, first a linear ordering of modules is obtained using the previous two algorithms to minimize wirelength, congestion, and critical path delay. Then a maximum matching between the existing inactive modules and the linear ordering is sought such that the maximum number of modules are reused while perturbations to the linear ordering are kept at a minimum. The algorithm is then extended to be applied to general graphs, and not just trees. To achieve better reuse, a maximum common subgraph problem is solved to find the largest subset of modules and their connections of the expression graphs that are already placed and those of the new basic block.

46.4.5 VARIATION-AWARE PLACEMENT

Hutton et al. proposed the first statistical timing analysis placement method for FPGAs [31]. They consider both inter- and intradie process variations in their modeling, but do not model spatial correlations among within-die variables. In other words, local variations are modeled as independent random variables.* In Ref. [31], they model delay of a circuit element as a Gaussian variable, which is a function of V_t and L_{eff}, each of which are broken into their global (systematic) and local (random) components. Block-based statistical timing analysis [33] is used to compute the timing criticality of nodes, which will be used instead of TVPR's timing-cost component (see Equations 46.3 and 46.5). SSTA (statistical static timing analysis) is performed only at each temperature, not at every move.

In their experiments, they compare their statistical timing-based placement to TVPR, and consider the effect of guard-banding and speed-binning. Guard-banding is achieved by adding $k.\sigma$ to the delay of every element, where k is a user-defined factor such as 3, 4, or 5, and σ is the standard deviation of the element's delay. Timing yield considering speed-binning is computed during Monte Carlo simulations by assuming that chips are divided into fast, medium, and slow critical path delays. Their statistical placement shows yield improvements over TVPR in almost all combinations of guard-banding and speed-binning scenarios. In a follow-up work, Lin and He [34] show

---

* Cheng et al. [32] show that by ignoring spatial correlations, we lose at least 14 percent in the accuracy of the estimated delay. The error in delay estimation accuracy is defined as the integration of the absolute error between the distributions obtained through Monte Carlo simulations and statistical sum and maximum computations of the circuit delay. See Section 46.3 of Ref. [32] for more details.

that combining statistical physical synthesis, statistical placement and statistical routing result in significant yield improvements (from 50 failed chips per 10,000 chips to 5 failed chips in their experimental setup).

Cheng et al. [32] propose a placement method that tailors the placement to individual chips, after the variation map for every chip is obtained. This is a preliminary work that tries to answer the question of given the exact map of FPGA element delays, how much improvement can we get by adapting the placement to individual chips. They show about 5.3 percent improvement on average in their experimental setup, although they do not address how the device parameter maps can be obtained in practice.

46.4.6 Low Power Placement

Low power FPGA placement and routing methods try to assign noncritical elements to low power resources on the FPGA. There have been many recent works targetting FPGA power minimization. We will only focus on two efforts: one deals with the placement problem [35] and the other addresses dual voltage assignment to routes [36], the latter will be discussed in Section 46.5.4.

The authors in Ref. [35] consider an architecture that is divided into physical regions, each of which can be independently power gated. To enable leakage power savings, designers must look into two issues carefully:

1. Region granularity: They should determine the best granularity of the power gating regions. Too small a region would have high circuit overheads both in terms of sleep transistors and configuration bits that must control them. On the other hand, a finer granularity gives more control over which logic units could shut down and could potentially harness more leakage savings.
2. Placement strategies: CAD developers should adopt placement strategies that constrain logic blocks with similar activity to the same regions. If all logic blocks placed in one region are going to be inactive for a long period of time, then the whole region can be power gated. However, architectural properties of the FPGA would influence the effectiveness of the placement strategy. For example, if the FPGA architecture has carry chains that run in the vertical direction, then the placement algorithm must place modules in regions that are vertically aligned. Not doing so could harm performance significantly.

By constraining the placement of modules with similar power activity, we can achieve two goals: power gate unused logic permanently, and power gate inactive modules for the duration of their inactive period. In their experiments, they consider various sizes of the power gating regions and also look into dynamic versus static powering down of unused/idle regions.

46.5 ROUTING

Versatile placement and routing [6] uses Dijkstra's algorithm (i.e., a maze router) to connect terminals of a net. Its router is based on the negotiation-based algorithm PathFinder [37]. PathFinder first routes all nets independently using the shortest route for each path. As a result, some routing regions will become overcongested. Then in an iterative process, nets are ripped-up and rerouted to alleviate congestion. Nets that are not timing-critical take detours away from the congested regions, and nets that are timing critical are likely to take the same route as round one.

There is a possibility that two routing channels show a thrashing effect, that is, nets are ripped-up from one channel and rerouted through the other, and then in the next iteration be ripped-up from the second and rerouted through the first. To avoid this, VPR use a history term that not only penalizes routing through a currently congested region, but it also uses the congestion data from the recent history to avoid thrashing. So the congestion of a channel is defined as its current resource (over-)usage plus a weighted sum of the previous congestion values from previous routing iterations.

Expansion wavefront

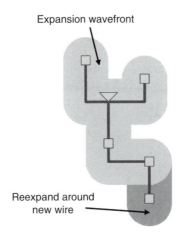

Reexpand around
new wire

FIGURE 46.15 Local expansion of the wavefront. (Based on Betz, V. and Rose, J., *Field-Programmable Logic and Applications* (W. Luk, P. Y. Cheung, and M. Glesner, eds.), pp. 213–222, Springer-Verlag, Berlin, Germany, 1997. With permission.)

To route a multiterminal net, VPR uses the maze routing algorithm, described in Chapter 23. After connecting two terminals of a k terminal net, VPR's maze router starts a wave from all points on the wire connecting the two terminals. The wave is propagated until the next terminal is reached. The process is repeated $k-1$ times. When a new terminal is reached, instead of restarting the wave from the new wiring tree from scratch, the maze routing algorithm starts a local wave from the new branch of wire that connected the new terminal to the rest of the tree. When the wavefront of the local wave gets as far out as the previous wavefront, the two waves are merged and expanded until a new terminal is reached. Figure 46.15 illustrates the process.

46.5.1 Hierarchical Routing

Chang et al. propose a hierarchical routing method for island-style FPGAs with segmented routing architecture in Ref. [38] (Section 45.4.1). Because nets are simultaneously routed, the net-ordering problem at the detailed routing level would not be an issue, in fact, global routing and detailed routing are performed at the same time in this approach. They model timing in their formulation as well, and estimate the delay of a route to be the number of programmable switches that it has to go through. This is a reasonable estimation because the delay of the switch points is much larger than the routing wires in a typical FPGA architecture. Each channel is divided into a number of subchannels, each subchannel corresponding to the set of segments of the same length within that channel.

After minimum spanning routing trees are generated, delay bounds are assigned to segments of the route and then the problems of channel assignment and delay bound recalculation are solved hierarchically. Figure 46.16 shows an example of a hierarchical routing step, in which connection i is generated by a minimum spanning tree algorithm. The problem is divided into two subproblems, one containing pin1 and the other containing pin2. The cutline between the two regions contains a number of horizontal subchannels. The algorithm tries to decide on the subchannel through which this net is going to be routed. Once the subchannel is decided (see the right part of Figure 46.16), then the routing problem can be broken into two smaller subproblems. While dividing the problem into smaller subproblems, the algorithm keeps updating the delay bounds on the nets, and keeps an eye on the congestion.

To decide on which subchannel j to use to route a routing segment i, the following cost function is used:

$$C_{ij} = C_{ij}^{(1)} + C_{ij}^{(2)} + C_{ij}^{(3)} \tag{46.6}$$

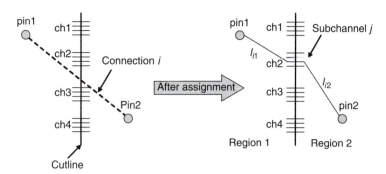

FIGURE 46.16 Delay bound redistribution after a hierarchical routing step. (Based on Chang, Y.-W. et al., *ACM Transactions on Design Automation of Electronic Systems*, 5, 433–450, 2000. With permission.)

where $C_{ij}^{(0)}$ is zero if connection i can reach subchannel j, and ∞ otherwise. Reachability can be determined by a breadth-first search on the connectivity graph. The second term intends to utilize the routing segments evenly according to the connection length and its delay bound:

$$C_{ij}^{(2)} = a \left| \frac{l_i}{U_i} - L_j \right| \tag{46.7}$$

where
l_i is the Manhattan distance of the connection i
U_i is the delay bound of the connection
L_j is the length of routing segments in the subchannel j
$a > 0$ is a constant

The term tries to maximize routing resource efficiency in routing. So, for example, if a net has a delay bound $U_i = 4$ and Manhattan distance $l_i = 8$, it can be routed through four switches, which means the ideal routing resource whose length is just right for this connection is $8/4 = 2$. For a subchannel that contains routing segments of length 2, the cost function will evaluate to zero, that is, segment length of 2 is ideal for routing this net. On the other hand, if a subchannel with segment length of 6 is considered, then the cost function will evaluate to 4, which means using segments of length 6 might be an overkill for this net, as its slack is high and we do not have to waste our length 6 routing resources on this net.

Cost component $C_{ij}^{(3)}$ in Equation 46.6 is shown in Figure 46.17. Figure 46.17b shows a typical nontiming driven routing, and Figure 46.17a shows the cost function used in Ref. [38]. The basic idea is to assign a lower cost to routes that are likely to use fewer bends. For example, in Figure 46.17a, if subchannel $s3$ is chosen, then chances are that when the subproblem of routing from a pin to $s3$ is being solved, more bends are introduced between the pin and $s3$. On the other hand, routing the net through $s1$ or $s5$ will guarantee that the route from the subchannel to at least one pin is going to use no bends. Note that the cost of routing outside the bounding box of the net increases linearly to discourage detours, which in turn hurt the delay of a net.

After a net is divided into two subnets, the delay bound of the net is distributed among the two subnets based on their lengths. So, for example, in Figure 46.17, if the original delay bound of connection i was U_i, then $U_{i1} = [l_{i1}/(l_{i1} + l_{i2})] \times U_i$, and $U_{i2} = [l_{i2}/(l_{i1} + l_{i2})] \times U_i$.

46.5.2 SAT-BASED ROUTING

Recent advances in SAT (Satisfiability problem) solvers have encouraged researchers to formulate various problems as SAT problems and utilize the efficiency of these solvers. Nam et al. [39] formulated the detailed routing on a fully segmented routing architecture (i.e., all routing segments

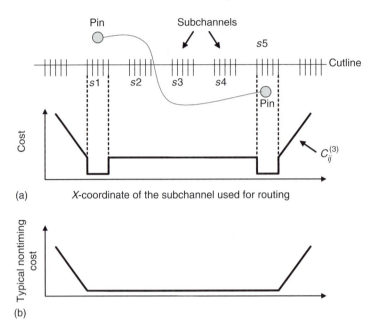

(a)   X-coordinate of the subchannel used for routing

(b)

FIGURE 46.17 Cost function. (Based on Chang, Y.-W. et al., *ACM Transactions on Design Automation of Electronic Systems*, 5, 433–450, 2000. With permission.)

are of length 1) as a SAT problem. The basic idea is shown in Figure 46.18. Figure 46.18a shows an instance of a global routing problem that includes three nets, *A, B,* and *C* and an FPGA with a channel width of three tracks. Figure 46.18b shows possible solutions for the routing of net *A*.

In a SAT problem, constraints are written in the form of conjunctive normal form (CNF) clauses. The CNF formulation of the constraints on net *A* are shown in Equation 46.8, where AH, BH, and *CH* are integer variables showing the horizontal track numbers that are assigned to nets *A, B,* and *C*, respectively. AV is the vertical track number assigned to net *A*. The conditions on the first line enforce that a unique track number is assigned to *A*, the second line ensures that the switchbox constraints are met (here it is assumed that a subset switchbox is used), and the third line enforces that a valid track number is assigned to the vertical segment of net *A*. These conditions state the connectivity constraints for net *A*.

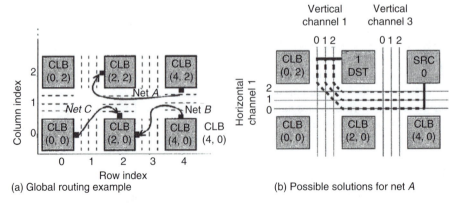

(a) Global routing example   (b) Possible solutions for net *A*

FIGURE 46.18 SAT formulation of a detailed routing problem. (From Nam, G.-J., Sakallah, K. A., and Rutenbar, R. A., *IEEE Trans. Comput. Aided Des. Integrated Circuits Syst.*, 21, 674, 2002. With permission.)

$$\begin{aligned} \text{Conn}(A) = &[(\text{AH} \equiv 0) \vee (\text{AH} \equiv 1) \vee (\text{AH} \equiv 2)] \wedge \\ &[(\text{AH} = \text{AV})] \wedge \\ &[(\text{AV} \equiv 0) \vee (\text{AV} \equiv 1) \vee (\text{AV} \equiv 2)] \end{aligned} \tag{46.8}$$

To ensure that different nets do not share the same track number in a channel (exclusivity constraint), conditions like Equation 46.9 must be added to the problem:

$$\text{Excl}\,(H1) = (\text{AH} \neq \text{BH}) \wedge (\text{AH} \neq \text{CH}) \tag{46.9}$$

where $H1$ refers to the horizontal channel shown in Figure 46.18a. The routability problem of the example of Figure 46.18a can be formulated as in Equation 46.10:

$$\text{Routable}\,(X) = \text{Conn}\,(A) \wedge \text{Conn}\,(B) \wedge \text{Conn}\,(C) \wedge \text{Excl}\,(H1) \tag{46.10}$$

where X is a vector of track variables AH, BH, CH, AV, BV, and CV. If Routable(X) is satisfiable, then a routing solution exists and can be derived from the values returned by the SAT solver. The authors extend the model so that doglegs can be defined too. Interested readers and referred to Ref. [39] for details.

Even though detailed routing can be elegantly formulated as a SAT problem, in practice its application is limited. If a solution does not exist (i.e., when there are not enough tracks), the SAT solver would take a long time exploring all track assignment possibilities and returning with a negative answer, that is, Routable(X) is not satisfiable. Furthermore, even if a solution exists but the routing instance is difficult (e.g., when there are barely enough routing tracks to route the given problem instance), the SAT solver might take a long time. In practice, the SAT solver could be terminated if the time spent on the problem is more than a prespecified limit. This could either mean that the problem instance is difficult, or no routing solution exists for the given number of tracks.

46.5.3 GRAPH-BASED ROUTING

The FPGA global routing problem can be modeled as a graph matching problem in which branches of a routing tree are assigned (matched) to sets of routing segments in a multisegment architecture to estimate the number of channels required for detailed routing. Lin et al. propose a graph-based routing method in Ref. [40]. The input to the problem is a set of globally routed nets. The goal is to assign each straight segment of each net to a track in the channel that it is globally routed so that a lower bound on the required number of tracks is obtained for each channel. Interactions between channels are ignored in this work, as a result, the bound on the number of tracks needed for each channel is calculated in isolation. The actual number of tracks needed for the whole design might be larger depending on the switchbox architecture and the way horizontal and vertical channels interact.

They model the track assignment problem within one channel as a weighted matching problem. Straight segments of nets are called subnets (e.g., a net routed in the shape of an "L" is divided into two subnets). Within a channel, subnets belonging to a maximum clique C of overlapping subnets* are assigned to tracks from a set of tracks H using a bipartite graph matching problem. Members of set C form the nodes on one side of the bipartite graph used in the matching problem, and the nodes on the other side of the matching graph are tracks in set H. The weight on the edges from subnets to routing tracks are determined based on the track length utilization. The track utilization $U_r(i_x, t)$ of a subnet i_x on track t is defined as

$$U_r\,(i_x, t) = \frac{\text{len}\,(i_x)}{\sum_{1 \leq y < k} \text{len}\,(s_y)} + \frac{\alpha}{k} \tag{46.11}$$

---

* Refer to Ref. [41] for more discussions on finding cliques of overlapping net intervals and calculating lower bounds on channel densities.

where
  len(i_x) and len(s_y) are the respective lengths of the subnet i_x and the segment s_y
  y is an FPGA routing segment in the track that i_x is globally routed in
  k is the number of segments needed to route the subnet on that track

Note that the first and the last FPGA routing segments used in routing the subnet might be longer than what the subnet needs, and hence some of the track length would go underutilized. The algorithm tries to maximize routing segment utilization by matching a subnet to a track that has segments whose lengths and starting points match closely to those of the span of the subnet. This is achieved by maximizing the sum of track utilizations $U_r(i_x, t)$ over all subnets. Parameter α in the equation above is used to enable simultaneous routability and timing optimization. They further extend the algorithm to consider timing as well as routability using an iterative process. After an initial routing, they distribute timing slacks to nets, and order channels based on how critical they are. A channel is critical if its density is the highest.

46.5.4 Low Power Routing

The authors in Ref. [36] assume that all switches and connection boxes in a modified island-style FPGA are Vdd-programmable. An SRAM bit can determine if the driver driving a particular switch or connection box will be in high or low Vdd. To avoid adding level converters, they enforce the constraint that no low-Vdd switch can drive a high-Vdd element. The result is each routing tree can be mapped either fully in high-Vdd, or fully in low-Vdd, or mapped to high-Vdd from the source up to a point in the routing tree, and then low-Vdd from that point to the sink. In terms of power consumption, it is desired to map as many routing resources to low-Vdd, as that would consume less power than high-Vdd. But because low-Vdd resources are slower, care must be taken not to slow down critical paths in the circuit.

They propose a heuristic sensitivity-based algorithm and a linear programming formulation for assigning voltage levels to programmable routing resources (switches and their associated buffers). The sensitivity-based method first calculates power sensitivity $\Delta P/\Delta V_{dd}$ for each routing resource, which is the power reduction by changing high-Vdd to low-Vdd. A resource with the highest sensitivity is tried with low-Vdd. If the path containing the switch does not violate the timing constraint, then the switch and all its downsteam routing resources are locked on low-Vdd. Otherwise, the switch is changed back to high-Vdd. The linear programming method tries to distribute path slacks among route segments such that the number of low-Vdd resources is maximized subject to the constraint that no low-Vdd switch drives a high-Vdd one.

46.5.5 Other Routing Methods

In this subsection, we review miscellaneous routing methods such as pipeline routing, congestion-driven routing, and statistical timing routing.

46.5.5.1 Pipeline Routing

Eguro and Hauck [42] propose a timing-driven pipeline-aware routing algorithm that reduces critical path delay. A pipeline-aware routing problem requires the connection from a source node to a sink node to pass through certain number of pipeline registers and each segment of the route (between source, sink, and registers) must satisfy delay constraints. The work by Eguro and Hauck adapts PathFinder [37]. When considering pipelining, the problem becomes more difficult compared to a traditional routing problem, because as registers move along a route, the criticality of the routing segments would change. For example, suppose a net is to connect logic block A to logic block B through one register R. In the first routing iteration, R might be placed close to A, which makes the subroute A–R not critical, but R–B would probably be critical. In the next iteration, R might move closer to B, and hence the two subroutes might be considered critical and noncritical in successive iterations.

To address the problem stated above, the authors in Ref. [42] perform simultaneous wave propagation maze routing searches, each assuming that the net has a distinct timing-criticality value. When the sink (or a register) is reached in the search process, the routing wave that best balances congestion and timing criticality is chosen. Interested readers are referred to Ref. [42] for more details.

46.5.5.2 Congestion-Driven Routing

Another work that deals with routability and congestion estimation is fGrep [43]. To estimate congestion, waves are started from a source node, and all possible paths are implicitly enumerated at every step of the wave propagation. The probability that the net passes through a particular routing element is the ratio of the total number of paths that pass through that routing element to the total number of paths that can route the net. Routing demand or congestion on a routing element is defined as the sum of these probabilities among all nets. Of course, performing full wave propagation for every net would be costly. As a trade-off, the authors trim the wave once it has passed a certain predetermined distance, which results in the speedup of the estimation at the cost of accuracy. Another speedup technique used by the authors is to start waves from all terminals of a net and stop when two waves reach each other.

46.5.5.3 Statistical Timing Routing

Statistical timing analysis has found its way into FPGA CAD tools in recent years. Sivaswamy et al. [44] showed that using SSTA during the routing stage could greatly improve timing yield over traditional static timing analysis methods with guard-banding. More specifically, in their experimental setup they could reduce the yield loss from about 8 per 10,000 chips to about 1 per 10,000 chips. They considered inter- and intradie variations and modeled spatial correlations in their statistical modeling of device parameters.

Matsumo et al. [45] proposed a reconfiguration methodology for yield enhancement in which multiple routing solutions are generated for a design and the one that yields the best timing for a particular FPGA chip is loaded on that chip. This can be done by performing at-speed testing of an individual FPGA chip using each of the n configurations that are generated and by picking the one that yields the best clock speed. The advantage of this method compared to a method that requires obtaining the delay map of all elements on the chip (e.g., the work by Cheng et al. [32]) is that extensive tests are not required to determine which configuration yields the best timing results.

In the current version of their method, Matsumo et al. [45] fix the placement and only explore different routing solutions. In each configuration, they try to avoid routing each critical path through the same regions used by other configurations, which means that ideally, each configuration routes a critical path through a unique set of routing resources that are spatially far away from the paths in other configurations. As a result, if a critical path in one configuration is slow due to process variations, chances are that other configurations would route the same path through regions that are faster, resulting in a faster clock frequency. Figure 46.19 shows three configurations with different routes for a critical path and the delay variation map of the switch matrix. Using the delay map in Figure 46.19, we can calculate the delay of the critical path in the first, second, and third configurations as 4.9, 4.5, and 5.1, respectively.

They ignore spatial correlations in their method, hence they can analytically calculate the probability that a design fails timing constraints given n configurations. The probability that none of the n configurations passes the timing test is

$$Y_n \left(\text{Target} \right) = 1 - \left[1 - Y_1 \left(\text{Target} \right) \right]^n \qquad (46.12)$$

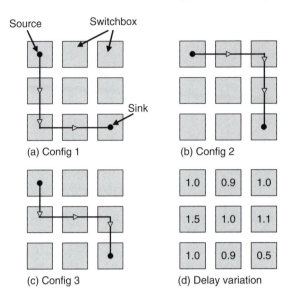

FIGURE 46.19 Three critical path configurations and delay variations of a switch matrix. (Based on Matsumoto, Y. et al., *Proceedings of the 2007 ACM/SIGDA 15th International Symposium on Field Programmable Gate Arrays*, ACM Press, New York, 2007. With permission.)

where Y_1(Target) is defined as

$$Y_1 \, (\text{Target}) = \int_{-\infty}^{T_{Target}} f_{\text{crit}}\,(t)\,\mathrm{d}t \tag{46.13}$$

In Equation 46.12, the likelihood that all n configurations fail is subtracted from 1. In their work, they assume complete independence between critical paths in different configurations, which enables them to analytically evaluate Equations 46.12 and 46.13. This assumption is not valid, as we know spatial correlations exist between circuit elements, and also critical paths across different configurations might share routing resources, especially close to the source and sink nodes.

They propose a routing algorithm that keeps track of the usage of routing resources by critical paths and tries to avoid them in consecutive configurations that are generated. The method is similar to the congestion avoidance procedure used in VPR, that is, resources that are used by critical paths in other configurations are penalized so that the router avoids them if other paths with the same delay exist.

REFERENCES

1. J. Cong and K. Minkovich, Optimality study of logic synthesis for Lut-based FPGAs, *IEEE Transactions on Computer-Aided Design of Integrated Circuits and Systems*, 26(2): 230–239, 2007.
2. D. Chen and J. Cong, Daomap: A depth-optimal area optimization mapping algorithm for FPGA designs, in *ICCAD '04: Proceedings of the 2004 IEEE/ACM International Conference on Computer-Aided Design*, pp. 752–759, IEEE Computer Society, Washington DC, 2004.
3. B. L. Synthesis and V. Group, Abc: A system for sequential synthesis and verification. Available at http://www.eecs.berkeley.edu/~alanmi/abc/.
4. Alan, S. Chatterjee, and R. Brayton, Improvements to technology mapping for Lut-based FPGAs, in *FPGA '06: Proceedings of the 2006 ACM/SIGDA 14th International Symposium on Field Programmable Gate Arrays*, pp. 41–49, ACM Press, New York, 2006.
5. J. Cong and Y. Ding, Flowmap: An optimal technology mapping algorithm for delay optimization in lookup-table based FPGA designs, *IEEE Transactions on Computer-Aided Design of Integrated Circuits and Systems (TCAD)*, 13(1): 1–12, 1994.

6. V. Betz and J. Rose, VPR: A new packing, placement and routing tool for FPGA research, in *Field-Programmable Logic and Applications* (W. Luk, P. Y. Cheung, and M. Glesner, eds.), pp. 213–222, Springer-Verlag, Berlin, Germany, 1997.

7. A. S. Marquardt, V. Betz, and J. Rose, Using cluster-based logic blocks and timing-driven packing to improve FPGA speed and density, in *Proceedings of the ACM/SIGDA International Symposium on Field Programmable Gate Arrays*, Monterey, CA, pp. 37–46, 1999.

8. E. Bozorgzadeh, S. Ogrenci-Memik, and M. Sarrafzadeh, Rpack: Routability-driven packing for cluster-based FPGAs, in *Proceedings of the Asia-South Pacific Design Automation Conference*, Yokohama, Japan, 2001, pp. 629–634.

9. A. Singh and M. Marek-Sadowska, Efficient circuit clustering for area and power reduction in FPGAs, in *Proceedings of the ACM/SIGDA International Symposium on Field Programmable Gate Arrays*, Monterey, CA, pp. 59–66, 2002.

10. A. DeHon, Balancing interconnect and computation in a reconfiguable computing array (or, why you don't really want 100% LUT utilization), in *Proceedings of the ACM/SIGDA International Symposium on Field Programmable Gate Arrays*, Monterey, CA, pp. 69–78, 1999.

11. L. Cheng and M. D. F. Wong, Floorplan design for multi-million gate FPGAs, in *Proceedings of the IEEE/ACM International Conference on Computer-Aided Design*, San Jose, CA, pp. 292–299, 2004.

12. Y. Sankar and J. Rose, Trading quality for compile time: Ultra-fast placement for FPGAs, in *Proceedings of the ACM/SIGDA International Symposium on Field Programmable Gate Arrays*, San Jose, CA, pp. 157–166, 1999.

13. J. M. Emmert and D. Bhatia, A methodology for fast FPGA floorplanning, in *Proceedings of the ACM/SIGDA International Symposium on Field Programmable Gate Arrays*, Monterey, CA, pp. 47–56, 1999.

14. K. Bazargan, R. Kastner, and M. Sarrafzadeh, Fast template placement for reconfigurable computing systems, *IEEE Design and Test—Special Issue on Reconfigurable Computing*, 17: 68–83, January 2000.

15. E. L. Horta, J. W. Lockwood, D. E. Taylor, and D. Parlour, Dynamic hardware plugins in an FPGA with partial runtime reconfiguration, in *Proceedings of the ACM/IEEE Design Automation Conference*, New Orleans, LA, pp. 343–347, 2002.

16. J. Chen, J. Moon, and K. Bazargan, A reconfigurable FPGA-based readback signal generator for hard-drive read channel simulator, in *Proceedings of the ACM/IEEE Design Automation Conference*, New Orleans, LA, pp. 349–354, 2002.

17. M. Handa and R. Vemuri, An efficient algorithm for finding empty space for online FPGA placement, in *Proceedings of the ACM/IEEE Design Automation Conference*, San Diego, CA, pp. 960–965, 2004.

18. L. Singhal and E. Bozorgzadeh, Multi-layer floorplanning on a sequence of reconfigurable designs, in *FPL'06: Proceedings of the 2006 International Conference on Field Programmable Logic and Applications*, Madrid, 2006.

19. J. Cong, M. Romesis, and M. Xie, Optimality and stability study of timing-driven placement algorithms, in *Proceedings of the IEEE/ACM International Conference on Computer-Aided Design*, San Jose, CA, p. 472, 2003.

20. C. -L. E. Cheng, Risa: Accurate and efficient placement routability modeling, in *Proceedings of the IEEE/ACM International Conference on Computer-Aided Design*, San Jose, CA, pp. 690–695, 1994.

21. A. Marquardt, V. Betz, and J. Rose, Timing-driven placement for FPGAs, in *Proceedings of the ACM/SIGDA International Symposium on Field Programmable Gate Arrays*, Monterey, CA, pp. 203–213, 2000.

22. S. Nag and R. A. Rutenbar, Performance-driven simultaneous placement and routing for FPGA's *IEEE Transactions on Computer-Aided Design of Integrated Circuits and Systems (TCAD)*, 17(6): 499–518, 1998.

23. P. Maidee, C. Ababei, and K. Bazargan, Timing-driven partitioning-based placement for island style FPGAs, *IEEE Transactions on Computer-Aided Design of Integrated Circuits and Systems (TCAD)*, 24(3): 395–406, 2005.

24. S. A. Senouci, A. Amoura, H. Krupnova, and G. Saucier, Timing driven floorplanning on programmable hierarchical targets, in *Proceedings of the ACM/SIGDA International Symposium on Field Programmable Gate Arrays*, Monterey, CA, pp. 85–92, 1998.

25. M. Hutton, K. Adibsamii, and A. Leaver, Timing-driven placement for hierarchical programmable logic devices, in *Proceedings of the ACM/SIGDA International Symposium on Field Programmable Gate Arrays*, Monterey, CA, pp. 3–11, 2001.

26. G. Chen and J. Cong, Simultaneous timing-driven placement and duplication, in *Proceedings of the ACM/SIGDA International Symposium on Field Programmable Gate Arrays*, Monterey, CA, pp. 51–59, 2005.

27. D. P. Singh and S. D. Brown, Incremental placement for layout-driven optimizations on FPGAs, in *Proceedings of the IEEE/ACM International Conference on Computer-Aided Design*, San Jose, CA, pp. 752–759, 2002.

28. S. -W. Hur and J. Lillis, Mongrel: Hybrid techniques for standard cell placement, in *Proceedings of the IEEE/ACM International Conference on Computer-Aided Design*, San Jose, CA, pp. 165–170, 2000.

29. T. J. Callahan, P. Chong, A. DeHon, and J. Wawrzynek, Fast module mapping and placement for datapaths in FPGAs, in *Proceedings of the ACM/SIGDA International Symposium on Field Programmable Gate Arrays*, Monterey, CA, pp. 123–132, 1998.

30. C. Ababei and K. Bazargan, Non-contiguous linear placement for reconfigurable fabrics, *International Journal of Embedded Systems (IJES)*—esp. issue on Reconfigurable Architectures Workshop (RAW), 2(1/2): 86–94, 2006.

31. M. Hutton, Y. Lin, and L. He, Placement and timing for FPGAs considering variations, in *FPL'06: Proceedings of the 2006 International Conference on Field Programmable Logic and Applications*, Madrid, 2006.

32. L. Cheng, J. Xiong, L. He, and M. Hutton, FPGA performance optimization via chipwise placement considering process variations, in *FPL'06: Proceedings of the 2006 International Conference on Field Programmable Logic and Applications*, Madrid, 2006.

33. C. Visweswariah, K. Ravindran, K. Kalafala, S. G. Walker, S. Narayan, D. K. Beece, J. Piaget, N. Venkateswaran, and J. G. Hemmett, First-order incremental block-based statistical timing analysis, *IEEE Transactions on Computer-Aided Design of Integrated Circuits and Systems*, 25: 2170–2180, October 2006.

34. Y. Lin and L. He, Stochastic physical synthesis for FPGAs with pre-routing interconnect uncertainty and process variation, in *FPGA '07: Proceedings of the 2007 ACM/SIGDA 15th International Symposium on Field Programmable Gate Arrays*, pp. 80–88, ACM Press, New York, 2007.

35. A. Gayasen, Y. Tsai, N. Vijaykrishnan, M. Kandemir, M. J. Irwin, and T. Tuan, Reducing leakage energy in fpgas using region-constrained placement, in *Proceedings of the ACM/SIGDA International Symposium on Field Programmable Gate Arrays*, Monterey, CA, pp. 51–58, 2004.

36. Y. Lin and L. He, Leakage efficient chip-level dual-vdd assignment with time slack allocation for FPGA power reduction, in *Proceedings of the ACM/IEEE Design Automation Conference*, Anaheim, CA, pp. 720–725, 2005.

37. L. McMuchie and C. Ebeling, Pathfinder: A negotiation-based performance-driven router for FPGAs, in *Proceedings of the ACM/SIGDA International Symposium on Field Programmable Gate Arrays*, Monterey, CA, pp. 473–482, 1995.

38. Y. -W. Chang, K. Zhu, and D. F. Wong, Timing-driven routing for symmetrical array-based FPGAs, *ACM Transactions on Design Automation of Electronic Systems*, 5(3): 433–450, 2000.

39. G. -J. Nam, K. A. Sakallah, and R. A. Rutenbar, A new FPGA detailed routing approach via search-based Boolean satisfiability, *IEEE Transactions on Computer-Aided Design of Integrated Circuits and Systems (TCAD)*, 21(6): 674–684, 2002.

40. J. -M. Lin, S. -R. Pan, and Y. -W. Chang, Graph matching-based algorithms for array-based FPGA segmentation design and routing, in *Proceedings of the Asia-South Pacific Design Automation Conference*, Kitakyushu, Japan, pp. 851–854, 2003.

41. N. Sherwani, *Algorithms for VLSI Physical Design Automation*, 2 edn. Kluwer Academic Publishers, Boston, MA, 1995.

42. K. Eguro and S. Hauck, Armada: Timing-driven pipeline-aware routing for FPGAs, in *Proceedings of the ACM/SIGDA International Symposium on Field Programmable Gate Arrays*, Monterey, CA, pp. 169–178, 2006.

43. P. Kannan, S. Balachandran, and D. Bhatia, On metrics for comparing routability estimation methods for FPGAs, in *Proceedings of the ACM/IEEE Design Automation Conference*, New Orleans, LA, pp. 70–75, 2002.

44. S. Sivaswamy and K. Bazargan, Variation-aware routing for FPGAs, in *FPGA '07: Proceedings of the 2007 ACM/SIGDA 15th International Symposium on Field Programmable Gate Arrays*, pp. 71–79, ACM Press, New York 2007.

45. Y. Matsumoto, M. Hioki, T. Kawanami, T. Tsutsumi, T. Nakagawa, T. Sekigawa, and H. Koike, Performance and yield enhancement of FPGAs with within-die variation using multiple configurations, in *FPGA '07: Proceedings of the 2007 ACM/SIGDA 15th International Symposium on Field Programmable Gate Arrays*, pp. 169–177, ACM Press, New York 2007.

47 Physical Design for Three-Dimensional Circuits

Kia Bazargan and Sachin S. Sapatnekar

CONTENTS

47.1 INTRODUCTION

Recent advances in process technology have brought three-dimensional (3D) circuits to the realm of reality. This new design paradigm will require a major change from contemporary design methodologies, because an optimal 3D design has very different characteristics from an optimal 2D design. The move from conventional 2D to 3D is inherently a topological change, and therefore, many of the problems that are unique to 3D circuits lie in the domain of physical design.

The essential idea of a 3D circuit is to place multiple tiers of active devices (transistors) above each other, as opposed to a conventional 2D circuit where all transistors and gates lie in a single tier. An example of 3D circuit is shown in Figure 47.1.

One of the primary motivators for 3D technologies is related to the dominant effects of interconnects in nanoscale technologies, and the addition of a third dimension provides significant relief in this respect. This is achieved by reductions in the average interconnect lengths (in comparison with 2D implementations, for the same circuit size), lower wire congestion, as well as by denser integration, which results in the replacement of chip-to-chip interconnections by intrachip connections. In addition, the increased packing density improves the computation per unit volume.

For instance, Figure 47.2 shows a 2D layout on a chip of dimension $2L \times 2L$ on the left, where the longest (nondetoured) wire, going from one end of the layout to the other, has a length of $4L$. If this design is built on four tiers, as shown at right, assuming the same total silicon area and a square aspect ratio for each tier, the silicon area in each tier is $L \times L$. Therefore, the longest possible

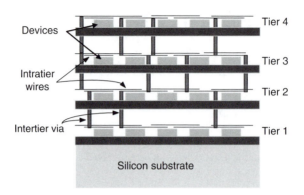

FIGURE 47.1   Schematic of a 3D integrated circuit.

undetoured wirelength, going from one end in the lowest tier to the other end in the uppermost tier, is approximately $2L$ (because the intertier thickness is negligible). Because, for a buffered two-pin interconnect, the delay of a wire is proportional to its length, this implies that the delay is halved. Moreover, the reduced wire lengths also reduce the likelihood of congestion bottlenecks, potentially reducing the need to detour wires. A more precise distribution of the wirelength has been reported in Ref. [1], which shows that the histogram of wirelength distributions moves progressively to the left as the number of tiers is increased.

In addition, 3D designs can result in new paradigms, for example, heterogeneous integration, where each tier could be a different material (e.g., a silicon-based circuit on one tier and a GaAs-based circuit on another). Even for purely silicon-based circuits, 3D designs permit analog/RF and digital circuits to be build on different tiers, which improves their noise behavior; additionally, it is possible to construct shielding structures such as Faraday cages between tiers for enhanced noise reduction.

Various flavors of 3D technologies have been proposed and are in use. One of the simplest forms involves wafer stacking, where the distance between active devices in the third dimension (or the "z dimension") equals the thickness of a wafer. However, the thickness of a wafer is of the order of several hundreds of microns, and the full potential of 3D is not achieved by this approach due to the long distance that a wire must traverse in the z dimension. Further progress has resulted in the development of integrated 3D circuits in industrial [2], government [3], and academic [4] settings, which have demonstrated 3D designs with intertier separations of the order of a few microns.

Today, it is only possible to build a few tiers in the third dimension, as a result of which many of these technologies are often referred to as 2.5D rather than fully 3D. Nevertheless, even the half dimension can provide the potential for substantial performance improvements, and perhaps future technological improvements will enable truly 3D integration.

In this chapter, we present an overview of physical design technologies for 3D circuits. We begin with a brief overview of a typical 3D technology, and then discuss physical design problems in the custom/ASIC design as well as the FPGA paradigms. Generally speaking, the number of tiers is taken in as a technology input by the 3D tools described in this chapter.

FIGURE 47.2   Comparison of the maximum wirelength in a 2D layout (left) and in its 3D counterpart (right). For clarity, the intertier thicknesses in the 3D circuit are shown to be exaggeratedly large.

47.2   STANDARD CELL-BASED DESIGNS

A typical cell-based flow begins with a floorplanning step, where the system is laid out at the level of macroblocks, detailed placement of the cells in the layout, and routing. In the 3D context, each of these must be modified to adapt to the constraints imposed by 3D circuits. In addition to conventional metrics, 3D-specific geometrical considerations must be used, for example, for wirelength metrics. In addition, temperature is treated as a first-class citizen during these optimizations.* Moreover, intertier via reduction is considered to be a desirable goal, because the number of available vias is restricted and must be shared between signal nets and supply and clock nets.

In addition to floorplanning, placement, and routing, a 3D-specific optimization that makes the temperature distribution more uniform is the judicious positioning of thermal vias within the layout. These vias correspond to intertier metal connections that have no electrical function, but instead, constitute a passive cooling technology that draws heat from the problem areas to the heat sink, and can be built into each of these steps or performed as an independent postprocessing step, depending on the design methodology.

It is instructive to view the result of a typical 3D thermally aware placement [5]: a layout for the benchmark circuit, IBM01, in a four-tier 3D process, is displayed in Figure 47.3. The cells are positioned in ordered rows on each tier, and the layout in each individual tier looks similar to a 2D standard cell layout. The heat sink is placed at the bottom of the 3D chip, and the lighter shaded regions are hotter than the darker shaded regions. The coolest cells are those in the bottom tier, next to the heat sink, and the temperature increases as we move to higher tiers. The thermal placement method consciously mitigates the temperature by making the upper tiers sparser, in terms of the percentage of area populated by the cells, than the lower tiers.

47.2.1   THERMAL VIAS

Although silicon is a good thermal conductor, with half or more of the conductivity of typical metals, many of the materials used in 3D technologies are strong insulators that place severe restrictions on the amount of heat that can be removed, even under the best placement solution. The materials include epoxy bonding materials used to attach 3D tiers, or field oxide, or the insulator in an SOI technology. Therefore, the use of deliberate metal lines that serve as heat-removing channels, called thermal vias, are an important ingredient of the total thermal solution. The second step in the flow determines the optimal positions of thermal vias in the placement that provide an overall improvement in the

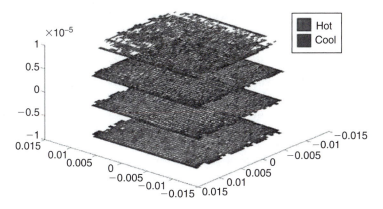

FIGURE 47.3   Placement for the benchmark ibm01 in a four-tier 3D technology. (From Ababei, C., et al., *IEEE Design and Test*, 22, 520, 2005. Copyright IEEE. With permission.)

---

* A description of techniques for thermal analysis is provided in Section 3.4

temperature distribution. In realistic 3D technologies, the footprints of these intertier vias are of the order 5×5 μm.

In principle, the problem of placing thermal vias can be viewed as one of determining one of two conductivities (corresponding to the presence or absence of metal) at every candidate point where a thermal via may be placed in the chip. However, in practice, it is easy to see that such an approach could lead to an extremely large search space that is exponential in the number of possible positions; note that the set of possible positions in itself is extremely large.

Quite apart from the size of the search space, such an approach is unrealistic for several other reasons. First, the wanton addition of thermal vias in any arbitrary region of the layout would lead to nightmares for a router, which would have to navigate around these blockages. Second, from a practical standpoint, it is unreasonable to perform full-chip thermal analysis, particularly in the inner loop of an optimizer, at the granularity of individual thermal vias. At this level of detail, individual elements would have to correspond to the size of a thermal via, and the size of the thermal simulation matrix would become extremely large.

Fortunately, there are reasonable ways to overcome each of these issues. The blockage problem may be controlled by enforcing discipline within the design, designating a specific set of areas within the chip as potential thermal via sites. These could be chosen as specific interrow regions in the cell-based layout, and the optimizer would determine the density with which these are filled with thermal vias. The advantage to the router is obvious, because only these regions are potential blockages, which is much easier to handle. To control the finite element analysis (FEA) stiffness matrix size, one could work with a two-level scheme with relatively large elements, where the average thermal conductivity of each region is a design variable. Once this average conductivity is chosen, it could be translated back into a precise distribution of thermal vias within the element that achieves that average conductivity.

Various published methods take different approaches to thermal via insertion. We now describe an algorithm to postfacto thermal via insertion [6]; other procedures perform thermal via insertion during floorplanning, placement or routing are discussed in the appropriate sections.

For a given placed 3D circuit, an iterative method was developed in which, during each iteration, the thermal conductivities of certain FEA elements (thermal via regions) are incrementally modified so that thermal problems are reduced or eliminated. Thermal vias are generically added to elements to achieve the desired thermal conductivities. The goal of this method is to satisfy given thermal requirements using as few thermal vias as possible, that is, keeping the thermal conductivities as low as possible.

The approach uses the finite element equations to determine a target thermal conductivity. A key observation in this work is that the insertion of thermal vias is most useful in areas with a high thermal gradient, rather than areas with a high temperature. Effectively, the thermal via acts as a pipe that allows the heat to be conducted from the higher temperature region to the lower temperature region; this, in turn, leads to temperature reductions in areas of high temperature.

This is illustrated in Figure 47.4, which shows the 3D layout of the benchmark `struct`, before and after the addition of thermal vias. The hottest region is the center of the uppermost tier, and a major reason for its elevated temperature is because the tier below it is hot. Adding thermal vias to remove heat from the second tier, therefore, effectively also significantly reduces the temperature of the top tier. For this reason, the regions where the insertion of thermal vias is most effective are those that have high thermal gradients.

Therefore the method in Ref. [6] employs an iterative update formula of the type

$$K_i^{\text{new}} = K_i^{\text{old}} \left(\frac{|g_i^{\text{old}}|}{g_{i,\text{ideal}}} \right) \quad i = x, y, z \tag{47.1}$$

is employed, where K_i^{new} and K_i^{old} are, respectively, the new and old thermal conductivities in each direction, before and after each iteration, g_i^{old} is the old thermal gradient, and $g_{i,\text{ideal}}$ is a heuristically selected ideal thermal gradient.

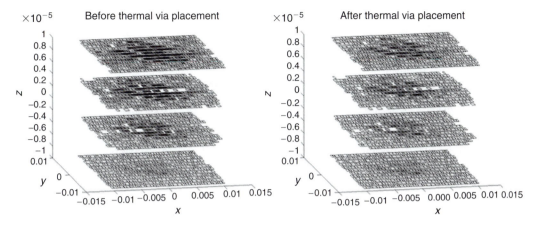

FIGURE 47.4 Thermal profile of struct before (left) and after (right) thermal via insertion. The top four layers of the figure at right correspond to the four layers in the figure at left. (From Goplen, B. and Sapatnekar, S. S., *IEEE Transactions on Computer-Aided Design*, 26, 692, 2006. Copyright IEEE. With permission.)

Each iteration begins with a distribution of the thermal vias; this distribution is corrected using the above update formula, and the K_i^{new} value is then translated to a thermal via density, and then a precise layout of thermal vias, using precharacterization. The iterations end when the desired temperature profile is achieved. This essential iterative idea has also been used in other methods for thermal-via insertion steps that are integrated within floorplanning, placement, and routing, as described in succeeding sections. This general framework has been used in several other published techniques that insert thermal vias either concurrently during another optimization, or as an independent step.

47.2.2 3D FLOORPLANNING

The 3D floorplanning problem is analogous to the 2D problem discussed in Chapters 8 through 13, with all the constraints and opportunities that arise with the move to the third dimension. Typical cost functions include a mix of the conventional wirelength and total area costs, and the temperature and the number of intertier vias.

The approach in Ref. [7] presented one of the first approaches to 3D floorplanning, and used the transitive closure graph (TCG) representation [8], described in Section 11.7, for each tier, and a bucket structure for the third dimension. Each bucket represents a 2D region over all tiers, and stores, for each tier, the indices of the blocks that intersect that bucket. In other words, the TCG and this bucket structure can quickly determine any adjacency information. A simulated annealing engine is then utilized, with the moves corresponding to perturbations within a tier and across tiers; in each such case, the corresponding TCGs and buckets are updated, as necessary.

A simple thermal analysis procedure is built into this solution, using a finite difference approximation of the thermal network to build an *RC* thermal network. Under the assumption that heat flows purely in the z direction and there is no lateral heat conduction, the *RC* model obtained from a finite difference approximation has a tree structure, and Elmore-like computations (Section 47.3.1) can be performed to determine the temperature. The optimization heuristically attempts to make this a self-fulfilling assumption, by discouraging lateral heat conduction, introducing a cost function parameter that discourages strong horizontal gradients. A hybrid approach performs an exact thermal analysis once every 20 iterations or so and uses the approximate approach for the other iterations.

The work in Ref. [9] expands the idea of thermally driven floorplanning by integrating thermal via insertion into the simulated annealing procedure. A thermal analysis procedure based on random walks [10] is built into the method, and an iterative formula, similar to Ref. [6], is used in a thermal-via insertion step between successive simulated annealing iterations.

47.2.3 3D PLACEMENT

In the placement step, the precise positions of cells in a layout are determined, and they are arranged in rows within the tiers of the 3D circuit. Because thermal considerations are particularly important in 3D cell-based circuits, this procedure must spread the cells to achieve a reasonable temperature distribution, while also capturing traditional placement requirements.

Several approaches to 3D placement have been proposed in the literature. The work in Ref. [11] embeds the netlist hypergraph into the layout area. A recursive bipartitioning procedure is used to assign nodes of the hypergraph to partitions, using mincut as the primary objective and under partition capacity constraints. Partitioning in the z direction corresponds to tier assignment, and xy partitions to assigning standard cells to rows. No thermal considerations are taken into account.

The procedure in Ref. [5] presents a 3D-specific force-directed placer that incorporates thermal objectives directly into the placer. Instead of the finite difference method that is used in many floorplanners, this approach employs FEA, which discretizes the design space into regions known as elements. For rectangular structures of the type encountered in integrated circuits, a rectangular cuboidal element can simulate heat conduction in the lateral directions without aberrations in the prime directions. As described in Chapter 3, FEA results in a matrix of the type

$$KT = P \qquad (47.2)$$

The left hand side matrix, K, known as the global stiffness matrix, can be constructed using stamps for the finite elements and the boundary conditions. The FEA equations are solved rapidly using an iterative linear solver, with clever adjustments of the convergence criteria to achieve greater or lesser accuracy, as required at different stages of the iterative placement process.

The placement engine is based on a force-directed approach, the key idea of which is described in Chapter 18. Attractive forces are created between interconnected cells, and these are proportional to the quadratic function of the cell coordinates that represents the Euclidean distance between the blocks. The constants of proportionality are chosen to be higher in the z direction to discourage intertier vias.

Apart from design criteria such as cell overlap, in the 3D context, thermal criteria are also used to generate repulsive forces, to prevent hot spots. The temperature gradient (which itself can be related to the stiffness matrix and its derivative) is used to determine the magnitudes and directions of these forces.

Once the entire system of attractive and repulsive forces is generated, repulsive forces are added, the system is solved for the minimum energy state, that is, the equilibrium location. Ideally, this minimizes the wirelengths while at the same time satisfying the other design criteria such as the temperature distribution. The iterative force-directed approach follows the following steps in the main loop. Initially, forces are updated based on the previous placement. Using these new forces, the cell positions are then calculated. These two steps of calculating forces and finding cell positions are repeated until the exit criteria are satisfied. The specifics of the force-directed approach to thermal placement, including the mathematical details, are presented in Ref. [5]. Once the iterations converge, a final postprocessing step is used to legalize the placement. Even though forces have been added to discourage overlaps, the force-directed engine solves the problem in the continuous domain, and the task of legalization is to align cells to tiers, and to rows within each tier.

Another method in Ref. [12] maps an existing 2D placement to a 3D placement through transformations based on dividing the layout into 2^k regions, for integer values of k, and then defining local transformations to heuristically refine the layout.

More recent work in Ref. [13] observes that because 3D layouts have very limited flexibility in the third dimension (with a small number of layers and a fixed set of discrete locations), partitioning works better than a force-directed method. Accordingly, this work performs global placement using recursive bisectioning. Thermal effects are incorporated through thermal resistance reduction nets, which are attractive forces that induce high power nets to remain close to the heat sink. The global placement step is followed by coarse legalization, in which a novel cell-shifting approach is proposed. This generalizes the methods in FastPlace, described in Chapter 18, by allowing shift moves to adjust the boundaries of both sparsely and densely populated cells using a computationally simple method. Finally, detailed legalization generates a final nonoverlapping layout. The approach is shown to provide excellent trade-offs between parameters such as the number of interlayer vias, wirelength, and temperature.

47.2.4 ROUTING ALGORITHMS

During routing, several objectives and constraints must be taken into consideration, including avoiding blockages due to areas occupied by thermal vias, incorporating the effect of temperature on the delays of the routed wires, and of course, traditional objectives such as wirelength, timing, congestion, and routing completion.

Once the cells have been placed and the locations of the thermal vias determined, the routing stage finds the optimal interconnections between the wires. As in 2D routing, it is important to optimize the wirelength, the delay, and the congestion. In addition, several 3D-specific issues come into play. First, the delay of a wire increases with its temperature, so that more critical wires should avoid the hottest regions, as far as possible. Second, intertier vias are a valuable resource that must be optimally allocated among the nets. Third, congestion management and blockage avoidance is more complex with the addition of a third dimension. For instance, a signal via or thermal via that spans two or more tiers constitutes a blockage that wires must navigate around.

Consider the problem of routing in a three-tier technology, as illustrated in Figure 47.5. The layout is gridded into rectangular tiles, each with a horizontal and vertical capacity that determines the number of wires that can traverse the tile, and an intertier via capacity that determines the number of free vias available in that tile. These capacities account for the resources allocated for nonsignal wires (e.g., power and clock wires) as well as the resources used by thermal vias. For a single net, as shown in the figure, the degrees of freedom that are available are in choosing the locations of the intertier vias, and selecting the precise routes within each tier. The locations of intertier vias will depend on the resource contention for vias within each grid. Moreover, critical wires should avoid the high-temperature tiles, as far as possible.

The work in Ref. [14] presents a thermally conscious router, using a multilevel routing paradigm similar to Ref. [15,16], with integrated intertier via planning and incorporating thermal considerations. An initial routing solution is constructed by building a 3D minimum spanning tree (MST) for each multipin net, and using maze routing to avoid obstacles.

At each level of the multilevel scheme, the intertier via planning problem assigns vias in a given region at level $k - 1$ of the multilevel hierarchy to tiles at level k. The problem is formulated as

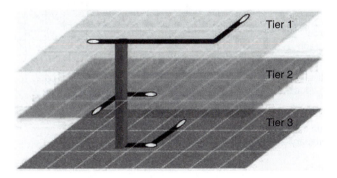

FIGURE 47.5 Example route for a net in a three-tier 3D technology. (From Ababei, C., et al., *IEEE Design and Test*, 22, 520, 2005. Copyright IEEE. With permission.)

a mincost maxflow problem, which has the form of a transportation problem. The flow graph is constructed as follows:

- Source node of the flow graph is connected through directed edges to a set of nodes v_i, representing candidate thermal vias; the edges have capacity 1 and cost 0.
- Directed edges connect a second set of nodes, T_j, from each tile to the sink node, with capacity equaling the number of vias that the tile can contain, and cost zero. The capacity is computed using a heuristic approach that takes into account the temperature difference between the tile and the one directly in the tier below it (under the assumption that heat flows downward toward the sink); the thermal analysis is based on a commercial FEA solver.
- Source and sink both have cost m, which equals the number of intertier vias in the entire region.
- Finally, a node v_i is connected to a tile T_j through an arc with infinite capacity and cost equaling the estimated wirelength of assigning an intertier via v_i to tile T_j.

Another approach to 3D routing, presented in Ref. [17], combines the problem of 3D routing with heat removal by inserting thermal vias in the z direction, and introduces the concept of thermal wires. Like a thermal via, a thermal wire is a dummy object: it has no electrical function, but is used to spread heat in the lateral direction. Each tier is tiled into a set of regions, as shown in Figure 47.6.

The global routing scheme goes through two phases. In phase I, an initial routing solution is constructed. A 3D MST is built for each multipin net, and based on the corresponding two-pin decomposition, the routing congestion is statistically estimated over each lateral routing edge using the method in Ref. [18]. This congestion model is extended to 3D by assuming that a two-pin net with pins on different tiers has an equal probability of utilizing any intertier via position within the bounding box defined by the pins.

A recursive bipartitioning scheme is then used to assign intertier vias. This is also formulated as a transportation problem, but the formulation is different from the multilevel method described above. Signal intertier via assignment is then performed across the cut in each recursive bipartition.

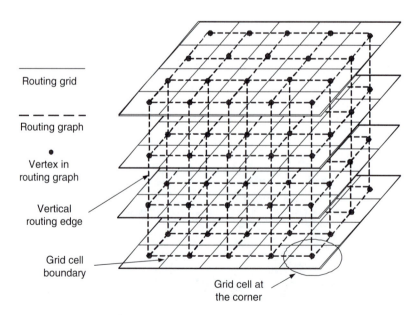

Routing grid

Routing graph

Vertex in
routing graph

Vertical
routing edge

Grid cell
boundary

Grid cell at
the corner

FIGURE 47.6 Routing grid and routing graph for a four-tier 3D circuit. (From Zhang, T., et al., In *Proceedings of the Asia-South Pacific Design Automation Conference*, 2006. Copyright IEEE. With permission.)

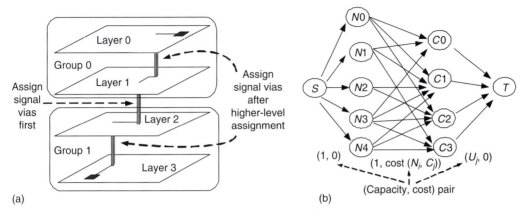

FIGURE 47.7 (a) Example of hierarchical signal via assignment for a four-tier circuit. (b) Example of min-cost network flow heuristics to solve signal via assignment problem at each level of hierarchy. (From Zhang, T., et al., In *Proceedings of the Asia-South Pacific Design Automation Conference*, 2006. Copyright IEEE. With permission.)

Figure 47.7a shows an example of signal intertier via assignment for a decomposed two-pin signal net in a four-tier circuit with two levels of hierarchy. The signal intertier via assignment is first performed at the boundary of group 0 and group 1 at topmost level, and then it is processed for tier boundary within each group. At each level of the hierarchy, the problem of signal intertier via assignment is formulated as a min-cost network flow.

Figure 47.7b shows the network flow graph for assigning signal intertier vias of five intertier nets to four possible intertier via positions. The idea is to assign each net that crosses the cut to an intertier via. Each intertier net is represented by a node N_i in the network flow graph; each possible intertier via position is indicated by a node C_j. If C_j is within the bounding box of the two-pin intertier net N_i, we build a directed edge from N_i to C_j, and set the capacity to be 1, the cost of the edge to be $\text{cost}(N_i, C_j)$. The $\text{cost}(N_i, C_j)$ is evaluated as the shortest path cost for assigning intertier via position C_j to net N_i when both pins of N_i are on the two neighboring tiers; otherwise it is evaluated as the average shortest path cost over all possible unassigned signal intertier via positions in lower levels of the hierarchy. The shortest path cost is obtained with Dijkstra's algorithm in the 2D congestion map generated from the previous estimation step, and the cost function for crossing a lateral routing edge is a combination of edge length and an overflow cost function similar to that in Ref. [19]. The supply at the source, equaling the demand at the sinks, is N, the number of nets.

Finally, once the intertier vias are fixed, the problem reduces to a 2D routing problem in each tier, and maze routing is used to route the design.

Next, in phase II, a linear programming approach is used to assign thermal vias and thermal wires. A thermal analysis is performed, and fast sensitivity analysis using the adjoint network method, which has the cost of a single thermal simulation. The benefit of adding thermal vias, for relatively small perturbations in the via density, is given by a product of the sensitivity and the via density, a linear function. The objective function is a sum of via densities and is also linear. Additional constraints are added in the formulation to permit overflows, and a sequence of linear programs is solved to arrive at the solution.

47.3 3D FPGA DESIGNS

As in the case of standard cell designs, the idea of building 3D designs using FPGAs is not new, and there has been some earlier work in this area. Alexander et al. [20] proposed using the MCM (multichip module) technology with through die vias to build 3D FPGAs, and enumerated a number of issues that should be considered in building 3D FPGAs such as yield, channel width, thermal issues, and placement and routing. A 3D FPGA architecture called Rothko, in which each RLB (routing and logic block) tile is connected to the RLB directly above and below it (i.e., no multilength segments in the z direction), was presented in Ref. [21]. The process technology that the authors assumed was that of Northeastern University's 3D fabrication technology, which was similar to that of MIT's [4]. A more advanced version of Rothko's work appears in Ref. [22] in which the authors propose placing the routing in one layer and logic on another for more efficient layer utilization. Other notable contributions include the work by Lin et al. [23] and Chiricescu et al. [24], who propose placing memory and routing elements functions in different tiers; Campenhout et al. [25], who proposes using optical interconnects to provide communications between tiers of a 3D FPGA; and Wu et al. [26], who propose a universal switchbox for 3D FPGAs.

Recent 3D FPGA CAD efforts can be classified into estimation methods and placement and routing algorithms. In the estimation methods, analytical models are developed to estimate 3D wirelength and channel width, and as a result estimating the power consumption and area of a 3D FPGA design. Because such methods do not require costly placement and routing steps, they can predict resource requirements very fast at the cost of estimation accuracy. In the placement and routing methods, specialized CAD algorithms are developed to target specific needs of a 3D architecture. In the following sections we discuss both categories: estimation and placement/routing.

47.3.1 ESTIMATION METHODS

Analytical models for estimating channel width in gate arrays were studied by Gamal [27]. He observed that the channel width follows a Poisson distribution and the average channel width W is estimated as

$$W = \frac{\gamma L}{2} \tag{47.3}$$

where
  γ is the average number of edges incident to logic blocks
  L is the average wirelength

Later studies have shown that better estimations can be obtained by considering multiterminal nets and their wirelength distributions. Rahman et al. [28] extend these models for a 2D FPGA with unit routing segments as follows:

$$W = \frac{\sum_{l=1}^{2\sqrt{N}-2} lf(l)X_{\text{fpgn}}}{2Ne_t} \tag{47.4}$$

where
  N is the number of CLBs (configurable logic block, or the basic unit of the FPGA logic)
  l is the wirelength
  $f(l)$ is the probability density function of the wirelength and can be derived from the Rent's rule

Parameters X_{fpga} and e_t are architecture and placement and routing dependent. X_{fpga} is a multi- to two-terminal routing adjustment factor and e_t is the channel utilization factor. Typically 5–10 percent of the routing segments are shared among multiple terminals of a multiterminal net, resulting in $X_{\text{fpga}} = 90$–95 percent. Channel utilization e_t is less than one because of detours in the routing.

For a 3D FPGA, they assume $F_s = 5$ for every switch (where F_s is as defined in Section 45.4.3.) where N_z is the number of 3D tiers. The maximum length in the third dimension is $(N_z - 1)t_z$ where

t_z is the distance between adjacent tiers. The average channel width in a 3D FPGA is estimated as the following:

$$W = \frac{\sum_{l=1}^{2\sqrt{N/N_z}-2+(N_z-1)t_z} lf_{3D}(l)\,X_{\text{fpga}}}{\left(2N + \frac{(N_z-1)N}{N_z}\right)e_t} \tag{47.5}$$

where $f_{3D}(l)$ is the 3D wirelength distribution function.

The analytical model for channel width estimation is further improved in Ref. [29] by factoring in the under-utilization of the CLBs, which changes the number of nets by a factor of u^{p+1} and the chip area by $1/u$, where u is the CLB utilization factor and p is the Rent's exponent. Interested readers are referred to Ref. [29] for details on the improved formulation. The authors validate their analytical model by comparing the estimated channel width to channel widths obtained by placement and detailed routing of benchmark circuits. They show an average of 11 percent error in their estimation. A brief description of their placement and routing algorithm is presented in Section 47.3.2.

The reduction in channel width of a 3D design compared to the 2D version could potentially result in fewer programmable switches per CLB/switchbox tile and smaller 2D distance between CLBs. The area of an FPGA tile is $A_L + A_c + A_s$ where A_L is the area of the logic blocks in a CLB, A_c is the area of the connection box, and A_s is the area of the switchbox. Comparing a 2D versus 3D implementation, A_L does not change. A_c reduces linearly with a decrease in channel width, and A_s is a linear function of the channel width and a quadratic function of F_s. The exact numbers depend on the sizing of the transistors and the implementation of the switches and connection box. For example, in Ref. [28], $A_c = (20 + 13.5 \times W) \times O + (6\log_2(W) + 35.5 \times W) \times I$ times the area of a minimum width transistor where O and I are the number of output and input pins connected to a CLB. Furthermore, in Ref. [28] $A_s = 13.5 \times W \times F_s \times (F_s + 1)/2$. Note that in a 3D FPGA, the channel width is likely to decrease compared to a 2D implementation, but $F_s = 5$ in a 3D architecture studied in Ref. [28] compared to a 2D implementation with $F_s = 3$. If the channel width reduction is significant (e.g., more than 1/3), then the area of a CLB/switchbox tile will be smaller in a 3D FPGA compared to a 2D FPGA.

The reduction of the tile area will likely result in a decrease in power consumption and increased clock frequency because the distance between adjacent CLBs decreases and hence the physical lengths of the wire segments reduce. Although a more detailed analysis would have to consider the countereffect of intertier via parasitics on delay and power. The authors in Ref. [28] use an approximate model in which they assume the delay of an intertier routing segment is comparable to that of a 2D wire segment. Furthermore, they ignore the under-utilization of long wire segments. As a result, their delay and power improvement estimations are on the optimistic side.

Another study that uses analytical models to estimate potential benefits of 3D fabrication technologies was presented by Lin et al. [23]. Assuming a monolithic 3D fabrication technology with short intertier vias, they propose a 2.5D FPGA architecture in which the logic and routing tiles are still placed in a 2D plane but the transistors implementing the tiles are stacked vertically. For example, if three device layers are provided by the fabrication technology, the SRAMs that hold the programming bits of the FPGA tiles could be placed on the top tier, pass transistors could be placed in the middle tier, and routing resource buffers and logic block transistors could be placed on the lower tier. Note that the CLB/switchbox tiles are still layed out in a 2D plane (unlike the 3D floorplan proposed by Rahman et al. [23]). See Figure 47.8a and b for two examples. If the area utilization of the three tiers is close to 100 percent, then the area of a three-tier FPGA could be 33 percent of a regular CMOS FPGA at best. The authors further argue that if a RAM technology with smaller area compared to 6T SRAM is used, then the area reduction would be even greater because a significant portion of the area of an FPGA is occupied by the SRAM cells holding the configuration bits. For example, in Figure 47.8c, the authors assume a RAM technology is used whose area is 0.7 times the area of a regular CMOS SRAM.

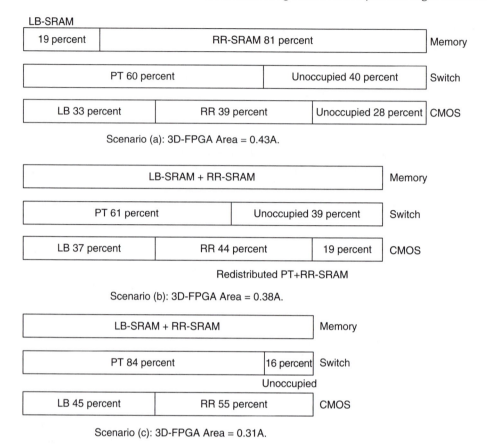

FIGURE 47.8 Using a monolithic 3D technology to distribute transistors of an FPGA. (From Lin, M., et al., In *Proceedings of the ACM/SIGDA International Symposium on Field Programmable Gate Arrays*, 2006.) A, area of a baseline 2D FPGA; LB, logic block; RR, routing resources; PT, pass transistor. In parts (a) and (b) regular CMOS SRAMs are used and in part (c) RAM cells with 0.7 times the area of an SRAM are used.

Note that this approach is not applicable to a technology similar to the one assumed in Ref. [28] because 3D vias need to be very small to produce any meaningful area savings. In the layout implementation of Ref. [23], significantly more intertier vias are used compared to Ref. [28].

Unlike Rahman's work [28], the layout in Lin's work [23] does not result in any channel width reduction because the underlying placement of the tiles does not change (but the size of the tiles reduces). Instead, the reduction in footprint area of a tile results in shorter physical distances between CLBs and hence smaller wirelengths, area and power consumption of a 3D implementation compared to a 2D FPGA. The amount of area reduction depends on the size of the RAM cells used to implement the configuration memory (e.g., in Figure 47.8b the area is 0.38 of a 2D FPGA, while in Figure 47.8c the area is 0.31 times the area of the 2D FPGA). They study area, performance and power benefits of a monolithic 3D technology as a function of the ratio of the RAM cell size compared to a regular 6T CMOS SRAM cell for a number of process technologies. Wirelength reduction is the square root of the area reduction, which in turn depends on the RAM size reduction. Hence, in the examples of Figure 47.8b and c wirelength is $\sqrt{0.38} = 0.61$ and $\sqrt{0.31} = 0.56$ times the wirelength of a 2D implementation.

Lin et al. consider 3D benefits for a number of technology nodes (180 nm, 130 nm, 90 nm, and 65 nm using the Berkeley Predictive Technology Model) and various wirelength reduction factors $0.56 \le r \le 0.61$. Because various circuit parameters such as pass transistor sizes, number of buffers on long segments, buffer sizes, and other circuit parameters should be optimized as functions of both technology node parameters and wiring parasitics, the authors develop analytical models for the delay of each segment type based on the Elmore delay model and circuit parameters. For any given combination of technology parameters and wirelength reduction, they optimize circuit parameters such as buffer sizes, and then use the optimized delay values to study performance and power benefits of 3D. Note that in their method they can plot the delay of each segment type (such as single, double, hex) as a function of technology node and wirelength reduction factor r. As a result, their estimations of delay improvements at the system level are more accurate compared to a method that only studies average wirelength reductions. Assuming the configuration of Figure 47.8c is used on a 65 nm technology, the authors report an estimated 3.2 times higher logic density, 1.7 times lower critical path delay, and 1.7 times lower total dynamic power consumption than the baseline 2D-FPGA fabricated in the same technology node.

47.3.2 PLACEMENT AND ROUTING ALGORITHMS

Spiffy [30,31] was the first 3D placement and routing tool for FPGAs. Assuming the MCM fabrication technology for 3D FPGAs proposed in Ref. [20], it uses a divide-and-conquer approach to recursively partition the netlist and assign the partitions to physical subregions on the (3D) chip. Terminal propagation is applied by fixing the location in which a net enters a partition from a neighboring partition and rectilinear Steiner tree global routing is attempted simultaneously. Such a strategy results in close interaction between global routing and recursive partitioning-based placement. In addition to partitioning-based placement, the authors improve the quality of placement using simulated annealing.

As mentioned in Section 47.3.1, Rahman et al. propose a modification of a 2D placement and routing CAD flow to target 3D designs. Their placement method consists of two phases. In phase 1, an hybrid simulated annealing (Chapter 16) and force-directed method (Chapter 18) is used to move CLBs across tiers. Basically, an individual move of the annealing process in phase 1 moves a CLB to the center of gravity of its adjacent CLBs. Phase 2 of the placement locks each CLB in its the tier it was placed at the end of phase 1 and only allows movements within tiers. The placement phase is followed by global and detailed routing steps, which are similar to their 2D counterparts.

Ababei et al. [32] proposed a 3D FPGA CAD flow called TPR (three-dimensional place and route) that uses a partitioning-base placement phase to distribute CLBs across partitions while simultaneously minimizing both cutsize (hence the number of required 3D vias) and wirelength (hence reducing circuit delay). One key difference between Ababei's work and previous work such as [31] and [28] is that in previous 3D FPGA studies, the authors assume that every track in a channel is 3D (i.e., $F_s = 5$), whereas in Ababei's work only a subset of tracks in a channel connect to 3D switches (i.e., the majority of switches route signals within a tier and have a switch flexibility of $F_s = 3$ and other switches have $F_s = 5$). This results in significant area, delay, and power savings.

Another difference between TPR and other 3D FPGA CAD efforts is the optimization steps that they use to explicitly minimize the number of intertier vias, and the assumption that multisegment routing is used in the third dimension as well as within tiers.

Figure 47.9a shows an example of a 3D FPGA where only a subset of the switches in the switchbox provide connections between tiers. Figure 47.9b shows such a switchbox with a mixture of switch flexibilities of $F_s = 5$ and $F_s = 3$. Note that the reduced area in the switchbox should be carefully balanced with switch flexibility so that routability does not degrade. Switchboxes with too much connectivity will excessively waste area, and meager intertier via counts will hurt the performance of the design.

TPR is an extension of the VPR [33] algorithm. The flow of the TPR CAD tool is shown in Figure 47.10. The placement algorithm first employs a partitioning step using the hMetis algorithm [34] to divide the circuit into a number of balanced partitions, equal to the number of tiers for 3D integration. The goal of this first mincut partitioning is to minimize the connections between tiers, which translates into reducing the number of vertical (i.e., intertier) wires and decreasing the area

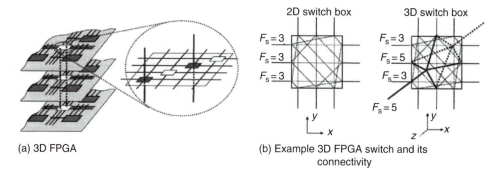

(a) 3D FPGA

(b) Example 3D FPGA switch and its connectivity

FIGURE 47.9 3D FPGA and switch example. (From Ababei, C., et al., *IEEE Transactions on Computer-Aided Design*, 25, 1132, 2006. Copyright IEEE. With permission.)

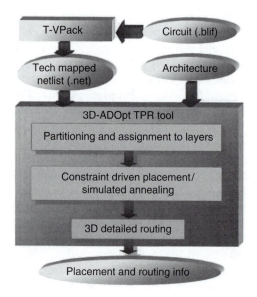

FIGURE 47.10 Flow of the TPR tool. (From Ababei, C., et al., *IEEE Transactions on Computer-Aided Design*, 25, 1132, 2006. Copyright IEEE. With permission.)

overhead associated with 3D switches as discussed before. After dividing the netlist into tiers, TPR continues with the placement of each tier using a hybrid approach that combines top-down partitioning and simulated annealing [35]. The annealing step moves cells mostly within tiers. Finally, the cells are routed to obtain a placed and routed solution. The routing algorithm is very similar to the VPR's routing algorithm except that intertier vias are heavily penalized to avoid excessive usage of them.

47.3.2.1 Partitioning the Circuit between Tiers

The TPR step that performs partitioning and tier assignment of the circuit is shown conceptually in Figure 47.11. After the netlist is partitioned using hMetis, a novel linear placement approach is used to arrange the tiers such that wirelength and the maximum cutsize between adjacent tiers is minimized. This is achieved by mapping this problem to that of minimizing the bandwidth of a matrix,* using an efficient matrix bandwidth minimization heuristic.

---

* The bandwidth of a matrix is defined as the maximum bandwidth of all its rows. The bandwidth of a row is defined as the distance between the first and last nonzero entries.

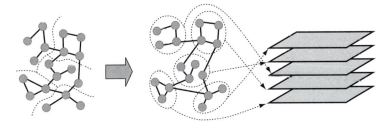

FIGURE 47.11   Partitioning of the netlist into tiers. (From Ababei, C., et al., *IEEE Transactions on Computer-Aided Design*, 25, 1132, 2006. Copyright IEEE. With permission.)

Figure 47.12 shows a graph in which each node corresponds to a cluster from the graph in Figure 47.11. An *E–V* matrix is formed in which each row corresponds to an edge, and the columns correspond to vertices. An entry a_{ij} in the matrix is nonzero if vertex j is incident to edge i, and zero otherwise, and the bandwidth of this matrix is sought to be minimized by choosing an optimal ordering of the vertices.

Intuitively, we would like to minimize the bandwidth of every row, because the bandwidth of a row represents how many tiers the net corresponding to that row spans. Furthermore, it is desirable to distribute the bands of different rows among all columns, because the number of bands enclosing a particular column translates into the number of vertical vias that have to pass through the tier corresponding to that column. Minimizing the matrix bandwidth achieves both goals: it minimizes the span of every row (intertier wirelength minimization), and distributes the bands across columns (cutsize minimization). Details of the bandwidth minimization problem can be found in Ref. [32]. When the bandwidth minimization algorithm is run on the example on the left of Figure 47.12, the linear arrangement on the right is created.

47.3.2.2   Partitioning-Based Placement within Tiers

After the initial tier assignment, placement is performed on each tier starting with the top tier, proceeding tier after tier. The placement of every tier is based on edge-weighted quad partitioning using the hMetis partitioning algorithm, and is similar to the approach in Ref. [35], which has the same quality as VPR but at three to four times shorter runtimes. Edge weights are usually computed inversely proportional to the timing slack of the corresponding nets. To improve timing, the bounding

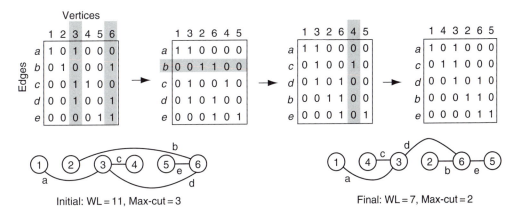

FIGURE 47.12   E-V matrix and steps to minimize both wire length and cutsize. (From Ababei, C., et al., *IEEE Transactions on Computer-Aided Design*, 25, 1132, 2006. Copyright IEEE. With permission.)

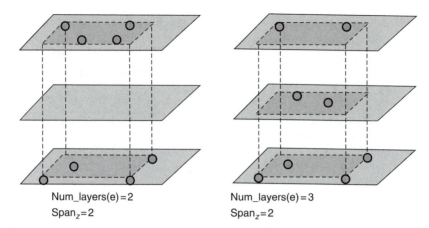

Num_layers(e)=2   Num_layers(e)=3
Span$_z$=2   Span$_z$=2

FIGURE 47.13 Example showing the difference between a net's span and number of tiers. (From Ababei, C., et al., *IEEE Transactions on Computer-Aided Design*, 25, 1132, 2006. Copyright IEEE. With permission.)

box of the terminals of a critical net placed on a tier is projected to the lower tiers and used as a placement constraint for other terminals. More details of the partitioning-based placement phase can be found in Ref. [32].

47.3.2.3 Simulated Annealing Placement Phase

Following the partitioning-based placement step, a 3D-adapted version of VPR [33] is used in the low-temperature annealing phase to further improve wirelength and routability. The following cost function is used for each net.

$$\text{Cost}_{3D}(e) = q.\text{Cost}_{2D}(e) + \alpha.\text{Span}_z(e) + \beta.\text{numTiers}(e) \qquad (47.6)$$

where

Cost$_{2D}$ is the half-perimeter size of the 2D projection of the bounding box of net e
Span$_z(e)$ is the total span of the net between tiers
numTiers(e) is the number of tiers on which the terminals of the net are distributed
parameters q, α, and β are tuning parameters (q has the same role as in VPR)

Figure 47.13 shows an example to illustrate why both Span$_z$ and numTiers should be used. In a 3D routing structure that employs multisegment intertier connections, the left figure is more likely to use fewer vertical connections (of length 2) to connect the terminals on the first and the third tiers.

REFERENCES

1. J. W. Joyner, P. Zarkesh-Ha, and J. D. Meindl. Global interconnect design in a three-dimensional system-on-a-chip. *IEEE Transactions on VLSI Systems*, 12(4):367–372, April 2004.
2. K. W. Guarini, A. W. Topol, M. Leong, R. Yu, L. Shi, M. R. Newport, D. J. Frank, D. V. Singh, G. M. Cohen, S. V. Nitta, D. C. Boyd, P. A. O'Neil, S. L. Tempest, H. B. Pogpe, S. Purushotharnan, and W. E. Haensch. Electrical integrity of state-of-the-art 0.13 μm SOI CMOS devices and circuits transferred for three-dimensional (3D) integrated circuit (IC) fabrication. In *Technical Digest of the IEEE International Electron Devices Meeting*, San Francisco, CA, pp. 943–945, 2002.
3. J. Burns, L. McIlrath, J. Hopwood, C. Keast, D. P. Vu, K. Warner, and P. Wyatt. An SOI-based three dimensional integrated circuit technology. In *IEEE International SOI Conference*, Williamsburg, VA, pp. 20–21, October 2000.

4. R. Reif, A. Fan, K. -N. Chen, and S. Das. Fabrication technologies for three-dimensional integrated circuits. In *Proceedings of the International Symposium on Quality Electronic Design (ISQED)*, Wakefield, MA, pp. 33–37, 2002.

5. B. Goplen and S. S. Sapatnekar. Efficient thermal placement of standard cells in 3D ICs using a force directed approach. In *Proceedings of the IEEE/ACM International Conference on Computer-Aided Design*, San Jose, CA, pp. 86–89, 2003.

6. B. Goplen and S. S. Sapatnekar. Thermal via placement in 3D ICs. In *Proceedings of the ACM International Symposium on Physical Design*, San Francisco, CA, pp. 167–174, 2005.

7. J. Cong, J. Wei, and Y. Zhang. A thermal-driven floorplanning algorithm for 3D ICs. In *Proceedings of the ACM International Symposium on Physical Design*, Phoenix, AZ, pp. 306–313, 2004.

8. J. -M. Lin and Y. -W. Chang. TCG: A transitive closure graph based representation for non-slicing floorplans. In *Proceedings of the ACM/IEEE Design Automation Conference*, Las Vegas, NV, pp. 764–769, 2001.

9. E. Wong and S. K. Lim. 3D floorplanning with thermal vias. In *Proceedings of Design, Automation and Test in Europe Conference*, Munich, Germany, pp. 878–883, 2006.

10. H. Qian, S. R. Nassif, and S. S. Sapatnekar. Power grid analysis using random walks. *IEEE Transactions on Computer-Aided Design*, 24(8):1204–1224, August 2005.

11. S. Das, A. Chandrakasan, and R. Reif. Design tools for 3-D integrated circuits. In *Proceedings of the Asia-South Pacific Design Automation Conference*, Kitakyushu, Japan, pp. 53–56, 2003.

12. J. Cong, G. Luo, J. Wei, and Y. Zhang. Thermal-aware 3D IC placement via transformation. In *Proceedings of the Asia-South Pacific Design Automation Conference*, Yokohama, Japan, pp. 780–785, 2007.

13. B. Goplen and S. S. Sapatnekar. Placement of 3D ICs with thermal and interlayer via considerations. In *Proceedings of the ACM/IEEE Design Automation Conference*, San Diego, CA, pp. 626–631, 2007.

14. J. Cong and Y. Zhang. Thermal-driven multilevel routing for 3-D ICs. In *Proceedings of the Asia-South Pacific Design Automation Conference*, Shanghai, China, pp. 121–126, 2005.

15. J. Cong, J. Fang, and Y. Zhang. Multilevel approach to full-chip gridless routing. In *Proceedings of the IEEE/ACM International Conference on Computer-Aided Design*, San Jose, CA, pp. 234–241, 2001.

16. J. Cong, M. Xie, and Y. Zhang. An enhanced multilevel routing system. In *Proceedings of the IEEE/ACM International Conference on Computer-Aided Design*, San Jose, CA, pp. 51–58, 2002.

17. T. Zhang, Y. Zhan, and S. S. Sapatnekar. Temperature-aware routing in 3D ICs. In *Proceedings of the Asia-South Pacific Design Automation Conference*, Yokohama, Japan, pp. 309–314, 2006.

18. J. Westra, C. Bartels, and P. Groeneveld. Probabilistic congestion prediction. In *Proceedings of the ACM International Symposium on Physical Design*, Phoenix, AZ, pp. 204–209, 2004.

19. R. T. Hadsell and P. H. Madden. Improved global routing through congestion estimation. In *Proceedings of the ACM/IEEE Design Automation Conference*, Anaheim, CA, pp. 28–34, 2003.

20. M. Alexander, J. Cohoon, J. Colflesh, J. Karro, and G. Robins. Three-dimensional field-programmable gate arrays. In *Proceedings of the International ASIC Conference*, Austin, TX, pp. 253–256, 1995.

21. M. Leeser, W. Meleis, M. Vai, S. Chiricescu, W. Xu, and P. Zavracky. Rothko: A three-dimensional FPGA. *IEEE Design and Test of Computers*, 15(1):16–23, January–March 1998.

22. S. Chiricescu, M. Leeser, and M. M. Vai. Design and analysis of a dynamically reconfigurable three-dimensional FPGA. *IEEE Transactions on VLSI Systems*, 9(1):186–196, 2001.

23. M. Lin, A. El Gamal, Y. -C. Lu, and S. Wong. Performance benefits of monolithically stacked 3D-FPGA. In *Proceedings of the ACM/SIGDA International Symposium on Field Programmable Gate Arrays*, Monterey, CA, pp. 113–122, 2006, New York, ACM Press.

24. S. M. S. A. Chiricescu and M. M. Vai. A three-dimensional FPGA with an integrated memory for in-application reconfiguration data. In *Proceedings of the IEEE International Symposium on Circuits and Systems*, volume 2, pp. 232–235, Monterey, CA, 1998.

25. J. van Campenhout, H. Van Marck, J. Depreitere, and J. Dambre. Optoelectronic FPGAs. *IEEE Journal of Selected Topics in Quantum Electronics*, 5(2):306–315, 1999.

26. G. -M. Wu, M. Shyu, and Y. -W. Chang. Universal switch blocks for three-dimensional FPGA design. In *Proceedings of the ACM/SIGDA International Symposium on Field Programmable Gate Arrays*, Monterey, CA, p. 254, 1999.

27. A. Gamal. Two dimensional model for interconnections in master slice integrated circuits. *IEEE Transactions on Circuits and Systems*, 28:127–138, February 1981.

28. A. Rahman, S. Das, A. P. Chandrakasan, and R. Reif. Wiring requirement and three-dimensional integration technology for field programmable gate arrays. *IEEE Transactions on VLSI Systems*, 11(1):44–54, 2003.

29. Y. -S. Kwon, P. Lajevardi, A. P. Chandrakasan, F. Honoré, and D. E. Troxel. A 3-D FPGA wire resource prediction model validated using a 3-D placement and routing tool. In *Proceedings of the 2005 International Workshop on System Level Interconnect Prediction (SLIP)*, San Francisco, CA, pp. 65–72, 2005.

30. M. Alexander, J. Cohoon, J. Colflesh, J. Karro, E. Peters, and G. Robins. Placement and routing for three-dimensional FPGAs. In *Fourth Canadian Workshop on Field-Programmable Devices*, Toronto, Canada, pp. 11–18, 1996.

31. J. Karro and J. P. Cohoon. A spiffy tool for the simultaneous placement and global routing for three-dimensional field-programmable gate arrays. In *Proceedings of the Great Lakes Symposium on VLSI*, Ann Arbor, MI, pp. 230–231, 1999.

32. C. Ababei, H. Mogal, and K. Bazargan. Three-dimensional place and route for FPGAs. *IEEE Transactions on Computer-Aided Design*, 25(6):1132–1140, June 2006.

33. V. Betz and J. Rose. VPR: A new packing placement and routing tool for FPGA research. In *Field-Programmable Logic and Applications*, London, U.K., pp. 213–222, 1997.

34. G. Karypis, R. Aggarwal, V. Kumar, and S. Shekhar. Multi-level hypergraph partitioning: Applications in VLSI design. In *Proceedings of the ACM/IEEE Design Automation Conference*, Anaheim, CA, pp. 526–529, 1997.

35. P. Maidee, C. Ababei, and K. Bazargan. Fast timing-driven partitioning-based placement for island style FPGAs. In *Proceedings of the ACM/IEEE Design Automation Conference*, Anaheim, CA, pp. 598–603, 2003.

36. C. Ababei, Y. Feng, B. Goplen, H. Mogal, T. Zhang, K. Bazargan, and S. Sapatnekar. Placement and routing in 3D integrated circuits. *IEEE Design and Test*, 22(6):520–531, November–December 2005.

37. B. Goplen and S. S. Sapatnekar. Placement of thermal vias in 3-D ICs using various thermal objectives. *IEEE Transactions on Computer-Aided Design*, 26(4):692–709, April 2006.

Index

A

Amplitude and intensity, for conventional mask, 709
Absorption metric, role of, 114
Abutment constraints, 172, 175–176, 199, 201
Accurate gate delay, steps of, 549
ACG, *see* Analytical constraint generation
Across chip linewidth variation (ACLV), 774
Actel ProASIC3 logic blocks, 947
Adaptive tree adjustment technique, 574
Adhesion metric, of logic network, 448–449
Ad hoc look-ahead floorplanning, 302–303
Adjacency graph, 140, 151, 158, 178, 217, 224–225
Adjacency matrix, of graph, 114
Adjacent constraint graph
　define, 224
　for floorplan, 224–225
　perturbations for, 226–227
　properties of
　　directed edges, 225
　　geometrical relations, 225–226
Admittance propagation, 547
ADS, *see* Attached dead-space
Advanced simulated annealing algorithm, 317
Advanced synthesis techniques, 823
Agglomerative clustering, 127–130
Aggressor net logic error, 42
Aggressor–victim pair, 44
AHHK spanning tree, 513
AHHK tree, euclidean plane, 513
Algebraic multigrid (AMG) technique, 378, 380, 923, 926
Algorithm for, buffer block planning, 661
Algorithmis complexity analysis, 73–74
Alpha 21264, 889, 901–904
　clock
　　grids, 903
　　hierarchy, 902
　GCLK grid, 901
　global clock, distribution network of, 902
American map, definition of, 339
Analog floorplanning, 250–251
Analytical constraint generation, 295, 456
Analytical placement
　algorithms, 284
　basic idea of, 327
　geometric partitioning, 337–341
　netlength minimization of
　　linear netlength minimization, 331–332
　　netlength definition, 328–330
　　objective functions of, 334–335
　　quadratic netlength minimization, 332–334
　parallelization technique and macros, 344
　partitioning information usages in, 341–343
　quadratic placement properties, 335–337
　repartitioning technique, 343–344
　steps of, 328

Annealing schedule, 312–313
Anticipated plot, acceptance rate *vs.* generated new
　configurations, 315
APlace, 365
　and log-sum-exp approximation, 366–369
　relaxation in, 392–393
Appending, 226; *see also* Adjacent constraint graph
Application specific integrated circuit, 179, 450, 628, 942
　counterparts, 957
　and system-on-chip (SOC) design, 427
Approximation scheme; *see also* Fractional global routing
　minimizing relative congestion, 635–638
　　advantages of approximation algorithm, 638
　　for any given approximation ratio $1 + \epsilon_0$, 635
　　inequality, use of, 636–637
　　by linear programming duality (theorem 1),
　　　expression, 636
　　maximum number of phases bounded by, 638
　　modified update rule for y_e and prove to theorem,
　　　635–638
　　theorem, with relative congestion at most 1, 635
　　upper bound on approximation ratio ρ, 637
　minimizing total weighted netlength, 639–640
　　additional dual variable y_L use of, 639
　　to minimize total weighted netlength, 639–640
　　minimum-cost multicommodity flow problem,
　　　use of, 639
　　Steiner tree and total increment expression, 639–640
Arbitraryweighted graphs, 519
Arc, capacity of, 124–125
Area-optimal slicing floorplans, 177–178
ASIC, *see* Application specific integrated circuit
Assignment problem
　constructive methods for, 13
　iterative methods for, 12–13
Asymptotic waveform evaluation technique, 586
Atomic test pattern generation (ATPG), 918
A-tree router, in congestion-driven placement
　techniques, 463
Attached dead-space, 654–655
Augmenting path, 83
Automated wire-routing, 476
Automatic move strategy, 321
Avoid blockages, rip-up and reroute, 574

B

Backend-of-line (BEOL), 792
Bakoglu's metric, 543
Balanced binary tree, 166–167
Basic blocks, 973; *see also* GAMA, linear-time simultaneous
　placement and mapping method
Basic logic element (BLE), 945
　cluster basic and, 946
　　LUT coupled with a flip-flop, 946
Batched greedy algorithm (BGA), 502